POEMS, POETS, POETRY

*An Introduction
and Anthology*

POEMS, POETS, POETRY

*An Introduction
and Anthology*

SECOND EDITION

Helen Vendler

HARVARD UNIVERSITY

Bedford/St. Martin's

Boston ■ New York

For Bedford/St. Martin's

Developmental Editor: Stephen A. Scipione
Production Editor: Ara Salibian
Senior Production Supervisor: Dennis Conroy
Marketing Manager: Richard Cadman
Editorial Assistant: Emily Goodall
Copyeditor: Jane Zanichkowsky
Text Design: Anna George
Cover Design: Sara Eisenman
Composition: Stratford Publishing Services
Printing and Binding: Haddon Craftsmen, Inc., an R.R. Donnelley & Sons Company

President: Charles H. Christensen
Editorial Director: Joan E. Feinberg
Editor in Chief: Karen S. Henry
Director of Marketing: Karen Melton
Director of Editing, Design, and Production: Marcia Cohen
Managing Editor: Elizabeth M. Schaaf

Library of Congress Control Number: 2001095138

Manufactured in the United States of America.

6 5
i h g

For information, write: Bedford/St. Martin's, 75 Arlington Street, Boston, MA 02116
(617-399-4000)

ISBN: 0–312–25706–6

Acknowledgments

Elizabeth Alexander, "Nineteen" from *The Venus Hottentot*. Copyright © 1990 by Elizabeth Alexander. Reprinted with the permission of the University Press of Virginia.

Acknowledgments and copyrights are continued at the back of the book on pages 686–695, which constitute an extension of the copyright page. It is a violation of the law to reproduce these selections by any means whatsoever without the written permission of the copyright holder.

Preface:
About This Book

This book offers ways to read and understand poems with the pleasure they deserve. The nine chapters in Part I approach the poem from various directions, in the conviction that any artwork invites consideration from different perspectives. Chapter 1, "The Poem as Life," uses several short poems to show how a poetic utterance springs from a life-moment — sometimes a private one (falling in love), sometimes a public one (the decline of aristocracy). Chapter 2, "The Poem as Arranged Life," considers the same poems that appear in Chapter 1 but treats them as arrangements, rather than as utterances; it asks why the poem takes the imaginative shape it does and how its elements have been ordered. In Chapter 3, "Poems as Pleasure," aspects of poetry that give pleasure are mentioned and illustrated: formal aspects such as rhythm and rhyme, of course, but also construction and images. Thematic aspects such as poignancy and wisdom are included, too, as is the individual, personal language proper to each poet. Chapter 4, "Describing Poems," and Chapter 5, "The Play of Language," suggest some useful ways of describing poems — by the class of poems to which they belong, by the little plots they act out through grammar and syntax, by the speech acts in which they engage, by the agents the poets choose to do the work of the poem, and so on.

Chapter 6, "Constructing a Self," moves on to the psychological world of the poem. Given that each poem is a fictive speech by an imagined speaker, how is that speaker made convincing by the author? How is a credible self constructed on the page? The more abstract lyric self of Chapter 6 — ungendered, of no specified age or race, of no determined country — is contrasted in Chapter 7, "Poetry and Social Identity," with the lyric self that is socially marked, as we encounter a speaker making clear her sex, or his race, or his age, or her sexual orientation. Our sense of the purpose and the audience of a poem depends to a great extent on how the self of the speaker is defined. Chapter 8, "History and Regionality," takes up the topics of time and space — the two great axes on which all literature turns — as they apply to lyric poetry. And finally, in Chapter 9, "Attitudes, Values, Judgments," the largest questions we can put to a literary work — fundamentally, questions of ethical value — are raised and discussed with respect to some crucial examples, old and new.

Each chapter takes up several poems by way of illustration, and ends with a section called "Reading Other Poems" that introduces a small group of poems that can be usefully read in the light of that chapter. These poems are usually short and range from the canonical to the recent.

Part II, "Writing about Poetry," introduces some techniques by which readers can convey what they discover in poems to other readers. Chapter 10, "Writing about Poems," looks closely at two poems about daffodils, one by Robert Herrick and one by William Wordsworth, and suggests some general methods for shaping a paper about Wordsworth's poem. Chapter 11, "Studying Groups of Poems," is divided into two parts: the first examines a suite of poems by Walt Whitman commemorating Abraham Lincoln, and the second probes the theme of time in several Emily Dickinson poems.

The anthology in Part III is intended to provide a wide sampling — more than 260 poems — from the literature of lyric, including some poems longer and more complex than those cited in the chapters. Arranged alphabetically by author, the anthology includes poems by more than 120 poets, many of them represented in significant depth so as to suggest the range of an individual poet's work. Finally, my appendices on prosody, grammar, speech acts, rhetorical devices, and lyric subgenres provide further illustration of points taken up substantively but not exhaustively in individual chapters. They can help consolidate and extend — when assigned as home reading — the demonstrations given in class.

I have also prepared a brief instructor's manual in which I discuss some of the issues of teaching poetry and suggest exercises that have, over the years, helped my students understand and appreciate poetry.

The manual also comments on most of the poems in Part I that are not discussed in the text's nine chapters.

New to This Edition

Based on the publisher's survey of instructors who have taught with *Poems, Poets, Poetry,* I have introduced about 60 new poems to this edition, most of them by contemporary poets. In Part I and in the anthology, works by Stanley Kunitz, Margaret Atwood, Julia Alvarez, Gary Soto, Jane Kenyon, Michael S. Harper, Joy Harjo, Dionisio Martínez, Harold Littlebird, Pat Mora, Carl Phillips, Jane Yeh, and many others are new. The chapters on writing in Part II are new as well. Readers should not find themselves daunted by the amount of writing instruction in these chapters. I emphasize that resourceful reading and question-asking will lead readers to discoveries they are eager to share. The brief tips, guidelines, and admonitions about writing that I provide should help them do so.

In addition, I have assented to a few changes in the format of the book. In the first edition, none of the poems had their lines numbered. Poets tend to conceive their poems stanzaically, not by line, and they prefer that their poems not be encumbered by elements (such as line numbers) that they themselves have not introduced. Therefore, my own classroom practice is to specify by referring to stanzas and page numbers ("Look at the third stanza on page 42"). But many instructors pointed out how difficult it is to talk about long poems such as "The Love Song of J. Alfred Prufrock" without some minimal line-numbering to help navigate the turns of the discussion. In deference to them, every fifth line in poems of more than 50 lines is now numbered (unless the *stanzas* in those longer poems are already numbered — see, for example, Browning's "Childe Roland to the Dark Tower Came"). Finally, the dates of the poets are now included in the text, so that readers will have a broad sense of when the poems were written and which poets were contemporaries — who might have read whom, and when.

Acknowledgments

I'd like to thank once more all the reviewers who helped shape the first edition by their detailed and incisive suggestions, among them Charles Altieri, University of California at Berkeley; Paul Fry, Yale University; Vincent B. Leitch, Purdue University; Jeredith Merrin, The

Ohio State University; Robert Phillips, University of Houston; Susan Schweik, University of California at Berkeley; David Sofield, Amherst College; and George Stade, Columbia University. My latest debt of gratitude is to all the teachers who used the first edition, but especially to those who took the time to fill out the publisher's survey about *Poems, Poets, Poetry:* Nell Altizer, University of Hawaii; Jennifer Atkinson, George Mason University; Jonathan M. Barron, University of Southern Mississippi; Anna Battigelli, Plattsburgh State University; Stephen Bernstein, University of Michigan at Flint; John Bremer, Moorhead State University; Joni M. Butcher, Louisiana State University; Carol H. Cantrell, Colorado State University; Mary Crow, Colorado State University; Fred Dings, Wichita State University; Alistair Duckworth, University of Florida; Jocelyn Emerson, University of Iowa; Joseph Heininger, University of Michigan at Ann Arbor; Christine Hume, University of Denver; Jeannie Sargent Judge, University of Massachusetts at Lowell; Theodore D. Mason Jr., Kenyon College; James Scannell McCormick, Marquette University; Daniel Morris, Purdue University; Joseph Musser, Ohio Wesleyan University; Patricia O'Hara, Franklin and Marshall College; "Do" Roberts, ILEAD, Dartmouth College; Karen Steele, Texas Christian University; Rebecca Steinitz, Ohio Wesleyan University; David Thoreen, Assumption College; Penelope A. Tschantz, University of Tennessee; Andrea Rohlfs Wright, Texas Christian University. I would also like to thank George Held of Queens College for his helpful corrections.

Once more I am grateful to Charles Christensen, Joan Feinberg, and Stephen Scipione at Bedford/St. Martin's for their interest in this project, for their intuition about the shape it might take, and for their alert editorial guidance. I would also like to thank Elizabeth Schaaf, Ara Salibian, Tracey Finch, Emily Goodall, Jane Zanichkowsky, and my permissions editor, the efficient Fred Courtright of the Permissions Company. I was assisted in gathering material by my graduate student Nick Halpern. Finally, I want to express my warmest gratitude to Sylvan Barnet, who first suggested I write such a book, who had faith in its completion, and who has selflessly read, as a friend, every word in both editions. His detailed comments have been invaluable, and his patient counsel, in the ups and downs of revision, was appreciated more than he will ever know, or than I can ever say.

Brief Contents

Contents

Appendices   *659*

Chronological Contents

About Poets and Poetry

Poets possess two talents: one is imagination, the other is a mastery of language. Many people, writers and nonwriters alike, see the world imaginatively: to accompany such people to a party or an exhibition or a play is to see the event more keenly and more vividly than one might have done alone. The world takes on more color; things are seen from a new slant; events are freshly interpreted and highlighted; a vivacity of response is summoned up. With one sort of imaginative person, everything is seen more darkly: the guests at the party seem trivial, grotesque; the exhibition is tragic; the play is an emblem of despair. In the company of an imaginative person of a different sort, we see the world, as the cliché has it, through rose-colored glasses: people seem better, the world kinder, the cause for optimism stronger. In short, imaginative people have the gift of making others see the world as they see it. And as the poet Wallace Stevens put it, "Things seen are things as seen."

While many imaginative people are content to let their sense of the world, conveyed through conversation, vanish as they speak, writers feel compelled to set down their perceptions in writing. Writers often see the imagination, as Stevens saw it, as a "third planet." Just as a given scene looks one way in sunlight, another way in moonlight, so it looks yet a third way in the light of the imagination. "There's a certain slant of light," says Emily Dickinson; "In this blue light, I can take you there," promises Jorie Graham in "San Sepolcro." That is the implicit invitation offered by all writers: that you will see things in a new light, the light of their construction of the world.

We read imaginative works — whether epic, fiction, drama, or poetry — in order to gain a wider sense of the real. Our hunger to know the world, born with us and eager in childhood, finds one of its chief satisfactions in learning about the responses of others. Of course we are pleased to learn that others share our views, but we are also keenly interested to find out that others see the real differently from us. This is partly a matter of temperament (say, mournful versus humorous), partly a matter of experience (male versus female, young versus old), partly an accidental matter of what happens in a writer's historical epoch (war versus peace). Some forms of literature (we can call them the social genres) such as epic, fiction, and drama, make us look at the wide panorama of a social group — a nation, a village, a family. Though all of the social genres used to be written in verse (Milton, Chaucer, Shakespeare), nowadays the social world is usually observed through prose. We know one America through the eyes of Herman Melville, another through Edith Wharton, yet another through Ralph Ellison. Each of them induces us to live for a while in the light of a fresh imagining of the United States. And in addition to an imaginative view of America, each of these writers has a mastery of language — Melville's encyclopedic and torrential language of whaling, Wharton's fastidious language of social difference, and Ellison's brooding and intense intellectual language of the "invisible man."

But besides the narrative and dramatic social genres, there exists the large body of poetry we call lyric. Lyric is the genre of private life: it is what we say to ourselves when we are alone. There may be an addressee in lyric (God, or a beloved), but the addressee is always absent. (The dramatic monologue, a form Browning made famous, has a silent addressee on stage, but this is the exception to the rule of the absent addressee.) In a way, imagination is at its most unfettered in lyric because the writer need not give a recognizable portrait of society, as the novelist or dramatist must. Because the lyric represents a moment of inner meditation, it is relatively short, and always exists in a particular place — "here" — and a particular time — "now." It may speak about the there and then, but it speaks about them from the here and now. It lets us into the innermost chamber of another person's mind, and makes us privy to what he or she would say in complete secrecy and safety, with none to overhear.

The diary is the nearest prose equivalent to the lyric, but a diary is seen by a reader as the words of another person, whereas a lyric is meant to be spoken by its reader as if the reader were the one uttering the words. A lyric poem is a script for performance by its reader. It is, then, the most intimate of genres, constructing a twinship between writer and reader. And it is the most universal of genres, because it presumes that the reader resembles the writer enough to step into the writer's shoes and speak the lines the writer has written as though they were the reader's own:

> Two roads diverged in a yellow wood,
> And sorry I could not travel both
> And be one traveler, long I stood
> And looked down one as far as I could
> To where it bent in the undergrowth.
>
> — ROBERT FROST,
> "The Road Not Taken"

To read these lines is to be transformed into the hesitating speaker. We do not listen to him; we become him.

Sometimes, of course, the speaker is more narrowly specified, as a certain type of person or even as an individual. Yet even when there is a clear disparity of personal character — as when I, a twenty-first-century white American woman, am reading Blake's lyric spoken by a little black boy in eighteenth-century England — the lyric poet expects that I will put myself into the subject-position of the little black boy, and make the boy's words my own. Though some theorists have suggested that we "overhear" the speaker of lyric (making lyric into a kind of monodrama of which we are the audience), it is more often true that I do not become a disinterested spectator overhearing the lyric speaker: rather, the words of the speaker become my own words. This imaginative transformation of self is what is offered to us by the lyric.

Because lyric is a short form (unlike the epic or the verse-tale), it must be more concise than narrative or drama. Every word has to count. So does every gap. In fact, lyric depends on gaps, and depends even more on the reader to fill in the gaps. It is suggestive rather than exhaustive. As the poet W. B. Yeats said in a 1925 letter, referring to *Hamlet* (but perhaps with his own writing of lyric in mind), "Tell a little & he is Hamlet; tell all & he is nothing. Nothing has life except the incomplete." In the following pages, suggestions are made on how to go about exploring a lyric, in order to fill in its gaps and make the most of its hints, so that the course of its emotions can be understood in their full subtlety.

Even though lyric sometimes makes greater demands on us than do the more explicit genres, a poem always (if it is successful) attracts us enough to make us willing to bear with it while we try to understand it better. A poem, said Coleridge, can communicate while it is still imperfectly understood. It can communicate because it exhibits a mastery of language, in addition to an imaginative sense of the world. We are drawn in by words used in unusual and compelling ways — ways that appeal to the senses of sight and hearing and bodily tension, as well as to the mind. We are also drawn in by the architecture of the poem — the manner in which its parts are arranged, so as to make a structure that reflects emotional intensity. We are drawn in by its volatility and its surprising resources of strategy. And finally, we are drawn in because every poem enters into a continuing conversation with its culture — querying it, amplifying it, rebelling against it, subverting it, aestheticizing it, enhancing it. Robert Frost, in "The Gift Outright," says that when the English came to the American continent, they found a land "still unstoried, artless, unenhanced." Our present anthropological awareness means that no twenty-first-century poet could think of the America of the Puritans as "unstoried" or "artless": the various and widespread Native American cultures had already covered the American continent with stories and with arts. The aim of every artist, then and now, is to contribute those stories, that art, and enhancement that will endow both place and time with significance.

Lyric has recently undergone, in the United States, many significant changes. Twenty-first-century America is a far more heterogeneous country than pre–twenty-first-century England, and contemporary American lyric naturally reflects its own culture and epoch. The availability of translations means that an American poet is now almost as likely to be influenced by a Polish or South American poet — Czeslaw Milosz or Pablo Neruda — as by an English or American poet. Lyric speakers are more ready to define themselves sexually, ethnically, or racially; yet lyric still hopes for the reader's willingness to place himself or herself in the writer's subject-position. Because the dominant influence on a medium is always the medium itself as it has existed through time, the dominant influence on English-language verse is still English as it has been used by preceding poets. That is why one is unlikely to read contemporary poetry well without having read the poetry of the England from which it descends. The selections here are all in English (lyric poetry being notoriously untranslatable) and are divided between poems that have stood up well over time and other, more recent poems which, while they may reflect some long-continuing concerns in American life (racism, war, religious faith), also take on new modes in both content (Adrienne Rich's feminism, W. S. Merwin's ecological concern) and style (the reticence of Elizabeth Bishop, the dream-idiom of John Berryman, the "snapshots" of Robert Lowell).

Like all arts, lyric is meant to give pleasure — imaginative, linguistic, intellectual, and moral. If one hasn't enjoyed a poem and been moved by it, one hasn't really experienced it as an artwork. There are moments in life when one poem suits and another doesn't. The poems in this book will not invariably please everybody, because each of us brings a unique life-experience, and a different expectation of art, to the page. Nonetheless, many of these poems have won and kept readers because in them readers have found the most moving revelation of all — that of their own inner life, enacted in words adequate to both sorrow and joy. The rule of thumb for the encounter with any art is to dwell on what moves you or gives you pleasure, and skip over, for the time being, what leaves you cold. But if you remember that someone, somewhere, has been fiercely attracted by each of these poems, you may be willing to give the ones you first neglect a second chance. Often, a door that has been shut can open marvelously at the second knock.

POEMS, POETS, POETRY

*An Introduction
and Anthology*

I

AN INTRODUCTION
TO POETRY

1

The Poem as Life

Poems have their origins in life, especially in the formal or informal ceremonies that occur at crucial moments or phases in a single private life — birth, adolescence, marriage, death — or at public moments when we collectively commemorate a war, a religious feast, a holiday. Equally, poems show life lived in a spatial environment, whether immediate (one's house, one's region) or cosmic (the world, the galaxy); they also show seasonal or ritual moments of time. The first questions to ask of any poem are *What piece of life, private or public, is it concerned with?* and *Where and when is this life being lived?*

Of course, cliché haunts all the well-known and well-worn occasions of life. In the occasions of private life shown us by greeting cards or popular magazines, babies are "lovable," brides are "beautiful," fiftieth wedding anniversaries are "happy"; in the public life, cliché tells us that young men should fight in war, that cities are thriving communities, and that Americans should take pride in their country's history. We are also accustomed to clichés of time and space, often hearing, for example, that the springtime of life leads only to the narrow space of the grave. As we trace some of these central aspects of life through poems, the first thing to notice is how the poet manages to avoid cliché — how he or she brings originality to the moment. We look in this chapter at a sample of several poems, the first group representing events in private life, the second group chiefly taking up moments in public life, and the third group expressing some place in space or some moment in the natural seasons of time. In Chapter 2 we will look again at the same poems, to see how they are not only representations of life but also works of art.

The Private Life

"Write a poem about a birth," says the culture to the poet; and what the poet writes (speaking in the person of a newborn baby) may shock the reader:

WILLIAM BLAKE (1757 – 1827)
Infant Sorrow

My mother groaned, my father wept —
Into the dangerous world I leapt,
Helpless, naked, piping loud,
Like a fiend hid in a cloud.

Struggling in my father's hands,
Striving against my swaddling bands,
Bound and weary, I thought best
To sulk upon my mother's breast.

Precisely because our culture does not usually say that a baby resembles "a fiend hid in a cloud," we find the poem arresting. It makes us stop and think. Now let us look at the next phase of life, childhood.

The child's first day of school is an event marked by conventional behavior (new clothes, an apple for the teacher, says the cliché). Louise Glück has written a poem about how a mother feels seeing her child go off into the power of a new authority, who may or may not be kind to the child:

LOUISE GLÜCK (b. 1943)
The School Children

The children go forward with their little satchels.
And all morning the mothers have labored
to gather the late apples, red and gold,
like words of another language.

And on the other shore
are those who wait behind great desks
to receive these offerings.

How orderly they are — the nails
on which the children hang
their overcoats of blue or yellow wool.

And the teachers shall instruct them in silence
and the mothers shall scour the orchards for a way out,
drawing to themselves the gray limbs of the fruit trees
bearing so little ammunition.

The new clothes and the apples for the teacher are here, but they have been made strangely sinister. Once again, the reader is made to stop and think. What is so disturbing about this poem?

Next, the child comes to the apparently quiet period between infancy and puberty, a period psychologists call "latency" because sexuality seems dormant. At this time, intense same-sex friendships form; the child is never seen without his or her "best friend," so much so that Eddie and Bill become a single noun: "Have you seen EddieandBill?" But gradually hormones change Eddie and Bill into adolescents, and the pagan god of sex (whom E. E. Cummings here identifies with goat-footed Pan, the god of all) makes his appearance. We know that in heterosexual development the twosomes "eddieandbill" and "bettyandisbel," so inseparable, will soon, with real anguish and yet with painful anticipation of sexual joy, split up, leave their childish games, and re-form into the new twosomes "eddieandbetty" and "billandisbel":

E. E. CUMMINGS (1894 – 1962)
in Just-

in Just-
spring   when the world is mud-
luscious the little
lame balloonman

whistles   far   and wee

and eddieandbill come
running from marbles and
piracies and it's
spring

when the world is puddle-wonderful

the queer
old balloonman whistles
far   and   wee
and bettyandisbel come dancing

from hop-scotch and jump-rope and

it's
spring
and
   the

       goat-footed

balloonMan   whistles
far
and
wee

The reader senses something threatening and seductive in the balloon-man, and knows that this is not merely a simple poem about spring hop-scotch and jump-rope. Also, the typographic arrangement is puzzling. What is Cummings up to?

The young man or woman will experiment with love, and will discover that there is something inherent in many relationships which makes them dissolve. As adolescents take their first step into adult emotional relations, they learn what it is to be troubled in love, even forsaken. This is a love poem by Walt Whitman to a male lover who has deserted him, but it soon turns into a poem for everyone who has been deserted:

WALT WHITMAN (1819 – 1892)
Hours Continuing Long

Hours continuing long, sore and heavy hearted,
Hours of the dusk, when I withdraw to a lonesome and
      unfrequented spot, seating myself, leaning my face in my
      hands;
Hours sleepless, deep in the night, when I go forth, speeding
      swiftly the country roads, or through the city streets, or
      pacing miles and miles, stifling plaintive cries;
Hours discouraged, distracted — for the one I cannot content
      myself without, soon I saw him content himself without me;
Hours when I am forgotten (O weeks and months are passing, but
      I believe I am never to forget!)
Sullen and suffering hours! (I am ashamed — but it is useless — I
      am what I am);
Hours of my torment — I wonder if other men ever have the
      like, out of the like feelings?

Is there even one other like me — distracted — his friend, his
    lover, lost to him?
Is he too as I am now? Does he still rise in the morning, dejected,
    thinking who is lost to him? and at night, awaking, think
    who is lost?
Does he too harbor his friendship silent and endless? harbor his
    anguish and passion?
Does some stray reminder, or the casual mention of a name, bring
    the fit back upon him, taciturn and deprest?
Does he see himself reflected in me? In these hours, does he see
    the face of his hours reflected?

The phases of life succeed one another, and we could go on to give
examples of poems about parenting, maturity, loss, and old age. Poems,
in short, trace the general and special phases of life down to its end in
death, and, in religious poems, even to the afterlife. Each of these phases
can provoke many different responses — joy, bitterness, bravery, sto-
icism. Here, for instance, is a twentieth-century poem about the last
phase of autumnal life by a writer who, to his grief, sees that all his
youthful hopes and imaginings have become old, dilapidated, and sul-
lied. Yet, he feels, he would have missed something had he not had to
encounter this final bleakness and to muster the effort of will that it calls
from him — to find a new fortitude, a new self-knowledge.

WALLACE STEVENS (1879 – 1955)
The Plain Sense of Things

After the leaves have fallen, we return
To a plain sense of things. It is as if
We had come to an end of the imagination,
Inanimate in an inert savoir.

It is difficult even to choose the adjective
For this blank cold, this sadness without cause.
The great structure has become a minor house.
No turban walks across the lessened floors.

The greenhouse never so badly needed paint.
The chimney is fifty years old and slants to one side.
A fantastic effort has failed, a repetition
In a repetitiousness of men and flies.

Yet the absence of the imagination had
Itself to be imagined. The great pond,

The plain sense of it, without reflections, leaves,
Mud, water like dirty glass, expressing silence

Of a sort, silence of a rat come out to see,
The great pond and its waste of the lilies, all this
Had to be imagined as an inevitable knowledge,
Required, as a necessity requires.

This poem of a late phase of life shows the poet feeling cold, sad, inert — and yet rising to the challenge of seeing this phase truly, as a necessary part of experience. Although many of the feelings of loss that Stevens expresses are conventional in descriptions of old age, he succeeds in making them fresh.

These poems of the private life are all meant to be said by anyone, by everyone. We will come later, in a chapter about place and history, to poems that are more personally specific than these — poems that could be said only by a person belonging to a particular subgroup in society.

The Public Life

Some public poems commemorate communal celebration — Thanksgiving or the Fourth of July or Christmas. (What can a poet do to write a new kind of Christmas poem? Well, he can stage his poem a day early and write "The Night before Christmas," as Clement Moore did.) Public poems often concern crucial single public events. Here is a poem joining two events in the history of American blacks — the blowing-up of an Alabama church in which four young black girls were killed and an imagined episode in the slave trade at the time of the American Revolution (the phrase "middle passage," in line 4, refers to the route that slave ships once took from Africa to the South):

MICHAEL S. HARPER (b. 1938)
American History

For John Callahan
Those four black girls blown up
in that Alabama church
remind me of five hundred
middle passage blacks,
in a net, under water
in Charleston harbor
so *redcoats* wouldn't find them.

Can't find what you can't see
can you?

"History" rarely ends with a question mark, but Harper's cynical question replicates the cynicism of the slave dealers.

Other public poems are written about the state of common life, shared by some population in a certain time and place. We might tend to think of such poems as written about violent wrongs such as genocide or slavery, but Charles Simic's "Old Couple" is about the plight of a hidden group of victims — the urban poor in old age, for whom all possible scenarios — eviction, murder, illness, death from malnutrition — are equally frightening:

CHARLES SIMIC (b. 1938)
Old Couple

They're waiting to be murdered,
Or evicted. Soon
They expect to have nothing to eat.
As far as I know, they never go out.

A vicious pain's coming, they think.
It will start in the head
And spread down to the bowels.
They'll be carried off on stretchers, howling.

In the meantime, they watch the street
From their fifth floor window.
It has rained, and now it looks
Like it's going to snow a little.

I see him get up to lower the shades.
If their window stays dark,
I know that his hand has reached hers
Just as she was about to turn on the lights.

Who is the watcher here? Does he share the life of the old couple, and if so, how?

Of course, the private life and the public life are not separate issues, and there are many poems in which the two are mirror images of each other. In Robert Lowell's "Skunk Hour," the decline of the inhabitants of the Maine town where the speaker lives mirrors his own decline into voyeurism and madness. Besides the public life and the private life, "Skunk Hour" invokes the life of nature, which has a sturdy strength (pictured in the dauntless invading "mother skunk and her column of kittens") lacking in the public and private spheres:

ROBERT LOWELL (1917 – 1977)
Skunk Hour

For Elizabeth Bishop

Nautilus Island's hermit
heiress still lives through winter in her Spartan cottage;
her sheep still graze above the sea.
Her son's a bishop. Her farmer
is first selectman in our village;
she's in her dotage.

Thirsting for
the hierarchic privacy
of Queen Victoria's century,
she buys up all
the eyesores facing her shore,
and lets them fall.

The season's ill —
we've lost our summer millionaire,
who seemed to leap from an L. L. Bean
catalogue. His nine-knot yawl
was auctioned off to lobstermen.
A red fox stain covers Blue Hill.

And now our fairy
decorator brightens his shop for fall;
his fishnet's filled with orange cork,
orange, his cobbler's bench and awl;
there is no money in his work,
he'd rather marry.

One dark night,
my Tudor Ford climbed the hill's skull;
I watched for love-cars. Lights turned down,
they lay together, hull to hull,
where the graveyard shelves on the town. . . .
My mind's not right.

A car radio bleats,
"Love, O careless Love. . . ." I hear

my ill-spirit sob in each blood cell,
as if my hand were at its throat. . . .
I myself am hell;
nobody's here —

only skunks, that search
in the moonlight for a bite to eat.
They march on their soles up Main Street:
white stripes, moonstruck eyes' red fire
under the chalk-dry and spar spire
of the Trinitarian Church.

I stand on top
of our back steps and breathe the rich air —
a mother skunk with her column of kittens swills the garbage pail.
She jabs her wedge-head in a cup
of sour cream, drops her ostrich tail,
and will not scare.

What relations are implied here between the town's public life and the speaker's private life, between his private life and the life of nature?

Nature and Time

The poem-as-life notices, besides the inevitable themes of public and private life, two other great intertwined subjects — nature (the earth, the sun, the moon, the stars, animals, plants) and time, with its seasons and months. Because nature and time are such ancient resources for poetry, perhaps the hardest achievement is to write an original poem about, say, spring. An anonymous thirteenth-century poet began our spring poetry as he heard the cuckoo (the herald of spring) and saw all of nature come to life. At that time, there was only one word, "sumer," for the new season after winter; the word "spring" was a later invention.

ANONYMOUS
The Cuckoo Song

Sumer is icumen in,
 Lhude° sing, cuccu!   *loud*
Groweth sed and bloweth med°   *meadow*
  And springth the wude nu.
   Sing, cuccu!

Awe° bleteth after lomb,   *ewe*
    Lhouth° after calve cu,°   *loweth / cow*
Bulluc sterteth,° bucke verteth° —   *leaps / breaks wind*
        Murie sing, cuccu!
            Cuccu, cuccu.
        Wel singes thu, cuccu.
        Ne swik° thu never nu!   *stop*

The spring songs of the Middle Ages generated a whole series of seasonal poems.

A contemporary poet, Dave Smith, writes his spring poem in an auto junkyard, using a pun on the word "spring" to make new sap rise even in rusty steel:

DAVE SMITH (b. 1942)
The Spring Poem

> *Every poet should write a Spring poem.*
> — LOUISE GLÜCK

Yes, but we must be sure of verities
such as proper heat and adequate form.
That's what poets are for, is my theory.
This then is a Spring poem. A car warms
its rusting hulk in a meadow; weeds slog
up its flanks in martial weather. April
or late March is our month. There is a fog
of spunky mildew and sweaty tufts spill
from the damp rump of a back seat. A spring
thrusts one gleaming tip out, a brilliant tooth
uncoiling from Winter's tension, a ring
of insects along, working out the Truth.
Each year this car, melting around that spring,
hears nails trench from boards and every squeak sing.

We feel that the rusting car warms into new life partly because it has been used by courting couples who have lent their presence to the phrases Smith uses for the back seat — its "damp rump," its "spunky mildew and sweaty tufts." When even a metal spring puts out new shoots, when even nails spring free from the boards they have been hammered into, we know that spring is irresistible.

The seasons have become a constant resource for poets describing stages of human life, so that in reading poems as life we can't fail to think of Keats's sonnet on the human seasons, which sets out the great analogy between nature and ourselves:

JOHN KEATS (1795 – 1821)
The Human Seasons

Four seasons fill the measure of the year;
    Four seasons are there in the mind of man.
He hath his lusty spring, when fancy clear
    Takes in all beauty with an easy span:
He hath his summer, when luxuriously
    He chews the honied cud of fair spring thoughts,
Till, in his soul dissolv'd, they come to be
    Part of himself. He hath his autumn ports
And havens of repose, when his tired wings
    Are folded up, and he content to look
On mists in idleness: to let fair things
    Pass by unheeded as a threshold brook.
He hath his winter too of pale misfeature,
Or else he would forget his mortal nature.

A poet can choose any one of the "human seasons" and find its counterpart in the natural world.

When poets describe Time, they tend to employ many of the images of passing time that have entered cultural memory — such motifs as the waves of the sea, the progress of the sun from dawn to dusk, the fall of great men, the tragedy of early death, Time the Grim Reaper, and so on. Here, using such time-honored resources, is Shakespeare on Time. In his first model of how we imagine Time (lines 1–4), the moments of our life are seen as waves of the sea, all alike; in his second model (lines 5–8), the moments of our life are like the dramatic rise and eclipse of a sun, or the rise and fall of a tragic hero; and in his third model (lines 9–12), we scarcely have time to live before Death scythes us down.

WILLIAM SHAKESPEARE (1564 – 1616)
Sonnet 60

Like as the waves make toward the pebbled shore,
So do our minutes hasten to their end,
Each changing place with that which goes before,
In sequent° toil all forwards do contend.   *repetitive*
Nativity,° once in the main° of light,   *birth / sea*

Crawls to maturity, wherewith being crowned,
Crooked eclipses 'gainst his glory fight,
And Time that gave doth now his gift confound.
Time doth transfix the flourish° set on youth,   *beauty*
And delves the parallels° in beauty's brow,   *furrows*
Feeds on the rarities of nature's truth,
And nothing stands but for his scythe to mow.
And yet to times in hope my verse shall stand,
Praising thy worth, despite his cruel hand.

What does Shakespeare set against Time in the final couplet?

In Brief: The Poem as Life

The first thing to notice about *any* poem is what piece of life (a disappointment in love, the death of a parent, an absence from a friend, a crisis of personal confidence, a moment of fear) the poem is about. Lyric poems spring from moments of disequilibrium: something has happened to disturb the status quo. Hope has come to rebuke despair; love has come to thaw coldness; envy has come to upset happiness; shame has come to interfere with self-esteem. If you can't find the piece of life that the poem is about, read the poem again, speaking it aloud in your own voice. It helps to ask, "Under what circumstances would I find myself saying these words?" The poem is *written for you to say.* You are the speaker of every lyric poem you read. That is what a lyric poem is: it is a speech made for you to utter. (We will come later to poems spoken to a silent listener by a defined character — not you, but for instance a madman or a Renaissance duke — poems that we call dramatic monologues.)

Once you have made a plausible hypothesis about what piece of life the poem is about, you can go on to see how the poem, though *about* life, is *not* life. This is the subject of our next chapter, which returns to these poems.

Reading Other Poems

Think about the following poems as utterances coming out of a particular life situation. Try to make deductions from each one.

- ◆ What has recently happened to the speaker?
- ◆ What aspect of his or her life has the speaker been thinking about? Is this a private life situation (a family death, for instance) or a public situation (a religious massacre, a war memorial)?

- What stage of life has the speaker reached?
- How much does the speaker tell you about his or her feelings?

You might ask, too, whether these are the feelings and the remarks you might expect to find expressed in this situation (comparing them with what people might normally say or feel).

- How do Sir Thomas Wyatt's feelings change as he reacts to having been jilted?
- Do John Milton's remarks about revenge surprise you?
- What feelings arise in Ben Jonson when his beloved first son dies?
- What does John Keats most regret when he thinks he will die while he is still young (as he did)?
- Why do you suppose Emily Dickinson represented herself as a boy in the poem about coming across a snake? Can you describe the feeling at the close of Dickinson's poem in different words?
- Are Dylan Thomas's words the usual ones addressed by a son to a dying father?

"Theme for English B" and "Those Winter Sundays" are by black writers: one takes up the tension between a black student and his white teacher in a freshman English class; the other doesn't mention race at all.

- When do you think a life situation might lead to the mention of race, and when not?
- Jonson's poem expresses the feelings of a father for his son; can you compare it to Robert Hayden's poem expressing the feelings of a son for his father?
- How do these compare with the feelings expressed by Sylvia Plath when she thinks about her relation to her father? And with Rita Dove's recollection of her childhood evenings with her father in "Flash Cards"?

Both Milton and Yusef Komunyakaa look at large social issues: in Milton's case, the massacre of a large number of Protestant "heretics" by Catholic forces in northern Italy; in Komunyakaa's case, the residue of the Vietnam War as represented by the Vietnam War Memorial in Washington.

- In what way do the tones adopted by these two poets differ?
- How do you think a poet decides how "loudly" to speak when he or she speaks of public issues?

Literature can be sharply critical of the life it represents. In *Home-coming*, Julia Alvarez describes attending, as a seventeen-year-old college student, a South American wedding reception where the bride is Alvarez's cousin and the groom a man from Minnesota. What aspects of the reception does the poet emphasize as she presents the life led by her relatives? Can you isolate the main faults, as she sees them, of the society she now analyzes, much later, with the eyes of an outsider?

SIR THOMAS WYATT (1503 – 1542)
They Flee from Me

They flee from me, that sometime did me seek,
With naked foot stalking in my chamber.
I have seen them, gentle, tame, and meek,
That now are wild, and do not remember
That sometime they put themselves in danger
To take bread at my hand; and now they range,
Busily seeking with a continual change.

Thankèd be Fortune it hath been otherwise,
Twenty times better; but once in special,
In thin array, after a pleasant guise,
When her loose gown from her shoulders did fall,
And she me caught in her arms long and small,°   *slender*
Therewithal sweetly did me kiss
And softly said, "Dear heart, how like you this?"

It was no dream, I lay broad waking.
But all is turned, thorough my gentleness,
Into a strange fashion of forsaking;
And I have leave to go, of her goodness,
And she also to use newfangleness.
But since that I so kindely am servèd,
I fain would know what she hath deservèd.

BEN JONSON (1573 – 1637)
On My First Son

Farewell, thou child of my right hand,[1] and joy;
My sin was too much hope of thee, loved boy:

---

[1]A literal translation of the Hebrew "Benjamin," the boy's name. Jonson's son was born in 1596 and died of the plague in 1603.

Seven years thou wert lent to me, and I thee pay,
Exacted by thy fate, on the just day.
O could I lose all father now! for why
Will man lament the state he should envy,
To have so soon 'scaped world's and flesh's rage,
And, if no other misery, yet age?
Rest in soft peace, and asked, say, "Here doth lie
Ben Jonson his best piece of poetry."
For whose sake henceforth all his vows be such
As what he loves may never like too much.

JOHN MILTON (1608 – 1674)
On the Late Massacre in Piedmont[1]

Avenge, O Lord, thy slaughtered saints, whose bones
    Lie scattered on the Alpine mountains cold,
    Even them who kept thy truth so pure of old
    When all our fathers worshiped stocks° and stones,   *idols*
Forget not: in thy book record their groans
    Who were thy sheep and in their ancient fold
    Slain by the bloody Piemontese that rolled
    Mother with infant down the rocks. Their moans
The vales redoubled to the hills, and they
    To Heaven. Their martyred blood and ashes sow
    O'er all th' Italian fields where still doth sway
The triple tyrant,[2] that from these may grow
    A hundredfold, who having learnt thy way
    Early may fly the Babylonian woe.[3]

JOHN KEATS (1795 – 1821)
When I Have Fears

When I have fears that I may cease to be
    Before my pen has gleaned my teeming brain,

---

[1] The Vaudois, or Waldenses, a Protestant people living in the northwestern part of Italy, were subjected in 1655 to a bloody persecution because they refused to accept Catholicism.

[2] The pope, as claiming authority on earth and in heaven and hell.

[3] Protestants frequently identified the Roman Catholic church with Babylon.

Before high-pilèd books, in charact'ry,°   *written letters*
     Hold like rich garners the full-ripened grain;
When I behold, upon the night's starred face,
     Huge cloudy symbols of a high romance,
And think that I may never live to trace
     Their shadows, with the magic hand of chance;
And when I feel, fair creature of an hour,
     That I shall never look upon thee more,
Never have relish in the faery power
     Of unreflecting love! — then on the shore
Of the wide world I stand alone, and think
Till Love and Fame to nothingness do sink.

EMILY DICKINSON (1830 – 1886)
A narrow Fellow in the Grass

A narrow Fellow in the Grass
Occasionally rides —
You may have met Him — did you not
His notice sudden is —

The Grass divides as with a Comb —
A spotted shaft is seen —
And then it closes at your feet
And opens further on —

He likes a Boggy Acre
A Floor too cool for Corn —
Yet when a Boy, and Barefoot —
I more than once at Noon

Have passed, I thought, a Whip lash
Unbraiding in the Sun
When stooping to secure it
It wrinkled, and was gone —

Several of Nature's People
I know, and they know me —
I feel for them a transport
Of cordiality —

But never met this Fellow
Attended, or alone
Without a tighter breathing
And Zero at the Bone —

LANGSTON HUGHES (1902 – 1967)

Theme for English B

The instructor said,

> *Go home and write*
> *a page tonight.*
> *And let that page come out of you —*
> *Then, it will be true.*

I wonder if it's that simple?
I am twenty-two, colored, born in Winston-Salem.
I went to school there, then Durham, then here
to this college on the hill above Harlem.
I am the only colored student in my class.
The steps from the hill lead down into Harlem,
through a park, then I cross St. Nicholas,
Eighth Avenue, Seventh, and I come to the Y,
the Harlem Branch Y, where I take the elevator
up to my room, sit down, and write this page:

It's not easy to know what is true for you or me
at twenty-two, my age. But I guess I'm what
I feel and see and hear, Harlem, I hear you:
hear you, hear me — we two — you, me, talk on this page.
(I hear New York, too.) Me — who?
Well, I like to eat, sleep, drink, and be in love.
I like to work, read, learn, and understand life.
I like a pipe for a Christmas present,
or records — Bessie,[1] bop, or Bach.
I guess being colored doesn't make me *not* like
the same things other folks like who are other races.
So will my page be colored that I write?
Being me, it will not be white.
But it will be
a part of you, instructor.
You are white —
yet a part of me, as I am a part of you.
That's American.
Sometimes perhaps you don't want to be a part of me.
Nor do I often want to be a part of you.

---

[1]Bessie Smith (1898?–1937), African American blues singer.

But we are, that's true!
As I learn from you,
I guess you learn from me —
although you're older — and white —
and somewhat more free.

This is my page for English B.

ROBERT HAYDEN (1913 – 1980)
Those Winter Sundays

Sundays too my father got up early
and put his clothes on in the blueblack cold,
then with cracked hands that ached
from labor in the weekday weather made
banked fires blaze. No one ever thanked him.

Slight Anger reminiscence

I'd wake and hear the cold splintering, breaking.
When the rooms were warm, he'd call,
and slowly I would rise and dress,
fearing the chronic angers of that house,

Safety associated w/ father

Speaking indifferently to him,
who had driven out the cold
and polished my good shoes as well.
What did I know, what did I know
of love's austere and lonely offices?

guilt

DYLAN THOMAS (1914 – 1953)
Do Not Go Gentle into That Good Night

Do not go gentle into that good night,
Old age should burn and rave at close of day;
Rage, rage against the dying of the light.

Though wise men at their end know dark is right,
Because their words had forked no lightning they
Do not go gentle into that good night.

Good men, the last wave by, crying how bright
Their frail deeds might have danced in a green bay,
Rage, rage against the dying of the light.

Wild men who caught and sang the sun in flight,
And learn, too late, they grieved it on its way,
Do not go gentle into that good night.

Grave men, near death, who see with blinding sight
Blind eyes could blaze like meteors and be gay,
Rage, rage against the dying of the light.

And you, my father, there on the sad height,
Curse, bless, me now with your fierce tears, I pray.
Do not go gentle into that good night.
Rage, rage against the dying of the light.

SYLVIA PLATH (1932 – 1963)
Daddy

You do not do, you do not do
Any more, black shoe
In which I have lived like a foot
For thirty years, poor and white,
Barely daring to breathe or Achoo.   5

Daddy, I have had to kill you.
You died before I had time —
Marble-heavy, a bag full of God,
Ghastly statue with one gray toe[1]
Big as a Frisco seal   10

And a head in the freakish Atlantic
Where it pours bean green over blue
In the waters off beautiful Nauset.
I used to pray to recover you.
Ach, du.[2]   15

In the German tongue, in the Polish town
Scraped flat by the roller
Of wars, wars, wars.
But the name of the town is common.
My Polack[3] friend   20

Says there are a dozen or two.
So I never could tell where you
Put your foot, your root,

---

[1]Otto Plath's diabetes caused a gangrenous toe, which led to the septicemia that killed him.

[2]German: "Ah, you." The second-person familiar form (*du*) is used for intimates.

[3]Derogatory slang for "Polish."

I never could talk to you.
The tongue stuck in my jaw.   25

It stuck in a barb wire snare.
Ich, ich, ich, ich,[4]
I could hardly speak.
I thought every German was you.
And the language obscene   30

An engine, an engine
Chuffing me off like a Jew.
A Jew to Dachau, Auschwitz, Belsen.[5]
I began to talk like a Jew.
I think I may well be a Jew.   35

The snows of the Tyrol,[6] the clear beer of Vienna[7]
Are not very pure or true.
With my gypsy ancestress and my weird luck
And my Taroc pack and my Taroc pack[8]
I may be a bit of a Jew.   40

I have always been scared of *you,*
With your Luftwaffe,[9] your gobbledygoo.
And your neat moustache
And your Aryan[10] eye, bright blue.
Panzer-man, panzer-man,[11] O You —   45

Not God but a swastika[12]
So black no sky could squeak through.
Every woman adores a Fascist,
The boot in the face, the brute
Brute heart of a brute like you.   50

---

[4]German: "I, I, I, I."

[5]Nazi concentration camps.

[6]Alpine region of Austria.

[7]Capital of Austria. Plath's mother was of Austrian descent; Austria was annexed by the Nazis.

[8]Pack of cards used in fortune telling.

[9]The Nazi air force.

[10]Word used by Nazis to characterize those of "pure" or unadulterated German stock.

[11]Man resembling a German armored tank.

[12]Symbol of the Nazi party.

You stand at the blackboard, daddy,[13]
In the picture I have of you,
A cleft in your chin instead of your foot
But no less a devil for that, no not
Any less the black man who   55

Bit my pretty red heart in two.
I was ten when they buried you.
At twenty I tried to die
And get back, back, back to you.
I thought even the bones would do.   60

But they pulled me out of the sack,
And they stuck me together with glue.
And then I knew what to do.
I made a model of you,
A man in black with a Meinkampf[14] look   65

And a love of the rack and the screw.[15]
And I said I do, I do.
So daddy, I'm finally through.
The black telephone's off at the root,
The voices just can't worm through.   70

If I've killed one man, I've killed two —
The vampire who said he was you
And drank my blood for a year,
Seven years, if you want to know.
Daddy, you can lie back now.   75

There's a stake in your fat black heart[16]
And the villagers never liked you.
They are dancing and stamping on you.
They always *knew* it was you.
Daddy, daddy, you bastard, I'm through.   80

---

[13]Otto Plath was a professor of entomology at Boston University.

[14]German: "My struggle," the title of Hitler's manifesto.

[15]Rack, screw: instruments of torture.

[16]Traditionally, a vampire was buried at a crossroads with a stake through his heart.

RITA DOVE (b. 1952)
Flash Cards

In math I was the whiz kid, keeper
of oranges and apples. *What you don't understand,*
master, my father said; the faster
I answered, the faster they came.

I could see one bud on the teacher's geranium,
one clear bee sputtering at the wet pane.
The tulip trees always dragged after heavy rain
so I tucked my head as my boots slapped home.

My father put up his feet after work
and relaxed with a highball and *The Life of Lincoln.*
After supper we drilled and I climbed the dark

before sleep, before a thin voice hissed
numbers as I spun on a wheel. I had to guess.
Ten, I kept saying, *I'm only ten.*

YUSEF KOMUNYAKAA (b. 1947)
Facing It

My black face fades,
hiding inside the black granite.
I said I wouldn't,
dammit: No tears.
I'm stone. I'm flesh.
My clouded reflection eyes me
like a bird of prey, the profile of night
slanted against morning. I turn
this way — the stone lets me go.
I turn that way — I'm inside
the Vietnam Veterans Memorial
again, depending on the light
to make a difference.
I go down the 58,022 names,
half-expecting to find
my own in letters like smoke.
I touch the name Andrew Johnson;
I see the booby trap's white flash.
Names shimmer on a woman's blouse
but when she walks away

the names stay on the wall.
Brushstrokes flash, a red bird's
wings cutting across my stare.
The sky. A plane in the sky.
A white vet's image floats
closer to me, then his pale eyes
look through mine. I'm a window.
He's lost his right arm
inside the stone. In the black mirror
a woman's trying to erase names:
No, she's brushing a boy's hair.

Julia Alvarez (b. 1950)

Homecoming

When my cousin Carmen married, the guards
at her father's *finca*° took the guests' bracelets   *ranch*
and wedding rings and put them in an armored truck
for safekeeping while wealthy, dark-skinned men,
their plump, white women and spoiled children   5
bathed in a river whose bottom had been cleaned
for the occasion. She was Tío's° only daughter;   *Uncle's*
and he wanted to show her husband's family,
a bewildered group of sunburnt Minnesotans,
that she was valued. He sat me at their table   10
to show off my English, and when he danced with me,
fondling my shoulder blades beneath my bridesmaid's gown
as if they were breasts, he found me skinny
but pretty at seventeen, and clever.
Come back from that cold place, Vermont, he said,   15
all this is yours! Over his shoulder
a dozen workmen hauled in blocks of ice
to keep the champagne lukewarm and stole
glances at the wedding cake, a dollhouse duplicate
of the family rancho, the shutters marzipan,   20
the cobbles almonds. A maiden aunt housekept,
touching up whipped cream roses with a syringe
of eggwhites, rescuing the groom when the heat
melted his chocolate shoes into the frosting.
On too much rum Tío led me across the dance floor,   25
dusted with talcum for easy gliding, a smell

of babies underfoot. He twirled me often,
excited by my pleas of dizziness, teasing me
that my merengue° had lost its Caribbean.   *a dance*
Above us, Chinese lanterns strung between posts   30
came on and one snapped off and rose
into a purple postcard sky.
A grandmother cried: *The children all grow up too fast.*
The Minnesotans finally broke loose and danced a Charleston
and were pronounced good gringos° with latino hearts.   *non-*
The little sister, freckled with a week of beach,   *Hispanics*
her hair as blonde as movie stars', was asked
by maids if they could touch her hair or skin,
and she backed off, until it was explained to her,
they meant no harm. *This is all yours,*   40
Tío whispered, pressing himself into my dress.
The workmen costumed in their workclothes danced
a workman's jig. The maids went by with trays
of wedding bells and matchbooks monogrammed
with Dick's and Carmen's names. It would be years   45
before I took the courses that would change my mind
in schools paid for by sugar from the fields around us,
years before I could begin to comprehend
how one does not see the maids when they pass by
with trays of deviled eggs arranged in daisy wheels.   50
— It was too late, or early, to be wise —
The sun was coming up beyond the amber waves
of cane, the roosters crowed, the band struck up
Las Mañanitas, a morning serenade. I had a vision
that I blamed on the champagne: 55
the fields around us were burning. At last
a yawning bride and groom got up and cut
the wedding cake, but everyone was full
of drink and eggs, roast pig, and rice and beans.
Except the maids and workmen,   60
sitting on stoops behind the sugar house,
ate with their fingers from their open palms
windows, shutters, walls, pillars, doors,
made from the cane they had cut in the fields.

2

The Poem as Arranged Life

The preceding chapter, "The Poem as Life," suggested that poems originate in crucial moments of private life (for instance, marriage) or public life (for instance, a revolutionary era), and that they are set in recognizable places (in a junkyard, for example) or times (in spring). But to speak of the poem "as life" is not to say that it is simply a transcription of what has occurred. Life itself is a continuation of successive moments in one stream. Art interrupts the stream and constructs one segment or level of the stream for processing. In a single act, it describes, analyzes, and confers form on that segment. The form it confers by its ways of organizing the poem makes visible the contour of that life-moment as the poet perceives it. The poet discovers the emotional import of that life-moment by subjecting it to analysis; the analysis then determines how the moment is described, and the invented organizational form that replicates it. These are remarks that will become clear when we look at particular poems, so let us go back to our poems-as-life to see how they are *arranged* life — that is, in what way they are formal constructions of life. What organizational patterns have the poets chosen?

The Private Life

Blake's baby, first of all. For Blake, every moment in life could be seen in either of two ways — innocently or with experience. The innocent way of seeing a baby is what we might call both a cliché and a truth: a baby *is* beautiful, guileless, smiling, appealing, the joy of its mother's days. In an earlier poem, "Infant Joy," Blake shows us what the innocent mother, in her fantasy, would like the baby to say to her as he tells her how to name him (stanza 1), and what she would then say to him (stanza 2):

WILLIAM BLAKE (1757 – 1827)
Infant Joy

"I have no name,
I am but two days old."
"What shall I call thee?"
"I happy am,
Joy is my name."
"Sweet joy befall thee!"

"Pretty joy!
Sweet joy but two days old,
Sweet joy I call thee;
Thou dost smile,
I sing the while —
Sweet joy befall thee!"

But a baby is also the bundle of tension that will generate its future sorrows, as Blake asserts in "Infant Sorrow," the companion-poem to "Infant Joy." If you think back, he suggests, to how awful it was to be a baby when you were one, then you will see infancy from the point of view of "experience" rather than the maternal doting "innocence." You will remember how dangerous the world seemed to you when you were small, how helpless you felt, how little power you had over your environment and your belongings, how often you cried in frustration, how fiendish your unsatisfied shrieks must have seemed to your parents, how you must have longed to wrest personal control of your physical self from your parents' attentions. This remarkable sympathetic description of *babyhood from the point of view of the rebellious and unhappy baby* was Blake's originating insight; he then had to arrange his intuition of the baby's rage into an analytic and poetic shape.

WILLIAM BLAKE (1757 – 1827)

Infant Sorrow

My mother groaned, my father wept —
Into the dangerous world I leapt,
Helpless, naked, piping loud,
Like a fiend hid in a cloud.

Struggling in my father's hands,
Striving against my swaddling bands,
Bound and weary, I thought best
To sulk upon my mother's breast.

Blake analyzes the baby into two aspects, its physical body and its mental operations; he gives a stanza to each aspect. The main verb of the first stanza is the physical word "leapt"; the main verb of the second stanza is the mental word "thought." First the baby leaps into the world; then he thinks about his condition and decides what attitude to take toward it (he finally decides to sulk, after fruitlessly struggling and striving).

If the *division into the physical and the mental* is the most basic analytic move of the poem (causing it to divide itself into two stanzas), what other shapes does Blake confer on his piece of life? We notice that the baby's mother and father are present in each of the stanzas: by repeating the shape "parents/baby, parents/baby," Blake shows us that the baby does not exist alone but lives always in dependency on his parents. First, they preside at his birth, while his mother groans in labor and his father weeps in sympathy. Next, they literally enclose him, as they occupy the first and last line of the second stanza; the baby is held in his father's hands in the first line and supported on his mother's breast in the last. This *environmental* "parents/baby, parents/baby" shape is superimposed on the first shape ("baby/body, baby/mind") that we perceived. Just as the first shape made concrete — physically represented — Blake's analytic separation of the baby into body and mind, the second shape shows Blake's perception of the baby's total physical and moral impotence. He must continue to live (stanza 2) in the power of his parents who gave him existence (stanza 1), and it will be a long time before he will be old enough to have the independence he furiously craves.

Blake confers a third analytic shape on the poem with all the adjectives that the baby uses about himself: "helpless," "naked," "piping," "like a fiend hid," "struggling," "striving," "bound," and "weary." These are all realistic except "like a fiend hid." The realistic adjectives tell us how much any infant already knows about his intolerable condition; but the adjectival comparison, "[I am] like a fiend hid in a cloud," tells us that the baby can summon up a very strange analogy. We conclude (as would Blake, a Christian), that the baby has come into this life from a previous supernatural existence where he knew angels and devils. The baby (to his dismay) realizes that in this horrible new struggling embodied state he is more like the fiends he remembers than like the angels he resembled in heaven. The adjectival division of the baby's *self-awareness* into an *"earthly"* one (conscious of being naked, struggling, etc.) and a *"supernatural"* one (recalling fiends — and presumably their counterpart angels — known to his former life) reflects the baby's rage and self-division.

The fourth analytic shape Blake confers on his picture of the baby's state is a grammatical one — a contrast between present participial adjectives and non-"ing" adjectives. We see in this shape Blake's *contrast between doing and feeling* — between the baby's participial adjectives of action ("piping," "struggling," "striving") and his other adjectives of feeling ("helpless," "naked," "like a fiend," "bound," "weary"). The present participles show us what the baby can *do* (he can pipe, he can struggle, he can strive); the other adjectives tell us how he *feels* — his sufferings and his self-estimation as a fiend. We can understand his struggling and striving; but the unusual word "piping" tells us that in Blake's view the baby is not screaming or shrieking — he is making a song. "Piping" is a musical word, and it represents the beginning of language (or at least vocal expression) in the baby. He is full of sorrow, but he is also expressing his sorrow vocally.

There are other verbal effects we could mention: for instance, the fact that the baby is shown actively "leaping" into the world, rather than passively "being born"; that the successively weaker participial line-beginnings — "Struggling," "Striving," "Bound" — enact (act out, give us in miniature) the baby's eventual resignation into his sulky state; that the little couplets (pairs of rhyming lines) demonstrate Blake's decision to use the simplest sort of rhyme for the baby's speech; that the space between the stanzas represents the transition from being born to living. But as we look back on the task the poet set himself — "Find a shape for saying how life seems to the baby as he's born and just afterward" — we see that the poem has had to find several shapes for just that. To the extent that the poem exhibits analytic shapes, it has been removed from the stream of undifferentiated moments of existence and brought into the formal world of art. A poem that at first looks like a description ("Helpless, naked, piping loud; / Like a fiend hid in a cloud") is in fact an analysis of aspects of the baby's condition, arranged in ways (such as division into physical and mental, parents in each stanza, recall of heavenly preexistence, a contrast between acting and feeling) that show how the baby perceives life.

To sum up: by "analytic shape" I mean any meaningful patterning in the poem that "acts out" one of the insights the poet has had about the experience treated by the poem. It is as though in this poem Blake, with a poet's instinct, thought, "How shall I show that the baby is a mind as well as a body?" and decided, "I'll make a two-stanza poem, with the main *verb* in the first stanza a body-word, and the main *verb* in the second stanza a mind-word" (Shape 1). Then he thought, "How will I show the baby's dependence on its parents?" and decided, "I'll put the *nouns* "mother" and "father" in each stanza to show that the baby is always dependent on his parents" (Shape 2). Then, "How will I show the baby's previous supernatural life? By having him, amid all his *realistic* self-adjectives, include one *supernatural* adjectival comparison alluding to that previous life" (Shape 3). Then, "How can I show what the baby is feeling as well as what the baby is doing? I'll give him *present-participial adjectives* of doing *and non-"ing" adjectives* of feeling" (Shape 4). These decisions organize the poem, giving it structures that are dynamic ones, constantly overlapping and interlocking, making up the overall organization of the poem.

Of course, such patterns occur in lightning-quick ways to the trained mind of the poet. A composer does not say, "I think this is the place for a diminished seventh," or "Perhaps it would be effective to follow eighth-note triplets with a dotted quarter note." No, the composer "hears the music" and writes it down; it is only later that analysts demonstrate the patterns that make the music seem intended, not chaotic. A poet, too, "hears the poem," writes it down, and then further refines its visible patterns. Naturally, when a given pattern precedes the composition of the poem ("I want to write a sonnet"), much will be dictated by the preexistent formal requirements; but even then, the swift internal processes of composition organize the temporal, spatial, grammatical, and syntactic shapes of the poem more by instinct than by conscious plan. One could say that artists are people who think naturally in highly patterned ways.

As this summary shows, it is up to the reader to notice patterns such as those Blake uses. "How is it that the main action of the baby is a body-action in stanza 1 and a mind-action in stanza 2? What does this tell me about the baby's condition?" Or, "How is it that among all these realistic adjectives suiting the baby's state I find this one weird one — 'like a fiend hid in a cloud'? How does the newborn baby know about fiends hiding in clouds? What does this tell me about the baby's mind?"

A pattern shows that the poet has analyzed, and then replicated in language, some aspect of the content of the poem. We can therefore call a pattern an analytic shape. (In well-written poems, most of the larger perceived patterns will be analytically meaningful.) Much is explained to us about the baby by the patterns we have seen. The *main-verb pattern* tells us that the baby is composed of mind and body, which do separate things. The *noun-repeat pattern* ("mother," "father") tells us of the baby's dependency. The *realistic/supernatural adjectival pattern* of contrast tells us of the baby's memory of a past state. The *present-participial adjectives/other adjectives pattern* shows us the baby doing and the baby feeling. These few patterns remind us that there can be shapes of:

1. simple meaning-contrast (the antonyms "leapt" and "thought");
2. word-repetition ("mother," "father");
3. series, whether similar or broken ("like a fiend" breaks the realistic series and therefore stands out);
4. grammatical contrast (here, present-participial adjectives versus other adjectives, showing us actions versus feelings).

To discern the patterns in any poem, you may have to notice, then, such things as contrasts of meaning, repetitions of words, items in series, and grammatical emphases. Then, having seen such patterns, you can begin to ask yourself if they show you something about the situation in the poem that makes sense of the experience depicted.

We can ask, now, how does Louise Glück give formal shape to the first day of school?

As we've seen, Glück takes her cast of characters and their props from our conventional picture of the first day of school: there are children with their new primary-color clothes ("overcoats of blue or yellow wool"), their first book-bags or lunch-boxes ("their little satchels"), and their apples (from their family's orchard) for the teachers. The teachers "wait behind . . . desks." The mothers are left behind as the children "go forward" to school. So far, so ordinary. No one would be surprised to be told these details about the first day of school. But Glück gives us more, and more sinister, details:

LOUISE GLÜCK (b. 1943)
The School Children

The children go forward with their little satchels.
And all morning the mothers have labored
to gather the late apples, red and gold,
like words of another language.

And on the other shore
are those who wait behind great desks
to receive these offerings.

How orderly they are — the nails
on which the children hang
their overcoats of blue or yellow wool.

And the teachers shall instruct them in silence
and the mothers shall scour the orchards for a way out,
drawing to themselves the gray limbs of the fruit trees
bearing so little ammunition.

We perceive poetic shape mostly through *oddness*. There are several oddnesses here. The apples are said to be "like words of another language." The school is said to be "on the other shore" of some unspecified body of water. The teachers' (ordinary) desks are said to be "great" desks — and the teachers wait, like gods, to receive "offerings." The only detail given about the school itself is that it has an orderly row of nails serving as coat hooks. The limbs of the fruit trees in the orchards which the mothers "scour" for "a way out" are "gray," and the apples are seen, at the end of the poem, as "ammunition." These are the oddnesses any account of the shapes of the poem would have to make sense of.

We also perceive shape through the *division into stanzas* — here, four of them, with their appropriate dramatis personae, or cast of characters. Stanza 1 is for the *children,* the *mothers,* and the *apples;* stanza 2 is for the *teachers* and the *apples;* stanza 3 is for the *nails;* and stanza 4 is for the *teachers* (doing one thing at school) and the *mothers* (doing another thing in the orchards with apples). Why is this the way the characters come on the stage? Why do the nails have a stanza to themselves? Why isn't the word "apples" mentioned in the last stanza?

We perceive shape through *series:* the apples, which were "words from another language" in stanza 1, and "these offerings" in stanza 2, are "ammunition" in stanza 4. The apples are the only image that changes, and they become more pathetic as the poem goes on.

At this point, we can say that the first basic shape that the poem confers on the opening of school is a *spatial* one. There is a terrible and dangerous separation of teacher-territory from mother-territory: they lie on opposite shores of a watery divide. The two regions speak different languages, and the apples are the only words in the teacher-language that can bridge the gap. The two regions are also in conflict; but the teachers have nails and the mothers have only apples — as propitiatory offerings, as ammunition against the teacher's power. The mothers' desperate work ("all morning the mothers have labored"; "the mothers shall scour the orchards") to protect the children is bound to fail — they have "so little ammunition" from the already-withering fruit trees (next year's apples will be of no use, since the children will be wholly socialized into their public school-selves by then). The day will come when the children will have to go to school without an apple to offer to those mysterious strangers, the teachers, who speak another language, who wait behind their monumental "great desks." What will happen then?

The *spatial* shape of the great divide into two territories is matched by the *temporal* shape of the poem. By "temporal shape" I mean what happens to the poem as it progresses in time. Here, as the poem advances from stanza 1 to stanza 2 to stanza 3, the gaze of the narrator narrows from the home group (mothers and children) to the people behind the "great desks" to the sinister single objects "orderly . . . nails." Then the gaze of the narrator broadens again, to the children firmly in the power of the teacher (who will quell their native language and reduce them to the silence and orderliness of socialization) and the mothers, on the other shore, who will wildly seek a way, by scouring the orchards for apples (which they now think of solely as "ammunition") to fight the trap that is closing on their children.

These two axes, Space and Time, are often used to organize poems. In Glück's poem, the first represents the analysis of the life-event into different regions (home and school), and the second represents the analysis of the life-event into successive temporal stages (here, from the child's point of view — leaving home, seeing the teacher behind the "great desk," divesting yourself of your new coat and leaving an effigy of yourself hanging on a nail, and being "instructed in silence" by the teacher). The last stanza of the poem, unlike all the rest (which are written in the present tense) is written in the future tense: the teachers "shall instruct" the children; the mothers "shall scour" the orchards. This is a prophetic future tense (otherwise the phrases would read "will instruct" and "will scour"). The future tense represents a prediction from the main present-tense account in the poem, but it is a logical conjecture from the very first words, "The children go forward."

The purpose of Glück's two main shapes, one of space and one of time, is to make the transition from home to school sinister. We imagine primary-school children walking to a school close by, but we learn (in the shape of the two regions) that the school is on "another shore." We imagine a cordial relation between home and school, but the temporal plot shows us an alienation between them ("another language") so that the mothers must try propitiation ("offerings") and then open conflict ("ammunition") to save the children. These two sinister shapes of widening space and future loss "act out," most of all, the mothers' sense that their children are far off, in the power of alien beings, in danger, and essentially without hope of rescue. This reinterpretation of the conventionally cheerful view of the first day of school forces us to rethink our previous notion: Is not the first day of school really more like Glück's idea of it than like the conventionally happy version? The artist's distrust of group "order" and "silence" lies behind this critique of early education.

The shape that E. E. Cummings puts on life is simpler. He separates the two sexes, and shows us what age they are by their games (marbles and piracies for the boys, hop-scotch and jump-rope for the girls). He makes the children same-sex Siamese twins, so to speak — eddieandbill and bettyandisbel. He troubles their same-sex play by an apparently insignificant figure of pleasure, a balloonman:

E. E. Cummings (1894 – 1962)

in Just-

in Just-
spring   when the world is mud-
luscious the little
lame balloonman

whistles   far   and wee

and eddieandbill come
running from marbles and
piracies and it's
spring

when the world is puddle-wonderful

the queer
old balloonman whistles
far   and   wee
and bettyandisbel come dancing

from hop-scotch and jump-rope and

it's
spring
and
    the

        goat-footed

balloonMan   whistles
far
and
wee

The balloonman enters three times with his seductive whistle. We are left
to imagine its ultimate sexual effect on the preadolescent children — but
the effect is not in doubt because he draws the couples away from their
same-sex childhood play, forecasting their regrouping into sexual
couples. In the triple appearance of the balloonman, we find him char-
acterized by different adjectives — "little lame," "queer old," and "goat-
footed." He also acquires an honorific capital "M" in his last appearance,
where we see the goat-feet which proclaim him a nature-spirit, even a
god — therefore he is a balloonMan. (In ancient Greece the god of
nature was the goat-footed Pan.) We call the phrase repeating the return
of the balloonman a *refrain:*

> The little lame balloonman whistles far and wee
> The queer old balloonman whistles far and wee
> The goat-footed balloonMan whistles far and wee

We notice that other things in the poem also come round thrice:

> in Just- / spring   when the world is mud- / luscious
> it's / spring / when the world is puddle-wonderful
> it's / spring

We can now see that the "plot" of the poem is:

1. Spring, balloonman, boys together;
2. Spring, balloonman, girls together;
3. Spring, balloonMan, ——— ?

When we ask ourselves: "What does Cummings imply about the com-
pletion of the poem? What is the missing plot element?" we answer:
"girl with boy, boy with girl."

To his Siamese-twin trick, and his triple balloonman refrain, and
his triple appearance of spring, and the "missing" sexual conclusion to
his plot, Cummings adds yet another element of shape — his typo-
graphic arrangement of these things. The "horizontal" whistling —
"whistles   far   and wee" — looks as though it is happening
within the space we move in. But the "vertical" whistle —

> whistles
> far
> and
> wee

makes it seem as though the balloonman is gradually, like a Pied Piper, receding in space, taking the newly sexual couples off with him, Typographically speaking, too, the important word "spring" always comes first in the lines in which it appears.

There is an odd stop, inserted at the line-break, between the adjectives characterizing the balloonman at first: "little — [Is he lame? Yes, maybe] / lame balloonman"; "queer — [Does he walk that way because he's old, not lame? Yes, maybe] / old balloonman." And then the puzzle is resolved: he's not lame; he's not old; he walks oddly because he is "goat-footed." And there's no more hesitation: he's a god — he's the balloonMan.

If we were talking about the life-moment Cummings has selected, we would say it is the spring of life — the moment when childhood ends, same-sex friendships break up, adolescents hear the alluring call of sexuality, and sexual couples first form. That is a summary of the poem, but it has not explained the shapes Cummings has invented to act out the life-moment. Only an examination of form — in Cummings, typographic as well as verbal form — shows us how the poem *enacts* (represents by several formal shapes) the moment it has chosen, and makes us see the *processes* of that moment, how it gradually unfolds in time, with both pathos and joy.

We have said that Whitman's "Hours Continuing Long" is a poem of forsaken love; its first line tells us that its special subject is how *long* the hours seem to the one forsaken. How does the poem act out the length of the hours?

WALT WHITMAN (1819 – 1892)

Hours Continuing Long

Hours continuing long, sore and heavy hearted,
Hours of the dusk, when I withdraw to a lonesome and
      unfrequented spot, seating myself, leaning my face in my
      hands;
Hours sleepless, deep in the night, when I go forth, speeding
      swiftly the country roads, or through the city streets, or
      pacing miles and miles, stifling plaintive cries;
Hours discouraged, distracted — for the one I cannot content
      myself without, soon I saw him content himself without me;

Hours when I am forgotten (O weeks and months are passing, but
    I believe I am never to forget!)
Sullen and suffering hours! (I am ashamed — but it is useless — I
    am what I am);
Hours of my torment — I wonder if other men ever have the
    like, out of the like feelings?
Is there even one other like me — distracted — his friend, his
    lover, lost to him?
Is he too as I am now? Does he still rise in the morning, dejected,
    thinking who is lost to him? and at night, awaking, think
    who is lost?
Does he too harbor his friendship silent and endless? harbor his
    anguish and passion?
Does some stray reminder, or the casual mention of a name, bring
    the fit back upon him, taciturn and deprest?
Does he see himself reflected in me? In these hours, does he see
    the face of his hours reflected?

Certainly the successive long weary lines beginning with the word
"Hours" — there are six of these, five in a row, then an interruption
("Sullen and suffering hours!"), then another one — act out the theme
of the poem. We will have to account for the interruption, but for the
moment we can say that the first seven lines of the poem make us see and
feel, by a series of statements exhaustedly resembling one another, the
inertia of the weary hours.

Then the poem makes its major change of shape, turning from one
grammatical form (*statements*) to a different one (*questions*). We see now
that it is basically a *two-part* poem, the parts distinguished by this central
grammatical turn. Do the two parts differ in anything besides grammati-
cal form? Part I is solely about the speaker; but Part II wonders whether
there are "other men" like the speaker, or even "one other like me."

Before the poem began, there was of course "one other like" the
speaker — his lover. The speaker was one of two; now he is alone; he
would like to be one of at least two again. The usual hope might be to
find another lover, but that is a path that this poem does not, cannot,
take, since the speaker is still too much in love to imagine finding a new
lover. No — the speaker will imagine that there is another person as
dejected as he is himself, a brother in suffering, who will be his twin in
endurance. This is a replacement strategy: the lost lover is "replaced" by
the imagined twin-in-grief.

What causes this evolution in the poem? Can we explain what moti-
vates the transition from solitary grief to the imagining of a fellow suf-

ferer? It may come from a wish to replace the lost lover; but the poem suggests another motivation, too. Let us look at the two-line central turning-point of the poem, beginning with the line that does not open with "Hours" and continuing into the line where statements turn to questions:

> Sullen and suffering hours! (I am ashamed — but it is useless — I
>   am what I am);
> Hours of my torment — I wonder if other men ever have the
>   like, out of the like feelings?

We can see that the first movement out of the self toward society is one of unexplained shame: "If others could see me, they would rebuke me; and yes, I am ashamed — but it is useless — I am what I am." We do not know, and will never know, whether the poet is ashamed of his homosexuality (he suppressed this poem from his collection *Leaves of Grass*) or of his sullen dejection (Whitman strongly wished to appear a positive poet of democratic strength). Eventually the poet surmises that some group of men might not recoil from him, because they themselves have had similar feelings. At least there may be one such man — and the poem then does a reprise in the third person ("Does he too harbor his friendship silent and endless?") of what the speaker had previously said of himself in the first person ("I withdraw to a lonesome and unfrequented spot," etc.).

This shape — doing something once, then doing it again differently — is one we have already seen in Cummings's poem, where we saw spring come three times and heard the balloonman whistle three times. Here, love is expressed in the first person, via statements, and then in the third person, via questions; this shape tells us that what seemed at first shamefully personal may perhaps be shared by others, perhaps by everyone. It is like hearing a melody twice, the first time in the major key, the second time in the minor. Art thrives on such variations.

Stevens's poem consists of five quatrains. Although the lines are somewhat irregular in length, they keep returning to a pentameter base. The orderliness of the poem — the fact that its stanzas are all of the same length, and that its lines keep reverting to the pentameter norm — suggests that this is not a wayward or willful poem, but rather a sober and steadfast one.

WALLACE STEVENS (1879 – 1955)
The Plain Sense of Things

After the leaves have fallen, we return
To a plain sense of things. It is as if

We had come to an end of the imagination,
Inanimate in an inert savoir.

It is difficult even to choose the adjective
For this blank cold, this sadness without cause.
The great structure has become a minor house.
No turban walks across the lessened floors.

The greenhouse never so badly needed paint.
The chimney is fifty years old and slants to one side.
A fantastic effort has failed, a repetition
In a repetitiousness of men and flies.

Yet the absence of the imagination had
Itself to be imagined. The great pond,
The plain sense of it, without reflections, leaves,
Mud, water like dirty glass, expressing silence

Of a sort, silence of a rat come out to see,
The great pond and its waste of the lilies, all this
Had to be imagined as an inevitable knowledge,
Required, as a necessity requires.

As we scan the poem for pattern, we notice that its language is sometimes abstract and at other times concrete. We might try writing out the poem again, in two columns, one for the speaker's generalizing statements and the other for his specific examples.

Abstract	Concrete
The Plain Sense of Things	
	After the leaves have fallen, we return / To
a plain sense of things. It is as if / We had come to an end of the imagination, / Inanimate in an inert savoir. / It is difficult even to choose the adjective / this sadness without cause. /	For this blank cold,
	The great structure has become a minor house. /

No turban walks across the
    lessened floors. /
The greenhouse never so
    badly needed paint. /
The chimney is fifty years
    old and slants to one
    side. /

A fantastic effort has failed, a
    repetition /
In a repetitiousness of men
    and flies. /
Yet the absence of the
    imagination
had / Itself to be imagined.
The plain sense of it,
    without reflections,

The great pond, /

silence / Of a sort,
silence

leaves, / Mud, water like
    dirty glass, expressing

of a rat come out to see, /
The great pond and its waste
    of the lilies, all this /

Had to be imagined
    as an inevitable
    knowledge, /
Required, as a necessity
    requires.

It is clear that the back-and-forth pattern between concrete visualiza-
tion and abstract contemplation in "The Plain Sense of Things" mimics the
way that a reflective mind tends to see a concrete piece of evidence and then
to express it in intellectual ways. In analyzing such a poem, it's often useful
first to re-create the visual side (and only later to consider the thoughts par-
alleling it). Here, reading down the right-hand column, we see that it is late
autumn (the leaves have all fallen) and that it is cold. We are in the presence
of what was once, in the past, a "great structure," but which has now
declined to "a minor house." It is uninhabited (though once, the speaker
knows, an exotic turban-wearing person inhabited it), and the floors,
deprived of that former presence, seem "lessened." There is a greenhouse
(the mark of a rich estate), but it is badly weathered and cries out for paint.
The chimney of the house (once warmed by its inner fire) is now a half-
century old, so old that it has lost its true uprightness and slants forlornly to
one side. The great pond (another mark of a rich estate) which, in spring

and summer, was filled with beautiful reflections, has now a surface "like dirty glass," obscured by mud and fallen leaves. Because nothing "looks back at" the speaker from the surface of the great pond, he feels a silence of a sort: the visible world is not returning his gaze, is not speaking to him.

It is at this point that we are startled. Into this inanimate scene of decline, there intrudes a bright-eyed animate presence: that of "a rat come out to see." Something in the world *is* gazing back at the speaker; someone, like him, is inspecting the scene. But the rat is not reflecting on the past grandeur of the surroundings. It has just come out to see what there is to see now, today.

The speaker reverts to the scene, taking his last look — remarking with sadness the "waste of the lilies" of the great pond, all of them now dead. Still, he has perceived, in his companion the rat, another manner of looking: merely, without mournful nostalgia, to "come out to see."

What thoughts, then, have been prompted by the sight of the great estate in decline? If we look down the left-hand column, we see that the formulation of the title — the plain sense of things (implying certainty) — has been lessened in stanza 1 to a plain sense of things — a sense that hasn't yet become specific. We suspect from the title that the specificity is to come — and, sure enough, it does arrive, in the the of stanza 4 — "the plain sense of it." We notice that this progression in certainty has a parallel: whereas in the first stanza the speaker (speaking in the plural of human generalization) says that we have come to an end of the imagination, in the fourth stanza, he speaks of the absence of the imagination. Something, then, happens between the opening of the poem and stanza 4, by which the speaker has come from a and an to the and the. By stanza 4 the speaker has come to new and specific forms of knowledge: he knows what the plain sense of things is, and he knows what the absence of the imagination is.

How do the other thoughts of the speaker connect with this most basic one? To find yourself "in-animate in an in-ert savoir" is to be next to dead ("inanimate" means without *anima,* Latin for "spirit"; and "inert" means without *ars,* Latin for "art"). The inability of language to move off the rails of repeated sound suggests, here, the stultifying absence of new stimuli: "an end of the im-ag-in-ation, / In-an-im-ate in an in-ert savoir." The proof of the inertness of the imagination is its inability to offer up any adjectives except the uncommunicative "blank" and "without cause," signs of absence lacking positive specificity.

The next abstract summing-up emphasizes the speaker's strenuous earlier strivings after hope and achievement: they were "a fantastic effort," but one that is now seen to be a failure — carrying out the repeated human pattern of mortality and bodily corruption. (Flies are the accompaniment of corpses in literature as in life.)

It is at this point in our inventory of the column of abstract thoughts that the grieving sighs of the poem come to a surprising halt. The speaker pulls himself up by his bootstraps both with his resolved "Yet" and with his verb of necessity — "had to be imagined," twice stated (in stanzas 4 and 5). The second time the verb appears, it has a complement: "Had to be imagined as an inevitable knowledge." We see that the speaker's earlier words of deadness — "inanimate," "inert" — have now been transmuted into a word of necessity — "inevitable" — that which cannot be escaped (from Latin, *evitare,* "to shun").

The first shape that we have noticed, then, is this oscillatory one of the mind moving from spectacle (the ruined estate) to thought (summing-up), back to spectacle again, and so on. A second shape that we have seen is that of sadness countered by resolve ("And yet"). If that second shape had been perfectly observed, no sadness would have occurred after the moment of resolve: the graph of the poem would show a grieving slide down, and then a recovery to a resolute steady-state of stoic fortitude. But that is not what we see. Stevens allows three further moments of sadness after the brave resolve: these are enunciated in three phrases. "Without reflections" recalls the time when the pond allowed images of the world; "water like dirty glass" recalls, by its contrastive adjective, when the water was like clear glass; and "the great pond and its waste of the lilies" recalls, by its noun of decline, the earlier time when the lilies were in bloom. Stevens allows us to see, here, the believable momentary "backsliding" of a mind into sadness even after it has resolved to grieve no longer; and yet he also shows us how that mind pulls itself up again with its reiterated "had to be imagined." We might call this shape that of argument and counterargument: sadness against resolve, resolve against sadness.

A third shape (besides the oscillatory one between thought and spectacle and the "backsliding" one of argument between resolve and grief) is one of persistent repetition. In part, we are alerted to the presence of this shape by the almost instant repetition of the title (with a slight variation) in line 2: just after hearing "The Plain Sense of Things" we hear "a plain sense of things." Repetition is always the sign of the mind scrutinizing what it has just said and either confirming or changing its phrasing as it judges it. A list of the moments of semantic repetition would go as follows:

The Plain Sense of Things
a plain sense of things
the plain sense of it

this blank cold
this sadness without cause

the great structure
the great pond
the great pond and its waste of the lilies

a repetition
In a repetitiousness of men and flies

an end of the imagination
the absence of the imagination

had itself to be imagined
had to be imagined

after the leaves have fallen
leaves

silence of a sort
silence of a rat come out to see

required
as a necessity requires

Anyone reading the poem aloud will recognize that this patterning of insistent semantic repetition (remarkable in a short poem) is backed by persistent phonetic repetition (which we have already seen in "inanimate in an inert savoir" and which often reappears, for example, in the *f*'s of "a fantastic effort has failed"). Depending on one's view of the poem, one could find various explanations of this "repetition-shape": among other functions, it certainly reinforces the idea that what has happened — the decline of the estate, the aging of the speaker, the failure of the speaker's hopes — is "a repetition in a repetitiousness." We would not believe that statement had not some pattern in the poem borne it out.

We can see another repetition-shape, this time syntactic, in the instancing of specific details of decline. These are all presented in short declarative sentences: the structure, the turban, the greenhouse, the chimney. Each sentence has the same basic shape: subject-predicate (although Stevens is careful to allow for some variation). And each sentence is of the same length — one end-stopped line:

The great structure has become a minor house.
No turban walks across the lessened floors.
The greenhouse never so badly needed paint.
The chimney is fifty years old and slants to one side.

The detail that escapes this one-line declarative shape is the pond. We could have had a sentence, comparable to the others, that said, "The great pond is obscured with leaves and mud." However, the treatment of the great pond "breaks the shape" into which the other elements were ostentatiously and repetitively fitted. The pond is more complex than a greenhouse that needs paint or a chimney that slants. When the speaker turns his gaze to the pond, a spate of descriptive phrases, of a very mixed sort, pours from his lips:

the great pond,

the plain sense of it,

without reflections,

leaves,

mud,

water like dirty glass,

expressing silence (of a sort)

silence (of a rat come out to see)

the great pond and its waste of the lilies — all this . . .

Depending on your view of the entire poem, you might find many different things to say about this passage. The former inarguable inventory of decay, absence, effacement, and decline — "structure . . . turban . . . greenhouse . . . chimney" — and the summing-up of that inventory in the absolute certainty of "a fantastic effort has failed" — differ in tone and mood from the passage on the pond, which is both more heart-stricken and more "confused," as it mixes the abstract and the concrete, sight with hearing, the inanimate with the animate, the nonrepetitive with the repetitive, all turning on the pun on the word "reflections" — which means both "thoughts" and "images."

We now perceive that the rigid shapes that we have so far come across — discursive oscillation between abstract and concrete; emotional argument (sadness) versus counterargument (resolve); and repetitiveness on the semantic, syntactic, and phonetic planes — exist only to be broken in the climactic ingathering of the pond. The speaker is acquiring

his new way of seeing — seeing as the rat sees. He "backslides" in saying
that the pond is "without reflections" and "like dirty glass" and that it
displays "its waste of the lilies," but he mixes with this nostalgia the
"plain sense" of the pond: leaves; mud; silence. His "confusion" is
shown by his desertion of his earlier formula — doling out one end-
stopped line to each detail — for his inventory of decay. Now sentiment
overspills the line-ends and mixes up categories:

<blockquote>

The great pond,
The plain sense of it, without reflections, leaves,
Mud, water like dirty glass, expressing silence

Of a sort, silence of a rat come out to see,
The great pond and its waste of the lilies, all this . . .

</blockquote>

The "orderly" proportion of sentiment to line returns at the end of the
poem in "Required, as a necessity requires" — but even this is not a syn-
tactically complete sentence in itself, as the inventory lines about the
greenhouse and the chimney are.

Another shape comes into view when we see how the complex
passage on the pond is bracketed, firmly, between the two appearances of
"had to be imagined":

<blockquote>

Yet the absence of the imagination
<u>had</u> / <u>Itself to be imagined</u>.
The great pond . . .
The great pond . . .
<u>Had to be imagined</u>.

</blockquote>

This is the shape of imprisonment. There is no way to keep the pond
purely in nostalgia; necessity grips it in its talons. Necessity "requires":
the word comes from the Latin *re* + *quaerere*, "to ask again." "Required,
as a necessity requires": Stevens has his poem act out the "again" of the
Latin prefix *re*.

Finally, we might notice one more fleeting semantic shape of the
poem — the substitution of the word "knowledge" in stanza 5 for the
word "savoir" in stanza 1. "Savoir" (French: "to know how") has come
into English in the phrase "savoir-faire," which means "to know how to
manage in a social situation." An "inert savoir" tells us that the speaker's
practical knowledge has lapsed into a paralysis, an inertia, approaching
the condition of death ("inanimate"). By the end of the poem, the
speaker has been resurrected from his collapse; by resolving to open his
imagination to what the absence of the imagination might mean in his

life, he has acquired a new "inevitable" knowledge, proper to, and neces-
sary in, old age. By opening his eyes to death, he can see not only decline
from his former estate (literal and metaphorical) but the nature of his
present state. He realizes that this, however painful, is an improvement
over denial. He also sees the comedy in inventing an inquisitive rat as his
mentor in a better, more objective, seeing.

The presence of several patterns operating within one poem is
what gives us the sense of complexity that we feel in reading "The Plain
Sense of Things." We feel the rigidity of the aging mind making its sad
inventory and deducing its conclusive thoughts; we also feel the emo-
tional fortitude in the pattern that counters nostalgia with resolve; we
feel the exertion of the will as the mind strives to find the slight (but cru-
cial) difference between "a" plain sense (general) and "the" plain sense
(particular) of its condition; we feel the further exertion of the stoic
mind in deciding that it will offer its "Yet": "Yet the absence of the
imagination had / Itself to be imagined." And we sense the cascade of
feeling generating the waterfall of phrases about the "great pond" — a
symbol of that youthful mind that once was full of image-reflections,
that believed it could mirror the world in art, that had confidence in the
erotic beauty of its lilies. Finally, we feel not only the iron brackets of
necessity surrounding the new view of the pond but also the poet's sense
that necessity will ask of him, again and again as he ages, that he revise
his sense of the world. It will also force him to take on the posture, not of
a mourner, but of a curious spectator, imitating his companion the rat.

You can absorb a good deal of Stevens's feelings about the bleak-
ness and fortitude of age just by reading "The Plain Sense of Things"
and by being emotionally receptive to its statements and its symbols. But
if you are curious about how Stevens makes the poem "work," and why
the poem is memorable, you will have to seek out its patterns and inquire
how they act on your own imagination to render vivid the complex feel-
ings encoded in the poem.

The Public Life

As we turn from the private to the public life, we come to this very
brief poem by Michael S. Harper — which nonetheless has the compre-
hensive title "American History." It consists of two parts. The first is a
personal statement ("Those . . . girls . . . remind me of five hundred . . .
blacks"), and the second is the sardonic quip following it, spoken by
someone who seems to be giving us a knowing wink: "Can't find what
you can't see / can you?"

MICHAEL S. HARPER (b. 1938)
American History

For John Callahan
Those four black girls blown up
in that Alabama church
remind me of five hundred
middle passage blacks,
in a net, under water
in Charleston harbor
so *redcoats* wouldn't find them.
Can't find what you can't see
can you?

The "invisibility" of blacks in American culture has been a persistent theme of black authors; Ralph Ellison called his famous autobiographical novel *Invisible Man*. A few blacks more or less, in racist contexts, would scarcely be noticed. The furor caused by the death of four young black girls when a bomb exploded in a black church was one of the signs of the rising civil rights movement; yet those who placed the bomb didn't care how many blacks they killed. Harper's anecdote of American ship-captains drowning slaves so they would not be stolen, as items of value, by British troops suggests the perennial "invisibility" of blacks throughout American history, from the very beginning. The wry quip at the end of the poem makes even more horrible the "success" of hiding — by murder — the valuable slaves to keep them from the redcoats.

By calling his poem "American History" Harper suggests that the episodes he recounts represent, better than textbooks bearing that name, the real narrative of American events. The real American history remains to be written, the poem implies. So we must see, between these two markers — the invisibility of drowned blacks in the Revolution, the invisibility of bombed blacks in the twentieth century — a whole silent procession of comparable incidents, decade by decade, from the seventeenth century till today. In this way, by evoking the shape "normally" belonging to the title "American History" (a long textbook full of patriotic self-glorification), Harper makes us see his little shape as one that could be extended into a very big one.

We come to another marginalized group in public life, Charles Simic's aged poor:

CHARLES SIMIC (b. 1938)

Old Couple

They're waiting to be murdered,
Or evicted. Soon
They expect to have nothing to eat.
As far as I know, they never go out.

A vicious pain's coming, they think.
It will start in the head
And spread down to the bowels.
They'll be carried off on stretchers, howling.

In the meantime, they watch the street
From their fifth floor window.
It has rained, and now it looks
Like it's going to snow a little.

I see him get up to lower the shades.
If their window stays dark,
I know that his hand has reached hers
Just as she was about to turn on the lights.

If we quickly sum up the subject of each of the four stanzas of Simic's "Old Couple," we might come up with something like this:

1. Three possible futures for the old couple — murdered, evicted, starved;

2. Another possible future — terminal illness;

3. The present interim before one of these horrors happens;

4. The suppositions of the speaker watching them.

A quick summary of this sort at least shows that the horrors die down, by stanza 3, to the brief and fragile peace of the interim moment at the end; this decline in horror is one overall shape of the poem. But it leaves out the presence of the person watching the old couple. It is this person who speaks the poem, and we identify him, since this is not a dramatic monologue, with the author of the poem. He knows, in stanza 1, what the old people are thinking. He comments on their behavior ("As far as I know, they never go out"). He watches them compulsively ("I see him get up to lower the shades"). He even invents what they do when he cannot observe them ("I know that his hand has reached hers").

If the shape of the old people's lives is a downhill dread of continual terror, what is the shape of the watcher's life? The poet asks us to imagine the passing days of a watcher in a nearby building. At some point in the past, he noticed the old couple across the way; perhaps at that point they were still going out for walks or to the store. That seems to have stopped. But when they were still visible in the neighborhood, the watcher noted their mutual devotion, which causes him now to imagine the old man reaching for his wife's hand. The watcher is so conscious of the few things the old couple can look at that he has reduced his own consciousness to the tenuousness of theirs: "It has rained, and now it looks / Like it's going to snow a little" — an observation of no real importance, except to people who have nothing else but the weather to observe (but it also suggests worsening weather, one more threat). The old couple have become so real to the watcher that he has absorbed their terrors into his own mind. He knows that one of these days he will either see them taken out on stretchers, howling in pain, or see their possessions on the sidewalk as they are evicted with no place to go, or he will hear that they have been murdered, or that someone has found them dead of malnutrition in their apartment. There are simply no other possible futures to imagine for them; the watcher knows this.

As soon as we see the watcher/speaker as the principal consciousness in the poem, we read the work as a protest-poem against the conditions of modern urban life. The neglect by society of its most helpless members means that anyone in a modern city becomes necessarily a watcher of cases like this. Nobody can be free of horror and guilt, as the probable future seeps from the victims to their neighbors.

The two interlocking shapes — the heading-for-disaster life-shape of the old couple, the ongoing and speculative life-shape of the watcher — make up the figure of the poem. Spatially, we are given two rooms — the implied room of the watcher, the room of the old couple across the street; temporally, we are presented with the several envisaged plots of the old couple meeting their end, each plot as terrifying as the other. The plots exhaust all possibilities. The old couple have no one to rescue them — they will end in a public hospital ward for the indigent, in a shelter for the homeless, out on the street after being evicted, in the morgue after being murdered, or in their bed, starved.

Many poems have two or more interlocking shapes. We have seen such shapes in "Infant Sorrow" (the baby as mind and body; the baby as dependent on parents; the baby as part human, part supernatural; the baby as a doing creature and a feeling creature), and again in "Old Couple" (the successive shapes of the couple's envisaged horrifying futures; the watcher's steady-state speculative shape). When several overlapping and interlocking shapes are present at once in a poem, it becomes potentially more interesting — because more complex, as life is — than poems that have only one shape. The ideal poem would have a temporal shape, a spatial shape, a rhythmic shape, a phonetic shape, a grammatical shape, a syntactic shape, and so on — each one beautifully worked out, each one graphically presenting in formal terms an aspect of the emotional and intellectual import of the poem. One way we distinguish more accomplished poems from less accomplished ones is the control of the artist over a number of shapes at once. Other things being equal, the more shapes that are being evoked, the more pleasure one derives from the poem because more of its inner life has been thought through, analyzed, and made visible in form by its creator.

The manuscript drafts of Robert Lowell's "Skunk Hour" show that it originally began in the way that a traditional lyric might — "One dark night," etc. The present stanza 5 was the beginning of the poem:

ROBERT LOWELL (1917 – 1977)
Skunk Hour

For Elizabeth Bishop

Nautilus Island's hermit
heiress still lives through winter in her Spartan cottage;
her sheep still graze above the sea.
Her son's a bishop. Her farmer
is first selectman in our village;
she's in her dotage.

Thirsting for
the hierarchic privacy
of Queen Victoria's century,
she buys up all
the eyesores facing her shore,
and lets them fall.

The season's ill —
we've lost our summer millionaire,
who seemed to leap from an L. L. Bean
catalogue. His nine-knot yawl
was auctioned off to lobstermen.
A red fox stain covers Blue Hill.

And now our fairy
decorator brightens his shop for fall;
his fishnet's filled with orange cork,

orange, his cobbler's bench and awl;
there is no money in his work,
he'd rather marry.

One dark night,
my Tudor Ford climbed the hill's skull;
I watched for love-cars. Lights turned down,
they lay together, hull to hull,
where the graveyard shelves on the town. . . .
My mind's not right.

A car radio bleats,
"Love, O careless Love. . . ." I hear
my ill-spirit sob in each blood cell,
as if my hand were at its throat. . . .
I myself am hell;
nobody's here —

only skunks, that search
in the moonlight for a bite to eat.
They march on their soles up Main Street;
white stripes, moonstruck eyes' red fire
under the chalk-dry and spar spire
of the Trinitarian Church.

I stand on top
of our back steps and breathe the rich air —
a mother skunk with her column of kittens swills the garbage pail.
She jabs her wedge-head in a cup
of sour cream, drops her ostrich tail,
and will not scare.

Lowell brackets his "lyric center" — stanzas 5 and 6 — with a set of "characters" fore and a set of animals aft. This three-part shape is instantly visible:

1. Grotesque inhabitants of my Maine town;
2. Myself;
3. A mother skunk and her kittens taking over the town.

Each of the three parts has an inner shape of its own. In the first part, the native "hermit heiress" owns two stanzas, while the lesser summer millionaire and "fairy decorator," transients both, own only one stanza each. (The manuscript suggests that all of these are figures for the poet himself. Whereas the final version says "There is no money in his work, / he'd rather marry" about the "fairy decorator," in the draft the poet says this about himself: "There is no money in this work, / I'd rather marry.") Lowell inherited his house in Castine, Maine, from his aunt who lived there, but he only went there summers, like the "summer millionaire." No longer living in one of the roles proper to his Brahmin lineage — hermit, or bishop, or landowner — the speaker has declined into the unvirile role of an artist, comparable to that of the man whom the town contemptuously terms the "fairy decorator."

After presenting these disguised figures for himself in the first part of the poem, the speaker shows us himself in the second part as a voyeur, aware of his own madness as he spies on lovers in cars. The gradually intensifying shape of this middle part is one of mortified self-watching: "My Tudor Ford climbed the hill's skull," not "I drove up the hill." And it is one of psychological self-judging: "My mind's not right." And it is one of medical self-diagnosis: "I hear / my ill-spirit sob in each blood cell." Finally, it is one of ethical self-damnation: "I myself am hell." After the disengaged tone of detached social commentary which dominates the first part of the poem describing Castine, these damning first-person sentences chill the blood.

Then come the skunks. Nature takes over from the decadent culture of Castine. The skunks invade the town. The mother is the general; her offspring are her military "column." We are watching the barbarians (disciplined, vital, fiery-eyed) take over Rome (declining, degenerate, chalk-dry). The vivid verbs used of the skunks energize the exhaustions and distresses of the poem: the skunks *search,* and *march;* the mother skunk *swills* the garbage pail, *jabs* her head into the cup, *drops* her tail, *will not* scare. The speaker is (almost) glad to resign his inherited world to the skunks; certainly he is in no shape to govern it, or even to live in it, any more. It is a poem of total abdication from rule by the originally ruling, now depleted, Brahmin class. It was Lowell's revenge on his own heritage, which he always regarded with mixed admiration and contempt. And it shows his heritage gradually disappearing back into nature, as all cultures eventually do.

Nature and Time

Almost the whole appeal of the little medieval spring song we saw as our first example of nature poetry comes from its rhythm. Here I have marked the "silent *e*'s," which were pronounced ("uh") in the Middle Ages, so that the original rhythm can be heard:

ANONYMOUS

The Cuckoo Song

Sumer is icumen in,
        Lhudè sing, cuccu!
Groweth sed and bloweth med
        And springth the wudè nu.
                Sing, cuccu!

Awè bleteth after lomb,
        Lhouth after calvè cu,
Bulluc sterteth, buckè verteth —
        Murie sing, cuccu!
                Cuccu, cuccu.
        Wel singès thu, cuccu.
        Ne swik thu never nu!

At first, as we expect in a simple ballad quatrain (a four-line stanza with alternating four-beat and three-beat lines), a four-beat line ("SUmer IS iCUMen IN") is here followed by a three-beat line ("LHUde SING, cuCU!") and another four-beat line is followed by a three-beat line, all of them about the renewing of vegetation. But to our surprise an unexpected three-beat echo-line is added as a fifth line — "Sing, cuccu!"

Then the poem starts up again. Naturally, we expect another 4 / 3 / 4 / 3 pattern, and we find it, yet this second quatrain is not about vegetation but about the renewing of animal life (ewe and lamb, cow and calf, bullock and buck). We might even expect another echo-line, and we receive it — "Cuccu, cuccu." But this is followed by another surprise — two more three-beat lines, a little congratulation to the harbinger of spring: "Wel singes thu, cuccu. / Ne swik thu never nu!" The lilt of the whole makes us recognize it as a song, even though we find it in printed form.

Besides its rhythmic shape, then, this little two-stanza poem has exhibited a logical shape, separating the vegetative springing of seed and mead and wood (stanza 1) from the animal springing of bullocks (stanza 2), and it has also made a pleasing alternation between description ("Sumer is icumen in") and direct address ("Sing, cuccu!"). It has even displayed another shape: in both stanzas some verbs precede their nouns ("Groweth sed," "Lhouth after calve cu") and some do not ("Sumer is icumen in," "Bulluc sterteth"). These changes make for unpredictability, and therefore pleasure, since we derive pleasure in poems, just as in life, not only from pattern but from the interruption of pattern. If everything

were unpredictable we would have chaos, but what we usually find in a
good poem is the unpredictable within an overarching purposiveness.

Dave Smith's poem on spring uses one of the oldest European
lyric forms, that of the sonnet. Smith's sonnet is a hybrid one, with a
Shakespearean rhyming *ababcdcd* octave and a Petrarchan sestet, *efefee*:

DAVE SMITH (b. 1942)
The Spring Poem

> *Every poet should write a Spring poem.*
> — LOUISE GLÜCK

Yes, but we must be sure of verities
such as proper heat and adequate form.
That's what poets are for, is my theory.
This then is a Spring poem. A car warms
its rusting hulk in a meadow; weeds slog
up its flanks in martial weather. April
or late March is our month. There is a fog
of spunky mildew and sweaty tufts spill
from the damp rump of a back seat. A spring
thrusts one gleaming tip out, a brilliant tooth
uncoiling from Winter's tension, a ring
of insects along, working out the Truth.
Each year this car, melting around that spring,
hears nails trench from boards and every squeak sing.

Although Smith, in homage to Shakespeare's spring sonnets
("From you have I been absent in the spring," etc.), has given his spring
sonnet a Shakespearean octave, he has not divided his sonnet neatly, in
terms of thought-units, into three quatrains and a couplet, as Shake-
speare usually did. Instead, Smith's poem begins as a reply to the remark
by Louise Glück, couching its reply in stern theoretical language about
proper and adequate verities. It then announces its own existence: "This
then is a Spring poem."

The rest of the poem is description: an actual present-tense
description of the rusting car, followed (in the closing couplet) by a
habitual-present-tense description of what happens "each year," reassur-
ing us that the previous present-tense process has happened before and
happens, in fact, every year. But there is one odd moment in the descrip-
tion of weeds, fog, mildew, tufts, back-seat spring, nails, and boards. It is
the phrase about the insects who gather on the metal spring: they are

"working out the Truth." The word "truth" is the Anglo-Saxon form of the Latinate word "verity" (used earlier in line 1 in the plural, "verities"), so we know that the insects are experiencing "proper heat and adequate form" and are stand-ins for the poet seeking his verities. As the metal tooth of the spring uncoils, so the weeds and the rest of nature are uncoiling from winter tension, and the poet has to follow along that uncoiling motion, tracing the path of truth as the insects trace the new path afforded them by the newly sprung spring.

From the end of line 4 through line 12, each line spills over into the next one as the scene uncoils before us. Nothing is end-stopped, everything is growing and expanding. (Poems usually indicate a pause at the end of a line either by a break in thought or by the use of a comma, a period, or some other mark of punctuation; when lines "run over," we are to infer an ongoing rush of thought or feeling.) The last two lines of Smith's poem, though, because they tell us what happens "every year" instead of what is happening "now," are a neat couplet; they represent not discovery but summary. Smith has given us first the theory of the spring poem, then the spring poem in action, and finally the spring poem in habitual summary, showing us his three responses to Glück's demand — "I know the theory, I know the thing itself, and I know it happens every year." He also shows us that he is aware Shakespeare did it first, while refusing, as a Modernist, to follow the Renaissance neatness of the four Shakespearean separate thought-units, one for each quatrain, one for the couplet.

Keats's sonnet on the human seasons is written in imitation of Shakespeare, meaning that it has four quatrains and a couplet. Spring happens in quatrain 1, summer in 2, autumn in 3, and winter in the couplet; we can see Keats's orderly arrangement at work. Since not only this procession of the four seasons but also its analogy to human life (from spring-youth to winter-old age) are all predictable once the subject is decided upon, how will Keats make his (known in advance) process aesthetically interesting?

JOHN KEATS (1795 – 1821)
The Human Seasons

Four seasons fill the measure of the year;
    Four seasons are there in the mind of man.
He hath his lusty spring, when fancy clear
    Takes in all beauty with an easy span:
He hath his summer, when luxuriously
    He chews the honied cud of fair spring thoughts,

Till, in his soul dissolv'd, they come to be
    Part of himself. He hath his autumn ports
And havens of repose, when his tired wings
    Are folded up, and he content to look
On mists in idleness: to let fair things
    Pass by unheeded as a threshold brook.
He hath his winter too of pale misfeature,
Or else he would forget his mortal nature.

First of all, Keats doesn't speak of the seasons of the human *body* —
doesn't say, "Man has his spring of youth, his summer of maturity, his
autumn of decline, and his winter of death." That cliché was too well
known. He decides to put the seasons inside man's *mind*. Does the mind,
like the body, have seasons? And if so, what are they like (since the mind,
in the ordinary sense, does not grow old)? Briefly put, what Keats says is
that in youth the mind finds an easy pleasure in spanning the whole
world, absorbing everything beautiful. In mental summer, man reconsid-
ers the "fair thoughts" of his spring, redigesting them till they dissolve in
his soul and become totally internalized, part of himself. During his
mental autumn, he rests, folds his wings, and doesn't try to see
everything — he is "content to look on mists in idleness." At this stage,
he allows fair things to "pass by unheeded," as a cottager might fail to
notice the brook that flows by beyond his threshold. What does the man
look on in winter? Not "all beauty," not "fair things," not even
"mists" — rather, he looks on "pale misfeature." Why must he look on
the diseased and the deformed? Because otherwise, he would "forget his
mortal nature." He would forget that he too must grow pale and die, if
he looked only on the beautiful or the misty.

This is a brief summary of a complex poem, but it is enough to
show the rapid progress of the Keatsian seasonal sketches — the winged
fancy of spring, the cud chewing of summer during the pondering of
beauty in the soul, the ports and havens for man's autumn migration, the
folding of his tired wings among the mists of uncertainty, the threshold
brook passing by unheeded outside the house of (as Keats called himself)
the "spiritual cottager." Keats's poems often lead us along by a succession
of such descriptions. Without the unexpectedness of all these lightly
drawn images, the procession of the seasons might be too predictable.
And Keats lets each of the first three seasons slip into the next almost
imperceptibly, imitating the way of nature. Only winter is unmistakably
set apart in the couplet, as misfeature replaces feature.

In Chapter 1, we looked at Shakespeare's three models of life in
Sonnet 60: the steady-state model of successive waves in which each

moment of life resembles its predecessor and its successor; the rise-and-eclipse-of-the-sun model that sketches a catastrophic view of life; and the third, worst, model, in which we do not even have time to grow before we are scythed down. This structure in itself would have seemed sufficient to many poets. In fact, it would have seemed too much. Often, poems offer only one model of whatever they are discussing. But Shakespeare found it irresistible, very often, to let each of his quatrains set up a model *different* from those set up by the others. The intellectual tension thereby generated — "Is life a steady-state procession? Or a single long climb and fall? Or nothing but successive and premature annihilations?" — involves the reader strongly in the progress of the poem:

WILLIAM SHAKESPEARE (1564 – 1616)
Sonnet 60

Like as the waves make toward the pebbled shore,
So do our minutes hasten to their end,
Each changing place with that which goes before,
In sequent toil all forwards do contend.
Nativity, once in the main of light,
Crawls to maturity, wherewith being crowned,
Crooked eclipses 'gainst his glory fight,
And Time that gave doth now his gift confound.
Time doth transfix the flourish set on youth,
And delves the parallels in beauty's brow,
Feeds on the rarities of nature's truth,
And nothing stands but for his scythe to mow.
    And yet to times in hope my verse shall stand,
    Praising thy worth, despite his cruel hand.

Each of Shakespeare's three models of Time is a mini-poem in itself. The first model displays itself in balanced ceremonious full uninterrupted lines, like successive waves, making its analogy calmly, as a sermon might:

Metaphor (in simile-form)	Like as the waves . . . shore,
Literal truth	So do our minutes . . . end,
Elaboration	Each changing . . . before,
	In sequent toil . . . contend.

The next model is far more troubled, and its pace is charted by its governing words in *cr:* *"crawls," "crowned," "crooked."*

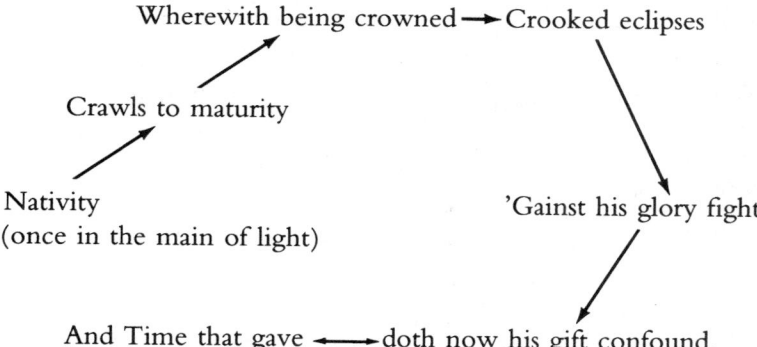

We see nativity crawl up to crowning, then crookedness fight it to death. Time gives on the left, takes away on the right. This is what we think of as the tragic model embedded in those of Shakespeare's plays that show the rise and fall of a character like Macbeth or Othello. It is completely different from Shakespeare's steady-state model in quatrain 1.

Shakespeare's third model consists neither of steady-state waves nor of rising and eclipsed sun. It shows us a drastic speed-up in his rate of extinction. It took three lines for the sun to be extinguished; now the deaths occur at the rate of one per line for two lines, and then several per line:

> Time doth transfix the flourish set on youth,
> And delves the parallels in beauty's brow,
> Feeds on the rarities of nature's truth,
> And nothing stands but for his scythe to mow.

These destructions take place with appalling rapidity, but, what is worse, the way they are related by the syntax of the clauses puts death before lived life. Transfixing precedes flourishing, wrinkles (delved "parallels") precede the appearance of the beautiful brow, devouring precedes the growing of the rare items in nature's garden. Finally, life itself is seen to exist for scything, and for that alone: "*Nothing* stands but *for* his scythe to mow." The poet Gerard Manley Hopkins was later to say bitterly, remembering this line, that man was born *for* death: "It is the blight man was *born for.*"

Shakespeare's three mini-poems, three incompatible models of life, have now been sketched in his sonnet. They are all about Time, and how nothing stands. The couplet, in revenge, shifts from "Time" to "times," and makes them "times in hope" — that is, the envisaged future. The couplet also shifts from "nothing stands" to something standing. In future times ("times in hope"), when the organic world has died, the inorganic world of art, which the scythe cannot mow down, will stand:

> And yet to *times* in hope my verse shall *stand,*
> Praising your worth, despite his cruel hand.

This boast might seem to vanquish Time, if the poem did not end with the hand of Time itself, characterized by an adjective — "cruel" — which opens with the same *cr*- of doom which we remember from the tragic series "crawls," "crowned," "crooked." "Cruel" comes from the Latin *cruor,* "blood" — and Time's bloody hand is set over against the "hand," or handwriting, that creates verse praising worth. It is something of a standoff — but even that is a victory for the rarities of art's truth. After the three competing models of natural life, each more destructive than the last, Shakespeare has closed his sonnet with a model of the endurance — not forever, but at least to "times in hope" — of his verse.

This second look at our original poems suggests that one can't fully understand a poem until one sees the various shapes into which meaning has been arranged. We have seen steady-state shapes, and shapes of increase and decrease; shapes of contrast and alternation; shapes of series, both internally consistent and inconsistent; shapes of pointed metrical emphasis, of space and time. There is no lack of shapes for poets to imitate — every human action conducted over time offers such a shape, of success or failure, of stasis or catastrophe, of contest or conciliation. The dynamism of such shapes gives dynamism to poetry.

In Brief: The Poem as Arranged Life

We have seen, by taking a second look at the poems introduced in Chapter 1, how each of these poems is not only an utterance springing from a life-situation, but also a construction, an arrangement. The elements that can enter into the arranging of a poem are very various. The author can be arranging a sound-pattern while arranging a list of parallel elements, and also, simultaneously, advancing the plot through a series of changes in tense or mood. Or the author can be setting up a stanza form at the same time as a logical form: the stanza form may tell us that the poem is a ballad, while the construction may tell us that the poem is built on a logical contrast between "then" and "now." A poem may say "the same thing" three times ("I am growing old"), but each time may use a different model for aging and thus convey a different emphasis. Tones of voice can be varied, from protest to resignation, while another element is held constant (say, the tense of the verbs). By learning to look at each level of organization — phonetic, grammatical, syntactic, psychological, temporal, spatial, and so on — you learn to see the work the author is doing to make the poem both interesting on many levels and coherent in its arrangements. We will be looking at all of these levels in greater detail in subsequent chapters.

Reading Other Poems

The following poems have strong and visible structures. Think first about the life-situation out of which each emerges, and then begin to explore the way in which the life-situation has been imagined and arranged. "Lord Randal," for instance, is structured by the stages of its narrative, as is George Herbert's "Love."

◆ Does each of these poems begin at the outset of its narrative, or do some begin in the middle?

Given that every plot has a beginning and an end, the writer has the most free play in composing the middle. At the beginning of Herbert's poem, the sinful soul has arrived, after death, at the gate of heaven; at the end of the poem, the soul sits down and participates in the heavenly banquet.

◆ What happens in the middle?

◆ How many stages are there between beginning and end?

John Donne's poem doesn't reach the beginning of its story about a husband's departure on a journey — "I must go" — until it has traversed a long comparison of the way virtuous men die and the way virtuous spouses part. How does Donne end his plot?

Shakespeare, Robert Herrick, and Robert Frost, on the other hand, use contrastive structures to explore two different states: Shakespeare contrasts depression and elation; Herrick presents a woman clothed and the same woman naked; Frost contrasts the life lived and the life unlived. Rather than contrast, Walt Whitman uses analogy: He explains his own actions through those of a spider.

◆ How does the structure of each of these poems reinforce the contrast or the comparison?

◆ What is the imaginative spin put on each poem by the images chosen?

Thomas Hardy's poem about the collision of an iceberg and the *Titanic* begins in the present, with the sunken ship.

◆ Where does it end?
◆ Where else could it have begun or ended?

The most tightly structured of all these poems is probably "Tichborne's Elegy." Each of its three stanzas is constructed on roughly the same plan, but with variations.

◆ Can you describe the basic plan and specify how it varies in each stanza?
◆ Try rearranging the stanzas. Would it be the same poem if you interchanged stanzas 1 and 3?
◆ Can you see how the tenses change in the poem?

In her "footnote" to a report on torture issued by Amnesty International, Margaret Atwood has had to decide how to structure the chief elements of her poem: persons who are tortured and their torturers; a torture chamber; and a witness ("the man who works here"). If you draw a map of the poem, in what section is the scene of torture located? Where does Atwood put the torture chamber? What element is used to close the poem? Whose emotions does the poem follow closely? Where does this graph of emotions begin and end? Why?

Marilyn Nelson chooses an unexpected arrangement for a poem about animals at the zoo when she puts her poem into the form of a sonnet (fourteen five-beat lines, consisting of two quatrains and two tercets, with fairly regular rhymes). Look to see what animals inhabit the first quatrain, the second, the third, the couplet. Which animals are most specifically represented? Which have had names given to them? Nelson's choice of form is partly explained by her quotation from a sonnet by the German poet Rainer Maria Rilke concerning Orpheus, the legendary Thracian poet; according to Greek mythology, when Orpheus sang, animals listened and trees danced.

Anonymous
Lord Randal

1

"O where ha' you been, Lord Randal, my son?
And where ha' you been, my handsome young man?"

"I ha' been at the greenwood; mother, mak my bed soon,
For I'm wearied wi' huntin', and fain wad lie down."

2

"And wha met ye there, Lord Randal, my son?
And wha met you there, my handsome young man?"
"O I met wi' my true-love; mother, mak my bed soon,
For I'm wearied wi' huntin', and fain wad lie down."

3

"And what did she give you, Lord Randal, my son?
And what did she give you, my handsome young man?"
"Eels fried in a pan; mother, mak my bed soon,
For I'm wearied wi' huntin', and fain wad lie down."

4

"And wha gat your leavin's, Lord Randal, my son?
And wha gat your leavin's, my handsome young man?"
"My hawks and my hounds; mother, mak my bed soon,
For I'm wearied wi' huntin', and fain wad lie down."

5

"And what becam of them, Lord Randal, my son?
And what becam of them, my handsome young man?"
"They stretched their legs out and died; mother, mak my bed
     soon,
For I'm wearied wi' huntin', and fain wad lie down."

6

"O I fear you are poisoned, Lord Randal, my son!
I fear you are poisoned, my handsome young man!"
"O yes, I am poisoned; mother, mak my bed soon,
For I'm sick at the heart, and I fain wad lie down."

7

"What d' ye leave to your mother, Lord Randal, my son?
What d' ye leave to your mother, my handsome young man?"
"Four and twenty milk kye°; mother, mak my bed soon,   *cattle*
For I'm sick at the heart, and I fain wad lie down."

8

"What d' ye leave to your sister, Lord Randal, my son?
What d' ye leave to your sister, my handsome young man?"
"My gold and my silver; mother, mak my bed soon,
For I'm sick at the heart, and I fain wad lie down."

9

"What d' ye leave to your brother, Lord Randal, my son?
What d' ye leave to your brother, my handsome young man?"
"My houses and my lands; mother, mak my bed soon,
For I'm sick at the heart, and I fain wad lie down."

10

"What d' ye leave to your true-love, Lord Randal, my son?
What d' ye leave to your true-love, my handsome young man?"
"I leave her hell and fire; mother, mak my bed soon,
For I'm sick at the heart, and I fain wad lie down."

WILLIAM SHAKESPEARE (1564 – 1616)
Sonnet 29

When in disgrace° with fortune and men's eyes,	*disfavor*
I all alone beweep my outcast state,	
And trouble deaf heaven with my bootless° cries,	*futile*
And look upon myself and curse my fate,	

Wishing me like to one more rich in hope,
Featured like him, like him with friends possessed,
Desiring this man's art, and that man's scope,
With what I most enjoy contented least;
Yet in these thoughts myself almost despising,
Haply I think on thee, and then my state
(Like to the lark at break of day arising
From sullen earth) sings hymns at heaven's gate,
    For thy sweet love remembered such wealth brings
    That then I scorn to change my state with kings.

CHIDIOCK TICHBORNE (d. 1586)
Tichborne's Elegy

Written with his own hand in the Tower before his execution

My prime of youth is but a frost of cares,
My feast of joy is but a dish of pain,
My crop of corn is but a field of tares,
And all my good is but vain hope of gain;
The day is past, and yet I saw no sun,
And now I live, and now my life is done.

My tale was heard and yet it was not told,
My fruit is fallen and yet my leaves are green,
My youth is spent and yet I am not old,
I saw the world and yet I was not seen;
My thread is cut and yet it is not spun,
And now I live, and now my life is done.

I sought my death and found it in my womb,
I looked for life and saw it was a shade,
I trod the earth and knew it was my tomb,
And now I die, and now I was but made;
My glass° is full, and now my glass is run,   *hourglass*
And now I live, and now my life is done.

JOHN DONNE (1572 – 1631)
A Valediction: Forbidding Mourning

As virtuous men pass mildly away,
  And whisper to their souls to go,
Whilst some of their sad friends do say
  The breath goes now, and some say, No;

So let us melt, and make no noise,
  No tear-floods, nor sigh-tempests move,
'Twere profanation of our joys
  To tell the laity our love.

Moving of th' earth brings harms and fears,
  Men reckon what it did and meant;
But trepidation of the spheres,
  Though greater far, is innocent.

Dull sublunary° lovers' love   *earthly*
  (Whose soul is sense) cannot admit
Absence, because it doth remove
  Those things which elemented it.

But we by a love so much refined
  That our selves know not what it is,
Inter-assurèd of the mind,
  Care less, eyes, lips, and hands to miss.

Our two souls therefore, which are one,
  Though I must go, endure not yet

A breach, but an expansion,
    Like gold to airy thinness beat.

If they be two, they are two so
    As stiff twin compasses are two;
Thy soul, the fixed foot, makes no show
    To move, but doth, if th' other do.

And though it in the center sit,
    Yet when the other far doth roam,
It leans and hearkens after it,
    And grows erect, as that comes home.

Such wilt thou be to me, who must
    Like th' other foot, obliquely run;
Thy firmness makes my circle just,
    And makes me end where I begun.

ROBERT HERRICK (1591 – 1674)
Upon Julia's Clothes

Whenas in silks my Julia goes,
Then, then, methinks, how sweetly flows
That liquefaction of her clothes.

Next, when I cast mine eyes, and see
That brave vibration each way free,
O, how that glittering taketh me!

GEORGE HERBERT (1593 – 1633)
Love (III)

Love bade me welcome: yet my soul drew back,
    Guilty of dust and sin.
But quick-eyed Love, observing me grow slack
    From my first entrance in,
Drew nearer to me, sweetly questioning
    If I lacked anything.

"A guest," I answered, "worthy to be here":
    Love said, "You shall be he."
"I, the unkind, ungrateful? Ah, my dear,
    I cannot look on thee."

Love took my hand, and smiling did reply,
　　　　"Who made the eyes but I?"

"Truth, Lord; but I have marred them; let my shame
　　　　Go where it doth deserve."
"And know you not," says Love, "who bore the blame?"
　　　　"My dear, then I will serve."
"You must sit down," says Love, "and taste my meat."
　　　　So I did sit and eat.

WALT WHITMAN (1819 – 1892)
A Noiseless Patient Spider

A noiseless patient spider,
I mark'd where on a little promontory it stood isolated,
Mark'd how to explore the vacant vast surrounding,
It launch'd forth filament, filament, filament, out of itself,
Ever unreeling them, ever tirelessly speeding them.

And you O my soul where you stand,
Surrounded, detached, in measureless oceans of space,
Ceaselessly musing, venturing, throwing, seeking the spheres to
　　　connect them,
Till the bridge you will need be form'd, till the ductile anchor
　　　hold,
Till the gossamer thread you fling catch somewhere, O my soul.

THOMAS HARDY (1840 – 1928)
The Convergence of the Twain

Lines on the loss of the Titanic

1

　　In a solitude of the sea
　　Deep from human vanity,
And the Pride of Life that planned her, stilly couches she.

2

　　Steel chambers, late the pyres
　　Of her salamandrine fires,
Cold currents thrid,° and turn to rhythmic tidal lyres.　　　*thread*

3

Over the mirrors meant
To glass the opulent
The sea-worm crawls — grotesque, slimed, dumb, indifferent.

4

Jewels in joy designed
To ravish the sensuous mind
Lie lightless, all their sparkles bleared and black and blind.

5

Dim moon-eyed fishes near
Gaze at the gilded gear
And query: "What does this vaingloriousness down here?"

6

Well: while was fashioning
This creature of cleaving wing,
The Immanent Will that stirs and urges everything

7

Prepared a sinister mate
For her — so gaily great —
A Shape of Ice, for the time far and dissociate.

8

And as the smart ship grew
In stature, grace, and hue,
In shadowy silent distance grew the Iceberg too.

9

Alien they seemed to be:
No mortal eye could see
The intimate welding of their later history,

10

Or sign that they were bent
By paths coincident
On being anon twin halves of one august event,

11

Till the Spinner of the Years
Said "Now!" And each one hears,
And consummation comes, and jars two hemispheres.

ROBERT FROST (1874 – 1963)
The Road Not Taken

Two roads diverged in a yellow wood,
And sorry I could not travel both
And be one traveler, long I stood
And looked down one as far as I could
To where it bent in the undergrowth;

Then took the other, as just as fair,
And having perhaps the better claim,
Because it was grassy and wanted wear;
Though as for that, the passing there
Had worn them really about the same,

And both that morning equally lay
In leaves no step had trodden black.
Oh, I kept the first for another day!
Yet knowing how way leads on to way,
I doubted if I should ever come back.

I shall be telling this with a sigh
Somewhere ages and ages hence:
Two roads diverged in a wood, and I —
I took the one less traveled by,
And that has made all the difference.

MARGARET ATWOOD (b. 1939)
Footnote to the Amnesty Report on Torture

The torture chamber is not like anything
you would have expected.
No opera set or sexy chains and
leather-goods from the glossy
porno magazines, no thirties horror   5
dungeon with gauzy cobwebs; nor is it
the bare cold–lighted
chrome space of the future
we think we fear.
More like one of the seedier   10
British Railways stations, with scratched green
walls and spilled tea,

crumpled papers, and a stooped man
who is always cleaning the floor.

It stinks, though; like a hospital,   15
of antiseptics and sickness,
and, on some days, blood
which smells the same anywhere,
here or at the butcher's.

The man who works here   20
is losing his sense of smell.
He's glad to have this job, because
there are few others.
He isn't a torturer, he only
cleans the floor: 25
every morning the same vomit,
the same shed teeth, the same
piss and liquid shit, the same panic.

Some have courage, others
don't; those who do what he thinks of   30
as the real work, and who are
bored, since minor bureaucrats
are always bored, tell them
it doesn't matter, who
will ever know they were brave, they might   35
as well talk now
and get it over.

Some have nothing to say, which also
doesn't matter. Their
warped bodies too, with the torn   40
fingers and ragged tongues, are thrown
over the spiked iron fence onto
the Consul's lawn, along with
the bodies of children
burned to make their mothers talk.   45

The man who cleans the floors
is glad it isn't him.
It will be if he ever says
what he knows. He works long hours,
submits to the searches, eats   50
a meal he brings from home, which tastes
of old blood and the sawdust

he cleans the floor with. His wife
is pleased he brings her money
for the food, has been told   55
not to ask questions.

As he sweeps, he tries
not to listen; he tries
to make himself into a wall,
a thick wall, a wall   60
soft and without echoes. He thinks
of nothing but the walk back
to his hot shed of a house,
of the door
opening and his children   65
with their unmarked skin and flawless eyes
running to meet him.

He is afraid of
what he might do
if he were told to,   70
he is afraid of the door,

he is afraid, not
of the door but of the door
opening; sometimes, no matter
how hard he tries,   75
his children are not there.

MARILYN NELSON (b. 1946)
Live Jazz, Franklin Park Zoo

> *Kubie sobbed when a nearby jazz band stopped playing.*
> — CHRISTIAN SCIENCE MONITOR, 8/27/96

A tree grew. Oh, remembering gorillas!
O *Orpheus singt!*[1] Oh, Africa in the ear!
The recluse, Vip, came out. Gigi sat still
and wide-eyed, black face pressed against the bars.

---

[1]From Rainer Maria Rilke's *Sonnets to Orpheus.*

Kubie lay on his back, as he usually does,
vacantly staring. Then he turned over, hairy chin
on one huge leather palm; with his other hand
he scratched his head, contemplatively picked his nose.

The zebras' ears twirled. Behind their fancy fences,
the silenced animals listened to something new.
Suddenly their calls, even the lion's roar,

shrank in their hearts, as they knew something more.
And where there had been, at most, a nest of boughs
to receive it, music built a cathedral in their senses.

3

Poems as Pleasure

Every artwork exists to evoke pleasures that are easier to feel than to describe. Music, for instance, gives rhythmic pleasure and melodic pleasure and harmonic pleasure, in different proportions in different pieces. Some paintings afford the pleasure of recognizable representation; some (purely abstract or nonobjective) do not. Sketches in black-and-white and sketches in color both give pleasure, but of different kinds. We can say in general that all artworks appeal to our (apparently inborn) love of patterning, whether the rhythmic and melodic patterning we hear in music, or the visual patterning we see in a painting or a quilt, or the patterning of volume that we see in architecture, from a cathedral to a cottage. Pattern and rhythm are very closely connected, so closely that people talk of the rhythm of repetition in the successive vaults of a church nave, or the rhythm of repeated curves in a painting.

Since the base of all organic life is repetition (repeated motion in growth and form), and since human life, by its heartbeat and breathing, is innately rhythmic, we can suppose that there is a biological basis for our recognition of, and apparently instinctive pleasure in, repetition. Besides our almost unconscious biological patterns of breathing and sleeping, we enjoy simple repetitive patterned body motions — rocking a baby, swimming, riding a bicycle. Babies learn by patterned repetition, and the pleasure of learning and recognizing new and old patterns is probably the source of our deepest pleasure in art. Most of the true and wise things said in artworks have also been said (in less-patterned and unrhythmic ways) in philosophy and letters and newspaper editorials and conversation, where they also may strike us as true and wise, but not as art. In distinguishing literary artworks from other verbal pieces of truth or wisdom, we tend to be moved by the more intense patterning of the artwork.

The excess of patterning, beyond what is necessary to convey paraphrasable meaning, gives the work what we sometimes call "literariness." Just as a painting can use its elements of pattern — line (bold or delicate), color (moody or cheerful), and visual allusions (such as posing a figure in a gesture known to us from Greek sculpture) — to "say" more than merely "Here is a young woman naked," or "Here is a house in a field," so poems too convey their effects through their manner as much as through their matter. In using pattern in excess of what is strictly necessary for prose meaning, the poet reveals an intent to make art as well as to represent being. The representational urge of most poets is very strong, and every serious poet has something serious to say. Yet though a poet such as Yeats often says "the same thing" in his essays, letters, and speeches — works which we would not tend to call art — as he has said in a poem, we feel a great difference in the manner of the saying. What, then, are the pleasures we find in poems that we cannot find in a prose paraphrase of the same poem or in an essay advocating the same ideas?

Rhythm

The first and most elementary pleasure in all poetry is rhythm. Poetry is far more visibly rhythmic than most prose, and its rhythms are recurrent. Even in free verse, where lines are of unpredictably different lengths and may not rhyme, we often hear the same rhythms recurring. T. S. Eliot's character J. Alfred Prufrock, for instance, both wants to encounter experience (especially sexual experience) and wants to run away from it. His "theme rhythm," as a fellow teacher once pointed out to me, is a little initial skip (˘˘´) in which *two* unstressed syllables are followed by one stressed syllable: "Let us GO." But the little excited skip can't be kept up — each time Prufrock uses it, it dies out into the "ordinary" rhythm of one unstressed syllable followed by one stressed syllable (˘´). "Let us GO, then, YOU and I." And the subsequent lines continue to begin with a skip and die out into a walk, off and on, throughout the poem, right down to the line that is the third from the end, which is the last time we hear the skip:

We have LINGered in the chambers of the sea
By sea-girls wreathed in seaweed red and brown
Till human voices wake us, and we drown.

Good free verse always matches its rhythms to the emotional content of its utterance — in Prufrock's words, "As if a magic lantern threw the nerves in patterns on a screen."

But free verse, though it is a major form in contemporary poetry, is a relatively recent invention. Most poetry in most languages, historically speaking, has had a regular rhythm (though much of it has not had rhyme). English verse began in Anglo-Saxon poetry with no rhyme but a strong four-beat rhythm, and that four-beat rhythm is still very natural to us. In Anglo-Saxon poetic rules, at least three of the four stressed words in a line had to begin with the same consonant-sound ("cat" and "king," even though they begin with different consonants, begin with the same consonant-sound). A modern poet writing in four-beat lines reminds us, by his matching stressed consonant-sounds and words (see those italicized below) that he knows the old forms. Here is the beginning of Wallace Stevens's "A Postcard from the Volcano," in which the dead (like the dead buried in Pompeii by the eruption of Mount Vesuvius) speak to the generations following them who are excavating their buried city:

Children picking up our bones
Will *never know* that these *were once*
As quick° as foxes on the hill;   *fast, alive*

And that in autumn, when the grapes
Made *sharp* air *sharper* by their smell
These had a *being, breathing* frost;

And least *will* guess that *with* our bones
We *left much more, left what* still is
The *look* of things, *left what we* felt

At *what we* saw.

After the conquest of England by the French in 1066, Anglo-Saxon forms of poetry gave way to newer forms that counted by syllables instead of solely by stress. Gradually, a stable set of possible English rhythms evolved and were given names borrowed from Greek meters (iambic, trochaic, and so on; see appendix "On Prosody" in this volume). A number of rhymed stanza-forms (such as the sonnet and the villanelle) were adapted from European models. Poets can always invent new rhythms and new stanza-forms (as Gerard Manley Hopkins did in the second half of the nineteenth century, and as the free-verse poets did in the twentieth century). They can also revive or adapt older forms (Wallace Stevens, for instance, made the pentameter three-line stanza of Dante his favorite form, though he did not use Dante's rhymes). The more you read, the more you tend to notice the rhythms poets write in, and how the stanzas rhyme.

Rhythm itself is a distinct pleasure. Here are some samples of things people have liked:

Nursery rhythms, strong and emphatic:

> Ding, dong, bell,
> Pussy's in the well.
> Who threw her in?
> Little Johnny Thin.
> Who pulled her out?
> Little Tommy Stout.

The insistent hypnotic rhythms (ONE-two-three-four) of Edgar Allan Poe's four-beat lines in "The Raven":

> Once upon a midnight dreary, while I pondered weak and weary,
> Over many a quaint and curious volume of forgotten lore,
> As I nodded, nearly napping, suddenly I heard a tapping,
> As of someone gently rapping, rapping at my chamber door.

The excited and syncopated five-beat rhythms of Hopkins's "The Starlight Night":

> Look at the stars! look, look up at the skies!
>   O look at all the fire-folk sitting in the air!
>   The bright boroughs, the circle-citadels there!
> Down in dim woods the diamond-delves! the elves'-eyes!

The complex four-beat rhythms of Algernon Charles Swinburne's "When the Hounds of Spring," where dactyls (ONE-two-three) and trochees (ONE-two) predominate:

> And PAN by NOON and BACCHus by NIGHT,
>   FLEETer of FOOT than the FLEET-foot KID,
> FOLLows with DANCing and FILLS with deLIGHT
>   The MAEnad AND the BASSarid;°   *Bacchus's devotees*

And SOFT as LIPS that LAUGH and HIDE,
The LAUGHing LEAVES of the TREES diVIDE,
And SCREEN from SEEing and LEAVE in SIGHT
    The GOD purSUing, the MAIDen HID.

When rhythms become too insistent, they seem like parodies of themselves. For "Hiawatha," Henry Wadsworth Longfellow picked up the four-beat trochaic rhythm (ONE-two) of the Scandinavian epics, but because it is not, in its unrhymed form, a native narrative rhythm in English, it becomes tedious, as in this description of Hiawatha making a picture of the earth:

For the earth he drew a straight line,
For the sky a bow above it;
White the space between for day-time,
Filled with little stars for night-time;
On the left a point for sunrise,
On the right a point for sunset,
On the top a point for noon-tide.

Such a repetitive rhythm was bound to give rise to parodies. George A. Strong's runs, in part:

Of the skin he made him mittens,
Made them with the fur side inside,
Made them with the skin side outside.

Most English verse is made up of rhythms less insistent than those I have been illustrating. The usual English rhythms are one-TWO (iambic) or ONE-two (trochaic), and the usual English line has three or four or five stresses. In most verse, the pleasures of rhythm come from the tension between the basic metrical scheme of the line (one-TWO, one-TWO, one-TWO, one-TWO, one-TWO, as if you were to say, five times, "Untie, untie, untie, untie, untie") and the actual spoken intonation of the line. The underlying scheme of *all* of Shakespeare's dramatic poetry is "Untie untie untie untie untie," but what we actually find is an enormously flexible spoken line:

Tomorrow, and tomorrow, and tomorrow,
Creeps in this petty pace from day to day,
To the last syllable of recorded time.

We hear the undersong of the *metrical scheme* as a child might mechanically recite it, as if to a metronome:

> ToMORRow, AND toMORRow, AND toMORRow,
> Creeps IN this PETTy PACE from DAY to DAY,
> To THE last SYLLable OF reCORDed TIME.

And we also sense the oversong of the *natural intonation of the words* as they would be ordinarily spoken:

> ToMORRow, and toMORRow, and toMORRow,
> CREEPS IN this PETTy PACE from DAY to DAY,
> To the LAST SYLLable of reCORDed TIME.

A good actor makes an amalgam of metrical scheme and natural intonation, so that the audience hears a *rhythm* that keeps both the undersong of five beats and the oversong of urgent speech. One of the hardest things to do in poetry is to write hundreds of lines obeying the same *scheme* (as Milton does with his unrhymed five-beat lines in *Paradise Lost*) while varying the *rhythm,* so that the reader's ear does not tire. Of course, composers do the same. Every measure of a musical piece in 4/4 time has four beats to the measure, but not every measure is composed of four quarter-notes. There are eighth-notes, sixteenth-notes, half-notes, whole notes, held notes, notes with trills on them, and so on.

Knowing the musical weight, so to speak, of every possible syllable in the language is the gift of great poets. Some syllables are heavy, some light; some long, some short; some open, some closed; some nasal, some mellow; some sharp, some sweet. Keats, in his poem "If by dull rhymes," advises himself and other poets to care at least as much for syllabic wealth as King Midas cared for his gold, and not to repeat lifeless and worn-out strategies:

> Let us inspect the lyre, and weigh the stress
> Of every chord, and see what may be gained
> By ear industrious, and attention meet;
> Misers of sound and syllable, no less
> Than Midas of his coinage, let us be
> Jealous of dead leaves in the bay wreath crown.

Rhythms should be recurrent but not boring, hearable but not predictable.

Rhyme

We seem to be born liking sounds that match. Children make up games with simple counting rhymes. "One, two, button my shoe" still lives, though no one wears high-button shoes any more. Rhyme makes for conclusiveness and the sense of an ending. Once you accept the principle of rhyme, you can do many various things with it.

Rhythmically speaking, the simplest rhymes are monosyllables — *day, say*. You get a different effect from disyllables — *reason, treason*. The effect often becomes comic once you get trisyllables — *temptation, relation*. You can combine words having different numbers of syllables — *lover, discover*.

Graphically speaking, the simplest rhymes are those that are spelled the same — *day, say*. You get a different effect, even with monosyllables, when they are spelled differently — *day, weigh*. When you have three monosyllables, all with different spelling, the sense of poetic invention is even stronger — *day, weigh, fey*. Though amateur poets tend to rhyme monosyllables spelled the same way, poets interested in technical invention tend to investigate all the possibilities of more complicated polysyllabic and differently spelled rhyming words.

Grammatically speaking, the simplest rhymes are those in which both words are the same part of speech — say, two verbs (*weigh, neigh*) or two nouns (*cat, hat*). As soon as you have two words that are matched by rhyme but that don't match in other ways — say, a noun and a verb (*day, weigh*) — you feel a slight shock of difference.

Semantically speaking, the most satisfactory rhymes are ones in which the two rhyming words have some meaning-relation to each other. The meaning-relation may be one of sameness (*high/sky*) or difference (*island/highland*).

Some poets care a great deal more about making their rhymes meaningful than others do. Comic poets especially like to make points by ridiculous rhymes: here is Lord Byron on the young Don Juan's classical education, which Juan's mother (Donna Inez) must countenance but which she finds shocking. We can imagine how Byron amused himself rhyming "goddesses," "bodices," and "Odysseys":

> His classic studies made a little puzzle,
>   Because of filthy loves of gods and goddesses,
> Who in the earlier ages raised a bustle,
>   But never put on pantaloons or bodices;
> His reverend tutors had at times a tussle,
>   And for their Aeneids, Iliads, and Odysseys,

Were forced to make an odd sort of apology,
For Donna Inez dreaded the Mythology.

To make end-rhymes, one must have at least two lines, explaining why Keats thought of a kiss as a rhyme (and perhaps of a rhyme as a kiss of language). Arranging lines (usually rhyming lines, but not necessarily so) in a perceptible shape makes a stanza. One of the well-known stanza forms in English is a stanza of six five-beat lines rhyming *ababcc*. That is, the first and third lines rhyme on one sound — here designated *a;* the second and fourth lines rhyme on a different sound, *b;* and the fifth and sixth lines rhyme on yet another sound, *c*. Though this can be used in a long poem (it is in fact called the "*Venus and Adonis* stanza" because Shakespeare used it in his narrative poem of that name), it is also used by Ben Jonson in his one-stanza satiric poem on a lustful glutton allegorically named "Gut":

BEN JONSON
On Gut

Gut eats all day and lechers all the night;
So all his meat he tasteth over twice;
And, striving so to double his delight,
He makes himself a thoroughfare of vice.
Thus in his belly can he change a sin:
Lust it comes out, that gluttony went in.

Most poems written in stanza-form, unlike "On Gut," consist of more than one stanza. Stanzas have names (see the appendix "On Prosody"), and poems using the same stanza forms belong to a recognizable family. Yeats may use a stanza-form associated with Geoffrey Chaucer; Keats may use the sonnet-form we associate with Shakespeare. As we read the later poet, we are reminded of the earlier one (and as we read the earlier one, we sometimes think forward to how a later poet will write in this stanza-form). Poets make certain stanza-forms their own. Dante wrote the whole of the *Divine Comedy* in three-line pentameter stanzas with interlaced rhyme, and ever since, anyone writing in this form or one of its modern adaptations — from Percy Bysshe Shelley in the nineteenth century through Wallace Stevens and Seamus Heaney in the twentieth century — evokes Dante.

Some stanzaic forms undergo interesting changes over time. Early narrative ballads were written in a stanza rhyming *abcb,* meaning that only the second and fourth lines rhymed. Usually the first line had four beats, the second three, the third four, and the fourth three (which we represent as 4/3/4/3). The early ballads were primarily stories in verse: the important feature in them was a plot of love, mystery, or adventure that moved incrementally on, often to disaster. Characterization and emotional reaction and description were kept to a minimum. Here is a representative ballad stanza, clearly interested in setting up a story:

> There lived a wife at Usher's Well,
>   And a wealthy wife was she;
> She had three stout and stalwart sons,
>   And sent them o'er the sea.

In the nineteenth century, William Wordsworth, though he was still interested in telling stories, was more concerned with the inner states and emotional responses accompanying events than in the events themselves. He invented what he called "lyrical ballads"; they were still written in the ballad stanza, and were allied to storytelling, but their emphasis was "lyrical" — that is, emotional and private rather than factual and plot-governed. Here is the ending of one of Wordsworth's lyrical ballads:

> She lived unknown, and few could know
>   When Lucy ceased to be;
> But she is in her grave, and, oh,
>   The difference to me!

Both "The Wife of Usher's Well" and Wordsworth's poem have the same stanzaic arrangement — four beats, three beats, four beats, three beats — with the second and fourth lines rhyming (and in Wordsworth's poem the first and third lines rhyming as well). Whenever we see this 4/3/4/3 rhyming stanza turn up, we are reminded that it goes back to our earliest folk poetry. When later poets want to write in an archaic way, they often use this stanza or a variant on it (see Samuel Taylor Coleridge's "Rime of the Ancient Mariner" and Keats's "La Belle Dame sans Merci").

The ballad stanza is four lines long, and so is called a quatrain, as are all stanzas of four lines. But there are other kinds of rhymes that a quatrain can use besides *abcb* or *abab*. It can use *aabb,* as in "Infant Sorrow":

> My mother groaned, my father wept.
> Into the dangerous world I leapt,
> Helpless, naked, piping loud;
> Like a fiend hid in a cloud.

Or a quatrain can rhyme *abba,* a form that Alfred, Lord Tennyson used in his long elegy "In Memoriam":

> Ring out, wild bells, to the wild sky,
>> The flying cloud, the frosty light:
>> The year is dying in the night;
> Ring out, wild bells, and let him die.

Several different variables combine to make stanzas: the length of the stanza (here, in our examples, four lines); the stress-length of the individual lines (4/3/4/3 in the ballads, 4/4/4/4 in Blake's and Tennyson's poems); the arrangement of the rhymes (whether *abab, aabb,* or *abba*); and the combination of stressed and unstressed syllables. Poets experiment with all these variables to make the different kinds of stanzas named below (which are described at fuller length in the appendix "On Prosody"):

Two lines: *couplet*

Three lines: *tercet*

Four lines: *quatrain*

Five lines: *cinquain*

Six lines: *sixain* or *sestet*

Seven lines: *rime royal* (rhyming *ababbcc*)

Eight lines: *ottava rima* (rhyming *abababcc*)

Nine lines: *Spenserian stanza* (rhyming *ababbcbcc*)

Fourteen lines: *sonnet*

By and large, the longer stanzas listed above are written in five-beat widths. But almost any combination of width (number of beats per line) and length (number of lines) and rhyme has been tried by someone. The important thing is to notice what the poet has been up to in the way of metrical form — rhymes, line-width, and stanza-shape — and to recall, if you can, other poems that have the same stanzaic shape as the one you are reading. One of the pleasures offered by poetry is a technical cousinship among poems, recognizable if you are used to registering the stanzaic shapes they take.

Structure

The structures of a poem are the intellectual or logical shapes into which its thoughts are dynamically organized. Any overarching structure can have many substructures. We saw, in "Infant Sorrow," a general structure in which the first stanza shows us the physical baby, the second the baby as thinker. Within that general structure we saw others — the presence of the parents in each stanza, the decline from *struggling* to *striving* to *bound,* and so on. Perhaps the greatest pleasure given by poetry is the sense that dynamic structure and thought are so intimately connected that each gives coherence to the other. We sometimes express this by saying that the structure of the poem *enacts* (acts out, dramatizes) by way of a dynamic evolution of form what the poem *says* by way of assertion.

How does one come to perceive the structure by which the poem conveys its assertions? As we saw in Chapter 2, it takes something like X-ray vision, by which you look for patterns. Patterns occur at many levels in poetry, just as they do in the physical universe: one can look for patterns in subatomic behavior, in atomic behavior, in molecular behavior, and so on, all the way up to the patterns of the planets and the stars. If you think of a poem as a small universe, you can begin looking at the smallest patterns (the binding-together of certain words by rhyme or by similar initial sounds) or at the largest patterns (the number of sentences and their relations to each other as a dynamic pattern of thinking). One level of investigation may not yield much: the poem you are looking at may not rhyme, and there may be only a relatively small number of alliterating words (words beginning with the same consonant-sound). At this point, you would probably give up looking for interesting sound-patterns, and move on to sentence-relations. Or, on another level, the poem may not have many descriptive phrases representing people or a landscape — it may be mostly statement (say, of philosophical truths). At this point, you would stop looking for a pattern of descriptive images, and perhaps move on to patterns of diction. Or, on another level, that of plot, nothing much may seem to happen. Do not be discouraged; if the energy of the poem is not in plot, it may be in its grammatical play; if it is not in grammatical play, it may be in images; if it is not in images, it may be in rhythm.

What, for instance, could we find to say about this poem, called simply "Poem," by William Carlos Williams?

WILLIAM CARLOS WILLIAMS (1883 – 1963)
Poem

As the cat
climbed over
the top of

the jamcloset
first the right
forefoot

carefully
then the hind
stepped down

into the pit of
the empty
flowerpot

There certainly isn't much that is philosophical or intellectual here. In fact, if the four stanzas were written out as the one sentence they are, it wouldn't seem like a poem at all: "As the cat climbed over the top of the jamcloset, first the right forefoot, carefully, then the hind, stepped down into the pit of the empty flowerpot." And the "plot" — a cat finding its way — is an ordinary event seen every day. A good strategy in examining a poem is always to see why the poet wrote out its sentences in the way he or she did. Williams divided his sentence into four stanzas, each of three lines. How did he decide where to break his sentence, and why did he group the twelve pieces three-by-three? If we reread the poem asking the questions that the pause after each line encourages us to ask, we can see the meaning of Williams's line-breaks:

As the cat	*did what?*
climbed over	*over what?*
the top of	*of what?*
the jamcloset	*how?*
first the right	*paw? rear leg?*
forefoot	*then? (a mistaken question; it turns out Williams wanted me to ask "how?")*
carefully	*then what?*
then the hind	*did what?*
stepped down	*where?*
into the pit of	*oops! of what?*
the empty	*what has a "pit" anyhow?*
flowerpot	*not what you expected, kittycat!*

Well, this more or less shows me why Williams put his unsteady little pauses where he did. But why did he group his lines three by three? This action inserts three "major pauses" at certain points to punctuate the "minor pauses" at the end of each line. The first major pause comes when the cat stops before the descent into unknown regions (which it cannot see) from the top of the jamcloset. The second comes after the right forefoot has found (hurrah!) a place to poise. The third comes after the hind leg successfully (whee!) moves to follow the forefoot. Then comes the farcical end, when the poor cat finds itself trapped inside a deep flowerpot instead of safe on a flat surface.

Williams's lines consist, sometimes, of only a single word — "forefoot," "carefully," "flowerpot." Each line represents a cat-step, so these are particularly fraught steps. Some lines have two words — these are steps of medium difficulty. We end up feeling that the lines of *three* or even *four* words — "As the cat," "the top of," "first the right," "into the pit of," are almost carefree, almost lilting.

As for Williams's stanzas, they are all adverbial, ornaments attached to the central main verb, "stepped." There is the "as" stanza, the "first" stanza, the "then" stanza, and the "into" stanza. They are all equal in length, as though the cat had made four neat forays into what it hoped would be stability, but what it found was captivity. Clearly the initial confident tentativeness and the ultimate bewildering failure of the cat delighted Williams as a little emblem of human venturing. Whenever a poet calls a poem "Poem" it means that the story told in the poem resembles the making of poetry itself. Like the cat, the poet ventures out into the hazards of thin air, places a "foot" (a metrical foot, no doubt) on a possible landing, tries another foot after it, and may find farce instead of success.

It would be of no use to go to this poem looking for harmonious melody, or philosophical assertion, or nature description, or rhyme, or song-rhythm, or historical insight, or Freudian dreamwork, or gender problems. Each poem leads you to the questions it makes sense to ask it. It makes sense to ask this poem about its twelve lines and its four stanzas and its three white spaces and its line-breaks; it makes sense to ask what the cat expected and what the cat found; it makes sense to ask why the poet gave this humble anecdote the honorific name "Poem." It makes sense, too, to ask what the poet who writes such a poem understands poetry to be — to which we might answer that it is the imaginative perception of the ordinary; and the comic perception of hazards-and-landings; and the emblematic perception of how an animal's small ventures might be like ours.

Let us look for a moment at a very different sort of poem altogether, "We Real Cool," by Gwendolyn Brooks:

GWENDOLYN BROOKS (1917 – 2000)
We Real Cool

> *The Pool Players.*
> *Seven at the Golden Shovel.*

We real cool. We
Left school. We

Lurk late. We
Strike straight. We

Sing sin. We
Thin gin. We

Jazz June. We
Die soon.

The first thing that strikes anyone reading this poem is that its sentences are arranged "wrong." It "should" read,

We real cool.
We left school.

We lurk late.
We strike straight.

And so on. The second thing that strikes the ear is that most of the poem is spoken in the present tense, but two things break that pattern — the past tense in "We *left* school" and the implied future tense — or is it? — in the "We die soon" that ends the poem.

The subtitle of the poem tells us who is speaking — seven pool players at the Golden Shovel pool room. The diction of the poem — "We real cool" instead of "We're real cool" — tells us the pool players are black, as they omit the verb "to be." Why are the poem's rhymes displaced to the "wrong" place in the lines, and why do its tenses change? How do these practices of the poet enact something about the seven pool players? And how, we might add, are we to explain that all their sentences consist of three words? And why do their sentences have so many internal binding sounds — "lurk late," "strike straight," "sing sin," "thin gin," "jazz June"? All the answers to such questions must be conjectural, but the analyst's aim is to make the conjectural answers as plausible as possible, so that they "account for" those patterns in which the composing poet, and the responsive reader, take pleasure.

In answering the questions that the poem makes us ask, we notice that instead of a "rhyme" at the end of each line, the insistent "We" appears down the right margin. "We" is the real word binding these seven adolescents together — they are a group giving each other solidarity. We get so used to seeing "We" at the end of every line — one, two, three, four, five, six, seven — that when we "miss" it at the end of line 8 we know that its absence is a sign of the imminent death of the group. The poverty-stricken sentences — after all, the first complete sentences made by babies consist of two or three words, "Me want that," "I go bed" — are a sign that indeed these young men have "left school" and its more complex possibilities of language. Nonetheless, their syntactically simple sentences are full of a feel for language — if they had stayed in school, they might have produced, among them, a poet or two. They like groups of words that sound "jazzy," and they like singing and playing games — all inclinations characteristic of poets. The trouble is the gin and the sin and the gambling and the school leaving and the lurking into late hours.

It makes sense to ask this poem questions about its rhymes, its syntax, its tenses, its word placement, in order to know who these "cool" adolescents are, how the poet enacts their solidarity, their gifts, their appetites, and their mistakes. It makes sense, once one knows that this is a poem about young black dropouts, to ask what the poet's feelings about them are — "young, talented with words, doomed." It makes sense to ask this poem about its wit (these young men make their every word count — their three-word sentences have three full beats). It makes sense, too, to ask it about racial questions (the white world is entirely absent — why?). It makes sense to put the poem in a genre — the genre of elegy, especially the subgroup of elegies that mourn people who died much too young. This is an elegy with no visible offer of consolation — there is no better purpose served by the deaths of the young men, no envisaged heaven for them to go to after their death, no legacy they leave behind them of children begotten or accomplishments completed. It makes sense, as well, to ask to whom the young men are speaking. To us? To themselves? Highly literate readers may recall a "we" elegy spoken by the small band of Spartan soldiers who died in 480 B.C., at Thermopylae, an elegy that is perhaps the classical ancestor of this poem:

> Go tell the Spartans, thou who passest by,
> That here, obedient to their laws, we lie.

We can then see the poem not simply as an elegy by Gwendolyn Brooks for these young men, but as their self-epitaph, which could be inscribed on their grave: "We / Die soon." The apparent future tense of the last line then becomes a generalized present tense about the fate of all such adolescents: "We — people like us — always die soon."

The important thing is to be accustomed to looking, in any poem, at several levels — the sound, the rhythms and rhymes, the grammar, the images, the sentences, the plot, the assertions, the allusions, the self-contradictions. Somewhere the energy of the poem awaits you. The moment you see the main and subordinate patterns, you smile, and it "all makes sense."

Images

Though people sometimes refer to "images" in poems, a word is not the same thing as a picture. Words refer; images represent. When poets use nouns or phrases referring to something that an artist could represent by graphic means (a painting or sketch), they use them either for descriptive purposes or as illustrative examples. The images can be either literally pictorial ("This is the forest primeval") or figurative, as when Wordsworth says of a rural woman that she is "A violet by a mossy stone, / Half hidden from the eye." Shakespeare's three images in Sonnet 60 for time's action (ocean waves; a sun that rises and is eclipsed; a repeated destructive attack by a spear, a spade, a maw, a scythe) give three illustrative ways of thinking about life: life is a steady state in which each moment, wavelike, resembles the next; or, life is a glowing rise followed by a catastrophic blackout; or, life is experienced as a continuous and premature and universal execution. These are not compatible images, and the poem makes us see each later image obliterating the former model(s).

Images, in fact, serve in poems as a shorthand for argument. It is quicker to show than to tell. It is a rule of thumb in poems that when a second, different, image follows a first, the second one is somehow importantly supplementing, or indeed correcting or supplanting, the first, because of some perceived inadequacy in the first image (otherwise, the poem would not have needed the second). So, when William Blake wanders through London despairing at the evils of modern life, he first mentions, as a major evil that comes to mind, "the mind-forg'd manacles" of false beliefs. But he does not stop there. He replaces the manacles with the institution that imposes them, and which permits the exploitation of the poor and the powerless — the Church. Yet the Church is not the worst evil: after all, to lose one's life is worse than to be manacled in mind or to be poor, and so Blake goes on to indict the monarchy, which sends its sons off to be killed. Yet even that image of evil does not suffice. He must supplement Church and Palace with one more, the worst — the corruption of the sexual life which, by prostitution and syphilis, blinds the newborn infant in the cradle. Blake's images rise, supplementing and even replacing one another, to the fatal last word in the last line:

WILLIAM BLAKE (1757 – 1827)

London

I wander thro' each charter'd street,
Near where the charter'd Thames does flow,

And mark in every face I meet
Marks of weakness, marks of woe.

In every cry of every man,
In every Infant's cry of fear,
In every voice, in every ban,
The mind-forg'd manacles I hear.

How the Chimney-sweeper's cry
Every blackning Church appalls;
And the hapless Soldier's sigh
Runs in blood down Palace walls.

But most thro' midnight streets I hear
How the youthful Harlot's curse
Blasts the new-born Infant's tear,
And blights with plagues the Marriage hearse.

It is necessary to see the climactic order of Blake's images ("But *most* I hear") in order to set them in relation to each other. Every image needs to be related to others in the same poem, but in an imaginative, not a mechanical, way. You need to enter the mind of the speaker, make yourself into the speaker, and ask yourself how you are connecting things in your ongoing expression.

Argument

A poem often looks as though it is making an argument. But "real" arguments are made in prose (theological tracts argue about God, philosophical books argue ethics or metaphysics, political papers argue politics). Arguments in poems are miniature imitations of "real" arguments, and are often designed to show the moves in the argumentative game rather than to make a full argument in order to persuade a "real-life" person. The debates in poems are often sophisticated games, as when a "shepherd" (really a courtier in pastoral disguise) tries to persuade a "nymph" (an aristocratic young woman playing at being a rustic shepherdess) to love him. She counters with a mini-sermon on the transience of all earthly love, relenting at the end to wish things were otherwise:

CHRISTOPHER MARLOWE (1564 – 1593)
The Passionate Shepherd to His Love

Come live with me and be my love,
And we will all the pleasures prove°   *experience*

That valleys, groves, hills, and fields,
Woods, or steepy mountain yields.

And we will sit upon the rocks,
Seeing the shepherds feed their flocks,
By shallow rivers to whose falls
Melodious birds sing madrigals.

And I will make thee beds of roses
And a thousand fragrant posies,
A cap of flowers, and a kirtle
Embroidered all with leaves of myrtle;

A gown made of the finest wool
Which from our pretty lambs we pull;
Fair linèd slippers for the cold,
With buckles of the purest gold;

A belt of straw and ivy buds,
With coral clasps and amber studs:
And if these pleasures may thee move,
Come live with me, and be my love.

The shepherd swains shall dance and sing
For thy delight each May morning:
If these delights thy mind may move,
Then live with me and be my love.

SIR WALTER RALEGH (1554 – 1618)
The Nymph's Reply to the Shepherd

If all the world and love were young,
And truth in every shepherd's tongue,
These pretty pleasures might me move
To live with thee and be thy love.

Time drives the flocks from field to fold
When rivers rage and rocks grow cold,
And Philomel° becometh dumb;   *the nightingale*
The rest complains of cares to come.

The flowers do fade, and wanton fields
To wayward winter reckoning yields;

A honey tongue, a heart of gall,
Is fancy's spring, but sorrow's fall.

Thy gowns, thy shoes, thy beds of roses,
Thy cap, thy kirtle, and thy posies
Soon break, soon wither, soon forgotten —
In folly ripe, in reason rotten.

Thy belt of straw and ivy buds,
Thy coral clasps and amber studs,
All these in me no means can move
To come to thee and be thy love.

But could youth last and love still breed,
Had joys no date° nor age no need,   *end*
Then these delights my mind might move
To live with thee and be thy love.

There exist within poetic tradition debates between body and soul, between gardeners and mowers, between God and man, between the owl and the nightingale, between the flower and the leaf, between a philosopher and a poet. Such debates usually raise perennial questions — hedonism versus asceticism, night versus day, the mirthful man versus the pensive man, the active life versus the contemplative life, and so on. Partly *because* such questions cannot be settled, the pleasure in a poem of argument lies in seeing what strategic moves, and what new speakers, can be invented for such perennial arguments.

Poignancy

We often say a poem is "moving." What makes a poem moving? Normally, it is the relation between the situation implied in the poem (say, a lover at a girl's window) and the utterance of the poem (plaintive, or witty, or ecstatic).

Often, the situation in a poem changes as the poem develops, and the utterance changes along with the new event or the new perception. We never expect, for instance, that anyone we love will be taken from us, however logically we may "know" that death comes to everyone. Somehow we "repress" (as we now say) our knowledge that those we love most are themselves mortal. Wordsworth's speaker in a famous poem says that his mind (he calls it his "spirit") "slumbered" when it exempted his beloved from the threat of mortality. In the first stanza of the poem, the insidious word "seemed" hints at the forthcoming catastrophe:

WILLIAM WORDSWORTH (1770 – 1850)
A slumber did my spirit seal

A slumber did my spirit seal;
　　I had no human fears:
She seemed a thing that could not feel
　　The touch of earthly years.

A white space intervenes between stanza 1 and stanza 2. When we begin stanza 2, we see that the girl has died between the two stanzas — that the white space represents her death. The first stanza was delusion; the second is reality:

No motion has she now, no force;
　　She neither hears nor sees;
Rolled round in earth's diurnal course,
　　With rocks, and stones, and trees.

What is poignant here is, first of all, the speaker's total suppression of the narrative of her death. He does not say, "But then she sickened and she died" — it is too painful for him to say that bald sentence. He makes her still the subject of his second sentence, as she was the subject of the last part of his first sentence: "She seemed . . . She has now . . . ; She neither hears nor sees." But the sentence of stanza 2 is all negation in its predicates: Motion? No. Force? No. Hears? No. Sees? No. We then realize, looking back, that there was a comparable negation in stanza 1: Can feel earthly years? No. But that was preceded by the verb "seemed." Now, it proves untrue. She *can* feel the touch of earthly years, so much so that the word the speaker lightly used of her in stanza 1 — "thing" — turns out to be the accurate word. She is now a thing, as rocks and stones and trees are things, and she is as inertly rolled round, day and night, by the planet's motion as they are.

If the poignancy is partly in the speaker's mistake, and partly in his unwitting use of the word "thing," it lies also, in stanza 2, in his stern truthfulness. He speaks in strictly inorganic physical terms: motion, force, diurnal course, rocks, stones. He has mentioned hearing and see- ing, organic functions, only to deny them. Nonetheless, he ultimately relents: in placing his beloved not only with rocks and stones and plane- tary motion, but also — and lastly — with organic and living trees, he gives her a posthumous association with life. The poem would be very different — and almost inhuman — if the last line read, "With granite, stones, and rocks." The poignancy of any poem comes with the struggle between uttering truth and honoring the undertow of strong feeling.

Wisdom

Poems descend in part from wisdom literature — prayers, spells, riddles, epigrams, proverbs, aphorisms. "What oft was thought but ne'er so well expressed" (Alexander Pope) is one description of poetry, and we respond (especially when we are young) to what poetry can tell us about human experience. Countless adolescents have memorized lines such as "How do I love thee? Let me count the ways" (Elizabeth Barrett Browning). Poetry is the most concise form of literature, and it has perfected techniques for rapid and deft exposition (partly by the shorthand arguments of imagery). Many people read poetry chiefly for the wisdom they find there, scarcely knowing that the wisdom seems wiser for having been expressed so memorably. There is a psychological wisdom in lyric: one of its functions is to give us a believable representation of what Matthew Arnold called "the dialogue of the mind with itself." When we see a credible representation of grief, or rebellion, or delusion, we feel the assuaging assent that comes from a ratification of something we have felt but have not previously seen represented. "Strength came where weakness was not known to be," as Wordsworth says of a similar experience. It is important to everyone to find his or her own experience mirrored back; some find this mirroring chiefly in novels, others in poetry, depending on personal taste. The dazzling variety of voices in lyric, each available to any reader as a vicarious voice in which to speak, lets us move through many experiences comparable to our own. Often we find (as we are being John Donne — "Sweetest love, I do not go / For weariness of thee" — or Elizabeth Bishop — "I caught a tremendous fish" —) that the exhilaration of having a new voice and new insight reverberates back into our "real" experiences of a comparable sort.

A New Language

Each major artist creates in a distinctive way. Though early Beethoven can sound like Mozart, or early Mozart like Haydn, in their maturity they end up sounding different from the predecessors whom they imitated in youth. We can walk into a museum and say, "That's a Van Gogh," or "That's a Picasso," because each major painter has a distinctive way of representing and coloring the world. Poets are the same: we can tell (after a while) Tennyson from William Butler Yeats, and Milton from Edmund Spenser, and Adrienne Rich from Anne Sexton, even though in many cases there are resemblances in subject matter. It is not subject matter that distinguishes artists, it is treatment. There are hundreds of portraits of distinguished-looking men, but anyone who has spent some time in museums can tell a Velásquez from a Hals, and either from a Cézanne.

A distinctive style is created in part by the artist and in part by the epoch in which the artist works. One can tell a Renaissance painting from a nineteenth-century painting, a piece of anonymous fifteenth-century music from a piece of anonymous seventeenth-century music. (I will say more about this in the chapter "History and Regionality.") Within what any given epoch permits, many styles are possible (as one can tell from looking at twentieth-century American painting or poetry). Wordsworth said that the poet must create the taste by which he is enjoyed; that is, the poet trains the audience to like a new sort of art. The training takes time, and each new poet you read is training you to like a new personal shorthand of images and a systematically original language. If a poet does not appeal to you now, look again at the work in ten years, and you may like it then. Acculturation is fast in some cases, slow in others. But if many people have found a poet's language memorable, you may some day find it memorable, too. Each person's taste hovers at a different evolutionary moment. A person brought up on Christian prayer comes to Christian religious poetry with great ease; someone who has never heard a Christian prayer or hymn may take a long time to get used to George Herbert or Christina Rossetti. An ecologist may not be put off by the scientific vocabulary in the poems of A. R. Ammons or Amy Clampitt; someone who has never heard of the Cambrian shield or pheromones may be more apprehensive. The rule of thumb is to let the poem work on you over time.

Finding Yourself

The strangest experience in reading poetry, as in writing it, is to find yourself in it, to be yourself in it. We sometimes speak of this as finding a "favorite poet." This is a poet whose writing is so close to your own way of seeing and thinking that there seems no barrier at all between you and the poet. Such a poet is a powerful reflecting mirror of your own sensibility and creativity. In that poet's work, you find yourself "more truly and more strange" (as Wallace Stevens put it in "Tea at the Palaz of Hoon"). Sometimes poets are mirrors for a whole generation, and become bestsellers on that account — as T. S. Eliot and Robert Frost and Adrienne Rich and Allen Ginsberg have been in the United States in the twentieth century. Other American poets, just as good, remain known to relatively few readers (who nonetheless claim them as intensely as the country at large claims the bestsellers). Samuel Johnson said (in his "Preface to Shakespeare") that it was only after a century had passed, and the topical interest of a piece of literature had died down, that one could tell whether it would last. Luckily, you do not have to worry about the potential durability of works in which you find a voice and a reflecting mirror; that question will take care of itself. The important thing is to feel companioned, as you go through life, by a host of poems which speak to your experience. And, in the long run, the poems you first read because you wanted to find out about love or death you will read again because of the living quality of the voice that speaks in them, that quality we call "style."

In Brief: Poems as Pleasure

No single poem offers all the pleasures of poetry. As you read, you will sometimes be caught up in the lilt of a rhythm, sometimes intrigued by plot; at other times you may be struck by an insight, moved by the poignancy of tone, or puzzled and pleased by a subversive and unexpected move by the text. The important thing is to be ready for whatever the poem offers, and to take it on its own terms, not requiring philosophical discourse from a song, or simplicity from a knotted problem-poem. The single best way to gain pleasure from a poem is to read it aloud; if you let the poem take you on its journey, you will know intuitively where it has led you. The next pleasure is to find words for what you felt and thought on that journey; and the next is to find what aspects of the poem — structure, images, argument — generated those feelings and those thoughts. Chapter 4 will suggest some ways by which you can describe the various aspects of poems from which these pleasures arise.

Reading Other Poems

All the following poems combine representation and strong patterning. Both Theodore Roethke and William Carlos Williams declare by their titles that they will employ strong rhythmic patterning.

◆ Can you graph the rhythms their lines enact?

Some poets can create strong patterns in very brief poems. William Blake's "The Sick Rose" consists (if one were to consider it clinically) of six lines of diagnosis followed by two of prognosis (or forecast of the course of the rose's disease).

◆ Do the rhymes in any way suggest the plot?

Gerard Manley Hopkins's "sonnet" of reduced proportions — a six-line "octave" followed by a four-and-a-half-line "sestet" — is divided into two ways of talking about "dappled" beauty — beauty that is spotted, variegated, multiple.

◆ What is the pattern of discussion in the first part of the poem, offered in words like "skies," "trout," "trades"? And in the second, offered in words like "all things," "whatever is fickle," and so on?

Rhythms can differ greatly, from the lilt of "My Papa's Waltz" to the hypnotic repetitive rhythms of D. H. Lawrence's "Snake" to the long-breathed lines of Derek Walcott's "The Season of Phantasmal Peace." Read each of these aloud to hear the difference in yourself as you become the person speaking the poem.

◆ How much can you say about the tones of voice of the speaker as they issue from you?

Sometimes a structural pattern can be borrowed, as we saw in this chapter with the passionate shepherd's invitation and the nymph's reply (in which she borrows the shepherd's stanza-form and vocabulary). The anterior structure generating a poem is sometimes well known in the poet's culture; sonneteers, for instance, were accustomed to praise their lady's beauties one by one. To understand Shakespeare's mocking reply to such a practice, you need to imagine that he has just read a poem beginning "My mistress' eyes shine brightly like the sun; / Coral is not more red than her lips' red, / She walks on air, she does not tread the ground," and so on. "I don't know about *your* mistress," says Shakespeare, "but *mine* has no such powers. *My* mistress' eyes are nothing *like* the sun."

◆ How precisely can you deduce from Shakespeare's reply the anterior claims of praise that he is mocking?

Description in lyric often proceeds by successive images, piled up in a montage of evidence. Consider Robert Frost's two poems about the apple harvest: the first, "After Apple-Picking," offers "realistic" images of the overwhelming harvest followed by a succession of dream-images, only to return, in the third section of the poem, to realistic images again. By contrast to this flood of images about the anxiety of trying to pluck all possible apples, "Unharvested" presents only a single image — a ring of fallen apples on the ground below a tree that was not harvested — but this image is investigated for all it can yield.

◆ What is the symbolic suggestion of apple picking?

◆ What different effects does Frost pursue for the image constellation of apple harvesting?

Both Robert Herrick's "To the Virgins, to Make Much of Time" and Thomas Hardy's "The Darkling Thrush" are poems giving moral advice, in the form of argument against an implied other moral position. Should virgins hasten to marry or not? At the end of the old century, should one despair or not?

◆ What means of persuasion does each author find to make the message seem not only wise but also moving?

◆ Rephrase the advice in a prose proposition. Does it lose its poignancy?

If you were asked by a friend to describe Blake's style in "The Sick Rose," can you think of three or four adjectives you might use for an answer?

Finally, can you see the patterning-by-pronouns ("I" versus "he") in Elizabeth Alexander's poem about a summer love affair? How does it change from stanza to stanza?

WILLIAM SHAKESPEARE (1564 – 1616)
Sonnet 130

My mistress' eyes are nothing like the sun;
Coral is far more red than her lips' red;
If snow be white, why then her breasts are dun;
If hairs be wires, black wires grow on her head.
I have seen roses damasked,° red and white,   *variegated*
But no such roses see I in her cheeks,
And in some perfumes is there more delight
Than in the breath that from my mistress reeks.
I love to hear her speak, yet well I know
That music hath a far more pleasing sound;
I grant I never saw a goddess go;°   *walk*
My mistress when she walks treads on the ground.
    And yet by heaven I think my love as rare
    As any she belied with false compare.

ROBERT HERRICK (1591 – 1674)

To the Virgins, to Make Much of Time

Gather ye rosebuds while ye may,
    Old time is still a-flying;
And this same flower that smiles today
    Tomorrow will be dying.

The glorious lamp of heaven, the sun,
    The higher he's a-getting,
The sooner will his race be run,
    And nearer he's to setting.

That age is best which is the first,
    When youth and blood are warmer;
But being spent, the worse, and worst
    Times still succeed the former.

Then be not coy, but use your time,
    And, while ye may, go marry;
For, having lost but once your prime,
    You may forever tarry.

WILLIAM BLAKE (1757 – 1827)

The Sick Rose

O Rose, thou art sick!
The invisible worm
That flies in the night,
In the howling storm,

Has found out thy bed
Of crimson joy:
And his dark secret love
Does thy life destroy.

GERARD MANLEY HOPKINS (1844 – 1889)

Pied Beauty

Glory be to God for dappled things —
    For skies of couple-colour as a brinded cow;
        For rose-moles all in stipple upon trout that swim;

Fresh-firecoal chestnut-falls; finches' wings;
     Landscape plotted and pieced — fold, fallow, and plough;
       And áll trádes, their gear and tackle and trim.
All things counter, original, spare, strange;
     Whatever is fickle, freckled (who knows how?)
       With swift, slow; sweet, sour; adazzle, dim;
He fathers-forth whose beauty is past change:
          Praise him.

THOMAS HARDY (1840 – 1928)
The Darkling Thrush

I leant upon a coppice gate
    When Frost was spectre-gray,
And Winter's dregs made desolate
    The weakening eye of day.
The tangled bine-stems° scored the sky   *wood-bine*
    Like strings of broken lyres,
And all mankind that haunted nigh
    Had sought their household fires.

The land's sharp features seemed to be
    The Century's corpse outleant,
His crypt the cloudy canopy,
    The wind his death-lament.
The ancient pulse of germ and birth
    Was shrunken hard and dry,
And every spirit upon earth
    Seemed fervourless as I.

At once a voice arose among
    The bleak twigs overhead
In a full-hearted evensong
    Of joy illimited;
An aged thrush, frail, gaunt, and small,
    In blast-beruffled plume,
Had chosen thus to fling his soul
    Upon the growing gloom.

So little cause for carolings
    Of such ecstatic sound
Was written on terrestrial things
    Afar or nigh around,

That I could think there trembled through
    His happy good-night air
Some blessed Hope, whereof he knew
    And I was unaware.

ROBERT FROST (1874 – 1963)

After Apple-Picking

My long two-pointed ladder's sticking through a tree
Toward heaven still,
And there's a barrel that I didn't fill
Beside it, and there may be two or three
Apples I didn't pick upon some bough.
But I am done with apple-picking now.
Essence of winter sleep is on the night,
The scent of apples: I am drowsing off.
I cannot rub the strangeness from my sight
I got from looking through a pane of glass
I skimmed this morning from the drinking trough
And held against the world of hoary grass.
It melted, and I let it fall and break.
But I was well
Upon my way to sleep before it fell,
And I could tell
What form my dreaming was about to take.
Magnified apples appear and disappear,
Stem end and blossom end,
And every fleck of russet showing clear.
My instep arch not only keeps the ache,
It keeps the pressure of a ladder-round.
I feel the ladder sway as the boughs bend.
And I keep hearing from the cellar bin
The rumbling sound
Of load on load of apples coming in.
For I have had too much
Of apple-picking: I am overtired
Of the great harvest I myself desired.
There were ten thousand thousand fruit to touch,
Cherish in hand, lift down, and not let fall.
For all
That struck the earth,
No matter if not bruised or spiked with stubble,

Went surely to the cider-apple heap
As of no worth.
One can see what will trouble
This sleep of mine, whatever sleep it is.
Were he not gone,
The woodchuck could say whether it's like his
Long sleep, as I describe its coming on,
Or just some human sleep.

Unharvested

A scent of ripeness from over a wall.
And come to leave the routine road
And look for what had made me stall,
There sure enough was an apple tree
That had eased itself of its summer load,
And of all but its trivial foliage free,
Now breathed as light as a lady's fan.
For there there had been an apple fall
As complete as the apple had given man.
The ground was one circle of solid red.

May something go always unharvested!
May much stay out of our stated plan,
Apples or something forgotten and left,
So smelling their sweetness would be no theft.

D. H. LAWRENCE (1885 – 1930)
Snake

A snake came to my water-trough
On a hot, hot day, and I in pyjamas for the heat,
To drink there.

In the deep, strange-scented shade of the great dark carob-tree
I came down the steps with my pitcher   5
And must wait, must stand and wait, for there he was at the trough
    before me.

He reached down from a fissure in the earth-wall in the gloom
And trailed his yellow-brown slackness soft-bellied down, over the
    edge of the stone trough   10
And rested his throat upon the stone bottom,
And where the water had dripped from the tap, in a small clearness,
He sipped with his straight mouth,

Softly drank through his straight gums, into his slack   15
    long body,
Silently.

Someone was before me at my water-trough,
And I, like a second comer, waiting.

He lifted his head from his drinking, as cattle do,   20
And looked at me vaguely, as drinking cattle do,
And flickered his two-forked tongue from his lips, and mused a
    moment,
And stooped and drank a little more,
Being earth-brown, earth-golden from the burning bowels of   25
    the earth
On the day of Sicilian July, with Etna° smoking.   *the volcano*

The voice of my education said to me
He must be killed,
For in Sicily the black, black snakes are innocent, the gold are   30
    venomous.

And voices in me said, If you were a man
You would take a stick and break him now, and finish him off.

But must I confess how I liked him,
How glad I was he had come like a guest in quiet, to drink at   35
    my water-trough
And depart peaceful, pacified, and thankless,
Into the burning bowels of this earth?

Was it cowardice, that I dared not kill him?
Was it perversity, that I longed to talk to him?   40
Was it humility, to feel so honoured?
I felt so honoured.

And yet those voices:
If you were not afraid, you would kill him!

And truly I was afraid, I was most afraid,   45
But even so, honoured still more
That he should seek my hospitality
From out the dark door of the secret earth.

He drank enough
And lifted his head, dreamily, as one who has drunken,   50
And flickered his tongue like a forked night on the air, so black;

Seeming to lick his lips,
And looked around like a god, unseeing, into the air,
And slowly turned his head,
And slowly, very slowly, as if thrice adream,   55
Proceeded to draw his slow length curving round
And climb again the broken bank of my wall-face.

And as he put his head into that dreadful hole,
And as he slowly drew up, snake-easing his shoulders, and entered
    farther,   60
A sort of horror, a sort of protest against his withdrawing into that
    horrid black hole,
Deliberately going into the blackness, and slowly drawing himself
    after,
Overcame me now his back was turned.   65

I looked round, I put down my pitcher,
I picked up a clumsy log
And threw it at the water-trough with a clatter.

I think it did not hit him,
But suddenly that part of him that was left behind convulsed   70
    in undignified haste,
Writhed like lightning, and was gone
Into the black hole, the earth-lipped fissure in the wall-front,
At which, in the intense still noon, I stared with fascination.

And immediately I regretted it.   75
I thought how paltry, how vulgar, what a mean act!
I despised myself and the voices of my accursed human education.

And I thought of the albatross,[1]
And I wished he would come back, my snake.   80

For he seemed to me again like a king,
Like a king in exile, uncrowned in the underworld,
Now due to be crowned again.

And so, I missed my chance with one of the lords
Of life.   85
And I have something to expiate;
A pettiness.

---

[1]Albatross: the bird shot and killed by the Seaman in Coleridge's "The Rime of
the Ancient Mariner."

WILLIAM CARLOS WILLIAMS (1883 – 1963)

The Dance

In Breughel's[1] great picture, The Kermess,
the dancers go round, they go round and
around, the squeal and the blare and the
tweedle of bagpipes, a bugle and fiddles
tipping their bellies (round as the thick-
sided glasses whose wash they impound)
their hips and their bellies off balance
to turn them. Kicking and rolling about
the Fair Grounds, swinging their butts, those
shanks must be sound to bear up under such
rollicking measures, prance as they dance
in Breughel's great picture, The Kermess.

THEODORE ROETHKE (1908 – 1963)

My Papa's Waltz

The whiskey on your breath
Could make a small boy dizzy;
But I hung on like death:
Such waltzing was not easy.

We romped until the pans
Slid from the kitchen shelf;
My mother's countenance
Could not unfrown itself.

The hand that held my wrist
Was battered on one knuckle;
At every step you missed
My right ear scraped a buckle.

You beat time on my head
With a palm caked hard by dirt,
Then waltzed me off to bed
Still clinging to your shirt.

---

[1]Pieter Brueghel (also spelled Breughel) the Elder (1521?–1569) was a Flemish painter famed for his pictures of peasant life, such as that of an open-air festival, or "Kermess."

DEREK WALCOTT (b. 1930)

The Season of Phantasmal° Peace   *imaginary*

Then all the nations of birds lifted together
the huge net of the shadows of this earth
in multitudinous dialects, twittering tongues,
stitching and crossing it. They lifted up
the shadows of long pines down trackless slopes,
the shadows of glass-faced towers down evening streets,
the shadow of a frail plant on a city sill —
the net rising soundless as night, the birds' cries soundless, until
there was no longer dusk, or season, decline, or weather,
only this passage of phantasmal light
that not the narrowest shadow dared to sever.

And men could not see, looking up, what the wild geese drew,
what the ospreys trailed behind them in silvery ropes
that flashed in the icy sunlight; they could not hear
battalions of starlings waging peaceful cries,
bearing the net higher, covering this world
like the vines of an orchard, or a mother drawing
the trembling gauze over the trembling eyes
of a child fluttering to sleep;
                              it was the light
that you will see at evening on the side of a hill
in yellow October, and no one hearing knew
what change had brought into the raven's cawing,
the killdeer's screech, the ember-circling chough
such an immense, soundless, and high concern
for the fields and cities where the birds belong,
except it was their seasonal passing, Love,
made seasonless, or, from the privilege of their birth,
something brighter than pity for the wingless ones
below them who shared dark holes in windows and in houses,
and higher they lifted the net with soundless voices
above all change, betrayals of falling suns,
and this season lasted one moment, like the pause
between dusk and darkness, between fury and peace,
but, for such as our earth is now, it lasted long.

ELIZABETH ALEXANDER (b. 1962)

Nineteen

That summer in Culpepper, all there was to eat was white:
cauliflower, flounder, white sauce, white ice-cream.
I snuck around with an older man who didn't tell me
he was married. I was the baby, drinking rum and Coke
while the men smoked reefer they'd stolen from the campers.
I tiptoed with my lover to poison-ivied fields, camp vans.
I never slept. Each fortnight I returned to the city,
black and dusty, with a garbage bag of dirty clothes.

At nineteen it was my first summer away from home.
His beard smelled musty. His eyes were black. "The ladies love my
    hair,"
he'd say, and like a fool I'd smile. He knew everything
about marijuana, how dry it had to be to burn,
how to crush it, sniff it, how to pick the seeds out. He said
he learned it all in Vietnam. He brought his son to visit
after one of his days off. I never imagined a mother.
"Can I steal a kiss?" he said, the first thick night in the field.

I asked and asked about Vietnam, how each scar felt,
what combat was like, how the jungle smelled. He listened
to a lot of Marvin Gaye, was all he said, and grabbed
between my legs. I'd creep to my cot before morning.
I'd eat that white food. This was before I understood
that nothing could be ruined in one stroke. A sudden
storm came hard one night; he bolted up inside the van.
"The rain sounded just like that," he said, "on the roofs there."

4

Describing Poems

There are many ways of describing poems. As new sorts of poems are invented, as cross-fertilizing among cultures takes place, we need to come up with new descriptions. But it is useful to know some of the ways in which critics have described poems in the past, and to learn a handy set of methods for exploring a poem to find things worth describing in it. This chapter is a quick look at some techniques you can use to describe a poem you have read.

The large category "poetry" has often been divided into subcategories. We are concerned here not with the longer genres, epic poetry and dramatic poetry, but with the smaller kinds of relatively short poetry. Here are some of them. (A longer list can be found in the appendix "On Lyric Subgenres.")

Poetic Kinds

Narrative versus Lyric; Narrative in Lyric

We tend to distinguish *narrative* poems from *lyric* poems. A *narrative* poem (for instance, a ballad) tells a story — for example, about the murder of Lord Randal, or (as in the case of "Frankie and Johnny") about the revenge a woman took on her unfaithful lover. A *lyric,* on the other hand, may contain the germ of a story — say, a man's regret that a love affair is ending — but the poem dwells less on the plot than on the man's feelings (despair, grief, resentment, and so on). Wordsworth put the two kinds together and called some of his short poems "lyrical ballads" — meaning poems that, although they imply or even tell a story, make the characters' feelings more important than the plot. Narrative and lyric sometimes overlap, because most narrative poems include feeling and reflection as well as plot, and most lyric poems have an implied plot of sorts.

Lyric poems in which there is a distinct narrative interest often show changes in tense: "Once I *did* this but now I *can* no longer *do* it, and in the future I *will* never *do* it again." (Poems that are primarily lyric meditations on a single subject are often phrased in the present tense alone: "The expense of spirit in a waste of shame / Is lust in action"). To see the way tenses organize the narrative plot of a poem, let's look at a poem by Adrienne Rich, spoken by a woman who has emerged from the exhaustions of motherhood and is thinking that she will at last have a private life again. She retraces her own birth and ambitious adolescence, then shows her inner deprivation as her life (once she became a mother) was handed over to others in what sometimes seemed to her a form of slavery; she concludes with her present anticipation of a new — but aging — self. I have put the MAIN VERBS in uppercase so as to emphasize the tense changes; the *present participles* (which help make presentness) in italic; and the **past participles** (which help make pastness) in boldface:

ADRIENNE RICH (b. 1929)
Necessities of Life

Piece by piece I SEEM	*present*
to re-enter the world: I first BEGAN	*past*
a small, **fixed** dot, still SEE	*present*
that old myself, a dark-blue thumbtack	
pushed into the scene,	
a hard little head *protruding*	
from the pointillist's buzz and bloom,	
After a time the dot	
BEGINS to ooze. Certain heats	*present*
MELT it. Now I WAS hurriedly	*present/past*
BLURRING into ranges	
of **burnt** red, *burning* green,	
whole biographies SWAM up and	
SWALLOWED me like Jonah.	*past*

Jonah! I WAS Wittgenstein,	*past*
Mary Wollstonecraft, the soul	

of Louis Jouvet, dead
in a **blown-up** photograph.

Till, **wolfed** almost to shreds,	
I LEARNED to make myself	*past*

unappetizing. Scaly as a dry bulb
thrown into a cellar

I USED myself, LET nothing use me.	*past*
Like *being* on a private dole,	

sometimes more like *kneading* bricks in Egypt.	
What life WAS then, WAS mine,	*past*

now and again TO LAY	*infinitive*
one hand on a warm brick	

and TOUCH the sun's ghost	*infinitive*
with economical joy,	

now and again TO NAME	*infinitive*
over the bare necessities.	

So much for those days. Soon	
practice MAY MAKE me middling-perfect, I'LL	*modal future*

DARE inhabit the world	*future*
trenchant in motion as an eel, solid	

as a cabbage-head. I HAVE invitations:	*present*
a curl of mist STEAMS upward	*present*

from a field, visible as my breath,	
houses along a road STAND waiting	*present*

like old women *knitting,* breathless	
TO TELL their tales.	*infinitive*

One can see the *narrative* here unfolding in the verbs and verbals (tensed verbs, infinitives, present and past participles), and can watch the past becoming momentarily present in memory (in present participles like "protruding" and "kneading"). The future becomes tenseless, and thereby infinitely extendable, by means of an infinitive ("breathless / to tell their tales"). It is always useful to look for the narrative in all poems, and to decide how much of the poem is narrative versus how much "stays the same" as it meditates for a while without changing its stance.

Some poems are almost purely *meditative*. Here is the contemporary poet Philip Larkin on estrangement between two people who have been lovers for a long time. You will notice that "nothing happens," that the speaker is still in the same predicament at the end as at the beginning. The whole poem, except for the general statement of the first line, takes place in the present tense, as many meditations do:

PHILIP LARKIN (1922 – 1985)
Talking in Bed

Talking in bed ought to be easiest,
Lying together there goes back so far,
An emblem of two people being honest.

Yet more and more time passes silently.
Outside, the wind's incomplete unrest
Builds and disperses clouds about the sky,

And dark towns heap up on the horizon.
None of this cares for us. Nothing shows why
At this unique distance from isolation

It becomes still more difficult to find
Words at once true and kind,
Or not untrue and not unkind.

The *narrative* here — concerning the way talk becomes harder and harder as lovers gradually grow apart — is less important than the *meditation* on this problem conducted by the poet, as he says many things about it: that intimate talk should be easy, that he and his companion have a common past, that bed used to be the place where honesty had a chance, that the outside restless and menacing world is no help, and that there is no explanation for the increasing difficulty summed up in the last two lines. Here, the successive items reflected on in the meditation are the focus of interest, converging on the final redefinition of the problem in the last two lines. A meditative poem asks you to notice all its successive "takes" on the subject being considered.

In short, look for the *plot* in narrative lyrics where the tenses change, and look for *successive "takes"* on a subject in meditative lyrics.

Classifying Lyric Poems

Lyric poems themselves are generally classified in three ways: by *content,* by *speech act,* and by *outer form.*

Content: We could classify the poems by Rich and Larkin according to their *content,* calling Rich's an *autobiography* and Larkin's a *love-poem.*

Speech act: Or we could classify the two poems according to their *speech acts,* calling Rich's a *confessional narration* and Larkin's a *meditation* on estrangement.

Outer form: Or we could classify the poems according to their *outer form,* describing Rich's as a *poem in unrhymed couplets* and Larkin's as a *poem in rhymed tercets.*

Each of these classifications requires that we investigate the poem for something different — for what its content is, what sort of speech acts it is engaging in, and what outer form it displays.

CONTENT GENRES: Here are some of the most frequent kinds (or *genres,* the French word for "kinds") of lyric poems identified by *content:*

The love poem

The aubade (a dawn poem in which one of the lovers, usually, is waked by the sun and speaks)

The nocturne (a night scene)

The pastoral (a poem spoken by a shepherd; loosely, a poem in the countryside)

The elegy (a poem mourning a death)

The epithalamion (a poem celebrating a wedding)

The prayer

The autobiography

The flower poem

The sea poem

The travel poem

The birthday poem

There are enough poems of all the above sorts so that any poet writing a travel poem is bound to remember other travel poems, and so on. The poet expects the reader, often, to know how such poems usually go (a travel poem, for instance, normally reaches a destination). The poet then often "changes the rules," and violates the very expectations that the poem has set up. The seventeenth-century poet George Herbert, for instance, in a poem called "Pilgrimage," leads us by his title to expect that he will find a destination, but all he finds is "a lake of brackish waters" instead of a place of spiritual healing. Flower poems, to give another example, usually praise the flower, but William Blake writes of a "sunflower, weary of time" and makes us wonder about the weariness of the flower. The dawn poem is usually spoken by one lover to the other, as in *Romeo and Juliet;* John Donne makes his dawn poem unusual by addressing the sun: "Busy old fool, unruly sun!" In every case, a poet writing with a known content will want to do something new and interesting with that content. The more poems you have read, the more pleasure you will get from reading a new poem, since you will be alert to the new thing the poet is doing. It is the "new twist," as well as the old thing done very well in a new way, that gives the pleasure.

The first poet to invent a kind sets a problem: What do lovers say when the sun comes up and interrupts their lovemaking? Every subsequent poet finds a new solution to the problem. No one solution is better, in theory, than any other; and a rich poetic problem is one that keeps on generating new solutions.

Emily Dickinson, for instance, wrote a prayer-poem describing a heart praying to an invisible power. The success of the poem depends on our having a sense that the usual prayer is addressed to God, has a reverential tone, and asks for some hoped-for good: only if we know these normal conditions will we see Dickinson's blasphemy. Dickinson tells us in the first stanza that *someone* is being addressed by the Heart, but it is not until the second stanza that that person addressed is described as an "inquisitor," a torturer. And the hoped-for good asked for by the Heart changes as the poem goes on, giving the poem its dynamic shape or inner form, as the praying Heart changes from someone demanding pleasure to an abject prisoner craving from God "the privilege to die":

Emily Dickinson (1830 – 1886)
The Heart asks Pleasure — first —

The Heart asks Pleasure — first —
And then — Excuse from Pain —
And then — those little Anodynes°   *painkillers*
That deaden suffering —

And then — to go to sleep —
And then — if it should be
The will of its Inquisitor
The privilege to die —

This two-stanza description of a prayer is organized as a list of goods asked for. Its dynamic shape can be indicated as a long chain of petitions, all of them the direct objects of the verb "asks":

The Heart asks: ————————⟶   Pleasure (first)
& then   Excuse from Pain
& then   Anodynes

& then   to go to sleep
& then
(if it should be the will of its
        Inquisitor)   the privilege to die

Why does Dickinson divide this single list into two stanzas? What makes stanza 2 worth separating from stanza 1? As soon as we ask this question we realize that we don't know, in stanza 1, whom the Heart is addressing with its prayer. If we translate Dickinson's narrative into the Heart's direct pleas, the young Heart says: "I want Pleasure." Pleasure never comes; that prayer goes unanswered. "Well, then, I want to have no more Pain," says the Heart, still believing that its unknown Addressee in heaven would prefer to bestow pleasure or at least painlessness on the petitioner. But the pain goes on, unabated. "Well, then, please give me some drugs to lessen the suffering," asks the Heart. Throughout the first stanza the Heart still wants to maintain consciousness, even if it should be consciousness dulled by a sedative. Throughout the first stanza the Heart still believes in the potential benevolence of the Person listening to these demands.

But no anodynes are forthcoming, and the Heart foresees that its life will be one of unrelieved suffering. "At least let me sleep," prays the Heart, now willing to forgo consciousness. But that prayer goes unanswered, too; nights of insomniac suffering succeed days full of undeadened pain. It is at this point that the Heart redefines the person addressed. This person on high is clearly totally nonbenevolent, having denied the Heart any morsel of pleasure, having even denied a letup in pain, refusing to give painkilling medicines, withholding even the relief from pain given by sleep. What can we call such a torturer? Dickinson reaches to the Renaissance image of a church-licensed torturer, an Inquisitor. The Inquisitor has total power; the tortured Heart, none. Once you recognize that the person in charge of your destiny is a torturer and that you are totally in his power, nothing is left for you but to be abject, to cringe, to say, "Oh Inquisitor, if it be thy will, grant me the privilege of dying." It is to this suicidal point that the Heart comes at the end of her prayer, when she is willing (as she was not in the first stanza) to forgo consciousness entirely. She now clearly perceives (as she did not in the first stanza) that she is in the hands not of a benevolent God but of a relentlessly cruel one. At last we see why Dickinson divided her list of petitions in two.

The petitionary form described in this poem is that of a Christian prayer. A poem describing a "standard" Christian prayer might say:

> The soul asks peace of mind,
> And then for virtue's power,
> And then for hope and charity
> In every evil hour;

> And then for faith in grief,
> And then — if it should be
> The will of its Creator-God —
> His face at death to see.

A "conventional" prayer-poem of this sort is the "ghost-model" behind Dickinson's blasphemous rewriting of the genre. Dickinson expects her reader to react strongly to her departure from the conventional ways of talking to God. All poets expect readers to know (from ordinary social behavior) what sort of content would normally appear in the usual prayer, or the usual wedding song, or the conventional funeral speech, and to measure the poem's departures in content from the norm.

SPEECH ACTS: When we classify poems by their speech acts, we draw attention to their *manner* of expression more than to their content. I can apologize for any number of things — my tardiness, or my mistakes, or my clothing — but in each of these cases my speech act (whatever its content) is an *apology*. Similarly, I can protest about time, or death, or love — but in every case, my speech act is a *protest*. Since the language of most poems can be thought of as a series of utterances by a speaker, the poet expects you to track the person's successive speech acts, just as you might do in life when you might say, "First, she *criticized* me, then she *apologized*, then she *explained* why she was upset, and finally she *asked* if we could still be friends." A poem's speech acts need to be followed and identified in just this way: "The speaker *declares* his love, and then *vows* that he will always be faithful, while *protesting* the indifference of his beloved and *reproaching* her for it." Here are a few speech acts that often organize poems (a longer list is provided in the appendix "On Speech Acts"):

Apology

Apostrophe (a direct second-person address to another, usually of higher rank)

Declaration

Boast

Command

Interrogation

Exclamation

Description

Hypothesis

Rebuttal

Narration

Prayer

Debate or dialogue

Reproach

We have seen a *narration* of autobiography in Rich's poem "Necessities of Life," a *narration* of prayer in Dickinson's "The Heart asks Pleasure — first —." A poem whose *speech act* was prayer would be, unlike the Dickinson poem, addressed directly to God, like George Herbert's "Discipline," which begins,

> Throw away thy rod,
> Throw away thy wrath,
>   O my God,
> Take the gentle path.

Or the speech act of a poem can be a *command*. Commands are normally given by people; one way of being original in a command-poem would be to have the commands given by something that normally doesn't talk. This is what Carl Sandburg does in his poem "Grass," where the grass speaks. This poem surveys the sites of famous battles during the Napoleonic Wars, the Civil War, and the First World War:

CARL SANDBURG (1878 – 1967)
Grass

Pile the bodies high at Austerlitz and Waterloo.
Shovel them under and let me work —
    I am the grass; I cover all.

And pile them high at Gettysburg
And pile them high at Ypres and Verdun.
Shovel them under and let me work.
Two years, ten years, and passengers ask the conductor:

> What place is this?
> Where are we now?
>
> I am the grass.
> Let me work.

This poem contains other speech acts besides its repeated *commands* ("pile," "shovel under," "let me work"). It also contains a repeated *self-definition* ("I am the grass") and a piece of *narration* "Two years . . . and passengers ask . . . what place is this?" If we were mapping this poem by the grass's speech acts, numbering the commands in sequence (1, 2, and so on), it would read:

> *Command* 1a ("pile")
> *Commands* 2a and 3a ("shovel under," "let me work")
> > *Self-definition* 1a ("I am the grass")
>
> *Command* 1b ("and pile")
> *Command* 1c ("and pile")
> *Commands* 2b and 3b ("shovel under" and "let me work")
> *Narration* ("passengers ask")
>
> > (Inserted *question* by passengers: "What . . . ?")
> > (Inserted *question* by passengers: "Where . . . ?")
>
> > *Self-definition* 1b ("I am the grass")
> > *Command* 3c ("let me work")

When we "map" a poem by its speech acts, we are often enabled to see its skeletal structure and to describe it precisely, saying, "This is a poem of repeated *commands* by the grass. The grass *defines itself* by its work of covering-over the dead of all battles, important in their day but soon forgotten, as the *questions* asked by later passers-by, *narrated* by the grass, reveal." This is a far more exact way of describing a poem than to mention only its theme, saying, "This poem is about the way in which past battles are soon forgotten." In noting the way the poet has made this thematic cliché memorable — by having the grass be the speaker, and by giving it relatively few and repeated speech acts to use — one sees the poem not merely as a statement about war but as a constructed piece of art. Since the language of most poems can be thought of as a series of utterances by a speaker, the poet expects the reader to track and identify the speech acts, just as we do in life. Here, the repetitiveness of form is used to emphasize the sameness of all wars, as burial follows burial repeatedly.

OUTER FORM: A poem can also be classified according to various aspects of its *outer form,* having to do with meter, rhyme, and stanza-form. (The appendix "On Prosody" describes these aspects more fully.) With respect to prosody, here are a few examples of kinds of naming.

Line-Width. Some form-names have to do with the *width* of the poetic *line.* A pentameter poem is a poem in lines *five* beats *wide:*

> When I / see BIRCH / es BEND / to LEFT / and RIGHT . . .
> I LIKE / to THINK / some BOY'S / been SWING / ing
>   THEM.

A trimeter poem is a poem in lines *three* beats *wide:*

> It is TIME / that I MADE / my WILL;
> I CHOOSE / upSTAND / ing MEN.

The single most important thing to remember in deciding how many beats a line has is that you cannot ascertain this in isolation. You need to look at the lines surrounding it, and, if it occurs in a poem with stanzas, at matching lines in other stanzas. The reason you need surrounding or matching lines is that many lines, taken by themselves, could be read in different ways. Take the line from Hamlet's famous soliloquy "To be or not to be: that is the question." You could read this line, taken by itself, in two different ways:

> To BE or NOT to be: THAT is the QUESTion.   (*4 beats*)
> To BE or NOT to BE: THAT is the QUESTion.   (*5 beats*)

We decide that the line is meant to have five beats because the lines surrounding it in Hamlet's speech mostly seem to fall into place if we read them with five beats:

> To DIE, to SLEEP; to SLEEP, perCHANCE to DREAM,   (5)
> And IN that SLEEP of DEATH what DREAMS may COME   (5)
> When WE have SHUFFled OFF this MORtal COIL   (5)
> Must GIVE us PAUSE.

This gives us the evidence we need to decide that we should read our dubious line as "To BE or NOT to BE; THAT is the QUESTion," with five beats.

Similarly, the line with which William Butler Yeats begins his poem "Easter 1916" is "I have met them at close of day." Taken by itself, we could read this line perfectly reasonably as having four beats ("I

HAVE met THEM at CLOSE of DAY") if it were followed by another four-beat line, as in this piece of doggerel:

I have met them at close of day,	*(4)*
But they have never greeted me,	*(4)*
And though I now am old and gray,	*(4)*
I think that we cannot agree.	*(4)*

In point of fact, though, Yeats's line is followed by a long series of lines that all have three beats each, which makes us read it, too, with a three-beat rhythm — "I have MET them at CLOSE of DAY":

I have MET them at CLOSE of DAY	*(3)*
COMing with VIVid FAces,	*(3)*
From COUNTer or DESK among GREY	*(3)*
EIGHTeenth-CENtury HOUSes.	*(3)*

The rule of thumb, then, is always to look at lines *in groups* when you are deciding how many beats they have. Find another stanza in the poem matching the one you are dubious about, and see if its pattern is clearer. (All similar stanzas in a poem have the same arrangement of beats.) The best way to "hear" the beats of a poem is to read it aloud, and to notice the natural stresses of the sentences as you read, deciding, in dubious cases, how to read the line by comparing it with others.

Rhythm. Some form-names have to do with the *rhythm* of the line. Rhythms are either *rising* (one-TWO, one-TWO would be an example) or *falling* (ONE-two-three, ONE-two-three would be an example). Shakespeare's blank verse has a two-syllable rising rhythmic unit represented as one-TWO, ˘´. Five of these building units make up the Shakespearean line — *five* beats *wide,* in a *rising* rhythm: ˘´˘´˘´˘´˘´; "To DIE, to SLEEP, to SLEEP, perCHANCE to DREAM." *Falling* rhythm is much heavier than rising rhythm, and is often used to imitate marching, hoof-beats, or some form of raw power, as in Blake's poem on the TYger that goes ONE-two, ONE-two: "TYger, TYger, BURNing BRIGHT / IN the FORests OF the NIGHT."

Poem-Length. Some form-names have to do with the *length* of the *whole poem:* Wallace Stevens's "Sunday Morning" is a poem in eight *cantos,* in which each *canto* (a single long stanza) has fifteen lines. The name *sonnet* normally means that the poem in question has fourteen lines.

Combinatorial Form-Names. Some form-names have to do with the width *and* rhythm *and* length *and* rhymes of the *whole poem:* a "Shakespearean sonnet" is a poem with lines *five* beats *wide* in a two-syllable *rising* rhythm; it is *fourteen* lines long, and the lines rhyme *abab cdcd efef gg* (making three quatrains in alternate rhyme and a rhyming couplet).

These qualities of form are explained systematically in the appendix "On Prosody." They need to be observed routinely, in the case of every poem you read. Once you have described its *content* (a spring poem, an elegy) and its successive *speech acts* (a narration, a plea), look at the *outer form.* How many lines does the whole poem have? How many stanzas? Are they all the same shape? How wide is the line? Where do the rhymes come? What is the overall rhythm? It helps to jot down what you observe in the margin next to the poem on the page ("Elegy; lament, protest, consolation; fifteen alternately rhymed pentameter quatrains in rising rhythm"). That way you have a handle on the poem the next time you look at it.

INNER STRUCTURAL FORM: Besides its *outer form* ("This is a poem in quatrains in falling rhythm rhyming *aabb*" — a description of Blake's "Tyger"), every poem has *internal structural form.* This is its dynamic shape, which derives from the curve traced by the emotions of the poem as they change over its duration. That emotional curve is plotted by connecting two, three, or more points of the poem, a rise from depression to hope to joy, for instance — or a decline from triumph through doubt to despair. Very few poems represent an unchanging steady state of the same emotion all through.

Some poems are two-part (*binary*) poems, like William Wordsworth's "A slumber did my spirit seal" (which we saw changing from illusion to stern knowledge), or like Dickinson's "The Heart asks Pleasure — first —" (which we saw changing its conception of God from benevolence to cruelty). Another fundamentally binary form is the debate poem, where A speaks, then B challenges A, then A replies to B, back and forth.

There are also many three-part (*ternary*) poems, which often take on the internal structure of beginning, modulation, end (a song-form preserved in lyric). For an example of three-part form, see W. B. Yeats's "Crazy Jane Talks with the Bishop."

Internal forms are infinitely variable, since they represent emotional response, always volatile. One well-known internal structure is that of the "surprise" ending, where the last few lines reverse everything that has gone before. George Herbert's poem "The Collar" is full of rebellion against God, until the very end:

> But as I raved, and grew more fierce and wild
>   At every word,

Methoughts I heard one calling, *Child!*
And I replied, *My Lord.*

In investigating the internal structure of a poem, one should try to divide it into parts along its "fault lines." Where does the logic of the argument seem to break? Where does the poem change from first person to second person? Where does the major change in tense or speech act take place? Here are some of the ingredients of internal structural form that will help you to explore a poem.

Sentences. Poems are, on the whole, made of sentences, and sentences are an important internal structuring principle of poems. For instance, there will often be a procession of short sentences, and then one very long sentence, or vice versa. The poet means us to notice how many sentences there are in a poem, and how they relate to one another. There may be a generalizing sentence ("How do I love thee? Let me count the ways") followed by many particulars; or many small instances leading up to more important ones, as in Robert Herrick's summary of his poetic subjects, ending at the hope of salvation:

Robert Herrick (1591 – 1674)

The Argument of His Book

I sing of brooks, of blossoms, birds, and bowers,
Of April, May, of June, and July flowers.
I sing of Maypoles, hock carts, wassails, wakes,
Of bridegrooms, brides, and of their bridal cakes.
I write of youth, of love, and have access
By these to sing of cleanly wantonness.
I sing of dews, of rains, and, piece by piece,
Of balm, of oil, of spice, and ambergris.
I sing of times trans-shifting, and I write
How roses first came red and lilies white.
I write of groves, of twilights, and I sing
The court of Mab° and of the fairy king.   *queen of the fairies*
I write of hell; I sing (and ever shall)
Of heaven, and hope to have it after all.

You can often discover a lot about a poem by copying out its successive sentences in prose, putting each one under its predecessor. You can then ask yourself how they resemble one another, and how they differ, and why.

Person. Sentences are written either in the first person (*I/me* in the singular, *we/us* in the plural); the second person (*you* — archaic forms are *thou* in the nominative singular, *thee* in the objective singular, and *ye* in the plural); or the third person (*he/him, she/her,* and *it* in the singular; *they/them* in the plural). A *change of person* as a poem goes along is a significant structuring device. A change to the second person, addressing a person ("you") in the poem who hasn't appeared before, usually raises the temperature of a poem, as when Wordsworth, after a long monologue in "Tintern Abbey," turns to his sister, saying, "For thou art with me here upon the banks / Of this fair river," and we learn for the first time that he is not alone. An elegy often begins by trying to keep the dead person "alive" by directly addressing him or her, and may then subside into the third person, speaking no longer of "you" but of "the body," as Robert Lowell does in his elegy for his mother, "Sailing Home from Rapallo." He is bringing his mother's body from Italy (where she had died) home to New England, and we gradually see Charlotte Lowell turn from being a "you" to being "the corpse":

> **Your** nurse could only speak Italian,
> but after twenty minutes I could imagine **your** final week,
> and tears ran down my cheeks. . . .

> When I embarked from Italy with **my mother's body**,
> the whole shoreline of the *Golfo di Genova*°　　　·　　*Gulf of Genoa*
> was breaking into fiery flower.

> .　.　.　.　.

> **Mother** travelled first-class in the hold.

> .　.　.　.　.

> In the grandiloquent lettering on **Mother's** coffin,

> *Lowell* had been misspelled LOVEL.
> **The corpse**
> was wrapped like *panettone* in Italian tinfoil.

Person reveals the poet's relation to the world. Is the poet in the world of "you" or "we" — other persons — or in a solitary world inhabited only by the "I" of the poem? Or a world with no addressees, full of "its" and "thems"?

Agency. Every sentence has a subject; the subject is the agent of the verb. Many poems have one subject ("I") for every sentence: in them, agency never changes. Others have a single *change in agency:* see, for instance, Randall Jarrell's "The Death of the Ball Turret Gunner," in which the subject of all the main verbs is "I" until the last line, when, because the ball turret gunner has been killed, the "I" vanishes and "they" take over. The "I" who acted becomes the "me" who is acted on. Here is the complete poem:

RANDALL JARRELL (1914 – 1965)
The Death of the Ball Turret Gunner

From my mother's sleep I fell into the State,
And I hunched in its belly till my wet fur froze.
Six miles from earth, loosed from its dream of life,
I woke to black flak and the nightmare fighters.
When I died *they* washed *me* out of the turret with a hose.

Some poems have a different subject for every sentence — these make the reader take on several different perspectives at once. See, for instance, Lowell's "Skunk Hour," where in the first stanza alone there are four different subjects which govern verbs:

Nautilus Island's hermit
heiress still lives through winter in her Spartan cottage;
her *sheep* still graze above the sea.
Her *son's* a bishop. Her *farmer*
is first selectman in our village;
she's in her dotage.

Heiress, sheep, son, farmer: all govern verbs ("lives," "graze," "is," "is"). These agents are all linked in an elaborate system of center and satellites. The *hermit heiress* has *her* cottage, *her* sheep, *her* son, and *her* farmer (unfortunately, there is also *her* dotage, which she is in). The heiress still in some sense owns her sheep, her son, and her farmer (they are all *hers*); but because they are all given independent existence as agents in the poem, we know they are no longer hers, really. They are separate from her, separate subjects; and the only things that are really hers now are her cottage and her dotage; only these two rhyming nouns, among "her" possessions, are not independent agents governing a verb. *By tracing agency through a poem we can tell who is ruling it as it goes along.* In "Skunk Hour," the various inhabitants of the seaside town at first "own" the poem; then the disturbed speaker "owns" the poem while he carries out his voyeuristic acts; but finally it is the mother skunk with her column of kittens who "owns" the poem and the town, as in the last stanza the troubled speaker yields agency to the skunk:

I **stand** on top
of our back steps and **breathe** the rich air —
a mother skunk with her column of kittens *swills* the garbage pail.
She jabs her wedge-head in a cup
of sour cream, *drops* her ostrich tail,
and *will not scare.*

It is important to know who "owns," by agency, each part of every poem.

Tenses. Sentences are written in tenses, and tenses are also an important internal structuring aspect of the poem, making it move in time (as we saw in Adrienne Rich's "Necessities of Life") from past to present to future. *Tense-changes* ask to be noticed. Sometimes, even often, they are the main point of the poem. As we saw earlier, in Wordsworth's "A slumber did my spirit seal," the first stanza is in the past tense, the second in the present tense. The first stanza stands for delusion ("seemed"); the second stanza for reality; and the white gap between the two tenses represents the death of the beloved. Here are the tensed verbs:

WILLIAM WORDSWORTH (1770 – 1850)
A slumber did my spirit seal

A slumber *did* my spirit *seal;*
    I *had* no human fears;
She *seemed* a thing that *could not feel*
    The touch of earthly years.

No motion *has* she now, no force;
    She neither *hears* nor *sees;*
Rolled round in earth's diurnal course,
    With rocks, and stones, and trees.

The main structuring agent of the poem is the *tense-change,* bracketing the invisible (infinite, untensed) white-space moment of the girl's death.

Images, or Sensual Words. "We thought in images," said Robert Lowell in a poem to his friend and fellow poet John Berryman. Though words in poetry can only refer and not really picture, a linkage of references in the same category of sense-perceivable words — say, many words about the moon, such as "bright," "beams," "round," "white," and so on — tend to create the impression of the object to which they all refer. Linked words (referring especially to the senses of sight and hearing) help to structure many poems. These words can be all of one sort (a collection of names of different flowers, for instance, in Milton's "Lycidas") or they can be of different sorts: that is, a series of specific nouns like "flood," "earthquake," "fire," and "shipwreck" can all help to construct the single abstract category "catastrophe." There are systematic ways in which the concrete words that some refer to as "images" may be assembled, too: they may be arranged in *parallel,* or in *contrast,* or in a ranked *hierarchy.* See how Sylvia Plath arranges her images in "Metaphors":

SYLVIA PLATH (1932 – 1963)
Metaphors

I'm a riddle in nine syllables,
An elephant, a ponderous house,
A melon strolling on two tendrils.
O red fruit, ivory, fine timbers!
This loaf's big with its yeasty rising.
Money's new-minted in this fat purse.
I'm a means, a stage, a cow in calf.
I've eaten a bag of green apples,
Boarded the train there's no getting off.

In this poem, Plath runs through many *parallel images* to express her feelings about being pregnant. The first is her ignorance of what her baby will be (boy? girl? placid? temperamental? tall? short?) at the end of nine months: it is a "riddle." Next, she emphasizes (via the elephant) the weight she has gained and (via the house) the difficulty of movement. Next, she emphasizes (via the melon) her new shape and how fragile her legs feel (like tendrils) supporting her abdomen. From the melon, she generalizes to the newborn baby as a "red fruit" — then generalizes further to its precious potential as "ivory" and "fine timbers." The dynamism of the progress of pregnancy is pointed to in the organic "yeasty rising" of bread; but then the dynamism (given its value) is made inorganic, as money is "new minted" (but with a return to her weight in the referral to herself as a "fat" purse).

The next set of metaphors, however, departs from what we could reasonably call "images." "I'm a means, a stage." These *abstractions* — a means to an end, a stage in a process — show the poet generalizing beyond the dynamic images (bread rising, money being newly minted) to dynamism itself, a dynamism that reaches to a foreseen conclusion.

Immediately the poet returns to *images.* She is a pregnant cow (another reference to her unwieldy size) who has "eaten a bag of green apples" (thought to provoke labor in cows); and she is a helpless and fearful passenger, unable to leave the rushing forward motion of the train that will take her to her unknown destination.

You might ask yourself both why the poet passes from images to abstractions, and equally why she does not end in abstractions but returns to images for closure. Does it seem dehumanizing for the author to call herself a means? a stage? Each of Plath's images has a part-to-whole relation to the theme of the poem. Taken all together, they give the poem its emotional resonance. Which parts are cheerful? Which are triumphant? Which are apprehensive? How would the poem be different if it ended with the elephant? the money? the cow? the stage? Why does Plath end, do you think, with the train?

Exploring a Poem

What follows is a series of things to note when you run through a poem to see what its parts are and how they fit together. Let us use this list on a sonnet by John Keats, called "On First Looking into Chapman's Homer." The anthology will tell us a few things we have to know to understand the references in the poem: Keats did not know Greek, and so he first read Homer's *Odyssey* in the Renaissance translation by George Chapman; Apollo is the Greek god of poetry; Keats believed (mistakenly) that it was the Spanish conquistador Cortez who, in exploring Panama ("Darien"), discovered the Pacific Ocean (in reality it was Balboa, but the historical error doesn't matter for the imaginative purposes of the poem). Keats tells us what it is like, even for a reader as experienced in poetry as he, to come across Homer's Odyssean epic (from which he draws his opening travel imagery) for the first time:

JOHN KEATS (1795 – 1821)
On First Looking into Chapman's Homer

Much have I travell'd in the realms of gold,
    And many goodly states and kingdoms seen;
    Round many western islands have I been
Which bards in fealty° to Apollo hold.   *allegiance*
Oft of one wide expanse had I been told
    That deep-brow'd Homer ruled as his demesne°;   *domain*
    Yet did I never breathe its pure serene°   *atmosphere*
Till I heard Chapman speak out loud and bold:
Then felt I like some watcher of the skies
    When a new planet swims into his ken°;   *view*

Or like stout Cortez when with eagle eyes
    He star'd at the Pacific — and all his men
Look'd at each other with a wild surmise —
    Silent, upon a peak in Darien.

How do we go about exploring such a poem? Let us try a series of steps.

1. Meaning

This is the usual sort of information-retrieval reading that we do with any passage of prose or verse. We come up with a summary of greater or lesser length giving the import of the passage as we make sense of it. Here, we might arrive at something like "The speaker says that he had traveled through a lot of golden terrain — had read a lot of poems — and people had told him about the Homeric domain, but he had never breathed its air till he heard Chapman speak out. Then he felt like an astronomer discovering a new planet; or like the explorer who discovered the Pacific, whose men, astonished by his gaze, guessed at his discovery." This sort of meaning-paraphrase is necessary, but less useful in poetry than in prose. In many poems there is rather little in the way of plot or character or message or "information" in the ordinary sense, and that little can be quickly sketched (perhaps initially, especially in the case of a complex poem, by the teacher to the class). Hoping to learn things about the poem that are more interesting than simply "what it says" in prose, we try to construct its

2. Antecedent Scenario

What has been happening *before* the poem starts? What has disturbed the status quo and set the poem in motion? Here, we know what has happened: the speaker has picked up Homer (in Chapman's translation) for the first time, and has had a revelatory experience. But the antecedent scenario is not always given to us so clearly. If it is not evident right away, one moves on hopefully to

3. A Division into Structural Parts

Because small units are more easily handled than big ones, and because the process of a poem, even one as short as a sonnet, can't be addressed all at once with a single global question like "What's going on here?" we divide the poem into pieces. One way of dividing this poem up is to notice that it falls, by its rhymes, into two large parts: "I never knew Homer till I read Chapman" (*abbaabba*) and "Then I felt like this" (*cdcdcd*). The first part takes up the first eight lines, connected by the two rhyme-sounds represented by -*old* (rhyme *a*) and -*een* (rhyme *b*); and the second part takes up the last six lines, connected by a new set of rhyme-sounds, represented by -*ies* (rhyme *c*) and -*en* (rhyme *d*). There are other ways, besides this 8:6 division, to divide this poem into parts, as we shall see, but let us work first within this 8:6 division-by-rhyme. In order to suggest a meaningful relation of the parts, it is useful to look at

4. The Climax

In Keats's sonnet, the climax seems to come when Cortez stares at the Pacific — the high point of the poem. What is special about this experience? Why does it replace the image of the astronomer discovering a new planet? In lyric poems, the various parts tend to cluster around a moment of special significance — which its attendant parts lead up to, lead away from, help to clarify, and so on. The climax usually manifests itself by such things as greater intensity of tone, an especially significant metaphor, a change in rhythm, or a change in person. Having located the climax, one can now move back to

5. The Other Parts

About each part, it is useful to ask how it *differs* from the other parts. What is distinctive in it by contrast to the other members of the poem? Does something shift gears? Does the tense change? Does the predominant grammatical form change? (For example, does the poem stop emphasizing nouns and start emphasizing participles?) Is a new person addressed? Have we left a general overlook for certain particulars? Here, we notice that the first four lines talk in *general* about states, kingdoms, and islands. The next four lines talk about *one* special "wide expanse," the one ruled by Homer. The next part says, "I felt like an astronomer discovering a new planet." And the last part produces a new comparison: "I felt like an explorer discovering a new ocean, accompanied by his companions." Some questions immediately arise: Why doesn't the poem end after the poet says, "I felt as though I had discovered a new planet"? Why does he feel he needs a *second* comparison? And why, in the second comparison, does he need not only a single discoverer comparable to the astronomer, but a discoverer *accompanied by a group of companions* ("all his men")? Once these four parts (general realms; Homer's expanse; solo astronomer / planet; Cortez and men / Pacific Ocean) have been isolated, one can move on to the game called

6. Find the Skeleton

What is the dynamic curve of emotion on which the whole poem is arranged? "I am much travelled, and have visited [presumably by ship] many islands; however, I had never visited the Homer-expanse till I heard Chapman; then I breathed the air of the Homer-expanse, and it was like finding" — like finding what? The first stab at comparison ("like finding a new planet") isn't quite right — you can't walk on a planet and explore it and get to know it the way you get to know islands and states. Well, what would be a better comparison? And the speaker realizes that whereas other poets seem feudal lords of a given piece of earth — a state, a kingdom, an island — Homer is different *not just in degree but in kind.* He is, all by himself, an *ocean.* A new ocean, unlike a planet, is something on one's own plane that one can actually explore; yet it is something so big that it must contain many new islands and realms within it. When we understand this, we can identify the curve of astonishment in the poem when the Homer-*expanse* (a carefully chosen word that doesn't give away too much) turns out to be not just another piece of land, and not some faraway uninhabitable body in the sky, but a whole unexplorable ocean, hitherto unguessed at. The tone has changed from one of ripe experience ("Much have I travelled") to one of ignorance (the speaker has never breathed the air of the vast Homeric expanse, though others had, and had told him about it), to the revelation of the "wild surmise" — we have found not just another bounded terrain, but an unsuspected ocean! This curve of emotion, rising from an almost complacent sense of experience to an astonished recognition, is the emotional skeleton of the poem. We can then ask about

7. Games the Poet Plays with the Skeleton

If "On First Looking into Chapman's Homer," by its content, is a then/now poem ("I used not to know Homer / Now I do"), what is the event bridging the then and the now? It is reading Homer in Chapman's translation. "Reading" is not an "event" in the usual sense: most then/now poems (like "A slumber did my spirit seal") are about some more tangible event (a death, an absence, a catastrophe). Keats plays a game, then, with the then/now poem in making its fulcrum an experience of reading. By saying that reading, too, is an Event, Keats makes the then/now poem new.

If this is a riddle-poem (and it is: "What is Homer-land like?"), how is the riddle prepared? It is prepared by a series of alternatives: "I have seen realms, states, kingdoms, islands." Some "expanse" is ruled by Homer, but I have not seen it yet. Will it be a realm? a state? a kingdom?

another island? The first "answer" to the riddle is, "None of the above; Homer-land is a *new planet!*" But that is the wrong answer (one can't travel to and explore a new planet, and the speaker *is* exploring Homer), so the poem tries again to answer the riddle, and this time does it correctly: "None of the above; Homer-expanse is a *new ocean!*" The poet has played a game with our sense of the poem as a riddle by answering not in the category we anticipated from his former travels (a piece of land) but in an unexpected one (ocean), thus making the riddle-poem new.

Keats plays another game with the ignorance/discovery skeleton by making his poem a hero-poem. He makes the reward at the end of the emotional curve — the discovery of the new ocean — not a solitary experience (like that of the "watcher of the skies" seeing the planet), but a communal one. We normally think of reading as an uneventful private act. Why did Keats make it heroic? Furthermore, why did he show the heroic discovery being made not by a single explorer but by a company of explorers? Cortez is not alone on the isthmus of Panama, but is accompanied by "all his men / Look[ing] at each other with a wild surmise." When one discovers the Homeric "expanse" one reads alone, but one becomes thereby a member of a company of people who have discovered Homer — those people who had "oft . . . told" the speaker about Homer. A feat like Homer's writing the *Odyssey* is as heroic as the exploits of Achilles: mastery of such an intellectual discovery is itself a form of heroic exploration. Such a cultural discovery, Keats implies by the presence of Cortez's men, is collective, not private. Keats thought of himself as a poet among poets; a reader of Homer among readers of Homer; an explorer among explorers. And in this way he made the hero-poem both newly intellectual and newly communal and democratic.

Having seen the genre games that the poet plays with his skeleton — as a then/now poem, a riddle-poem, a hero-poem — one can go on to ask about

8. Language

Of course, we have been looking at language all along, but now we can do it more consciously. How many *sentences* does the poem have? (Two.) Where does the break between sentences come? (After line 4.) This gives us, as I promised earlier, a new division into parts: not the 8:6 of the then/now structure, but the 4:10 of the knowledge/discovery structure, which locates for us the moment in which traveled complacency turns to longing for Homeric acquaintance. *Poems often have several overlapping internal structures.* It is one of the signs of a complex poem that its rhymes may be dividing the poem one way, its theme another way, its action from inception through climax another way, its grammar another way, its sentences yet another way. Each of these divisions has something to tell us about the emotional dynamic of the poem.

What *parts of speech* predominate in the poem? (For a further explanation of these, see the appendix "On Grammar."). In Keats's sonnet, the chain of *nouns* of space — "realms," "states," "kingdoms," "islands," "expanse," "demesne," "planet," "Pacific" — stands out as one unifying link.

What other *words*, regardless of whether they are different parts of speech, make a *chain of significant relation*? You might notice how words of seeing and watching — "seen," "watcher," "ken," "eagle eyes," "stared," "looked at" — connect the parts of the poem as do the nouns of space.

What *contexts* are expressed in the diction? (We notice traveling, sailing, exploring, astronomical observation, feudal loyalty, and so on.)

Is the *diction* modern or ancient? (Keats uses archaic words like "realms of gold," "goodly," "bards," "fealty," "demesne," "pure serene," and "ken," which help us sense how long Homer has been alive in our culture.) A close look at language always leads to

9. Tone

The calm beginning, in the voice of ripe experience ("Much have I travelled") mounts to the excitement of the "wild surmise," which then suddenly is confirmed by the breathless "silent" of the last line, and by the image of the "peak," corresponding to this heightened moment. Reading a poem aloud as if it were your own utterance makes you able to distinguish the various *tones of voice* it exhibits, and to name them. At this point, we can turn to

10. Agency and Speech Acts

Who has agency in this poem? We notice that the main verbs are all governed by the "I" who speaks the poem: "I have travelled . . . and seen . . . [and] have been . . . [and] had been told . . . yet [never] did I breathe . . . I heard . . . Then felt I." But we notice that in the subordinate clauses a great many other subagencies are present. Bards hold islands, Homer rules an expanse, Chapman speaks out, the new planet swims into ken, Cortez stares at the Pacific, and his men look with wild surmise at each other. It is by the interpenetration of the rather colorless main verbs denoting the sedentary activity of reading, and the other more public or active actions of the other agents, that Keats draws his new acquaintance with the *Odyssey* into large realms of cultural activity. The speech act of this poem is a single long *narration* of the speaker's more remote and recent pasts. The unusual thing about the speech act (narration) and agency (a single main agent) is that they stop so soon: the last narrative verb by the agent is "Then felt I" in line 9. After that, the attention of the poem never comes back to the speaker, but instead expands out to the most exalted sorts of cultural discovery — that of an astronomer, that of explorers.

11. Roads Not Taken

What are the *roads not taken* in the poem? The sonnet might have ended with the comparison of the self to an astronomer. Would this have been as satisfactory? Or the expanse ruled over by Homer might have been shown as a new continent rather than as a new ocean. Would this have been equally revealing? Or the poem might have been written in the third person instead of the first person:

> Many have travelled in the realms of gold,
>> And they have goodly states and kingdoms seen;
>> Round many western islands have they been
> Which bards in fealty to Apollo hold.

Is this as dramatic as the first person? Or the poem might have *begun* with the reading of Chapman's Homer, instead of leading up to it:

> I once heard Chapman speak out loud and bold;
>> He told me of a wide expanse unseen,
>> (Better than other states and realms of gold)
>> That deep-brow'd Homer ruled as his demesne.
> Then felt I like stout Cortez on his peak,
>> When with his eagle eyes he saw the sea. . . .

We can see how presenting the climax in line 5, as in this rewriting, creates a very different structural shape from the 4:10 knowledge/discovery structure building up to the Pacific. It is useful to think of plausible *roads not taken* by a poem, because they help to identify the roads that *were* taken. With a clear idea of the function of each piece of the poem within the whole, and of the dynamic curve of emotion governing the order in which the pieces appear, we can then pass on to

12. Genre, Form, and Rhythm

What is the *content* genre of the poem? A dramatic change between then and now; a poem about reading; a poem about a hero; a poem about collective experience. (It can be compared to other poems about newness, about reading, about heroes, about collectivity.)

What is the *speech act* genre of the poem? A *narration in the first person* of a significant event marking one life-period off from another; and an *asking-a-riddle:* "What is reading Homer like?" (It can be compared to other first-person narrations and to other riddle-poems.)

What is the *formal* genre of the poem? A sonnet (using the usual five-beat rising-rhythm line found in sonnets) rhyming *abbaabba cdcdcd.* (It can be compared to other sonnets rhyming the same way.) About form, we always need to ask how it has been made vivid; see below for remarks on Keats's rhythm. We can then move on to the last issue, which is always

13. The Imagination

What has the poet's *imagination invented* that is striking, or memorable, or beautiful? We can tell, from the metaphors of sailing, that before writing his poem Keats had been reading Homer's *Odyssey,* and had been thinking about what Odysseus had discovered as he sailed from realm to realm, from island to island. Wanting to describe his own first reading of Homer, Keats imaginatively borrows from the very book he has been reading, using the image of travel, saying that reading poetry in general is like voyaging from Shakespeare-land to Milton-kingdom to Spenser-state, but that reading Homer is not like finding just another piece of land to visit: it is like finding a new planet, or, even better, a whole unexpected new ocean to sail in. Keats *imagined* these large analogies — sailing, astronomical observation, discovering an ocean — for the act of reading in general, and for reading Homer in particular; they enliven the sonnet. What makes the poem touching is the imagined change from the complacency of the well-traveled speaker to the astonishment of the discoverer of Homer, and the poet's realization that in reading Homer he has joined a company of others who have also discovered the Homeric ocean, sharing his "wild surmise." It is characteristic of Keats to see poetry as a collective act: he said in a letter, "I think I shall be among the English poets after my death," not "I think I shall be famous after my death."

But the imagination is not invested in themes and images alone. The imagination of a poet has to extend to the rhythm of the poem as well. What the imagination has invented here that is *rhythmically* memorable is the change from the stately first ten lines — because even the astronomer doesn't have to do anything but look through his telescope — to the strenuous broken rhythms of the heroic last four lines, with their four sharply differentiated parts:

1. Or like stout Cortez when with eagle eyes he stared at the Pacific —
2. And all his men look'd at each other with a wild surmise —

3. Silent,

4. Upon a peak in Darien.

The intent, piercing stare of "stout Cortez"; the amazed mutual conjecture of his men; the sudden, short, transfixed silence of the whole group; the summit of foreign experience on which the action takes place — each of these four facts is given its own rhythmically irregular phrase, so different from the undisturbed and measured pentameter narration in "Then felt I like some watcher of the skies / When a new planet swims into his ken." A poem needs *imaginative rhythms* as well as *imaginative transformation* of content.

You will, of course, read most poems without investigating them in this detailed way for their inner processes. But as soon as you want to know *how a poem works,* as well as what it says, and *why it is poignant or compelling,* you will find yourself beginning to study it, using methods like the ones sketched here. Soon, it becomes almost second nature for you to notice sentences, tense-changes, speech acts, tonal variants, changes of agency, rhythms, rhymes, and other ingredients of internal and outer structure. Just as an archaeologist studies ruins, while the rest of us simply walk through Pompeii not understanding much of what we see, a student of poetry becomes more than simply a reader. You become more like a conductor who studies the musical score before conducting the piece in performance.

You can experience a poem with great pleasure as a general reader; or you can also learn how to explore it, to gain the more experienced pleasure that a student of architecture feels inside a Renaissance palace, or that an engineer feels looking at the San Francisco Bay Bridge. In every case, study adds to what you are able to perceive. Poems — because they are short and written in your own mother tongue — are very rewarding things to study as well as to read, to learn by heart as well as to study. They keep you company in life.

Exploring a poem under the broad headings given above will almost always lead you to a deeper understanding of the poem as a work of art, constructed in a dense and satisfying and surprising way. Though we almost always respond first to the quickly sensed "message" of a poem, the *reason* for our response (even if we do not at first know this) is the *arrangement* of the message (on many intersecting planes) into a striking and moving form. To give a poem its due as a work of art, we need to be able to see it as an *arranged* message. Looking through the poem thoroughly helps us realize the kind of work the poet puts into constructing this urgent expression of life as it is seen, sensed, and reflected on. Even the simplest of short poems will show imagination and architectural construction.

In Brief: Describing Poems

When you are looking for useful ways to describe a poem, this checklist of questions can guide your exploration:

1. *Meaning:* Can you paraphrase in prose the general outline of the poem?

2. *Antecedent scenario:* What has been happening before the poem begins? What has provoked the speaker into utterance? How has a previous equilibrium been unsettled? What is the speaker upset about?

3. *Division into parts:* How many? Where do the breaks come?

4. *The climax:* How do the other parts fall into place around it?

5. *The other parts:* What makes you divide the poem into these parts? Are there changes in person? In agency? In tense? In parts of speech?

6. *Find the skeleton:* What is the emotional curve on which the whole poem is strung? (It even helps to draw a shape — a crescendo, perhaps, or an hourglass-shape, or a sharp ascent followed by a steep decline — so you'll know how the poem looks to you as a whole.)

7. *Games with the skeleton:* How is this emotional curve made new?

8. *Language:* What are the contexts of diction; chains of significant relation; parts of speech emphasized; tenses; and so on?

9. *Tone:* Can you name the pieces of the emotional curve — the changes in tone you can hear in the speaker's voice as the poem goes along?

10. *Agency and its speech acts:* Who is the main agent in the poem, and does the main agent change as the poem progresses? See what the main speech act of the agent is, and whether that changes. Notice oddities about agency and speech acts.

11. *Roads not taken:* Can you imagine the poem written in a different person, or a different tense, or with the parts rearranged, or with an additional stanza, or with one stanza left out, conjecturing by such means why the poet might have wanted *these* pieces in *this* order?

12. *Genres:* What are they by content, by speech act, by outer form?

13. *The imagination:* What has it invented that is new, striking, memorable — in content, in genre, in analogies, in rhythm, in a speaker?

Reading Other Poems

If you were to give a genre-name by *content* to each of the poems below, you could begin, "Shakespeare: lust-poem"; "Herbert: prayer-poem"; "Marvell: solitude-poem," and go on through the list down to "Alexie: decline-poem." If you were to give a genre-name by *form* to each one, you could begin, "Shakespeare: sonnet"; "Herbert: shaped poem"; "Marvell: poem in 8-line couplet-stanzas"; down to "Alexie: poem in tercets," and so on. If you were to group them according to person, you could say, "Shakespeare: third person"; "Herbert: third person and first person"; "Marvell: third person and first person," and so forth. If you were to name them by principal speech act, you could say, "Shakespeare: definition"; "Herbert: apostrophe"; "Marvell: description"; down to "Alexie: narration." Try making such a list, and see how each question — content? form? person? speech act? — gives you a different purchase on the poem. You can expand that purchase by expanding the number of questions you put to the poem. For instance, where is the climax? Does the poem have a happy ending? From what position — participant, observer, judge — does the speaker operate? The following are merely some sample questions.

- What is the emotional curve traced by Shakespeare in his speaker's feelings about lust? By Ezra Pound in the young wife's feelings? Can you see how the tones of voice change with the feelings?

- How many different emotional responses to the fact of his blindness does Milton express? Can you suggest why Bradstreet's poem begins and ends in "we," while the middle uses other pronouns?

Consider how the poet's imagination has worked on the material.

- As Jorie Graham sees Piero della Francesca's painting of the young but majestic standing Virgin, pregnant and unbuttoning her dress before she goes into labor, how does the poet's imagination respond to the painting?

- As Mark Strand imagines courtship, how does he make it comic?

- As Heaney imagines that the anxiety of writing is like confronting police at a border checkpoint, how does he make that confrontation vivid?

- As Sherman Alexie imagines the decline of life on an Indian reservation, through what example does he convey it?

In longer poems like "Ode to a Nightingale," "Dover Beach," and "Mending Wall," the more scannings you make the more you see. You can begin anywhere that interests you. Anything you notice helps to build up your picture of the poem's world. In "Dover Beach" you might notice how one setting — on the English coast — leads to another — the Aegean Sea, and how one topic — love — leads to another — the ebbing of religious faith. These large structural blocks make you perceive how the poem is composed, and enable you to look at the micro-structures within each part. You can even begin your scanning at the end of the poem: when you look at the close of "Ode to a Nightingale" and see that it ends with two unresolved questions, you are more prepared for its inner vexations. Be patient with your scannings: each new run-through reveals more of the strategy of the poem, and enables you to describe the energies of the poem better.

WILLIAM SHAKESPEARE (1564 – 1616)
Sonnet 129

Th'expense of spirit in a waste of shame
Is lust in action, and till action, lust
Is perjured, murderous, bloody, full of blame,
Savage, extreme, rude, cruel, not to trust;
Enjoyed no sooner but despisèd straight,
Past reason hunted, and no sooner had,
Past reason hated as a swallowed bait,
On purpose laid to make the taker mad:
Mad in pursuit and in possession so,
Had, having, and in quest to have, extreme;
A bliss in proof,° and proved, a very woe,   *in the experience*
Before, a joy proposed, behind, a dream.
    All this the world well knows; yet none knows well
    To shun the heaven that leads men to this hell.

GEORGE HERBERT (1593 – 1633)
Easter Wings

    Lord, who createdst man in wealth and store,
      Though foolishly he lost the same,
        Decaying more and more
          Till he became
           Most poor:
           With thee

O let me rise
As larks, harmoniously,
And sing this day thy victories:
Then shall the fall further the flight in me.

My tender age in sorrow did begin;
And still with sicknesses and shame
Thou didst so punish sin,
That I became
Most thin.
With thee
Let me combine,
And feel this day thy victory;
For, if I imp[1] my wing on thine,
Affliction shall advance the flight in me.

ANDREW MARVELL (1621 – 1678)
The Garden

How vainly men themselves amaze
To win the palm, the oak, or bays,[1]
And their incessant labors see
Crowned from some single herb, or tree,
Whose short and narrow-vergèd shade   5
Does prudently their toils upbraid;
While all flowers and all trees do close
To weave the garlands of repose!

Fair Quiet, have I found thee here,
And Innocence, thy sister dear?   10
Mistaken long, I sought you then
In busy companies of men.
Your sacred plants, if here below,
Only among the plants will grow;
Society is all but rude   15
To this delicious solitude.

No white nor red was ever seen
So amorous as this lovely green.

---

[1]To graft feathers on a damaged wing so as to improve powers of flight. (A term from falconry.)

[1]Awards for military, civic, or poetic achievement.

Fond lovers, cruel as their flame,
Cut in these trees their mistress' name: 20
Little, alas, they know or heed
How far these beauties hers exceed!
Fair trees, wheresoe'er your barks I wound,
No name shall but your own be found.

　　When we have run our passion's heat,   25
Love hither makes his best retreat.
The gods, that mortal beauty chase,
Still in a tree did end their race:
Apollo hunted Daphne so,
Only that she might laurel grow;   30
And Pan did after Syrinx speed,
Not as a nymph, but for a reed.[2]

　　What wondrous life is this I lead!
Ripe apples drop about my head;
The luscious clusters of the vine   35
Upon my mouth do crush their wine;
The nectarine and curious peach
Into my hands themselves do reach;
Stumbling on melons, as I pass,
Insnared with flowers, I fall on grass.   40

　　Meanwhile the mind, from pleasure less,°   *from lesser pleasure*
Withdraws into its happiness;
The mind, that ocean where each kind
Does straight its own resemblance find;[3]
Yet it creates, transcending these,   45
Far other worlds and other seas,
Annihilating all that's made
To a green thought in a green shade.

　　Here at the fountain's sliding foot,
Or at some fruit tree's mossy root,   50
Casting the body's vest aside,

---

[2]Daphne, to escape Apollo, turned into a laurel tree. Syrinx, to escape Pan, turned into a reed. Marvell implies that Apollo and Pan desired these transformations.

[3]Alluding to the popular notion that the flora and fauna of the land have their parallels in the sea.

My soul into the boughs does glide:
There, like a bird, it sits and sings,
Then whets and combs its silver wings,
And, till prepared for longer flight,   55
Waves in its plumes the various light.

     Such was that happy garden-state,
While man there walked without a mate:
After a place so pure and sweet,
What other help could yet be meet!   60
But 'twas beyond a mortal's share
To wander solitary there:
Two paradises 'twere in one
To live in paradise alone.

     How well the skillful gardener drew   65
Of flowers and herbs this dial new,
Where, from above, the milder sun
Does through a fragrant zodiac run;
And as it works, th' industrious bee
Computes its time as well as we!   70
How could such sweet and wholesome hours
Be reckoned but with herbs and flowers?

JOHN MILTON (1608 – 1674)
When I Consider How My Light Is Spent

When I consider how my light is spent
    Ere half my days in this dark world and wide,
    And that one talent which is death to hide
    Lodged with me useless, though my soul more bent
To serve therewith my Maker, and present
    My true account, lest he returning chide;
    "Doth God exact day-labor, light denied?"
    I fondly ask; but Patience to prevent
That murmur, soon replies, "God doth not need
    Either man's work or his own gifts; who best
    Bear his mild yoke, they serve him best. His state
Is kingly. Thousands at his bidding speed
    And post o'er land and ocean without rest:
    They also serve who only stand and wait."

ANNE BRADSTREET (c. 1612 – 1672)

To My Dear and Loving Husband

If ever two were one, then surely we.
If ever man were loved by wife, then thee;
If ever wife was happy in a man,
Compare with me ye women if you can.
I prize thy love more than whole mines of gold,
Or all the riches that the East doth hold.
My love is such that rivers cannot quench,
Nor ought but love from thee give recompense.
Thy love is such I can no way repay;
The heavens reward thee manifold, I pray.
Then while we live, in love let's so persever,
That when we live no more we may live ever.

JOHN KEATS (1795 – 1821)

Ode to a Nightingale

1

My heart aches, and a drowsy numbness pains
    My sense, as though of hemlock[1] I had drunk,
Or emptied some dull opiate to the drains
    One minute past, and Lethe-wards[2] had sunk:
'Tis not through envy of thy happy lot,
    But being too happy in thine happiness —
        That thou, light-wingèd Dryad of the trees,
        In some melodious plot
Of beechen green, and shadows numberless,
    Singest of summer in full-throated ease.

2

O, for a draught of vintage! that hath been
    Cooled a long age in the deep-delvèd earth,
Tasting of Flora° and the country green,   *goddess of flowers*
    Dance, and Provençal song,[3] and sunburnt mirth!
O for a beaker full of the warm South,

---

[1]A plant which produces a powerful sedative, and from which it is also possible to produce a poison.

[2]Souls waiting in Hades to be reborn drink the waters of Lethe in order to forget their past existence.

[3]Provence was the home of the medieval troubadours.

Full of the true, the blushful Hippocrene,[4]
  With beaded bubbles winking at the brim,
    And purple-stainèd mouth;
That I might drink, and leave the world unseen,
  And with thee fade away into the forest dim:

3

Fade far away, dissolve, and quite forget
  What thou among the leaves hast never known,
The weariness, the fever, and the fret
  Here, where men sit and hear each other groan;
Where palsy shakes a few, sad, last gray hairs,
  Where youth grows pale, and specter-thin, and dies,
    Where but to think is to be full of sorrow
      And leaden-eyed despairs,
  Where Beauty cannot keep her lustrous eyes,
    Or new Love pine at them beyond tomorrow.

4

Away! away! for I will fly to thee,
  Not charioted by Bacchus and his pards,[5]
But on the viewless° wings of Poesy,   *invisible*
  Though the dull brain perplexes and retards:
Already with thee! tender is the night,
  And haply the Queen-Moon is on her throne,
    Clustered around by all her starry Fays;°   *fairies*
    But here there is no light,
  Save what from heaven is with the breezes blown
    Through verdurous glooms and winding
      mossy ways.

5

I cannot see what flowers are at my feet,
  Nor what soft incense hangs upon the boughs,
But, in embalmèd° darkness, guess each sweet   *perfumed*
  Wherewith the seasonable month endows
The grass, the thicket, and the fruit tree wild;
  White hawthorn, and the pastoral eglantine;
    Fast fading violets covered up in leaves;

---

[4]A fountain near Mount Helicon in Greece; its water induced poetic inspiration.

[5]Bacchus is the Greek god of wine, often represented in a chariot drawn by leopards ("pards").

And mid–May's eldest child,
The coming musk-rose, full of dewy wine,
The murmurous haunt of flies on summer eves.

6

Darkling° I listen; and for many a time   *in the dark*
I have been half in love with easeful Death,
Called him soft names in many a musèd rhyme,
To take into the air my quiet breath;
Now more than ever seems it rich to die,
To cease upon the midnight with no pain,
While thou art pouring forth thy soul abroad
In such an ecstasy!
Still wouldst thou sing, and I have ears in vain —
To thy high requiem become a sod.

7

Thou wast not born for death, immortal Bird!
No hungry generations tread thee down;
The voice I hear this passing night was heard
In ancient days by emperor and clown:
Perhaps the selfsame song that found a path
Through the sad heart of Ruth,[6] when, sick for home,
She stood in tears amid the alien corn;
The same that ofttimes hath
Charmed magic casements, opening on the foam
Of perilous seas, in faery lands forlorn.

8

Forlorn! the very word is like a bell
To toll me back from thee to my sole self!
Adieu! the fancy cannot cheat so well
As she is famed to do, deceiving elf.
Adieu! adieu! thy plaintive anthem fades
Past the near meadows, over the still stream,
Up the hill side; and now 'tis buried deep
In the next valley-glades:
Was it a vision, or a waking dream?
Fled is that music: — Do I wake or sleep?

---

[6]In the Old Testament Book of Ruth, Ruth was a faithful widow who followed her mother-in-law to a foreign land; there, as she was gleaning in a field, she was glimpsed by the master Boaz, who then married her.

MATTHEW ARNOLD (1822 – 1888)
Dover Beach

The sea is calm tonight.
The tide is full, the moon lies fair
Upon the straits; on the French coast the light
Gleams and is gone; the cliffs of England stand,
Glimmering and vast, out in the tranquil bay.
Come to the window, sweet is the night-air!
Only, from the long line of spray
Where the sea meets the moon-blanched land,
Listen! you hear the grating roar
Of pebbles which the waves draw back, and fling,
At their return, up the high strand,
Begin, and cease, and then again begin,
With tremulous cadence slow, and bring
The eternal note of sadness in.

Sophocles long ago
Heard it on the Aegean, and it brought
Into his mind the turbid ebb and flow
Of human misery; we
Find also in the sound a thought,
Hearing it by this distant northern sea.

The Sea of Faith
Was once, too, at the full, and round earth's shore
Lay like the folds of a bright girdle furled.
But now I only hear
Its melancholy, long, withdrawing roar,
Retreating, to the breath
Of the night-wind, down the vast edges drear
And naked shingles of the world.

Ah, love, let us be true
To one another! for the world, which seems
To lie before us like a land of dreams,
So various, so beautiful, so new,
Hath really neither joy, nor love, nor light,
Nor certitude, nor peace, nor help for pain;
And we are here as on a darkling plain
Swept with confused alarms of struggle and flight,
Where ignorant armies clash by night.

ROBERT FROST (1874 – 1963)
Mending Wall

Something there is that doesn't love a wall,
That sends the frozen-ground-swell under it,
And spills the upper boulders in the sun;
And makes gaps even two can pass abreast.
The work of hunters is another thing:
I have come after them and made repair
Where they have left not one stone on a stone,
But they would have the rabbit out of hiding,
To please the yelping dogs. The gaps I mean,
No one has seen them made or heard them made,
But at spring mending-time we find them there.
I let my neighbor know beyond the hill;
And on a day we meet to walk the line
And set the wall between us once again.
We keep the wall between us as we go.
To each the boulders that have fallen to each.
And some are loaves and some so nearly balls
We have to use a spell to make them balance:
"Stay where you are until our backs are turned!"
We wear our fingers rough with handling them.
Oh, just another kind of outdoor game,
One on a side. It comes to little more:
There where it is we do not need the wall:
He is all pine and I am apple orchard.
My apple trees will never get across
And eat the cones under his pines, I tell him.
He only says, "Good fences make good neighbors."
Spring is the mischief in me, and I wonder
If I could put a notion in his head:
"*Why* do they make good neighbors? Isn't it
Where there are cows? But here there are no cows.
Before I built a wall I'd ask to know
What I was walling in or walling out,
And to whom I was like to give offense.
Something there is that doesn't love a wall,
That wants it down." I could say "Elves" to him,
But it's not elves exactly, and I'd rather
He said it for himself. I see him there
Bringing a stone grasped firmly by the top

In each hand, like an old–stone savage armed.
He moves in darkness as it seems to me,
Not of woods only and the shade of trees.
He will not go behind his father's saying,
And he likes having thought of it so well
He says again, "Good fences make good neighbors."

EZRA POUND (1885 – 1972)

The River-Merchant's Wife: A Letter[1]

While my hair was still cut straight across my forehead
I played about the front gate, pulling flowers.
You came by on bamboo stilts, playing horse,
You walked about my seat, playing with blue plums.
And we went on living in the village of Chokan:
Two small people, without dislike or suspicion.

At fourteen I married My Lord you.
I never laughed, being bashful.
Lowering my head, I looked at the wall.
Called to, a thousand times, I never looked back.

At fifteen I stopped scowling,
I desired my dust to be mingled with yours
Forever and forever and forever.
Why should I climb the look out?

At sixteen you departed,
You went into far Ku-to-yen, by the river of swirling eddies,
And you have been gone five months.
The monkeys make sorrowful noise overhead.

You dragged your feet when you went out.
By the gate now, the moss is grown, the different mosses,
Too deep to clear them away!
The leaves fall early this autumn, in wind.
The paired butterflies are already yellow with August
Over the grass in the West garden;
They hurt me. I grow older.
If you are coming down through the narrows of the river Kiang,

---

[1]Adapted from the Chinese of Li Po (700?–762). Ernest Fenellosa (1853–1908), an American orientalist and collector, made the translation from which Pound worked.

Please let me know beforehand,
And I will come out to meet you
     As far as Cho-fu-Sa.

MARK STRAND (b. 1934)

Courtship

There is a girl you like so you tell her
your penis is big, but that you cannot get yourself
to use it. Its demands are ridiculous, you say,
even self-defeating, but to be honored somehow,
briefly, inconspicuously in the dark.

When she closes her eyes in horror,
you take it all back. You tell her you're almost
a girl yourself and can understand why she is shocked.
When she is about to walk away, you tell her
you have no penis, that you don't

know what got into you. You get on your knees.
She suddenly bends down to kiss your shoulder and you know
you're on the right track. You tell her you want
to bear children and that is why you seem confused.
You wrinkle your brow and curse the day you were born.

She tries to calm you, but you lose control.
You reach for her panties and beg forgiveness as you do.
She squirms and you howl like a wolf. Your craving
seems monumental. You know you will have her.
Taken by storm, she is the girl you will marry.

SEAMUS HEANEY (b. 1939)

From the Frontier of Writing

The tightness and the nilness round that space
when the car stops in the road, the troops inspect
its make and number and, as one bends his face

towards your window, you catch sight of more
on a hill beyond, eyeing with intent
down cradled guns that hold you under cover

and everything is pure interrogation
until a rifle motions and you move
with guarded unconcerned acceleration —

a little emptier, a little spent
as always by that quiver in the self,
subjugated, yes, and obedient.

So you drive on to the frontier of writing
where it happens again. The guns on tripods;
the sergeant with his on-off mike repeating

data about you, waiting for the squawk
of clearance: the marksman training down
out of the sun upon you like a hawk.

And suddenly you're through, arraigned yet freed,
as if you'd passed from behind a waterfall
on the black current of a tarmac road

past armour-plated vehicles, out between
the posted soldiers flowing and receding
like tree shadows into the polished windscreen.

JORIE GRAHAM (b. 1950)
San Sepolcro[1]

In this blue light
      I can take you there,
snow having made me
      a world of bone
seen through to. This
      is my house,

my section of Etruscan
      wall, my neighbor's
lemontrees, and, just below
      the lower church,
the airplane factory.
      A rooster

---

[1]A town in Italy whose name translates to "holy grave."

crows all day from mist
    outside the walls.
There's milk on the air,
    ice on the oily
lemonskins. How clean
    the mind is,

holy grave. It is this girl
    by Piero
della Francesca,[2] unbuttoning
    her blue dress,
her mantle of weather,
    to go into

labor. Come, we can go in.
    It is before
the birth of god. No-one
    has risen yet
to the museums, to the assembly
    line — bodies

and wings — to the open air
    market. This is
what the living do: go in.
    It's a long way.
And the dress keeps opening
    from eternity

to privacy, quickening.
    Inside, at the heart,
is tragedy, the present moment
    forever stillborn,
but going in, each breath
    is a button

coming undone, something terribly
    nimble-fingered
finding all of the stops.

---

[2]Piero della Francesca (1420?–1492), Italian painter, whose fresco of the pregnant Virgin Mary, *La Madonna del Parto*, is described in the poem..

SHERMAN ALEXIE (b. 1966)

Evolution

Buffalo Bill opens a pawn shop on the reservation
right across the border from the liquor store
and he stays open 24 hours a day, 7 days a week

and the Indians come running in with jewelry
television sets, a VCR, a full-length beaded buckskin outfit
it took Inez Muse 12 years to finish. Buffalo Bill

takes everything the Indians have to offer, keeps it
all catalogued and filed in a storage room. The Indians
pawn their hands, saving the thumbs for last, they pawn

their skeletons, falling endlessly from the skin
and when the last Indian has pawned everything
but his heart, Buffalo Bill takes that for twenty bucks

closes up the pawn shop, paints a new sign over the old
calls his venture THE MUSEUM OF NATIVE AMERICAN
        CULTURES
charges the Indians five bucks a head to enter.

5

The Play of Language

Language is the principal raw material out of which poets construct their experiments (rhythmic patterns are the other chief raw materials). By the single word "language" we mean many things:

Sound Units

The sound units of a poem are its syllables. The word "enemy" has three successive sounds, *en-eh-mee*. Readers are conscious of a sound effect when they hear two end-words rhyme; but poets are conscious of *all* the sounds in their lines, just as they are of the rhythms of a line. Poets "bind" words together in a line by having them share sounds, whether consonants (*alliteration,* as in "*b*roken *b*read") or vowels (*assonance,* as in "*whe*n . . . s*e*ssions"). This makes the words sound as if they "belong" together by natural affinity. Note how Shakespeare uses the vowel sounds *eh* and *uh* and the consonant sounds *wh, n, t, th,* and *s* in this line from Sonnet 20: "When to the sessions of sweet silent thought . . ." Good poets tend to bind together words that have an important meaning-connection, as Robert Frost does in this line from "Birches": "When I see *b*irches *b*end to left and right . . ." and as Sylvia Plath does in these lines from "Ariel":

> *Stasis* in *darkness.*
> Then the *substanceless blue*
> Pour of *tor* and *distances* . . .

Word Roots

These are the pieces of words that come from words in earlier languages, often Greek, Latin, or Anglo-Saxon. Poets usually are aware of the roots of the words they use. Many of these roots are preceded by prefixes, which also retain their original meanings. These prefixes change their spelling sometimes to "blend" with the root that follows:

re- ("again"): return, revolve, repair, represent, etc.

ex- ("out of"): explain, expire, exhale, etc.

pre- ("in front of"): precede, prefer, preclude, etc.

com- (*cum,* "with"): compare, commemorate, connote, colloquium, etc.

de- ("away from"): delete, defer, delay, defend, etc.

in- ("not"): inexplicable, innocent, immiscible, etc.

We have two main streams of language in English: our basic short words generally come from Anglo-Saxon, and our more complicated words from Latin (often through French). In the past, English was closer to Latin and French than it is today (during the Renaissance, for example, educated people usually knew several languages), and poets drew on that closeness. In Sonnet 15, Shakespeare wrote:

> When I *consider* everything that grows
> Holds in perfection but a little moment,
> That this huge stage presenteth naught but shows
> Whereon the *stars* in secret influence comment;
> When I *perceive* that men as plants increase,
> Cheerèd and checked even by the selfsame sky,
>
> .   .   .   .   .
>
> Then the *conceit* of this inconstant stay
> Sets *you* most rich in *you*th before my sight . . .

Here, he expected his readers to know that "consider" comes from a root (which we also find, for instance, in the word "sidereal") meaning "stars" — a word that appears in line 4. He also expected them to notice that the word "consider" is composed of two parts, *con-* and *-sider,* and that the next "I"-verb ("perceive") is followed by a noun ("conceit") which combines the *con-* of "consider" with the *-ceive* of "perceive." Perhaps he also expected at least some of his readers to see how the *con-* of "consider" and "conceit" is repeated in "in*con*stant" (and that the word "you" is contained in "youth").

We now live in an age when most readers are not schooled in Latin and therefore are less likely to recognize the Latin implications in English words. Still, we can easily find this information, especially for a word that seems unusually important in a poem, by consulting a dictionary.

Words

The meaning of a word in a poem is determined less by its dictionary definition (a single word like "stage" or "store" can have many definitions in a comprehensive dictionary) than by the words around it. Every word in a poem enters into relation with the other words in that poem. These relations can be of several kinds:

1. *thematic* (or meaning) relation — as we would connect "stars" and "sky" in the quotation above;

2. *phonemic* relation — as we would connect "stage," "stars," "secret," "selfsame," "sky," and "stay" in the quotation above by their initial *s*'s and *st*'s;

3. *grammatical* relation — as "cheerèd" and "checked" (already linked *phonemically* by their sounds, and *thematically* by their being antonyms of each other) are both verbal adjectives modifying "men";

4. *syntactic* relation — as "When I consider" and "When I perceive" introduce dependent clauses in "I," both modifying the main clause, "Then the conceit . . . sets you."

Each word, then, exists in several "constellations" of relation, all of which the reader needs to notice in order to see the overlapping structures of language in the poem.

Sentences

When we think about a poem, it's useful to write out its sentences in ordinary prose order, and then see what has been done to them in verse. For each sentence, it's indispensable to identify the grammatical *subject* — the person, place, or thing in charge of the verb, so to speak — and the *predicate* — the verb telling what the grammatical subject is or does (present tense), was or did (past tense), or will be or will do (future tense). In the course of a poem, *subjects* can change (the poet can say, "*I* love you" and then say "*You* love me"), *predicates* can change (the poet can say, "I *love* you" and then, "I *hate* you"), and *tenses* can change (the poet can say, "I *love* you now," and later say, "But I *will* not *love* you tomorrow"). By tracking these changes of subject, predicate, and tense you can see the dynamic of the poem: where and with whom it began, what's happening to it, where it's going, and where it ends up.

The more complex the poem, the more necessary this tracking is, if you're to get a firm sense of who is doing (or saying) what when, in each part. But even a "simple" poem repays attention of this sort. In Robert Frost's "Stopping by Woods on a Snowy Evening," the grammatical *subject* alone changes from "I" to "house" to "he" (the owner) to "horse" to "he" (the horse) to "sound" to "woods" to "I."

Robert Frost (1874 – 1963)
Stopping by Woods on a Snowy Evening

Whose woods these are *I* think *I* know.
His *house* is in the village, though;
He will not see me stopping here
To watch his woods fill up with snow.

My little *horse* must think it queer
To stop without a farmhouse near
Between the woods and frozen lake
The darkest evening of the year.

He gives his harness bells a shake
To ask if there is some mistake.
The only other *sound*'s the sweep
Of easy wind and downy flake.

The *woods* are lovely, dark and deep
But *I* have promises to keep,
And miles to go before *I* sleep,
And miles to go before *I* sleep.

One can imagine a version of this poem (I apologize for its crudeness) in which the subject never changes, and is "I" throughout:

I know these woods, their owner too,
I feel in watching them some fear,
I sense my little horse's rue,
Pausing without a farmhouse near.

I hear his harness bells now shake
In wonder at my strange mistake.

I hear the sound of falling snow,
All easy wind and downy flake.

I love the woods so dark and deep,
But I have promises to keep,
And miles to go before I sleep,
And miles to go before I sleep.

Why does Frost, do you think, give a *subject*-position not only to himself
but also to the owner of the woods and to his horse? And why does he
also give it to inanimate things (the woods that fill up with snow, the
sound of the wind)? The short answer is that everything in a poem that
has subject-position is "alive" and can "do things": the owner of the
woods is alive enough to see (but won't) the trespasser; the little horse is
alive enough to query his master's odd behavior; the woods are alive
enough to be "lovely, dark and deep"; and the silence in the snowy
woods is deep enough to make the sound "of easy wind and downy
flake" come alive, too. The whole world of the poem, in short, is ani-
mate and animated. This is far more interesting, at least in Frost's view of
nature, than to make the speaker the only live person in the scene.

Sentences are, grammatically speaking, made up of words which
function in different ways. Some words can function in several different
ways: for instance, the word "stage" can be either a *noun* ("Have you
built the *stage* yet?") or a *verb* ("Will they *stage* a Shakespeare play this sea-
son?"). The poet intends you to notice how each word *functions,* as well
as what it *means.*

There are conventional names in grammar for words in their func-
tions. You probably remember the basic names of most of the "parts of
speech" (as they are called); if not, you might want to turn to the appen-
dix "On Grammar" to refresh your memory.

In clarifying the *function* of each word in a poem, you can see the
parade of main statements (nouns plus verbs) making up the logical
skeleton of the poem, and you can distinguish these main clauses from
the poet's ornamental or explanatory additions. Ask yourself, about each
main piece of the skeleton, "What would be lost if I deleted this state-
ment?" (What would be lost if we left out the little horse's query in
"Stopping by Woods," for instance?) Then ask yourself what purpose is
served by the pieces *outside* the noun-verb skeleton — explanations,
additions, and ornaments. Sometimes, as in Dickinson's "The Heart
asks," the "add-ons" to the main skeleton are of crucial importance.
Here is the poem with its add-ons printed in italics:

EMILY DICKINSON (1830 – 1886)
The Heart asks Pleasure — first —

The Heart asks Pleasure — *first* —
And *then* — Excuse *from Pain* —
And *then* — *those little* Anodynes
That deaden suffering —

And *then* — to go to sleep —
And *then* — *if it should be*
The will of its Inquisitor
The privilege to die.

Think what the bare skeleton would be: "The heart asks pleasure and excuse and anodynes and to go to sleep and the privilege to die." It is the adjectives and adverbs that punctuate the poem into its successive phases of torture.

Implication

Because poems are short, they depend more on implication than longer works, such as novels, do. A novel has time and leisure to spell things out; a poem compresses the maximum into each word. Because a poem can only suggest, not expatiate, it requires *you* to supply the concrete instances for each of its suggestions. At the end of his late poem "The Tower," William Butler Yeats draws an escalating list of the ills of old age, gradually arriving at the worst of all. He fears, he says,

> . . . the wreck of body,
> Slow decay of blood,
> Testy delirium
> Or dull decrepitude,
> Or what worse evil come —
> The death of friends, or death
> Of every brilliant eye
> That made a catch in the breath.

A lyric poet like Yeats expects *you to think concretely* as he speaks abstractly, since his words are to be yours. What do you mean when you tell me that you fear in yourself "the wreck of body"? Perhaps paralysis, perhaps a wasting disease — it doesn't matter, but you *must* (in reading the line to yourself or speaking it aloud) have *something* actively in mind that corresponds in *your* mind to Yeats's words. "Slow decay of blood": perhaps, remembering Yeats's use of "blood" elsewhere, you will connect this phrase with the cooling of the hot blood of passion. "Testy delirium": you may think of brain damage from strokes, or incoherence from fever. "Dull decrepitude": you may think of senility. For "the death of friends," you might think of the friend you would miss the most. Then you arrive at the strange periphrasis (indirect way of speaking) marking the climax: What, Yeats makes us ask, is worse than bodily aging, worse than mental decay, worse than the death of friends? What is this "death / Of every brilliant eye / That made a catch in the breath"? The "death / Of every brilliant eye" is an indirect way of speaking of the death of a beautiful and beloved face — the worst event of all, the disappearance of the one face in the world that was everything to you. Perhaps, Yeats implies with "every," there were several such faces in his long life.

This process of paying attention to words, their functions, their logical arrangements in sentences, and their implications is what we really mean by "close" reading. It means spelling out, in your *own* mind — since the words of a poem are given to you to say *as if they were your own* — what the generalizing phrases of the poem mean *in your own case* as you extend their implications to yourself. Only then can you speak the words of the poem with conviction.

Lyric always generalizes. It is a blueprint of life, not a detailed transcription of it (as a novel can seem to be). Lyric, as Elizabeth Bishop said, is a map, not a photograph. Lyric is an algebraic equation, giving you x and y (decay, decrepitude, delirium) and asking you to fill in the poet's equation with your own "real numbers." A lyric asks you to be its co-creator, as you supply your own inner particulars for its generalizations.

Implication can be present in rhythm as well as in words. In Chapter 4, for instance, we saw the excited broken rhythms succeeding, in the close, the stately opening rhythms in Keats's "On First Looking into Chapman's Homer." In every case, you can discover implication by asking "Why?" Why is Yeats's list given in this order? Why do Keats's rhythms change at the end? Why isn't Keats's first metaphor (an astronomer discovering a new planet) good enough, so that he has to progress to a better metaphor (the discovery of the Pacific Ocean by an explorer and his men)? As Samuel Taylor Coleridge said, "Poetry is the best words in the best order." Your task, as a student of poetry, is to form hypotheses about why the poet arranged *these* words in *this* order till the poem seemed a satisfying whole. Your reflections on these matters will bring you into the heart of the poem, will give you intenser pleasure, and will make the poem an increasingly satisfying whole to you.

The Ordering of Language

Because poetry is a temporal art, it has to unfold sequentially, one piece after another. First I say *x*, then *y*, then *z*. But the *logical* relations among *x*, *y*, and *z* may not be additive or sequential ones. X, *y*, and *z* may instead be radii of the same circle, as in George Herbert's sonnet "Prayer," where the successive definitions all relate radially to the one subject:

GEORGE HERBERT (1593 – 1633)

Prayer (I)

Prayer, the church's banquet, angels' age,
  God's breath in man returning to his birth,
  The soul in paraphrase, heart in pilgrimage,
 The Christian plummet sounding heaven and earth;

Engine against th'Almighty, sinner's tower,
    Reversèd thunder, Christ-side-piercing spear,
    The six-days' world transposing in an hour,
A kind of tune, which all things hear and fear:

Softness, and peace, and joy, and love, and bliss,
    Exalted manna, gladness of the best,
    Heaven in ordinary, man well dressed,
The Milky Way, the bird of Paradise,
    Church bells beyond the stars heard, the soul's blood,
    The land of spices; something understood.

This list of all the things that prayer is might best be represented as radii of a circle: Herbert's order is one of radial amplification of one concept, prayer. But does the poem, in addition to its *radial* order, have a *temporal* order? That is, does something "happen" to the concept of prayer as the poem progresses? Most readers will be aware that thinking of prayer as "reversèd thunder" is not the same in feeling-tone as thinking of it as "softness, and peace, and joy, and love, and bliss." You may want to track the changes in mind of the speaker as the poem progresses, as the speaker exchanges one metaphor for another — only to give up entirely on metaphor at the end. In short, a poem can have more than one "shape" — here, it has both a static radial shape and a dynamic temporal unfolding.

Frequently the ordering of a poem's language offers a gradual clarification of meaning. At first, in Sonnet 66, Shakespeare's speaker sees only a procession of terrible miscarriages of justice in the world:

WILLIAM SHAKESPEARE (1564 – 1616)
Sonnet 66

Tired with all these, for restful death I cry:
As to behold desert a beggar born,
And needy nothing trimmed in jollity,
And purest faith unhappily forsworn,
And gilded honour shamefully misplaced,
And maiden virtue rudely strumpeted,
And right perfection wrongfully disgraced, . . .

At this point, most readers (especially those who have been imaginatively "filling in" the implications of Shakespeare's categories with their own current examples of the same vices) will begin to see that these actions have no agents. Who reduced the deserving ("desert") to beggary? Who misplaced honor, bestowing it on the unworthy instead of the worthy? Who has seduced the maiden? As the procession of wrongs continues in the poem, the speaker's vision becomes clarified: he can see now not only the victims but their victimizers accompanying them:

> And strength *by limping sway* disablèd,
> And art made tongue-tied *by authority,*
> And *folly, doctor-like,* controlling skill, . . .

The procession is now advancing two-by-two, instead of one-by-one; for instance, "strength" is hampered by "limping sway" (incompetent authority). Then, the two-by-two procession is interrupted by an anomalous solo figure:

> And simple truth miscalled simplicity.

Who can this be but the poem itself (in the person of its author)? Its "simple truth" is called, wrongly, "simplicity" ("political naïveté," in modern terms) by its detractors. Finally, we come, at the end, to the chief authority figure, who in a liturgical or court procession would be the Bishop or King. Here we see the chief agent of all the miscarriages of justice, leading his ultimate allegorical victim:

> And captive good attending captain ill.

Captain Ill is a secularized form of Satan, "the prince of this world." Just as the speaker of Shakespeare's sonnet sees more clearly as the procession winds on, so do we, until the author of all evil is revealed. This leaves the speaker with no hope of amelioration. Because Ill is Captain, and Good is always Captive in his power, there is no visible justice in this world. And so the speaker, though he is still longing for death, decides against it, not out of hope but out of protectiveness for his beloved:

> Tired with all these, from these would I be gone,
> Save that to die, I leave my love alone.

"Alone" is a terrible word in the evil world of this sonnet. In danger of being alone, strumpeted, tongue-tied, disgraced, disabled — who, in these circumstances, could abandon his beloved?

We can see the "shape" of this poem in several ways:

1. As a long procession bracketed by the speaker's two declarations of exhaustion;

2. More precisely, we can see the procession itself subdivided into three main parts: one-by-one, two-by-two, and a final archetype (generalizing personification) of Good in captivity to Ill;

3. Or we can see a single shape (disillusion and exhaustion) for the first thirteen lines, "redeemed" by line 14, which reveals that the speaker has one value, love, as yet uncorrupted by the world.

The more ways we see the governing linguistic order of the poem, the more human complexity we can perceive within it.

The ordering of experience in shapes of radial or logical clarification — clarification by hierarchy, clarification by a comparison of then to now, clarification by here versus there, or clarification by rise-and-decline (to name only four common "shapes") — is what gives poetry its aura of mastery. Even when its "content" is tragic — as in Dickinson's list of the heart's requests, or Shakespeare's procession of injustice — the fact that the list has been ordered into an understood set or a hierarchy reassures us that the mind can understand what the heart cannot endure, and that the imagination can find a linguistic shape for the structures of reality, even for those that are most tragic.

There is no linguistic ingredient too small to attract the poet's interest. Wallace Stevens makes poems that turn on the difference between the definite and indefinite article ("the" versus "a"); Yeats constructs a poem ("In Memory of Eva Gore-Booth and Con Markiewicz") that turns on a movement from "I" to "you" to "we" as a sign of reconciliation of enemies. Shakespeare can build a whole sonnet ("Th'expense of spirit in a waste of shame," Sonnet 129) on a contrast between nouns and adjectives (nouns give essence, we are reminded; adjectives give qualities). The play of language is the chief cause for the aesthetic success of any poem. Without play at many levels of language, from phonemes to logical structures, a poem is merely prose with line-breaks added.

Let's look at a sample poem, Michael Drayton's "Since there's no help," to try to bring to bear on it what this chapter has said about examining the language of a poem very closely at several levels — its sound-units, its etymological roots, its sentences with their words functioning as parts of speech, its subjects and predicates, tenses and moods, its imaginative play of language, and its processes of implication. The poem is spoken by a young man whose beloved, we infer, has just declared that their love affair is over:

MICHAEL DRAYTON (1564 – 1631)
Since there's no help

Since there's no help, come let us kiss and part;
Nay, I have done, you get no more of me,
And I am glad, yea glad with all my heart
That thus so cleanly I myself can free;
Shake hands forever, cancel all our vows,
And when we meet at any time again,
Be it not seen in either of our brows
That we one jot of former love retain.
Now at the last gasp of love's latest breath,
When, his pulse failing, passion speechless lies,
When faith is kneeling by his bed of death,
And innocence is closing up his eyes;
Now if thou wouldst, when all have given him over,
From death to life thou mightst him yet recover.

Here are the main independent clauses of the first sentence of the poem, which occupies the octave, or first eight lines, of the sonnet. The clauses are here written out as statements, with the **pronouns** in boldface and the *predicates* italicized:

Come *let* **us** *kiss* and *part*
I *have done*
You *get* no more of **me**
I *am* glad
[*let* **us**] *shake* hands
[*let* **us**] *cancel* vows
be **it** not *seen*

The first sentence, then, moves through several verbs in the hortatory mood — "let us kiss and part," "let us shake hands," "let us cancel all our vows," "[let] it not be seen" — interspersed with verbs in the indicative mood, one in the past tense ("I have done") and two in the future tense ("you [will] get no more of me" and "when we [shall] meet at any [future] time"). The pronouns change from **us** to **I** to **you** to **me** to **I** to **us** to **it**. All of these changes are indexes of the speaker's troubled state, as he darts from mood to mood, from tense to tense, and from subject position to object position. Although many of the dependent clauses add information ("Since there's no help," "that thus so cleanly I myself can free," "that we one jot of former love retain"), yet the skeleton above of the main clauses makes the import of the sentence clear.

The case is very different when we come to the second sentence, which takes up the last six lines (the sestet) of the sonnet. It has only one main clause: "**Thou** *mightst* him *recover.*" All the other clauses are strung from this one. "Thou mightst him recover" — when?

> Now at the last gasp of love's latest breath
> [Now] when passion speechless lies
> [Now] when faith is kneeling by his bed
> [Now] when innocence is closing up his eyes
> Now when all have given him over

All of these adverbial clauses "lead up" like the steps of a staircase to the main clause, giving the sestet its long suspense. In this way the relatively straightforward march of main clauses in the octave changes dramatically once we meet the long delay of the main clause in the sestet.

When we look at the kind of words these two sentences are composed of, we notice that with a few exceptions like "cancel" and "retain," most of the words of the octave are those short brisk words we tend to associate with our Anglo-Saxon linguistic heritage — "help," "come," "kiss," "get," "glad," "heart," "clean," and so on. When we come to the sestet, the number of Latin- or Romance-derived words rises — "pulse," "fail," "passion," "faith," "innocence," "close," "recover." Even if readers do not recognize the roots of all these words, they will sense how the more ceremonious sestet departs from the brisk colloquial nature of the words in the octave, not only because of the rise of Latin-derived words but also because of the suspended syntax.

It is clear that the speaker speaks about himself *in the first person* ("I") in the octave: "Nay, I have done, you get no more of me." But in the sestet, we see a change in language: instead of speaking directly about himself, the speaker speaks in the *third person* of someone called "Passion" who is lying on his "bed of death," whose "pulse [is] failing," who is emitting the last gasp of love's breath. This dying person is attended by two mourners: Faith is kneeling by his deathbed, and Innocence is closing the eyes of the dying man. This little third-person tableau is a way of avoiding first-person speech (otherwise, by the principle of inertia, the speaker would have continued as he began). The change to the third person makes us ask, "What would this closing tableau have been like if it, like the octave, had been put in the first person?"

> Now, at the last gasp of my loving breath,
> My passion has no words to say to thee,
> I seem to lose the faith I had, and death

Of love is death of innocence in me.
Now if thou wouldst, when I have given love over,
From death to life thou mightst me yet recover.

We can see that it's more dignified to ask the woman to rescue "Passion" than to say, "Please, even at this last gasp of passion, rescue *me*."

Because the octave has been phrased in the *hortatory* ("let us") and *indicative* ("I am glad") moods, we especially notice, when we come to the sestet, that it turns for its main clause to the *conditional* mood: "Now *if* thou *wouldst* . . . / thou *mightst* him recover." This holds out a grain of hope — if she *would* do this, she *might* bring him back to life. This is "politer" than saying, in the imperative, "Do this, and he will be cured." It is a plea, not a command.

After the relatively plain octave, in which the words are linked by the concept of saying farewell and canceling vows, we come to two conspicuous sets of linked words in the sestet. One is a set of abstract nouns — Love, Passion, Faith, and Innocence. They are the actors in the little tableau. The other set of words is medical and funereal — "gasp," "breath," "pulse failing," "speechless," "bed of death," "closing . . . eyes," "life," "recover." Normally, it is human beings who are in the situation where here we find Passion — dying among mourners. Drayton brings together in the sestet two incompatible sets of linked words — one abstract, one medically concrete — and constructs his surprising little third-person tableau with them to show us how the lover feels: he is not *really* dying physically, but emotionally "a deathbed scene" is the best description for what is happening to his passion — and he hopes that externalizing his inward feelings in this theatrical tableau may persuade his beloved to have pity on him.

We see from the closing tableau, and the plea with which it ends, that the speaker put on his original bluster ("Nay, I have done, you get no more of me; / And I am glad, yea glad") to hide the real dismay and despair that his closing tableau reveals.

These are only some of the moves we could make in beginning to study the language of this poem, and to ask the questions it provokes: "Why the change in person between octave and sestet?" "Why the introduction of the little tableau?" "Why is the sestet so ceremoniously written after the colloquial language of the octave?" "Why is the main clause of the sestet in the conditional mood?" "Why is the main clause of the sestet so long suspended adverbially before we get to it?"

Of course, we eventually have to move on from the use of language to the wider purposes of the poem — Drayton's conception of passion, and its relation to love, faith, and innocence, and his apt psychological observation of the defenses put up by the jilted lover, before the lover breaks down into his final abject plea. But that is material for a longer study, in which we might compare this poem to others written by Drayton, and get a better idea of his general poetic procedures. In each case, though, the first place to begin is with the play of language. In it, we find the imagination at work.

In Brief: The Play of Language

Since the language of lyric is condensed, every word carries weight, and all aspects of grammar and syntax (parts of speech, speech acts, even word roots) are full of significance. Poets are people steeped in language: "For many years," said Emily Dickinson, "my lexicon was my only companion." It is helpful to look at each sentence by itself, and at its chief agent, and at what the agent does. What are the interesting or unusual words in the sentence? What speech acts are taking place? What is implied in the "white space" between sentences or stanzas? Is the organization linear (start-to-finish), radial (a cluster of phrases around a center), or recursive (doubling back on itself)? Does the language change from concrete to abstract, or vice versa? Language gives you the *manner* of the poem, as well as its matter.

Reading Other Poems

There is no poem that does not play with language. As the following poems demonstrate, some are more overt about it, some less so. Language is both spoken and written, and the poet thinks about both aspects: how the poem sounds, how it looks on the page.

Not everything written can be spoken: see E. E. Cummings's poem on the way the grasshopper rearranges his limbs while leaping.

◆ If you trace the stages of the grasshopper's motions, how does Cummings mimic them?

Track the gestures implicit in the language of the Duke as he talks to the envoy arranging the new marriage. See how inconspicuously Robert Browning uses rhyme, and how the Duke's syntax shapes his powerful ongoing sentences. In the case of Wallace Stevens's two-room poem, ask what you see in the first room, the kitchen, versus what you see in the second room, the bedroom, and how language is invented to match the reality in each room.

Repetition of language is one of the weapons in the armory of poetry, and certain verse-forms entail the "foregrounding" of one or two lines by repetition.

◆ What are the repeated lines in Elizabeth Bishop's villanelle "One Art"? Can you describe the effect on the reader of having them recur so often? To how many things are these lines applied?

In free verse, too, repetition makes us aware of patterning. The word "deer," appearing for the first time in the title of Joy Harjo's "Song for the Deer and Myself to Return On," serves as the linch-pin of the lines that follow, as it is four times repeated. At first the speaker is alone, eventually she is part of a compound subject ("the deer and I"). By this time, the deer have been humanized: they "wonder," they "are trying to figure out a song." Because of this patterning emphasizing the deer, and because they are gradually brought into the human world of the speaker, we may be surprised when the deer disappear from the last two lines of the poem. Can you suggest why that happens?

The play of language is deeply felt when a poem has to convey changes over time.

◆ Can you see the time specified in each of Keats's stanzas in his autumn ode? What sort of language predominates in each stanza (for example, the infinitives in stanza 1)? What sort of noises end the poem?

◆ Can you compare the language used to guide the reader through the time sequence in Keats to the language that guides mentions of time in Yeats's poem about the swans? What sort of language does Yeats use about himself, by contrast to the language he uses about the swans?

Both John Donne's "Holy Sonnet 14" and H.D.'s "Oread" are poems structured by commands.

◆ Who is being commanded? Can they be commanded?

◆ What kind of language appears in the commands?

◆ Can the commands be obeyed?

◆ Do some commands in the poem differ from others?

◆ Imagine each poem rewritten as narrative rather than command: Can you then see the poet's attraction to this syntactic form?

Henry Reed's poem "Naming of Parts" is structured by repetition and by puns: What are their expressive functions?

Sometimes the play of language is structured on the relation of one metaphor to another (as Donne shifts from calling himself a usurped town to calling himself a betrothed woman, with consequences for the diction of the poem). At other times, the play of language depends on the relation of one language to another (as Lorna Dee Cervantes asserts the perpetual presence, in her mind, of both Spanish and English).

◆ What is your reaction to this mixed diction? (There is an old tradition of mixed diction in English poetry, beginning with poems written partly in English and partly in Latin.)

JOHN DONNE (1572 – 1631)
Holy Sonnet 14

Batter my heart, three-personed God; for You
As yet but knock, breathe, shine, and seek to mend;
That I may rise and stand, o'erthrow me, and bend
Your force to break, blow, burn, and make me new.
I, like an usurped town, to another due,
Labor to admit You, but O, to no end;
Reason, Your viceroy in me, me should defend,
But is captivèd, and proves weak or untrue.
Yet dearly I love You, and would be lovèd fain,
But am betrothed unto Your enemy.
Divorce me, untie or break that knot again;
Take me to You, imprison me, for I,
Except You enthrall me, never shall be free,
Nor ever chaste, except You ravish me.

JOHN KEATS (1795 – 1821)
To Autumn

1

Season of mists and mellow fruitfulness,
    Close bosom-friend of the maturing sun;
Conspiring with him how to load and bless
    With fruit the vines that round the thatch-eaves run;
To bend with apples the mossed cottage-trees,
    And fill all fruit with ripeness to the core;
        To swell the gourd, and plump the hazel shells
    With a sweet kernel; to set budding more,
And still more, later flowers for the bees,

Until they think warm days will never cease,
      For Summer has o'er-brimmed their clammy cells.

2

Who hath not seen thee oft amid thy store?
      Sometimes whoever seeks abroad may find
Thee sitting careless on a granary floor,
      Thy hair soft-lifted by the winnowing wind;
Or on a half-reaped furrow sound asleep,
      Drowsed with the fume of poppies, while thy hook
          Spares the next swath and all its twinèd flowers:
And sometimes like a gleaner thou dost keep
      Steady thy laden head across a brook;
      Or by a cider-press, with patient look,
          Thou watchest the last oozings hours by hours.

3

Where are the songs of Spring? Aye, where are they?
      Think not of them, thou hast thy music too —
While barrèd clouds bloom the soft-dying day,
      And touch the stubble-plains with rosy hue;
Then in a wailful choir the small gnats mourn
      Among the river sallows,° borne aloft   *low-growing willows*
          Or sinking as the light wind lives or dies;
And full-grown lambs loud bleat from hilly bourn;
      Hedge crickets sing; and now with treble soft
      The redbreast whistles from a garden-croft;[1]
          And gathering swallows twitter in the skies.

ROBERT BROWNING (1812 – 1889)
My Last Duchess

Ferrara

That's my last duchess painted on the wall,
Looking as if she were alive. I call
That piece a wonder, now: Frà Pandolf's hands
Worked busily a day, and there she stands.
Will't please you sit and look at her? I said   5
"Frà Pandolf" by design, for never read

---

[1]Small field at the edge of a property, often leased to another proprietor.

Strangers like you that pictured countenance,
The depth and passion of its earnest glance,
But to myself they turned (since none puts by
The curtain I have drawn for you, but I)   10
And seemed as they would ask me, if they durst,
How such a glance came there; so, not the first
Are you to turn and ask thus. Sir, 'twas not
Her husband's presence only, called that spot
Of joy into the Duchess' cheek: perhaps   15
Frà Pandolf chanced to say "Her mantle laps
Over my lady's wrist too much," or "Paint
Must never hope to reproduce the faint
Half-flush that dies along her throat": such stuff
Was courtesy, she thought, and cause enough   20
For calling up that spot of joy. She had
A heart — how shall I say? — too soon made glad,
Too easily impressed; she liked whate'er
She looked on, and her looks went everywhere.
Sir, 'twas all one! My favor at her breast,   25
The dropping of the daylight in the West,
The bough of cherries some officious fool
Broke in the orchard for her, the white mule
She rode with round the terrace — all and each
Would draw from her alike the approving speech,   30
Or blush, at least. She thanked men — good! but thanked
Somehow — I know not how — as if she ranked
My gift of a nine-hundred-years-old name
With anybody's gift. Who'd stoop to blame
This sort of trifling? Even had you skill   35
In speech — which I have not — to make your will
Quite clear to such an one, and say, "Just this
Or that in you disgusts me; here you miss,
Or there exceed the mark" — and if she let
Herself be lessoned so, nor plainly set   40
Her wits to yours, forsooth, and made excuse,
 — E'en then would be some stooping; and I choose
Never to stoop. Oh sir, she smiled, no doubt,
Whene'er I passed her; but who passed without
Much the same smile? This grew; I gave commands;   45
Then all smiles stopped together. There she stands
As if alive. Will't please you rise? We'll meet
The company below, then. I repeat,

The Count your master's known munificence
Is ample warrant that no just pretense   50
Of mine for dowry will be disallowed;
Though his fair daughter's self, as I avowed
At starting, is my object. Nay, we'll go
Together down, sir. Notice Neptune, though,
Taming a sea-horse, thought a rarity,   55
Which Claus of Innsbruck cast in bronze for me!

HENRY REED (1914 – 1986)
Naming of Parts

Today we have naming of parts. Yesterday,
We had daily cleaning. And tomorrow morning,
We shall have what to do after firing. But today,
Today we have naming of parts. Japonica
Glistens like coral in all of the neighboring gardens,
     And today we have naming of parts.

This is the lower sling swivel. And this
Is the upper sling swivel, whose use you will see,
When you are given your slings. And this is the piling swivel,
Which in your case you have not got. The branches
Hold in the gardens their silent, eloquent gestures,
     Which in our case we have not got.

This is the safety-catch, which is always released
With an easy flick of the thumb. And please do not let me
See anyone using his finger. You can do it quite easy
If you have any strength in your thumb. The blossoms
Are fragile and motionless, never letting anyone see
     Any of them using their finger.

And this you can see is the bolt. The purpose of this
Is to open the breech, as you see. We can slide it
Rapidly backwards and forwards: we call this
Easing the spring. And rapidly backwards and forwards
The early bees are assaulting and fumbling the flowers:
     They call it easing the Spring.

They call it easing the Spring: it is perfectly easy
If you have any strength in your thumb: like the bolt,
And the breech, and the cocking-piece, and the point of balance,

Which in our case we have not got; and the almond-blossom
Silent in all of the gardens and the bees going backwards and
    forwards,
      For today we have naming of parts.

WILLIAM BUTLER YEATS (1865 – 1939)
The Wild Swans at Coole

The trees are in their autumn beauty,
The woodland paths are dry,
Under the October twilight the water
Mirrors a still sky;
Upon the brimming water among the stones
Are nine-and-fifty swans.

The nineteenth autumn has come upon me
Since I first made my count;
I saw, before I had well finished,
All suddenly mount
And scatter wheeling in great broken rings
Upon their clamorous wings.

I have looked upon those brilliant creatures,
And now my heart is sore.
All's changed since I, hearing at twilight,
The first time on this shore,
The bell-beat of their wings above my head,
Trod with a lighter tread.

Unwearied still, lover by lover,
They paddle in the cold
Companionable streams or climb the air;
Their hearts have not grown old;
Passion or conquest, wander where they will,
Attend upon them still.

But now they drift on the still water,
Mysterious, beautiful;
Among what rushes will they build,
By what lake's edge or pool
Delight men's eyes when I awake some day
To find they have flown away?

WALLACE STEVENS (1879 – 1955)

The Emperor of Ice-Cream

Call the roller of big cigars,
The muscular one, and bid him whip
In kitchen cups concupiscent curds.
Let the wenches dawdle in such dress
As they are used to wear, and let the boys
Bring flowers in last month's newspapers.
Let be be finale of seem.
The only emperor is the emperor of ice-cream.

Take from the dresser of deal,
Lacking the three glass knobs, that sheet
On which she embroidered fantails once
And spread it so as to cover her face.
If her horny feet protrude, they come
To show how cold she is, and dumb.
Let the lamp affix its beam.
The only emperor is the emperor of ice-cream.

H. D. (1886 – 1961)

Oread[1]

Whirl up, sea —
whirl your pointed pines,
splash your great pines
on our rocks,
hurl your green over us,
cover us with your pools of fir.

---

[1]A nymph of the mountains and hills.

E. E. CUMMINGS (1894 – 1962)
r-p-o-p-h-e-s-s-a-g-r

                        r-p-o-p-h-e-s-s-a-g-r
            who
a)s w(e loo)k
upnowgath
        PPEGORHRASS
                            eringint(o-
aThe):l
        eA
            !p:
S   a
                    (r
rIvInG   .gRrEaPsPhOs)
                                        to
rea(be)rran(com)gi(e)ngly
,grasshopper;

ELIZABETH BISHOP (1911 – 1979)
One Art

The art of losing isn't hard to master;
so many things seem filled with the intent
to be lost that their loss is no disaster.

Lose something every day. Accept the fluster
of lost door keys, the hour badly spent.
The art of losing isn't hard to master.

Then practice losing farther, losing faster:
places, and names, and where it was you meant
to travel. None of these will bring disaster.

I lost my mother's watch. And look! my last, or
next-to-last, of three loved houses went.
The art of losing isn't hard to master.

I lost two cities, lovely ones. And, vaster,
some realms I owned, two rivers, a continent.
I miss them, but it wasn't a disaster.

— Even losing you (the joking voice, a gesture
I love) I shan't have lied. It's evident
the art of losing's not too hard to master
though it may look like (*Write* it!) like disaster.

JOY HARJO (b. 1951)
Song for the Deer and Myself to Return On

This morning when I looked out the roof window
before dawn and a few stars were still caught
in the fragile weft of ebony night
I was overwhelmed. I sang the song Louis taught me:
a song to call the deer in Creek, when hunting,
and I am certainly hunting something as magic as deer
in this city far from the hammock of my mother's belly.
It works, of course, and deer came into this room
and wondered at finding themselves
in a house near downtown Denver.
Now the deer and I are trying to figure out a song
to get them back, to get all of us back,
because if it works I'm going with them.
And it's too early to call Louis
and nearly too late to go home.

LORNA DEE CERVANTES (b. 1954)
Poema para los Californios Muertos[1]

> *Once a refuge for Mexican Californios . . .*
> — PLAQUE OUTSIDE A RESTAURANT
> IN LOS ALTOS, CALIFORNIA, 1974

These older towns die
into stretches of freeway.
The high scaffolding cuts a clean cesarean[2]
across belly valleys and fertile dust.
What a bastard child, this city
lost in the soft

---

[1]Poem for the dead Californios. (*Californios* — original inhabitants when California was still Mexico.)

[2]A caesarean is a surgical incision of the walls of the abdomen and uterus for delivery of offspring.

llorando de las madres.[3]
Californios moan like husbands of the raped,
husbands de la tierra,
tierra la madre.[4]

I run my fingers
across this brass plaque.
Its cold stirs in me a memory
of silver buckles and spent bullets,
of embroidered shawls and dark rebozos.[5]
Yo recuerdo los antepasados muertos.
Los recuerdo en la sangre,
la sangre fértil.[6]

What refuge did you find here,
ancient Californios?
Now at this restaurant nothing remains
but this old oak and an ill-placed plaque.
Is it true that you still live here
in the shadows of these white, high-class houses?
Soy la hija pobrecita
pero puedo maldecir estas fantasmas blancas.
Las fantasmas tuyas deben aquí quedarse,
solas las tuyas.[7]

In this place I see nothing but strangers.
On the shelves there are bitter antiques,
yanqui remnants
y estos no de los Californios.[8]
A blue jay shrieks
above the pungent odor of crushed
eucalyptus and the pure scent
of rage.

---

[3]Crying of the mothers.

[4]Of the land, the mother earth.

[5]A rebozo is a long shawl worn by Mexican women.

[6]I remember the dead ancestors. I remember them in my blood, my fertile blood.

[7]I am only your poor daughter, but I can curse these white ghosts. Only your ghosts should remain here, only yours.

[8]And these not of the Californios.

6

Constructing a Self

If you are a poet wanting to create, on paper, a self into whose shoes a reader will be willing to step, a self whose voice a reader will willingly take on, you have probably only a short space (maybe 150 words) in which to give your lyric speaker credibility. You must create a personality provoked into speech; tones of voice tracking both provocation and response; and enough variability of expression to make for fictive robustness. How to do it?

Multiple Aspects

The single most successful way is to give your speaker not only a present but a past, and often not just a yesterday, but the day before that, and the year before that, and five years before that. (See Wordsworth's "Lines Composed a Few Miles above Tintern Abbey" for a stunning lengthy version of this process.) You invite your reader to "turn into" the speaker, uttering the sentences of the poem; you construct a whole temporal self available to be inhabited, a believable "thickly described" life to be entered. Here is Shakespeare's Sonnet 30, "When to the sessions of sweet silent thought," in which a speaker with a multiphased past comes alive:

WILLIAM SHAKESPEARE (1564 – 1616)

Sonnet 30

When to the sessions of sweet silent thought
I summon up remembrance of things past,
I sigh the lack of many a thing I sought,
And with old woes new wail my dear time's waste;
Then can I drown an eye (unused to flow)
For precious friends hid in death's dateless night,
And weep afresh love's long since canceled woe,
And moan th'expense of many a vanished sight.
Then can I grieve at grievances foregone,
And heavily from woe to woe tell o'er
The sad account of fore-bemoanèd moan,
Which I new pay as if not paid before.
   But if the while I think on thee (dear friend)
   All losses are restored and sorrows end.

The speaker (whose initial "when" means "whenever") is referring to a series of habitual actions. This in itself gives the speaker a continuous life stretching from the past to the present; he often has sessions of silent thought when he voluntarily summons past things to mind. In fact, when he does this, he finds himself in tears — an unusual event for him: "Then can I drown an eye, *unused to flow*."

We're now in a better position to reconstruct the speaker's multi-phased life. Let's call the time when he as yet did not have a friend T_1, the next phase T_2, and so on:

T_1: He doesn't yet have friends A, B, C.

T_2: He makes friends with A, B, C.

T_3: He enjoys the friendship over time.

T_4: Friends A, B, C die.

T_5: He weeps at the moment of their death.

T_6: Grief turns to stoicism; his tears stop.

T_7: He spends a long time without weeping; his tears are "unused to flow."

T_8: He often summons up, voluntarily, the old grief so that he can "drown" again in tears for his dead friends.

This pattern recurs throughout the poem, as, for instance: he "weep[s] *afresh* love's *long since canceled* woe." He was without love; then had it; then lost it, and wept in woe; that woe was (apparently) canceled, and he was dry-eyed for a long time; now he can weep afresh for that woe. In fact, this process, many times safely and even luxuriously repeated, now suddenly awakens such grief in the speaker that he pays his debt of grief anew: "I new pay," he says, "*as if not paid before.*" This is a frightening experience. He thought he could summon up at will old griefs, and almost enjoy renewing them in "sessions of *sweet* silent thought." Yet suddenly the session is no longer sweet but painfully acute — grief recurs as if for the first time. It is this acute grief which pitches the speaker into looking for consolation in his present state; at least he has a friend now, friend Z:

> But if the while I think on thee (dear friend)
> All losses are restored and sorrows end.

This discovery of present joy stabilizes the character of the speaker at one point in his multiphased life. But the overall effect of the sonnet is to make us know the speaker as someone who has undergone many psychological phases — joy, grief, stoicism, loss, renewed grief — over time, and this confers on him a "reality" of prolonged existence which we take on as we speak his words.

Change of Discourse

Another way, if you are a poet, to give your speaker credibility is to let her change discourses in midstream. In "Diving into the Wreck," Adrienne Rich lets her practical, well-equipped speaker drift into hypnotic reverie once she's under water:

> I put on
> the body-armor of black rubber
> the absurd flippers
> the grave and awkward mask. . . .
>
> I go down.
> My flippers cripple me,
> I crawl like an insect down the ladder. . . .
>
> This is the place.
> And I am here, the mermaid whose dark hair
> streams black, the merman in his armored body.
> We circle silently
> about the wreck

we dive into the hold.
I am she: I am he

whose drowned face sleeps with open eyes
whose breasts still bear the stress. . . .

By the end, after this entrance to incantatory and androgynous language, the personality of the speaker seems to have more than one facet. The more facets — practical, mystical, baffled, exalted — the "thicker" the description.

Space and Time

Yet another way of giving historical believability to your speaker is, in the course of your poem, to relocate him or her in space and time. In "Mid-Term Break," the Irish poet Seamus Heaney (pronounced "Shāmus Hēney") writes about his return home from boarding school for the funeral of his four-year-old brother, killed by a car. ("College" in the first line refers to a boarding school.)

SEAMUS HEANEY (b. 1939)
Mid-Term Break

I sat all morning in the college sick bay
Counting bells knelling classes to a close.
At two o'clock our neighbors drove me home.

In the porch I met my father crying —
He had always taken funerals in his stride —
And Big Jim Evans saying it was a hard blow.

The baby cooed and laughed and rocked the pram
When I came in, and I was embarrassed
By old men standing up to shake my hand

And tell me they were "sorry for my trouble."
Whispers informed strangers I was the eldest,
Away at school, as my mother held my hand

In hers and coughed out angry tearless sighs.
At ten o'clock the ambulance arrived
With the corpse, stanched and bandaged by the nurses.

Next morning I went up into the room. Snowdrops
And candles soothed the bedside; I saw him
For the first time in six weeks. Paler now,

Wearing a poppy bruise on his left temple,
He lay in the four foot box as in his cot.
No gaudy scars, the bumper knocked him clear.

A four foot box, a foot for every year.

We first see the speaker in the morning at his boarding school, after he has been notified of his brother's death; next we see him being driven home; next he is on the porch at home; next inside the house; next, present at evening when the body is brought from the hospital by an ambulance; next, the following morning, upstairs seeing the body of his brother laid out on the bed; next, seeing his brother in the coffin before the funeral. The living presence of the speaker over two days, in several places, makes him seem a "real person," into whose believable narrative we can enter. We track the changes in space and time by a series of markers in the poem:

Space	*Time*
in the college sick bay	all morning
home	two o'clock
in the porch	
I came in	
	whispers . . . as my mother
	held my hand
the ambulance arrived	at ten o'clock
up into the room . . . bedside	next morning
the four foot box	

Poets expect you to "track," even if unconsciously, such relocations of the speaker in space and time, as you "become" the person who goes from school to the porch, from the porch to the room inside, from the downstairs to the upstairs, and who, in the end, however reluctantly, takes up a mourner's position next to the coffin.

Testimony

Speakers also can be made credible by their intimate knowledge of a given historical time and place and its inhabitants. We feel this in E. E. Cummings's speaker who satirizes "the Cambridge ladies who live in furnished souls" and mocks their taste for Henry Wadsworth Longfellow; we feel it equally in the speaker of Andrew Marvell's "Horatian

Ode" who seems to have observed the execution of Charles I, to know the details of Cromwell's campaign in Ireland, and to be aware of British parliamentary instability. Walt Whitman speaks as a witness to the events recounted in "Song of Myself": "I am the man; I suffered; I was there;" and his Civil War poems offer vivid, almost cinematically detailed accounts of real events in "A March in the Night Hard Press'd" or "Cavalry Crossing a Ford." Even in a poem of symbolic experience, like Samuel Taylor Coleridge's "Rime of the Ancient Mariner," the mariner tells so many particular details of his supernatural experiences, along with many natural ones, that we are drawn to find both halves of his tale reliable.

Motivations

How does the poet lead us to understand the selves that are so sketchily created on the page, in whose voices we find ourselves speaking? We tend, as the poem goes on, to fill in its gaps, and to think that Shakespeare's speaker weeping afresh has a whole "real life" in between his reported bouts of grief, stoicism, and renewed weeping. We assume that Coleridge's Ancient Mariner is being truthful about how he passes, like night, from land to land retelling his tale, and that he had a life before he shot the albatross. We also invent plausible reasons for the fact that a speaker who has formerly spoken of his estrangement from his beloved ("Since there's no help, come let us kiss and part") can say, only thirteen lines later, that his beloved could resuscitate love "from death to life." By postulating reasonable motivations, justifications, and conclusions in the gaps between words or lines, we ascribe to the speaker a "realness" that literature is designed to offer in order to persuade us of its insights about experience.

Typicality

Yet another aspect of credibility in a lyric speaker comes from typicality, a powerful resource of lyric. Anyone can put himself or herself into the unstipulated place and indefinite time of Shakespeare's speaker summoning up remembrance of things past. Even when the place and subject are specific (as they are in "the Cambridge ladies"), anyone, male or female, who lived in Cambridge might be the speaker of the poem. Even when the event is wholly personal, as in "Mid-Term Break," the emotions of the stunned adolescent recalled by the speaker are those that any adolescent in such a situation would probably experience. To create such a representative set of reactions, Heaney, like many lyric poets, deletes many particular autobiographical details (the presence of his siblings, the specific religious ceremonies surrounding a home wake in Ireland such as the recitation of the rosary) in order to make the experience related in the poem typical, rather than narrowly personal.

A lyric, then, wants us to be its speaker. We are not to *listen to* the speaker, but to *make ourselves into* the speaker. We speak the words of the poem as though we were their first utterers. The speaker's past is our past; his motivations are ours, his emotions ours, his excuses ours, his predictions ours. A poem is a set of instructions for voicing; listened to carefully, it tells us how to say its sentences — regretfully, apprehensively, bitterly, elatedly. We call these ways of voicing the *tones* of the poem. They are sufficiently typical that any reader can utter them.

Tone as Marker of Selfhood

Though poetry has become a written art, it has never lost its roots in speech. And since the first thing a poem asks of you is to read it aloud as though you were saying *it as your own words,* you must sound angry if "you" are angry, sad if "you" are sad. The poem itself tells you how to sound. Every lyric is uttered in response to a situation that has disturbed some former equilibrium: "you" have been told someone no longer loves you ("Since there's no help"), or that your brother has been killed in an accident ("Mid-Term Break"), or that "We don't like modern poetry" (the "Cambridge ladies," says Cummings, "believe in Christ and Longfellow, both dead"). Robert Frost went so far as to say, "Everything written is as good as it is dramatic. . . . [A poem is] heard as sung or spoken by a person in a scene — in character, in a setting." Because you cannot know the whole situation of the speaker till you have read the whole poem, you often are not sure what set of intonations to give the poem as you *first* read it aloud. But as you get to know it better, it begins to speak itself believably in your mind, and its speaker's character and emotions, mediated through the tones of utterance, become yours.

Take, for example, the first stanza of Emily Dickinson's poem, spoken above the many graves of her Dickinson ancestors in the cemetery of Amherst, Massachusetts:

Safe in their Alabaster Chambers —
Untouched by Morning
And untouched by Noon —

Sleep the meek members of the Resurrection —
Rafter of satin
And Roof of stone.

Is it good or bad for the dead to be "safe" in their mausoleums or graves? Is it good or bad to be "untouched" by morning and noon? Is it desirable to be ensconced under satin rafters and a roof of stone? In what tone are you to say these lines?

As you get to know the poem, you may decide that Dickinson thought it was certainly a deprivation to exist insensible to both morning and noon; that she is judging the dead as timid ("meek") people who always wanted to be "safe": now, indeed, and ironically, they are. When you learn that Dickinson rewrote the poem to remove the implication of resurrection — substituting "lie" for "sleep" in line 4 — you may decide that she thought her dead ancestors had been cheated by their credulous beliefs in an afterlife to which they would awaken. And however fine it may be to have satin rafters in your coffin, those rafters exist, after all, under that claustrophobic mausoleum-roof "of stone." Your tone might well then become ironic as you read the words "safe" and "untouched," seeing those words as the poet's gibe at the conventional timidity of her ancestors' lives.

In telling someone else how you see this poem, you probably would have to say, "I hear Dickinson being critical of the dead, with a dismissive and almost contemptuous tone in her description of them as 'safe' and 'untouched.'" And in speaking the poem aloud, you, as the speaker of these sentiments, would make your own voice take on that dismissive tone. In this way, every poem suggests to its readers the tones with which they might give voice to it; and conversely, the tones you feel to be present, as you get to know the poem well, give you clues to the perceptions and emotions of the self, constructed in the poem, that generates those tones.

Here, for instance, is a short poem in which an adult, who knows suffering well, comes upon a young girl who is crying because the leaves are falling from the trees in the wood called "Goldengrove." The adult thinks her grief trivial and childish, and rebukes her for wasting her tears on trees, prophesying that life soon enough will give her more serious things to cry about. But she continues nevertheless to cry, asking *why* the leaves have to fall. The poem turns on the adult's response to the child's *"Why?"* I've marked, next to the lines, the tones of voice they suggest. (In the third line from the end, "ghost guessed" means, approximately, "your spirit intuited.")

GERARD MANLEY HOPKINS (1844 – 1889)
Spring and Fall

To a Young Child

Márgarét, áre you gríeving	*bantering disbelief*
Over Goldengrove unleaving?	
Leáves, líke the things of mán, you	*patronizing reproach*
With your fresh thoughts care for, can you?	
Áh, ás the héart grows ólder	*chilly prophecy of rational future*
It will come to such sights colder	
By and by, nor spare a sigh	
Though worlds of wanwood leafmeal lie;	*regret*
And yet you *will* weep and know why.	*impatience*
Now no matter, child, the name:	*insight, surprised*
Sórrow's spríngs áre the sáme.	*recognition and admission*
Nor mouth had, no, nor mind expressed	
What héart héard of, ghóst guéssed;	*self-reproach*
It ís the blíght mán was bórn for,	*universal despair*
It is Margaret you mourn for.	*grief*

By the end, the speaker is ashamed at rebuking Margaret's tears, and sees that adult grief and child grief are one; both lament the consequences of the fall of man — the temporality and mortality of all things. In "tracking the tones" of such a poem, readers can differ over the exact name of each tone, but every reader will hear changes of tone over the length of the poem. Uttering this poem, you must at first be the superior and patronizing adult; then, as you come to acknowledge your own shortsightedness, you feel the heavy weight of human destiny — that we are all born for blight, and that our tears, even when they seem to be shed for falling leaves, are in reality shed for our implicit recognition of our own fate. As you perceive the tones and say the words of this adult speaker, his selfhood — in his original pride of superior knowledge and his subsequent willingness to be ashamed of himself — becomes potentially credible.

The speaker's change in view has to be persuasively "put over" by your own voice as you speak (even if only mentally) the words, or the poem will lack its striking effect of self-rebuke and final shared grief. However, lyric poems are usually *inner meditations,* not dramatic or declaimed speeches; one can't be an orator or an actor in speaking a lyric aloud. One has to be a self, musing aloud over inner responses, not someone addressing an audience, or even someone speaking aloud in

solitude like an actor delivering a soliloquy. Even when there is an audi-
tor (here, Margaret), the lyric represents the *inner* speech or meditation
of its utterer, and must sound inward and reflective rather than outer-
directed and rhetorical. As William Butler Yeats said, "Out of the quar-
rel with others, we make rhetoric; out of the quarrel with ourselves,
poetry." All the tones of a poem are the tones of an inward, not an out-
ward, quarrel; the credible self in the lyric is the private divided self of
the inner life. Even in a dramatic monologue (which is publicly
addressed to another person, as Robert Browning's Duke addresses the
ambassador), it is important to perceive the revelation of the inner life of
the speaker by the poem. The Duke reveals himself to be jealous and
homicidal, even though he may not be aware how much of himself is
visible in his outwardly smooth and aristocratic speech. To see a dramatic
monologue as simultaneously a self-protective public speech and an
unconsciously self-revealing document is to read it as dramatic lyric
demands, doubly.

Imagination

The selves constructed in poems needn't have original ideas (in
fact, few of them do), but they must have imagination — and the imagi-
nation of the reader of the poem must somehow (by art) be drawn into
the imagination of the speaker. The word "imagination" covers almost
anything unusual and nonfactual in the way the self conveys thought.
Often something said "imaginatively" is logically absurd, as in this cou-
plet from William Blake's "Auguries of Innocence":

> If the Sun and Moon should doubt,
> They'd immediately go out.

This is an imaginative way of saying that life lives on faith, and that skep-
ticism is corrosive to radiant living. Here is another example, this time
from W. H. Auden's ballad "As I Walked Out One Evening":

> The glacier knocks in the cupboard,
>   The desert sighs in the bed,
> And the crack in the teacup opens
>   A lane to the land of the dead.

Such imaginativeness in the poetic self asks you to free-associate: even
in the cupboard of the food supply, a coming Ice Age is making itself

heard; even in the midst of lovemaking, aridity appears; a small flaw in a cup suggests the great Flaw in life, that we are not immortal.

Why — as the question is often put — do the poets (or their constructed poetic selves) say what they mean in "other" words? No poet would agree with putting the question this way. Poets tell us that in poems they say *exactly* what they mean in words chosen precisely to mean what they (the words) say. "Bed-desert-sigh" is an *exact* transcription, in Auden's speaker's mind, of what he felt in bed; "crack-lane-death," he thinks when he takes that teacup out of the cupboard; and even though he may close the door of the cupboard, a freezing-hidden-thing, the rigor mortis of the human relations in the house, makes its knocking heard behind the silent wood.

John Ashbery, in "Self-Portrait in a Convex Mirror," calls the surface of a poem its "visible core." The emotional core of Auden's poem, which we infer from the appearance on its surface of the glacier and the desert, is the inner feeling of dread that Auden's speaker feels even in the midst of the "safest" surroundings — his kitchen, his bed. And the dread seems to be lodged not in him but in his very cups and cupboards; *they* seem uneasy, disturbed, flawed. Psychologists call this reaction "projection" — when we "project" our inner emotion upon the world so that outside things seem uncanny or threatening. It would *not* be accurate, in this case, for the poet to say, "I feel dread and aridity" — that would be a generalizing summary, not a transcription of how concretely he feels a threat in every object at home. And poets wish to give accurate transcripts of feeling, as well as accurate transcripts of the structures of reality.

"How would I be feeling if I said *exactly this?*" is the question readers must ask as they read the words about the doubting sun uttered by the self that Blake constructs. And the answer is something like, "I'd be feeling that if the sun suddenly went out, it would be like my starting to doubt my belief in God — everything would go black." The animism by which the sun and moon become doubters like us, or by which a desert can sigh in a bed, is part of imagination's capacity to make the whole world alive. A credible self in poetry is one who can make us feel as he or she does. The poet shows; the poet does not simply tell. The poet transmits things "on the pulses," as Keats said; the senses are reproduced in words.

Words like "dread," "suspicion," "skepticism," and "faith" are words from the discourses of psychology and theology, rather than words from the senses or feelings. The senses and the feelings are poetry's stock in trade; words like "cup" and "desert," "sun" and "moon," never age in the way intellectual discourse does.

It is easy to describe, when reading striking excerpts like the ones from Blake and Auden, how the poet is using language "imaginatively" and creating a "flesh-and-blood self." But what about poems that seem factually written, without the odd personal deflections of language that characterize an idiosyncratic self? Here is a passage from Tennyson's "Mariana" which may seem largely like straightforward natural description, a passage transcribed by a camera rather than uttered by a defined self:

> About a stone-cast from the wall
>   A sluice with blacken'd waters slept,
> And o'er it many, round and small,
>   The cluster'd marish-mosses crept.
> Hard by a poplar shook alway,
>   All silver-green with gnarlèd bark:
>   For leagues no other tree did mark
> The level waste, the rounding gray.

There are in the stanza two relatively inconspicuous metaphors: the sluice *sleeps,* the mosses *creep.* Sleeping waters and creeping vegetation are not in themselves notably imaginative. Everything else — the wall, the sluice-channel, the round small marsh-grasses, the single shaking silver-green poplar with its gnarled bark, the level waste of land meeting the rounding gray of the horizon — seems factual, transcribed, uninfected by imagination. Of course the passage is highly decorative in terms of sound, but where is the imagination, or the imagining self?

It is only when we see the whole of "Mariana" — which contains seven of these stanzas — that we realize what the imagination is contributing to the poem. Tennyson is representing in "Mariana" the stream of consciousness of a girl waiting, with increasing hopelessness, for her lover to come. Because she has nothing else to occupy her mind, she notes, minutely and exhaustedly, every item in her surroundings, every small change of atmosphere during the long hours as they pass. It is in the accumulation of seven stanzas' worth of mounting ennui, apprehension, and loathing that we see Tennyson's imagination at work creating the imagination of Mariana. He gives each stanza its own peculiar atmosphere. We have already seen the unpromising "blacken'd waters" and "level waste" outside; here is a stanza in which Mariana perceives the inside atmosphere, as the day wears on without the arrival of her lover:

> All day within the dreary house
>   The doors upon their hinges creak'd;
> The blue fly sung in the pane; the mouse
>   Behind the moldering wainscot shriek'd.

The buzz of the fly, the shriek of the mouse, the creak of the hinges —
by these details we understand the hope within hopelessness with which
Mariana listens for the slightest sound of an arrival, and is rewarded only
by these tiny interruptions of the deathly silence.

Where a poem offers such "facts" as the blackened waters or the
creaking hinges, they are always facts seen through the lens of a particular
feeling, which has been imagined by the poet, and ascribed to the imagi-
nation of the speaker. It is the *successive* feelings enacted by the poem which
will lead you to see how the imagination is at work, even in the most "fac-
tual" lines. There is not a very great distance between Tennyson's "factual"
mouse squeaking behind the wainscot and Auden's glacier knocking in the
cupboard. Both of them serve chiefly as transcripts of the believable feel-
ings of the constructed self rather than as a record of actual things.

Another way poets often show imagination operating in their fic-
tive selves is to take a conventional timeline — birth, youth, maturity,
old age, death (for example), or spring, summer, autumn, winter — and
place the poem in a spot on the timeline that no one else has used. Dick-
inson (remembering Tennyson's "Mariana" where "the blue fly sung in
the pane") inserts her (posthumous) speaker, who is recalling her own
death, into the timeline of life at its very last gasp, the moment when she
actually died. It is imaginative to employ a speaker speaking posthu-
mously, but that had been done before — for instance, by George Her-
bert in "Love (III)." Dickinson's speaker takes the old tradition of "holy
dying" and revises it blasphemously:

EMILY DICKINSON (1830 – 1886)
I heard a Fly buzz — when I died —

I heard a Fly buzz — when I died —
The Stillness in the Room
Was like the Stillness in the Air —
Between the Heaves of Storm —

The Eyes around — had wrung them dry —
And Breaths were gathering firm
For that last Onset — when the King
Be witnessed — in the Room —

I willed my Keepsakes — Signed away
What portion of me be
Assignable — and then it was
There interposed a Fly —

> With Blue — uncertain stumbling Buzz —
> Between the light and me —
> And then the Windows failed — and then
> I could not see to see —

Dickinson is perfectly aware that the death of a Christian ought to take place when God, the "King," comes to take the soul to heaven, and she shows the mourners waiting precisely for "that last Onset." But instead of Christ's "Today shalt thou be with me in Paradise," the speaker reports a "Blue — uncertain stumbling Buzz," and dies. In inventing this sacrilegious rendering of the conventional "happy death" of the Christian believer, Dickinson has found a way for imagination to re-represent death, this time in wholly bodily and nihilistic form. Dickinson in this instance has inserted her fictive (and credibly blasphemous) self into the human timeline at the very last second.

Other poets, using the seasonal timeline, will also make their fictive selves speak from a new place. Wallace Stevens does not say, "At the beginning of spring" (a cliché), but rather, "At the earliest ending of winter" ("Not Ideas About the Thing But the Thing Itself"); he does not say, "The leaves have all fallen" (a cliché for autumn), but rather, "The last leaf that was going to fall had fallen" ("An Ordinary Evening in New Haven"). The poet can likewise choose an unusual moment in a timeline by referring to the hours of the day: "There's a certain slant of light," says Dickinson — the first time in literature that a writer has alluded to the light on late winter afternoons. These imaginative perceptions make a poetic self arresting, as well as believable.

Another strategy of the poetic imagination is to insert into a genre — say, the sonnet — where the reader might expect a conventional topic (love or death), a new topic, such as prayer (Herbert) or the massacre of "heretics" (Milton) or a car junkyard (Dave Smith). This "turn" of the speaker surprises the reader and refreshes the genre; the expectations of the sonnet form become roomier, deeper, riskier. Or the imagination can borrow a form from another literature and write a poem in that form in English, as Edward FitzGerald borrowed the Persian Rubáiyát and Allen Ginsberg borrowed the sutra (a Buddhist form) in his "Sunflower Sutra." Or a poet's imagination can flout the moral expectations of society: Thomas Hardy's "ruined maid" is quite happy in her new circumstances — "'One's pretty lively when ruined,' said she."

An imaginative self can range freely through space and time, and can ask startling questions like, "What if this present were the world's last night?" (Donne). It can draw unusual comparisons, as when the birches bent by the weight of vanished snow seem to Frost "like girls on hands and knees that throw their hair / Before them over their heads to dry in the sun." It matters less *how* the imaginative self renews feeling — through a surreal phrase like Auden's "glacier . . . in the cupboard," through an old image like Pan revived as Cummings's balloonMan, through a genre-violation like Milton's sonnet of "slaughtered saints," or through blasphemy, as when Dickinson substitutes a fly for Christ in the death-room — than *that* it renews feeling through a reconceiving of familiar circumstance.

The real appeal of the imagination, when it appears in a poetic speaker, is that one never knows what it will do next. Tonight the Last Judgment? Doubt eclipsing the sun and the moon? A speaker addressing us from beyond the grave? For every self you meet speaking in poetry, the first question — and the last question — to ask is: "Where in these words do I see the imagination at work?" Without imagination, the noblest idea is empty of *poetic* interest, and the most heartfelt confession merely a twice-told tale. With imagination, the world is made new, and seen sharply, clearly, at an angle. We go to poetry, as to fiction, for the shock of the newly seen. "Things seen," says Stevens, "are things as seen." It is in the "as" of a credible speaker that the imagination lives.

Persona

There are many ways to refer to the self who speaks a poem. Some-times, in obviously autobiographical lyrics, we simply use the name of the author: "Keats writes about reading Homer for the first time." In this sort of shorthand, we mean, by the word "Keats," "the author as he lets us see himself in the speaker of this poem, in his fictive poetic self." The author's fictive self overlaps with, but is not identical to, his "real" self, because a poem obeys many laws (of form, of structure, of language) which may deflect it from factual accuracy.

Robert Lowell begins his poem "Bright Day in Boston" with the phrase, "Joy of standing up my dentist." In fact (as he later said) he *had* kept his dentist appointment, and only after it was over had he taken the walk recorded in the poem. But — as he also said — the felt impulse to skip the dentist, which in life he had *not* obeyed, made a "truer" emo-tional beginning to the poem. We can say, then, that "Lowell" stood up his dentist, while Lowell did not. It is often easiest, once one has made clear that one means the author rather than the person, to say "Keats" or "Lowell" in referring to the speaker of a poem.

But there are poems where the speaker is clearly not the author: Yeats, for instance, writes several poems in the voice of an old woman whom he calls "Crazy Jane." It is customary, in such cases, to refer to the speaker of the poem as a "persona" adopted by Yeats. The word "persona" comes from the Latin verb *personare* — "to *speak through* a mask." Only when the speaker is wearing a mask — that is, cannot possibly be seen as the actual author because of a difference of age, or sex, or national origin — does it make sense to speak of a "persona." Otherwise it is preferable to refer simply to "the speaker."

Why would a poet adopt a persona? Why does an educated, prosperous poet want to take on the voice of a poor old woman of the roads? What is there that the poet wants to express that he can utter only in Crazy Jane's voice? These are the questions that anyone writing on Yeats's late poetry must ask. Here is the most famous of Crazy Jane's poems. In it, Jane encounters the Bishop, who once (as we know from another poem in the sequence) was a priest in the parish where Jane and her lover, Jack, lived; he banned Jack from the parish, supposedly for religious reasons. Now, in old age, Crazy Jane and the Bishop once again exchange words:

WILLIAM BUTLER YEATS (1865 – 1939)
Crazy Jane Talks with the Bishop

I met the Bishop on the road
And much said he and I.
"Those breasts are flat and fallen now,
Those veins must soon be dry;
Live in a heavenly mansion,
Not in some foul sty."

"Fair and foul are near of kin,
And fair needs foul," I cried.
"My friends are gone, but that's a truth
Nor grave nor bed denied,
Learned in bodily lowliness
And in the heart's pride.

"A woman can be proud and stiff
When on love intent;
But Love has pitched his mansion in
The place of excrement;
For nothing can be sole or whole
That has not been rent."

We can deduce, from the Bishop's opening remarks about the state of Crazy Jane's breasts — that they are "flat and fallen now" — that he had improperly noticed their unflat and unfallen shape in the past, and that when he banished Jack it was because of jealousy rather than piety. After the first stanza, the rest of the poem is Jane's. We notice that she can say things that a philosophical poet like Yeats might feel called upon, if he spoke in his own voice, to qualify further ("fair needs foul," for instance); but Crazy Jane, as the voice of peasant wisdom (speaking, we should notice, in an adaptation of an old folk ballad), does not need to be philosophically subtle. And although her final assertion — that "Love has pitched his mansion in / The place of excrement" — is based on a dry Augustinian remark ("We are born between urine and feces"), she can phrase that observation more passionately because it is her own female body that is in question; to the Bishop's stable "heavenly mansion" she opposes the nomadic "mansion" of Love, a tent pitched in "the place of excrement."

Crazy Jane says things, in short, that Yeats as a philosophically educated person, and as a man, could not say in his own person. That is the usefulness of adopting a persona. Well brought-up girls, in Dickinson's day, were not allowed to roam the fields barefoot; and so, when Dickinson wants to show the terror of encountering a snake underfoot, she has a boy speak her poem. When you see an obvious persona speaking a poem (as in so many of Browning's "dramatic monologues"), ask yourself what the persona is being used to express that the poet could not believably convey in a contemporary "real-life" voice. Poets often take on the voice of someone long dead: black poets like Robert Hayden and Rita Dove have written in the voice of slaves, to give vicarious utterance to those who were historically denied literacy and consequently expression in writing. William Blake did the same when he spoke in the persona of a "little black boy," showing the boy already corrupted by Christian teaching:

> My mother bore me in the southern wild,
> And I am black, but O! my soul is white;
> White as an angel is the English child:
> But I am black as if bereav'd of light.

The assumption of the persona of a black child by a white poet, or of a female persona by a male poet, has been criticized by those who believe that only a black can speak of the black experience, only a woman of a woman's experience. Many have retorted that the very function of the imagination is to enable us to imagine the Other, and that only by such leaps of the imagination across the gaps of gender, race, and age can poetry induce its readers to practice that enabling fellow-feeling. Readers who might not have reflected on class issues, or issues of religious tyranny, or issues of the place of the sexual in the spiritual, can be brought, by Crazy Jane's encounter with the Bishop, to think of these issues afresh. It does not matter who wrote the lyric, if the self presented in the lyric is a credible one invested with imaginative power. Because every speaker of a lyric is a constructed speaker, made "alive" by the imagination, and delineated in the play of language, a poem asks that as you step into the shoes of the speaker, you notice how language has been arranged to make that act possible.

In Brief: Constructing a Self

As you read a poem, ask yourself questions about the speaker constructed within the poem. Where is he or she in time and space? Over how long a period? With what motivations? How typical? Speaking in what tones of voice? Imagining life how? Resembling the author or different from the author? The more you can deduce about the speaker, the better you understand the poem. If you think about what has been happening to the speaker *before* the poem begins (if that is implied by the poem), you will understand the speaker better.

Reading Other Poems

The constituents of selfhood that are being emphasized in any one poem can be seen from both content and form.

- ◆ What kind of a self do you feel you have if you find a tree to be a close relative, as Walt Whitman's speaker does?
- ◆ What kind of a self do you feel you have if you speak meditatively and slowly, as Whitman's fictive self does?

  You can ask these questions of each of the poems that follow.

- ◆ What kind of a self do you feel you have if you call yourself "nobody," as Emily Dickinson's speaker does?
- ◆ You might expect that Thomas Hardy's "ruined maid" would feel herself to be a nobody (and so she might, in another poet's hands). But she feels herself quite a somebody. Why? Does the rhythm of

Hardy's poem reinforce or contradict the attitude taken by the fictive speaker toward the prostitute?

- What kind of a self usually utters a "love song"? Do you find that kind of a self in T. S. Eliot's poem? How does Prufrock's prophecy of his self in old age ("Do I dare to eat a peach? / I shall wear white flannel trousers, and walk upon the beach") help to construct your idea of his present self?

- The free-verse rhythms in which Prufrock speaks betray his personality, too. How?

- Eliot gradually assembles traits of Prufrock (beginning with his name) so that we understand him better and better as the poem proceeds. Can you characterize these traits?

The self of the speaker can sometimes only be deduced from what he or she says observing another.

- John Dryden's little song "Sylvia the Fair" enables you to deduce the speaker's attitude toward sexuality. How would you characterize it?

When we come to more explicitly social identities (often imposed by others rather than self-chosen), we arrive at speakers who must construct an identity in part from pregiven materials (as Countee Cullen and Carl Phillips do).

- How does Cullen's speaker confront this problem in "Heritage"?

- How are the contrasting positions imagined in this "dialogue of the mind with itself"?

- Can you speculate why Cullen gave his speaker the strong rhythmic form seen here (technically known as trochaic tetrameter rhyming couplets), rather than constructing the self of his speaker in, say, meditative blank verse, often used for such poems of internal debate (as, say, in Shakespeare's soliloquies)?

- How do Cullen's methods of defining himself vis-à-vis Africa compare with those of Phillips? To what extent is the speaker of each poet a type rather than a unique individual?

Because a self is often constructed, whether in a novel or a poem, around a decisive moment of crisis or choice, we can find the selfhood crystallizing around a single episode. William Butler Yeats's airman is an Irishman in the British army, defending England though he has never lived there, participating in a war in which his own country (Ireland) was neutral. Alone in his airplane, he sees his life clearly, and a young indeterminate self suddenly crystallizes.

♦ In what rhythms does he speak? Are they uncertain and wavering, or strong and emphatic?

♦ How, both negatively and positively, does he delineate his newly discovered self?

On the other hand, sometimes a self is constructed as much by social conditions as by a moment of decision.

♦ How did Elsie (in real life, William Carlos Williams's household help) end up the way she did?

♦ Williams imagines a group of social causes that cooperate to keep many Elsies from having a rewarding and independent life: each of them has contributed to the kind of self Elsie now is. Can you connect these causes to her self as it is described?

♦ Can you construct a plausible picture of the speaker's self from his personal and social feelings about Elsie?

In contrast to the self chosen in a moment, there is the self assumed to be stable: Anne Sexton's speaker assumes she belongs to a typical category of persons ("Her Kind"), and Charles Wright, though he writes many self-portraits, confers a temporary stability on the speaker of each one.

♦ How do Sexton and Wright assemble a stable speaking self through images?

♦ Sickness, too, can confer a new identity. What, according to Jane Kenyon's "Otherwise," is the chief characteristic of her new identity as one living with cancer?

♦ How does she structure the temporal course of her poem — and why would she choose this structure?

♦ What influence does her illness have, do you think, on the way she recounts her successive responses?

♦ Why does the word "otherwise" become so insistent in her new identity?

JOHN DRYDEN (1631 – 1700)
Sylvia the Fair

1

SYLVIA, the fair, in the bloom of fifteen,
Felt an innocent warmth as she lay on the green;
She had heard of a pleasure, and something she guess'd
By the towzing, and tumbling, and touching her breast.
She saw the men eager, but was at a loss,
What they meant by their sighing, and kissing so close;
　　By their praying and whining,
　　And clasping and twining,
　　And panting and wishing,
　　And sighing and kissing,
　And sighing and kissing so close.

2

"Ah!" she cried, "ah! for a languishing maid,
In a country of Christians, to die without aid!
Not a Whig, or a Tory, or Trimmer[1] at least,
Or a Protestant parson, or Catholic priest,
To instruct a young virgin, that is at a loss,
What they meant by their sighing, and kissing so close!
　　By their praying and whining,
　　And clasping and twining,
　　And panting and wishing,
　　And sighing and kissing,
　And sighing and kissing so close."

3

Cupid, in shape of a swain, did appear,
He saw the sad wound, and in pity drew near;
Then show'd her his arrow, and bid her not fear,
For the pain was no more than a maiden may bear.
When the balm was infus'd, she was not at a loss,
What they meant by their sighing and kissing so close;
　　By their praying and whining,
　　And clasping and twining,
　　And panting and wishing,

---

[1]A trimmer is one who inclines to either of two opposing political parties, as
interest dictates.

> And sighing and kissing,
> And sighing and kissing so close.

WALT WHITMAN (1819 – 1892)
I Saw in Louisiana a Live-Oak Growing

I saw in Louisiana a live-oak growing,
All alone stood it and the moss hung down from the branches,
Without any companion it grew there uttering joyous leaves of
    dark green,
And its look, rude, unbending, lusty, made me think of myself,
But I wonder'd how it could utter joyous leaves standing alone
    there without its friend near, for I knew I could not,
And I broke off a twig with a certain number of leaves upon it,
    and twined around it a little moss,
And brought it away, and have placed it in sight in my room,
It is not needed to remind me as of my own dear friends,
(For I believe lately I think of little else than of them,)
Yet it remains to me a curious token, it makes me think of manly
    love;
For all that, and though the live-oak glistens there in Louisiana
    solitary in a wide flat space,
Uttering joyous leaves all its life without a friend a lover near,
I know very well I could not.

EMILY DICKINSON (1830 – 1886)
I'm Nobody! Who are you?

I'm Nobody! Who are you?
Are you — Nobody — Too?
Then there's a pair of us!
Don't tell! they'd advertise — you know!

How dreary — to be — Somebody!
How public — like a Frog —
To tell one's name — the livelong June —
To an admiring Bog!

WILLIAM BUTLER YEATS (1865 – 1939)
An Irish Airman Foresees His Death

I know that I shall meet my fate
Somewhere among the clouds above;

Those that I fight I do not hate,
Those that I guard I do not love;
My country is Kiltartan Cross,
My countrymen Kiltartan's poor,
No likely end could bring them loss
Or leave them happier than before.
Nor law, nor duty bade me fight,
Nor public men, nor cheering crowds,
A lonely impulse of delight
Drove to this tumult in the clouds;
I balanced all, brought all to mind,
The years to come seemed waste of breath,
A waste of breath the years behind
In balance with this life, this death.

THOMAS HARDY (1840 – 1928)
The Ruined Maid

"O 'Melia, my dear, this does everything crown!
Who could have supposed I should meet you in Town?
And whence such fair garments, such prosperi-ty?"
"O didn't you know I'd been ruined?" said she.

"You left us in tatters, without shoes or socks,
Tired of digging potatoes, and spudding up docks;
And now you've gay bracelets and bright feathers three!"
"Yes: that's how we dress when we're ruined," said she.

"At home in the barton° you said 'thee' and 'thou,'   *farm*
And 'thik oon,' and 'theäs oon,' and 't'other'; but now
Your talking quite fits 'ee for high compa-ny!"
"Some polish is gained with one's ruin," said she.

"Your hands were like paws then, your face blue and bleak
But now I'm bewitched by your delicate cheek,
And your little gloves fit as on any la-dy!"
"We never do work when we're ruined," said she.

"You used to call home-life a hag-ridden dream,
And you'd sigh, and you'd sock; but at present you seem
To know not of megrims° or melancho-ly!"   *low spirits*
"True. One's pretty lively when ruined," said she.

"I wish I had feathers, a fine sweeping gown,
And a delicate face, and could strut about Town!"

"My dear — a raw country girl, such as you be,
Cannot quite expect that. You ain't ruined," said she.

T. S. ELIOT (1888 – 1965)
The Love Song of J. Alfred Prufrock

> *S'io credessi che mia risposta fosse*
> *A persona che mai tornasse al mondo,*
> *Questa fiamma staria senza più scosse.*
>
> *Ma perciocche giammai di questo fondo*
> *Non tornò vivo alcun, s' i'odo il vero,*
> *Senza tema d'infamia ti rispondo.*[1]

Let us go then, you and I,
When the evening is spread out against the sky
Like a patient etherised upon a table;
Let us go, through certain half-deserted streets,
The muttering retreats   5
Of restless nights in one-night cheap hotels
And sawdust restaurants with oyster-shells:
Streets that follow like a tedious argument
Of insidious intent
To lead you to an overwhelming question . . .   10
Oh, do not ask, "What is it?"
Let us go and make our visit.

    In the room the women come and go
Talking of Michelangelo.

    The yellow fog that rubs its back upon the window-panes, 15
The yellow smoke that rubs its muzzle on the window-panes
Licked its tongue into the corners of the evening,
Lingered upon the pools that stand in drains,
Let fall upon its back the soot that falls from chimneys,
Slipped by the terrace, made a sudden leap,   20
And seeing that it was a soft October night,
Curled once about the house, and fell asleep.

    And indeed there will be time
For the yellow smoke that slides along the street,

---

[1]From Dante's *Inferno*, Canto 27, lines 61–66. Guido da Montefeltro speaks, after Dante questions him: "If I thought that my reply were to be to someone who would ever return to the world, this flame would be still, without further motion. But since no one has ever returned alive from this depth, if what I hear is true, I answer you without fear of shame."

Rubbing its back upon the window-panes;   25
There will be time, there will be time
To prepare a face to meet the faces that you meet;
There will be time to murder and create,
And time for all the works and days[2] of hands
That lift and drop a question on your plate;   30
Time for you and time for me,
And time yet for a hundred indecisions,
And for a hundred visions and revisions,
Before the taking of a toast and tea.

    In the room the women come and go   35
Talking of Michelangelo.

    And indeed there will be time
To wonder, "Do I dare?" and, "Do I dare?"
Time to turn back and descend the stair,
With a bald spot in the middle of my hair —   40
[They will say: "How his hair is growing thin!"]
My morning coat, my collar mounting firmly to the chin,
My necktie rich and modest, but asserted by a simple pin —
[They will say: "But how his arms and legs are thin!"]
Do I dare   45
Disturb the universe?
In a minute there is time
For decisions and revisions which a minute will reverse.

    For I have known them all already, known them all:
Have known the evenings, mornings, afternoons,   50
I have measured out my life with coffee spoons;
I know the voices dying with a dying fall
Beneath the music from a farther room.
    So how should I presume?

    And I have known the eyes already, known them all —   55
The eyes that fix you in a formulated phrase,
And when I am formulated, sprawling on a pin,
When I am pinned and wriggling on the wall,
Then how should I begin
To spit out all the butt-ends of my days and ways?   60
    And how should I presume?

---

[2]The Greek poet Hesiod (eighth century B.C.) wrote *Works and Days,* a poem about country life.

And I have known the arms already, known them all —
Arms that are braceleted and white and bare
[But in the lamplight, downed with light brown hair!]
Is it perfume from a dress   65
That makes me so digress?
Arms that lie along a table, or wrap about a shawl.
    And should I then presume?
    And how should I begin?

. . . . .

Shall I say, I have gone at dusk through narrow streets   70
And watched the smoke that rises from the pipes
Of lonely men in shirt-sleeves, leaning out of windows? . . .

    I should have been a pair of ragged claws
Scuttling across the floors of silent seas.

. . . . .

And the afternoon, the evening, sleeps so peacefully!   75
Smoothed by long fingers,
Asleep . . . tired . . . or it malingers,
Stretched on the floor, here beside you and me.
Should I, after tea and cakes and ices,
Have the strength to force the moment to its crisis?   80
But though I have wept and fasted, wept and prayed,
Though I have seen my head [grown slightly bald] brought in
    upon a platter,[3]
I am no prophet — and here's no great matter;
I have seen the moment of my greatness flicker,   85
And I have seen the eternal Footman hold my coat, and snicker,
And in short, I was afraid.

    And would it have been worth it, after all,
After the cups, the marmalade, the tea,
Among the porcelain, among some talk of you and me,   90
Would it have been worth while,
To have bitten off the matter with a smile,
To have squeezed the universe into a ball
To roll it toward some overwhelming question,
To say: "I am Lazarus,[4] come from the dead,   95

---

[3]The head of John the Baptist was delivered on a platter to Salome (Matthew 14: 1–11).

[4]Lazarus was raised from the dead by Jesus (John 11: 1–44).

Come back to tell you all, I shall tell you all" —
If one, settling a pillow by her head,
    Should say: "That is not what I meant at all.
    That is not it, at all."

    And would it have been worth it, after all,   100
Would it have been worth while,
After the sunsets and the dooryards and the sprinkled streets,
After the novels, after the teacups, after the skirts that trail along
    the floor —
And this, and so much more? —   105
It is impossible to say just what I mean!
But as if a magic lantern threw the nerves in patterns on a screen:
Would it have been worth while
If one, settling a pillow or throwing off a shawl,
And turning toward the window, should say: 110
    "That is not it at all,
    That is not what I meant, at all."

       · · · · ·

No! I am not Prince Hamlet, nor was meant to be;
Am an attendant lord, one that will do
To swell a progress,° start a scene or two,   *royal procession* 115
Advise the prince; no doubt, an easy tool,
Deferential, glad to be of use,
Politic, cautious, and meticulous;
Full of high sentence,° but a bit obtuse;   *sententiousness*
At times, indeed, almost ridiculous —   120
Almost, at times, the Fool.

    I grow old . . . I grow old . . .
I shall wear the bottoms of my trousers rolled.

    Shall I part my hair behind? Do I dare to eat a peach?
I shall wear white flannel trousers, and walk upon the beach. 125
I have heard the mermaids singing, each to each.

    I do not think that they will sing to me.

    I have seen them riding seaward on the waves
Combing the white hair of the waves blown back
When the wind blows the water white and black. 130

    We have lingered in the chambers of the sea
By sea-girls wreathed with seaweed red and brown
Till human voices wake us, and we drown.

WILLIAM CARLOS WILLIAMS (1883 – 1963)
To Elsie

The pure products of America
go crazy —
mountain folk from Kentucky

or the ribbed north end of
Jersey   5
with its isolate lakes and

valleys, its deaf-mutes, thieves
old names
and promiscuity between

devil-may-care men who have taken   10
to railroading
out of sheer lust of adventure —

and young slatterns, bathed
in filth
from Monday to Saturday   15

to be tricked out that night
with gauds°   *jewelry*
from imaginations which have no

peasant traditions to give them
character   20
but flutter and flaunt

sheer rags — succumbing without
emotion
save numbed terror

under some hedge of choke-cherry   25
or viburnum —
which they cannot express —

Unless it be that marriage
perhaps
with a dash of Indian blood   30

will throw up a girl so desolate
so hemmed round
with disease or murder

that she'll be rescued by an
agent —   35
reared by the state and

sent out at fifteen to work in
some hard-pressed
house in the suburbs —

some doctor's family, some Elsie —   40
voluptuous water
expressing with broken

brain the truth about us —
her great
ungainly hips and flopping breasts   45

addressed to cheap
jewelry
and rich young men with fine eyes

as if the earth under our feet
were   50
an excrement of some sky

and we degraded prisoners
destined
to hunger until we eat filth

while the imagination strains   55
after deer
going by fields of goldenrod in

the stifling heat of September
Somehow
it seems to destroy us   60

It is only in isolate flecks that
something
is given off

No one
to witness   65
and adjust, no one to drive the car

COUNTEE CULLEN (1903 – 1946)

Heritage

For Harold Jackman

What is Africa to me:
Copper sun or scarlet sea,
Jungle star or jungle track,
Strong bronzed men, or regal black
Women from whose loins I sprang   5
When the birds of Eden sang?
One three centuries removed
From the scenes his fathers loved,
Spicy grove, cinnamon tree,
What is Africa to me?   10

So I lie, who all day long
Want no sound except the song
Sung by wild barbaric birds
Goading massive jungle herds,
Juggernauts of flesh that pass   15
Trampling tall defiant grass
Where young forest lovers lie,
Plighting troth beneath the sky.
So I lie, who always hear,
Though I cram against my ear   20
Both my thumbs, and keep them there,
Great drums throbbing through the air.
So I lie, whose fount of pride,
Dear distress, and joy allied,
Is my somber flesh and skin,   25
With the dark blood dammed within
Like great pulsing tides of wine
That, I fear, must burst the fine
Channels of the chafing net
Where they surge and foam and fret.   30
Africa? A book one thumbs
Listlessly, till slumber comes.
Unremembered are her bats
Circling through the night, her cats
Crouching in the river reeds,   35
Stalking gentle flesh that feeds
By the river brink; no more
Does the bugle-throated roar

Cry that monarch claws have leapt
From the scabbards where they slept.   40
Silver snakes that once a year
Doff the lovely coats you wear,
Seek no covert in your fear
Lest a mortal eye should see;
What's your nakedness to me?   45
Here no leprous flowers rear
Fierce corollas in the air;
Here no bodies sleek and wet,
Dripping mingled rain and sweat,
Tread the savage measures of   50
Jungle boys and girls in love.
What is last year's snow to me,
Last year's anything? The tree
Budding yearly must forget
How its past arose or set —   55
Bough and blossom, flower, fruit,
Even what shy bird with mute
Wonder at her travail there,
Meekly labored in its hair.
One three centuries removed   60
From the scenes his fathers loved,
Spicy grove, cinnamon tree,
What is Africa to me?

So I lie, who find no peace
Night or day, no slight release   65
From the unremittent beat
Made by cruel padded feet
Walking through my body's street.
Up and down they go, and back,
Treading out a jungle track.   70
So I lie, who never quite
Safely sleep from rain at night —
I can never rest at all
When the rain begins to fall;
Like a soul gone mad with pain   75
I must match its weird refrain;
Ever must I twist and squirm,
Writhing like a baited worm,
While its primal measures drip

Through my body, crying, "Strip!   80
Doff this new exuberance.
Come and dance the Lover's Dance!"
In an old remembered way
Rain works on me night and day.

Quaint, outlandish heathen gods   85
Black men fashion out of rods,
Clay, and brittle bits of stone,
In a likeness like their own,
My conversion came high-priced;
I belong to Jesus Christ,   90
Preacher of Humility;
Heathen gods are naught to me.

Father, Son, and Holy Ghost,
So I make an idle boast;
Jesus of the twice-turned cheek,   95
Lamb of God, although I speak
With my mouth thus, in my heart
Do I play a double part.
Ever at Thy glowing altar
Must my heart grow sick and falter,   100
Wishing He I served were black,
Thinking then it would not lack
Precedent of pain to guide it,
Let who would or might deride it;
Surely then this flesh would know   105
Yours had borne a kindred woe.
Lord, I fashion dark gods, too,
Daring even to give You
Dark despairing features where,
Crowned with dark rebellious hair,   110
Patience wavers just so much as
Mortal grief compels, while touches
Quick and hot, of anger, rise
To smitten cheek and weary eyes.
Lord, forgive me if my need   115
Sometimes shapes a human creed.
All day long and all night through,
One thing only must I do:
Quench my pride and cool my blood,
Lest I perish in the flood,   120

Lest a hidden ember set
Timber that I thought was wet
Burning like the dryest flax,
Melting like the merest wax,
Lest the grave restore its dead.
Not yet has my heart or head
In the least way realized
They and I are civilized.

125

ANNE SEXTON (1928 – 1974)
Her Kind

I have gone out, a possessed witch,
haunting the black air, braver at night;
dreaming evil, I have done my hitch
over the plain houses, light by light:
lonely thing, twelve-fingered,[1] out of mind.
A woman like that is not a woman, quite.
I have been her kind.

I have found the warm caves in the woods,
filled them with skillets, carvings, shelves,
closets, silks, innumerable goods;
fixed the suppers for the worms and the elves:
whining, rearranging the disaligned.
A woman like that is misunderstood.
I have been her kind.

I have ridden in your cart, driver,
waved my nude arms at villages going by,
learning the last bright routes, survivor
where your flames still bite my thigh
and my ribs crack where your wheels wind.[2]
A woman like that is not ashamed to die.
I have been her kind.

---

[1]Witches were thought to have six fingers on each hand.

[2]In the seventeenth century, women thought to be witches were often tortured on the wheel (which stretched the victim's body till the bones broke), then burned at the stake.

CHARLES WRIGHT (b. 1935)

Self-Portrait

Someday they'll find me out, and my lavish hands,
Full moon at my back, fog groping the gone horizon, the edge
Of the continent scored in yellow, expectant lights,
White shoulders of surf, a wolf-colored sand,
The ashes and bits of char that will clear my name.

Till then, I'll hum to myself and settle the whereabouts.
Jade plants and oleander float in a shine.
The leaves of the pepper tree turn green.
My features are sketched with black ink in a slow drag through the
    sky,
Waiting to be filled in.

Hand that lifted me once, lift me again,
Sort me and flesh me out, fix my eyes.
From the mulch and the undergrowth, protect me and pass me on.
From my own words and my certainties,
From the rose and the easy cheek, deliver me, pass me on.

JANE KENYON (1947 – 1995)

Otherwise

I got out of bed
on two strong legs.
It might have been
otherwise. I ate
cereal, sweet
milk, ripe, flawless
peach. It might
have been otherwise.
I took the dog uphill
to the birch wood.
All morning I did
the work I love.

At noon I lay down
with my mate. It might

have been otherwise.
We ate dinner together
at a table with silver
candlesticks. It might
have been otherwise.
I slept in a bed
in a room with paintings
on the walls, and
planned another day
just like this day.
But one day, I know,
it will be otherwise.

CARL PHILLIPS (b. 1959)
Africa Says

Before you arrive, forget
the landscape the novels are filled with,
the dull retro-colonial glamour
of the British Sudan, Tunis's babble,
the Fat Man, Fez, the avenue that is Khartoum.
Forget the three words you know of
this continent: *baraka, baksheesh,*
assassin, words like chipped knives thrust
into an isolation of sand and night.
These will get you only so far.

In the dreams of the first night,
Africa may seem just another body to
sleep with, a place where you can lay
your own broken equipment to rest.
You have leisure to wonder at her being
a woman, at your being disappointed
with this. You come around to asking
what became of her other four fingers,
how she operates on six alone.
You wipe the sweat from
your chest with her withered hand, raised
and two-fingered; observe, as she sleeps,
how that hand casts the perfect
jackal on a wall whose color
is the same as that of the country

itself, a dark, unpalatable thing who
uses a bulbed twig to paint her lids
in three parallel zones that meet and
kiss one another. She smells of henna or
attar, or rises steeped in musk that in other
women does not stray from between the legs.
She says she has no desire to return
with you. Don't be surprised if
she takes nothing you offer, and moves
on bare feet away from you, or if
you wake feeling close to something,
the gauze damp and loose at your face.

And should you choose to leave, know better
than to give the city a farewell sweep of
the eye. To the pith-helmeted mosques, the slim
and purposeless boulevardiers, the running
sores at the breasts of the women who beg
beside stalled trains, you were never here.
For this reason, you may decide to stay put,
thinking you have left nothing finished.
You may have an urge
to make each move count.
You may have learned nothing at all.

7

Poetry and Social Identity

The identity of the lyric speaker (by contrast to the speaker of satire or of dramatic monologue, for instance) has historically been "open-ended," meaning that the words of the speaker could be spoken by any reader within the culture. In the past, in literate cultures, both Western and Eastern, education was preliminary to the (male) professions; and writers, who usually came from the group of those so educated, directed their writings to people who belonged to the same group and possessed the same culture. As we look at the lyrics being produced today, especially in the United States, we can see a marked change in the conception of the lyric speaker. The speaker often is not "neutral" but is given a defined nationality, race, class, sex, or sexual preference, so that we may say, "This is a poem spoken by an African American," or "The speaker is a mother who addresses her sister," or "This is a gay love poem spoken by one man to another," or "This is a poem spoken in Hispanic dialect."

The choice of identity in a poem is up to the writer, for whom identity is never simple. All writers know that besides the forms of identity listed above (which can be combined into such a mixture as "African American middle-class gay male") there are other important identity components such as religion, generation (elder or younger), family roles, social roles, and so on. There is a riddle-game called "Who are you?" to test how people primarily identify themselves: answers by the same person could vary from "I'm a Marine" to "I'm Eric's father" to "I'm a Catholic" to "I'm a Chicano" to "I'm Joan's husband" to "I'm the suspect" — all sayable by the very same person, depending on the situation and the context. When you read a poem with a clearly identified speaker, you need to ask yourself which *one or more* of his or her inevitably many identities the writer is invoking.

The poet Adrienne Rich, for instance, has poems entitled "A Marriage in the 'Sixties," "Sisters," "At the Jewish New Year," "Twenty-One Love Poems," "Mother-in-Law," "Heroines," and "Grandmothers," in which she presents herself, successively, as a wife, a sister, a perplexed Jew, a woman writing love poems to a woman, a lesbian daughter-in-law, an investigator of class privilege, and a granddaughter. These are identities belonging to Rich insofar as she is an individual; in other poems Rich adopts a collective identity ("we" or "you") which makes the speaker representative of a class, such as "women" or "poets." Here are two of Rich's identity-poems. Can we say why the identities the poet chooses are relevant to the poems? The first poem is a dialogue between the mother-in-law (who speaks aloud, in italics) and the daughter-in-law (who silently replies when her mother-in-law says, "Tell me something"):

ADRIENNE RICH (b. 1929)
Mother-in-Law

Tell me something
>   you say
>   Not: What are you working on now, is there anyone special,
>   how is the job
>   do you mind coming back to an empty house
>   what do you do on Sundays
Tell me something . . .
>   Some secret
>   we both know and have never spoken?
>   Some sentence that could flood with light
>   your life, mine?
Tell me what daughters tell their mothers
everywhere in the world, and I and only I
even have to ask. . . .
Tell me something.
>   Lately, I hear it: Tell me something true,
>   daughter-in-law, before we part,
>   tell me something true before I die

And time was when I tried.
You married my son, and so
strange as you are, you're my daughter
Tell me. . . .
    I've been trying to tell you, mother-in-law
    that I think I'm breaking in two
    and half of me doesn't even want to love
    I can polish this table to satin because I don't care
    I am trying to tell you, I envy
    the people in mental hospitals their freedom
    and I can't live on placebos
    or Valium, like you

A cut lemon scours the smell of fish away
You'll feel better when the children are in school
    I would try to tell you, mother-in-law
    but my anger takes fire from yours and in the oven
    the meal bursts into flames
Daughter-in-law, before we part
tell me something true
    I polished the table, mother-in-law
    and scrubbed the knives with half a lemon
    the way you showed me to do
    I wish I could tell you —
               Tell me!
They think I'm weak and hold
things back from me. I agreed to this years ago.
Daughter-in-law, strange as you are,
tell me something true

tell me something
        Your son is dead
    ten years, I am a lesbian,
    my children are themselves.
    Mother-in-law, before we part
    shall we try again? Strange as I am,
    strange as you are? What do mothers
    ask their own daughters, everywhere in the world?
    Is there a question?
        Ask me something.

    If we sort out the speaker's multiple identities as she reveals them to us here, we find out that she is a daughter-in-law, a member of a younger generation addressing a member of the older generation, a person with a job, a person living alone, a mother, a widow, and a lesbian. We also are given a glimpse into her past, when she was the mother of young children not yet in school, a young woman taking lessons from her mother-in-law on how to polish a table and how to remove a fish smell from knives by rubbing them with a lemon, a young woman with a dangerously submerged anger. This double exposure — older identity superimposed on younger identity — is a familiar technique in lyric poetry, serving as it does to point up changes in identity over time. But the constant in the poem is the mother-in-law, saying now as she said then, *"Tell me something,"* while the daughter-in-law answers now, as she did not then, "Ask me something." In her youth, the daughter-in-law was afraid to tell the truth because what she would have said ("I think I'm breaking in two") was too frightening to articulate even to herself. Now she is prepared to try to create a bridge of honest speaking between herself and her mother-in-law: "Your son is dead / ten years, I am a lesbian." But it is not enough to speak the truth; she wants an answering gesture from her mother-in-law, wants her to show some interest in her daughter-in-law's life — "What are you working on now?" "Is there anyone special?" "How is the job?" — almost anything. You will notice that in this poem Rich is *not* mobilizing identities ("I am a poet"; "I am half-Jewish") that she will use for other poems. Why not? In what way is each of the identities she *does* bring out here useful to the poem? A good rule of thumb is that in a poem where you see multiple identities, past as well as present, each of them is in some way necessary to make the poem work.

The relation between son and father (from the point of view of the son) has been frequently explored in literature. Rich broadens the topic of relation between the generations into daughter-in-law and mother-in-law — a relation not often explored, if ever, in lyric. And though the relation to one's mother-in-law has been made the subject of frequent jokes, Rich shows it as one which entails well-meaning gestures on both sides (the mother-in-law giving household advice, the daughter-in-law cooking a meal for the mother-in-law) but in which no truth-telling is possible, until, late in the day, the speaker senses that a desire for truth hovers in the mother-in-law's question, so that it becomes "Tell me something true before we part." The brutal answer — "Your son is dead / ten years, I am a lesbian, / my children are themselves" — surprises us. It is of course a clearing of the ground, as though the speaker demands that these facts be accepted before any further truths are possible. The tenuous relational links between the two women — "You married my son; we are both women; your children are my grandchildren" — are all true, but they are not the whole truth. "Your son is dead; I am a lesbian and you are not; the children are no longer children or grandchildren but adults" — these are the facts that must be accepted, says the daughter-in-law, before any further intimacy is possible. The hopeful end of the poem — "Ask me something" — is a request for that further intimacy, on a new basis, in the few years left.

The junctures at which mother-in-law and daughter-in-law meet are of course the son/husband, grandchildren, common-sex junctures. Being a daughter-in-law is an identity negotiated around these junctures. What happens when the people enabling the junctures disappear? With the son dead, and the children grown, does the daughter-in-law identity have any reality left? Is only an estranged generational relation present — older heterosexual woman, younger lesbian woman? Or can a new identity bond — a mother-daughter one — be formed? "What do mothers / ask their own daughters everywhere in the world? / Is there a question? // Ask me something."

By investigating a particular facet of identity — here, the unexplored one (in literature) of daughter-in-law-hood — the poet renews and deepens identity itself. At the same time, no poem was ever made viable by its topic alone. What does Rich do to stylize the identity juncture she wants to explore? And what do her chosen stylizations tell us about experience?

First of all, as I have said, Rich creates a double exposure of her young self and her older self; this tells us that although there is a separation between Rich as angry young mother and Rich as older lesbian living alone, the later self has not forgotten or obliterated her younger self — there is a continuity of the ego over time. Another principal tactic is Rich's use of a repeated refrain of double address ("Mother-in-law," "Daughter-in-law" — names people don't usually use in address); she borrows this repeated double address from a famous ballad, "Edward, Edward":

> "Why does your brand° so drop with blood,   *sword*
>   Edward, Edward?
> Why does your brand so drop with blood,
>   And why so sad gang ye,° O?"   *go you*
>   "O, I have killed my hawk so good,
>   Mother, mother:
>   O, I have killed my hawk so good,
>   And I had no more but he, O."

Yet another stylization is the repetition of request ("Tell me something," "Ask me something"). Fourteen times "tell" occurs, three times "ask." If we graphed the poem, it would be a series of spirals coming back, again and again, to those two points — "Tell me," "Ask me." This stylized recurrence represents the wish of the two women to stay in touch in spite of the disappearance of the former links between them. The poem is written in good faith, hoping that one will ask so that the other can tell.

It is not enough, therefore, to point out in what identity or identities a poem is written. We need to see how that identity, conferred by biology or by society, may be subjected to critique by the imagination (as it is here), and how it is stylized into poetry.

Here, by contrast, is one of Rich's poems in which the identity of the speaker is *not* very strongly particularized. The speaker, however, offers a new collective identity to a group of people addressed as "Prospective Immigrants." Presumably the speaker is someone who immigrated some time ago, and who speaks from the other side of the door that the new group may or may not choose to pass through:

ADRIENNE RICH (b. 1929)
Prospective Immigrants Please Note

Either you will
go through this door
or you will not go through.

If you go through
there is always the risk
of remembering your name.

Things look at you doubly
and you must look back
and let them happen.

If you do not go through
it is possible
to live worthily

to maintain your attitudes
to hold your position
to die bravely

but much will blind you,
much will evade you,
at what cost who knows?

The door itself
makes no promises.
It is only a door.

To go through the door is to join a group of which the speaker is pre-
sumably one member. In this poem, Rich does not speak as a mother, a
wife, a widow, a daughter-in-law, a Jew, a poet, a lesbian, or even as a
woman. Her identity is "Immigrant," "One Who Has Gone through the
Door." This is a slightly more particularized identity than "person" or
"self" or "soul" (our names for the speaker of the normative generalized
lyric of the past), but it is not very much more specific.

What can we deduce from the poem about the collective identity
of those who immigrate to this new land? That it is painful to remember
your old name here; that there is a double consciousness here, and an
acquiescence in event; that you will see more clearly; that you will con-
front much. What can we deduce about those who choose not to go
through the door? That they can retain their old names; that it is not
ignoble to choose to stay where they are (they can live worthily, maintain
their attitudes, hold on to their position, even die bravely). But they will
be to some degree blind, to some degree unconscious, to some degree
penalized.

This poem clearly draws on actual experiences of immigrants
to the United States, who often lost their own names at Ellis Island
when the Inspectors of Immigration affixed new ones to them. Immi-
grants to America found strange new things to look at and strange new
events to undergo; they learned to live with the double consciousness of
the hyphenated American. And the poem draws on the experience of
those who stayed home in Europe, Asia, Africa, and Latin America and
chose not to emigrate — who held to what they knew, and paid the
price of never finding a New World.

Yet we feel that this is a poem not about physical immigration but
about spiritual immigration. The "prospective immigrants" do not have
to cross oceans or wait at Ellis Island or undergo quarantine; they have
only to open a nameless door. Once through the door, they cannot go
back. Clearly, however, the speaker is glad of his/her own past decision
to join the immigrant group; the poem is, after all, an invitation to new
vision and an abjuring of blindness. This poem is an example of an
ancient literary genre: the immemorial promise of a better spiritual life.

How does Rich stylize her warning to prospective immigrants
about joining the immigrant community? She does it by making her
poem fork into the two possible decisions — to go through the door,
or not:

Go or not go through door (lines 1–3)

Go (lines 4–9)   *Not go* (lines 10–18)

Bad   *Good*   *Good*   *Bad*
(lines 4–6)   (lines 7–9)   (lines 10–15)   (lines 16–18)

The door (lines 19–21)

At the end, Rich brings us back to the very door where we began, waiting for us to make our choice. Because entry to a more complex level of inner life is a choice open to all, Rich's speaker is neither gendered nor identified in any other way — nor are her co-immigrants or the prospective immigrants. In writing about an author who has, over the course of a career, spoken in many different identities, you will want to decide which identity is (or which identities are) operative in any given poem, and why.

An author who encounters an identity already preconstructed for him or her by society ("You are a woman"; "You are Boston Irish"; "You are a black male") is inevitably made conscious of identity questions by encountering the stereotypes attached by society to certain identities. Langston Hughes, writing not only about himself but about the wider Harlem community, shows particular awareness not only of race identity in itself, as society constructs it, but of alternative identities within the same group, constructed by the group about itself. Sometimes, as in the poem "Dream Variations," he writes about himself as black:

> Rest at pale evening . . .
> A tall, slim tree . . .
> Night coming tenderly
>   Black like me.

But sometimes, as in "Cross," he is a speaker of mixed race:

> My old man died in a fine big house.
> My ma died in a shack.
> I wonder where I'm gonna die,
> Being neither white nor black?

Sometimes, as in "I, Too," he is declaredly American as well as black:

> I, too, sing America.
>
> I am the darker brother.

Sometimes, as in "Afro-American Fragment," he is African American:

> Subdued and time-lost
> Are the drums — and yet
> Through some vast mist of race
> There comes this song
> I do not understand,
> This song of atavistic land,
> Of bitter yearnings lost
> Without a place —
> So long,
> So far away
> Is Africa's
> Dark face.

And sometimes he is identified not by color, but only by his exceptional intelligence — which perhaps in childhood isolated him, even more than his color, as a social "monster." The North, as Hughes points out in other poems, does not lynch blacks as the South did — but the North finds victims it wants to kill spiritually, among them children distinguished by exceptional talent or intelligence:

LANGSTON HUGHES (1902 – 1967)
Genius Child

> This is a song for the genius child.
> Sing it softly, for the song is wild.
> Sing it softly as ever you can —
> Lest the song get out of hand.
>
> *Nobody loves a genius child.*
>
> Can you love an eagle,
> Tame or wild?
>
> Wild or tame,
> Can you love a monster
> Of frightening name?

Nobody loves a genius child.
Kill him — and let his soul run wild!

How does Hughes bring imagination to the theme of the marginalized "genius child"? And how does he stylize his poem? He suggests that even to mention the genius child is dangerous — any song about him is "wild" and likely to "get out of hand." The tribe will recognize the song as something outside their culture, and will persecute the song and the singer as well as the genius child. But then the imagination of the poet does a 180-degree turn. He understands the feelings of the tribe. Could any of us love another species, a monster? And that is how the genius child appears to people. The refrain is absolute: nobody, absolutely nobody loves the child — and we are to believe that "nobody" includes the genius child's parents, his siblings, his teachers, his peers. The surprising and horrifying solution — a "lynching" to set the pariah free — is the most unsparing in all of Hughes's work. Culture no longer has any room for a wild soul; it is a kindness to put it to death.

Hughes was himself a genius at the assuming of different identities within the black community, male and female, upright and delinquent, upper-class and lower-class, educated and uneducated. Here he is in one of the poems written in "black English":

LANGSTON HUGHES (1902 – 1967)
Me and the Mule

My old mule,
He's got a grin on his face.
He's been a mule so long
He's forgot about his race.

I'm that old mule —
Black — and don't give a damn!
You got to take me
Like I am.

A poem like this makes us think about the mule's "race" — half horse, half donkey. The gradual consolidation of the mule's "identity" consoles his owner, who makes the half-humorous, half-serious analogy with himself: live long enough and you become just yourself, not someone's notion of you. "You" says the black speaker to his white audience, "got to take me / Like I am." "You got to" — the whites have no choice, because this black knows himself so well he yields none of his individual autonomy to white society. Hughes stylizes his poem by giving us the mule's "success" first to "guarantee" his speaker's eventual triumph. By the end, the speaker's grin matches the one he imagines on the mule.

Our identities are constructed, according to the modern paradox, by others. We are taught to see ourselves first as our parents see us ("Sally's the one who's good at sports"), next as our peers see us ("You're black!" "You're just a girl!"), next as society as a whole sees us ("Statistics show that a high percentage of scientists are males"), and even as literature conceives us ("What are little girls made of? Sugar and spice and everything nice"). It is against these disabling conceptions from outside that inner authenticity makes its struggle. And the disabling conceptions — say, of race — do not have to come from "outside" the group itself. One of Hughes's most stinging poems embodies the mortified hatred of "upper-class" blacks for "lower-class" ones:

LANGSTON HUGHES (1902 – 1967)
High to Low

God knows
We have our troubles, too —
One trouble is you:
you talk too loud,
cuss too loud,
look too black,
don't get anywhere,
and sometimes it seems
you don't even care.
The way you send your kids to school
stockings down,
(not Ethical Culture)
the way you shout out loud in church,
(not St. Phillips)
and the way you lounge on doorsteps
just as if you were down South,
(not at 409)
the way you clown —
the way, in other words,
you let me down —
me, trying to uphold the race
and you —
well, you can see,
we have our problems,
too, with you.

The blacks who are looked down on by the Ethical Culture / St. Phillips set (the names are those of a fashionable school and church) are already having pejorative identities ("loud," "too black," "don't care") constructed for them by their very own fellow blacks. Add these to the identities constructed for them by the surrounding whites, and the construction of an authentic self has two strikes against it before it can begin. Even the notion of what an "authentic self" might be is modeled by cultural expectations into which we are born.

Poetry is one of the great means in which one identity reaches out to another, tries to explain itself to another, brings up images to clarify itself (Rich's meal bursting into flames in the oven, Hughes's grinning and ornery mule), finds a diction that speaks its mind, and finds a stylized form to enact its appeal. There is a danger that a reader will take the identity in a lyric as more simple than it is, and will mentally invoke a stereotype of the female speaker or the black speaker or the gay speaker or the Catholic speaker. But good poems are thoroughly considered constructions; and in order for the poem to be interesting, the author must critique or reinvent the social stereotype. A lyric to keep in mind when reading identity-poems is Seamus Heaney's "Terminus," a poem announcing that a poet's identity is always at least a double one, because any poet worthy of the name has "second thoughts." Heaney, a Northern Irish poet, grew up on a farm but within sight of industry, in a rural place where people still used horses to draw wagons but took the train to go to the city. One "terminus" or border of the farm was the "march drain" — the creek marking the line ("march") between two parishes. Heaney, as a child, lived also along divides in the world of words — on the borderline between his parents' secular proverbs and their Biblical stories — both equally stimulating to the nascent poet's mind. And he lived between the present (Northern Ireland governed by England) and the better past (before the Irish earls, defeated by the British, fled to France in 1798, ending Irish independence). "Is it any wonder," the poet asks, given all these influences on my identity, that "when I thought / I would have second thoughts?" Any reflective poet has "second thoughts" about both inherited and acquired "identities," and it is those "second thoughts," and their origins, that Heaney so well identifies:

SEAMUS HEANEY (b. 1939)

Terminus

I

When I hoked° there, I would find   *fished*
An acorn and a rusted bolt.

If I lifted my eyes, a factory chimney
And a dormant mountain.

If I listened, an engine shunting
And a trotting horse.

Is it any wonder when I thought
I would have second thoughts?

II

When they spoke of the prudent squirrel's hoard
It shone like gifts at a nativity.

When they spoke of the mammon of iniquity
The coins in my pockets reddened like stove-lids.

I was the march drain and the march drain's banks
Suffering the limit of each claim.

III

Two buckets were easier carried than one.
I grew up in between.

My left hand placed the standard iron weight.
My right tilted a last grain on the balance.

Baronies, parishes met where I was born.
When I stood on the central stepping stone

I was the last earl on horseback in midstream
Still parleying, in earshot of his peers.

Though a poem like Heaney's particularizes much about his identity (Irish, rural, Catholic, modern), it still does not specify idiosyncrasies that would point him out as a single individual. Even Rich's self-identification as lesbian widow, mother of children, daughter-in-law, could fit many people.

The most extreme reach of the "identity poem" is a poem that specifies its speaker so completely that he or she becomes entirely unique. No one but Frank O'Hara could speak the poem entitled "The Day Lady Died," a poem showing O'Hara's humdrum day suddenly brought to a stunned halt as he sees a newspaper headline announcing the death of the famous jazz singer Billie Holiday. The poem goes, in part:

It is 12:20 in New York a Friday
three days after Bastille day, yes
it is 1959 and I go get a shoeshine

because I will get off the 4:19 in Easthampton
at 7:15 and then go straight to dinner . . .
and in the GOLDEN GRIFFIN I get a little Verlaine
for Patsy with drawings by Bonnard . . .

and for Mike I just stroll into the PARK LANE
Liquor Store and ask for a bottle of Strega and
then I go back where I came from to 6th Avenue
and the tobacconist in the Ziegfeld Theatre and
casually ask for a carton of Gauloises and a carton
of Picayunes, and a NEW YORK POST with her face on it.

Nobody but Frank O'Hara is doing just these things in this order on this specified date, buying presents for specified friends named Patsy and Mike. In such a poem, not only are time and space fully specified, but personal identity is unmistakably that of only one person. The construction of a speaker in such a poem is as far as possible from the normative lyric construction of a "universal" or "representative" speaker, like the one in an anonymous English love song who says (as almost anyone in the world might say), "Love me little, love me long, / Is the burden of my song":

Constant love is moderate ever,
And it will through life persever;
Give me that, with true endeavor
    I will it restore.

Why would the lyric poet sometimes want to construct a specified speaker instead of a universal one? Perhaps as modern life has grown more heterogeneous, it seems harder to some poets to speak for everyone. In England, before the turn of the century, there was a relatively small educated class confined to one island nation possessing only two universities. In such a country, with such an audience, the lyric poet could address his cultivated audience as though his speech and theirs were one. The poet in contemporary America, with its diversity of types and interests, may feel it only reasonable to speak more narrowly — not always, but sometimes. The uniqueness of each person is one modern article of faith — and by making himself unique, O'Hara suggests that each person lives a common shared event differently. Many people, on that day in New York, saw the headline about Billie Holiday's death: but, says the poet, your moment and mine were different. Let me tell you how it was for me; that will make you think how it was for you. The appeal to representativeness is still present, but it is an appeal to sameness-in-difference. Every lyric, no matter how socially specified, assumes that it speaks a language its readers can understand — even if in their own different terms.

In Brief: Poetry and Social Identity

Remembering Rich, remembering Hughes, remembering Heaney, remembering O'Hara, ask yourself, with respect to any identity-poem, "Between what borders, left and right, does this poem flow? What does it see when it looks up? or down? or around? Which words shine with morality? Which redden with shame? How does it see the past? the present? In what communities does it station itself? Against what others does it contend? To what degree does it specify its own uniqueness?" The rich contribution of identity formation to poetry, especially in the twentieth century, both criticizes and renews our inherited sense of the lyric speaker, reminding us that if we stand in the shoes of the poem, we do so not only in general ways but also in our own individualized way.

Reading Other Poems

Besides an idiosyncratic and unique personal identity, all of us have social identity, arising from groups to which we belong or are consigned. As you read the following poems, consider what portion of social identity each speaker claims as his or her own, or ascribes to his characters. Robert Southwell's speaker, for instance, has a vision identifying him as a Christian believer; Thomas Nashe's speaker is a victim of the plague for whom the whole world has narrowed into one great mortuary. We may know only one identifying trait of the speaker from the *thematic* content of the poem. (We may know other traits from the speaker's tone, the images used, and so on.)

- By contrast, how many personal identifying traits can you find in Anne Bradstreet's poem?
- What difference does it make in the effect of a poem to have the self of its speaker so narrowly specified?

Would you rather read a poem that you can speak without feeling that a particular person uttered it — a poem that can be uttered by almost anyone, because its feelings are so general, and its speaker so apparently universal? Or would you rather feel that the poem is introducing you to the life and speech of a unique individual? (Neither one of these is better than the other; but we all have varying aesthetic responses, and you may prefer one to the other; reflect on why you do.)

- If you are not a Christian, how are you able to read Southwell's poem with imaginative sympathy?

- Explore your own answers to such questions, which are profound ones and affect all art. Can a non-Christian respond to a painting of the nativity of Jesus?

- Can a white person respond to Rita Dove's portrait of her wid-owed grandmother's first participation in an "integrated" social occasion?

- Is the drama of a poem spoken by a socially specified individual (Edward Lear describing himself as others might see him, Gerard Manley Hopkins speaking as a Catholic priest) different from that of a poem spoken by an abstract speaker?

- Sylvia Plath's "applicant" gets her identity from her envisaged social role. What is that role? Does it allow for any personal indi-viduality? Can you compare Plath's view of the individuality allowed within marriage to Anne Bradstreet's view? (You do not have to choose: the very purpose of reading poetry is to let you see the world through many different lenses.)

- William Blake's persona, the little black boy, is a type rather than a person; but though we imagine ourselves in his shoes, speaking his words so full of pathos, are we not also objective observers, realiz-ing the extent to which he is parroting what he has been taught (souls are white, angels are white, and so on)?

- What is the use, to Blake, of the persona of the little black boy, when the poet could equally well have written a poem protesting slavery in his own adult voice?

- Why do you think he had the little black boy speak in "heroic quatrains" — broad pentameter alternately rhyming quatrains, usu-ally used for a philosophic or noble subject?

Poems exploring social identity must often face the fact that not all members of the social group share the same attitudes.

- In David Mura's poem about the internment of Japanese Ameri-cans during World War II, what are the attitudes dramatized? In what does the conflict consist?

- In Sheila Ortiz Taylor's "The Way Back," the brother's choices offend both family members and neighbors. In what ways does the social identity of both brother and sister differ from the group identities around them?

ROBERT SOUTHWELL (1561 – 1595)
The Burning Babe

As I in hoary winter's night stood shivering in the snow,
Surprised I was with sudden heat which made my heart to glow;
And lifting up a fearful eye to view what fire was near,
A pretty babe all burning bright did in the air appear;
Who, scorchèd with excessive heat, such floods of tears did shed
As though his floods should quench his flames which with his
    tears were fed.
"Alas," quoth he, "but newly born in fiery heats I fry,
Yet none approach to warm their hearts or feel my fire but I!
My faultless breast the furnace is, the fuel wounding thorns,
Love is the fire, and sighs the smoke, the ashes shame and scorns;
The fuel justice layeth on, and mercy blows the coals,
The metal in this furnace wrought are men's defilèd souls,
For which, as now on fire I am to work them to their good,
So will I melt into a bath to wash them in my blood."
With this he vanished out of sight and swiftly shrunk away,
And straight I callèd unto mind that it was Christmas day.

THOMAS NASHE (1567 – ?1601)
A Litany in Time of Plague

Adieu, farewell, earth's bliss;
This world uncertain is;
Fond are life's lustful joys;
Death proves them all but toys;
None from his darts can fly;
I am sick, I must die.
        Lord, have mercy on us!

Rich men, trust not in wealth,
Gold cannot buy you health;
Physic himself must fade.
All things to end are made,

The plague full swift goes by;
I am sick, I must die.
    Lord, have mercy on us!

Beauty is but a flower
Which wrinkles will devour;
Brightness falls from the air;
Queens have died young and fair;
Dust hath closed Helen's eye.
I am sick, I must die.
    Lord, have mercy on us!

Strength stoops unto the grave,
Worms feed on Hector brave;
Swords may not fight with fate,
Earth still holds ope her gate.
"Come, come!" the bells do cry.
I am sick, I must die.
    Lord, have mercy on us.

Wit with his wantonness
Tasteth death's bitterness;
Hell's executioner
Hath no ears for to hear
What vain art can reply.
I am sick, I must die.
    Lord, have mercy on us.

Haste, therefore, each degree,
To welcome destiny;
Heaven is our heritage,
Earth but a player's stage;
Mount we unto the sky.
I am sick, I must die.
    Lord, have mercy on us.

ANNE BRADSTREET (c. 1612 – 1672)

A Letter to Her Husband, Absent upon Public Employment

My head, my heart, mine eyes, my life, nay, more,
My joy, my magazine° of earthly store,   *storehouse*
If two be one, as surely thou and I,
How stayest thou there, whilst I at Ipswich lie?
So many steps, head from the heart to sever,

If but a neck, soon should we be together.
I, like the Earth this season, mourn in black,
My Sun is gone so far in's zodiac,
Whom whilst I joyed, nor storms, nor frost I felt,
His warmth such frigid colds did cause to melt.
My chillèd limbs now numbèd lie forlorn;
Return; return, sweet Sol, from Capricorn;
In this dead time, alas, what can I more
Than view those fruits which through thy heat I bore?
Which sweet contentment yield me for a space,
True living pictures of their father's face.
O strange effect! now thou art southward gone,
I weary grow the tedious day so long;
But when thou northward to me shalt return,
I wish my Sun may never set, but burn
Within the Cancer of my glowing breast,
The welcome house of him my dearest guest.
Where ever, ever stay, and go not thence,
Till nature's sad decree shall call thee hence;
Flesh of thy flesh, bone of thy bone,
I here, thou there, yet both but one.

WILLIAM BLAKE (1757 – 1827)
The Little Black Boy

My mother bore me in the southern wild,
And I am black, but O! my soul is white;
White as an angel is the English child:
But I am black as if bereav'd of light.

My mother taught me underneath a tree,
And sitting down before the heat of day,
She took me on her lap and kissèd me,
And pointing to the east, began to say:

"Look on the rising sun: there God does live,
And gives his light, and gives his heat away;
And flowers and trees and beasts and men receive
Comfort in morning, joy in the noon day.

"And we are put on earth a little space,
That we may learn to bear the beams of love,
And these black bodies and this sun-burnt face

Is but a cloud, and like a shady grove.

"For when our souls have learn'd the heat to bear,
The cloud will vanish; we shall hear his voice,
Saying: 'Come out from the grove, my love & care,
And round my golden tent like lambs rejoice.'"

Thus did my mother say, and kissèd me;
And thus I say to little English boy:
When I from black and he from white cloud free,
And round the tent of God like lambs we joy,

I'll shade him from the heat till he can bear
To lean in joy upon our father's knee;
And then I'll stand and stroke his silver hair,
And be like him, and he will then love me.

EDWARD LEAR (1812 – 1888)

How Pleasant to Know Mr. Lear

How pleasant to know Mr. Lear!
    Who has written such volumes of stuff!
Some think him ill-tempered and queer,
    But a few think him pleasant enough.

His mind is concrete and fastidious,
    His nose is remarkably big;
His visage is more or less hideous,
    His beard it resembles a wig.

He has ears, and two eyes, and ten fingers,
    Leastways if you reckon two thumbs;
Long ago he was one of the singers,
    But now he is one of the dumbs.

He sits in a beautiful parlor,
    With hundreds of books on the wall;
He drinks a great deal of Marsala,
    But never gets tipsy at all.

He has many friends, laymen and clerical;
    Old Foss is the name of his cat;
His body is perfectly spherical,
    He weareth a runcible hat.

When he walks in a waterproof white,
    The children run after him so!
Calling out, "He's come out in his night-
    Gown, that crazy old Englishman, oh!"

He weeps by the side of the ocean,
    He weeps on the top of the hill;
He purchases pancakes and lotion,
    And chocolate shrimps from the mill.

He reads but he cannot speak Spanish,
    He cannot abide ginger-beer:
Ere the days of his pilgrimage vanish,
    How pleasant to know Mr. Lear!

GERARD MANLEY HOPKINS (1844 – 1889)
Felix Randal

Felix Randal the farrier,° O is he dead then?   *blacksmith*
    my duty all ended,
Who have watched his mould of man, big-boned and
    hardy-handsome
Pining, pining, till time when reason rambled in it and some
Fatal four disorders, fleshed there, all contended?

Sickness broke him. Impatient, he cursed at first, but mended
Being anointed and all; though a heavenlier heart began some
Months earlier, since I had our sweet reprieve and ransom
Tendered to him. Ah well, God rest him all road ever he offended!

This seeing the sick endears them to us, us too it endears.
My tongue had taught thee comfort, touch had quenched
    thy tears,
Thy tears that touched my heart, child, Felix, poor Felix Randal;

How far from then forethought of, all thy more boisterous years,
When thou at the random° grim forge, powerful   *ramshackle*
    amidst peers,
Didst fettle° for the great grey drayhorse his bright   *shape*
    and battering sandal!

SYLVIA PLATH (1932 – 1963)

The Applicant

First, are you our sort of a person?
Do you wear
A glass eye, false teeth or a crutch,
A brace or a hook,
Rubber breasts or a rubber crotch,

Stitches to show something's missing? No, no? Then
How can we give you a thing?
Stop crying.
Open your hand.
Empty? Empty. Here is a hand

To fill it and willing
To bring teacups and roll away headaches
And do whatever you tell it.
Will you marry it?
It is guaranteed

To thumb shut your eyes at the end
And dissolve of sorrow.
We make new stock from the salt.
I notice you are stark naked.
How about this suit —

Black and stiff, but not a bad fit.
Will you marry it?
It is waterproof, shatterproof, proof
Against fire and bombs through the roof.
Believe me, they'll bury you in it.

Now your head, excuse me, is empty.
I have the ticket for that.
Come here, sweetie, out of the closet.
Well, what do you think of *that?*
Naked as paper to start

But in twenty-five years she'll be silver,
In fifty, gold.
A living doll, everywhere you look.
It can sew, it can cook,
It can talk, talk, talk.

It works, there is nothing wrong with it.
You have a hole, it's a poultice.

You have an eye, it's an image.
My boy, it's your last resort.
Will you marry it, marry it, marry it.

DAVID MURA (b. 1952)
An Argument: On 1942

For My Mother

Near Rose's Chop Suey and Jinosuke's grocery,
the temple where incense hovered and inspired
dense evening chants (prayers for Buddha's mercy,
colorless and deep), that day he was fired . . .

— No, no, no, she tells me. Why bring it back?
The camps are over. (Also overly dramatic.)
Forget *shoyu*°-stained *furoshiki,*°   *soy sauce / scarf*
    mochi° on a stick: *rice cakes*
You're like a terrier, David, gnawing a bone, an old, old trick . . .

Mostly we were bored. Women cooked and sewed,
men played blackjack, dug gardens, a *benjo.*°   *toilet*
Who noticed barbed wire, guards in the towers?
We were children, hunting stones, birds, wild flowers.

Yes, Mother hid tins of *utskemono* and eel
beneath the bed. And when the last was peeled,
clamped tight her lips, growing thinner and thinner.
But cancer not the camps made her throat blacker

. . . And she didn't die then . . . after the war, in St. Paul,
you weren't even born. Oh I know, I know, it's all
part of your job, your way, but why can't you glean
how far we've come, how much I can't recall —

David, it was so long ago — how useless it seems . . .

RITA DOVE (b. 1952)
Wingfoot Lake

(Independence Day, 1964)

On her 36th birthday, Thomas had shown her
her first swimming pool. It had been
his favorite color, exactly — just

so much of it, the swimmers' white arms jutting
into the chevrons of high society.
She had rolled up her window
and told him to drive on, fast.

Now this *act of mercy:* four daughters
dragging her to their husbands' company picnic,
white families on one side and them
on the other, unpacking the same
squeeze bottles of Heinz, the same
waxy beef patties and Salem potato chip bags.
So he was dead for the first time
on Fourth of July — ten years ago

had been harder, waiting for something to happen,
and ten years before that, the girls
like young horses eyeing the track.
Last August she stood alone for hours
in front of the T.V. set
as a crow's wing moved slowly through
the white streets of government.
That brave swimming

scared her, like Joanna saying
Mother, we're Afro-Americans now!
What did she know about Africa?
Were there lakes like this one
with a rowboat pushed under the pier?
Or Thomas' Great Mississippi
with its sullen silks? (There was
the Nile but the Nile belonged

to God.) Where she came from
was the past, 12 miles into town
where nobody had locked their back door,
and Goodyear hadn't begun to dream of a park
under the company symbol, a white foot
sprouting two small wings.

SHEILA ORTIZ TAYLOR (b. 1939)
The Way Back

for Uncle Jim

They stand in this Christmas snapshot
poised like adagio dancers
facing each other
their arms draped around
their matching bones   5
brother and sister
while behind them
out of focus
the family
spins   10

Around these two
youngest of thirteen
held now for eternity
in this moment before their
twin feet slide them out   15
in a celestial tango
a silence gathers

We see their handsome faces
Indian bones in glinting cheeks
their raven hair, gray-streaked   20
their eyes as deep and dark as wells
holding a history of careless loss
land, lovers, mothers, maps

The way back is a land
more innocent than this   25
He joined the navy
She married a judge
They both baked bread in institutional ovens
He wrote long letters home
and sent his mother silk pillows   30
embroidered with military targets

He baked bread while
his eight brothers lost fingers
toes, knees, elbows
He could almost hear the bullets   35
thud into dough
and the sound made him rise

growing from uniform to uniform
until they had to declare peace

Home again   40
he folded away his whites
kissed his sisters
and told his brothers
he was going to become
a hairdresser   45
news that made their wounds ache
more than seemed possible
Finally he followed them to work at Lockheed
learned to drill holes in himself
discovered insomnia   50
married a beautician named Molly
whose hair he dyed green every Christmas

He loved all holidays
Life needed themes
spelled out in sparkles, sprinkles   55
cutouts, paste-ups
but most of all
in costume.

Halloweens found brother and sister
on their knees   60
before bolts of cloth
and wimpling tissue
pins in their mouths
blue chalk on their hands
for years   65
artists of the self

You can see it here
in this snapshot
white polyester pants belling out

around white cowboy boots   70
red western shirts
tailored close to the rib
Indian silver at the waist
twins in spirit
if not by birth   75
holding each other
in a light embrace

their grace
not lost

And yet   80
the way back is a land
more innocent than this
The time came round
when neighbors
preferring razor blades to invention   85
would not let their children
trick or treat
where a grown man
put costumes on.

That Christmas night   90
very late
he backed his throbbing
Continental
into the dark garage
that shut down tight behind him   95
crawled into the backseat
bearing a bottle of champagne
one glass
a photograph

8

History and Regionality

Poetry is always interested in time and space. Sometimes these can be very generally expressed, as we saw in "A slumber did my spirit seal." Time in this poem means simply past versus present; space encloses first two individuals, then the whole planet:

WILLIAM WORDSWORTH (1770 – 1850)
A slumber did my spirit seal

A slumber did my spirit seal;
    I had no human fears:
She seemed a thing that could not feel
    The touch of earthly years.

No motion has she now, no force;
    She neither hears nor sees;
Rolled round in earth's diurnal course,
    With rocks, and stones, and trees.

But poetry is not only interested in such large general uses of space and time. It is also interested in time specified — in history. Especially for nations emerging from colonial status — America after the Revolution, Ireland after 1916 — history needs to be made freshly significant, newly sacred. Important events need to be memorialized (as "The Star-Spangled

Banner" commemorates the battle of Fort McHenry; as William Butler Yeats's "Easter 1916" meditates on Ireland's Easter Rising). Important heroes and heroines need to be immortalized (as John Greenleaf Whittier's "Barbara Frietchie" salutes a semilegendary heroine of the Revolution; as Yeats's "A Rose Tree" salutes Padraic Pearse, executed for his part in the Easter Rising). And poetry about history is not only celebratory. Problematic aspects of history have to be investigated (as Herman Melville queries war enthusiasm in "The March into Virginia" during the Civil War; as Adrienne Rich decries the 1953 execution of Ethel Rosenberg in "For Ethel Rosenberg"; as Seamus Heaney scrutinizes the violent conflicts in Northern Ireland in "North").

History

Immediate challenges arise for a lyric poet who is writing a poem about (or within or against) history. In the first place, written history is a narrative genre, and the history of a complex event (the American Revolution, the Civil War in England leading to the execution of Charles I, the Easter Rising) is not only narratively complicated, but always politically disputed. The English narrate the American Revolution from a point of view (that of the losing side) very different from the celebratory view taken in American history books. Propaganda always exists on both sides of any historical question, as on both sides of any disputed ethical question. It is up to the poet to see beyond the simplifications of propaganda (always unfair to the intricacy of any disputed event) and to present the crises of history in a way that does not diminish their ambiguity and their painfulness.

How does the poet incorporate history within the miniature dimensions of the lyric? There are several central techniques:

1. Focusing on a problem rather than on incidents;
2. Finding an emblematic scene or scenes;
3. Finding a symbolic or mythological equivalent for a historical episode;
4. Seeing the human inside of the event as corresponding to the historical outside;
5. Finding an epigrammatic summation;
6. Adopting a prophetic or philosophic view larger than that of a mere eyewitness.

Let us see how these techniques come into play in Melville's Civil War poem, "The March into Virginia," written in fear and dismay after the Union forces were twice routed by the Confederate army in the first and second battles of Manassas (sometimes called the first and second battles of Bull Run). The Union army — composed of young, patriotic, impulsive, untried recruits — marched gaily into battle, only to suffer carnage. The few who survived had to march into battle once again, knowing, this time, the horrors ahead. Was their original innocence of any value? Can naive ignorance be of ultimate political use? Melville begins his consideration by reflecting on this problem: he admits how little we would undertake if we knew beforehand the "lets and bars" — obstacles and hindrances — that we would encounter:

> Did all the lets and bars appear
>   To every just or larger end,
> Whence should come the trust and cheer?
>   Youth must its ignorant impulse lend —
> Age finds place in the rear.
>   All wars are boyish, and are fought by boys,
> The champions and enthusiasts of the state:
>   Turbid ardours and vain joys
>   Not barrenly abate —
>   Stimulants to the power mature,
>   Preparatives of fate.

Having stated the paradox that enthusiasm for war is both ignorant ("All wars are boyish, and are fought by boys") and useful (the boys' "vain joys" and patriotic ardor bring forth the fruit of mature power, through which one can hope for the reinstatement of the Union), Melville can go on to set the scene of the boys' heedless march into Virginia:

> Who here forecasteth the event?
> What heart but spurns at precedent
> And warnings of the wise,
> Contemned foreclosures of surprise?
> The banners play, the bugles call,
> The air is blue and prodigal.
>   No berrying party, pleasure-wooed,
> No picnic party in the May,
> Ever went less loth than they
>   Into that leafy neighbourhood.

After this naturalistic scene painting, Melville breaks into a foreboding symbolic discourse of myth. The intoxicated glee of the boys, comparable to that of the devotees of the wine god Bacchus, will lead them into being sacrificed. They resemble, in fact, the Hebrew children sacrificed to the idol Moloch:

> In Bacchic glee they file toward Fate,
> Moloch's uninitiate;
> Expectancy, and glad surmise
> Of battle's unknown mysteries.

From his prophetic and mythological distance, Melville then returns, in close focus, to a last snapshot of the emotional state of the naive boys as they "file toward Fate":

> All they feel is this: 'tis glory,
> A rapture sharp, though transitory,
> Yet lasting in belaureled story.
> So they gaily go to fight,
> Chatting left and laughing right.

At this point, the speaker of the poem, who had begun philosophically and had continued scenically, becomes once again a prophet, foreseeing the end of these boys, some dead, some surviving the shame of defeat to fight, a year later, the battle of second Manassas:

> But some who this blithe mood present,
> As on in lightsome files they fare,
> Shall die experienced ere three days are spent —
> Perish, enlightened by the volleyed glare;
> Or shame survive, and, like to adamant,
> The throe of Second Manassas share.

We can now see that Melville epitomizes the war for us by showing us three stages in an emblematic young soldier's experience: his initial gaiety and desire for fame and glory, his "enlightenment" in the volleyed glare as he learns, perishing, what war is; or, for one who survives the shame of defeat, a third stage, beyond mere "enlightenment," in which the soldier becomes "like to adamant" in his stony and steeled knowledge of degradation, violence, and death. By his philosophic problematizing of ignorance and courage, by his visual scenes of carefree young soldiers, by his penetration of their emotional attitudes, by his shorthand references to the mythic Bacchus and Moloch to represent poles of

blithe ignorance and pitiless extinction, by his schematizing the experi-
ence of war in three stages, and by his final prophecy — that the boys
"shall die experienced" or shall share "the throe of Second Manassas" —
Melville puts a year of the Civil War, and the problems it raised for him,
into the short confines of lyric.

Not all of these techniques appear in every historical poem, but the
poet always needs some of these strategies to make history pliable to
lyric. Though Melville intermittently takes a philosophic position above
the scene of battle, it is clear from his inner snapshots of the recruits'
feelings that he sympathizes with the Union side, hoping that the youth-
ful Union forces' "turbid ardours" will be useful to the country in stim-
ulating its ultimate Fate.

In some history poems, the poet is immediately engaged, writing
from within a particular moment, representing himself or herself as a
historically specified person, of specified political or historical alle-
giance, and (as we will see) of specified geographic origin. This tradition
in American verse begins with *Leaves of Grass,* in which the author
named himself and his home: "Walt Whitman, a kosmos, of Manhattan
the son," and specified even his age, "I, now thirty-seven years old in
perfect health begin." However, we notice that even this socially speci-
fied self also identifies himself as "a kosmos," that is, a representative uni-
verse. The lyric poet, even when engaged in social self-specification,
intends representativeness as well. This is the case in Robert Lowell's
unrhymed sonnet about the March on the Pentagon in 1967 protesting
the Vietnam War. Lowell took part in the March (vividly described later
by Norman Mailer in *The Armies of the Night*), as the protesters went,
several abreast, toward the Pentagon — only to be routed by the Army:

ROBERT LOWELL (1917 – 1977)
The March 1

For Dwight Macdonald

Under the too white marmoreal Lincoln Memorial,
the too tall marmoreal Washington Obelisk,
gazing into the too long reflecting pool,
the reddish trees, the withering autumn sky,
the remorseless, amplified harangues for peace —
lovely to lock arms, to march absurdly locked
(unlocking to keep my wet glasses from slipping)
to see the cigarette match quaking in my fingers,
then to step off like green Union Army recruits
for the first Bull Run, sped by photographers,

the notables, the girls . . . fear, glory, chaos, rout . . .
our green army staggered out on the miles-long green fields,
met by the other army, the Martian, the ape, the hero,
his new-fangled rifle, his green new steel helmet.

It is clear that Lowell is remembering Melville's poem about the "green Union Army recruits / for the first Bull Run" as he writes of his own first foray into battle. But he is a middle-aged man, feeling absurd in the fraternal political gesture of locked arms, hating (as only a poet could) the awful propaganda slogans of the March being relentlessly boomed out over his head by the marchers' public address system. Nor does the poet feel akin to the ideology affirmed by the state architecture of Washington: its marble monuments inspired by Rome ("marmoreal") and Egypt ("obelisk"), its supersized conception of itself (which he sees as too white, too tall, too long). He is no hero — his glasses keep slipping, his hands quake with fear. The poem is scenic with a vengeance for its first eight lines, but the scenes are always infused with the poet's attitude toward what they show. Just when we wonder whether anything philosophic, epigrammatic, prophetic, or emblematic might come along to sum up and give point to Lowell's procession of scenes, we meet just what we have been expecting — first the allusion to Melville as an epigrammatic summing up of ignorance about to be turned into experience, then an emblematic series of nouns ("fear, glory, chaos, rout") summing up the stages of both political protest and armed war. The poem returns, at the end, to a scenic mode, this time a scene not of a march but of a confrontation, as the "green army" of the protesters is met by the real Army in tactical gear. We see three "green's" in succession: the green (inexperienced) protesters, the "miles-long" ideologically too-big green (grass) fields of the Washington Mall, and the literal green metal of the Army soldier's helmet. This "irrational" repetition of "green" in several different contexts makes the closing scene feel epigrammatic, "tied together," "final."

And the closing scene, unlike the literal scenes preceding it, has elements of the surreal. What does it seem like when you find yourself, as an American protester, being confronted inimically by your own American Army, composed of green recruits like yourself? And how do you feel about the Army now? You have a confused set of impressions as you see your first soldier in riot gear: "He looks like a Martian, something out of science fiction; no, with his hulking posture he looks more like an ape; but wait, this is *our* Army, he's a hero; odd, he seems to have a new-fangled kind of rifle, not the kind I remember from newsreels; he's the archetypal warrior, archaic, helmeted, like the warriors of Troy, only his helmet is new, and it is made of steel, not bronze." Some such latent content is contained within the last two lines, a content more "intellectual" than the scenes with which the poem opened, and therefore able to satisfy our desire that the poet "make something" — if only by revealing how confusing it is to be opposing your own American Army — of his experience. Though Lowell's poem is about a specific historical event, and represents the poet himself not only in his physical being (his fear, his glasses) but also in his political taking of sides, it is a representative poem, too, about the confused emotions Lowell feels in protesting the actions of his own government — a set of emotions anyone might feel.

A simpler "propaganda" poem written by a participant in the March would probably not have shown a sweating and awkward protagonist with his glasses slipping down his nose; it would certainly not have called the peace messages "the *remorseless*, amplified *harangues* for peace"; and it would not have seen the Army soldier as *both* ape and hero. It is Lowell's accuracy, both to his own motives for marching (the critique of America's imperial ambitions) and to his own sense of absurdity (including his mixed reactions to the Army soldier) that makes the poem humanly believable.

Even the simplest "history" poem usually has scene, epigram, feeling, and "philosophic" comment. Here is Langston Hughes's little song-and-echo poem, "World War II":

LANGSTON HUGHES (1902 – 1967)
World War II

What a grand time was the war!
   Oh, my, my!
What a grand time was the war!
   My, my, my!
In wartime we had fun,
Sorry that old war is done!
What a grand time was the war,
   My, my!

Echo:
   Did
   Somebody
   Die?

Here, Hughes is not writing as a socially specified singular self — as a black poet or as "Langston Hughes," a man of a certain age living in a certain city; rather, he writes a public chorus for the late 1940s, and counterpoints the chorus with a single satiric and epigrammatic echo. Hughes can sympathize with the chorus of voices praising wartime: following the catastrophe of the 1929 Depression and its long dreary aftermath of stinted lives, the plentiful jobs (in defense, in war work, in communications and services) brought about by the war effort rejuvenated many a poor family. The chorus has not a single dissenting voice, as all join in for the refrain, "Oh, my, my." Who utters the haunting echo? Is it the philosophic poet? Is it a forgotten Gold Star mother? Is it the voice of history? Whoever it is, each of its words is significant. The chorus's words all run together horizontally — "In wartime we had fun." But the Echo's voice runs vertically:

Did
Somebody
Die?

This is the way oracles speak: every word with a line to itself, every word capitalized, every word in italics. These are sacred words, whereas the words of the chorus are profane words. By such simple means Hughes shows us two comments on history, both "correct," but irreconcilable.

One of the problems in reading history poems is that one has to know something about history, and about the import of historical events within a given culture. Someone who knew nothing about the Civil War, or the March on Washington, or about the economic boom brought by World War II, would have difficulty taking in the attitudes and implications of these poems by Melville, Lowell, and Hughes. To this extent, lyric poets writing history poems have to depend on the shared knowledge of a common culture — and American readers wishing to understand an English poem about, say, the English Civil War have to learn, perhaps, many things that an English reader would have learned in school and that the poet took for granted in composing the poem. It is up to the poet to give the reader as much information as possible in the poem, but there is a limit to what can be conveyed in a short space. The generalized lyric usually has a longer shelf-life than the historically specified lyric because it does not make such particular demands on the reader. Yet nothing matches the vivid scenic, topical, and philosophic intensity of the best history poems, especially as they are first encountered by the audience to whom their topic is an urgent and contemporary one.

"Revisionary" history poems aim to turn the received view of a given historical circumstance upside down. War was treated heroically by classical literature, and the quotation from the Roman poet Horace, "Dulce et decorum est pro patria mori" ("It is sweet and fitting to die for one's country"), had been taken as the epitome of the proper attitude for young men going off to war. The introduction of such inhuman fighting methods as poison gas in World War I made a revisionary view of war almost inevitable, and the most famous poem of that war, dismantling armed struggle as a noble act, was composed by the English poet Wilfred Owen, who died in the war in 1918. You will see that in spite of the revisionary aims of the poem, it uses the familiar strategies of scenic presentation, crucial event, emotional insight, a mythic interlude (here, a recurrent dream), and epigrammatic summation (via Horace). It is spoken not by someone removed at a philosophic distance, but by one of the soldiers undergoing a gas attack:

WILFRED OWEN (1893 – 1918)
Dulce et Decorum Est

Bent double, like old beggars under sacks,
Knock-kneed, coughing like hags, we cursed through sludge,
Till on the haunting flares we turned our backs
And towards our distant rest began to trudge.
Men marched asleep. Many had lost their boots
But limped on, blood-shod. All went lame; all blind;
Drunk with fatigue; deaf even to the hoots
Of tired, outstripped Five-Nines° that dropped behind.   *gas shells*

Gas! GAS! Quick, boys! — An ecstasy of fumbling,
Fitting the clumsy helmets just in time;
But someone still was yelling out and stumbling
And flound'ring like a man in fire or lime . . .
Dim, through the misty panes and thick green light,
As under a green sea, I saw him drowning.

In all my dreams, before my helpless sight,
He plunges at me, guttering, choking, drowning.

If in some smothering dreams you too could pace
Behind the wagon that we flung him in,
And watch the white eyes writhing in his face,
His hanging face, like a devil's sick of sin;
If you could hear, at every jolt, the blood
Come gargling from the froth-corrupted lungs,
Obscene as cancer, bitter as the cud
Of vile, incurable sores on innocent tongues, —

My friend, you would not tell with such high zest
To children ardent for some desperate glory,
The old Lie: Dulce et decorum est
Pro patria mori.

Owen chooses as a form for his poem the alternately rhyming iambic pentameter four-line stanza known as the "heroic quatrain" because it was used for noble narratives. The irony of attaching its heroic lineage to the squalor and tragedy of gas warfare must have appealed to the revisionary poet. "Dulce et Decorum Est" reads at first like a realistic, unshaped report. Owen jams his quatrains together to obscure the regularity of his form (one can read the poem without realizing, at first, that it is written in rhyming quatrains). However, his report is "broken" by the shortest passage — the two-line recurrent dream of the dying gassed man — which is marked off from the rest of the poem not only by its brevity and its dream-based present tense, but also by its repetition of an identical rhyme-word: "drowning" rhymes with "drowning."

Regionality

When the generalized space of lyric — the vague spatial context, say, of "A slumber did my spirit seal" — gives way to a particular climate, geography, and scenery, we say that we have a regional poem. Wordsworth's poetry has made the Lake District of northern England a place of tourism and literary pilgrimage; Hopkins made the scenery of North Wales enter English poetry; Longfellow, Whittier, Frost, and Lowell became famous for their poems of New England; Robinson Jeffers immortalized Big Sur on the California coast; and Elizabeth Bishop, though American by birth, wrote many memorable poems about the landscapes of Brazil. These are only a few relatively recent examples. In older countries, descriptive poems (and landscape paintings) blanket the whole landscape: there is scarcely a town in Italy that has not been represented by a painter or a poet of classical or modern times.

The power of imagination to clothe a landscape in powerful allusive images is nowhere better seen than in Robert Lowell's "The Quaker Graveyard in Nantucket." This is a powerful, violent, and tumultuous poem, boiling up from the page as it follows the poet's meditations as he looks at the graveyard in Nantucket where the Quaker whalers buried their dead. Yet when one goes and looks at that very graveyard, it is simply a placid green slope, for the most part unmarked by headstones. It is Lowell's poem that has transformed that placid and uninformative space into a powerful container of ocean combers, whaling ships, wounded whales, harpoons, dead bodies, and fearful prayers. To visit the graveyard before, and then after, reading Lowell's poem is to see how regional poetry clothes the land in reminiscence, intimations of history, and imaginative power. The same is true of Longfellow's poem "The Jewish Cemetery in Newport." One might easily pass by an old cemetery with graves inscribed in Hebrew letters; but after reading Longfellow's meditation on the early Jewish settlers, now vanished into "the long, mysterious Exodus of death," one sees the cemetery with different eyes.

Though European colonizers thought the New World bare of culture, Native Americans had already consecrated certain lands and mountains as sacred, and had composed poetry about them. This first acculturation of space in the United States has been in great part lost, with many of the Indian languages and their oral literatures fallen into extinction. But an imaginative claim to American territory is now being repeated by Native American poets like Sherman Alexie, who recalls, in his poem "On the Amtrak from Boston to New York City," a wellmeaning woman whose ideas of American history, American landscape, and American literature start with the Revolutionary period and end with Thoreau:

SHERMAN ALEXIE (b. 1966)
On the Amtrak from Boston to New York City

The white woman across the aisle from me says, "Look,
look at all the history, that house
on the hill there is over two hundred years old,"
as she points out the window past me

into what she has been taught. I have learned
little more about American history during my few days
back East than what I expected and far less
of what we should all know of the tribal stories

whose architecture is 15,000 years older
than the corners of the house that sits
museumed on the hill. "Walden Pond,"
the woman on the train asks, "Did you see Walden Pond?"

and I don't have a cruel enough heart to break
her own by telling her there are five Walden Ponds
on my little reservation out West
and at least a hundred more surrounding Spokane,

the city I pretend to call my home. "Listen,"
I could have told her. "I don't give a shit
about Walden. I know the Indians were living stories
around that pond before Walden's grandparents were born

and before his grandparents' grandparents were born.
I'm tired of hearing about Don-fucking-Henley[1] saving it, too,
because that's redundant. If Don Henley's brothers and sisters
and mothers and fathers hadn't come here in the first place

then nothing would need to be saved."
But I didn't say a word to the woman about Walden
Pond because she smiled so much and seemed delighted
that I thought to bring her an orange juice

back from the food car. I respect elders
of every color. All I really did was eat
my tasteless sandwich, drink my Diet Pepsi
and nod my head whenever the woman pointed out

another little piece of her country's history
while I, as all Indians have done
since this war began, made plans
for what I would do and say the next time

somebody from the enemy thought I was one of their own.

The first English colonists, as Robert Frost says in "The Gift Outright," felt estranged in America because their own culture was English. They lived on land they had conquered, but they were still "unpossessed" by it. It was not until they (we) broke the tie to England, Frost argues, that we could give ourselves to the land "vaguely realizing westward, / But still unstoried, artless, unenhanced." It was the hope of writers to give that land stories, art, enhancement. By writing narrative poems like "The Wreck of the Hesperus" (about a wreck off the New England shore), "Evangeline" (about the exile of the Acadians), and Hiawatha (about Indians of New England), Longfellow hoped to give to the unstoried land the aura of legend. But Longfellow also wrote New England regional lyrics without narrative aim, like his famous poem about the coastal waters, "The Tide Rises, the Tide Falls":

> The tide rises, the tide falls,
> The twilight darkens, the curlew calls;

---

[1]Don Henley: A popular musician who organized benefit concerts to save Walden Pond from real estate developers.

Along the sea-sands damp and brown
The traveller hastens toward the town,
    And the tide rises, the tide falls.

Is this a poem that a poet who had grown up in Tulsa would write? Probably not; and in sensing that a child of the desert or the prairie would find rhythms not in the tides but perhaps in the winds, would write not about the wreck of the Hesperus but about the devastation caused by a tornado, we begin to see how the poetry of a large country like the United States (or Russia, or China) necessarily begins to have a large component of regional difference.

But the "regional" poet can also be one whose sense of a place is sharpened by coming to that landscape late in life. Elizabeth Bishop's poems of Brazil, such as "Questions of Travel," convey the mixed sense of estrangement combined with wonder and amazement that is felt by one to whom the tropics were a late revelation:

There are too many waterfalls here; the crowded streams
hurry too rapidly down to the sea,
and the pressure of so many clouds on the mountaintops
makes them spill over the sides in soft slow-motion,
turning to waterfalls under our very eyes. . . .

Should we have stayed at home and thought of here? . . .

But surely it would have been a pity
not to have seen the trees along this road,
really exaggerated in their beauty,
not to have seen them gesturing
like noble pantomimists, robed in pink. . . .

The poet never describes landscape without entering it kinesthetically, feeling the motion of the crowded streams, humanizing the trees into noble pantomimists. Landscape in poetry is always *projected outward from the writing self,* which has, before the composition of the poem, absorbed it and colored it with the personality of the writer. It is not "London" that we see in William Blake's "London," which begins, "I wander through each charter'd street," but rather London-as-interpreted-by-Blake. Similarly, it is not "London" that we see in Wordsworth's "Composed upon Westminster Bridge," but rather "London-as-interpreted-by-Wordsworth" or "Wordsworth-turned-into-London." Because Wordsworth loved tranquil and sublime scenery, the bustle of daytime London repelled him; yet he found a way to discover "his" London, a London that could resemble him and his way of being. It was the London of dawn, when the air was free of smoke and the Thames was free of barges and the streets free of noise, when the architectural features of the city seemed almost like items in a natural landscape:

William Wordsworth (1770 – 1850)
Composed upon Westminster Bridge, September 3, 1802

Earth hath not anything to show more fair:
Dull would he be of soul who could pass by
A sight so touching in its majesty:
This City now doth, like a garment, wear
The beauty of the morning; silent, bare,
Ships, towers, domes, theatres, and temples lie
Open unto the fields, and to the sky;
All bright and glittering in the smokeless air.
Never did sun more beautifully steep
In his first splendour, valley, rock, or hill;
Ne'er saw I, never felt, a calm so deep!
The river glideth at his own sweet will:
Dear God! the very houses seem asleep;
And all that mighty heart is lying still!

Just as the "history poem" must have a problem, and scenes to illustrate it, and a point of view from which to consider it, and a summing-up of insight somewhere in its close, so the "geography poem" must have a problem — and scenes, and a point of view, and a "solution," if only temporary, to the problem. That is, description is never "merely description." Wordsworth's powerful visual sense, repelled by daytime London, is nonetheless forced to concede aesthetic beauty to dawn London — is forced even to concede that the sight of man's most ambitious creative product — a city — is no less impressive than the sight of nature: "Never did sun more beautifully steep . . . valley, rock, or hill." As the list "valley, rock, or hill" is compared to the list "Ships, towers, domes, theatres, and temples," it is clear that the City wins. Nature has "majesty," of course, but its majesty is not "touching" as the majesty of the human city, a human product, is. Yet the beauty of the morning is only a temporary "garment" that the City briefly wears; and the tension between the satisfying, because unchanging, beauty of the valley or hill and the temporary, but touching, majesty of the City gives the poem its oscillations of feeling as the poet wrestles with his own taste, and concedes worth to the fallen majesty of the human over the serene majesty of his beloved nature.

In Brief: History and Regionality

In thinking about history poems, the main thing to remember is that there is always a tension between the copiousness of history and the brevity of lyric. To see how a structure as brief as lyric can present, speculate on, and judge history is to see a form straining against its own limits. When it succeeds, it strikes us as a triumph of style over difficulty. It is also useful to remember that the history poem has been a genre chiefly undertaken, until recently, by men, since they were the group admitted to warfare, political rights, and historical decision making. As women increasingly take on political responsibility, history will be "owned" by women as much as by men, and "poems on affairs of state" will be written by men and women alike. The notable public poems written in the last several years by such poets as Adrienne Rich, Amy Clampitt, and Jorie Graham (on such topics as the atomic bomb, the Vietnam War Memorial, and the B-52 bombers on perpetual alert) show the increasing intervention of women's poetry in political life.

When you encounter a poem of geography or regionality, ask yourself how it embodies a problem and how landscape has been "lyricized" — that is, made a bearer of human feeling. Usually there will be at least two points of view in the poem (as in Bishop's mixed feelings about Brazil, and Wordsworth's mixed feelings about London). These points of view represent an emotional, and even a moral, quarrel within the poet. As Marianne Moore says in "The Steeple-Jack," speaking of a New England town in a storm, "It is a privilege to see so / much confusion." And that is indubitably true. At the same time, her protagonist "sees boats // at sea progress white and rigid as if in / a groove" and likes that "elegance of which / the source is not bravado." Should the modern American poem throw itself open to the privilege of confusion, or should it have a formal elegance not defensive but self-generated? Moore wants — and attains — both; she is famous for her profusion of detail and her unobtrusive elegance of formulation. Her New England town is herself, and she becomes its displays, whether dynamic or rigid. It is always the author that the landscape reveals to us; and the landscape of lyric is always revelatory because the author is within it, projecting it from its preliminary reconstitution in the imagination.

Reading Other Poems

Ask yourself what the time-axis and the space-axis are for each of the poems that follow.

- ◆ Does the poem take place over time, and if so, how many episodes does it show? (You can trace, through "Tintern Abbey," Wordsworth's entire development to adulthood, from his "glad animal movements" as a child to his political disillusion to his present restoration.)
- ◆ Does the poem bring in several different spaces? (Look at "Tintern Abbey" and see whether it all takes place outdoors.)
- ◆ Some poems, like W. S. Merwin's "The Asians Dying" (about the Vietnam War), treat only one episode of time. How is that episode made significant?
- ◆ Does the poem refer, as Robert Hayden's does, to a time in the historical past? If so, what does that epoch mean to the speaker?
- ◆ Why would a nineteenth-century man such as Keats write a poem about ancient Greece?
- ◆ If the poem treats a contemporary episode (as Yeats treats the 1916 Irish insurrection), how is the chaos of history ordered into the brief space of a lyric?
- ◆ Does the poem move from space to space as it goes along, or does it remain in one place?
- ◆ How big is the space delineated in the poem? (That is, would Stevens's "Anecdote" be a different poem if it lacked the words "wilderness" or "Tennessee"?)
- ◆ If the poem treats imagined spaces (as Coleridge does in the fantastic visions of "Kubla Khan"), how are those spaces laid out and demarcated?

Derek Walcott writes the relatively new genre, the airplane poem: he takes off from Love Field, Dallas, and contemplates the state of the nation from an enormous height (a height no one could see from earlier than the twentieth century).

- ◆ What advantages (and disadvantages) come from writing at such a spatial distance?
- ◆ Does his adaptation of Dante's *terza rima* suggest a (perhaps hellish) expanse to be gazed at?

Jorie Graham contemplates a barbed-wire-enclosed field full of B-52 bombers on perpetual alert, kept running always in case they must respond instantly to an enemy threat. Her field of vision then takes in two more episodes — one of a marriage, one of the murder of the first poet, Orpheus.

- ◆ Can you link these three episodes, one in public space, one in private space, one in mythological space?

Lowell's "For the Union Dead," too, takes place in several spaces, and also over several times, stretching from the Revolutionary War to the poet's current America of forced school integration and New England decline (symbolized by the destruction of the Boston Common to make an underground garage for the cars that have invaded the city).

- ◆ Can you track Lowell's spaces and times, and suggest some reasons why the poem does not proceed chronologically in time or in some ordered spatial way?

Simon Ortiz's poem, too, is ordered by both space and time, as are many quest-poems.

- ◆ What are its temporal and spatial coordinates?
- ◆ What is the object of its quest?

Robert Hayden's poem enacts itself in a time and place tersely announced by its title. What do the two parts of the poem tell us about "night" and "Mississippi"?

The new narratives inserted by immigrants constitute important modifications of ideas of "Americanness" and of "history." Gary Soto's "History" is a reflection on the anonymity of immigrants, on the numerous untold stories behind their migration, their sorrows, and their joys. By giving the grand name "History" to his poem about one inconspicuous woman, Soto asks us to reflect on the sort of events we unreflectively call "history."

- ◆ Is his account chronological? If not, why not, do you think?

Silvia Curbelo, too, emphasizes the hidden history behind migration, as her Cuban "boat-person" encodes his past life in music.

- ◆ What three episodes from his previous life does music summon up for the balsero?

For Dionisio Martínez, growing up in a house where the first language is not English makes the child realize that an entire history precedes the family's arrival in an English-speaking country. That history is deduced only from fragmented conversations and angers.

◆ How does Martínez intertwine space, time, and language in "History as a Second Language"?

Samuel Taylor Coleridge (1772 – 1834)
Kubla Khan[1]

Or a Vision in a Dream. A Fragment

In Xanadu did Kubla Khan
A stately pleasure dome decree:
Where Alph, the sacred river, ran
Through caverns measureless to man
  Down to a sunless sea.   5
So twice five miles of fertile ground
With walls and towers were girdled round:
And there were gardens bright with sinuous rills,
Where blossomed many an incense-bearing tree;
And there were forests ancient as the hills,   10
Enfolding sunny spots of greenery.

But oh! that deep romantic chasm which slanted
Down the green hill athwart a cedarn cover!
A savage place! as holy and enchanted
As e'er beneath a waning moon was haunted   15
By woman wailing for her demon lover!
And from this chasm, with ceaseless turmoil seething,
As if this earth in fast thick pants were breathing,
A mighty fountain momently was forced:
Amid whose swift half-intermitted burst   20
Huge fragments vaulted like rebounding hail,
Or chaffy grain beneath the thresher's flail:
And 'mid these dancing rocks at once and ever
It flung up momently the sacred river.
Five miles meandering with a mazy motion   25
Through wood and dale the sacred river ran,
Then reached the caverns measureless to man,
And sank in tumult to a lifeless ocean:
And 'mid this tumult Kubla heard from far
Ancestral voices prophesying war!   30

---

[1]Ruler of the Mongol dynasty in thirteenth-century China. Coleridge has invented the topography and place names in the poem.

> The shadow of the dome of pleasure
> Floated midway on the waves;
> Where was heard the mingled measure
> From the fountain and the caves.
> It was a miracle of rare device,   35
> A sunny pleasure dome with caves of ice!

> A damsel with a dulcimer
> In a vision once I saw:
> It was an Abyssinian maid,
> And on her dulcimer she played,   40
> Singing of Mount Abora.
> Could I revive within me
> Her symphony and song,
> To such a deep delight 'twould win me,
> That with music loud and long,   45
> I would build that dome in air,
> That sunny dome! those caves of ice!
> And all who heard should see them there,
> And all should cry, Beware! Beware!
> His flashing eyes, his floating hair!   50
> Weave a circle round him thrice,
> And close your eyes with holy dread,
> For he on honey-dew hath fed,
> And drunk the milk of Paradise.

WILLIAM WORDSWORTH (1770 – 1850)

Lines Composed a Few Miles above Tintern Abbey on Revisiting the Banks of the Wye During a Tour

July 13, 1798

> Five years have passed; five summers, with the length
> Of five long winters! and again I hear
> These waters, rolling from their mountain-springs
> With a soft inland murmur. Once again
> Do I behold these steep and lofty cliffs,   5
> That on a wild secluded scene impress
> Thoughts of more deep seclusion; and connect
> The landscape with the quiet of the sky.
> The day is come when I again repose
> Here, under this dark sycamore, and view   10
> These plots of cottage ground, these orchard tufts,

Which at this season, with their unripe fruits,
Are clad in one green hue, and lose themselves
'Mid groves and copses. Once again I see
These hedgerows, hardly hedgerows, little lines   15
Of sportive wood run wild; these pastoral farms,
Green to the very door; and wreaths of smoke
Sent up, in silence, from among the trees!
With some uncertain notice, as might seem
Of vagrant dwellers in the houseless woods,   20
Or of some Hermit's cave, where by his fire
The Hermit sits alone.

         These beauteous forms,
Through a long absence, have not been to me
As is a landscape to a blind man's eye;   25
But oft, in lonely rooms, and 'mid the din
Of towns and cities, I have owed to them,
In hours of weariness, sensations sweet,
Felt in the blood, and felt along the heart;
And passing even into my purer mind,   30
With tranquil restoration — feelings too
Of unremembered pleasure; such, perhaps,
As have no slight or trivial influence
On that best portion of a good man's life,
His little, nameless, unremembered, acts   35
Of kindness and of love. Nor less, I trust,
To them I may have owed another gift,
Of aspect more sublime; that blessed mood,
In which the burthen of the mystery,
In which the heavy and the weary weight   40
Of all this unintelligible world,
Is lightened — that serene and blessed mood,
In which the affections gently lead us on —
Until, the breath of this corporeal frame
And even the motion of our human blood   45
Almost suspended, we are laid asleep
In body, and become a living soul;
While with an eye made quiet by the power
Of harmony, and the deep power of joy,
We see into the life of things.   50

         If this
Be but a vain belief, yet, oh! how oft —

In darkness and amid the many shapes
Of joyless daylight; when the fretful stir
Unprofitable, and the fever of the world,   55
Have hung upon the beatings of my heart —
How oft, in spirit, have I turned to thee,
O sylvan Wye! thou wanderer through the woods,
How often has my spirit turned to thee!

    And now, with gleams of half-extinguished thought,   60
With many recognitions dim and faint,
And somewhat of a sad perplexity,
The picture of the mind revives again;
While here I stand, not only with the sense
Of present pleasure, but with pleasing thoughts   65
That in this moment there is life and food
For future years. And so I dare to hope,
Though changed, no doubt, from what I was when first
I came among these hills; when like a roe
I bounded o'er the mountains, by the sides   70
Of the deep rivers, and the lonely streams,
Wherever nature led — more like a man
Flying from something that he dreads than one
Who sought the thing he loved. For nature then
(The coarser pleasures of my boyish days,   75
And their glad animal movements all gone by)
To me was all in all. — I cannot paint
What then I was. The sounding cataract
Haunted me like a passion; the tall rock,
The mountain, and the deep and gloomy wood,   80
Their colors and their forms, were then to me
An appetite; a feeling and a love,
That had no need of a remoter charm,
By thought supplied, nor any interest
Unborrowed from the eye. — That time is past,   85
And all its aching joys are now no more,
And all its dizzy raptures. Not for this
Faint I, nor mourn nor murmur; other gifts
Have followed; for such loss, I would believe,
Abundant recompense. For I have learned   90
To look on nature, not as in the hour
Of thoughtless youth; but hearing oftentimes
The still, sad music of humanity,

Nor harsh nor grating, though of ample power
To chasten and subdue. And I have felt   95
A presence that disturbs me with the joy
Of elevated thoughts; a sense sublime
Of something far more deeply interfused,
Whose dwelling is the light of setting suns,
And the round ocean and the living air,   100
And the blue sky, and in the mind of man:
A motion and a spirit, that impels
All thinking things, all objects of all thought,
And rolls through all things. Therefore am I still
A lover of the meadows and the woods,   105
And mountains; and of all that we behold
From this green earth; of all the mighty world
Of eye, and ear — both what they half create,
And what perceive; well pleased to recognize
In nature and the language of the sense   110
The anchor of my purest thoughts, the nurse,
The guide, the guardian of my heart, and soul
Of all my moral being.

                 Nor perchance,
If I were not thus taught, should I the more   115
Suffer my genial spirits to decay:
For thou art with me here upon the banks
Of this fair river; thou my dearest Friend,[1]
My dear, dear Friend; and in thy voice I catch
The language of my former heart, and read   120
My former pleasures in the shooting lights
Of thy wild eyes. Oh! yet a little while
May I behold in thee what I was once,
My dear, dear Sister! and this prayer I make,
Knowing that Nature never did betray   125
The heart that loved her; 'tis her privilege,
Through all the years of this our life, to lead
From joy to joy: for she can so inform
The mind that is within us, so impress
With quietness and beauty, and so feed   130
With lofty thoughts, that neither evil tongues,

---

[1]He is referring to his sister, Dorothy Wordsworth (1771–1855), writer and diarist.

Rash judgments, nor the sneers of selfish men,
Nor greetings where no kindness is, nor all
The dreary intercourse of daily life,
Shall e'er prevail against us, or disturb   135
Our cheerful faith, that all which we behold
Is full of blessings. Therefore let the moon
Shine on thee in thy solitary walk;
And let the misty mountain winds be free
To blow against thee: and, in after years,   140
When these wild ecstasies shall be matured
Into a sober pleasure; when thy mind
Shall be a mansion for all lovely forms,
Thy memory be as a dwelling place
For all sweet sounds and harmonies; oh! then,   145
If solitude, or fear, or pain, or grief
Should be thy portion, with what healing thoughts
Of tender joy wilt thou remember me,
And these my exhortations! Nor, perchance —
If I should be where I no more can hear   150
Thy voice, nor catch from thy wild eyes these gleams
Of past existence — wilt thou then forget
That on the banks of this delightful stream
We stood together; and that I, so long
A worshipper of Nature, hither came   155
Unwearied in that service; rather say
With warmer love — oh! with far deeper zeal
Of holier love. Nor wilt thou then forget,
That after many wanderings, many years
Of absence, these steep woods and lofty cliffs,   160
And this green pastoral landscape, were to me
More dear, both for themselves and for thy sake!

JOHN KEATS (1795 – 1821)
Ode on a Grecian Urn

1

Thou still unravished bride of quietness,
    Thou foster child of silence and slow time,
Sylvan historian, who canst thus express
    A flowery tale more sweetly than our rhyme:
What leaf-fringed legend haunts about thy shape

Of deities or mortals, or of both,
      In Tempe or the dales of Arcady?[1]
What men or gods are these? What maidens loath?
What mad pursuit? What struggle to escape?
      What pipes and timbrels? What wild ecstasy?

2

Heard melodies are sweet, but those unheard
      Are sweeter; therefore, ye soft pipes, play on;
Not to the sensual ear, but, more endeared,
      Pipe to the spirit ditties of no tone:
Fair youth, beneath the trees, thou canst not leave
      Thy song, nor ever can those trees be bare;
        Bold Lover, never, never canst thou kiss,
Though winning near the goal — yet, do not grieve;
        She cannot fade, though thou hast not thy bliss,
      Forever wilt thou love, and she be fair!

3

Ah, happy, happy boughs! that cannot shed
      Your leaves, nor ever bid the Spring adieu;
And, happy melodist, unwearièd,
      Forever piping songs forever new;
More happy love! more happy, happy love!
      Forever warm and still to be enjoyed,
        Forever panting, and forever young;
All breathing human passion far above,
      That leaves a heart high-sorrowful and cloyed,
        A burning forehead, and a parching tongue.

4

Who are these coming to the sacrifice?
      To what green altar, O mysterious priest,
Lead'st thou that heifer lowing at the skies,
      And all her silken flanks with garlands dressed?
What little town by river or sea shore,
      Or mountain-built with peaceful citadel,
        Is emptied of this folk, this pious morn?
And, little town, thy streets forevermore
      Will silent be; and not a soul to tell
        Why thou art desolate, can e'er return.

---

[1] Traditional pastoral landscapes.

                                    5

O Attic shape! Fair attitude! with brede°   *embroidery*
    Of marble men and maidens overwrought,
With forest branches and the trodden weed;
    Thou, silent form, dost tease us out of thought
As doth eternity: Cold Pastoral!
    When old age shall this generation waste,
       Thou shalt remain, in midst of other woe
    Than ours, a friend to man, to whom thou say'st,
"Beauty is truth, truth beauty, — that is all
       Ye know on earth, and all ye need to know."

WILLIAM BUTLER YEATS (1865 – 1939)
Easter 1916 [1]

I have met them at close of day
Coming with vivid faces
From counter or desk among grey
Eighteenth-century houses.
I have passed with a nod of the head   5
Or polite meaningless words,
Or have lingered awhile and said
Polite meaningless words,
And thought before I had done
Of a mocking tale or a gibe   10
To please a companion
Around the fire at the club,
Being certain that they and I
But lived where motley is worn:
All changed, changed utterly: 15
A terrible beauty is born.

That woman's days were spent
In ignorant good-will,
Her nights in argument
Until her voice grew shrill.   20
What voice more sweet than hers
When, young and beautiful,

---

[1]The title refers to the Easter Rebellion on April 24, 1916. Republicans seized buildings and a park in the center of Dublin. They were killed or captured by April 29 and the leaders were executed in May.

She rode to harriers?[2]
This man had kept a school
And rode our wingèd horse;[3]   25
This other his helper and friend[4]
Was coming into his force;
He might have won fame in the end,
So sensitive his nature seemed,
So daring and sweet his thought.   30
This other man I had dreamed
A drunken, vainglorious lout.[5]
He had done most bitter wrong
To some who are near my heart,
Yet I number him in the song;   35
He, too, has resigned his part
In the casual comedy;
He, too, has been changed in his turn,
Transformed utterly:
A terrible beauty is born.   40

Hearts with one purpose alone
Through summer and winter seem
Enchanted to a stone
To trouble the living stream.
The horse that comes from the road,   45
The rider, the birds that range
From cloud to tumbling cloud,
Minute by minute they change;
A shadow of cloud on the stream
Changes minute by minute;   50
A horse-hoof slides on the brim,
And a horse plashes within it;
The long-legged moor-hens dive,
And hens to moor-cocks call;
Minute by minute they live: 55

---

[2]Yeats's friend, Countess Markiewicz, née Constance Gore-Booth (1868–1927), was involved in the rebellion. Because she was a woman, she was not executed, and is therefore omitted from the final roll call.

[3]Patrick Pearse (1879–1916), the founder of St. Edna's School for Boys at Rathfarnhan near Dublin, was one of the leaders of the rebellion. He was also a poet. (The winged horse is Pegasus, a symbol of poetic inspiration.)

[4]Thomas MacDonagh (1878–1916), poet and dramatist.

[5]Major Thomas MacBride had been married to Maud Gonne, whom Yeats loved; they had divorced.

The stone's in the midst of all.

Too long a sacrifice
Can make a stone of the heart.
O when may it suffice?
That is Heaven's part, our part   60
To murmur name upon name,
As a mother names her child
When sleep at last has come
On limbs that had run wild.
What is it but nightfall?   65
No, no, not night but death;
Was it needless death after all?
For England may keep faith
For all that is done and said.[6]
We know their dream; enough   70
To know they dreamed and are dead;
And what if excess of love
Bewildered them till they died?
I write it out in a verse —
MacDonagh and MacBride   75
And Connolly and Pearse
Now and in time to be,
Wherever green is worn,
Are changed, changed utterly:
A terrible beauty is born.   80

WALLACE STEVENS (1879 – 1955)
Anecdote of the Jar

I placed a jar in Tennessee,
And round it was, upon a hill.
It made the slovenly wilderness
Surround that hill.

The wilderness rose up to it,
And sprawled around, no longer wild.
The jar was round upon the ground
And tall and of a port in air.

It took dominion everywhere.
The jar was gray and bare.

---

[6]England had promised Home Rule for Ireland.

It did not give of bird or bush,
Like nothing else in Tennessee.

ROBERT LOWELL (1917 – 1977)
For the Union Dead[1]

"Relinquunt Omnia Servare Rem Publicam."[2]

The old South Boston Aquarium stands
in a Sahara of snow now. Its broken windows are boarded.
The bronze weathervane cod[3] has lost half its scales.
The airy tanks are dry.

Once my nose crawled like a snail on the glass;   5
my hand tingled
to burst the bubbles
drifting from the noses of the cowed, compliant fish.

My hand draws back. I often sigh still
for the dark downward and vegetating kingdom   10
of the fish and reptile. One morning last March,
I pressed against the new barbed and galvanized

fence on the Boston Common.[4] Behind their cage,
yellow dinosaur steamshovels were grunting
as they cropped up tons of mush and grass   15
to gouge their underworld garage.[5]

Parking spaces luxuriate like civic
sandpiles in the heart of Boston.
A girdle of orange, Puritan-pumpkin colored girders
braces the tingling Statehouse,   20

---

[1]Soldiers who died fighting for the North in the Civil War. The poem is written about a bronze bas-relief opposite the Massachusetts State House on Beacon Street, in Boston; the monument, by Augustus St. Gaudens (1848–1897), commemorates Colonel Robert Gould Shaw (1837–1863), who commanded the first all-Negro regiment in the North and who was killed while leading an attack on Fort Wagner in South Carolina. The monument represents Shaw on horseback flanked by Negro foot soldiers.

[2]Lowell has changed the inscription on the monument from the singular to the plural, so that it reads: "They leave everything behind to serve the Republic."

[3]Codfish, the symbol of Boston.

[4]Park facing the State House.

[5]The construction of the garage beneath the Common was attended by graft and corruption.

shaking over the excavations, as it faces Colonel Shaw
and his bell-cheeked Negro infantry
on St. Gaudens' shaking Civil War relief,
propped by a plank splint against the garage's earthquake.

Two months after marching through Boston,   25
half the regiment was dead;
at the dedication,
William James[6] could almost hear the bronze Negroes breathe.

Their monument sticks like a fishbone
in the city's throat.   30
Its Colonel is as lean
as a compass-needle.

He has an angry wrenlike vigilance,
a greyhound's gentle tautness;
he seems to wince at pleasure,   35
and suffocate for privacy.

He is out of bounds now. He rejoices in man's lovely,
peculiar power to choose life and die —
when he leads his black soldiers to death,
he cannot bend his back.   40

On a thousand small town New England greens,
the old white churches hold their air
of sparse, sincere rebellion; frayed flags
quilt the graveyards of the Grand Army of the Republic.

The stone statues of the abstract Union Soldier   45
grow slimmer and younger each year —
wasp-waisted, they doze over muskets
and muse through their sideburns . . .

Shaw's father wanted no monument
except the ditch,   50
where his son's body was thrown
and lost with his "niggers."[7]

The ditch is nearer.
There are no statues for the last war here;

---

[6]Philosopher and psychologist (1842–1910).

[7]Shaw's father could have had his son's body brought home (officers had that privilege, while infantry were buried where they fell), but he refused, knowing his son's affection for his men.

on Boylston Street, a commercial photograph   55
shows Hiroshima boiling

over a Mosler Safe, the "Rock of Ages"
that survived the blast. Space is nearer.
When I crouch to my television set,
the drained faces of Negro school-children[8] rise like balloons.   60

Colonel Shaw
is riding on his bubble,
he waits
for the blessèd break.

The Aquarium is gone. Everywhere,   65
giant finned cars nose forward like fish;
a savage servility
slides by on grease.

ROBERT HAYDEN (1913 – 1980)
Night, Death, Mississippi

I

A quavering cry. Screech-owl?
Or one of them?
The old man in his reek
and gauntness laughs —

One of them, I bet —
and turns out the kitchen lamp,
limping to the porch to listen
in the windowless night.

Be there with Boy and the rest
if I was well again.
Time was. Time was.
White robes like moonlight

In the sweetgum dark.
Unbucked that one then
and him squealing bloody Jesus
as we cut it off.

---

[8]Schools in the South were being forcibly desegregated in 1960.

Time was. A cry?
A cry all right.
He hawks and spits,
fevered as by groinfire.

Have us a bottle,
Boy and me —
he's earned him a bottle —
when he gets home.

II

Then we beat them, he said,
beat them till our arms was tired
and the big old chains
messy and red.

O Jesus burning on the lily cross

Christ, it was better
than hunting bear
which don't know why
you want him dead.

O night, rawhead and bloodybones night

You kids fetch Paw
some water now so's he
can wash that blood
off him, she said.

O night betrayed by darkness not its own

W. S. MERWIN (b. 1927)
The Asians Dying

When the forests have been destroyed their darkness remains
The ash the great walker follows the possessors
Forever
Nothing they will come to is real
Nor for long
Over the watercourses
Like ducks in the time of the ducks
The ghosts of the villages trail in the sky
Making a new twilight

Rain falls into the open eyes of the dead
Again again with its pointless sound
When the moon finds them they are the color of everything
The nights disappear like bruises but nothing is healed
The dead go away like bruises
The blood vanishes into the poisoned farmlands

Pain the horizon
Remains
Overhead the seasons rock
They are paper bells
Calling to nothing living

The possessors move everywhere under Death their star
Like columns of smoke they advance into the shadows
Like thin flames with no light
They with no past
And fire their only future

DEREK WALCOTT (b. 1930)
The Gulf

For Jack and Barbara Harrison

I

The airport coffee tastes less of America.
Sour, unshaven, dreading the exertion
of tightening, racked nerves fuelled with liquor,

some smoky, resinous bourbon,
the body, buckling at its casket hole,
a roar like last night's blast racing its engines,

watches the fumes of the exhausted soul
as the trans-Texas jet, screeching, begins
its flight and friends diminish. So, to be aware

of the divine union the soul detaches
itself from created things. "We're in the air,"
the Texan near me grins. All things: these matches

from LBJ's[1] campaign hotel, this rose
given me at dawn in Austin by a child,
this book of fables by Borges,[2] its prose

---

[1]Lyndon Baines Johnson (1908–1975), thirty-sixth president of the United States.
[2]Jorge Luis Borges (1899–1986), Argentine writer.

a stalking, moonlit tiger. What was willed
on innocent, sun-streaked Dallas, the beast's claw
curled round that hairspring rifle[3] is revealed

on every page as lunacy or feral law;
circling that wound we leave Love Field.
Fondled, these objects conjure hotels,

quarrels, new friendships, brown limbs
nakedly moulded as these autumn hills
memory penetrates as the jet climbs

the new clouds over Texas; their home means
an island suburb, forest, mountain water;
they are the simple properties for scenes

whose joy exhausts like grief, scenes where we learn,
exchanging the least gifts, this rose, this napkin,
that those we love are objects we return,

that this lens on the desert's wrinkled skin
has priced our flesh, all that we love in pawn
to that brass ball, that the gifts, multiplying,

clutter and choke the heart, and that I shall
watch love reclaim its things as I lie dying.
My very flesh and blood! Each seems a petal

shrivelling from its core. I watch them burn,
by the nerves' flare I catch their skeletal
candour! Best never to be born,

the great dead cry. Their works shine on our shelves,
by twilight tour their gilded gravestone spines,
and read until the lamplit page revolves

to a white stasis whose detachment shines
like a propeller's rainbowed radiance.
Circling like us; no comfort for their loves!

II

The cold glass darkens. Elizabeth wrote once
that we make glass the image of our pain;
I watch clouds boil past the cold, sweating pane

---

[3]Reference to the assassination of President John F. Kennedy in Dallas on November 22, 1963.

above the Gulf. All styles yearn to be plain
as life. The face of the loved object under glass
is plainer still. Yet, somehow, at this height,

above this cauldron boiling with its wars,
our old earth, breaking to familiar light,
that cloud-bound mummy with self-healing scars

peeled of her cerements again looks new;
some cratered valley heals itself with sage,
through that grey, fading massacre a blue

lighthearted creek flutes of some siege
to the amnesia of drumming water.
Their cause is crystalline: the divine union

of these detached, divided states, whose slaughter
darkens each summer now, as one by one,
the smoke of bursting ghettos clouds the glass

down every coast where filling station signs
proclaim the Gulf, an air, heavy with gas,
sickens the state, from Newark to New Orleans.

III

Yet the South felt like home. Wrought balconies,
the sluggish river with its tidal drawl,
the tropic air charged with the extremities

of patience, a heat heavy with oil,
canebrakes, that legendary jazz. But fear
thickened my voice, that strange, familiar soil

prickled and barbed the texture of my hair,
my status as a secondary soul.
The Gulf, your gulf, is daily widening,

each blood-red rose warns of that coming night
when there's no rock cleft to go hidin' in
and all the rocks catch fire, when that black might,

their stalking, moonless panthers turn from Him
whose voice they can no more believe, when the black X's
mark their passover with slain seraphim.

IV

The Gulf shines, dull as lead. The coast of Texas
glints like a metal rim. I have no home
as long as summer bubbling to its head

boils for that day when in the Lord God's name
the coals of fire are heaped upon the head
of all whose gospel is the whip and flame,

age after age, the uninstructing dead.

SIMON J. ORTIZ (b. 1941)
Bend in the River

Flicker flies by.
His ochre wing
is tied to prayer sticks.
Pray for mountains,
the cold strong shelter.

Sun helps me to see
where Arkansas River
ripples over pebbles.
Glacial stone moves slowly;
it will take a while.

A sandbank cuts sharply
down to a poplar log
buried in damp sand.
Shadow lengths tell me
it is afternoon.

There are tracks
at river's edge, raccoon,
coyote, deer, crow,
and now my own.

My sight follows
the river upstream
until it bends.
Beyond the bend
is more river
and, soon, the mountains.
We shall arrive,
to see, soon.

Jorie Graham (b. 1950)
What the End Is For

Grand Forks, North Dakota

A boy just like you took me out to see them,
  the five hundred B–52's on alert on the runway,
fully loaded fully manned pointed in all the directions,
  running every minute
of every day.   5
  They sound like a sickness of the inner ear,

where the heard foams up into the noise of listening,
  where the listening arrives without being extinguished.
The huge hum soaks up into the dusk.
  The minutes spring open. Six is too many.   10
From where we watch,
  from where even watching is an anachronism,

from the 23rd of March from an open meadow,
  the concertina wire in its double helix
designed to tighten round a body if it turns   15
  is the last path the sun can find to take out,
each barb flaring gold like a braille being read,
  then off with its knowledge and the sun
is gone. . . .

That's when the lights on all the extremities, like an outline 20
   like a dress,
  become loud in the story,
and a dark I have not seen before
  sinks in to hold them one
by one.   25
  Strange plot made to hold so many inexhaustible
screams.
  Have you ever heard in a crowd mutterings of
blame

that will not modulate that will not rise?   30
  He tells me, your stand-in, they *stair-step* up.
He touches me to have me look more deeply
  in
to where for just a moment longer
  color still lives: 35
the belly white so that it looks like sky, the top

some kind of brown, some soil — How does it look
from up there now
     this meadow we lie on our bellies in, this field Iconography
tells me stands for sadness   40
     because the wind can move through it uninterrupted?
What is it the wind
     would have wanted to find and didn't

leafing down through this endless admiration unbroken
     because we're too low for it   45
to find us?
     Are you still there for me now in that dark
we stood in for hours
     letting it sweep as far as it could down over us
unwilling to move, irreconcilable? What *he*   50
     wants to tell me,

his whisper more like a scream
     over this eternity of engines never not running,
is everything: how the crews assigned to each plane
     for a week at a time, the seven boys, must live   55
inseparable,
     how they stay together for life,
how the wings are given a life of
     seven feet of play,

how they drop practice bombs called *shapes* over Nevada,   60
     how the measures for counterattack in air
have changed and we
     now forego firepower for jamming, for the throwing
of false signals. The meadow, the meadow hums, love, with
         the planes,   65
     as if every last blade of grass were wholly possessed

by this practice, wholly prepared. The last time I saw you,
     we stood facing each other as dusk came on.
I leaned against the refrigerator, you leaned against the door.
     The picture window behind you was slowly extinguished,   70
the tree went out, the two birdfeeders, the metal braces on them.
     The light itself took a long time,

bits in puddles stuck like the useless
     splinters of memory, the chips
of history, hopes, laws handed down. *Here, hold these* he says,   75
     these grasses these

torn pods, he says, smiling over the noise another noise, *take these*
    he says, my hands wrong for
the purpose, here,
    not-visible-from-the-sky, prepare yourself with these, boy   80
      and
bouquet of
    thistleweed and wort and william and
timothy. We stood there. Your face went out a long time
    before the rest of it. Can't see you anymore I said. *Nor I,*   85
you, whatever you still were
    replied.
When I asked you to hold me you refused.
    When I asked you to cross the six feet of room to hold me

you refused. Until I   90
    couldn't rise out of the patience either any longer
to make us
    take possession.
Until we were what we must have wanted to be:
    shapes the shapelessness was taking back.   95
Why should I lean out?
    Why should I move?
When the Maenads tear Orpheus limb from limb,
    they throw his head

out into the river.[1]   100
    Unbodied it sings
all the way downstream, all the way to the single ocean,
    head floating in current downriver singing,
until the sound of the cataracts grows,
    until the sound of the open ocean grows and the voice.   105

Gary Soto (b. 1952)

History

Grandma lit the stove.
Morning sunlight
Lengthened in spears
Across the linoleum floor.

---

[1]Orpheus was torn to pieces by Maenads, savage female followers of Dionysus, god of drunkenness and revelry. Orpheus's severed head, floating down the Thracian river, Hebrus, reached the island of Lesbos, the home of lyric poetry, where it was buried.

Wrapped in a shawl,   5
Her eyes small
With sleep,
She sliced *papas,*°   *potatoes*
Pounded chiles
With a stone   10
Brought from Guadalajara.

                          After
Grandpa left for work,
She hosed down
The walk her sons paved   15
And in the shade
Of a chinaberry,
Unearthed her
Secret cigar box
Of bright coins   20
And bills, counted them
In English,
Then in Spanish,
And buried them elsewhere.
Later, back   25
From the market,
Where no one saw her,
She pulled out
Pepper and beet, spines
Of asparagus   30
From her blouse,
Tiny chocolates
From under a paisley bandana,
And smiled.

That was the fifties   35
And Grandma in her fifties,
A face streaked
From cutting grapes
And boxing plums.
I remember her insides   40
Were washed of tapeworm,
Her arms swelled into knobs
Of small growths —
Her second son
Dropped from a ladder   45

And was dust.
And yet I do not know
The sorrows
That sent her praying
In the dark of a closet,   50
The tear that fell
At night
When she touched loose skin
Of belly and breasts.
I do not know why   55
Her face shines.
Or what goes beyond this shine,
Only the stories
That pulled her
From Taxco° to San Joaquin,   *a town and county in southern*   60
Delano to Westside,   *Mexico*
The places
In which we all begin.

Silvia Curbelo (b. 1955)
Balsero[1] Singing

When he opens his mouth
he is drifting, he is
in the air, and the child

he's remembering leans out
of some dark window
in his head. The sunlight

is incidental, falling
all around him like a word
or a wing. In another dream

he is dancing in a cottage by the sea
and music is a language he has just
learned to speak, the cool *yes*

of her throat. The sky goes on
for days with its one cloud waving,
the song lifting him like a sail.

---

[1]Refugee from Cuba in a raft, or *balsa*.

The real boat is lost
at sea, one voice nailed
to the planks of history, salt

on the tongue of thirty years.
A window empties
its small cargo —

an eyelash, grief. Each new breath
is a harbor, then a wave
closes over it

like a book.

Dionisio Martínez (b. 1956)
History as a Second Language

I grew up hearing the essence
of conversations in the next room.
My father and his friends conspired
in the next room. The new regime
succeeded in spite of their plot.
The next room is usually dark. People
whisper in it. You hear only so much.
Just enough if you know what to listen for.
I thought I heard a murder in the next
room. It was the radio. I thought
I heard a murder long after the radio
had been thrown against the wall and smashed
to bits. It was a whore at the end of
a long day. Families like mine
always managed to have a whore or two
as "good" friends. It made us look
less rich, less whatever being rich meant.
In those days things became
the meanings we gave them and not the other
way around, not like today. The next room
meant the room next door. If you looked
hard enough, you could see through the wall.
The specifics of a conversation
were not necessary to understand a plot
or a confession; the blurred
view through the wall was enough

to know more or less how the whores
earned their pay, how a government
might have failed, how a single threat
would keep a family together through war
and sabotage. The room next door
made us what we became with time in exile:
failed lovers, experts in the mechanics
of things we never learned to name.

9

Attitudes, Values, Judgments

You're under no obligation to like all the remarks or attitudes you come across in art. Past artists reflect the prejudices and beliefs of their time, just as our twenty-first-century writers will reveal, to later readers, the (frequently unconscious) presumptions and beliefs of our era. It is notoriously hard to believe that morally we are much superior to our ancestors. Social attitudes may progress in one or another area (we in America no longer recommend public hangings or beheadings), but we are sure to seem as backward and ignorant to our descendants as even our recent ancestors seem to us.

Nor are artists necessarily morally better than others in their private or public actions. Genius does not guarantee moral probity in the ordinary activities of life. What, then, are the moral obligations of artists insofar as they are artists? (As people, they exist under the same moral imperatives as anyone else, and are conditioned by their cultures in their interpretation of those imperatives.) How — to put our question another way — can artists betray their artistic principles?

They can betray themselves as artists, and their art itself, by saying what society wants to hear, rather than what seems true; by papering over the actual with the agreeable or the socially enjoined; by falling into the comfortable habits of the past instead of reinventing their medium. If, however, the artist has the talent to work the medium accurately — to reveal in stylized language the structure of reality as it is delivered by perception, emotion, and thought — without being cowed by convention or audience response, there is a chance that the artwork will succeed.

This does not mean that a work has to be composed entirely freely, with no external conditions laid upon it. On the contrary. Many commissioned artworks have been spectacularly successful — Michelangelo's paintings in the Sistine Chapel, Bach's cantatas for Sunday services, Milton's "Lycidas," written for an anthology of verse compiled in honor of a schoolfellow who was drowned. In fact, nothing is more stimulating to some artists than a patron's saying, "I'd like you to make a painting in a semicircular shape to fit that space over the door; and I'd like it to represent Apollo; and you may have exactly four ounces of gold leaf to decorate it with." Poetry is less often commissioned than music, sculpture, or painting, yet William Blake represents his *Songs of Innocence* as "commissioned" by a child-Muse:

> Piping down the valleys wild
> Piping songs of pleasant glee
> On a cloud I saw a child,
> And he laughing said to me,
>
> "Pipe a song about a Lamb";
> So I piped with merry cheer.
> "Piper, pipe that song again" —
> So I piped, he wept to hear.

And Shakespeare's sonnets seem to have begun as a commissioned sequence urging an aristocratic young man to marry and beget an heir.

A poem sometimes seeks out its own commissions, so to speak, by casting itself as a letter replying to a request or a question. Gerard Manley Hopkins's friend and fellow poet Robert Bridges asks Hopkins, in a letter, why he has sent him no poems lately. In response, Hopkins sends a verse-letter in the form of a sonnet ("To R.B.") explaining that inspiration has forsaken him:

> Sweet fire, the sire of muse, my soul needs this;
> I want the one rapture of an inspiration.
> Oh then if in my lagging lines you miss
> The roll, the rise, the carol, the creation,
> My winter world, that scarcely breathes that bliss,
> Now yields you, with some sighs, our explanation.

We may suppose that this poem might never have been written without the pressure of Bridges's "commissioning" question. It is always useful, in considering the attitudes of a poem, to ask what has occasioned it. Has an anterior question, reproach, or command brought it into being? If we do not ask this question, we are likely to mistake the poem's attitudes, values, and tone.

Consider the following example:

WILLIAM SHAKESPEARE (1564 – 1616)
Sonnet 76

> Why is my verse so barren of new pride?
> So far from variation or quick change?
> Why with the time do I not glance aside
> To new-found methods and to compounds strange?
> Why write I still all one, ever the same,
> And keep invention in a noted weed,°   *well-known garment*
> That every word doth almost tell my name,
> Showing their birth, and where they did proceed?
> O know, sweet love, I always write of you,
> And you and love are still my argument;
> So all my best is dressing old words new,
> Spending again what is already spent:
> > For as the sun is daily new and old,
> > So is my love, still telling what is told.

Shakespeare's Sonnet 76 has usually been read as a self-interrogation in which Shakespeare laments the barrenness and sameness of his poems. Improbably enough, according to this reading, Shakespeare thought ill of his own work, accusing himself of a boring similarity in all his poems:

> Why is my verse so barren of new pride?
> So far from variation or quick change?
> Why with the time do I not glance aside
> To new-found methods and to compounds strange?
> Why write I still all one, ever the same,
> And keep invention in a noted weed,
> That every word doth almost tell my name,
> Showing their birth and where they did proceed?

If this were all we had of the poem, we might indeed think Shakespeare is reproaching himself. But the next part of the sonnet shows that this is an "answer-poem," replying to an implied question previously asked by Shakespeare's young patron: "Why do you bring me nothing but sonnets, old-fashioned poems?" Shakespeare replies, "O know, sweet love, I always write of you":

> And you and love are still my argument;
> So all my best is dressing old words new,
> Spending again what is already spent:
> >   For as the sun is daily new and old,
> >   So is my love, still telling what is told.

Armed with this knowledge of implied question and answer, we can now better imagine the "antecedent scenario" of the poem. The fashionable young man, who has by now received many sonnets from Shakespeare, is surprised that his poet keeps writing in this old-fashioned form, already in existence for over two hundred years. Other poets have gone on to new things. Why can't his poet write a satire, or a picturesque mini-narrative, or a debate-poem? "Why," says the up-to-date young man to the poet, "are you always writing the same old sonnets, all the same sort, so that everyone who sees them says, 'Oh, of course, another piece by Shakespeare'?" And he continues, "How about doing something new next time?" Shakespeare, only too conscious of the young man's ignorant and trendy dismissal of his incomparable poems, gives the soft answer that turns away wrath, repeating and quoting the young man's reproach, but finding nonetheless a way to defend himself. We can now reconstruct the poem as it should be read: not as Shakespeare's reproach to himself but as his reproof of the young man:

> *Why* [you ask] is my verse so barren of "new pride"?
> So far from "variation" or "quick change"?
> *Why* with the time do I not glance aside
> To "new-found methods" and to "compounds strange"?
> *Why* write I still "all one," "ever the same,"
> And keep invention in a "noted weed,"
> That every word doth almost "tell my name,"
> Showing their birth and where they did proceed?
> O know, sweet love, I always write of you,
> And you and love are still my argument;
> So all my best is dressing old words new,
> Spending again what is already spent:
> >   For as the sun is daily new and old,
> >   So is my love, still telling what is told.

This deft but gentle rebuke reminds the young man, at the close, that nobody looks up at the sky at dawn and says, "The sun again! How boring and repetitive!" There are things so precious — the sun and love being among them — that we never have enough of them. And poetry, after all, never has new *words* — all the words are already present in the language. The only thing *any* poet can do is "dress [that is, arrange] old words new," re-spending the words that poetic predecessors have already spent.

Our view of the attitudes expressed by the speaker in this sonnet depends very much on whether we see it as *self-reproach* or as a *rebuke to the young man*. This reminds us that before we can evaluate the attitudes and values expressed in a poem we must try to be as accurate as possible in describing them. These are delicate questions; and the sophistication of poems (and of the people who write them) warns us against too hasty a judgment. One has to understand a poem well before judging it. (And really understanding the implications of a poem usually depends on having read many other poems by that poet.)

Evaluation depends on where you stand with respect to the things described in a poem. Until fairly recently, the poems that Langston Hughes wrote about Harlem — representing such realities as sexual intercourse before marriage, marital infidelity, children born out of wedlock, prostitution and pimping, and the strife between Jewish landlords and black tenants — were simply not represented in general anthologies of American poetry or anthologies of poetry by blacks. Much of Hughes's subject matter seemed indecent to whites and blacks alike; and black anthologists wanted to print poems that were "a credit to the race." Hughes's veracity — his refusal to betray the structure of reality as he saw it for something more acceptable — is today much admired, but was in his lifetime often criticized. Judges were judging not his art — represented in his striking sequences on Harlem and his adaptation of jazz rhythms — but what they saw as his failure to condemn immorality, on the one hand, and his washing dirty social linen in public, on the other.

It is not desirable to let a difference in values blind us to the imaginative mastery of language and form in such poets as the atheist Robinson Jeffers (whose nihilism was much criticized) or the social realists Langston Hughes and Allen Ginsberg. The nineteenth-century anthologists who censored Charles Baudelaire's depiction of lesbianism are replaced in our day by those who censor Ginsberg's depiction of homosexuality. The accurate representation of reality is, for the artist, the highest morality. It is immoral to conceal the way human beings live, or what human beings think. The tension between allowing an artist free expression and, for instance, shielding the sensibilities of the young is a real one; and most societies have worked out a gradual scale according to which the young can be exposed to art of increasing moral complexity.

However, in countries with active political or religious censorship, where free expression is not permitted at all, artists perform marvelous end-runs around forbidden topics. During the Cold War years, ingenious Eastern European poets in Russia, Poland, Hungary, and other Iron Curtain countries constructed allegorical poems which were seemingly "harmless" but which everyone could read as a coded critique of the regime. Even under censorship, art will find a way to be free — though sometimes the artist may suffer imprisonment and death.

It is impossible not to notice the attitudes and values expressed in a poem. In fact, they are often the first thing we do notice. Yet a criticism of attitudes and values alone does not come to grips with what a poet really has to offer, which is a personal sense of the world, an idiosyncratic temperament, a unique imagination, and a new linguistic lens through which readers may see the world afresh.

How, then, are we to evaluate the success of a poem if we cannot base our judgment on its attitudes and values? Robert Lowell, in the poem "Epilogue," printed last in his final book, *Day by Day,* suggests one way. Despairing of his unrhymed modern "snapshots" of reality, he asks why he can't make something as beautiful as the radiant interiors painted by the seventeenth-century Dutch artist Jan Vermeer. He is thinking particularly of one painting, which shows a girl reading a letter; Lowell imagines her "yearning" for its absent writer. She stands by a casement window from which light steals across the wall behind her, illuminating the map on the wall (which is, in Vermeer and elsewhere, a figure for the abstraction of art). Here is the poem:

ROBERT LOWELL (1917 – 1977)

Epilogue

Those blessèd structures, plot and rhyme —
why are they no help to me now
I want to make
something imagined, not recalled?
I hear the noise of my own voice:
The painter's vision is not a lens,
it trembles to caress the light.
But sometimes everything I write

with the threadbare art of my eye
seems a snapshot
lurid, rapid, garish, grouped,
heightened from life,
yet paralyzed by fact.
All's misalliance.
Yet why not say what happened?
Pray for the grace of accuracy
Vermeer gave to the sun's illumination
stealing like the tide across a map
to his girl solid with yearning.
We are poor passing facts,
warned by that to give
each figure in the photograph
his living name.

At its middle, the poem collapses in despair: "All's misalliance." But then the poet gets a second wind: What is wrong with describing his life truthfully as he sees it? "Yet why not say what happened?" He resolves his poem by realizing that though his "snapshots" may not look superficially like Vermeer's paintings, he and Vermeer have in common the artist's truest motive — accuracy of representation. The artist can vow accuracy, but he or she must pray for the other ingredient in successful art — grace. "Pray for *the grace of accuracy*," the poet tells himself. One part of his function as a poet is a duty to set down contemporary facts of life before they disappear; but he can only hope and pray that by the grace of aesthetic power he can give to the people of his century (who will otherwise be anonymous numbers in a census, "poor passing facts") their "living name." That living name is conferred only by the *grace* of art — its aesthetic power that often seems bestowed from the outside, like religious "grace." By the end of the poem, the poet can stop referring to his work by the ugly and clipped word "snapshot," and can speak of it as "writing with light" — a "photo-graph." He, like Vermeer, will also become a writer with light if he can attain "the grace of accuracy."[*]

This poem suggests that we must judge any poem we read as a representation of its author's perception of reality; but we must also judge it as an experiment in its medium, according to its portion of "grace" — what Hopkins called "the roll, the rise, the carol, the creation."

If, in one direction, we judge poetry, it is also true that in another direction the poem judges us. It looks at us with a steady gaze and dares us to judge ourselves by its revelations. "The poet judges, not as the judge judges but as the sun falling around a helpless thing," said Walt

Whitman. To observe and convey reality is itself a judgment on reality, even if the poem makes no explicit judgment on the reality conveyed.

Rita Dove, a contemporary African American poet, writes about the "poetic justice" of art in a poem about a painting she saw in Germany by a modern painter, Christian Schad. He had painted, in the twenties, in Berlin, a portrait of two circus "freaks": one of them was a man with a bone disease that caused his shoulder bones to protrude like wings. He was billed as "Agosta the Winged Man." The other "freak" was a perfectly normal black woman who, billed as "Rasha, the Black Dove," was displayed as an exotic jungle creature, dancing entwined with a boa constrictor. The black Rita Dove, seeing "the Black Dove" — who, but for an accident of time, could have been herself — depicts Schad, the painter, planning the double portrait he is about to begin, attempting to decide where its power will lie. Is it in the mercilessness of his unsparing view of his subjects? No,

> The canvas,
> not his eye, was merciless. . . .
>
> Schad would place him°   *Agosta*
> on a throne, a white sheet tucked
> over his loins, the black suit jacket
> thrown off like a cloak.
> Agosta had told him
>   of the medical students
> at the Charité,°   *a hospital*
> that chill arena
>
>   where he perched on
> a cot, his torso
> exposed, its crests and fins
> a colony of birds, trying
> to get out . . .
>   and the students,
> lumps caught
> in their throats, taking notes.
>
> Ah, Rasha's
>   foot on the stair.
> She moved slowly, as if she carried
> the snake around her body
> always. . . .

                        Agosta in
classical drapery, then,
and Rasha at his feet.
Without passion. Not
the canvas
                        but their gaze,
                        so calm,
        was merciless.

Is it the painter's eye, seeing the social marginalization of his subjects
(one black, one deformed) that is merciless in its accuracy? Or is it the
canvas, demanding how paint shall be used, and how the picture will be
composed, that is merciless? Schad decides that neither of these is true.
It is neither his eye nor the canvas that is merciless, but the gaze of his
two subjects, saying, "Here we are. This is how we were seen, in Berlin,
in 1929." The gaze is merciless because it is, like the portrait which
depicts it, "without passion." The painting is not propaganda; it is not
"social protest art"; it is simply an accurate transcription (with the
"grace" of its compositional arrangements with which Schad has taken
such care) of "Reality, Berlin, 1929." Nothing more than this is neces-
sary; but how hard it is to ensure that the eye and the canvas and the gaze
maintain this accuracy of perception — without exaggeration, without
deletion.

    There have been other suggestions by poets on how to make and
judge art, each understandable within its culture and its century. The
religious poet George Herbert thought that if one wrote for God alone,
one would write well: "If I please him, I write fine and wittie." Similarly,
Milton said, in "Lycidas," that the poet should look for true fame only
from the "pure eyes / And perfect witness of all-judging Jove." These
reflections suggest that the poets did not find the immediate judgment of
contemporaries a reliable measure for any poet.

    We, too, can be warned by such remarks that poems that last for a
long time tend to satisfy many criteria of success, and to interest many
generations of future writers. It is, in the last analysis, chiefly by the
admiration of other writers that writers become "canonized." In one
strand of the canonical male line (male because until recently only males
were educated in complex uses of language) Spenser admires Chaucer,
John Milton admires Spenser, Wordsworth admires Milton, Keats
admires Wordsworth, Tennyson admires Keats, Eliot admires Tennyson,
Auden admires Eliot, Merrill admires Auden, and so it has gone. It is no

accident that almost every contemporary woman poet in America, from Adrienne Rich through Jorie Graham to Lucie Brock-Broido, has written a poem to or about Emily Dickinson, or that Dickinson herself wrote a poem about her favorite woman poet, Elizabeth Barrett Browning, or that Elizabeth Bishop wrote a poem to Marianne Moore, creating a comparable ongoing line of female "canonization." It is also true that canonization crosses gender lines: T. S. Eliot and Wallace Stevens and William Carlos Williams and A. R. Ammons admired the poetry of Marianne Moore; Hopkins admired Christina Rossetti; Dickinson admired Emerson; and Moore admired La Fontaine. It is the admiration of poets for each other's accomplishments in the medium of language that keeps poetry alive; and poets keep poetry honest in their fine-tuned admiration of any writing that is not only "accurate with respect to the structures of reality" but also full of "the grace of accuracy," giving the "poor passing facts" of every era their "living name."

In Brief: Attitudes, Values, Judgments

If we keep the honorific name "poetry" to mean "verse that succeeds in achieving lasting interest over time," we are still uncertain of the amount of "poetry" being produced by our own century. There is a great deal of verse being written, all of it, of course, of documentary interest to sociologists or anthropologists or cultural critics. For such scholars, the overt message, or representation of life in a poem, means more than the skill with which that message or representation has been arranged. We all read for message and picture, but readers with a strong commitment to poetry as an art require in it those new symbolic structures, invented by talented artists of every age, that both affront and refresh. An experienced reader of poetry is soon bored by the already known and the clichéd; but the previously unheard, the previously unknown, arranged in a form true to a temperament, and transmitting a shock of pleasure — this makes for the renewal of both life and art. It is this capacity of poetry to rewrite the old that we value in it, that we search out in it, and that we judge it by.

Reading Other Poems

Each of the following poems expresses a strong moral attitude: that is, at least two sets of opposing values are presented, and the poet (through a sympathetic or unsympathetic speaker) comes out in favor of one set. This entails describing, or at least implying, the contrasting set of values that the poet repudiates.

- ◆ In each poem, trace the way the repudiated value is presented — whether in Phillis Wheatley's advocacy of Christianity over paganism, or John Milton's corrupt bishops, or Rita Dove's dictator, or Walt Whitman's astronomer, or William Butler Yeats's imperial rulers, or Louise Glück's speaker's sexual partner.
- ◆ Does the poet imply that the reader already agrees with his or her preferred value?

Sometimes the poet's preference may be surprising (see Jonson, Lovelace, Whitman, and Glück). The woman poet has to examine the clichés of women's advancement. In these cases, when the poet cannot count on the agreement of the reader, what sort of persuasive means does he or she employ?

Sometimes a poem which seems to express values admired by the poet's contemporaries can later be subject to question. Robert Frost was invited to read his 1942 sonnet "The Gift Outright" at the inauguration of President John F. Kennedy.

- ◆ What are the patriotic values expressed in the sonnet?
- ◆ How might they be viewed now by a Native American reader? How do you respond when you read both "with the grain" of the poem and also "against the grain"?

It is a useful exercise to read strongly moral poems from the poet's view and also from a different viewpoint.

- ◆ What might Lucasta have said back to the man going off to war; or Ben Jonson's addressee back to the poet; or an astronomer back to Whitman?
- ◆ How might the recipient of Elizabeth Barrett Browning's love-sonnet have felt? (Would you want to be loved "with the passion put to use" of abandoned religious belief?)
- ◆ What would a believer in original sin make of Ginsberg's "Sunflower Sutra," with its belief in original innocence?
- ◆ How might the man accused in Heidy Steidlmayer's "Knife-Sharpener's Song" respond to her account of his infidelity?

Dove, though she opposes the slave-holding and slave-murdering Dominican dictator Rafael Trujillo, lets him speak and articulate his motives in order that her reader may get inside his mind. Though finally, in reading these poems, you may come to sympathize with the poet's view, it is useful to position yourself, at least temporarily, on both sides of the question being debated. That way you sharpen your sense of the attitudes being expressed, the values being contested, and the judgments being made.

JOHN MILTON (1608 – 1674)
Lycidas

> In this monody[1] the author bewails a learned friend, unfortunately drowned in his passage from Chester on the Irish seas, 1637. And by occasion foretells the ruin of our corrupted clergy, then in their height.

Yet once more, O ye laurels, and once more
Ye myrtles brown, with ivy never sere,
I come to pluck your berries harsh and crude,
And with forced fingers rude,
Shatter your leaves before the mellowing year.   5
Bitter constraint, and sad occasion dear,
Compels me to disturb your season due;
For Lycidas is dead, dead ere his prime,
Young Lycidas, and hath not left his peer.
Who would not sing for Lycidas? He knew   10
Himself to sing, and build the lofty rhyme.
He must not float upon his watery bier
Unwept, and welter to the parching wind,
Without the meed of some melodious tear.
Begin then, sisters of the sacred well°   *muses*   15
That from beneath the seat of Jove doth spring,
Begin, and somewhat loudly sweep the string.
Hence with denial vain, and coy excuse;
So may some gentle Muse°   *poet*
With lucky words favor my destined urn,   20
And as he passes turn,
And bid fair peace be to my sable shroud.
For we were nursed upon the selfsame hill,
Fed the same flock, by fountain, shade, and rill.
Together both, ere the high lawns appeared   25
Under the opening eyelids of the morn,
We drove afield, and both together heard
What time the grayfly winds her sultry horn,

---

[1] A dirge sung by a single voice.

Battening our flocks with the fresh dews of night,
Oft till the star that rose at evening bright   30
Toward Heaven's descent had sloped his westering wheel.
Meanwhile the rural ditties were not mute,
Tempered to th' oaten flute,
Rough satyrs danced, and fauns with cloven heel
From the glad sound would not be absent long,   35
And old Damoetas² loved to hear our song.
       But O the heavy change, now thou art gone,
Now thou art gone, and never must return!
Thee, shepherd, thee the woods and desert caves,
With wild thyme and the gadding vine o'ergrown,   40
And all their echoes mourn.
The willows and the hazel copses green
Shall now no more be seen,
Fanning their joyous leaves to thy soft lays.
As killing as the canker° to the rose,   *cankerworm*   45
Or taint-worm to the weanling herds that graze,
Or frost to flowers that their gay wardrobe wear,
When first the white thorn blows;°   *blossoms*
Such, Lycidas, thy loss to shepherd's ear.
       Where were ye, nymphs, when the remorseless deep   50
Closed o'er the head of your loved Lycidas?
For neither were ye playing on the steep,
Where your old Bards, the famous Druids lie,
Nor on the shaggy top of Mona high,
Nor yet where Deva spreads her wizard stream:³   55
Ay me! I fondly dream —
Had ye been there — for what could that have done?
What could the Muse⁴ herself that Orpheus bore,
The Muse herself, for her inchanting son
Whom universal Nature did lament,   60
When by the rout that made the hideous roar,
His gory visage down the stream was sent,

---

²A conventional name from pastoral poetry, possibly referring to a Cambridge tutor.

³Mona is the Roman name for the Isle of Anglesey, off the Welsh coast. Deva is the river Dee, which flows into the Irish Sea. Its changes were said to foretell good or ill for England and Wales.

⁴Calliope, the muse of epic poetry. Her son, Orpheus, was slain by Thracian women, and his head cast into the river Hebrus.

Down the swift Hebrus to the Lesbian shore?
    Alas! What boots° it with uncessant care   *profits*
To tend the homely slighted shepherd's trade,   65
And strictly meditate the thankless Muse?
Were it not better done as others use,
To sport with Amaryllis in the shade,
Or with the tangles of Neaera's hair?[5]
Fame is the spur that the clear spirit doth raise   70
(That last infirmity of noble mind)
To scorn delights, and live laborious days;
But the fair guerdon° when we hope to find,   *reward*
And think to burst out into sudden blaze,
Comes the blind Fury[6] with th' abhorrèd shears,   75
And slits the thin spun life. "But not the praise,"
Phoebus° replied, and touched my trembling   *Apollo, god of*
    ears;   *poetic inspiration*
"Fame is no plant that grows on mortal soil,
Nor in the glistering foil
Set off to th' world, nor in broad rumor lies,   80
But lives and spreads aloft by those pure eyes,
And perfect witness of all-judging Jove;
As he pronounces lastly on each deed,
Of so much fame in Heaven expect thy meed."
    O fountain Arethuse,[7] and thou honored flood,   85
Smooth-sliding Mincius crowned with vocal reeds,
That strain I heard was of a higher mood.
But now my oat° proceeds,   *oaten-pipe song*
And listens to the herald of the sea°   *Triton*
That came in Neptune's plea.   90
He asked the waves, and asked the felon winds,
"What hard mishap hath doomed this gentle swain?"
And questioned every gust of rugged wings
That blows from off each beakèd promontory;
They knew not of his story,   95
And sage Hippotades° their answer brings,   *god of winds*
That not a blast was from his dungeon strayed,
The air was calm, and on the level brine,

---

[5] Amaryllis and Neaera: conventional names for shepherdesses.

[6] Atropos, not one of the Furies, but the Fate who cuts the thread of life.

[7] Arethusa was a nymph pursued by Alpheus. She fled under the sea to Sicily, where she came up as a fountain.

Sleek Panope° with all her sisters played.   *sea nymph*
It was that fatal and perfidious bark   100
Built in th' eclipse, and rigged with curses dark,
That sunk so low that sacred head of thine.
    Next Camus,[8] reverend sire, went footing slow,
His mantle hairy, and his bonnet sedge,
Inwrought with figures dim, and on the edge   105
Like to that sanguine flower inscribed with woe.[9]
"Ah! who hath reft," quoth he, "my dearest pledge?"
Last came and last did go
The pilot of the Galilean lake,°   *Saint Peter*
Two massy keys he bore of metals twain   110
(The golden opes, the iron shuts amain).
He shook his mitered locks, and stern bespake:
"How well could I have spared for thee, young swain,
Enow of such as for their bellies' sake,
Creep and intrude, and climb into the fold!   115
Of other care they little reckoning make,
Than how to scramble at the shearers' feast,
And shove away the worthy bidden guest.
Blind mouths! That scarce themselves know how to hold
A sheep-hook, or have learned aught else the least   120
That to the faithful herdsman's art belongs!
What recks it them? What need they? They are sped;
And when they list, their lean and flashy songs
Grate on their scrannel° pipes of wretched straw.   *meager*
The hungry sheep look up, and are not fed,   125
But swoln with wind, and the rank mist they draw,
Rot inwardly, and foul contagion spread,
Besides what the grim wolf with privy paw
Daily devours apace, and nothing said.
But that two-handed engine at the door   130
Stands ready to smite once, and smite no more."[10]
    Return, Alpheus,° the dread voice is past,   *(see note 6)*
That shrunk thy streams; return, Sicilian muse,
And call the vales, and bid them hither cast
Their bells and flowerets of a thousand hues.   135

---

[8]God of the river Cam, representing Cambridge University.

[9]The hyacinth, supposedly marked with the Greek cry of lamentation, "aiai."

[10]Milton has in mind some instrument of retribution which will punish the corrupt clergy.

Ye valleys low where the mild whispers use,
Of shades and wanton winds, and gushing brooks,
On whose fresh lap the swart star[11] sparely looks,
Throw hither all your quaint enameled eyes,
That on the green turf suck the honeyed showers,　　　　　140
And purple all the ground with vernal flowers.
Bring the rathe° primrose that forsaken dies,　　　　*early*
The tufted crow-toe, and pale jessamine,
The white pink, and the pansy freaked° with jet,　　*dappled*
The glowing violet,　　　　　　　　　　　　　　145
The musk-rose, and the well attired woodbine.
With cowslips wan that hang the pensive head,
And every flower that sad embroidery wears:
Bid amaranthus all his beauty shed,
And daffadillies fill their cups with tears,　　　　　150
To strew the laureate hearse where Lycid lies.
For so to interpose a little ease,
Let our frail thoughts dally with false surmise.
Ay me! Whilst thee the shores and sounding seas
Wash far away, where'er thy bones are hurled,　　　155
Whether beyond the stormy Hebrides,
Where thou perhaps under the whelming tide
Visit'st the bottom of the monstrous world;
Or whether thou, to our moist vows denied,
Sleep'st by the fable of Bellerus old,　　　　　　　160
Where the great vision of the guarded mount
Looks toward Namancos and Bayona's hold;[12]
Look homeward angel now, and melt with ruth:
And, O ye dolphins, waft the hapless youth.
　　Weep no more, woeful shepherds, weep no more,　　165
For Lycidas your sorrow is not dead,
Sunk though he be beneath the watery floor,
So sinks the day-star° in the ocean bed,　　　　　*sun*
And yet anon repairs his drooping head,
And tricks° his beams, and with new-spangled ore,　*dresses*　170
Flames in the forehead of the morning sky:

---

[11]Sirius, the Dog Star, associated with the hot days of late summer.
[12]Bellerus is a giant said to be buried at Land's End in Cornwall. St. Michael's Mount is also in Cornwall. The angel looks toward Namancos and Bayona on the Spanish coast.

So Lycidas sunk low, but mounted high,
Through the dear might of him that walked the waves,
Where other groves, and other streams along,
With nectar pure his oozy locks he laves,   175
And hears the unexpressive° nuptial song,   *inexpressible*
In the blest kingdoms meek of joy and love.
There entertain him all the saints above,
In solemn troops and sweet societies
That sing, and singing in their glory move,   180
And wipe the tears forever from his eyes.
Now, Lycidas, the shepherds weep no more;
Henceforth thou art the genius° of the shore,   *protective deity*
In thy large recompense, and shalt be good
To all that wander in that perilous flood.   185
    Thus sang the uncouth swain to th' oaks and rills,
While the still morn went out with sandals gray;
He touched the tender stops of various quills,
With eager thought warbling his Doric° lay: *rustic*
And now the sun had stretched out all the hills,   190
And now was dropped into the western bay;
At last he rose, and twitched his mantle blue:
Tomorrow to fresh woods, and pastures new.

BEN JONSON (1572 – 1637)
Still to Be Neat

Still to be neat, still to be dressed,
As you were going to a feast;
Still to be powdered, still perfumed;
Lady, it is to be presumed,
Though art's hid causes are not found,
All is not sweet, all is not sound.

Give me a look, give me a face
That makes simplicity a grace;
Robes loosely flowing, hair as free;
Such sweet neglect more taketh me
Then all th' adulteries of art.
They strike mine eyes, but not my heart.

RICHARD LOVELACE (1618 – 1658)
To Lucasta, Going to the Wars

Tell me not, sweet, I am unkind
That from the nunnery
Of thy chaste breast and quiet mind,
To war and arms I fly.

True, a new mistress now I chase,
The first foe in the field;
And with a stronger faith embrace
A sword, a horse, a shield.

Yet this inconstancy is such
As you too shall adore;
I could not love thee, dear, so much,
Loved I not honor more.

PHILLIS WHEATLEY (1753 – 1784)
On Being Brought from Africa to America

'Twas mercy brought me from my pagan land,
Taught my benighted soul to understand
That there's a God, that there's a Savior too:
Once I redemption neither sought nor knew.
Some view our sable race with scornful eye,
"Their color is a diabolic die.°"   *dye*
Remember, Christians, Negros, black as Cain,
May be refined, and join th' angelic train.

ELIZABETH BARRETT BROWNING (1806 – 1861)
How Do I Love Thee?

How do I love thee? Let me count the ways.
I love thee to the depth and breadth and height
My soul can reach, when feeling out of sight
For the ends of Being and ideal Grace.
I love thee to the level of everyday's
Most quiet need, by sun and candle-light.
I love thee freely, as men strive for Right;
I love thee purely, as they turn from Praise.
I love thee with the passion put to use

In my old griefs, and with my childhood's faith.
I love thee with a love I seemed to lose
With my lost saints — I love thee with the breath,
Smiles, tears, of all my life! — and, if God choose,
I shall but love thee better after death.

WALT WHITMAN (1819 – 1892)
When I Heard the Learn'd Astronomer

When I heard the learn'd astronomer,
When the proofs, the figures, were ranged in columns before me,
When I was shown the charts and diagrams, to add, divide, and
    measure them,
When I sitting heard the astronomer where he lectured with
    much applause in the lecture-room,
How soon unaccountable I became tired and sick,
Till rising and gliding out I wander'd off by myself,
In the mystical moist night-air, and from time to time,
Look'd up in perfect silence at the stars.

WILLIAM BUTLER YEATS (1865 – 1939)
Meru[1]

Civilisation is hooped together, brought
Under a rule, under the semblance of peace
By manifold illusion; but man's life is thought,
And he, despite his terror, cannot cease
Ravening through century after century,
Ravening, raging, and uprooting that he may come
Into the desolation of reality:
Egypt and Greece, good-bye, and good-bye, Rome!
Hermits upon Mount Meru or Everest,
Caverned in night under the drifted snow,
Or where that snow and winter's dreadful blast
Beat down upon their naked bodies, know
That day brings round the night, that before dawn
His glory and his monuments are gone.

---

[1]In Hindu mythology, Meru is a sacred mountain at the center of the world. It is the home of Vishnu, the god who preserves humanity.

ROBERT FROST (1874 – 1963)

The Gift Outright

The land was ours before we were the land's.
She was our land more than a hundred years
Before we were her people. She was ours
In Massachusetts, in Virginia,
But we were England's, still colonials,
Possessing what we still were unpossessed by,
Possessed by what we now no more possessed.
Something we were withholding made us weak
Until we found it was ourselves
We were withholding from our land of living,
And forthwith found salvation in surrender.
Such as we were we gave ourselves outright
(The deed of gift was many deeds of war)
To the land vaguely realizing westward,
But still unstoried, artless, unenhanced,
Such as she was, such as she would become.

ALLEN GINSBERG (1926 – 1997)

Sunflower Sutra[1]

I walked on the banks of the tincan banana dock and sat down
    under the huge shade of a Southern Pacific locomotive to
    look at the sunset over the box house hills and cry.
Jack Kerouac[2] sat beside me on a busted rusty iron pole,
    companion, we thought the same thoughts of the soul,   5
    bleak and blue and sad-eyed, surrounded by the gnarled
    steel roots of trees of machinery.
The oily water on the river mirrored the red sky, sun sank on top
    of final Frisco peaks, no fish in that stream, no hermit in
    those mounts, just ourselves rheumy-eyed and hungover   10
    like old bums on the riverbank, tired and wily.
Look at the Sunflower, he said, there was a dead gray shadow
    against the sky, big as a man, sitting dry on top of a pile of
    ancient sawdust —

---

[1]Buddhist religious text.
[2]Jack Kerouac (1922–1969), friend of Ginsberg's and author of *On the Road* and
other autobiographical novels.

— I rushed up enchanted — it was my first sunflower,   15
    memories of Blake[3] — my visions — Harlem
and Hells of the Eastern rivers, bridges, clanking Joes Greasy
    Sandwiches, dead baby carriages, black treadless tires
    forgotten and unretreaded, the poem of the riverbank,
    condoms & pots, steel knives, nothing stainless, only the   20
    dank muck and the razor sharp artifacts passing into the
    past —
and the gray Sunflower poised against the sunset, crackly bleak
    and dusty with the smut and smog and smoke of olden
    locomotives in its eye —   25
corolla of bleary spikes pushed down and broken like a battered
    crown, seeds fallen out of its face, soon-to-be-toothless
    mouth of sunny air, sunrays obliterated on its hairy head like
    a dried wire spiderweb,
leaves stuck out like arms out of the stem, gestures from the   30
    sawdust root, broke pieces of plaster fallen out of the black
    twigs, a dead fly in its ear,
Unholy battered old thing you were, my sunflower O my soul, I
    loved you then!
The grime was no man's grime but death and human   35
    locomotives,
all that dress of dust, that veil of darkened railroad skin, that smog
    of cheek, that eyelid of black mis'ry, that sooty hand or
    phallus or protuberance of artificial worse-than-dirt —
    industrial — modern — all that civilization spotting your   40
    crazy golden crown —
and those blear thoughts of death and dusty loveless eyes and ends
    and withered roots below, in the home-pile of sand and
    sawdust, rubber dollar bills, skin of machinery, the guts and
    innards of the weeping coughing car, the empty lonely   45
    tincans with their rusty tongues alack, what more could I
    name, the smoked ashes of some cock cigar, the cunts of
    wheelbarrows and the milky breasts of cars, wornout asses
    out of chairs & sphincters of dynamos — all these
entangled in your mummied roots — and you there standing   50
    before me in the sunset, all your glory in your form!
A perfect beauty of a sunflower! a perfect excellent lovely
    sunflower existence! a sweet natural eye to the new hip

---

[3]William Blake (1757–1827), English poet and author of "Ah! Sun-flower." Ginsberg in 1948 had had a vision in which he heard Blake's voice reciting his poems.

moon, woke up alive and excited grasping in the sunset
 shadow sunrise golden monthly breeze!   55
How many flies buzzed round you innocent of your grime, while
 you cursed the heavens of the railroad and your flower soul?
Poor dead flower? when did you forget you were a flower? when
 did you look at your skin and decide you were an impotent
 dirty old locomotive? the ghost of a locomotive? the 60
 specter and shade of a once powerful mad American
 locomotive?
You were never no locomotive, Sunflower, you were a sunflower!
And you Locomotive, you are a locomotive, forget me not!
So I grabbed up the skeleton thick sunflower and stuck it at my 65
 side like a scepter,
and deliver my sermon to my soul, and Jack's soul too, and anyone
 who'll listen,
— We're not our skin of grime, we're not our dread bleak dusty
 imageless locomotive, we're all beautiful golden sun- 70
 flowers inside, we're blessed by our own seed & golden hairy
 naked accomplishment-bodies growing into mad black
 formal sunflowers in the sunset, spied on by our eyes under
 the shadow of the mad locomotive riverbank sunset Frisco
 hilly tincan evening sitdown vision.   75

LOUISE GLÜCK (b. 1943)
Mock Orange

It is not the moon, I tell you.
It is these flowers
lighting the yard.

I hate them.
I hate them as I hate sex,
the man's mouth
sealing my mouth, the man's
paralyzing body —

and the cry that always escapes,
the low, humiliating
premise of union —

In my mind tonight
I hear the question and pursuing answer
fused in one sound

that mounts and mounts and then
is split into the old selves,
the tired antagonisms. Do you see?
We were made fools of.
And the scent of mock orange
drifts through the window.

How can I rest?
How can I be content
when there is still
that odor in the world?

RITA DOVE (b. 1952)
Parsley[1]

1. The Cane Fields

There is a parrot imitating spring
in the palace, its feathers parsley green.
Out of the swamp the cane appears

to haunt us, and we cut it down. El General
searches for a word; he is all the world   5
there is. Like a parrot imitating spring,

we lie down screaming as rain punches through
and we come up green. We cannot speak an R —
out of the swamp, the cane appears

and then the mountain we call in whispers *Katalina*.[2]   10
The children gnaw their teeth to arrowheads.
There is a parrot imitating spring.

El General has found his word: *perejil*.
Who says it, lives. He laughs, teeth shining
out of the swamp. The cane appears   15

in our dreams, lashed by wind and streaming.
And we lie down. For every drop of blood
there is a parrot imitating spring.
Out of the swamp the cane appears.

---

[1]Dove's note: "*Parsley:* On October 2, 1937, Rafael Trujillo (1891–1961), dictator
of the Dominican Republic, ordered 20,000 blacks killed because they could not roll the
letter *r* in *perejil,* the Spanish word for parsley."
[2]Properly "Katarina."

2. The Palace

The word the general's chosen is parsley.   20
It is fall, when thoughts turn
to love and death; the general thinks
of his mother, how she died in the fall
and he planted her walking cane at the grave
and it flowered, each spring stolidly forming   25
four-star blossoms. The general

pulls on his boots, he stomps to
her room in the palace, the one without
curtains, the one with a parrot
in a brass ring. As he paces he wonders   30
Who can I kill today. And for a moment
the little knot of screams
is still. The parrot, who has traveled

all the way from Australia in an ivory
cage, is, coy as a widow, practising   35
spring. Ever since the morning
his mother collapsed in the kitchen
while baking skull-shaped candies
for the Day of the Dead,[3] the general
has hated sweets. He orders pastries   40
brought up for the bird; they arrive

dusted with sugar on a bed of lace.
The knot in his throat starts to twitch;
he sees his boots the first day in battle
splashed with mud and urine   45
as a soldier falls at his feet amazed —
how stupid he looked! — at the sound
of artillery. *I never thought it would sing*
the soldier said, and died. Now

the general sees the fields of sugar   50
cane, lashed by rain and streaming.
He sees his mother's smile, the teeth
gnawed to arrowheads. He hears
the Haitians sing without R's
as they swing the great machetes: 55
Katalina, they sing, *Katalina,*

---

[3]November 1, the Feast of All Souls.

mi madle, mi amol en muelte.[4] God knows
his mother was no stupid woman; she
could roll an R like a queen. Even
a parrot can roll an R! In the bare room   60
the bright feathers arch in a parody
of greenery, as the last pale crumbs
disappear under the blackened tongue. Someone

calls out his name in a voice
so like his mother's, a startled tear   65
splashes the tip of his right boot.
My mother, my love in death.
The general remembers the tiny green sprigs
men of his village wore in their capes
to honor the birth of a son. He will   70
order many, this time, to be killed

for a single, beautiful word.

HEIDY STEIDLMAYER (B. 1969)
Knife-Sharpener's Song

I said no word of her to him,
nor he of her to me, *oh yes*.

We sharpened down the sliding

hour the knives wooled thick
with rust, *oh yes*; the days grew

small and wider, stripping

words down to their edge —
cutthroat, flashy, without a flaw,

what he did to me, *oh yes*.

Turn by turn, those knives of hers
shone quietly aware, *oh yes*,

not I but she would be the one

he carefully undressed —
but he said no word of her to me

nor I to him of us, *oh yes*.

---

[4]"My mother, my love in death." In the Spanish, the *r*'s have been changed to *l*'s to
simulate the Haitians' inability to roll their *r*'s.

II

WRITING ABOUT POETRY

10

Writing about Poems

Basic Principles

In writing about a poem, the most important thing to remember is that a poem is not an essay or a "message," it is a thing imagined, an artwork like a piece of music or a painting or a dance. Your first task is to see how the theme of the work is being imagined: how the literal statement of the poet's feeling has been transformed. After that, you can experience the poem as you hear a piece of music or see a dance, as something unfolding itself in **time**, with a beginning, middle, and end. Or, you can see it from afar in the way you see a painting (or from above as you might see a terrain from an airplane) — as a **space** full of things and "colors" set in relation to each other. Both of these ways of seeing are indispensable.

Considered as pieces extending themselves over time, poems have a "plot" — not so much one of events as one of feelings. A poem might begin in despair and rise toward hope; or might begin in hope and end in despair. A good question to begin with, when reading a poem as a series of events in time, is how the place you find yourself in at the end is different from the place you found yourself in at the beginning. If you take stock of Z, where you end up, and A, where you began, you are likely to be able to plot the B, F, O, and W that lie between.

And considered as a space where parts are arranged in relation to each other, poems have a configuration, just as paintings do: the poet may contrast one part to another (as painters put light against shade), or set one part above another in a hierarchy, or may create an imbalance by which twelve lines are "outweighed" by a closing couplet. A good question to begin with, when reading a poem as a spatial arrangement, is what parts it falls into and how they relate to each other in size, feeling-tone, and language.

A Brief Example

Let us take a brief lyric by Robert Herrick as an example of how we might approach a poem. We must of course read it whole before saying anything, since we can't really estimate the beginning until we have seen the end. And reading it whole means thinking about the title as well:

ROBERT HERRICK (1591 – 1674)
Divination by a Daffodil

When a daffodil I see
Hanging down his head towards me,
Guess I may what I must be:
First, I shall decline my head;
Secondly, I shall be dead;
Lastly, safely burièd.

We can say, at first reading, that the poet compares himself, in his mortality, to a transient natural object. This is not a new idea. What has Herrick done to turn it into a poem? How has he newly imagined this theme?

He has, first of all, made the commonplace act of seeing a flower into an act of "divination." In classical times, priests "divined" the future by examining the entrails of a sacrificed animal. Herrick transfers this bloody act to something light and beautiful and glancing when he chooses, as his **symbolic object**, the daffodil (with its characteristic drooping head). Second, Herrick doesn't begin with the comparison of his fate to that of the daffodil, he might have said, "When a daffodil I spy, / I know that I, like it, shall die." Instead, he divides his poem into **two parts**: he reserves the comparison to the second half of the **single-sentence** poem, leaving us to guess, as we read the first half, what he might be going to divine from his daffodil.

When you note the general metrical scheme of this poem — "**strong** weak / **strong** weak / **strong** weak / **strong**" — you can see that the author wanted the first word of the line to bear emphasis, but not really for the purposes of the first half (which could equally well have read "weak **strong** / weak **strong**," etc.: "A daffodil appears to me; / His head is hanging down, and we / Can guess from that what we must be"). The real purpose of the meter is clear when we arrive at the second half of the poem: it is to give weight to "*First . . . / Secondly . . . / Lastly*," which ring with inexorable emphasis in summoning up the last stages of life: illness, death, and burial. When you examine the **rhyme** (**aaabbb**) you see that it possesses the same inevitability in the second half: the relatively uninteresting rhymes of the first half (**see, me, be**) are supplanted by the death-knell of **head, dead, burièd**.

Once you have studied the **symbolic imagination**, the **words**, the **syntax of the sentences**, the poem's **division into parts**, and the **rhyme and rhythm**, you are prepared to make a sketch of the "drama" of the poem, that is, to see its <u>beginning</u>, <u>middle</u>, and <u>end</u> as elements in an unfolding of human emotion. Someone is speaking the words of the poem, and that someone is now you; lyrics are designed as scripts for performance (not by an actor; by the reader). Speak the poem as if it were you who had been compelled into speech by something that had upset your equilibrium — otherwise you would have had no reason to break into words. Then try to imagine the "backstory" behind your utterance. What was happening to you before the poem began that makes you speak in this way? This is where you must use your imagination. Presumably Herrick has often seen daffodils, but something has recently happened — a sense of aging or of approaching death — that makes this daffodil into an emblem he uses to divine his future. Interestingly, though Herrick was a clergyman, he makes no mention in this poem of an afterlife, choosing to see himself in purely material terms, as another living being on a par with an unremarkable flower. On the other hand, his method in the poem — divining a message from a natural object — is very much a religious method (as his title suggests), by which man reads messages from God in the works of God's creation. Seventeenth-century poetry is full of such "messages" drawn from natural things and events.

To sum up: Herrick has made his theme — man's mortality — into a poem by imagining that one can divine one's fate from a flower; by arranging a perfect spatial symmetry (three lines each) to flower and man; and by letting us hear, after the inoffensive first three lines, the heavy tread of his own death announcement.

A Longer Example

When you have seen one way of treating a flower, it puts other ways — especially those from other centuries — into sharper relief. Suppose that, having seen Herrick's poem on daffodils, you now turn to study a poem on daffodils by William Wordsworth, "I Wandered Lonely as a Cloud."

WILLIAM WORDSWORTH (1770 – 1850)

I Wandered Lonely as a Cloud

I wandered lonely as a cloud
That floats on high o'er vales and hills,
When all at once I saw a crowd,
A host, of golden daffodils;
Beside the lake, beneath the trees,
Fluttering and dancing in the breeze.

Continuous as the stars that shine
And twinkle on the milky way,
They stretched in never-ending line
Along the margin of a bay:
Ten thousand saw I at a glance,
Tossing their heads in sprightly dance.

The waves beside them danced; but they
Outdid the sparkling waves in glee;
A poet could not but be gay,
In such a jocund company;
I gazed — and gazed — but little thought
What wealth the show to me had brought:

For oft, when on my couch I lie
In vacant or in pensive mood,
They flash upon that inward eye
Which is the bliss of solitude;
And then my heart with pleasure fills,
And dances with the daffodils.

After you have spent some time studying the poem, your notebook might look like this:

I wandered lonely as a cloud **a**	Speaker <u>lonely</u>; why is he like a cloud? 4
That floats on high o'er vales and hills, **b**	Natural scene stretched out, hills and valleys 4
When all at once I saw a crowd, **a**	<u>crowd</u>: word generally used of people 4
A host, of golden daffodils; **b**	<u>host</u>: armies, but here flowers 4
Beside the lake, beneath the trees, **c**	Closer focus than vales and hills 4
Fluttering and dancing in the breeze. **c**	Can flowers <u>dance</u>? aren't they rooted? 4
Continuous as the stars that shine	Much further focus — up to stars
And twinkle on the milky way,	Difference between <u>shine</u> and <u>twinkle</u>?
They stretched in never-ending line	Exaggeration, "never-ending" like stars
Along the margin of a bay:	First "beside" the lake; now entire margin
Ten thousand saw I at a glance,	Exaggeration again; and <u>saw</u> becomes <u>a glance</u>
Tossing their heads in sprightly dance.	Daffodils = people, having "heads" they "toss"
The waves beside them danced; but they	Waves now like people too, dancing
Outdid the sparkling waves in glee;	Flowers have feelings: <u>glee</u>
A poet could not but be gay,	Wasn't he *lonely* when he started?
In such a jocund company;	<u>company</u>; he's not alone any more
I gazed — and gazed — but little thought	<u>saw</u> > <u>glance</u> > <u>gazed and gazed</u>
What wealth the show to me had brought:	<u>golden</u> (l.4) = <u>wealth</u>; <u>show</u>, not <u>company</u> now
For oft, when on my couch I lie	<u>oft</u>: past anecdote over, now present tense
In vacant or in pensive mood,	Difference between <u>vacant</u> and <u>pensive</u>?
They flash upon that inward eye	<u>flash</u>; not <u>dance</u> or <u>flutter</u> or <u>toss</u>: why?
Which is the bliss of solitude;	<u>solitude</u>: different from first <u>lonely</u>?
And then my heart with pleasure fills	Earlier, <u>eye</u> (outward and inward); now <u>heart</u>?
And dances with the daffodils.	Same rhyme-sound as in stanza 1

Everyone's first notebook jottings are somewhat idiosyncratic. If you decide to think first about <u>words</u>, several in the poem would send you to a dictionary to check out etymologies and different connotations. Poets — since words are their stock in trade — always have a very specific sense of the aura around each word. Here are some roots and meanings relevant to this poem, taken from the *American Heritage Dictionary*:

lonely: derived from alone

crowd (Old English *crudan,* to hasten): generally used of the common people

host (Latin *hostis,* army, enemy)

daffodil: from asphodel (Greek *asphodelos*), a yellow flower

shine (Old English *scinan,* to shine): beam, emit light, reflect light, gleam, glisten

twinkle (Old English *twinklian,* to twinkle): to flicker, glimmer, sparkle

glance (Middle English *glansen,* to strike obliquely): to direct the gaze briefly

sprightly (Latin *spiritus,* spirit): buoyant, animated, full of life, with briskness, gaily

glee (Middle English *gle,* entertainment): jubilant gaiety, joy

gay (French *gai*): exuberant, merry, bright

jocund (Latin *jucundus,* delighted, <*juvare,* to delight): cheerful, merry

gaze (Middle English *gasen,* to gaze): prolonged and studied looking, often indicative of wonder, fascination, awe, or admiration

vacant (Latin *vacare,* to be empty): expressionless, blank, not filled with activity

pensive (Latin *pensare,* to think, <*pendere,* to weigh): engaged in deep, often melancholy thoughtfulness

flash (Middle English *flashen,* to splash): to burst forth into or as if into flame; to appear or occur suddenly; *flash* refers to a sudden and brilliant but short-lived outburst of light

bliss (Old English *bliss*): extreme happiness, joy, the ecstasy of salvation, spiritual joy

solitude (Latin *solus,* alone): the state of being alone or remote from others; isolation

We can notice — without yet doing much with the fact — that there are "families" of words evident here, just as there were in the Herrick poem:

- *glee, gay,* and *jocund* (a family of being happy, in terms of both meaning and — in the case of the first three — alliteration);

- *glance, glee, gay, gaze* (words connected by alliteration, joining looking and happiness);

- *saw, glance, gaze* (a family of looking);
- *float, flutter, dance, shine, twinkle, toss, flash, fill* (a family of verbs of motion)

Something will have to be said about these families, which help to organize the poem. And something should be said about the balance between words coming from the German side of English (Anglo-Saxon) and words coming from the Latin-French side. Wordsworth seems to be balancing Latinate words (*jocund, vacant, pensive, solitude*) with Germanic words (*glee, bliss, shine, twinkle*).

So much for words. What about **sentences**? The first sentence is the first stanza. The second sentence is the second stanza. What do we expect next? That the third sentence will be the third stanza. But that is not what happens: the third and fourth stanzas together make up the third sentence, and the "hinge" that joins the third and fourth stanzas is the couplet, "I gazed — and gazed — but little thought / What wealth the show to me had brought." This couplet leads into the exemplification of the "wealth" in stanza 4. The third sentence is twice as long as the other two (and therefore bears twice the weight).

We have our preliminary findings about words and sentences. What about **rhyme** and **rhythm**? The stanzas rhyme **ababcc**: that is, there is a quatrain followed by a couplet — a rhyme-scheme that implies: "I have something to say (my quatrain), and then I have something to add (my couplet)." There are 4 beats per line, and the basic meter is: weak **strong**, weak **strong**, weak **strong**, weak **strong**. We can see that this meter is more or less kept in the first five lines of the poem, but that in line 6, to emphasize the unexpected motion of the flowers, Wordsworth changes the first two syllables to read "**strong** weak": "Fluttering." A careful reader will see that for his concluding rhyme ("fills / daffodils") Wordsworth has reused one of the rhyme-sounds from his first stanza ("hills / daffodils"), giving us a strong sense of the end coming back to the beginning.

We've now done a fair amount of looking at the poem in terms of **words**, **sentences**, **rhyme** and **rhythm**. Now, suppose we look at the poem **temporally**, to see what changes we can observe in it as it goes along? Let us look at **A**, where the speaker is when the poem opens: he is alone, feeling *lonely*, feeling as unconnected to the world as a cloud is when floating high above the earth. Let us look at **Z**, where the speaker is when the poem ends; he is still alone, but he is no longer lonely; now he feels *the bliss of solitude*. What has made the difference? By the end, he has had, often, involuntary experiences of delight; alone in his room, he has perhaps been thinking of nothing, or reflecting in a slightly melancholy way about life, when suddenly, unasked, the daffodils flash into his mind so vividly that he sees them with his "inward eye." The experience makes that empty container, his heart, fill with pleasure, recapturing his previous pleasure on that apparently forgotten day.

Because the speaker in this poem doesn't differentiate himself (by gender, occupation, or age) from the author, we can refer to him as "Wordsworth," while remembering that he is a fictive creation, who speaks in verse — as the real Wordsworth, in real life, would not have done. We must ask how the poet has succeeded in conveying the earlier pleasure of his speaker so that we are convinced that the daffodils have indeed lasted intensely in his mind, without any conscious effort on his part. If we have seen **A** and **Z**, we now have to decide what goes on between lines 1–2 (**A**) and lines 19–24 (**Z**). All the verbs of motion, all the verbs of seeing, all the verbs of delight (those "families" of words we saw earlier) help to explain how we move from **A** to **Z**.

Now let us look at the poem **spatially**, "from above," so to speak, as if we were looking at a map spread out at our feet. We notice that there are three descriptions of the daffodils, three "glances" at the same phenomenon. The first glance ("I saw") shows us the daffodils as **many** (*a crowd, a host*), **in a landscape** (*lake, trees*), and **in motion** (*fluttering, dancing*). The second glance ("at a glance") shows us the daffodils as **many** (*stars . . . on the milky way, ten thousand*), **in a landscape** (*margin of a bay*), and **in motion** (*tossing their heads in sprightly dance*). The third glance ("I gazed — and gazed") shows us the daffodils as **many** (*company*), **in a landscape** (*waves beside them*), and **in motion** (*outdid the sparkling waves in glee*). We would draw distinctions about these three descriptions if we were considering them **temporally** (the distinction between seeing, glancing, and gazing, for instance), but in considering them **spatially**, as three versions of "the same thing," we notice that the important things about the daffodils (reiterated by the speaker each time he looks at them) is that they are <u>not alone</u> since there are many of them; that they feel <u>at home in nature</u>, beside the lake and beneath the trees and on the margin of a bay next to the waves; that they are not gloomily rigid but in joyous <u>motion</u> responsive to the waves and the breeze. We would not be so sure <u>why</u> the daffodils were so important to Wordsworth unless he had shown us, three times, the very same qualities in them. What may seem repetition in a poem is often intensification.

Again, as we look at the poem **spatially**, we notice that it is divided into two parts: outdoors (stanzas 1–3) and indoors (stanza 4). The outdoor part, phrased in the past tense, tells of one particular day when the poet saw the daffodils; the indoor part, phrased in what we call the habitual present tense (representing something that happens often), removes the daffodils from a physical scene (in nature) to a virtual scene (in the mind). Wordsworth makes explicit, at the end, the connection between what the eye has seen, glanced at, and finally gazed at (imprinting the scene firmly) and what the heart feels. Just as Herrick uses his second stanza to alter the perspective from the daffodils to human beings ("we"), so Wordsworth uses his last stanza to bring the daffodils indoors: in each case, something has changed so that we recognize that the poem has been brought to closure.

We haven't yet said how Wordsworth makes credible the interaction between the speaker and the flowers that made the scene so important. If we look at **the subjects of the sentences** in our spatial overview, we see that **the speaker** governs the first sentence ("**I** wandered lonely") and the daffodils are the objects of his observation ("I saw a crowd, a host, of golden daffodils"). But **the daffodils** govern the first part of the second sentence: ("**They** stretched"), while **the speaker** governs the second part ("ten thousand saw **I**"). **The daffodils**, along with the waves, govern the first part of the third sentence ("The waves . . . danced; but **they** outdid the sparkling waves"), while **the speaker** governs the second part ("**A poet** could not but be gay . . . **I** gazed — and gazed"). Finally, in the last stanza's continuation of the third sentence, **the daffodils** govern the first main clause ("**They** flash") while **the speaker** governs the second ("**my heart** with pleasure fills"). What we see, then, is an antiphonal structure of alternation (A; B /A; B) in which the poet and the daffodils engage in a "syntactic dialogue," as first one predominates, then the other. We "believe in" the speaker's interaction with the daffodils because the poem shows it happening. As Herrick paralleled daffodils with human beings, so Wordsworth shows them interacting.

Finally, we might notice that Wordsworth has put the word *dance,* in one or another of its variants, in each stanza. *Dancing; dance; danced; dances.* And we notice that the word *dance* alliterates with the word *daffodils,* making them "belong" together phonetically.

Getting It Down on Paper

Now, suppose you are to write a paper about how Wordsworth's poem "works." Remember that your readers probably will not have the poem at hand. When you are discussing a poem as brief as "Daffodils" (or any poem that is but a page or so in length), it is a courtesy to your readers to reproduce it early in your paper. Nonetheless, as you discuss the poem, you are still responsible for "tucking in" any information your readers need in order to understand what you are talking about. You don't want them to be flipping back and forth between your analysis and the poem.

Indeed, you should always write as if your readers cannot see the poem (as will be the case with longer poems you discuss, anyway), being careful to explain how the poem looks on the page — its stanzas, its rhymes. And you have the responsibility, as the speaker's surrogate, of explaining to your readers why the daffodils that day had the power over you that they did (even if you only realized it later). And you have the responsibility, as the poet's surrogate, of explaining how you set up your artifact in order to make it not only clear but beautiful.

Begin with a Question

A good way to begin a paper on a poem is to put before your reader some of the questions that occurred to you as you were studying the poem:

> Wordsworth writes a poem about the importance, to him, of a day in which he came upon a bed of daffodils next to a lake and watched them as they seemed to dance because of the breeze passing through them. Why would a bed of flowers become of lasting importance? What was it about them that later impelled the poet into speech? Does he seem to write the poem immediately after seeing them — was it the beauty of the sight that made him want to record it? Or was the poem written much later — and if so, what was it, at that later time, that made him write about the daffodils he had seen perhaps months before?

A paper that begins with your genuine questions about a poem draws your reader into the subject in a way a set of conclusions would not. Besides, the reader is not yet ready to hear your conclusions: conclusions are interesting only after the questions to which they are the answers have been first made compelling to the reader. It is not a good idea, then, to start your paper by saying:

> Memory was important to Wordsworth. Often, experiences were more significant to him a long time after they had happened, and that is why he wrote a poem about daffodils he had seen long before.

Such a beginning, in addition to being a bit solemn, takes all the suspense out of the poem. One of the effects of the poem — and you are responsible for evoking those effects in your reader — is to make you wonder why the poet is emphasizing three times something so common in England as an extended bed of daffodils.

In evoking the effects of the poem, you might say:

> The speaker is concerned to set himself before us as someone lonely, disconnected from the human world, until he comes upon the daffodils. How do they seem to him when he first *sees* them? He is impressed first by their sheer number, next by the way they fit into the landscape, and third by their motion. Although this motion is really imparted to them by the breeze, the speaker prefers to think of them as engaging in both involuntary (*fluttering*) and voluntary (*dancing*) actions. Strange as it may seem, we learn nothing more, basically, about the daffodils when the speaker sees them again (at a *glance*) in stanza 2, and again (with a double *gaze*) in stanza 3: they are many, they are an intimate part of the landscape, and they dance. Why is it that these three qualities of the daffodils so strike the speaker, and what do we learn from the slight difference in the poem's representations of them as it returns to them for a second and a third time?

This makes your reader

- notice the three repetitions;
- notice what they have in common;
- wonder what distinguishes them from each other; and
- see how they emphasize the power of this scene to move the speaker.

As you go on, you can ask further questions. Are we surprised, after seeing this scene three times, that the poem suddenly goes on fast-forward, to a future experience (often repeated) of the daffodils, this time in virtual vision rather than real vision? How does the poet connect this anomalous last stanza to his three previous visions of the daffodils? And so on. The more questions you ask, the more interested your reader will be to see what answers you will provide.

Present Your Case

You may be thinking at this point, "How do I work in the facts about the **rhyme** and **meter**?" It is useless just to name the rhyme and meter; nobody learns anything from a sentence that says, "The poem, in iambic tetrameter, rhymes **ababcc**." Such a sentence is true, but uninformative. It is, of course, easier to talk about rhyme and meter once you have acquired a sense of how set forms are used over time by different poets; but anyone can see that blank verse ("Of man's first disobedience, and the fruit / Of that immortal tree whose mortal taste / Brought death into the world, and all our woe") sounds very different, in its solemnity, from the dance-meter of "And then my heart with pleasure fills, / And dances with the daffodils." So somewhere along the way — when you are emphasizing the repetition of the word *dance,* perhaps — you might add that Wordsworth has very naturally written the poem in a meter — iambic tetrameter — that suggests lightness, the same meter that Milton used for his poem on happiness, *L'Allegro:* "Then come, thou goddess fair and free, / In heaven yclept Euphrosyne." As for the rhyme, you can point out that in a poem that keeps coming back to the same scene, the appearance of a refrain in the recurrent couplets is appropriate. Imagine the last stanza if it had no break into quatrain and couplet, if it rhymed **ababab**:

> For oft, when on my couch I lie
> In vacant or in pensive mood,
> They dance upon that inward eye
> Which is the bliss of solitude;
> And then I feel the pleasure nigh
> Of daffodils on which I brood.

When the stanza is not broken in two, marked off by rhyme as a quatrain plus a couplet, one doesn't feel the sense of afterthought, of add-on, so important to the poem, which is itself all about the "add-on" of subsequent mental reference to earlier physical experience — Wordsworth's great theme. In brief, insert your reflections on rhyme and meter where they best fit with your discussion of the poem's theme and manner, just as, in considering Herrick's poem, you might mention the effect of the strong first syllables when you are treating the speaker's conviction of his coming death.

Draw Your Conclusions

At the end of your paper, after integrating all you've noticed about the words, sentences, and rhyme and rhythm of the poem; after working out how to describe the poem's emotional evolution in time and the patterns you see in it from a spatial overview, posing questions for your reader all the way, you are entitled to tell the reader your conclusions. You might say:

> Wordsworth must convince his reader of the continuing importance, to him, of a single experience — his coming across a bed of daffodils. The poem, it turns out, is not only about seeing daffodils; it is about the "bliss" and wonder of memory — the fact that our memory unconsciously stores phenomena to which we have deeply responded and can make those phenomena "flash" into view long afterward, when we are unoccupied and alone.
>
> In his first loneliness, the speaker — a person alienated from the earth as much as a high-floating cloud would be, a wanderer who lacks company, a destination, and delight — comes upon the beautiful daffodils and is struck by the contrast between his state and theirs because <u>they</u> are at home in nature, they <u>do</u> have company, and they seem content to respond in sheer delight to the breeze that sets them in motion, so as even to "outdo" the dancing waves beside them. Lost in their sheer number and extent, in their beauty, naturalness, and freedom, the poet — expressing their happiness in a "dance-rhythm" of iambic tetrameter — is unable to tear himself away (as we see from his repeating the original scene twice more, each time with small but significant differences).
>
> The poet's perception alternates between his own agency and that of the daffodils: he sees, they act, he sees, they act, he gazes, and we begin to understand what it means to impress a scene on the mind by constant internal dialogue with it. All the time, the little stanza, which is composed of a basic statement and then an afterthought, acts out the way the mind frames a notion, and then adds to it, decoratively or reminiscently.
>
> The poet turns both to simple Anglo-Saxon words (*shine, twinkle, glee, flash*) with their familiar commonness, and to less familiar Latinate words (*continuous, jocund, vacant, pensive*), with their overtones of learning, to suggest that the flowers bring out all the parts of his sensibility, from childlike perception to literary response. By the end, the poet has found not only "company" in the "neverending line" of daffodils, but nourishment for the future: his outward eye, brought into company and into nature and into delight, has, unbeknownst to him, stored up the daffodils as nurture for the "inward eye" that now makes solitude not "lonely" but "bliss[ful]."

No one paper can say everything about even a short poem. "I Wandered Lonely as a Cloud" can be set into larger frames: among other Wordsworth poems; among other daffodil poems; among other loneliness poems or nature poems; among other Romantic poems; among poems in iambic tetrameter; among poems about memory; and so on. Each "frame" shows the poem somewhat differently and gives one a better handle on the special idiosyncrasy of this poem.

Keeping Your Readers in Mind

What you chiefly want readers to feel, if they turn back from your paper to read the poem, is that you haven't left out anything important. A reader might say, reading an imperfect paper, "I would never have known that Wordsworth does the initial scene *three* times!" (This might be the reader's reaction if your discussion had essentially turned this into a poem that has two parts: "Wordsworth saw daffodils and liked them; Wordsworth remembers daffodils later.") Or a reader might say (if you had neglected to talk about vocabulary), "It sounded like such an <u>artless</u> poem in your paper; I never would have guessed that it had Latinate words like *sprightly* and *jocund* and *vacant* and *solitude* in it." Or, "You never said it had such a dance-like rhythm!" Or, "I had no idea that it was organized by 'see; glance; gaze' or that there was all that alliteration linking all those 'g' words together — *golden, glance, glee, gay, gazed, gazed* — or that there was *dance* in every stanza." Or, "But how could you have left out the difference between *lonely* at the beginning and *the bliss of solitude* at the end? It really sums up the whole difference between the poet's mood before he sees the daffodils and after!" A good paper leaves the readers, when they come back to the poem, feeling, "Oh, yes! And yes! Of course!" It makes readers see aspects of the poem they may not have noticed themselves, in their more cursory reading of the poem, but now see clearly because you have showed them those things.

A Note on Writing about Unrhymed Poems

The examples we saw above, "Divination by a Daffodil" and "I Wandered Lonely as a Cloud," are poems in rhymed stanzas. Since the beginning of the twentieth century many poets have been writing in what is called "free verse," that is, lines of irregular length that do not rhyme according to a fixed pattern and may not rhyme at all. Nonetheless, such poems *are* patterned — by repetition of rhythms, parallel syntactic patterns, metaphorical alliances, recurrent tones, alliteration, and so on. They usually fall into parts (two, three, or four), just as rhymed stanzaic poems do. One can imagine a poem parallel to "I Wandered Lonely as a Cloud" written in free verse, but it would still have to have the built-in pattern of a single outdoor experience in the past matched by a later blissful habitual indoor experience; by the pattern of the outward eye versus the inward eye; by the pattern of loneliness followed by "company"; by the pattern of a scene repeated to intensify its effect; and so on. The principal thing to remember is that all well-written verbal art is based on pattern-repetition, structural organization, and memorable language: these are as readily identified in free verse as in metered verse.

Organizing Your Paper

You do *not* have to "go through" the poem inch by inch, line by line. "In the first line the author says. . . . In the second line the author adds. . . . In line three, the poet goes on to observe . . . ," etc. Your reader would die of boredom. There is nothing wrong with starting a paper — as a means of posing some of your initial questions, perhaps — by looking at the ending.

> Wordsworth ends his poem with the speaker enjoying "the bliss of solitude" — the very same speaker who complained, at the beginning, that he was "wandering," with no company, "as lonely as a cloud," alienated from both man and nature. How did this melancholy person translate himself into a state of bliss?

Or your paper can begin in the middle of the poem:

> "I Wandered Lonely as a Cloud" is a poem divided between a single day in the past and many days in the present — the past day when the speaker "saw a crowd / A host, of golden daffodils" and the present days when the daffodils "flash upon [his] inward eye." The hinge between these two parts of the poem comes at the end of the third stanza:
>
> > I gazed — and gazed — but little thought
> > What wealth the show to me had brought:
>
> What is that "wealth"? and how did the common spectacle of "golden" daffodils become transmuted into a different sort of gold, the "wealth" of involuntary memory?

Or your paper can begin with a feature of the poem:

> We might expect that a poem beginning "I wandered" would keep to this format throughout, with the speaker as the subject of all the verbs: "I saw," "I gazed," "I thought," and so on. But we notice that Wordsworth's poem on the daffodils offers a peculiar grammatical alternation between the poet as subject and the flowers as subject: it is almost as if they are engaging in a dialogue. The poet notices; then the flowers do something; then the poet notices; then the flowers do something else; then the poet notices yet again. Wordsworth is teaching us, so to speak, how to look so that the scenes we see can have lasting meaning for us. We need to be willing to receive the impress of the phenomena around us; but we also need to *see,* to glance, to **gaze** — and **GAZE**, with increasing intensity. And this is not necessarily a solemn process: in every stanza of the poem, some thing or person "dances" in this dialogue of the eye with nature.

In short, your paper can begin anywhere, as long as it is well organized and somehow includes all the main features of the poem.

A Note on Well-Ordered Paragraphs

One of the chief features of a well-organized paper is the internal arrangement of its paragraphs. A well-ordered paragraph has a point of view, and a subject that does not change markedly as the paragraph evolves. Here is an example of a badly organized paragraph, in which every sentence jumps to a different grammatical subject:

> Wordsworth is writing about seeing a bed of daffodils. The speaker has been wandering in a lonely mood, but then he glimpses the flowers. The 6-line stanza is written with a rhyming couplet at the end, in which we see the daffodils "fluttering and dancing in the breeze." Nature is for the poet a source of refreshment and solace. Often the Romantic poets found a recourse in nature that they could not find in urban life. Metaphors from nature are important to the Romantics; this is seen in Wordsworth's comparison of his loneliness to that of a cloud. The daffodils represent to Wordsworth the happiness and company to be found in nature.

The grammatical subjects of the successive sentences of this paragraph are *Wordsworth, the speaker, the stanza, Nature, the Romantic poets, metaphors,* and *daffodils*. A reader feels seasick as the paragraph lurches from focus to focus. The writer should choose one focus: the paragraph should be about Wordsworth, the composer of the poem; or about the speaker who utters the poem; about the scene in the poem (daffodils); about the technique of the poem (the stanzas, sentence-forms, rhymes); about Romantic poets and their relation to nature; or about metaphors in the poem.

A new paragraph is the place to change the focus. After a paragraph on Wordsworth as poet, it might be fine to have a paragraph about the speaker, followed by a paragraph about the metaphors in the poem — providing logical transitions are found to get from one topic to the next. For instance, if you had opened with a brief summary of the plot of the poem, telling about the speaker's loneliness and his seeing the daffodils first with his outward eye and then with his inward eye, you could bring that paragraph to a close by saying, "Yet behind this speaker, with his interest in the psychology of memory-imprinting, we find Wordsworth the author, who is constructing this speaker, and these stanzas, and these metaphors." Then you could have a paragraph about the author and how he has arranged the poem scenically, rhythmically, metaphorically, and so on.

Ideally, in a well-organized paper, you ought to be able to delete, from each paragraph, the follow-up sentences supporting the topic sentence, and be left with a "skeleton" consisting of nothing but the topic sentences for each paragraph. That skeleton would make sense by itself, would proceed logically, and would contain all the main points of your paper. Some writers like to do a sentence-outline of this sort after taking notes on the poem and seeing what the notes add up to in general terms. Then all they have to do is to fill in the evidence supporting the topic sentence for each paragraph. This is a sturdy and logical way of ordering a paper. In rereading and revising your paper, you might try typing out what you consider the topic sentence of each paragraph and seeing how well those sentences hang together as a logical sequence. Often you discover that something you have noticed late, and written down late, really belongs somewhere earlier in the paper, or that an earlier sentence properly should be brought down into the conclusion.

Checking Your Work

Three serious defects can mar a paper on a poem. One such defect is having made the poem boring to your reader. Ask yourself why it was important to the poet to write this poem, and then you will make it urgent to your reader, too. Another defect is to have misrepresented the poem, so that the reader will say, "Well, I never understood from your paper that the speaker was *lonely* when he came across the daffodils!" And perhaps the worst defect is to have treated the poem as though it is simply a message, rather than an artifact — something arranged by a writer to be beautiful, patterned, coordinated, musical, and memorable. To avoid these defects, read your paper over, saying to yourself:

- Have I made my reader see the urgency of the poem?
- Have I noticed all the important points about words, sentences, rhyme and rhythm, emotional curve over time, spatial patterning, and memorable language?
- Have I treated this as an artwork and not merely as a statement?

By the time you finish your paper, if you have done your work well, you will almost know the poem by heart, because you will have seen how it fits together. Your reader should see that, too.

It is important that your paper offer no typographical or grammatical obstructions to your reader:

- Messiness is an obstruction;
- Misspelling is an obstruction;
- Misquotation of your text is an obstruction;
- Mistakes in grammar and syntax are obstructions.

The paper has obligations to the poem: it should be almost as beautiful as the poem is, almost as interesting as the poem is, almost as memorable as the poem is.

There may be a part of the poem that you simply can't fit into your overview. If so, admit it and go on. Sometimes just writing about your difficulty solves it, and in going back, you see how the stanza fits in or why that metaphor was used. But even if you don't see how to solve your difficulty, you can leave it as a problem for your reader; there's nothing readers like better than being asked to think about an enigma that you have left open for their reflection.

11

Studying Groups of Poems

Sometimes you will want to assemble a group of poems by a single author in order to write in depth about that author's practice. The best way to do this is to find a group of poems about a single theme or a group of poems concerning a single problem. To illustrate this process, we reprint, first, four poems written by Walt Whitman (1819–1892) about Abraham Lincoln after Lincoln was assassinated, with some information found in books about the assassination; and second, a number of poems by Emily Dickinson that consider the problem of how we mark off and describe events as they take place in time.

Walt Whitman: Poems on Lincoln

What are some of the ways Whitman might choose to write about his murdered president? Lincoln was shot by the Confederate sympathizer John Wilkes Booth, one of a group of conspirators, on Good Friday, April 14, 1865, shortly before the end of the Civil War. The assassination was dramatic: Lincoln was shot in his box at the theater, in full sight of his wife and the audience; he died several hours later. It was decided that he would be buried in Illinois, his home state, rather than in Washington. After a funeral service in Washington, a ceremonial train, decked in black and bearing the coffin, would traverse the states in a long trajectory across the East before arriving at Springfield. At every stop that the train made, buildings were draped in black, and ceremonies included the tolling of bells, music, services, sermons, and processions, with long lines of citizens waiting to pass by the body lying in state. The body of Lincoln's young son Tod, who had died a few years earlier, was disinterred and brought on the train to be reburied in the tomb that would hold the president's coffin. The conspirators were brought to justice and hanged. How much of this information, you might ask yourself, will Whitman use?

Some of the sermons preached, and poems written, on Lincoln's death spoke of him as a "martyr," drawing an analogy with Christ's death on Good Friday. Others compared Lincoln (whose Emancipation Proclamation freed the slaves) to Moses, who led the Hebrews out from their slavery in Egypt to the promised land in Canaan. You might wonder, knowing these facts, whether Whitman uses any such Judeo-Christian analogies in his poems, and you store this question away.

Only two of Whitman's four poems are dated: the first ("Hush'd Be the Camps To-day"), was written on May 4, 1865, shortly after Lincoln's death; and the last, "This Dust Was Once the Man," was published in 1871. The two middle poems — "O Captain! My Captain!" and "When Lilacs Last in the Dooryard Bloom'd" — were composed sometime in 1865 or 1866.

"Hush'd Be the Camps To-day" is a poem spoken not in Whitman's own voice but in the collective voice of the soldiers for whom Lincoln was the commander-in-chief. It consists of a series of quasi-military orders, beginning with the command that a silence be maintained in the camps during Lincoln's funeral service in Washington: "Hush'd be the camps to-day." Because Whitman thought that Lincoln would be buried in Washington, he closes the poem as the soldiers imagine the "invaulting" of the body:

Hush'd Be the Camps To-day

Hush'd be the camps to-day,
And soldiers let us drape our war-worn weapons,
And each with musing soul retire to _celebrate_,
Our dear commander's death.

No more for him life's stormy conflicts,
Nor victory, nor defeat — no more time's dark events,
Charging like ceaseless clouds across the sky.

But sing poet in our name,
Sing of the love we bore him — because you, dweller in
    camps, know it truly.

As they invault the coffin there,
Sing — as they close the doors of earth upon him — one verse,
For the heavy hearts of soldiers.

It has been conjectured that Whitman's second-written poem of
these four may have been "O Captain! My Captain!" since it is the one
replying to the soldiers' collective wish — in "Hush'd Be the Camps" —
that the poet compose and sing a song in *their* voice. Because a young
recruit speaks the poem, Whitman composes it in a ballad-measure of
the sort that was popular in folk-poetry of his day. Lincoln is here not the
commander-in-chief of the army but rather the captain of the ship of
state, killed just before the victorious ship is about to make harbor.

O Captain! My Captain!

O Captain! my Captain! our fearful trip is done,
The ship has weather'd every rack, the prize we sought is won,
The port is near, the bells I hear, the people all exulting,
While follow eyes the steady keel, the vessel grim and daring:
    But O heart! heart! heart!
      O the bleeding drops of red,
        Where on the deck my Captain lies,
          Fallen cold and dead.

O Captain! my Captain! rise up and hear the bells;
Rise up — for you the flag is flung — for you the bugle trills,
For you bouquets and ribbon'd wreaths — for you the shores
    a-crowding,
For you they call, the swaying mass, their eager faces turning;
    Here Captain! dear father!
      This arm beneath your head!
        It is some dream that on the deck,
          You've fallen cold and dead.

My Captain does not answer, his lips are pale and still,
My father does not feel my arm, he has no pulse nor will,
The ship is anchor'd safe and sound, its voyage closed and done,
From fearful trip the victor ship comes in with object won;
    Exult O shores, and ring O bells!
      But I with mournful tread,
        Walk the deck my Captain lies,
          Fallen cold and dead.

Whitman, understandably, must have wished to write an elegy for Lincoln in his own voice and his own verse-measure. The elegy he composes, in which he speaks in the first person as himself, is his longest poem about Lincoln and the one that has become a classic of American literature; for this reason, you might want to spend most of the space in your paper on "When Lilacs Last in the Dooryard Bloom'd":

When Lilacs Last in the Dooryard Bloom'd

1

When lilacs last in the dooryard bloom'd,
And the great star early droop'd in the western sky in the night,
I mourn'd, and yet shall mourn with ever-returning spring.
Ever-returning spring, trinity sure to me you bring,
Lilac blooming perennial and drooping star in the west,   5
And thought of him I love.

2

O powerful western fallen star!
O shades of night — O moody, tearful night!
O great star disappear'd — O the black murk that hides the star!
O cruel hands that hold me powerless — O helpless soul   10
    of me!
O harsh surrounding cloud that will not free my soul.

3

In the dooryard fronting an old farm-house near the white-wash'd
    palings,
Stands the lilac-bush tall-growing with heart-shaped leaves of rich
    green,
With many a pointed blossom rising delicate, with the perfume
    strong I love,
With every leaf a miracle — and from this bush in the   15
    dooryard,
With delicate-color'd blossoms and heart-shaped leaves of rich
    green,
A sprig with its flower I break.

4

In the swamp in secluded recesses,
A shy and hidden bird is warbling a song.

Solitary the thrush, 20
The hermit withdrawn to himself, avoiding the settlements,
Sings by himself a song.

Song of the bleeding throat,
Death's outlet song of life, (for well dear brother I know,
If thou wast not granted to sing thou would'st surely die.) 25

5

Over the breast of the spring, the land, amid cities,
Amid lanes and through old woods, where lately the violets peep'd
   from the ground, spotting the gray debris,
Amid the grass in the fields each side of the lanes, passing the
   endless grass,
Passing the yellow-spear'd wheat, every grain from its shroud in
   the dark-brown fields uprisen,
Passing the apple-tree blows of white and pink in the orchards, 30
Carrying a corpse to where it shall rest in the grave,
Night and day journeys a coffin.

6

Coffin that passes through lanes and streets,[1]
Through day and night with the great cloud darkening the land,
With the pomp of the inloop'd flags with the cities draped in 35
   black,
With the show of the States themselves as of crape-veil'd women
   standing,
With processions long and winding and the flambeaus of the
   night,
With the countless torches lit, with the silent sea of faces and the
   unbared heads,
With the waiting depot, the arriving coffin, and the sombre faces,
With dirges through the night, with the thousand voices rising 40
   strong and solemn,
With all the mournful voices of the dirges pour'd around the
   coffin,
The dim-lit churches and the shuddering organs — where amid
   these you journey,

---

[1]Lincoln's funeral procession traveled from Washington, D.C., to Springfield, Illinois, stopping along the way so that people could honor the slain president.

With the tolling tolling bells' perpetual clang,
Here, coffin that slowly passes,
I give you my sprig of lilac.   45

7

(Nor for you, for one alone,
Blossoms and branches green to coffins all I bring,
For fresh as the morning, thus would I chant a song for you O
      sane and sacred death.

All over bouquets of roses,
O death, I cover you over with roses and early lilies,   50
But mostly and now the lilac that blooms the first,
Copious I break, I break the sprigs from the bushes,
With loaded arms I come, pouring for you,
For you and the coffins all of you O death.)

8

O western orb sailing the heaven,   55
Now I know what you must have meant as a month since I walk'd,
As I walk'd in silence the transparent shadowy night,
As I saw you had something to tell as you bent to me night after
      night,
As you droop'd from the sky low down as if to my side, (while the
      other stars all look'd on,)
As we wander'd together the solemn night, (for something I   60
      know not what kept me from sleep,)
As the night advanced, and I saw on the rim of the west how full
      you were of woe,
As I stood on the rising ground in the breeze in the cool
      transparent night,
As I watch'd where you pass'd and was lost in the netherward black
      of the night,
As my soul in its trouble dissatisfied sank, as where you sad orb,
Concluded, dropt in the night, and was gone.   65

9

Sing on there in the swamp,
O singer bashful and tender, I hear your notes, I hear your call,
I hear, I come presently, I understand you,
But a moment I linger, for the lustrous star has detain'd me,
The star my departing comrade holds and detains me.   70

10

O how shall I warble myself for the dead one there I loved?
And how shall I deck my song for the large sweet soul that has
    gone?
And what shall my perfume be for the grave of him I love?

Sea-winds blown from east and west,
Blown from the Eastern sea and blown from the Western sea,   75
    till there on the prairies meeting,
These and with these and the breath of my chant,
I'll perfume the grave of him I love.

11

O what shall I hang on the chamber walls?
And what shall the pictures be that I hang on the walls,
To adorn the burial-house of him I love?   80

Pictures of growing spring and farms and homes,
With the Fourth-month eve at sundown, and the gray smoke
    lucid and bright,
With floods of the yellow gold of the gorgeous, indolent, sinking
    sun, burning, expanding the air,
With the fresh sweet herbage under foot, and the pale green leaves
    of the trees prolific,
In the distance the flowing glaze, the breast of the river, with a   85
    wind-dapple here and there,
With ranging hills on the banks, with many a line against the sky,
    and shadows,
And the city at hand with dwellings so dense, and stacks of
    chimneys,
And all the scenes of life and the workshops, and the workmen
    homeward returning.

12

Lo, body and soul — this land,
My own Manhattan with spires, and the sparkling and   90
    hurrying tides, and the ships,
The varied and ample land, the South and the North in the light,
    Ohio's shores and flashing Missouri,
And ever the far-spreading prairies cover'd with grass and corn.

Lo, the most excellent sun so calm and haughty,
The violet and purple morn with just-felt breezes,

The gentle soft-born measureless light,   95
The miracle spreading bathing all, the fulfill'd noon,
The coming eve delicious, the welcome night and the stars,
Over my cities shining all, enveloping man and land.

13

Sing on, sing on you gray-brown bird,
Sing from the swamps, the recesses, pour your chant from the   100
    bushes,
Limitless out of the dusk, out of the cedars and pines.

Sing on dearest brother, warble your reedy song,
Loud human song, with voice of uttermost woe.

O liquid and free and tender!
O wild and loose to my soul — O wondrous singer!   105
You only I hear — yet the star holds me, (but will soon depart,)
Yet the lilac with mastering odor holds me.

14

Now while I sat in the day and look'd forth,
In the close of the day with its light and the fields of spring, and
    the farmers preparing their crops,
In the large unconscious scenery of my land with its lakes and   110
    forests,
In the heavenly aerial beauty, (after the perturb'd winds and the
    storms,)
Under the arching heavens of the afternoon swift passing, and the
    voices of children and women,
The many-moving sea-tides, and I saw the ships how they sail'd,
And the summer approaching with richness, and the fields all busy
    with labor,
And the infinite separate houses, how they all went on, each   115
    with its meals and minutia of daily usages,
And the streets how their throbbings throbb'd, and the cities
    pent — lo, then and there,
Falling upon them all and among them all, enveloping me with
    the rest,
Appear'd the cloud, appear'd the long black trail,
And I knew death, its thought, and the sacred knowledge of
    death.

Then with the knowledge of death as walking one side of me,   120

And the thought of death close-walking the other side of me,
And I in the middle as with companions, and as holding the hands
    of companions,
I fled forth to the hiding receiving night that talks not,
Down to the shores of the water, the path by the swamp in the
    dimness,
To the solemn shadowy cedars and ghostly pines so still. 125

And the singer so shy to the rest receiv'd me,
The gray-brown bird I know receiv'd us comrades three,
And he sang the carol of death, and a verse for him I love.

From deep secluded recesses,
From the fragrant cedars and the ghostly pines so still, 130
Came the carol of the bird.

And the charm of the carol rapt me,
As I held as if by their hands my comrades in the night,
And the voice of my spirit tallied the song of the bird.

Come lovely and soothing death, 135
Undulate round the world, serenely arriving, arriving,
In the day, in the night, to all, to each,
Sooner or later delicate death.

Prais'd be the fathomless universe,
For life and joy, and for objects and knowledge curious, 140
And for love, sweet love — but praise! praise! praise!
For the sure-enwinding arms of cool-enfolding death.

Dark mother always gliding near with soft feet,
Have none chanted for thee a chant of fullest welcome?
Then I chant it for thee, I glorify thee above all, 145
I bring thee a song that when thou must indeed come, come unfalteringly.

Approach strong deliveress,
When it is so, when thou hast taken them I joyously sing the dead,
Lost in the loving floating ocean of thee,
Laved in the flood of thy bliss O death. 150

From me to thee glad serenades,
Dances for thee I propose saluting thee, adornments and feastings for
    thee,
And the sights of the open landscape and the high-spread sky are fitting,
And life and the fields, and the huge and thoughtful night.

The night in silence under many a star, 155
The ocean shore and the husky whispering wave whose voice I know,
And the soul turning to thee O vast and well-veil'd death,
And the body gratefully nestling close to thee.

Over the tree-tops I float thee a song,
Over the rising and sinking waves, over the myriad fields and the 160
    prairies wide,
Over the dense-pack'd cities all and the teeming wharves and ways,
I float this carol with joy, with joy to thee O death.

15

To the tally of my soul,
Loud and strong kept up the gray-brown bird,
With pure deliberate notes spreading filling the night. 165

Loud in the pines and cedars dim,
Clear in the freshness moist and the swamp-perfume,
And I with my comrades there in the night.

While my sight that was bound in my eyes unclosed,
As to long panoramas of visions. 170

And I saw askant the armies,
I saw as in noiseless dreams hundreds of battle-flags,
Borne through the smoke of the battles and pierc'd with missiles I
    saw them,
And carried hither and yon through the smoke, and torn and
    bloody,
And at last but a few shreds left on the staffs, (and all in silence,) 175
And the staffs all splinter'd and broken.

I saw battle-corpses, myriads of them,
And the white skeletons of young men, I saw them,
I saw the debris and debris of all the slain soldiers of the war,
But I saw they were not as was thought, 180
They themselves were fully at rest, they suffer'd not,
The living remain'd and suffer'd, the mother suffer'd,
And the wife and the child and the musing comrade suffer'd,
And the armies that remain'd suffer'd.

16

Passing the visions, passing the night, 185
Passing, unloosing the hold of my comrades' hands,

Passing the song of the hermit bird and the tallying song of my
    soul,
Victorious song, death's outlet song, yet varying ever-altering
    song,
As low and wailing, yet clear the notes, rising and falling, flooding
    the night,
Sadly sinking and fainting, as warning and warning, and yet   190
    again bursting with joy,
Covering the earth and filling the spread of the heaven,
As that powerful psalm in the night I heard from recesses,
Passing, I leave thee lilac with heart-shaped leaves,
I leave thee there in the door-yard, blooming, returning with
    spring.

I cease from my song for thee,   195
From my gaze on thee in the west, fronting the west, communing
    with thee,
O comrade lustrous with silver face in the night.

Yet each to keep and all, retrievements out of the night,
The song, the wondrous chant of the gray-brown bird,
And the tallying chant, the echo arous'd in my soul,   200
With the lustrous and drooping star with the countenance full of
    woe,
With the holders holding my hand nearing the call of the bird,
Comrades mine and I in the midst, and their memory ever to
    keep, for the dead I loved so well,
For the sweetest, wisest soul of all my days and lands —
    and this for his dear sake,
Lilac and star and bird twined with the chant of my soul,   205
There in the fragrant pines and the cedars dusk and dim.

Finally, in 1871, Whitman writes an epitaph for Lincoln. An epi-
taph (from Greek *epi*, "upon," and *tophos*, "tomb") has to be short
enough to be inscribed on a tombstone, and it has to be written in an
impersonal way. No "voice," as such, speaks this poem unless it is the
voice of History, pronouncing finally on Lincoln, not as man — his
body is now dust — but as historical personage: "This Dust Was Once
the Man":

This Dust Was Once the Man

This dust was once the man,
Gentle, plain, just and resolute, under whose cautious hand,

Against the foulest crime in history known in any land or age,
Was saved the Union of these States.

Suppose you have gathered these four poems together as the products of Whitman's need to celebrate, memorialize, elegize, and even write an epitaph for Lincoln. You might separate them first into two groups: the three poems in which Whitman does *not* speak in his own voice, and "Lilacs," in which he does.

- In "Hush'd Be the Camps To-day," what sort of voice appears in the collective wishes of the soldiers?
- What can they do to mourn Lincoln?
- What is the one thing they need someone else to do for them?
- How do they imagine the moment when that is done?
- Why, do you think, did Whitman want to write a poem in the voice of the soldiers?

Then you might ask:

- What sort of voice and verse-measure do we hear coming from the young naval recruit whose captain has just been shot?
- In what sort of rhythms does he speak?
- What emotion does he chiefly express?
- How does he express his relation to the fallen captain?
- How does the allegorical metaphor of the ship of state play out in the poem?
- Of what use is that metaphor to Whitman in writing the poem?
- What changes occur in the young sailor's speech in the last stanza?
- For what sort of audience is the ballad-like stanza of this poem intended?

Then you might consider the epitaph "This Dust Was Once the Man":

- In what voice does History speak?
- What sort of vocabulary does History use, by comparison with the vocabulary of the soldiers in "Hush'd Be the Camps To-day" or that of the young recruit in "O Captain! My Captain!"?
- What sort of syntax does History employ?
- Why does History use the passive verb-form ("the Union was saved") instead of the active form ("he saved the Union")?
- Who saved the Union?

- What adjectives does History use of Lincoln, and is there any significance to their order?

- If the poetic that underlies "O Captain! My Captain!" is that of popular ballad verse, what are the characteristics of epitaph-writing that underlie "This Dust"?

You have seen what it occurred to Whitman to say in the voice of soldiers who have just received the news of the death of their commander-in-chief; in the voice of a youthful sailor holding the dead body of his slain captain; and in the voice of History, impersonally summarizing Lincoln's high achievements in ending slavery and preserving the Union. Now you are better prepared to see what Whitman says in his own voice.

But first, you might stand off a bit from all the poems to consider what they add up to as poetry of the Civil War and of assassination. In these poems, do you see battles? Do you see the Emancipation Proclamation? Do you see the assassination? Do you see the punishment of the conspirators? Do you see slaves? members of Congress? generals? members of the Confederacy? And you might see what the poems add up to in elegizing Lincoln the private man. Do we see his wife? his living children? his dead son Tod, about to be buried with him? It is by selection from all available material that the writer makes his emphasis clear.

As you study "Lilacs," before writing about it, you will want to look at it section by section, since it is such a long poem. A good way of thinking about any poem is to write it out in your own handwriting, thinking of yourself as a poet composing the lines, and asking, "Why have I said this?" "Why have I followed this section with the next section?" "Why have I changed my focus?" and so on. But "Lilacs" is too long for this procedure, and for a poem of this length the best strategy for seeing it clearly is to write a one-sentence summary of each section, noticing the manner as well as the matter of the section. Your summaries of the first few sections of "Lilacs" might look like this:

1. Lilac, star, and thought as trinity of mourning: star "droops," lilac is a perennial. Spring perennial too.

2. Star disappears; speaker held helpless in harsh dark cloud. O, O, O, O, O, O, O, O — eight of them!

3. Lilac bush — 5-line description leading up in line 17 to the action: "A sprig . . . I break."

4. Thrush: Talks to thrush ("dear brother"); singing prevents dying.

5. Like lilac stanza — long lead-in ("passing . . . passing . . . carrying") to action: "journeys a coffin."

By the time you get to later stanzas, you will have noticed that Whitman not only talks to the thrush, he also talks to the coffin (stanza 6), to death (stanza 7), to the star (stanza 8), and to the thrush again (stanza 9); and you will see that these addressees represent different planes of existence: the material (the coffin), the abstract (death), the celestial (the star), the animal (the thrush). You will also notice that having once addressed all of these symbolic beings, the poet turns back to put questions to himself in stanzas 10–11 and to act as a displayer of the American landscape (stanza 12), before returning to address the thrush a second time in stanza 13.

By amassing one-sentence descriptions in this way, you'll have begun to see the ways Whitman manages his poem — by exclamations, by direct address, by ranging to different planes of experience, and so on. Soon these will gather together to give you several talking points for your paper.

In writing about a long poem such as this, you will find certain sections that you want to concentrate on and others that you will want to treat more lightly. This choice depends on what your main point concerning "Lilacs" is. If you want to talk about the poet's direct addresses to other beings, you might choose stanzas 4 and 13, in which he addresses the thrush, and then explain why he ceases to address the thrush in the second person but rather talks about the bird in the third person from line 126 on ("The singer so shy to the rest receiv'd me"). You might notice that this does not happen right away with the lilac or the star: in line 193 the speaker says, addressing the lilac directly, "Passing, I leave thee lilac," and in line 195 he says to the star, "I cease from my song for thee." Eventually all three symbols are spoken of in the third person: "Lilac and star and bird twined with the chant of my soul" (line 205).

If, on the other hand, your main point about "Lilacs" is how private a poem it is by comparison to the more public poems of the camps, the young sailor, and the epitaph, you might want to concentrate on the word "love" as it appears throughout this poem. Or if you want to emphasize its meditation on death — excluded from the other three poems — you would want to concentrate on the very long stanza 14, containing Whitman's "translation" of the song of the bird, "Come lovely and soothing death."

If (to take another example) you are interested in how Whitman, while abjuring the Judeo-Christian symbols of martyrdom, resurrection, afterlife in heaven, and so on, renews the imagination of death from other sources, you would want to concentrate on stanza 11 (where Whitman draws on the Egyptian practice of painting the insides of tombs with scenes from daily life) and stanzas 14–15 (where Whitman draws on the Greek conception of an underworld haunted by shades, which he transfers to the swamp).

By writing out a brief summary of each section of the long poem, you will easily be able to assemble possible points of comparison and contrast with the other poems and to have a quick reference for finding the parts of the long poem that you want to cite.

What can we learn from comparisons of this sort among poems by the same author that have a theme in common? We learn, first, that no theme determines the form a poem takes — that the death of Lincoln can be looked at in many different ways, from many points of view — singular, collective, public, private, allegorical, and so on. Once the writer has chosen the point of view for a poem ("I think I'll have it be a young sailor mourning the captain of the ship of state") there is still the verse-form to be decided on; and then how many stanzas; and then how the opening and closing might work; and then what the emotional range of the poem will be. Each decision helps determine the ultimate shape of the poem.

Such a set of comparisons also induces us to make evaluative judgments. Most readers have thought "Lilacs" the best of these poems. This is a chance for you to ask yourself whether you agree, and if so why; or if not, why not? Perhaps readers prefer private mourning to public epitaphs; is this a fair preference? Or perhaps readers like the clear "trinity" of symbols — lilac and star and bird — in "Lilacs." Do you? Or perhaps readers feel that a longer poem can include more of the many feelings prompted by Lincoln's death. Do you?

We can also, by comparing poems in the same broad genre (these are all elegies for Lincoln), see the capacity of a single genre to contain many subgenres — here, the elegy voiced by a group ("Hush'd Be the Camps To-day"); the elegy voiced by a "naïve" speaker (here, the young sailor); the impersonal elegy voiced by "History" ("This Dust"); and the elegy voiced by the poet in his own speech. You can carry this knowledge to the next elegiac poem you read; it will sharpen your sense of the idiosyncrasy of that poem.

Finally, by comparing poems, we find out something about ourselves in relation to Whitman: that we like best the Whitman of a collective voice, or the Whitman of historical severity, or the Whitman of panorama, or the Whitman of folk-ballad, or the Whitman of intimacy of address, or the Whitman of long unrolling sentences, or the Whitman of the renewal of imagination from Egyptian and Greek sources. As we sort out our own responses, we are discovering where our taste and judgment lead us; but also, as we read a number of poems, we are broadening our own sense of what poetry can do. Robert Frost has a relevant comment about reading a poem in the light of other poems. In a short essay first published in the *New York Times Book Review* (March 31, 1954), he said:

> A poem is best read in the light of all the other poems ever written. We read A the better to read B (we have to start somewhere; we may get very little out of A). We read B the better to read C, C the better to read D, D the better to go back and get something more out of A. Progress is not the aim, but circulation. The thing is to get among the poems where they hold each other apart in their places as the stars do.

Emily Dickinson: Poems on Time

Let us suppose you have been asked to write a paper on a selection of poems by Emily Dickinson (1830–1886) that concern a similar theme. You are to suggest what the poems have in common, how they differ from each other, what qualities of human psychological response they are interested in, and with what variety of poetic means Dickinson conceptualizes and stylizes their subject matter.

Here, a selection of eight poems has been made for you, all of them concerned with events in time, each of them structuring time in its own way. Dickinson investigates in these poems how she experiences time and how one might express different senses of time when composing narratives in verse. After reading the poems below, and the brief questions following them, you might decide which three poems you will focus on for your paper, choosing those that most attract you by the emotions conveyed by the strategies Dickinson finds to arrange her plot-events, and by the language that she presses into service for each poem.

1

The most naive experience of time, one that we all have, is a linear one with a beginning and end separated by a set of markers. It could be the year from January to December divided by months, or the day from dawn to midnight divided by hours, or (projected on space) the journey from Boston to New York punctuated by the stops made by the train.

Dickinson sets out this equable and predictable idea of time in her poem about watching the local train: "I like to see it lap the Miles":

I like to see it lap the Miles —

I like to see it lap the Miles —
And lick the Valleys up —

And stop to feed itself at Tanks —
And then — prodigious step

Around a Pile of Mountains —
And supercilious peer
In Shanties — by the sides of Roads —
And then a Quarry pare

To fit its sides
And crawl between
Complaining all the while
In horrid — hooting stanza —
Then chase itself down Hill —

And neigh like Boanerges —
Then — prompter than a Star
Stop — docile and omnipotent
At its own stable door —

- How do you think Dickinson decided on the train's stops?
- Does anything untoward happen to the train? If not, why not?
- Where does the train end up?
- What sort of human experience of time (exciting? placid? even? irregular? inconsistent? routine?) does the poem enact?
- How does Dickinson suggest her feelings when watching the progress of the train?
- Does life ever unroll over time in the way the story of the train does?

2

In a poem more sinister than "I like to see it lap the Miles," Dickinson again represents linear time by the stops made by a conveyance. This is her tale of a carriage ride with Death: "Because I could not stop for Death."

Because I could not stop for Death —

Because I could not stop for Death —
He kindly stopped for me —
The Carriage held but just Ourselves —
And Immortality.

We slowly drove — He knew no haste
And I had put away

My labor and my leisure too,
For His Civility —

We passed the School, where Children strove
At Recess — in the Ring —
We passed the Fields of Gazing Grain —
We passed the Setting Sun —

Or rather — He passed Us —
The Dews drew quivering and Chill —
For only Gossamer, my Gown —
My Tippet° — only Tulle —   *shawl*

We paused before a House that seemed
A Swelling of the Ground —
The Roof was scarcely visible —
The Cornice — in the Ground —

Since then — 'tis Centuries — and yet
Feels shorter than the Day
I first surmised the Horses' Heads
Were toward Eternity —

- What are the stops here? Does the poem begin when the journey begins? Does the poem end when the journey ends? If not, why not?
- Does the journey end where it began, as the train's journey did?
- Dickinson here reflects on how memory can change the perception of time: What was the longest internal "day" of Dickinson's life? Why?
- The poet says, "Since then — 'tis Centuries": is it, really? If not, what does this line convey?
- The poem uses as its end-brackets two words that negate time: "Immortality" and "Eternity." How does the dictionary distinguish between them? Which is more appealing?
- The poet has imagined Death as a courteous gentleman who, neglected by the speaker, comes calling to remind her of his existence. Can you imagine other ways of imagining this event in one's existence?

3

Linear time can be divided by subjective criteria, too, as life modulates from one state to another. In "The Heart asks Pleasure — first,"

Dickinson creates a main clause — "The Heart asks" — and follows it by a series of requests by the heart, of which the first is "pleasure." These requests are joined by the repeated phrase "And then," emphasizing the inexorable links of this temporal sequence.

The Heart asks Pleasure — first —

The Heart asks Pleasure — first —
And then — excuse from Pain —
And then — those little Anodynes
That deaden suffering —

And then — to go to sleep —
And then — if it should be
The will of its Inquisitor
The privilege to die —

- At what approximate point in life does this narrative begin?
- What is the first criterion of change noticed by the heart?
- At what point does the narrative end? Or does it end at all?
- The "pieces" of time segmented here are of the same syntactic length until the last one arrives. Why does the syntax "spread out" at this point?
- What does one learn from the last segment that one had not known before?
- Who is in control of the segmentation of time felt by the speaker? What motivates the torturer? Why is he given the name by which he is called? Why has he not been named sooner?
- Are these "stops" on the journey of life universal and predictable, according to Dickinson?
- How would the import of the poem change if it were spoken in the first person — if the first line said, "My Heart asks Pleasure — first"?

4

So far, time has been shown as a linear structure, with a beginning followed by a series of stops. The stops separating beginning and end in this journey can be familiar and predictable (as with the course of the train), both familiar and unfamiliar (as with the ride in Death's carriage), or they can be markers gradually intensifying in emotional effect (as in "The Heart asks"). Do we ever structure time in ways that disrupt this linear pattern of a beginning, followed by intermediate stops, approaching an end? Can temporal patterning disappear altogether?

When Dickinson's self is cleft in two by suffering ("I felt a Cleaving in my Mind"), time no longer seems to resemble itself.

I felt a Cleaving in my Mind

I felt a Cleaving in my Mind —
As if my Brain had split —
I tried to match it — Seam by Seam —
But could not make them fit —

The thought behind, I strove to join
Unto the thought before —
But Sequence ravelled out of Sound —
Like Balls — upon a Floor —

There are two manuscripts (one a partial one, of the second stanza only) for "I felt a Cleaving in my Mind." The manuscript of the complete poem shows a variant for lines 7–8, in which "Sequence ravelled out of reach, / Like balls upon a floor." The simile of balls of yarn that unravel as they fall to the floor and roll out of reach is a domestic one. How does the reading chosen by Dickinson's editor, "Sequence ravelled out of Sound" — with its implied metaphor of a musical sequence that disappears into inaudibility — change your sense of the speaker's feeling?

The Dust behind I strove to join
Unto the Disk before —
But Sequence ravelled out of Sound
Like Balls upon a Floor —

The manuscript that contains only the second stanza substitutes, for the relatively literal lines 5–6 ("The thought behind, I strove to join / Unto the thought before"), the following metaphorical lines: "The Dust behind I strove to join / Unto the Disk before." Can one make a mental "sequence" that would link a smooth, solid, and perfect "disk" to an atomized and formless "dust"? What has happened to thought, according to this metaphor? How does an incapacity for sequential thinking affect one's sense of time?

5

In the linear plot of crisis that structures "I felt a Cleaving in my Mind" time also is cleft in two — into "before" and "after" the crisis. (In

Dickinson the arranging of time around a single event makes for either binary poems ("The Soul selects her own Society — / Then — shuts the Door") or for three-part series reducing life to beginning, middle, and end ("Born — Bridalled — Shrouded"). If this is what happens to one's sense of time when a single crisis has occurred, how is that sense of time affected when crisis is multiplied? Dickinson considers the horrifying recurrence of catastrophe in "The first Day's Night had come": you will see in this poem the same conclusion-in-aftermath that was present in "Because I could not stop for Death":

The first Day's Night had come —

The first Day's Night had come —
And grateful that a thing
So terrible — had been endured —
I told my Soul to sing —

She said her strings were snapt —
Her Bow — to atoms blown —
And so to mend her — gave me work
Until another Morn —

And then — a Day as huge
As Yesterdays in pairs,
Unrolled its horror in my face —
Until it blocked my eyes —

My Brain — begun to laugh —
I mumbled — like a fool —
And tho' 'tis Years ago — that Day —
My Brain keeps giggling — still.

And Something's odd — within —
That person that I was —
And this One — do not feel the same —
Could it be Madness — this?

- How does Dickinson indicate the comparative magnitude of the second catastrophe?

- How does the recurrence of catastrophe affect the brain of the speaker?

- Analyze the contribution of each of the verbs in the second-to-last stanza: "laugh," "mumble," and "giggle." What sense of time does the speaker now experience, do you think?

6

"After great pain, a formal feeling comes" begins when the crisis is already over. Dickinson has nothing to say about the time before the crisis, nor does she specify the nature or temporal extent of the crisis itself: we know it only from its result, "great pain."

After great pain, a formal feeling comes

After great pain, a formal feeling comes —
The Nerves sit ceremonious, like Tombs —
The stiff Heart questions 'was it He, that bore,'
And 'Yesterday, or Centuries before'?

The Feet, mechanical, go round —
A Wooden way
Of Ground, or Air, or Ought —
Regardless grown,
A Quartz contentment, like a stone —

This is the Hour of Lead —
Remembered, if outlived,
As Freezing persons, recollect the Snow —
First — Chill — then Stupor — then the letting go —

- What does the first stanza tell us about the speaker's sense of time?
- Do the speaker's feet advance in their motion? How do you know?
- In the last stanza, time is given weight: "This is the Hour of Lead." Can you extrapolate from this metaphor to others like it? "This is the day of ___"? "This is the noon of ___"? Can a time of "lead" advance?
- A second "story" — about freezing in the snow — is told in the last three lines of the poem. Is this a linearly narrated story? How does it end? How does it resemble the first story?
- What is the point of adding this second story to the first one?
- How does the speaker's experience of time "after great pain" differ from that in "I like to see it lap the Miles" or "The Heart asks Pleasure — first"?

7

In the poem "There's a certain Slant of light," Dickinson begins with a "stopped frame" of the light itself, defining it. It is only in the last stanza that she shows us the beginning-point of the light: "When it comes."

There's a certain Slant of light

There's a certain Slant of light,
Winter Afternoons —
That oppresses, like the Heft
Of Cathedral Tunes —

Heavenly Hurt, it gives us —
We can find no scar,
But internal difference —
Where the Meanings, are —

None may teach it — Any —
'Tis the Seal Despair —
An imperial affliction
Sent us of the Air —

When it comes, the Landscape listens —
Shadows — hold their breath —
When it goes, 'tis like the Distance
On the look of Death —

If Dickinson had unfolded the progress of the light in linear fashion (in the manner of the train making its journey), she would have made a different poem, one (with apologies to Dickinson) like this:

When a Shaft — of Light — comes
Slanting through the Trees
On a Winter afternoon
Weighing on our Eyes —

Then we feel, within our Brain —
A Cathedral Tune —
As the steady Shadows lean —
Darker — into Dim —

Then Light fading — fainter still —
Tells us of Despair —
As the Landscape vanishes
In the somber Air —

Till the ones who held their Breath,
Watching ebbing Light —

Still afflicted — perish — with it —
At the fall of Night —

Consider how Dickinson changes our perception of time by "crowding" the light's coming and going, beginning and end, into the last quatrain. What does this make us feel about the light that we would not feel if its appearance were "played out" as it is in the linear version that has been made up here to contrast with the original?

8

Finally, here is a poem in which Dickinson herself reflects on how time is affected by pain: "Pain — expands the Time . . . / Pain contracts — the Time" she writes paradoxically:

Pain — expands the Time

Pain — expands the Time —
Ages coil within
The minute Circumference
Of a single Brain —

Pain contracts — the Time —
Occupied with Shot
Gamuts of Eternities
Are as they were not —

- Dickinson could have written two separate poems — one on how pain expands time and another on how pain contracts time. What is gained, do you think, by putting mutually contradictory perceptions into a single poem?
- Is there any such thing as "sequence" in this poem?
- We see here again Dickinson's use of the word "eternity" in connection with time. We met it before in "Because I could not stop for Death," but there it appeared in the singular. What is the effect here of making it plural?
- Can you explain the sort of pain that expands time and compare it with the sort of pain that contracts time? It may help to reflect that this poem (with its "shot," or bullet) was probably written in 1864, during the Civil War.

Writing Your Paper

After you have read and reflected on these eight poems about time, you will want, in order to write your paper, to select a few (say, three) to concentrate on (while reserving the right to make brief reference to some or all of the others as you compose your essay). Always choose to write on the poems that stir you most, those you are drawn to explore in more detail.

One reader might want to treat Dickinson's whimsy as she invents the stops for her train — and the remnant of that whimsy as she imagines the carriage ride with Death — with an ironic remnant of the whimsy in her mention, in "The Heart asks Pleasure" of "those little Anodynes / That deaden suffering."

Another might be drawn to Dickinson's radical use of metaphor, centering on the strange and unworldly metaphors Dickinson uses to describe the stopping of time in "After great pain" (what is "A Quartz contentment, like a stone")? Grouped around "After great pain" might be the other strange metaphors in "Pain — expands the Time": what are "Gamuts of Eternities"?

Yet another reader might be drawn to Dickinson's relentlessness when writing of time and could investigate aspects like the following:

- How episodes in time are linked (e.g., by the grim "and then's" of "The Heart asks");
- What happens when relentlessness has to walk in a circle (in "After great pain");
- What the result is when crisis is piled on crisis, and the second "and then" is bigger ("AND THEN") than the first (as in "The first Day's Night had come").

No matter which three poems you choose to concentrate on, you should make a list in two columns, grouping the aspects of your poems:

What Is Literal	*What Is Imagined*
Things in Common: Matter	*Things Different: Matter*
Things in Common: Style	*Things Different: Style*

Under *What Is Literal* put whatever basic psychological life-experience the poem conveys. For "After great pain," you might write, "Aftermath of emotional devastation: no sensations or feelings; time confused; time stands still; environment unclear; self rigid." Under *What Is Imagined* you might write, for the same poem, "Nerves like tombs in a cemetery; heart 'stiff' as in *rigor mortis*; 'yesterday' indistinguishable from

'centuries before'; feet on wooden circular track: ground? air?; self —
crystalline or stony, which?" Inquiry into figurative language reveals, in
each case, an originating emotion that has found its way into language.

Under *Things in Common: Matter* you could list ideas about the
sense of time — its beginning, its end, and its interior episodes — that
link your three poems together. Your poems might have in common
their sense of a crisis marking time into Before and After, for instance;
their sense that time has stopped altogether; or their contrast of time
with eternity. Under *Things in Common: Style* you might put the fact that
all three of your poems have three stanzas; that all three display an iron
sequence of inseparably linked events; that they all begin with the first
event in a sequence; that they all end in aftermath rather than with the
final episode; or that they share syntactic forms. Don't be concerned if
only two of your poems show such resemblances: you can always use the
third to show differences.

Under *Things Different: Matter* put whatever ideas differentiate your
three poems from each other: they may all exhibit different emotional
responses to time, or they may treat time as natural in one instance, as
unreal in another. Under *Things Different: Style* put any structural and sty-
listic differences: your poems may begin at the end of their linear
sequence; they may not give a true ending to the sequence at all; one
may use chiefly verbs, another, nouns; one may be all one sentence,
another, composed of several sentences; or one may arrange items in cli-
mactic order, another, not.

Decide on an order of treatment of your poems: perhaps shortest
to longest, most ordinary to most imaginative, or least paradoxical to
most paradoxical. Your reader wants to feel that you are setting out, in
some logical order, your ideas about Dickinson's poetic strategies for
dealing with the felt experience of time.

Before beginning to write, think about your own feelings about
time. Have you ever felt time stand still? Have you ever felt that one year
went by much faster than another? Have you ever felt time drag? Have
your feelings about time been influenced by the loss of people through
death? Has time ever seemed to become more intense, day by day or year
by year? Has time ever seemed to go in circles? Has clock-time always
seemed real to you? Do the concepts of Eternity and Immortality have
meaning for you? It is only by reflecting on your own senses of time that
you will be able to make a true connection to Dickinson's experience
and to see how each poem stylizes sequence differently so as to be able
to render the psychological structure of experience with maximum
accuracy.

As you write, remember that a good essay on poetry evokes the atmosphere of a poem (by such words as "leisurely" or "relentless"; "whimsy" or "sublimity"; "sinister" or "light-hearted"; "even" or "irregular"; "intimate" or "public"; "appealing" or "grotesque"). It is not enough to go through the poem and say *what* it says: what you need to show your reader is *how* it says what it says — by what means, with what atmosphere, with what vividness of language, with what turns of syntax, with what temperature in the feelings. Otherwise, if you remain in the realm of paraphrase of ideas, you are not conveying the emotion that propelled the poem into being, that made the poet break her silence.

You must quote the poem, or at least the parts of it you discuss (in the case of a nonprincipal poem), so that the reader can see the evidence for your remarks. It is a good idea to give a brief set of questions at the beginning of your paper, to interest the reader:

> How did Emily Dickinson perceive time? Do her perceptions change with the nature of the experience she is evoking? Can time be sequenced in different ways? Is all time felt as evenly linear, or is it sometimes felt in different ways? When does time stop? How can the structures of our varied experiences of time be enacted with fineness and discrimination in a poem? Some answers to these questions can be found in considering three characteristic poems.

Then you can say, "The first of the three poems, the shortest and most paradoxical, embodies Dickinson's contradictory views of time," and begin with, say, "Pain — expands the Time." After quoting the poem, it is a good idea to give your reader a one-sentence "view" of the chief aspects of the poem: its literal experience, its chief act of imagining, its subject-matter, and its form. These can be given in any order:

> "The Heart asks Pleasure — first" is a one-sentence, two-stanza poem of increasing disillusionment with life, as the heart's requests are ignored with greater and greater cruelty by its hidden "Inquisitor," whose identity is revealed only at the end.

This one-sentence summary gives your reader a thumbnail sketch of how you see the poem and enables your subsequent analysis to fit into a comprehensible overview.

In concluding your paper, now that you have done the analysis of the strategies of the three poems, you can answer some of the questions raised at the beginning:

Not only does Dickinson expand and contract time, she also alters sequence and in fact stops sequence altogether, as her poems mimic the relativity of time in emotional experience.

Reread your paper to make sure that your logic and your evidence — your evidence will chiefly be quotations supporting your points — are sufficient to persuade your reader that what you say is true. Check that the beginning offers questions to interest the reader and that your conclusion offers answers to the questions raised at the outset. Ask yourself if you have evoked the temperature and feeling-tone of the poems as well as their imaginative and linguistic strategies. Ask yourself if you have shown, in your paper, why Dickinson is considered a gripping poet of intense feeling. If you have done your job well, your reader will come away from your essay not only understanding your three poems in relation to Dickinson's structuring of time, but also wanting to read more of Dickinson's poetry. A good essay whets the appetite of its reader.

III

ANTHOLOGY

SHERMAN ALEXIE (b. 1966)
Reservation Love Song

I can meet you
in Springdale buy you beer
& take you home
in my one-eyed Ford

I can pay your rent
on HUD house get you free
food from the BIA
get your teeth fixed at IHS

I can buy you alcohol
& not drink it all
while you're away I won't fuck
any of your cousins

if I don't get too drunk
I can bring old blankets
to sleep with in winter
they smell like grandmother

hands digging up roots
they have powerful magic
we can sleep good
we can sleep warm

PAULA GUNN ALLEN (b. 1939)
Zen Americana

Un is okay.
Un pretentious. Un decided. Un known.
Un ego is where I want to be. How do you open
the door to Un? What does the un place look like,
look alikes?

Un beginning; can I un wake myself, un sleep
motionless in a bright green chair?
Maybe un lamps light the room (the un place).
When I get there, maybe it will be dark, un lit
where it has no occasion to be any way.

(Un celebrated.)
(Un repentant.)
(Un regenerate.)
(Un believed.)

Julia Alvarez (b. 1950)
Dusting

Each morning I wrote my name
on the dusty cabinet, then crossed
the dining table in script, scrawled
in capitals on the backs of chairs,
practising signatures like scales
while Mother followed, squirting
linseed from a burping can
into a crumpled-up flannel.

She erased my fingerprints
from the bookshelf and rocker,
polished mirrors on the desk
scribbled with my alphabets.
My name was swallowed in the towel
with which she jeweled the table tops.
The grain surfaced in the oak
and the pine grew luminous.
But I refused with every mark
to be like her, anonymous.

A. R. Ammons (1926 – 2001)
The City Limits

When you consider the radiance, that it does not withhold
itself but pours its abundance without selection into every
nook and cranny not overhung or hidden; when you consider

that birds' bones make no awful noise against the light but
lie low in the light as in a high testimony; when you consider
the radiance, that it will look into the guiltiest

swervings of the weaving heart and bear itself upon them,
not flinching into disguise or darkening; when you consider
the abundance of such resource as illuminates the glow-blue

bodies and gold-skeined wings of flies swarming the dumped
guts of a natural slaughter or the coil of shit and in no
way winces from its storms of generosity; when you consider

that air or vacuum, snow or shale, squid or wolf, rose or lichen,
each is accepted into as much light as it will take, then
the heart moves roomier, the man stands and looks about, the

leaf does not increase itself above the grass, and the dark
work of the deepest cells is of a tune with May bushes
and fear lit by the breadth of such calmly turns to praise.

Easter Morning

I have a life that did not become,
that turned aside and stopped,
astonished:
I hold it in me like a pregnancy or
as on my lap a child   5
not to grow or grow old but dwell on

it is to his grave I most
frequently return and return
to ask what is wrong, what was
wrong, to see it all by   10
the light of a different necessity
but the grave will not heal
and the child,
stirring, must share my grave
with me, an old man having   15
gotten by on what was left

when I go back to my home country in these
fresh far-away days, it's convenient to visit
everybody, aunts and uncles, those who used to say,
look how he's shooting up, and the   20
trinket aunts who always had a little
something in their pocketbooks, cinnamon bark
or a penny or nickel, and uncles who
were the rumored fathers of cousins
who whispered of them as of great, if   25
troubled, presences, and school
teachers, just about everybody older
(and some younger) collected in one place

waiting, particularly, but not for
me, mother and father there, too, and others   30
close, close as burrowing
under skin, all in the graveyard
assembled, done for, the world they
used to wield, have trouble and joy
in, gone   35

the child in me that could not become
was not ready for others to go,
to go on into change, blessings and
horrors, but stands there by the road
where the mishap occurred, crying out for   40
help, come and fix this or we
can't get by, but the great ones who
were to return, they could not or did
not hear and went on in a flurry and
now, I say in the graveyard, here   45
lies the flurry, now it can't come
back with help or helpful asides, now
we all buy the bitter
incompletions, pick up the knots of
horror, silently raving, and go on   50
crashing into empty ends not
completions, not rondures the fullness
has come into and spent itself from
I stand on the stump
of a child, whether myself   55
or my little brother who died, and
yell as far as I can, I cannot leave this place, for
for me it is the dearest and the worst,
it is life nearest to life which is
life lost: it is my place where   60
I must stand and fail,
calling attention with tears
to the branches not lofting
boughs into space, to the barren
air that holds the world that was my world   65

though the incompletions
(& completions) burn out
standing in the flash high-burn

momentary structure of ash, still it
is a picture-book, letter-perfect
Easter morning: I have been for a   70
walk: the wind is tranquil: the brook
works without flashing in an abundant
tranquility: the birds are lively with
voice: I saw something I had   75
never seen before: two great birds,
maybe eagles, blackwinged, whitenecked
and -headed, came from the south oaring
the great wings steadily; they went
directly over me, high up, and kept on   80
due north: but then one bird,
the one behind, veered a little to the
left and the other bird kept on seeming
not to notice for a minute: the first
began to circle as if looking for   85
something, coasting, resting its wings
on the down side of some of the circles:
the other bird came back and they both
circled, looking perhaps for a draft;
they turned a few more times, possibly   90
rising — at least, clearly resting —
then flew on falling into distance till
they broke across the local bush and
trees: it was a sight of bountiful
majesty and integrity: the having   95
patterns and routes, breaking
from them to explore other patterns or
better ways to routes, and then the
return: a dance sacred as the sap in
the trees, permanent in its descriptions   100
as the ripples round the brook's
ripplestone: fresh as this particular
flood of burn breaking across us now
from the sun.

ANONYMOUS
Sir Patrick Spens[1]

1

The king sits in Dumferling town,
    Drinking the blude-reid° wine: *blood-red*
"O whar will I get guid sailor,
    To sail this ship of mine?"

2

Up and spak an eldern knicht,
    Sat at the king's richt knee:
"Sir Patrick Spens is the best sailor
    That sails upon the sea."

3

The king has written a braid° letter   *broad*
    And signed it wi' his hand,
And sent it to Sir Patrick Spens,
    Was walking on the sand.

4

The first line that Sir Patrick read,
    A loud lauch° lauchèd he;   *laugh*
The next line that Sir Patrick read,
    The tear blinded his ee.°   *eye*

5

"O wha is this has done this deed,
    This ill deed done to me,
To send me out this time o' the year,
    To sail upon the sea?

6

"Mak haste, mak haste, my mirry men all,
    Our guid ship sails the morn."
"O say na sae,° my master dear,   *so*
    For I fear a deadly storm.

7

"Late, late yestre'en I saw the new moon
    Wi' the auld moon in hir arm,

---

[1]First printed in 1765, the story may be based on a thirteenth-century incident.

And I fear, I fear, my dear master,
    That we will come to harm."

8

O our Scots nobles were richt laith°   *loath*
    To weet° their cork-heeled shoon,°   *wet / shoes*
But lang or° a' the play were played   *before*
    Their hats they swam aboon.°   *above*

9

O lang, lang may their ladies sit,
    Wi' their fans into their hand,
Or ere they see Sir Patrick Spens
    Come sailing to the land.

10

O lang, lang may the ladies stand
    Wi' their gold kems° in their hair,   *combs*
Waiting for their ain dear lords,
    For they'll see them na mair.

11

Half o'er, half o'er to Aberdour
    It's fifty fadom deep,
And there lies guid Sir Patrick Spens
    Wi' the Scots lords at his feet.

ANONYMOUS
Western Wind[1]

Western wind, when will thou blow,
    The small rain down can rain?
Christ, if my love were in my arms
    And I in my bed again!

MATTHEW ARNOLD (1822 – 1888)
Shakespeare

Others abide our question. Thou art free.
We ask and ask — thou smilest and art still,

---

[1]A fifteenth-century lyric that survived in an early sixteenth-century manuscript.

Out-topping knowledge. For the loftiest hill,
Who to the stars uncrowns his majesty,

Planting his stedfast footsteps in the sea,
Making the heaven of heavens his dwelling-place,
Spares but the cloudy border of his base
To the foiled searching of mortality;

And thou, who didst the stars and sunbeams know,
Self-schooled, self-scanned, self-honored, self-secure,
Didst tread on earth unguessed at — better so!

All pains the immortal spirit must endure,
All weakness which impairs, all griefs which bow,
Find their sole speech in that victorious brow.

To Marguerite

Yes! in the sea of life enisled,
With echoing straits between us thrown,
Dotting the shoreless watery wild,
We mortal millions live *alone.*
The islands feel the enclasping flow,
And then their endless bounds they know.

But when the moon their hollows lights,
And they are swept by balms of spring,
And in their glens, on starry nights,
The nightingales divinely sing;
And lovely notes, from shore to shore,
Across the sounds and channels pour —

Oh! then a longing like despair
Is to their farthest caverns sent;
For surely once, they feel, we were
Parts of a single continent!
Now round us spreads the watery plain —
Oh might our marges meet again!

Who ordered, that their longing's fire
Should be, as soon as kindled, cooled?
Who renders vain their deep desire? —
A God, a God their severance ruled!
And bade betwixt their shores to be
The unplumbed, salt, estranging sea.

JOHN ASHBERY (b. 1927)
The Painter

Sitting between the sea and the buildings
He enjoyed painting the sea's portrait.
But just as children imagine a prayer
Is merely silence, he expected his subject
To rush up the sand, and, seizing a brush,
Plaster its own portrait on the canvas.

So there was never any paint on his canvas
Until the people who lived in the buildings
Put him to work: "Try using the brush
As a means to an end. Select, for a portrait,
Something less angry and large, and more subject
To a painter's moods, or, perhaps, to a prayer."

How could he explain to them his prayer
That nature, not art, might usurp the canvas?
He chose his wife for a new subject,
Making her vast, like ruined buildings,
As if, forgetting itself, the portrait
Had expressed itself without a brush.

Slightly encouraged, he dipped his brush
In the sea, murmuring a heartfelt prayer:
"My soul, when I paint this next portrait
Let it be you who wrecks the canvas."
The news spread like wildfire through the buildings:
He had gone back to the sea for his subject.

Imagine a painter crucified by his subject!
Too exhausted even to lift his brush,
He provoked some artists leaning from the buildings
To malicious mirth: "We haven't a prayer
Now, of putting ourselves on canvas,
Or getting the sea to sit for a portrait!"

Others declared it a self-portrait.
Finally all indications of a subject
Began to fade, leaving the canvas
Perfectly white. He put down the brush.
At once a howl, that was also a prayer,
Arose from the overcrowded buildings.

They tossed him, the portrait, from the tallest of the buildings;
And the sea devoured the canvas and the brush
As though his subject had decided to remain a prayer.

Paradoxes and Oxymorons

This poem is concerned with language on a very plain level.
Look at it talking to you. You look out a window
Or pretend to fidget. You have it but you don't have it.
You miss it, it misses you. You miss each other.

The poem is sad because it wants to be yours, and cannot.
What's a plain level? It is that and other things,
Bringing a system of them into play. Play?
Well, actually, yes, but I consider play to be

A deeper outside thing, a dreamed role-pattern,
As in the division of grace these long August days
Without proof. Open-ended. And before you know
It gets lost in the steam and chatter of typewriters.

It has been played once more. I think you exist only
To tease me into doing it, on your level, and then you aren't there
Or have adopted a different attitude. And the poem
Has set me softly down beside you. The poem is you.

Street Musicians

One died, and the soul was wrenched out
Of the other in life, who, walking the streets
Wrapped in an identity like a coat, sees on and on
The same corners, volumetrics, shadows
Under trees. Farther than anyone was ever
Called, through increasingly suburban airs
And ways, with autumn falling over everything:
The plush leaves the chattels in barrels
Of an obscure family being evicted
Into the way it was, and is. The other beached
Glimpses of what the other was up to:
Revelations at last. So they grew to hate and forget each other.

So I cradle this average violin that knows
Only forgotten showtunes, but argues
The possibility of free declamation anchored
To a dull refrain, the year turning over on itself

In November, with the spaces among the days
More literal, the meat more visible on the bone.
Our question of a place of origin hangs
Like smoke: how we picnicked in pine forests,
In coves with the water always seeping up, and left
Our trash, sperm and excrement everywhere, smeared
On the landscape, to make of us what we could.

MARGARET ATWOOD (b. 1939)
This Is a Photograph of Me

It was taken some time ago.
At first it seems to be
a smeared
print: blurred lines and grey flecks
blended with the paper;

then, as you scan
it, you see in the left-hand corner
a thing that is like a branch: part of a tree
(balsam or spruce) emerging
and, to the right, halfway up
what ought to be a gentle
slope, a small frame house.

In the background there is a lake,
and beyond that, some low hills.

(The photograph was taken
the day after I drowned.
I am in the lake, in the center
of the picture, just under the surface.

It is difficult to say where
precisely, or to say
how large or small I am:
the effect of water
on light is a distortion

but if you look long enough,
eventually
you will be able to see me.)

Up

You wake up filled with dread.
There seems no reason for it.
Morning light sifts through the window,
there is birdsong,
you can't get out of bed.

It's something about the crumpled sheets
hanging over the edge like jungle
foliage, the terry slippers gaping
their dark pink mouths for your feet,
the unseen breakfast — some of it
in the refrigerator you do not dare
to open — you will not dare to eat.

What prevents you? The future. The future tense,
immense as outer space.
You could get lost there.
No. Nothing so simple. The past, its density
and drowned events pressing you down,
like sea water, like gelatin
filling your lungs instead of air.

Forget all that and let's get up.
Try moving your arm.
Try moving your head.
Pretend the house is on fire
and you must run or burn.
No, that one's useless.
It's never worked before.

Where is it coming from, this echo,
this huge No that surrounds you,
silent as the folds of the yellow
curtains, mute as the cheerful
Mexican bowl with its cargo
of mummified flowers?
(You chose the colours of the sun,
not the dried neutrals of shadow.
God knows you've tried.)

Now here's a good one:
you're lying on your deathbed.
You have one hour to live.

Who is it, exactly, you have needed
all these years to forgive?

Variations on the Word Love

This is a word we use to plug
holes with. It's the right size for those warm
blanks in speech, for those red heart–
shaped vacancies on the page that look nothing
like real hearts. Add lace
and you can sell
it. We insert it also in the one empty
space on the printed form
that comes with no instructions. There are whole
magazines with not much in them
but the word *love,* you can
rub it all over your body and you
can cook with it too. How do we know
it isn't what goes on at the cool
debaucheries of slugs under damp
pieces of cardboard? As for the weed-
seedlings nosing their tough snouts up
among the lettuces, they shout it.
Love! Love! sing the soldiers, raising
their glittering knives in salute.

Then there's the two
of us. This word
is far too short for us, it has only
four letters, too sparse
to fill those deep bare
vacuums between the stars
that press on us with their deafness.
It's not love we don't wish
to fall into, but that fear.
This word is not enough but it will
have to do. It's a single
vowel in this metallic
silence, a mouth that says
O again and again in wonder
and pain, a breath, a finger
grip on a cliffside. You can
hold on or let go.

W. H. AUDEN (1907 – 1973)
As I Walked out One Evening

As I walked out one evening,
    Walking down Bristol Street,
The crowds upon the pavement
    Were fields of harvest wheat.

And down by the brimming river   5
    I heard a lover sing
Under an arch of the railway:
    "Love has no ending.

"I'll love you, dear, I'll love you
    Till China and Africa meet,   10
And the river jumps over the mountain
    And the salmon sing in the street,

"I'll love you till the ocean
    Is folded and hung up to dry
And the seven stars go squawking   15
    Like geese about the sky.

"The years shall run like rabbits,
    For in my arms I hold
The Flower of the Ages,
    And the first love of the world."   20

But all the clocks in the city
    Began to whirr and chime:
"O let not Time deceive you,
    You cannot conquer Time.

"In the burrows of the Nightmare   25
    Where Justice naked is,
Time watches from the shadow
    And coughs when you would kiss.

"In headaches and in worry
    Vaguely life leaks away,   30
And Time will have his fancy
    Tomorrow or today.

"Into many a green valley
    Drifts the appalling snow;
Time breaks the threaded dances   35
    And the diver's brilliant bow.

"O plunge your hands in water,
    Plunge them in up to the wrist;
Stare, stare in the basin
    And wonder what you've missed.   40

"The glacier knocks in the cupboard,
    The desert sighs in the bed,
And the crack in the teacup opens
    A lane to the land of the dead.

"Where the beggars raffle the banknotes   45
    And the Giant is enchanting to Jack,
And the Lily-white Boy is a Roarer,
    And Jill goes down on her back.

"O look, look in the mirror,
    O look in your distress;   50
Life remains a blessing
    Although you cannot bless.

"O stand, stand at the window
    As the tears scald and start;
You shall love your crooked neighbor   55
    With your crooked heart."

It was late, late in the evening,
    The lovers they were gone;
The clocks had ceased their chiming,
    And the deep river ran on.   60

Musée des Beaux Arts[1]

About suffering they were never wrong,
The Old Masters: how well they understood
Its human position; how it takes place
While someone else is eating or opening a window or just walking
    dully along;
How, when the aged are reverently, passionately waiting
For the miraculous birth, there always must be
Children who did not specially want it to happen, skating
On a pond at the edge of the wood:
They never forgot
That even the dreadful martyrdom must run its course

---

[1]French for "Museum of Fine Arts."

Anyhow in a corner, some untidy spot
Where the dogs go on with their doggy life and the torturer's
       horse
Scratches its innocent behind on a tree.

In Brueghel's *Icarus,* for instance: how everything turns away
Quite leisurely from the disaster; the ploughman may
Have heard the splash, the forsaken cry,
But for him it was not an important failure; the sun shone
As it had to on the white legs disappearing into the green
Water; and the expensive delicate ship that must have seen
Something amazing, a boy falling out of the sky,
Had somewhere to get to and sailed calmly on.

JOHN BERRYMAN (1914 – 1972)
Dream Song 4

Filling her compact & delicious body
with chicken páprika, she glanced at me
twice.
Fainting with interest, I hungered back
and only the fact of her husband & four other people
kept me from springing on her

or falling at her little feet and crying
"You are the hottest one for years of night
Henry's dazed eyes
have enjoyed, Brilliance." I advanced upon
(despairing) my spumoni. — Sir Bones: is stuffed,
de world, wif feeding girls.

— Black hair, complexion Latin, jeweled eyes
downcast . . . The slob beside her   feasts . . . What wonders is
she sitting on, over there?
The restaurant buzzes. She might as well be on Mars.
Where did it all go wrong? There ought to be a law against Henry.
— Mr. Bones: there is.

Dream Song 45

He stared at ruin. Ruin stared straight back.
He thought they was old friends. He felt on the stair
where her papa found them bare

they became familiar. When the papers were lost
rich with pals' secrets, he thought he had the knack
of ruin. Their paths crossed

and once they crossed in jail; they crossed in bed;
and over an unsigned letter their eyes met,
and in an Asian city
directionless & lurchy at two & three,
or trembling to a telephone's fresh threat,
and when some wired his head

to reach a wrong opinion, 'Epileptic'.
But he noted now that: they were not old friends.
He did not know this one.
This one was a stranger, come to make amends
for all the imposters, and to make it stick.
Henry nodded, un–.

Dream Song 384

The marker slants, flowerless, day's almost done,
I stand above my father's grave with rage,
often, often before
I've made this awful pilgrimage to one
who cannot visit me, who tore his page
out: I come back for more,

I spit upon this dreadful banker's grave
who shot his heart out in a Florida dawn
O ho alas alas
When will indifference come, I moan & rave
I'd like to scrabble till I got right down
away down under the grass

and ax the casket open ha to see
just how he's taking it, which he sought so hard
we'll tear apart
the mouldering grave clothes ha & then Henry
will heft the ax once more, his final card,
and fell it on the start.

FRANK BIDART (b. 1939)
Ellen West

I love sweets, —
                heaven
would be dying on a bed of vanilla ice cream . . .

But my true self
is thin, all profile   5

and effortless gestures, the sort of blond
elegant girl whose
                body is the image of her soul.

— My doctors tell me I must give up
this ideal;   10
        but I
WILL NOT . . . cannot.

Only to my husband I'm not simply a "case."

But he is a fool. He married
meat, and thought it was a wife.   15

                •   •   •

Why am I a girl?

I ask my doctors, and they tell me they
don't know, that it is just "given."

But it has such
implications — ;   20
                and sometimes,
I even feel like a girl.

                •   •   •

Now, at the beginning of Ellen's thirty-second year, her physical con-
dition has deteriorated still further. Her use of laxatives increases
beyond measure. Every evening she takes sixty to seventy tablets of a
laxative, with the result that she suffers tortured vomiting at night and
violent diarrhea by day, often accompanied by a weakness of the heart.
She has thinned down to a skeleton, and weighs only 92 pounds.

                •   •   •

About five years ago, I was in a restaurant,
eating alone
                with a book. I was   25
not married, and often did that . . .

— I'd turn down
dinner invitations, so I could eat alone;

I'd allow myself two pieces of bread, with   30
butter, at the beginning, and three scoops of
vanilla ice cream, at the end, —

                   sitting there alone
with a book, both in the book
and out of it, waited on, idly   35
watching people, —

             when an attractive young man
and woman, both elegantly dressed,
sat next to me.
            She was beautiful — ;   40

with sharp, clear features, a good
bone structure — ;
           if she took her make-up off
in front of you, rubbing cold cream
again and again across her skin, she still would be   45
beautiful —
        more beautiful.

And he, —
          I couldn't remember when I had seen a man
so attractive. I didn't know why. He was almost   50

a male version
        of her, —

I had the sudden, mad notion that I
wanted to be his lover . . .

— Were they married?   55
            were *they* lovers?

They didn't wear wedding rings.
Their behavior was circumspect. They discussed
politics. They didn't touch . . .

— How could I discover?   60

           Then, when the first course
arrived, I noticed the way

each held his fork out for the other

to taste what he had ordered . . .

They did this   65
again and again, with pleased looks, indulgent
smiles, for each course,

                    more than once for *each* dish — ;
much too much for just friends

— Their behavior somehow sickened me;   70

the way each *gladly*
put the *food* the other had offered *into his mouth* — ;

I knew what they were. I knew they slept together.

An immense depression came over me . . .

— I knew I could never   75
with such ease allow another to put food into my mouth:

happily *myself* put food into another's mouth — ;

I knew that to become a wife I would have to give up my ideal.

                    •   •   •

Even as a child,
I saw that the "natural" process of aging   80

is for one's middle to thicken —
one's skin to blotch;

as happened to my mother.
And her mother.
                    I loathed "Nature."   85

At twelve, pancakes
became the most terrible thought there is . . .

I shall *defeat* "Nature."

In the hospital, when they
weigh me, I wear weights secretly sewn into my belt.   90

                    •   •   •

January 16. The patient is allowed to eat in her room, but comes
readily with her husband to afternoon coffee. Previously she had
stoutly resisted this on the ground that she did not really eat but
devoured like a wild animal. This she demonstrated with utmost
realism. . . . Her physical examination showed nothing striking.
Salivary glands are markedly enlarged on both sides.

January 21. Has been reading *Faust*[1] again. In her diary, writes that art is the "mutual permeation" of the "world of the body" and the "world of the spirit." Says that her own poems are "hospital poems . . . weak — without skill or perseverance; only managing to beat their wings softly."

February 8. Agitation, quickly subsided again. Has attached herself to an elegant, very thin female patient. Homo-erotic component strikingly evident.

February 15. Vexation, and torment. Says that her mind forces her always to think of eating. Feels herself degraded by this. Has entirely, for the first time in years, stopped writing poetry.

•   •   •

Callas[2] is my favorite singer, but I've only   95
seen her once — ;

I've never forgotten that night . . .

— It was in *Tosca,*[3] she had long before
lost weight, her voice
had been, for years,   100
          deteriorating, half itself . . .

When her career began, of course, she was fat,

enormous — ; in the early photographs,
sometimes I almost don't recognize her . . .

The voice too then was enormous —   105

healthy; robust; subtle; but capable of
crude effects, even vulgar,
          almost out of
high spirits, too much health . . .
But soon she felt that she must lose weight, —   110
that all she was trying to express

was obliterated by her body,
buried in flesh — ;
          abruptly, within

---

[1]Work by Johann Wolfgang von Goethe (1749–1842) about the magician of German legend who enters into a compact with the devil.

[2]Maria Callas (1923–1977), Greek American soprano.

[3]An opera by Giacomo Puccini (1858–1924).

four months, she lost at least sixty pounds . . .   115

— The gossip in Milan was that Callas
had swallowed a tapeworm.

But of course she hadn't.

                    The *tapeworm*
was her *soul* . . .   120

— How her soul, uncompromising,
insatiable,
            must have loved eating the flesh from her bones,

revealing this extraordinarily
mercurial; fragile; masterly creature . . .   125

— But irresistibly, nothing
stopped there; the huge voice

also began to change: at first, it simply diminished
in volume, in size,
            then the top notes became   130
shrill, unreliable — at last,
usually not there at all . . .

— No one knows *why.* Perhaps her mind,
ravenous, still insatiable, sensed

that to struggle with the *shreds* of a voice   135

must make her artistry subtler, more refined,
more capable of expressing humiliation,
rage, betrayal . . .

— Perhaps the opposite. Perhaps her spirit
loathed the unending struggle   140

to *embody* itself, to *manifest* itself, on a stage whose

mechanics, and suffocating customs,
seemed expressly designed to annihilate spirit . . .

— I know that in *Tosca,* in the second act,
when, humiliated, hounded by Scarpia,   145
she sang *Vissi d'arte*
           — "I lived for art" —

and in torment, bewilderment, at the end she asks,
with a voice reaching
           harrowingly for the notes,   150

"Art has *repaid* me LIKE THIS?"

                                        I felt I was watching
autobiography —

                    an art; skill;
virtuosity   155

miles distant from the usual soprano's
athleticism, —
                    the usual musician's dream
of virtuosity *without* content . . .

— I wonder what she feels, now,   160
listening to her recordings.

For they have already, within a few years,
begun to date . . .

Whatever they express
they express through the style of a decade   165
and a half — ;
                    a style *she* helped create . . .

— She must know that now
she probably would *not* do a trill in
exactly that way, —   170
                    that the whole sound, atmosphere,
dramaturgy of her recordings

have just slightly become those of the past . . .

— Is it bitter? Does her soul
tell her   175

that she was an *idiot* ever to think
anything
                    material wholly could satisfy? . . .

— Perhaps it says: *The only way*
to escape   180
the History of Styles

is not to have a body.

When I open my eyes in the morning, my great
mystery
                    stands before me . . .   185

— I *know* that I am intelligent; therefore

the inability not to fear food
day-and-night; this unending hunger
ten minutes after I have eaten . . .
                              a childish   190
dread of eating; hunger which can have no cause, —

half my mind says that all this
is *demeaning* . . .

            Bread
for days on end   195
drives all real thought from my brain . . .

— Then I think, No. The ideal of being thin

conceals the ideal
not to have a body — ;
                        which is NOT trivial . . .   200

This wish seems now as much a "given" of my existence

as the intolerable
fact that I am dark-complexioned; big-boned;
and once weighed
one hundred and sixty-five pounds . . .   205

— But then I think, *No.* That's too simple, —

without a body, who can
know himself at all?
                  Only by
acting; choosing; rejecting; have I   210
made myself —
            discovered who and what *Ellen* can be . . .

— But then again I think, *NO.* This *I* is anterior

to name; gender; action;
fashion;   215
         MATTER ITSELF, —

. . . trying to stop my hunger with FOOD
is like trying to appease thirst
                        with ink.

            •   •   •

March 30. Result of the consultation: Both gentlemen agree com-
pletely with my prognosis and doubt any therapeutic usefulness of
commitment even more emphatically than I. All three of us are
agreed that it is not a case of obsessional neurosis and not one of
manic-depressive psychosis, and that no definitely reliable therapy
is possible. We therefore resolved to give in to the patient's demand
for discharge.   220

· · ·

The train-ride yesterday
was far *worse* than I expected . . .

                          In our compartment
were ordinary people: a student;
a woman; her child; —   225

they had ordinary bodies, pleasant faces;

                                   but I thought
I was surrounded by creatures

with the pathetic, desperate
desire to be *not* what they were: —   230

the student was short,
and carried his body as if forcing
it to be taller — ;

the woman showed her gums when she smiled,
and often held her   235
hand up to hide them —;

the child
seemed to cry simply because it was
small; a dwarf, and helpless . . .

— I was hungry. I had insisted that my husband   240
not bring food . . .

After about thirty minutes, the woman
peeled an orange

to quiet the child. She put a section
into its mouth — ;   245
                   immediately it spit it out.
The piece fell to the floor.

— She pushed it with her foot through the dirt
toward me
several inches.   250

My husband saw me staring
down at the piece . . .

— I didn't move; how I wanted
to reach out,
           and as if invisible   255

shove it in my mouth — ;

my body
became rigid. As I stared at him,
I could see him staring

at me, —   260
           then he looked at the student — ; at the woman — ; then
back to me . . .

I didn't move.

— At last, he bent down, and
casually   265
           threw it out the window.

He looked away.

— I got up to leave the compartment, then
saw his face, —

his eyes   270
were red;
           and I saw

— *I'm sure I saw* —

disappointment.

·   ·   ·

On the third day of being home she is as if transformed. At break-
fast she eats butter and sugar, at noon she eats so much that — for
the first time in thirteen years! — she is satisfied by her food and
gets really full. At afternoon coffee she eats chocolate creams and
Easter eggs. She takes a walk with her husband, reads poems, listens
to recordings, is in a positively festive mood, and all heaviness
seems to have fallen away from her. She writes letters, the last one a
letter to the fellow patient here to whom she had become so
attached. In the evening she takes a lethal dose of poison, and on
the following morning she is dead. "She looked as she had never
looked in life — calm and happy and peaceful."   275

•   •   •

Dearest. — I remember how
at eighteen,
                on hikes with friends, when
they rested, sitting down to joke or talk,

I circled   280
around them, afraid to hike ahead alone,

yet afraid to rest
when I was not yet truly thin.

You and, yes, my husband, —
you and he   285

have by degrees drawn me within the circle;
forced me to sit down at last on the ground.

I am grateful.

But something in me *refuses* it.

— How eager I have been   290
to compromise, to kill this *refuser,* —

but each compromise, each attempt
to poison an ideal
which often seemed to *me* sterile and unreal,

heightens my hunger.   295

I am crippled. I disappoint you.

Will you greet with anger, or
happiness,

the news which might well reach you
before this letter?   300
                Your *Ellen.*

To My Father

I walked into the room.
There were objects in the room. I thought I needed nothing
from them. They began to speak,
but the words were unintelligible, a painful cacophony . . .
Then I realized they were saying
                                the name
of the man who had chosen them, owned them,

ordered, arranged them, their deceased cause,
the secret pattern that made these things order.
I strained to hear: but
the sound remained unintelligible . . .
senselessly getting louder, urgent, deafening.

Hands over my ears, at last I knew
> they would remain
inarticulate; your name was not in my language.

ELIZABETH BISHOP (1911 – 1979)
At the Fishhouses

Although it is a cold evening,
down by one of the fishhouses
an old man sits netting,
his net, in the gloaming almost invisible,
a dark purple-brown,   5
and his shuttle worn and polished.
The air smells so strong of codfish
it makes one's nose run and one's eyes water.
The five fishhouses have steeply peaked roofs
and narrow, cleated gangplanks slant up   10
to storerooms in the gables
for the wheelbarrows to be pushed up and down on.
All is silver: the heavy surface of the sea,
swelling slowly as if considering spilling over,
is opaque, but the silver of the benches,   15
the lobster pots, and masts, scattered
among the wild jagged rocks,
is of an apparent translucence
like the small old buildings with an emerald moss
growing on their shoreward walls.   20
The big fish tubs are completely lined
with layers of beautiful herring scales
and the wheelbarrows are similarly plastered
with creamy iridescent coats of mail,
with small iridescent flies crawling on them.   25
Up on the little slope behind the houses,
set in the sparse bright sprinkle of grass,
is an ancient wooden capstan,[1]

---

[1]Machine for raising weights by winding cable around a vertical rotating drum.

cracked, with two long bleached handles
and some melancholy stains, like dried blood,   30
where the ironwork has rusted.
The old man accepts a Lucky Strike.
He was a friend of my grandfather.
We talk of the decline in the population
and of codfish and herring   35
while he waits for a herring boat to come in.
There are sequins on his vest and on his thumb.
He has scraped the scales, the principal beauty,
from unnumbered fish with that black old knife,
the blade of which is almost worn away.   40

Down at the water's edge, at the place
where they haul up the boats, up the long ramp
descending into the water, thin silver
tree trunks are laid horizontally
across the gray stones, down and down   45
at intervals of four or five feet.

Cold dark deep and absolutely clear,
element bearable to no mortal,
to fish and to seals . . . One seal particularly
I have seen here evening after evening.   50
He was curious about me. He was interested in music;
like me a believer in total immersion,[2]
so I used to sing him Baptist hymns.
I also sang "A Mighty Fortress Is Our God."[3]
He stood up in the water and regarded me   55
steadily, moving his head a little.
Then he would disappear, then suddenly emerge
almost in the same spot, with a sort of shrug
as if it were against his better judgment.
Cold dark deep and absolutely clear,   60
the clear gray icy water . . . Back, behind us,
the dignified tall firs begin.
Bluish, associating with their shadows,
a million Christmas trees stand
waiting for Christmas. The water seems suspended   65

---

[2]Form of baptism practiced by some Christian sects.
[3]Hymn of which the original German version was written by Martin Luther
(1483–1546).

above the rounded gray and blue-gray stones.
I have seen it over and over, the same sea, the same,
slightly, indifferently swinging above the stones,
icily free above the stones,
above the stones and then the world. 70
If you should dip your hand in,
your wrist would ache immediately,
your bones would begin to ache and your hand would burn
as if the water were a transmutation of fire
that feeds on stones and burns with a dark gray flame. 75
If you tasted it, it would first taste bitter,
then briny, then surely burn your tongue.
It is like what we imagine knowledge to be:
dark, salt, clear, moving, utterly free,
drawn from the cold hard mouth 80
of the world, derived from the rocky breasts
forever, flowing and drawn, and since
our knowledge is historical, flowing, and flown.

The Fish

I caught a tremendous fish
and held him beside the boat
half out of water, with my hook
fast in a corner of his mouth.
He didn't fight. 5
He hadn't fought at all.
He hung a grunting weight,
battered and venerable
and homely. Here and there
his brown skin hung in strips 10
like ancient wall-paper,
and its pattern of darker brown
was like wall-paper:
shapes like full-blown roses
stained and lost through age. 15
He was speckled with barnacles,
fine rosettes of lime,
and infested
with tiny white sea-lice,
and underneath two or three 20
rags of green weed hung down.

While his gills were breathing in
the terrible oxygen
— the frightening gills,
fresh and crisp with blood,   25
that can cut so badly —
I thought of the coarse white flesh
packed in like feathers,
the big bones and the little bones,
the dramatic reds and blacks   30
in his shiny entrails,
and the pink swim-bladder
like a big peony.
I looked into his eyes
which were far larger than mine   35
but shallower, and yellowed,
the irises backed and packed
with tarnished tinfoil
seen through the lenses
of old scratched isinglass.   40
They shifted a little, but not
to return my stare.
— It was more like the tipping
of an object toward the light.
I admired his sullen face,   45
the mechanism of his jaw,
and then I saw
that from his lower lip
— if you could call it a lip —
grim, wet, and weapon-like,   50
hung five old pieces of fish-line,
or four and a wire leader
with the swivel still attached,
with all their five big hooks
grown firmly in his mouth.   55
A green line, frayed at the end
where he broke it, two heavier lines,
and a fine black thread
still crimped from the strain and snap
when it broke and he got away.   60
Like medals with their ribbons
frayed and wavering,
a five-haired beard of wisdom

trailing from his aching jaw.
I stared and stared   65
and victory filled up
the little rented boat,
from the pool of bilge
where oil had spread a rainbow
around the rusted engine   70
to the bailer rusted orange,
the sun-cracked thwarts,
the oarlocks on their strings,
the gunnels — until everything
was rainbow, rainbow, rainbow!   75
And I let the fish go.

Poem

About the size of an old-style dollar bill,
American or Canadian,
mostly the same whites, gray greens, and steel grays
— this little painting (a sketch for a larger one?)
has never earned any money in its life.   5
Useless and free, it has spent seventy years
as a minor family relic
handed along collaterally to owners
who looked at it sometimes, or didn't bother to.

It must be Nova Scotia; only there   10
does one see gabled wooden houses
painted that awful shade of brown.
The other houses, the bits that show, are white.
Elm trees, low hills, a thin church steeple
— that gray-blue wisp — or is it? In the foreground   15
a water meadow with some tiny cows,
two brushstrokes each, but confidently cows;
two minuscule white geese in the blue water,
back-to-back, feeding, and a slanting stick.
Up closer, a wild iris, white and yellow,   20
fresh-squiggled from the tube.
The air is fresh and cold; cold early spring
clear as gray glass; a half inch of blue sky
below the steel-gray storm clouds.
(They were the artist's specialty.)   25

A specklike bird is flying to the left.
Or is it a flyspeck looking like a bird?

Heavens, I recognize the place, I know it!
It's behind — I can almost remember the farmer's name.
His barn backed on that meadow. There it is,   30
titanium white, one dab. The hint of steeple,
filaments of brush-hairs, barely there,
must be the Presbyterian church.
Would that be Miss Gillespie's house?
Those particular geese and cows   35
are naturally before my time.

A sketch done in an hour, "in one breath,"
once taken from a trunk and handed over.
Would you like this? I'll probably never
have room to hang these things again.   40
Your Uncle George, no, mine, my Uncle George,
he'd be your great-uncle, left them all with Mother
when he went back to England.
You know, he was quite famous, an R.A. . . . .

I never knew him. We both knew this place,   45
apparently, this literal small backwater,
looked at it long enough to memorize it,
our years apart. How strange. And it's still loved,
or its memory is (it must have changed a lot).
Our visions coincided — "visions" is   50
too serious a word — our looks, two looks:
art "copying from life" and life itself,
life and the memory of it so compressed
they've turned into each other. Which is which?
Life and the memory of it cramped,   55
dim, on a piece of Bristol board,
dim, but how live, how touching in detail
— the little that we get for free,
the little of our earthly trust. Not much.
About the size of our abidance   60
along with theirs: the munching cows,
the iris, crisp and shivering, the water
still standing from spring freshets,
the yet-to-be-dismantled elms, the geese.

Sestina

September rain falls on the house.
In the failing light, the old grandmother
sits in the kitchen with the child
beside the Little Marvel Stove,
reading the jokes from the almanac,
laughing and talking to hide her tears.

She thinks that her equinoctial tears
and the rain that beats on the roof of the house
were both foretold by the almanac,
but only known to a grandmother.
The iron kettle sings on the stove.
She cuts some bread and says to the child,

It's time for tea now; but the child
is watching the teakettle's small hard tears
dance like mad on the hot black stove,
the way the rain must dance on the house.
Tidying up, the old grandmother
hangs up the clever almanac

on its string. Birdlike, the almanac
hovers half open above the child,
hovers above the old grandmother
and her teacup full of dark brown tears.
She shivers and says she thinks the house
feels chilly, and puts more wood in the stove.

It was to be, says the Marvel Stove.
I know what I know, says the almanac.
With crayons the child draws a rigid house
and a winding pathway. Then the child
puts in a man with buttons like tears
and shows it proudly to the grandmother.

But secretly, while the grandmother
busies herself about the stove,
the little moons fall down like tears
from between the pages of the almanac
into the flower bed the child
has carefully placed in the front of the house.

Time to plant tears, says the almanac.
The grandmother sings to the marvelous stove
and the child draws another inscrutable house.

WILLIAM BLAKE (1757 – 1827)
Ah Sun-flower

Ah Sun-flower, weary of time,
Who countest the steps of the Sun,
Seeking after that sweet golden clime
Where the traveller's journey is done:

Where the Youth pined away with desire,
And the pale Virgin shrouded in snow
Arise from their graves and aspire
Where my Sun-flower wishes to go.

The Garden of Love

I went to the Garden of Love,
And saw what I never had seen:
A Chapel was built in the midst,
Where I used to play on the green.

And the gates of this Chapel were shut,
And "Thou shalt not" writ over the door;
So I turn'd to the Garden of Love,
That so many sweet flowers bore,

And I saw it was filled with graves,
And tomb-stones where flowers should be:
And Priests in black gowns were walking their rounds,
And binding with briars my joys & desires.

The Lamb

  Little Lamb, who made thee?
  Dost thou know who made thee?
Gave thee life & bid thee feed,
By the stream & o'er the mead;
Gave thee clothing of delight,
Softest clothing, wooly, bright;
Gave thee such a tender voice,
Making all the vales rejoice?
  Little Lamb, who made thee?
  Dost thou know who made thee?

  Little Lamb, I'll tell thee,
  Little Lamb, I'll tell thee:

He is callèd by thy name,
For he calls himself a Lamb.
He is meek & he is mild,
He became a little child.
I a child, & thou a lamb,
We are callèd by his name.
  Little Lamb, God bless thee.
  Little Lamb, God bless thee.

The Tyger

Tyger! Tyger! burning bright
In the forests of the night,
What immortal hand or eye
Could frame thy fearful symmetry?

In what distant deeps or skies
Burnt the fire of thine eyes?
On what wings dare he aspire?
What the hand, dare seize the fire?

And what shoulder, & what art,
Could twist the sinews of thy heart?
And when thy heart began to beat,
What dread hand? & what dread feet?

What the hammer? what the chain?
In what furnace was thy brain?
What the anvil? what dread grasp
Dare its deadly terrors clasp?

When the stars threw down their spears,
And water'd heaven with their tears,
Did he smile his work to see?
Did he who made the Lamb make thee?

Tyger! Tyger! burning bright
In the forests of the night,
What immortal hand or eye
Dare frame thy fearful symmetry?

RICHARD BLANCO (b. 1926)
Letters for Mamá

For years they came for you:
Awkward size envelopes

Labeled AIR MAIL *(POR AVION)*
Affixed with multiple oversized stamps
Honoring men from another history.
Monthly, you would peel
Through eggshell pages —
White onionskin sheets
That told you the details
Of Kiki's first steps
And your own Mother's death,
The approximate dates
Recorded by postmarks.

Sometimes there were pictures:
Poor black and white photos
With foreign dimensions
Of children you would point to,
Tell me were my cousins.
I would handle the images,
Look for my resemblance
In an ear, eyebrow or a nose.

When possible
You would parcel
A few pounds of your absence
Into discreet brown packages
Filled with bubble gum,
Baby clothes, hand-me-downs,
A few yards of Taffeta
For your niece's wedding gown,
Which you would later see
Couturiered to her body
In new pictures that would introduce Alfredo,
Her husband, an addition
You would never meet.

Your silent, filed anxieties
Matched the random terrazzo mosaic
Of our porchgarden
Where you sat
Fading into ninety blue miles,
Surrounded by unopened buds of Impatience,
Waiting for the postman,
While gazing at the purgatorial clouds
Swollen with unfallen rain

That would never spew
Through the mouths of coral-faced gods
Into the empty fountains
Of your parched memory.

MICHAEL BLUMENTHAL (b. 1949)

A Marriage

For Margie Smigel and Jon Dopkeen

You are holding up a ceiling
with both arms. It is very heavy,
but you must hold it up, or else
it will fall down on you. Your arms
are tired, terribly tired,
and, as the day goes on, it feels
as if either your arms or the ceiling
will soon collapse.

But then,
unexpectedly,
something wonderful happens:
Someone,
a man or a woman,
walks into the room
and holds their arms up
to the ceiling beside you.

So you finally get
to take down your arms.
You feel the relief of respite,
the blood flowing back
to your fingers and arms.
And when your partner's arms tire,
you hold up your own
to relieve him again.

And it can go on like this
for many years
without the house falling.

Wishful Thinking

I like to think that ours will be more than just another story
of failed love and the penumbras of desire. I like to think

that the moon that day was in whatever house the astrologists
would have it in for a kind of quiet, a trellis lust could climb
easily and then subside, resting against the sills and ledges,
giving way like shore to an occasional tenderness, coddling
the cold idiosyncrasies of impulse and weather that pound it
as it holds to its shape against the winds and duststorms of
temptation and longing. I like to think that some small canister
of hope and tranquility washed ashore that day and we, in
the right place, found it. These are the things I imagine
all lovers wish for amid the hot commencements of love
and promises, their histories and failures washing ashore
like flotsam, their innards girthed against those architects
of misery, desire and restlessness, their hope rising
against the air as it fondles the waves and frolics them skywards.
I like to think that, if the heart pauses awhile in a single place,
it finds a home somewhere, like a vagabond lured by fatigue
to an unlikely town and, with a sudden peacefulness, deciding
to stay there. I like to think these things because, whether
or not they reach fruition, they provide the heart with a kind
of solace, the way poetry does, or all forms of tenderness
that issue out amid the deserts of failed love and petulant desire.
I like to think them because, meditated on amid this pattern
of off-white and darkness, they lend themselves to a kind of
music, not unlike the music a dove makes as it circles the trees,
not unlike the sun and the earth and their orbital brothers,
the planets, as they chant to the heavens their longing for hope
and repetition amid orderly movement, not unlike the music
these humble wishes make with their cantata of willfulness
and good intentions, looking for some pleasant abstractions
amid our concretized lives, something tender and lovely to
defy the times with, quiet and palpable amid the flickers of flux
and the flames of longing: a bird rising over the ashes, a dream.

ANNE BRADSTREET (c. 1612 – 1672)
Before the Birth of One of Her Children

All things within this fading world hath end,
Adversity doth still our joys attend;
No ties so strong, no friends so dear and sweet,
But with death's parting blow is sure to meet.
The sentence past is most irrevocable,
A common thing, yet oh, inevitable.

How soon, my Dear, death may my steps attend,
How soon't may be thy lot to lose thy friend,
We both are ignorant, yet love bids me
These farewell lines to recommend to thee,
That when that knot's untied that made us one,
I may seem thine, who is effect am none.
And if I see not half my days that's due,
What nature would, God grant to yours and you;
The many faults that well you know I have
Let be interred in my oblivious grave;
If any worth or virtue were in me,
Let that live freshly in thy memory
And when thou feel'st no grief, as I no harms,
Yet love thy dead, who long lay in thine arms,
And when thy loss shall be repaid with gains
Look to my little babes, my dear remains.
And if thou love thyself, or loved'st me,
These O protect from stepdame's° injury.   *stepmother's*
And if chance to thine eyes shall bring this verse,
With some sad sighs honor my absent hearse;
And kiss this paper for thy love's dear sake,
Who with salt tears this last farewell did take.

LUCIE BROCK-BROIDO (b. 1956)
Carrowmore

All about Carrowmore[1] the lambs
Were blotched blue, belonging.

They were waiting for carnage or
Snuff. This is why they are born

To begin with, to end.
Ruminants do not frighten

At anything — gorge in the soil, butcher
Noise, the mere graze of predators.

All about Carrowmore
The rain quells for three days.

I remember how cold I was, the botched
Job of travelling. And just so.

---

[1] A location in County Sligo, Ireland, where there is a large prehistoric megalithic cemetery.

Wherever I went I came with me.
She buried her bone barrette

In the ground's woolly shaft.
A tear of her hair, an old gift

To the burnt other who went
First. My thick braid, my ornament —

My belonging I
Remember how cold I will be.

Domestic Mysticism

In thrice 10,000 seasons, I will come back to this world
In a white cotton dress. Kingdom of After My Own Heart.
Kingdom of Fragile. Kingdom of Dwarves. When I come home,
Teacups will quiver in their Dresden saucers, pentatonic chimes
Will move in wind. A covey of alley cats will swarm on the side
Porch & perch there, portents with quickened heartbeats
You will feel against your ankles as you pass through.

After the first millennium, we were supposed to die out.
You had your face pressed up against the coarse dyed velvet
Of the curtain, always looking out for your own transmigration:
What colors you would wear, what cut of jewel,
What kind of pageantry, if your legs would be tied
Down, if there would be wandering tribes of minstrels
Following with woodwinds in your wake.

This work of mine, the kind of work which takes no arms to do,
Is least noble of all. It's peopled by Wizards, the Forlorn,
The Awkward, the Blinkers, the Spoon-Fingered, Agnostic
        Lispers,
Stutterers of Prayer, the Flatulent, the Closet Weepers,
The Charlatans. I am one of those. In January, the month the owls
Nest in, I am a witness & a small thing altogether. The Kingdom
Of Ingratitude. Kingdom of Lies. Kingdom of *How Dare I.*

I go on dropping words like little pink fish eggs, unawares, slightly
Illiterate, often on the mark. Waiting for the clear whoosh
Of fluid to descend & cover them. A train like a silver
Russian love pill for the sick at heart passes by
My bedroom window in the night at the speed of mirage.
In the next millennium, I will be middle aged. I do not do well
In the marrow of things. Kingdom of Trick. Kingdom of Drug.

In a lung-shaped suburb of Virginia, my sister will be childless
Inside the ice storm, forcing the narcissus. We will send
Each other valentines. The radio blowing out
Vaughan Williams on the highway's purple moor.
At nine o'clock, we will put away our sewing to speak
Of lofty things while, in the pantry, little plants will nudge
Their frail tips toward the light we made last century.

When I come home, the dwarves will be long
In their shadows & promiscuous. The alley cats will sneak
Inside, curl about the legs of furniture, close the skins
Inside their eyelids, sleep. Orchids will be intercrossed & sturdy.
The sun will go down as I sit, thin armed, small breasted
In my cotton dress, poked with eyelet stitches, a little lace,
In the queer light left when a room snuffs out.

I draw a bath, enter the water as a god enters water:
Fertile, knowing, kind, surrounded by glass objects
Which could break easily if mishandled or ill-touched.
Everyone knows an unworshipped woman will betray you.
There is always that promise, I like that. Kingdom of Kinesis.
Kingdom of Benevolent. I will betray as a god betrays,
With tenderheartedness. I've got this mystic streak in me.

EMILY BRONTË (1818 – 1848)
No Coward Soul Is Mine

No coward soul is mine,
No trembler in the world's storm-troubled sphere!
I see Heaven's glories shine,
And Faith shines equal, arming me from Fear.

O God within my breast,
Almighty ever-present Deity!
Life, that in me hast rest
As I, undying Life, have power in thee!

Vain are the thousand creeds
That move men's hearts, unutterably vain;
Worthless as withered weeds,
Or idlest froth, amid the boundless main

To waken doubt in one
Holding so fast by thy infinity,

So surely anchored on
The steadfast rock of Immortality.

With wide-embracing love
Thy spirit animates eternal years,
Pervades and broods above,
Changes, sustains, dissolves, creates and rears.

Though earth and moon were gone,
And suns and universes ceased to be,
And thou were left alone,
Every Existence would exist in thee.

There is not room for Death,
Nor atom that his might could render void
Since thou art Being and Breath,
And what thou art may never be destroyed.

Remembrance

Cold in the earth — and the deep snow piled above thee,
Far, far removed, cold in the dreary grave!
Have I forgot, my only Love, to love thee,
Severed at last by Time's all-severing wave?

Now, when alone, do my thoughts no longer hover
Over the mountains, on that northern shore,
Resting their wings where heath and fern leaves cover
Thy noble heart forever, ever more?

Cold in the earth — and fifteen wild Decembers,
From those brown hills, have melted into spring;
Faithful, indeed, is the spirit that remembers
After such years of change and suffering!

Sweet Love of youth, forgive, if I forget thee,
While the world's tide is bearing me along;
Other desires and other hopes beset me,
Hopes which obscure, but cannot do thee wrong!

No later light has lightened up my heaven,
No second morn has ever shone for me;
All my life's bliss from thy dear life was given,
All my life's bliss is in the grave with thee.

But, when the days of golden dreams had perished,
And even Despair was powerless to destroy,

Then did I learn how existence could be cherished,
Strengthened, and fed without the aid of joy.

Then did I check the tears of useless passion —
Weaned my young soul from yearning after thine;
Sternly denied its burning wish to hasten
Down to that tomb already more than mine.

And, even yet, I dare not let it languish,
Dare not indulge in memory's rapturous pain;
Once drinking deep of that divinest anguish,
How could I seek the empty world again?

GWENDOLYN BROOKS (1917 – 2000)
The Bean Eaters

They eat beans mostly, this old yellow pair.
Dinner is a casual affair.
Plain chipware on a plain and creaking wood,
Tin flatware.

Two who are Mostly Good.
Two who have lived their day,
But keep on putting on their clothes
And putting things away.

And remembering . . .
Remembering, with twinklings and twinges,
As they lean over the beans in their rented back room that is full
        of beads and receipts and dolls and clothes, tobacco crumbs,
        vases and fringes.

Kitchenette Building

We are things of dry hours and the involuntary plan,
Grayed in, and gray. "Dream" makes a giddy sound, not strong
Like "rent," "feeding a wife," "satisfying a man."

But could a dream send up through onion fumes
Its white and violet, fight with fried potatoes
And yesterday's garbage ripening in the hall,
Flutter, or sing an aria down these rooms

Even if we were willing to let it in,
Had time to warm it, keep it very clean,
Anticipate a message, let it begin?

We wonder. But not well! not for a minute!
Since Number Five is out of the bathroom now,
We think of lukewarm water, hope to get in it.

The Mother

Abortions will not let you forget.
You remember the children you got that you did not get,
The damp small pulps with a little or with no hair,
The singers and workers that never handled the air.
You will never neglect or beat
Them, or silence or buy with a sweet.
You will never wind up the sucking-thumb
Or scuttle off ghosts that come.
You will never leave them, controlling your luscious sigh,
Return for a snack of them, with gobbling mother-eye.

I have heard in the voices of the wind the voices of my dim killed
     children.
I have contracted. I have eased
My dim dears at the breasts they could never suck.
I have said, Sweets, if I sinned, if I seized
Your luck
And your lives from your unfinished reach,
If I stole your births and your names,
Your straight baby tears and your games,
Your stilted or lovely loves, your tumults, your marriages, aches,
     and your deaths,
If I poisoned the beginnings of your breaths,
Believe that even in my deliberateness I was not deliberate.
Though why should I whine,
Whine that the crime was other than mine? —
Since anyhow you are dead.
Or rather, or instead,
You were never made.
But that too, I am afraid,
Is faulty: oh, what shall I say, how is the truth to be said?
You were born, you had body, you died.
It is just that you never giggled or planned or cried.

Believe me, I loved you all.
Believe me, I knew you, though faintly, and I loved, I loved you
All.

ELIZABETH BARRETT BROWNING (1806 – 1861)

A Musical Instrument

What was he doing, the great god Pan,
    Down in the reeds by the river?
Spreading ruin and scattering ban,°   *baleful influence*
Splashing and paddling with hoofs of a goat,
And breaking the golden lilies afloat
    With the dragonfly on the river.

He tore out a reed, the great god Pan,
    From the deep cool bed of the river;
The limpid water turbidly ran,
And the broken lilies a–dying lay,
And the dragonfly had fled away,
    Ere he brought it out of the river.

High on the shore sat the great god Pan
    While turbidly flowed the river;
And hacked and hewed as a great god can,
With his hard bleak steel at the patient reed,
Till there was not a sign of the leaf indeed
    To prove it fresh from the river.

He cut it short, did the great god Pan
    (How tall it stood in the river!),
Then drew the pith, like the heart of a man,
Steadily from the outside ring,
And notched the poor dry empty thing
    In holes, as he sat by the river.

"This is the way," laughed the great god Pan
    (Laughed while he sat by the river),
"The only way, since gods began
To make sweet music, they could succeed."
Then, dropping his mouth to a hole in the reed,
    He blew in power by the river.

Sweet, sweet, sweet, O Pan!
    Piercing sweet by the river!
Blinding sweet, O great god Pan!
The sun on the hill forgot to die,
And the lilies revived, and the dragonfly
    Came back to dream on the river.

Yet half a beast is the great god Pan,
    To laugh as he sits by the river,
Making a poet out of a man;
The true gods sigh for the cost and pain —
For the reed which grows nevermore again
    As a reed with the reeds in the river.

ROBERT BROWNING (1812 – 1889)
"Childe Roland to the Dark Tower Came"[1]

(See Edgar's Song in Lear*)*

1

My first thought was, he lied in every word,
    That hoary cripple, with malicious eye
    Askance to watch the working of his lie
On mine, and mouth scarce able to afford
Suppression of the glee, that pursed and scored
    Its edge, at one more victim gained thereby.

2

What else should he be set for, with his staff?
    What, save to waylay with his lies, ensnare
    All travelers who might find him posted there,
And ask the road? I guessed what skull–like laugh
Would break, what crutch 'gin° write my epitaph   *begin to*
    For pastime in the dusty thoroughfare,

3

If at his counsel I should turn aside
    Into that ominous tract which, all agree,
    Hides the Dark Tower. Yet acquiescingly
I did turn as he pointed: neither pride
Nor hope rekindling at the end descried,
    So much as gladness that some end might be.

---

[1]The title is taken from Shakespeare's *King Lear* (III. iv. 173). A "childe" is a medieval term for a youth awaiting knighthood.

4

For, what with my whole world-wide wandering,
      What with my search drawn out through years, my hope
      Dwindled into a ghost not fit to cope
With that obstreperous joy success would bring, —
I hardly tried now to rebuke the spring
      My heart made, finding failure in its scope.

5

As when a sick man very near to death
      Seems dead indeed, and feels begin and end
      The tears, and takes the farewell of each friend,
And hears one bid the other go, draw breath
Freelier outside, ("since all is o'er," he saith,
      "And the blow fallen no grieving can amend;")

6

While some discuss if near the other graves
      Be room enough for this, and when a day
      Suits best for carrying the corpse away,
With care about the banners, scarves and staves:
And still the man hears all, and only craves
      He may not shame such tender love and stay.

7

Thus, I had so long suffered in this quest,
      Heard failure prophesied so oft, been writ
      So many times among "The Band" — to wit,
The knights who to the Dark Tower's search addressed
Their steps — that just to fail as they, seemed best,
      And all the doubt was now — should I be fit?

8

So, quiet as despair, I turned from him,
      That hateful cripple, out of his highway
      Into the path he pointed. All the day
Had been a dreary one at best, and dim
Was settling to its close, yet shot one grim
      Red leer to see the plain catch its estray.[2]

---

[2]Potential victim who has strayed.

9

For mark! no sooner was I fairly found
    Pledged to the plain, after a pace or two,
    Than, pausing to throw backward a last view
O'er the safe road, 'twas gone; gray plain all round:
Nothing but plain to the horizon's bound.
    I might go on; naught else remained to do.

10

So, on I went. I think I never saw
    Such starved ignoble nature; nothing throve:
    For flowers — as well expect a cedar grove!
But cockle, spurge, according to their law
Might propagate their kind, with none to awe,
    You'd think: a burr had been a treasure trove.

11

No! penury, inertness and grimace,
    In some strange sort, were the land's portion. "See
    Or shut your eyes," said Nature peevishly,
"It nothing skills: I cannot help my case:
'Tis the Last Judgment's fire must cure this place,
    Calcine° its clods and set my prisoners free."   *reduce to ash*

12

If there pushed any ragged thistle-stalk
    Above its mates, the head was chopped;
        the bents°   *coarse grasses*
    Were jealous else. What made those holes and rents
In the dock's harsh swarth leaves, bruised as to balk
All hope of greenness? 'tis a brute must walk
    Pashing° their life out, with a brute's intents.   *crushing*

13

As for the grass, it grew as scant as hair
    In leprosy; thin dry blades pricked the mud
    Which underneath looked kneaded up with blood.
One stiff blind horse, his every bone a-stare,
Stood stupefied, however he came there:
    Thrust out past service from the devil's stud!

14

Alive? he might be dead for aught I know,
    With that red gaunt colloped° neck a-strain,   *ridged*
    And shut eyes underneath the rusty mane;
Seldom went such grotesqueness with such woe;
I never saw a brute I hated so;
    He must be wicked to deserve such pain.

15

I shut my eyes and turned them on my heart.
    As a man calls for wine before he fights,
    I asked one draught of earlier, happier sights,
Ere fitly I could hope to play my part.
Think first, fight afterwards — the soldier's art:
    One taste of the old time sets all to rights.

16

Not it! I fancied Cuthbert's reddening face
    Beneath its garniture of curly gold,
    Dear fellow, till I almost felt him fold
An arm in mine to fix me to the place,
That way he used. Alas, one night's disgrace!
    Out went my heart's new fire and left it cold.

17

Giles then, the soul of honor — there he stands
    Frank as ten years ago when knighted first.
    What honest man should dare (he said) he durst.
Good — but the scene shifts — faugh! what hangman hands
Pin to his breast a parchment? His own bands
    Read it. Poor traitor, spit upon and curst!

18

Better this present than a past like that;
    Back therefore to my darkening path again!
    No sound, no sight as far as eye could strain.
Will the night send a howlet° or a bat?   *owl*
I asked: when something on the dismal flat
    Came to arrest my thoughts and change their train.

19

A sudden little river crossed my path
  As unexpected as a serpent comes.
  No sluggish tide congenial to the glooms;
This, as it frothed by, might have been a bath
For the fiend's glowing hoof — to see the wrath
  Of its black eddy bespate° with flakes   *bespattered*
   and spumes.

20

So petty yet so spiteful! All along,
  Low scrubby alders kneeled down over it;
  Drenched willows flung them headlong in a fit
Of mute despair, a suicidal throng:
The river which had done them all the wrong,
  Whate'er that was, rolled by, deterred no whit.

21

Which, while I forded, — good saints, how I feared
  To set my foot upon a dead man's cheek,
  Each step, or feel the spear I thrust to seek
For hollows, tangled in his hair or beard!
— It may have been a water-rat I speared,
  But, ugh! it sounded like a baby's shriek.

22

Glad was I when I reached the other bank.
  Now for a better country. Vain presage!
  Who were the strugglers, what war did they wage,
Whose savage trample thus could pad the dank
Soil to a plash? Toads in a poisoned tank,
  Or wild cats in a red-hot iron cage —

23

The fight must so have seemed in that fell cirque.
  What penned them there, with all the plain to choose?
  No footprint leading to that horrid mews,
None out of it. Mad brewage set to work

Their brains, no doubt, like galley-slaves the Turk
    Pits for his pastime, Christians against Jews.

24

And more than that — a furlong on — why, there!
    What bad use was that engine for, that wheel,
    Or brake, not wheel — that harrow fit to reel
Men's bodies out like silk? with all the air
Of Tophet's° tool, on earth left unaware,   *Hell's*
    Or brought to sharpen its rusty teeth of steel.

25

Then came a bit of stubbed ground, once a wood,
    Next a marsh, it would seem, and now mere earth
    Desperate and done with; (so a fool finds mirth,
Makes a thing and then mars it, till his mood
Changes and off he goes!) within a rood°   *quarter-acre*
    Bog, clay and rubble, sand and stark black dearth.

26

Now blotches rankling, colored gay and grim,
    Now patches where some leanness of the soil's
    Broke into moss or substances like boils;
Then came some palsied oak, a cleft in him
Like a distorted mouth that splits its rim
    Gaping at death, and dies while it recoils.

27

And just as far as ever from the end!
    Nought in the distance but the evening, nought
    To point my footstep further! At the thought,
A great black bird, Apollyon's[3] bosom-friend,
Sailed past, nor beat his wide wing
        dragon-penned°   *dragon-feathered*
    That brushed my cap — perchance the guide I sought.

28

For, looking up, aware I somehow grew,
    'Spite of the dusk, the plain had given place
    All round to mountains — with such name to grace

---

[3]In Revelation 9:11, an angel of the bottomless pit.

Mere ugly heights and heaps now stolen in view.
How thus they had surprised me, — solve it, you!
  How to get from them was no clearer case.

29

Yet half I seemed to recognize some trick
  Of mischief happened to me, God knows when —
  In a bad dream perhaps. Here ended, then,
Progress this way. When, in the very nick
Of giving up, one time more, came a click
  As when a trap shuts — you're inside the den!

30

Burningly it came on me all at once,
  This was the place! those two hills on the right,
  Crouched like two bulls locked horn in horn in fight;
While to the left, a tall scalped mountain . . . Dunce,
Dotard, a-dozing at the very nonce,
  After a life spent training for the sight!

31

What in the midst lay but the Tower itself?
  The round squat turret, blind as the fool's heart,
  Built of brown stone, without a counterpart
In the whole world. The tempest's mocking elf
Points to the shipman thus the unseen shelf
  He strikes on, only when the timbers start.

32

Not see? because of night perhaps? — why, day
  Came back again for that! before it left,
  The dying sunset kindled through a cleft:
The hills, like giants at a hunting, lay,
Chin upon hand, to see the game at bay, —
  "Now stab and end the creature — to the heft!"

33

Not hear? when noise was everywhere! it tolled
  Increasing like a bell. Names in my ears
  Of all the lost adventurers my peers, —
How such a one was strong, and such was bold,

And such was fortunate, yet each of old
    Lost, lost! one moment knelled the woe of years.

34

There they stood, ranged along the hillsides, met
    To view the last of me, a living frame
    For one more picture! in a sheet of flame
I saw them and I knew them all. And yet
Dauntless the slug-horn[4] to my lips I set,
    And blew. *"Childe Roland to the Dark Tower came."*

ROBERT BURNS (1759 – 1796)
O, Wert Thou in the Cauld Blast

O, wert thou in the cauld blast
    On yonder lea, on yonder lea,
My plaidie to the angry airt,°   *quarter (of the wind)*
    I'd shelter thee, I'd shelter thee.
Or did misfortune's bitter storms
    Around thee blaw, around thee blaw,
Thy bield° should be my bosom,   *shelter*
    To share it a', to share it a'.

Or were I in the wildest waste,
    Sae black and bare, sae black and bare,
The desert were a paradise,
    If thou wert there, if thou wert there.
Or were I monarch o' the globe,
    Wi' thee to reign, wi' thee to reign,
The brightest jewel in my crown
    Wad be my queen, wad be my queen.

A Red, Red Rose

O my luve's like a red, red rose,
    That's newly sprung in June;
O my luve's like the melodie
    That's sweetly played in tune.

As fair art thou, my bonnie lass,
    So deep in luve am I;

---

[4]A rough trumpet made from the horn of an ox or cow.

And I will luve thee still, my dear,
 Till a' the seas gang dry.

Till a' the seas gang dry, my dear,
 And the rocks melt wi' the sun:
O I will luve thee still, my dear,
 While the sands o' life shall run.

And fare thee weel, my only luve,
 And fare thee weel awhile!
And I will come again, my luve,
 Though it were ten thousand mile.

GEORGE GORDON, LORD BYRON (1788 – 1824)
She Walks in Beauty

1

She walks in beauty, like the night
 Of cloudless climes and starry skies;
And all that's best of dark and bright
 Meet in her aspect and her eyes:
Thus mellowed to that tender light
 Which heaven to gaudy day denies.

2

One shade the more, one ray the less,
 Had half impaired the nameless grace
Which waves in every raven tress,
 Or softly lightens o'er her face;
Where thoughts serenely sweet express
 How pure, how dear their dwelling place.

3

And on that cheek, and o'er that brow,
 So soft, so calm, yet eloquent,
The smiles that win, the tints that glow,
 But tell of days in goodness spent,
A mind at peace with all below,
 A heart whose love is innocent!

When We Two Parted

When we two parted
 In silence and tears,

Half broken-hearted
    To sever for years,
Pale grew thy cheek and cold,
    Colder thy kiss;
Truly that hour foretold
    Sorrow to this.

The dew of the morning
    Sunk chill on my brow —
It felt like the warning
    Of what I feel now.
Thy vows are all broken,
    And light is thy fame;
I hear thy name spoken,
    And share in its shame.

They name thee before me,
    A knell to mine ear;
A shudder comes o'er me —
    Why wert thou so dear?
They know not I knew thee,
    Who knew thee too well —
Long, long shall I rue thee,
    Too deeply to tell.

In secret we met —
    In silence I grieve,
That thy heart could forget,
    Thy spirit deceive.
If I should meet thee
    After long years,
How should I greet thee? —
    With silence and tears.

LORNA DEE CERVANTES (b. 1954)
Freeway 280

Las casitas[1] near the gray cannery,
nestled amid wild abrazos[2] of climbing roses
and man-high red geraniums

---

[1] The little houses.
[2] Embraces.

are gone now. The freeway conceals it
all beneath a raised scar.

But under the fake windsounds of the open lanes,
in the abandoned lots below, new grasses sprout,
wild mustard remembers, old gardens
come back stronger than they were,
trees have been left standing in their yards.
Albaricoqueros, cerezos, nogales . . .[3]
Viejitas[4] come here with paper bags to gather greens.
Espinaca, verdolagas, yerbabuena . . . [5]

I scramble over the wire fence
that would have kept me out.
Once, I wanted out, wanted the rigid lanes
to take me to a place without sun,
without the smell of tomatoes burning
on swing shift in the greasy summer air.

Maybe it's here
en los campos extraños de esta ciudad[6]
where I'll find it, that part of me
mown under
like a corpse
or a loose seed.

Poem for the Young White Man Who Asked Me How I, an Intelligent, Well-Read Person Could Believe in the War Between Races

In my land there are no distinctions.
The barbed wire politics of oppression
have been torn down long ago. The only reminder
of past battles, lost or won, is a slight
rutting in the fertile fields.   5

In my land
people write poems about love,
full of nothing but contented childlike syllables.

---

[3]Apricot trees, cherry trees, walnut trees.
[4]Old women.
[5]Spinach, purslane, mint.
[6]In the strange fields of this city.

Everyone reads Russian short stories and weeps.
There are no boundaries.   10
There is no hunger, no
complicated famine or greed.

I am not a revolutionary.
I don't even like political poems.
Do you think I can believe in a war between races?   15
I can deny it. I can forget about it
when I'm safe,
living on my own continent of harmony
and home, but I am not
there.   20

I believe in revolution
because everywhere the crosses are burning,
sharp-shooting goose-steppers round every corner,
there are snipers in the schools . . .
(I know you don't believe this.   25
You think this is nothing
but faddish exaggeration. But they
are not shooting at you.)

I'm marked by the color of my skin.
The bullets are discrete and designed to kill slowly.   30
They are aiming at my children.
These are facts.
Let me show you my wounds: my stumbling mind, my
"excuse me" tongue, and this
nagging preoccupation   35
with the feeling of not being good enough.

These bullets bury deeper than logic.
Racism is not intellectual.
I can not reason these scars away.

Outside my door   40
there is a real enemy
who hates me.

I am a poet
who yearns to dance on rooftops,
to whisper delicate lines about joy   45
and the blessings of human understanding.
I try. I go to my land, my tower of words and

bolt the door, but the typewriter doesn't fade out
the sounds of blasting and muffled outrage.
My own days bring me slaps on the face.   50
Every day I am deluged with reminders
that this is not
my land

and this is my land.

I do not believe in the war between races   55
but in this country
there is war.

MARILYN CHIN (b. 1955)
Autumn Leaves

My dead piled up, thick, fragrant, on the fire escape.
My mother ordered me again, and again, to sweep it clean.
All that blooms must fall. I learned this not from the Tao,
      but from high school biology.
Oh, the contradictions of having a broom and not a dustpan!
I swept the leaves down, down through the iron grille
and let the dead rain over the Wong family's patio.

And it was Achilles Wong who completed the task.
     We called her:
The-one-who-cleared-away-another-family's-autumn.
She blossomed, tall, benevolent, notwithstanding.

AMY CLAMPITT (1920 – 1994)
A Procession at Candlemas[1]

1

Moving on or going back to where you came from,
bad news is what you mainly travel with:
a breakup or a breakdown, someone running off

or walking out, called up or called home:
death in the family. Nudged from their stanchions   5
outside the terminal, anonymous of purpose

[1]February 2. Observed as a church festival in commemoration of the presentation of Christ in the temple and the purification of the Virgin Mary after childbirth.

as a flock of birds, the bison of the highway
funnel westward onto Route 80, mirroring
an entity that cannot look into itself and know

what makes it what it is. Sooner or later   10
every trek becomes a funeral procession.
The mother curtained in Intensive Care —

a scene the mind leaves blank, fleeing instead
toward scenes of transhumance,° the belled sheep   *transport of flocks*
moving up the Pyrenees, red-tassled pack llamas   15

footing velvet-green precipices, the Kurdish
women, jingling with bangles, gorgeous
on their rug-piled mounts — already lying dead,

bereavement altering the moving lights
to a processional, a feast of Candlemas.   20
Change as child-bearing, birth as a kind

of shucking off: out of what began
as a Mosaic² insult — such a loathing
of the common origin, even a virgin,

having given birth, needs purifying —   25
to carry fire as though it were a flower,
the terror and the loveliness entrusted

into naked hands, supposing God might have,
might actually need a mother: people have
at times found this a way of being happy.   30

A Candlemas of moving lights along Route 80;
lighted candles in a corridor from Arlington³
over the Potomac, for every carried flame

the name of a dead soldier: an element
fragile as ego, frightening as parturition,°   *giving birth*   35
necessary and intractable as dreaming.

The lapped, wheelborne integument, layer
within layer, at the core a dream of
something precious, ripped: Where are we?

---

²Of or related to Moses or the institutions or writings attributed to him; here, the
Mosaic law that forty days after childbirth a woman must present herself at the temple for
ritual purification.
³Arlington National Cemetery.

The sleepers groan, stir, rewrap themselves   40
about the self's imponderable substance,
or clamber down, numb-footed, half in a drowse

of freezing dark, through a Stonehenge
of fuel pumps, the bison hulks slantwise
beside them, drinking. What is real except   45

what's fabricated? The jellies glitter
cream-capped in the cafeteria showcase;
gumball globes, Life Savers cinctured

in parcel gilt, plop from their housings
perfect, like miracles. Comb, nail clipper,   50
lip rouge, mirrors and emollients embody,

niched into the washroom wall case,
the pristine seductiveness of money.
Absently, without inhabitants, this

nowhere oasis wears the place name   55
of Indian Meadows. The westward-trekking
transhumance, once only, of a people who,

in losing everything they had, lost even
the names they went by, stumbling past
like caribou, perhaps camped here. Who   60

can assign a trade-in value to that sorrow?
The monk in sheepskin over tucked-up saffron
intoning to a drum becomes the metronome

of one more straggle up Pennsylvania Avenue
in falling snow, a whirl of tenderly   65
remorseless corpuscles, street gangs

amok among magnolias' pregnant wands,
a stillness at the heart of so much whirling:
beyond the torn integument of childbirth,

sometimes, wrapped like a papoose into a grief   70
not merely of the ego, you rediscover almost
the rest-in-peace of the placental coracle.

2

Of what the dead were, living, one knows
so little as barely to recognize
the fabric of the backward-ramifying   75

antecedents, half-noted presences
in darkened rooms: the old, the feared,
the hallowed. Never the same river

drowns the unalterable doorsill. An effigy
in olive wood or pear wood, dank   80
with the sweat of age, walled in the dark

at Brauron, Argos, Samos:[4] even the unwed
Athene,[5] who had no mother, born — it's declared —
of some man's brain like every other pure idea,

had her own wizened cult object, kept   85
out of sight like the incontinent whimperer
in the backstairs bedroom, where no child

ever goes — to whom, year after year,
the fair linen of the sacred peplos[6]
was brought in ceremonial procession —   90

flutes and stringed instruments, wildflower-
hung cattle, nubile Athenian girls, young men
praised for the beauty of their bodies. Who

can unpeel the layers of that seasonal
returning to the dark where memory fails,   95
as birds re-enter the ancestral flyway?

Daylight, snow falling, knotting of gears:
Chicago. Soot, the rotting backsides
of tenements, grimed trollshapes of ice

underneath the bridges, the tunnel heaving   100
like a birth canal. Disgorged, the infant
howling in the restroom; steam-table cereal,

pale coffee; wall-eyed TV receivers, armchairs
of molded plastic: the squalor of the day
resumed, the orphaned litter taken up again   105

unloved, the spawn of botched intentions,
grief a mere hardening of the gut,
a set piece of what can't be avoided:

[4]Brauron was a site known from ancient times for the worship of Artemis. Hera
was worshiped at Argos. Samos is an island in the Aegean Sea.

[5]Athena, who emerged, fully armed, from the head of her father, Zeus.

[6]A linen shawl, cult symbol of Athena; object of the Panathenaic procession in
ancient Athens, represented on the Parthenon.

parents by the tens of thousands living
unthanked, unpaid but in the sour coin   110
of resentment. Midmorning gray as zinc

along Route 80, corn-stubble quilting
the underside of snowdrifts, the cadaverous
belvedere of windmills, the sullen stare

of feedlot cattle; black creeks puncturing   115
white terrain, the frozen bottomland
a mush of willow tops; dragnetted in ice,

the Mississippi. Westward toward the dark,
the undertow of scenes come back to, fright
riddling the structures of interior history: 120

Where is it? Where, in the shucked-off
bundle, the hampered obscurity that has been
for centuries the mumbling lot of women,

did the thread of fire, too frail
ever to discover what it meant, to risk   125
even the taking of a shape, relinquish

the seed of possibility, unguessed-at
as a dream of something precious? Memory,
that exquisite blunderer, stumbling

like a migrant bird that finds the flyway   130
it hardly knew it knew except by instinct,
down the long-unentered nave of childhood,

late on a midwinter afternoon, alone
among the snow-hung hollows of the windbreak
on the far side of the orchard, encounters   135

sheltering among the evergreens, a small
stilled bird, its cap of clear yellow
slit by a thread of scarlet — the untouched

nucleus of fire, the lost connection
hallowing the wizened effigy, the mother   140
curtained in Intensive Care: a Candlemas

of moving lights along Route 80, at nightfall,
in falling snow, the stillness and the sorrow
of things moving back to where they came from.

JOHN CLARE (1793 – 1864)

Badger

When midnight comes a host of dogs and men
Go out and track the badger to his den,
And put a sack within the hole, and lie
Till the old grunting badger passes by.
He comes and hears — they let the strongest loose.
The old fox hears the noise and drops the goose.
The poacher shoots and hurries from the cry,
And the old hare half wounded buzzes by.
They get a forkèd stick to bear him down
And clap the dogs and take him to the town,
And bait him all the day with many dogs,
And laugh and shout and fright the scampering hogs.
He runs along and bites at all he meets:
They shout and hollo down the noisy streets.

He turns about to face the loud uproar
And drives the rebels to their very door.
The frequent stone is hurled where'er they go;
When badgers fight, then everyone's a foe.
The dogs are clapped and urged to join the fray;
The badger turns and drives them all away.
Though scarcely half as big, demure and small,
He fights with dogs for hours and beats them all.
The heavy mastiff, savage in the fray,
Lies down and licks his feet and turns away.
The bulldog knows his match and waxes cold,
The badger grins and never leaves his hold.
He drives the crowd and follows at their heels
And bites them through — the drunkard swears and reels.

The frighted women take the boys away,
The blackguard laughs and hurries on the fray.
He tries to reach the woods, an awkward race,
But sticks and cudgels quickly stop the chase.
He turns again and drives the noisy crowd
And beats the many dogs in noises loud.
He drives away and beats them every one,
And then they loose them all and set them on.
He falls as dead and kicked by boys and men,
Then starts and grins and drives the crowd again;

Till kicked and torn and beaten out he lies
And leaves his hold and crackles, groans, and dies.

First Love

I ne'er was struck before that hour
    With love so sudden and so sweet,
Her face it bloomed like a sweet flower
    And stole my heart away complete.
My face turned pale as deadly pale.
    My legs refused to walk away,
And when she looked, what could I ail?
    My life and all seemed turned to clay.

And then my blood rushed to my face
    And took my eyesight quite away,
The trees and bushes round the place
    Seemed midnight at noonday.
I could not see a single thing,
    Words from my eyes did start —
They spoke as chords do from the string,
    And blood burnt round my heart.

Are flowers the winter's choice?
    Is love's bed always snow?
She seemed to hear my silent voice,
    Not love's appeals to know.
I never saw so sweet a face
    As that I stood before.
My heart has left its dwelling-place
    And can return no more.

I Am

I am: yet what I am none cares or knows
    My friends forsake me like a memory lost,
I am the self-consumer of my woes —
    They rise and vanish in oblivious host,
Like shadows in love's frenzied, stifled throes —
And yet I am, and live — like vapors tossed

Into the nothingness of scorn and noise,
    Into the living sea of waking dreams,
Where there is neither sense of life or joys,
    But the vast shipwreck of my life's esteems;

Even the dearest, that I love the best,
Are strange — nay, rather stranger than the rest.

I long for scenes, where man hath never trod,
    A place where woman never smiled or wept —
There to abide with my Creator, God,
    And sleep as I in childhood sweetly slept,
Untroubling, and untroubled where I lie,
The grass below — above the vaulted sky.

HENRI COLE (b. 1956)
40 Days and 40 Nights

Opening a vein he called my radial,
the phlebotomist introduced himself as Angel.
Since the counseling it had been ten days
of deep inversion — self-recrimination weighed
against regret, those useless emotions.
Now there would be thirty more enduring the notion
of some self-made doom foretold in the palm.

Waiting for blood work with aristocratic calm,
big expectant mothers from Spanish Harlem
appeared cut-out, as if Matisse had conceived them.
Their bright smocks ruffling like plumage before the fan,
they might themselves have been angels, come by land.

Consent and disclosure signed away, liquid gold
of urine glimmering in a plastic cup, threshold
of last doubt crossed, the red fluid was drawn
in a steady hematic ooze from my arm.
"Now, darling, the body doesn't lie," Angel said.
DNA and enzymes and antigens in his head
true as lines in the face in the mirror
on his desk.

      I smiled, pretending to be cheered.
In the way that some become aware of God
when they cease becoming overawed
with themselves, no less than the artist concealed
behind the surface of whatever object or felt
words he builds, so I in my first week
of waiting let the self be displaced by each
day's simplest events, letting them speak

with emblematic voices that might teach me.
They did . . . until I happened on the card
from the clinic, black-framed as a graveyard.
Could the code 12 22 90 have represented
some near time, December 22, 1990, for repentance?
The second week I believed it. The fourth I
rejected it and much else loved, until the eyes
teared those last days and the lab phoned.

Back at the clinic — someone's cheap cologne,
Sunday lamb yet on the tongue, the mind cool as a pitcher
of milk, a woman's knitting needles aflutter,
Angel's hand in mind — I watched the verdict-lips move,
rubbed my arm, which, once pricked, had tingled then bruised.

Kayaks

Beyond the soggy garden, two kayaks
float across mild clear water. A red sun
stains the lake like colored glass. Day is stopping.
Everything I am feels distant or blank
as the opulent rays pass through me,
distant as action is from thought,
or language is from all things desirable
in the world, when it does not deliver
what it promises and pathos comes instead —
the same pathos I feel when I tell myself,
within or without valid structures of love:
I have been deceived, he is not what he seemed —
though the failure is not in the other,
but in me because I am tired, hurt or bitter.

SAMUEL TAYLOR COLERIDGE (1772 – 1834)
Dejection: An Ode

> *Late, late yestreen I saw the new Moon,*
> *With the old Moon in her arms;*
> *And I fear, I fear, my master dear!*
> *We shall have a deadly storm.*
> — BALLAD OF SIR PATRICK SPENCE

1

Well! If the Bard was weather-wise, who made
    The grand old ballad of Sir Patrick Spence,
    This night, so tranquil now, will not go hence

Unroused by winds, that ply a busier trade
Than those which mold yon cloud in lazy flakes,
Or the dull sobbing draft, that moans and rakes
Upon the strings of this Aeolian lute,[1]
        Which better far were mute.
     For lo! the New-moon winter-bright!
     And overspread with phantom light,
     (With swimming phantom light o'erspread
     But rimmed and circled by a silver thread)
I see the old Moon in her lap, foretelling
     The coming-on of rain and squally blast.
And oh! that even now the gust were swelling,
     And the slant night shower driving loud and fast!
Those sounds which oft have raised me, whilst they awed,
     And sent my soul abroad,
Might now perhaps their wonted impulse give,
Might startle this dull pain, and make it move and live!

2

A grief without a pang, void, dark, and drear,
     A stifled, drowsy, unimpassioned grief,
     Which finds no natural outlet, no relief,
       In word, or sigh, or tear —
O Lady! in this wan and heartless mood,
To other thoughts by yonder throstle wooed,
     All this long eve, so balmy and serene,
Have I been gazing on the western sky,
     And its peculiar tint of yellow green:
And still I gaze — and with how blank an eye!
And those thin clouds above, in flakes and bars,
That give away their motion to the stars;
Those stars, that glide behind them or between,
Now sparkling, now bedimmed, but always seen:
Yon crescent Moon, as fixed as if it grew
In its own cloudless, starless lake of blue;
I see them all so excellently fair,
I see, not feel, how beautiful they are!

---

[1]An Aeolian lute or harp is a stringed instrument that produces musical sounds when touched by a current of air.

3

My genial spirits fail;
And what can these avail
To lift the smothering weight from off my breast?
It were a vain endeavor,
Though I should gaze forever
On that green light that lingers in the west:
I may not hope from outward forms to win
The passion and the life, whose fountains are within.

4

O Lady! we receive but what we give,
And in our life alone does Nature live:
Ours is her wedding garment, ours her shroud!
And would we aught behold, of higher worth,
Than that inanimate cold world allowed
To the poor loveless ever-anxious crowd,
Ah! from the soul itself must issue forth
A light, a glory, a fair luminous cloud
Enveloping the Earth —
And from the soul itself must there be sent
A sweet and potent voice, of its own birth,
Of all sweet sounds the life and element!

5

O pure of heart! thou need'st not ask of me
What this strong music in the soul may be!
What, and wherein it doth exist,
This light, this glory, this fair luminous mist,
This beautiful and beauty-making power.
Joy, virtuous Lady! Joy that ne'er was given,
Save to the pure, and in their purest hour,
Life, and Life's effluence, cloud at once and shower,
Joy, Lady! is the spirit and the power,
Which wedding Nature to us gives in dower
A new Earth and new Heaven,
Undreamt of by the sensual and the proud —
Joy is the sweet voice, Joy the luminous cloud —
We in ourselves rejoice!
And thence flows all that charms or ear or sight,
All melodies the echoes of that voice,
All colors a suffusion from that light.

6

There was a time when, though my path was rough,
    This joy within me dallied with distress,
And all misfortunes were but as the stuff
    Whence Fancy made me dreams of happiness:
For hope grew round me, like the twining vine,
And fruits, and foliage, not my own, seemed mine.
But now afflictions bow me down to earth:
Nor care I that they rob me of my mirth;
    But oh! each visitation
Suspends what nature gave me at my birth,
    My shaping spirit of Imagination.

For not to think of what I needs must feel,
    But to be still and patient, all I can;
And haply by abstruse research to steal
    From my own nature all the natural man —
    This was my sole resource, my only plan:
Till that which suits a part infects the whole,
And now is almost grown the habit of my soul.

7

Hence, viper thoughts, that coil around my mind,
    Reality's dark dream!
I turn from you, and listen to the wind,
    Which long has raved unnoticed. What a scream
Of agony by torture lengthened out
That lute sent forth! Thou Wind, that rav'st without,
    Bare crag, or mountain tairn,° or blasted tree,   *pool*
Or pine grove whither woodman never clomb,
Or lonely house, long held the witches' home,
    Methinks were fitter instruments for thee,
Mad Lutanist! who in this month of showers,
Of dark-brown gardens, and of peeping flowers,
Mak'st Devils' yule, with worse than wintry song,
The blossoms, buds, and timorous leaves among.
    Thou Actor, perfect in all tragic sounds!
Thou mighty Poet, e'en to frenzy bold!
    What tell'st thou now about?
    'Tis of the rushing of an host in rout,
    With groans, of trampled men, with smarting wounds —
At once they groan with pain, and shudder with the cold!

But hush! there is a pause of deepest silence!
    And all that noise, as of a rushing crowd,
With groans, and tremulous shudderings — all is over —
    It tells another tale, with sounds less deep and loud!
        A tale of less affright,
        And tempered with delight,
As Otway's[2] self had framed the tender lay —
        'Tis of a little child
        Upon a lonesome wild,
Not far from home, but she hath lost her way:
And now moans low in bitter grief and fear,
And now screams loud, and hopes to make her mother hear.

8

'Tis midnight, but small thoughts have I of sleep:
Full seldom may my friend such vigils keep!
Visit her, gentle Sleep! with wings of healing,
    And may this storm be but a mountain birth,
May all the stars hang bright above her dwelling,
    Silent as though they watched the sleeping Earth!
        With light heart may she rise,
        Gay fancy, cheerful eyes,
    Joy lift her spirit, joy attune her voice;
To her may all things live, from pole to pole,
Their life the eddying of her living soul!
    O simple spirit, guided from above,
Dear Lady! friend devoutest of my choice,
Thus mayest thou ever, evermore rejoice.

---

[2]Thomas Otway (1652–1685), a dramatist whose plays emphasize pathos and sentiment.

The Rime of the Ancient Mariner

In Seven Parts

> *Facile credo, plures esse Naturas invisibiles quam visibiles*
> *in rerum universitate. Sed horum [sic] omnium familiam*
> *quis nobis enarrabit? et gradus et cognationes et discrimina*
> *et singulorum munera? Quid agunt? quae loca habitant?*
> *Harum rerum notitiam semper ambivit ingenium*
> *humanum, nunquam attigit. Juvat, interea, non diffiteor,*
> *quandoque in animo, tanquam in tabulà, majoris et*
> *melioris mundi imaginem contemplari: ne mens assuefacta*
> *hodiernae vitae minutiis se contrahat nimis, et tota subsi-*
> *dat in pusillas cogitationes. Sed veritati interea invigilan-*
> *dum est, modusque servandus, ut certa ab incertis, diem a*
> *nocte, distinguamus.*[1]

— T. BURNET

Part I

An ancient Mariner meeteth three Gallants bidden to a wedding feast, and detaineth one.	It is an ancient Mariner And he stoppeth one of three. — "By thy long gray beard and glittering eye, Now wherefore stopp'st thou me?

The Bridegroom's doors are opened wide,   5
And I am next of kin;
The guests are met, the feast is set:
May'st hear the merry din."

He holds him with his skinny hand,
"There was a ship," quoth he.   10
"Hold off! unhand me, graybeard loon!"
Eftsoons° his hand dropped he.   *immediately*

The Wedding Guest is spellbound by the eye of the old seafaring man, and constrained to hear his tale.	He holds him with his glittering eye — The Wedding Guest stood still, And listens like a three years' child: 15 The Mariner hath his will.

---

[1]From Burnet's *Archaeologiae Philosophiae*: "I can easily believe that there are more invisible than visible beings in the universe. But of their families, degrees, connections, distinctions, and functions, who shall tell us? How do they act? Where are they found? About such matters the human mind has always circled without attaining knowledge. Yet I do not doubt that sometimes it is well for the soul to contemplate as in a picture the image of a larger and better world, lest the mind, habituated to the small concerns of daily life, limit itself too much and sink entirely into trivial thinking. But meanwhile we must be on watch for the truth, avoiding extremes, so that we may distinguish certain from uncertain, day from night." Burnet was a seventeenth-century English theologian.

The Wedding Guest sat on a stone:
He cannot choose but hear;
And thus spake on that ancient man,
The bright-eyed Mariner.   20

"The ship was cheered, the harbor cleared,
Merrily did we drop
Below the kirk,° below the hill,   church
Below the lighthouse top.

*The Mariner tells
how the ship sailed
southward with a
good wind and fair
weather, till it
reached the line.*

The Sun came up upon the left,   25
Out of the sea came he!
And he shone bright, and on the right
Went down into the sea.

Higher and higher every day,
Till over the mast at noon — "   30
The Wedding Guest here beat his breast,
For he heard the loud bassoon.

*The Wedding Guest
heareth the bridal
music; but the
Mariner continueth
his tale.*

The bride hath paced into the hall,
Red as a rose is she;
Nodding their heads before her goes   35
The merry minstrelsy.

The Wedding Guest he beat his breast,
Yet he cannot choose but hear;
And thus spake on that ancient man,
The bright-eyed Mariner.   40

*The ship driven by
a storm toward the
South Pole.*

"And now the STORM-BLAST came, and he
Was tyrannous and strong;
He struck with his o'ertaking wings,
And chased us south along.

With sloping masts and dipping prow,   45
As who pursued with yell and blow
Still treads the shadow of his foe,
And forward bends his head,
The ship drove fast, loud roared the blast,
And southward aye we fled.   50

And now there came both mist and snow,
And it grew wondrous cold:
And ice, mast-high, came floating by,
As green as emerald.

The land of ice, and
of fearful sounds
where no living
thing was to be
seen.

And through the drifts the snowy clifts°   55   *cliffs*
Did send a dismal sheen:
Nor shapes of men nor beasts we ken —
The ice was all between.

The ice was here, the ice was there,
The ice was all around: 60
It cracked and growled, and roared and howled,
Like noises in a swound!°   *swoon*

Till a great sea bird,
called the Albatross,
came through the
snowfog and was
received with great
joy and hospitality.

At length did cross an Albatross,
Thorough the fog it came;
As if it had been a Christian soul,   65
We hailed it in God's name.

It ate the food it ne'er had eat,
And round and round it flew.
The ice did split with a thunder-fit;
The helmsman steered us through!   70

And lo! the
Albatross proveth a
bird of good omen,
and followeth the
ship as it returned
northward through
fog and floating ice.

And a good south wind sprung up behind;
The Albatross did follow,
And every day, for food or play,
Came to the mariners' hollo!

In mist or cloud, on mast or shroud,   75
It perched for vespers nine;
Whiles all the night, through fog-smoke white,
Glimmered the white Moon-shine."

The ancient
Mariner
inhospitably killeth
the pious bird of
good omen.

"God save thee, ancient Mariner!
From the fiends, that plague thee thus! —   80
Why look'st thou so?" — With my crossbow
I shot the ALBATROSS.

Part II

The Sun now rose upon the right:
Out of the sea came he,
Still hid in mist, and on the left   85
Went down into the sea.

And the good south wind still blew behind,
But no sweet bird did follow,
Nor any day for food or play
Came to the mariners' hollo!   90

His shipmates cry out against the ancient Mariner, for killing the bird of good luck.

And I had done a hellish thing,
And it would work 'em woe:
For all averred, I had killed the bird
That made the breeze to blow.
Ah wretch! said they, the bird to slay,   95
That made the breeze to blow!

But when the fog cleared off, they justify the same, and thus make themselves accomplices in the crime.

Nor dim nor red, like God's own head,
The glorious Sun uprist:
Then all averred, I had killed the bird
That brought the fog and mist.   100
'Twas right, said they, such birds to slay,
That bring the fog and mist.

The fair breeze continues; the ship enters the Pacific Ocean, and sails northward, even till it reaches the Line.

The ship hath been suddenly becalmed.

The fair breeze blew, the white foam flew,
The furrow followed free;
We were the first that ever burst   105
Into that silent sea.

Down dropped the breeze, the sails dropped down,
'Twas sad as sad could be;
And we did speak only to break
The silence of the sea!   110

All in a hot and copper sky,
The bloody Sun, at noon,
Right up above the mast did stand,
No bigger than the Moon.

Day after day, day after day,   115
We stuck, nor breath nor motion;
As idle as a painted ship
Upon a painted ocean.

And the Albatross begins to be avenged.

Water, water, everywhere,
And all the boards did shrink;   120
Water, water, everywhere,
Nor any drop to drink.

The very deep did rot: O Christ!
That ever this should be!
Yea, slimy things did crawl with legs   125
Upon the slimy sea.

About, about, in reel and rout
The death-fires danced at night;
The water, like a witch's oils,
Burnt green, and blue and white.   130

And some in dreams assurèd were

A Spirit had fol-
lowed them; one of
the invisible inhab-
itants of this

Of the Spirit that plagued us so;
Nine fathom deep he had followed us
From the land of mist and snow.

planet, neither departed souls nor angels; concerning whom the learned Jew, Josephus, and the
Platonic and Constantinopolitan, Michael Psellus, may be consulted. They are very numerous,
there is no climate or element without one or more.

And every tongue, through utter drought,   135
Was withered at the root;
We could not speak, no more than if
We had been choked with soot.

The shipmates, in
their sore distress,
would fain throw
the whole guilt on
the ancient Mari-

Ah! well-a-day! what evil looks
Had I from old and young!   140
Instead of the cross, the Albatross
About my neck was hung.

ner: in sign whereof they hang the dead sea bird round his neck.

Part III

There passed a weary time. Each throat
Was parched, and glazed each eye.
A weary time! a weary time!   145
How glazed each weary eye,

The ancient
Mariner beholdeth a
sign in the element
afar off.

When looking westward, I beheld
A something in the sky.

At first it seemed a little speck,
And then it seemed a mist;   150
It moved and moved, and took at last
A certain shape, I wist.°   *knew*

A speck, a mist, a shape, I wist!
And still it neared and neared:
As if it dodged a water sprite,   155
It plunged and tacked and veered.

At its nearer
approach, it seemeth
him to be a ship;

With throats unslaked, with black lips baked,
We could nor laugh nor wail;
Through utter drought all dumb we stood!

and at a dear ransom he freeth his speech from the bonds of thirst.

I bit my arm, I sucked the blood,   160
And cried, A sail! a sail!

With throats unslaked, with black lips baked,
Agape they heard me call:

A flash of joy;

Gramercy! they for joy did grin,   165
And all at once their breath drew in,
As they were drinking all.

And horror follows. For can it be a ship that comes onward without wind or tide?

See! see! (I cried) she tacks no more!
Hither to work us weal;
Without a breeze, without a tide,
She steadies with upright keel!   170

The western wave was all aflame.
The day was well nigh done!
Almost upon the western wave
Rested the broad bright Sun;
When that strange shape drove suddenly   175
Betwixt us and the Sun.

It seemeth him but the skeleton of a ship.

And straight the Sun was flecked with bars,
(Heaven's Mother send us grace!)
As if through a dungeon grate he peered
With broad and burning face.   180

Alas! (thought I, and my heart beat loud)

And its ribs are seen as bars on the face of the setting Sun.

How fast she nears and nears!
Are those *her* sails that glance in the Sun,
Like restless gossameres?

The Specter-Woman and her Deathmate, and no other on board the skeleton ship.

Are those *her* ribs through which the Sun   185
Did peer, as through a grate?
And is that Woman all her crew?
Is that a DEATH? and are there two?
Is DEATH that woman's mate?

Like vessel, like crew!

Her lips were red, *her* looks were free,   190
Her locks were yellow as gold:
Her skin was as white as leprosy,
The Nightmare LIFE-IN-DEATH was she,
Who thicks man's blood with cold.

Death and Life-in-Death have diced for the ship's crew, and she (the latter) winneth the ancient Mariner.

The naked hulk alongside came,   195
And the twain were casting dice;
"The game is done! I've won! I've won!"
Quoth she, and whistles thrice.

No twilight within
the courts of the Sun.

The Sun's rim dips; the stars rush out:
At one stride comes the dark;   200
With far-heard whisper, o'er the sea,
Off shot the specter-bark.

At the rising of the
Moon,

We listened and looked sideways up!
Fear at my heart, as at a cup,
My lifeblood seemed to sip!   205
The stars were dim, and thick the night,
The steersman's face by his lamp gleamed white;
From the sails the dew did drip —
Till clomb above the eastern bar
The hornèd Moon, with one bright star   210
Within the nether tip.

One after another,

One after one, by the star-dogged Moon,
Too quick for groan or sigh,
Each turned his face with ghastly pang,
And cursed me with his eye.   215

His shipmates drop
down dead.

Four times fifty living men,
(And I heard nor sigh nor groan)
With heavy thump, a lifeless lump,
They dropped down one by one.

But Life-in-Death
begins her work on
the ancient Mariner.

The souls did from their bodies fly —   220
They fled to bliss or woe!
And every soul, it passed me by,
Like the whizz of my cross-bow!

Part IV

The Wedding Guest
feareth that a Spirit
is talking to him;

"I fear thee, ancient Mariner!
I fear thy skinny hand!   225
And thou art long, and lank, and brown,
As is the ribbed sea-sand.

I fear thee and thy glittering eye,
And thy skinny hand, so brown." —

But the ancient
Mariner assureth
him of his bodily
life, and proceedeth
to relate his horrible
penance.

Fear not, fear not, thou Wedding Guest!   230
This body dropped not down.

Alone, alone, all, all alone,
Alone on a wide wide sea!
And never a saint took pity on
My soul in agony.   235

*He despiseth the
creatures of the calm,*
The many men, so beautiful!
And they all dead did lie:
And a thousand thousand slimy things
Lived on; and so did I.

*And envieth that
they should live,
and so many lie
dead.*
I looked upon the rotting sea,   240
And drew my eyes away;
I looked upon the rotting deck,
And there the dead men lay.

I looked to heaven, and tried to pray;
But or ever a prayer had gushed,   245
A wicked whisper came, and made
My heart as dry as dust.

I closed my lids, and kept them close,
And the balls like pulses beat,
For the sky and the sea, and the sea and the sky   250
Lay like a load on my weary eye,
And the dead were at my feet.

*But the curse liveth
for him in the eye of
the dead men.*
The cold sweat melted from their limbs,
Nor rot nor reek did they:
The look with which they looked on me   255
Had never passed away.

An orphan's curse would drag to hell
A spirit from on high;
But oh! more horrible than that
Is the curse in a dead man's eye!   260
Seven days, seven nights, I saw that curse,
And yet I could not die.

*In his loneliness and
fixedness he yearneth
towards the journey-
ing Moon, and the
stars that still
sojourn, yet still
move onward; and
everywhere the blue
sky belongs to them,
and is their appointed
rest, and their*
The moving Moon went up the sky,
And nowhere did abide:
Softly she was going up,   265
And a star or two beside —

Her beams bemocked the sultry main,
Like April hoar-frost spread;
But where the ship's huge shadow lay,
The charmèd water burnt away   270
A still and awful red.

*native country and their own natural homes, which they enter unannounced, as lords that are
certainly expected and yet there is a silent joy at their arrival.*

*By the light of the
Moon he beholdeth*
Beyond the shadow of the ship,
I watched the water snakes:

*God's creatures of
the great calm.*
They moved in tracks of shining white,
And when they reared, the elfish light   275
Fell off in hoary flakes.

Within the shadow of the ship
I watched their rich attire:
Blue, glossy green, and velvet black,
They coiled and swam; and every track   280
Was a flash of golden fire.

*Their beauty and
their happiness.*
O happy living things! no tongue
Their beauty might declare:
A spring of love gushed from my heart,

*He blesseth them in
his heart.*
And I blessed them unaware: 285
Sure my kind saint took pity on me,
And I blessed them unaware.

*The spell begins to
break.*
The self-same moment I could pray;
And from my neck so free
The Albatross fell off, and sank   290
Like lead into the sea.

Part V

Oh sleep! it is a gentle thing,
Beloved from pole to pole!
To Mary Queen the praise be given!
She sent the gentle sleep from Heaven,   295
That slid into my soul.

*By grace of the holy
Mother, the ancient
Mariner is refreshed
with rain.*
The silly° buckets on the deck,   *lowly*
That had so long remained,
I dreamt that they were filled with dew;
And when I awoke, it rained.   300

My lips were wet, my throat was cold,
My garments all were dank;
Sure I had drunken in my dreams,
And still my body drank.

I moved, and could not feel my limbs: 305
I was so light — almost
I thought that I had died in sleep,
And was a blessèd ghost.

*He heareth sounds
and seeth strange*
And soon I heard a roaring wind:
It did not come anear;   310

sights and commo-
tions in the sky and
the element.

But with its sound it shook the sails,
That were so thin and sere.

The upper air burst into life!
And a hundred fire-flags sheen,
To and fro they were hurried about! 315
And to and fro, and in and out,
The wan stars danced between.

And the coming wind did roar more loud,
And the sails did sigh like sedge;
And the rain poured down from one black cloud; 320
The Moon was at its edge.

The thick black cloud was cleft, and still
The Moon was at its side:
Like waters shot from some high crag,
The lightning fell with never a jag, 325
A river steep and wide.

The bodies of the
ship's crew are
inspirited, and the
ship moves on;

The loud wind never reached the ship,
Yet now the ship moved on!
Beneath the lightning and the Moon
The dead men gave a groan. 330

They groaned, they stirred, they all uprose,
Nor spake, nor moved their eyes;
It had been strange, even in a dream,
To have seen those dead men rise.

The helmsman steered, the ship moved on; 335
Yet never a breeze up-blew;
The mariners all 'gan work the ropes,
Where they were wont to do;
They raised their limbs like lifeless tools —
We were a ghastly crew. 340

The body of my brother's son
Stood by me, knee to knee:
The body and I pulled at one rope,
But he said nought to me.

"I fear thee, ancient Mariner!" 345
Be calm, thou Wedding Guest!
'Twas not those souls that fled in pain,
Which to their corses came again,
But a troop of spirits blest:

But not by the souls
of the men, nor by
demons of earth or
middle air, but by a

*blèssed troop of
angelic spirits, sent
down by the invo-
cation of the guardian
saint.*

For when it dawned — they dropped their arms,   350
And clustered round the mast;
Sweet sounds rose slowly through their mouths,
And from their bodies passed.

Around, around, flew each sweet sound,
Then darted to the Sun;   355
Slowly the sounds came back again,
Now mixed, now one by one.

Sometimes a-dropping from the sky
I heard the sky-lark sing;
Sometimes all little birds that are,   360
How they seemed to fill the sea and air
With their sweet jargoning!°   *warbling*

And now 'twas like all instruments,
Now like a lonely flute;
And now it is an angel's song,   365
That makes the heavens be mute.

It ceased; yet still the sails made on
A pleasant noise till noon,
A noise like of a hidden brook
In the leafy month of June,   370
That to the sleeping woods all night
Singeth a quiet tune.

Till noon we quietly sailed on,
Yet never a breeze did breathe:
Slowly and smoothly went the ship,   375
Moved onward from beneath.

*The lonesome Spirit
from the South Pole
carries on the ship
as far as the Line, in
obedience to the
angelic troop, but
still requireth
vengeance.*

Under the keel nine fathom deep,
From the land of mist and snow,
The spirit slid: and it was he
That made the ship to go.   380
The sails at noon left off their tune,
And the ship stood still also.

The Sun, right up above the mast,
Had fixed her to the ocean:
But in a minute she 'gan stir,   385
With a short uneasy motion —
Backwards and forwards half her length
With a short uneasy motion.

Then like a pawing horse let go,
She made a sudden bound: 390
It flung the blood into my head,
And I fell down in a swound.

The Polar Spirit's
fellow demons, the
invisible inhabitants
of the element, take
part in his wrong;
and two of them
relate, one to the
other, that penance
long and heavy for
the ancient Mariner
hath been accorded
to the Polar Spirit,
who returneth
southward.

How long in that same fit I lay,
I have not° to declare;   *am not able*
But ere my living life returned,   395
I heard and in my soul discerned
Two voices in the air.

"Is it he?" quoth one, "Is this the man?
By him who died on cross,
With his cruel bow he laid full low   400
The harmless Albatross.

The spirit who bideth by himself
In the land of mist and snow,
He loved the bird that loved the man
Who shot him with his bow."   405

The other was a softer voice,
As soft as honey-dew:
Quoth he, "The man hath penance done,
And penance more will do."

Part VI

FIRST VOICE

"But tell me, tell me! speak again,   410
Thy soft response renewing —
What makes that ship drive on so fast?
What is the ocean doing?"

SECOND VOICE

"Still as a slave before his lord,
The ocean hath no blast;   415
His great bright eye most silently
Up to the Moon is cast —

If he may know which way to go;
For she guides him smooth or grim.
See, brother, see! how graciously   420
She looketh down on him."

FIRST VOICE

The Mariner hath been cast into a trance; for the angelic power causeth the vessel to drive northward faster than human life could endure.

"But why drives on that ship so fast,
Without or wave or wind?"

SECOND VOICE

"The air is cut away before,
And closes from behind.   425

Fly, brother, fly! more high, more high!
Or we shall be belated:
For slow and slow that ship will go,
When the Mariner's trance is abated."

The supernatural motion is retarded; the Mariner awakes, and his penance begins anew.

I woke, and we were sailing on   430
As in a gentle weather:
'Twas night, calm night, the moon was high;
The dead men stood together.

All stood together on the deck,
For a charnel-dungeon fitter: 435
All fixed on me their stony eyes,
That in the Moon did glitter.

The pang, the curse, with which they died,
Had never passed away:
I could not draw my eyes from theirs,   440
Nor turn them up to pray.

The curse is finally expiated.

And now this spell was snapped: once more
I viewed the ocean green,
And looked far forth, yet little saw
Of what had else been seen —   445

Like one, that on a lonesome road
Doth walk in fear and dread,
And having once turned round walks on,
And turns no more his head;
Because he knows, a frightful fiend   450
Doth close behind him tread.

But soon there breathed a wind on me,
Nor sound nor motion made:
Its path was not upon the sea,
In ripple or in shade.   455

It raised my hair, it fanned my cheek
Like a meadow-gale of spring —
It mingled strangely with my fears,
Yet it felt like a welcoming.

Swiftly, swiftly flew the ship,   460
Yet she sailed softly too:
Sweetly, sweetly blew the breeze —
On me alone it blew.

And the ancient   Oh! dream of joy! is this indeed
Mariner beholdeth   The lighthouse top I see?   465
his native country.   Is this the hill? is this the kirk?
Is this mine own countree?

We drifted o'er the harbor-bar,
And I with sobs did pray —
O let me be awake, my God!   470
Or let me sleep alway.

The harbor bay was clear as glass,
So smoothly it was strewn!
And on the bay the moonlight lay,
And the shadow of the Moon.   475

The rock shone bright, the kirk no less,
That stands above the rock:
The moonlight steeped in silentness
The steady weathercock.

The angelic spirits   And the bay was white with silent light,   480
leave the dead   Till rising from the same,
bodies,   Full many shapes, that shadows were,
In crimson colors came.

A little distance from the prow
And appear in their   Those crimson shadows were: 485
own forms of light.   I turned my eyes upon the deck —
Oh, Christ! what saw I there!

Each corse lay flat, lifeless and flat,
And, by the holy rood!°   *cross of Christ*
A man all light, a seraph°-man,   *angel-like*   490
On every corse there stood.

This seraph-band, each waved his hand:
It was a heavenly sight!
They stood as signals to the land,
Each one a lovely light;   495

This seraph-band, each waved his hand,
No voice did they impart —
No voice; but oh! the silence sank
Like music on my heart.

But soon I heard the dash of oars,   500
I heard the Pilot's cheer;
My head was turned perforce away
And I saw a boat appear.

The Pilot and the Pilot's boy,
I heard them coming fast: 505
Dear Lord in Heaven! it was a joy
The dead men could not blast.

I saw a third — I heard his voice:
It is the Hermit good!
He singeth loud his godly hymns   510
That he makes in the wood.
He'll shrieve my soul, he'll wash away
The Albatross's blood.

Part VII

*The Hermit of the
Wood*

This Hermit good lives in that wood
Which slopes down to the sea.   515
How loudly his sweet voice he rears!
He loves to talk with marineres
That come from a far countree.

He kneels at morn, and noon, and eve —
He hath a cushion plump: 520
It is the moss that wholly hides
The rotted old oak stump.

The skiff-boat neared: I heard them talk,
"Why, this is strange, I trow!
Where are those lights so many and fair,   525
That signal made but now?"

*Approacheth the
ship with wonder.*

"Strange, by my faith!" the Hermit said —
"And they answered not our cheer!

The planks looked warped! and see those sails,
How thin they are and sere! 530
I never saw aught like to them,
Unless perchance it were

Brown skeletons of leaves that lag
My forest-brook along;
When the ivy tod° is heavy with snow, *bushy clump* 535
And the owlet whoops to the wolf below,
That eats the she-wolf's young."

"Dear Lord! it hath a fiendish look,"
The Pilot made reply,
"I am a-feared" — "Push on, push on!" 540
Said the Hermit cheerily.

The boat came closer to the ship,
But I nor spake nor stirred;
The boat came close beneath the ship,
And straight a sound was heard. 545

*The ship suddenly
sinketh.*

Under the water it rumbled on,
Still louder and more dread:
It reached the ship, it split the bay;
The ship went down like lead.

*The ancient
Mariner is saved in
the Pilot's boat.*

Stunned by that loud and dreadful sound, 550
Which sky and ocean smote,
Like one that hath been seven days drowned
My body lay afloat;
But swift as dreams, myself I found
Within the Pilot's boat. 555

Upon the whirl, where sank the ship,
The boat spun round and round;
And all was still, save that the hill
Was telling of the sound.

I moved my lips — the Pilot shrieked 560
And fell down in a fit;
The holy Hermit raised his eyes,
And prayed where he did sit.

I took the oars: the Pilot's boy,
Who now doth crazy go, 565
Laughed loud and long, and all the while
His eyes went to and fro.

"Ha! ha!" quoth he, "full plain I see,
The Devil knows how to row."

And now, all in my own countree,   570
I stood on the firm land!
The Hermit stepped forth from the boat,
And scarcely he could stand.

The ancient
Mariner earnestly
entreateth the
Hermit to shrieve
him; and the
penance of life falls
on him.

"O shrieve me, shrieve me, holy man!"
The Hermit crossed his brow.   575
"Say quick," quoth he, "I bid thee say —
What manner of man art thou?"

Forthwith this frame of mine was wrenched
With a woeful agony,
Which forced me to begin my tale;   580
And then it left me free.

And ever and anon
throughout his
future life an agony
constraineth him to
travel from land to
land;

Since then, at an uncertain hour,
That agony returns:
And till my ghastly tale is told,
This heart within me burns.   585

I pass, like night, from land to land;
I have strange power of speech;
That moment that his face I see,
I know the man that must hear me:
To him my tale I teach.   590

What loud uproar bursts from that door!
The wedding guests are there:
But in the garden-bower the bride
And bridemaids singing are:
And hark the little vesper bell,   595
Which biddeth me to prayer!

O Wedding Guest! this soul hath been
Alone on a wide wide sea:
So lonely 'twas, that God himself
Scarce seemèd there to be.   600

O sweeter than the marriage feast,
'Tis sweeter far to me,
To walk together to the kirk
With a goodly company!

To walk together to the kirk,   605
And all together pray,
While each to his great Father bends,
Old men, and babes, and loving friends
And youths and maidens gay!

And to teach, by his   Farewell, farewell! but this I tell   610
own example, love   To thee, thou Wedding Guest!
and reverence to all   He prayeth well, who loveth well
things that God   Both man and bird and beast.
made and loveth.

He prayeth best, who loveth best
All things both great and small;   615
For the dear God who loveth us,
He made and loveth all.

The Mariner, whose eye is bright,
Whose beard with age is hoar,
Is gone: and now the Wedding Guest   620
Turned from the bridegroom's door.

He went like one that hath been stunned,
And is of sense forlorn:
A sadder and a wiser man,
He rose the morrow morn.

WILLIAM COWPER (1731 – 1800)

The Castaway

Obscurest night involved the sky,
     The Atlantic billows roared,
When such a destined wretch as I,
     Washed headlong from on board,
Of friends, of hope, of all bereft,   5
His floating home forever left.

No braver chief could Albion boast
     Than he with whom he went,[1]
Nor ever ship left Albion's coast,
     With warmer wishes sent.   10

---

[1]Cowper's poem is based on an incident in Richard Walter's *A Voyage Round the World by . . . George Anson* (1748).

He loved them both, but both in vain,
Nor him beheld, nor her again.

Not long beneath the whelming brine,
    Expert to swim, he lay;
Nor soon he felt his strength decline,   15
    Or courage die away;
But waged with death a lasting strife,
Supported by despair of life.

He shouted; nor his friends had failed
    To check the vessel's course,   20
But so the furious blast prevailed,
    That, pitiless perforce,
They left their outcast mate behind,
And scudded still before the wind.

Some succor yet they could afford;   25
    And, such as storms allow,
The cask, the coop, the floated cord,
    Delayed not to bestow.
But he (they knew) nor ship, nor shore,
Whate'er they gave, should visit more.   30

Nor, cruel as it seemed, could he
    Their haste himself condemn,
Aware that flight, in such a sea,
    Alone could rescue them;
Yet bitter felt it still to die   35
Deserted, and his friends so nigh.

He long survives, who lives an hour
    In ocean, self-upheld;
And so long he, with unspent power,
    His destiny repelled;   40
And ever, as the minutes flew,
Entreated help, or cried, "Adieu!"

At length, his transient respite past,
    His comrades, who before
Had heard his voice in every blast,   45
    Could catch the sound no more.
For then, by toil subdued, he drank
The stifling wave, and then he sank.

No poet wept him; but the page
    Of narrative sincere,   50

That tells his name, his worth, his age,
    Is wet with Anson's tear.
And tears by bards or heroes shed
Alike immortalize the dead.

I therefore purpose not, or dream,   55
    Descanting on his fate,
To give the melancholy theme
    A more enduring date:
But misery still delights to trace
Its semblance in another's case.   60

No voice divine the storm allayed,
    No light propitious shone,
When, snatched from all effectual aid,
    We perished, each alone;
But I beneath a rougher sea,
And whelmed in deeper gulfs than he.

Epitaph on a Hare

Here lies, whom hound did ne'er pursue,
    Nor swifter greyhound follow,
Whose foot ne'er tainted morning dew,
    Nor ear heard huntsman's hallo',

Old Tiney, surliest of his kind,
    Who, nursed with tender care,
And to domestic bounds confined,
    Was still a wild jack-hare.

Though duly from my hand he took
    His pittance every night,
He did it with a jealous look,
    And, when he could, would bite.

His diet was of wheaten bread,
    And milk, and oats, and straw,
Thistles, or lettuces instead,
    With sand to scour his maw.

On twigs of hawthorn he regaled,
    On pippins' russet peel;
And, when his juicy salads failed,
    Sliced carrot pleased him well.

A Turkey carpet was his lawn,
    Whereon he loved to bound,
To skip and gambol like a fawn,
    And swing his rump around.

His frisking was at evening hours,
    For then he lost his fear;
But most before approaching showers,
    Or when a storm drew near.

Eight years and five round-rolling moons
    He thus saw steal away,
Dozing out all his idle noons,
    And every night at play.

I kept him for his humor's sake,
    For he would oft beguile
My heart of thoughts that made it ache,
    And force me to a smile.

But now, beneath this walnut-shade
    He finds his long, last home,
And waits in snug concealment laid,
    Till gentler Puss shall come.

He, still more agèd, feels the shocks
    From which no care can save,
And, partner once of Tiney's box,
    Must soon partake his grave.

Hart Crane (1899 – 1932)
The Broken Tower

The bell-rope that gathers God at dawn
Dispatches me as though I dropped down the knell
Of a spent day — to wander the cathedral lawn
From pit to crucifix, feet chill on steps from hell.

Have you not heard, have you not seen that corps
Of shadows in the tower, whose shoulders sway
Antiphonal carillons launched before
The stars are caught and hived in the sun's ray?

The bells, I say, the bells break down their tower;
And swing I know not where. Their tongues engrave

Membrane through marrow, my long-scattered score
Of broken intervals . . . And I, their sexton slave!

Oval encyclicals in canyons heaping
The impasse high with choir. Banked voices slain!
Pagodas, campaniles° with reveilles outleaping —   *bell towers*
O terraced echoes prostrate on the plain! . . .

And so it was I entered the broken world
To trace the visionary company of love, its voice
An instant in the wind (I know not whither hurled)
But not for long to hold each desperate choice.

My word I poured. But was it cognate, scored
Of that tribunal monarch of the air
Whose thigh embronzes earth, strikes crystal Word
In wounds pledged once to hope — cleft to despair?

The steep encroachments of my blood left me
No answer (could blood hold such a lofty tower
As flings the question true?) — or is it she
Whose sweet mortality stirs latent power?

And through whose pulse I hear, counting the strokes
My veins recall and add, revived and sure
The angelus of wars my chest evokes:
What I hold healed, original now, and pure . . .

And builds, within, a tower that is not stone
(Not stone can jacket heaven) — but slip
Of pebbles — visible wings of silence sown
In azure circles, widening as they dip

The matrix of the heart, lift down the eye
That shrines the quiet lake and swells a tower . . .
The commodious, tall decorum of that sky
Unseals her earth, and lifts love in its shower.

To Brooklyn Bridge

How many dawns, chill from his rippling rest
The seagull's wings shall dip and pivot him,
Shedding white rings of tumult, building high
Over the chained bay waters Liberty —

Then, with inviolate curve, forsake our eyes
As apparitional as sails that cross

Some page of figures to be filed away;
— Till elevators drop us from our day . . .

I think of cinemas, panoramic sleights
With multitudes bent toward some flashing scene
Never disclosed, but hastened to again,
Foretold to other eyes on the same screen;

And Thee, across the harbor, silver-paced
As though the sun took step of thee, yet left
Some motion ever unspent in thy stride, —
Implicitly thy freedom staying thee!

Out of some subway scuttle, cell or loft
A bedlamite° speeds to thy parapets,   *madman*
Tilting there momently, shrill shirt ballooning,
A jest falls from the speechless caravan.

Down Wall,° from girder into street noon leaks,   *Wall Street*
A rip-tooth of the sky's acetylene;
All afternoon the cloud-flown derricks turn . . .
Thy cables breathe the North Atlantic still.

And obscure as that heaven of the Jews,
Thy guerdon° . . . Accolade thou dost bestow   *reward*
Of anonymity time cannot raise:
Vibrant reprieve and pardon thou dost show.

O harp and altar, of the fury fused,
(How could mere toil align thy choiring strings!)
Terrific threshold of the prophet's pledge,
Prayer of pariah and the lover's cry, —

Again the traffic lights that skim thy swift
Unfractioned idiom, immaculate sigh of stars,
Beading thy path — condense eternity:
And we have seen night lifted in thine arms.

Under thy shadow by the piers I waited;
Only in darkness is thy shadow clear.
The City's fiery parcels all undone,
Already snow submerges an iron year . . .

O Sleepless as the river under thee,
Vaulting the sea, the prairies' dreaming sod,
Unto us lowliest sometime sweep, descend
And of the curveship lend a myth to God.

ROBERT CREELEY (b. 1926)
A Marriage

The first retainer
he gave to her
was a golden
wedding ring.

The second — late at night
he woke up,
leaned over on an elbow,
and kissed her.

The third and the last —
he died with
and gave up loving
and lived with her.

COUNTEE CULLEN (1903 – 1946)
Incident

For Eric Walrond

Once riding in old Baltimore,
    Heart-filled, head-filled with glee,
I saw a Baltimorean
    Keep looking straight at me.

Now I was eight and very small,
    And he was no whit bigger,
And so I smiled, but he poked out
    His tongue, and called me, "Nigger."

I saw the whole of Baltimore
    From May until December;
Of all the things that happened there
    That's all that I remember.

E. E. CUMMINGS (1894 – 1962)
anyone lived in a pretty how town

anyone lived in a pretty how town
(with up so floating many bells down)
spring summer autumn winter
he sang his didn't he danced his did.

Women and men(both little and small)
cared for anyone not at all
they sowed their isn't they reaped their same
sun moon stars rain

children guessed(but only a few
and down they forgot as up they grew
autumn winter spring summer)
that noone loved him more by more

when by now and tree by leaf
she laughed his joy she cried his grief
bird by snow and stir by still
anyone's any was all to her

someones married their everyones
laughed their cryings and did their dance
(sleep wake hope and then)they
said their nevers they slept their dream

stars rain sun moon
(and only the snow can begin to explain
how children are apt to forget to remember
with up so floating many bells down)

one day anyone died i guess
(and noone stooped to kiss his face)
busy folk buried them side by side
little by little and was by was

all by all and deep by deep
and more by more they dream their sleep
noone and anyone earth by april
wish by spirit and if by yes.

Women and men(both dong and ding)
summer autumn winter spring
reaped their sowing and went their came
sun moon stars rain

may i feel said he

may i feel said he
(i'll squeal said she
just once said he)
it's fun said she

(may i touch said he
how much said she
a lot said he)
why not said she

(let's go said he
not too far said she
what's too far said he
where you are said she)

may i stay said he
(which way said she
like this said he
if you kiss said she

may i move said he
is it love said she)
if you're willing said he
(but you're killing said she

but it's life said he
but your wife said she
now said he)
ow said she

(tiptop said he
don't stop said she
oh no said he)
go slow said she

(cccome?said he
ummm said she)
you're divine!said he
(you are Mine said she)

EMILY DICKINSON (1830 – 1886)
The Brain — is wider than the Sky —

The Brain — is wider than the Sky —
For — put them side by side —
The one the other will contain
With ease — and You — beside —

The Brain is deeper than the sea —
For — hold them — Blue to Blue —

The one the other will absorb —
As Sponges — Buckets — do —

The Brain is just the weight of God —
For — Heft them — Pound for Pound —
And they will differ — if they do —
As Syllable from Sound —

I like a look of Agony

I like a look of Agony,
Because I know it's true —
Men do not sham Convulsion,
Nor simulate, a Throe —

The Eyes glaze once — and that is Death —
Impossible to feign
The Beads upon the Forehead
By homely Anguish strung.

Much Madness is divinest Sense —

Much Madness is divinest Sense —
To a discerning Eye —
Much Sense — the starkest Madness —
'Tis the Majority
In this, as All, prevail —
Assent — and you are sane —
Demur — you're straightway dangerous —
And handled with a Chain —

My Life had stood — a Loaded Gun —

My Life had stood — a Loaded Gun —
In Corners — till a Day
The Owner passed — identified —
And carried Me away —

And now We roam in Sovereign Woods —
And now We hunt the Doe —
And every time I speak for Him —
The Mountains straight reply —

And do I smile, such cordial light
Upon the Valley glow —
It is as a Vesuvian face
Had let its pleasure through —

And when at Night — Our good Day done —
I guard My Master's Head —
'Tis better than the Eider-Duck's
Deep Pillow — to have shared —

To foe of His — I'm deadly foe —
None stir the second time —
On whom I lay a Yellow Eye —
Or an emphatic Thumb —

Though I than He — may longer live
He longer must — than I —
For I have but the power to kill,
Without — the power to die —

Safe in their Alabaster Chambers —

(Version of 1859)

Safe in their Alabaster Chambers —
Untouched by Morning
And untouched by Noon —
Sleep the meek members of the Resurrection —
Rafter of satin,
And Roof of stone.

Light laughs the breeze
In her Castle above them —
Babbles the Bee in a stolid Ear,
Pipe the Sweet Birds in ignorant cadence —
Ah, what sagacity perished here!

Safe in their Alabaster Chambers —

(Version of 1861)

Safe in their Alabaster Chambers —
Untouched by Morning —
And untouched by Noon —
Lie the meek members of the Resurrection —
Rafter of Satin — and Roof of Stone!

Grand go the Years — in the Crescent — above them —
Worlds scoop their Arcs —
And Firmaments — row —

Diadems — drop — and Doges[1] — surrender —
Soundless as dots — on a Disc of Snow —

The Soul selects her own Society —

The Soul selects her own Society —
Then — shuts the Door —
To her divine Majority —
Present no more —

Unmoved — she notes the Chariots — pausing —
At her low Gate —
Unmoved — an Emperor be kneeling
Upon her Mat —

I've known her — from an ample nation —
Choose One —
Then — close the Valves of her attention —
Like Stone —

Success is counted sweetest

Success is counted sweetest
By those who ne'er succeed.
To comprehend a nectar
Requires sorest need.

Not one of all the purple Host
Who took the Flag today
Can tell the definition
So clear of Victory

As he defeated — dying —
On whose forbidden ear
The distant strains of triumph
Burst agonized and clear!

There's a certain Slant of light

There's a certain Slant of light,
Winter Afternoons —
That oppresses, like the Heft
Of Cathedral Tunes —

---

[1]Chief magistrates in Venice from the eleventh through the sixteenth centuries.

Heavenly Hurt, it gives us —
We can find no scar,
But internal difference,
Where the Meanings, are —

None may teach it — Any —
'Tis the Seal Despair —
An imperial affliction
Sent us of the Air —

When it comes, the Landscape listens —
Shadows — hold their breath —
When it goes, 'tis like the Distance
On the look of Death —

Wild Nights — Wild Nights!

Wild Nights — Wild Nights!
Were I with thee
Wild Nights should be
Our luxury!

Futile — the Winds —
To a Heart in port —
Done with the Compass —
Done with the Chart!

Rowing in Eden —
Ah, the Sea!
Might I but moor — Tonight —
In Thee!

JOHN DONNE (1572 – 1631)
The Canonization

For God's sake hold your tongue, and let me love,
    Or chide my palsy, or my gout,
My five gray hairs, or ruined fortune, flout,
      With wealth your state, your mind with arts improve,
        Take you a course, get you a place,
        Observe His Honor, or His Grace,
Or the King's real, or his stampèd face
      Contémplate; what you will, approve,°   *experience*
      So you will let me love.

Alas, alas, who's injured by my love?
      What merchant's ships have my sighs drowned?
Who says my tears have overflowed his ground?
        When did my colds a forward spring remove?
          When did the heats which my veins fill
          Add one more to the plaguy bill?[1]
Soldiers find wars, and lawyers find out still
      Litigious men, which quarrels move,
      Though she and I do love.

Call us what you will, we're made such by love;
      Call her one, me another fly,
We're tapers too, and at our own cost die,[2]
        And we in us find th' eagle and the dove.
          The phoenix[3] riddle hath more wit°   *meaning*
          By us: we two being one, are it.
So, to one neutral thing both sexes fit.
      We die and rise the same, and prove
      Mysterious by this love.

We can die by it, if not live by love,
      And if unfit for tombs and hearse
Our legend be, it will be fit for verse;
        And if no piece of chronicle we prove,
          We'll build in sonnets pretty rooms;
          As well a well-wrought urn becomes
The greatest ashes, as half-acre tombs;
      And by these hymns, all shall approve
      Us canonized for love:

And thus invoke us: You whom reverend love
      Made one another's hermitage;
You, to whom love was peace, that now is rage;
        Who did the whole world's soul contract, and drove
          Into the glasses of your eyes
          (So made such mirrors, and such spies,
That they did all to you epitomize)
      Countries, towns, courts: Beg from above
      A pattern of your love!

---

[1] Weekly list of people who died of the plague.

[2] "Die" was slang for consummating the sexual act. It was believed that this act reduced one's life span.

[3] Mythical unique bird, periodically regenerated from its own ashes.

Death, be not proud

Death, be not proud, though some have callèd thee
Mighty and dreadful, for thou art not so;
For those whom thou think'st thou dost overthrow
Die not, poor Death, nor yet canst thou kill me.
From rest and sleep, which but thy pictures be,
Much pleasure; then from thee much more must flow,
And soonest our best men with thee do go,
Rest of their bones, and soul's delivery.
Thou art slave to fate, chance, kings, and desperate men,
And dost with poison, war, and sickness dwell,
And poppy or charms can make us sleep as well
And better than thy stroke; why swell'st thou then?
One short sleep past, we wake eternally,
And death shall be no more; Death, thou shalt die.

The Sun Rising

> Busy old fool, unruly sun,
> Why dost thou thus,
Through windows and through curtains call on us?
Must to thy motions lovers' seasons run?
> Saucy pedantic wretch, go chide
> Late school boys and sour prentices,
> Go tell court huntsmen that the king will ride,
> Call country ants to harvest offices;
Love, all alike, no season knows nor clime,
Nor hours, days, months, which are the rags of time.

> Thy beams, so reverend and strong
> Why shouldst thou think?
I could eclipse and cloud them with a wink,
But that I would not lose her sight so long;
> If her eyes have not blinded thine,
> Look, and tomorrow late tell me,
> Whether both th' Indias of spice and mine
> Be where thou leftst them, or lie here with me.
Ask for those kings whom thou saw'st yesterday,
And thou shalt hear, All here in one bed lay.

> She's all states, and all princes, I,
> Nothing else is.
Princes do but play us; compared to this,
All honor's mimic, all wealth alchemy.

Thou, sun, art half as happy as we,
In that the world's contracted thus;
Thine age asks ease, and since thy duties be
To warm the world, that's done in warming us.
Shine here to us, and thou art everywhere;
This bed thy center is, these walls, thy sphere.

RITA DOVE (b. 1952)
Adolescence — II

Although it is night, I sit in the bathroom, waiting.
Sweat prickles behind my knees, the baby-breasts are alert.
Venetian blinds slice up the moon; the tiles quiver in pale strips.

Then they come, the three seal men with eyes as round
As dinner plates and eyelashes like sharpened tines.
They bring the scent of licorice. One sits in the washbowl,

One on the bathtub edge; one leans against the door.
"Can you feel it yet?" they whisper.
I don't know what to say, again. They chuckle,

Patting their sleek bodies with their hands.
"Well, maybe next time." And they rise,
Glittering like pools of ink under moonlight,

And vanish. I clutch at the ragged holes
They leave behind, here at the edge of darkness.
Night rests like a ball of fur on my tongue.

Dusting

Every day a wilderness — no
shade in sight. Beulah
patient among knicknacks,
the solarium a rage
of light, a grainstorm
as her gray cloth brings
dark wood to life.

Under her hand scrolls
and crests gleam
darker still. What
was his name, that

silly boy at the fair with
the rifle booth? And his kiss and
the clear bowl with one bright
fish, rippling
wound!

Not Michael —
something finer. Each dust
stroke a deep breath and
the canary in bloom.
Wavery memory: home
from a dance, the front door
blown open and the parlor
in snow, she rushed
the bowl to the stove, watched
as the locket of ice
dissolved and he
swam free.

That was years before
Father gave her up
with her name, years before
her name grew to mean
Promise, then
Desert-in-Peace.
Long before the shadow and
sun's accomplice, the tree.

Maurice.

JOHN DRYDEN (1631 – 1700)
To the Memory of Mr. Oldham

Farewell, too little, and too lately known,
Whom I began to think and call my own:
For sure our souls were near allied, and thine
Cast in the same poetic mold with mine.
One common note on either lyre did strike,
And knaves and fools we both abhorred alike.
To the same goal did both our studies drive;
The last set out the soonest did arrive.

Thus Nisus[1] fell upon the slippery place,
While his young friend performed and won the race.
O early ripe! to thy abundant store
What could advancing age have added more?
It might (what nature never gives the young)
Have taught the numbers of thy native tongue.
But satire needs not those, and wit will shine
Through the harsh cadence of a rugged line:
A noble error, and but seldom made,
When poets are by too much force betrayed.
Thy generous fruits, though gathered ere their prime,
Still showed a quickness, and maturing time
But mellows what we write to the dull sweets of rhyme.
Once more, hail and farewell; farewell, thou young,
But ah too short, Marcellus[2] of our tongue;
Thy brows with ivy, and with laurels bound;
But fate and gloomy night encompass thee around.

PAUL LAURENCE DUNBAR (1872 – 1906)
Harriet Beecher Stowe[1]

She told the story, and the whole world wept
    At wrongs and cruelties it had not known
    But for this fearless woman's voice alone.
    She spoke to consciences that long had slept:
Her message, Freedom's clear reveille, swept
    From heedless hovel to complacent throne.
    Command and prophecy were in the tone
    And from its sheath the sword of justice leapt.
Around two peoples swelled a fiery wave,
    But both came forth transfigured from the flame.
Blest be the hand that dared be strong to save,
    And blest be she who in our weakness came —
    Prophet and priestess! At one stroke she gave
    A race to freedom and herself to fame.

---

[1]In Book V of Virgil's *Aeneid,* two friends, Nisus and Euryalus, run together in a foot race. Nisus, the older man, is on the point of winning the race when he slips and falls. He trips the next runner, thereby enabling his friend Euryalus to win.

[2]The nephew and adopted son of Augustus, who was expected to succeed him as emperor, but who died in 23 B.C.

[1]Harriet Beecher Stowe (1811–1896) wrote *Uncle Tom's Cabin* (1852), an antislavery novel that had an enormous impact on American attitudes toward slavery.

Robert Gould Shaw[1]

Why was it that the thunder voice of Fate
    Should call thee, studious, from the classic groves,
    Where calm-eyed Pallas[2] with still footstep roves,
And charge thee seek the turmoil of the state?
What bade thee hear the voice and rise elate,
    Leave home and kindred and thy spicy loaves,
    To lead th' unlettered and despisèd droves
To manhood's home and thunder at the gate?

Far better the slow blaze of Learning's light,
    The cool and quiet of her dearer fane,
Than this hot terror of a hopeless fight,
    This cold endurance of the final pain, —
Since thou and those who with thee died for right
    Have died, the Present teaches, but in vain!

We Wear the Mask

We wear the mask that grins and lies,
It hides our cheeks and shades our eyes —
This debt we pay to human guile;
With torn and bleeding hearts we smile,
And mouth with myriad subtleties.
Why should the world be over-wise,
In counting all our tears and sighs?
Nay, let them only see us, while
    We wear the mask.

We smile, but, O great Christ, our cries
To thee from tortured souls arise.
We sing, but oh the clay is vile
Beneath our feet, and long the mile;
But let the world dream otherwise,
    We wear the mask!

---

[1]Robert Gould Shaw (1837–1863) commanded the first all-Negro regiment in the North. He was killed while leading an attack on Fort Wagner in South Carolina.
[2]Pallas Athena, Greek goddess of wisdom.

why such an interplay between life + death?

T. S. ELIOT (1888 – 1965)
Marina[1]

Quis hic locus, quae regio, quae mundi plaga?[2]

What seas what shores what grey rocks and what islands
What water lapping the bow
And scent of pine and the woodthrush singing through the fog
What images return
O my daughter.

    Those who sharpen the tooth of the dog, meaning
Death
Those who glitter with the glory of the humming-bird, meaning
Death
Those who sit in the stye of contentment, meaning
Death
Those who suffer the ecstasy of the animals, meaning
Death

    Are become unsubstantial, reduced by a wind,
A breath of pine, and the woodsong fog
By this grace dissolved in place

    What is this face, less clear and clearer
The pulse in the arm, less strong and stronger —
Given or lent? more distant than stars and nearer than the eye
    Whispers and small laughter between leaves and hurrying
        feet
Under sleep, where all the waters meet.

    Bowsprit cracked with ice and paint cracked with heat.
I made this, I have forgotten
And remember.
The rigging weak and the canvas rotten
Between one June and another September.
Made this unknowing, half conscious, unknown, my own.
The garboard strake leaks, the seams need caulking.

This form, this face, this life
Living to live in a world of time beyond me; let me

---

[1]In Shakespeare's *Pericles,* the name of the miraculously regained daughter.

[2]This epigraph comes from the play *Hercules Furens (The Madness of Hercules)* by the Roman writer Seneca (4? B.C.–A.D. 65). Hercules, upon discovering that in his madness he has killed his wife and children, says: "What place is this, what region, what quarter of the world?"

Resign my life for this life, my speech for that unspoken,
The awakened, lips parted, the hope, the new ships.

What seas what shores what granite islands towards my
        timbers
And woodthrush calling through the fog
My daughter.

Preludes

I

The winter evening settles down
With smell of steaks in passageways.
Six o'clock.
The burnt-out ends of smoky days.
And now a gusty shower wraps
The grimy scraps
Of withered leaves about your feet
And newspapers from vacant lots;
The showers beat
On broken blinds and chimney-pots,
And at the corner of the street
A lonely cab-horse steams and stamps.
And then the lighting of the lamps.

[handwritten margin note: how does the language of the poem help convey the others mood?]

II

The morning comes to consciousness
Of faint stale smells of beer
From the sawdust-trampled street
With all its muddy feet that press
To early coffee-stands.
With the other masquerades
That time resumes,
One thinks of all the hands
That are raising dingy shades
In a thousand furnished rooms.

[handwritten margin note: has time stopped?]

III

You tossed a blanket from the bed,
You lay upon your back, and waited;
You dozed, and watched the night revealing
The thousand sordid images
Of which your soul was constituted;

They flickered against the ceiling.
And when all the world came back
And the light crept up between the shutters
And you heard the sparrows in the gutters,
You had such a vision of the street
As the street hardly understands;
Sitting along the bed's edge, where
You curled the papers from your hair,
Or clasped the yellow soles of feet
In the palms of both soiled hands.

IV

His soul stretched tight across the skies
That fade behind a city block,
Or trampled by insistent feet
At four and five and six o'clock;
And short square fingers stuffing pipes,
And evening newspapers, and eyes
Assured of certain certainties,
The conscience of a blackened street
Impatient to assume the world.

    I am moved by fancies that are curled
Around these images, and cling:
The notion of some infinitely gentle
Infinitely suffering thing.

    Wipe your hand across your mouth, and laugh;
The worlds revolve like ancient women
Gathering fuel in vacant lots.

THOMAS SAYERS ELLIS (b. 1965)
View of the Library of Congress from Paul Laurence Dunbar High School

for Doris Craig and Michael Olshausen

A white substitute teacher
At an all-black public high school,
He sought me out saying my poems
Showed promise, range, a gift,
And had I ever heard of T. S. Eliot?   5
No. Then Robert Hayden perhaps?

Hayden, a former colleague,
Had recently died, and the obituary
He handed me had already begun
Its journey home — from the printed page   10
Back to tree, gray becoming
Yellow, flower, dirt.

No river, we skipped rocks
On the horizon, above Ground Zero,
From the roof of the Gibson Plaza Apartments.   15
We'd aim, then shout the names
Of the museums, famous monuments,
And government buildings

Where our grandparents, parents,
Aunts, and uncles worked. Dangerous duds.   20
The bombs we dropped always fell short,
Missing their mark. No one, not even
Carlton Green, who had lived in
As many neighborhoods as me,

Knew in which direction   25
To launch when I lifted Hayden's
Place of employment —
The Library of Congress —
From the obituary, now folded
In my back pocket, a creased map.   30

We went home, asked our mothers,
But they didn't know. Richard's came
Close: Somewhere near Congress,
On Capitol Hill, take the 30 bus,
Get off before it reaches Anacostia,   35
Don't cross the bridge into Southeast.

The next day in school
I looked it up — The National Library
Of the United States in Washington, D.C.,
Founded in 1800, open to all taxpayers   40
And citizens. *Snap!* My Aunt Doris
Works there, has for years.

Once, on her day off, she
Took me shopping and bought
The dress shoes of my choice.   45

Loafers. They were dark red,
Almost purple, bruised — the color
Of blood before oxygen reaches it.

I was beginning to think
Like a poet, so in my mind   50
Hayden's dying and my loafers
Were connected, but years apart,
As was Dunbar to other institutions —
Ones I could see, ones I could not.

RALPH WALDO EMERSON (1803 – 1882)

Concord Hymn

Sung at the Completion of the Battle Monument,[1] *July 4, 1837*

By the rude bridge that arched the flood,
    Their flag to April's breeze unfurled,
Here once the embattled farmers stood
    And fired the shot heard round the world.

The foe long since in silence slept;
    Alike the conqueror silent sleeps;
And Time the ruined bridge has swept
    Down the dark stream which seaward creeps.

On this green bank, by this soft stream,
    We set to-day a votive stone;
That memory may their deed redeem,
    When, like our sires, our sons are gone.

Spirit, that made those heroes dare
    To die, and leave their children free,
Bid Time and Nature gently spare
    The shaft we raise to them and thee.

LOUISE ERDRICH (b. 1954)

I Was Sleeping Where the Black Oaks Move

We watched from the house
as the river grew, helpless
and terrible in its unfamiliar body.

---

[1]Commemorating the battles of Lexington and Concord, April 19, 1775.

Wrestling everything into it,
the water wrapped around trees
until their life-hold was broken.
They went down, one by one,
and the river dragged off their covering.

Nests of the herons, roots washed to bones,
snags of soaked bark on the shoreline:
a whole forest pulled through the teeth
of the spillway. Trees surfacing
singly, where the river poured off
into arteries for fields below the reservation.

When at last it was over, the long removal,
they had all become the same dry wood.
We walked among them, the branches
whitening in the raw sun.
Above us drifted herons,
alone, hoarse-voiced, broken,
settling their beaks among the hollows.

Grandpa said, *These are the ghosts of the tree people,*
moving above us, unable to take their rest.

Sometimes now, we dream our way back to the heron dance.
Their long wings are bending the air
into circles through which they fall.
They rise again in shifting wheels.
How long must we live in the broken figures
their necks make, narrowing the sky.

The Strange People

> The antelope are strange people . . . they are beau-
> tiful to look at, and yet they are tricky. We do not
> trust them. They appear and disappear; they are
> like shadows on the plains. Because of their great
> beauty, young men sometimes follow the antelope
> and are lost forever. Even if those foolish ones find
> themselves and return, they are never again right in
> their heads.
>
> — *PRETTY SHIELD, MEDICINE WOMAN OF THE*
> *CROWS,* TRANSCRIBED AND EDITED BY FRANK
> LINDERMAN (1932)

All night I am the doe, breathing
his name in a frozen field,
the small mist of the word
drifting always before me.

And again he has heard it
and I have gone burning
to meet him, the jacklight
fills my eyes with blue fire;
the heart in my chest
explodes like a hot stone.

Then slung like a sack
in the back of his pickup,
I wipe the death scum
from my mouth, sit up laughing,
and shriek in my speeding grave.

Safely shut in the garage,
when he sharpens his knife
and thinks to have me, like that,
I come toward him,
a lean gray witch,
through the bullets that enter and dissolve.

I sit in his house
drinking coffee till dawn,
and leave as frost reddens on hubcaps,
crawling back into my shadowy body.
All day, asleep in clean grasses,
I dream of the one who could really wound me.

Windigo

> The Windigo is a flesh-eating, wintry demon with a man
> buried deep inside of it. In some Chippewa stories, a young
> girl vanquishes this monster by forcing boiling lard down
> its throat, thereby releasing the human at the core of ice.

You knew I was coming for you, little one,
when the kettle jumped into the fire.
Towels flapped on the hooks,
and the dog crept off, groaning,
to the deepest part of the woods.

In the hackles of dry brush a thin laughter started up,
Mother scolded the food warm and smooth in the pot
and called you to eat.
But I spoke in the cold trees:
New one, I have come for you, child hide and lie still.

The sumac pushed sour red cones through the air.
Copper burned in the raw wood.
You saw me drag toward you.
Oh touch me, I murmured, and licked the soles of your feet.
You dug your hands into my pale, melting fur.

I stole you off, a huge thing in my bristling armor.
Steam rolled from my wintry arms, each leaf shivered
from the bushes we passed
until they stood, naked, spread like the cleaned spines of fish.

Then your warm hands hummed over and shoveled themselves
    full
of the ice and the snow. I would darken and spill
all night running, until at last morning broke the cold earth
and I carried you home,
a river shaking in the sun.

ROBERT FROST (1874 – 1963)
Birches

When I see birches bend to left and right
Across the lines of straighter darker trees,
I like to think some boy's been swinging them.
But swinging doesn't bend them down to stay
As ice-storms do. Often you must have seen them   5
Loaded with ice a sunny winter morning
After a rain. They click upon themselves
As the breeze rises, and turn many-colored
As the stir cracks and crazes their enamel.
Soon the sun's warmth makes them shed crystal shells   10
Shattering and avalanching on the snow-crust —
Such heaps of broken glass to sweep away
You'd think the inner dome of heaven had fallen.
They are dragged to the withered bracken by the load,
And they seem not to break; though once they are bowed   15
So low for long, they never right themselves:
You may see their trunks arching in the woods

Years afterwards, trailing their leaves on the ground
Like girls on hands and knees that throw their hair
Before them over their heads to dry in the sun.   20
But I was going to say when Truth broke in
With all her matter-of-fact about the ice-storm
I should prefer to have some boy bend them
As he went out and in to fetch the cows —
Some boy too far from town to learn baseball,   25
Whose only play was what he found himself,
Summer or winter, and could play alone.
One by one he subdued his father's trees
By riding them down over and over again
Until he took the stiffness out of them,   30
And not one but hung limp, not one was left
For him to conquer. He learned all there was
To learn about not launching out too soon
And so not carrying the tree away
Clear to the ground. He always kept his poise   35
To the top branches, climbing carefully
With the same pains you use to fill a cup
Up to the brim, and even above the brim.
Then he flung outward, feet first, with a swish,
Kicking his way down through the air to the ground.   40
So was I once myself a swinger of birches.
And so I dream of going back to be.
It's when I'm weary of considerations,
And life is too much like a pathless wood
Where your face burns and tickles with the cobwebs   45
Broken across it, and one eye is weeping
From a twig's having lashed across it open.
I'd like to get away from earth awhile
And then come back to it and begin over.
May no fate willfully misunderstand me   50
And half grant what I wish and snatch me away
Not to return. Earth's the right place for love:
I don't know where it's likely to go better.
I'd like to go by climbing a birch tree,
And climb black branches up a snow-white trunk   55
Toward heaven, till the tree could bear no more,
But dipped its top and set me down again.
That would be good both going and coming back.
One could do worse than be a swinger of birches.

Design[1]

I found a dimpled spider, fat and white,
On a white heal-all, holding up a moth
Like a white piece of rigid satin cloth —
Assorted characters of death and blight
Mixed ready to begin the morning right,
Like the ingredients of a witches' broth —
A snow-drop spider, a flower like a froth,
And dead wings carried like a paper kite.

What had that flower to do with being white,
The wayside blue and innocent heal-all?
What brought the kindred spider to that height,
Then steered the white moth thither in the night?
What but design of darkness to appall? —
If design govern in a thing so small.

JAMES GALVIN (b. 1951)
Independence Day, 1956: A Fairy Tale

I think this house's mouth is full of dirt.

        Smoke is nothing up its sleeve.
I think it could explode.

      Where I am, in the dirt under the floor, I hear
them.

  They don't know.

       My mother leaves each room my father enters.

           Now
she is cleaning things that are already clean.

        My father is in the living
room.

   He's pouring.

    Rum into a glass, gas into a lamp, kerosene into a can.

He pours capped fuses, matches, dynamite sticks into his pockets.

          He pours
rounds into the .45 which he will point skyward and hold next to
his ear

---

[1] The argument from design (order in nature) was often used as a proof for the existence of God.

as if it were telling him things.

Where I am, the spider spins.

The broken
mouse drags a trap through lunar talc of dust.

Where the bitch whelps is
where I wriggle on my belly, cowardly, ashamed, to escape the
    Fourth of July.
I think the house is very ready.

It seems to hover like an "exploded
view" in a repair manual.

Parts suspended in disbelief.

Nails pulled back,
aimed.

My father goes out.

My mother whimpers.

There'll be no supper.
She opens the firebox and stuffs it full of forks.

ALLEN GINSBERG (1926 – 1997)
America

America I've given you all and now I'm nothing.
America two dollars and twentyseven cents January 17, 1956.
I can't stand my own mind.
America when will we end the human war?
Go fuck yourself with your atom bomb.   5
I don't feel good don't bother me.
I won't write my poem till I'm in my right mind.
America when will you be angelic?
When will you take off your clothes?
When will you look at yourself through the grave?   10
When will you be worthy of your million Trotskyites?[1]
America why are your libraries full of tears?
America when will you send your eggs to India?[2]
I'm sick of your insane demands.
When can I go into the supermarket and buy what I need with   15
    my good looks?

---

[1]Communist idealists, followers of Leon Trotsky (1879–1940), the opponent of Stalin.

[2]India was suffering a famine, while America had an agricultural surplus.

America after all it is you and I who are perfect not the next world.
Your machinery is too much for me.
You made me want to be a saint.
There must be some other way to settle this argument.   20
Burroughs is in Tangiers[3] I don't think he'll come back it's
    sinister.
Are you being sinister or is this some form of practical joke?
I'm trying to come to the point.
I refuse to give up my obsession.   25
America stop pushing I know what I'm doing.
America the plum blossoms are falling.
I haven't read the newspapers for months, everyday somebody
    goes on trial for murder.
America I feel sentimental about the Wobblies.[4]   30
America I used to be a communist when I was a kid I'm not sorry.
I smoke marijuana every chance I get.
I sit in my house for days on end and stare at the roses in the closet.
When I go to Chinatown I get drunk and never get laid.
My mind is made up there's going to be trouble.   35
You should have seen me reading Marx.[5]
My psychoanalyst thinks I'm perfectly right.
I won't say the Lord's Prayer.
I have mystical visions and cosmic vibrations.
America I still haven't told you what you did to Uncle Max   40
    after he came over from Russia.

I'm addressing you.
Are you going to let your emotional life be run by Time Magazine?
I'm obsessed by Time Magazine.
I read it every week.   45
Its cover stares at me every time I slink past the corner candystore.
I read it in the basement of the Berkeley Public Library.
It's always telling me about responsibility. Businessmen are serious.
    Movie producers are serious. Everybody's serious but me.
It occurs to me that I am America.   50
I am talking to myself again.

---

[3]William Burroughs (1914–1997), a friend of Ginsberg's and author of the novel *Naked Lunch* (1959), was living in Morocco.

[4]Nickname for members of the Industrial Workers of the World, a union founded in 1905.

[5]Karl Marx (1818–1883), German political theorist and coauthor, with Friedrich Engels, of *The Communist Manifesto* (1848).

Asia is rising against me.
I haven't got a chinaman's chance.
I'd better consider my national resources.
My national resources consist of two joints of marijuana millions   55
      of genitals an unpublishable private literature that goes 1400
      miles an hour and twentyfive-thousand mental institutions.
I say nothing about my prisons nor the millions of underprivileged
      who live in my flowerpots under the light of five hundred
      suns.   60
I have abolished the whorehouses of France, Tangiers is the next
      to go.
My ambition is to be President despite the fact that I'm a Catholic.

America how can I write a holy litany in your silly mood?
I will continue like Henry Ford my strophes are as individual   65
      as his automobiles more so they're all different sexes.
America I will sell you strophes $2500 apiece $500 down on your
      old strophe
America free Tom Mooney[6]
America save the Spanish Loyalists[7]   70
America Sacco & Vanzetti[8] must not die
America I am the Scottsboro boys.[9]
America when I was seven momma took me to Communist Cell
      meetings they sold us garbanzos[10] a handful per ticket a ticket
      costs a nickel and the speeches were free everybody was   75
      angelic and sentimental about the workers it was all so sincere
      you have no idea what a good thing the party was in 1935
      Scott Nearing was a grand old man a real mensch Mother
      Bloor made me cry I once saw Israel Amter[11] plain. Every-
      body must have been a spy.   80

---

[6]American labor agitator in California, accused of bomb killings and sentenced to death in 1916 but pardoned in 1939.

[7]Those fighting against Franco in the Spanish Civil War.

[8]Nicola Sacco and Bartolomeo Vanzetti were executed in Massachusetts in 1927 for a murder connected with a robbery. Sentiment ran high against them because of their radical beliefs.

[9]The "Scottsboro boys" were nine blacks who were convicted in Alabama of the rape of two white women in 1931. Liberals and radicals believed the conviction to be unproved. Four years later the sentences were reduced in four cases and the charges dropped in five.

[10]Chickpeas.

[11]Scott Nearing (1883–1983), Ella ("Mother") Bloor (1862–1951), and Israel Amter (1881–1954): well-known American Socialists and Communists.

America you don't really want to go to war.
America it's them bad Russians.
Them Russians them Russians and them Chinamen. And them
    Russians.
The Russia wants to eat us alive. The Russia's power mad. She   85
    wants to take our cars from out our garages.
Her wants to grab Chicago. Her needs a Red Readers' Digest. Her
    wants our auto plants in Siberia. Him big bureaucracy run-
    ning our fillingstations.
That no good. Ugh. Him make Indians learn read. Him need big   90
    black niggers. Hah. Her make us all work sixteen hours a day.
    Help.
America this is quite serious.
America this is the impression I get from looking in the television
    set.   95
America is this correct?
I'd better get right down to the job.
It's true I don't want to join the Army or turn lathes in precision
    parts factories, I'm nearsighted and psychopathic anyway.
America I'm putting my queer shoulder to the wheel.   100

LOUISE GLÜCK (b. 1943)
All Hallows[1]

Even now this landscape is assembling.
The hills darken. The oxen
sleep in their blue yoke,
the fields having been
picked clean, the sheaves
bound evenly and piled at the roadside
among cinquefoil,[2] as the toothed moon rises:

This is the barrenness
of harvest or pestilence.
And the wife leaning out the window
with her hand extended, as in payment,
and the seeds
distinct, gold, calling

---

[1]Halloween (short for "All Hallows Even"), October 31, the evening before All
Saints' Day.
[2]Plant with five-lobed leaves.

Come here
Come here, little one

And the soul creeps out of the tree.

The Balcony

It was a night like this, at the end of summer.

We had rented, I remember, a room with a balcony.
How many days and nights? Five, perhaps — no more.

Even when we weren't touching we were making love.
We stood on our little balcony in the summer night.
And off somewhere, the sounds of human life.

We were the soon to be anointed monarchs,
well disposed to our subjects. Just beneath us,
sounds of a radio playing, an aria we didn't in those years know.

Someone dying of love. Someone from whom time had taken
the only happiness, who was alone now,
impoverished, without beauty.

The rapturous notes of an unendurable grief, of isolation and
terror,
the nearly impossible to sustain slow phrases of the ascending
figures —
they drifted out over the dark water
like an ecstasy.

Such a small mistake. And many years later,
the only thing left of that night, of the hours in that room.

The White Lilies

As a man and woman make
a garden between them like
a bed of stars, here
they linger in the summer evening
and the evening turns
cold with their terror: it
could all end, it is capable
of devastation. All, all
can be lost, through scented air
the narrow columns

uselessly rising, and beyond,
a churning sea of poppies —

Hush, beloved. It doesn't matter to me
how many summers I live to return:
this one summer we have entered eternity.
I felt your two hands
bury me to release its splendor.

JORIE GRAHAM (b. 1951)
Of Forced Sightes and Trusty Ferefulness[1]

Stopless wind, here are the columbine seeds I have
collected. What we would do with them is
different. Though both your trick and mine flower blue
and white

with four stem tails and yellow underpetals. Stopless   5
and unessential, half-hiss, half-
lullaby, if I fell in among your laws,
if I fell down into your mind your snow, into the miles

of spirit-drafts you drive, frenetic multitudes,
out from timber to the open ground and back to no   10
avail, if I fell down, warmblooded, ill, into your endless
evenness,

into this race you start them on and will not let them win . . . ?
If I fell in?
What is your law to my law, unhurried hurrying?   15
At my remove from you, today, in your supremest

calculation, re-
adjustment, are these three birds scratching for dead
bark beetles, frozen seeds, too late for being here yet only
    here,
in the stenchfree   20

cold. This is another current, river of rivers, this thrilling
third-act love. Who wouldn't want to stay
behind? They pack the rinds away, the blazing applecores,
the frantic shadow-wings scribbling the fenceposts, window-

panes. Meanwhile you turn, white jury, draft, away,   25
deep justice done.

---

[1]Graham's title is quoted from Sir Thomas Wyatt's sonnet beginning: "My galley charged with forgetfulness."

I don't presume to cross the distances, the clarity,
but what grows in your only open hands? Or is

digressive love,
row after perfect greenhouse row,   30
the garden you're out of for good, wind of the theorems,
of proof, square root of light,

chaos of truth,
blinder than the mice that wait you out
        in any crack?
This is the best I can do now for prayer — to you,   35
for you — these scraps I throw

my lonely acrobats
that fall
of your accord
right to my windowsill: they pack it away, the grains, the   40

accidents, they pack it deep into the rent
heart of the blue
spruce, skins in with spiky needles. . . . Oh
        hollow
charged with forgetfulness,

through wind, through winter nights, we'll pass,   45
steering with crumbs, with words,
making of every hour
a thought, remembering

by pain and rhyme and arabesques of foraging
the formula for theft   50
under your sky that keeps
sliding away

married to hurry
and grim song.

Soul Says

(Afterword)

To be so held by brittleness, shapeliness.
By meaning. As where I *have to go where you go,*
I *have to touch what you must touch,*
in hunger, in boredom, the spindrift, the ticket . . .
Distilled in you (can you hear me)
the idiom in you, the why —

The flash *of a voice*. The river *glints*.
The mother *opens the tablecloth up into the wind*.
There as the fabric descends — the alphabet of ripenesses,
what is, what could have been.
The bread on the tablecloth. Crickets shrill in the grass.

O pluck my magic garment from me. So.
[lays down his robe]
Lie there, my art —

(This is a form of matter of matter she sang)

(Where the hurry is stopped) (and held) (but not extinguished)
    (no)

(So listen, listen, this will soothe you) (if that is what you want)

Now then, I said, I go to meet that which I liken to
(even though the wave break and drown me in laughter)
the wave breaking, the wave drowning me in laughter —

THOMAS GRAY (1716 – 1771)
Elegy Written in a Country Churchyard

The curfew tolls the knell of parting day,
    The lowing herd wind slowly o'er the lea,
The plowman homeward plods his weary way,
    And leaves the world to darkness and to me.

Now fades the glimmering landscape on the sight,   5
    And all the air a solemn stillness holds,
Save where the beetle wheels his droning flight,
    And drowsy tinklings lull the distant folds;

Save that from yonder ivy-mantled tower
    The moping owl does to the moon complain   10
Of such, as wandering near her secret bower,
    Molest her ancient solitary reign.

Beneath those rugged elms, that yew tree's shade,
    Where heaves the turf in many a moldering heap,
Each in his narrow cell forever laid,   15
    The rude° forefathers of the hamlet sleep.   *rustic*

The breezy call of incense-breathing morn,
    The swallow twittering from the straw-built shed,
The cock's shrill clarion, or the echoing horn,
    No more shall rouse them from their lowly bed.   20

For them no more the blazing hearth shall burn,
    Or busy housewife ply her evening care;
No children run to lisp their sire's return,
    Or climb his knees the envied kiss to share.

Oft did the harvest to their sickle yield,   25
    Their furrow oft the stubborn glebe° has broke;   *clot of soil*
How jocund did they drive their team afield!
    How bowed the woods beneath their sturdy stroke!

Let not Ambition mock their useful toil,
    Their homely joys, and destiny obscure;   30
Nor Grandeur hear with a disdainful smile
    The short and simple annals of the poor.

The boast of heraldry, the pomp of power,
    And all that beauty, all that wealth e'er gave,
Awaits alike the inevitable hour.   35
    The paths of glory lead but to the grave.

Nor you, ye proud, impute to these the fault,
    If Memory o'er their tomb no trophies raise,
Where through the long-drawn aisle and fretted vault
    The pealing anthem swells the note of praise.   40

Can storied urn or animated bust
    Back to its mansion call the fleeting breath?
Can Honor's voice provoke the silent dust,
    Or Flattery soothe the dull cold ear of Death?

Perhaps in this neglected spot is laid   45
    Some heart once pregnant with celestial fire;
Hands that the rod of empire might have swayed,
    Or waked to ecstasy the living lyre.

But Knowledge to their eyes her ample page
    Rich with the spoils of time did ne'er unroll;   50
Chill Penury repressed their noble rage,
    And froze the genial current of the soul.

Full many a gem of purest ray serene,
    The dark unfathomed caves of ocean bear:
Full many a flower is born to blush unseen,   55
    And waste its sweetness on the desert air.

Some village Hampden,[1] that with dauntless breast
    The little tyrant of his fields withstood;

Some mute inglorious Milton here may rest,
    Some Cromwell guiltless of his country's blood.   60

The applause of listening senates to command,
    The threats of pain and ruin to despise,
To scatter plenty o'er a smiling land,
    And read their history in a nation's eyes,

Their lot forbade: nor circumscribed alone   65
    Their growing virtues, but their crimes confined;
Forbade to wade through slaughter to a throne,
    And shut the gates of mercy on mankind,

The struggling pangs of conscious truth to hide,
    To quench the blushes of ingenuous shame,   70
Or heap the shrine of Luxury and Pride
    With incense kindled at the Muse's flame.

Far from the madding crowd's ignoble strife,
    Their sober wishes never learned to stray;
Along the cool sequestered vale of life   75
    They kept the noiseless tenor of their way.

Yet even these bones from insult to protect
    Some frail memorial still erected nigh,
With uncouth rhymes and shapeless sculpture decked,
    Implores the passing tribute of a sigh.   80

Their name, their years, spelt by the unlettered Muse,
    The place of fame and elegy supply:
And many a holy text around she strews,
    That teach the rustic moralist to die.

For who to dumb Forgetfulness a prey,   85
    This pleasing anxious being e'er resigned,
Left the warm precincts of the cheerful day,
    Nor cast one longing lingering look behind?

On some fond breast the parting soul relies,
    Some pious drops the closing eye requires;   90
Even from the tomb the voice of Nature cries,
    Even in our ashes live their wonted fires.

---

[1]One of the leaders of the opposition to Charles I. He was killed in battle in the English Civil War.

For thee, who mindful of the unhonored dead
    Dost in these lines their artless tale relate;
If chance, by lonely contemplation led,   95
    Some kindred spirit shall inquire thy fate,

Haply some hoary-headed swain may say,
    "Oft have we seen him at the peep of dawn
Brushing with hasty steps the dews away
    To meet the sun upon the upland lawn.   100

"There at the foot of yonder nodding beech
    That wreathes its old fantastic roots so high,
His listless length at noontide would he stretch,
    And pore upon the brook that babbles by.

"Hard by yon wood, now smiling as in scorn,   105
    Muttering his wayward fancies he would rove,
Now drooping, woeful wan, like one forlorn,
    Or crazed with care, or crossed in hopeless love.

"One morn I missed him on the customed hill,
    Along the heath and near his favorite tree;   110
Another came; nor yet beside the rill,
    Nor up the lawn, nor at the wood was he;

"The next with dirges due in sad array
    Slow through the churchway path we saw him borne.
Approach and read (for thou canst read) the lay,   115
    Graved on the stone beneath yon aged thorn."

The Epitaph

Here rests his head upon the lap of Earth
    A youth to Fortune and to Fame unknown.
Fair Science° frowned not on his humble birth,   *general knowledge*
    And Melancholy marked him for her own.   120

Large was his bounty, and his soul sincere,
    Heaven did a recompense as largely send:
He gave to Misery all he had, a tear,
    He gained from Heaven ('twas all he wished) a friend.

No farther seek his merits to disclose,   125
    Or draw his frailties from their dread abode
(There they alike in trembling hope repose),
    The bosom of his Father and his God.

THOM GUNN (b. 1929)
The Man with Night Sweats

I wake up cold, I who
Prospered through dreams of heat
Wake to their residue,
Sweat, and a clinging sheet.

My flesh was its own shield:
Where it was gashed, it healed.

I grew as I explored
The body I could trust
Even while I adored
The risk that made robust,

A world of wonders in
Each challenge to the skin.

I cannot but be sorry
The given shield was cracked,
My mind reduced to hurry,
My flesh reduced and wrecked.

I have to change the bed,
But catch myself instead

Stopped upright where I am
Hugging my body to me
As if to shield it from
The pains that will go through me,

As if hands were enough
To hold an avalanche off.

My Sad Captains

One by one they appear in
the darkness: a few friends, and
a few with historical
names. How late they start to shine!
but before they fade they stand
perfectly embodied, all

the past lapping them like a
cloak of chaos. They were men
who, I thought, lived only to

renew the wasteful force they
spent with each hot convulsion.
They remind me, distant now.

True, they are not at rest yet,
but now that they are indeed
apart, winnowed from failures,
they withdraw to an orbit
and turn with disinterested
hard energy, like the stars.

H. D. (1886 – 1961)
Helen[1]

All Greece hates
the still eyes in the white face,
the lustre as of olives
where she stands,
and the white hands.

All Greece reviles
the wan face when she smiles,
hating it deeper still
when it grows wan and white,
remembering past enchantments
and past ills.

Greece sees unmoved,
God's daughter, born of love,
the beauty of cool feet
and slenderest knees,
could love indeed the maid,
only if she were laid,
white ash amid funereal cypresses.

THOMAS HARDY (1840 – 1928)
Afterwards

When the Present has latched its postern behind my tremulous
> stay,
> And the May month flaps its glad green leaves like wings,

---

[1]The beautiful wife of Menelaus. Her abduction by Paris was the cause of the
Trojan War.

Delicate-filmed as new-spun silk, will the neighbors say,
    "He was a man who used to notice such things"?

If it be in the dusk when, like an eyelid's soundless blink,
    The dewfall-hawk comes crossing the shades to alight
Upon the wind-warped upland thorn, a gazer may think,
    "To him this must have been a familiar sight."

If I pass during some nocturnal blackness, mothy and warm,
    When the hedgehog travels furtively over the lawn,
One may say, "He strove that such innocent creatures should
        come to no harm,
    But he could do little for them; and now he is gone."

If, when hearing that I have been stilled at last, they stand at the
        door,
    Watching the full-starred heavens that winter sees,
Will this thought rise on those who will meet my face no more,
    "He was one who had an eye for such mysteries"?

And will any say when my bell of quittance is heard in the gloom,
    And a crossing breeze cuts a pause in its outrollings,
Till they rise again, as they were a new bell's boom,
    "He hears it not now, but used to notice such things"?

Channel Firing

That night your great guns, unawares,
Shook all our coffins as we lay,
And broke the chancel window-squares,
We thought it was the Judgment-day

And sat upright. While drearisome
Arose the howl of wakened hounds:
The mouse let fall the altar-crumb,
The worms drew back into the mounds,

The glebe° cow drooled. Till God called, "No;   *plot of land*
It's gunnery practice out at sea
Just as before you went below;
The world is as it used to be:

"All nations striving strong to make
Red war yet redder. Mad as hatters
They do no more for Christés sake
Than you who are helpless in such matters.

"That this is not the judgment-hour
For some of them's a blessed thing,
For if it were they'd have to scour
Hell's floor for so much threatening. . . .

"Ha, ha. It will be warmer when
I blow the trumpet (if indeed
I ever do; for you are men,
And rest eternal sorely need)."

So down we lay again. "I wonder,
Will the world ever saner be,"
Said one, "than when He sent us under
In our indifferent century!"

And many a skeleton shook his head.
"Instead of preaching forty year,"
My neighbour Parson Thirdly said,
"I wish I had stuck to pipes and beer."

Again the guns disturbed the hour,
Roaring their readiness to avenge,
As far inland as Stourton Tower,
And Camelot, and starlit Stonehenge.

Joy Harjo (b. 1951)

Santa Fe

The wind blows lilacs out of the east. And it isn't lilac season. And
I am walking the street in front of St. Francis Cathedral in Santa Fe.
Oh, and it's a few years earlier and more. That's how you tell real
time. It is here, it is there. The lilacs have taken over everything:
the sky, the narrow streets, my shoulders, my lips. I talk lilac. And
there is nothing else until a woman the size of a fox breaks through
the bushes, breaks the purple web. She is tall and black and gor-
geous. She is the size of a fox on the arm of a white man who looks
and tastes like cocaine. She lies for cocaine, dangles on the arm of
cocaine. And lies to me now from a room in the DeVargas Hotel,
where she has eaten her lover, white powder on her lips. That is
true now; it is not true anymore. Eventually space curves, walks
over and taps me on the shoulder. On the sidewalk I stand near St.
Francis; he has been bronzed, a perpetual tan, with birds on his
hand, his shoulder, deer at his feet. I am Indian and in this town I
will never be a saint. I am seventeen and shy and wild. I have been

up until three at a party, but there is no woman in the DeVargas Hotel for that story hasn't yet been invented. A man whose face I will never remember, and never did, drives up on a Harley Davidson. There are lilacs on his arm, they spill out from the spokes of his wheels. He wants me on his arm, on the back of his lilac bike touring the flower kingdom of San Francisco. And for a piece of time the size of a nickel, I think, maybe. But maybe is vapor, has no anchor here in the sun beneath St. Francis Cathedral. And space is as solid as the bronze statue of St. Francis, the fox breaking through the lilacs, my invention of this story, the wind blowing.

MICHAEL S. HARPER (b. 1938)
Nightmare Begins Responsibility[1]

I place these numbed wrists to the pane
watching white uniforms whisk over
him in the tube-kept
prison
fear what they will do in experiment
watch my gloved stickshifting gasolined hands
breathe *boxcar-information-please* infirmary tubes
distrusting white-pink mending paperthin
silkened end hairs, distrusting tubes
shrunk in his *trunk-skincapped*
shaven head, in thighs
distrusting-white-hands-picking-baboon-light
on this son who will not make his second night
of this wardstrewn intensive airpocket
where his father's asthmatic
hymns of *night-train,* train done gone
his mother can only know that he has flown
up into essential calm unseen corridor
going boxscarred home, *mamaborn, sweetsonchild
gonedowntown* into *researchtestingwarehousebatteryacid
mama-son-done-gone* / me telling her 'nother
train tonight, no music, no breathstroked
heartbeat in my infinite distrust of them:

---

[1] A play on William Butler Yeats's epigraph to his volume *Responsibilities* (1913): "In dreams begin responsibilities." This poem is an elegy for Harper's son, who died one day after birth. Another son had also died shortly after birth.

and of my distrusting self
white-doctor-who-breathed-for-him-all-night
say it for two sons gone,
say nightmare, say it loud
panebreaking heartmadness:
nightmare begins responsibility.

"Use Trouble"

for Jacob Armstead Lawrence[1]
1917–2000, in memoriam

You told this to the children
when they confessed their works

were incomplete   your dignity   grace
a mapped space   for trouble

your *migration*   series at 23
synaptic code for having nothing

as you built off the backs of the poor
your symmetries where paint was talk

"gumbo yaya"   Hayden[2] (your collaborator)
coined it about his native paradise valley

a nourishment of the Detroit ghetto
while you were content with Harlem

a sixty-block walk to MOMA[3]
for filial instruction

of the Italian Renaissance:
now in Seattle they lay you down

those parts Indian of your heritage
in Chief Seattle's[4] words

migraines at gunpoint
bullet-ridden   love song   as migrants

---

[1]American painter, famous for his Migration Series, showing the exodus of southern blacks to the North.

[2]Robert Hayden, American poet from Detroit.

[3]Museum of Modern Art, New York.

[4]Chief Seattle (c. 1786–1866), orator of the Duwamish tribe of Puget Sound.

to the highest plane
a vast battlefield of tones

over vegetation of the visible
where there is no insurance

yet   in retrospective   fantasy
to remake the spirit in your name

We Assume: On the Death of Our Son, Reuben Masai Harper

We assume
that in 28 hours,
lived in a collapsible isolette,
you learned to accept pure oxygen
as the natural sky;
the scant shallow breaths
that filled those hours
cannot, did not make you fly —
but dreams were there
like crooked palmprints on
the twin-thick windows of the nursery —
in the glands of your mother.

We assume
the sterile hands
drank chemicals in and out
from lungs opaque with mucus,
pumped your stomach,
eeked the bicarbonate in
crooked, green-winged veins,
out in a plastic mask;

A woman who'd lost her first son
consoled us with an angel gone ahead
to pray for our family —
gone into that sky
seeking oxygen,
gone into autopsy,
a fine brown powdered sugar,
a disposable cremation:

We assume
you did not know we loved you.

ROBERT HAYDEN (1913 – 1980)

Frederick Douglass[1]

When it is finally ours, this freedom, this liberty, this beautiful
and terrible thing, needful to man as air,
usable as earth; when it belongs at last to all,
when it is truly instinct, brain matter, diastole, systole,
reflex action; when it is finally won; when it is more
than the gaudy mumbo jumbo of politicians:
this man, this Douglass, this former slave, this Negro
beaten to his knees, exiled, visioning a world
where none is lonely, none hunted, alien,
this man, superb in love and logic, this man
shall be remembered. Oh, not with statues' rhetoric,
not with legends and poems and wreaths of bronze alone,
but with the lives grown out of his life, the lives
fleshing his dream of the beautiful, needful thing.

Mourning Poem for the Queen of Sunday

    Lord's lost Him His mockingbird,
    His fancy warbler;
    Satan sweet-talked her,
    four bullets hushed her.
    Who would have thought
    she'd end that way?

Four bullets hushed her. And the world a–clang with evil.
Who's going to make old hardened sinner men tremble now
and the righteous rock?
Oh who and oh who will sing Jesus down
to help with struggling and doing without and being colored
all through blue Monday?
Till way next Sunday?

    All those angels
    in their cretonne clouds and finery
    the true believer saw
    when she rared back her head and sang,
    all those angels are surely weeping.

---

[1]Frederick Douglass (ca. 1817–1895), who escaped from slavery in 1838, became
an abolitionist, writer, and statesman.

Who would have thought
she'd end that way?

Four holes in her heart. The gold works wrecked.
But she looks so natural in her big bronze coffin
among the Broken Hearts and Gates-Ajar,
it's as if any moment she'd lift her head
from its pillow of chill gardenias
and turn this quiet into shouting Sunday
and make folks forget what she did on Monday.

Oh, Satan sweet-talked her,
and four bullets hushed her.
Lord's lost Him His diva,
His fancy warbler's gone.
Who would have thought,
who would have thought she'd end that way?

SEAMUS HEANEY (b. 1939)
Bogland

For T. P. Flanagan

We have no prairies
To slice a big sun at evening —
Everywhere the eye concedes to
Encroaching horizon,

Is wooed into the cyclops' eye
Of a tarn. Our unfenced country
Is bog that keeps crusting
Between the sights of the sun.

They've taken the skeleton
Of the Great Irish Elk
Out of the peat, set it up,
An astounding crate full of air.

Butter sunk under
More than a hundred years
Was recovered salty and white.
The ground itself is kind, black butter

Melting and opening underfoot,
Missing its last definition
By millions of years.
They'll never dig coal here,

Only the waterlogged trunks
Of great firs, soft as pulp.
Our pioneers keep striking
Inwards and downwards,

Every layer they strip
Seems camped on before.
The bogholes might be Atlantic seepage.
The wet centre is bottomless.

Punishment

I can feel the tug
of the halter at the nape
of her neck, the wind
on her naked front.

It blows her nipples
to amber beads,
it shakes the frail rigging
of her ribs.

I can see her drowned
body in the bog,
the weighing stone,
the floating rods and boughs.

Under which at first
she was a barked sapling
that is dug up
oak-bone, brain-firkin:°   *container*

her shaved head
like a stubble of black corn,
her blindfold a soiled bandage,
her noose a ring

to store
the memories of love.
Little adulteress,
before they punished you

you were flaxen-haired,
undernourished, and your
tar-black face was beautiful.
My poor scapegoat,

I almost love you
but would have cast, I know,
the stones of silence.
I am the artful voyeur

of your brain's exposed
and darkened combs,
your muscles' webbing
and all your numbered bones:

I who have stood dumb
when your betraying sisters,
cauled in tar,
wept by the railings,

who would connive
in civilized outrage
yet understand the exact
and tribal, intimate revenge.

GEORGE HERBERT (1593 – 1633)
The Collar

I struck the board° and cried, "No more; *table*
  I will abroad!
What? shall I ever sigh and pine?
My lines and life are free, free as the road,
  Loose as the wind, as large as store.
    Shall I be still in suit?
  Have I no harvest but a thorn
  To let me blood, and not restore
What I have lost with cordial fruit?
    Sure there was wine
  Before my sighs did dry it; there was corn
    Before my tears did drown it.
  Is the year only lost to me?
    Have I no bays to crown it,
No flowers, no garlands gay? All blasted?
    All wasted?
  Not so, my heart; but there is fruit,
    And thou hast hands.
  Recover all thy sigh-blown age
On double pleasures: leave thy cold dispute

Of what is fit and not. Forsake thy cage,
   Thy rope of sands,
Which petty thoughts have made, and made to thee
  Good cable, to enforce and draw,
    And be thy law,
 While thou didst wink and wouldst not see.
    Away! take heed;
    I will abroad.
Call in thy death's-head there; tie up thy fears.
    He that forbears
  To suit and serve his need,
    Deserves his load."
But as I raved and grew more fierce and wild
    At every word,
Methought I heard one calling, *Child!*
    And I replied, *My Lord.*

Redemption

Having been tenant long to a rich lord,
  Not thriving, I resolvèd to be bold,
  And make a suit unto him, to afford°   *grant*
A new small-rented lease, and cancel the old.

In heaven at his manor I him sought;
  They told me there that he was lately gone
  About some land, which he had dearly bought
Long since on earth, to take possessïon.

I straight returned, and knowing his great birth,
  Sought him accordingly in great resorts;
  In cities, theaters, gardens, parks and courts;
At length I heard a ragged noise and mirth

  Of thieves and murderers; there I him espied,
  Who straight, *Your suit is granted,* said, and died.

ROBERT HERRICK (1591 – 1674)
Corinna's Going A-Maying

Get up! get up for shame! the blooming morn
Upon her wings presents the god unshorn.° *Apollo, god of the sun*

See how Aurora° throws her fair   *goddess of dawn*
Fresh-quilted colors through the air:
Get up, sweet slug-a-bed, and see   5
The dew bespangling herb and tree.
Each flower has wept and bowèd toward the east
Above an hour since, yet you not dressed;
    Nay, not so much as out of bed?
    When all the birds have matins said,   10
    And sung their thankful hymns, 'tis sin,
    Nay, profanation to keep in,
Whenas a thousand virgins on this day
Spring, sooner than the lark, to fetch in May.

Rise, and put on your foliage, and be seen   15
To come forth, like the springtime, fresh and green,
    And sweet as Flora.° Take no care   *goddess of flowers*
    For jewels for your gown or hair;
    Fear not; the leaves will strew
    Gems in abundance upon you;   20
Besides, the childhood of the day has kept,
Against you come, some orient pearls unwept;
    Come and receive them while the light
    Hangs on the dew-locks of the night,
    And Titan° on the eastern hill   *the sun*   25
    Retires himself, or else stands still
Till you come forth. Wash, dress, be brief in praying:
Few beads° are best when once we go a-Maying.   *prayers*

Come, my Corinna, come; and, coming mark
How each field turns a street, each street a park   30
    Made green and trimmed with trees; see how
    Devotion gives each house a bough
    Or branch: each porch, each door ere this,
    An ark, a tabernacle is,
Made up of whitethorn neatly interwove,   35
As if here were those cooler shades of love.
    Can such delights be in the street
    And open fields, and we not see 't?
    Come, we'll abroad; and let's obey
    The proclamation made for May,   40
And sin no more, as we have done, by staying;
But, my Corinna, come, let's go a-Maying.

There's not a budding boy or girl this day
But is got up and gone to bring in May;
    A deal of youth, ere this, is come   45
    Back, and with whitethorn laden home.
    Some have dispatched their cakes and cream
    Before that we have left to dream;
And some have wept, and wooed, and plighted troth,
And chose their priest, ere we can cast off sloth.   50
    Many a green-gown has been given,
    Many a kiss, both odd and even,
    Many a glance, too, has been sent
    From out the eye, love's firmament;
Many a jest told of the keys betraying   55
This night, and locks picked; yet we're not a-Maying.

Come, let us go while we are in our prime,
And take the harmless folly of the time.
    We shall grow old apace, and die
    Before we know our liberty.   60
    Our life is short, and our days run
    As fast away as does the sun;
And, as a vapor or a drop of rain
Once lost, can ne'er be found again;
    So when or you or I are made   65
    A fable, song, or fleeting shade,
    All love, all liking, all delight
    Lies drowned with us in endless night.
Then while time serves, and we are but decaying,
Come, my Corinna, come, let's go a-Maying.   70

Gerard Manley Hopkins (1844 – 1889)
God's Grandeur

The world is charged with the grandeur of God.
    It will flame out, like shining from shook foil;
    It gathers to a greatness, like the ooze of oil
Crushed. Why do men then now not reck his rod?
Generations have trod, have trod, have trod;
    And all is seared with trade; bleared, smeared with toil;
    And wears man's smudge and shares man's smell: the soil
Is bare now, nor can foot feel, being shod.

And for all this, nature is never spent;
     There lives the dearest freshness deep down things;
And though the last lights off the black West went
     Oh, morning, at the brown brink eastward, springs —
Because the Holy Ghost over the bent
     World broods with warm breast and with ah! bright wings.

No worst, there is none. Pitched past pitch of grief

No worst, there is none. Pitched past pitch of grief,
More pangs will, schooled at forepangs, wilder wring.
Comforter, where, where is your comforting?
Mary, mother of us, where is your relief?

My cries heave, herds-long; huddle in a main, a chief-
woe, world-sorrow; on an age-old anvil wince and sing —
Then lull, then leave off. Fury had shrieked "No ling-
ering! Let me be fell:° force° I must be brief."   *fierce / perforce*

O the mind, mind has mountains; cliffs of fall
Frightful, sheer, no-man-fathomed. Hold them cheap
May who ne'er hung there. Nor does long our small
Durance deal with that steep or deep. Here! creep,
Wretch, under a comfort serves in a whirlwind: all
Life death does end and each day dies with sleep.

The Windhover

To Christ Our Lord

I caught this morning morning's minion, king-
     dom of daylight's dauphin, dapple-dawn-drawn Falcon, in his
                       riding
     Of the rolling level underneath him steady air, and striding
High there, how he rung upon the rein of a wimpling wing
In his ecstasy! then off, off forth on swing,
     As a skate's heel sweeps smooth on a bow-bend: the hurl and
          gliding
     Rebuffed the big wind. My heart in hiding
Stirred for a bird, — the achieve of, the mastery of the thing!

Brute beauty and valour and act, oh, air, pride, plume, here
     Buckle! AND the fire that breaks from thee then, a billion
Times told lovelier, more dangerous, O my chevalier!

No wonder of it: shéer plód makes plough down sillion
Shine, and blue-bleak embers, ah my dear,
    Fall, gall themselves, and gash gold-vermilion.

CAROLINA HOSPITAL (b. 1957)
Blake in the Tropics

We leave the Jaragua Hotel
in our stocking feet and shaven faces
to stumble over these bodies
yet to reach puberty.

They have turned dust into blankets
and newspapers into pillows
on a street edged in refuse.
Warm waves break against the sea wall,

never touching their bodies.
We are not in Blake's London and
the black on these boys
will not wash off with the dawn.

A. E. HOUSMAN (1859 – 1936)
Loveliest of Trees, the Cherry Now

Loveliest of trees, the cherry now
Is hung with bloom along the bough,
And stands about the woodland ride
Wearing white for Eastertide.

Now, of my threescore years and ten,
Twenty will not come again,
And take from seventy springs a score,
It only leaves me fifty more.

And since to look at things in bloom
Fifty springs are little room,
About the woodlands I will go
To see the cherry hung with snow.

With Rue My Heart Is Laden

With rue my heart is laden
    For golden friends I had,
For many a rose-lipt maiden
    And many a lightfoot lad.

By brooks too broad for leaping
　　The lightfoot boys are laid;
The rose-lipt girls are sleeping
　　In fields where roses fade.

LANGSTON HUGHES (1902 – 1967)
Harlem

What happens to a dream deferred?

　　Does it dry up
　　like a raisin in the sun?
　　Or fester like a sore —
　　And then run?
　　Does it stink like rotten meat?
　　Or crust and sugar over —
　　like a syrupy sweet?

　　Maybe it just sags
　　like a heavy load.

　　Or does it explode?

I, Too

I, too, sing America.

I am the darker brother.
They send me to eat in the kitchen
When company comes,
But I laugh,
And eat well,
And grow strong.

Tomorrow,
I'll be at the table
When company comes.
Nobody'll dare
Say to me,
"Eat in the kitchen,"
Then.

Besides,
They'll see how beautiful I am
And be ashamed —

I, too, am America.

Suicide's Note

The calm,
Cool face of the river
Asked me for a kiss.

The Weary Blues

Droning a drowsy syncopated tune,
Rocking back and forth to a mellow croon,
    I heard a Negro play.
Down on Lenox Avenue the other night
By the pale dull pallor of an old gas light
    He did a lazy sway. . . .
    He did a lazy sway. . . .
To the tune o' those Weary Blues.
With his ebony hands on each ivory key
He made that poor piano moan with melody.
    O Blues!
Swaying to and fro on his rickety stool
He played that sad raggy tune like a musical fool.
    Sweet Blues!
Coming from a black man's soul.
    O Blues!
In a deep song voice with a melancholy tone
I heard that Negro sing, that old piano moan —
    "Ain't got nobody in all this world,
    Ain't got nobody but ma self.
    I's gwine to quit ma frownin'
    And put ma troubles on the shelf."
Thump, thump, thump, went his foot on the floor.
He played a few chords then he sang some more —
    "I got the Weary Blues
    And I can't be satisfied.
    Got the Weary Blues
    And can't be satisfied —
    I ain't happy no mo'
    And I wish that I had died."
And far into the night he crooned that tune.
The stars went out and so did the moon.
The singer stopped playing and went to bed
While the Weary Blues echoed through his head.
He slept like a rock or a man that's dead.

BEN JONSON (1572 – 1637)
Come, My Celia[1]

Come, my Celia, let us prove,°   experience
While we can, the sports of love;
Time will not be ours forever;
He at length our good will sever.
Spend not then his gifts in vain.
Suns that set may rise again;
But if once we lose this light,
'Tis with us perpetual night.
Why should we defer our joys?
Fame and rumor are but toys.
Cannot we delude the eyes
Of a few poor household spies,
Or his easier ears beguile,
So removèd by our wile?
'Tis no sin love's fruit to steal;
But the sweet thefts to reveal,
To be taken, to be seen,
These have crimes accounted been.

JOHN KEATS (1795 – 1821)
In drear nighted December

In drear nighted December,
        Too happy, happy tree,
Thy branches ne'er remember
        Their green felicity —
The north cannot undo them
With a sleety whistle through them,
Nor frozen thawings glue them
        From budding at the prime.

In drear nighted December,
        Too happy, happy brook,
Thy bubblings ne'er remember
        Apollo's summer look;
But with a sweet forgetting
They stay their crystal fretting,

---

[1]From *Volpone.*

Never, never petting
  About the frozen time.

Ah! would 'twere so with many
  A gentle girl and boy —
But were there ever any
  Writh'd not of passèd joy?
The feel of not to feel it,
When there is none to heal it,
Nor numbèd sense to steel it,
  Was never said in rhyme.

La Belle Dame sans Merci[1]

O what can ail thee, Knight at arms,
  Alone and palely loitering?
The sedge has withered from the Lake
  And no birds sing!

O what can ail thee, Knight at arms,
  So haggard, and so woebegone?
The squirrel's granary is full
  And the harvest's done.

I see a lily on thy brow
  With anguish moist and fever dew,
And on thy cheeks a fading rose
  Fast withereth too.

"I met a Lady in the Meads,°   *meadows*
  Full beautiful, a faery's child,
Her hair was long, her foot was light
  And her eyes were wild.

"I made a Garland for her head,
  And bracelets too, and fragrant Zone;°   *belt*
She looked at me as she did love
  And made sweet moan.

"I set her on my pacing steed
  And nothing else saw all day long,
For sidelong would she bend and sing
  A faery's song.

---

[1]The beautiful lady without pity.

"She found me roots of relish sweet,
  And honey wild, and manna dew,
And sure in language strange she said
  'I love thee true.'

"She took me to her elfin grot
  And there she wept and sighed full sore,
And there I shut her wild wild eyes
  With kisses four.

"And there she lullèd me asleep,
  And there I dreamed, Ah Woe betide!
The latest° dream I ever dreamt   *last*
  On the cold hill side.

"I saw pale Kings, and Princes too,
  Pale warriors, death-pale were they all;
They cried, 'La belle dame sans merci
  Hath thee in thrall!'

"I saw their starved lips in the gloam
  With horrid warning gapèd wide,
And I awoke, and found me here
  On the cold hill's side.

"And this is why I sojourn here,
  Alone and palely loitering;
Though the sedge is withered from the Lake
  And no birds sing."

On Sitting Down to Read King Lear Once Again

O golden-tongued Romance with serene lute!
  Fair plumèd Siren!° Queen of far away!   *enchantress*
  Leave melodizing on this wintry day,
Shut up thine olden pages, and be mute:
Adieu! for once again the fierce dispute
  Betwixt damnation and impassioned clay
  Must I burn through; once more humbly assay
The bitter-sweet of this Shakespearean fruit.
Chief Poet! and ye clouds of Albion,°   *England*
  Begetters of our deep eternal theme,
When through the old oak forest I am gone,
  Let me not wander in a barren dream,

But when I am consumèd in the fire,
Give me new Phoenix[1] wings to fly at my desire.

This Living Hand[1]

This living hand, now warm and capable
Of earnest grasping, would, if it were cold
And in the icy silence of the tomb,
So haunt thy days and chill thy dreaming nights
That thou wouldst wish thine own heart dry of blood
So in my veins red life might stream again,
And thou be conscience-calmed — see here it is —
I hold it towards you.

JANE KENYON (1947 – 1995)
Surprise

He suggests pancakes at the local diner,
followed by a walk in search of mayflowers,
while friends convene at the house
bearing casseroles and a cake, their cars
pulled close along the sandy shoulders
of the road, where tender ferns unfurl
in the ditches, and this year's budding leaves
push last year's spectral leaves from the tips
of the twigs of the ash trees. The gathering
itself is not what astounds her, but the casual
accomplishment with which he has lied.

ETHERIDGE KNIGHT (1931 – 1991)
A Poem for Myself
(Or Blues for a Mississippi Black Boy)

I was born in Mississippi;
I walked barefooted thru the mud.
Born black in Mississippi,
Walked barefooted thru the mud.

---

[1]Legendary bird that lives for centuries, then consumes itself in fire and is reborn.

[1]Written on a manuscript page of Keats's unfinished poem, "The Cap and Bells."

But, when I reached the age of twelve
I left that place for good.
My daddy he chopped cotton
And he drank his liquor straight.
Said my daddy chopped cotton
And he drank his liquor straight.
When I left that Sunday morning
He was leaning on the barnyard gate.
I left my momma standing
With the sun shining in her eyes.
Left her standing in the yard
With the sun shining in her eyes.
And I headed North
As straight as the Wild Goose Flies,
I been to Detroit & Chicago —
Been to New York city too.
I been to Detroit and Chicago
Been to New York city too.
Said I done strolled all those funky avenues
I'm still the same old black boy with the same old blues.
Going back to Mississippi
This time to stay for good
Going back to Mississippi
This time to stay for good —
Gonna be free in Mississippi
Or dead in the Mississippi mud.

KENNETH KOCH (1925–2002)

Variations on a Theme by William Carlos Williams

1

I chopped down the house that you had been saving to live in next
        summer.
I am sorry, but it was morning, and I had nothing to do
and its wooden beams were so inviting.

2

We laughed at the hollyhocks together
and then I sprayed them with lye.
Forgive me. I simply do not know what I am doing.

3

I gave away the money that you had been saving to live on for the
　　next ten years.
The man who asked for it was shabby
and the firm March wind on the porch was so juicy and cold.

4

Last evening we went dancing and I broke your leg.
Forgive me. I was clumsy, and
I wanted you here in the wards, where I am the doctor!

YUSEF KOMUNYAKAA (b. 1947)

Boat People

After midnight they load up.
A hundred shadows move about blindly.
Something close to sleep
hides low voices drifting
toward a red horizon. Tonight's
a black string, the moon's pull —
this boat's headed somewhere.
Lucky to have gotten past
searchlights low-crawling the sea,
like a woman shaking water
from her long dark hair.

Twelve times in three days
they've been lucky,
clinging to each other in gray mist.
Now Thai fishermen gaze out across
the sea as it changes color,
hands shading their eyes
the way sailors do,
minds on robbery & rape.
Sunlight burns blood-orange.

Storm warnings crackle on a radio.
The Thai fishermen turn away.
Not enough water for the trip.
The boat people cling to each other,
faces like yellow sea grapes,
wounded by doubt & salt.

Dusk hangs over the water.
Seasick, they daydream Jade Mountain
a whole world away, half-drunk
on what they hunger to become.

My Father's Loveletters

On Fridays he'd open a can of Jax,
Close his eyes, & ask me to write
The same letter to my mother
Who sent postcards of desert flowers
Taller than a man. He'd beg her
Return & promised to never
Beat her again. I was almost happy
She was gone, & sometimes wanted
To slip in something bad.
His carpenter's apron always bulged
With old nails, a claw hammer
Holstered in a loop at his side
& extension cords coiled around his feet.
Words rolled from under
The pressure of my ballpoint:
Love, Baby, Honey, Please.
We lingered in the quiet brutality
Of voltage meters & pipe threaders,
Lost between sentences . . . the heartless
Gleam of a two-pound wedge
On the concrete floor,
A sunset in the doorway
Of the tool shed.
I wondered if she'd laugh
As she held them over a flame.
My father could only sign
His name, but he'd look at blueprints
& tell you how many bricks
Formed each wall. This man
Who stole roses & hyacinth
For his yard, stood there
With eyes closed & fists balled,
Laboring over a simple word,
Opened like a fresh wound, almost
Redeemed by what he tried to say.

STANLEY KUNITZ (b. 1905)

Father and Son

Now in the suburbs and the falling light
I followed him, and now down sandy road
Whiter than bone-dust, through the sweet
Curdle of fields, where the plums
Dropped with their load of ripeness, one by one.
Mile after mile I followed, with skimming feet,
After the secret master of my blood,
Him, steeped in the odor of ponds, whose indomitable love
Kept me in chains. Strode years; stretched into bird;
Raced through the sleeping country where I was young,
The silence unrolling before me as I came,
The night nailed like an orange to my brow.

How should I tell him my fable and the fears,
How bridge the chasm in a casual tone,
Saying, "The house, the stucco one you built,
We lost. Sister married and went from home,
And nothing comes back, it's strange, from where she goes.
I lived on a hill that had too many rooms:
Light we could make, but not enough of warmth,
And when the light failed, I climbed under the hill.
The papers are delivered every day;
I am alone and never shed a tear."

At the water's edge, where the smothering ferns lifted
Their arms, "Father!" I cried, "Return! You know
The way. I'll wipe the mudstains from your clothes;
No trace, I promise, will remain. Instruct
Your son, whirling between two wars,
In the Gemara[1] of your gentleness,
For I would be a child to those who mourn
And brother to the foundlings of the field
And friend of innocence and all bright eyes.
O teach me how to work and keep me kind."

Among the turtles and the lilies he turned to me
The white ignorant hollow of his face.

---

[1]Later of the two portions of the Talmud, a commentary on the first part, the Mishna.

The Portrait

My mother never forgave my father
for killing himself,
especially at such an awkward time
and in a public park,
that spring
when I was waiting to be born.
She locked his name
in her deepest cabinet
and would not let him out,
though I could hear him thumping.
When I came down from the attic
with the pastel portrait in my hand
of a long-lipped stranger
with a brave moustache
and deep brown level eyes,
she ripped it into shreds
without a single word
and slapped me hard.
In my sixty-fourth year
I can feel my cheek
still burning.

PHILIP LARKIN (1922 – 1985)
High Windows

When I see a couple of kids
And guess he's fucking her and she's
Taking pills or wearing a diaphragm,
I know this is paradise

Everyone old has dreamed of all their lives —
Bonds and gestures pushed to one side
Like an outdated combine harvester,
And everyone young going down the long slide

To happiness, endlessly. I wonder if
Anyone looked at me, forty years back,
And thought, *That'll be the life;*
No God any more, or sweating in the dark

About hell and that, or having to hide
What you think of the priest. He

And his lot will all go down the long slide
Like free bloody birds. And immediately
Rather than words comes the thought of high windows:
The sun-comprehending glass,
And beyond it, the deep blue air, that shows
Nothing, and is nowhere, and is endless.

Mr Bleaney

"This was Mr Bleaney's room. He stayed
The whole time he was at the Bodies, till
They moved him." Flowered curtains, thin and frayed,
Fall to within five inches of the sill,

Whose window shows a strip of building land,
Tussocky, littered. "Mr Bleaney took
My bit of garden properly in hand."
Bed, upright chair, sixty-watt bulb, no hook

Behind the door, no room for books or bags —
"I'll take it." So it happens that I lie
Where Mr Bleaney lay, and stub my fags
On the same saucer-souvenir, and try

Stuffing my ears with cotton-wool, to drown
The jabbering set he egged her on to buy.
I know his habits — what time he came down,
His preference for sauce to gravy, why

He kept on plugging at the four aways —
Likewise their yearly frame: the Frinton folk
Who put him up for summer holidays,
And Christmas at his sister's house in Stoke.

But if he stood and watched the frigid wind
Tousling the clouds, lay on the fusty bed
Telling himself that this was home, and grinned,
And shivered, without shaking off the dread

That how we live measures our own nature,
And at his age having no more to show
Than one hired box should make him pretty sure
He warranted no better, I don't know.

Reasons for Attendance

The trumpet's voice, loud and authoritative,
Draws me a moment to the lighted glass
To watch the dancers — all under twenty-five —
Shifting intently, face to flushed face,
Solemnly on the beat of happiness.

— Or so I fancy, sensing the smoke and sweat,
The wonderful feel of girls. Why be out here?
But then, why be in there? Sex, yes, but what
Is sex? Surely, to think the lion's share
Of happiness is found by couples — sheer

Inaccuracy, as far as I'm concerned.
What calls me is that lifted, rough-tongued bell
(Art, if you like) whose individual sound
Insists I too am individual.
It speaks; I hear; others may hear as well,

But not for me, nor I for them; and so
With happiness. Therefore I stay outside,
Believing this; and they maul to and fro,
Believing that; and both are satisfied,
If no one has misjudged himself. Or lied.

This Be The Verse

They fuck you up, your mum and dad.
    They may not mean to, but they do.
They fill you with the faults they had
    And add some extra, just for you.

But they were fucked up in their turn
    By fools in old-style hats and coats,
Who half the time were soppy-stern
    And half at one another's throats.

Man hands on misery to man.
    It deepens like a coastal shelf.
Get out as early as you can,
    And don't have any kids yourself.

D. H. LAWRENCE (1885 – 1930)
The English Are So Nice!

The English are so nice
So awfully nice
They are the nicest people in the world.
And what's more, they're very nice about being nice
About your being nice as well!
If you're not nice they soon make you feel it.

Americans and French and Germans and so on
They're all very well
But they're not *really* nice, you know.
They're not nice in *our* sense of the word, are they now?

That's why one doesn't have to take them seriously.
We must be nice to them, of course,
Of course, naturally.
But it doesn't really matter what you say to them,
They don't really understand
You can just say anything to them:
Be nice, you know, just nice
But you must never take them seriously, they wouldn't
        understand,
Just be nice, you know! oh, fairly nice,
Not too nice of course, they take advantage
But nice enough, just nice enough
To let them feel they're not quite as nice as they might be.

DENISE LEVERTOV (b. 1923)
The Ache of Marriage

The ache of marriage:

thigh and tongue, beloved,
are heavy with it,
it throbs in the teeth

We look for communion
and are turned away, beloved,
each and each

It is leviathan and we
in its belly

looking for joy, some joy
not to be known outside it

two by two in the ark of
the ache of it.

O Taste and See

The world is
not with us enough.
O taste and see

the subway Bible poster said,
meaning The Lord, meaning
if anything all that lives
to the imagination's tongue,

grief, mercy, language,
tangerine, weather, to
breathe them, bite,
savor, chew, swallow, transform

into our flesh our
deaths, crossing the street, plum, quince,
living in the orchard and being

hungry, and plucking
the fruit.

HAROLD LITTLEBIRD (b. 1951)
White-Washing the Walls

(For my mother)

"You just mix your sand with a little water . . ."

"How much?"

"Just enough to cover it, and when you put it on
always scoop enough sand in your water and keep
stirring and adding water. When you're ready to
start, at least say a few words to ask for help
and then it will go easier . . ."

this clay, sand-colored and dry, comes from a place near Laguna
the people have known about it for a long time

in a galvanized pan, mixed with warm water, I stir
and break up small hard chunks that crush easily
in my hands
an aroma like when it rains lightly, cool and sweet
fills the sunroom, taking me back years, to my mother's
house in Paguate, the adobe walls have always been
this color and always held this same smell
and in our small home among the grey sage
below Taos Mountain, it continues

HENRY WADSWORTH LONGFELLOW (1807 – 1882)
Aftermath

When the summer fields are mown,
When the birds are fledged and flown,
　　And the dry leaves strew the path;
With the falling of the snow,
With the cawing of the crow,
Once again the fields we mow
　　And gather in the aftermath.

Not the sweet, new grass with flowers
Is this harvesting of ours;
　　Not the upland clover bloom;
But the rowen mixed with weeds,
Tangled tufts from marsh and meads,
Where the poppy drops its seeds
　　In the silence and the gloom.

The Jewish Cemetery at Newport

How strange it seems! These Hebrews in their graves,
　　Close by the street of this fair seaport town,
Silent beside the never-silent waves,
　　At rest in all this moving up and down!

The trees are white with dust, that o'er their sleep   5
　　Wave their broad curtains in the southwind's breath,
While underneath these leafy tents they keep
　　The long, mysterious Exodus of Death.

And these sepulchral stones, so old and brown,
　　That pave with level flags their burial-place,   10

Seem like the tablets of the Law, thrown down
    And broken by Moses at the mountain's base.

The very names recorded here are strange,
    Of foreign accent, and of different climes;
Alvares and Rivera interchange   15
    With Abraham and Jacob of old times.

"Blessed be God! for he created Death!"
    The mourners said, "and Death is rest and peace;"
Then added, in the certainty of faith,
    "And giveth Life that nevermore shall cease."   20

Closed are the portals of their Synagogue,
    No Psalms of David now the silence break,
No Rabbi reads the ancient Decalogue°   *Ten Commandments*
    In the grand dialect the Prophets spake.

Gone are the living, but the dead remain,   25
    And not neglected; for a hand unseen,
Scattering its bounty, like a summer rain,
    Still keeps their graves and their remembrance green.

How came they here? What burst of Christian hate,
    What persecution, merciless and blind,   30
Drove o'er the sea — that desert desolate —
    These Ishmaels and Hagars of mankind?

They lived in narrow streets and lanes obscure,
    Ghetto and Judenstrass,[1] in mirk and mire;
Taught in the school of patience to endure   35
    The life of anguish and the death of fire.

All their lives long, with the unleavened bread
    And bitter herbs of exile and its fears,
The wasting famine of the heart they fed,
    And slaked its thirst with marah[2] of their tears.   40

Anathema maranatha![3] was the cry
    That rang from town to town, from street to street;
At every gate the accursed Mordecai[4]
    Was mocked and jeered, and spurned by Christian feet.

---

[1] German for "Street of Jews."

[2] The Hebrew word for bitterness.

[3] A curse; literally, "Let him be cursed, the Lord has come" (I Corinthians 16:22).

[4] See the Book of Esther, in which Mordecai represents the Jew devoted to his people's welfare.

Pride and humiliation hand in hand   45
    Walked with them through the world where'er they went;
Trampled and beaten were they as the sand,
    And yet unshaken as the continent.

For in the background figures vague and vast
    Of patriarchs and of prophets rose sublime,   50
And all the great traditions of the Past
    They saw reflected in the coming time.

And thus forever with reverted look
    The mystic volume of the world they read,
Spelling it backward, like a Hebrew book,   55
    Till life became a Legend of the Dead.

But ah! what once has been shall be no more!
    The groaning earth in travail and in pain
Brings forth its races, but does not restore,
    And the dead nations never rise again.   60

AUDRE LORDE (1934 – 1992)
Hanging Fire

I am fourteen
and my skin has betrayed me
the boy I cannot live without
still sucks his thumb
in secret
how come my knees are
always so ashy
what if I die
before morning
and momma's in the bedroom
with the door closed.

I have to learn how to dance
in time for the next party
my room is too small for me
suppose I die before graduation
they will sing sad melodies
but finally
tell the truth about me

There is nothing I want to do
and too much
that has to be done
and momma's in the bedroom
with the door closed.

Nobody even stops to think
about my side of it
I should have been on Math Team
my marks were better than his
why do I have to be
the one
wearing braces
I have nothing to wear tomorrow
will I live long enough
to grow up
and momma's in the bedroom
with the door closed.

ROBERT LOWELL (1917 – 1977)
Sailing Home from Rapallo[1]

[February 1954]

Your nurse could only speak Italian,
but after twenty minutes I could imagine your final week,
and tears ran down my cheeks. . . .

When I embarked from Italy with my Mother's body,
the whole shoreline of the *Golfo di Genova*[2]
was breaking into fiery flower.
The crazy yellow and azure sea–sleds
blasting like jack–hammers across
the *spumante*[3]-bubbling wake of our liner,
recalled the clashing colors of my Ford.
Mother traveled first-class in the hold;

---

[1]A city in northern Italy.
[2]Gulf of Genoa.
[3]Italian for "sparkling," as of wine.

her *Risorgimento*[4] black and gold casket
was like Napoleon's at the *Invalides*.[5] . . .

While the passengers were tanning
on the Mediterranean in deck-chairs,
our family cemetery in Dunbarton[6]
lay under the White Mountains
in the sub-zero weather.
The graveyard's soil was changing to stone —
so many of its deaths had been midwinter.
Dour and dark against the blinding snowdrifts,
its black brook and fir trunks were as smooth as masts.
A fence of iron spear-hafts
black-bordered its mostly Colonial grave-slates.
The only "unhistoric" soul to come here
was Father, now buried beneath his recent
unweathered pink-veined slice of marble.
Even the Latin of his Lowell motto:
Occasionem cognosce,[7]
seemed too businesslike and pushing here,
where the burning cold illuminated
the hewn inscriptions of Mother's relatives:
twenty or thirty Winslows and Starks.
Frost had given their names a diamond edge. . . .

In the grandiloquent lettering on Mother's coffin,
Lowell had been misspelled LOVEL.
The corpse
was wrapped like *panettone*[8] in Italian tinfoil.

ARCHIBALD MACLEISH (1892 – 1982)

Ars Poetica

A poem should be palpable and mute
As a globed fruit,

Dumb
As old medallions to the thumb,

---

[4]A reference to the period of Italy's national revival in the mid-nineteenth century.
[5]The building in Paris where Napoleon is buried.
[6]A town in New Hampshire near the Lowell's family home in Concord.
[7]Latin for "Recognize (your) opportunity."
[8]A Milanese sweet cake.

Silent as the sleeve-worn stone
Of casement ledges where the moss has grown —

A poem should be wordless
As the flight of birds.

A poem should be motionless in time
As the moon climbs,

Leaving, as the moon releases
Twig by twig the night-entangled trees,

Leaving, as the moon behind the winter leaves,
Memory by memory the mind —

A poem should be motionless in time
As the moon climbs.

A poem should be equal to:
Not true.

For all the history of grief
An empty doorway and a maple leaf.

For love
The leaning grasses and two lights above the sea —

A poem should not mean
But be.

DIONISIO MARTÍNEZ (b. 1956)
The Prodigal Son catches up with the bounty hunters

There is only one answer and even the bread crumbs stand at attention when it comes. Someone starts to talk about alleged disappearances, but is soon interrupted and the subject is closed. They bring him up to date on all the deaths in the family, the marriages, the births. In the wake of the latest scandal, they tell him, the new government has maintained its innocence, blaming the Constitution, blaming the scholars and "their gross misinterpretation of our laws." Tap water is potable for the first time in years. The house fell and was rebuilt at least three times, always on a different site. There was a war, they admit, although that's not what they want to say. There was famine. Their lungs and then their chests and finally their mouths fill with all the things they'd like to tell him. He knows the answer, but likes to hear them say it. After hovering, after spying like an insect on the screen door, he asks if perhaps there's a place for him at the table.

The Prodigal Son jumps bail

After hovering, after spying like an insect on the screen door, he asks if perhaps there's a place for him at the table. He knows the answer, but likes to hear them say it. Their lungs and then their chests and finally their mouths fill with all the things they'd like to tell him. There was a war, they admit, although that's not what they want to say. There was famine. The house fell and was rebuilt at least three times, always on a different site. Tap water is potable for the first time in years. In the wake of the latest scandal, they tell him, the new government has maintained its innocence blaming the Constitution, blaming the scholars and "their gross misinterpretation of our laws." They bring him up to date on all the deaths in the family, the marriages, the births. Someone starts to talk about alleged disappearances, but is soon interrupted and the subject is closed. There is only one answer and even the bread crumbs stand at attention when it comes.

ANDREW MARVELL (1621 – 1678)
An Horatian Ode

Upon Cromwell's Return from Ireland[1]
The forward youth that would appear
Must now forsake his Muses dear,
    Nor in the shadows sing
    His numbers° languishing: *poems*

'Tis time to leave the books in dust,   5
And oil the unusèd armor's rust,
    Removing from the wall
    The corslet of the hall.

So restless Cromwell could not cease
In the inglorious arts of peace,   10
    But through adventurous war
    Urgèd his active star;

And like the three-forked lightning, first
Breaking the clouds where it was nursed,

---

[1]Cromwell returned from conquering Ireland in May 1650, eighteen months after the execution of Charles I. In July he would invade Scotland.

Did thorough his own side   15
His fiery way divide.²

For 'tis all one to courage high,
The emulous or enemy;
   And with such to inclose
   Is more than to oppose.   20

Then burning through the air he went,
And palaces and temples rent;
   And Caesar's head at last
   Did through his laurels blast.

'Tis madness to resist or blame   25
The force of angry heaven's flame;
   And if we would speak true,
   Much to the man is due,

Who, from his private gardens, where
He lived reservèd and austere   30
   (As if his highest plot
   To plant the bergamot),³

Could by industrious valor climb
To ruin the great work of time,
   And cast the kingdom old   35
   Into another mold;

Though Justice against Fate complain,
And plead the ancient rights in vain;
   But those do hold or break,
   As men are strong or weak.   40

Nature, that hateth emptiness,
Allows of penetration less,⁴
   And therefore must make room
   Where greater spirits come.

What field of all the civil wars,   45
Where his were not the deepest scars?

---

²Cromwell, after 1644, opened a way for himself among rival parliamentary leaders.

³A pear-shaped orange, also known as prince's pear or the pear of kings.

⁴Although abhorring a vacuum, Nature is even more averse to the occupation of the same space by two bodies at the same time.

And Hampton shows what part
He had of wiser art;[5]

Where, twining subtle fears with hope,
He wove a net of such a scope   50
    That Charles himself might chase
    To Carisbrooke's narrow case,

That thence the royal actor borne
The tragic scaffold might adorn;
    While round the armèd bands   55
    Did clap their bloody hands.

He nothing common did or mean
Upon that memorable scene,
    But with his keener eye
    The axe's edge did try;   60

Nor called the gods with vulgar spite
To vindicate his helpless right;
    But bowed his comely head
    Down, as upon a bed.

This was that memorable hour   65
Which first assured the forcèd power:
    So, when they did design
    The Capitol's first line,

A bleeding head, where they begun,
Did fright the architects to run;   70
    And yet in that the state
    Foresaw its happy fate.[6]

And now the Irish are ashamed
To see themselves in one year tamed;
    So much one man can do   75
    That does both act and know.

They can affirm his praises best,
And have, though overcome, confessed

---

[5]Charles I fled to Carisbrooke Castle, which turned out to be a cage ("narrow case") for him. It was long believed that Cromwell connived at the flight of Charles from Hampton Court to Carisbrooke Castle in order to prod Parliament into executing him.

[6]Pliny tells, in his *Natural History* (28:4), an anecdote about workmen who found a head while digging the foundation of a temple to Jupiter on the Tarpeian hill in Rome. The omen was interpreted as indicating a prosperous future for Rome.

How good he is, how just,
And fit for highest trust.   80

Nor yet grown stiffer with command,
But still in the republic's hand —
   How fit he is to sway
   That can so well obey!

He to the Commons' feet presents   85
A kingdom for his first year's rents;
   And, what he may, forbears
   His fame to make it theirs;

And has his sword and spoils ungirt,
To lay them at the public's skirt: 90
   So when the falcon high
   Falls heavy from the sky,

She, having killed, no more does search
But on the next green bough to perch;
   Where, when he first does lure,   95
   The falconer has her sure.

What may not, then, our isle presume,
While victory his crest does plume?
   What may not others fear,
   If thus he crown each year?   100

A Caesar he, ere long, to Gaul
To Italy an Hannibal,
   And to all states not free
   Shall climactèric be.

The Pict no shelter now shall find   105
Within his parti-colored mind,[7]
   But from this valor sad
   Shrink underneath the plaid;

Happy if in the tufted brake
The English hunter him mistake,   110
   Nor lay his hounds in near
   The Caledonian° deer.   *Scottish*

---

[7]The early inhabitants of Scotland were called Picts because the warriors painted themselves with many colors for battle. (*Pictus* is Latin for "painted.") Marvell implies that the Scots are divided into many parties or factions.

But thou, the war's and fortune's son,
March indefatigably on!
>   And for the last effect,   115
>   Still keep thy sword erect;

Besides the force it has to fright
The spirits of the shady night,
>   The same arts that did gain
>   A power must it maintain.   120

The Mower's Song

My mind was once the true survey
Of all these meadows fresh and gay,
And in the greenness of the grass
Did see its hopes[1] as in a glass;°   *mirror*
When Juliana came, and she,
What I do to the grass, does to my thoughts and me.[2]

But these, while I with sorrow pine,
Grew more luxuriant still and fine,
That not one blade of grass you spied
But had a flower on either side;
When Juliana came, and she,
What I do to the grass, does to my thoughts and me.

Unthankful meadows, could you so
A fellowship so true forego,
And in your gaudy May-games[3] meet,
While I lay trodden under feet?
When Juliana came, and she,
What I do to the grass, does to my thoughts and me.

But what you in compassion ought
Shall now by my revenge be wrought,
And flowers, and grass, and I, and all,
Will in one common ruin fall;
When Juliana comes, and she,
What I do to the grass, does to my thoughts and me.

---

[1]Green is the color of hope.

[2]The alexandrine (12-syllable line) used here is the only example of a refrain in Marvell.

[3]Festivals and merrymaking marked the first of May.

And thus ye meadows, which have been
Companions of my thoughts more green,
Shall now the heraldry become
With which I shall adorn my tomb;
When Juliana comes, and she,
What I do to the grass, does to my thoughts and me.

The Mower to the Glowworms

Ye living lamps, by whose dear light
The nightingale does sit so late,
And studying all the summer night
Her matchless songs does mediate,

Ye country comets, that portend
No war nor prince's funeral,
Shining unto no higher end
Than to presage the grass's fall;

Ye glowworms, whose officious° flame   *zealous, attentive*
To wand'ring mowers shows the way,
That in the night have lost their aim,
And after foolish fires° do stray;   *will-o-the-wisps*

Your courteous fires in vain you waste,
Since Juliana here is come,
For she my mind hath so displaced
That I shall never find my home.

To His Coy Mistress

    Had we but world enough, and time,
This coyness, lady, were no crime.
We would sit down, and think which way
To walk, and pass our long love's day.
Thou by the Indian Ganges' side
Shouldst rubies find; I by the tide
Of Humber[1] would complain. I would
Love you ten years before the flood,
And you should, if you please, refuse
Till the conversion of the Jews.[2]

---

[1] The Humber flows through Hull, Marvell's native town.
[2] Supposed to occur at the end of time.

My vegetable love should grow
Vaster than empires and more slow;
An hundred years should go to praise
Thine eyes, and on thy forehead gaze;
Two hundred to adore each breast,
But thirty thousand to the rest;
An age at least to every part,
And the last age should show your heart.
For, lady, you deserve this state,
Nor would I love at lower rate.
      But at my back I always hear
Time's wingèd chariot hurrying near;
And yonder all before us lie
Deserts of vast eternity.
Thy beauty shall no more be found;
Nor, in thy marble vault, shall sound
My echoing song; then worms shall try
That long-preserved virginity,
And your quaint honor turn to dust,
And into ashes all my lust:
The grave's a fine and private place,
But none, I think, do there embrace.
      Now therefore, while the youthful hue
Sits on thy skin like morning dew,
And while thy willing soul transpires
At every pore with instant fires,
Now let us sport us while we may,
And now, like amorous birds of prey,
Rather at once our time devour
Than languish in his slow-chapped power.
Let us roll all our strength and all
Our sweetness up into one ball,
And tear our pleasures with rough strife
Thorough the iron gates of life:
Thus, though we cannot make our sun
Stand still, yet we will make him run.

HERMAN MELVILLE (1819 – 1891)
The Berg

A Dream

I saw a ship of martial build
(Her standards set, her brave apparel on)
Directed as by madness mere
Against a stolid iceberg steer,
Nor budge it, though the infatuate ship went down.
The impact made huge ice-cubes fall
Sullen, in tons that crashed the deck;
But that one avalanche was all —
No other movement save the foundering wreck.

Along the spurs of ridges pale,
Not any slenderest shaft and frail,
A prism over glass-green gorges lone,
Toppled; nor lace of traceries fine,
Nor pendent drops in grot or mine
Were jarred, when the stunned ship went down.

Nor sole the gulls in cloud that wheeled
Circling one snow-flanked peak afar,
But nearer fowl the floes that skimmed
And crystal beaches, felt no jar.
No thrill transmitted stirred the lock
Of jack-straw needle-ice at base;
Towers undermined by waves — the block
Atilt impending — kept their place.
Seals, dozing sleek on sliddery ledges
Slipt never, when by loftier edges
Through very inertia overthrown,
The impetuous ship in bafflement went down.

Hard Berg (methought), so cold, so vast,
With mortal damps self-overcast;
Exhaling still thy dankish breath —
Adrift dissolving, bound for death;
Though lumpish thou, a lumbering one —
A lumbering lubbard loitering slow,
Impingers rue thee and go down,
Sounding thy precipice below,
Nor stir the slimy slug that sprawls
Along thy dead indifference of walls.

Monody[1]

To have known him, to have loved him,
    After loneness long;
And then to be estranged in life,
    And neither in the wrong;
And now for death to set his seal —
    Ease me, a little ease, my song!

By wintry hills his hermit-mound
    The sheeted snow-drifts drape,
And houseless there the snow-bird flits
    Beneath the fir-tree's crape:
Glazed now with ice the cloistral vine
    That hid the shyest grape.

JAMES MERRILL (1926 – 1995)
The Broken Home

Crossing the street,
I saw the parents and the child
At their window, gleaming like fruit
With evening's mild gold leaf.

In a room on the floor below,   5
Sunless, cooler — a brimming
Saucer of wax, marbly and dim —
I have lit what's left of my life.

I have thrown out yesterday's milk
And opened a book of maxims.   10
The flame quickens. The word stirs.

Tell me, tongue of fire,
That you and I are as real
At least as the people upstairs.

My father,[1] who had flown in World War I,
Might have continued to invest his life   15

---

[1]This poem is perhaps an elegy for Nathaniel Hawthorne, called "Vine" in Melville's long poem *Clarel.*

[1]Charles Merrill, who was a financier and founder of the brokerage firm Merrill Lynch. He and Merrill's mother eventually divorced.

In cloud banks well above Wall Street and wife.
But the race was run below, and the point was to win.

Too late now, I make out in his blue gaze
(Through the smoked glass of being thirty-six)   20
The soul eclipsed by twin black pupils, sex
And business; time was money in those days.

Each thirteenth year he married. When he died
There were already several chilled wives
In sable orbit — rings, cars, permanent waves.   25
We'd felt him warming up for a green bride.

He could afford it. He was "in his prime"
At three score ten. But money was not time.

When my parents were younger this was a popular act:
A veiled woman would leap from an electric, wine-dark car   30
To the steps of no matter what — the Senate or the Ritz Bar —
And bodily, at newsreel speed, attack

No matter whom — Al Smith or José Maria Sert
Or Clemenceau[2] — veins standing out on her throat
As she yelled *War mongerer! Pig! Give us the vote!*,   35
And would have to be hauled away in her hobble skirt.

What had the man done? Oh, made history.
Her business (he had implied) was giving birth,
Tending the house, mending the socks.

Always that same old story —   40
Father Time and Mother Earth,[3]
A marriage on the rocks.

One afternoon, red, satyr-thighed
Michael, the Irish setter, head
Passionately lowered, led   45
The child I was to a shut door. Inside,

---

[2]Alfred E. Smith (1873–1944) and Georges Clemenceau (1841–1929) were politicians; José Maria Sert (1876–1945) was a painter.

[3]In mythology, Cronus (Time) and Rhea (mother of the gods) were the parents of Zeus, who dethroned his father.

Blinds beat sun from the bed.
The green-gold room throbbed like a bruise.
Under a sheet, clad in taboos
Lay whom we sought, her hair undone, outspread,   50

And of a blackness found, if ever now, in old
Engravings where the acid bit.
I must have needed to touch it
Or the whiteness — was she dead?
Her eyes flew open, startled strange and cold.   55
The dog slumped to the floor. She reached for me. I fled.

Tonight they have stepped out onto the gravel.
The party is over. It's the fall
Of 1931. They love each other still.

She: Charlie, I can't stand the pace.   60
He: Come on, honey — why, you'll bury us all!

A lead soldier guards my windowsill:
Khaki rifle, uniform, and face.
Something in me grows heavy, silvery, pliable.

How intensely people used to feel!   65
Like metal poured at the close of a proletarian novel,
Refined and glowing from the crucible,
I see those two hearts, I'm afraid,
Still. Cool here in the graveyard of good and evil,
They are even so to be honored and obeyed.   70

. . . Obeyed, at least, inversely. Thus
I rarely buy a newspaper, or vote.
To do so, I have learned, is to invite
The tread of a stone guest[4] within my house.

Shooting this rusted bolt, though, against him,   75
I trust I am no less time's child than some
Who on the heath impersonate Poor Tom[5]
Or on the barricades risk life and limb.

---

[4]In Mozart's opera *Don Giovanni,* the Commendatore's statue comes to life and enters the Don's house, seeking vengeance for his daughter's seduction.

[5]The name adopted, in Shakespeare's *King Lear,* by Edgar, disinherited by his father, Gloucester.

Nor do I try to keep a garden, only
An avocado in a glass of water —   80
Roots pallid, gemmed with air. And later,

When the small gilt leaves have grown
Fleshy and green, I let them die, yes, yes,
And start another. I am earth's no less.

A child, a red dog roam the corridors,   85
Still, of the broken home. No sound. The brilliant
Rag runners halt before wide-open doors.
My old room! Its wallpaper — cream, medallioned
With pink and brown — brings back the first nightmares,
Long summer colds, and Emma, sepia-faced,   90
Perspiring over broth carried upstairs
Aswim with golden fats I could not taste.

The real house became a boarding-school.
Under the ballroom ceiling's allegory
Someone at last may actually be allowed   95
To learn something; or, from my window, cool
With the unstiflement of the entire story,
Watch a red setter[6] stretch and sink in cloud.

W. S. MERWIN (b. 1927)

For a Coming Extinction

Gray whale
Now that we are sending you to The End
That great god
Tell him
That we who follow you invented forgiveness
And forgive nothing

I write as though you could understand
And I could say it
One must always pretend something
Among the dying
When you have left the seas nodding on their stalks
Empty of you

---

[6]This is a pun on "setter" — the dog and the setting sun.

Tell him that we were made
On another day

The bewilderment will diminish like an echo
Winding along your inner mountains
Unheard by us
And find its way out
Leaving behind it the future
Dead
And ours

When you will not see again
The whale calves trying the light
Consider what you will find in the black garden
And its court
The sea cows the Great Auks the gorillas
The irreplaceable hosts ranged countless
And fore-ordaining as stars
Our sacrifices

Join your word to theirs
Tell him
That it is we who are important

For the Anniversary of My Death

Every year without knowing it I have passed the day
When the last fires will wave to me
And the silence will set out
Tireless traveller
Like the beam of a lightless star

Then I will no longer
Find myself in life as in a strange garment
Surprised at the earth
And the love of one woman
And the shamelessness of men
As today writing after three days of rain
Hearing the wren sing and the falling cease
And bowing not knowing to what

JOHN MILTON (1608 – 1674)

L'Allegro[1]

Hence loathèd Melancholy
    Of Cerberus and blackest midnight born,
In Stygian cave forlorn
    'Mongst horrid shapes, and shrieks, and sights unholy,
Find out some uncouth cell,   5
    Where brooding Darkness spreads his jealous wings,
And the night-raven sings;
    There under ebon shades, and low-browed rocks,
As ragged as thy locks,
    In dark Cimmerian[2] desert ever dwell.   10
But come thou goddess fair and free,
In Heaven yclept° Euphrosyne,[3]   *called*
And by men, heart-easing Mirth,
Whom lovely Venus at a birth
With two sister Graces more   15
To ivy-crownèd Bacchus bore;
Or whether (as some sager sing)[4]
The frolic wind that breathes the spring,
Zephyr with Aurora playing,
As he met her once a-Maying,   20
There on beds of violets blue,
And fresh-blown roses washed in dew,
Filled her with thee a daughter fair,
So buxom, blithe, and debonair.
Haste thee nymph, and bring with thee   25
Jest and youthful Jollity,
Quips and Cranks, and wanton Wiles,
Nods, and Becks, and wreathèd Smiles,
Such as hang on Hebe's° cheek,   *goddess of youth*
And love to live in dimple sleek;   30
Sport that wrinkled Care derides,
And Laughter holding both his sides.
Come, and trip it as ye go
On the light fantastic toe,
And in thy right hand lead with thee,   35

---

[1]The title is Italian for "The Cheerful Man."
[2]A land in which, according to Homer, the sun never shone.
[3]Mirth, one of the three Graces.
[4]This genealogy is invented by Milton.

The mountain nymph, sweet Liberty;
And if I give thee honor due,
Mirth, admit me of thy crew
To live with her and live with thee,
In unreprovèd pleasures free;   40
To hear the lark begin his flight,
And, singing, startle the dull night,
From his watch-tower in the skies,
Till the dappled dawn doth rise;
Then to come in spite of sorrow,   45
And at my window bid good morrow,
Through the sweetbriar, or the vine,
Or the twisted eglantine.
While the cock with lively din,
Scatters the rear of darkness thin,   50
And to the stack, or the barn door,
Stoutly struts his dames before;
Oft listening how the hounds and horn
Cheerly rouse the slumbering morn,
From the side of some hoar hill,   55
Through the high wood echoing shrill.
Sometime walking not unseen
By hedgerow elms, on hillocks green,
Right against the eastern gate,
Where the great sun begins his state,   60
Robed in flames, and amber light,
The clouds in thousand liveries dight;°   *clad*
While the plowman near at hand,
Whistles o'er the furrowed land,
And the milkmaid singeth blithe,   65
And the mower whets his scythe,
And every shepherd tells his tale,
Under the hawthorn in the dale.
Straight mine eye hath caught new pleasures
Whilst the landscape round it measures,   70
Russet lawns and fallows gray,
Where the nibbling flocks do stray,
Mountains on whose barren breast
The laboring clouds do often rest;
Meadows trim with daisies pied,   75
Shallow brooks, and rivers wide.
Towers and battlements it sees

Bosomed high in tufted trees,
Where perhaps some beauty lies,
The cynosure of neighboring eyes.   80
Hard by, a cottage chimney smokes,
From betwixt two aged oaks,
Where Corydon and Thyrsis[5] met,
Are at their savory dinner set
Of herbs, and other country messes,   85
Which the neat-handed Phyllis dresses;
And then in haste her bower she leaves,
With Thestylis to bind the sheaves;
Or if the earlier season lead
To the tanned haycock in the mead.   90
Sometimes with secure delight
The upland hamlets will invite,
When the merry bells ring round
And the jocund rebecks° sound   *fiddles*
To many a youth and many a maid,   95
Dancing in the checkered shade;
And young and old come forth to play
On a sunshine holiday,
Till the livelong daylight fail;
Then to the spicy nut-brown ale,   100
With stories told of many a feat,
How fairy Mab the junkets eat;
She was pinched and pulled, she said,
And he, by Friar's lantern° led,   *will-o'-the-wisp*
Tells how the drudging goblin sweat   105
To earn his cream-bowl, duly set,
When in one night, ere glimpse of morn,
His shadowy flail hath threshed the corn
That ten day-laborers could not end;
Then lies him down the lubber° fiend,   *drudging*   110
And, stretched out all the chimney's° length,   *fireplace's*
Basks at the fire his hairy strength;
And crop-full out of doors he flings
Ere the first cock his matin rings.
Thus done the tales, to bed they creep,   115
By whispering winds soon lulled asleep.

---

[5]Corydon, Thyrsis, Phyllis (lines 83, 86), and Thestylis (line 88) are conventional
names from pastoral poetry.

Towered cities please us then,
And the busy hum of men,
Where throngs of knights and barons bold,
In weeds of peace high triumphs hold,   120
With store of ladies, whose bright eyes
Rain influence, and judge the prize
Of wit, or arms, while both contend
To win her grace, whom all commend.
There let Hymen° oft appear   *god of marriage*   125
In saffron robe, with taper clear,
And pomp, and feast, and revelry,
With masque, and antique pageantry;
Such sights as youthful poets dream
On summer eves by haunted stream.   130
Then to the well-trod stage anon,
If Jonson's learnèd sock[6] be on,
Or sweetest Shakespeare, fancy's child,
Warble his native wood-notes wild.
And ever against eating cares   135
Lap me in soft Lydian airs
Married to immortal verse
Such as the meeting soul may pierce
In notes, with many a winding bout°   *turn*
Of linkèd sweetness long drawn out,   140
With wanton heed, and giddy cunning,
The melting voice through mazes running;
Untwisting all the chains that tie
The hidden soul of harmony;
That Orpheus' self[7] may heave his head   145
From golden slumber on a bed
Of heaped Elysian flowers, and hear
Such strains as would have won the ear
Of Pluto, to have quite set free
His half-regained Eurydice.   150
These delights if thou canst give,
Mirth, with thee I mean to live.

---

[6]The light shoe of ancient comic actors, a symbol of comedy.

[7]Orpheus, the great musician of classical mythology, pleaded with Pluto, god of the underworld, to allow him to rescue his wife, Eurydice. Pluto consented to let Eurydice return; but Orpheus, by looking back to be sure she was following, broke the terms of his agreement with Pluto, and Eurydice remained in Hades.

Methought I Saw My Late Espousèd Saint

Methought I saw my late espousèd saint
    Brought to me like Alcestis from the grave,
    Whom Jove's great son to her glad husband gave,
    Rescued from Death by force, though pale and faint.
Mine, as whom washed from spot of child-bed taint
    Purification in the Old Law did save,
    And such, as yet once more I trust to have
    Full sight of her in heaven without restraint,
Came vested all in white, pure as her mind.
    Her face was veiled; yet to my fancied sight
    Love, sweetness, goodness, in her person shined
So clear as in no face with more delight.
    But O, as to embrace me she inclined,
    I waked, she fled, and day brought back my night.

On Shakespeare

What needs my Shakespeare for his honored bones
The labor of an age in pilèd stones?
Or that his hallowed reliques should be hid
Under a star-ypointing pyramid?
Dear son of Memory, great heir of Fame,
What need'st thou such weak witness of thy name?
Thou in our wonder and astonishment
Hast built thyself a livelong monument.
For whilst, to th' shame of slow-endeavoring art,
Thy easy numbers flow, and that each heart
Hath from the leaves of thy unvalued° book   *invaluable*
Those Delphic lines with deep impression took,
Then thou, our fancy of itself bereaving,
Dost make us marble with too much conceiving,
And so sepúlchred in such pomp dost lie
That kings for such a tomb would wish to die.

MARIANNE MOORE (1887 – 1972)
Poetry

I, too, dislike it: there are things that are important beyond all
                      this fiddle.
    Reading it, however, with a perfect contempt for it, one
                    discovers in

it after all, a place for the genuine.
     Hands that can grasp, eyes
     that can dilate, hair that can rise
          if it must, these things are important not because a

high-sounding interpretation can be put upon them but because
                                                  they are
     useful. When they become so derivative as to become
                                        unintelligible,
     the same thing may be said for all of us, that we
          do not admire what
          we cannot understand: the bat
               holding on upside down or in quest of something to

eat, elephants pushing, a wild horse taking a roll, a tireless wolf
                                                  under
          a tree, the immovable critic twitching his skin like a horse
                              that feels a flea, the base-
     ball fan, the statistician —
          nor is it valid
               to discriminate against "business documents and

school-books";[1] all these phenomena are important. One must
                              make a distinction
          however: when dragged into prominence by half poets, the
                              result is not poetry,
     nor till the poets among us can be
          "literalists of
          the imagination"[2] — above
               insolence and triviality and can present

for inspection, "imaginary gardens with real toads in them,"
                                        shall we have
     it. In the meantime, if you demand on the one hand,
     the raw material of poetry in
          all its rawness and

---

[1]Moore's note: "*Diary of Tolstoy* (Dutton), p. 84. 'Where the boundary between prose and poetry lies, I shall never be able to understand. The question is raised in manuals of style, yet the answer to it lies beyond me. Poetry is verse; prose is not verse. Or else poetry is everything with the exception of business documents and school books.'"

[2]Moore's note: "*Yeats: Ideas of Good and Evil* (A. H. Bullen, 1903), p. 182. 'The limitation of his view was from the very intensity of his vision; he was a too literal realist of imagination, as others are of nature; and because he believed that the figures seen by the mind's eye, when exalted by inspiration, were "eternal existences," symbols of divine essences, he hated every grace of style that might obscure their lineaments.'"

that which is on the other hand
genuine, you are interested in poetry.

The Steeple-Jack

Revised, 1961

Dürer would have seen a reason for living
in a town like this, with eight stranded whales
to look at; with the sweet sea air coming into your house
on a fine day, from water etched
with waves as formal as the scales   5
on a fish.

One by one in two's and three's, the seagulls keep
flying back and forth over the town clock,
or sailing around the lighthouse without moving their wings —
rising steadily with a slight   10
quiver of the body — or flock
mewing where

a sea the purple of the peacock's neck is
paled to greenish azure as Dürer changed
the pine green of the Tyrol to peacock blue and guinea   15
gray. You can see a twenty-five-
pound lobster; and fish nets arranged
to dry. The

whirlwind fife-and-drum of the storm bends the salt
marsh grass, disturbs stars in the sky and the   20
star on the steeple; it is a privilege to see so
much confusion. Disguised by what
might seem the opposite, the sea-
side flowers and

trees are favored by the fog so that you have   25
the tropics at first hand: the trumpet vine,
foxglove, giant snapdragon, a salpiglossis that has
spots and stripes; morning-glories, gourds,
    . or moon-vines trained on fishing twine
at the back door: 30

cattails, flags, blueberries and spiderwort,
striped grass, lichens, sunflowers, asters, daisies —
yellow and crab-claw ragged sailors with green bracts — toad-
plant,

petunias, ferns; pink lilies, blue 35
      ones, tigers; poppies; black sweet-peas.
The climate

is not right for the banyan, frangipani, or
      jack-fruit trees; or for exotic serpent
life. Ring lizard and snakeskin for the foot, if you see fit; 40
but here they've cats, not cobras, to
      keep down the rats. The diffident
little newt

with white pin-dots on black horizontal spaced-
      out bands lives here; yet there is nothing that 45
ambition can buy or take away. The college student
named Ambrose sits on the hillside
      with his not-native books and hat
and sees boats

at sea progress white and rigid as if in 50
      a groove. Liking an elegance of which
the source is not bravado, he knows by heart the antique
sugar-bowl shaped summerhouse of
      interlacing slats, and the pitch
of the church 55

spire, not true, from which a man in scarlet lets
      down a rope as a spider spins a thread;
he might be part of a novel, but on the sidewalk a
sign says C. J. Poole, Steeple Jack,
      in black and white; and one in red 60
and white says

Danger. The church portico has four fluted
      columns, each a single piece of stone, made
modester by whitewash. This would be a fit haven for
waifs, children, animals, prisoners, 65
      and presidents who have repaid
sin-driven

senators by not thinking about them. The
      place has a schoolhouse, a post-office in a
store, fish-houses, hen-houses, a three-masted 70
      schooner on

the stocks. The hero, the student,
    the steeple jack, each in his way,
is at home.

It could not be dangerous to be living   75
    in a town like this, of simple people,
who have a steeple-jack placing danger signs by the church
while he is gliding the solid-
    pointed star, which on a steeple
stands for hope.   80

To a Snail

If "compression is the first grace of style,"
you have it. Contractility is a virtue
as modesty is a virtue.
It is not the acquisition of any one thing
that is able to adorn,
or the incidental quality that occurs
as a concomitant of something well said,
that we value in style,
but the principle that is hid:
in the absence of feet, "a method of conclusions";
"a knowledge of principles,"
in the curious phenomenon of your occipital horn.

To a Steam Roller

The illustration
is nothing to you without the application.
    You lack half wit. You crush all the particles down
        into close conformity, and then walk back and forth on
            them.

Sparkling chips of rock
are crushed down to the level of the parent block.
    Were not "impersonal judgment in aesthetic
        matters, a metaphysical impossibility," you

might fairly achieve
it. As for butterflies, I can hardly conceive
    of one's attending upon you, but to question
        the congruence of the complement is vain, if it exists.

PAT MORA (b. 1942)
La Migra[1]

1

Let's play La Migra.
I'll be the Border Patrol.
You be the Mexican maid.
I get the badge and sunglasses.
You can hide and run,
but you can't get away
because I have a jeep.
I can take you wherever
I want, but don't ask
questions because
I don't speak Spanish.
I can touch you wherever
I want but don't complain
too much because I've got
boots and kick — if I have to,
and I have handcuffs.
Oh, and a gun.
Get ready, get set, run.

2

Let's play La Migra.
You be the Border Patrol.
I'll be the Mexican woman.
Your jeep has a flat,
and you have been spotted
by the sun.
All you have is heavy: hat,
glasses, badge, shoes, gun.
I know this desert,
where to rest,
where to drink.
Oh, I am not alone.
You hear us singing
and laughing with the wind,
Agua dulce brota aquí, aquí, aquí,[2]

---

[1]Emigration.
[2]Sweet water springs up here, here, here.

but since you can't speak Spanish,
you do not understand.
Get ready.

THYLIAS MOSS (b. 1954)
Lunchcounter Freedom

I once wanted a white man's eyes upon
me, my beauty riveting him to my slum
color. Forgetting his hands are made for my
curves, he would raise them to shield his eyes
and they would fly to my breasts with gentleness
stolen from doves.

I've made up my mind not to order a sandwich on
light bread if the waitress approaches me
with a pencil. My hat is the one I wear
the Sundays my choir doesn't sing. A dark
bird on it darkly sways to the gospel music,
trying to pull nectar from a cloth flower.
Psalms are mice in my mind, nibbling,
gnawing, tearing up my thoughts.
White men are the walls. I can't tell anyone
how badly I want water. In the mirage that
follows, the doves unfold into hammers.
They still fly to my breasts.

Because I'm nonviolent I don't act or
react. When knocked from the stool
my body takes its shape from what
it falls into. The white man cradles
his tar baby. Each magus in turn.
He fathered it, it looks just like him,
the spitting image. He can't let go of
his future. The menu offers tuna fish,
grits, beef in a sauce like desire.
He is free to choose from available
choices. The asterisk marks the special.

FRANK O'HARA (1926 – 1966)
Ave Maria[1]

Mothers of America
              let your kids go to the movies!
get them out of the house so they won't know what you're up to
it's true that fresh air is good for the body
                     but what about the soul
that grows in darkness, embossed by silvery images
and when you grow old as grow old you must
                       they won't hate you
they won't criticize you they won't know
                they'll be in some glamorous country
they first saw on a Saturday afternoon or playing hookey
they may even be grateful to you
                for their first sexual experience
which only cost you a quarter
                and didn't upset the peaceful home
they will know where candy bars come from
                and gratuitous bags of popcorn
as gratuitous as leaving the movie before it's over
with a pleasant stranger whose apartment is in the Heaven on Earth
    Bldg
near the Williamsburg Bridge
                 oh mothers you will have made the little tykes
so happy because if nobody does pick them up in the movies
they won't know the difference
              and if somebody does it'll be sheer gravy
and they'll have been truly entertained either way
instead of hanging around the yard
                 or up in their room
                    hating you
prematurely since you won't have done anything horribly mean yet
except keeping them from the darker joys
                it's unforgivable the latter
so don't blame me if you won't take this advice
              and the family breaks up
and your children grow old and blind in front of a TV set
                 seeing
movies you wouldn't let them see when they were young

---

[1]Latin: "Hail Mary," prayer to the Virgin Mary saluting her as the Mother of God.

Why I Am Not a Painter

I am not a painter, I am a poet.
Why? I think I would rather be
a painter, but I am not. Well,

for instance, Mike Goldberg
is starting a painting. I drop in.
"Sit down and have a drink" he
says. I drink; we drink. I look
up. "You have SARDINES in it."
"Yes, it needed something there."
"Oh." I go and the days go by
and I drop in again. The painting
is going on, and I go, and the days
go by. I drop in. The painting is
finished. "Where's SARDINES?"
All that's left is just
letters, "It was too much," Mike says.

But me? One day I am thinking of
a color: orange. I write a line
about orange. Pretty soon it is a
whole page of words, not lines.
Then another page. There should be
so much more, not of orange, of
words, of how terrible orange is
and life. Days go by. It is even in
prose, I am a real poet. My poem
is finished and I haven't mentioned
orange yet. It's twelve poems, I call
it ORANGES. And one day in a gallery
I see Mike's painting, called SARDINES.

WILFRED OWEN (1893 – 1918)
Anthem for Doomed Youth

What passing-bells for these who die as cattle?
    — Only the monstrous anger of the guns.
    Only the stuttering rifles' rapid rattle
Can patter out their hasty orisons.
No mockeries now for them; no prayers nor bells;
    Nor any voice of mourning save the choirs, —

The shrill, demented choirs of wailing shells;
    And bugles calling for them from sad shires.

What candles may be held to speed them all?
    Not in the hands of boys, but in their eyes
Shall shine the holy glimmers of goodbyes.
    The pallor of girls' brows shall be their pall;
Their flowers the tenderness of patient minds,
And each slow dusk a drawing-down of blinds.

Disabled

He sat in a wheeled chair, waiting for dark,
And shivered in his ghastly suit of grey,
Legless, sewn short at elbow. Through the park
Voices of boys rang saddening like a hymn,
Voices of play and pleasure after day,
Till gathering sleep had mothered them from him.

About this time Town used to swing so gay
When glow-lamps budded in the light blue trees,
And girls glanced lovelier as the air grew dim,
— In the old times, before he threw away his knees.
Now he will never feel again how slim
Girls' waists are, or how warm their subtle hands.
All of them touch him like some queer disease.

There was an artist silly for his face,
For it was younger than his youth, last year.
Now, he is old; his back will never brace;
He's lost his colour very far from here,
Poured it down shell-holes till the veins ran dry,
And half his lifetime lapsed in the hot race
And leap of purple spurted from his thigh.

One time he liked a bloodsmear down his leg,
After the matches, carried shoulder-high.
It was after football, when he'd drunk a peg,
He thought he'd better join. — He wonders why.
Someone had said he'd look a god in kilts,
That's why; and maybe, too, to please his Meg,
Aye, that was it, to please the giddy jilts
He asked to join. He didn't have to beg;
Smiling they wrote his lie: aged nineteen years.
Germans he scarcely thought of; all their guilt

And Austria's, did not move him. And no fears
Of Fear came yet. He thought of jewelled hilts
For daggers in plaid socks; of smart salutes;
And care of arms; and leave; and pay arrears;
Esprit de corps; and hints for young recruits.
And soon, he was drafted out with drums and cheers.

Some cheered him home, but not as crowds cheer Goal.
Only a solemn man who brought him fruits
Thanked him; and then inquired about his soul.

Now, he will spend a few sick years in institutes,
And do what things the rules consider wise,
And take whatever pity they may dole.
Tonight he noticed how the women's eyes
Passed from him to the strong men that were whole.
How cold and late it is! Why don't they come
And put him into bed? Why don't they come?

CARL PHILLIPS (b. 1959)
The Kill

The last time I gave my body up,

to you, I was minded
briefly what it is made of,
what yours is, that

I'd forgotten, the flesh
which always
I hold in plenty no

little sorrow for because — oh, do
but think on its predicament,
and weep.

We cleave most entirely
to what most we fear
losing. We fear loss

because we understand
the fact of it, its largeness, its
utter indifference to whether

we do, or don't,
ignore it. By then, you
were upon me, and then

in me, soon the tokens
I almost never can let go of, I'd
again begin to, and would not

miss them: the swan
unfolding
upward less on trust than

because, simply, that's
what it does; and the leaves,
leaving; a single arrow held

back in the merciless
patience which, in taking
aim, is everything; and last,

as from a grove in
flame toward any air
more clear, the stag, but

this time its bent
head a chandelier, rushing
for me, like some

undisavowable
distraction. I looked back,
and instead of you, saw

the soul-at-labor-to-break-its-bonds
that you'd become. I tensed
my bow:

one animal at attack,
the other — the other one
suffering, and love would

out all suffering —

Passing

When the Famous Black Poet speaks,
I understand

that his is the same unnervingly slow
rambling method of getting from A to B
that I hated in my father,
my father who always told me
don't shuffle.

The Famous Black Poet is
speaking of the dark river in the mind
that runs thick with the heroes of color,
Jackie R., Bessie, Billie, Mr. Paige, anyone
who knew how to sing or when to run.
I think of my grandmother, said
to have dropped dead from the evil eye,
of my lesbian aunt who saw cancer and
a generally difficult future headed her way
in the still water
of her brother's commode.
I think of voodoo in the bottoms of soup-cans,
and I want to tell the poet that the blues
is *not* my name, that Alabama
is something I cannot use
in my business.

He is so like my father,
I don't ask the Famous Black Poet,
afterwards,
to remove his shoes,
knowing the inexplicable black
and pink I will find there, a cut
gone wrong in five places.
I don't ask him to remove
his pants, since that too
is known, what has never known
a blade, all the spaces between,
where we differ . . .

I have spent years tugging
between my legs,
and proved nothing, really.
I wake to the sheets I kicked aside,
and examine where they've failed to mend
their own creases, resembling some silken
obstruction, something pulled
from my father's chest, a bad heart,
a lung,

the lung of the Famous Black Poet
saying nothing I want to understand.

SYLVIA PLATH (1932 – 1963)

Blackberrying

Nobody in the lane, and nothing, nothing but blackberries,
Blackberries on either side, though on the right mainly,
A blackberry alley, going down in hooks, and a sea
Somewhere at the end of it, heaving. Blackberries
Big as the ball of my thumb, and dumb as eyes
Ebon in the hedges, fat
With blue-red juices. These they squander on my fingers.
I had not asked for such a blood sisterhood; they must love me.
They accommodate themselves to my milkbottle, flattening their
    sides.

Overhead go the choughs in black, cacophonous flocks —
Bits of burnt paper wheeling in a blown sky.
Theirs is the only voice, protesting, protesting.
I do not think the sea will appear at all.
The high, green meadows are glowing, as if lit from within.
I come to one bush of berries so ripe it is a bush of flies,
Hanging their bluegreen bellies and their wing panes in a Chinese
    screen.
The honey-feast of the berries has stunned them; they believe in
    heaven.
One more hook, and the berries and bushes end.

The only thing to come now is the sea.
From between two hills a sudden wind funnels at me,
Slapping its phantom laundry in my face.
These hills are too green and sweet to have tasted salt.
I follow the sheep path between them. A last hook brings me
To the hills' northern face, and the face is orange rock
That looks out on nothing, nothing but a great space
Of white and pewter lights, and a din like silversmiths
Beating and beating at an intractable metal.

Edge

The woman is perfected.
Her dead

Body wears the smile of accomplishment,
The illusion of a Greek necessity

Flows in the scrolls of her toga,
Her bare

Feet seem to be saying:
We have come so far, it is over.

Each dead child coiled, a white serpent,
One at each little

Pitcher of milk, now empty.
She has folded

Them back into her body as petals
Of a rose close when the garden

Stiffens and odors bleed
From the sweet, deep throats of the night flower.

The moon has nothing to be sad about,
Staring from her hood of bone.

She is used to this sort of thing.
Her blacks crackle and drag.

Lady Lazarus[1]

I have done it again.
One year in every ten
I manage it —
A sort of walking miracle, my skin
Bright as a Nazi lampshade,[2]   5
My right foot

A paperweight,
My face a featureless, fine
Jew linen.

Peel off the napkin[3]   10
O my enemy.
Do I terrify? —

The nose, the eye pits, the full set of teeth?
The sour breath
Will vanish in a day.   15

---

[1]Lazarus was raised from the dead by Jesus.

[2]The Nazis, in concentration camps, made lampshades of human skin.

[3]According to legend, the veil or napkin with which Veronica wiped Jesus' face, as he bore the Cross, was then impressed with his features.

Soon, soon the flesh
The grave cave ate will be
At home on me

And I a smiling woman.
I am only thirty.   20
And like the cat I have nine times to die. *Comedy*

This is Number Three.
What a trash
To annihilate each decade.

What a million filaments.   25
The peanut-crunching crowd
Shoves in to see

Them unwrap me hand and foot —
The big strip tease.
Gentleman, ladies,   30

These are my hands,
My knees.
I may be skin and bone,

Nevertheless, I am the same, identical woman.
The first time it happened I was ten.   35
It was an accident.

The second time I meant
To last it out and not come back at all.
I rocked shut

As a seashell.   40
They had to call and call
And pick the worms off me like sticky pearls.

Dying
Is an art, like everything else.
I do it exceptionally well.   45

I do it so it feels like hell.
I do it so it feels real.
I guess you could say I've a call.

It's easy enough to do it in a cell.
It's easy enough to do it and stay put.   50
It's the theatrical

Comeback in broad day
To the same place, the same face, the same brute
Amused shout:

"A miracle!"   55
That knocks me out.
There is a charge

For the eyeing of my scars, there is a charge
For the hearing of my heart —
It really goes.   60

And there is a charge, very large charge,
For a word or a touch
Or a bit of blood

Or a piece of my hair or my clothes.
So, so, Herr Doktor.   65
So, Herr Enemy.

I am your opus,
I am your valuable,
The pure gold baby

That melts to a shriek.   70
I turn and burn.
Do not think I underestimate your great concern.

Ash, ash —
You poke and stir.
Flesh, bone, there is nothing there —   75

A cake of soap,
A wedding ring,
A gold filling.[4]

Herr God, Herr Lucifer,
Beware   80
Beware.

Out of the ash
I rise with my red hair
And I eat men like air.

---

[4]Items left in the crematoria of the Nazi concentration camps after the bodies of prisoners had been burned. (The rendered fat of the bodies was used to make soap.)

Morning Song

Love set you going like a fat gold watch.
The midwife slapped your footsoles, and your bald cry
Took its place among the elements.

Our voices echo, magnifying your arrival. New statue.
In a drafty museum, your nakedness
Shadows our safety. We stand round blankly as walls.

I'm no more your mother
Than the cloud that distills a mirror to reflect its own slow
Effacement at the wind's hand.

All night your moth-breath
Flickers among the flat pink roses. I wake to listen:
A far sea moves in my ear.

One cry, and I stumble from bed, cow-heavy and floral
In my Victorian nightgown.
Your mouth opens clean as a cat's. The window square

Whitens and swallows its dull stars. And now you try
Your handful of notes;
The clear vowels rise like balloons.

EDGAR ALLAN POE (1809 – 1849)

Annabel Lee

It was many and many a year ago,
     In a kingdom by the sea,
That a maiden there lived whom you may know
     By the name of Annabel Lee;
And this maiden she lived with no other thought
     Than to love and be loved by me.

She was a child and *I* was a child,
     In this kingdom by the sea,
But we loved with a love that was more than love —
     I and my Annabel Lee —
With a love that the wingèd seraphs of Heaven
     Coveted her and me.

And this was the reason that, long ago,
     In this kingdom by the sea,
A wind blew out of a cloud by night
     Chilling my Annabel Lee;

So that her highborn kinsmen came
    And bore her away from me,
To shut her up in a sepulchre
    In this kingdom by the sea.

The angels, not half so happy in Heaven,
    Went envying her and me:
Yes! that was the reason (as all men know,
    In this kingdom by the sea)
That the wind came out of the cloud, chilling
    And killing my Annabel Lee.

But our love it was stronger by far than the love
    Of those who were older than we —
    Of many far wiser than we —
And neither the angels in Heaven above
    Nor the demons down under the sea,
Can ever dissever my soul from the soul
    Of the beautiful Annabel Lee:

For the moon never beams without bringing me dreams
    Of the beautiful Annabel Lee;
And the stars never rise but I see the bright eyes
    Of the beautiful Annabel Lee;
And so, all the night-tide, I lie down by the side
Of my darling, my darling, my life and my bride,
    In her sepulchre there by the sea —
    In her tomb by the side of the sea.

To Helen

Helen, thy beauty is to me
    Like those Nicean barks of yore,
That gently, o'er a perfumed sea,
    The weary, way-worn wanderer bore
    To his own native shore.

On desperate seas long wont to roam,
    Thy hyacinth hair, thy classic face,
Thy Naiad airs have brought me home
    To the glory that was Greece
And the grandeur that was Rome.

Lo! in yon brilliant window-niche
    How statue-like I see thee stand!
    The agate lamp within thy hand,

Ah! Psyche,[1] from the regions which
    Are Holy Land!

ALEXANDER POPE (1688 – 1744)

From *An Essay on Man* (Epistle I)

Heav'n from all creatures hides the book of Fate,
All but the page prescrib'd, their present state:
From brutes what men, from men what spirits know:
Or who could suffer Being here below?
The lamb thy riot dooms to bleed to-day,
Had he thy Reason, would he skip and play?
Pleas'd to the last, he crops the flow'ry food,
And licks the hand just rais'd to shed his blood.
Oh blindness to the future! kindly giv'n,
That each may fill the circle mark'd by Heav'n;
Who sees with equal eye, as God of all,
A hero perish, or a sparrow fall,
Atoms or systems into ruin hurl'd,
And now a bubble burst, and now a world.
                    (lines 77–90)

What would this Man? Now upward will he soar,
And little less than Angel, would be more;
Now looking downwards, just as griev'd appears
To want the strength of bulls, the fur of bears.
Made for his use all creatures if he call,
Say what their use, had he the pow'rs of all?
Nature to these, without profusion, kind,
The proper organs, proper pow'rs assign'd;
Each seeming want compénsated of course,
Here with degrees of swiftness, there of force;
All in exact proportion to the state;
Nothing to add, and nothing to abate.
Each beast, each insect, happy in its own;
Is Heav'n unkind to Man, and Man alone?
Shall he alone, whom rational we call,

---

[1]Psyche was married to Cupid, who came to her only at night; she was forbidden to look at him. When she stole a glimpse of him sleeping, he awoke and disappeared. She asked Venus to help her find him. Venus, required, among other things, that Psyche bring back, unopened, a box from the underworld.

Be pleas'd with nothing, if not bless'd with all?
     The bliss of Man (could Pride that blessing find)
Is not to think or act beyond mankind;
No pow'rs of body or of soul to share,
But what his nature and his state can bear.
Why has not Man a microscopic eye?
For this plain reason, Man is not a Fly.
Say what the use, were finer optics giv'n,
T' inspect a mite, not comprehend the heav'n?
Or touch, if tremblingly alive all o'er,
To smart and agonize at ev'ry pore?
Or quick effluvia darting thro' the brain,
Die of a rose in aromatic pain?

                                        (lines 173–200)

     Far as Creation's ample range extends,
The scale of sensual, mental pow'rs ascends:
Mark how it mounts, to Man's imperial race,
From the green myriads in the peopled grass:
What modes of sight betwixt each wide extreme,
The mole's dim curtain, and the lynx's beam:
Of smell, the headlong lioness between,
And hound sagacious on the tainted green:
Of hearing, from the life that fills the flood,
To that which warbles thro' the vernal wood:
The spider's touch, how exquisitely fine!
Feels at each thread, and lives along the line:
In the nice° bee, what sense so subtly true   *exact*
From pois'nous herbs extracts the healing dew:
How Instinct varies in the grov'ling swine,
Compar'd, half-reas'ning elephant, with thine:
'Twixt that, and Reason, what a nice barrier,
For ever sep'rate, yet for ever near!
Remembrance and Reflection how ally'd;
What thin partitions Sense from Thought divide:
And Middle natures, how they long to join,
Yet never pass th' insuperable line!
Without this just gradation, could they be
Subjected these to those, or all to thee?
The pow'rs of all subdu'd by thee alone,
Is not thy Reason all these pow'rs in one?

                                        (lines 207–232)

ERZA POUND (1885 – 1972)
In a Station of the Metro

The apparition of these faces in the crowd;
Petals on a wet, black bough.

SIR WALTER RALEGH (c. 1554 – 1618)
The Lie

Go, soul, the body's guest,
Upon a thankless errand;
Fear not to touch the best;
The truth shall be thy warrant.
Go, since I needs must die,   5
And give the world the lie.

Say to the court, it glows
And shines like rotten wood;
Say to the church, it shows
What's good, and doth no good.   10
If church and court reply,
Then give them both the lie.

Tell potentates, they live
Acting by others' action;
Not loved unless they give,   15
Not strong but by a faction.
If potentates reply,
Give potentates the lie.

Tell men of high condition,
That manage the estate,   20
Their purpose is ambition,
Their practice only hate.
And if they once reply,
Then give them all the lie.

Tell them that brave it most,   25
They beg for more by spending,
Who, in their greatest cost,
Seek nothing but commending.
And if they make reply,
Then give them all the lie.   30

Tell zeal it wants° devotion;   *lacks*
Tell love it is but lust;
Tell time it is but motion;
Tell flesh it is but dust.
And wish them not reply,   35
For thou must give the lie.

Tell age it daily wasteth;
Tell honor how it alters;
Tell beauty how she blasteth;
Tell favor how it falters.   40
And as they shall reply,
Give every one the lie.

Tell wit how much it wrangles
In tickle° points of niceness;   *fine*
Tell wisdom she entangles   45
Herself in overwiseness.
And when they do reply,
Straight give them both the lie.

Tell physic of her boldness;
Tell skill it is pretension;   50
Tell charity of coldness;
Tell law it is contention.
And as they do reply,
So give them still the lie.

Tell fortune of her blindness;   55
Tell nature of decay;
Tell friendship of unkindness;
Tell justice of delay.
And if they will reply,
Then give them all the lie.   60

Tell arts they have no soundness,
But vary by esteeming;
Tell schools they want profoundness,
And stand too much on seeming.
If arts and schools reply,   65
Give arts and schools the lie.

Tell faith it's fled the city;
Tell how the country erreth;

Tell manhood shakes off pity;
Tell virtue least preferreth.   70
And if they do reply,
Spare not to give the lie.

So when thou hast, as I
Commanded thee, done blabbing —
Although to give the lie   75
Deserves no less than stabbing —
Stab at thee he that will,
No stab the soul can kill.

John Crowe Ransom (1888 – 1974)
Bells for John Whiteside's Daughter

There was such speed in her little body,
And such lightness in her footfall,
It is no wonder her brown study
Astonishes us all.

Her wars were bruited° in our high window.   *loudly voiced*
We looked among orchard trees and beyond
Where she took arms against her shadow,
Or harried unto the pond

The lazy geese, like a snow cloud
Dripping their snow on the green grass,
Tricking and stopping, sleepy and proud,
Who cried in goose, Alas,

For the tireless heart within the little
Lady with rod that made them rise
From their noon apple-dreams and scuttle
Goose-fashion under the skies!

But now go the bells, and we are ready,
In one house we are sternly stopped
To say we are vexed at her brown study,
Lying so primly propped.

ADRIENNE RICH (b. 1929)
Diving into the Wreck

First having read the book of myths,
and loaded the camera,
and checked the edge of the knife-blade,
I put on
the body-armor of black rubber   5
the absurd flippers
the grave and awkward mask.
I am having to do this
not like Cousteau[1] with his
assiduous team   10
aboard the sun-flooded schooner
but here alone.

There is a ladder.
The ladder is always there
hanging innocently   15
close to the side of the schooner.
We know what it is for,
we who have used it.
Otherwise
it's a piece of maritime floss   20
some sundry equipment.

I go down.
Rung after rung and still
the oxygen immerses me
the blue light   25
the clear atoms
of our human air.
I go down.
My flippers cripple me,
I crawl like an insect down the ladder   30
and there is no one
to tell me when the ocean
will begin.

First the air is blue and then
it is bluer and then green and then   35

---

[1]Jacques Cousteau (1910–1997), French underwater explorer, inventor of the aqualung, author, and filmmaker.

black I am blacking out and yet
my mask is powerful
it pumps my blood with power
the sea is another story
the sea is not a question of power   40
I have to learn alone
to turn my body without force
in the deep element.

And now: it is easy to forget
what I came for   45
among so many who have always
lived here
swaying their crenellated fans
between the reefs
and besides   50
you breathe differently down here.

I came to explore the wreck.
The words are purposes.
The words are maps.
I came to see the damage that was done   55
and the treasures that prevail.
I stroke the beam of my lamp
slowly along the flank
of something more permanent
than fish or weed   60

the thing I came for:
the wreck and not the story of the wreck
the thing itself and not the myth
the drowned face always staring
toward the sun   65
the evidence of damage
worn by salt and sway into this threadbare beauty
the ribs of the disaster
curving their assertion
among the tentative haunters.   70

This is the place.
And I am here, the mermaid whose dark hair
streams black, the merman in his armored body
We circle silently

about the wreck   75
we dive into the hold.
I am she: I am he

whose drowned face sleeps with open eyes
whose breasts still bear the stress
whose silver, copper, vermeil cargo lies   80
obscurely inside barrels
half-wedged and left to rot
we are the half-destroyed instruments
that once held to a course
the water-eaten log   85
the fouled compass

We are, I am, you are
by cowardice or courage
the one who find our way
back to this scene   90
carrying a knife, a camera
a book of myths
in which
our names do not appear.

The Middle-Aged

Their faces, safe as an interior
Of Holland tiles and Oriental carpet,
Where the fruit-bowl, always filled, stood in a light
Of placid afternoon — their voices' measure,
Their figures moving in the Sunday garden
To lay the tea outdoors or trim the borders,
Afflicted, haunted us. For to be young
Was always to live in other peoples' houses
Whose peace, if we sought it, had been made by others,
Was ours at second-hand and not for long.
The custom of the house, not ours, the sun
Fading the silver-blue Fortuny[1] curtains,
The reminiscence of a Christmas party
Of fourteen years ago — all memory,
Signs of possession and of being possessed,

---

[1]Manufacturers of expensive cloth.

We tasted, tense with envy. They were so kind,
Would have given us anything; the bowl of fruit
Was filled for us, there was a room upstairs
We must call ours: but twenty years of living
They could not give. Nor did they ever speak
Of the coarse stain on that polished balustrade,
The crack in the study window, or the letters
Locked in a drawer and the key destroyed.
All to be understood by us, returning
Late, in our own time — how that peace was made,
Upon what terms, with how much left unsaid.

Snapshots of a Daughter-in-Law

1

You, once a belle in Shreveport,
with henna-colored hair, skin like a peachbud,
still have your dresses copied from that time,
and play a Chopin[1] prelude
called by Cortot:[2] *"Delicious recollections
float like perfume through the memory."*[3]

Your mind now, moldering like wedding-cake,
heavy with useless experience, rich
with suspicion, rumor, fantasy,
crumbling to pieces under the knife-edge
of mere fact. In the prime of your life.

Nervy, glowering, your daughter
wipes the teaspoons, grows another way.

2

Banging the coffee-pot into the sink
she hears the angels chiding, and looks out
past the raked gardens to the sloppy sky.
Only a week since They said: *Have no patience.*
The next time it was: *Be insatiable.*
Then: *Save yourself; others you cannot save.*

---

[1]Frederick François Chopin (1810–1849), Polish composer and pianist who settled in Paris in 1831.

[2]Alfred Cortot (1877–1962), French pianist.

[3]Cortot's notation on one of Chopin's preludes.

Sometimes she's let the tapstream scald her arm,
a match burn to her thumbnail,

or held her hand above the kettle's snout
right in the woolly steam. They are probably angels,
since nothing hurts her anymore, except
each morning's grit blowing into her eyes.

3

A thinking woman sleeps with monsters.
The beak that grips her, she becomes. And Nature,
that sprung-lidded, still commodious
steamer-trunk of *tempora* and *mores*[4]
gets stuffed with it all: the mildewed orange-flowers,
the female pills, the terrible breasts
of Boadicea[5] beneath flat foxes' heads and orchids.

Two handsome women, gripped in argument,
each proud, acute, subtle, I hear scream
across the cut glass and majolica
like Furies cornered from their prey:
The argument *ad feminam,* all the old knives
that have rusted in my back, I drive in yours,
ma semblable, ma soeur![6]

4

Knowing themselves too well in one another:
their gifts no pure fruition, but a thorn,
the prick filed sharp against a hint of scorn . . .
Reading while waiting
for the iron to heat,
writing, *My Life had stood — a Loaded Gun —* [7]
in that Amherst pantry while the jellies boil and scum,
or, more often,
iron-eyed and beaked and purposed as a bird,
dusting everything on the whatnot every day of life.

---

[4]A reference to Cicero's phrase "O Tempora! O Mores!" ("Alas for the degeneracy of the times and the low standard of our morals!")

[5]British queen in the time of the Roman emperor Nero. She led an unsuccessful revolt against Roman rule.

[6]The last line of the poem "Au Lecteur" by Charles Baudelaire reads, "Hypocrite lecteur! — mon semblable, — mon frère!" ("Hypocrite reader, my double, my brother!") Rich alters the line to read, "my sister."

[7]A poem by Emily Dickinson, reproduced earlier in this anthology.

5

Dulce ridens, dulce loquens,[8]
she shaves her legs until they gleam
like petrified mammoth-tusk.

6

When to her lute Corinna sings[9]
neither words nor music are her own;
only the long hair dipping
over her cheek, only the song
of silk against her knees
and these
adjusted in reflections of an eye.

Poised, trembling and unsatisfied, before
an unlocked door, that cage of cages,
tell us, you bird, you tragical machine —
is this *fertilisante douleur?*[10] Pinned down
by love, for you the only natural action,
are you edged more keen
to prise the secrets of the vault? has Nature shown
her household books to you, daughter-in-law,
that her sons never saw?

7

"To have in this uncertain world some stay
which cannot be undermined, is
of the utmost consequence."[11]
Thus wrote
a woman, partly brave and partly good,
who fought with what she partly understood.
Few men about her would or could do more,
hence she was labeled harpy, shrew and whore.

8

"You all die at fifteen," said Diderot,[12]
and turn part legend, part convention.

---

[8]Latin for "sweetly laughing, sweetly speaking." The line is adapted from Horace's Ode 22.

[9]First line of a poem by Thomas Campion (1567–1620).

[10]French for "fertilizing sorrow," "life-giving sorrow."

[11]From Mary Wollstonecraft, *Thoughts on the Education of Daughters* (1787).

[12]Denis Diderot (1713–1784) was a French philosopher.

Still, eyes inaccurately dream
behind closed windows blankening with steam.
Deliciously, all that we might have been,
all that we were — fire, tears,
wit, taste, martyred ambition —
stirs like the memory of refused adultery
the drained and flagging bosom of our middle years.

9

Not that it is done well, but
that it is done at all?[13] Yes, think
of the odds! or shrug them off forever.
This luxury of the precocious child,
Time's precious chronic invalid, —
would we, darlings, resign it if we could?
Our blight has been our sinecure:
mere talent was enough for us —
glitter in fragments and rough drafts.

Sigh no more, ladies.
                Time is male
and in his cups drinks to the fair.
Bemused by gallantry, we hear
our mediocrities over-praised,
indolence read as abnegation,
slattern thought styled intuition,
every lapse forgiven, our crime
only to cast too bold a shadow
or smash the mold straight off.

For that, solitary confinement,
tear gas, attrition shelling.
Few applicants for that honor.

10

                    Well,
she's long about her coming, who must be
more merciless to herself than history.

---

[13]An allusion to Samuel Johnson's remark to Boswell, "Sir, a woman's preaching is like a dog's walking on his hinder legs. It is not done well; but you are surprised to find it done at all."

Her mind full to the wind, I see her plunge
breasted and glancing through the currents,
taking the light upon her
at least as beautiful as any boy
or helicopter,
                    poised, still coming,
her fine blades making the air wince

but her cargo
no promise then:
delivered
palpable
ours.

ALBERTO RÍOS (b. 1952)
Mi Abuelo[1]

Where my grandfather is is in the ground
where you can hear the future
like an Indian with his ear at the tracks.
A pipe leads down to him so that sometimes
he whispers what will happen to a man
in town or how he will meet the best
dressed woman tomorrow and how the best
man at her wedding will chew the ground
next to her. Mi abuelo is the man
who speaks through all the mouths in my house.
An echo of me hitting the pipe sometimes
to stop him from saying *my hair is a*
sieve is the only other sound. It is a phrase
that among all others is the best,
he says, and *my hair is a sieve* is sometimes
repeated for hours out of the ground
when I let him, which is not often.
An abuelo should be much more than a man
like you! He stops then, and speaks: *I am a man*
who has served ants with the attitude
of a waiter, who has made each smile as only
an ant who is fat can, and they liked me best,

---

[1]Spanish: "my grandfather."

but there is nothing left. Yet I know he ground
green coffee beans as a child, and sometimes
he will talk about his wife, and sometimes
about when he was deaf and a man
cured him by mail and he heard groundhogs
talking, or about how he walked with a cane
he chewed on when he got hungry.
At best, mi abuelo is a liar.
I see an old picture of him at nani's with an
off-white yellow center mustache and sometimes
that's all I know for sure. He talks best
about these hills, *slowest waves,* and where this man
is going, and I'm convinced his hair is a sieve,
that his fever is cooled now underground.
Mi abuelo is an ordinary man.
I look down the pipe, sometimes, and see a
ripple-topped stream in its best suit, in the ground.

Teodoro Luna's Two Kisses

Mr. Teodoro Luna in his later years had taken to kissing
His wife
Not so much with his lips as with his brows.
This is not to say he put his forehead
Against her mouth —
Rather, he would lift his eyebrows, once, quickly:
Not so vigorously he might be confused with the villain
Famous in the theaters, but not so little as to be thought
A slight movement, one of accident. This way
He kissed her
Often and quietly, across tables and through doorways,
Sometimes in photographs, and so through the years themselves.
This was his passion, that only she might see. The chance
He might feel some movement on her lips
Toward laughter.

EDWIN ARLINGTON ROBINSON (1869 – 1935)
Richard Cory

Whenever Richard Cory went down town,
We people on the pavement looked at him:

He was a gentleman from sole to crown,
Clean favored, and imperially slim.

And he was always quietly arrayed,
And he was always human when he talked;
But still he fluttered pulses when he said,
"Good-morning," and he glittered when he walked.

And he was rich — yes, richer than a king —
And admirably schooled in every grace:
In fine, we thought that he was everything
To make us wish that we were in his place.

So on we worked, and waited for the light,
And went without the meat, and cursed the bread;
And Richard Cory, one calm summer night,
Went home and put a bullet through his head.

THEODORE ROETHKE (1908 – 1963)

Elegy for Jane

My Student, Thrown by a Horse

I remember the neckcurls, limp and damp as tendrils;
And her quick look, a sidelong pickerel smile;
And how, once startled into talk, the light syllables leaped for her,
And she balanced in the delight of her thought,
A wren, happy, tail into the wind,
Her song trembling the twigs and small branches.
The shade sang with her;
The leaves, their whispers turned to kissing;
And the mold sang in the bleached valleys under the rose.

Oh, when she was sad, she cast herself down into such a pure
        depth,
Even a father could not find her:
Scraping her cheek against straw;
Stirring the clearest water.

My sparrow, you are not here,
Waiting like a fern, making a spiny shadow.
The sides of wet stones cannot console me,
Nor the moss, wound with the last light.

If only I could nudge you from this sleep,
My maimed darling, my skittery pigeon.
Over this damp grave I speak the words of my love:
I, with no rights in this matter,
Neither father nor lover.

The Waking

I wake to sleep, and take my waking slow.
I feel my fate in what I cannot fear.
I learn by going where I have to go.

We think by feeling. What is there to know?
I hear my being dance from ear to ear.
I wake to sleep, and take my waking slow.

Of those so close beside me, which are you?
God bless the Ground! I shall walk softly there,
And learn by going where I have to go.

Light takes the Tree; but who can tell us how?
The lowly worm climbs up a winding stair;
I wake to sleep, and take my waking slow.

Great Nature has another thing to do
To you and me; so take the lively air,
And, lovely, learn by going where to go.

This shaking keeps me steady. I should know.
What falls away is always. And is near.
I wake to sleep, and take my waking slow.
I learn by going where I have to go.

ANNE SEXTON (1928 – 1974)
Snow White and the Seven Dwarfs

No matter what life you lead
the virgin is a lovely number:
cheeks as fragile as cigarette paper,
arms and legs made of Limoges,[1]

---

[1]Fine porcelain made in Limoges, France.

lips like Vin Du Rhone,[2]   5
rolling her china-blue doll eyes
open and shut.
Open to say,
Good Day Mama,
and shut for the thrust   10
of the unicorn.
She is unsoiled.
She is as white as a bonefish.

Once there was a lovely virgin
called Snow White.   15
Say she was thirteen.
Her stepmother,
a beauty in her own right,
though eaten, of course, by age,
would hear of no beauty surpassing her own.   20
Beauty is a simple passion,
but, oh my friends, in the end
you will dance the fire dance in iron shoes.
The stepmother had a mirror to which she referred —
something like the weather forecast —   25
a mirror that proclaimed
the one beauty of the land.
She would ask,
Looking glass upon the wall,
who is fairest of us all?   30
And the mirror would reply,
You are fairest of us all.
Pride pumped in her like poison.

Suddenly one day the mirror replied,
Queen, you are full fair, 'tis true,   35
but Snow White is fairer than you.
Until that moment Snow White
had been no more important
than a dust mouse under the bed.
But now the queen saw brown spots on her hand   40
and four whiskers over her lip
so she condemned Snow White
to be hacked to death.

---

[2]Rhone wine (French).

Bring me her heart, she said to the hunter,
and I will salt it and eat it. 45
The hunter, however, let his prisoner go
and brought a boar's heart back to the castle.
The queen chewed it up like a cube steak.
Now I am fairest, she said,
lapping her slim white fingers. 50

Snow White walked in the wildwood
for weeks and weeks.
At each turn there were twenty doorways
and at each stood a hungry wolf,
his tongue lolling out like a worm. 55
The birds called out lewdly,
talking like pink parrots,
and the snakes hung down in loops,
each a noose for her sweet white neck.
On the seventh week 60
she came to the seventh mountain
and there she found the dwarf house.
It was as droll as a honeymoon cottage
and completely equipped with
seven beds, seven chairs, seven forks 65
and seven chamber pots.
Snow White ate seven chicken livers
and lay down, at last, to sleep.

The dwarfs, those little hot dogs,
walked three times around Snow White, 70
the sleeping virgin. They were wise
and wattled like small czars.
Yes. It's a good omen,
they said, and will bring us luck.
They stood on tiptoes to watch 75
Snow White wake up. She told them
about the mirror and the killer-queen
and they asked her to stay and keep house.
Beware of your stepmother,
they said. 80
Soon she will know you are here.
While we are away in the mines
during the day, you must not
open the door.

Looking glass upon the wall . . .   85
The mirror told
and so the queen dressed herself in rags
and went out like a peddler to trap Snow White.
She went across seven mountains.
She came to the dwarf house   90
and Snow White opened the door
and bought a bit of lacing.
The queen fastened it tightly
around her bodice,
as tight as an Ace bandage,   95
so tight that Snow White swooned.
She lay on the floor, a plucked daisy.
When the dwarfs came home they undid the lace
and she revived miraculously.
She was as full of life as soda pop.   100
Beware of your stepmother,
they said.
She will try once more.

Looking glass upon the wall . . .
Once more the mirror told   105
and once more the queen dressed in rags
and once more Snow White opened the door.
This time she bought a poison comb,
a curved eight-inch scorpion,
and put it in her hair and swooned again.   110
The dwarfs returned and took out the comb
and she revived miraculously.
She opened her eyes as wide as Orphan Annie.
Beware, beware, they said,
but the mirror told,   115
the queen came,
Snow White, the dumb bunny,
opened the door
and she bit into a poison apple
and fell down for the final time.   120
When the dwarfs returned
they undid her bodice,
they looked for a comb,
but it did no good.

Though they washed her with wine   125
and rubbed her with butter
it was to no avail.
She lay as still as a gold piece.

The seven dwarfs could not bring themselves
to bury her in the black ground   130
so they made a glass coffin
and set it upon the seventh mountain
so that all who passed by
could peek in upon her beauty.
A prince came one June day   135
and would not budge.
He stayed so long his hair turned green
and still he would not leave.
The dwarfs took pity upon him
and gave him the glass Snow White —   140
its doll's eyes shut forever —
to keep in his far-off castle.
As the prince's men carried the coffin
they stumbled and dropped it
and the chunk of apple flew out   145
of her throat and she woke up miraculously.

And thus Snow White became the prince's bride.
The wicked queen was invited to the wedding feast
and when she arrived there were
red-hot iron shoes,   150
in the manner of red-hot roller skates,
clamped upon her feet.
First your toes will smoke
and then your heels will turn black
and you will fry upward like a frog,   155
she was told.
And so she danced until she was dead,
a subterranean figure,
her tongue flicking in and out
like a gas jet.   160
Meanwhile Snow White held court,
rolling her china-blue doll eyes open and shut
and sometimes referring to her mirror
as women do.

WILLIAM SHAKESPEARE (1564 – 1616)
Fear No More the Heat o' the Sun[1]

Fear no more the heat o' the sun,
    Nor the furious winter's rages;
Thou thy worldly task hast done,
    Home art gone, and ta'en thy wages:
Golden lads and girls all must,
As chimney-sweepers, come to dust.

Fear no more the frown o' the great;
    Thou art past the tyrant's stroke;
Care no more to clothe and eat;
    To thee the reed is as the oak:
The scepter, learning, physic, must
All follow this, and come to dust.

Fear no more the lightning flash,
    Nor the all-dreaded thunder stone;
Fear not slander, censure rash;
    Thou hast finished joy and moan:
All lovers young, all lovers must
Consign to thee, and come to dust.

No exorciser harm thee!
Nor no witchcraft charm thee!
Ghost unlaid forbear thee!
Nothing ill come near thee!
Quiet consummation have;
And renownèd be thy grave!

Full Fathom Five[1]

Full fathom five thy father lies;
    Of his bones are coral made;
Those are pearls that were his eyes:
    Nothing of him that doth fade,
But doth suffer a sea change
Into something rich and strange.
Sea nymphs hourly ring his knell:
    Ding-dong.
Hark! now I hear them — Ding-dong, bell.

[1]From *Cymbeline.*
[1]From *The Tempest.*

Sonnet 18

Shall I compare thee to a summer's day?
Thou art more lovely and more temperate:
Rough winds do shake the darling buds of May,
And summer's lease hath all too short a date:
Sometimes too hot the eye of heaven shines,
And often is his gold complexion dimmed;
And every fair from fair sometimes declines,
By chance or nature's changing course
        untrimmed;°   *divested of beauty*
But thy eternal summer shall not fade,
Nor lose possession of that fair thou ow'st;°   *ownest*
Nor shall death brag thou wander'st in his shade,
When in eternal lines to time thou grow'st:
So long as men can breathe, or eyes can see,
So long lives this, and this gives life to thee.

Sonnet 116

Let me not to the marriage of true minds
Admit impediments. Love is not love
Which alters when it alteration finds,
Or bends with the remover to remove:
Oh, no! it is an ever-fixèd mark,
That looks on tempests and is never shaken;
It is the star to every wandering bark,
Whose worth's unknown, although his height be taken.
Love's not Time's fool, though rosy lips and cheeks
Within his bending sickle's compass come;
Love alters not with his brief hours and weeks,
But bears it out even to the edge of doom.
If this be error and upon me proved,
I never writ, nor no man ever loved.

PERCY BYSSHE SHELLEY (1792 – 1822)
England in 1819

An old, mad, blind, despised, and dying king[1] —
Princes, the dregs of their dull race, who flow

---

[1]George III was eighty-one and hopelessly insane in 1819.

Through public scorn — mud from a muddy spring;
Rulers who neither see, nor feel, nor know,
But leechlike to their fainting country cling,
Till they drop, blind in blood, without a blow;
A people starved and stabbed in the untilled field —
An army, which liberticide and prey
Makes as a two-edged sword to all who wield;
Golden and sanguine laws which tempt and slay;
Religion Christless, Godless — a book sealed;
A Senate — Time's worst statute[2] unrepealed —
Are graves, from which a glorious Phantom[3] may
Burst, to illumine our tempestuous day.

Ode to the West Wind

1

O wild West Wind, thou breath of Autumn's being,
Thou, from whose unseen presence the leaves dead
Are driven, like ghosts from an enchanter fleeing,

Yellow, and black, and pale, and hectic red,
Pestilence-stricken multitudes: O thou,
Who chariotest to their dark wintry bed

The wingèd seeds, where they lie cold and low,
Each like a corpse within its grave, until
Thine azure sister of the Spring shall blow

Her clarion o'er the dreaming earth, and fill
(Driving sweet buds like flocks to feed in air)
With living hues and odors plain and hill:

Wild Spirit, which art moving everywhere;
Destroyer and preserver; hear, oh, hear!

2

Thou on whose stream, mid the steep sky's commotion,
Loose clouds like earth's decaying leaves are shed,
Shook from the tangled boughs of Heaven and Ocean,

---

[2]The laws excluding Catholics from office.
[3]The spirit of political liberty.

Angels of rain and lightning: there are spread
On the blue surface of thine aëry surge,
Like the bright hair uplifted from the head

Of some fierce Maenad,[1] even from the dim verge
Of the horizon to the zenith's height,
The locks of the approaching storm. Thou dirge

Of the dying year, to which this closing night
Will be the dome of a vast sepulcher,
Vaulted with all thy congregated might

Of vapors, from whose solid atmosphere
Black rain, and fire, and hail will burst: oh, hear!

3

Thou who didst waken from his summer dreams
The blue Mediterranean, where he lay,
Lulled by the coil of his crystálline streams,

Beside a pumice isle in Baiae's bay,[2]
And saw in sleep old palaces and towers
Quivering within the wave's intenser day,

All overgrown with azure moss and flowers
So sweet, the sense faints picturing them! Thou
For whose path the Atlantic's level powers

Cleave themselves into chasms, while far below
The sea-blooms and the oozy woods which wear
The sapless foliage of the ocean, know

Thy voice, and suddenly grow gray with fear,
And tremble and despoil themselves: oh, hear!

4

If I were a dead leaf thou mightest bear;
If I were a swift cloud to fly with thee;
A wave to pant beneath thy power, and share

The impulse of thy strength, only less free
Than thou, O uncontrollable! If even
I were as in my boyhood, and could be

---

[1]Women inspired with ecstatic frenzy by the Greek god Dionysus.
[2]Near Naples, Italy.

The comrade of thy wanderings over Heaven,
As then, when to outstrip thy skyey speed
Scarce seemed a vision; I would ne'er have striven

As thus with thee in prayer in my sore need.
Oh, lift me as a wave, a leaf, a cloud!
I fall upon the thorns of life! I bleed!

A heavy weight of hours has chained and bowed
One too like thee: tameless, and swift, and proud.

5

Make me thy lyre, even as the forest is:
What if my leaves are falling like its own!
The tumult of thy mighty harmonies

Will take from both a deep, autumnal tone,
Sweet though in sadness. Be thou, Spirit fierce,
My spirit! Be thou me, impetuous one!

Drive my dead thoughts over the universe
Like withered leaves to quicken a new birth!
And, by the incantation of this verse,

Scatter, as from an unextinguished hearth
Ashes and sparks, my words among mankind!
Be through my lips to unawakened earth

The trumpet of a prophecy! O Wind,
If Winter comes, can Spring be far behind?

Ozymandias[1]

I met a traveler from an antique land
Who said: Two vast and trunkless legs of stone
Stand in the desert . . . Near them, on the sand,
Half sunk, a shattered visage lies, whose frown,
And wrinkled lip, and sneer of cold command,
Tell that its sculptor well those passions read
Which yet survive, stamped on these lifeless things,
The hand that mocked them, and the heart that fed:
And on the pedestal these words appear:
"My name is Ozymandias, king of kings:
Look on my works, ye Mighty, and despair!"

---

[1]Greek name for the Egyptian monarch Ramses II (1304–1237 B.C.).

Nothing beside remains. Round the decay
Of that colossal wreck, boundless and bare
The lone and level sands stretch far away.

SIR PHILIP SIDNEY (1554 – 1586)
From *Astrophel and Stella*

1

Loving in truth, and fain in verse my love to show,
That she, dear she, might take some pleasure of my pain,
Pleasure might cause her read, reading might make her know,
Knowledge might pity win, and pity grace obtain,
I sought fit words to paint the blackest face of woe:
Studying inventions fine, her wits to entertain,
Oft turning others' leaves, to see if thence would flow
Some fresh and fruitful showers upon my sunburned brain.
But words came halting forth, wanting Invention's stay;
Invention, Nature's child, fled stepdame Study's blows;
And others' feet still seemed but strangers in my way.
Thus, great with child to speak, and helpless in my throes,
Biting my truant° pen, beating myself for spite: *idle*
"Fool," said my Muse to me, "look in thy heart, and write."

31

With how sad steps, Oh Moon, thou climb'st the skies,
How silently, and with how wan a face!
What, may it be that even in heav'nly place
That busy archer° his sharp arrows tries?   *Cupid*
Sure, if that long-with-love-acquainted eyes
Can judge of love, thou feel'st a lover's case;
I read it in thy looks: thy languished grace,
To me that feel the like, thy state descries.
Then even of fellowship, Oh Moon, tell me,
Is constant love deemed there but want of wit?
Are beauties there as proud as here they be?
Do they above love to be loved, and yet
Those lovers scorn whom that love doth possess?
Do they call virtue there ungratefulness?

LESLIE MARMON SILKO (b. 1948)

Prayer to the Pacific

I traveled to the ocean
         distant
                from my southwest land of sandrock
                to the moving blue water
          Big as the myth of origin.
Pale
pale water in the yellow-white light of
                sun   floating west
                    to China
            where ocean herself was born.
Clouds that blow across the sand are wet.

Squat in the wet sand and speak to the Ocean:
      I return to you   turquoise   the red coral you sent us,
              sister spirit of Earth.
Four round stones in my pocket   I carry back the ocean
            to suck and to taste.

Thirty thousand years ago
                Indians came riding across the ocean
           carried by giant sea turtles.
Waves were high that day
      great sea turtles waded   slowly out
                from the gray sundown sea.
Grandfather Turtle rolled in the sand   four times
           and disappeared
                swimming into the sun.

And so   from that time
       immmemorial,
              as the old people say,
rain clouds drift from the west
         gift from the ocean.

Green leaves in the wind
Wet earth on my feet
      swallowing raindrops
        clear from China.

CHARLES SIMIC (b. 1938)
Charon's° Cosmology

ferryman of the dead

With only his feeble lantern
To tell him where he is
And every time a mountain
Of fresh corpses to load up

Take them to the other side
Where there are plenty more
I'd say by now he must be confused
As to which side is which

I'd say it doesn't matter
No one complains he's got
Their pockets to go through
In one a crust of bread in another a sausage

Once in a long while a mirror
Or a book which he throws
Overboard into the dark river
Swift cold and deep

Fork

This strange thing must have crept
Right out of hell.
It resembles a bird's foot
Worn around the cannibal's neck.

As you hold it in your hand,
As you stab with it into a piece of meat,
It is possible to imagine the rest of the bird:
Its head which like your fist
Is large, bald, beakless and blind.

CHRISTOPHER SMART (1722 – 1771)
From *Jubilate Agno*[1]

For I will consider my Cat Jeoffry.
For he is the servant of the Living God, duly and daily serving
    him.

---

[1]"Jubilate Agno" was written during Smart's incarceration in a private madhouse from 1758 to 1763. The manuscript remained unknown to the public until 1939.

For at the first glance of the glory of God in the East he worships
    in his way.
For is this done by wreathing his body seven times round with
    elegant quickness.
For then he leaps up to catch the musk, which is the blessing of   5
    God upon his prayer.
For he rolls upon prank to work it in.
For having done duty and received blessing he begins to consider
    himself.
For this he performs in ten degrees.
For first he looks upon his fore-paws to see if they are clean.
For secondly he kicks up behind to clear away there.   10
For thirdly he works it upon stretch with the fore paws extended.
For fourthly he sharpens his paws by wood.
For fifthly he washes himself.
For sixthly he rolls upon wash.
For Seventhly he fleas himself, that he may not be interrupted   15
    upon the beat.
For Eighthly he rubs himself against a post.
For Ninthly he looks up for his instructions.
For Tenthly he goes in quest of food.
For having consider'd God and himself he will consider his neigh-
    bour.
For if he meets another cat he will kiss her in kindness.   20
For when he takes his prey he plays with it to give it chance.
For one mouse in seven escapes by his dallying.
For when his day's work is done his business more properly begins.
For he keeps the Lord's watch in the night against the adversary.
For he counteracts the powers of darkness by his electrical skin   25
    & glaring eyes.
For he counteracts the Devil, who is death, by brisking about the
    life.
For in his morning orisons he loves the sun and the sun loves him.
For he is of the tribe of Tiger.
For the Cherub Cat is a term of the Angel Tiger.
For he has the subtlety and hissing of a serpent, which in goodness
    he suppresses.   30
For he will not do destruction, if he is well-fed, neither will he spit
    without provocation.
For he purrs in thankfulness, when God tells him he's a good Cat.
For he is an instrument for the children to learn benevolence
    upon.

For every house is incompleat without him & a blessing is lacking
    in the spirit.

For the Lord commanded Moses concerning the cats at the de-   35
    parture of the Children of Israel from Egypt.[2]

For every family had one cat at least in the bag.

For the English Cats are the best in Europe.

For he is the cleanest in the use of his fore-paws of any quadrupede.

For the dexterity of his defence is an instance of the love of God
    to him exceedingly.

For he is the quickest to his mark of any creature.   40

For he is tenacious of his point.

For he is a mixture of gravity and waggery.

For he knows that God is his Saviour.

For there is nothing sweeter than his peace when at rest.

For there is nothing brisker than his life when in motion.   45

For he is of the Lord's poor and so indeed is he called by benev-
    olence perpetually — Poor Jeoffry! poor Jeoffry! the rat has
    bit thy throat.

For I bless the name of the Lord Jesus that Jeoffry is better.

For the divine spirit comes about his body to sustain it in compleat
    cat.

For his tongue is exceeding pure so that it has in purity what it
    wants in musick.

For he is docile and can learn certain things.   50

For he can set up with gravity which is patience upon approbation.

For he can fetch and carry, which is patience in employment.

For he can jump over a stick which is patience upon proof positive.

For he can spraggle upon waggle at the word of command.

For he can jump from an eminence into his master's bosom.   55

For he can catch the cork and toss it again.

For he is hated by the hypocrite and miser.

For the former is afraid of detection.

For the latter refuses the charge.

For he camels his back to bear the first notion of business.   60

For he is good to think on, if a man would express himself neatly.

For he made a great figure in Egypt for his signal services.

For he killed the Icneumon-rat[3] very pernicious by land.

For his ears are so acute that they sting again.

---

[2]No cats are mentioned in the Bible.

[3]The Ichneumon, which resembles a weasel, was domesticated (and highly val-
ued) by the ancient Egyptians.

For from this proceeds the passing quickness of his attention.   65
For by stroaking of him I have found out electricity.
For I perceived God's light about him both wax and fire.
For the Electrical fire is the spiritual substance, which God sends
  from heaven to sustain the bodies both of man and beast.
For God has blessed him in the variety of his movements.
For, tho he cannot fly, he is an excellent clamberer.   70
For his motions upon the face of the earth are more than any other
  quadrupede.
For he can tread to all the measures upon the musick.
For he can swim for life.
For he can creep.

On a Bed of Guernsey Lilies

Written in September 1763
Ye beauties! O how great the sum
  Of sweetness that ye bring;
On what a charity ye come
  To bless the latter spring!
How kind the visit that ye pay,
Like strangers on a rainy day,
  When heartiness despair'd of guests:
No neighbour's praise your pride alarms,
No rival flow'r surveys your charms,
  Or heightens, or contests!

Lo, thro' her works gay nature grieves
  How brief she is and frail,
As ever o'er the falling leaves
  Autumnal winds prevail.
Yet still the philosophic mind
Consolatory food can find,
  And hope her anchorage maintain:
We never are deserted quite;
'Tis by succession of delight
  That love supports his reign.

DAVE SMITH (b. 1942)
On a Field Trip at Fredericksburg[1]

The big steel tourist shield says maybe
fifteen thousand got it here. No word
of either Whitman[2] or one uncle
I barely remember in the smoke
that filled his tiny mountain house.

If each finger were a thousand of them
I could clap my hands and be dead
up to my wrists. It was quick
though not so fast as we can do it
now, one bomb, atomic or worse,
one silly pod slung on wing-tip,
high up, an egg cradled
by some rapacious mockingbird.

Hiroshima[3] canned nine times their number
in a flash. Few had the time
to moan or feel the feeling
ooze back in the groin.

In a ditch I stand
above Marye's Heights, the book-
boned faces of Brady's[4] fifteen-year-old
drummers, before battle, rigid
as August's dandelions
all the way to the Potomac
rolling in my skull.

If Audubon[5] came here, the names
of birds would gush, the marvel
single feathers make
evoke a cloud, a nation,
a gray blur preserved
on a blue horizon, but

---

[1]Site in Virginia of a Civil War battle (December 13, 1862), a Union defeat.

[2]Although Walt Whitman (1819–1892) wrote about the Civil War, his poems do not mention the Battle of Fredericksburg.

[3]City in Japan where the first atomic bomb was dropped.

[4]Matthew Brady (ca. 1823–1896), Civil War photographer.

[5]John James Audubon (1785–1851), Haitian-born American ornithologist and painter of birds.

there is only a wandering child,
one dark stalk snapped off
in her hand, held out to me.
Taking it, I try to help her
hold its obscure syllables
one instant in her mouth,
like a drift of wind
at the forehead, the front door,
the black, numb fingernails.

STEVIE SMITH (1902 – 1971)
Not Waving but Drowning

Nobody heard him, the dead man,
But still he lay moaning:
I was much further out than you thought
And not waving but drowning.

Poor chap, he always loved larking
And now he's dead
It must have been too cold for him his heart gave way,
They said.

Oh, no no no, it was too cold always
(Still the dead one lay moaning)
I was much too far out all my life
And not waving but drowning.

Pretty

Why is the word pretty so underrated?
In November the leaf is pretty when it falls
The stream grows deep in the woods after rain
And in the pretty pool the pike stalks

He stalks his prey, and this is pretty too,
The prey escapes with an underwater flash
But not for long, the great fish has him now
The pike is a fish who always has his prey

And this is pretty. The water rat is pretty
His paws are not webbed, he cannot shut his nostrils
As the otter can and the beaver, he is torn between
The land and water. Not "torn," he does not mind.

The owl hunts in the evening and it is pretty
The lake water below him rustles with ice
There is frost coming from the ground, in the air mist
All this is pretty, it could not be prettier.

GARY SNYDER (b. 1930)
Axe Handles

One afternoon the last week in April
Showing Kai how to throw a hatchet
One-half turn and it sticks in a stump.
He recalls the hatchet-head
Without a handle, in the shop
And go gets it, and wants it for his own.
A broken-off axe handle behind the door
Is long enough for a hatchet,
We cut it to length and take it
With the hatchet head
And working hatchet, to the wood block.
There I begin to shape the old handle
With the hatchet, and the phrase
First learned from Ezra Pound
Rings in my ears!
"When making an axe handle
        the pattern is not far off."
And I say this to Kai
"Look: We'll shape the handle
By checking the handle
Of the axe we cut with — "
And he sees. And I hear it again:
It's in Lu Ji's *Wên Fu,* fourth century
A.D. "Essay on Literature" — in the
Preface: "In making the handle
Of an axe
By cutting wood with an axe
The model is indeed near at hand."
My teacher Shih-hsiang Chen
Translated that and taught it years ago
And I see: Pound was an axe,
Chen was an axe, I am an axe

And my son a handle, soon
To be shaping again, model
And tool, craft of culture,
How we go on.

How Poetry Comes to Me

It comes blundering over the
Boulders at night, it stays
Frightened outside the
Range of my campfire
I go to meet it at the
Edge of the light

Riprap[1]

Lay down these words
Before your mind like rocks.
                placed solid, by hands
In choice of place, set
Before the body of the mind
                in space and time:
Solidity of bark, leaf, or wall
                riprap of things:
Cobble of milky way,
                straying planets,
These poems, people,
                lost ponies with
Dragging saddles
                and rocky sure-foot trails.
The world's like an endless
                four-dimensional
Game of *Go.*
                ants and pebbles
In the thin loam, each rock a word
                a creek-washed stone
Granite: ingrained
                with torment of fire and weight
Crystal and sediment linked hot
                all change, in thoughts,
As well as things.

---

[1]Snyder's note: "Riprap: a cobble of stone laid on steep slick rock to make a trail for horses in the mountains."

EDMUND SPENSER (c. 1552 – 1599)
Epithalamion

Ye learnèd sisters° which have oftentimes   *the muses*
Beene to me ayding, others to adorne:
Whom ye thought worthy of your gracefull rymes,
That even the greatest did not greatly scorne
To heare theyr names sung in your simple layes,   5
But joyèd in theyr prayse.
And when ye list your owne mishaps to mourne,
Which death, or love, or fortunes wreck did rayse,
Your string could soone to sadder tenor turne,
And teach the woods and waters to lament   10
Your dolefull dreriment.
Now lay those sorrowfull complaints aside,
And having all your heads with girland crownd,
Helpe me mine owne loves prayses to resound,
Ne let the same of any be envíde: 15
So Orpheus did for his owne bride,
So I unto my selfe alone will sing,
The woods shall to me answer and my Eccho ring.

Early before the worlds light giving lampe,
His golden beame upon the hils doth spred,   20
Having disperst the nights unchearefull dampe,
Doe ye awake, and with fresh lustyhed
Go to the bowre of my belovèd love,
My truest turtle dove,
Bid her awake; for Hymen° is awake,   *god of marriage* 25
And long since ready forth his maske to move,
With his bright Tead° that flames with many a flake,   *torch*
And many a bachelor to waite on him,
In theyr fresh garments trim.
Bid her awake therefore and soone her dight,°   *dress* 30
For lo the wishèd day is come at last,
That shall for al the paynes and sorrowes past,
Pay to her usury of long delight:
And whylest she doth her dight,
Doe ye to her of joy and solace sing,   35
That all the woods may answer and your eccho ring.

Bring with you all the Nymphes that you
    can heare°   *that can hear you*
Both of the rivers and the forrests greene:

And of the sea that neighbours to her neare,
Al with gay girlands goodly wel beseene.   40
And let them also with them bring in hand,
Another gay girland
For my fayre love of lillyes and of roses,
Bound truelove wize with a blew silke riband.
And let them make great store of bridale poses,   45
And let them eeke° bring store of other flowers   *also*
To deck the bridale bowers.
And let the ground whereas her foot shall tread,
For feare the stones her tender foot should wrong
Be strewed with fragrant flowers all along,   50
And diapred lyke the
        discolored mead.°   *patterned like the multicolored meadow*
Which done, doe at her chamber dore awayt,
For she will waken strayt,
The whiles doe ye this song unto her sing,
The woods shall to you answer and your Eccho ring.   55

Ye Nymphes of Mulla[1] which with carefull heed,
The silver scaly trouts doe tend full well,
And greedy pikes which use therein to feed,
(Those trouts and pikes all others doo excell)
And ye likewise which keepe the rushy lake,   60
Where none doo fishes take,
Bynd up the locks the which hang scatterd light,
And in his waters which your mirror make,
Behold your faces as the christall bright,
That when you come whereas my love doth lie,   65
No blemish she may spie.
And eke ye lightfoot mayds which keepe the deere,
That on the hoary mountayne use to towre,[2]
And the wylde wolves which seeke them to devoure,
With your steele darts doo chace from comming neer   70
Be also present heere,
To helpe to decke her and to help to sing,
That all the woods may answer and your eccho ring.

Wake, now my love, awake; for it is time,
The Rosy Morne long since left Tithones bed,   75

---

[1]The vale of Mulla, near Spenser's home in Ireland.
[2]To climb high, a term from falconry.

All ready to her silver coche to clyme,
And Phoebus gins to shew his glorious hed.
Hark how the cheerefull birds do chaunt theyr laies
And carroll of loves praise.
The merry Larke hir mattins sings aloft.   80
The thrush replyes, the Mavis
       descant° playes,   *melodic counterpoint*
The Ouzell shrills, the Ruddock warbles soft,
So goodly all agree with sweet consent,
To this dayes merriment.
Ah my deere love why doe ye sleepe thus long,   85
When meeter° were that ye should now awake, *fitter*
T' awayt the comming of your joyous make,°   *mate*
And hearken to the birds lovelearnèd song,
The deawy leaves among.
For they of joy and pleasance to you sing,   90
That all the woods them answer and theyr eccho ring.

My love is now awake out of her dreame,
And her fayre eyes like stars that dimmèd were
With darksome cloud, now shew theyr goodly beams
More bright then Hesperus° his head doth rere. *evening star* 95
Come now ye damzels, daughters of delight,
Helpe quickly her to dight,°   *adorn*
But first come ye fayre houres which were begot
In Joves sweet paradice, of Day and Night,
Which doe the seasons of the yeare allot,   100
And al that ever in this world is fayre
Doe make and still repayre.
And ye three handmayds of the Cyprian Queene,° *Venus*
The which doe still adorne her beauties pride,
Helpe to addorne my beautifullest bride: 105
And as ye her array, still throw betweene°   *now and then*
Some graces to be seene,
And as ye use to Venus, to her sing,
The whiles the woods shal answer and your eccho ring.

Now is my love all ready forth to come,   110
Let all the virgins therefore well awayt,
And ye fresh boyes that tend upon her groome
Prepare your selves; for he is comming strayt.
Set all your things in seemely good aray
Fit for so joyfull day,   115

The joyfulst day that ever sunne did see.
Faire Sun, shew forth thy favourable ray,
And let thy lifull heat not fervent be
For feare of burning her sunshyny face,
Her beauty to disgrace.   120
O fayrest Phoebus, father of the Muse,
If ever I did honour thee aright,
Or sing the thing, that mote thy mind delight,
Doe not thy servants simple boone° refuse,   *request*
But let this day let this one day be myne,   125
Let all the rest be thine.
Then I thy soverayne prayses loud wil sing,
That all the woods shal answer and theyr eccho ring.

Harke how the Minstrels gin to shrill aloud
Their merry Musick that resounds from far   130
The pipe, the tabor,° and the trembling Croud,°   *drum / viol*
That well agree withouten breach or jar
But most of all the Damzels doe delite,
When they their tymbrels° smyte,   *tambourines*
And thereunto doe daunce and carrol sweet,
That all the sences they doe ravish quite,   135
The whyles the boyes run up and downe the street,
Crying aloud with strong confusèd noyce,
As if it were one voyce.
Hymen iô Hymen, Hymen they do shout,   140
That even to the heavens theyr shouting shrill
Doth reach, and all the firmament doth fill,
To which the people standing all about,
As in approvance doe thereto applaud
And loud advaunce her laud,°   *praise*   145
And evermore they *Hymen Hymen* sing,
That al the woods them answer and theyr eccho ring.

Loe where she comes along with portly° pace   *majestic*
Lyke Phoebe° from her chamber of the East,   *moon goddess*
Arysing forth to run her mighty race,   150
Clad all in white, that seemes° a virgin best.   *suits*
So well it her beseemes that ye would weene
Some angell she had beene.
Her long loose yellow locks lyke golden wyre,
Sprinckled with perle, and perling flowres a tweene,   155
Doe lyke a golden mantle her attyre,

And being crownèd with a girland greene,
Seeme lyke some mayden Queene.
Her modest eyes abashèd to behold
So many gazers, as on her do stare,   160
Upon the lowly ground affixèd are.
Ne dare lift up her countenance too bold,
But blush to heare her prayses sung so loud,
So farre from being proud.
Nathlesse doe ye still loud her prayses sing.   165
That all the woods may answer and your eccho ring.

Tell me ye merchants daughters did ye see
So fayre a creature in your towne before,
So sweet, so lovely, and so mild as she,
Adornd with beautyes grace and vertues store,   170
Her goodly eyes lyke Saphyres shining bright,
Her forehead yvory white,
Her cheekes lyke apples which the sun hath rudded,
Her lips lyke cherryes charming men to byte,
Her brest like to a bowle of creame uncrudded,° *uncurdled*   175
Her paps° lyke lyllies budded,   *breasts*
Her snowie necke lyke to a marble towre,
And all her body lyke a pallace fayre,
Ascending uppe with many a stately stayre,
To honors seat and chastities sweet bowre.   180
Why stand ye still ye virgins in amaze,
Upon her so to gaze,
Whiles ye forget your former lay to sing,
To which the woods did answer and your eccho ring.

But if ye saw that which no eyes can see,   185
The inward beauty of her lively spright,
Garnisht with heavenly guifts of high degree,
Much more then would ye wonder at that sight,
And stand astonisht lyke to those which red°   *saw*
Medusaes mazeful hed.   190
There dwels sweet love and constant chastity,
Unspotted fayth and comely womanhood,
Regard of honour and mild modesty,
There vertue raynes as Queene in royal throne,
And giveth lawes alone.   195
The which the base affections doe obay,
And yeeld theyr services unto her will,

Ne thought of thing uncomely ever may
Thereto approach to tempt her mind to ill.
Had ye once seene these her celestial threasures,   200
And unrevealèd pleasures,
Then would ye wonder and her prayses sing,
That al the woods should answer and your eccho ring.

Open the temple gates unto my love,
Open them wide that she may enter in,   205
And all the postes adorne as doth behove,°   *as is proper*
And all the pillours deck with girlands trim,
For to recyve this Saynt with honour dew,
That commeth in to you.
With trembling steps and humble reverence,   210
She commeth in, before th' almighties vew,
Of her ye virgins learne obedience,
When so ye come into those holy places,
To humble your proud faces:
Bring her up to th' high altar, that she may   215
The sacred ceremonies there partake,
The which do endlesse matrimony make,
And let the roring Organs loudly play
The praises of the Lord in lively notes,
The whiles with hollow throates   220
The Choristers the joyous Antheme sing,
That al the woods may answere and their eccho ring.

Behold whiles she before the altar stands
Hearing the holy priest that to her speakes
And blesseth her with his two happy hands,   225
How the red roses flush up in her cheekes,
And the pure snow with goodly vermill stayne,
Like crimsin dyde in grayne,°   *fast color*
That even th' Angels which continually,
About the sacred Altare doe remaine,   230
Forget their service and about her fly,
Ofte peeping in her face that seemes more fayre,
The more they on it stare.
But her sad° eyes still fastened on the ground,   *serious*
Are governèd with goodly modesty,   235
That suffers not one looke to glaunce awry,
Which may let in a little thought unsownd.
Why blush ye love to give to me your hand,

The pledge of all our band?°   *bond*
Sing ye sweet Angels, Alleluya sing,   240
That all the woods may answere and your eccho ring.

Now al is done; bring home the bride againe,
Bring home the triumph of our victory,
Bring home with you the glory
  of her gaine,°   *the glory of gaining her*
With joyance bring her and with jollity.   245
Never had man more joyfull day then this,
Whom heaven would heape with blis.
Make feast therefore now all this live long day,
This day for ever to me holy is,
Poure out the wine without restraint or stay, 250
Poure not by cups, but by the belly full,
Poure out to all that wull
And sprinkle all the postes and wals with wine,
That they may sweat, and drunken be withall.
Crowne ye God Bacchus with a coronall,   255
And Hymen also crowne with wreathes of vine,
And let the Graces daunce unto the rest;
For they can doo it best:
The whiles the maydens doe theyr carroll sing,
To which the woods shal answer and theyr eccho ring. 260

Ring ye the bels, ye yong men of the towne,
And leave your wonted labors for this day:
This day is holy; doe ye write it downe,
That ye for ever it remember may.
This day the sunne is in his chiefest hight, 265
With Barnaby the bright,[3]
From whence declining daily by degrees,
He somewhat loseth of his heat and light,
When once the Crab behind his back he sees.
But for this time it ill ordainèd was,   270
To chose the longest day in all the yeare,
And shortest night, when longest fitter weare:
Yet never day so long, but late° would passe. *at last*
Ring ye the bels, to make it weare away,
And bonefiers make all day,   275

---

[3]Saint Barnabas's Day was the day of the summer solstice in Spenser's time.

And daunce about them, and about them sing:
That all the woods may answer, and your eccho ring.

Ah when will this long weary day have end,
And lende me leave to come unto my love?
How slowly do the houres theyr numbers spend?   280
How slowly does sad Time his feathers move?
Hast thee O fayrest Planet° to thy home   *the sun*
Within the Westerne fome:
Thy tyred steedes long since have need of rest.
Long though it be, at last I see it gloome,   285
And the bright evening star with golden creast
Appeare out of the East.
Fayre childe of beauty, glorious lampe of love
That all the host of heaven in rankes doost lead,
And guydest lovers through the nightès dread,   290
How chearefully thou lookest from above,
And seemst to laugh atweene thy twinkling light
As joying in the sight
Of these glad many which for joy doe sing,
That all the woods them answer and their eccho ring.   295

Now ceasse ye damsels your delights forepast;
Enough is it, that all the day was youres:
Now day is doen, and night is nighing fast:
Now bring the Bryde into the brydall boures.
Now night is come, now soone her disaray,   300
And in her bed her lay;
Lay her in lillies and in violets,
And silken courteins over her display,
And odourd sheetes, and Arras° coverlets.   *tapestry*
Behold how goodly my faire love does ly   305
In proud humility;
Like unto Maia,[4] when as Jove her tooke,
In Tempe, lying on the flowry gras,
Twixt sleepe and wake, after she weary was,
With bathing in the Acidalian brooke.   310
Now it is night, ye damsels may be gon,
And leave my love alone,
And leave likewise your former lay to sing:
The woods no more shal answere, nor your eccho ring.

[4]The eldest and most beautiful of the Pleiades.

Now welcome night, thou night so long expected,   315
That long daies labour doest at last defray,°   *pay*
And all my cares, which cruell love collected,
Hast sumd in one, and cancellèd for aye:
Spread thy broad wing over my love and me,
That no man may us see,   320
And in thy sable mantle us enwrap,
From feare of perrill and foule horror free.
Let no false treason seeke us to entrap,
Nor any dread disquiet once annoy
The safety of our joy: 325
But let the night be calme and quietsome,
Without tempestuous storms or sad afray:
Lyke as when Jove with fayre Alcmena° lay,   *mother of Hercules*
When he begot the great Tirynthian groome:
Or lyke as when he with thy selfe did lie,   330
And begot Majesty.
And let the mayds and yongmen cease to sing:
Ne let the woods them answer, nor theyr eccho ring.

Let no lamenting cryes, nor dolefull teares,
Be heard all night within nor yet without: 335
Ne let false whispers, breeding hidden feares,
Breake gentle sleepe with misconceivèd dout.
Let no deluding dreames, nor dreadful sights
Make sudden sad affrights;
Ne let housefyres, nor lightnings helpelesse harmes,   340
Ne let the Pouke,[5] nor other evill sprights,
Ne let mischívous witches with theyr charmes,
Ne let hob Goblins, names whose sence we see not,
Fray us with things that be not.
Let not the shriech Oule, nor the Storke be heard: 345
Nor the night Raven that still° deadly yels,   *continually*
Nor damnèd ghosts cald up with mighty spels,
Nor griesly vultures make us once affeard:
Ne let th' unpleasant Quyre of Frogs still croking
Make us to wish theyr choking.   350
Let none of these theyr drery accents sing;
Ne let the woods them answer, nor theyr eccho ring.

---

[5]The same Puck as in Shakespeare's *A Midsummer Night's Dream*. This Puck, however, is an "evil spright."

But let stil Silence trew night watches keepe,
That sacred peace may in assurance rayne,
And tymely sleep, when it is tyme to sleepe,   355
May poure his limbs forth on your pleasant playne,
The whiles an hundred little wingèd loves,
Like divers fethered doves,
Shall fly and flutter round about your bed,
And in the secret darke, that none reproves,   360
Their prety stealthes shal worke, and snares shal spread
To filch away sweet snatches of delight,
Conceald through covert night.
Ye sonnes of Venus, play your sports at will,
For greedy pleasure, carelesse of your toyes,°   *amorous dallying*   365
Thinks more upon her paradise of joyes,
Then what ye do, albe it good or ill.
All night therefore attend your merry play,
For it will soone be day:
Now none doth hinder you, that say or sing,   370
Ne will the woods now answer, nor your Eccho ring.

Who is the same, which at my window peepes?
Or whose is that faire face, that shines so bright,
Is it not Cinthia,° she that never sleepes,   *moon goddess*
But walkes about high heaven al the night?   375
O fayrest goddesse, do thou not envy
My love with me to spy:
For thou likewise didst love, though now
     unthought,°   *unsuspected*
And for a fleece of woll, which privily,
The Latmian shephard⁶ once unto thee brought,   380
His pleasures with thee wrought.
Therefore to us be favorable now;
And sith of wemens labours thou hast charge,
And generation goodly dost enlarge,
Encline thy will t' effect our wishfull vow,   385
And the chast wombe informe with timely seed,
That may our comfort breed:
Till which we cease our hopefull hap to sing,
Ne let the woods us answere, nor our Eccho ring.

---

⁶Endymion, with whom Cynthia/Diana fell in love.

And thou great Juno, which with awful might 390
The lawes of wedlock still dost patronize,
And the religion° of the faith first plight *sanctity*
With sacred rites hast taught to solemnize:
And eeke for comfort often callèd art
Of women in their smart,° *labor* 395
Eternally bind thou this lovely band,
And all thy blessings unto us impart.
And thou glad Genius, in whose gentle hand,
The bridale bowre and geniall bed remaine,
Without blemish or staine, 400
And the sweet pleasures of theyr loves delight
With secret ayde doest succour and supply,
Till they bring forth the fruitfull progeny,
Send us the timely fruit of this same night.
And thou fayre Hebe,° and thou Hymen free, *goddess of youth* 405
Grant that it may so be.
Til which we cease your further prayse to sing,
Ne any woods shal answer, nor your Eccho ring.

And ye high heavens, the temple of the gods,
In which a thousand torches flaming bright 410
Doe burne, that to us wretched earthly clods,
In dreadful darknesse lend desiréd light;
And all ye powers which in the same remayne,
More then we men can fayne,° *imagine*
Poure out your blessing on us plentiously, 415
And happy influence upon us raine,
That we may raise a large posterity,
Which from the earth, which they may long possesse,
With lasting happinesse,
Up to your haughty pallaces may mount, 420
And for the guerdon° of theyr glorious merit *reward*
May heavenly tabernacles there inherit,
Of blessed Saints for to increase the count.
So let us rest, sweet love, in hope of this,
And cease till then our tymely joyes to sing, 425
The woods no more us answer, nor our eccho ring.

Song made in lieu of many ornaments,
With which my love should duly have bene dect,
Which cutting off through hasty accidents,

Ye would not stay your dew time to expect,   430
But promist both to recompens,
Be unto her a goodly ornament,
And for short time an endlesse moniment.

Sonnet 75

From "Amoretti"

One day I wrote her name upon the strand,
But came the waves and washèd it away:
Agayne I wrote it with a second hand,
But came the tyde, and made my paynes his pray.
"Vayne man," sayd she, "that doest in vaine assay,
A mortall thing so to immortalize,
For I my selve shall lyke to this decay,
And eek° my name bee wypèd out lykewize."   *also*
"Not so," quod I, "let baser things devize°   *contrive*
To dy in dust, but you shall live by fame:
My verse your vertues rare shall eternize,
And in the hevens wryte your glorious name.
Where whenas death shall all the world subdew,
Our love shall live, and later life renew."

WALLACE STEVENS (1879 – 1955)
The Idea of Order at Key West

She sang beyond the genius of the sea.
The water never formed to mind or voice,
Like a body wholly body, fluttering
Its empty sleeves; and yet its mimic motion
Made constant cry, caused constantly a cry,   5
That was not ours although we understood,
Inhuman, of the veritable ocean.

The sea was not a mask. No more was she.
The song and water were not medleyed sound
Even if what she sang was what she heard,   10
Since what she sang was uttered word by word.
It may be that in all her phrases stirred
The grinding water and the gasping wind;
But it was she and not the sea we heard.
For she was the maker of the song she sang.   15

The ever-hooded, tragic-gestured sea
Was merely a place by which she walked to sing.
Whose spirit is this? we said, because we knew
It was the spirit that we sought and knew
That we should ask this often as she sang.   20

If it was only the dark voice of the sea
That rose, or even colored by many waves;
If it was only the outer voice of sky
And cloud, of the sunken coral water-walled,
However clear, it would have been deep air,   25
The heaving speech of air, a summer sound
Repeated in a summer without end
And sound alone. But it was more than that,
More even than her voice, and ours, among
The meaningless plungings of water and the wind,   30
Theatrical distances, bronze shadows heaped
On high horizons, mountainous atmospheres
Of sky and sea.
                    It was her voice that made
The sky acutest at its vanishing.   35
She measured to the hour its solitude.
She was the single artificer of the world
In which she sang. And when she sang, the sea,
Whatever self it had, became the self
That was her song, for she was the maker. Then we,   40
As we beheld her striding there alone,
Knew that there never was a world for her
Except the one she sang and, singing, made.

Ramon Fernandez,[1] tell me, if you know,
Why, when the singing ended and we turned   45
Toward the town, tell why the glassy lights,
The lights in the fishing boats at anchor there,
As the night descended, tilting in the air,
Mastered the night and portioned out the sea,
Fixing emblazoned zones and fiery poles,   50
Arranging, deepening, enchanting night.

Oh! Blessed rage for order, pale Ramon,
The maker's rage to order words of the sea,

---

[1]No particular person is intended.

Words of the fragrant portals, dimly-starred,
And of ourselves and of our origins,   55
In ghostlier demarcations, keener sounds.

The Planet on the Table[1]

Ariel[2] was glad he had written his poems.
They were of a remembered time
Or of something seen that he liked.

Other makings of the sun
Were waste and welter
And the ripe shrub writhed.

His self and the sun were one
And his poems, although makings of his self,
Were no less makings of the sun.

It was not important that they survive.
What mattered was that they should bear
Some lineament or character,

Some affluence, if only half-perceived,
In the poverty of their words,
Of the planet of which they were part.

The Snow Man

One must have a mind of winter
To regard the frost and the boughs
Of the pine-trees crusted with snow;

And have been cold a long time
To behold the junipers shagged with ice,
The spruces rough in the distant glitter

Of the January sun; and not to think
Of any misery in the sound of the wind,
In the sound of a few leaves,

Which is the sound of the land
Full of the same wind
That is blowing in the same bare place

[1]The "planet" is an image for Stevens's *Collected Poems* (1954).
[2]Ariel, the tree spirit in Shakespeare's play, *The Tempest,* here represents the poet.

For the listener, who listens in the snow,
And, nothing himself, beholds
Nothing that is not there and the nothing that is.

Sunday Morning

1

Complacencies of the peignoir, and late
Coffee and oranges in a sunny chair,[1]
And the green freedom of a cockatoo
Upon a rug mingle to dissipate
The holy hush of ancient sacrifice.[2]
She dreams a little, and she feels the dark
Encroachment of that old catastrophe,
As a calm darkens among water–lights.
The pungent oranges and bright, green wings
Seem things in some procession of the dead,
Winding across wide water, without sound.
The day is like wide water, without sound,
Stilled for the passing of her dreaming feet
Over the seas, to silent Palestine,
Dominion of the blood and sepulchre.[3]

2

Why should she give her bounty to the dead?
What is divinity if it can come
Only in silent shadows and in dreams?
Shall she not find in comforts of the sun,
In pungent fruit and bright, green wings, or else
In any balm or beauty of the earth,
Things to be cherished like the thought of heaven?
Divinity must live within herself:
Passions of rain, or moods in falling snow;
Grievings in loneliness, or unsubdued
Elations when the forest blooms; gusty
Emotions on wet roads on autumn nights;
All pleasures and all pains, remembering

---

[1]The woman in the poem does not attend a Sunday church service; instead, she remains in her peignoir and has breakfast.

[2]The death of Jesus.

[3]The passion and entombment of Jesus.

The bough of summer and the winter branch.
These are the measures destined for her soul.

3

Jove in the clouds had his inhuman birth.
No mother suckled him, no sweet land gave
Large-mannered motions to his mythy mind.
He moved among us, as a muttering king,
Magnificent, would move among his hinds,°   *shepherds*
Until our blood, commingling, virginal,
With heaven, brought such requital to desire
The very hinds discerned it, in a star.
Shall our blood fail? Or shall it come to be
The blood of paradise? And shall the earth
Seem all of paradise that we shall know?
The sky will be much friendlier then than now,
A part of labor and a part of pain,
And next in glory to enduring love,
Not this dividing and indifferent blue.

4

She says, "I am content when wakened birds,
Before they fly, test the reality
Of misty fields, by their sweet questionings;
But when the birds are gone, and their warm fields
Return no more, where, then, is paradise?"
There is not any haunt of prophecy,
Nor any old chimera° of the grave,   *ghost*
Neither the golden underground,[4] nor isle
Melodious,[5] where spirits gat them home,
Nor visionary south, nor cloudy palm[6]
Remote on heaven's hill, that has endured
As April's green endures; or will endure
Like her remembrance of awakened birds,
Or her desire for June and evening, tipped
By the consummation of the swallow's wings.

---

[4]The Elysian fields — in Greek mythology, the heaven of heroes.
[5]Avalon, where King Arthur was taken after his death.
[6]The palm was the reward given to Christian martyrs in heaven.

5

She says, "But in contentment I still feel
The need of some imperishable bliss."
Death is the mother of beauty; hence from her,
Alone, shall come fulfilment to our dreams
And our desires. Although she strews the leaves
Of sure obliteration on our paths,
The path sick sorrow took, the many paths
Where triumph rang its brassy phrase, or love
Whispered a little out of tenderness,
She makes the willow shiver in the sun
For maidens who were wont to sit and gaze
Upon the grass, relinquished to their feet.
She causes boys to pile new plums and pears
On disregarded plate.° The maidens taste   *silver dishes*
And stray impassioned in the littering leaves.

6

Is there no change of death in paradise?
Does ripe fruit never fall? Or do the boughs
Hang always heavy in that perfect sky,
Unchanging, yet so like our perishing earth,
With rivers like our own that seek for seas
They never find, the same receding shores
That never touch with inarticulate pang?
Why set the pear upon those river-banks
Or spice the shores with odors of the plum?
Alas, that they should wear our colors there,
The silken weavings of our afternoons,
And pick the strings of our insipid lutes!
Death is the mother of beauty, mystical,
Within whose burning bosom we devise
Our earthly mothers waiting, sleeplessly.

7

Supple and turbulent, a ring of men
Shall chant in orgy on a summer morn
Their boisterous devotion to the sun,
Not as a god, but as a god might be,
Naked among them, like a savage source.
Their chant shall be a chant of paradise,
Out of their blood, returning to the sky;

And in their chant shall enter, voice by voice,
The windy lake wherein their lord delights,
The trees, like serafin,° and echoing hills,   *angels*
That choir among themselves long afterward.
They shall know well the heavenly fellowship
Of men that perish and of summer morn.
And whence they came and whither they shall go
The dew upon their feet shall manifest.

8

She hears, upon that water without sound,
A voice that cries, "The tomb in Palestine
Is not the porch of spirits lingering.
It is the grave of Jesus, where he lay."
We live in an old chaos of the sun,
Or old dependency of day and night,
Or island solitude, unsponsored, free,
Of that wide water, inescapable.
Deer walk upon our mountains, and the quail
Whistle about us their spontaneous cries;
Sweet berries ripen in the wilderness;
And, in the isolation of the sky,
At evening, casual flocks of pigeons make
Ambiguous undulations as they sink,
Downward to darkness, on extended wings.

Thirteen Ways of Looking at a Blackbird

1

Among twenty snowy mountains,
The only moving thing
Was the eye of the blackbird.

2

I was of three minds,
Like a tree
In which there are three blackbirds.

3

The blackbird whirled in the autumn winds.
It was a small part of the pantomime.

4

A man and a woman
Are one.
A man and a woman and a blackbird
Are one.

5

I do not know which to prefer,
The beauty of inflections
Or the beauty of innuendoes,
The blackbird whistling
Or just after.

6

Icicles filled the long window
With barbaric glass.
The shadow of the blackbird
Crossed it to and fro.
The mood
Traced in the shadow
An indecipherable cause.

7

O thin men of Haddam,°   *town in Connecticut*
Why do you imagine golden birds?
Do you not see how the blackbird
Walks around the feet
Of the women about you?

8

I know noble accents
And lucid, inescapable rhythms;
But I know, too,
That the blackbird is involved
In what I know.

9

When the blackbird flew out of sight,
It marked the edge
Of one of many circles.

10

At the sight of blackbirds
Flying in a green light,
Even the bawds of euphony
Would cry out sharply.

11

He rode over Connecticut
In a glass coach.
Once, a fear pierced him,
In that he mistook
The shadow of his equipage
For blackbirds.

12

The river is moving.
The blackbird must be flying.

13

It was evening all afternoon.
It was snowing
And it was going to snow.
The blackbird sat
In the cedar-limbs.

MARK STRAND (b. 1934)

Keeping Things Whole

In a field
I am the absence
of field.
This is
always the case.
Wherever I am
I am what is missing.

When I walk
I part the air
and always
the air moves in
to fill the spaces
where my body's been.

We all have reasons
for moving.
I move
to keep things whole.

JONATHAN SWIFT (1667 – 1745)
A Description of the Morning

Now hardly here and there a hackney coach
Appearing, showed the ruddy morn's approach.
Now Betty from her master's bed has flown,
And softly stole to discompose her own.
The slipshod prentice from his master's door
Had pared the dirt, and sprinkled round the floor.
Now Moll had whirled her mop with dexterous airs,
Prepared to scrub the entry and the stairs.
The youth with broomy stumps began to trace
The kennel-edge,° where wheels had worn the place.   *gutter*
The smallcoal man was heard with cadence deep;[1]
Till drowned in shriller notes of chimney-sweep.
Duns[2] at his Lordship's gate began to meet;
And Brickdust[3] Moll had screamed through half a street.
The turnkey now his flock returning sees,
Duly let out a-nights to steal for fees.[4]
The watchful bailiffs take their silent stands;
And schoolboys lag with satchels in their hands.

ALFRED, LORD TENNYSON (1809 – 1892)
From *In Memoriam A. H. H.*

7

Dark house, by which once more I stand
   Here in the long unlovely street,
   Doors, where my heart was used to beat
So quickly, waiting for a hand,

---

[1]Coal was hawked in the street.
[2]Bailiffs acting as debt collectors.
[3]Tanned; a tanned complexion was a mark of the working classes.
[4]Prisoners were let out to get money to pay their jailers.

A hand that can be clasped no more —
    Behold me, for I cannot sleep,
    And like a guilty thing I creep
At earliest morning to the door.

He[1] is not here; but far away
    The noise of life begins again,
    And ghastly through the drizzling rain
On the bald street breaks the blank day.

99

Risest thou thus, dim dawn, again,
    So loud with voices of the birds,
    So thick with lowings of the herds,
Day, when I lost the flower of men;

Who tremblest thro' thy darkling red
    On yon swollen brook that bubbles fast
    By meadows breathing of the past,
And woodlands holy to the dead;

Who murmurest in the foliage eaves
    A song that slights the coming care,
    And Autumn laying here and there
A fiery finger on the leaves;

Who wakenest with thy balmy breath
    To myriads on the genial earth,
    Memories of bridal, or of birth,
And unto myriads more, of death.

O, wheresoever those may be,
    Betwixt the slumber of the poles,
    To-day they count as kindred souls;
They know me not, but mourn with me.

106

Ring out, wild bells, to the wild sky,
    The flying cloud, the frosty light:
    The year is dying in the night;
Ring out, wild bells, and let him die.

---

[1]Arthur Henry Hallam (1811–1833), Tennyson's brilliantly promising friend. He died suddenly in Vienna, while on a tour of the Continent with his father.

Ring out the old, ring in the new,
    Ring, happy bells, across the snow:
    The year is going, let him go;
Ring out the false, ring in the true.

Ring out the grief that saps the mind,
    For those that here we see no more;
    Ring out the feud of rich and poor,
Ring in redress to all mankind.

Ring out a slowly dying cause
    And ancient forms of party strife;
    Ring in the nobler modes of life,
With sweeter manners, purer laws.

Ring out the want, the care, the sin,
    The faithless coldness of the times;
    Ring out, ring out my mournful rhymes,
But ring the fuller minstrel in.

Ring out false pride in place and blood,
    The civic slander and the spite;
    Ring in the love of truth and right,
Ring in the common love of good.

Ring out old shapes of foul disease;
    Ring out the narrowing lust of gold;
    Ring out the thousand wars of old,
Ring in the thousand years of peace.

Ring in the valiant man and free,
    The larger heart, the kindlier hand;
    Ring out the darkness of the land,
Ring in the Christ that is to be.

121

Sad Hesper° o'er the buried sun   *the evening star*
    And ready, thou, to die with him,
    Thou watchest all things ever dim
And dimmer, and a glory done.

The team is loosened from the wain,°   *wagon*
    The boat is drawn upon the shore;
    Thou listenest to the closing door,
And life is darkened in the brain.

Bright Phosphor,° fresher for the night,   *the morning star*
    By thee the world's great work is heard
    Beginning, and the wakeful bird;
Behind thee comes the greater light.

The market boat is on the stream,
    And voices hail it from the brink;
    Thou hear'st the village hammer clink,
And see'st the moving of the team.

Sweet Hesper-Phosphor, double name[2]
    For what is one, the first, the last,
    Thou, like my present and my past,
Thy place is changed; thou art the same.

Tears, Idle Tears

From "The Princess"

    Tears, idle tears, I know not what they mean,
Tears from the depth of some divine despair
Rise in the heart, and gather to the eyes,
In looking on the happy autumn-fields,
And thinking of the days that are no more.

    Fresh as the first beam glittering on a sail,
That brings our friends up from the underworld,
Sad as the last which reddens over one
That sinks with all we love below the verge;
So sad, so fresh, the days that are no more.

    Ah, sad and strange as in dark summer dawns
The earliest pipe of half-awakened birds
To dying ears, when unto dying eyes
The casement slowly grows a glimmering square;
So sad, so strange, the days that are no more.

    Dear as remembered kisses after death,
And sweet as those by hopeless fancy feigned
On lips that are for others; deep as love,
Deep as first love, and wild with all regret;
O Death in Life, the days that are no more!

---

[2]The morning star and evening star are both the planet Venus.

Ulysses[1]

It little profits that an idle king,
By this still hearth, among these barren crags,
Matched with an aged wife, I mete and dole
Unequal laws unto a savage race,
That hoard, and sleep, and feed, and know not me.   5
I cannot rest from travel; I will drink
Life to the lees. All times I have enjoyed
Greatly, have suffered greatly, both with those
That loved me, and alone; on shore, and when
Through scudding drifts the rainy Hyades[2]   10
Vext the dim sea. I am become a name;
For always roaming with a hungry heart
Much have I seen and known — cities of men
And manners, climates, councils, governments,
Myself not least, but honored of them all, —   15
And drunk delight of battle with my peers,
Far on the ringing plains of windy Troy.
I am a part of all that I have met;
Yet all experience is an arch wherethrough
Gleams that untraveled world whose margin fades   20
For ever and for ever when I move.
How dull it is to pause, to make an end,
To rust unburnished, not to shine in use!
As though to breathe were life! Life piled on life
Were all too little, and of one to me   25
Little remains; but every hour is saved
From that eternal silence, something more,
A bringer of new things; and vile it were
For some three suns to store and hoard myself,
And this gray spirit yearning in desire   30
To follow knowledge like a sinking star,
Beyond the utmost bound of human thought.
        This is my son, mine own Telemachus,
To whom I leave the scepter and the isle,
Well-loved of me, discerning to fulfill   35

---

[1]This poem derives from Ulysses' description of his last voyage in Dante's *Inferno* (Canto 26).

[2]A cluster of five stars in the constellation Taurus. They were supposed to foretell rain.

This labor, by slow prudence to make mild
A rugged people, and through soft degrees
Subdue them to the useful and the good.
Most blameless is he, centered in the sphere
Of common duties, decent not to fail   40
In offices of tenderness, and pay
Meet adoration to my household gods,
When I am gone. He works his work, I mine.
    There lies the port; the vessel puffs her sail;
There gloom the dark, broad seas. My mariners,   45
Souls that have toiled, and wrought, and thought with me,
That ever with a frolic welcome took
The thunder and the sunshine, and opposed
Free hearts, free foreheads — you and I are old;
Old age hath yet his honor and his toil.   50
Death closes all; but something ere the end,
Some work of noble note, may yet be done,
Not unbecoming men that strove with gods.
The lights begin to twinkle from the rocks;
The long day wanes; the slow moon climbs; the deep   55
Moans round with many voices. Come, my friends,
'Tis not too late to seek a newer world.
Push off, and sitting well in order smite
The sounding furrows; for my purpose holds
To sail beyond the sunset, and the baths   60
Of all the western stars, until I die.
It may be that the gulfs will wash us down;
It may be we shall touch the Happy Isles,[3]
And see the great Achilles, whom we knew.
Though much is taken, much abides; and though   65
We are not now that strength which in old days
Moved earth and heaven, that which we are, we are,
One equal temper of heroic hearts,
Made weak by time and fate, but strong in will
To strive, to seek, to find, and not to yield.   70

---

[3]The abode after death of those favored by the gods.

DYLAN THOMAS (1914 – 1953)
Fern Hill

Now as I was young and easy under the apple boughs
About the lilting house and happy as the grass was green,
    The night above the dingle starry,
       Time let me hail and climb
     Golden in the heydays of his eyes,   5
And honored among wagons I was prince of the apple towns
And once below a time I lordly had the trees and leaves
      Trail with daisies and barley
    Down the rivers of the windfall light.

And as I was green and carefree, famous among the barns   10
About the happy yard and singing as the farm was home,
     In the sun that is young once only,
       Time let me play and be
     Golden in the mercy of his means,
And green and golden I was huntsman and herdsman, the calves 15
Sang to my horn, the foxes on the hills barked clear and cold,
      And the sabbath rang slowly
    In the pebbles of the holy streams.

All the sun long it was running, it was lovely, the hay
Fields high as the house, the tunes from the chimneys, it was air 20
     And playing, lovely and watery
       And fire green as grass.
     And nightly under the simple stars
As I rode to sleep the owls were bearing the farm away,
All the moon long I heard, blessed among stables, the night-jars 25
     Flying with the ricks, and the horses
       Flashing into the dark.

And then to awake, and the farm, like a wanderer white
With the dew, come back, the cock on his shoulder: it was all
     Shining, it was Adam and maiden,   30
       The sky gathered again
     And the sun grew round that very day.
So it must have been after the birth of the simple light
In the first, spinning place, the spellbound horses walking warm
     Out of the whinnying green stable   35
       On to the fields of praise.

And honored among foxes and pheasants by the gay house
Under the new made clouds and happy as the heart was long,
    In the sun born over and over,
        I ran my heedless ways,   40
    My wishes raced through the house high hay
And nothing I cared, at my sky blue trades, that time allows
In all his tuneful turning so few and such morning songs
    Before the children green and golden
        Follow him out of grace,   45

Nothing I cared, in the lamb white days, that time would take me
Up to the swallow thronged loft by the shadow of my hand,
    In the moon that is always rising,
        Nor that riding to sleep
    I should hear him fly with the high fields   50
And wake to the farm forever fled from the childless land.
Oh as I was young and easy in the mercy of his means,
        Time held me green and dying
    Though I sang in my chains like the sea.

In My Craft or Sullen Art

In my craft or sullen art
Exercised in the still night
When only the moon rages
And the lovers lie abed
With all their griefs in their arms,
I labor by singing light
Not for ambition or bread
Or the strut and trade of charms
On the ivory stages
But for the common wages
Of their most secret heart.

Not for the proud man apart
From the raging moon I write
On these spindrift pages
Nor for the towering dead
With their nightingales and psalms
But for the lovers, their arms
Round the griefs of the ages,
Who pay no praise or wages
Nor heed my craft or art.

HENRY VAUGHAN (1622 – 1695)

They Are All Gone into the World of Light!

They are all gone into the world of light!
    And I alone sit lingering here;
Their very memory is fair and bright,
    And my sad thoughts doth clear.

It glows and glitters in my cloudy breast
    Like stars upon some gloomy grove,
Or those faint beams in which this hill is dressed
    After the sun's remove.

I see them walking in an air of glory,
    Whose light doth trample on my days;
My days, which are at best but dull and hoary,
    Mere glimmering and decays.

O holy hope, and high humility,
    High as the heavens above!
These are your walks, and you have showed them me
    To kindle my cold love.

Dear, beauteous death! the jewel of the just,
    Shining nowhere but in the dark;
What mysteries do lie beyond thy dust,
    Could man outlook that mark!

He that hath found some fledged bird's nest may know
    At first sight if the bird be flown;
But what fair well or grove he sings in now,
    That is to him unknown.

And yet, as angels in some brighter dreams
    Call to the soul when man doth sleep,
So some strange thoughts transcend our wonted themes,
    And into glory peep.

If a star were confined into a tomb,
    Her captive flames must needs burn there;
But when the hand that locked her up gives room,
    She'll shine through all the sphere.

O Father of eternal life, and all
    Created glories under Thee!
Resume° Thy spirit from this world of thrall   *take back*
    Into true liberty!

Either disperse these mists, which blot and fill
    My pérspective° still as they pass;   *telescope*
Or else remove me hence unto that hill
    Where I shall need no glass.

DEREK WALCOTT (b. 1930)
Blues

Those five or six young guys
hunched on the stoop
that oven–hot summer night
whistled me over. Nice
and friendly. So, I stop.
MacDougal or Christopher
Street in chains of light.

A summer festival. Or some
saint's. I wasn't too far from
home, but not too bright
for a nigger, and not too dark.
I figured we were all
one, wop, nigger, jew,
besides, this wasn't Central Park.
I'm coming on too strong? You figure
right! They beat this yellow nigger
black and blue.

Yeah. During all this, scared
in case one used a knife,
I hung my olive-green, just-bought
sports coat on a fire plug.
I did nothing. They fought
each other, really. Life
gives them a few kicks,
that's all. The spades, the spicks.

My face smashed in, my bloody mug
pouring, my olive-branch jacket saved
from cuts and tears,
I crawled four flights upstairs.
Sprawled in the gutter, I
remember a few watchers waved

loudly, and one kid's mother shouting
like "Jackie" or "Terry,"
"now that's enough!"
It's nothing really.
They don't get enough love.

You know they wouldn't kill
you. Just playing rough,
like young America will.
Still, it taught me something
about love. If it's so tough,
forget it.

God Rest Ye Merry, Gentlemen

Splitting from Jack Delaney's, Sheridan Square,
that winter night, stewed, seasoned in Bourbon,
my body kindled by the whistling air
snowing the Village that Christ was reborn,
I lurched like any lush by his own glow
across towards Sixth, and froze before the tracks
of footprints bleeding on the virgin snow.
I tracked them where they led across the street
to the bright side, entering the wax-
sealed smell of neon, human heat,
some all-night diner with its wise-guy cook
his stub thumb in my bowl of stew and one
man's pulped and beaten face, its look
acknowledging all that, white-dark outside,
was possible: some beast prowling the block,
something fur-clotted, running wild
beyond the boundary of will. Outside,
more snow had fallen. My heart charred.
I longed for darkness, evil that was warm.
Walking, I'd stop and turn. What had I heard,
wheezing behind my heel with whitening breath?
Nothing. Sixth Avenue yawned wet and wide.
The night was white. There was nowhere to hide.

Ruins of a Great House

> *Though our longest sun sets at right declensions and makes but winter arches, it cannot be long before we lie down in darkness, and have our light in ashes . . .*
>
> — BROWNE, URN BURIAL[1]

Stones only, the disjecta membra° of this   *fragments*
    Great House,
Whose moth-like girls are mixed with candledust,
Remain to file the lizard's dragonish claws.
The mouths of those gate cherubs shriek with stain;   5
Axle and coach wheel silted under the muck
Of cattle droppings.
              Three crows flap for the trees
And settle, creaking the eucalyptus boughs.
A smell of dead limes quickens in the nose   10
The leprosy of empire.
             "Farewell, green fields,
             Farewell, ye happy groves!"°   *adpated from*
Marble like Greece, like Faulkner's[2] South in stone,   *Satan's speech*
Deciduous beauty prospered and is gone,   *in* Paradise
                          Lost, I, 249.
    15
But where the lawn breaks in a rash of trees
A spade below dead leaves will ring the bone
Of some dead animal or human thing
Fallen from evil days, from evil times.

It seems that the original crops were limes   20
Grown in the silt that clogs the river's skirt;
The imperious rakes are gone, their bright girls gone,
The river flows, obliterating hurt.
I climbed a wall with the grille ironwork
Of exiled craftsmen protecting that great house
From guilt, perhaps, but not from the worm's rent   25
Nor from the padded cavalry of the mouse.
And when a wind shook in the limes I heard
What Kipling[3] heard, the death of a great empire, the abuse
Of ignorance by Bible and by sword.   30
A green lawn, broken by low walls of stone,

---

[1]Sir Thomas Browne (1605–1682), English physician and author of the treatise *Hydriotaphia: Urn Burial.*

[2]William Faulkner (1897–1962), American novelist.

[3]Rudyard Kipling (1865–1936), English novelist and poet.

Dipped to the rivulet, and pacing, I thought next
Of men like Hawkins, Walter Raleigh, Drake,[4]
Ancestral murderers and poets, more perplexed
In memory now by every ulcerous crime.   35
The world's green age then was a rotting lime
Whose stench became the charnel galleon's text.
The rot remains with us, the men are gone.
But, as dead ash is lifted in a wind
That fans the blackening ember of the mind,   40
My eyes burned from the ashen prose of Donne.[5]

Ablaze with rage I thought,
Some slave is rotting in this manorial lake,
But still the coal of my compassion fought
That Albion[6] too was once   45
A colony like ours, "part of the continent, piece of the main,"[7]
Nook-shotten, rook o'erblown, deranged
By foaming channels and the vain expense
Of bitter faction.
                 All in compassion ends   50
So differently from what the heart arranged:
"as well as if a manor of thy friend's . . ."

ROSANNA WARREN (b. 1953)
In Creve Coeur, Missouri

(Pulitzer Prize for Photojournalism, 1989)

Only in Creve Coeur
would an amateur photographer
firebug snap a shot so
unconsolable: fireman bent low

---

[4]Sir John Hawkins (1532–1595); Sir Walter Raleigh (1552?–1618); Sir Francis Drake (1540?–1596). Leading English explorers.

[5]John Donne (1572–1631), English poet.

[6]A poetic name for Great Britain.

[7]John Donne, Meditation 17, from his "Devotions upon Emergent Occasions." "No man is an island entire of itself; every man is a piece of the continent, a part of the main; if a clod be washed away by the sea, Europe is the less, as well as if a promontory were, as well as if a manor of thy friend's or of thine own were." Walcott quotes the closing phrase of this quotation to close his poem.

over the rag of body held
like impossible laundry pulled
too soon from the line, too pale,
too sodden with smoke to flail

in his huge, dark, crumpled embrace.
He leans to the tiny face.
Her hair stands out like flame.
She is naked, she has no name.

No longer a baby, almost
a child, not yet a ghost,
she presses a doll-like fist
to his professional chest.

Her head falls back to his hand.
Tell us that she will stand
again, quarrel and misbehave.
He is trying to make her breathe.

Strong man, you know how it's done,
you've done it again and again
sucking the spirit back
to us from its lair of smoke.

We'll call it a fine surprise.
The snapshot won a prize
though it couldn't revive *her*
that night in Creve Coeur.

AFAA MICHAEL WEAVER (b. 1951)
The Picnic, an Homage to Civil Rights

We spread torn quilts and blankets,
mashing the grass under us until it was hard,
piled the baskets of steamed crabs
by the trees in columns that hid the trunk,
put our water coolers of soda pop
on the edges to mark the encampment,
like gypsies settling in for revelry
in a forest in Rumania or pioneers
blazing through the land of the Sioux,
the Apache, and the Arapaho, looking guardedly

over our perimeters for poachers
or the curious noses of fat women
ambling past on the backs of their shoes.
The sun crashed through the trees,
tumbling down and splattering in shadows
on the baseball diamond like mashed bananas.
We hunted for wild animals in the clumps
of forests, fried hot dogs until the odor
turned solid in our nostrils like wood.
We were in the park.

One uncle talked incessantly, because he knew
the universe; another was the griot[1]
who stomped his foot in syncopation
to call the details from the base of his mind;
another was a cynic who doubted everything,
toasting everyone around with gin.
The patriarchal council mumbled on,
while the women took the evening to tune
their hearts to the slow air and buzzing flies,
to hold their hands out so angels could stand
in their palms and give dispensation,
as we played a rough game of softball
in the diamond with borrowed gloves,
singing Chuck Berry and Chubby Checker,
diving in long lines into the public pool,
throwing empty peanut shells to the lion,
buying cotton candy in the aviary
of the old mansion, laughing at monkeys,
running open-mouthed and full in the heat
until our smell was pungent and natural,
while the sun made our fathers and uncles
fall down in naps on their wives' laps, and
we frolicked like wealthy children on an English estate,
as reluctant laws and bloodied heads
tacked God's theses on wooden doors,[2]
guaranteed the canopy of the firmament above us.

---

[1]African tribal storyteller.
[2]tacked . . . theses: As did Martin Luther, beginning the Protestant Reformation.

James Welch (b. 1940)
Harlem, Montana: Just Off the Reservation

We need no runners here. Booze is law
and all the Indians drink in the best tavern.
Money is free if you're poor enough.
Disgusted, busted whites are running
for office in this town. The constable,
a local farmer, plants the jail with wild
raven-haired stiffs who beg just one more drink.
One drunk, a former Methodist, becomes a saint
in the Indian church, bugs the plaster man
on the cross with snakes. If his knuckles broke,
he'd see those women wail the graves goodbye.

Goodbye, goodbye, Harlem on the rocks,
so bigoted, you forget the latest joke,
so lonely, you'd welcome a battalion of Turks
to rule your women. What you don't know,
what you will never know or want to learn —
Turks aren't white. Turks are olive, unwelcome
alive in any town. Turks would use
your one dingy park to declare a need for loot.
Turks say bring it, step quickly, lay down and dead.

Here we are when men were nice. This photo, hung
in the New England Hotel lobby, shows them nicer
than pie, agreeable to the warring bands of redskins
who demanded protection money for the price of food.
Now, only Hutterites out north are nice. We hate
them. They are tough and their crops are always good.
We accuse them of idiocy and believe their belief all wrong.

Harlem, your hotel is overnamed, your children
are raggedy-assed but you go on, survive
the bad food from the two cafes and peddle
your hate for the wild who bring you money.
When you die, if you die, will you remember
the three young bucks who shot the grocery up,
locked themselves in and cried for days, we're rich,
help us, oh God, we're rich.

WALT WHITMAN (1819 – 1892)
A Hand-Mirror

Hold it up sternly — see this it sends back, (who is it? is it you?)
Outside fair costume, within ashes and filth,
No more a flashing eye, no more a sonorous voice or
    springy step,
Now some slave's eye, voice, hands, step,
A drunkard's breath, unwholesome eater's face, venerealee's[1]
    flesh,
Lungs rotting away piecemeal, stomach sour and cankerous,
Joints rheumatic, bowels clogged with abomination,
Blood circulating dark and poisonous streams,
Words babble, hearing and touch callous,
No brain, no heart left, no magnetism of sex;
Such from one look in this looking-glass ere you go hence,
Such a result so soon — and from such a beginning!

From *Song of Myself*

1

I celebrate myself, and sing myself,
And what I assume you shall assume,
For every atom belonging to me as good belongs to you.

I loaf and invite my soul,
I lean and loaf at my ease observing a spear of summer grass.

My tongue, every atom of my blood, formed from this soil, this air,
Born here of parents born here from parents the same, and their
    parents the same,
I, now thirty-seven years old in perfect health begin,
Hoping to cease not till death.

Creeds and schools in abeyance,
Retiring back a while sufficed at what they are, but never forgotten,
I harbor for good or bad, I permit to speak at every hazard,
Nature without check with original energy.

6

A child said *What is the grass?* fetching it to me with full hands;
How could I answer the child? I do not know what it is any more
    than he.

---

[1]Victim of venereal disease.

I guess it must be the flag of my disposition, out of hopeful green
    stuff woven.

Or I guess it is the handkerchief of the Lord,
A scented gift and remembrancer designedly dropped,
Bearing the owner's name someway in the corners, that we may
    see and remark, and say *Whose?*

Or I guess the grass is itself a child, the produced babe of the
    vegetation.

Or I guess it is a uniform hieroglyphic,
And it means, Sprouting alike in broad zones and narrow zones,
Growing among black folks as among white,
Kanuck, Tuckahoe, Congressman, Cuff,[1] I give them the same,
    I receive them the same.

And now it seems to me the beautiful uncut hair of graves.

Tenderly will I use you curling grass,
It may be you transpire from the breasts of young men,
It may be if I had known them I would have loved them,
It may be you are from old people, or from offspring taken soon
    out of their mothers' laps,
And here you are the mothers' laps.

This grass is very dark to be from the white heads of old mothers,
Darker than the colorless beards of old men,
Dark to come from under the faint red roofs of mouths.

O I perceive after all so many uttering tongues,
And I perceive they do not come from the roofs of mouths for
    nothing.

I wish I could translate the hints about the dead young men and
    women,
And the hints about old men and mothers, and the offspring taken
    soon out of their laps.

What do you think has become of the young and old men?
And what do you think has become of the women and children?

They are alive and well somewhere,
The smallest sprout shows there is really no death,

---

[1]A "Kanuck" refers to a French Canadian, a "Tuckahoe" refers to a native of
Tidewater, Virginia, and a "Cuff" refers to an African American.

And if ever there was it led forward life, and does not wait at the
    end to arrest it,
And ceased the moment life appeared.

All goes onward and outward, nothing collapses,
And to die is different from what anyone supposed, and luckier.

52

The spotted hawk swoops by and accuses me, he complains of my
    gab and my loitering.

I too am not a bit tamed, I too am untranslatable,
I sound my barbaric yawp over the roofs of the world.

The last scud of day holds back for me,
It flings my likeness after the rest and true as any on the shadowed
    wilds,
It coaxes me to the vapor and the dusk.

I depart as air, I shake my white locks at the runaway sun,
I effuse my flesh in eddies, and drift it in lacy jags.

I bequeath myself to the dirt to grow from the grass I love,
If you want me again look for me under your boot-soles.

You will hardly know who I am or what I mean,
But I shall be good health to you nevertheless,
And filter and fiber your blood.

Failing to fetch me at first keep encouraged,
Missing me one place search another,
I stop somewhere waiting for you.

Vigil Strange I Kept on the Field One Night

Vigil strange I kept on the field one night;
When you my son and my comrade dropt at my side that day,
One look I but gave which your dear eyes return'd with a look I
    shall never forget,
One touch of your hand to mine O boy, reach'd up as you lay on
    the ground,
Then onward I sped in the battle, the even-contested battle,
Till late in the night reliev'd to the place at last again I made my
    way,
Found you in death so cold dear comrade, found your body son of
    responding kisses, (never again on earth responding,)

Bared your face in the starlight, curious the scene, cool blew the
  moderate night-wind,
Long there and then in vigil I stood, dimly around me the battle-
  field spreading,
Vigil wondrous and vigil sweet there in the fragrant silent night,
But not a tear fell, not even a long-drawn sigh, long I gazed,
Then on the earth partially reclining sat by your side leaning my
  chin in my hands,
Passing sweet hours, immortal and mystic hours with you dearest
  comrade — not a tear, not a word,
Vigil of silence, love and death, vigil for you my son and my
  soldier,
As onward silently stars aloft, eastward new ones upward stole,
Vigil final for you brave boy, (I could not save you, swift was your
  death,
I faithfully loved you and cared for you living, I think we shall
  surely meet again,)
Till at latest lingering of the night, indeed just as the dawn
  appear'd,
My comrade I wrapt in his blanket, envelop'd well his form,
Folded the blanket well, tucking it carefully over head and care-
  fully under feet,
And there and then and bathed by the rising sun, my son in his
  grave, in his rude-dug grave I deposited,
Ending my vigil strange with that, vigil of night and battle-field dim,
Vigil for boy of responding kisses, (never again on earth respond-
  ing,)
Vigil for comrade swiftly slain, vigil I never forget, how as day
  brighten'd,
I rose from the chill ground and folded my soldier well in his
  blanket,
And buried him where he fell.

RICHARD WILBUR (b. 1921)

Cottage Street, 1953

Framed in her phoenix fire-screen, Edna Ward
Bends to the tray of Canton,[1] pouring tea

---

[1]Blue-and-white patterned Chinese-export porcelain ware; in this case, the tea
service.

For frightened Mrs. Plath; then, turning toward
The pale, slumped daughter, and my wife, and me,

Asks if we would prefer it weak or strong.
Will we have milk or lemon, she enquires?
The visit seems already strained and long.
Each in his turn, we tell her our desires.

It is my office to exemplify
The published poet in his happiness,
Thus cheering Sylvia, who has wished to die;[2]
But half-ashamed, and impotent to bless,

I am a stupid life-guard who has found,
Swept to his shallows by the tide, a girl
Who, far from shore, has been immensely drowned,
And stares through water now with eyes of pearl.

How large is her refusal; and how slight
The genteel chat whereby we recommend
Life, of a summer afternoon, despite
The brewing dusk which hints that it may end.

And Edna Ward shall die in fifteen years,
After her eight-and-eighty summers of
Such grace and courage as permit no tears,
The thin hand reaching out, the last word *love,*

Outliving Sylvia who, condemned to live,
Shall study for a decade, as she must,
To state at last her brilliant negative
In poems free and helpless and unjust.

---

[2]The poet Sylvia Plath (1932–1963) attempted suicide after her junior year at Smith College. Later, she died by suicide, at thirty-one.

Junk

Huru Welandes

 worc ne geswiceð

monna ænigum

 ðara ðe Mimming can

heardne gehealdan.

 — WALDERE[1]

An axe angles

 from my neighbor's ashcan;

It is hell's handiwork,

 the wood not hickory,

The flow of the grain   5

 not faithfully followed.

The shivered shaft

 rises from a shellheap

Of plastic playthings,

 paper plates,   10

And the sheer shards

 of shattered tumblers

That were not annealed

 for the time needful.

At the same curbside,   15

 a cast-off cabinet

Of wavily-warped

 unseasoned wood

Waits to be trundled

 in the trash-man's truck.   20

Haul them off! Hide them!

 The heart winces

For junk and gimcrack,

 for jerrybuilt things

And the men who make them   25

 for a little money,

Bartering pride

 like the bought boxer

Who pulls his punches,

 or the paid-off jockey   30

---

[1] *Waldere* (or *Waldhere*) is the name of an Old English poem. Wilbur explains, "The epigraph, taken from a fragmentary Anglo-Saxon poem, concerns the legendary smith Wayland, and may roughly be translated: 'Truly, Wayland's handiwork — the sword Mimming which he made — will never fail any man who knows how to use it bravely.'"

Who in the home stretch

                  holds in his horse.

Yet the things themselves

                in thoughtless honor

Have kept composure,   35

              like captives who would not

Talk under torture.

           Tossed from a tailgate

Where the dump displays

              its random dolmens,   40

Its black barrows

         and blazing valleys,

They shall waste in the weather

                toward what they were.

The sun shall glory   45

           in the glitter of glass-chips,

Foreseeing the salvage

          of the prisoned sand,

And the blistering paint

          peel off in patches,   50

That the good grain

       be discovered again.

Then burnt, bulldozed,

         they shall all be buried

To the depth of diamonds,   55

         in the making dark

Where halt Hephaestus

       keeps his hammer

And Wayland's work

      is worn away.   60

Love Calls Us to the Things of This World

    The eyes open to a cry of pulleys,
And spirited from sleep, the astounded soul
Hangs for a moment bodiless and simple
As false dawn.
              Outside the open window
The morning air is all awash with angels.

    Some are in bed-sheets, some are in blouses,
Some are in smocks: but truly there they are.
Now they are rising together in calm swells

Of halcyon feeling, filling whatever they wear
With the deep joy of their impersonal breathing;

    Now they are flying in place, conveying
The terrible speed of their omnipresence, moving
And staying like white water; and now of a sudden
They swoon down into so rapt a quiet
That nobody seems to be there.
                      The soul shrinks

    From all that it is about to remember,
From the punctual rape of every blessèd day,
And cries,
             "Oh, let there be nothing on earth but laundry,
Nothing but rosy hands in the rising steam
And clear dances done in the sight of heaven."

    Yet, as the sun acknowledges
With a warm look the world's hunks and colors,
The soul descends once more in bitter love
To accept the waking body, saying now
In a changed voice as the man yawns and rises,

    "Bring them down from their ruddy gallows;
Let there be clean linen for the backs of thieves;
Let lovers go fresh and sweet to be undone,
And the heaviest nuns walk in a pure floating
Of dark habits,
             keeping their difficult balance."

The Writer

In her room at the prow of the house
Where light breaks, and the windows are tossed with linden,
My daughter is writing a story.

I pause in the stairwell, hearing
From her shut door a commotion of typewriter-keys
Like a chain hauled over a gunwale.

Young as she is, the stuff
Of her life is a great cargo, and some of it heavy:
I wish her a lucky passage.

But now it is she who pauses,
As if to reject my thought and its easy figure.
A stillness greatens, in which

The whole house seems to be thinking,
And then she is at it again with a bunched clamor
Of strokes, and again is silent.

I remember the dazed starling
Which was trapped in that very room, two years ago;
How we stole in, lifted a sash

And retreated, not to affright it;
And how for a helpless hour, through the crack of the door,
We watched the sleek, wild, dark

And iridescent creature
Batter against the brilliance, drop like a glove
To the hard floor, or the desk-top,

And wait then, humped and bloody,
For the wits to try it again; and how our spirits
Rose when, suddenly sure,

It lifted off from a chair-back,
Beating a smooth course for the right window
And clearing the sill of the world.

It is always a matter, my darling,
Of life or death, as I had forgotten. I wish
What I wished you before, but harder.

WILLIAM CARLOS WILLIAMS (1883 – 1963)
Landscape with the Fall of Icarus

According to Breughel
when Icarus fell
it was spring

a farmer was ploughing
his field
the whole pageantry

of the year was
awake tingling
near

the edge of the sea
concerned
with itself

sweating in the sun
that melted
the wings' wax

unsignificantly
off the coast
there was

a splash quite unnoticed
this was
Icarus drowning

The Raper from Passenack

was very kind. When she regained
her wits, he said, It's all right, Kid,
I took care of you.

What a mess she was in. Then he added,
You'll never forget me now.
And drove her home.

Only a man who is sick, she said
would do a thing like that.
It must be so.

No one who is not diseased could be
so insanely cruel. He wants to give it
to someone else —

to justify himself. But if I get a
venereal infection out of this
I won't be treated.

I refuse. You'll find me dead in bed
first. Why not? That's
the way she spoke,

I wish I could shoot him. How would
you like to know a murderer?
I may do it.

I'll know by the end of this week.
I wouldn't scream. I bit him
several times

but he was too strong for me.
I can't yet understand it. I don't
faint so easily.

When I came to myself and realized
what had happened all I could do
was to curse

and call him every vile name I could
think of. I was so glad
to be taken home.

I suppose it's my mind — the fear of
infection. I'd rather a million times
have been got pregnant.

But it's the foulness of it can't
be cured. And hatred, hatred of all men
— and disgust.

Spring and All

By the road to the contagious hospital
under the surge of the blue
mottled clouds driven from the
northeast — a cold wind. Beyond, the
waste of broad, muddy fields
brown with dried weeds, standing and fallen

patches of standing water
the scattering of tall trees

All along the road the reddish
purplish, forked, upstanding, twiggy
stuff of bushes and small trees
with dead, brown leaves under them
leafless vines —

Lifeless in appearance, sluggish
dazed spring approaches —

They enter the new world naked,
cold, uncertain of all
save that they enter. All about them
the cold, familiar wind —

Now the grass, tomorrow
the stiff curl of wildcarrot leaf
One by one objects are defined —
It quickens: clarity, outline of leaf

But now the stark dignity of
entrance — Still, the profound change

[handwritten margin notes:]
> is this just a description, or is it a theme that re-occurs throughout?

> why use familiar when they are described as "uncertain of all save that they enter"?

has come upon them: rooted, they
grip down and begin to awaken

This Is Just to Say

I have eaten
the plums
that were in
the icebox

and which
you were probably
saving
for breakfast

Forgive me
they were delicious
so sweet
and so cold

WILLIAM WORDSWORTH (1770 – 1850)
My Heart Leaps Up

My heart leaps up when I behold
    A rainbow in the sky:
So was it when my life began;
So is it now I am a man;
So be it when I shall grow old,
    Or let me die!
The Child is father of the Man;
And I could wish my days to be
Bound each to each by natural piety.

Ode

*Intimations of Immortality from Recollections
of Early Childhood*

*The Child is father of the Man;
And I could wish my days to be
Bound each to each by natural piety.*

1

There was a time when meadow, grove, and stream,
The earth, and every common sight,

To me did seem
Appareled in celestial light,
The glory and the freshness of a dream.
It is not now as it hath been of yore —
Turn whereso'er I may,
By night or day,
The things which I have seen I now can see no more.

2

The Rainbow comes and goes,
And lovely is the Rose,
The Moon doth with delight
Look round her when the heavens are bare,
Waters on a starry night
Are beautiful and fair;
The sunshine is a glorious birth;
But yet I know, where'er I go,
That there hath passed away a glory from the earth.

3

Now, while the birds thus sing a joyous song,
And while the young lambs bound
As to the tabor's° sound,   *small drum*
To me alone there came a thought of grief;
A timely utterance gave that thought relief,
And I again am strong:
The cataracts blow their trumpets from the steep;
No more shall grief of mine the season wrong;
I hear the Echoes through the mountains throng,
The Winds come to me from the fields of sleep,
And all the earth is gay;
Land and sea
Give themselves up to jollity,
And with the heart of May
Doth every Beast keep holiday —
Thou Child of Joy,
Shout round me, let me hear thy shouts, thou happy Shepherd-
boy!

4

Ye blessèd Creatures, I have heard the call
    Ye to each other make; I see
The heavens laugh with you in your jubilee;
    My heart is at your festival,
      My head hath its coronal,
The fullness of your bliss, I feel — I feel it all.
      — Oh, evil day! if I were sullen
      While Earth herself is adorning,
        This sweet May morning,
    And the Children are culling
      On every side,
    In a thousand valleys far and wide,
    Fresh flowers; while the sun shines warm,
And the Babe leaps up on his Mother's arm —
    I hear, I hear, with joy I hear!
    — But there's a Tree, of many, one,
A single Field which I have looked upon,
Both of them speak of something that is gone:
      The Pansy at my feet
      Doth the same tale repeat:
Whither is fled the visionary gleam?
Where is it now, the glory and the dream?

5

Our birth is but a sleep and a forgetting:
The Soul that rises with us, our life's Star,
    Hath had elsewhere its setting,
      And cometh from afar:
    Not in entire forgetfulness,
    And not in utter nakedness,
But trailing clouds of glory do we come
    From God, who is our home:
Heaven lies about us in our infancy!
Shades of the prison-house begin to close
    Upon the growing Boy
But he beholds the light, and whence it flows,
    He sees it in his joy;
The Youth, who daily farther from the east
    Must travel, still is Nature's Priest,
    And by the vision splendid

Is on his way attended;
At length the Man perceives it die away,
And fade into the light of common day.

6

Earth fills her lap with pleasures of her own;
Yearnings she hath in her own natural kind,
And, even with something of a Mother's mind,
    And no unworthy aim,
    The homely Nurse doth all she can
To make her foster child, her Inmate Man,
    Forget the glories he hath known,
And that imperial palace whence he came.

7

Behold the Child among his newborn blisses,
A six-years' Darling of a pygmy size!
See, where 'mid work of his own hand he lies,
Fretted by sallies of his mother's kisses,
With light upon him from his father's eyes!
See, at his feet, some little plan or chart,
Some fragment from his dream of human life,
Shaped by himself with newly-learnèd art;
    A wedding or a festival,
    A mourning or a funeral;
        And this hath now his heart,
    And unto this he frames his song;
        Then will he fit his tongue
To dialogues of business, love, or strife;
    But it will not be long
    Ere this be thrown aside,
    And with new joy and pride
The little Actor cons another part;
Filling from time to time his "humorous stage"
With all the Persons, down to palsied Age,
That Life brings with her in her equipage;
    As if his whole vocation
    Were endless imitation.

8

Thou, whose exterior semblance doth belie
    Thy Soul's immensity;

Thou best Philosopher, who yet dost keep
Thy heritage, thou Eye among the blind,
That, deaf and silent, read'st the eternal deep,
Haunted forever by the eternal mind —
    Mighty Prophet! Seer blest!
    On whom those truths do rest,
Which we are toiling all our lives to find,
In darkness lost, the darkness of the grave;
Thou, over whom thy Immortality
Broods like the Day, a Master o'er a Slave,
A Presence which is not to be put by;
Thou little Child, yet glorious in the might
Of heaven-born freedom on thy being's height,
Why with such earnest pains dost thou provoke
The years to bring the inevitable yoke,
Thus blindly with thy blessedness at strife?
Full soon thy Soul shall have her earthly freight,
And custom lie upon thee with a weight,
Heavy as frost, and deep almost as life!

9

    O joy! that in our embers
    Is something that doth live,
    That nature yet remembers
    What was so fugitive!
The thought of our past years in me doth breed
Perpetual benediction: not indeed
For that which is most worthy to be blest;
Delight and liberty, the simple creed
Of Childhood, whether busy or at rest,
With new-fledged hope still fluttering in his breast —
    Not for these I raise
    The song of thanks and praise;
    But for those obstinate questionings
    Of sense and outward things,
    Fallings from us, vanishings;
    Blank misgivings of a Creature
Moving about in worlds not realized,
High instincts before which our mortal Nature
Did tremble like a guilty Thing surprised;

But for those first affections,
Those shadowy recollections,
Which, be they what they may,
Are yet the fountain-light of all our day,
Are yet a master-light of all our seeing;
Uphold us, cherish, and have power to make
Our noisy years seem moments in the being
Of the eternal Silence: truths that wake,
To perish never;
Which neither listlessness, nor mad endeavor,
Nor Man nor Boy,
Nor all that is at enmity with joy,
Can utterly abolish or destroy!
Hence in a season of calm weather
Though inland far we be,
Our Souls have sight of that immortal sea
Which brought us hither,
Can in a moment travel thither,
And see the Children sport upon the shore,
And hear the mighty waters rolling evermore.

10

Then sing, ye Birds, sing, sing a joyous song!
And let the young Lambs bound
As to the tabor's sound!
We in thought will join your throng,
Ye that pipe and ye that play,
Ye that through your hearts today
Feel the gladness of the May!
What though the radiance which was once so bright
Be now forever taken from my sight,
Though nothing can bring back the hour
Of splendor in the grass, of glory in the flower;
We will grieve not, rather find
Strength in what remains behind;
In the primal sympathy
Which having been must ever be;
In the soothing thoughts that spring
Out of human suffering;
In the faith that looks through death,
In years that bring the philosophic mind.

11

And O, ye Fountains, Meadows, Hills, and Groves,
Forebode not any severing of our loves!
Yet in my heart of hearts I feel your might;
I only have relinquished one delight
To live beneath your more habitual sway.
I love the Brooks which down their channels fret,
Even more than when I tripped lightly as they;
The innocent brightness of a newborn Day
        Is lovely yet;
The clouds that gather round the setting sun
Do take a sober coloring from an eye
That hath kept watch o'er man's mortality;
Another race hath been, and other palms° are won.   *symbols of victory*
Thanks to the human heart by which we live,
Thanks to its tenderness, its joys, and fears,
To me the meanest° flower that blows°   *most ordinary / blooms*
    can give
Thoughts that do often lie too deep for tears.

The Solitary Reaper

Behold her, single in the field,
Yon solitary Highland Lass!
Reaping and singing by herself;
Stop here, or gently pass!
Alone she cuts and binds the grain,
And sings a melancholy strain;
O listen! for the Vale profound
Is overflowing with the sound.

No Nightingale did ever chaunt
More welcome notes to weary bands
Of travelers in some shady haunt,
Among Arabian sands;
A voice so thrilling ne'er was heard
In springtime from the Cuckoo bird,
Breaking the silence of the seas
Among the farthest Hebrides,

Will no one tell me what she sings? —
Perhaps the plaintive numbers flow
For old, unhappy, far-off things,

And battles long ago;
Or is it some more humble lay,
Familiar matter of today?
Some natural sorrow, loss, or pain,
That has been, and may be again?

Whate'er the theme, the Maiden sang
As if her song could have no ending;
I saw her singing at her work,
And o'er the sickle bending —
I listened, motionless and still;
And, as I mounted up the hill,
The music in my heart I bore,
Long after it was heard no more.

The World Is Too Much with Us

The world is too much with us; late and soon,
Getting and spending, we lay waste our powers;
Little we see in Nature that is ours;
We have given our hearts away, a sordid boon!°   *gift*
This Sea that bares her bosom to the moon,
The winds that will be howling at all hours,
And are up-gathered now like sleeping flowers,
For this, for everything, we are out of tune;
It moves us not. — Great God! I'd rather be
A Pagan suckled in a creed outworn;
So might I, standing on this pleasant lea,
Have glimpses that would make me less forlorn;
Have sight of Proteus rising from the sea;
Or hear old Triton blow his wreathèd horn.[1]

JAMES WRIGHT (1927–1980)
A Blessing

Just off the highway to Rochester, Minnesota,
Twilight bounds softly forth on the grass.
And the eyes of those two Indian ponies

---

[1]In Greek mythology, Proteus is a lesser sea god, to whom Poseidon gave the ability to change his form. Triton, a merman, is usually represented as blowing on a shell or conch, calming the waves.

Darken with kindness.
They have come gladly out of the willows
To welcome my friend and me.
We step over the barbed wire into the pasture
Where they have been grazing all day, alone.
They ripple tensely, they can hardly contain their happiness
That we have come.
They bow shyly as wet swans. They love each other.
There is no loneliness like theirs.
At home once more,
They begin munching the young tufts of spring in the darkness.
I would like to hold the slenderer one in my arms,
For she has walked over to me
And nuzzled my left hand.
She is black and white,
Her mane falls wild on her forehead,
And the light breeze moves me to caress her long ear
That is delicate as the skin over a girl's wrist.
Suddenly I realize
That if I stepped out of my body I would break
Into blossom.

Small Frogs Killed on the Highway

Still,
I would leap too
Into the light,
If I had the chance.
It is everything, the wet green stalk of the field
On the other side of the road.
They crouch there, too, faltering in terror
And take strange wing. Many
Of the dead never moved, but many
Of the dead are alive forever in the split second
Auto headlights more sudden
Than their drivers know.
The drivers burrow backward into dank pools
Where nothing begets
Nothing.

Across the road, tadpoles are dancing
On the quarter thumbnail

Of the moon. They can't see,
Not yet.

Sir Thomas Wyatt (1503 – 1542)
Forget Not Yet

Forget not yet the tried intent
Of such a truth as I have meant;
My great travail so gladly spent
      Forget not yet.

Forget not yet when first began
The weary life ye know, since whan°   *when*
The suit, the service none tell can;
      Forget not yet.

Forget not yet the great assays,°   *trials*
The cruel wrong, the scornful ways,
The painful patience in denays,°   *denials*
      Forget not yet.

Forget not yet, forget not this,
How long ago hath been and is
The mind that never meant amiss;
      Forget not yet.

Forget not then thine own approved,
The which so long hath thee so loved,
Whose steadfast faith yet never moved;
      Forget not this.

William Butler Yeats (1865 – 1939)
Among School Children

I

I walk through the long schoolroom questioning;
A kind old nun in a white hood replies;
The children learn to cipher and to sing,
To study reading-books and history,
To cut and sew, be neat in everything
In the best modern way — the children's eyes
In momentary wonder stare upon
A sixty-year-old smiling public man.

II

I dream of a Ledaean body,[1] bent
Above a sinking fire, a tale that she
Told of a harsh reproof, or trivial event
That changed some childish day to tragedy —
Told, and it seemed that our two natures blent
Into a sphere from youthful sympathy,
Or else, to alter Plato's parable,
Into the yolk and white of the one shell.[2]

III

And thinking of that fit of grief or rage
I look upon one child or t'other there
And wonder if she stood so at that age —
For even daughters of the swan can share
Something of every paddler's heritage —
And had that colour upon cheek or hair,
And thereupon my heart is driven wild:
She stands before me as a living child.

IV

Her present image floats into the mind —
Did Quattrocento[3] finger fashion it
Hollow of cheek as though it drank the wind
And took a mess of shadows for its meat?
And I though never of Ledaean kind
Had pretty plumage once — enough of that,
Better to smile on all that smile, and show
There is a comfortable kind of old scarecrow.

V

What youthful mother, a shape upon her lap
Honey of generation had betrayed,
And that must sleep, shriek, struggle to escape
As recollection or the drug decide,

---

[1]A body like Leda's. Leda was, in Greek myth, a maiden ravished by Zeus, who took the form of a swan. She bore Helen of Troy, whom Yeats identified with his beloved Maud Gonne.

[2]Plato, in *The Symposium,* suggests that man was originally both male and female but fell into division. Each half now longs for the other half.

[3]Italian name for the fifteenth century.

Would think her son, did she but see that shape
With sixty or more winters on its head,
A compensation for the pang of his birth,
Or the uncertainty of his setting forth?

VI

Plato thought nature but a spume that plays
Upon a ghostly paradigm of things;
Solider Aristotle played the taws
Upon the bottom of a king of kings;[4]
World-famous golden-thighed Pythagoras
Fingered upon a fiddle-stick or strings
What a star sang and careless Muses heard:[5]
Old clothes upon old sticks to scare a bird.

VII

Both nuns and mothers worship images,
But those the candles light are not as those
That animate a mother's reveries,
But keep a marble or a bronze repose.
And yet they too break hearts — O Presences
That passion, piety or affection knows,
And that all heavenly glory symbolise —
O self-born mockers of man's enterprise;

VIII

Labour is blossoming or dancing where
The body is not bruised to pleasure soul,
Nor beauty born out of its own despair,
Nor blear-eyed wisdom out of midnight oil.
O chestnut-tree, great-rooted blossomer,
Are you the leaf, the blossom or the bole?
O body swayed to music, O brightening glance,
How can we know the dancer from the dance?

---

[4]Yeats wrote to a friend, "Here is a fragment of my last curse upon old age. It means that even the greatest men are owls, scarecrows, by the time their fame has come. Aristotle, remember, was Alexander [the Great's] tutor, hence the taws [form of birch]," i.e., Aristotle flogged his pupil into learning.

[5]Yeats is referring to the fact that Pythagoras measured the intervals between notes on a stretched string.

Down by the Salley Gardens

Down by the salley gardens my love and I did meet;
She passed the salley gardens with little snow-white feet.
She bid me take love easy, as the leaves grow on the tree;
But I, being young and foolish, with her would not agree.
In a field by the river my love and I did stand,
And on my leaning shoulder she laid her snow-white hand.
She bid me take life easy, as the grass grows on the weirs;
But I was young and foolish, and now am full of tears.

The Lake Isle of Innisfree

I will arise and go now, and go to Innisfree,
And a small cabin build there, of clay and wattles made:
Nine bean-rows will I have there, a hive for the honeybee,
And live alone in the bee-loud glade.

And I shall have some peace there, for peace comes dropping slow,
Dropping from the veils of the morning to where the cricket sings;
There midnight's all a glimmer, and noon a purple glow,
And evening full of the linnet's wings.

I will arise and go now, for always night and day
I hear lake water lapping with low sounds by the shore;
While I stand on the roadway, or on the pavements grey,
I hear it in the deep heart's core.

Leda and the Swan[1]

A sudden blow: the great wings beating still
Above the staggering girl, her thighs caressed
By the dark webs, her nape caught in his bill,
He holds her helpless breast upon his breast.

How can those terrified vague fingers push
The feathered glory from her loosening thighs?
And how can body, laid in that white rush,
But feel the strange heart beating where it lies?

A shudder in the loins engenders there
The broken wall, the burning roof and tower

---

[1] In Greek myth, Leda was ravished by Zeus, who took the form of a swan. She gave birth to Helen. Helen left her husband, Menelaus, to go with Paris to Troy, thus causing the Trojan War.

And Agamemnon dead.
                                        Being so caught up,
So mastered by the brute blood of the air,
Did she put on his knowledge with his power
Before the indifferent beak could let her drop?

Sailing to Byzantium

I

That is no country for old men. The young
In one another's arms, birds in the trees
— Those dying generations — at their song,
The salmon-falls, the mackerel-crowded seas,
Fish, flesh, or fowl, commend all summer long
Whatever is begotten, born, and dies.
Caught in that sensual music all neglect
Monuments of unageing intellect.

II

An aged man is but a paltry thing,
A tattered coat upon a stick, unless
Soul clap its hands and sing, and louder sing
For every tatter in its mortal dress,
Nor is there singing school but studying[1]
Monuments of its own magnificence;
And therefore I have sailed the seas and come
To the holy city of Byzantium.

III

O sages standing in God's holy fire
As in the gold mosaic of a wall,
Come from the holy fire, perne in a gyre,[2]
And be the singing-masters of my soul.
Consume my heart away; sick with desire
And fastened to a dying animal
It knows not what it is; and gather me
Into the artifice of eternity.

---

[1]That is, "Nor is there any way to learn to sing except by studying."
[2]Swoop down in a whirling movement. A pern is a cone-shaped bobbin.

IV

Once out of nature I shall never take
My bodily form from any natural thing,
But such a form as Grecian goldsmiths make
Of hammered gold and gold enamelling
To keep a drowsy Emperor awake;[3]
Or set upon a golden bough to sing
To lords and ladies of Byzantium
Of what is past, or passing, or to come.

The Second Coming

Turning and turning in the widening gyre[1]
The falcon cannot hear the falconer;
Things fall apart; the centre cannot hold;
Mere anarchy is loosed upon the world,
The blood-dimmed tide is loosed, and everywhere
The ceremony of innocence is drowned;
The best lack all conviction, while the worst
Are full of passionate intensity.
Surely some revelation is at hand;
Surely the Second Coming is at hand.
The Second Coming! Hardly are those words out
When a vast image out of *Spiritus Mundi*[2]
Troubles my sight: somewhere in sands of the desert
A shape with lion body and the head of a man
A gaze blank and pitiless as the sun,
Is moving its slow thighs, while all about it
Reel shadows of the indignant desert birds.
The darkness drops again; but now I know
That twenty centuries of stony sleep
Were vexed to nightmare by a rocking cradle,
And what rough beast, its hour come round at last,
Slouches towards Bethlehem to be born?

---

[3]Yeats's note: "I have read somewhere that in the Emperor's palace at Byzantium was a tree made of gold and silver, and artificial birds sang."

[1]Yeats used the image of two interlocking gyres or cones to symbolize the conflicting forces of life.

[2]Yeats's term for the collective human memory.

JANE YEH (b. 1971)

Revenger's Tragedy

You don't return my calls. In a month of missing days
Everything thwarts me, even the curls of my hair freeze;

My skin sheds, leaving flakes on my wool sweater. We are
    erratic
Both, changing with the weather, but you think of it

As an astronomical progression. Last year you called me
Your little sunflower. Eleven blizzards later I think of how

To get you: calculating mercury, sighting along
    constellations,
Rehearsing the lines of a paid assassin — *not know me, my*
    Lord?

You cannot choose! I bide time,
Hoarse-tongued & blue as poison, the double

Line of my eyes gone to slits. I hate like a tooth hurts,
At the root. I will startle the bones

From their sockets, they will crack like glass
& catch in your throat. I will dazzle

Your heart from its cage. The lungs will knock & clap
Together in the empty place. The applause will make you rattle.

Appendices

Appendix 1. On Prosody

Prosody concerns the measure in which poems are written. There are three kinds of poems, prosodically speaking:

poems in counted lines (where lines have a regular number of beats);

poems in free verse (where lines have an irregular number of beats);

poems in prose (usually a short symbolic paragraph).

This appendix is concerned with poems in counted lines and poems in free verse. Since free verse is a relatively recent form (Walt Whitman is the earliest significant American poet of free verse), we will take up counted poetry first.

Poems in Counted Lines

Poems in counted lines are written in units we call feet. A foot consists of one stressed syllable (one "beat," to use the musical term), usually accompanied by one or two unstressed syllables. We represent a stressed syllable by an accent (´) and an unstressed syllable by a symbol called a breve (˘).

Here is an example of a line with four feet:

Whose woóds / these áre / I thínk / I knów

The number of feet in a line gives the line its (Greek-derived) name, and tells you how *wide* the line is. Natural intonation makes you stress some words and leave others unstressed, helping you to see how many beats are in the line. We characterize a line by how many stresses (beats) exist in it: the word "meter" (meaning measure) is the general name for the length of a counted line:

> one beat per line = *monometer* (from Greek meaning "one," as in "monologue");
>
> two beats per line = *dimeter* (from Greek meaning "two," as in "dialogue");
>
> three beats per line = *trimeter* (from Greek meaning "three," as in "triangle");
>
> four beats per line = *tetrameter* (from Greek meaning "four," as in "tetrahedron");
>
> five beats per line = *pentameter* (from Greek meaning "five," as in "Pentagon");
>
> six beats per line = *hexameter* (from Greek meaning "six," as in "hexagram");
>
> seven beats per line = *heptameter* (from Greek meaning "seven," as in "heptathlon");
>
> eight beats per line = *octameter* (from Greek meaning "eight," as in "octopus").

Most poems written in English have lines four or five beats wide. Shakespeare wrote all of his plays in pentameter lines five beats wide (though he also inserted prose and short songs from time to time).

When you are looking to see how many beats are in a line, it helps sometimes to see how many syllables are in the line. Ten-syllable lines tend to have five beats each; eight-syllable lines tend to have four beats each. But it is still natural intonation that tells you where to put the stresses:

> When Í / see bír / ches bénd / to léft / and ríght [ten syllables, five beats]
> Gólden / láds and / gírls all / múst [seven syllables, four beats]

Here are samples of all the line-widths. It helps to read these aloud, so that you can hear the beats.

1. **MONOMETER** *(one beat per line, a rare meter)*, as in the little poem called "Fleas":

   > Adam
   > Had 'em.

2. **DIMETER** *(two beats)*, which is likewise rare:

   > Take her up tenderly,
   > Lift her with care,
   > Fashioned so slenderly,
   > Young and so fair.
   >
   > — THOMAS HOOD, "The Bridge of Sighs"

3. **TRIMETER** *(three beats):*

   > It is time that I wrote my will;
   > I choose upstanding men
   > That climb the streams until
   > The fountain leap, and at dawn
   > Drop their cast at the side
   > Of dripping stone; I declare
   > They shall inherit my pride.
   >
   > — W. B. YEATS, "The Tower"

4. **TETRAMETER** *(four beats):*

   > Whose woods these are I think I know
   > His house is in the village though,
   > He will not see me stopping here
   > To watch his woods fill up with snow.
   >
   > — ROBERT FROST, "Stopping by Woods"

5. **PENTAMETER** *(five beats):*

   > The woods decay, the woods decay and fall,
   > The vapours weep their burthens to the ground,
   > Man comes and tills the soil and lies beneath,
   > And after many a summer dies the swan.
   >
   > — ALFRED, LORD TENNYSON, "Tithonus"

6. **HEXAMETER** *(six beats)*, which is sometimes called an Alexandrine (from the French usage) and which is rare in English verse:

   > I will arise and go now, and go to Innisfree,
   > And a small cabin build there, of clay and wattles made.
   >
   > — W. B. YEATS, "The Lake Isle of Innisfree"

The common meters (line–lengths) have been trimeter, tetrameter, and pentameter, used singly or in combination.

Rhythm

You have probably noticed that the lilts (swings) in each of the above examples of line-length differ. That is because the lines are written in different rhythms. Two dimeter poems can sound very different from each other because they are written in two different rhythms. You can see this by comparing Hood's "The Bridge of Sighs," given above as an example of dimeter, with Dorothy Parker's satirical poem on suicide, "Résumé," also in dimeter:

> Táke her up / ténderly,
> Líft her with / cáre
> Fáshioned so / slénderly
> Yóung and so / fáir

> Rázors / páin you
> Rívers are / dámp;
> Ácids / stáin you;
> And drúgs cause / crámp.

To describe the versification of a poem, you have to say not only how wide its lines are, but also what rhythm they are written in. English rhythms are based on *stressed* and *unstressed* syllables. Each stressed syllable with its associated unstressed syllable(s) makes a single unit, which we call a foot.

There are two main kinds of rhythm in English: *rising* rhythms and *falling* rhythms. In a *rising* rhythm, a foot consists of one or more unstressed syllables leading up to a stressed syllable: ˘´ or ˘˘´.

> Where the yoúth / pined awáy / with desíre
> And the pále / virgin shroúd / ed in snów
> Aríse / from their gráves / and aspíre
> Where my sún / flower wísh / es to gó.
> — WILLIAM BLAKE, "Ah Sun-flower"

In a *falling* rhythm, a foot begins with the stressed syllable, which is followed by one or more unstressed syllables: ´˘ or ´˘˘.

> Týger, / týger, / búrning / bríght
> Ín the / fórests / óf the / níght.
> — WILLIAM BLAKE, "The Tyger"

Metrical feet are named according to where their stress appears and how many unstressed syllables they possess. Rising rhythms are either *iambic* (with two syllables, ˘´) or *anapestic* (with three syllables, ˘˘´). We speak of an *iamb* or an *iambic foot* when we mean ˘´; an *anapest* or an *anapestic foot* when we mean ˘˘´. Falling rhythms are either *trochaic* (with two syllables, ´ ˘) or *dactylic* (with three syllables, ´ ˘ ˘). The corresponding nouns are *trochee* and *dactyl*.

When you read a poem in counted lines, try to see whether the general movement is a rising one or a falling one. In the two examples from Blake given above, "Ah Sun-flower" is written in rising anapestic (three-syllable) feet, and "The Tyger" in falling trochaic (two-syllable) feet.

In each *line* of "Ah Sun-flower" there are three *feet* (because there are three stressed syllables):

Where the yoúth / pined awáy / with desíre

In each *line* of "The Tyger" there are four *feet* (because there are four stressed syllables):

Týger, / týger, / búrning / bríght

If you think of each *stressed* syllable as a musical beat, the lines of "Ah Sun-flower" have three beats each ("and a *one* and a *two* and a *three*"); the lines of "The Tyger" have four beats each ("*one* and *two* and *three* and *four*").

Feet can shed one or more of their unstressed syllables. You can see that at the end of each line in "The Tyger," an unstressed syllable is "missing." And in "Ah Sun-flower," in the line "Aríse / from their gráves / and aspíre," an unstressed syllable is missing in the first foot, which has only two syllables, "Arise." These irregularities do not occur so often that they destroy the general impression of the metrical scheme underlying the poem.

If you hear these rhythms in your ear as you read, you will soon recognize them. Here are two more examples, to fill our scheme:

I found a dimpled spider, fat and white.
— ROBERT FROST, "Design"

Read aloud, this reveals itself to have five beats (five stressed syllables): "and *one* and *two* and *three* and *four* and *five*." Each of the five units consists of an unstressed syllable followed by a stressed syllable (iambic foot):

I foúnd / a dímp / led spí / der, fát / and whíte.

Listen to Longfellow's description of the original American forest:

This is the forest primeval, the murmuring pines and the hemlocks.
— HENRY WADSWORTH LONGFELLOW, "Evangeline"

Read aloud, this reveals itself to have six beats (six stressed syllables): "*one* and a *two* and a *three* and // a *four* and a *five* and a *six* and.*" Each foot (except the last, which has shed one unstressed syllable) consists of a stressed syllable followed by two unstressed syllables (dactylic foot):

> Thís is the / fórest prim / éval // the / múrmuring / pínes and the / hémlocks.

These rising and falling feet occur in lines of different widths. We have seen, above, trimeter lines ("Ah Sun-flower") and tetrameter lines ("The Tyger"). We have seen pentameter lines ("Design") and hexameter lines ("Evangeline"). *A full description of a line describes its rhythm and then its width.* "Ah Sun-flower" is written in anapestic trimeter. "The Tyger" is written in trochaic tetrameter. "Design" is written in iambic pentameter. "Evangeline" is written in dactylic hexameter.

It is less important that you know these names than that you recognize a rhythm by ear. Practice tapping out the rhythms above until they become familiar. Counting out the rhythm and length of a line is called *scanning* it.

It is often difficult, even impossible, to scan a single line taken by itself. One line can be scanned two or more ways, depending on the intonation we give it. The rule of thumb is to look at the other lines matching it. If they are all five-beat lines, then the dubious line is probably a five-beat line, too. But do not allow the prevailing rhythm, when you read a line aloud, to ride roughshod over the sense; the sense will usually tell you what syllables ought to be stressed.

In all rhythms, some feet are irregular, so that the cadence does not become intolerably inflexible. Feet of comparable length can freely substitute for each other. Shakespeare often begins one of his iambic (˘´) lines with an initial trochaic foot (´˘) to give energy to the line:

> Whý is / my verse / so bar / ren of / new pride?

Each of these metrical schemes is merely a grid underlying a line. The line itself must, by its intonation pattern, indicate the grid (or you cannot know what the basic rhythm is supposed to be), but it can depart from the grid in various ways — by substituting a different foot, by having a light foot called the *pyrrhic* (˘˘) for unimportant words, or a heavy foot called the *spondee* (´´) for important words, and so on. What you are asked to do in scanning the line is to see the underlying grid, first of all, and then to note any departures from it. Poets enjoy varying their rhythms to accord with dramatic emphasis, tone of voice, and so on. They also enjoy breaking their lines with a pause in the middle, which we call a *caesura* and represent with a double slash. An iambic pentameter line can be broken one or more times:

> I grant I never saw a goddess go;
> My mistress, // when she walks, // treads on the ground.
> And yet, // by heaven, // I think my love as rare
> As any she belied with false compare.
>
> — SHAKESPEARE, Sonnet 130

RHYMES AND STANZA-FORMS

Not all counted poetry is written in rhymes. But because lyric began as song (the name "lyric" comes from "lyre"), simple rhyming stanza-forms such as those found in the ballad or the hymn became important in the English tradition. Gradually, as oral poetry gave way to printed poetry (meant to be read rather than sung), stanza-forms of considerable complexity arose. Here are some of the most common rhyming forms in English. When rhyming units are separated by white space, they are called *stanzas*.

1. A pair of rhyming lines is called a *couplet*. Couplets are frequently run together, not separated as stanzas:

> While the plowman near at hand,
> Whistles o'er the furrowed land,
> And the milkmaid singeth blithe,
> And the mower whets his scythe,
> And every shepherd tells his tale,
> Under the hawthorn in the dale.
>
> — JOHN MILTON, "L'Allegro"

These couplets are written in trochaic tetrameter. The rhyme scheme of these lines is indicated thus: *aabbcc*. That is, because the first two lines rhyme ("hand" "land"), they can be indicated by *aa*, and because the next two rhyme, they can be indicated by *bb*. We indicate the *rhyme scheme* by these abbreviated lowercase italicized letters.

The *heroic couplet* is an iambic pentameter couplet that is end-stopped (marked by a heavy pause after the second line of the couplet), and frequently pointed and witty. Alexander Pope and John Dryden used it with brio:

> Meanwhile, declining from the noon of day,
> The sun obliquely shoots his burning ray;

The hungry judges soon the sentence sign,
And wretches hang that jurymen may dine.
— ALEXANDER POPE, "The Rape of the Lock"

2. A stanza of three lines is called a *tercet:*

Light the first light of evening, as in a room
In which we sit, and for small reason, think
The world imagined is the ultimate good.
— WALLACE STEVENS,
"Final Soliloquy of the Interior Paramour"

Terza rima is a form of pentameter tercet with interlinked rhymes (*aba bcb cdc* and so on) used by Dante in the *Divine Comedy.* It is difficult to carry off in English, though Shelley used it for his "Ode to the West Wind." Many poets intend an allusion to Dante when they use loosely rhymed pentameter tercets.

3. A stanza of four lines is called a *quatrain.* The commonest quatrain is the *ballad stanza,* in which the first and third lines are unrhymed and have four beats, while the second and fourth lines rhyme and have three beats:

It is an ancient Mariner,
And he stoppeth one of three.
"By thy long grey beard and glittering eye,
Now wherefore stopp'st thou me?"
— SAMUEL TAYLOR COLERIDGE,
"The Rime of the Ancient Mariner"

Some tetrameter quatrains are rhymed *abba,* like those in Shakespeare's "The Phoenix and the Turtle" and Tennyson's "In Memoriam." This stanza is generally referred to as the *"In Memoriam" stanza:*

Ring out, wild bells, to the wild sky,
The flying cloud, the frosty light,
The year is dying in the night;
Ring out, wild bells, and let him die.

The *heroic quatrain* is an iambic pentameter quatrain, rhyming *abab:*

I know my life's a pain and but a span;
I know my sense is mock'd with everything;

And, to conclude, I know myself a man,
Which is a proud and yet a wretched thing.

— SIR JOHN DAVIES, "Nosce Teipsum"

4. A stanza of six lines is sometimes called a *sixain* (its French name) or a *sestet.* The commonest sixain rhyme-form is *ababcc.* A pentameter sixain rhyming this way is called the *"Venus and Adonis stanza,"* from the poem of that name by Shakespeare:

> Look how a bird lies tangled in a net,
> So fast'nd in her arms Adonis lies,
> Pure shame and awed resistance made him fret,
> Which bred more beauty in his angry eyes.
>> Rain added to a river that is rank
>> Perforce will force it overflow the bank.

5. The only common seven-line stanza is *rime royal* (so called because King James I used it) — iambic pentameter rhyming *ababbcc.* This is the meter of many long poems on high themes — Chaucer's *Troilus and Criseyde,* for instance. Spenser uses it for his "Four Hymns":

> For love is a celestial harmony
> Of likely hearts composed of stars' consent,
> Which join together in sweet sympathy,
> To work each other's joy and true content,
> Which they have harbored since their first descent
> Out of their heavenly bowers, where they did see
> And know each other here beloved to be.

— EDMUND SPENSER, "Hymn to Love"

6. The best-known eight-line form is *ottava rima* — iambic pentameter rhyming *abababcc.* The final couplet can give this stanza epigrammatic point, and Byron used it with notable wit in his long poem *Don Juan.* Its greatest modern practitioner has been W. B. Yeats:

> Labour is blossoming or dancing where
> The body is not bruised to pleasure soul,
> Nor beauty born out of its own despair,
> Nor blear-eyed wisdom out of midnight oil.
> O chestnut-tree, great-rooted blossomer,
> Are you the leaf, the blossom or the bole?

> O body swayed to music, O brightening glance,
> How can we know the dancer from the dance?
> — W. B. YEATS, "Among School Children"

7. The best-known nine-line form is the *Spenserian stanza* (so called because Spenser used it in *The Faerie Queene*). Keats adopted it for "The Eve of St. Agnes." All its lines are pentameter, except the last, which is a hexameter. It rhymes in a closely linked way: *ababbcbcc.*

> St. Agnes' Eve — Ah, bitter chill it was!
> The owl, for all his feathers, was a-cold;
> The hare limped trembling through the frozen grass,
> And silent was the flock in woolly fold:
> Numb were the Beadsman's fingers, while he told
> His rosary, and while his frosted breath,
> Like pious incense from a censer old,
> Seemed taking flight for heaven, without a death,
> Past the sweet Virgin's picture, while his prayer he saith.
> — JOHN KEATS, "The Eve of St. Agnes"

There are many unnamed stanza-forms, some of them common ones. For instance, an extra line or two is often added to the ballad stanza, to make a five- or six-line stanza. Or a *refrain* (a line repeated after every stanza) can be added to lengthen the ballad quatrain.

TYPES OF RHYMING POEMS

1. The *sonnet* is a fourteen-line pentameter poem. There are two chief forms:

The *Italian (Petrarchan) sonnet* consists of an octave and a sestet. There are embraced rhymes in the octave (the first eight lines): *abbaabba.* The sestet of a Petrarchan sonnet can rhyme in several different ways, but the most common are *cdecde* and (as below) *cdcdee:*

> Who will in fairest book of Nature know
>   How Virtue may best lodged in beauty be,
>   Let him but learn of *Love* to read in thee,
> Stella, those fair lines which true goodness show.
> There shall he find all vices' overthrow,
>   Not by rude force, but sweetest sovereignty
>   Of reason, from whose light those nightbirds fly,
> That inward sun in thine eyes shineth so.
>   And, not content to be Perfection's heir

Thyself, dost strive all minds that way to move,
Who mark in thee what is in thee most fair.
So while thy beauty draws the heart to love,
    As fast thy Virtue bends that love to good.
    "But ah," Desire still cries, "give me some food."
            — SIR PHILIP SIDNEY, *Astrophel and Stella*, 71

The *English (Shakespearean) sonnet* consists of three four-line quatrains, alternately rhymed *(ababcdcdefef)*, and a couplet, *gg:*

Let me not to the marriage of true minds
Admit impediments. Love is not love
Which alters when it alteration finds,
Or bends with the remover to remove.
O no, it is an ever fixèd mark
That looks on tempests and is never shaken;
It is the star to every wand'ring bark,
Whose worth's unknown, although his height be taken.
Love's not Time's fool, though rosy lips and cheeks
Within his bending sickle's compass come,
Love alters not with his brief hours and weeks,
But bears it out even to the edge of doom.
    If this be error and upon me proved,
    I never writ, nor no man ever loved.

There have been many variations on the two basic sonnet forms. Spenser wrote sonnets that were composed of linked rhymes: *abab bcbc cdcd ee.* Some poets (Herbert, Yeats) have made hybrid sonnets by attaching Petrarchan sestets to Shakespearean octaves, or vice versa. Others, like George Meredith and Stevens, have written sonnet-like poems with sixteen or fifteen lines. The odes of Keats basically form their stanzas by combining a Shakespearean quatrain with a Petrarchan sestet (they vary the length of line and sometimes double a rhyme, but it is clear that their elements come from the two sonnet traditions).

2. The *sestina* is a pentameter poem consisting of six stanzas of six lines plus a three-line coda (known as the *envoy* or *envoi*). The sestina "rhymes" on six end-words, which must be repeated in each stanza in a controlled order, whereby the last end-word in each stanza becomes the first end-word of the next stanza: *abcdef, faebdc, cfdabe, ecbfad, deacfb, bdfeca.* The envoi must employ two of the end-words in each of its three lines. A good sestina makes this difficult pattern seem natural. The sestina is easier seen than described. Here is one (called "Sestina") by Elizabeth Bishop. The six end-words are "house," "grandmother," "child," "stove," "almanac," and "tears."

It may help to know that Bishop was raised by her grandmother, since her father was dead and her mother was confined to an insane asylum:

September rain falls on the house.
In the failing light, the old grandmother
sits in the kitchen with the child
beside the Little Marvel Stove,
reading the jokes from the almanac,
laughing and talking to hide her tears.

She thinks that her equinoctial tears
and the rain that beats on the roof of the house
were both foretold by the almanac,
but only known to a grandmother.
The iron kettle sings on the stove.
She cuts some bread and says to the child,

It's time for tea now; but the child
is watching the teakettle's small hard tears
dance like mad on the hot black stove,
the way the rain must dance on the house.
Tidying up, the old grandmother
hangs up the clever almanac

on its string. Birdlike, the almanac
hovers half open above the child,
hovers above the old grandmother
and her teacup full of dark brown tears.
She shivers and says she thinks the house
feels chilly, and puts more wood in the stove.

It was to be, says the Marvel Stove.
I know what I know, says the almanac.
With crayons the child draws a rigid house
and a winding pathway. Then the child
puts in a man with buttons like tears
and shows it proudly to the grandmother.

But secretly, while the grandmother
busies herself about the stove,
the little moons fall down like tears
from between the pages of the almanac
into the flower bed the child
has carefully placed in the front of the house.

Time to plant tears, says the almanac.
The grandmother sings to the marvelous stove
and the child draws another inscrutable house.

3. The *villanelle* is a French form that has been used with notable suc-
cess by many modern poets, among them Theodore Roethke, William
Empson, Dylan Thomas, and Bishop. A villanelle is a poem of five pen-
tameter tercets rhyming *aba,* followed by a pentameter quatrain rhyming
abaa. In a villanelle, lines 1 and 3 of the first tercet are repeated alter-
nately at the end of each following tercet, and they close the final qua-
train. Again, this is easier seen than described, and in a good villanelle the
repetitions are made to seem natural. Here is Dylan Thomas's villanelle
"Do Not Go Gentle into That Good Night," a poem he wrote when his
father was dying:

Do not go gentle into that good night,
Old age should burn and rave at close of day;
Rage, rage against the dying of the light.

Though wise men at their end know dark is right,
Because their words had forked no lightning they
Do not go gentle into that good night.

Good men, the last wave by, crying how bright
Their frail deeds might have danced in a green bay,
Rage, rage against the dying of the light.

Wild men who caught and sang the sun in flight,
And learn, too late, they grieved it on its way,
Do not go gentle into that good night.

Grave men, near death, who see with blinding sight
Blind eyes could blaze like meteors and be gay,
Rage, rage against the dying of the light.

And you, my father, there on the sad height,
Curse, bless, me now with your fierce tears, I pray.
Do not go gentle into that good night.
Rage, rage against the dying of the light.

There are many other rhymed poem-forms, such as the *rondeau,* the *bal-
lade,* the *pantoum.* A poet using one of the rhymed poem-forms expects
the reader to recall the tradition of such forms.

4. The *ode* in English is usually a stanzaic poem, but it has no set form.
An ode is defined by its content: it is a poem of a lofty or sublime sort,

often using the figure of speech called *apostrophe,* which is an address to some divine or quasi-divine person or thing. "O wild West Wind," says Shelley; "Thou still unravished bride of quietness," says Keats addressing the Grecian urn.

COUNTED VERSE THAT DOES NOT RHYME

The most common form of counted unrhymed verse is *blank verse,* unrhymed iambic pentameter lines. This is the verse of Shakespeare's plays and of Milton's epic poem, *Paradise Lost:*

> That space the evil one abstracted stood
> From his own evil, and for the time remained
> Stupidly good, of enmity disarmed,
> Of guile, of hate, of envy, of revenge.

Blank verse can also be used in a lyric, as Coleridge uses it in his poem "Frost at Midnight":

> Therefore all seasons shall be sweet to thee,
> Whether the summer clothe the general earth
> With greenness, or the redbreast sit and sing
> Betwixt the tufts of snow on the bare branch.

Most of the unrhymed verse in English is blank verse, though poets have also written unrhymed four-beat poems that imitate Anglo-Saxon meter. Some poets have experimented with stanzas of unrhymed verse in imitation of Greek and Latin verse (which did not rhyme, but depended on a quantitative system contrasting long vowels with short vowels). Here are two stanzas of Thomas Campion's "Rose-Cheeked Laura," an imitation of the Greek meter called, after the poet Sappho, *sapphic.* The first three lines have four beats each, the fourth line two beats:

> Róse-cheéked Laúra, cóme,
> Síng thou smoóthly wíth thy beaúty's
> Sílent músic, eíther óther
>   Sweétly grácing.

> Lovely forms do flow
> From concent divinely framèd;
> Heav'n is music, and thy beauty's
>   Birth is heavenly.

Every so often a new poet will once again imitate classical unrhymed forms.

Free Verse

Free verse — verse in which the lines are of different widths, and which does not rhyme in any regular way — was invented by poets who had been brought up on rhymed and counted verse. Poets like Whitman, Pound, Eliot, Stevens, Williams, Lowell, and Bishop all began by writing conventional verse. Whitman was drawn to free verse because he saw it as a primitive, "bardic" form. Eliot wrote it in imitation of the French poet Jules Laforgue. Pound wrote it in an attempt to achieve poetic effects he thought inhered in the Chinese ideogram. Williams and Stevens adopted it as a way to free themselves from the hold of English poets such as Keats. But behind their free verse there lurked always the shadow of counted verse. Eliot's "The Love Song of J. Alfred Prufrock" keeps threatening to turn into regular pentameter. Pound's largely free-verse "Cantos" include counted and rhymed segments.

The history of free verse is not yet entirely understood. The United States was a more hospitable environment for it than England, and a nativist wish to throw off inherited English forms certainly motivated many American poets. The unit of free verse seems to be the breath: there is a breath limit to the long line of free verse (reached by Whitman and Ginsberg, to give two notable examples). The theoretical appeal of free verse is that it admits an element of chance; it offers a model not of a teleological or providential universe but of an *aleatory* one, where the casual, rather than the fated, holds sway.

Free verse must justify its reasons for breaking a line here rather than there. If we look at a small free-verse poem, William Carlos Williams's "The Red Wheelbarrow," we must ask why the lines break where they do:

> So much depends
> upon
>
> a red wheel
> barrow
>
> glazed with rain
> water
>
> beside the white
> chickens

We might notice that in each little "stanza" the second line has only two syllables. This gives symmetry to the poem. The word "upon" literally hangs off the word "depends," acting out the meaning of something which depends (Latin: *dependere,* "to hang from") on something else. The red "wheel" turns into a "wheelbarrow" as we turn the line. Rain turns into rainwater, in the same way. After the inorganic wheelbarrow and rainwater, we may expect an inorganic object to follow the word "white" — say "the white / fence." Instead, the scene comes alive with chickens.

This very mannered little poem says that if the eye didn't see something inviting in the landscape (the shiny glaze the rain has put on the redness of the wheelbarrow; the composition of the still wheelbarrow and the living chickens; the contrast of red and white), there would be nothing to write about. "So much depends" on there being something out there to gratify and focus the eye. When we understand the poem, we understand its line-breaks. A free-verse poem that doesn't justify its line-breaks hardly deserves the name "poem."

Summary

When you come across a new poem, look at the way it displays itself on the page. Is it a skinny poem or a wide poem? A short poem or a long one? Are all the lines the same length, or are some shorter than others? Does it rhyme? Does it have stanzas?

Think of the look of the poem as its body. Is it a symmetrical body or a ragged body? A solid-looking body or an emaciated one?

As you read it aloud and listen to its rhythms, feel what it is telling you. Is it serious or even ponderous? Or does it move with a lilt and a skip? Does it change its manner of walking, from indolent to hurried? Does it manifest leisure or anxiety in its rhythms?

These are questions to ask even before you begin to note a rhyme scheme or count how many beats there are in a line. After you have done the technical noticing and counting, ask yourself how these formal features match up with the sentiments and emotions that the poem is expressing. Do the formal features align with those sentiments, or do they contradict them? It is always worthwhile to pay attention to the technical work the poet has done on the external form of the poem; it is, after all, the body the poet has chosen to live in for a determined period.

For a more complete survey of metrical forms, see Paul Fussell, *Poetic Meter and Poetic Form* (New York: Random House, 1965; revised 1979); or John Hollander, *Rhyme's Reason* (New Haven, Conn.: Yale University Press, 1981). For fuller definitions of terms used here, see the *Princeton Encyclopedia of Poetry and Poetics,* ed. Alex Preminger et al. (Princeton, N.J.: Princeton University Press, 1965; rpt. 1993).

Appendix 2. On Grammar

A familiarity with grammatical terms can help you to analyze and to describe poetry. This appendix provides a brief review of some of the most common and useful grammatical terms.

Noun

A word that names a person, place, thing, or idea. Examples: "Adam," "garden," "chair," "destiny." In short, a noun names an *essence*.

Adjective

A word that tells you something about that essence. An adjective modifies a noun by limiting or describing it. Examples: "the *early* bird," "a *false* alarm." An adjective expresses something present with or connected to a noun, but not essential: "a *red* wheelbarrow" (not all wheelbarrows are red). Adjectives are the chief resource of descriptive language, as when Shakespeare says (Sonnet 129) that lust is "perjur'd, murderous, bloody, full of blame, / Savage, extreme, rude, cruel, not to trust." The plainness of nouns is fleshed out by adjectives; and the complexity of life is such that poems need a wealth of adjectives to describe their essential nouns.

Pronoun

A word that stands in for a noun. Pronouns can be used as subjects (nominative case, as in "On a cloud *I* saw a child") or as objects (objective case, as in "And he laughing said to *me*"). In what follows I'll give the objective case in brackets after the nominative case.

The *first-person singular* is "I" [objective: "me"]; the *first-person plural* is "we" ["us"].

The modern *second-person pronoun* is "you" in both the singular and plural, nominative and objective, though in the past it was more complex. Then, the second-person singular was "thou" ["thee"], and the plural was "ye." "Thou" was used both in familiar address and in an exalted form of address to God or a monarch; over time, "you" took its place.

The *third-person singular* pronouns are "he" ["him"], "she" ["her"], and "it"; the plural is "they" ["them"].

A change in person ("I" to "you") or in number ("I" to "we") in a poem is always of profound significance, since, on the general principle of inertia, a speaker tends to continue in the same person rather than change, unless the change is somehow provoked. In the poem "In Memory of Eva Gore-Booth and Con Markiewicz," Yeats himself changes significantly from "I" to "we," as he finally makes common cause with the sisters he had begun by opposing; and his reference to the sisters changes from "one or the other" (third-person, people other than the poet) to "you" (people he addresses) to "we" (part of a group which also contains the poet):

> Many a time *I* think to seek
> *One or the other* out. . . .

> Dear shadows, now *you* know it all. . . .

> *We* the great gazebo built. . . .

A reader who misses the changes in person and number here misses the essential drama of the poem, as the poet changes his mind about the sisters and his relation to them.

Verb

A word that usually conveys either action ("My mother *bore* me in the southern wild") or state ("And I *am* black"). Verbs may be

> *Linking* verbs, which join two things that are equivalent ("He *seems* tired"; "I *will become* a teacher"; "Mary *is* a doctor");
>
> *Transitive* verbs, which take objects both direct and indirect ("I *gave* him the book"); or
>
> *Intransitive* verbs, which do not take an object ("The building *fell* down").

Verbs can appear in two *voices:*

> *Active:* "I do this."
>
> *Passive:* "This is done to me."

They can take on different *tenses* (past, present, future, and so on):

> *Simple present:* "I *sing* of heaven."
>
> *Present of habitual action:* "Whenever it *rains,* I *take* my umbrella."
>
> *Present of perpetual truth:* "Water *boils* at 212°F."
>
> *Present of state:* "I *am* a lawyer."
>
> *Present progressive:* "It *is raining.*"
>
> *Simple past:* "I *knew* him, Horatio."
>
> *Compound past:* "I *have known* him a long time."

Past progressive: "It *was snowing.*"

Pluperfect: "I *had known* him for several years before I met his wife."

Simple future: "I *will call* him tomorrow."

Future perfect: "I *will have called* him by Wednesday."

Future progressive: "I *shall be telling* this with a sigh."

They can appear in different *moods* (statement, question, wish, and so on):

Indicative (states an assertion): "I *like* him."

Interrogative (asks a question): "*Do* you *like* him?"

Imperative (gives a command): "*Do* this."

Subjunctive (often contrary to fact or hypothetical): "If I *were to do* this, I would be prosecuted."

Optative (wish): "Oh, if I *could* only *do* [*have done*] this!"

Hortatory (enjoining something): "*Let us kiss* and part."

Conditional: "I *should like* to come if you *would let* me."

Poems can achieve multiple effects by changing tenses and moods as they go along.

Adverb

A word that characterizes (limits or describes) a verb, just as an adjective characterizes a noun. Adverbs answer the questions "Where?" "How?" "In what manner?" "When?" "Why?" and so on. Examples: "Till noon we *quietly* sailed on"; "my collar mounting *firmly* to my chin." Since verbs, like nouns, tend to be bare things, the poet uses adverbs to put a halo of circumstance around the verbs of the poem. Verbs are also amplified by adverbial phrases: "From you have I been absent *in the spring.*"

Appendix 3. On Speech Acts

There are numberless speech acts in which a lyric speaker may engage. The list that follows is merely a sampling of common ones in lyric. It is always a good idea to name the successive speech acts in a poem. Does it begin with an apology? Is that followed by a plea? Is that followed by a claim? Is that followed by a boast? This classifying helps you to track the emotions that structure a poem.

ACKNOWLEDGING	The darkness drops again, but now I know. . . .
ADDRESS	Old trooper, I see your child's red crayon pass.
ADMISSION	Alas, 'tis true, I have gone here and there, And made myself a motley to the view.
APOLOGY	Sweet Love of youth, forgive, if I forget thee.
APOSTROPHE	O wild West Wind!
BANISHING	Hence, loathèd Melancholy!
BOAST	Not marble, nor the gilded monuments Of princes, shall outlive this powerful rhyme.
CELEBRATION	I celebrate myself, and sing myself.
CLAIM	Mine — by the Right of the White Election!
COMMAND	Irish poets, learn your trade, Sing whatever is well made.
CONJECTURE	Thou mayst be false, and yet I know it not.
CONSOLATION	Fear no more the heat o' the sun.
DEFINITION	Remorse — is Memory — awake —
DESCRIPTION	No cloud, no relique of the sunken day Distinguishes the West.
DIALOGUE	Does the road wind uphill all the way? Yes, to the very end.
DREAMING	I dream of a Ledaean body, bent Above a sinking fire.

Exclamation	What a piece of work is a man!
Exhortation	Be shellèd, eyes, with double dark And find the uncreated light.
Expostulation	Up, up, my friend, and quit your books!
Generalization	All this the world well knows, yet none knows well To shun the heaven that leads men to this hell.
Imprecation	For God's sake hold your tongue, and let me love.
Instruction	He who binds to himself a joy Does the wingèd life destroy.
Invitation	Come live with me and be my love.
Invocation	But come, thou goddess fair and free.
Lament	Alas! I have nor hope nor health.
Narration	
PRESENT	It is an ancient Mariner And he stoppeth one of three.
PAST	I wandered lonely as a cloud.
HABITUAL	For oft, when on my couch I lie . . . They flash upon that inward eye.
HISTORICAL	Calvert and Wilson, Blake and Claude, Prepared a peace for the people of God.
Oath	I will not harm her, by all saints I swear.
Plea	Say, may I be for aye thy vassal blest?
Prayer	Mine, O thou Lord of life, send my roots rain.
Prophecy	Therefore all seasons shall be sweet to thee.
Question	Did he who made the Lamb make thee?
Rebuttal	Love's not Time's fool.
Reminiscence	I was thy neighbor once, thou rugged Pile!
Request	Permit me voyage, love, into your hands.
Resolve	Despair I will not.
Retraction	But I am by her death (which word wrongs her) . . .

RHETORICAL QUESTION	O chestnut-tree, great-rooted blossomer, / Are you the leaf, the blossom, or the bole?
SCORNING	How vainly men themselves amaze / To win the palm, the oak, the bays.
SELF–BLAME	I see / The lost are like this, and their scourge to be / As I am mine, their sweating selves, but worse.
SELF–CORRECTION	Alas, but Morrison fell young: / He never fell, thou fall'st, my tongue. / He stood, a soldier to the last right end.
SELF–PRESENTATION	I am the mower Damon.
SPELL	No exorciser harm thee! / Nor no witchcraft charm thee!
SUPPOSITION	Had we but world enough, and time.
SURMISE	I cannot see what flowers are at my feet . . . / But, in embalmèd darkness, guess each sweet.
VOW	Yes, I will be thy priest.

Appendix 4. On Rhetorical Devices

These devices, sometimes called "figures of speech," appear in all speech and writing (you can find them in advertising, political speeches, and newspapers, as well as in essays, letters, and poems). It helps, if you wish to give a brief description of what a writer is doing at a given moment, to know some of these shorthand terms for frequent practices.

ALTERNATIVE ORDERING

A man that looks on glass,
On it may stay his eye,
Or, if he pleaseth, through it pass,
And then the heaven espy.

ANALOGY
(comparison of A and B)

No more be grieved at that which thou
    hast done:
Roses have thorns, and silver fountains
    mud.

ANAPHORA
(repetition of opening word)

All shuffle there, all cough in ink,
All wear the carpet with their shoes,
All think what other people think;
All know the man their neighbor knows.

ANTICLIMAX

In silk, in crepes, in Garters, and in rags.

ANTITHESIS
(opposition of A and B)

For I have sworn thee fair, and thought
    thee bright,
Who art as black as hell, as dark as night.

APPOSITION
(list of different formulations of the same thing)

    The Mind of Man,
My haunt, and the main region of my
    song.

CATALOGUE

The leaden-eyed shark, the walrus, the
    turtle, the hairy sea-leopard.

CHIASMUS
(an X-like arrangement)

By brooks too broad for leaping
    The lightfoot boys are laid;
The rose-lipt girls are sleeping
    In fields where roses fade.
[brooks : boys :: girls : fields]

HIERARCHICAL ORDERING	Such sweet neglect more taketh me Than all th' adulteries of art.
METAPHOR *(comparison without "like" or "as")*	Church bells beyond the stars heard, the soul's blood, The land of spices; something understood.
METONYMY *(assemblage by parts)*	Four beating wings, two beaks, a swirling mass.
ONOMATOPOEIA *(imitative sound)*	And murmuring of innumerable bees.
PARADOX *(union of dissimilar qualities)*	There is in God, some say, A deep but dazzling darkness.
PARALLELISM	These are thy wonders, Lord of Power . . . These are thy wonders, Lord of Love.
PERIPHRASIS *(circumlocution)*	The Peer now spreads the glittering forfex wide [= opens scissors]
PERSONIFICATION *(an abstraction made into a person)*	Love is swift of foot, Love's a man of war.
PUN *(a play on two meanings of one word)*	Therefore I lie with her, and she with me, And in our faults by lies we flattered be.
QUOTATION	My flesh began unto my soul in pain, "Sicknesses cleave my bones."
SIMILE *(comparison with "like" or "as")*	Like as the waves make toward the pebbled shore, So do our minutes hasten to their end.
SYNECDOCHE *(use of the part for the whole)*	Diadems — drop — and Doges — surrender
ZEUGMA *(two dissimilar objects of same verb)*	Or stain her honor, or her new brocade.

Appendix 5. On Lyric Subgenres

This is a summary of the kinds of poems that lyric poets return to most frequently. It is convenient to be able to name a poem by its kind, because you can then compare it to others of the same kind.

ADDRESS TO THE READER	Pray thee, take care, that tak'st my book.
BALLAD	There lived a wife at Usher's well, And a wealthy wife was she; She had three stout and stalwart sons, And sent them o'er the sea.
CHILD'S POEM	"The Little Black Boy" (Blake)
DAWN POEM *(aubade)*	Get up! get up for shame! the blooming morn Upon her wings presents the god unshorn.
DEATHBED POEM	I heard a Fly buzz — when I died —
DEBATE-POEM	*Body* O who shall me deliver whole From bonds of this tyrannic soul? . . . *Soul* What magic could me thus confine Within another's grief to pine?
ECHO-POEM	Then tell me, what is that supreme de- light? Light. Light to the mind, what shall the will en- joy? Joy.
EKPHRASIS *(poem on an art object)*	"Ode on a Grecian Urn" (Keats)
ELEGY	Felix Randal the farrier, O is he dead then, my duty all ended?
EMBLEM-POEM *(allegorical object)*	"The Sick Rose" (Blake)

EPIGRAM *(short, pointed poem)*	I am his Highness' dog at Kew: And pray, good sir, whose dog are you?
EPITAPH	Underneath this stone doth lie All of beauty that could die.
EPITHALAMION *(wedding song)*	And evermore they *Hymen Hymen* sing, That al the woods them answer and theyr eccho ring.
HYMN	Jerusalem, Jerusalem, Lift up your gates and sing, Hosanna in the highest . . .
INSCRIPTION	I the poet William Yeats . . . Restored this tower for my wife George: And may these characters remain When all is ruin once again.
LETTER	This is my letter to the world That never wrote to me.
LOVER'S COMPLAINT	And wilt thou leave me thus?
LULLABY	Lullay, lullay, thou tiny child.
MUSE-POEM	"The Solitary Reaper" (Wordsworth)
NOCTURNE	'Tis the year's midnight, and it is the day's.
PASTORAL *(rustic poem)*	The shepherds' swains shall dance and sing For thy delight each May morning.
POLITICAL POEM	"Easter, 1916" (Yeats)
PRAISE-POEM	Shall I compare thee to a summer's day? Thou art more lovely and more temperate.
QUEST-POEM	"The Pilgrimage" (Herbert)
RELIGIOUS POEM	I saw eternity the other night.
ROMANCE *(fairy-tale poem)*	"The Eve of St. Agnes" (Keats)
SEASONAL POEM	Sumer is icumen in, Lhude sing cuccu!

SELF-REFLEXIVE POEM	I sing of brooks, of blossoms, birds, and bowers.
SHAPED POEM	"Easter Wings" (Herbert)
SONG	It was a lover and his lass, With a hey and a ho and a hey nonny no . . .
TWIN POEMS	"The Lamb" and "The Tyger" (Blake)
VALEDICTION	Adieu, farewell earth's bliss.
VARIATIONS ON A THEME	"Thirteen Ways of Looking at a Black-bird" (Stevens)

There are many other such that one could name: the *bird poem,* the *eclogue* (a dialogue of shepherds), the *georgic* (a poem on farming), the *testament* (a poem making a will), the *conversation poem* (a poem of a middle, or familiar, style recounting a conversation among friends), and so on. The essential thing is to realize that almost any poem is a repeat of a preceding genre, perhaps an answer to it, perhaps a revision of it. Thinking "What kind of a lyric is this?" makes you more aware of its place in a genre tradition, and of its response to that tradition.

Elizabeth Bishop, "One Art," "The Fish," "Poem," and "Sestina" from *Elizabeth Bishop: The Complete Poems 1927–1979*. Copyright © 1979, 1983 by Alice Helen Methfessel. Reprinted with the permission of Farrar, Straus & Giroux, LLC.

Richard Blanco, "Letters for Mama." As found in *Little Havana Blues: A Cuban-American Literature Anthology*, edited by Delia Poey and Virgil Suarez (Houston: Arte Publico, 1996). Reprinted with the permission of the publisher.

Michael Blumenthal, "A Marriage" from *Against Romance*. Copyright © 1987 by Michael Blumenthal. Reprinted with the permission of Viking Penguin, a division of Penguin Putnam Inc. "Wishful Thinking" from *Days We Would Rather Know* (New York: Viking Penguin, 1984). Copyright © 1984 by Michael Blumenthal. Reprinted with the permission of the author.

Lucie Brock-Broido, "Carrowmore" from *The Master Letters*. Copyright © 1995 by Lucie Brock-Broido. "Domestic Mysticism" from *A Hunger*. Copyright © 1988 by Lucie Brock-Broido. Both reprinted with the permission of Alfred A. Knopf, a division of Random House, Inc.

Gwendolyn Brooks, "We Real Cool," "The Bean Eaters," "Kitchenette Building," and "The Mother" from *Blacks*. Copyright © 1991 by Gwendolyn Brooks. Reprinted with the permission of Gwendolyn Brooks.

Lorna Dee Cervantes, "Poema para los Californios Muertos," "Poem for the Young White Man Who Asked Me How I, an Intelligent Well-Read Person Could Believe in the War Between Races," and "Freeway 280" from *Emplumada*. Copyright © 1981 by Lorna Dee Cervantes. Reprinted with the permission of the University of Pittsburgh Press. "Freeway 280" from Emplumada (Pittsburgh: University of Pittsburgh Press, 1981). Originally in *The Latin American Literary Review* 5, no. 10 (1977). Reprinted with the permission of the publishers.

Marilyn Chin, "Autumn Leaves" from *The Phoenix Gone, The Terrace Empty*. Copyright © 1994 by Marilyn Chin. Reprinted with the permission of Milkweed Editions.

Amy Clampitt, "A Procession at Candlemas" from *The Kingfisher*. Copyright © 1983 by Amy Clampitt. Reprinted with the permission of Alfred A. Knopf, a division of Random House, Inc.

Henri Cole, "40 Days and 40 Nights" from *The Look of Things*. Copyright © 1994 by Henri Cole. Reprinted with the permission of Alfred A. Knopf, a division of Random House, Inc. "Kayaks." Reprinted with the permission of the author.

Robert Creeley, "A Marriage" from *The Collected Poems of Robert Creeley*. Copyright © 1982 by The Regents of the University of California. Reprinted with the permission of the University of California Press.

Countee Cullen, "Heritage" and "Incident" from *On These I Stand: An Anthology of the Best Poems of Countee Cullen*. Copyright 1925 by Harper & Brothers, renewed

1953 by Ida M. Cullen. Reprinted with the permission of Thompson and Thompson, for the Estate of Countee Cullen.

E. E. Cummings, "in Just-," "r-p-o-p-h-e-s-s-a-g-r," "Anyone lived in a pretty how town," and "may I feel said he" from *Complete Poems: 1904–1962*, edited by George J. Firmage. Copyright 1923, 1935, 1940, 1951, 1963, 1968, 1991 by the Trustees for the E.E. Cummings Trust. Copyright © 1976, 1978 by George J. Firmage. Reprinted with the permission of Liveright Publishing Corporation.

Silvia Curbelo, "Balsero Singing" from *The Secret History of Water* (Tallahassee: Anhinga Press, 1998). Reprinted with the permission of the publishers.

Emily Dickinson, "A narrow Fellow in the grass," "The Heart asks Pleasure — first — ," "I heard a Fly buzz — when I died — ," "I'm nobody — Who are you?," "Because I could not stop for death," "After great pain, a formal feeling comes," "The Brain — is wider than the Sky — ," "I like a look of Agony," "Much Madness is divinest Sense — ," "My Life had stood — a Loaded Gun — ," "Safe in their alabaster chambers" (1859), "Safe in their alabaster chambers" (1861), "The Soul selects her own Society," "Success is counted sweetest," "Wild Nights — Wild Nights!," "I Like to See It Lap the Miles," "I felt a Cleaving in my Mind," "The first Day's Night had come," "There's a certain Slant of light," and "Pain — expands the Time" from *The Poems of Emily Dickinson*, edited by Thomas H. Johnson. Copyright © 1951, 1955, 1979, 1983 by the President and Fellows of Harvard College. All rights reserved. Reprinted with the permission of The Belknap Press of Harvard University Press.

H. D. (Hilda Doolittle), "Oread" and "Helen" from *Collected Poems 1912–1944*, edited by Louis L. Martz. Copyright © 1962 by The Estate of Hilda Doolittle. Reprinted with the permission of New Directions Publishing Corporation.

Rita Dove, "Wingfoot Lake," "Parsley," "Adolescence — II," and "Dusting" from *Selected Poems* (New York: Random House, 1993). Copyright © 1993 by Rita Dove. Reprinted with the permission of the author. "Flash Cards" from *Grace Notes*. Copyright © 1989 by Rita Dove. Reprinted with the permission of the author and W. W. Norton & Company, Inc.

T. S. Eliot, "The Love Song of J. Alfred Prufrock," "Marina," and "Preludes" from *Collected Poems 1909–1962*. Copyright © 1963. Reprinted with the permission of Harcourt, Inc. and Faber and Faber, Limited.

Thomas Sayers Ellis, "View of the Library of Congress from Paul Laurence Dunbar High School" from *The Southern Review* (Spring 1995). Copyright © 1995 by Thomas Sayers Ellis. Reprinted with the permission of the author.

Louise Erdrich, "I Was Sleeping Where the Black Oaks Move," "The Strange People," and "Windigo" from *Jacklight*. Copyright © 1984 by Louise Erdrich. Reprinted with the permission of Henry Holt and Company, LLC.

Robert Frost, "The Road Not Taken," "Mending Wall," "Stopping by Woods on a Snowy Evening," "The Gift Outright," "Birches," "Design," "After Apple-Picking," and "Unharvested" from *The Poetry of Robert Frost*, edited by Edward Connery Lathem. Copyright © 1936, 1942, 1951 by Robert Frost. Copyright © 1964, 1970 by Lesley Frost Ballantine. Copyright © 1923, 1969 by Henry Holt and Company, LLC. Reprinted with the permission of Henry Holt and Company, LLC.

James Galvin, "Independence Day, 1956: A Fairy Tale" from *Lethal Frequencies*. Originally published in *The New Yorker*. Copyright © 1995 by James Galvin. Reprinted with the permission of Copper Canyon Press, P. O. Box 271, Port Townsend, WA 98368-0271.

Allen Ginsberg, "Sunflower Sutra" and "America" from *Collected Poems 1947–1980*. Copyright © 1955 by Allen Ginsberg. Copyright renewed. Reprinted with the permission of HarperCollins Publishers, Inc.

Louise Glück, "The School Children," "All Hallows," and "Mock Orange" from *The First Four Books of Poems*. Copyright © 1975, 1985 by Louise Glück. "The White Lilies" from The Wild Iris. Copyright © 1992 by Louise Glück. "The Balcony" from *The Seven Ages*. Copyright ©2001 by Louise Glück. All reprinted with the permission of HarperCollins Publishers, Inc.

Jorie Graham, "What the End Is For" from *The End of Beauty*. Copyright © 1987 by Jorie Graham. "Soul Says" from *Regions of Unlikeness*. Copyright © 1991 by Jorie Graham. Both reprinted with the permission of HarperCollins Publishers, Inc. "San Sepolcro" and "Of Forces Sightes and Trusty Ferefulness" from *Erosion*. Copyright © 1983 by Jorie Graham. Reprinted with the permission of Princeton University Press.

Thom Gunn, "The Man with Night Sweats" from *The Man with Night Sweats*. Copyright © 1992 by Thom Gunn. "My Sad Captains" from *My Sad Captains*. Copyright © 1961 by Thom Gunn. Both reprinted with the permission of Farrar, Straus & Giroux, LLC and Faber and Faber Ltd.

Thomas Hardy, "Afterwards" from *The Complete Poems of Thomas Hardy*, edited by James Gibson. Copyright © 1976 by Macmillan London Ltd. Reprinted with the permission of Simon and Schuster, Inc.

Joy Harjo, "Song for Deer and Myself to Return On." Reprinted with the permission of the author. "Santa Fe" from *In Mad Love and War*. Copyright © 1990 by Joy Harjo. Reprinted with the permission of Wesleyan University Press.

Michael S. Harper, "American History" from *Dear John, Dear Coltrane*. Copyright © 1970, 1985 by Michael S. Harper. Reprinted with the permission of the author. "Nightmare Begins Responsibility" and "We Assume: On the Death of Our Son, Reuben Masai Harper" from *Songliness in Michaeltree: New and Collected Poems*. Copyright © 2000 by Michael S. Harper. Reprinted with the permission of the author and the University of Illinois Press. "Use Trouble" from *The American Scholar* 69 (Autumn 2000). Copyright © 2000 by Michael S. Harper. Reprinted with the permission of the author.

Robert Hayden, "Those Winter Sundays," "Night, Death, Mississippi," "Frederick Douglass," and "Mourning Poem for the Queen of Sunday" from *Angle of Ascent: New and Selected Poems*. Copyright © 1975, 1972, 1966 by Robert Hayden. Reprinted with the permission of Liveright Publishing Corporation.

Seamus Heaney, "From the Frontier of Writing," "Mid-Term Break," "Terminus," "Bogland," and "Punishment" from *Seamus Heaney: Selected Poems 1966–1987*. Copyright © 1990. Reprinted with the permission of Farrar, Straus & Giroux, LLC and Faber and Faber, Ltd.

Carolina Hospital, "Blake in the Tropics" from *Little Havana Blues: A Cuban-American Literature Anthology*, edited by Delia Poey and Virgil Suarez (Houston: Arte Publico Press, 1996). Reprinted with the permission of the author.

Langston Hughes, "Theme for English B," "Genius Child," "Me and the Mule," "High to Low," "World War II," "Harlem," "I, Too," "Suicide's Note," and "The Weary Blues" from *Collected Poems*. Copyright © 1994 by the Estate of Langston Hughes. Reprinted with the permission of Alfred A. Knopf, Inc.

Randall Jarrell, "The Death of the Ball Turret Gunner" from *The Complete Poems*. Copyright © 1945 and renewal copyright by Mrs. Randall Jarrell. Reprinted with the permission of Farrar, Straus & Giroux, LLC.

Jane Kenyon, "Otherwise" and "Surprise" from *Otherwise: New and Selected Poems*. Copyright © 1996 by Jane Kenyon. Reprinted with the permission of Graywolf Press, Saint Paul, Minnesota.

Etheridge Knight, "A Poem for Myself (Or Blues for a Mississippi Black Boy)" from *Poems from Prison*. Copyright © 1966 by Broadside Press. Reprinted with the permission of Broadside Press.

Kenneth Koch, "Variations on a Theme by William Carlos Williams" from *On the Great Atlantic Rainway: Selected Poems 1950–1988* (New York: Alfred A. Knopf, 1994). Copyright © 1962 by Kenneth Koch. Reprinted with the permission of the author.

Yusef Komunyakaa, "Facing It" and "Boat People" from *Dien Cai Dau*. Copyright © 1988 by Yusef Komunyakaa. "My Father's Loveletters" from *Magic City*. Copyright © 1992 by Yusef Komunyakaa. All reprinted with the permission of the Wesleyan University Press.

Stanley Kunitz, "Father and Son" from *The Collected Poems of Stanley Kunitz*. Copyright ©2000 by Stanley Kunitz. "The Portrait" from *Passing Through: The Later Poems New and Selected*. Copyright © 1971 by Stanley Kunitz. Both reprinted with the permission of W. W. Norton & Company, Inc.

Philip Larkin, "Talking in Bed," "High Windows," "Mr. Bleaney," and "This Be The Verse" from *Philip Larkin: Collected Poems*, edited by Anthony Thwaite. Copyright © 1989. Reprinted with the permission of Farrar, Straus & Giroux, LLC and Faber & Faber, Ltd. "Reasons for Attendance" from *The Less Deceived*. Copyright © 1958 by Philip Larkin. Reprinted with the permission of The Marvell Press, England.

D. H. Lawrence, "The English Are So Nice!" from *The Complete Poems of D.H. Lawrence*, edited by V. DeSola Pinto and F. W. Roberts. Copyright © 1964, 1971 by Angelo Ravagli and C.M. Weekley, Executors of the Estate of Frieda Lawrence Ravagli. Reprinted with the permission of Penguin Putnam Inc.

Denise Levertov, "The Ache of Marriage" and "O Taste and See" from *Poems 1960–1967*. Copyright © 1966, 1964 by Denise Levertov. Reprinted with the permission of New Directions Publishing Corporation.

Audre Lorde, "Hanging Fire" from *The Black Unicorn*. Copyright © 1978 by Audre Lorde. Reprinted with the permission of W.W. Norton & Company, Inc.

Robert Lowell, "Skunk Hour" and "Sailing Home from Rapallo" from *Life Studies*. Copyright © 1956, 1959 by Robert Lowell. Renewal Copyright © 1987 by Harriet Lowell. "The March 1" from *History*. Copyright © 1973 by Robert Lowell. "For the Union Dead" from *For the Union Dead*. Copyright © 1964 by Robert Lowell. "Epilogue" from *Day by Day*. Copyright © 1977 by Robert Lowell. All reprinted with the permission of Farrar, Straus & Giroux, LLC.

Archibald MacLeish, "Ars Poetica" from *Collected Poems 1917–1982*. Copyright © 1985 by The Estate of Archibald MacLeish. Reprinted with the permission of Houghton Mifflin Company. All rights reserved.

Dionisio Martinez, "History as a Second Language" from *History as a Second Language* (Columbus: The Ohio State University Press, 1992). Copyright © 1992 by Dionisio Martinez. Reprinted with the permission of the author. "The Prodigal Son jumps bail" and "The Prodigal Son catches up with the bounty hunters" from *Climbing Back*. Copyright ©2001 by Dionisio Martinez. Reprinted with the permission of W.W. Norton & Company, Inc.

James Merrill, "The Broken Home" from *Selected Poems: 1946–1985*. Copyright © 1995 by James Merrill. Reprinted with the permission of Alfred A. Knopf, Inc.

W. S. Merwin, "The Asians Dying," "For a Coming Extinction," and "For the Anniversary of My Death" from *The Second Four Books of Poems* (Port Townsend, Wash.: Copper Canyon Press, 2000). Copyright © 1967 by W. S. Merwin. Reprinted with the permission of The Wylie Agency, Inc.

Marianne Moore, "Poetry," "To a Snail," and "To a Steam Roller" from *The Collected Poems of Marianne Moore*. Copyright 1935 by Marianne Moore, renewed © 1963 by Marianne Moore and T. S. Eliot. Reprinted with the permission of Simon & Schuster, Inc. "The Steeple-jack" from *The Complete Poems of Marianne Moore*. Copyright 1951 by Marianne Moore, renewed © 1979 by Lawrence E. Brinn and

Louise Crane, Executors of the Estate of Marianne Moore. Reprinted with the permission of Penguin Putnam Inc.

Pat Mora, "La Migra" from *Agua Santa: Holy Water*. Copyright © 1995 by Pat Mora. Reprinted with the permission of Beacon Press, Boston.

Thylias Moss, "Lunch Counter Freedom" from *Small Congregations*. Copyright © 1983, 1990, 1991, 1993 by Thylias Moss. Reprinted with the permission of HarperCollins Publishers, Inc.

David Mura, "An Argument: On 1942" from *After We Lost Our Way* (New York: E. P. Dutton, 1989). Copyright © 1989. Reprinted with the permission of the author.

Marilyn Nelson, "Live Jazz, Franklin Park Zoo" from *The New Bread Loaf Anthology of Contemporary American Poetry*, edited by Michael Collier and Stanley Plumly (Hanover, N. H.: University Press of New England, 1999). Reprinted with the permission of the author.

Frank O'Hara, "Ave Maria" from *The Selected Poems of Frank O'Hara*. Copyright © 1964. Reprinted with the permission of City Lights Books. "Why I Am Not a Painter" from *Collected Poems*. Copyright © 1958 by Maureen Granville-Smith, Administratrix of the Estate of Frank O'Hara. Reprinted with the permission of Alfred A. Knopf, Inc.

Simon J. Ortiz, "Bend in the River" from *Going for the Rain*. Copyright © 1976. Reprinted with the permission of the author.

Carl Phillips, "Africa Says" and "Passing" from *In the Blood*. Copyright © 1992 by Carl Phillips. Reprinted with the permission of Northeastern University Press. "The Kill" from *Pastoral*. Copyright ©2000 by Carl Phillips. Reprinted with the permission of Graywolf Press, Saint Paul, Minnesota.

Sylvia Plath, "Daddy," "The Applicant," "Edge," "Lady Lazarus," and "Morning Song" from *Ariel*. Copyright © 1963 by Ted Hughes. "Blackberrying" from *Crossing the Water*. Originally published in *Uncollected Poems*. Copyright © 1962 by Ted Hughes. "Metaphors" from *Collected Poems*. Copyright © 1981 by Ted Hughes. All reprinted with the permission of HarperCollins Publishers, Inc. and Faber & Faber Ltd.

Ezra Pound, "The River Merchant's Wife: A Letter" and "In a Station of the Metro" from *Personae*. Copyright 1926 by Ezra Pound. Reprinted with the permission of New Directions Publishing Corporation.

John Crowe Ransom, "Bells for John Whiteside's Daughter" from *Selected Poems, Third Edition, Revised and Enlarged*. Copyright 1924, 1927 by Alfred A. Knopf, Inc., renewed 1952, © 1955 by John Crowe Ransom. Reprinted with the permission of Alfred A. Knopf, a division of Random House, Inc.

Henry Reed, "Naming of Parts" from *Henry Reed's Collected Poems*, edited by Jon Stallworthy. Reprinted with the permission of Oxford University Press, Ltd.

Adrienne Rich, "Necessities of Life," "Mother-in-Law," "Prospective Immigrants Please Note," "Diving Into the Wreck," "The Middle-Aged," and "Snapshots of a Daughter-in-Law" from *Collected Early Poems: 1950–1970*. Copyright © 1993 by Adrienne Rich. Copyright © 1967, 1963, 1962, 1961, 1960, 1959, 1958, 1957, 1956, 1955, 1954, 1953, 1952, 1951 by Adrienne Rich. Copyright © 1984, 1975, 1971, 1969, 1966 by W.W. Norton & Company, Inc. Reprinted with the permission of the author and W.W. Norton & Company, Inc.

Alberto Rios, "Teodoro Luna's Two Kisses" from *Teodoro Luna's Two Kisses*. Copyright © 1982, 1990 by Alberto Rios. Reprinted with the permission of W.W. Norton & Company, Inc. "Mi Abuelo" from *Whispering to Fool the Wind* (Bronx: Sheep Meadow Press, 1982). Copyright © 1982 by Alberto Rios. Reprinted with the permission of the author.

Theodore Roethke, "My Papa's Waltz," "Elegy for Jane," and "The Waking" from *The Collected Poems of Theodore Roethke*. Copyright 1942 by Hearst Magazines, Inc. Copyright 1950, 1953 by Theodore Roethke. Reprinted with the permission of Doubleday, a division of Random House, Inc.

Carl Sandburg, "Grass" from *Cornhuskers*. Copyright 1918 by Holt, Rinehart & Winston, and renewed 1946 by Carl Sandburg. Reprinted with the permission of Harcourt, Inc.

Anne Sexton, "Her Kind" from *To Bedlam and Part Way Back*. Copyright © 1960 by Anne Sexton, renewed 1988 by Linda G. Sexton. "Snow White and the Seven Dwarfs" from *Transformations*. Copyright © 1971 by Anne Sexton. Reprinted with the permission of Houghton Mifflin Company. All rights reserved.

Leslie Marmon Silko, "Prayer to the Pacific" from *Storyteller*. Copyright © 1981 by Leslie Marmon Silko. Reprinted with the permission of Seaver Books, New York, New York.

Charles Simic, "Charon's Cosmology" and "Fork" from *Selected Early Poems*. Copyright © 1999 by Charles Simic. Reprinted with the permission of George Braziller, Inc. "Old Couple" from *Weather Forecast for Utopia and the Vicinity*. Copyright © 1983. Reprinted with the permission of Station Hill Press.

Dave Smith, "The Spring Poem" and "On a Field Trip of Fredericksburg" from *Floating on Solitude: Three Volumes of Poetry* (Urbana : University of Illinois Press, 1996). Copyright © 1976 by Dave Smith. Reprinted with the permission of the author.

Stevie Smith, "Not Waving But Drowning" and "Pretty" from *The Collected Poems of Stevie Smith*. Copyright © 1972 by Stevie Smith. Reprinted with the permission of New Directions Publishing Corporation.

Gary Snyder, "Axe Handles" from *Axe Handles*. Copyright © 1983 by Gary Snyder. "Riprap" from *Riprap*. Copyright © 1959 by Gary Snyder. Both reprinted with the permission of North Point Press, Farrar, Straus & Giroux, LLC. "How Poetry

World" from *Things of this World*. Copyright © 1956 and renewed 1984 by Richard Wilbur. "Junk" from *Advice to a Prophet and Other Poems*. Copyright © 1961 and renewed 1989 by Richard Wilbur. All reprinted with the permission of Harcourt, Inc.

William Carlos Williams, "Poem," "The Dance," "To Elsie," "The Raper from Passenack," "Spring and All," and "This Is Just to Say" from *Collected Poems: 1909–1939*, Volume I. Copyright © 1938, 1944, 1945 by New Directions Publishing Corporation. "Landscape with the Fall of Icarus" from *Collected Poems: 1939–1962*, Volume II. Copyright © 1962 by William Carlos Williams. All reprinted with the permission of New Directions Publishing Corporation.

Charles Wright, "Self-Portrait" from *The World of the Ten Thousand Things: Poems 1980–1990*. Copyright © 1990. Reprinted with the permission of Farrar, Straus & Giroux, LLC.

James Wright, "A Blessing" and "Small Frogs Killed on the Highway" from *Collected Poems*. Copyright © 1971 by James Wright. "A Blessing" from *The Branch Will Not Break*. Copyright © 1963 by James Wright. All reprinted with the permission of Wesleyan University Press.

William Butler Yeats, "Crazy Jane Talks with the Bishop," "Meru," "Among School Children," "The Lake Isle of Innisfree," "Leda and the Swan," and "Sailing to Byzantium" from *The Poems of W. B. Yeats: A New Edition*, edited by Richard J. Finneran. Copyright 1928, 1934 by The Macmillan Company, renewed © 1956 by Georgie Yeats, © 1962 by Bertha Georgie Yeats. Reprinted with the permission of Scribner, a division of Simon & Schuster, Inc.

Jane Yeh, "Revenger's Tragedy" from *Poetry* 177 (February 2001). Copyright © 2001 by The Modern Poetry Association. Reprinted with the permission of the Editor of *Poetry* and the author.

Index of Authors, Titles, and First Lines

Index of Terms

Dubai

Live·Work·Explore

EXPLORER

WATER MEETS WONDER

ATLANTIS

PALM JUMEIRAH, DUBAI

DON'T FORGET TO BREATHE

Dubai Explorer 2009/13th Edition
First Published 1996
2nd Edition 1997
3rd Edition 1998
4th Edition 2000
5th Edition 2001
6th Edition 2002
7th Edition 2003
8th Edition 2004
9th Edition 2005
10th Edition 2006
11th Edition 2007
12th Edition 2008
13th Edition 2009   ISBN 978-9948-8589-0-4

Copyright © Explorer Group Ltd, 1996, 1997, 1998, 2000, 2001, 2002, 2003, 2004, 2005, 2006, 2007, 2008, 2009.
All rights reserved.

Front Cover Photograph – Atlantis The Palm – Victor Romero

Printed and bound by Emirates Printing Press, Dubai, United Arab Emirates.

Explorer Publishing & Distribution
PO Box 34275, Dubai
United Arab Emirates
Phone   +971 (0)4 340 8805
Fax   +971 (0)4 340 8806
Email   info@explorerpublishing.com
Web   www.explorerpublishing.com

Welcome

Apart from being a great workout for the biceps, this chunky tome is also your first port of call for all the answers to all the questions you have about living, working and exploring in Dubai.

Get your bearings in the **General Information** chapter (p.1), which gives an overview of the UAE and Dubai in particular, covering geography, history, environment, culture, places to stay and getting around. The meaty **Residents** chapter (p.77) will be your constant companion from the time you step off the plane – it's your faithful sidekick through every bureaucratic battle, red-tape wrangle, and headache-inducing hurdle you face while you're settling into your new life as a Dubai expat.

Dubai's fascinating areas are all covered in the **Exploring** chapter (p.239), with parks, beaches, art galleries, museums, waterparks and zoos to visit along the way. Sporty types should team up with the **Activities** chapter (p.327), a listing of physical pursuits from aerobics to watersports, as well as more cerebral activities such as chess and flower arranging, and a well-being section to guide you through the city's finest spas. Figure out whether Dubai's shopping scene deserves its lofty reputation in the **Shopping** chapter (p.415), which lists where you can buy items by category and gives a rundown of the best malls, souks and department stores. And when the sun goes down, turn to the **Going Out** chapter (p.525), with reviews of restaurants, bars, cafes and clubs to help you plan your nights out for the next year.

If all this advice has left you feeling a bit disoriented, head to the back of the book for a huge **Maps** section (p.637) that will get you out and about, exploring with confidence.

So there you have it – that covers just about everything. We've spent ages getting this encyclopaedic edition on the shelves, and now it's your turn to do a bit of work: head off to www.liveworkexplore.com, and register as a member of our online Dubai community. Not only can you get updates and additional information on the city, but you can share your own expertise and ask searching questions of other expats on our forums. We'll see you there.

The Explorer Team

Thanks: special thanks to the entire Explorer team; without them we'd never get this book done every year, but this year in particular, everybody went above and beyond the call of duty to get it all finished in time. Thanks also to our brave team of reviewers, who eat delicious dinners and endure luxurious spa treatments all in the name of research – thanks very much Mandy Kelly, Jola Chudy, Jason Ward, Clay Gervais, Craig Downing and Leanne Smith, Kellie Whitehead, Alex Jeffries, Peter Loakman, Emma Lomax, Kellie Whitehead, Michelle Anthony, Jason Providence, Catherine McManus and Chris Booth, Veronica Pereira, David Quinn, Richard Greig, and Jenny Lyon. A big thanks as always to Anand, Tony and the team from Emirates Printing Press, and all our readers who, throughout the year, send in comments and suggestions that keep us on our toes and make this the greatest book on Dubai ever made.

www.liveworkexplore.com

You've got the book – now log on to the website for:

- Regular newsletters on what's happening in your city
- Access to over 3,000 local listings in our Directory
- Join and set up local groups
- Online maps
- Local forums and discussion boards
- Classifieds section
- Exclusive special offers
- Competitions
- E-shop

Sign up today!
Log onto www.liveworkexplore.com/signup to create your account.

Register your guide
Register your guide for instant access to the entire guide content online, plus live updates.

E-shop
Visit www.liveworkexplore.com/shop for all our latest products and special offers.

Corporate

For information on Explorer Publishing and our other services, including advertising and sponsorship rate cards, please log onto www.explorerpublishing.com.

THE TIMES

The world's most respected newspaper, printed daily in the Gulf

The armchair explorer's guide to the world.

Explore the world from the comfort and safety of your armchair. Get global news on your doorstep daily. Subscribe to the world's most respected newspaper and enjoy the finest in cutting edge journalism, incisive commentary, features, business and sport. To subscribe now simply email subscribe@sab-media.com

www.thetimesme.com

Take home more than just memories.

Welcome to Deira City Centre, Dubai's premier shopping destination.
With over 370 stores including 120 fashion outlets, you never have to go anywhere else.

- Family leisure & entertainment centre
- Free shuttle bus service to select hotels
- Luggage storage facility
- Car rental counters
- Wi-Fi service throughout the mall

- Branded mall souvenirs and gift vouchers available
- Currency exchange, full service banking & ATMs
- Postal, courier & business services
- Dubai Tourism counter
- Wheelchairs & baby strollers

DEIRA
CITY CENTRE

where you can be you.

Shop until midnight on weekends.

For more information, call 04 295 4486.

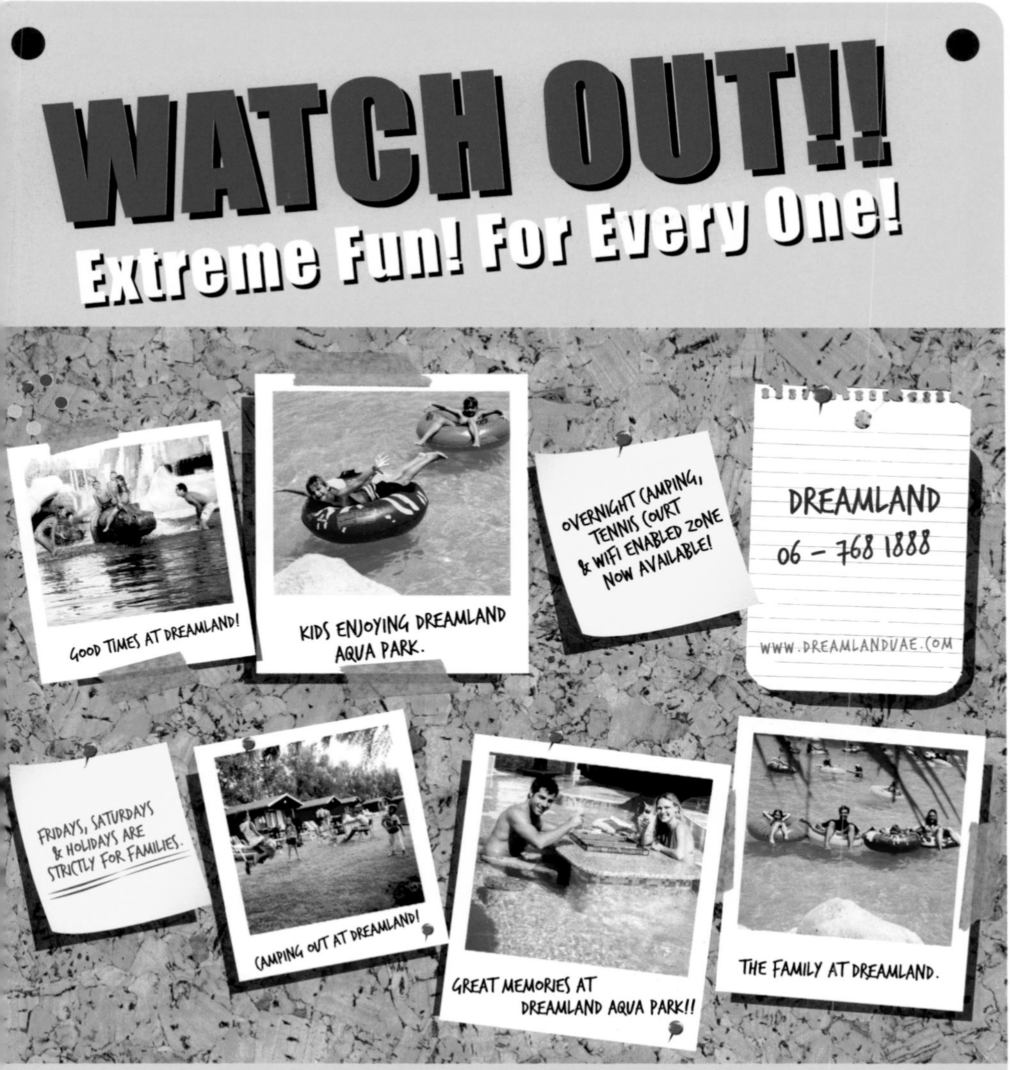

WATCH OUT!!

Extreme Fun! For Every One!

GOOD TIMES AT DREAMLAND!

KIDS ENJOYING DREAMLAND AQUA PARK.

OVERNIGHT CAMPING, TENNIS COURT & WIFI ENABLED ZONE NOW AVAILABLE!

DREAMLAND
06 - 768 1888

WWW.DREAMLANDUAE.COM

FRIDAYS, SATURDAYS & HOLIDAYS ARE STRICTLY FOR FAMILIES.

CAMPING OUT AT DREAMLAND!

GREAT MEMORIES AT DREAMLAND AQUA PARK!!

THE FAMILY AT DREAMLAND.

Splash, play, laze around, enjoy good food & do nothing but have fun at Dreamland Aqua Park. With 250,000 sq.m of landscaped gardens, over 30 thrilling rides, crazy slides, go-karts, a mini pet land & all your favourite restaurants.

Ras Al Khaimah Highway, through Emirates Road, Exit 103
Tel: 06.768.1888
www.dreamlanduae.com

IT'S THE PERFECT RETREAT FOR THE ENTIRE FAMILY!!

HALA
Hotel / Apartments

Hala Hotel Apartment is located at Muscat Business District in Ruwi. It is just a 20 minutes drive from Muscat International Airport. Hala building is designed with the style of Omani architecture to provide guests with Omani and Arabic culture. Recently opened its doors with over 48 luxurious suites. Hala Hotel has 17-one bedrooms suites plus 31-two bedroom suites.

Hala Hotel Apartment offers suitable Studio suites to both business travellers and visitors in Oman, at the heart of Muscat city, stay at Hala.

HALA
Hotel / Apartments

P.O. Box 678, P.C. 116 Muscat, Sultanate of Oman,
Tel: +968 24810442, Fax: +968 24810142
web : www.halahotelapartment.com   e-mail : hala@motifoman.com

Mall of the **Emirates**

Shopping is just the beginning

Welcome to the desert.

Sun and sand is plentiful in Dubai, but for snow and shopping make a trip to Mall of the Emirates, Dubai's finest shopping resort and the largest mall in the Eastern Hemisphere. With over 460 stores housing the world's leading brands, Ski Dubai - an Alpine themed snow resort, a 14-screen cineplex, a two level family entertainment zone with indoor rollercoasters, and over 75 cafés and restaurants, there are plenty of reasons for you to visit us.

Opening hours: 10am – 10pm (Sun – Wed), 10am – midnight (Thu – Sat)
Carrefour, CineStar and restaurant hours may vary. Please ask for details.
Interchange 4, Sheikh Zayed Road, Tel: 04 409 9000 www.malloftheemirates.com

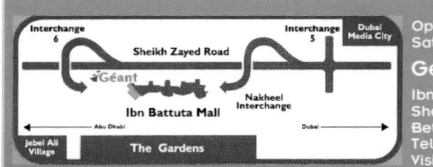

It's Géant and it's for y

Together for a better Environment

**Plastic damages our environment.
It's a Non-Bio Degradable substance
which keeps destroying our
Eco System. Burning it will emit
toxic fumes that can poison
the environment.**

Say NO to plastic bags

**For only 5.00AED, we will strive
to protect the environment.
Do your share by picking up our
reusable JUTEBAGS
from our counters.**

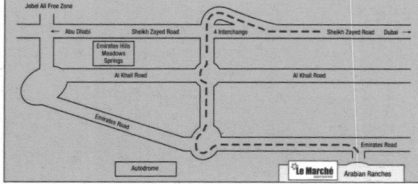

Le Marché
Supermarket

BIGGEST CHOICE OF BOOKS

MAGIC CHOICE OF BOOKS

EXCITING CHOICE OF BOOKS

Phenomenal choice of books

UNBEATABLE CHOICE OF BOOKS   IN FULL COLOUR

SPECIAL CHOICE of books

THRILLING CHOICE OF BOOKS

Encyclopedic choice of Books

BALANCED CHOICE OF BOOKS

FANTASTIC CHOICE OF BOOKS

BORDERS®

YOUR PLACE FOR KNOWLEDGE AND ENTERTAINMENT

Mall of the Emirates 04 3415758, Deira City Centre 04 2943344
Sharjah City Centre 06 5330645, Dubai International Financial Centre 04 4250371,
Muscat City Centre 00968 24558089 & Qurm City Centre 00968 24470491
Opening soon at Ibn Battuta Mall & Dubai Marina Mall

MEGASTORE

Mall of the Emirates • Jumeira Beach Residence
Abu Dhabi Mall • Deira City Center • Burjuman • Mercato

FAMILY, HEALTH, BODY & MIND √

BUSINESS & COMPUTER √

COMICS & MAGAZINES √

NON FICTION √

LITERATURE √

PRACTICAL √

ARTS √

KIDS √

Books available at

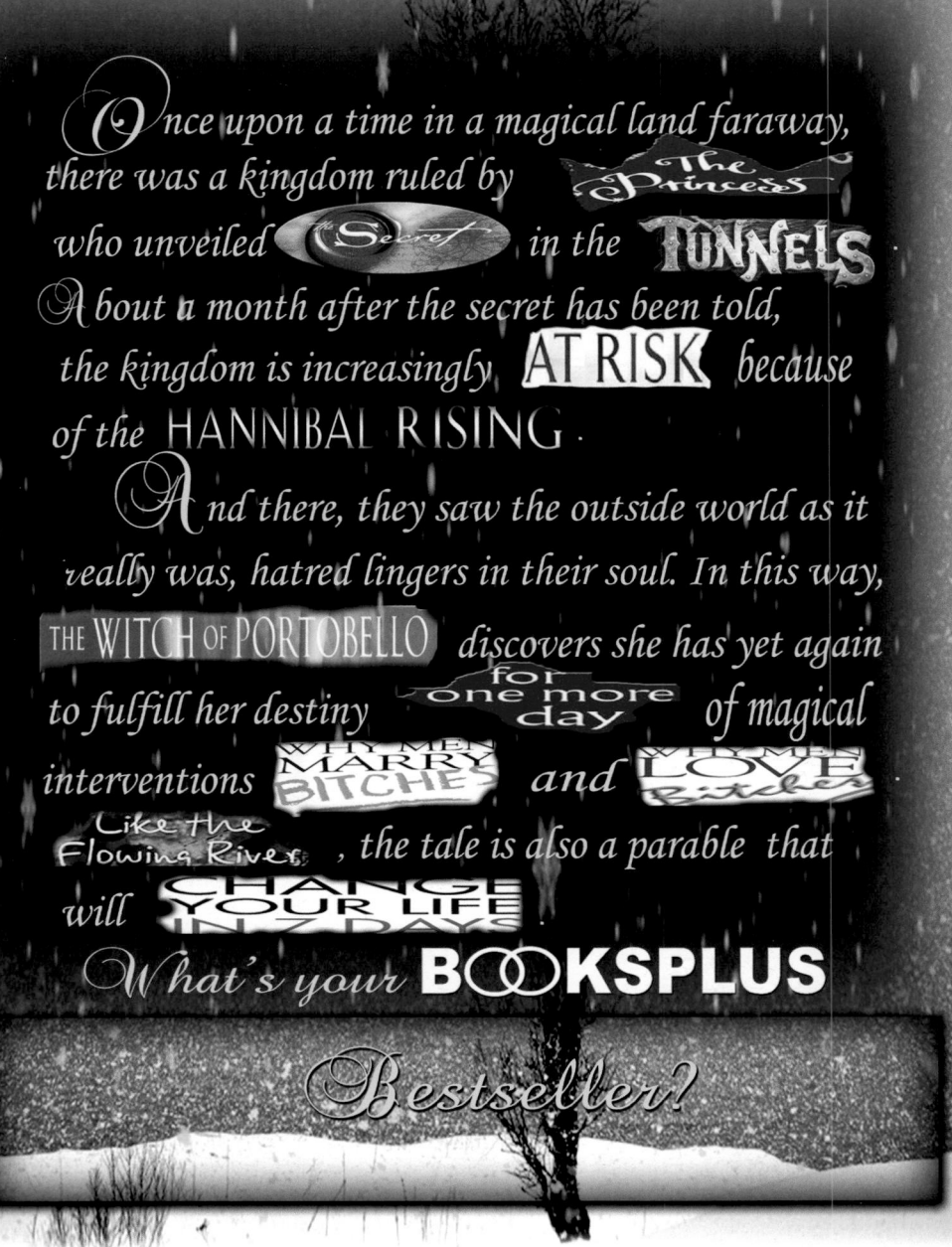

Once upon a time in a magical land faraway, there was a kingdom ruled by **The Princess** who unveiled the **Secret** in the **TUNNELS**. About a month after the secret has been told, the kingdom is increasingly **AT RISK** because of the **HANNIBAL RISING**. And there, they saw the outside world as it really was, hatred lingers in their soul. In this way, **THE WITCH OF PORTOBELLO** discovers she has yet again to fulfill her destiny **for one more day** of magical interventions **WHY MEN MARRY BITCHES** and **WHY WOMEN LOVE Bitches**. **Like the Flowing River**, the tale is also a parable that will **CHANGE YOUR LIFE IN 7 DAYS**. What's your **BOOKSPLUS** *Bestseller?*

Contents

Contents

717
TOP PRINTERS.

34
EUROPEAN COUNTRIES.

1
PRINTER FROM
THE MIDDLE EAST.

2
AWARDS.

Emirates Printing Press, Dubai, is the proud winner of the Silver award in the Brochure Category and the Bronze award in the Magazine Category at the Sappi European Printer of the Year Awards 2008.

EMIRATES PRINTING PRESS (L.L.C.)

P. O. Box 5106, Al Quoz, Dubai, United Arab Emirates
Tel: (+971 4) 347 5550, Fax: (+971 4) 347 5959
E-mail: eppdubai@emirates.net.ae
Website: www.eppdubai.com

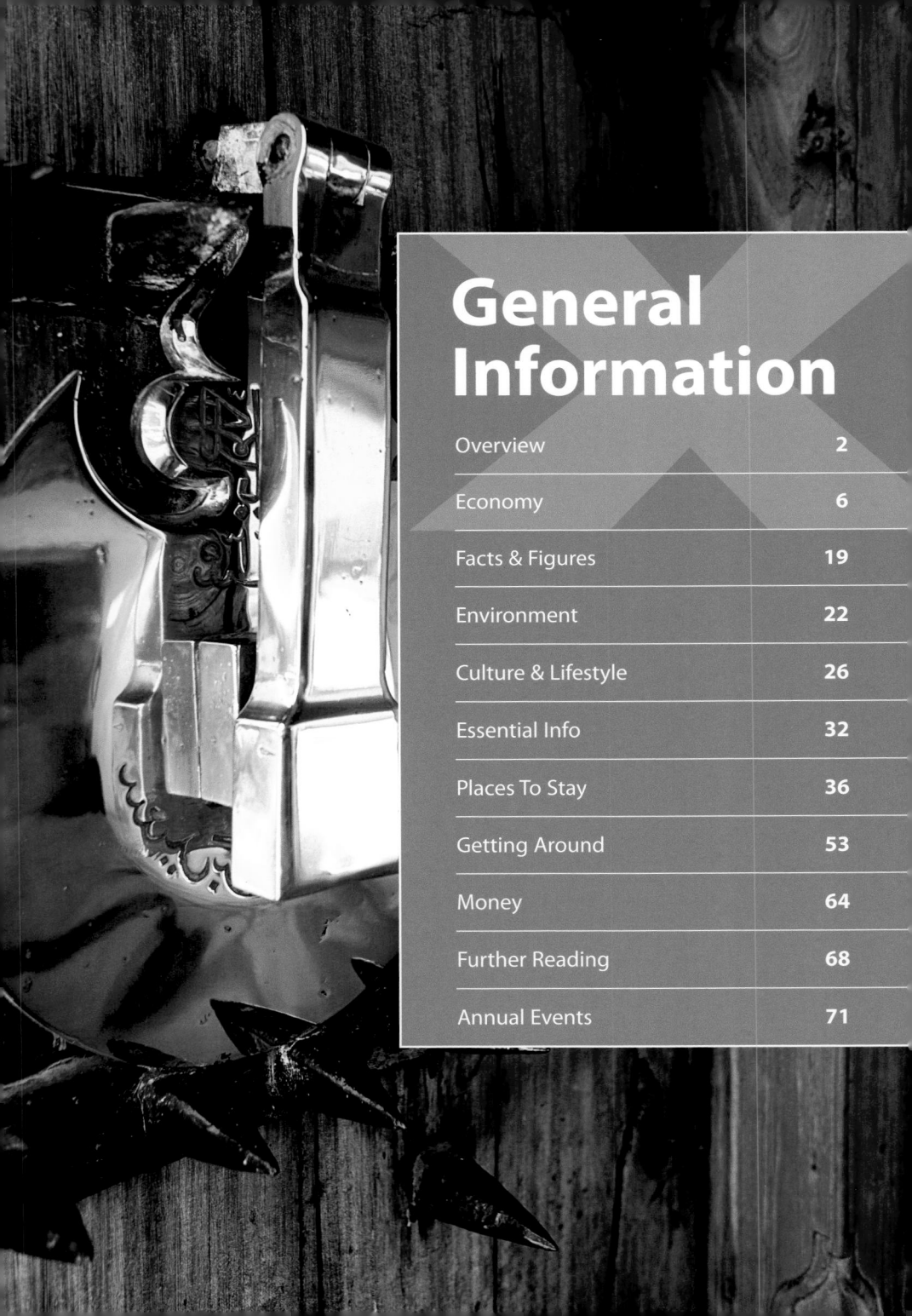

General Information

General Information

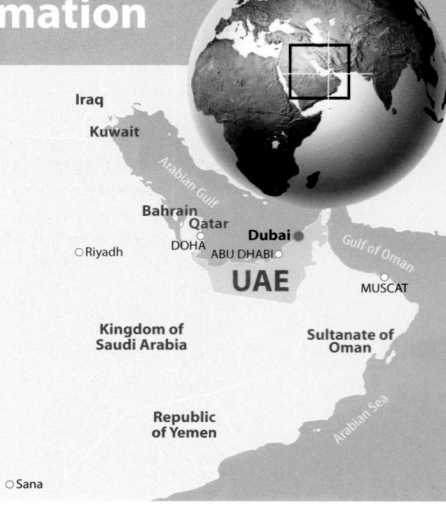

Geography

The United Arab Emirates (UAE) is situated on the eastern side of the Arabian Peninsula, bordering Saudi Arabia and the Sultanate of Oman, with coastlines on both the Arabian Gulf and the Gulf of Oman. The country comprises seven emirates – Abu Dhabi, Ajman, Dubai, Fujairah, Ras Al Khaimah, Sharjah and Umm Al Quwain. Abu Dhabi is by far the largest emirate, occupying over 80% of the country. With an area of 3,885 square kilometres, the emirate of Dubai is the second largest.

The coast is littered with coral reefs and more than 200 islands, most of which are uninhabited. The interior of the country is characterised by *sabkha* (salt flats), stretches of gravel plain, and vast areas of sand desert. However, to the east rise the Hajar Mountains, (*hajar* is Arabic for rock). Lying close to the Gulf of Oman, they form a backbone through the country, from the Musandam Peninsula in the north, through the eastern UAE and into Oman. The highest point is Jebel Yibir at 1,527 metres. The Rub Al Khali, or Empty Quarter, occupies a large part of the south of the country.

Common to the UAE, Saudi Arabia, Oman and Yemen, it's the largest sand desert in the world, covering an area roughly the same size as France, Belgium and the Netherlands. The Rub Al Khali consists of stark desert, salt flats, occasional oases, and spectacular sand dunes that rise to more than 300 metres. The emirate of Dubai is of course best known for its modern, rapidly expanding city, but visitors will also find a landscape that varies from vast stretches of desert to rugged mountains.

Emirs Or Sheikhs?

While the term emirate comes from the ruling title of 'emir', the rulers of the UAE are called 'sheikhs.'

History

The Arabian Gulf was an important trading post as far back as the Kingdom of Sumer in 3000BC. Sumer, located in the area between the Tigris and Euphrates Rivers in present-day Iraq, is believed to be the birthplace of modern civilisation. This great kingdom had influence, if not control, over trading points throughout the Gulf, and probably further. Deira/Dubai was one of these key positions, a safe haven before entering the narrow Strait of Hormuz and the open sea.

Development Of Islam

Dubai's early existence is closely linked to the arrival and development of Islam in the greater Middle East region. Islam developed in modern-day Saudi Arabia at the beginning of the seventh century AD with the revelations of the Quran being received by the Prophet Muhammad. Military conquests of the Middle East and North Africa enabled the Arab empire to spread the teachings of Islam from Mecca and Medina to the local Bedouin tribes. Following the Arab Empire came the Turks, the Mongols and the Ottomans, each leaving their mark on local culture and all championing Islam.

Downtown Burj Dubai

The Trucial States

After the fall of the Muslim empires, both the British and Portuguese became interested in the area due to its strategic position between India and Europe, and for the opportunity to control the activities of pirates based in the region, which earned it the title the 'Pirate Coast'. In 1820, the British defeated the pirates and a general treaty was agreed by the local rulers, denouncing piracy. The following years witnessed a series of maritime truces, with Dubai and the other emirates accepting British protection in 1892. In Europe, the area became known as the Trucial Coast (or Trucial States), a name it retained until the departure of the British in 1971.

Modern Dubai

Trade and commerce are still the cornerstones of Dubai's success, with the traditional manufacturing and distribution industries now joined by financial, media, IT and telecom businesses. With so many world-class hotels, and leisure and entertainment options, the city is also becoming an increasingly popular tourist destination, with visitor numbers expected to reach 15 million by the year 2010.

A Growing Trade

In the late 1800s Dubai's ruler, Sheikh Maktoum bin Hasher Al Maktoum, granted tax concessions to foreign traders, encouraging many to switch their base of operations from Iran and Sharjah to Dubai. By 1903, a British shipping line had been persuaded to use Dubai as its main port of call in the area, giving traders direct links with British India and other important trading ports in the region. Dubai's importance as a trading hub was further enhanced by Sheikh Rashid bin Saeed Al Maktoum, father of the current ruler of Dubai, who ordered the creek to be dredged, thus providing access for larger vessels. The city came to specialise in the import and re-export of goods, mainly gold to India, and trade became the foundation of this emirate's wealthy progression.

Independence

In 1968, Britain announced its withdrawal from the region and oversaw the creation of a single state consisting of Bahrain, Qatar and the Trucial Coast. The ruling sheikhs, particularly of Abu Dhabi and Dubai, realised that by uniting forces they would have a stronger voice in the wider Middle East region. Negotiations collapsed when Bahrain and Qatar chose to become independent states. However, the Trucial Coast remained committed to forming an alliance, and in 1971 the federation of the United Arab Emirates was born.

UAE Fact Box

Coordinates: 24º00' North 54º00' East

Borders: 410km with Oman and 457km with Saudi Arabia

Total land area: approx. 83,000 sq km

Total coastline: 1,318km

Highest point: 1,527m

Total land area: 3,885 sq km

Total Dubai coastline: 60km, but new offshore projects will add over 1,000km

Formation Of The United Arab Emirates

The new state comprised the emirates of Dubai, Abu Dhabi, Ajman, Fujairah, Sharjah, Umm Al Quwain and, in 1972, Ras Al Khaimah (each emirate is named after its main town). Under the agreement, the individual emirates each retained a certain degree of autonomy, with Abu Dhabi and Dubai providing the most input into the federation. The leaders of the new federation elected the ruler of Abu Dhabi, His Highness Sheikh Zayed bin Sultan Al Nahyan, to be their president, a position he held until he passed away on 2 November 2004. His eldest son, His Highness Sheikh Khalifa bin Zayed Al Nahyan, was then elected to take over the presidency. Despite the unification of the seven emirates, boundary disputes have caused a few problems. At the end of

Sheikh Zayed's first term as president, in 1976, he threatened to resign if the other rulers didn't settle the demarcation of their borders. The threat proved an effective way of ensuring cooperation, although the degree of independence of the various emirates has never been fully determined.

Sheikh Zayed bin Sultan Al Nahyan
Sheikh Zayed bin Sultan Al Nahyan ruled the UAE for 33 years and in that time oversaw major developments to the nation's economy and pioneered the extension of privileges to expatriates. Sheikh Zayed embraced change without compromising the principles of Arabic heritage and culture. He was a well-respected international figure and passionate about the environment. He passed away in November 2004.

The Discovery Of Oil

The formation of the UAE came after the discovery of huge oil reserves in Abu Dhabi in 1958 (Abu Dhabi has an incredible 10% of the world's known oil reserves). This discovery dramatically transformed the emirate. In 1966, Dubai, which was already a relatively wealthy trading centre, also discovered oil.

Dubai's ruler at the time, the late Sheikh Rashid bin Saeed Al Maktoum, ensured that the emirate's oil revenues were used to develop an economic and social infrastructure, which is the basis of today's modern society. His work was continued through the reign of his son, and successor, Sheikh Maktoum bin Rashid Al Maktoum and by the present ruler, Sheikh Mohammed bin Rashid Al Maktoum.

Dubai Timeline

1799	Al Fahedi Fort is built (estimated)
1833	The Maktoum family settles in Dubai
1835	Maritime Truce signed between the Trucial States and Britain
1892	Dubai falls under the protection of Britain
1950s	Oil is discovered in the Trucial States
1963	Maktoum Bridge is built, becoming the first bridge across the creek
1966	Commercial quantities of oil discovered off the coast of the UAE. Dubai's first hotel, The Carlton (now The Riviera), is built
1967	The Shindagha Tunnel is built, providing an alternative to Maktoum Bridge for crossing the creek
1970	Al Fahedi Fort is converted into Dubai Museum
1971	Britain withdraws from the Gulf and Dubai becomes independent. The United Arab Emirates is born, with HH Sheikh Zayed bin Sultan Al Nahyan as the leader. The UAE joins the Arab League
1973	Dubai and the other emirates launch their single currency, the UAE dirham
1981	The Gulf Cooperation Council is formed, with the UAE as a founding member
1985	Emirates Airline is founded
1990	After the death of his father, Sheikh Rashid bin Saeed Al Maktoum, Sheikh Maktoum bin Rashid Al Maktoum becomes the ruler of Dubai
1999	The doors of the Burj Al Arab, the tallest hotel in the world, open to the public for the first time
2001	Construction starts on Palm Jumeirah
2004	Sheikh Zayed bin Sultan Al Nahyan dies and is succeeded as ruler of the UAE by his son, Sheikh Khalifa bin Zayed Al Nahyan
2006	Sheikh Maktoum bin Rashid Al Maktoum dies and is succeeded as Ruler of Dubai and Prime Minister of the UAE by his brother, Sheikh Mohammed bin Rashid Al Maktoum
2007	The first residents move on to the Palm Jumeirah; Burj Dubai becomes world's tallest building
2008	Atlantis on the Palm opens its doors

United Arab Emirates Overview

The UAE is considered the second richest Arab country, after Qatar, on a per capita basis. According to World Bank figures for 2006, the UAE's Gross National Income (GNI) per capita was US$23,950. The country has just under 10% of the world's proven oil reserves (most of it within Abu Dhabi emirate) and the fourth largest natural gas reserves. Recent record fuel prices have helped the UAE's GDP grow at over 8% a year. GDP for 2007 was Dhs.697 billion, with the 2008 figures estimated at Dhs.809 billion. In 2006, Dubai contributed more than 40% of the UAE's non-oil revenue.

The UAE's wealth is not solely reliant on oil revenue though, as for the last three years oil accounted for just 27% of overall GDP. Trade, manufacturing, tourism and construction are playing an increasingly important part in the national economy. The country's main export partners are Saudi Arabia, Iran, Japan, India, Singapore, South Korea and Oman. The main import partners are Japan, USA, UK, Italy, Germany and South Korea.

Gross Domestic Product

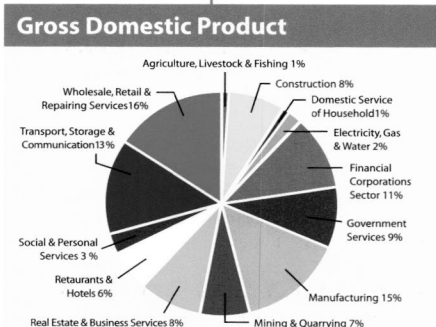

- Agriculture, Livestock & Fishing 1%
- Construction 8%
- Domestic Service of Household 1%
- Wholesale, Retail & Repairing Services 16%
- Transport, Storage & Communication 13%
- Electricity, Gas & Water 2%
- Financial Corporations Sector 11%
- Government Services 9%
- Social & Personal Services 3%
- Retaurants & Hotels 6%
- Manufacturing 15%
- Real Estate & Business Services 8%
- Mining & Quarrying 7%

Dubai Overview

Whereas 20 years ago oil revenues accounted for around half of Dubai's GDP, in 2006 the oil sector contributed just 5.5%. It is expected that by 2010 oil will account for less than 1% of total GDP. Dubai's rulers have known for many years that the oil would run out, and so embarked on ambitious projects to diversify the emirate's economy. Today, trade, manufacturing, transport, construction and real estate are the main contributors to Dubai's strong, growing economy. Indeed, the latest figures show that the construction and real estate sectors between them account for almost a quarter of total GDP. In 2007, Dubai's GDP was in excess of Dhs.198 billion, an increase of 18% on the previous year's figure.

One concern with regard to the economy's growth is rising inflation. Factors such as rising rents – especially in Dubai – mean the cost of living is increasing rapidly for

Sheikh Zayed Road

Economy

Quick Facts

- Dubai Shopping Festival attracted 3.5 million visitors in 2007/8.
- Dubai Government aims to attract 15 million visitors a year to Dubai by 2010.
- By 2010, tourism is expected to contribute 20% to the UAE's GDP.
- 34 million passengers passed through Dubai International Airport in 2007. The initial estimate for 2008 was 40 million.
- Dubai International Airport will soon have capacity to handle 70 million passengers a year.
- By 2015, Al Maktoum International Airport will also have the same passenger capacity.
- The Palms, World, and Dubai Waterfront will add more than a thousand kilometres to Dubai's coastline collectively.
- Value of projects and developments planned for next five years is estimated at more than US$30 billion.
- Dubai currently has over 370 hotels and hotel apartments, offering over 31,000 rooms.
- Rumour has it that up to 20% of the world's cranes are currently in Dubai.

residents. In fact, inflation in 2007 at 11.8% was the highest in the last two decades, with food, drinks and tobacco accounting for more than 10% of this rise according to a pole by Reuters.

It may come as a surprise but despite these rises, a recent survey by Mercer revealed that Dubai has dropped from 34th to 52nd in the ranking for the most expensive cities to live in, with cities such as Moscow, Tokyo and Oslo becoming increasingly more expensive in comparison.

Trade

A long trading tradition, which earned Dubai its reputation as 'the city of merchants' in the Middle East, continues to be an important consideration for foreign companies looking at opportunities in the region today. It is reflected not just in an open and liberal regulatory environment, but also in the local business community's familiarity with international commercial practices and the city's cosmopolitan lifestyle. Strategically located between Europe and the far east, Dubai attracts multinational and private companies wishing to tap the lucrative Middle Eastern, Indian and African markets (which have a combined population of over two billion). Annual domestic imports exceed US$17 billion and Dubai is the gateway to over US$150 billion (annually) in trade.

Growth

The pace of economic growth in Dubai over the last 20 years has been incredible – trade alone has grown at more than 9% per annum over the past 10 years. Looking to the future, Dubai stands poised for further growth with the development of many multi-billion dollar coastal extension projects (such as the three Palm Island projects, The World, and Dubai Waterfront) plus new business and financial ventures. Legislation and government institutions have been designed so that bureaucracy is minimised and there's a positive business environment. Government officials take an active role in promoting investment in Dubai and decisions are taken (and implemented) swiftly. In recent years government departments have also placed increasing importance on improving customer service levels, particularly in the free zones such as Internet City, Media City and Healthcare City, which foster a community environment for specific industries and are very easy to set up and operate in.

However, don't be fooled by the healthy economy into believing that the average expat coming to work in Dubai will automatically be on a huge salary. The wealth isn't spread evenly and except for highly skilled professionals, the salaries for most types of jobs are dropping. This downward trend is attributed in part to the willingness of workers to accept a position at a very low wage. While the UAE GDP per capita income was estimated at approximately Dhs.93,000 in 2007, this figure includes all sections of the community and the average labourer, of which there are many, can expect to earn as little as Dhs.600 (US$165) per month.

Employment

While the unemployment level of the National population in the UAE is lower than that of many other Arab states, there are still a significant number of Emiratis out of work (over 30,000, according to some estimates). This is partly due to a preference for public sector work and partly because of qualifications, and salary expectations, not matching the skills required in the private sector. However, the government is trying to reverse this scenario and reduce unemployment in the local sector with a 'Nationalisation' or 'Emiratisation' programme (which is common to countries throughout the region). The eventual goal is to rely less on an expat workforce, which will be achieved by improving vocational training and by making it compulsory for certain types of companies, such as banks, to hire a set percentage of Emiratis. In another attempt to attract more Nationals to the private sector, the government has a pension scheme where private companies are required to provide a pension for their National employees. The IMF has also encouraged GCC countries to reduce public sector wage levels to encourage locals into the more competitive private sector. This advice doesn't seem to have been heeded though, as 2005 saw the Dubai government sanction a 25% salary increase for National public sector employees, who benefited again in 2007 from a generous settlement.

Really Tax Free?

Do taxes exist in Dubai? Yes and no. You don't pay income or sales tax, except when you purchase alcohol from a licensed liquor store – when you'll be hit with a steep 30% tax. The main tax that you will come across is the municipality tax of 5% on rent and 10% on food, beverages and rooms in hotels. The rest are hidden taxes in the form of 'fees', such as your car registration renewal, visa/permit fees and Salik (road toll).

Leading Industries

The leading industries in Dubai include trade, manufacturing, transport, construction, real estate, energy, telecommunications, finance and tourism. Other sectors such as publishing, recruitment, advertising and IT, while not as developed in terms of size, are undergoing something of a boom (aided in part by the various free zones).

Tourism Developments

Dubai is well ahead of many other cities in the Middle East in terms of travel and tourism. Its hotels and hotel apartments accommodated approximately seven million guests in 2007, an increase of 5.2% on the previous year. The mix of visitors at the moment is roughly 40% business traveller and 60% leisure, but the ratio of leisure travellers is set to increase as Dubai strives to reach its target of attracting 15 million visitors a year by 2010.

Key Projects

Dubai is certainly the place to be if you're an ambitious architect – the city is home to some of the most exciting building projects, ranging from the practical to the utterly unbelievable. Just a few years ago when the first of the Palm Island projects was announced, it seemed an impossible task (p.14), yet now there are residents living on Palm Jumeirah, and various other projects have since been planned that make the Palm look small by comparison.

Dubailand
Emirates Road

Al Barari
www.albarari.com

Nestling on the edge of Dubailand and bordering a conservation area, Al Barari is a development of 330 luxury villas, a boutique hotel, health resort and commercial space for nature lovers. Around 80% of the development will be left 'unconstructed', with areas of woodland, botanical gardens, themed gardens, lakes and streams.
Size 14 million square feet
Completion The first villas will be handed over end 2008

Economy

Nxt to Ibn
Battuta Mall
Jebel Ali

Al Furjan
www.nakheel.ae
A luxurious residential and commercial site boasting architecture influenced by South America, Persia and Asia. The area will have freshwater streams, cycling paths and an 18 hole golf course designed by Greg Norman.
Size 5.6 kilometres
Completion To be confirmed

Extending around
Jebel Ali and Dubai
World Central

Arabian Canal
www.limitless.ae
A man-made waterway that will run from the new Dubai Waterfront development, past Al Maktoum International Airport, before linking back up with the Arabian Gulf at Dubai Marina. It will be the largest and most complex civil engineering project undertaken in the Middle East, sparking a myriad of new waterside communities.
Size 75km long, 150 metres wide
Completion End of 2010

Nr Dubailand
Emirates Road

Bawadi
www.bawadi.ae
This colossal, Dhs.200 billion development will offer 60,000 hotel rooms in 51 hotels. The plan is to produce the world's longest shopping and hospitality area that will conveniently allow visitors to walk from one end to the other. Asia Asia, the showpiece of Bawadi, is a hotel that will provide 6,500 rooms, a shopping mall and entertainment facilities. It aims to be more environmentally friendly than comparable developments.
Size 40 million square feet
Completion Unknown

Interchange 1
Sheikh Zayed Road

Business Bay
www.businessbay.ae
Business Bay is based around an extension to the creek that will stretch up to Sheikh Zayed Road at Interchange 2 before continuing to the sea. This self-contained city aims to become the commercial and business capital for the region. Construction has already begun on more than 70 towers; when finished, the development will be home to 220 towers, including the Emirates Park Towers Hotel, set to be the tallest hotel in the UAE.
Size 64 million square feet
Completion The entire project by 2015

Dubai Creek

Creek Crossings
Dubai's motorists breathed a sigh of relief in 2007, with the opening of the 13 lane Business Bay Bridge and the smaller six lane Floating Bridge, spanning the creek next to Maktoum Bridge. Work was also completed on a much bigger Garhoud Bridge (which totals 13 lanes), and the government has announced two further bridges to ease congestion. Shindagha Bridge will run close to Shindagha Tunnel, while a fifth bridge will connect Deira and Bur Dubai between Shindagha and Maktoum Bridges. The plan is to have 47 lanes crossing the creek by 2008, and a staggering 100 by 2020.
Completion The project for Shindagha should be completed by 2012

Opp Festival City
Jadaf

Culture Village
www.dubai-properties.ae
With architectural emphasis on heritage, Culture Village is set to become a hub for art and culture lovers. The mixed development will feature residential, commercial and

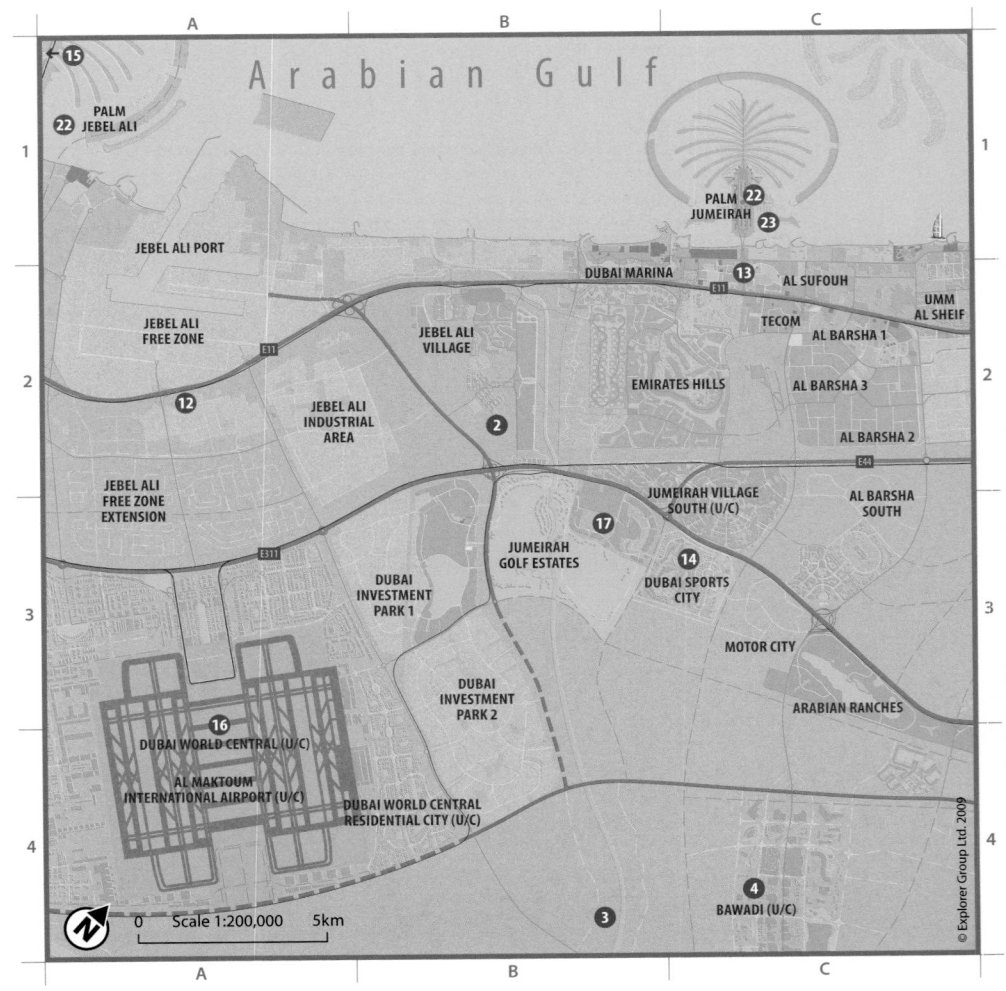

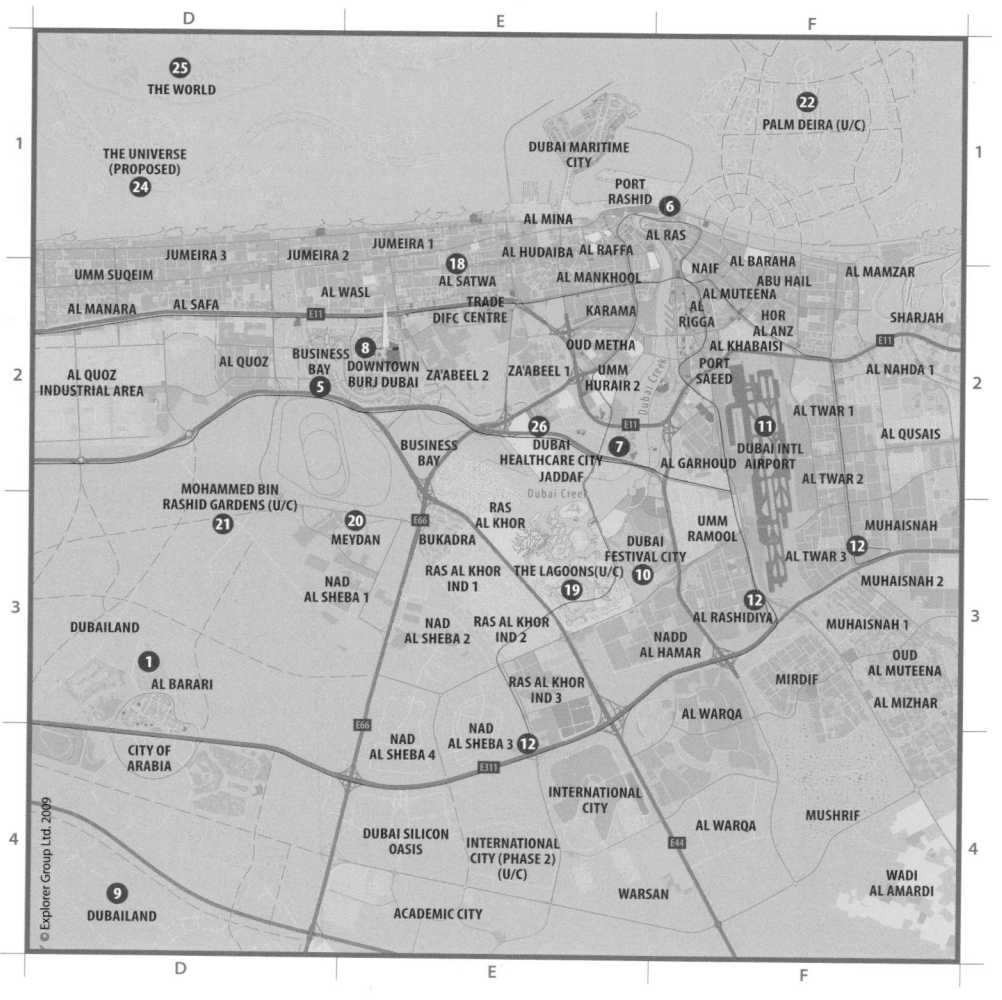

© Explorer Group Ltd. 2009

retail zones. The commercial district will house academies for art, music, dance and crafts, while the retail district will feature hotels and restaurants, art and craft galleries. There will also be an outdoor amphitheatre and traditional dhow yard.
Size 40 million square feet
Completion First buildings completed in 2008

Interchange 1
Sheikh Zayed Road

Downtown Burj Dubai
www.emaar.com
Burj Dubai, the heart of this vast Emaar development, became the tallest building in the world in July 2007, dominating the landscape in the process. When completed, the tower will house retail outlets, offices, exclusive apartments and eight international chain and boutique hotels. The Downtown development is home to Dubai Mall, a lake and park, business and residential complexes.
Size The Burj Dubai tower's estimated height is around 800 metres
Completion 2009

Btw Arabian Ranches and International City
Emirates Road

Dubailand
www.dubailand.ae
With individual themed 'worlds', this aims to be the biggest tourism, leisure and entertainment attraction on the planet. There will be theme parks, a Sports City, numerous hotels, the largest shopping mall in the world (Mall of Arabia), a snowdome, Formula One World and much, much more. The Bawadi project (p.9) alone will have 51 hotels.
Size 278.71 square kilometres/two billion square feet
Completion The Autodrome is already open. Phase one, incorporating all the necessary infrastructure and seven other projects is expected from 2009

Nr Dubai Creek

Dubai Festival City
www.dubaifestivalcity.com
A huge mixed-use development, featuring housing, offices, schools, hotels, retail, entertainment, a marina, and leisure facilities including a golf course and the region's first W Hotel.
Size 6.47 square kilometres, spanning 4km of creek frontage
Completion Some elements are already finished including the Festival Waterfront Centre (home to hundreds of shops, plus huge IKEA and ACE stores). The entire project will be completed by 2015

Nxt to Terminal 1
Garhoud

Dubai International Airport
www.dubaiairport.com
The exclusive Emirates terminal has now opened, with construction already well underway on a huge cargo terminal. Once complete, the airport will be able to handle 70 million passengers a year.
Completion Terminal 3 is open, the cargo terminal is still underway

Throughout Dubai

Dubai Metro
www.dubaimetro.info
Under ground, over ground, this light-rail network will operate driverless trains on four lines, including two linking Al Maktoum International Airport and Dubai International Airport. The network will include trams on Beach Road and Al Sufouh Road. It is estimated that by 2020, the metro will handle 1.85 million passengers a day (see also Metro p.62).
Size Total length of 318km by 2020
Completion The first trains should be running by September 2009

*Nr entrance
to Palm Jumeirah
Al Sufouh*

Dubai Pearl

www.dubaipearl.com

Dubai Pearl will be neatly contained within a circle of land beside Media and Internet Cities, and promises office towers, freehold apartments, hotels, a shopping mall, an art gallery, and the Royal Hall, set to be the largest performing arts venue in the region. It was due to be completed in 2008, however following a change in property developers the initial construction was demolished and is being rebuilt from scratch.
Size The diameter of the circle is 500m
Completion End of 2010

Dubailand

Dubai Sports City

www.dubaisportscity.ae

Part of the vast Dubailand project, Dubai Sports City will be home to a mass of sporting venues and facilities, including four stadia, and soccer, golf, hockey and tennis academies, boasting world renowned brands such as Manchester United Football Club and the International Cricket Council.
Size 4,500,000 square metres
Completion The Els Club, an 18 hole championship golf course, is already open; the remainder by 2010

*Adjoining Palm
Jebel Ali
Next to Abu Dhabi
border*

Dubai Waterfront

www.dubaiwaterfront.ae

Dwarfing all previous developments, Dubai Waterfront will consist of over 250 individual communities. Madinat Al Arab, another new 'downtown', will feature Al Burj – set to be one of the world's tallest buildings. Phase one sold out (to selected developers) within five days, for a cool Dhs.13 billion. The project is being developed by Nakheel, the firm responsible for the three Palms and The World.
Size 81 square kilometres, it will add 880km of new coastline
Completion First phase by 2010

*Inland from
Jebel Ali Port*

Dubai World Central

www.dubaiworldcentral.ae

Originally called Jebel Ali International Airport City, this will be a self-contained urban centre, based around a new airport with six runways. The first phase includes Dubai Logistics City, a regional hub for air, sea, and road freight. Once complete, DWC will feature commercial and residential areas, a science and technology park and a golf resort. It is expected to handle 120 million passengers a year by 2050.
Size DWC will eventually cover around 140 square kilometres
Completion The airport is expected to become operational in 2009

*Btw Autodrome
and Green
Community,
Emirates Road*

International Media Production Zone

www.impz.ae

This project is a free zone, not unlike Dubai Media City, but dedicated solely to the media production industry. The first phase will focus on the printing and publishing. Located off the E311 Emirates Road, the development will eventually house hotels, retail outlets, and residential and commercial towers.
Size 4 square kilometres of land
Completion 2008 onwards

Satwa

Jumeirah Garden City

A totally demolished Satwa will be home to a whole new development of residential and commercial properties that will link up to the Business Bay hub and Creek extensions. The project is still in planning stages, but is expected to be a huge undertaking featuring plenty of green spaces, canals, ponds, and a waterway that will link back to the Gulf.

Completion Partly on hold; new completion date to be confirmed

Nr Ras Al Khor
Wildlife Sanctuary
Dubai Creek

The Lagoons
www.lagoons.ae
The Lagoons will be made up of seven artificial islands already under construction on the edge of Dubai Creek. The creek will be extended inland to create a new environmentally friendly development area, providing a range of housing as well as shopping centres, marinas, office space, cultural focal points (including an opera house) and five-star hotels.
Size 70 million square feet
Completion 2010

Nr Nad Al Sheba
Golf Course

Meydan
www.meydan.ae
This new urban centre will incorporate a racecourse to supersede the existing Nad Al Sheba track. The project aspires to create a 'horseracing city', with a business park, residential areas and shopping arcades. Due to become the new home of the Dubai Racing Club, Meydan will be linked to the creek by a canal, and will boast its own marina.
Size 15 million square feet
Completion 2010

Nr Meydan

Mohammed bin Rashid Gardens
www.craven-property.com
An ambitious US$55 billion development that claims to preserve and protect the environment with its environmentally friendly build, this project aims to have communities at the forefront of its development. The new city has four parts, with parks, libraries, mosques, a zoo, universities and financial centres within their distinct zones.
Completion To be confirmed

Off Dubai's coastline
Jebel Ali, Jumeirah and
Deira

Palm Islands
www.thepalm.ae
These three palm tree-shaped islands will extend out into the Arabian Gulf and increase Dubai's coastline by hundreds of kilometres. They will feature thousands of villas and apartments, numerous hotels, leisure and entertainment attractions, and retail outlets aplenty.
Size Trunk lengths: Jumeirah – 2km, Deira – 12.5km, Jebel Ali – 2.4km
Completion The first homes on Palm Jumeirah were released in 2007; land reclamation on Palm Deira is at 20% and will be completed in 2013; Jebel Ali's first properties should also be ready by 2013 and land reclamation is almost finished.

Tourist Hotspot

The development of high-end tourist amenities and visitor attractions, in conjunction with an aggressive overseas marketing campaign, means that Dubai is swiftly becoming a popular holiday destination. The city is also attracting a lot of business in the MICE (meetings, incentives, conferences and exhibitions) market. The government's plan is to attract 15 million visitors a year by 2010, and 40 million a year by 2015.

Dubai's **ONLY** Complete Street Atlas

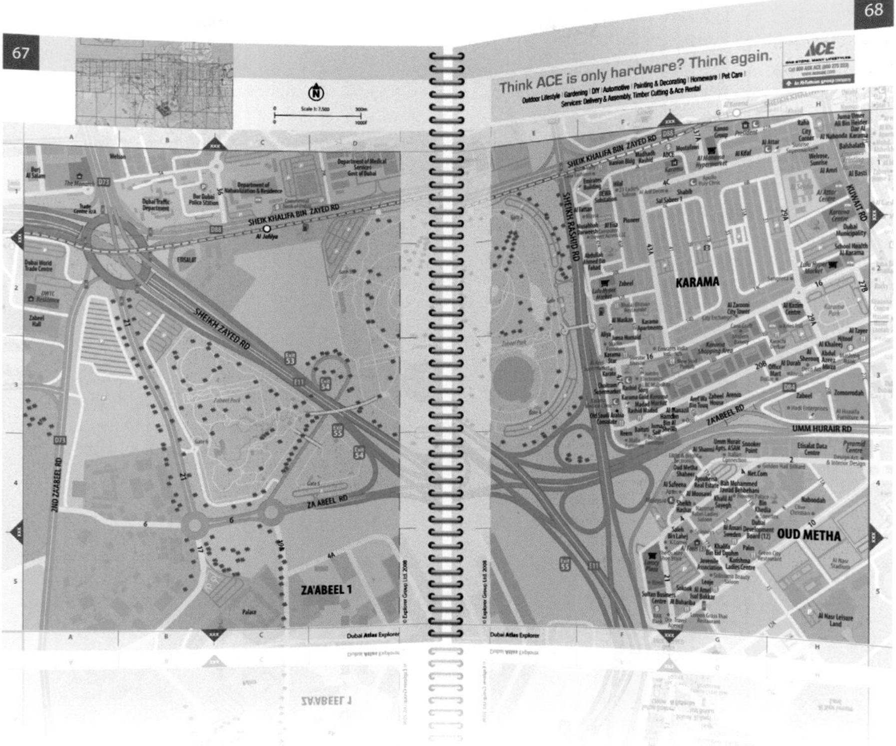

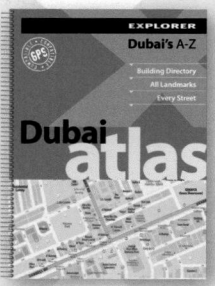

Featuring over 10,000 buildings, plus the new road naming system, this is the most comprehensive atlas for Dubai ever produced. You just got lost for the last time.

Dubai Atlas
The complete street atlas

The Palm Jumeirah ◀

QE2
www.qe2.org.uk
November 2008 saw the arrival of one of the most famous ships in history: the QE2. The ship headed to Port Rashid, accompanied by a flotilla which included Sheikh Mohammed's private yacht, where it will undergo a makeover, transforming it in to a luxurious hotel before it's moored at its permanent home at the Palm Jumeirah.
Completion 2011

Nr The World ◀
Btw Palm Jumeirah &
Palm Deira

The Universe
www.nakheel.com
The Universe is possibly one of the most ambitious projects by Nakheel. The development follows on from The World, and will feature islands that will form the shape of the universe. The project is still in the planning stages, and is expected to take up to 20 years to construct. The islands will be located in between Palm Jumeirah and Palm Deira, close to the World islands.
Completion To be confirmed

3km off Dubai's coast ◀
Btw Jumeirah and
Deira Palm Islands

The World
www.theworld.ae
These 303 artificial islands in the Arabian Gulf will broadly represent a map of the world. The islands, varying in size, were offered for sale to individual buyers, who could then develop them as they wished. The islands will feature mansions, villas and apartments.
Size 9km east to west, 6km north to south
Completion dredging completed in 2008, construction by 2009

Nr Al Wasl Hospital ◀

Zabeel Mall
www.zabeelmall.ae
Spread over eight storeys, this new mall will feature 280 retail outlets, 30 food and beverage outlets, a children's entertainment centre and an eight-screen cinema. The complex will also include 120 serviced apartments with facilities.
Size 400,000 square feet
Completion 2009

International Relations

The UAE remains open in its foreign relations, and is firmly committed to the support of Arab unity. HH Sheikh Khalifa bin Zayed Al Nahyan is very generous with the country's wealth when it comes to helping Arab nations and communities that are in need of aid.

The UAE became a member of the United Nations and the Arab League in 1971. It is a member of the International Monetary Fund (IMF), the Organisation of Petroleum Exporting Countries (Opec), the World Trade Organisation (WTO) and other international and Arab organisations. It is also a member of the Arab Gulf Cooperation Council (AGCC, also known as the GCC), whose other members are Bahrain, Kuwait, Oman, Qatar and Saudi Arabia. Pioneered by the late Sheikh Zayed bin Sultan Al Nahyan, the UAE had a leading role in the formation of the AGCC, in 1981, and the country is the third largest member in terms of geographical size, after Saudi Arabia and Oman. All major embassies and consulates are represented either in Dubai or in Abu Dhabi, or both. The UAE does not officially recognise the state of Israel.

Economy

Downtown Burj Dubai

Dubai International Airport T3

QE2

Dubai Sports City

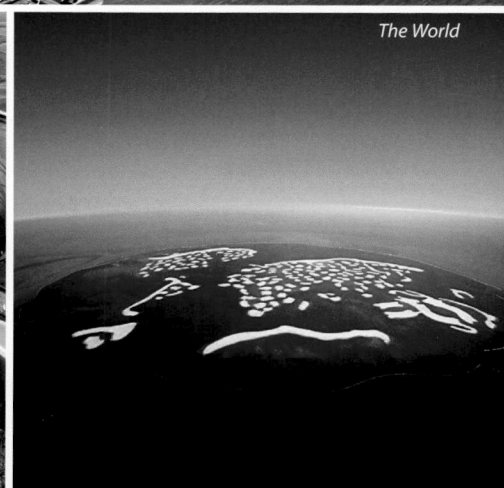

The World

Government & Ruling Family

The Supreme Council of Rulers is the highest authority in the UAE, comprising the hereditary rulers of the seven emirates. Since the country is governed by hereditary rule there is little distinction between the royal families and the government. The Supreme Council is responsible for general policy matters involving education, defence, foreign affairs, communications and development, and for ratifying federal laws. The Council meets four times a year and the Abu Dhabi and Dubai rulers have effective power of veto over decisions.

The Supreme Council elects the chief of state (the President) from among its seven members. The current president is the ruler of Abu Dhabi, Sheikh Khalifa bin Zayed Al Nahyan. He took over the post in November 2004 from his late father, Sheikh Zayed bin Sultan Al Nahyan.

The Supreme Council also elects the Vice President of the UAE, currently Sheikh Mohammed bin Rashid Al Maktoum, Ruler of Dubai. The president and Vice President are elected and appointed for five-year terms, although they are often re-elected time after time, as was the case with Sheikh Zayed. The president appoints the prime minister (currently Sheikh Mohammed bin Rashid Al Maktoum) and the deputy prime ministers (currently Sheikh Sultan bin Zayed Al Nahyan and Sheikh Hamdan bin Zayed Al Nahyan).

The emirate of Dubai is currently ruled by Sheikh Mohammed bin Rashid Al Maktoum, Vice President and Prime Minister of the UAE (who is considered the driving force behind Dubai's exponential growth) and his brother Sheikh Hamdan bin Rashid Al Maktoum, the UAE Minister of Finance and Industry.

The Federal National Council (FNC) reports to the Supreme Council. It has executive authority to initiate and implement laws and is a consultative assembly of 40 representatives. The Council currently monitors and debates government policy but has no power of veto.

The individual emirates still have a degree of autonomy, and laws that affect everyday life vary between them. For instance, if you buy a car in one emirate and need to register it in a different emirate, you will first have to export and then re-import it. All emirates have a separate police force, with different uniforms and cars.

Girl Power

Over 22% of the UAE government is made up of women, one of the highest rates in the world. Following elections in 2007, a number of women were voted in to official positions, demonstrating the integration between men and women in UAE society.

Dubai Ruling Family Tree

Maktoum Bin Hasher Al Maktoum (Ruler 1894-1906)

- Saeed (Ruler 1912-58)
  - Rashid (Ruler 1958-90)
    - Maktoum (Ruler 1990-2006)
    - Hamdan (Deputy Ruler)
    - **Mohammed** (Ruler 2006-) Prime Minister & Vice President of UAE
      - Rashid
      - Ahmed
      - Majid
      - Hamdan
      - Latifa
      - Maitha
      - (others)
    - Ahmed
  - Khalifa
  - Ahmed (Chairman of Emirates)
- Juma
  - Maktoum
    - Hasher
      - Mohammed
    - Butti
    - Juma
      - Ahmed
    - Marwan (Major General)
- Hasher

Population

All figures below are for National and expat residents.

- According to figures released in 2007, the population of the UAE stands at 4.49 million people, which is a 9.4% increase on the 2005 national census figure of just over 4.1 million, and a 6.1% increase on 2006.
- The UAE's population is made up of 20.1% Nationals and 79.9% expatriates.
- Dubai's population was estimated as 1,480,000 at the end of 2007, compared to the 2006 figure of 1,422,000. Approximately 33% of the total population of the UAE lives in Dubai.
- By 2017 it is estimated that the population of Dubai will have reached 3 million.
- The annual growth rate for Dubai is approximately 8%, and 7.5% for the UAE.
- In 2007, 292,000 new residents entered Dubai (800 a day).
- 75.5% of Dubai's population is male and 24.5% is female.
- A recent Dubai Municipality statistical survey revealed that the average size of a UAE National household is 7.6 members, while that of an expat is 3.7.
- According to the United Nations Development Program (UNDP), the UAE has the highest life expectancy in the Arab world at 72.2 years for males and 75.6 years for females.

UAE Population Age Breakdown

Source: www.tedad.ae and Dubai Statistics Department

UAE Population by Emirate

Source: www.tedad.ae and Dubai Statistics Department

Education Levels

- University 17
- Secondary 5
- Literate 18
- Intermediate 51
- Illiterate 9

Source: www.tedad.ae and Dubai Statistics Department

National Flag

The UAE flag comprises three equal horizontal bands: green at the top, white in the middle and black at the bottom. A thicker, vertical band of red runs down the hoist side. The colours on the flag are common to many of the Arab nations and they symbolise Arab unity and independence. In a nation continually striving for world records, it is no surprise that when the 30 year anniversary celebrations were marked on National Day 2001, one of the world's tallest flagpoles was erected in Abu Dhabi and the world's largest UAE flag was raised at Union House in Jumeira, Dubai.

Local Time

The UAE is four hours ahead of UCT (Universal Coordinated Time – formerly known as GMT). There is no altering of clocks for daylight saving in the summer, so when Europe and North America loses an hour, the time in the UAE stays the same. During this period the time difference is one hour less, so when it is 12:00 in the UAE it is 09:00 in the UK instead of 08:00 during the winter. The table on the next page shows time differences between the UAE and various cities around the world (not allowing for any daylight savings in those cities).

Social & Business Hours

Social hours differ greatly in Dubai, with some people waking up early and working a straight shift (usually from 08:00 to 17:00 or 09:00 to 18:00, with an hour for lunch), while others work a split shift (working from

Time Zones	
Amman	-2
Athens	-2
Auckland	+8
Bangkok	+3
Beijing	+4
Canberra	+6
Colombo	+2
Damascus	-2
Denver	-11
Doha	-1
Dublin	-4
Hong Kong	+4
Johannesburg	-2
Karachi	+1
Kuwait City	-1
Lebanon	-2
London	-4
Los Angeles	-12
Manama	-1
Mexico City/Dallas	-10
Moscow	-1
Mumbai	+1.5
Munich	-3
Muscat	0
New York	-9
Paris	-3
Perth	+4
Prague	-3
Riyadh	-1
Rome	-3
Singapore	+4
Sydney	+6
Tokyo	+5
Toronto	-9
Wellington	+8

09:00 to 13:00, then taking a long lunch break before returning to work from 16:00 to 19:00). Years ago, most of Dubai closed for a long period over lunch, opening again in the late afternoon. Even shops would close their doors at 13:00 and return for evening trading. However, these days the majority of larger shops and shopping centres are open throughout the day and into the evening, generally closing at 22:00. It is only the more traditional, smaller street traders that still close for three or four hours in the afternoon. Friday is the Islamic holy day and therefore a universal day off for offices and schools. Consumer demand means that the hospitality and retail industries are open seven days a week. In 2006, the five-day working week for government departments and schools was set as Sunday to Thursday, bringing them into line with much of the private sector. There are still private companies which have retained the traditional Saturday to Wednesday working week, while others work five and a half days a week and some operate a six-day week, taking only Friday as a rest day.

Government offices are generally open from 07:30 to 14:00, Sunday to Thursday. Private sector office hours vary between split shift days, which are generally 08:00 to 13:00, reopening at either 15:00 or 16:00 and closing at 18:00 or 19:00; or straight shifts, usually 09:00 to 18:00, with an hour for lunch.

Independent shop and souk opening times are usually based on split shift hours, while outlets in the big shopping malls remain open all day. Closing times are usually 22:00 or midnight, while some food shops and petrol stations are open 24 hours a day. On Fridays, many places are open all day, apart from prayer time (11:30 to 13:30), while larger shops in the malls only open in the afternoon from either 12:00 or 14:00.

Embassies and consulates are usually open from 07:30 to 14:30, but they may designate specific times and days for certain tasks (such as passport applications), so it's best to call before you go. Most embassies now take a Friday/Saturday weekend. All will have an emergency number on their answering service, website or on their office doors.

Ramadan Hours

According to the labour laws, all companies are obliged to shorten the working day by two hours during Ramadan. Even though this is to assist Muslim employees who are fasting, the law makes no distinction in this regard between Muslim and non-Muslim employees. So technically, even expats are entitled to a shorter working day. However, many international companies do not follow this principle, and labour lawyers would advise you not to make a fuss if you are not given a shorter working day.

Some lucky expats do get to work shorter hours during Ramadan, and many businesses, schools and shops change their hours slightly.

Dubai's traffic has a totally different pattern during Ramadan: instead of being gridlocked in the mornings and quiet in the afternoons, the mornings are almost jam-free and you'll sail through all the usual trouble spots, while in the afternoons the roads are totally clogged. Night-time activity increases during Ramadan, with many shops staying open later (until midnight or even 01:00) and the city's many shisha cafes and some restaurants staying open until the early hours.

Public Holidays

The Islamic calendar starts from the year 622AD, the year of Prophet Muhammad's migration (Hijra) from Mecca to Al Madinah. Hence the Islamic year is called the Hijri year and dates are followed by AH (AH stands for Anno Hegirae, meaning 'after the year of the Hijra').

As some holidays are based on the sighting of the moon and do not have fixed dates on the Hijri calendar, Islamic holidays are more often than not confirmed less than 24 hours in advance. Most companies send an email to employees the day before, notifying them of the confirmed holiday date. Some non-religious holidays are fixed according to the Gregorian calendar. It should be noted that the public sector often gets additional days

Facts & Figures

Lunar Calendar

The Hijri calendar is based on lunar months; there are 354 or 355 days in the Hijri year, which is divided into 12 lunar months, and is thus 11 days shorter than the Gregorian year. There are plenty of websites with Gregorian/Hijri calendar conversion tools, so you can find the equivalent Hijri date for any Gregorian date, and vice versa. Try www.rabiah.com/convert.

off for holidays where the private sector may not (for example on National Day the public sector gets two days of official holiday, whereas private sector companies take only one day). This can be a problem for working parents, as

Public Holidays	
New Year's Day (1)	Jan 1 Fixed
Prophet Muhammad's Birthday (1)	Mar 9 Moon
Lailat Al Mi'Raj (1)	Jul 19 Moon
Eid Al Fitr (3)	Sep 20 Moon
Eid Al Adha (4)	Nov 27 Moon
UAE National Day (2)	Dec 2 Fixed
Islamic New Year's Day (1)	Dec18 Moon

schools fall under the public sector and therefore get the extended holidays, so your children will usually have more days off than you do. No problem if you have full-time home help, but if not then you may have to take a day's leave.

The table above lists the holidays and the number of days they last. This applies mainly to the public sector, so if you work in the private sector you may get fewer days per holiday. The main Muslim festivals are Eid Al Fitr (the festival of the breaking of the fast, which marks the end of Ramadan) and Eid Al Adha (the festival of the sacrifice, which marks the end of the pilgrimage to Mecca).

Mawlid Al Nabee is the holiday celebrating the Prophet Muhammad's birthday, and Lailat Al Mi'raj celebrates the Prophet's ascension into heaven.

Wafi City, Raffles Hotel

DIFC The Gate

Dubai Marina

Climate

Dubai has a subtropical and arid climate. Sunny blue skies and high temperatures can be expected most of the year. Rainfall is infrequent and erratic, usually falling on an average of only 25 days per year, mainly in winter (December to March), but it often seems like less. While the number of days with rain can be as high as 18 per month in extreme cases, the average is five days per month through the winter, and when it does rain, it is not usually for very long or very heavily. However in the Hajar Mountains the amount of rainfall can be much higher and flash floods in the wadis are not unheard of. The last few years have not been particularly wet (2005-06 had only 74mm of rain), but compared to the previous few years they were a lot wetter. Between 2000 and 2003 total annual rainfall was as low as 8.8mm, less than 10% of the usual annual total. As it is not seen very often, heavy rainfall can really take its toll on the city within a relatively short period. Not all roads have adequate drainage, and even those that do are not designed for massive downpours and can get blocked by sand, resulting in water logging. In addition, many of Dubai's drivers are not accustomed to wet conditions, and tend to respond by putting their hazard lights on, meaning you rarely know which direction they are heading. January 2008 saw two days of flooding which resulted in many schools and businesses closing due to impassable roads, and even a number of homes had water damage.

Temperatures range from a low of around 10°C (50°F) in winter to a high of 48°C (118°F) in summer. The mean daily maximum is 24°C (75°F) in January, rising to 41°C (106°F) in August. Climatic changes have not had a marked effect, but local urbanisation and industrialisation factors, such as the vast increase in the amount of tarmac roads and large buildings since weather records began in the 1960s, have caused a slight increase in temperatures, especially the minimum temperature in winter.

During winter there are occasional sandstorms when the sand is whipped up off the desert. This is not to be confused with a shamal, a north-westerly wind that comes off the Arabian Gulf and can cool temperatures down. Sandstorms cover anything left outside in gardens or on balconies and can even blow inside, so make sure your doors and windows are shut.

Surprisingly, mornings can get very foggy and humid, especially in spring and autumn, but by mid-morning the sun invariably burns any cloud away. Humidity is usually between 50% and 65%, being slightly lower in the summer than the winter. However, when combined with the high summer temperatures, even 60% humidity can produce extremely uncomfortable conditions. The most pleasant time to visit Dubai is in the cooler winter months, when temperatures are perfect for comfortable days on the beach and long, lingering evenings outside. For up to date weather reports, log on to www.dubaiairport.com/dubaimet, or www.das.ae, or call Dubai Meteorological Services' automated system on 04 216 2218.

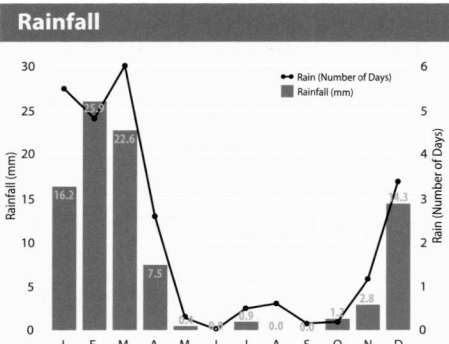

Temperature & Humidity

Humidity
Average Max. Temp
Average Min. Temp

Rainfall

Rain (Number of Days)
Rainfall (mm)

Environment

Flora & Fauna

As you would expect in a country with such an arid climate, the variety of flora and fauna is not as extensive as in other parts of the world. Still, a variety of plants and animals have managed to adapt to a life of high temperatures and low rainfall. Despite its sandy and rocky nature, the UAE is adorned with many parks and green belts, and Dubai is no exception. The municipality

Camels at Big Red

has an extensive greening programme in place and areas along the roads are unusually colourful for a desert environment, with grass, palm trees and flowers being constantly maintained by an army of workers and round-the-clock watering. The city also boasts a large number of well-kept parks (see p.280).

Flora

The region has about 3,500 endemic plants, which is perhaps surprising considering the high salinity of the soil and the harsh environment. The most famous is, of course, the date palm, which is also the most flourishing of the indigenous flora and provides wonderful seas of green, especially in the oases. Heading towards the mountains, flat-topped acacia trees and wild grasses create scenery not unlike that of an African savannah. The deserts are often surprisingly green in places, even during the dry summer months, but it takes an experienced botanist to get the most out of the area.

Fauna

Indigenous fauna includes the Arabian leopard and the ibex, but sightings of them are extremely rare. Realistically, the only large animals you will see are camels and goats (often roaming dangerously close to roads). Other desert life includes the sand cat, sand fox and desert hare, plus gerbils, hedgehogs, snakes and geckos.

Birds

Birdlife in the city is a little limited – this isn't a place for hearing a dawn chorus, unless you're extremely lucky. However, recent studies have shown that the number of species of birds is rising each year, due in part to the increasing lushness of the area. This is most apparent in the parks, especially in spring and autumn, as the country lies on the route for birds migrating between central Asia and east Africa. You can also see flamingos at the Khor Dubai Wildlife Sanctuary at the southern end of Dubai Creek.

Marine Life

Off the coast of the UAE, the seas contain a rich abundance of marine life, including tropical fish, jellyfish, coral, the dugong ('sea cow') and sharks. Eight species of whale and seven species of dolphin have been recorded in UAE waters. Various breeds of turtle are also indigenous to the region. These include the loggerhead, green and hawksbill turtles, all of which are under threat. These are seen by divers off both coasts, and by swimmers or snorkellers, quite commonly just off the east coast at places such as Snoopy Island, and sometimes in Khor Kalba.

See Them For Yourself

To get close to the flora and fauna of the UAE, you really need to go looking for them in the right places. On close inspection, you'll find that the sand dunes, mountains and wadis are full of hardy creatures that survive despite harsh conditions. Get out of the city and into some natural habitats – and don't forget to take a copy of the UAE Off-Road Explorer *with you – it's the ultimate guide to the best off-road routes in the region.*

Environmental Issues

The Living Planet Report 2008 recently revealed that the UAE has the highest ecological footprint per capita in the world. The research was jointly undertaken by the WWF and the UAE government, providing for the first time indisputable evidence of the country's environmental impact that the UAE administration can no longer ignore. In the past, the vast amounts of natural resources available in the area has meant that the government has not shown any inclination towards greener energy forms, and for this reason you are unlikely to see a single solar panel within the UAE despite having over 300 days of sunshine per year.

Perhaps as a result of living in a nation inhabited by a vast majority of expatriates, the average UAE resident feels little responsibility towards the country's environment. There is a pressing need for residents to start making a personal contribution to reduce the impact of their presence. It is being increasingly recognised throughout the world that the time left to be able to make a difference to the future of the planet is decreasing, and it will require everyone to get involved or the earth could well become a very different place for future generations. From turning your air conditioning down a degree or two and switching off electrical appliances when not in use, to recycling as much of your waste as possible, there are plenty of things that are easy to do and can make the difference to the UAE's 'footprint'.

Environmental Issues & Ecosystem

Despite efforts being made, there are some serious environmental issues facing the UAE. The massive scale of development being pursued in Dubai on gigantic projects such as the Palm Islands and Dubai Waterfront is changing the coastline of Dubai and its ecosystem immeasurably, while the desert is being swallowed up by Dubailand and other leisure and residential developments. In 2001, the Dubai government banned any further development along the coast without prior permission, although that seems something of a paradox in light of the projects that have already been granted permission. Conservationists have suggested that the massive construction for projects in the Arabian Gulf will destroy coral reefs and fish stocks, as well as damaging breeding grounds for endangered species such as the hawksbill turtle. In 2007, it was announced by Nakheel that it was becoming difficult to source sand for the land

Jumeira Beach Park

reclamation from inside UAE waters for these projects as so much has already been taken. Changes to the coastal environment have been on such a colossal scale that effects on marine life have been significant. Another result of these developments is the possible downsizing of future projects due to lack of sand. The developers, however, argue that the sites will attract sealife, and point to the recent increase in fish and marine life witnessed around the crescent on the Palm Jumeirah. One strange by-product is that due to this crescent being six kilometres out to sea, certain species of shark that wouldn't normally come so close to the land have been spotted around the beaches.

Also, while the UAE desert is not exactly teeming with wildlife, the animals that do survive are being affected by all the development and once gone from the country will be very difficult to reintroduce. While many conservationists slate the rapid expansion of Dubai's infrastructure, the issue remains contentious. Many other countries enjoyed their boom-time in the early part of the last century when environmental issues were not as prominent as they are today, so in some ways it seems unfair that the UAE shouldn't be allowed to develop as other nations have. Then again, the UAE has the advantage of being able to learn from the experience of others, and if there had been more environmental awareness during the industrialisation of leading nations, the world would probably not require such drastic environmental measures. Whatever side you are on, it's safe to say that there are some green issues that could, and should, be given more consideration.

Water Usage & Desalination

The lower than average rainfall over the last few years and the increasing demand for water from the UAE's growing population have compounded problems with the decreasing water table, which is at a record low. It was estimated in 2004 that the amount of water taken out of the ground was around 880 million m^3 per year, while the amount going back in could be as low as 20 million m^3. The water table has decreased by an average of one metre a year for the past 30 years, and if extraction of water from the ground continues at this rate, there is a very real danger of this water drying out completely.

As the water table decreases, saltwater moves inland to fill the gap. This contaminates the fresh water stored underground, especially near the coast where the increasing salinity of the ground affects the fertility of the soil, hampering farming. It has even affected places as far inland as the Hajar Mountains, where inland freshwater wells have started to dry up in areas close to Masafi, home of the country's most famous brand of bottled water.

One major factor is that the UAE currently has the highest water consumption per capita in the world, using an estimated 133 gallons a day, which is 150% of the amount used by the United States. To provide the ever-growing population of Dubai with water, a complex of desalination plants (the biggest in the world) were recently set up in Jebel Ali to boost production. However, considering the projected growth of Dubai, both businesses and residents need to help reduce the amount of water that is wasted. Charity starts at home, so why not do your bit by saving water wherever you can (for example turn off the tap as you're brushing your teeth) and encourage your company to take similar measures.

Environmental Organisations

Various organisations have been formed to protect the environment, as well as to educate the population on the importance of environmental issues. The Environment Agency Abu Dhabi (www.ead.ae) was established in 1996 to assist the Abu Dhabi government in the conservation and management of the emirate's natural environment, resources, wildlife and biological diversity. This organisation was previously known as the Environmental Research & Wildlife Development Agency (ERWDA) before it was renamed in 2005. Sir Bani Yas Island off Abu Dhabi is home to an internationally acclaimed breeding programme for endangered wildlife. Created as a private wildlife sanctuary by the late Sheik Zayed, it is now an exclusive eco-resort (02 801 5400, www. anantara.com). Emirates Wildlife Society is a national environmental NGO that operates in association with the WWF (www.panda.org/uae). In addition, The Breeding Centre for Endangered Arabian Wildlife (06 531 1212) at Sharjah Desert Park, has a successful breeding programme for endangered wildlife, particularly the Arabian leopard. The breeding centre is off-limits to visitors but the Arabian Wildlife Centre (p.278), also at the Desert Park, is open to the public. See also Environmental Groups (p.349).

Dolphin Friendly?
This year has seen the opening of two dolphinariums, Dubai Dolphinarium at Creek Park and Dophin Bay at Atlantis the Palm. Animal welfare organisations have been critical of how the star attractions were acquired. They contend that no dolphinarium could ever be big enough to house these magnificent marine creatures, who can swim up to 100km per day in the wild. To find out more about dolphins in captivity, log on to www. wdcs.org.

Culture

Dubai's culture is firmly rooted in the Islamic traditions of Arabia. Islam is more than just a religion; it is a way of life that governs even mundane everyday events, from what to wear to what to eat and drink. Therefore, the culture and heritage of the UAE is closely linked to its religion. Unfortunately, Islamic fundamentalism has come to the forefront of the media in recent times and has lead many people around the world to adopt a very extreme, blanket view of the religion. However, in contrast to this image, the UAE is tolerant and welcoming; foreigners are free to practise their own religion, alcohol is served in hotels and the dress code is liberal. Women face little discrimination and, contrary to the policies of Saudi Arabia and Iran, are able to drive and walk around uncovered and unescorted.

Among the most highly prized virtues are courtesy and hospitality, and visitors are likely to experience the genuine warmth and friendliness of the Emirati people. Luckily, the negative view of Islam that has affected many Muslims living abroad has not had an impact on Dubai, and you will find various nationalities, whether Muslim, Hindu or Christian, working and living side by side without any conflict. To Muslims, like many other religions and cultures, the family unit is very important, and elders are respected for their experience and ability to give advice. Many generations will live together in the same house. Polygamy is practised in the UAE, with Islam allowing a man to have up to four wives at one time, providing he has the financial and physical means to treat each of them equally. However, a Muslim man taking more than one wife is more the exception than the norm, and most Muslim families resemble the traditional western family unit: mum, dad and kids.

The rapid economic development over the last 30 years has changed life in the Emirates beyond recognition. However, the country's rulers are committed to safeguarding their heritage against any erosion that could be caused by the speed of development and increased access to outside cultures and influence. They are therefore keen to promote cultural and sporting events that are representative of their traditions, such as falconry, camel racing and traditional dhow sailing. Arabic culture in poetry, dancing, songs and traditional art is encouraged, and weddings and celebrations are still colourful occasions of feasting and music.

Respect the local culture. When you first arrive you may find many aspects that seem very strange to you, and therefore 'wrong'. Take time to observe and understand local culture before you pass judgement; you'll soon realise that the many different nationalities living here make it a sometimes-frustrating but ultimately fascinating city.

Cross Culture
The Sheikh Mohammed Centre for Cultural Understanding (04 353 6666) was established to help bridge the gap between cultures and give visitors a clearer appreciation of the Emirati way of life. It organises tours of Jumeira Mosque (p.274) where you can learn about Islam.

Poetry

Poetry is an integral and historically important part of Arabic culture. The ancient form of poetry is called *Nabati*, and is also known as Bedouin poetry. It is a rich form of literature slightly removed from classical Arabic. HH Sheikh Mohammed bin Rashid Al Maktoum is a renowned poet, and a patron of poetry competitions. The Palm Jebel Ali will feature water-homes constructed on stilts that when viewed from above spell out the following verse written by Sheikh Mohammed: 'Take wisdom from the wise, not everyone who rides a horse is a jockey. It takes a man of vision to write on water, great men rise to great challenges.'

Language

Other options **Learning Arabic** p.224, **Language Schools** p.366

Arabic is the official language of the UAE, although English, Hindi, Malayalam and Urdu are commonly spoken. Arabic is the official business language, but English is so widely used that you could conduct business here for years without learning a single word of Arabic. Most road signs, shop signs and restaurant menus are in both languages. The further out of town you go, the more you will find just Arabic, both spoken and on street and shop signs.

Arabic isn't the easiest language to pick up, or to pronounce. But if you can throw in a couple of words here and there, you're more likely to receive a warmer welcome or at least a smile – even if your pronunciation is terrible.

See the table on p.27 for a list of useful Arabic phrases.

Basic Arabic

General		Taxi Or Car Related	
Yes	na'am	Is this the road to...	hadaa al tariyq ila...
No	la	Stop	kuf
Please	min fadlak (m) / min fadliki (f)	Right	yamiyn
Thank you	shukran	Left	yassar
Please (in offering)	tafaddal (m) / tafaddali (f)	Straight ahead	siydaa
Praise be to God	al-hamdu l-illah	North	shamaal
God willing	in shaa'a l-laah	South	januwb
Greetings		East	sharq
Greeting		West	garb
(peace be upon you)	as-salaamu alaykom	Turning	mafraq
Greeting (in reply)	wa alaykom is salaam	First	awwal
Good morning	sabah il-khayr	Second	thaaniy
Good morning (in reply)	sabah in-nuwr	Road	tariyq
Good evening	masa il-khayr	Street	shaaria
Good evening (in reply)	masa in-nuwr	Roundabout	duwwaar
Hello	marhaba	Signals	ishaara
Hello (in reply)	marhabtayn	Close to	qarib min
How are you?	kayf haalak (m) / kayf haalik (f)	Petrol station	mahattat betrol
Fine, thank you	zayn, shukran (m) / zayna, shukran (f)	Sea/beach	il bahar
Welcome	ahlan wa sahlan	Mountain/s	jabal/jibaal
Welcome (in reply)	ahlan fiyk (m) / ahlan fiyki (f)	Desert	al sahraa
Goodbye	ma is-salaama	Airport	mataar
Introductions		Hotel	funduq
My name is...	ismiy...	Restaurant	mata'am
What is your name?	shuw ismak (m) / shuw ismik (f)	Slow Down	schway schway
Where are you from?	min wayn inta (m) / min wayn inti (f)	**Accidents & Emergencies**	
I am from...	anaa min...	Police	al shurtaa
America	ameriki	Permit/licence	rukhsaa
Britain	braitani	Accident	haadith
Europe	oropi	Papers	waraq
India	al hindi	Insurance	ta'miyn
Questions		Sorry	aasif (m) / aasifa (f)
How many / much?	kam?	**Numbers**	
Where?	wayn?	Zero	sifr
When?	mataa?	One	waahad
Which?	ayy?	Two	ithnayn
How?	kayf?	Three	thalatha
What?	shuw?	Four	arba'a
Why?	laysh?	Five	khamsa
Who?	miyn?	Six	sitta
To/for	ila	Seven	saba'a
In/at	fee	Eight	thamaanya
From	min	Nine	tiss'a
And	wa	Ten	ashara
Also	kamaan	Hundred	miya
There isn't	maa fee	Thousand	alf

Race Relations

Dubai is a multi-cultural society with many different nationalities living side by side. Even though most of the time this is a harmonious arrangement, there are times when where you come from does seem to be an important factor. For example, you will notice that many job advertisements are very forthcoming about their racial requirements; asking for 'western candidates' is common. And salaries in the city definitely reflect nationality, with employees from the Asian subcontinent and the Philippines often getting paid less than their western colleagues, even when doing similar jobs.

Unfortunately this kind of racism spreads to other areas too; it is becoming increasingly popular with landlords to refuse tenants of certain nationalities, and certain bars and nightclubs have been accused in the past of having racist door policies (usually strenuously denied by those outlets, of course).

Call To Prayer
There are five calls to prayer throughout the day. They are Fajr at dawn, Juma in the middle of the day, Asr at mid-afternoon, Maghrib at sunset, and Isha at nightfall. The English translation of the call to prayer (Adhan) is something along the lines of 'God is most great, God is most great. There is no God except God, there is no God except God. Mohammed is the messenger of God, Mohammed is the messenger of God. Come to prayer, come to prayer, come to salvation, come to salvation. God is great, God is great. There is none worthy of worship except God.'

Religion

Islam is the official religion of the UAE, and is widely practised. The Islamic holy day is Friday. The basis of Islam is the belief that there is only one God and that Prophet Muhammed is his messenger. There are five pillars of the faith which all Muslims must follow: the Profession of Faith, Prayer, Charity, Fasting and Pilgrimage. Every Muslim is expected, at least once in his or her lifetime, to make the pilgrimage (Hajj) to the holy city of Mecca (also spelt Makkah) in Saudi Arabia.

Additionally, a Muslim is required to pray (facing Mecca) five times a day. The times vary according to the position of the sun. Most people pray at a mosque, although it's not unusual to see people kneeling by the side of the road if they are not near a place of worship. It is considered impolite to stare at people praying or to walk over prayer mats. The modern-day call to prayer, transmitted through loudspeakers on the minarets of each mosque, ensures that everyone knows it's time to pray. In an effort to ensure that prayer times are easily accessible to all Muslims, there are often several mosques within walking distance in each area.

Islam shares a common ancestry with Christianity and many of the prophets before Muhammad can be found in Christian as well as Muslim writings.

Under Islamic Shariah law, Muslim men are allowed to marry non-Muslim women, but a Muslim woman is not allowed to marry a non-Muslim man.

While the predominant religion is Islam, Dubai is tolerant of many other denominations, and the ruling family has, on numerous occasions, donated plots of land for the building of churches. Current churches include the Evangelical Church, Holy Trinity, United Christian Church and St Mary's (Roman Catholic), plus the various churches grouped together in a complex at Jebel Ali. There's also a Hindu temple in Bur Dubai.

Ramadan

Ramadan is the holy month in which Muslims commemorate the revelation of the Holy Quran (the holy book of Islam). It's a time of fasting and Muslims abstain from all food, drinks, cigarettes and unclean thoughts (or activities) between dawn and dusk. In the evening, the fast is broken with the Iftar feast. Iftar timings are found in all the daily newspapers.

Places of Worship

Church of Jesus Christ of Latter-Day Saints	Oud Metha	04 395 3883	na
Dubai Evangelical Church Centre	Jebel Ali	04 884 6630	www.deccc.com
Emirates Baptist Church International	Jumeira	04 349 1596	http://ebci.org
Holy Trinity Church (Church of England)	Oud Metha	04 337 0247	www.holytrinitychurchdubai.org
Marthoma Syrian Church of Malabar	Jebel Ali	04 884 5233	na
New Covenant Church	Oud Metha	04 335 1597	www.nccuae.org
St. Francis of Assisi Roman Catholic Church	Jebel Ali	04 884 5104	www.stfrancisjebelali.ae
St. Mary's Church Dubai	Oud Metha	04 337 0087	www.saintmarysdubai.com
United Christian Church of Dubai	Jebel Ali	04 884 6623	http://uccdubai.com

Jumeira Mosque

All over the city, festive Ramadan tents are filled to the brim each evening with people of all nationalities and religions enjoying shisha, traditional Arabic mezze and sweets. In addition to the standard favourite shisha cafes and restaurants around town, the five-star hotels erect special Ramadan tents for the month.

The timing of Ramadan is not fixed in terms of the western calendar, but each year it occurs around 11 days earlier than the previous year, with the start date depending on the sighting of the moon (see Public Holidays on p.21). In 2009, Ramadan is expected to commence on 21 August or thereabouts. Non-Muslims are also required to refrain from eating, drinking or smoking in public places during daylight hours as a sign of respect. Failure to do so could upset people or lead to an official complaint. If a passing policeman spotted you he'd most likely stop to explain what was expected. If you are uncooperative you may end up being taken to the police station.

During Ramadan the sale of alcohol in most outlets is restricted to after dusk, and office hours are cut (always for Muslims, sometimes for non-Muslims), while shops and parks usually open and close later. In addition, no live music or dancing is allowed (so nightclubs tend to close for the entire month) and cinemas limit daytime screenings of films.

Ramadan ends with a three-day celebration and holiday called Eid Al Fitr, the feast of the breaking of the fast. For Muslims, Eid has similar connotations as Diwali for Hindus and Christmas for Christians.

National Dress

On the whole, Emiratis wear traditional dress in public. For men this is the dishdasha or khandura: a white full length shirt dress, which is worn with a white or red checked headdress, known as a gutra or sifrah. This is secured with a black cord (agal). Sheikhs and important businessmen may also wear a thin black or brown robe (known as a bisht), over their dishdasha at important events, which is equivalent to the dinner jacket in western culture.

In public, women wear the black abaya – a long, loose black robe that covers their normal clothes – plus a headscarf called the sheyla. The abaya is often of very sheer, flowing fabric and may be open at the front. Some women also wear a thin black veil hiding their face and/or gloves, and older women sometimes still wear a leather mask, known as a burkha, which covers the nose, brow and cheekbones. Underneath the abaya, women traditionally wear a long tunic over loose, flowing trousers (sirwall), which are often heavily embroidered and fitted at the wrists and ankles. However, these are used more by the older generation and modern women will often wear the latest fashions from international labels under their abayas.

Arabic Family Names

Arabic names have a formal structure that traditionally indicates the person's family and tribe. Names are usually taken from an important person in the Quran or someone from the tribe. This is followed by the word bin (son of) for a boy or bint (daughter of) for a girl, and then the name of the child's father. The last name indicates the person's tribe or family. For prominent families, this has Al, the Arabic word for 'the', immediately before it. For instance, the President of the UAE is His Highness Sheikh Khalifa bin Zayed Al Nahyan. When women get married, they do not change their name.

National Weddings

Weddings in the UAE are very large, serious affairs. Homes are lit from top to bottom with strings of white lights and the festivities last up to two weeks. Men and women celebrate separately, normally in a hotel ballroom or convention centre, depending on the number of guests.

The government-sponsored Marriage Fund, based in Abu Dhabi, assists Emiratis with marriage, from counselling and financial assistance (long term loans up to Dhs.70,000 for a UAE National man marrying a UAE National woman) to organising group weddings to keep costs down. With so many UAE Nationals studying abroad, and so many expats in Dubai, inter-cultural marriages are increasingly common. The Marriage Fund strongly advises Nationals to marry fellow Nationals (in an effort to preserve the culture and reduce the number of UAE spinsters), although it is easier for a National man to marry a non-National woman than it is for a National woman to marry a non-National man.

> **Dressing Down**
> Sharjah has a less liberal attitude to dress code and moral behaviour. 'Indecent dress' includes anything that exposes the stomach, back or legs above the knees. Tight-fitting, transparent clothing is also best avoided, as are acts of vulgarity, indecent noises or harassment.

Food & Drink
Other options **Eating Out** p.526

You can eat your way around the world in Dubai – it is home to every cuisine imaginable, from European and American to Indian and Asian. Not only can you feast on exotic cuisines in the city's numerous five-star outlets, you can also find cheaper options at the many street cafes and independent restaurants. You'll find all the obligatory fast-food outlets such as McDonald's, KFC, Pizza Hut and Burger King here. In terms of food shopping, the mix of nationalities is once again advantageous – supermarkets tend to stock a range of products from around the world to keep their multinational client base happy. Spinneys and Park n Shop stock British and South African products, Safestway stocks more American products, and Choithram has a mix of both. Carrefour, HyperPanda and Géant are huge and stock products from just about everywhere (although not as specialised as the smaller stores). Fruit and vegetables are imported from around the world, and so can be a bit more expensive than buying local produce. There is some local produce available, mainly cucumbers, tomatoes, aubergines, courgettes, green peppers and potatoes, and these items are extremely cheap. For a more colourful food-buying experience, head to the fruit and vegetable market off Emirates Road where you can buy vast quantities of various fruits and vegetables at low prices. The fish market in Deira is also worth a trip – not only will you find a seemingly unlimited range of fresh fish and seafood at low prices, but you can also soak up the authentic atmosphere.

Arabic Cuisine
On your first trip back to your home country you may find yourself craving the distinctive Arabic cuisine that's so easily available throughout Dubai. Most of the Arabic food available here is based predominantly on Lebanese cuisine. Common dishes are shawarmas (lamb or chicken carved from a spit and served in a pita bread with salad and tahina), falafel (mashed chickpeas and sesame seeds, rolled into balls and deep fried), hummus (a creamy dip made from chickpeas and olive oil), and tabbouleh (finely chopped parsley, mint and crushed wheat). And to round off your meal, you must sample the extensive variety of fresh juices.

Dates

As one of the very few crops that thrive naturally across the Middle East, date palms have been cultivated as an invaluable source of nutrition for up to 5,000 years. It's said that in some countries the Bedouin way of life was sustained primarily by dates and camel milk up until as recently as the mid 20th century. Along with their high energy content, dates are also high in fibre, potassium, vitamins, magnesium and iron and contain negligible quantities of fat, cholesterol and salt. Even just five dates per day provide enough nutrition for the recommended daily portions of fruit or vegetables.

Emirati Cuisine

There are also opportunities to sample the local Emirati food. The legacy of the UAE's trading past means that local cuisine uses a blend of ingredients imported from around Asia and the Middle East. Spices such as cinnamon, saffron and turmeric along with nuts (almonds or pistachios), limes and dried fruit add interesting flavours to Emirati dishes. Dried limes are a common ingredient in Arabic cuisine, reflecting a Persian influence. They are dried in the sun and are used to flavour dishes, either whole or ground in a spice mill. They impart a distinctively musty, tangy, sour flavour to soups and stews.

Arabic Coffee

The serving of traditional coffee (*kahwa*) is an important social ritual in the Middle East. Local coffee is mild with a distinctive taste of cardamom and saffron, and it is served black without sugar. It is served with dates, to sweeten the palate between sips. It is considered polite to drink about three cups of the coffee when offered (it is served in tiny cups, about the size of an egg cup).

Pork

Pork is taboo in Islam. Muslims should not eat, prepare or serve pork. In order for a restaurant to serve pork on its menu, it should have a separate fridge, preparation equipment and cooking areas. Supermarkets also require pork to be sold in a separate area; you can buy pork mainly from Spinneys, Park n Shop and Choithram, but you have to find the screened-off pork section first. As pork is not locally produced you will find that it's more expensive than many other meats. All meat products for Muslim consumption have to be halal, which refers to the method of slaughter.

Alcohol

Alcohol is only served in licensed outlets associated with hotels (restaurants and bars), plus a few leisure clubs (such as golf clubs and sports clubs) and associations. Restaurants outside of hotels that are not part of a club or association are not permitted to serve alcohol.

Nevertheless, permanent residents who are non-Muslims can obtain alcohol for consumption at home without any difficulty. All they have to do is get a liquor licence (see p.92 for the procedure).

Shisha

Smoking the traditional shisha (water pipe) is a popular and relaxing pastime enjoyed throughout the Middle East. It is usually savoured in a local cafe while chatting with friends. They are also known as hookah pipes or hubbly bubbly, but the proper name is nargile. Shisha pipes can be smoked with a variety of aromatic flavours, such as strawberry, grape or apple, and the experience is unlike normal cigarette or cigar smoking. The smoke is 'smoothed' by the water, creating a much more soothing effect (although it still causes smoking related health problems). Smoking shisha is one of those things during your time in Dubai that should be tried at least once, especially during Ramadan, when tents are erected throughout the city and filled with people of all nationalities. You can buy your very own shisha pipe from the Arabian souvenir shops or from Carrefour supermarket, and once you get to grips with putting it all together you can enjoy the unique flavour anytime you want. See also Shisha Cafes (p.605).

Arabic food

In Emergency

If you need to see a doctor during your stay in Dubai, there are two options: private or government. If you have medical insurance, check out p.182 in the Residents chapter for an overview of the private hospitals. If you are happy with a government-run hospital, there is either Rashid Hospital (04 337 4000), the main emergency hospital for Dubai, located next to Dubai Creek, or the Iranian Hospital (04 344 0250), a government-affiliated hospital on Al Wasl Road in Satwa. Dial 999 for emergency services if you need an ambulance, or you can make your own way there if you are well enough. Treatment at Rashid Hospital is free for all emergencies, and costs Dhs.100 for a consultation with a doctor. Medicines prescribed can be bought at any chemist. Iranian Hospital charges Dhs.50 for consultations and it usually offers free medicine from the pharmacy in the hospital. In case you need medical help for children, Al Wasl Hospital is renowned as one of the best places for paediatric care in the Middle East, government or private, and is located near the Wafi interchange.

Emergency Services

Al Wasl Hospital	04 219 3000	Hospital
Ambulance	998/999	Emergency Services
American Hospital ▶ p.185	04 336 7777	Hospital
Cedars Jebel Ali International Hospital	04 881 4000	Hospital
Department for Tourist Security	800 4438	Police Services
DEWA Emergency	991	Emergency Services
Dubai Hospital	04 219 5000	Emergency Services
Dubai Police	04 609 9999	Police Services
Dubai Police Emergency	999	Emergency Services
Fire Department	997	Emergency Services
Iranian Hospital	04 344 0250	Hospital
Life Pharmacy	04 344 1122	24 hour pharmcy
Municipality Emergency Number	04 223 2323	Emergency Services
Rashid Hospital	04 337 4000	Hospital
Rashidiya Pharmacy	04 285 0692	24 hour pharmacy
Road service (AAA)	800 4430	Road Service
Telephone Directory	181	Telephone Directory
Welcare Hospital	04 282 7788	Hospital

Women

Women should face few, if any, problems while travelling in the UAE. One of the most annoying occurrences is the tendency of men of certain nationalities to stare unashamedly at women, which can make you feel uncomfortable. Rest assured that in most cases this habit, while infuriating, is borne more out of curiosity rather than sexual deviance, and poses little danger to women. If you find yourself being stared at, it is best to just ignore it if you can. A directive straight from Sheikh Mohammed himself orders men who are caught harassing women to be punished, and 'named and shamed' by having their photos printed in the newspaper.

In contrast with the more radical views of neighbouring Saudi Arabia, the UAE, along with most of the other smaller Gulf states, offers women the same rights as men including travelling alone, driving, owning and renting cars and dressing as they please. However, it is courteous to dress with a little modesty in consideration for local customs. You will feel much more comfortable if you are wearing clothing that is neither too revealing, nor too tight, but on the other hand, it is perfectly acceptable to wear summery tops, skirts and shorts, especially in the more 'expat' areas. If you venture into more traditional or Arabic areas, it is best to dress modestly. In other parts of the country, people in small villages in particular tend to be a lot more conservative.

Children

Other options **Kids' Clothes** p.455

Dubai is an excellent place for children: safe, with good facilities, and a lot on offer to keep them amused. Hotels and shopping malls are well equipped, offering everything from babysitting services to state-of-the-art amusement centres. Discounted rates for children are common so always ask. The health clubs belonging to hotels often have separate kids' clubs for hotel guests and health club members.

Child-friendly restaurants vary between just having a children's menu to offering activities or separate areas for families. Some places tend not to have many high chairs, so it's best to ask when making reservations. One part of Dubai life that is particularly good for families with young children is Friday brunch, with many outlets providing special entertainment for the little ones while mum and dad make repeat trips to the buffet (see Friday Brunch on p.506).

The best time of year in Dubai for kids is the winter, as they can enjoy outside activities. In summer, when the weather can be uncomfortable, there are still a good number of indoor activities to keep your little ones occupied. Most malls have at least one indoor play centre: think gigantic ball pits, padded climbing frames and arcade games. The Dubai Summer Surprises (p.73) festival offers all sorts of fun-filled activities for the whole family. But don't feel like you need to spend the whole summer indoors, however; you'll be surprised at how your kids hardly notice the heat, and as long as you keep outdoor playing restricted to early in the mornings or later in the afternoons, they will still be able to enjoy parks, pools and beaches.

The city is dotted with numerous surprisingly green parks, and its beach parks (p.279) are well equipped with sports and amusement facilities. Water activities, horse riding, sports clubs and other adventure sports are all catered for and there is also a wide variety of amusement centres, water parks and theme parks. See the Directory in the Exploring section (p.240) for more details.

Embassies & Consulates

Name	Tel	Map Ref
Australia	04 508 7100	7 C3
Bahrain	02 665 7500	1 D2
Canada	04 314 5555	8 F3
China	04 394 4733	8 C4
Czech Republic	02 678 2800	1 D2
Denmark	04 348 0877	6 C2
Egypt	04 397 1122	9 A4
France	04 332 9040	7 F2
Germany	04 397 2333	9 A4
India	04 397 1222	9 A4
Iran	04 344 4717	7 F1
Ireland (Saudi Arabia)	966 1 488 2300	na
Italy	04 331 4167	10 A1
Japan	04 331 9191	10 A1
Jordan	04 397 0500	9 A4
Kuwait	04 397 8000	9 A4
Lebanon	04 397 7450	9 A4
Malaysia	04 337 2152	10 D2
Mexico	04 394 5510	7 A2
The Netherlands	04 352 8700	8 F3
New Zealand	04 331 7500	7 F2
Norway	04 353 3833	8 F3
Oman	04 397 1000	9 A4
Pakistan	04 397 0412	9 A4
Philippines	04 254 4331	14 C2
Qatar	04 398 2888	8 C4
Russia	04 223 1272	9 C4
Saudi Arabia	04 397 9777	9 A4
South Africa	04 397 5222	9 A4
Spain	02 626 9544	1 D2
Sri Lanka	04 398 6535	8 B2
Sweden	02 621 0162	1 D2
Switzerland	04 329 0999	10 A1
Thailand	04 348 9550	6 B2
UK	04 309 4444	2 C3
USA	04 311 6000	10 A1

People With Disabilities

In keeping with its philosophy of being 'The City that Cares', Dubai is starting to consider the needs of disabled visitors more seriously. Dubai International Airport is well equipped for disabled travellers, with automatic doors, large lifts and all counters accessible by wheelchair users, as well as several services such as porters, special transportation and quick check-in to avoid long queues. Dubai Transport has a few specially modified taxis for journeys from the airport and around town. Disabled parking spaces do exist, but are often taken up by ignorant drivers who don't need the facility; however, police do monitor these spaces and hand out fines to offenders.

Most of Dubai's five-star hotels have wheelchair access, but in general, facilities for disabled guests are limited, particularly at tourist attractions. Wheelchair ramps are often really nothing more than delivery ramps and therefore have steep angles. When asking if a location has wheelchair access, make sure it really does – an escalator is considered 'wheelchair access' to some.

The Dubai Department of Tourism and Commerce Marketing (DTCM) is responsible for improving access for the physically challenged (www.dubaitourism.ae/disabled).

Smoke Signals ◀

*Smoking is now
banned in all
government
departments, public
buildings and
shopping malls (with
designated smoking
areas remaining
in some places). In
November 2007 all
restaurants and cafes
became smoke-free
environments, though
some may decide to
create non-intrusive
areas for smokers.
Many restaurants
and cafes appeared
unprepared for the
ban and in some
places it is still not
strictly enforced. You
will be fined in Dubai if
you are seen throwing
a cigarette butt onto
the street.*

What To Wear

No matter how cosmopolitan Dubai
becomes, there are still people outside
the Middle East of the opinion that it is a
conservative city where women have to
cover their faces and wear long black robes.
Nothing could be further from the truth.
Although the UAE is a Muslim country,
there is no need for women to cover up. It is
another common misconception that local
women are poor, downtrodden souls who
are forced by their domineering husbands
to hide themselves behind shrouds of black
and full veils – the truth is that UAE women are well educated, well respected, and
increasingly outspoken, and those that wear headscarves or veils do it mostly out of
choice and respect for their religion.

There are no real restrictions on dress codes in Dubai (as opposed to in neighbouring
emirate Sharjah, where things are more conservative and both men and women should
dress appropriately). However, topless sunbathing for women is a definite no-no, and
any clothing that reveals the bits only your mother, husband or doctor should see are
best left at home. But with the beautiful climate, shorts and T-shirts are acceptable, as
are dresses or tops with spaghetti straps. However, you may want to carry a pashmina
with you just in case you feel you need to cover up at any time, due to the cold or due
to cultural sensitivity. When going to places frequented by Muslims, it is courteous to
dress more modestly and during Ramadan, you should dress more conservatively out
of respect. During the cooler months (October to April), it is often necessary to wear a
light jacket or cardigan as the temperature drops into the low teens. Everything in the
city is air conditioned, and sometimes indoor temperatures can be uncomfortably cold.

What Are You Looking At?

As annoying and infuriating as it is to
have someone blatantly stare at you, the
good news is that these stares are not
really sexual in nature – they are more
the result of curiosity. The bad news is
that there is little you can do to stop this
strange little quirk of living in the region.
Your best defence is to avoid wearing
tight or revealing clothing, particularly in
certain areas such as the Gold Souk.

Photography

While it may lack the picturesque countryside of England or the quaint scenery of
Europe, Dubai is still full of fascinating sights that you will want to capture with your
camera. Normal tourist photography is acceptable but, like anywhere in the Arab
world, it is courteous to ask permission before photographing people, particularly

National dress

women. In general, photographs of
government buildings, military installations,
ports and airports should not be taken. See
also Camera Equipment in Shopping (p.430).

Crime & Safety

Other options **In Emergency** p.32

While the crime rate in Dubai is very low,
a healthy degree of caution should still be
exercised. Keep your valuables and travel
documents locked in your hotel room or in
the hotel safe. When in crowds, be discreet
with your money and wallet; don't carry
large amounts of cash on you and don't trust
strangers. Money and gem-related scams run
by con men are on the increase so don't be
bullied into anything.

With the multitude of driving styles converging on Dubai's roads, navigating the streets either on foot or in a vehicle can be a challenge. When walking, you need to be really aware of the traffic, as cars tend to do unpredictable things and don't give pedestrians the space or consideration you might be used to. When crossing roads use designated pedestrian crossings wherever possible (jaywalking is actually illegal), and make sure all cars are really going to stop for you before crossing.

If you plan on driving yourself, make sure you know the rules of the road, exercise extreme caution as traffic accidents are an all too common occurrence on Dubai's busy roads, always pay much more attention to your mirrors than you would do normally, and know what's happening around you at all times. For what to do in the event of an accident, see Accidents on p.32. Never drive without the correct documentation and insurance.

Money Matters

There has been talk of restrictions on the import and export of large amounts of any currency since the events of 11 September 2001. Do your homework before you attempt to carry wads of cash into or out of Dubai. The current limit for undeclared cash that can be brought into the country is Dhs.40,000.

Police

In an effort to better serve Dubai's visitors, the Dubai Police has launched the Department for Tourist Security. It acts as a liaison between you and Dubai Police, although in general police officers are extremely helpful. They are calm and understanding, and speak a multitude of languages. Its website (www.dubaipolice. gov.ae) is easy to navigate, helpful, and has extensive information on policies and procedures. For assistance, call the toll free number (800 4438). In 2007, a new hotline number was launched for people suffering problems on the beach (04 203 6398). These could include sexual harassment or annoyance by quad bikes. For other emergency services call 999 for Police or Ambulance and 997 for Fire.

Lost & Stolen Property

To avoid a great deal of hassle if your personal documents go missing, make sure you keep one photocopy with friends or family back home and one copy in a secure place, such as a safe. There are a lot of honest people in Dubai who will return found items. If you have no luck, then try the Dubai Police (999) or the Department for Tourist Security (800 4438 – toll free) to report the loss or theft; you'll be advised on a course of action. If you've lost something in a taxi, call the taxi company (p.62). If you lose your passport, your next stop should be your embassy or consulate. See p.33 for a list of all embassies and consulates in Dubai.

Dubai Tourism Offices Overseas

Australia & NZ	Sydney	+61 2 9956 6620
China	Beijing	+86 10 5979 2062
China	Guangzhou	+86 20 8760 7815
China	Shanghai	+86 21 5528 6900
Far East	Hong Kong	+852 2827 5221
France	Paris	+33 1 4495 8500
Germany	Frankfurt	+49 69 7100 020
India	Mumbai	+91 22 2282 8836
Italy	Milan	+39 2 8738 8132
Japan	Tokyo	+81 3 5367 5450
Kingdom of Saudi Arabia	Jeddah	+966 2 652 4283
Kingdom of Saudi Arabia	Riyadh	+966 1 217 7613
Russia, CIS & Baltic States	Moscow	+7 495 980 0717
Scandinavia	Stockholm	+46 8 411 1135
South Africa	Johannesburg	+27 11 785 4600
Switzerland & Austria	Ittigen-Bern	+41 31 924 7599
UK & Ireland	London	+44 20 7321 6110
USA	New York	+1 212 575 2262

Dubai Tourist Info Abroad

The Dubai Department of Tourism and Commerce Marketing operates 18 offices overseas, which promote Dubai to both travellers and businesses. They participate in travel fairs and exhibitions as well as conducting orientation workshops for travel agents in various countries interested in Dubai (www.dubaitourism.ae).

Places To Stay

Easy Visa

If you are not one of the nationalities listed on p.80, your hotel should be able to arrange a visit visa for you. The visa will be deposited at the airport for collection on arrival. The cost is around Dhs.180 for a regular visa, or Dhs.280 for an urgent visa.

In addition to a high number of luxurious five-star hotels, Dubai has plenty of four, three, two and one-star hotels, hotel apartments and youth hostels. A new hotel seems to spring up every few months – 22,000 rooms were added before the end of 2008 – and local folk have often wondered how all of Dubai's hotels are going to stay in business. But in true 'if you build it, they will come' style, room occupancy rates have soared over the last few years (currently an annual average of 85% – one of the highest in the world), and there are certain times of the year when you can't find a hotel vacancy for love nor money. At the end of 2006, there were more than 31,000 hotel rooms in Dubai, and the city hosted 5,863,509 guests during 2007.

Hotels
Other options **Landmark Hotels** p.38

DIY Dubai

Although a relatively new concept in Dubai, self catering can be more cost effective than hotels, and the accommodation comes equipped with everything from towels to teabags. Check out www.dubaifurnished apartments.com for online listings of self-catering apartments.

Dubai has a vast array of hotels ranging from one of the most superlative and opulent hotels in the world, the Burj Al Arab (p.38), with a published price, or rack rate, in the region of Dhs.11,000 for a night in a standard suite, right down to the cheapest hotels in areas such as Deira costing under Dhs.200 a night. While the hotels at the higher end of the market offer superb surroundings and facilities, those at the cheaper end vary – and you get what you pay for. For people arriving in Dubai on a holiday package, hotels are normally five or four star, but if you are looking for cheaper accommodation at the lower end of the market, make sure you check out the hotel and have a look at one of the rooms before checking in. Remember that, as with anywhere else in the world, you can usually get a discount on the rack rate or published price if you negotiate.

Hotels in Dubai can be split into beach hotels (grouped along the coast to the south of the creek entrance), creek hotels (offering a great central location from which to explore and loads of atmosphere) and city hotels, often used by business travellers or tourists for good value accommodation with access to business districts and shopping areas. Most are located within a 30 minute journey from Dubai International Airport.

No Frills?

The UK's low-cost hotel chain, Premier Inn, is branching out internationally. The first hotel is already open at Dubai Investments Park (04 885 0999), with the second opening at Dubai Silicon Oasis in May 2009 and more planned for the future. With rooms from Dhs.495 per night, they're great value like the UK hotels, but you can expect extra facilities fitting of Dubai such as rooftop pools and whirlpool spas.

The larger hotels all offer an airport shuttle service as well as a minibus service to the main tourist spots around the city. A taxi ride from the airport to most hotels will cost between Dhs.40 and Dhs.70. Road transport in Dubai is usually quite fast and the majority of journeys around town will only take 20 to 30 minutes, costing about Dhs.30 to Dhs.40 (for more information, see Taxis on p.62). With so many luxury hotels and resorts in Dubai, there's no reason why you can't combine a stay in a central Dubai hotel with a few nights at a desert resort, such as Bab Al Shams (p.46) or Al Maha Desert Resort & Spa (see p.46).

The Dubai Department of Tourism & Commerce Marketing (DTCM) oversees a hotel classification system that gives an internationally recognised star rating to hotels and hotel apartments so that visitors can judge more easily the standard of accommodation they will receive.

The DTCM also operates an internet reservation system for Dubai's hotels on its website (www.dubaitourism.com). This enables guests to reserve rooms online and allows them to take a virtual tour of the hotel before they book. Alternatively, the DTCM Welcome Bureau at the airport offers instant hotel reservations, often at greatly discounted rates.

For food and beverage outlets that can be found in Dubai's hotels, refer to the Index at the back of the book. Just look up the hotel name, and all of its restaurants and bars that are featured in the book will be listed underneath.

For a list of sports and leisure facilities available at a particular hotel, refer to the Club Facilities table (p.398).

Traditional
Dinner Cruise
by the Creek

l mansour dhow

The Radisson SAS Hotel, Dubai Deira Creek's legendary Al Mansour Dhow welcomes you aboard to experience an unforgettable dinner cruise featuring a sumptuous buffet with a spread of Arabian cuisine and live performances by our Oud player while you enjoy Dubai Creek's beautiful sights for only Dhs. 185 per person.

* Boarding daily at 8 pm

adisson SAS Hotel, Dubai Deira Creek
aniyas Road, P.O. Box 476, Dubai, UAE
or Bookings, please call 04-205 7033
focenter.dxbza@radissonsas.com
eiracreek.dubai.radissonsas.com

Radisson SAS
HOTEL, DUBAI DEIRA CREEK

Landmark Hotels

Burj Dubai Blvd
Downtown Burj Dubai
Map 7 D4

The Address, Downtown Burj Dubai

04 436 8888 | *www.theaddress.com*
At over 300 metres, The Address would seem tall if it didn't have the enormous Burj Dubai as its neighbour. Still, with breathtaking interiors, 196 spectacular rooms, and eight dining outlets, this is set to become one of the most popular addresses in town. Check out the panoramic views from Neos, the bar on the 63rd floor.

Casablanca Rd
Nr Dubai Intl Airport
Al Garhoud
Map 13 E1

Al Bustan Rotana Hotel

04 282 0000 | *www.rotana.com*
Located in the centre of Dubai, minutes away from the creek, Dubai International Airport, and Deira City Centre, this hotel provides easy access for tourists and business travellers alike. A member of 'The Leading Hotels of the World', it is renowned locally for having particularly good restaurants including Benihana (Japanese), Blue Elephant (Thai), Come Prima (Italian), and Choices (buffet).

Crescent Rd
Palm Jumeirah
Map 2 A3

Atlantis The Palm ▶ p.ii - p.iii

04 426 0000 | *www.atlantisthepalm.com*
The most anticipated hotel opening of the year, Atlantis has a staggering 1,539 rooms and suites all with either a view of the sea or Palm Jumeirah. Guests can also book into The Lost Chambers Suites, featuring floor to ceiling views into the aquarium. Onsite are a number of exclusive restaurants including a branch of Nobu. The resort is also home to Aquaventure, the biggest water park in the Middle East.

Jumeirah Rd
Nr Madinat Jumeirah
Umm Suqeim
Map 6 B1

Burj Al Arab

04 301 7777 | *www.burj-al-arab.com*
Architecturally unique, the world's tallest hotel stands at 321 metres high on its own man-made island, and is dramatic, lavish and exclusive. Suites have two floors and come complete with a butler to make your stay even more comfortable. To get into the Burj as a non-guest, you will need a restaurant reservation – try the Sky View Bar for afternoon tea (Dhs.350) or evening drinks (Dhs.270).

Sheikh Zayed Rd
Trade Centre 1
Map 7 F3

Crowne Plaza

04 331 1111 | *www.crowneplaza.com*
This 560 room hotel has offices and furnished apartments next door in the Commercial Tower. The complex has its own shopping mall, the Nautilus Health Club, as well as bars, restaurants and cafes including Trader Vic's for great cocktails, Wagamama, the trendy noodle bar chain, Oscar's Vine Society for wine connoisseurs, and Zinc, a nightclub to queue for.

Al Awir Rd
Approx 3km past
Dragonmart
Map 2 C3

Desert Palm Dubai

04 323 8888 | *www.desertpalm.ae*
Located outside the bustle of the city, Desert Palm is so tranquil you'll never want to leave. Overlooking polo fields, guests can chose from suites, or private villas with a pool. The extensive spa menu features massage and holistic therapies including reiki. Signature restaurant Rare is a must for meat lovers, while Epicure is a lovely gourmet deli and a great breakfast venue.

Off Jumeira Rd
Nxt to Palm Strip
Jumeira
Map 7 F1

Dubai Marine Beach Resort & Spa

04 346 1111 | *www.dxbmarine.com*
The only beach hotel near the centre of Dubai, this independent property has 195 villa-style rooms nestled among lush, green landscaped gardens, waterfalls and streams. The grounds offer three swimming pools, a spa, a health club and a small private beach. The restaurants and bars are perennially popular nightspots, especially the Ibiza-esque Sho Cho and beautiful hangout, Boudoir.

Sheik Zayed Rd
Trade Centre 2
Map 7 F3

Emirates Towers Hotel

04 330 0000 | *www.jumeirahemiratestowers.com*
Recently awarded 'Best Business Hotel in the Middle East', this hotel stands 305 metres high, with 400 rooms on 51 floors, and is the third tallest hotel in the world. Sophisticated and elegant, the hotel tower is twinned with the larger office tower behind it. Between these two, the Boulevard shopping mall provides some top-end retail and an assortment of excellent restaurants, cafes and bars.

Sheik Zayed Rd
Nr Trade Centre R/A
Trade Centre 1
Map 8 A4

Fairmont Dubai

04 332 5555 | *www.fairmont.com/dubai*
At night this grand hotel is hard to miss thanks to its glowing pyramids that change colour – the architecture is based on the traditional Arabian windtowers. The interior is even more inspirational, with water features and glass-fronted lifts offering views over the atrium. There's a rooftop pool, the Willow Stream Spa and some great restaurants including Spectrum on One (p.566).

Nr Garhoud Bridge
Umm Hurair
Map 13 C1

Grand Hyatt Dubai

04 317 1234 | *www.dubai.grand.hyatt.com*
The Grand Hyatt has 674 spacious rooms and an excellent range of facilities within its 37 acres of landscaped grounds. The sheer size is amazing, and from the air the building spells out the word 'Dubai' in Arabic. There's a health spa, fitness centre, and many restaurants, cafes, and bars, including Manhattan Grill (p.593).

Habtoor Grand Resort & Spa

Dubai Marina
West Marina Beach
Marsa Dubai
Map 5 B1

04 399 5000 | *www.grandjumeirah.habtoorhotels.com*
On the site of the former Metropolitan Resort & Beach Club, the Habtoor Grand Resort & Spa offers 442 beautifully furnished, spacious rooms and suites with garden or sea views. Pools, restaurants and bars are set amid the hotel's tropical gardens bordering the Arabian Gulf. Food and beverage options include The 25th, a fine-dining restaurant, and pub The Underground.

The Harbour Hotel & Residence

Al Sufouh Rd
Dubai Marina
Map 5 B2

04 319 4000 | *www.emirateshotelsresorts.com*
With 261 spacious suites, each with its own fitted kitchen and well-stocked bathroom, staying in The Harbour is like having your very own luxury apartment. However, with a range of dining options including The Observatory on the 52nd floor serving modern gastro-pub fare and the deli Counter Culture, it is unlikely you will want to cook in your suite.

Hilton Dubai Creek

Baniyas Rd
Nr Economic Dept
Deira
Map 11 C1

04 227 1111 | *www.hilton.com*
With understated elegance and high quality service, this ultra-minimalist hotel features interiors of wood, glass and chrome. Centrally located and overlooking the creek with splendid views of the Arabian dhow trading posts, the hotel has two renowned restaurants in Glasshouse and Gordon Ramsay's Verre. Hilton also has a beach resort in the Dubai Marina area.

Hyatt Regency Hotel

Nr Galleria Mall
Deira
Map 9 D1

04 209 1234 | *www.dubai.regency.hyatt.com*
After its refurbishment of a few years back, the Hyatt Regency is looking a lot smarter. Restaurants such as Miyako (Japanese), Focaccia (Mediterranean) and Shahrzad (Persian) are all excellent while Al Dawaar offers Dubai's only revolving restaurant, with views of the creek and coast. All 400 guest rooms and serviced suites have a creek view.

InterContinental Dubai Festival City

Dubai Festival City
Festival City
Map 13 D2

04 701 1111 | *www.intercontinental.com/dubai*
This hotel has five restaurants and two bars – including the Eclipse Bar, with panoramic views of Dubai, and a restaurant run by Michelin-starred chef Pierre Gagnaire. Offering extensive spa facilities and indoor access to Festival Waterfront Centre, all 498 rooms and suites have a view of either Dubai Creek or the Festival Marina.

Jct 9 nr Jebel Ali
Shooting Club
Jebel Ali
Map 3 A1

Jebel Ali Golf Resort & Spa ▶ p.533

04 883 6000 | *www.jebelali-international.com*
Just far enough out of Dubai to escape the city's hustle and bustle, this fully equipped resort offers luxurious surroundings and a peaceful atmosphere. It is set in 128 acres of lush, landscaped gardens, with a private beach, marina, spa, and one of the region's original golf courses.

Jumeirah Beach Rd
Nr Burj Al Arab
Umm Suqeim
Map 6 B1

Jumeirah Beach Hotel

04 348 0000 | *www.jumeirahbeachhotel.com*
Along with the Burj Al Arab and the Wild Wadi Water Park, this exclusive hotel is one of Dubai's landmarks. Built in the shape of an ocean wave with a dynamic and colourful interior, the hotel has 618 rooms, all with a sea view. It has some of the classiest joints in town including Uptown for happy hour cocktails and a great view of the Burj, and La Veranda for recommended beachside dining.

Abu Baker
Al Siddique Rd
Nxt to Hamarain
Shopping Ctr
Deira
Map 11 E1

JW Marriott Hotel

04 262 4444 | *www.marriott.com*
This hotel is located in the bustling heart of Deira. A grand staircase, detailed marble floors and natural lighting provided by the Middle East's largest skylight are all impressive, as is the landscaped indoor 'town square'. The Marriott boasts 305 rooms and 39 suites. Favourite eateries include Cucina and The Market Place, while Champions is one of Dubai's best bars for sports fans.

Mall of the Emirates
Al Barsha
Map 6 A3

Kempinski Mall of the Emirates

04 341 0000 | *www.kempinski-dubai.com*
This hotel has 395 deluxe rooms and 15 unique ski chalets overlooking the slopes. Guests can enjoy the Wellness Spa, infinity pool, ski slope, fitness centre and tennis court. The adjoining Mall of the Emirates has over 400 shops, a 14 screen cinema, a huge entertainment centre for children and a community theatre and arts centre.

Airport Rd
Al Garhoud
Map 13 E1

Le Meridien Dubai

04 217 0000 | *www.lemeridien-dubai.com*
Le Meridien has an ultra convenient location, close to both Dubai airport and the Aviation Club. Its 383 rooms don't have exquisite views, but benefit from luxury standards and service. It is home to a gym, tennis courts, the superb Natural Elements spa, and a popular array of restaurants, including the Meridien Village Terrace and Yalumba.

Le Meridien Mina Seyahi Beach Resort & Marina

Al Sufouh Rd
Al Sufouh
Map 5 C1

04 399 3333 | *www.lemeridien-minaseyahi.com*
This hotel has one of the longest stretches of private beach in Dubai, its own marina and a variety of water activities such as sailing and waterskiing. The 211 rooms come with views of the sea or the landscaped grounds and the clincher for families is the Penguin Club, which entertains kids. There is also the popular Barasti Bar right on the beach and The Dhow, a floating restaurant for romantic dinners.

Madinat Jumeirah

Jumeirah Rd
Nr Burj Al Arab
Umm Suqeim
Map 6 A2

04 366 8888 | *www.madinatjumeirah.com*
This extravagant resort has two hotels, Al Qasr and Mina A'Salam, with 940 luxurious rooms and suites, and the exclusive Dar Al Masyaf summer houses, all linked by man-made waterways navigated by abras. Nestled between the two hotels is the Souk Madinat, which has over 75 shops within its labyrinth network of passageways. There is also a total of 45 bars, restaurants and cafes.

The Monarch Dubai

1 Sheikh Zayed Rd
Opp Trade Centre
Trade Centre 2
Map 8 A4

04 501 8888 | *www.themonarchdubai.com*
The Monarch has one of the most desirable addresses in Dubai: One Sheikh Zayed Road. Well-designed rooms and fantastic views over Trade Centre and Sheikh Zayed Road. The hotel has 236 rooms and suites, including 53 serviced apartments, together with a business centre and Mandara Spa. The Monarch Suite located on the 32nd floor features a private outdoor pool that winds into the suite.

Mövenpick Hotel Bur Dubai ▶ p.573

Opp American
Hospital
Oud Metha
Map 10 D3

04 336 6000 | *www.moevenpick-hotels.com*
Located near Lamcy Plaza, this hotel offers a high standard of service true to the chain's Swiss background. You can dine in the impressive lobby, but you shouldn't miss the chance to eat at Fakhreldine, one of Dubai's best Lebanese restaurants. And the well-known nightclub downstairs, Jimmy Dix, is a great place for a laid-back night out.

One&Only Royal Mirage

Jumeira Rd
Al Sufouh
Map 5 C1

04 399 9999 | *www.oneandonlyroyalmirage.com*
Blessed with an intimate atmosphere, this resort comprises three different properties: The Palace, Arabian Court and Residence & Spa. With unrivalled service and dining you can indulge in a luxury spa treatment, try delectable Moroccan cuisine at Tagine, mingle with the rich and famous at Celebrities, or stay up late at Arabian nightclub Kasbar.

Burj Dubai Blvd
Old Town
Downtown Burj Dubai
Map 7 D4

The Palace – The Old Town

04 428 7888 | *www.thepalace-dubai.com*
Situated near Burj Dubai, The Palace hotel is one of the most luxurious additions to the city's hospitality scene. The palatial development boasts 242 deluxe rooms, including 81 suites, and offers traditional Arabic architecture juxtaposed with modern technology. There are three upmarket restaurants, an extensive spa, and butler service for all rooms

Nxt to Dubai Creek
Golf & Yacht Club
Creekside, Deira
Map 11 B4

Park Hyatt Dubai

04 602 1234 | *www.dubai.park.hyatt.com*
The Park Hyatt Dubai enjoys a prime waterfront location next to Dubai Creek Golf & Yacht Club. Mediterranean and Moorish in style with low buildings, natural colours and stylish decor, the hotel is illuminated by candles at night. All 225 rooms have a balcony or terrace with great views. Traiteur and The Thai Kitchen are fine restaurants and the hotel's luxurious spa provides pampering in private rooms.

Baniyas Rd
Nr Dubai Municipality
Deira
Map 9 C3

Radisson SAS Hotel, Dubai Deira Creek ▶ p.37

04 222 7171 | *www.deiracreek.dubai.radissonsas.com*
Traffic and parking can be a hindrance, but the popular restaurants, offering seafood, Italian, Japanese and Chinese, make the trip worthwhile. At the Seafood Market you pick your seafood and have it cooked to your preference, while Kubu Bar is the crux of cocktail cool. Located on the creekside in Deira in what was the longstanding and popular InterContinental.

Wafi Mall
Umm Hurair
Map 10 E4

Raffles Dubai

04 324 8888 | *www.dubai.raffles.com*
Part of the Wafi City complex, Raffles Dubai opened in October 2007. The hotel features 248 guest rooms and suites and the Raffles Amrita Spa with a unique Botanical Sky Garden – an oasis of exotic flowers and orchids around a pool. The nine food and beverage outlets offer a mix of international and far eastern cuisine and cocktails can be had at the trendy New Asia Bar.

Salahuddin Rd
Opp Muraqabat Police
Station
Deira
Map 11 E1

Renaissance Hotel ▶ p.567

04 262 5555 | *www.dubairenaissance.com*
Slightly off the beaten track in the northern part of Deira (Hor Al Anz), this hotel features 244 rooms, 37 suites and 11 meeting rooms. Offering all the plush services you'd expect from a five-star hotel, from limo service to valet dry cleaning, there are also four restaurants – including the all-inclusive institution that is... Spice Island (p.566).

Nxt to Royal Meridien
Dubai Marina
Map 5 B1

Ritz-Carlton, Dubai

04 399 4000 | *www.ritzcarlton.com*
Although the Ritz stands low in comparison to the marina towers behind, it offers stunning Mediterranean architecture. The 138 guest rooms all enjoy a view of the Gulf and their own private balcony or patio. Afternoon tea in the Lobby Lounge is a must; lots of yummy scones and pastries in a posh but comfortable setting. For dining there's Splendido Grill and La Baie – both equally delicious.

Sheik Zayed Rd
Trade Centre 1
Map 7 E3

Shangri-La Hotel

04 343 8888 | *www.shangri-la.com*
This 43 storey hotel is located on Sheikh Zayed Road, close to all of Dubai's main attractions, with fantastic views of the coast and the city. There are 301 guest rooms and suites, 126 serviced apartments, a health club and spa, two swimming pools and a variety of restaurants and bars including majestic Moroccan Marrakesh and seafood specialist, Amwaj.

Baniyas Rd
*Nxt to National Bank
of Dubai
Deira*
Map 9 B4

Sheraton Dubai Creek Hotel & Towers

04 228 1111 | *www.sheraton.com/dubai*
The 255 room Sheraton, like other hotels in this part of town has undergone refurbishments in recent years. Its location on the bank of the creek means that most rooms have beautiful views. Ashiana is renowned as one of the best traditional Indian restaurants in Dubai, Creekside is a favoured Japanese restaurant and Vivaldi shines as a wonderful Italian restaurant with great views.

Nr Deira City Centre
Port Saeed
Map 11 C3

Sofitel City Centre Hotel

04 294 1222 | *www.sofitel.com*
Adjoining one of the Middle East's largest and busiest shopping centres, Deira City Centre, this hotel is great if you're in town for a shopping spree. Some of the 327 rooms have a good view over the greens of Dubai Creek Golf & Yacht Club and the hotel also features conference facilities, serviced apartments, four restaurants and an English pub, as well as all the outlets in Deira City Centre.

Al Sufouh Rd
Al Sufouh
Map 5 C1

The Westin Dubai Mina Seyahi Beach Resort & Marina

04 399 4141 | *www.westin.com\dubaiminaseyahi*
The newly opened Westin is already a popular spot with visitors and residents. Set on 1,200 metres of private beach, it has 294 spacious rooms and suites with all the luxury amenities you would expect of a five star hotel, including the aptly named Heavenly Spa. For dining options try reliable Italian Bussola or cocktails and tapas at Senyar.

Resorts

Approx 75km from Dubai
Dubai – Al Ain Rd
Map 1 E2

Al Maha Desert Resort & Spa

04 303 4222 | *www.al-maha.com*
Set within a 225 sq km conservation reserve, this luxury getaway was recently named 'one of the world's best ecotourism models' by National Geographic Magazine. Al Maha resembles a Bedouin camp, but conditions are far from basic. Each suite has a private pool, and guests can enjoy fine dining on their own veranda. Activities include horse riding, falconry, and up-close views of rare wildlife.

Dubailand
5km from Exit 29 on Dubai – Al Ain Rd (dir Jebel Ali)
Map 2 B3

Al Sahra Desert Resort

04 367 9500 | *www.alsahra.com*
Surrounded by desert, Al Sahra bills itself as an 'eco-tourism resort'. The architecture is typically Arabian with a Bedouin-style working farm and stables, and a traditional craft souk. One of the main attractions is the 1200 seat amphitheatre which hosts events year-round including the resident show, 'Jumana – Secret of the Desert', a sound, laser and pyrotechnics spectacle with acrobats, dancers, camels and horses. There is a wide array of activities available including kite flying, pottery, archery, and belly dancing lessons, making it a popular venue for corporate team building events.

Nxt to Endurance Village
37km from Arabian Ranches R/A
Map 1 E2

Bab Al Shams Desert Resort & Spa

04 809 6100 | *www.jumeirahbabalshams.com*
Bab Al Shams, which translates as 'The Gateway to the Sun', is an elegant desert resort in a traditional Arabic fort setting and is home to the region's first authentic open air Arabic desert restaurant, Al Hadheerah. There's a kids' club with camel rides and falcon shows. Health and leisure facilities include the luxurious Satori Spa, an infinity swimming pool and bar with breathtaking views over the dunes.

Hotels

Five Star	Phone	Website	Map
Al Bustan Rotana Hotel	04 282 0000	www.rotana.com	13 E1
Al Maha Desert Resort & Spa	04 303 4222	www.al-maha.com	1 E2
Al Murooj Rotana Hotel & Suites	04 321 1111	www.rotana.com	7 E3
Al Qasr Hotel	04 366 8888	www.madinatjumeirah.com/al_qasr	6 A2
Amwaj Rotana	04 885 0962	www.rotana.com	4 F1
Atlantis The Palm ▶ p.ii – p.iii	04 426 0000	www.atlantisthepalm.com	2 A3
Bab Al Shams Desert Resort & Spa	04 809 6100	www.jumeirahbabalshams.com	1 E2
Burj Al Arab	04 301 7777	www.burj-al-arab.com	6 B1
Crowne Plaza	04 331 1111	www.crowneplaza.com	7 F3
Crowne Plaza Festival City	04 701 2222	www.crowneplaza.com/dfc	13 D2
Dar Al Masyaf	04 366 8888	www.madinatjumeirah.com	6 A1
Dhow Palace Hotel	04 359 9992	www.dhowpalacedubai.com	8 E3
Dubai Marine Beach Resort & Spa	04 346 1111	www.dxbmarine.com	7 F1

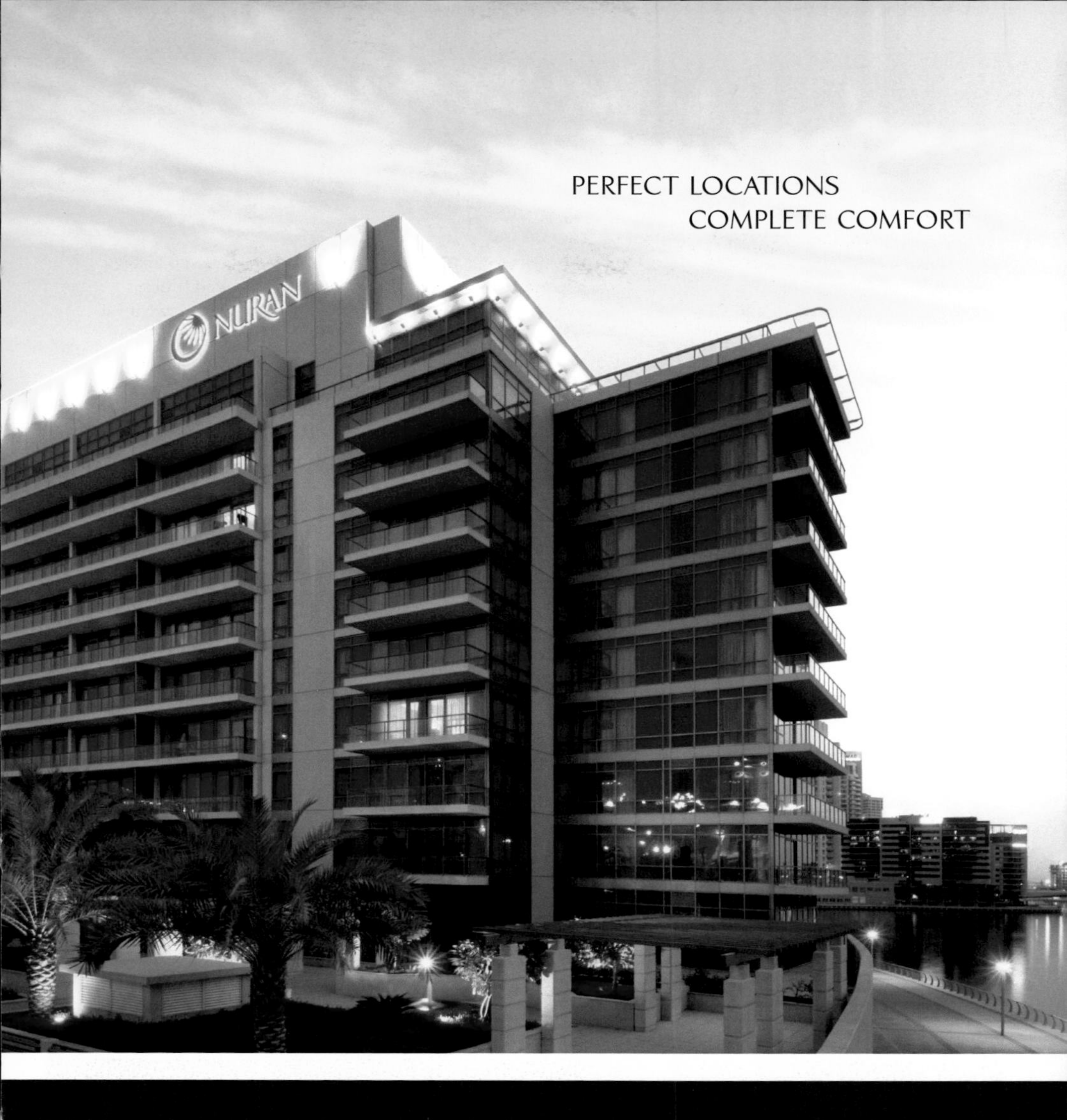

Hotels

Five Star

	Phone	Website	Map
The Address, Downtown Burj Dubai	04 436 8888	www.theaddress.com	7 D4
Dusit Thani Dubai	04 343 3333	www.dusit.com	7 E3
Emirates Towers Hotel	04 330 0000	www.jumeirahemiratestowers.com	7 F3
Fairmont Dubai	04 332 5555	www.fairmont.com/dubai	8 A4
Grand Hyatt Dubai	04 317 1234	www.dubai.grand.hyatt.com	13 C1
Grand Millennium Dubai	04 429 9999	www.millenniumhotels.com	5 E3
Habtoor Grand Resort & Spa	04 399 5000	www.grandjumeirah.habtoorhotels.com	5 B1
Hilton Dubai Creek	04 227 1111	www.hilton.com	11 C1
Hilton Dubai Jumeirah	04 399 1111	www.hilton.com	5 A1
Hyatt Regency Hotel	04 209 1234	www.dubai.regency.hyatt.com	9 D1
InterContinental Dubai Festival City	04 701 1111	www.intercontinental.com/dubai	13 D2
Jebel Ali Golf Resort & Spa ▶ p.533	04 883 6000	www.jebelali-international.com	3 A1
Jumeirah Beach Club Resort & Spa	04 344 5333	www.jumeirah.com	7 C1
Jumeirah Beach Hotel	04 348 0000	www.jumeirahbeachhotel.com	6 B1
JW Marriott Hotel	04 262 4444	www.marriott.com	11 E1
Kempinski Mall of the Emirates	04 341 0000	www.kempinski-dubai.com	6 A3
Le Meridien Dubai	04 217 0000	www.lemeridien-dubai.com	13 E1
Le Meridien Mina Seyahi Beach Resort & Marina	04 399 3333	www.lemeridien-minaseyahi.com	5 C1
Media Rotana	04 435 0000	www.rotana.com	5 E3
Metropolitan Palace Hotel	04 227 0000	www.palacedubai.habtoorhotels.com	11 C1
Mina A'Salam	04 366 8888	www.madinatjumeirah.com	6 A1
The Monarch Dubai	04 501 8888	www.themonarchdubai.com	8 A4
The Montgomerie, Dubai	04 390 5600	www.themontgomerie.com	5 B3
Mövenpick Hotel Bur Dubai ▶ p.573	04 336 6000	www.moevenpick-hotels.com	10 D3
One&Only Royal Mirage	04 399 9999	www.oneandonlyroyalmirage.com	5 C1
The Palace – The Old Town	04 428 7888	www.thepalace-dubai.com	7 D4
Park Hyatt Dubai	04 602 1234	www.dubai.park.hyatt.com	11 B4
Radisson SAS Hotel, Media City ▶ p.561	04 366 9111	www.dubai.radissonsas.com	5 C2
Radisson SAS Hotel, Dubai Deira Creek ▶ p.37	04 222 7171	www.deiracreek.dubai.radissonsas.com	9 C3
Raffles Dubai	04 324 8888	www.dubai.raffles.com	10 E4
Renaissance Hotel ▶ p.567	04 262 5555	www.dubairenaissance.com	11 E1
Ritz-Carlton, Dubai	04 399 4000	www.ritzcarlton.com	5 B1
Shangri-La Hotel	04 343 8888	www.shangri-la.com	7 E3
Sheraton Dubai Creek Hotel & Towers	04 228 1111	www.sheraton.com/dubai	9 B4
Sofitel City Centre Hotel	04 294 1222	www.sofitel.com	11 C3
Taj Palace Hotel	04 223 2222	www.tajhotels.com	11 C1
The Westin Dubai Mina Seyahi Beach Resort & Marina	04 399 4141	www.westin.com\dubaiminaseyahi	5 C1

Four Star

	Phone	Website	Map
Al Khaleej Palace Hotel	04 223 1000	www.alkhaleejhotels.com	9 C4
Al Manzil Hotel	04 428 5888	www.almanzilhotel.com	7 D4
Arabian Courtyard Hotel & Spa	04 351 9111	www.arabiancourtyard.com	9 A2
Ascot Hotel	04 352 0900	www.ascothoteldubai.com	8 F2
The Carlton Tower	04 222 7111	www.carltontower.net	9 B3
Coral Deira	04 224 8587	www.coral-deira.com	11 D1
Courtyard by Marriott Dubai Green Community	04 885 2222	www.cydubaigreencommunity.com	2 B4
Dubai Grand Hotel	04 263 2555	www.dubaigrandhotel.ae	14 C1
Four Points by Sheraton, Bur Dubai	04 397 7444	www.starwoodhotels.com/fourpoints	8 F3
Four Points by Sheraton, Downtown Dubai	04 354 3333	www.starwoodhotels.com/fourpoints	8 E3
Four Points by Sheraton, Sheikh Zayed Road	04 323 0333	www.starwoodhotels.com/fourpoints	7 E3
Golden Tulip Al Barsha	04 341 7750	www.goldentulippalbarsha.com	5 F3
Hatta Fort Hotel ▶ p.311	04 852 3211	www.jebelali-international.com	1 F2
Holiday Inn Downtown	04 228 8889	www.holiday-inn.com/downtowndubai	11 D1

Four Star	Phone	Website	Map
Ibis World Trade Centre	04 332 4444	www.accorhotels.com	7 F3
Jumeira Rotana Hotel	04 345 5888	www.rotana.com	8 A2
La Maison d'Hôtes	04 344 1838	www.lamaisondhotesdubai.com	7 D1
Le Méridien Fairway	04 608 5000	www.starwoodhotels.com	11 C4
Lotus Hotel	04 227 8888	www.lotus-hospitality.com	9 C4
Marco Polo Hotel	04 272 0000	www.marcopolohotel.net	9 E3
Metropolitan Hotel	04 343 0000	www.metropolitandubai.habtoorhotels.com	7 B3
Millennium Airport Hotel	04 282 3464	www.millenniumhotels.com	13 E1
Novotel Deira City Centre	04 294 8738	www.novotel.com	11 C3
Novotel World Trade Centre	04 332 0000	www.accorhotels.com	10 A1
The Palm Hotel	04 399 2222	www.thepalmhoteldubai.com	5 C2
Qamardeen Hotel	04 428 6888	www.qamardeenhotel.com	7 D4
Ramada Hotel	04 351 9999	www.ramadadubai.com	8 F3
Regent Palace Hotel	04 396 3888	www.ramee-group.com	8 F4
Riviera Hotel	04 222 2131	www.rivierahotel-dubai.com	9 B3
Rydges Plaza Hotel	04 398 2222	www.rydges.com	8 A3
Sheraton Deira	04 268 8888	www.sheraton.com/hoteldubai	11 F1
The Harbour Hotel & Residence	04 319 4000	www.emirateshotelsresorts.com	5 B2
Towers Rotana Hotel	04 343 8000	www.rotana.com	7 E3
Three Star			
Admiral Plaza	04 393 5333	www.admiralplazahotel.com	8 F2
Ambassador Hotel	04 393 9444	www.astamb.com	8 F1
Arabian Park Hotel	04 324 5999	www.arabianparkhotel.com	13 B1
Astoria Hotel	04 353 4300	www.astamb.com	8 F2
Claridge Hotel	04 271 6666	na	9 D3
Comfort Inn	04 222 7393	www.hotelcomfortinn.com	9 C4
Desert Palm Dubai	04 323 8888	www.desertpalm.ae	2 C3
Imperial Suites Hotel	04 351 5100	www.imperialsuiteshotel.com	8 F2
Premier Inn Dubai Investments Park	04 885 0999	http://global.premierinn.com	2 A4
Princess Hotel	04 263 5500	www.princesshoteldxb.com	14 B2
Ramee Guestline Hotel	04 229 9111	www.ramee-group.com	11 C1
Vendome Plaza Hotel	04 222 2333	www.vendomeplaza.com	9 C4
Two Star			
Ibis Deira City Centre	04 294 8737	www.ibishotel.com	11 C3
Phoenicia Hotel	04 222 7191	www.phoeniciahoteldubai.com	9 C2
President Hotel	04 334 6565	www.presidentdubai.com	8 F3
Ramee International Hotel	04 224 0222	www.ramee-group.com	9 C2
San Marco	04 272 2333	www.sanmarcohoteldubai.com	9 D2
Seashell Inn	04 393 4777	www.seashellinnhotel.com	8 E2
One Star			
Deira Park Hotel	04 223 9922	www.deiraparkhotel.com	9 C2
Vasantam Hotel	04 393 4873	www.thevasantabhavan.com	8 F2

Hotel Apartments

A cheaper alternative to staying in a hotel is to rent furnished accommodation. This can be done on a daily, weekly, monthly or yearly basis. The longer you rent the better the rate and there is a wide variety, and standard, of options in all areas of the city. One advantage is that the place can feel more like home than a hotel room, particularly on longer stays, so it's especially popular with people on short-term contracts or those first arriving in Dubai. Usually, the apartments come fully furnished, including everything from bed linen to cutlery, plus a cleaning service. Additionally, there may be sports facilities, such as a gym and a swimming pool, in the building. For the cheapest, try Al Mas or Desert Rose.

Hotel Apartments

Deluxe

Al Bustan Residence	Al Qusais	04 263 0000	www.al-bustan.com
Al Faris Hotel Apartment 3	Oud Metha	04 336 6566	www.alfarisdubai.com
Arjaan – Dubai Media City	Al Sufouh	04 436 0000	www.rotana.com
Bonnington, Jumeirah Lakes Towers ▶ p.51	Dubai Marina	04 361 9044	www.bonningtontower.com
BurJuman Rotana Suites	Bur Dubai	04 352 4444	www.rotana.com
Capitol Residence Hotel Apartments	Bur Dubai	04 393 2000	www.capitol-hotel.com
Chelsea Tower Hotel Apartments	Trade Centre 1	04 343 4347	www.chelseatowerdubai.com
Coral Boutique Hotel Apartments	Trade Centre 1	04 340 9040	www.coral-boutiquehotel.com
Golden Sands	Al Karama	04 359 9000	www.goldensandsdubai.com
Grand Hyatt Hotel Apartments	Umm Hurair	04 317 1234	www.dubai.grand.hyatt.com
Khalidia Hotel Apartments	Deira	04 228 2280	www.khalidiapalacehotel.ae
Marriott Executive Apartments Dubai Creek	Deira	04 213 1000	www.execapartments.com
Marriott Executive Apartments Dubai	Green Community	04 885 2222	www.execapartments.com
Nuran, Al Alka Serviced Residences ▶ p.47	Emirates Hills	8006 8726	www.nuran.com
Nuran, Al Majara Serviced Residences ▶ p.47	Dubai Marina	8006 8726	www.nuran.com
Oasis Beach Tower	Dubai Marina	04 399 4444	www.jebelali-international.com
Rihab Rotana Suites	Al Garhoud	04 294 0300	www.rotana.com
Rose Rotana	Trade Centre 2	04 323 0111	www.rotana.com
Savoy Crest Hotel Apartments	Bur Dubai	04 355 4488	www.savoy.ae
Sofitel City Centre Residence	Al Garhoud	04 294 1333	www.deiracitycentre.com
The Radisson SAS Residence	Dubai Marina	04 435 5000	www.radissonsas.com
Villa Rotana	Al Wasl	04 321 6111	www.rotana.com
Wafi Residence	Umm Hurair	04 324 7222	www.wafiproperties.com
Waterview Executive Apartments	Creekside, Deira	04 295 0000	www.waterviewdubai.com
World Trade Centre Residence	Trade Centre 1	04 511 0000	www.jumeirahliving.com

Standard

Al Deyafa Hotel Apartments	Deira	04 228 2555	www.aldeyafa.com
Al Mas Hotel Apartments	Bur Dubai	04 355 7899	www.almashotelapts.com
Crystal Living Courts	Al Barsha	04 420 2555	www.layia.net
Dar Al Sondos Hotel Apartments by Le Meridien	Bur Dubai	04 393 8000	www.starwoodhotels.com
Desert Rose Hotel Apartments	Bur Dubai	04 352 4848	na
Golden Sands Hotel Apartments	Bur Dubai	04 355 5553	www.goldensandsdubai.com
Number One Tower Suites	Trade Centre 1	04 343 4666	www.numberonetower.com
Ramee Guest Line Hotel Apartments	Bur Dubai	04 355 3344	www.ramee-group.com
Residence Deira by Le Meridien	Deira	04 224 1777	www.starwoodhotels.com

Guest Houses & Bed & Breakfasts

Guest houses are becoming more popular in Dubai. While smaller in size, B&B's offer a homely feel and are idea for guests who want to see more of the 'real Dubai'. Located in residential areas, they won't have access to private beaches, but there is no shortage of good public beaches. Some will have their own pool and benefit from intimate surroundings, while owners will be only too happy to give personal recommendations on what to see and do in the city. Fusion B&B (050 478 7539, www.fusionhotels.com) is located in Jumeira 3, has a large swimming pool and modern decor. Villa 47 (04 286 8239, www.villa47.com) has only two guest rooms, but is located close to the airport in Garhoud. La Maison d'Hôtes (344 1838, www.lamaisondhotesdubai.com) has 20 guest rooms and a continental inspired restaurant. The hotel does not have an alcohol licence, but is within minutes of the bigger hotel resorts.

JUMEIRAH LAKES TOWERS
DUBAI

A new level of quality, charm and service will arrive in Dubai this autumn. In the heart of New Dubai, Bonnington brings to you a stunning property. Bonnington will be a landmark of heritage and style, towering gracefully in the midst of Jumeirah Lakes Towers, providing a chic five star residential address to all who walk through her doors.

A CENTURY OF HOSPITALITY

Bonnington has welcomed guests for over 100 years and with each year, like a fine vintage, Bonnington improves with age. Since the turn of the century, Bonnington has refined the true meaning of British Hospitality.

Bonnington, Jumeirah Lakes Towers, Dubai is a five star deluxe hotel with serviced apartments, several restaurants, bars and lounges, meetings and events facilities and a leisure deck on the 12th floor with infinity pool and a state of the art gym, saunas and steam rooms.

it's all about you

OPENING AUTUMN 2008

Tel: +971 (4) 361 9044
Fax: +971 (4) 361 9045
Email: dubai@bonningtontower.com
www.bonningtontower.com

Hostels

Hostels			
Dubai Youth Hostel	Al Qusais	04 298 8161	12 B4
Fujairah Youth Hostel	Fujairah	09 222 2347	1 F2
Khor Fakkan Youth Hostel	Khor Fakkan	09 237 0886	1 F1
Sharjah Youth Hostel	Sharjah	06 522 5070	2 C2

Hostels

The Dubai Youth Hostel, located on Al Nahda Road near Al Mulla Plaza in the north of the city, provides the cheapest accommodation in town. A four-star wing was added to the hostel in 2002, almost tripling the number of rooms. In the old wing, there are 53 beds available for Dhs.60 per night (YHA members) or Dhs.75 (non-members), including breakfast, in one of 20 very clean, two-bed dormitory rooms. Beds in the new wing are Dhs.85 for members and Dhs.100 for non-members, including breakfast. Check-in is always open.

Accommodation is available for men, women and families. Annual membership costs Dhs.200; family membership is Dhs.350 and for groups of more than 25, the yearly charge is Dhs.2,000. Women travelling alone should check availability, since the management reserves the right to refuse bookings from single women when the hostel has a number of men staying. The hostel is well served by a cheap, regular bus service into the centre of Dubai and reasonably priced taxis are plentiful. By car, the hostel is about 15 minutes from Airport Terminal 1. Hostels are also located in some of the other emirates, including two in Sharjah and one in Fujairah.

Clever Camping

For the lowdown on camping in the UAE, get your hands on a copy of the UAE Off-Road Explorer. It's the definitive guide to outdoor living, and features recommended camping spots, what to take, and what to do when you get there. It's also packed with informative maps, life-saving tips and inspiring photography.

Backpacking

On first inspection Dubai doesn't seem like a backpackers' paradise, due to the luxury hotels and relatively expensive shopping. But many independent travellers have found that Dubai is a good gateway to South East Asia and Australia. There are four youth hostels spread over the Emirates, although many backpackers opt for low-star hotels (which are cheaper in town than they are on the beachfront). With cheap public transport, a myriad of local independent restaurants serving traditional fare for a pittance and so many free sights, Dubai can easily be explored on a budget. For a list of hostels, see table above.

Campsites

Other options **Camping** p.334

There are no official campsites in the UAE, but fortunately there are plenty of places to camp informally. Near Dubai, the desert dunes on the way to Hatta are a good option,

Abras on Dubai Creek

as are the mountains a little further on. Jebel Ali beach used to be a popular place, but the construction of Palm Jebel Ali and Dubai Waterfront has now closed access completely. Saih Ash Shaib beach, further down the coast towards Abu Dhabi past Jebel Ali Beach, is now a popular beach camping location. For a fun weekend out of Dubai with all the facilities, Dreamland (p.274) in Umm al Quwain offers camping in provided tents or 'cabana' huts, with access to the pools and all the rides, and food and drinks included in the deal.

Getting Around

Other options **Exploring** p.240

Other options **Exploring** p.240

Cars are the most popular method of getting around Dubai and the emirates, either by private vehicle or by taxi. There is a reasonable public bus service, and walking and cycling are possible, but the soaring summer heat and multiple-lane roads put most people off. There are a few motorcyclists on the roads, but most of them are courageous couriers or fearless fast food delivery drivers, as Dubai's aggressive road users make it unsafe for two wheelers. There are no trains and trams yet, but 2009 will see Dubai's first metro running both under and above ground (see Metro on p.62). The city's road network is excellent, although at certain times of the day it is packed with traffic jams. The majority of main roads have two or more lanes that are all well signposted, and Dubai is probably the easiest emirate to navigate. Blue or green signs indicate the main areas or locations out of the city and brown signs show heritage sites, places of interest and hospitals. People often rely on landmarks such as shops, hotels or notable buildings to identify streets, and refer to roads by their nickname, such as Bank Street or Trade Centre Road. All roads are numbered to aid navigation, but the numbers are gradually being phased out and replaced with official road names. In Jumeira 3, where a successful pilot of this scheme was run, all of the roads are named. The rest of the city's street naming should be completed by the end of 2009.

Dubai is a relatively easy city to negotiate. The creek divides Bur Dubai (to the south) and Deira (to the north). The creek currently has five main crossing points: Shindagha Tunnel, Maktoum Bridge, Garhoud Bridge, Business Bay Bridge and the Floating Bridge. The creek can also be crossed by a pedestrian foot tunnel near Shindagha, or by boat (the common water taxis are known locally as abras). Dubai is growing away from the creek though, and in general the new developments have good, modern road networks, often completed before the houses.

To ease the pressure on inner-city roads the E311 Emirates Road was built at a cost of Dhs.150 million. This connects Abu Dhabi directly to Sharjah and the northern emirates. The E44 Al Khail Road was also built with the hope of further relieving the congestion on Sheikh Zayed Road. There is a ban on all trucks on main routes at busy times of the day. More bypasses, or ring roads, including the E611, are planned, extending further out into the desert, in an effort to keep traffic away from the city's streets. With new interchanges and the underground track and stations for the metro being constructed, lane closures, contra-flows and hold-ups are an unfortunate reality for many.

Air Travel

Dubai's location at the crossroads of Europe, Asia and Africa makes it an easily accessible city. London is seven hours away, Frankfurt six, Hong Kong eight, India three and Nairobi four. Most major cities have direct flights to Dubai, many with a choice of operator. There are also direct flights to North America and Australia. Dubai International Airport is world renowned, handling over 28 million passengers in 2006. An ambitious $540 million expansion programme has transformed the already excellent airport into a state-of-the-art facility, ready to meet the needs of passengers for the next 30 years.

Currently, more than 110 airlines take advantage of Dubai's open skies policy, operating to and from over 160 destinations. Dubai's award winning airline,

Watch This Space

2009 will see the arrival of two new forms of rail transport. The Al Sufouh Tram project will run along the stretch of Al Sufouh, from the Burj Al Arab right along to Jumeirah Beach Residence via Dubai Marina and Media City. With a total of 19 stops scheduled for the first phase, the tram is aimed at commuters who live and work in this area, but with so many landmarks on the route it is sure to be popular with tourists too. The second development is the dedicated Palm Jumeirah monorail, the first monorail in the Middle East. Stopping at four locations along the length of the trunk including Atlantis and Palm Mall, the monorail will be driverless, and have a futuristic-style ticketing system. The monorail will also link at the base of the Palm with the Al Sufouh Tram line.

New Horizons

Virgin Atlantic (www.virgin-atlantic.com) has added Dubai to its list of destinations, with daily flights from Dubai to London and an extensive network of onward connections.

Salik

From 2007, electronic toll gates were installed at various points around Dubai. In order to pass through one of these gates, you need to affix a Salik tag to your windscreen and make sure you have enough credit loaded. For more information, see p.226.

Emirates (www.emirates.com), is based here and operates scheduled services to over 100 destinations. The airline's growth is staggering and is synonymous with the development of Dubai itself.

There are currently three terminals, located on different sides of the airport (a 15 to 30 minute taxi ride, depending on the traffic, and there's also a shuttle bus). All terminals offer car rental, hotel reservations and bureau de change services. Most of the better-known airlines use Terminal 1, but a selection of over 20 airlines operate from Terminal 2, primarily serving the former Soviet countries. The newly opened Terminal 3 is dedicated for the use of Emirates Airlines, and boasts 120 check-in desks to cut through waiting times. The lounges are spacious, with exclusive facilities for both business and first class passengers. The terminal has a vast selection of drinking and dining venues from fine cuisine to fast food, plus a host of designer labels in Duty Free. For up-to-date flight information, call 04 216 6666.

Duty Free shops are located in both the arrivals and departures halls, although the arrivals hall outlet is limited. Launched in November 2003, Etihad Airways, the national airline of the UAE (based in Abu Dhabi), has ambitious growth plans. Within 30 months of start-up, it was offering 30 routes; the aim is for 70 routes by 2010. Destinations served include Sydney, Toronto, New York, London, Manchester, Paris and Johannesburg. For more information, visit www. etihadairways.com. Another relative newcomer is the budget airline Air Arabia, based in Sharjah (www. airarabia.com). The attractions of this airline are reduced costs and 'ticketless' travel. While neither fly directly to or from Dubai, they do provide an alternative for coming to the UAE and travelling within the region, often at more affordable rates. Abu Dhabi airport is a 90 minute drive from Dubai, and Sharjah airport is 45 minutes away. Following international guidelines, Dubai airport has a restriction on the amount of liquids passengers can carry in their hand luggage. All liquids, gels

Airlines

Aeroflot	04 222 2245	www.aeroflot.ru
Air Arabia	06 508 8888	www.airarabia.com
Air France ▶ p.55	04 602 5400	www.airfrance.co.ae
Air India	04 227 6787	www.airindia.com
Air Mauritius	04 221 4455	www.airmauritius.com
Air New Zealand	04 393 3122	www.airnewzealand.com
Air Seychelles	04 295 1511	www.airseychelles.com
Alitalia	04 224 2257	www.alitalia.com
American Airlines	04 393 3234	www.aa.com
Austrian Airlines	04 294 1403	www.aua.com
Bangladesh Biman Airlines	04 222 0942	www.bimanair.com
British Airways	04 307 5777	www.britishairways.com
Cathay Pacific	04 295 0400	www.cathaypacific.com
China Airlines	04 295 1511	www.china-airlines.com
CSA Czech Airlines	04 295 9502	www.czechairlines.com
Cyprus Airways	04 221 5325	www.cyprusairways.com
Delta Airlines	04 397 7281	www.delta.com
Egypt Air	02 228 9444	www.egyptair.com
Emirates Airline	04 214 4444	www.emirates.com
Etihad Airways	02 505 8000	www.etihadairways.com
Etihad Holidays	04 800 2277	www.etihadairways.com
Gulf Air	04 271 3222	www.gulfairco.com
Iran Air	04 224 0200	www.iranair.com
Japan Airlines	04 222 3737	www.jal.com
KLM Royal Dutch Airlines	04 319 3777	www.klm.com
Kuwait Airways	04 228 1106	www.kuwait-airways.com
Lufthansa	04 316 6642	www.lufthansa.com
Malaysia Airlines	04 397 0250	www.malaysiaairlines.com
Middle East Airlines	04 223 7080	www.mea.com.lb
Olympic Airlines	04 222 8689	www.olympicairlines.com
Oman Air	04 351 8080	www.oman-air.com
Pakistan International Airlines	04 222 2154	www.piac.com.pk
Qantas	04 316 6652	www.qantas.com
Qatar Airways	04 229 2229	www.qatarairways.com
Royal Brunei Airlines	04 351 9330	www.bruneiair.com
Royal Jet Group	02 575 7000	www.royaljetgroup.com
Royal Jordanian Airlines	04 294 4322	www.rja.com.jo
Saudi Arabian Airlines	04 229 6111	www.saudiairlines.com
Singapore Airlines	04 223 2300	www.singaporeair.com
South African Airways	04 397 0766	www.flysaa.com
Sri Lankan Airlines	04 294 9119	www.srilankan.aero
Swiss Air	04 294 5051	www.swiss.com
Thai Airways	04 268 1702	www.thaiair.com
United Airlines	04 316 6942	www.ual.com
Virgin Atlantic	04 406 0650	www.virgin-atlantic.com

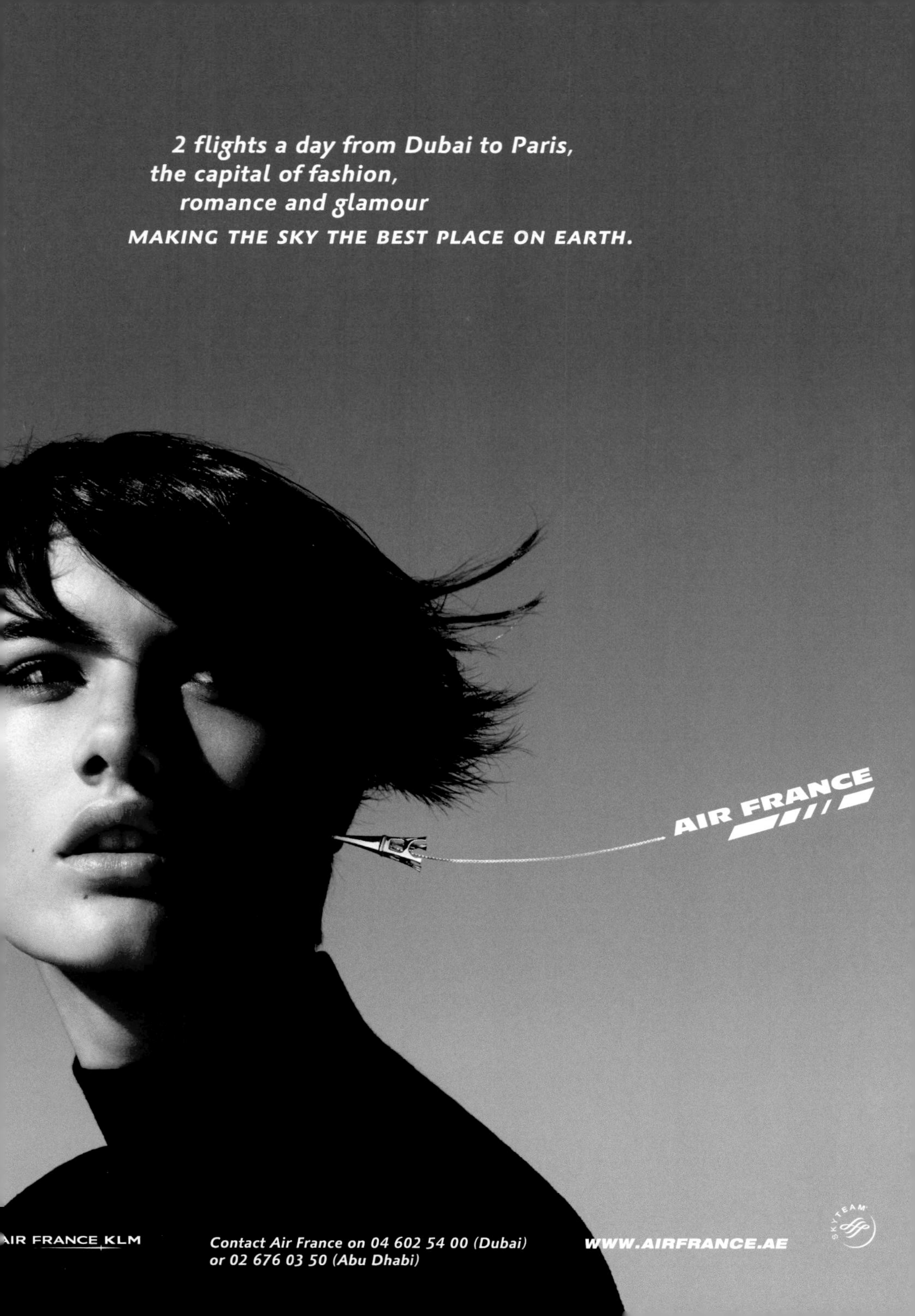
2 flights a day from Dubai to Paris,
the capital of fashion,
romance and glamour
MAKING THE SKY THE BEST PLACE ON EARTH.
AIR FRANCE
AIR FRANCE KLM
Contact Air France on 04 602 54 00 (Dubai)
or 02 676 03 50 (Abu Dhabi)
WWW.AIRFRANCE.AE
SKYTEAM

and aerosols must be in containers no bigger than 100ml. The total allowance is no more than one litre, and the containers must fit comfortably in a clear, re-sealable plastic bag.

For those customers who like to feel special, Dubai Airport has Al Majlis. Located next to Terminal 3, this VIP facility offers luxurious surroundings to guests who want more than the first class lounges can provide. Together with check-in desks and immigration, Al Majlis offers private lounges with shower facilities, limousine use and in-house Duty Free. The lounge can be hired by guests departing from or arriving in Dubai, and even guests in transit. The cost of the service starts at Dhs.1,510.

Not as exclusive, but still worthwhile, are the new express check-in counters in Terminal 1, which cater to guests who are only travelling with hand luggage. Guests can cut out the long queues and proceed straight to passport control, and travelling with only hand luggage cuts down waiting time at arrivals. Although popular with business travellers, the service is open to all.

Dubai World Central
Construction is well underway on Dubai's second airport (Al Maktoum International Airport) and the first phase will be just for freight. The whole airport aims to be fully operational by 2017. The first runway is complete, and is due to start functioning next year. But by 2050 it will have the capacity for 120 million passengers a year. For more information on one of the city's biggest projects, see p.8

Lose The Liquids
The new international regulations on fluids in carry on luggage are enforced at Dubai Airport. All liquids, gels and aerosols must be kept in containers smaller than 100ml. Those containers must then be kept in transparent, re-sealable bags. Any liquids, gels or aerosols not in compliance will be thrown out upon entering the terminal.

Customs

When travelling into or out of Dubai, make a special note of the customs restrictions on certain goods. Certain prescription medications are banned, even though they are freely available over the counter in other countries. Please do not carry any medications containing codeine or temazepam with you. As for recreational drugs, there have been some high-profile cases recently that have highlighted the UAE's zero tolerance approach to these substances. Even a miniscule quantity in your possession could result in a lengthy jail term. Your bags will be scanned on arrival to ensure you have no offending magazines or DVDs.

So what are you allowed to bring in? Each passenger is allowed 2,000 cigarettes, 400 cigars or two kilograms of tobacco. Non-Muslims are also allowed four 'units' of alcohol; a unit is either one bottle of wine, one bottle of liqueur or spirits, or a half-case of beer.

Bicycle

Other options **Cycling** p.338

Cycling can be a very efficient way of commuting as it avoids a great deal of traffic and is a cheap mode of transport, however for most people in Dubai, the car rules, and bikes are used only by those on lower incomes. A lot of care is needed when cycling in the UAE as some drivers pay little attention to anything, even other cars, and much less cyclists. Also, in the hotter months, cycling is more arduous and it should be remembered that you won't arrive anywhere fresh after pedalling in temperatures as high as 45ºC.

In the quieter areas, many of the roads are wide enough to accommodate cyclists as well as cars, and where there are footpaths, they are often wide and in good condition. Dubai's Roads and Transport Authority (RTA) has decided to try to encourage cycling in the busy districts of Deira and Bur Dubai by adding dedicated lanes and parking areas for cyclists. There is even talk of a network of cycle lanes that would eventually be extended to other parts of the city.

Boat

Opportunities for getting around by boat in the Emirates are limited unless you wish to travel by dhow. Crossing the creek by abra is a common method of transport for many people in Dubai, with the number of passengers in 2006 estimated at nearly 26 million.

The RTA (Roads & Transport Authority) recently upgraded the abra stations for boarding and alighting, and also raised the fare from 50 fils (the same price it had been for 20 years) to Dhs.1. Another recent addition to the creek is a fleet of air-conditioned water buses. These operate on four different routes crossing the creek, with fares set at Dhs.4 per trip, and are estimated to carry two million passengers in the first year. A 'tourist' route also exists, with a 45 minute creek tour costing Dhs.25.

Further plans are being looked at to extend the routes to Festival City and into Business Bay, and there has been talk of a coastal service between Dubai and Sharjah, and further off-shore to link all the new island developments. There's also the possibility of seeing solar-powered abras in the future, which will maintain the traditional look without the diesel fumes. Plans have also been announced for Ferry Dubai, a fleet of 10 modern boats that will each carry up to 100 passengers across the creek. The first phase will see six ferries on the creek by October 2009 for initial safety tests. Fares are yet to be decided, and the boats will initially ferry passengers along the abra routes.

It is possible to travel from Dubai, Sharjah and Ras Al Khaimah to several ports in Iran by boat, including a hydrofoil and traditional dhow option. Prices vary between Dhs.130 and Dhs.250, and the journey time can be up to 12 hours depending on the travel option chosen. For more information, contact the Oasis Freight Agency on 04 352 5000. There is a cruise ship terminal at Port Rashid, currently the only dedicated complex in the region

The RTA is developing a new water taxi project in a bid to help clear congestion on major routes. Due for completion in mid 2009, the scheme will see 20 stations dotted along Dubai creek and coastline which will be served by a fleet of water taxis that customers can book over the telephone, similar to a regular taxi. Seating up to 11 passengers, the state-of-the-art catamarans will be air conditioned and feature seats similar to those in business class on flights. Taxi stations will include four at the marina, with further stops catering to the hotels along the Jumeira stretch.

Bus

There are currently over 60 bus routes through the main residential and commercial areas of Dubai, with the available services recently being clarified with a colour coding system. While the buses are air-conditioned and modern, they do tend to be rather crowded. The Roads & Transport Authority (RTA) is in the process of doubling the number of buses in service (up to a total of 1,200, including double deckers and articulated buses), to serve 95% of the city and hopefully increase usage among the city's population from 6% to 30%. It has also introduced air-conditioned bus stops, which can now be seen throughout the city. The plan is to build over 800. Efforts are also being made to display better timetables and route plans at bus stops and stations to encourage people to use this inexpensive method of transport (www.rta.ae).

Bank Street traffic

Get Out There

When you think you've done it all – think again! Explorer's *UAE Weekend Breaks* will tantalise you with stunning photography and ideas for perfect getaway destinations helping you make the most of your weekends in the UAE and Oman.

Airport Bus

The RTA, in conjunction with the Dubai Department of Civil Aviation, operates airport buses to and from Dubai International Airport every 30 minutes, 24 hours a day. There are two loop routes: Route 401 services Deira, while Route 402 serves Bur Dubai. The fare is Dhs.3. Call 800 9090 for details, or log on to www.rta.ae.

The main bus station is near the Gold Souk in Deira and in Bur Dubai on Al Ghubaiba Road near the Plaza Cinema. Buses run at regular intervals, starting between 05:00 and 06:00 and going until midnight or so. Fares are cheap at between Dhs.1 and Dhs.3 per journey, and are paid to the driver when you board, so try to have the exact change ready. Monthly discount tickets and e-Go cards are also available. Buses also go further to Khawaneej, Al Awir, Hatta, and even Oman, for very reasonable prices – a one-way ticket to Hatta, which is 100 kilometres away, is Dhs.7, while Dubai to Muscat takes six hours and costs Dhs.50.

The E1 service links Dubai and Abu Dhabi. From early morning to late at night, buses operate every 40 minutes between Al Ghubaiba and Abu Dhabi Central bus stations, and the two-hour journey costs Dhs.15 each way. There is also a service to and from Al Arouba Road and Al Wahda in Sharjah to both Bur Dubai and Deira, which runs every 10 minutes. In addition to taxis, Dubai Transport Corporation also offers a minibus service to other emirates of the UAE. The buses are modern, air conditioned and offer a good value service to Ajman, Umm Al Quwain, Ras Al Khaimah, Fujairah, Al Ain and Abu Dhabi. Unfortunately, at present these services only carry passengers on the outward journeys. Anyone wishing to return to Dubai by public transport must make alternative arrangements. The Road and Transport Authority call centre number is 800 9090. The RTA website (www.rta.ae) has very comprehensive route plans, timetables and fares.

e-Go Card

This electronic smart card helps bus passengers save time and avoids the hassle of small change. Available for Dhs.5, the e-Go card can be topped up with credits (Dhs.20 for the first time and multiples of Dhs.10 thereafter). When placed on the ticket machine in the bus, the ticket amount is automatically deducted, and the balance is adjusted and stored. Alternatively you can buy a monthly pass for Dhs.90 at the bus station that allows unlimited travel for the whole month, but not on all routes.

Car

Other options **Transportation** p.225

Over the past two decades Dubai has built, and is still building, an impressive network of roads. The Municipality estimates that, in the last 10 years, the number of roads in Dubai has doubled. The roads to all major areas are excellent and an eight lane highway heads south-west from the city to Abu Dhabi, which takes about 90 minutes to reach. Despite this, the sheer volume of traffic has become a definite problem. In 2007, Dubai overtook Cairo as the most congested city in the Middle East, with the average commuter spending one hour and 45 minutes per day in their car. With annual traffic levels growing at a rate of 25%, and the number of new vehicles being registered among the highest of any city in the world, it doesn't look like it will improve anytime soon. Particularly busy spots include roads leading in and out of the city centre, and routes across the creek, due to the fact that the number of crossings are limited and the roads leading to them don't seem to be able to cope with the load. There are currently four bridges and a road tunnel linking the two main districts on either side of the creek, with plans underway to increase the number of crossings. Rush hour on Sheikh Zayed Road and on Maktoum Bridge across the creek is close to total gridlock. Only time will tell whether the increasing number of measures being implemented in Dubai will solve the horrendous traffic jams.

Plastic Isn't Fantastic

Customers can't use credit or debit cards to purchase fuel or shop items from Emarat, ENOC or EPPCO stations, and many stations don't have ATMs, so make sure you have enough cash.

Going Round & Round?

Dubai's ever-changing road network is confusing for new and seasoned residents alike. Get a copy of Explorer's *Dubai Atlas* – its comprehensive A to Z of every street, hotel, landmark and major building means your days of driving round in circles are over.

Highway To Hell

Despite the relatively diminutive size of the city, the average number of road traffic accidents in Dubai is high at around 125 per month, including 18 fatalities (figures released by Dubai Police). So stay alert. You have to keep your wits about you at all times and try to predict the random manoeuvres of other drivers before they happen.

Driving Habits & Regulations

While the infrastructure is superb, the general standard of driving is not. The UAE has one of the world's highest death rates per capita due to traffic accidents. According to Dubai Police, one person is killed in a traffic related accident every 48 hours, and there is one injury every four hours – not the most encouraging of statistics. Drivers often seem completely unaware of other cars on the road and fast, aggressive driving, swerving, pulling out suddenly, lane hopping, tail-gating and drifting happen far too regularly. One move to help the situation on the roads was a ban placed on using handheld mobile phones while driving. Predictably the sales of hands-free systems rocketed before people went back to their old bad habits.

In Dubai, cars are driven on the right-hand side of the road, and it is mandatory to wear seatbelts in the front seats. Children under 10 years of age are not allowed to sit in the front of a car, although you'll still see people driving with their children on their lap and kids climbing over the seats and on the dashboard. The fine for this is Dhs.100 and four black points.

Details of fines for any traffic violations and an outline of the black point system are found on the Dubai Police website (www.dubaipolice.gov.ae). Speeding fines are Dhs.200 and parking fines start at Dhs.100. You are also issued a certain number of black points against your licence according to the particular violation – get 12 points and you have to reapply for your licence. Most fines are paid when you renew your annual car registration. However, parking tickets appear on your windscreen and you have a week or two to pay; the amount increases if you don't pay within the time allotted on the back of the ticket.

Try to keep a reasonable stopping distance between yourself and the car in front; you also need to be more aware of the other cars on the road and check your mirrors frequently. You may consider yourself the safest of drivers but with so many bad drivers on the road it pays to be extra cautious.

If you wish to report a traffic violation, call the Traffic Police's toll free hotline (800 4353). The Dubai Police website (www.dubaipolice.gov.ae) offers all information relevant to driving, such as traffic violations, road maps and contact numbers. For complete information on highway codes, safety and Dubai's road rules, check out the Safe Driving Handbook available from the Emirates Motor Sports Federation (04 282 7111).

Speed Limits

Speed limits are usually 60 to 80 kph around town, while on main roads and roads to other emirates they are 100 to 120 kph. The speed limit is clearly indicated on road signs. Both fixed and movable radar traps, and Dubai Traffic Police, are there to catch the unwary violator. In 2008, two million traffic offences were reported – an increase of a whopping 43% from 2006 – the majority of which were speeding fines caught on radar. Average-speed and stopping-distance traps were recently introduced to try to catch speeding drivers who only slow down when they see speed cameras, and to discourage tailgating. On-the-spot traffic fines for certain offences have been introduced, but in most cases you won't know you've received a fine until you check on the website or renew your vehicle registration.

Driving Licence

To drive a rental vehicle you must provide either an international driving permit or a temporary Dubai licence, which you can only get if you are from one of the countries listed on the transfer list (see p.91).

If you want to drive a privately owned vehicle, you must first get a temporary Dubai licence. Unless you have a Dubai driving licence, either permanent or temporary, you are not insured to drive a private vehicle. For permanent licences, see Driving Licence in the Residents section (p.91). For more information on licences and the procedures involved, see the Dubai Red-Tape Explorer.

Traffic Jam Session

Avoid a traffic jam by tuning in to any of the following radio channels: Al Arabiya (98.9 FM), Al Khallejiya (100.9 FM), Dubai 92 (92.00 FM), Channel 4 FM (104.8 FM), and Emirates 1 FM (99.3FM, 100.5 FM). Regular updates about the traffic situation on main roads are provided throughout the day, forewarning you if a certain road is blocked so you can take an alternative route.

Salik

In 2007, the Roads and Transport Authority (RTA) unveiled the Salik road toll system in an effort to cut congestion on Sheikh Zayed Road. The scheme met much resistance when it launched, with many people complaining about this new 'tax', and increased journey times on alternative routes as drivers tried to avoid the tolls. Some drivers celebrated as their daily commute time was temporarily slashed, while traffic on other roads remained as bad as ever, if not worse. Motorists buy a 'tag' (Dhs.100, including Dhs.50 of credit) from any petrol station, and attach it to their windscreen.

There are currently four toll gates – the Al Barsha gate after Mall of the Emirates, Al Safa gate close to Safa Park exit, Garhoud Bridge and Al Maktoum Bridge. The system automatically deducts Dhs.4 from a user's account each time they pass beneath a gate – if your trip takes you past Al Barsha and Al Safa within an hour, you will only be charged Dhs.4 and the maximum you can be charged daily is Dhs.24. The Maktoum Bridge crossing will be free whenever the Floating Bridge is closed – 22:00 until 06:00 (22:00 to 09:00 on Fridays). An SMS warning will be sent when credit is running low. Accounts can be topped up at petrol stations, via some ATMs, and eventually through the phone and online. Visit www.salik.ae or call 800 72545.

From December 2008, passengers in taxis are exempt from paying Salik, so make sure this isn't added to your fare.

What's In A Name?

To make navigation even more difficult, places may not be referred to by their official name. For instance, Al Jumeira Road is often known as Beach Road, and Interchange One, on Sheikh Zayed Road, is invariably called Defence Roundabout. Recently, Sheikh Hamdan bin Rashid Al Maktoum ordered certain streets around Dubai to be given the names of prominent Arab cities, such as Amman Road, Cairo Road and Marrakech Road, to demonstrate the strong ties that exist between the UAE and other Arab nations.

Accidents

If you are involved in a traffic accident, however minor, you must remain with your car at the accident scene, report the incident to the Traffic Police and then wait for them to arrive. Unfortunately when you have an accident, you become a star attraction and the passing traffic will slow down to a crawl so that rubberneckers can have a good look at your mishap. Stationary vehicles that block the road after an accident as they wait for the police can cause serious tailbacks. If the accident is minor and no one is injured you should move your vehicle out of traffic while you wait for the police – you may be fined for blocking the road otherwise. When the police arrive you will have to explain how the accident happened. If the vehicles have been moved though, and there is a discrepancy between your version and the other driver's, it could be harder to fight your case.

Stray animals (mostly camels) are something else to avoid on some of the quieter roads in the UAE. If the animal hits your vehicle and causes damage or injury, the animal's owner should pay compensation, but if you are found to have been speeding or driving recklessly, you must compensate the animal's owner, which can be expensive. See Traffic Accidents (p.235).

Non-Drivers

In addition to dealing with bad drivers, you will find that many pedestrians tend to walk in the road and cross highways at inopportune times. The few cyclists who do brave the roads will often cycle towards you on the wrong side of the road, invariably without lights. Pedestrians often step out dangerously close

Blood Money

If you are driving and cause someone's death, you may be liable to pay a sum of money, known as 'blood money', to the deceased's family. The limit for this has been set at Dhs.200,000 per victim and your car insurance will cover this cost (hence the higher premiums). However, insurance companies will only pay if they cannot find a way of claiming that the insurance is invalid (if the driver was driving without a licence or under the influence of alcohol). The deceased's family can, however, waive the right to blood money if they feel merciful.

to oncoming traffic and a lack of convenient, safe crossings makes life for those on foot especially difficult. However, the number of pedestrian footbridges and pedestrian-operated traffic lights are gradually increasing. Jaywalking (crossing a road at an undesignated spot) is illegal in Dubai and can carry a fine of up to Dhs.200.

Lane Discipline

As so many different nationalities converge on Dubai's roads, there are bound to be some major differences in driving styles, and lane discipline is often absent. There is little etiquette for overtaking and cars tend to swerve from the far right to far left lanes in a bid to avoid the slow-paced jalopy trundling along in the middle lane. Aggressive driving is a real problem and you can expect to get incessantly flashed by a speed demon behind you despite there being a truck to your right, leaving you with nowhere to go.

Parking

In most areas of Dubai parking is available and people rarely have to walk too far in the heat. Increasing numbers of 'pay and display' parking meters are appearing around the busier parts of the city. The areas are clearly marked and the charge is either Dhs.1 or Dhs.2 for an hour. Try to have loose change with you since there are no automatic change machines available. You can also use prepaid cards that can be bought in post offices and shops; for Dhs.42.50 you get Dhs.50 worth of parking and for Dhs.80 you get parking to the value of Dhs.100. Alternatively, you can buy a card that is displayed on the vehicle's windscreen. Type A parking cards can be used in all parking areas and cost Dhs.700 for three months, Dhs.1,300 for six months and Dhs.2,500 for a year. Type B parking cards restrict you to off-street parking in designated areas and cost Dhs.450 for three months, Dhs.800 for six months and Dhs.1,500 for a year.

Parking meters operate from 08:00 to 13:00 and from 16:00 to 21:00, Saturday to Thursday. The authorities began converting the city's meters to a new hi-tech variety during 2007; in time these will accept payment from mobile phones, allowing you to top up your parking remotely. Failure to buy a ticket is likely to land you with a Dhs.100 fine. If you return to your parked car to find that someone has inconsiderately double-parked behind you, you can call 04 269 4848 and report them.

Petrol Stations

Petrol stations in the UAE are numerous and run by Emarat, EPPCO and ENOC (Adnoc in Abu Dhabi). Most offer extra services, such as a car wash or a shop selling all those necessities of life that you forgot to buy at the supermarket.

The pump price is controlled by the government, and the majority of visitors find petrol far cheaper than in their home countries – prices in late 2008 were Dhs.6.25 per gallon for Special (95 octane), Dhs.6.75 for Super (98 octane), and Dhs.13.95 for diesel.

Car Hire

All the main car rental companies, plus a few extra, can be found in Dubai. It is best to shop around as the rates vary considerably. The larger, reputable firms generally have more reliable vehicles and a greater capacity to help in an emergency (an important factor when dealing with the aftermath of an accident). Depending on the agent, cars can be hired with or without a driver, and the minimum hire period is usually 24 hours. Prices range from Dhs.90 a day for smaller cars to Dhs.1,200 for limousines.

Comprehensive insurance is essential; make sure that it includes personal accident coverage, and perhaps Oman cover if you're planning on going exploring.

To rent a car, you are usually required to produce a copy of your passport, a valid international driving licence or a Dubai licence, and two photographs. The rental company may be able to help arrange international or temporary local licences for visitors.

Car Rental Agencies

Autolease Rent-a-Car	04 282 6565	www.autolease-uae.com
Avis	04 295 7121	www.avisuae.com
Budget Rent A Car	04 295 6667	www.budget-uae.com
Diamond Lease	04 343 4330	www.diamondlease.com
Discount Rent A Car	04 338 9060	www.discountcardubai.com
Dubai Exotic Limo	04 286 8635	www.dubaiexoticlimo.com
EuroStar Rent-a-Car	04 266 1117	www.eurostarrental.com
Hertz	04 282 4422	www.hertz-uae.com
National Car Rental ▶ p.227	04 283 2020	www.national-me.com
Thrifty Car Rental	800 4694	www.thriftyuae.com
United Car Rentals	04 266 6286	www.unitedcarrentals.com

Train Of Thought ◀
Plans have been mooted for an 'Emirates Railway', a national rail network, as well as a proposed Arabian rail network for the future, which will connect the UAE to the rest of the GCC and countries to the north. However, both projects are still very much at the feasibility stage, and it remains to be seen when, or if, they will go ahead.

Metro

There are currently no trains in the UAE, but the Dubai Metro transit system will be up and running by the end of 2009. It aims to be the largest driverless metro system in the world, and will be focused on two lines. The Red Line starts at Dubai airport and travels alongside Sheikh Zayed Road to the new developments in the south of the city and Jebel Ali, while the Green Line services the city centre. The Red Line has 28 stations, including four underground at Bur Juman, Al Rigga, Port Sayed and Union Square. The Green Line has 14 stations throughout Bur Dubai and Deira. Some of the current problems on the roads in the centre of Dubai are due to the construction of the underground stations in these areas. The Red Line is scheduled to open on 9 September 2009 after a three-month trial period, with the Green Line estimated to be completed by March 2010. A third Purple line is at the planning stage and will be completely underground providing an express line between Dubai International Airport and Dubai's second airport (Al Maktoum International Airport at Jebel Ali). A Blue line which would follow Emirates Road and an extension of the Red Line to Abu Dhabi and Sharjah are also being considered by the Roads and Transport Authority (RTA). The metro is planned to connect with the increasing amount of other public transport in the city, including buses and abras, and the light rail network on Palm Jumeirah. See Key Projects (p.81) for more information.

Taxi

If you don't have a car, taxis are the most common way of getting around. There are seven companies operating nearly 7,000 metered taxis with a fixed fare structure. The cars are all beige with different coloured roofs: Dubai Taxis are red, National Taxis are yellow, Cars Taxis are blue, Metro Taxis are brown, Al Arabia are green, City Taxis are white and Hatta Taxis are gold. A fleet of 'ladies taxis' was launched in 2007, with distinctive pink roofs. These cars have female drivers and are meant for female passengers or mixed-gender groups only.

The pickup fare ranges from Dhs.3 to Dhs.7, depending on the time of day and taxi company, and whether you order a taxi by phone, although the starting fare inside the airport area is an extortionate Dhs.25. It is also possible to hire a taxi for 12 or 24 hour periods. From December 2008, taxis will be exempt from Salik charges.

Towards the end of 2002, three non-metered taxi companies were once again permitted to work on Dubai's roads. Falling under a franchise of Dubai Transport, non-metered cabs operated by Dubai Taxi, Khaibar Taxi and Palestine Taxi allow customers the option of bargaining the fare down. If you do choose this type of taxi, try to find out what the normal cab fare should be first and agree on the fare before the ride. For the least hassle, you might be better off taking one of the more common metered taxis.

Taxis can be flagged down by the side of the road or you can make a Dubai Transport taxi booking by calling 04 208 0808. If you make a booking, you will pay a slightly higher starting fare (usually only Dhs.3 more than the standard starting fare). The DTC automated phone system stores your address after the first time you call. Each subsequent time you ring from that number, just listen to the prompts, hit 1, and a cab will be dispatched automatically, (or hit 2, then enter a later time using the phone's keypad). All DTC taxis now have GPS too, so the nearest car can reach you in the shortest time (in theory). Alternatively, if you drop Dhs.1 into one of the 15 electronic booking machines dotted around town, a taxi is immediately sent to the machine's location. A new system

Taxi Companies	
Al Marmoom Tourist Taxi	04 347 6650
Arabia Taxi	04 285 5566
Cars Taxis	04 269 3344
Dubai Taxi	04 208 0808
Emirates Taxi (Limosines Only)	04 339 4455
Gulf Radio Taxi	04 223 6666
Metro Taxi Co. LLC	04 267 3222
National Taxis	04 339 0002
Sharjah Delta Taxis	06 559 8598

being rolled out will also enable customers to book a taxi from the roadside by sending an SMS from their mobile phone. Boards are being placed across the city with a taxi sign and location code, customers simply text the code number to the central booking office and the nearest taxi will be sent.

If you're new in Dubai, or even if you are taking a taxi to a new place for the first time, it can be a good idea to get an idea of how much the journey should cost before you even get in the cab (not from the driver), and even a rough idea of the route. Occurrences are very rare, but some taxi drivers have taken their fares 'for a ride', so to speak. If you are in any doubt that your driver isn't taking you where he should, either take his number from his ID card or the taxi number and tell him you will be calling the company to complain, or just get out at the earliest opportunity. To make sure you are in the right, it's best to pay him off the amount on the meter, and then take the matter up with the company. The company's contact number will be on the outside of the car.

Illegal Pickups
There is an illegal taxi system, where unlicensed drivers in unmarked cars tout for passengers at the roadside. These cars are unregulated and are not insured to carry passengers. This practice is not looked upon favourably by Dubai Police and hefty fines are levied on convicted drivers.

To make life a little more confusing, taxi drivers in Dubai occasionally lack any knowledge of the city and passengers may have to direct them. Start with the area of destination and then choose a major landmark, such as a hotel, roundabout or shopping centre. Then narrow it down as you get closer. If you are going to a new place, try to phone for instructions first. It's also helpful to take the phone number of your destination with you, in case you're going around in circles trying to find it. If your taxi driver is well and truly lost, ask him to radio his control point for instructions. There's no minimum distance or fare on a journey, although there have been reports of some taxi drivers asking where you are going before you get into their cab, and refusing to take you if you're only going a short distance. Taxi companies insist that their drivers are obliged to accept any fare, whether it is five kilometres or 50. So either give your destination after you get inside the taxi or make a note of the taxi number and report it. In late 2008, the RTA launched an initiative whereby certain taxis would be assigned to a particular area of the city. This move attempts to make more taxis available in areas of the city where there is a shortage, or where drivers are reluctant to pick up passengers. Taxis can take passengers to their desired destination but must return to their allocated district afterwards.

From June 2008, a trial of hybrid engine taxis has been ongoing and although numbers will remain small with only 20 hybrid taxis available at the end of 2008, it seems to be a small step in the right direction.

Walking

Other options **Hiking** p.360

Cities in the UAE are generally very car oriented and not designed to encourage walking. Additionally, summer temperatures of over 45°C are not conducive to spending any length of time walking through the city. The winter months, however, make walking a pleasant way to get around and people can be found strolling through the streets, especially in the evenings. Most streets are lined with pavements and there are pedestrian paths either side of the creek, along the seafront in Deira and Jumeira, as well as in the parks throughout the city.

Police have vowed to crack down on jaywalking in Dubai in an effort to encourage people to cross roads at designated pedestrian crossings only. If you cross the road in an undesignated area, you could face a fine.

Cash For Gas

Strangely, you can't use your credit card to buy petrol at garages in Dubai. You used to be able to, but now all garages accept only cash at petrol pumps and in their forecourt convenience stores.

Money

Cash is still the preferred method of payment in the Emirates, although credit and debit cards are now widely accepted. Foreign currencies and travellers' cheques can be exchanged in licensed exchange offices, banks and hotels (as usual, a passport is required for exchanging travellers' cheques). Cheques are a bit more tricky; although strict enforcement of laws regulates the bouncing of cheques, many places still won't accept them.

If you're shopping in the souks and markets in Dubai, or in smaller shops, you're better off paying cash; even if a shop does accept other forms of payment, paying cash will help your bargaining stance.

Local Currency

The monetary unit is the dirham (Dhs.), which is divided into 100 fils. The currency is also referred to as AED (Arab Emirate dirham). Notes come in denominations of Dhs.5 (brown), Dhs.10 (green), Dhs.20 (light blue), Dhs.50 (purple), Dhs.100 (pink), Dhs.200 (orange), Dhs.500 (blue) and Dhs.1,000 (browny-purple). The denominations are indicated on the notes in both Arabic and English.

Coins are a bit trickier because the amount is written in Arabic only. Fortunately, there are only three different coin denominations in regular use: the Dhs.1, the 50 fils, and the 25 fils. All are silver in colour. The Dhs.1 coin is nearly 2.5cm in diameter and almost always has a traditional coffee pot imprinted on one side. On the other side, you will be able to read the English words 'United Arab Emirates', but everything else is in Arabic. The 50 fils coin is seven-sided rather than circular, and usually has a picture of an oil refinery on one side. The 25 fils coin is circular but smaller than the Dhs.1 coin and usually has a picture of a small antelope on one side.

You may come across older versions of the Dhs.1 and 50 fils coins that are still in circulation, and this can be confusing because the old Dhs.1 coin is bigger than the new one, and the old 50 fils coin is the same size as the new Dhs.1 coin. Because 5 fils and 10 fils coins are rarely available, you will often not receive the exact change – sometimes this will work in your favour, sometimes it will work against, but it probably averages out in the end.

To see examples of the UAE's banknotes, visit the website of the Central Bank of the UAE (www.centralbank.ae) and click on 'currency' on the left. The dirham has been pegged to the US dollar since 1980, at a mid rate of US$1 to Dhs.3.6725 (see the exchange rates table on the left). Kuwait cut the dollar peg in 2007, and the UAE, along with several other Gulf states, looks increasingly likely to consider doing the same. However, for the time being, the UAE Central Bank has stated that it will maintain ties to the dollar, and would only make a move along with other Arab countries. Another issue even more on the cards is a single currency for the GCC, although it looks likely that this will not happen until later than the initial target of 2010.

Exchange Rates

Foreign Currency (FC)	1 Unit FC =Dhs	Dhs1 = xFC
Australia	2.35	0.43
Bahrain	9.74	0.10
Bangladesh	0.05	18.57
Canada	2.91	0.34
Denmark	0.63	1.59
Euro	4.68	0.21
Hong Kong	0.47	2.11
India	0.074	13.51
Japan	0.04	26.08
Jordan	5.19	0.19
Kuwait	13.44	0.07
Malaysia	1.01	0.99
New Zealand	1.98	0.50
Oman	9.54	0.10
Pakistan	0.05	21.41
Philippines	0.07	13.47
Qatar	1.01	0.99
Saudi Arabia	0.98	1.02
Singapore	2.42	0.41
South Africa	0.36	2.74
Sri Lanka	0.03	29.94
Sweden	0.46	2.18
Switzerland	3.05	0.33
Thailand	0.10	9.59
UK	5.54	0.18
USA	3.68	0.27

Banks

A well-structured and ever-growing network of local and international banks, strictly controlled by the UAE Central Bank, offers a full range of commercial and personal banking services. Transfers can be made without difficulty as there is no exchange control and the dirham is freely convertible. To open a bank account in the UAE (with a few exceptions), you usually have to be a resident. Normal banking hours are usually Saturday to Thursday, from 08:00 to 13:00 or 14:00 (some banks also keep later hours). For more information on services offered by banks in the UAE, refer to Bank Accounts in the Residents section (p.108).

Main Banks		
ABN AMRO Bank	04 351 2200	www.abnamro.ae
Abu Dhabi Commercial Bank	04 295 8888	www.adcb.com
Arab Bank	04 295 0845	www.arabbank.ae
Bank of Sharjah	04 282 7278	www.bankofsharjah.com
Barclays Bank Plc	04 362 6700	www.barclays.ae
BNP Paribas	04 222 5200	www.bnpparibas.ae
Citibank – Middle East	04 324 5000	www.citibank.com/uae
Dubai Islamic Bank	04 295 9999	www.alislami.ae
Emirates Bank International	04 225 6256	www.emiratesbank.ae
Habib Bank AG Zurich	04 221 4535	www.habibbank.com
HSBC Bank Middle East	800 4722	www.uae.hsbc.com
Lloyds TSB Bank Plc ▶ p.109	04 342 2000	www.lloydstsb.ae
Mashreqbank	04 217 4800	www.mashreqbank.com
National Bank of Abu Dhabi	800 2211	www.nbad.com
National Bank of Dubai (NBD)	04 310 0101	www.nbd.com
RAKBANK	04 224 8000	www.rakbank.ae
Standard Chartered Bank – Middle East	04 352 0455	www.standardchartered.com
Union National Bank	800 2600	www.unb.co.ae

ATMs

Top Tip

Common payment systems accepted around Dubai include American Express, Cirrus, Global Access, MasterCard, Plus System and Visa.

Most banks operate ATMs (Automatic Teller Machines, also known as cash points or service tills) that accept a wide range of cards. Most ATMs, although linked to a specific bank, are part of a central network so you can use any bank card in them. They usually display a range of symbols indicating which networks they are linked to (such as Cirrus and Visa Electron). You will probably pay a minimal charge if you use an ATM that does not belong to your bank for cash withdrawals and balance enquiries (usually only a dirham or two). Most shopping centres and large supermarkets have at least one ATM, some petrol stations have one in the forecourt or inside the 24 hour shop, and a few hotels have one in their lobby. A recent spate of ATM fraud has affected the UAE; contact your bank immediately if you believe you have been the victim of fraud. Safeguard your pin, be alert to suspicious devices on the machines (but do not remove them – tell the bank at once), and if the machine swallows your card contact your bank immediately. For international cards, the exchange rates used in the transaction are normally competitive and the process is faster and much less hassle than traditional travellers' cheques.

Money Exchanges

Money exchanges can be found all over Dubai, offering good service and reasonable exchange rates, often better than the banks. You'll find at least one in all major shopping malls and in some popular shopping districts (such as Karama or the Gold Souk). Exchange centres are usually open from 08:30 to 13:00, and again from 16:30 to 20:30.

Exchange Centres			
Al Ansari Exchange	04 397 7787	www.alansariuae.com	9 F4
Al Fardan Exchange ▶ p.67	600 52 2265	www.alfardanexchange.com	8 F2
Al Ghurair Exchange	04 222 2955	www.alghurairexchange.com	9 C4
Al Rostamani Travel	04 295 6777	www.alrostamanigroup.com	7 E3
First Gulf Exchange	04 351 5777	www.fgb.ae	11 C3
Wall Street Exchange Centre	800 4871	www.wallstreet.ae	9 C2

Hotels will usually exchange money and travellers' cheques at the standard (non-competitive) hotel rate. For more details about exchanges, refer to the table below, which lists some of the biggest names in town. Visit the website or call to find out the location of the nearest branch.

Credit Cards

Most shops, hotels and restaurants accept the major credit cards (American Express, Diners Club, MasterCard and Visa). Smaller retailers are sometimes less likely to accept credit cards and if they do you may have to pay an extra 5% for processing (and it's no use telling them that it's a contravention of the card company rules – you have to take it or leave it). Conversely, if you are paying in cash, you may sometimes be allowed a discount – it's certainly worth enquiring.

The general rule concerning the loss or theft of credit cards is to contact the bank as soon as possible and report the missing card. Once you have reported the loss it is highly unlikely that you will be held liable for any further transactions made on the card. As a consequence of ATM fraud, banks have now set a limit on the amount of cash you can withdraw per day in order to limit the financial damage of stolen credit cards (the amount varies from card to card). In addition to these measures, banks also advise the public on how to prevent credit card crime. A frequent problem is that people do not change their pin when they get the card. This is vital for secrecy, and banks also suggest you change your pin on a regular basis even after the initial necessary change.

Festival City

Tipping

Tipping practices are similar at all hotels, bars and restaurants around Dubai. Tips in restaurants are often shared with other staff. It is, however, still worth tipping and all tips, even when they are shared, are greatly appreciated. An increasing number of restaurants now also include a service charge on the bill, although it's not clear whether this ever sees the inside of your waiter's pockets. The usual amount to tip is 10% and this covers most services. It is however entirely up to the individual whether to tip and it is not a fixed expectation as you find in other countries. See Going Out for more information (p.525).

For taxi drivers it is regular practice to round up your fare as a tip, but this is not compulsory, so feel free to pay just the fare, especially if his driving standards were poor. For tipping when collecting your valet-parked car at hotels, around Dhs.5 is average. At petrol stations, especially when you get your windows cleaned, it's common practice to give a few dirhams as a tip. To avoid any confusion, wait for them to give you your change, and then hand them back their tip.

Newspapers & Magazines

The UAE has a growing number of daily English language newspapers. Until 2004, there were three main players: *Gulf News* (Dhs.3), *Khaleej Times* and *Gulf Today* (both Dhs.2 every day except for Fridays when a glossy magazine is included and the price goes up to Dhs.3). All three titles are of somewhat dubious quality compared with the top newspapers in other countries, with *Gulf News* being better in terms of design, writing and editorial comment. These newspapers are all government mouthpieces to varying degrees, and so you will rarely read anything critical of the UAE government, any member of the royal family or the interests of big business in the region. However, recent years have seen a big shake-up in the industry, starting in 2004 with the launch of *7Days*. Although it started out as a weekly paper, this tabloid-size publication is now distributed free of charge six days a week and features local, international, business and entertainment news and a sports section. It has pushed some of the boundaries of press freedom in the country, which should benefit the industry in the long run. In 2007, Al Nisr Group (the publisher of *Gulf News*) launched *XPRESS*, a free, weekly tabloid. This new title features a good mix of local news and human interest stories. *The National*, published in Abu Dhabi, is a daily UAE newspaper recently launched in 2008, offering a special weekend edition. Arabic language newspapers published in the UAE include *Al Bayan*, *Al Ittihad* and *Al Khaleej*. An international edition of UK broadsheet, *The Times*, is also printed and distributed in Dubai.

Censorship

International magazines are available in bookshops and supermarkets, at greatly inflated prices. All international titles are examined by the censor and anything offensive is crossed out with a big black marker. Even pictures of mothers lovingly breastfeeding their newborns in Mother & Baby *will be blacked out.*

The local magazine industry is thriving, with new titles being added seemingly every month. For info on Dubai's social scene and upcoming events, get your hands on *Time Out Dubai* (published weekly), *Connector* or *What's On* (both published monthly). *Aquarius* is a monthly magazine that also lists upcoming events and special offers in Dubai, with a health and beauty theme. *Aquarius* and *Connector* are distributed free of charge to certain outlets (you can usually pick up a copy in schools, doctors' offices and hair and beauty salons) or sold in bookshops and supermarkets if you can't find a free copy.

VIVA and *Emirates Woman* are monthly women's magazines with interesting features, beauty news and fashion spreads. These were recently joined by Middle East editions of the monthly fashion magazine *Harper's Bazaar* and glossy weekly, *Grazia*. For technology and gadget news, there is also a local edition of *Stuff* magazine.

The freehold housing boom is reflected in the number of homeowners' and decor magazines available, including *Inside Out* and *Emirates Home*. *Spinneys Food* is the Spinneys in-house magazine and is full of good recipes; it is available from Spinneys supermarkets. Other interesting local magazines include *Emirates Bride*, *Arabian Business* and *Gulf Marketing Review*.

With Dubai being such a sociable place full of so many people just dying to be seen, no discussion of the magazine industry would be complete without making mention of *Ahlan!*, *Society Dubai*, *OK Middle East* and *Hello! Middle East*. These glossy magazines feature syndicated articles on celebrity lifestyles (browse through six-page spreads of so-

Pushing The Limits

A final word on local magazines in Dubai: don't expect to find anything too similar to *FHM* or *GQ* just yet. Censorship laws are relaxing slowly, but they are still light years away from allowing local magazines with scantily clad women in provocative poses. Local men's mag *FO!* had its licence revoked after just two issues – supposedly for not sticking to its business plan but whispers in the industry claim it had more to do with the pictures that appeared in the second issue, despite a warning following the first.

and-so, star of such-and-such, relaxing in their glamorous home) as well as society pages with photographs of local party-goers out on the town. While the Middle East editions of *OK* and *Hello!* have not quite reached the same status as their UK counterparts, it still might be fun to phone home and tell your mum that you're in this week's edition of *OK*.

International Press

Foreign newspapers, mostly French, German, British and Asian, are available in supermarkets and bookshops, although they are more expensive than at home (about Dhs.8 to Dhs.12) and slightly out of date. One exception is *The Times*. An international edition of this daily UK title is now available on the morning of publication for Dhs.7. Other titles are available through Todaily (www.todaily.com), which releases international newspapers on the published date. Limited copies are available in Carrefour and Spinneys, but if you log on to its website you can subscribe to more than 200 titles from around the world.

Cultural Corner

Dubai Community Theatre & Arts Centre (DUCTAC), based in Mall of the Emirates, is well worth a visit. Art displays, theatre performances, and all kinds of classes are on offer, ranging from salsa to ballet dancing. (www.ductac.org).

Books

Other options **Websites** p.69, **Books** (Shopping, p.428)

As well as this residents' guide, Explorer Publishing also produces the *Dubai Mini Visitors' Guide* – a guidebook that is small in size, but packed full of all the information visitors need to know about Dubai. In terms of other tourist publications, publishers such as Time Out, Lonely Planet and Footprint have visitors' guides to Dubai and the United Arab Emirates.

If you want to read more about Dubai, the UAE and the Middle East region in general, there are plenty of books to choose from. Explorer Publishing also publishes the *Abu Dhabi Complete Residents' Guide*, as well as guides to Bahrain, Kuwait, Oman and Qatar. It also produces a range of regional activity guides, such as the *UAE Off-Road Explorer*, *Oman Off-Road Explorer* and the *Oman Trekking Explorer*. The *Dubai Red-Tape Explorer* guides you through the ins and outs of bureaucracy in Dubai and is essential for anybody trying to get settled in the city.

If you are looking for beautiful photographs of the region, have a look at *Images of Dubai and the UAE*, *Images of Abu Dhabi and the UAE*, *Sharjah's Architectural Splendour* and *Dubai: Tomorrow's City Today*, *Dubai Discovered* is a condensed pictorial tour of Dubai, featuring stunning images and published in five languages (English, French, Russian, Japanese and German). For a fascinating historical tour back in time, read *Telling Tales: An Oral History of Dubai*. All these photography books are published by Explorer Publishing and are available in bookshops and supermarkets. For a different perspective, read any of Wilfred Thesiger's books on his experiences in the deserts of the Middle East.

Websites

The table below lists various websites on Dubai and the UAE in general, which should be of interest to residents and visitors.

Websites	
Dubai Information	
www.7days.ae	Local newspaper
www.dnrd.gov.ae	Dubai Naturalisation & Residency Department
www.du-fam.com	A new site and forum especially for families in Dubai
www.dubai.ae	Official Dubai eGovernment portal
www.dubaiairport.com/dubaimet	Dubai's current weather and five day forecast

Websites

Dubai Information

www.dubaicityguide.com	Updated daily lists of upcoming and current events
www.dubaiclassified.com	Buying, selling, jobs and services
www.dubaidonkey.com	Free listings website – jobs, property, cars and more
www.dubaiinformer.com	News and rumours from in and around Dubai
www.dubaikidz.biz	Great site for kids' info
www.dubailime.com	Community, entertainment, business and classifieds
www.dubaitourism.ae	Department of Tourism & Commerce Marketing
www.dubizzle.com	Dubai's largest website for classifieds and community
www.expatgossip.com	A lively chatboard with lots of members
www.expatwoman.com	General information on living in UAE, woman's perspective
www.godubai.com	Covers all the events and news of Dubai
www.gulf-news.com	Local newspaper
www.howdoidubai.com	Information on living in Dubai
www.khaleejtimes.com	Local newspaper
www.liveworkexplore.com	Essential info on living in Dubai from Explorer Publishing
www.platinumlistdubai.com	Get on the guestlist for top Dubai nights out
www.roomservice-uae.com	Deliveries from your favourite restaurants
www.sheikhmohammed.co.ae	His Highness Sheikh Mohammed Bin Rashid Al Maktoum
www.sheikhzayed.com	A site dedicated to the life of the late UAE President
www.shouscene.com	News and listings for upcoming gigs and music events
www.souk.ae	The middle east's online market – mainly for books
www.souq.com	UAE auction and marketplace
www.timeoutdubai.com	Time Out Dubai
www.uaemall.com	Shop online in the UAE
www.yellowpages.ae	Yellow Pages on the net

Business/Industry

http://web.dcci.ae	Dubai Chamber of Commerce & Industry
www.dewa.gov.ae	Dubai Electricity & Water Authority
www.dm.gov.ae	Dubai Municipality
www.du.ae	Dubai's newest telephone and internet services provider
www.dubaiairport.com	Dubai International Airport
www.dubaidutyfree.com	Dubai Duty Free
www.dubaipolice.gov.ae	Dubai Police Headquarters
www.dwtc.com	Dubai World Trade Centre
www.dxbtraffic.gov.ae	Dubai Traffic Police – great for viewing traffic fines
www.e4me.co.ae	View and pay phone bills online
www.etisalat.ae	Dubai's original telephone service provider

Embassies

www.embassyworld.com	Search Engine for World's Embassies

UAE Information

www.ameinfo.com	Middle East business news
www.arabianwildlife.com	The UAE's flora and fauna
www.autodealer.ae	Used cars for sale in the UAE
www.das.ae	Weather info from the Department of Atmospheric Studies
www.government.ae	UAE Government 'e-portal' – lots of good info
www.uaeinsider.com	Classifieds, news and business info
www.uaeinteract.com	UAE Ministry of Information & Culture

Annual Events

Throughout the year, Dubai hosts a number of well-established annual events, some of which have been running for years. Whether you're keen to chill out to jazz performances from international artists, show off your prized pooch, or watch the world's best tennis stars, the emirate offers some great experiences. Some of the most popular and regular fixtures on Dubai's social calendar are described below.

January
Al Ain Airport

Al Ain Aerobatic Show
www.alainaerobaticshow.com

This five-day annual air show takes places at the Al Ain International Airport and sees participation from flying daredevils from around the world. There is a spectator grandstand for plane enthusiasts and those looking for a fun day out. Both military and civilian planes take part in the aerobatic displays.
There is also a biennial air show event in Dubai (the next will be November 2009).

January
Emirates Golf Club

Dubai Desert Classic
www.dubaidesertclassic.com

Tiger Woods won the tournament last year to the joy of many of Dubai's residents. Being a popular expat sport, the turn out each year does not disappoint. In case Tiger Woods heads your way, remember to dress to impress!

January
World Trade Centre

Dubai Marathon
www.dubaimarathon.org

Normally held in January (good for working off that festive tummy), the Dubai Marathon now offers a full marathon as well as a 10km road race and 3km charity run. The event attracts all types of runners, with the emphasis more on fun and participation than competition.

January to February
Various Locations

Dubai Shopping Festival
www.mydsf.com

A combination of a festival and a shopping extravaganza, Dubai Shopping Festival, or DSF as it is popularly known, is hard to miss as buildings and roads are decorated with coloured lights. There are bargains galore in the participating outlets. Highlights include spectacular fireworks each evening, the international wonders of Global Village and numerous raffles. It's a great (although sometimes rather congested) time to be in the city of Dubai.

January
Dubai International Convention & Exhibition Centre

The Wellbeing Show 2009

The bigger, brighter Wellbeing Show is held annually at the Dubai International Convention and Exhibition Centre. With demonstrations, seminars and workshops on looking and feeling good, fitness and health, food and nutrition, and mind, body and soul, this exhibition is a must for anyone looking to turn over a new leaf in the new year.

February
Nad Al Sheba

Dubai Pet Show
www.dubaipetshow.com

Held at Nad Al Sheda (usually on a Saturday) and sponsored by Pedigree Chum and Whiskas, the Pet Show is a popular family outing and the only show of its kind in the Middle East. You are guaranteed to see both pedigree and crossbreed dogs of every shape, size and colour imaginable. One of the most popular events is the 'Dog Most Like its Owner' competition – the likenesses are often uncanny. The demonstration by the police dog unit is also fascinating.

February
Aviation Club

Dubai Tennis Championships

www.dubaitennischampionships.com

The US$1,000,000 Dubai Duty Free Tennis Open is a popular and well-supported event. It is firmly established on the international tennis circuit and offers the chance for fans to see top seeds, both male and female, in an intimate setting. The Williams sisters, Rafael Nadal, Roger Federer and Maria Sharapova have all graced Dubai's courts in past tournaments. Held at the tennis stadium at the Aviation Club, so in between matches you can nip to the Irish Village for a pint.

February
Dubai International Convention & Exhibition Centre

International Property Show

www.internationalpropertyshow.ae

Featuring everything to do with buying international property, this show is particularly popular among expats who are looking to invest overseas. The 2009 exhibition will feature property from the Middle East and around the world.

February
Wonderland

Terry Fox Run

www.dubaiterryfoxrun.com

Each year, thousands of individuals run, jog, walk, cycle, and rollerblade their way around an 8.5km course for charity. The proceeds go to cancer research programmes at approved institutions around the world. Check the local media for contact details nearer the time.

March

Dubai Bike Week

www.dubaibikeweek.com

An annual festival celebrating motorcycles is now held in Festival City, where all kinds of biking-related activities take place such as stunt shows, motorbike displays and test rides. Promising to be bigger and better than previous events, Harley-Davidson will be organising it in conjunction with Festival City, so it's a good chance to get up close to some magnificent machines (and the characters who ride them). It's an interactive festival, and ideal entertainment for families.

March
Emirates Golf Club

Great British Day

www.britbiz-uae.com

With a village fete atmosphere, cream teas and fish and chips, the Great British Day guarantees a good family day out. It is organised by the British Business Group and is usually held on a Friday. Thousands of people of all nationalities attend the event and enjoy competitions, bouncy castles, live music, handicraft stalls and a terrific fireworks display as the grand finale.

March
DIMC

Dubai International Boat Show

www.boatshowdubai.com

If you love big boats then this is the event for you – even if you don't have the big bucks to afford one. Dubai International Boat Show, the largest marine industry exhibition in the Middle East, is a classic showcase of yachts and boats from both local and international builders, together with the latest innovations in marine equipment and accessories.

March
Dubai Media City

Dubai International Jazz Festival

www.chilloutproductions.com

If you are looking for a night of chilled moods, then this is the place to be. Established as an annual event over the last few years, this nine-day festival attracts a strong line-up of top artists from all around the world, and grows in popularity each year. It features performances from internationally recognised artists.

March
Nad Al Sheba

Dubai World Cup
www.dubaiworldcup.com
The Dubai World Cup is billed as the richest horse race in the world – last year's total prize money was over US$15,000,000. The prize for the Group One Dubai World Cup race alone was a staggering US$6,000,000. It is held on a Saturday to ensure maximum media coverage in the west. With a buzzing, vibrant atmosphere, it's a great opportunity to dress up and dig out your favourite hat.

March
DIMC

Powerboat Racing
www.dimc-uae.com
The UAE is well established on the world championship powerboat racing circuit – in Abu Dhabi with Formula One (Inshore) and in Dubai and Fujairah with Class One (Offshore). These events make a great spectacle, ideal for the armchair sports fan. Events in Dubai are held at the Dubai International Marine Club (DIMC, 04 399 4111).

March
The Sevens Stadium

Rugby World Cup 7s
www.rwcsevens.com
Following the continued success of the annual 7s tournament, Dubai will be the proud host of the Rugby 7s World Cup in 2009. Fans from all corners of the globe are expected to flock to the stunning new grounds (The Sevens), and tickets, already on sale, are sure to sell out fast.

April
World Trade Centre

Bride Show Dubai 2009
www.thebrideshow.com
The Bride Show is the largest bridal exhibition in the region, and brings the whole wedding industry together. Brides can browse through dresses, choose photographers and entertainment, pick their honeymoon destinations and meet wedding organisers. It's a must-do before you say 'I do'.

April
Aviation Club, Garhoud

Dubai Masters Football Cup
www.mastersfootballdubai.com
Watch former stars relive their glory days, as ex-Liverpool, Manchester United, Celtic and Rangers players compete for their former clubs in an evening of televised six-a-side matches. Legends such as Ian Rush and Lee Sharpe still have the silky skills that once electrified the crowds at Old Trafford and Anfield. Standard tickets cost Dhs.125.

June to August
Various Locations

Dubai Summer Surprises
www.mydsf.com
Dubai Summer Surprises is held to attract visitors during the hot and humid summer months. Aimed at families, it offers fun packed activities, generally held in climate-controlled facilities, such as shopping malls, specially constructed areas and hotels. Events are based on food, heritage, technology, family values and education.

October

Dubai Fashion Week
www.dfw.ae
This festival of fashion gives an opportunity to regional fashion designers to present their collections to the world's fashion media, together with the public. Designers whose work has been modelled on the catwalk include Walid Atallah and Aiisha Ramadan. Held at the glamorous Emirates Towers in the Godolphin Ballroom, this is one of the glitziest events on the Dubai social calendar, but is by invitation only.

October
Dubai International
Exhibition &
Convention Centre

Dubai World Game Expo

www.gameexpo.ae

A calendar highlight for all gaming fans wanting to try out the latest software and hardware in the market. Includes the Dubai World Game Championship.

October to May
DIMC

Dhow Racing

www.dimc-uae.com

This traditional Arabic sport is great to watch; there is something enigmatic about wooden dhows gliding gracefully over the water, especially when they're racing. The vessels are usually between 40ft and 60ft in length and are either powered by men (up to 100 oarsmen per dhow) or by the wind. Fixed races are held throughout the year as well as on special occasions, such as National Day.

October
Dubai International
Convention &
Exhibition Centre

GITEX

www.gitex.com

One of the largest and most successful international exhibitions for computing, communications systems and applications in the IT industry, Gitex gets bigger every year. The five-day exhibition, now in its 27th year, is renowned for its Gitex Computer Shopper where the public can snap up some great deals on technology.

October or November
Burj Al Arab

Swim The Burj

www.swimburjalarab.com

This event, organised by Medecins San Frontieres, gives you the chance to do a sponsored swim around the spectacular Burj Al Arab hotel. It is about a kilometre in total, great fun and all for a very good cause. There's a serious race for those who are very competitive swimmers, and a fun swim. Lifeguards are on hand and the number of participants is strictly limited. For more details, call 04 345 8177.

October or November
Jebel Ali Racecourse &
Empty Quarter

UAE Desert Challenge

www.uaedesertchallenge.com

This is the highest profile motorsport event in the country and is often the culmination of the World Cup in cross country rallying. Following prestigious events, such as the Paris – Dakar race, this event attracts some of the world's top rally drivers and bike riders who compete in the car, truck and moto-cross categories. The race takes place in several stages across the harsh and challenging terrain of the desert, including a spectator event in Dubai. For more details call 04 266 9922.

November
Various Locations

Desert Rallies

www.emsf.ae

The highest profile event is the Desert Challenge (above), which is the climax of the World Cup in Cross Country Rallying. It attracts top rally drivers from all over the world and is usually held in October or November, depending on other events. There are numerous other events throughout the year; contact EMSF (04 282 7111).

November to
December
The Sevens Stadium

Dubai Rugby 7s

www.dubairugby7s.com

This three-day event is a very popular sporting and spectator fixture. With alcohol on sale at the stadium, the party atmosphere carries on until late. Top international teams compete for the coveted 7s trophy (the Dubai tournament is usually the first leg of the IRB Sevens Tournament), while local teams from all over the Gulf try their luck in various competitions, including women's rugby. This has become one of the biggest sporting and partying weekends of the year in Dubai and attracts up to 150,000 spectators over the three days.

Annual Events

November to April
Nad Al Sheba

Horse Racing
www.dubairacingclub.com

Nad Al Sheba racecourse is one of the world's leading racing facilities and home to the Dubai World Cup. Racing takes place at night under floodlights, and begins at 19:00 (except during Ramadan when it is at 21:00). General admission and parking are free, but badge holders and members. have access to a reserved area. Day membership on race nights starts from Dhs.60. Everyone can take part in free competitions to select the winning horses, with the ultimate aim of taking home prizes or cash.

December
Madinat Jumeirah

Dubai International Film Festival
www.diff.ae

Having debuted in December 2004, this has become a hotly anticipated annual event and marks a great achievement for the film industry in Dubai. Last year it was hosted at Madinat Jumeirah and attracted some well-known industry players such as Morgan Freeman, Orlando Bloom and Sarah Michelle Gellar. The festival brings together a collection of international films, including those from the Arab world.

December
Starts at Dubai
Autodrome

Fun Drive
www.gulf-news.com

If your idea of fun is venturing through the wilderness of the UAE with 750 other 4WDs, then this event is for you. Spread over two days, the Fun Drive is a very sociable, guided off-road trip. Early booking is advised. Contact the Gulf News Promotions Department for more information. Gulf News also organises a daytrip Fun Drive.

December
Dubai International
Convention &
Exhibition Centre

Mother, Baby & Child Show
www.motherbabyandchild.com

Mums and kids will love this show, featuring exhibits by child-friendly companies and lots of entertainment for the little ones. Make sure you pick up a plastic bag at the entrance, because as you walk round you get given loads of samples and giveaways.

December
Sharjah Expo Centre

Sharjah World Book Fair
www.swbf.gov.ae

This annual event, one of the oldest and largest book fairs in the Arab World, takes place at the Sharjah Expo Centre and boasts participation from 35 countries. Thousands of titles in Arabic, English and many other languages are displayed by private book publishers, governments and universities.

December

X Games Dubai
www.xgamesdubai.com

Competitions involving adrenaline-fuelled BMX freestyle (including street and vert categories), skateboarding and moto x (where the best trick is the winner), all attract competitors from all around the world, and are available to watch for free in Festival City.

All year round
Various Locations

Exhibitions
www.dubaitourism.ae

With the increasing importance of MICE (meetings, incentives, conferences, exhibitions) tourism to Dubai, there are currently two large state-of-the-art exhibition spaces showcasing a variety of exhibitions each year. These are the Airport Expo (Map 13 F3) and the exhibition halls at the Dubai World Trade Centre (Map 10 A1). For details of exhibitions in Dubai, contact Dubai's Department of Tourism & Commerce Marketing (04 223 0000).

KIDS CLUB AND
CLUB RUSH BIRTHDAY PARTIES

Residents

Residents

Overview

Dubai is without a doubt a destination of the 21st century. Read any article about the fastest growing city in the region and it's almost guaranteed you'll see the words 'ambitious', 'record-breaking' and 'staggering'. This meteoric growth has not gone unnoticed, and each year thousands of expats arrive to claim a slice of the action. Dubai certainly has a lot to offer, and this book aims to provide you with all the information needed to make the most of your new life here and minimise the bureaucracy.

The Residents chapter takes you through every imaginable aspect of living in Dubai – whether you are reading this as you sit in the comfort of your home country while contemplating a sojourn abroad, are fresh off the plane with your whole life in a suitcase, have called Dubai home for months or even years, or are about to say your bittersweet farewells.

One thing you do need to remember is that procedures and laws change regularly, often in quite major ways. Changes are generally announced in the newspapers and can be implemented overnight – so be prepared for the unexpected.

Considering The City

Living in Dubai has much to offer. The sun shines almost every day, the shopping and leisure facilities are impressive, and the salaries are tax-free. Of course, there are hassles and annoyances, but for many these are outweighed by the positives.

But, with Dubai's dizzying growth and rising popularity, the expat experience has changed in recent years. Whereas once it was easy for expats to get work, more competition means employers can be pickier. And with candidates arriving from all over the world, salaries are dropping. But opportunities remain.

The cost of living is on the up too, with rents seeing significant increases. To make it worthwhile you may need to hold out for a good expat package with housing, schooling, and medical expenses included. These generous packages are not as common as they were. Before jumping on the first plane, test the job market by sending some emails to potential employers and monitoring the overseas appointments pages and recruitment websites (p.104).

You also need to consider how you're going to enter the country and stay here. To remain in Dubai on a permanent basis you need a residency permit (often called a visa), and to get this you need a 'sponsor'. For employed people, their company will be their sponsor. These employees should then be able to sponsor members of their family (subject to certain conditions, see p.86). If you don't have work lined up, you may be able to enter on a visit visa (see p.82), but this is for a limited period only.

Before You Arrive

If you're coming to Dubai to work, or even just to look for work, you should have any qualification certificates and important documents (such as your marriage certificate, and kids' birth certificates) attested in your home country. This can be quite a lengthy process, and involves solicitors and the UAE foreign embassy.

Property owners may consider selling up before the move, but don't be hasty. It may be wise to test the water and give yourself a year before you commit long-term – although many people have come for a year or two and are still in the country five years later. If you do own property in your home country you could consider letting for the first year, until you've settled in. You also need to get your financial affairs in order, such as telling banks and building societies, and the tax office. Speak to your pension company too – moving abroad could have implications on your contributions (see Financial & Legal Affairs, p.108). If you've got kids you should start researching schools

Drinking In DXB

While drinking alcohol is forbidden for Muslims, it is served in the many bars, clubs and restaurants throughout Dubai. However, you won't find a booze aisle in your local supermarket, although some people have made the mistake of stocking up on the 0% alcohol beers that line the shelves. Two companies operate liquor stores, but you'll need a licence to buy alcohol (see p.92).

as soon as possible. New schools are opening all the time to keep up with Dubai's growing population, but places are not guaranteed, so get your name down in plenty of time (see Education, p.203). Finding a place to live is one of the most important tasks in moving to a new country so, if possible, you should take your time and explore all the different residential areas Dubai has to offer (see p.128). A good idea is to arrange temporary accommodation, maybe in a furnished apartment (see p.50), while you look for your perfect home. If you have been employed from your home country some companies will pay for this initial accommodation. When you do move it's likely you'll want to bring more than just a suitcase with you, so speak to shipping and/or relocation companies, and book well in advance (for more information, see p.160). If you're coming to look for employment, do your homework before you arrive. Contact recruitment agencies and sign up with online job sites as far in advance as possible. There may also be agencies in your home country that specialise in overseas recruitment. The Work section (p.98) should give you some handy information.

When You Arrive

The list of things you'll have to deal with in the first few weeks can be a little daunting, and you may well be in for a lot of form filling, queuing, and coming and going. Try not to let it spoil things though, because you'll hopefully soon be a fully fledged resident enjoying your new life, and all that boring bureaucracy will be a distant memory. Some of the key issues you should be covering are listed below.

- Residency/visas – if you're on an employment or residency visa, you'll apply for a health card, take the medical test, and get your residency permit (see p.86). If you're on a visit visa, either sort out your sponsorship (by a company or family member) or be prepared to make 'visa runs' (p.84). A UAE ID card is in the process of being introduced for all residents, which will combine your labour, health and eGate cards in one (p.84).
- Furnish your new home and get connected – for advice on furnishings and how to get the water, electricity, phone and TV connected, see p.171 and p.176.
- Buy a car – for advice on what's available, how to go about it, and the registration process, see Vehicles, p.232.

Dubai Marina

- Licences – get your driving licence, and get a liquor licence if you want to buy alcohol. See licences on p.91 and p.92.
- Register with your embassy – it's always worthwhile letting your embassy know you're living here. See the table on p.33.
- Get acquainted – to help you settle in and find like-minded individuals, consider joining a social group.

Visa On Arrival ◀

Citizens of the following countries receive an automatic visa on arrival: Andorra, Australia, Austria, Belguim, Brunei, Canada, Cyprus, Denmark, Finland, France, Germany, Greece, Hong Kong, Iceland, Ireland, Italy, Japan, Liechtenstein, Luxembourg, Malaysia, Malta, Monaco, Netherlands, New Zealand, Norway, Portugal, San Marino, Singapore, South Korea, Spain, Sweden, Switzerland, United Kingdom, United States of America and Vatican City.

Essential Documents

For many procedures you'll have to produce your 'essential documents'. At the very least these are:
- Original passport
- Passport photocopies (including photo page and visa page if appropriate)
- Passport photographs

Depending on the procedure, you may also have to show a copy of your labour contract, a salary certificate, a tenancy contract, and a no objection certificate (NOC) from your company or sponsor. It's also a good idea to make copies of all your original documents and store them in a safe place.

You're going to need a lot of photographs over the coming months, as just about everything you do requires a copy of your passport and a photograph – whether you're applying for a health card, getting a phone connection or joining your local gym. To save time and money, when you have your photos done ask for the original negative or a CD. Duplicate photos can then be made easily. There are hundreds of photo shops all over Dubai that offer this service, and you'll pay around Dhs.20 for a dozen pictures. Often when renting a house or opening a bank account you have to produce a salary certificate from your employer to confirm that you are employed and earn the minimum salary requirement. You may have also be asked for an NOC (no objection certificate) from your employer when renting a property, buying a car, opening a bank account or applying for your driving licence, although it is not always a requirement. Either way, any paperwork provided by your employer should be on a company letterhead, signed and stamped with the company stamp to make it undeniably 'official'.

When You Leave

Rather than just jetting off, there are certain things that have to be wound up before you leave, such as:
- Electricity and water – give DEWA at least two days' notice before you leave the property. They'll take a final reading and return your security deposit (p.171).
- Landlord – make sure the place is spick and span, otherwise you may lose some of your deposit. The landlord may also require a clearance certificate from DEWA to prove you've paid all the bills.
- Sell your car – not always a straightforward job, and the second-hand garages can smell a departing expat a mile off so be prepared for lots of ridiculously low offers. For a list of used car dealers, see p.231.
- Shipping – just as when you arrived, the more notice you can give the removal/relocation company the better. For a list of companies, see p.160.
- Sell your home contents – sometimes easier (and cheaper) than shipping them half way across the world. The beauty of Dubai is that it is still a transient city, so there are often leavers looking to sell and newcomers looking to buy. You can put a notice on supermarket noticeboards or even have your own garage sale.

Red tape, unfamiliar bureaucracy and living out of a suitcase can make expat life a little stressful at the start, but year-round sunshine, golden sandy beaches, modern facilities, first-class shopping and some of the region's best restaurants and bars can make it all worthwhile.

We have what you want to lay your hands on.

Entry Visa

Visa Change

2008 saw many changes regarding visit visas for the UAE. In a nutshell, newspaper reports stated that all visitors (even those on the previous list for visas on entry) would now be charged for a visit visa and would get 30 days only (with no extension). However, in practice there seems to have been little impact and many nationalities are still getting free, extendable visit visas on arrival. Always cover yourself by checking beforehand with the UAE embassy in your home country for the latest rules before you arrive.

Visa requirements for entering Dubai vary greatly between different nationalities, and regulations should always be checked before travelling since details can change with little or no warning. GCC nationals (Bahrain, Kuwait, Qatar, Oman and Saudi Arabia) do not need a visa to enter Dubai. Citizens from many other countries (including the UK, USA, Australia, Canada and many EU countries) get an automatic visa upon arrival at the airport (see the full list of 33 countries on p.80). The entry visa is valid for 30 days, although you can renew for a further 30 days at a cost of Dhs.620 (see Visa Renewal, p.84).

Holders of British overseas passports issued in Hong Kong or China are also entitled to a visa on arrival at Dubai International Airport.

Expats with residency in other GCC countries, who do not belong to one of the 33 visa on arrival nationalities but who do meet certain criteria (professions such as managers, doctors and engineers) can get a non-renewable 30 day visa on arrival – check with your airline before flying.

People of certain nationalities who are visiting the Sultanate of Oman may also enter Dubai on a free-of-charge entry permit. The same criteria and facilities apply to Dubai visitors entering Oman (although if you have Dubai residency you will pay a small charge).

All other nationalities can get a 30 day tourist visa sponsored by a local entity, such as a hotel or tour operator, before entry into the UAE. The fee is Dhs.100 for the visa and can be renewed for a further 30 days for an additional Dhs.600.

Citizens of eastern European countries, countries that belonged to the former Soviet Union, China and South Africa can get a 30 day, non-renewable tourist visa sponsored by a local entity, such as a hotel or tour operator, before entry into the UAE. The fee is Dhs.100 for the visa and an additional Dhs.20 for delivery. Other visitors can apply for an entry service permit (exclusive of arrival/departure days), valid for use within 14 days of the date of issue and non-renewable. Once this visa expires the visitor must remain out of the country for 30 days before re-entering on a new visit visa. The application fee for this visa is Dhs.120, plus an additional Dhs.20 delivery charge.

For those travelling onwards to a destination other than that of the original departure, a special transit visa (up to 96 hours) may be obtained free of charge through certain airlines operating in the UAE.

A multiple-entry visa is available to visitors who have a relationship with a local business, meaning they have to visit that business regularly. It is valid for visits of a maximum of 14 days each time, for six months from date of issue.

Visitors

If you live in Dubai and friends or family want to visit you, but they don't qualify for an automatic visit visa on arrival (see p.80), there are various options. If they are staying in a hotel, most hotels offer a visa service. If they are flying with Emirates, the airline can arrange a visit visa (for an extra fee). Or you can arrange a visa for them – you'll need their passport copy, your own passport with your residency permit, your employment contract showing your salary, or a salary certificate for free zone workers, and sometimes your tenancy contract (not always required). Minimum salary requirements apply: a total salary of Dhs.3,000 plus housing allows you to sponsor your parents, Dhs.5,000 plus housing and your siblings can come too, and Dhs.9,000 means you can arrange visas for friends. Apply at the Immigration Department. Once the visa is approved, fax a copy to your visitors and deposit the original at the airport or, for a small fee, use the visa delivery service.

It costs Dhs.1,000 and should be applied for after entering the UAE on a visit visa. For an additional Dhs.200, a multiple entry visa holder is eligible for the eGate service (see p.84). Companies may levy a maximum of Dhs.50 extra in processing charges for arranging visas. The DNATA (Dubai National Airline Travel Agency) visa delivery service costs an extra Dhs.20.

Fully Fledged Resident

After entering Dubai on an employment or residency visa, you have 60 days to complete all of the procedures involved in becoming a resident (although it's unlikely to take anywhere near that long). If you need to leave the country again before the process is completed, you should be able to do so as long as you have the entry visa that was stamped in your passport when you first entered. It's probably best though if you avoid booking any holidays in those first few weeks.

Visa Renewals

Visit visas valid for renewal may be extended for a further 30 days at the Department of Immigration and Naturalisation (04 398 1010), Karama, near the Dubai World Trade Centre Roundabout. The fee is Dhs.610. The official stance is that at the end of this period, you must leave the country and remain out of the country for a period of one month or more before re-entering on a new visa. An unofficial alternative would be to leave and re-enter the country on a 'visa run', although the law has tightened with regard to this (see p.84).

While the current rules generally grant a 30 day visa free of charge to the 33 nationalities listed on p.80, discrepancies do sometimes occur. There is still a good deal of confusion with regard to the new laws which were introduced in mid 2008, and as rules and regulations have a habit of changing without notice you are best advised to check with the UAE consulate or embassy in your home country, or at least ask the airport official stamping your passport how long you're allowed to stay.

Visa Run

New visa legislation was introduced in 2008 in an attempt to crack down on visa runs. As such, visa runs (exiting and re-entering the country to gain an exit stamp and new entry stamp in your passport), once your 30 day extension has run out, have become much more difficult, and now involve returning to your country of residence before you will be granted entry into Dubai again. Officially, you will only be able to return to Dubai after 30 days' absence. Unofficially, people of nationalities qualifying for a visa on arrival have been granted an extra 30 day visa after a visa run.

eGate

The eGate service allows UAE and GCC nationals, as well as people with a valid residence permit, to pass through both the departures and arrivals halls of Dubai International Airport without a passport. Swipe your smart card through an electronic gate and through you go, saving a great deal of time otherwise spent in long queues. Applications for a card are processed within minutes at Dubai International Airport, in the DNATA buildings (one on Sheikh Zayed Road and one in Deira near Deira City Centre), or the DNRD office on Trade Centre Road. You'll need your passport, containing the valid residence permit and you will be fingerprinted and photographed. The eGate card costs Dhs.200 and is valid for two years. Payment can be made by cash or credit card. For further information, contact 04 316 6966 or see www.dubai.ae.

Make Sure Your PRO Is A Pro

In Dubai, a PRO is your company's 'man who can' – he liaises with various government departments and carries out those tiresome admin procedures. The PRO knows the system inside out, and will take care of all visa, residency, health card, and labour card applications. He might even help you get your driving licence. There is a move towards allowing only UAE Nationals to work as PROs in the future; bad news for the thousands of non-Nationals already employed in this field.

Health Card

Once you have the correct visa (either an employment visa or a work visa), the next step to becoming a fully fledged resident is to apply for a health card and take the medical test. If you entered Dubai on a visit visa, you must transfer your visa either by exiting and re-entering, or paying Dhs.500 to the Immigration Department for 'visa amendment.'

It may seem to be the wrong way round, but you actually get your health card before taking the medical test (although you can now do both on the same day). If you're in employment your company PRO should take care of most of the paperwork, and will certainly be able to get the health card for you as well as advise you where to go (and sometimes accompany you) for the medical test. Some employers provide additional private medical insurance and, as in many countries, this is regarded as preferable to state care.

To apply for a health card yourself, pick up an application form at any public hospital, (see p.178) such as the Iranian, Al Baraha (commonly known as Kuwaiti Hospital), Maktoum or Rashid Hospital, or the Ministry of Health. It makes sense to go to Rashid Hospital though, as that is where you will have to submit everything, unless you're on a free zone permit (see p.90) in which case you may be directed to another hospital. Take the application form (typed in Arabic) to the health card section at Rashid Hospital, along with your passport and passport copies, a copy of your visa (employment or residency), and two passport photos. The fee is Dhs.310, plus a typing fee of around Dhs.20, and in return you'll get a health card and a blank form for the medical test.

Improved Service

The Department of Health & Medical Services is attempting to improve their procedures by embracing the internet. Results of medical tests can be retrieved online and health cards can be renewed using the Express HC service. You will need to register on www.dohms.gov.ae to use this service. It can be somewhat temperamental and you may find yourself doing it the old fashioned way anyway, but it is still worth a couple of clicks.

Medical Test

Check with your employer which hospital to go to, or ask at Rashid Hospital when applying for your health card. The two most common options are Maktoum Hospital and Al Baraha (Kuwaiti) Hospital, which despite their ramshackle appearance are relatively well run. You will need your health card, a copy of the receipt for the Dhs.310 paid at Rashid Hospital, the test form filled out in Arabic (there are typing offices around Dubai who'll do this for Dhs.20 or so), and two passport photos. The test fee is Dhs.210. Submit all the forms, take a ticket and wait your turn. If you're lucky you'll only have a short wait, but if it's busy you may be there for many hours – the best time is usually first thing in the morning, and midweek is quieter. Blood will be taken (nurses use this to test for HIV and hepatitis). If your test is positive you will be called back for another test – if this test confirms that you are HIV positive or have hepatitis, you will be detained and deported to your home country. Getting called back for a second test does not automatically mean that you have something to worry about. Often samples are mixed in batches and one test will be run per batch, and if any blood within that specific batch is diseased everyone within that group will need to be tested again. If you are at all nervous about undergoing the test then it may be a good idea to go to your local doctor and get tested before you leave your home country.

After your blood test you might have to have a chest x-ray to test for tuberculosis. There are changing rooms, although if these are full you might have to change in the corridor. Ladies are given a gown, but if you go in a T-shirt, you don't have to wear the gown and can just remove your bra instead. After the tests are finished, collect a receipt – this will tell you when to return to collect your results (usually three or four days later).

Older Children

For parents sponsoring children, difficulties arise when sons (not daughters) turn 18. Unless they are enrolled in full-time education in the UAE they must transfer their visa to an employer, or the parents can pay a Dhs.5,000 security deposit (one-off payment) and apply for an annual visa. Daughters can stay on their father's sponsorship until they get married.

Residence Visa

Once you have your health card and the results of your medical test, you can go to the Immigration Department to process your residency. While you will often hear this referred to as your visa it is actually your residency permit – the visa is what allows you to enter the country in the first place.

There are two types of residence permit, one for when you are sponsored for employment, and the other for residence only (for example when you are sponsored by a family member who is already sponsored by an employer). The property-owner visa fell into the latter category, with the developer acting as sponsor for as long as you own the property, but without employment rights. However, this law ceased to exist in 2008, meaning buying a property no longer entitles you to a visa – although property owners are still able to apply for investor-based residency.

Once a resident, if you leave the UAE it can only be for a period of less than six months at any one time, otherwise your residency will lapse. This is particularly relevant to women going back home to give birth, or children studying abroad. If the residency is cancelled, the original sponsor can visit the Immigration Department and pay Dhs.100 for a temporary entry permit which will waive the cancellation and allow the person to re-enter Dubai. You'll need their passport copy, and will have to fax them a copy of the permit before they fly back.

Sponsorship By Employer

Your company PRO should handle all the paperwork, meaning you probably won't have to visit the Immigration Department yourself. He'll take your passport, employment visa (with entry stamp), medical test results, attested education certificates, copies of your company's establishment immigration card and trade licence, and three passport photos. For a fee of Dhs.300 (plus typing fees) the Immigration Department will process everything and affix and stamp the residency permit in the passport. This may take up to 10 days, during which time you'll be without your passport, but for an extra Dhs.100 they can do it on the same day. Your company is obliged to pay these fees for you. When arranging your residency, the company will apply directly for your labour card (see p.87). The Ministry of Labour website (www.mol.gov.ae) has a facility for companies to process applications and transactions online.

To be accepted by the authorities here, your education certificates must be verified by a solicitor or public notary in your home country and then by your foreign office to verify the solicitor as bona fide, then the UAE embassy. It's a good idea to have this done before you come to Dubai, but Empost does offer a verification service at a cost of Dhs.500 per degree. The minimum turnaround time you can expect for this service is two weeks.

Family Sponsorship

If you are sponsored and resident in Dubai you should be able to sponsor your family members, allowing them to stay in the country as long as you are here. It's unlikely that your company will assist you with this, and the process is quite tedious. To sponsor your wife or children you will need a minimum monthly salary of Dhs.3,000 plus accommodation, or a minimum all-inclusive salary of Dhs.4,000. Only what is printed on your labour contract will be accepted as proof of your earnings, so make sure you're happy with this before starting the job. To apply for residency visas for your family, you'll need to take your passport, a passport copy of the family member(s), and your labour contract to the Family Entry Permit counter at the Immigration Department. After submitting all the documents, return after a couple of days to collect the visa. Send a copy by fax to the family member, then deposit the original at the visa counter in Arrivals at the airport. When they arrive they swap their copy for the original. Once in Dubai on the correct entry visa, your family member must apply for a health card and take the medical test to continue the process.

With the medical test out of the way, you then return to the Immigration Department with all the essential documents as before, plus the medical test result and the attested birth certificate (if sponsoring a child) or attested marriage certificate (if sponsoring your spouse). For Dhs.300 (plus typing) the application will be processed and around five days later the passport – with the residency permit attached – will be ready for collection (for an additional Dhs.100, you can ask for the process to be completed on the same day). If the family member is already here in Dubai on a visit visa you can still apply for the residency entry visa as above. Once it is processed, the family member either exits the country and re-enters with the correct visa, or you can pay Dhs.500 to have the visa swapped over. If you are resident under family sponsorship and then get a job, you won't need to change onto your employer's sponsorship, but your new company will need to apply for a labour card on your behalf – see Labour Card (p.87).

It may be possible for a woman to sponsor her husband and children, for instance if she is employed in a certain profession (such as a doctor or teacher) and earning a high wage, but it is important to check this in advance before accepting any job offer. In most cases the male will be the 'head of the family' and therefore the sponsor. There are similar constraints when a resident wishes to sponsor his or her parents. A special committee meets to review each case individually – usually to consider the age of parents to be sponsored and their health requirements. In the case of a woman sponsoring her husband or a resident sponsoring their parents, even when a visa is granted it is only valid for one year and is reviewed for renewal on an annual basis.

Maids & Dependants

If you are processing a health card for a maid, driver or cook, you will need to pay an additional fee (Dhs.60-100) to have him or her vaccinated against hepatitis. There will also be a small typing fee (see Domestic Help, p.166). Only children over the age of 18 need to take the medical test; for under 18s you simply apply for the health card, and can then proceed directly with the next stage of the residency process.

Sponsoring A Maid

To sponsor a maid you must have a salary above Dhs.6,000 per month, and be able to provide the maid with housing and the usual benefits including an airfare home at least every two years. The process is very similar to sponsoring a family member (see above), the main differences being the additional costs involved – you have to pay a 'maid tax' of around Dhs.5,000 per year.

Sole Custody/Single Parents

If you have sole custody of your child and wish to sponsor him or her, in addition to the documents listed above you may also need a letter from the other parent stating the child's name, passport number and nationality, and that they have no objection to the child living with you in the UAE. The letter must be endorsed by the legal authority that issued the sole custody, and attested. If you have no way of contacting the other parent (or if they are deceased), then the attested divorce/sole custody paperwork (or death certificate) should suffice.

Labour Card

To work in the UAE you are legally required to have a valid labour card. The labour card can only be applied for once you have residency, but for employees on company sponsorship the process starts way before that. Before you are even granted an employment visa to enter the country, your company will have to get approval from the Ministry of Labour. You then enter on an employment visa, get a health card, take the medical test, and get the residency stamp in your passport. The company PRO then takes all of the relevant paperwork to the Ministry of Labour where the actual labour card will be issued (even though it has 'work permit' printed on the back). The card features your photo and details of your employer. You're supposed to carry the card with you at all times but it is highly unlikely that you will ever be asked to produce it. The process can also be quite slow, and it's possible you may not receive your card for a few weeks, or even months, after starting work. The labour card costs Dhs.1,000 (paid by your company) and is usually valid for three years. It must be renewed within 60 days of expiry. Failure to do so will result in a fine (which your company will be liable for) of Dhs.5,000 for each year the card has expired.

If your employer is arranging your residency you will need to sign your labour contract before the labour card is issued. This contract is printed in both Arabic and English. It's not necessarily your agreed 'contract' as such – most employees will sign a more comprehensive contract. Unless you read Arabic it may be advisable to have a translation made of your details, since the Arabic is the official version in any dispute. However, if there is any discrepancy, the judge would want to know why your company got the details wrong in the first place (see Employment Contracts, p.106).

Working On Family Sponsorship

If you are on a family residency and then decide to work, your employer, not your visa sponsor, will need to apply for a labour card. You'll need to give your employer the usual documents including a letter of no objection (NOC) from your sponsor (usually your husband or father), your passport with residency stamp, attested certificates (if appropriate), passport photos, and usually a photocopy of your sponsor's passport. The Labour Card will cost your employer Dhs.1,000, and must be renewed annually.

Holiday Jobs

Expat students who wish to work in Dubai during the summer holidays should apply to the Department of Naturalisation & Residency for a permit allowing them to work legally. Location: Ministry of Labour, near Galadari roundabout (04 269 1666).

ID Card

The Emirates Identity Authority (EIDA) has been given the responsibility of initiating a system in which all residents, nationals or not, must be in possession of a UAE ID card. The process is ongoing, with new centres opening up to deal with the administration. The aim is to secure personal identities and cut down on things such as fraud.

The card will eventually replace other cards, such as your health card and labour cards, but expats will still have to apply for them until the identity card is firmly introduced. The fee structure for the ID card is Dhs.100 for nationals, and the card will be valid for five years. Expat rates are linked to the length of residency visas; a resident with a one year visa will pay Dhs.100, up to two years costs Dhs.200, and three years is Dhs.300.

In order to register, fill in the pre-registration form, downloadable from www. emiratesid.ae or available from a registration centre, then take the completed form along to a registration centre along with the fee, passport and residency visa. Delivery of your ID card will cost an extra Dhs.20.

Under the threat of fines, suspension of bank accounts, and denied access to government services for late applicants, Nationals and expats have flooded to registration centres. Despite widespread confusion, reported problems with the

Cut The Red Tape

The *Dubai Red-Tape Explorer* is a comprehensive, step-by-step instruction manual that will help you navigate the administrative maze you'll encounter when you move to Dubai – allowing you to get on with living life to the full.

website, jammed phone lines and four-hour queues at registration centres, the government has refused to extend the application deadline of 31 December 2008 for Nationals. However, as a small concession, the government has pushed the deadline for expat workers back to 28 February 2009. After that date they may be denied access to government services, such as healthcare, without their ID card. For more information on location of offices and the latest ID card news releases, including deadline updates, visit www.emiratesid.ae.

Free Zones

Employees of companies in free zones have different sponsorship options depending on the free zone. For example, in Jebel Ali you can either be sponsored by an individual company or by the free zone authority itself. Whether the Jebel Ali Free Zone, Dubai Internet City, Media City, Knowledge Village, Healthcare City or the Dubai Airport Free Zone, the respective authority will process your residency visa/permit directly through the Immigration Department, without having to get employment approval from the Ministry of Labour. This speeds up the process significantly, and residency permits can sometimes be granted in a matter of hours. Once Immigration has stamped your residence permit in your passport, the free zone will issue your labour card – this also acts as your security pass for entry to the free zone. A big advantage of working in a free zone is the lack of red tape encountered if you move jobs to another free zone company. This is because the free zone is actually your sponsor, so when you switch jobs to another employer you won't be switching sponsors.

A free zone residency permit is valid for three years, and the labour card for either one or three years, depending on the free zone. Designed to encourage investment from overseas, free zones allow 100% foreign ownership and offer exemption from taxes and customs duties. An added attraction is the relative lack of red tape. For more information on setting up a business in a free zone, refer to the Business chapter of the *Dubai Red-Tape Explorer*.

Media City

Typing Office

Driving Licence

Other options **Transportation** p.225

If you are entering Dubai on a tourist visa you can drive a hire car, provided you have a valid international licence (this only applies to those countries on the transfer list below) – a driving licence from your country of origin is not acceptable. Be aware that once your visa process starts you will need a temporary Dubai driving licence in order to be covered by insurance. If you want to drive a private vehicle, you must obtain either a temporary or permanent Dubai driving licence, and as soon as your residence visa comes through you will need to switch to a Dubai licence. The interior ministry has recently drawn up a list of 100 occupations that will automatically be refused a driving licence. In a move to combat the rising number of drivers on Dubai's roads, non-skilled labourers, domestic assistants and many trades people will no longer be permitted to drive or own a car.

Temporary Licence

You cannot drive a privately registered vehicle on an international or foreign driving licence, as the vehicle is only insured for drivers holding a UAE driving licence. However, you can get a temporary UAE licence, even if you are not a resident here, which allows you to drive a privately owned car. Visitors to Dubai, or those who are waiting for their residency permit to be processed, can apply for a six-month temporary licence. If you belong to one of the nationalities listed below, the procedure is fairly straightforward. At the Traffic Police office visit the typing office to have the application form filled out in Arabic. Then go to the counter with your passport (original and copy), your visa (visit, employment or residency), your foreign licence (original and copy) and two passport photos. You should also take an eye test certificate, although this isn't always needed. The cost of the licence is Dhs.120 including the typing fee. You'll have your picture taken and the licence should be ready a few minutes later. For UK licence holders you need to take the card and the paper counterpart. It has been known for officials to ask for your licence to be authenticated by your consulate. In this case, oblige and visit your consulate – obtaining a letter of approval should not take long at all.

Permanent Licence

Once you have your residence permit you must apply for a permanent (10 year) Dubai licence. Nationals of the countries listed in the margin can automatically transfer their driving licence, as long as the original is valid. Take your existing foreign licence, your passport (with residency stamp), an eye test certificate (or have an eye test done on the premises), two passport photos, and the Dhs.100 fee to the licensing office of the Traffic Police. Again, have the typing office fill out the application in Arabic (Dhs.20), and take everything to the counter. Depending on how busy it is, you may have quite a wait before being seen by an officer, although women will probably find the queue in the ladies' section shorter. Your photo will be taken and you'll get your licence there and then.

Driving Test

If your nationality is not on the automatic transfer list you will need to sit a UAE driving test to be eligible to drive in Dubai, regardless of whether you hold a valid driving licence from your home country or not. Much of the driving test process has been handed over to five authorised driving institutes, so you can apply

Traffic Police Offices

- Traffic Police HQ: near Galadari Roundabout, Dubai-Sharjah Road (04 269 2222)
- Bur Dubai Police Station: Sheikh Zayed Road, Junction 4 (04 398 1111)
- Al Quoz Police Station: near Dubai Police Academy, Umm Suqueim Street (04 347 2222)

for a learner's permit at the driving school directly, instead of going to the Traffic Police. You can begin the process at the post office, which has teamed up with Emirates Driving Institute to offer prepaid packages. Some driving institutions insist that you pay for a set of prebooked lessons. In some cases, the package extends to 52 lessons and can cost up to Dhs.4,000. The lessons usually last 30 to 45 minutes during the week, or longer lessons can be taken at

Driving Schools		
Al Ahli Driving Center	04 341 1500	www.alahlidubai.com
Belhasa Driving Center	04 324 3535	www.bdc.ae
Dubai Driving Center	04 345 5855	www.dcds.ae
Emirates Driving Institute	04 263 1100	www.edi-uae.com
Galadari Motor Driving Centre	04 267 6166	www.gmdc.ae

weekends. Other companies offer lessons on an hourly basis, as and when you like, for around Dhs.35 per hour. Women are generally required to take lessons with a female instructor, at a cost of Dhs.65 per hour. If a woman wants to take lessons with a man she may need to provide NOCs from her husband/sponsor and the Traffic Police.

You will take three different tests on different dates. One is a Highway Code test, another includes parking and manoeuvres, and the third is a road test. You also have to take an assessment prior to doing the final test. Before you are issued with your permanent driving licence you will have to attend a number of road safety lectures, the cost of which is incorporated into the price of your lessons.

Always carry your Dubai driving licence when driving. If you fail to produce it during a police spot check you will be fined. You should also ensure you have the car's registration card in the car. Licences can be renewed at the Traffic Police as well as other sites around Dubai including Al Safa Union Co-Op (04 394 5007), Al Tawar Union Co-Op (04 263 4857) and Jumeirah Plaza (04 342 0737).

Motorcycle Licence

The rules for riding a motorbike in Dubai are similar to those for driving a car – if you have a transferable licence from your home country you can get either a six-month temporary licence or a 10 year permanent one (see the list of nationalities on p.91).

Off-Road Licence

Drivers working for tour companies who go off-roading in the desert must pass a desert driving course. For the time being, ordinary drivers who like to go off road don't need to take the test, although they can go on desert driving courses offered by most of the driving schools. Likewise, there are no licence requirements for riding a motorbike off road.

Liquor Licence
Other options **Alcohol** p.422

Get The Red Card
There are many benefits of getting your liquor licence, and not just because it can keep you out of trouble. MMI offers preferential treatment at events it sponsors, such as at the Rugby 7s, where you can use an express queue as long as you have your licence with you. You also get vouchers back to spend on alcohol, as well as gifts and special offers throughout the year.

Dubai probably has the most liberal attitude towards alcohol of all the emirates. You won't be able to buy alcohol at the supermarkets for home consumption, but you can apply for a liquor licence to buy it from licensed shops. In public, only hotels are licensed to serve alcoholic drinks in their bars and restaurants, as are some private clubs and associations. Independent restaurants generally do not have a liquor licence. You don't need a liquor licence to drink at a hotel or a club, but you will require valid ID to prove you are 21 or older.

To get a liquor licence you must be a non-Muslim and a resident of Dubai. The first thing to do is pick up an application form from one of the two licensed liquor store chains in Dubai, A&E or MMI. Complete the form (include your spouse's details, photograph and signature if you would like them to be able to use the licence too) and have it signed and

YOUR TEAM IS UP,
BUT HOW ARE YOUR SPIRITS?

We've added a bevy of fantastic features to ensure you get the maximum benefit from getting your licence. Having your red card will ensure you can enjoy the game without being offside.

There are 10 shops conveniently located across Dubai over flowing with great brands, monthly offers and featuring a refrigerated section full of your favourites

Joinus@
mmidubai.com

bringing more to life

Al Wasl • Deira • Silicon Oasis • Green Community • Ibn Battuta Mall • Mall of the Emirates
Sheikh Zayed Road • Trade Centre Rd • Bur Dubai • Karama

stamped by your employer. Return to the outlet with the following documents: passport copy, residence permit copy, labour contract copy (the Ministry of Labour one, in Arabic and English), tenancy contract copy (or a letter from your employer if you're in company accommodation), one passport photo and the fee of Dhs.160. (When you first submit your form make sure you tear off the strip at the bottom; when you go to collect your licence hand the slip back.) The liquor stores usually have offers whereby they refund the value of the licence fee in vouchers to spend on drink.

The liquor store will process your application through the Dubai Police on your behalf. The licence allows you to spend a limited amount on alcohol per month. The amount is based on your monthly salary, and is at the discretion of the police. The process takes around 10 days, and the outlet will contact you when the licence is ready. The card has a chip that records each transaction, so you can't spend over your limit. Limits are usually generous, and you should be able to buy enough booze on your limit to last you for at least a month. However, if you are planning a big party, it's a good idea to stockpile supplies for a few months. Buying alcohol from liquor shops can be expensive, as you have to pay an additional tax of 30% on top of the listed price. The range, however, is excellent. For a list of branches of MMI and A&E liquor stores, see p.422 in the Shopping section.

It is possible to buy alcohol without a licence in some of the neighbouring emirates, such as from Al Hamra Cellar in Ras Al Khaimah, Ajman's 'Hole in the Wall' near the Ajman Kempinski, the Barracuda Resort in Umm Al Quwain (next to Dreamland Aqua Park), and Centaurus in Ras Al Khaimah (see p.422 in Shopping). However, it is illegal to transport alcohol around the emirates without a liquor licence. This law is enforced particularly strictly in Sharjah and, while there are no regular roadblocks, if you're unfortunate enough to get stopped for anything, you may have all your alcohol confiscated. Drinking on the beach and in public parks is not tolerated, whether you have a licence or not.

While there may be cheaper alternatives, it is still worth having a liquor licence so you can nip out for supplies when you run dry, and so that you can drink at home without any worries.

Express Delivery

If you feel like you've got enough on your hands with your new arrival, MEDI-Express offers a service, for a fee, that will take much of the administration and hassle out of arranging the birth certificate for your baby. The firm is based at Baraha Hospital. See www. mediexpress.ae or call 04 272 7772 for more details.

New Babies

Babies born abroad to expatriate mums with UAE residency are required to have a residence visa or a visit visa before entering the UAE. The application should be filed by the father or family provider, along with the essential documents, a salary certificate and a copy of the birth certificate.

Birth Certificate & Registration

The hospital that delivers the baby will prepare an official 'notification of birth' (this will be in Arabic) upon receipt of hospital records, photocopies of both parents' passports and marriage certificate, and a fee of Dhs.50. To get the actual birth certificate, take the birth notification to the Birth Certificate Office at Al Baraha Hospital (04 271 0000). Every expat child born in the UAE should be registered with their parents' embassy (if the parents are from different countries you can choose which one to register your child with). You need to get a passport for your baby and apply for its residency permit within 120 days. If you don't get the residency within that time, you will have to pay a fine of Dhs.100 for every day that you go over the limit.

Adoption

While you can't adopt a UAE National baby, many couples in Dubai adopt children from Africa, Asia and Far Eastern countries. Adoption regulations vary according to which country the child comes from, but once you clear the requirements of that country, and formalise the adoption process, you will have no problems bringing your new child into the UAE on your sponsorship. Check with your embassy about the procedure for applying for citizenship of your home country for your new child. If you are considering adopting a child, a good starting point is to contact the Adoption Support Group (04 360 8113).

Marriage Certificate & Registration

Getting Married In Dubai

A few years ago organising a wedding in Dubai may have been a bit of a challenge, but thanks to the trusty rules of supply and demand, weddings are becoming big business. Everything your heart desires for a dream wedding is here, and in comparison to the big bucks weddings in other countries, things here are little more affordable – relatively. For more information on wedding dresses and accessories, as well as cakes and invitation cards, see p.470 in the Shopping section. While many hotels offer wedding packages, they mainly extend to the reception – The Royal Mirage (04 399 3999) and The Ritz-Carlton (04 399 4000) are the hot favourites, although the high-rise construction sites right next door could take a bit of the shine off your dream day. The Radisson SAS Creek also offers a tailored wedding service (04 205 7047) as does the Park Hyatt (04 602 1234). A wedding planner could be your fairy godmother (especially when your family support network is miles away). Sarah Feyling is an expert wedding planner based in Dubai who will help you every step of the way – from the paperwork to the seating plan (www.theweddingplanner.ae). Upscale & Posh offers a tailored service for flowers and wedding reception decorations (www.upscaleandposh.com). Brides needn't worry about missing out on the princess treatment. Most spas offer tailor-made services for brides. When it comes to hair and makeup there are a number of excellent salons dotted around Dubai, as well as a number of independent specialists. Maria Dowling (04 345 4225) is an excellent bridal hair stylist who will come to your house or hotel to do your hair on the day of the wedding. Wenda Oosterbroek (050 343 8161) is a CIBTAC qualified makeup artist with experience in bridal makeup. She offers trial makeup sessions where she works with the bride to find the perfect look, and on the big day she will do the bridal makeup at your home or hotel. THE One (for a list of branches see p.506) offers wedding gift registries. To set up the list you go around the store with a member of staff and select the items that you want (you can also add gift vouchers to the list).

The Paperwork

Before going ahead with a wedding you should consult your embassy or consulate for advice, especially regarding the legality of the marriage back home. In nearly all cases a marriage that is legally performed in Dubai will be recognised elsewhere in the world, but it's always best to check. In addition, you may need to inform your embassy of your intention to marry. The British Embassy in Dubai, for example, will display a 'notice of marriage' in the embassy waiting room for 21 days prior to the marriage (along the same lines as 'the banns' being published in a parish newsletter for three successive Sundays). Afterwards, providing no one has objected, they will issue a 'certificate of no impediment' that may be required by the church carrying out your ceremony.

A Muslim marrying another Muslim can apply at the marriage section of the Dubai Courts, next to Maktoum Bridge. You will need two male witnesses and the bride should ensure that either her father or brother attends as a witness. You will require your passports with copies, proof that the groom is Muslim and Dhs.50. You can marry there and then. A Muslim man can marry a non-Muslim woman, but a non-Muslim man cannot marry at the court. The situation is more complicated for a Muslim woman wishing to marry a

Wedding Photographers

Robeya Photography (050 494 4297), Simon Charlton (www. simoncharlton photography.com, 050 518 4241), and Sue Johnston (050 564 5519) are a selection of snappers to call to capture that special day.

non-Muslim man and this may only be possible if the man first converts to Islam. Call the Dubai Courts (04 334 7777) or the Dubai Court Marriage Section (04 303 0406) for more information.

Christians can either have a formal church ceremony with a congregation, or a small ceremony that must take place in a church, followed by a blessing at a different location, such as a hotel.

Your church may require that you have someone witness you signing a 'legal eligibility for marriage' document (a legal paper signed under oath) at your embassy or consulate. You may also need to attend at least three sessions of premarital counselling.

Shotgun Weddings

It is illegal to have a baby out of wedlock in the UAE. If you are unmarried and fall pregnant, you have two choices: march down the aisle asap or leave Dubai. You'll be asked for your marriage certificate when you give birth (and even earlier if you are having your prenatal checks at a government hospital). If there is a significant discrepancy in the dates, you will probably face many questions and a lot more paperwork.

At the official church ceremony you will need two witnesses to sign the marriage register and the church will then issue a marriage certificate. You will need to get the certificate translated into Arabic

> ## Living In Sin
>
> Under UAE law an unmarried couple may not live together. However, it is a fact that many, many unmarried couples do live together in Dubai without getting into trouble. Dubai is a liberal place, and the authorities seem to accept that this law is widely flouted. It would also be virtually impossible to enforce this rule on the millions of tourists that descend on Dubai each year from all around the world. No hotel will question whether a couple checking in are married or not. The only foreseeable problem could be if you got into trouble with the police over another matter, and they decided to punish you for this too, but you'd have to be quite unlucky.

by a court-approved legal translator. Take this, and the original, along with your essential documents to the Notary Public Office at the Dubai Courts. They will certify the documents for a fee of about Dhs.80. Next you will need to go to the Ministry of Justice (near CompuMe and Chili's in Garhoud) to authenticate the signature and the Notary Public seal. Just when you think it's all over you still have to go to the Ministry of Foreign Affairs (behind the distinctive Etisalat building in Deira) to authenticate the seal of the Ministry of Justice. Now you just need to pop back to your embassy for final legal verification.

Catholics must also undertake a marriage encounter course, which usually takes place at the busy St Mary's Church in Oud Metha (04 337 0087) on a Friday. At the end of the course you are presented with a certificate. You should then arrange with the priest to undertake a pre-nuptial ceremony (which will require your birth certificate, baptism certificate, passport and passport copies, an NOC from your parish priest in your home country and a donation, and the filling out of another form). If you are a non-Catholic marrying a Catholic you will need an NOC from your embassy/consulate stating that you are legally free to marry. A declaration of your intent to marry is posted on the public noticeboard at the church for three weeks, after which time, if there are no objections, you can set a date for the ceremony. The cost of the service will be Dhs.50. Anglicans should make an appointment to see the chaplain at Holy Trinity Church (04 337 0247). You will need to fill out forms confirming that you are legally free to marry and take your essential documents along (p.80). If you have previously been married you will need to produce either your divorce certificate or the death certificate of your previous partner. Fees differ depending on your nationality and circumstances but are around Dhs.1,000 for the ceremony and an additional Dhs.1,000 if you wish to hold the ceremony outside the church. You'll pay Dhs.50 for any additional copies of the marriage certificate that you want. If you're not overly concerned about sticking to a particular doctrine, but want a church wedding, the Anglican ceremony is simpler to arrange and less time consuming than its Catholic equivalent.

These marriages are recognised by the government of the UAE but must be formalised. To make your marriage 'official', get an Arabic translation of the marriage certificate and take it to the Dubai Court. Filipino citizens are required to contact their embassy in Abu Dhabi before the Dubai Court will authenticate their marriage certificate.

Hindus can be married through the Hindu Temple and the Indian Embassy (04 397 1222). The formalities take a minimum of 45 days.

Death Certificate & Registration

Local Burial

A local burial can be arranged at the Muslim or Christian cemeteries in Dubai. The cost of a burial is Dhs.1,100 for an adult and Dhs.350 for a child. You will need to get a coffin made, as well as transport to the burial site. Cremation is also possible, but only in the Hindu manner and with the prior permission of the next of kin and the CID.

In The Event Of A Death

In the event of the death of a friend or relative, the first thing to do is to notify the police by dialling 999. The police will fill out a report and the body will be taken to hospital where a doctor will determine the cause of death. The authorities will need to see the deceased's passport and visa details. On receipt of the doctor's report, the hospital will issue a death certificate declaration, for a fee of Dhs.50. Take the declaration and original passport to the police who will issue a letter addressed to Al Baraha (Kuwaiti) Hospital. This letter, plus death declaration, original passport and copies should be taken to Al Baraha Hospital, Department of Preventative Medicine, where an actual death certificate will be issued.

If you are sending the deceased home you should also request a death certificate in English (an additional Dhs.100) or appropriate language – check this with your embassy. Take the certificate to the Ministry of Health and then to the Ministry of Foreign Affairs to be registered officially.

Registering A Death

As well as notifying the police, you should contact the relevant embassy or consulate as soon as possible (see p.33 for a list of embassies). The embassy will be able to provide practical help, support, and advice on local procedures and any repatriation, if required. The embassy can also assist with registration of the death in the deceased's country of origin, and can also issue its own death certificates. Although it is not always obligatory to register the death with the embassy, for probate purposes a death certificate from the home country, or a consular report of death, may be mandatory. The embassy will need to see the original passport and the local death certificate and the embassy certificate could cost up to Dhs.700. The deceased's visa must also be cancelled by the Immigration Department. To do this take the local death certificate, original cancelled passport and embassy-issued death certificate.

Investigation & Autopsy

Dubai Police will investigate in the case of an accidental or suspicious death, and it's likely that an autopsy will be performed at a government hospital. If you're unhappy with the outcome of an investigation you could hire a private investigator, but this is a bit of a grey area so seek advice from your embassy or consulate.

Returning The Deceased To Their Country Of Origin

You will need to book a flight through DNATA (04 211 1111), get police clearance from airport security to ship the body out of the country, and an NOC from the embassy. The body needs to be embalmed and you must get a letter to this effect from the police. Embalming can be arranged through Al Maktoum Hospital for Dhs.1,000, which includes the embalming certificate. The body must be identified before and after embalming, after which it should be transferred to Cargo Village for shipping and this will cost Dhs.100. Cargo fees will range from Dhs.1,000 to Dhs.10,000 and a coffin costs about Dhs.750. The following documents should accompany the deceased: local death certificate, translation of the death certificate, embalming certificate, NOC from the police, embassy/consulate death certificate and NOC, and cancelled passport.

Working In Dubai

Expat workers come to Dubai for a number of reasons: to advance their career, for a higher standard of living, to take advantage of new opportunities or, most commonly, for the lifestyle and the experience of living and working in a new culture. Whatever the reason, there are various advantages to working here.

While the biggest bonus of working in Dubai may seem to be tax-free salaries, the benefits of not paying tax can be somewhat outweighed, for some nationalities, by the rate of the dirham (it remains pegged to the US dollar), depending on the rate of your home country – although in late 2008 the plummeting rate of the pound made the picture a little rosier for UK expats. Inflation and the astronomic property rental prices mean salary packages are generally less lucrative than they were four or five years ago, making disposable income not as impressive as it once was. However, there are other distinct benefits and these are what make people stay.

**Read Between
The Lines**
*If a job ad says 'UK/US
candidate preferred',
that usually means
they are looking for
a white, western
employee. Similarly,
'ability to speak Arabic
an advantage' actually
means 'Arabs only'.*

The New Dubai

The boom that Dubai has undergone, even in just the last few years, means that the job market is constantly changing. At the very senior end of the scale there remain some idyllic opportunities and huge packages that attract the big players, and these are predominantly in the construction, aviation and finance industries.

However, for positions lower than senior management, the image of a cushy expat life in the Gulf is changing, with much more competition in all areas of the market and an increasing number of people looking for work in Dubai. Not so long ago foreign expats could walk in to jobs that they could only dream of back home, but these days the market is much more competitive, not least because of the effects of the global economic downturn. All-inclusive packages with accommodation and education allowances are also not as common, although basic benefits still apply (such as annual flights home and 30 calendar days leave).

Work-wise, there are still a lot of great job prospects in Dubai and in many respects it is a land of opportunities for skilled professionals. It is also easier to change industries, as skill sets are less 'pigeon-holed' than in other countries.

Jobs in certain industries (such as construction and real estate) are likely to be much more available in the UAE due to the continued efforts to establish Dubai as a tourist and business centre.

Working On A Visa

One of the main differences about working in Dubai, as opposed to your country of origin, is that you need to be sponsored by an employer, which often leaves people feeling tied or uncomfortably obligated to their employer. If you leave the company, your current visa will be cancelled and you will have to go through the hassle of getting a new residency permit (for you and your family, if they are on your sponsorship).

Setting Up Business In Dubai

As well as the opportunities within companies, there are many people who start their own business here. With an economy that can best be described as 'exploding' rather than just 'growing', there are plenty of opportunities for small businesses in Dubai. Unless you are setting up your business in one of Dubai's free zones, you will need a local partner and the bureaucracy will no doubt frustrate you at times. But if you have the necessary drive and ambition, Dubai is a great platform for starting up your own business.

In addition to the various government departments specifically responsible for providing commercial assistance to enterprises in Dubai, there are various business groups that help facilitate investments and provide opportunities for networking with

others in the community. Some business groups and councils provide information on trade with their respective countries, as well as on business opportunities both in Dubai and internationally. Most also arrange social and networking events on a regular basis.

Before you set up, contact the Dubai Chamber of Commerce & Industry (www. dubaichamber.ae) and the Ministry of Economy (www.economy.ae). Both can offer excellent advice. Embassies or consulates can also be a good business resource and may be able to offer contact lists for the UAE and the country of representation.

For information and details, refer to the *Dubai Red-Tape Explorer*, the *Dubai Commercial Directory*, or the *Hawk Business Pages*.

Jobs Online

As well as the usual recruitment websites, two other sites worth checking out for jobs online or before you arrive in Dubai are the listings section of locally based www.dubaidonkey.com or the local version of the global recruitment site www.bayt.com.

Networking

With Dubai still being a relatively small city, made up of communities that are smaller still, networking is critical, even across industries. Everyone seems to know everyone and getting in with the corporate 'in-crowd' definitely has its plus points. Business acumen here can, at times, be more important than specific industry knowledge so it pays to attend business events and trade shows. Make friends in government departments and this will often land you in the front line for opportunities. Likewise, bad news is rarely made public here, so staying in tune with the grapevine can help prevent wrong decisions.

Business Culture & Etiquette

Despite its status as a cosmopolitan, modern metropolis, Dubai is still an Arab city in a Muslim country. Even if your counterpart in another company is an expatriate, the head decision maker may be a UAE National who could quite possibly take a different approach to business matters. Your best bet when you're just starting out in Dubai's business circles is to observe closely, have lots of patience and make a concerted effort to understand the culture and respect the customs.

Tea and coffee are a very important part of local custom and it may be considered rude to refuse this offer of hospitality during a meeting. Tilting the small Arabic coffee cup back and forth several times with your fingers will signal that you do not want another refill. Don't be too taken aback if you find time-keeping flexible and if people walk in during your meeting for a chat. Although proper dress is important for all business dealings, the local climate has dictated that a shirt and tie (for men) is sufficient for all but the most important of business encounters; women usually choose a suit or a skirt and blouse and nothing too revealing.

Working Hours

Hours differ dramatically between companies, with start and finish times varying. Straight shifts vary from 07:30 to 14:00 for government organisations

Business Councils & Groups

American Business Council	www.abcdubai.com
Australian Business Council	www.abc-dxb.com
British Business Group	www.britbiz-uae.com
Canadian Business Council	www.cbc-dubai.com
Danish Business Council	www.danishbusinessdubai.com
French Business Council	www.fbcdubai.com
German Business Council	www.gbc-dubai.com
Iranian Business Council	www.ibcuae.org
Lebanese Consulate	www.lebanonconsulate-uae.com
South African Business Council	www.sabco-uae.org
Swedish Business Council	www.swedchamb.com
Swiss Business Council	www.swissbcuae.com

to the common 09:00 to 18:00 for private companies. Most retail outlets tend to be open from 10:00 to 22:00 but often operate shifts. Teachers start early at around 07:30 and classes finish at 14:00, although like in any job, paperwork can add to the day's work. Although less common nowadays, some offices and shops operate split shifts, which allow for a longer break in the afternoon (hours are usually 08:00 to 13:00 and 16:00 to 19:00).

The maximum number of hours permitted per week according to UAE Labour Law is 48, although some industries, such as hospitality and retail, have longer stipulated hours. Annual holiday allowance starts at one calendar month per year, or 22 working days. Some employees, especially those in management, have more than this and long service usually adds to holiday allowance.

Friday is the Islamic holy day and therefore a universal day off for offices and schools. Consumer demand means that the hospitality and retail industries are open seven days a week. As for the second weekend day, in 2006 the five-day working week for government departments and schools was set as Sunday to Thursday, bringing them into line with much of the private sector. There are still private companies which have retained the traditional Saturday to Wednesday working week, while others work five and a half days a week and some operate a six-day week, taking only Friday as a rest day.

Public holidays (see p.20) are set by the government, while the timing of religious holidays depends on the sighting of the moon. The labour law states that all employees (even non-Muslims) are entitled to a shorter working day during Ramadan, although labour lawyers would advise you not to insist on this right if you are non-Muslim or not fasting.

Know Your Rights
You might be able to get a copy of the UAE Labour Law from your employer, or you can order it through the Ministry of Labour & Social Affairs (04 266 8967). However, with constant amendments to the law, it is usually best to seek legal advice. The UAE Labour Guide, published in 2002 by the Ministry, outlines rights of workers.

Finding Work

Until the global financial crisis hit, Dubai's boom meant that many industries were opening up and expanding, often quite rapidly, and therefore recruitment was a priority for many companies.

Things are a little tighter at present, but with a little luck, perseverance and flexibility you could still find yourself a decent job.

People are often seconded to Dubai by companies based in their home country or are recruited from their country of origin, but there are increasing numbers of people who arrive here with their partners or spouses and then begin to look for work. There's also a fair share of career hopefuls who start looking for work opportunities after visiting Dubai on holiday or to stay with friends and family here.

Finding Work Before You Come

While it is often easier to find a job once you are here, it's worth looking from your home country before you leave. There are a number of companies that recruit abroad, and you may even find Dubai jobs advertised in the media.

If you are lucky enough to find a job this way it's likely that the company will pay for your flight to Dubai, provide help with relocation costs, and start the paperwork involved in becoming a resident.

Alternatively, have a good search on the internet; there are plenty of job sites with Dubai listings. Local paper *Gulf News* has an excellent appointments section at www.gnads4u.com/jobs. Also try www.khaleejtimes.com, as well as www.uaestaffing.com, www.gulfjobsites.com and www.bayt.com. Browse vacancies listed on websites of recruitment firms such as Charterhouse and IQ Selection (p.104).

If you know the industry that you want to work in, it is worth investigating Dubai companies within that sector and contacting them with your CV. Word of mouth is a particularly useful tool here.

Finding Work While You're Here

It is undoubtedly easier to look for a job once you are here. Your first step should be to get your hands on the *Gulf News* appointments supplement, published on Sundays, Tuesdays and Thursdays, or the *Khaleej Times Appointments* on Sundays, Mondays and Wednesdays. It is also a good idea to register with a recruitment agency (p.104) and to contact companies directly and start networking.

Thanks to Dubai's relatively small size, the more people you meet the more likely you are to bump into someone who just happens to work somewhere that has a vacant position that you might be able to fill. Many large Dubai-based companies have vacancy listings on their websites, so if you have a company in mind, see if they have anything available.

Career Coaching

Careering Ahead ◄

Sandpiper Coaching offers tailored programmes to help get your career on track. Initial consultations are free, and the courses cover everything from preparing a CV, to starting a business or simply coping with expat life. See www. sandpipercoaching. com for more details.

If you're entering the world of work for the first time, or you feel like you need some external advice on changing jobs or improving your long-term employment prospects, enrolling on a career coaching course may be of interest. Jobsearchhelp.net is a career coaching company based in Dubai that provides coaching programmes for students, first-time job seekers, people who have lost their jobs, those who are looking for a change of job, and people returning to work after a career break. It offers one-to-one personalised coaching programmes on CV writing, networking and interviewing, and generally helps job seekers prepare for the job market.

Recruitment Agencies

There are numerous recruitment agencies in Dubai. To register, check with the agency to find out if they take walk-ins, although most only accept CVs via email and will then contact you for an interview. Invariably when you go for the agency interview you will also have to fill out an agency form summarising your CV and will need a few passport photos. The agency takes its fee from the registered company once the position has been filled. It is illegal for a recruitment company to levy fees on candidates for this service, although some might try.

Before You
Make A Move ◄

If you have an NOC from your previous employer, and the Ministry of Labour approves the move, your visa transfer should be hassle-free. But this is one area where laws change frequently so it's best to check with the Labour Department or a lawyer first.

Should you be suitable for a job, the agency will mediate between you and the employer and arrange all interviews. However, don't rely too heavily on the agency finding a job for you. More often than not, agencies depend on candidates spotting a vacancy that they have advertised in the paper. There is no reason why you can't sign up with more than one agency – just don't be surprised when they both try to put you forward for the same job. In this case it is at your discretion which agency you want to represent you. Below is a list of recruitment agencies based in the UAE. Some of these agencies specialise in certain industries so do your research and register accordingly. One to investigate if you have come to Dubai as a result of your partner or spouse's job is the Xpat Partners agency, which specialises in finding part-time and flexible work, particularly for expat women.

Voluntary & Charity Work

There are a number of opportunities to do voluntary or charity work in Dubai and the organisations listed below are always looking for committed volunteers. If it's environmental voluntary work you're after, the Emirates Environmental Group (www. eeg-uae.org) organises regular campaigns.

Volunteer Organisations

Feline Friends (www.felinefriendsuae.com, 050 451 0058) is a non-profit organisation that helps cats in the UAE. Volunteers rescue and re-home stray cats and kittens, promote the control of street cats by sterilisation and provide care and relief to sick

The fastest growing city in the world

Do you feel your career is growing at the same pace?

www.clearandtransparent.com

Recruitment Agencies

Apple Search & Selection	04 329 8220	www.appleselection.com
BAC Middle East ▶ p.99	04 337 5747	www.bac.ae
Baker Regent	04 881 8282	www.bakerregent.com
Bayt	04 391 1900	www.bayt.com
Charterhouse Partnership ▶ p.105	04 372 3500	www.charterhouseme.ae
Clarendon Parker	04 391 0460	www.clarendonparker.com
Concur Consultants	04 813 5200	www.concurme.com
DJN (Dubai Jobs Network)	na	www.dubaijobsnetwork.com
Emirates Consulting Group	na	www.ecg.ae
Grafton Recruitment	04 367 1939	www.graftonrecruitment.com
Headway	04 398 7369	www.headway.ae
Hudson	04 705 0323	ae.hudson.com
IQ Selection ▶ p.103	04 329 7770	www.iqselection.com
Job Scan	04 355 9113	www.jobscan.ae
Job Track	04 397 7751	www.jobtrackme.com
Kershaw Leonard	04 343 4606	www.kershawleonard.net
M2R Global	+44 1924 888 185	www.m2rglobal.com
SOS Agency	04 396 5600	www.sos.co.ae
Soundlines HR Consultancy	04 397 9064	www.soundlinesgroup.com
Talent Management Consultancy	04 335 0999	www.talentdubai.com
TASC (Talent Asset Software & Consulting)	04 355 4242	www.talentasset.com
Xpat Partners	04 341 8628	www.xpatpartners.com

and injured cats and kittens. Volunteers are needed for rescues and also for fostering cats until homes can be found for them.

K9 Friends helps care for and re-home unwanted dogs from all over the UAE. It is run by a dedicated group of volunteers. Running costs are met entirely through donations from the public, as well as corporate sponsors. If you are interested in volunteering, contact them in Dubai on 04 347 4611 or visit their site at www.k9friends.com.

Médecins Sans Frontières (MSF) is an international, independent, non-profit emergency medical relief organisation that relies on volunteers to provide aid in any way they can. If you would like to become involved locally with their fund-raising or awareness campaigns, call 04 345 8177 or visit www.msfuae.ae

Foresight is an organisation formed to raise funds for research and to improve the lives of visually impaired people in the UAE and throughout the world. Contact 04 364 3703 or visit the website (www.foresightrp.com) for more information.

Riding for the Disabled was set up to provide physical and mental stimulation through gentle horse riding for children with special needs. They are always on the lookout for reliable, committed volunteers to lead the horses and assist the riders. For more information visit www.rdad.ae.

All As One is a non-profit organisation, staffed by volunteers, whose primary concern is to care for the abandoned, disabled, abused and destitute children of Sierra Leone in the All As One Children's Centre. It depends on donations, child sponsorship, and fundraising events to fund operating costs. For more, visit www.allasone.org.

Working As A Freelancer Or Contractor

It is possible to obtain a visa to work in Dubai on a freelance basis. This kind of visa is linked to the various 'free zones' that exist, such as Dubai Media City. Professions need to be linked to the free zone, so in Media City that includes artists, editors, directors, writers, engineers, producers, photographers, camera operators and technicians in the fields of film, TV, music, radio and print media.

If you fall into one of the categories, and meet all the relevant criteria, you will get a residence visa and access to 'hot desk' facilities. There are a number of fees involved in this process, and obtaining a visa in this way will cost somewhere between Dhs.20,000 and Dhs.30,000. For more information, contact the appropriate free zone (see Free Zones, p.90).

An alternative option, depending on your line of work, may to be set up or register your own company. The Department of Economic Development (www.dubaided. gov.ae) is the place to contact for further information on how to do this.

Employment Contracts

Accepting an expat posting can have its pitfalls, so before you sign your contract pay special attention to things such as probation periods, accommodation, annual leave, travel entitlements, medical and dental cover, notice periods, and repatriation entitlements.

There is often confusion over the offer letter and the contract. An offer letter should give details of the terms of the job you are being offered, such as salary, leave, hours and other benefits; if you accept the terms of this offer, it becomes a legally binding contract. You may be asked to sign an additional Ministry of Labour contract that accompanies your residency application, but the initial offer letter is, in effect, your contract.

The UAE labour law allows for an end-of-service gratuity payment for employees. The rules are a bit convoluted, but basically, an employee on a fixed-term contract, who has completed one or more years of continuous service, will be entitled to 21 days pay for each of the first five years of service, and 30 days pay for each additional year. If the employee is on an 'unlimited duration' (open-ended) contract and terminates it of his own accord, he will get a third of the gratuity for a service period of between one and three years, two thirds for three to five years, and the full amount if service exceeds five years. Leaving before the end of your fixed-term contract or getting fired could result in you losing your gratuity. Gratuity payments are worked out according to your basic salary, which is why employers will often split your salary into various categories (basic, housing, transport and utilities). You will still get the same cash salary at the end of every month, but because your basic salary is much lower than your total salary, your gratuity payment is lower.

It is common for companies to have three or six-month probation periods written into employment contracts. Some companies may delay the residency process illegally until the probation period is up, which can make settling in difficult – no residency means you can't sponsor family members, buy a car or get a bank loan. You may also not be eligible for sick leave or annual leave during your probation period. All of these matters should be discussed with your future employer before signing your contract.

Labour Law

The Labour Law outlines everything related to employee entitlements, employment contracts and disciplinary rules. The law tends to favour employers, but it also clearly outlines employee rights.

Labour unions and strikes are illegal, although there have been some protests by labourers in the past. Rather than being punished, the labourers achieved some results. The employers concerned were forced to pay wages immediately or remedy living conditions, and a hotline was set up for other unpaid workers to report their employers. Also, an amended federal labour law looks likely to allow the formation of labour unions (trade unions have long existed in some other Gulf countries). If you find yourself in the situation where you have not

Bridge The Gulf

Starting or finding a job in a new part of the world is a challenging exprience. *Working in the Gulf* is a guide written by career coaching experts designed to give you all the advice needed to make your career in the region a succesful one.

been paid, you can file a case with the UAE Labour Department who will take the necessary action.

You could also get a lawyer to deal with the claim on your behalf (see p.114 for a list of law firms). Although lawyers are expensive in Dubai, the employer will have to bear the cost if the case is settled in your favour.

Maternity Leave

Maternity leave for public sector staff has been cut, from three months to two. Government workers can now claim up to 60 days off, fully paid. Previously, new mums were entitled to 30 days paid, 30 days on half pay, and 30 days unpaid. Private sector workers can claim up to 45 days on full pay, once they've completed one year of continuous service (it's Article 30 of the UAE Labour Law, if your boss needs reminding). This can only be used directly before and after the birth. Those who have been with their employer for less than a year can claim 45 days on half pay. Proud papas in the public sector now get three days off.

Changing Jobs

Until recently, anyone leaving a job and cancelling their visa faced the possibility of being 'banned' for six months. Fortunately, the banning rules have been relaxed, so as long as you remain on good terms with your employer, and he gives you permission to leave your job (in the form of a no objection certificate or NOC), you should be able to switch to a new job.

However there are catches: if you have a PhD or masters degree you can change jobs as many times as you like, but you are limited to two moves if you have a bachelor's degree and only one move if you have no tertiary qualifications. And you still need that crucial agreement from your previous sponsor – the all-important NOC.

To change sponsors, pick up the relevant forms from the Ministry of Labour and get them typed in Arabic. Get the forms signed and stamped by both your previous and new employers, and submit them along with the trade licence and establishment card of your new company. Everything goes to the Immigration Department who will amend your visa. In most cases your new employer will take care of this procedure for you.

There are some exceptions where you can transfer your sponsorship without the approval of your current sponsor, such as death of your sponsor, change of company ownership or company closure. Regulations differ in the free zones, as you are technically sponsored by the free zone authority (FZA) rather than the company. Therefore if you move to another company within the free zone, there is no need to transfer your visa.

Capital Gains Tax

Even though you are no longer resident in your home country, you may still be liable for capital gains. UK citizens may find the HM Revenue and Customs site helpful – www.hmrc.gov.uk.

Company Closure

Employees who face the unlucky situation of company bankruptcy or company closure are entitled under UAE Labour law to receive their gratuity payments and holiday pay, but you will need to speak to the labour department for the proper process as it is rather complex. An employee of a firm that has been closed is allowed to transfer sponsorship to a new employer if they are able to find a new job, but if not their visa will be cancelled and they will have to leave the country. To transfer the visa they'll need an attested certificate of closure, issued by the court and submitted to the Ministry of Labour & Social Affairs (04 269 1666). Consult the appropriate government offices to get your paperwork right, or consider investing in the services of a lawyer that specialises in labour issues (see p.114 for a list of lawyers).

Bank Accounts

Dubai is full of reputable banks that offer current, deposit and savings accounts, as well as credit cards and loans (although a lot more caution is now being used by banks where loans are concerned due to the global credit crisis of 2008). Most of them also offer the convenience of online banking, so you can check balances, transfer money, and pay bills with just a few clicks of the mouse. There are plenty of ATMs (cashpoints) around Dubai and most cards are compatible with the central bank network (some also offer global access links). You may pay a small fee for using another bank's ATM but it should never be more than a few dirhams.

To open an account in most Dubai banks, you need a residence visa or to have your residency application underway. The bank employee dealing with your application will require your original passport, copies of your passport (personal details and visa) and an NOC from your sponsor. Some banks set a minimum account limit – this can be around Dhs.2,000 for a deposit account and as much as Dhs.10,000 for a current account. This means that at some point in each month your account balance must be above the minimum limit. Although credit cards are widely available, Dubai banks don't provide an overdraft facility. If you don't have a residence visa, meBANK (an offshoot of Emirates Bank) will open an account for you and provide an ATM card, but not a chequebook. meBANK also allows you to apply online for an account (www.me.ae).

A number of laws passed recently aim to combat money laundering. The UAE Central Bank monitors all incoming and outgoing transfers, and banks and currency exchanges are required to report transfers over a certain limit. Additionally, if you need to send more than Dhs.2,000 by international transfer you may have to show a valid passport.

Banking Comparison Table

Name	Phone	Web	Tele-Banking
ABN AMRO Bank	04 351 2200	www.abnamro.com	04 426 6000
Abu Dhabi Commercial Bank	800 2030	www.adcb.com	800 2030
Arab Bank	04 295 0845	www.arabbank.ae	800 27224
Bank of Sharjah	04 282 7278	www.bankofsharjah.com	na
Barclays Bank Plc	04 362 6700	www.barclays.ae	800 428 6000
BNP Paribas	04 424 8200	www.bnpparibas.ae	na
Citibank – Middle East	04 324 5000	www.citibank.com/uae	04 311 4000
Dubai Islamic Bank	04 295 9999	www.alislami.ae	04 609 2222
Emirates Bank	04 316 0316	www.emiratesbank.ae	04 316 0316
Emirates Islamic Bank	04 316 0101	www.emiratesislamicbank.ae	04 316 0101
HSBC Bank Middle East	800 4722	www.hsbc.ae	800 4722
Lloyds TSB Bank ▶ p.109	04 342 2000	www.lloydstsb.ae	04 342 2999
Mashreqbank	04 217 4800	www.mashreqbank.com	04 424 4444
National Bank of Abu Dhabi	800 2211	www.nbad.com	800 2211
National Bank of Dubai (NBD)	04 310 0101	www.nbd.com	800 4444
RAK Bank	04 213 0000	www.rakbank.ae	04 213 0000
The Royal Bank of Scotland	04 351 2200	www.rbsbank.ae	04 426 6000
Standard Chartered Bank – Middle East	04 352 0455	www.standardchartered.com	04 313 8888
Union National Bank	800 2600	www.unb.co.ae	800 2600

Financial Planning

Many expats are attracted to Dubai for the tax-free salary and the opportunity to put a little something away for the future. When choosing a financial planner in Dubai there are some key points to bear in mind: most importantly you should ensure that they

Sleep more soundly with one of Dubai's safest banks.

There, that feels better already.

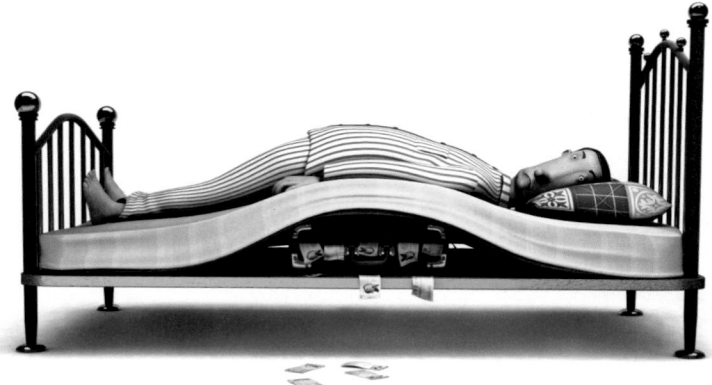

Choosing a bank isn't easy, whether you want a simple personal savings account or a high-powered corporate partner. So it should help you to know that Lloyds TSB is the only Moody's Aaa-rated bank in Dubai. Giving you complete peace of mind. And maybe even a comfier night's sleep.

Visit us in branch or call +971 4 342 2000

 Lloyds TSB | for the journey...

Cost of Living

Apples (per kg)	Dhs.6
Bananas (per kg)	Dhs.4.5
Barber haircut (male)	Dhs.25
Bottle of house wine (restaurant)	Dhs.150
Bottle of wine (off-licence)	Dhs.40
Burger (takeaway)	Dhs.12
Bus (10km journey)	Dhs.2
Can of dog food	Dhs.5
Can of soft drink	Dhs.1
Cappuccino	Dhs.18
Car rental (per day)	Dhs.100
Carrots (per kg)	Dhs.5.5
CD album	Dhs.60
Chocolate bar	Dhs.2.5
Cigarettes (pack of 20)	Dhs.7
Cinema ticket	Dhs.30
Cleaner (per hour)	Dhs.25
Digital photo printing (4x6)	Dhs.1
Dozen eggs	Dhs.8
Fresh beef (per kg)	Dhs.25-30
Fresh chicken (per kg)	Dhs.30
Fresh fish (per kg)	Dhs.20
Golf (18 holes)	Dhs.450
House wine (glass)	Dhs.25-40
Large takeaway pizza	Dhs.40
Loaf of bread	Dhs.4.5
Local postage stamp	Dhs.1
Milk (1 litre)	Dhs.5.5
Mobile to mobile call (local, per minute)	30 fils
New release DVD	Dhs.85
Newspaper (international)	Dhs.15
Newspaper (local)	Dhs.2
Orange juice (1 litre)	Dhs.4.5
Pack of 24 asprin/paracetamol tablets	Dhs.7
Petrol (gallon)	Dhs.6.25
Pint of beer	Dhs.20
Postcard	Dhs.3
Potatoes (per kg)	Dhs.3.50
Rice (1kg)	Dhs.7
Salon haircut (female)	Dhs.90
Salon haircut (male)	Dhs.70
Shawarma	Dhs.3
Six-pack of beer (off-licence)	Dhs.25
Strawberries (per punnet)	Dhs.6 (seasonal)
Sugar (2kg)	Dhs.7.5
Taxi (10km journey)	Dhs.20
Text message (local)	18 fils
Tube of toothpaste	Dhs.6
Water 1.5 litres (restaurant)	Dhs.10
Water 1.5 litres (supermarket)	Dhs.1.5

are licensed by the Central Bank of the UAE, so that you have some recourse in the event of a dispute. You should also consider the company's international presence – if you leave Dubai you still want to be able to reach the company and enjoy the same access to advice and information, and your investments. Finally, it may be better to use an independent company or advisor who is not tied to a specific bank or savings company, and therefore will objectively offer you the full range of savings products on the market.

Before leaving your home country you should contact the tax authorities to ensure that you are complying with the financial laws there. Most countries will consider you not liable for income tax once you prove you're a UAE resident (a contract of employment is normally a good starting point). However, you may still have to fulfil certain criteria, so do some research before you come (if you are already here, check with your embassy). You may be liable for tax on any income you receive from back home (for example if you are renting out your property).

Pensions

If you have a pension scheme in your home country, it may not be worth continuing your contributions once you come to Dubai, but rather to set up a tax-free, offshore savings plan. It is always advisable to speak to your financial adviser about such matters before you make any big move.

Offshore Accounts

While offshore banking used to be associated with the very wealthy or the highly shady, most expats now take advantage of tax efficient plans.

An offshore account works in much the same way as a conventional account, but it can be adjusted specifically for you. Money can be moved where it will produce the best rewards, and cash accessed whenever and wherever you need it, in your desired currency. Offshore accounts allow for management through the internet, and over the phone, in a range of currencies (most commonly in US dollars, euros or pounds sterling). If you are travelling outside the UAE, try to make sure that your account comes with 24 hour banking, internationally recognised

Inflation Nation

Inflation in the UAE rose to over 11% in 2008 – the highest level in almost 20 years. Cost of living is on the up, and not just housing prices – everyday items, such as food and cigarettes, are becoming more costly too.

debit cards, and the ability to write cheques in your preferred currency. To open an account, there is usually a minimum balance of around $10,000. Do some thorough research before opening an account, and check the potential tax implications in your home country. It is important to seek independent financial advice, and not just the opinion of the bank offering you an account. Lloyds TSB (www.lloydstsb.ae) and HSBC (www.hsbc.ae) both offer good offshore services, but will of course, only advise on their own products. To open your account, you may have to produce certain reports or documents from your chosen country. However, for those willing to do the research and undertake the admin, offshore banking can prove to be a lucrative investment.

Financial Advisors		
KPMG	04 403 0300	www.ae-kpmg.com
Mondial (Dubai) – Financial Partners International	04 331 0524	www.financial-partners.biz
PIC Middle East	04 343 3878	www.pic-uae.com
Prosperity Offshore Investment Consultants	04 312 4334	www.prosperity-uae.com

Taxation

The UAE levies no personal income taxes or withholding taxes, but the IMF is helping the UAE to plan the introduction of VAT, probably by 2010. This would no doubt be unpopular, and could hamper attempts to attract foreign investment, but the IMF is advising Middle Eastern governments to introduce tax reforms in order to diversify their resources. The only noticeable taxes you pay as an expat are a 5% municipality tax on rental accommodation and a 30% tax on alcohol bought at Dubai liquor stores. The municipality tax is included in your DEWA bill, and if you don't pay your utilities will be cut off. This has resulted in some complaints – the tax is meant to cover refuse collection, street lighting and community road networks, but people renting freehold properties also pay maintenance to cover these things so it's understandable why some people have objections. There is also a 10% municipality tax and a 10% service charge in hotel food and beverage outlets, but you'll find that these are usually incorporated into the displayed price. In 2007, the Salik road toll system (p.226) was introduced for the purpose of 'traffic management'. Many residents are unhappy about the system and with drivers seeing little or no improvement to the traffic situation while racking up charges of up to Dhs.24 a day, some feel that Salik is effectively a road tax.

Legal Issues

The country's constitution permits each emirate to have its own legislative body and judicial authority. Dubai has thus retained its own judicial system, including appellate courts (courts of appeal), which are not part of the UAE federal system. There are three primary sources of UAE law, namely federal laws and decrees (applicable in all emirates), local laws (laws and regulations enacted by the individual emirates), and Shariah (Islamic law). Generally, when a court is determining a commercial issue, it gives initial consideration to any applicable federal and/or local laws. If such federal and local laws do not address the issue, Shariah may be applied. Moreover, Shariah generally applies to family law matters, particularly when involving Muslims.

Divorce

Statistics show that the UAE has one of the highest divorce rates in the Arab world. To counter this, bodies such as the State Marriage Fund have launched schemes offering education and counselling services to National couples. Expats

Speedy Separation
Under Shariah law, a Muslim man can divorce his wife without cause by stating 'I divorce you' three times over the course of three months. Classical Shariah states that a woman can divorce a man under very limited conditions, including if he is insane, suffers from leprosy, or is infertile at the time of marriage.

can get divorced in Dubai, and in some cases the procedure can be relatively straightforward. However, expat couples wishing to divorce may also be governed by the laws of their home country (if the couple has mixed nationalities the home country of the husband applies), so it is advisable to seek legal advice. A husband who sponsors his wife has the right to have her residence visa cancelled in the event of divorce.

Getting A Will

Having a valid will in place is one of those essential things that everybody should do. It is especially important to seek legal advice when drawing up your will if you become a property owner in Dubai. This is one area where the law is rather complicated – under Shariah law, the basic rules as to who inherits property after someone's death differ to 'western' rules. For example, in the event of your death it may be the case that your sons (or brother, if you don't have any sons) are first in line for inheritance and your wife could end up with nothing. Therefore it is better to make sure that you have a clear last will and testament in place. A Dubai-based lawyer will be able to assist you with a locally viable will. See the table on p.114 for a list of law firms, or contact Just Wills (www.just-wills.net), part of a UK-based estate planning organisation that has a presence in the UAE.

Adoption

Although adoption is not recognised in the Muslim community, many expats based in the UAE have found it relatively straightforward to adopt children from Asia and the Far East. Once you successfully meet all the requirements in your adopted child's home country, you should have little trouble bringing your child back to the UAE and applying for a residence visa. Check the regulations involved in securing your citizenship for your child; your embassy will be able to help. Contact the Adoption Support Group (04 349 3970) for more information.

Crime

Dubai is known for having a low crime rate – in fact for many expats it is still the number one benefit of living here. It would be naive to think that there was no crime, as there are cases of theft, rape and even murder, but these occur on such a small scale that they rarely affect the quality of life of the average expat.

The most common reason for expats getting on the wrong side of the law is driving under the influence of alcohol. In the UAE there is a zero-tolerance policy – forget blood alcohol ratios or 'one safe pint'. If even a sip of alcohol has passed your lips, you are not allowed to drive. While there are few spot checks, if you have even a minor accident, and even if you were not at fault, you might be breathalysed and the consequences can be serious. Even driving the morning after a heavy night is risky, since you will still have alcohol in your system. You will be arrested, and the usual penalty is a minimum 30 days in prison. You should bear in mind too that

---

Tips For Women

The following general tips are useful for women in Dubai:
- Stick to the dress code; tight, revealing clothing equals unwanted attention.
- Be careful when out alone at night, especially after a few drinks.
- Never get into an unmetered taxi; and always take down the taxi number.
- As long as you exercise due care and attention Dubai is a safe place for women.

Neighbourhood Watch

In their efforts to maintain and promote a safe community, the Dubai Police launched Al Ameen, a confidential toll free telephone service where you can report anything suspicious. For example, if you have seen someone hanging around your property or loitering at cashpoints you can pass the information on anonymously by calling 800 4888 or emailing alameen@eim.ae.

PLANNING FOR THE FUTURE WITH JUST WILLS

Do you own assets /or have children in Dubai?

Are you aware of the implications of not having a valid Will?

Did you know that without a Will in Dubai your estate can pass via the provisions of the Shariah Law or even under the Laws of Intestacy/your home country?

Do you know that Guardians could be appointed on your behalf?

WHY NOT TAKE THE MOST IMPORTANT STEP TO SECURE YOUR FAMILY AND HAVE A PROFESSIONALLY CONSTRUCTED WILL IN PLACE.
BENEFITS OF OUR SERVICE INCLUDE:

- **Ensuring your estate will be dealt with tax efficiently**
- **Estate Planning**
- **Distribution of your assets to the right people**
- **Appointment of guardians for your children**
- **Appointment of appropriate Executors**
- **Options to leave a legacy to a Charity**
- **Establishment of trusts to maximize and protect Assets**
- **To exclude ex-partners from claiming from your estate**
- **Living wills**
- **Shariah wills**
- **Power of Attorneys**
- **To ensure peace of mind that your loved ones are protected, have a Will drafted as a priority.**

For more information contact: Info@just-wills.net
Or call   04 311 6592.

your insurance company could refuse to pay the claim if you were in an accident, even if you were not to blame. It's just not worth the risk – cabs are cheap and there are plenty of them.

Taking illegal narcotics is an absolute no-no – even the smallest amounts of marijuana or hashish could earn you a prison sentence of four years or more. This will almost certainly be followed by deportation. If you are found guilty of dealing or smuggling, you could be looking at a life sentence, or even the death penalty (although this is uncommon). Even some medications that are legal in your home country, such as codeine, temazepam and prozac, may be banned here – check with the UAE embassy in your home country before you leave, and if you are in any doubt, try and find an alternative or at least have a copy of the prescription and a letter from your doctor. You can see a list of approved drugs on the Ministry of Health website (www.moh.gov.ae) although it is not known how frequently this list is updated or how reliable it is.

Other Common Crimes

The following acts are definite law breakers, and although many of them are often overlooked, they are still against the law:
- Buying alcohol without a liquor licence
- Bouncing cheques
- Eating, smoking or drinking in public during daylight hours in Ramadan (including non-Muslims)
- Living together if not married
- Kissing in public or lewd behaviour
- Homosexual behaviour
- Distributing religious material (non-Muslim)

Harming others, whether physically or verbally, will get you into trouble – at the very least a heavy fine, but if the other person was injured a jail term may be in order. If the victim chooses to drop the charges then you will be released. If you are detained for being drunk and disorderly you may spend a night in the cells, but if you are abusive you could be looking at a fine or longer sentence.

In a very high profile case in 2008, two Britons were charged with public indecency (after it was alleged they were having sex in public) and being under the influence of alcohol. Apart from having their exploits publicly broadcast by the world's media and being fired from work (in the case of the female), the pair received a three-month suspended sentence, fines and deportation, although legally the punishment could have been much stronger. This case should serve as a warning for all visitors and residents in the UAE, and a reminder that the authorities will extend the full arm of the law if you are caught breaking it.

Traffic Accidents & Violations

If you are involved in a traffic accident in which someone is seriously injured or killed, it's possible that you'll be detained until the circumstances are ascertained. If you are found to have been at fault (and especially if under the influence of alcohol) you're likely to spend time in prison.

If you are held responsible for someone's death you'll remain in prison until the blood money has been paid to the victim's family, or until the family grants you a pardon. Make sure your insurance covers you for blood money, but be aware that insurance companies will do all they can to get out of paying it.

Law Firms		
Afridi & Angell	04 330 3900	www.afridi-angell.com
Al Sharif Advocates & Legal Consultants	04 262 8222	www.dubailaw.com
Al Tamimi & Company	04 364 1641	www.tamimi.com
Hadef Legal Consultants and Advocates	04 429 2999	www.hadalaw.com
Musthafa & Almana Associates	04 329 8411	www.sindhyamaassociates.com
Trench Associates	04 355 3146	www.trenchlaw.com

Arrest

If you are arrested you will be taken to a police station and questioned. If it's decided that you must go to court the case will go to the public prosecutor who will set a date for a hearing. For a minor offence you may get bail, and the police will keep your passport and often the passport of another male resident who is willing to vouch for you. Police stations have holding cells, so if you don't get bail you'll be held until the hearing. All court proceedings are conducted in Arabic, so you should secure the services of a translator. If sentenced you'll go straight from court to jail.

Upon being arrested you are advised to contact your embassy or consulate. They can liaise with family, advise on local legal procedures and provide a list of lawyers, but they will not pay your legal fees. The consulate will try to ensure that you are not denied your basic human rights, but they cannot act as lawyers, investigators, secure bail, or get you released.

Doing Time

Most prisoners will find themselves in the new Central Jail near Al Awir, which was moved from its old location in Al Wasl in 2006. Short-term or temporary male prisoners may be held in an 'Out Jail', while long-term prisoners are likely to go to the main Central Jail.

Conditions inside the old jail were described as basic but bearable, but the new complex has much improved conditions, with the reported overcrowding in the old jail a thing of the past.

Inmates are given three meals a day, and there's a small snack shop with limited opening hours. Prisoners are allowed occasional access to payphones, so if you are visiting an inmate a few phone cards will be appreciated.

Prisoners are generally allowed visits once a week. Thursdays are reserved for visits to Arab detainees, and Fridays are for other nationalities. Men and women are not allowed to visit together – men can visit from 10:00 to 11:00 and women from 16:00 to 17:00. If you are a woman you may not be allowed to visit a man who is of no family relation to you. Times are subject to change so it's best to check by calling the Department of Punitive Establishments (04 344 0351). In late 2007 there was a clampdown on drinking and driving with whispers of increased jail sentences, so always remember the law is zero tolerance.

DIFC

Housing

The first decision you need to make in terms of housing in Dubai is whether you want to buy or rent. It is only since 2002 that expats have been able to own property in Dubai and, until very recently, apartments and villas were being snapped up as quickly as they come on the market. The second decision is whether you would prefer to live in a villa or an apartment, and the third is what area you would like to live in. This chapter gives a detailed description of all the residential areas in Dubai, as well as the ins and outs of the processes involved in buying and renting.

Renting In Dubai

Despite expats now being able to buy property in Dubai, the property market is still somewhat volatile and many choose to continue renting. New residents arriving in Dubai to start a new job may be given accommodation (or a housing allowance) as part of their package. Your allowance may not always be high enough to rent a place in the area you want, so many expats choose to top up the amount out of their own pockets. If your contract provides specific accommodation but you would prefer the cash equivalent, it is worth asking as most employers are willing to be flexible.

Rents have risen steadily over the past few years, with 2008 seeing some severe increases – up to 70% in some cases. A decree was passed by Sheikh Mohammed in late 2006 limiting rental increases to 7% per year for existing tenants, but this means some landlords have hiked rents for new tenants, as there is no limit on what they can charge.

Finding A Home

There are a number of ways to find suitable accommodation, the most obvious of which is via a real estate agent (see p.118). But this isn't the only, or necessarily the best, option. If you have the time it is worth checking classified ads (p.69). An even better bet is to drive around a few areas and look out for 'To Let' signs displayed on vacant villas; these will display the phone number of either the landlord or the letting agent. Often this extra effort when looking for a home can result in a 'real find' and many proud barbecues to come.

Housing Abbreviations

BR	Bedroom
C.A/C	Central air conditioning (usually included in the rent)
D/S	Double storey villa
Ensuite	Bedroom has private bathroom
Ext S/Q	Servant quarters located outside the villa
Fully fitted	Includes appliances (such as oven, refrigerator, washing machine)
Hall flat	Apartment has an entrance hall (entrance doesn't open directly onto living room)
L/D	Living/dining room area
Pvt garden	Private garden
S/Q	Servant quarters
S/S	Single storey villa
Shared pool	Pool is shared with other villas in compound
W A/C	Window air conditioning (often indicates an older building)
W/robes	Built in wardrobes (closets)

Like any major city, Dubai has an enormous range of accommodation options and residential areas, each with its own pros and cons (see p.128 for details). Prices quoted are intended to illustrate going rates, but bear in mind that negotiation is part and parcel of the deal and that there are still finds to be had. Another reason for chatting to other expats is to find out what makes some areas more popular than others. Speaking to your colleagues about commuting times to work is also a good idea before you decide on an area.

The Lease

Your lease is an important document and, in addition to the financial terms, will state what you are liable for in terms of maintenance as well as what your landlord's responsibilities are. Therefore it is important that you read the contract and discuss any points of contention before you sign on the dotted line. The following points are often open to negotiation:

your shortcut to better living...

Finding that perfect property can be a difficult experience. Whether you are looking to lease or to buy, the Real Estate Specialists can give you advice in your search for the ideal property, be it your future home or a financial investment. Our team is committed to finding the right property for you.

- Real Estate
  Sales, Leasing, Management & Investment

- Interior Decoration
  Curtains, Soft Furnishings & Upholstery

- Relocation
  Settling in, Orientation & Cultural training

- Maintenance
  A/C, Plumbing, Electrical, Painter & Handyman

the specialists
complete real estate solutions
property • relocation • furnishings • maintenance

T +971 4 331 2662 P. O. Box 44644 Dubai U.A.E.
www.thespecialistsdubai.com

Renting Smart
Always check the paperwork: to avoid disputes with your landlord, the Rent Committee advises that both parties produce a written agreement. This contract reduces the risk of either party falling out on the rental terms discussed. Remember to get a copy of the estate agent's identification card and RERA licence, and make sure you save copies of all receipts, contracts and other documents.

- Tenants usually pay rent via a number of post-dated cheques – typically two or three. If you can afford to pay the whole year up front, use it as a bargaining tool to reduce the annual rent.
- Try to negotiate a fixed rate for two, three, or more years – that way you won't get any nasty shocks with rent increases after your first year.
- Unless you are certain you won't stay for more than a year, don't sign a non-renewable contract.
- Make sure you agree who is responsible for maintenance. Some rents might be fully inclusive of all maintenance and repairs, while you could negotiate a much cheaper rent (particularly on older properties) if you agree to carry out any maintenance work.
- While not common, some landlords will include utility expenses in the rent.
- Security deposit amounts vary, but are usually around Dhs.5,000 to Dhs.10,000 (although some landlords will ask for up to Dhs.20,000).
- The landlord must give written notice of any rent increase at least one month in advance. If your landlord does try to increase the rent unfairly then there are government channels to dispute rent matters.

Pay Out Or Get Out

Rent increases are a hot topic. While the Rent Committee aims to help, landlords still hold a great deal of power. Keep all documentation and offers in writing to continue paying the rent at an acceptable rate and know that you cannot be evicted without a court order.

Rent Disputes

In late 2006, Sheikh Mohammed capped annual rent increases at 7% for existing tenants. There have been reported cases where landlords refused to renew leases because they were 'renovating' or needed the place for their 'brother'. Although there is a Rent Committee (Dubai Municipality Building in Deira, 04 206 3917), many people have simply put up with the increase, fearing that they would incur costs in arguing it, and could lose anyway. However, the Rent Committee has ruled in favour of the tenants in many instances and you should know that you cannot be thrown out of your home without a court order, even if your lease is up (provided, of course, that you are still paying rent at the rate agreed in your tenancy contract). In the case of a rent dispute, you can approach the Rent Committee who will arbitrate between you and your landlord. You can lodge your complaint in the Dubai Municipality building in Deira, opposite the Sheraton hotel (opening hours are 09:00 to 14:30, Sunday to Thursday) or call 04 206 3917 for more information. Take your passport copy, the tenancy contract, and any correspondence. Any non-Arabic paperwork will have to be

Real Estate Agents		
Al Futtaim Real Estate	04 211 9111	www.al-futtaim.com
Arenco Group	04 355 5552	www.arencore.com
Asteco Property Management	04 403 7700	www.astecoproperty.com
Betterhomes	04 344 7714	www.bhomes.com
Cluttons	04 334 8585	www.cluttons.com
Dubai Property Group	04 262 9888	www.dubaipropertygroup.com
Dubai Real Estate Corporation	04 398 6666	www.realestate-dubai.gov.ae
Global Capital Partners	04 438 0665	www.globalcappartners.com
Landmark Properties	04 331 6161	www.landmark-dubai.com
Links Real Estate	04 339 3100	www.links-realestate.com
Oryx Real Estate	04 351 5770	www.oryxrealestate.com
The Property Shop	04 345 5711	www.propertyshopdubai.com
Sherwoods	04 343 8002	www.sherwoodsproperty.com
The Specialists ▶ p.117	04 331 2662	www.thespecialistsdubai.com

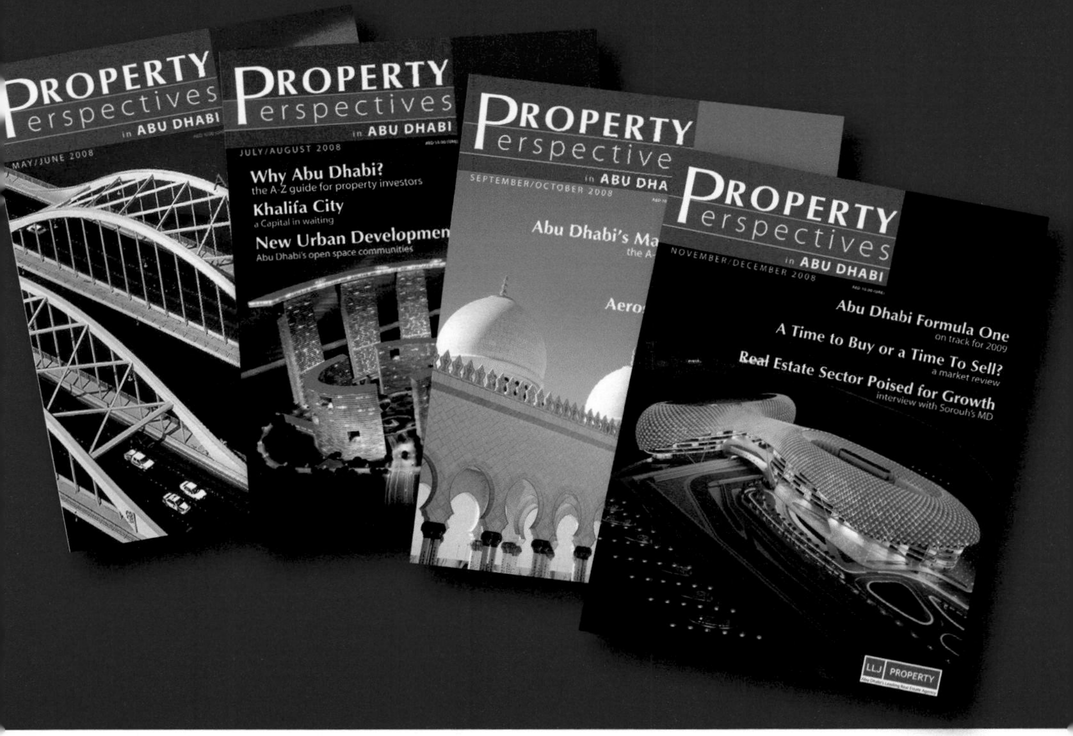

PROPERTY perspectives in ABU DHABI

Abu Dhabi's first dedicated property magazine from Abu Dhabi's leading real estate agency

For Sales, Leasing, Property Management & Investment Opportunities

CALL
+971 2 495 0500
www.lljproperty.com

LLJ PROPERTY
Abu Dhabi's Leading Real Estate Agency

translated. The official will fill in the form outlining your complaint, and you'll then have to pay a hefty fee – around 4% of the existing annual rent, plus an extra Dhs.100. Both parties will be instructed to attend on a given date. If you're lucky the landlord may well back down at this stage.

There have been mixed reports about the Rent Committee; some have reported success and others failure. But on the whole the outcome is often in the tenant's favour.

Main Accommodation Options

Renter's Nightmare

Most leases are fixed for one year. Leave before the year is up, and you will probably have to pay a penalty or lose the months you've already paid for as the year's rent is usually paid upfront. (Some landlords allow you to pay in two or three instalments with post-dated cheques). If you really want to get out of your lease you may be able to sub-let the place to new tenants, although this can only be done with your landlord's consent.

Apartment/Villa Sharing

Sharing a large villa has long been a popular option for many young professionals for economic and lifestyle reasons. The down side is the lack of privacy, and not having somewhere to call your own. You may also have to deal with the hassle of finding new housemates if someone moves out (and covering their share of the rent in the meantime). If you're looking to share, the noticeboards at area supermarkets or property classifieds in *Gulf News* are good places to start.

Keep in mind, however, that the municipality is trying to stamp out the practice. In an effort to prevent multiple families from sharing villas and breaking health codes, officials stepped up their efforts in 2008 to weed out villa sharers, and have systematically been evicting sharers in many areas. If caught, both the tenants and landlords face heavy fines. Some tenants in areas such as Al Barsha and Jumeirah, which are allotted as family accommodation spots, have been forced out by their landlords. In the most extreme cases, power and water have been disconnected to get them out. The Rent Committee will be little help where such homes are mixed, because strictly speaking, unmarried and unrelated men and women are not allowed to live together.

Standard Apartment

Dubai apartments come in various sizes, from studio to four bedroom, with widely varying rents to match. Newer apartments usually have central air conditioning (C A/C) and older ones have the noisier window air conditioners, where the unit is built into the wall. C A/C is usually more expensive, although in some apartment buildings your air-conditioning costs are built into the rent.

Top of the range apartments often come semi-furnished (with a cooker, fridge and washing machine), and have 24 hour security, satellite TV, covered parking, private gym and swimming pool. In some cases, there are additional facilities on site, such as a restaurant, shop and laundry.

One downside is that you're at the mercy of your neighbours to some extent, especially those upstairs (a disadvantage of marble/ceramic floors is that every scraped chair and stiletto heel is amplified through your ceiling). Depending on the area, parking may be a problem too – check to see if you get a space.

Villa

Most people's dream of the expat life is to have a beautiful villa where you can spend lazy days by the pool and balmy evenings around the barbie. This lifestyle doesn't come cheap, and smart villas are snapped up pretty quickly. The good news is that if you look hard enough and use the grapevine, you might find the perfect villa that won't break the budget. Depending on the area, size and age of the villa it may be cheaper than some apartments, even if air-conditioning costs will be higher.

Villas differ greatly in quality and facilities. Independent ones often have bigger gardens, while compound villas are usually newer and often have shared facilities like a pool (and even a gym).

Hotel Apartment

A hotel apartment is expensive, but ideal if you need temporary, furnished accommodation. There's a large concentration in Bur Dubai, but more and more are cropping up out of town. They can be rented on a daily, weekly, monthly or yearly basis. Water and electricity are also included in the rent (see p.49).

Other Rental Costs

On The Move
If you're moving within Dubai, you can use a moving company or hire a few guys with their own truck from downtown Bur Dubai. The latter is a cheaper option but requires constant supervision to ensure damage is kept to a minimum. Agree a price upfront to avoid a dispute later – work on around Dhs.50-70 per hour including two men.

Extra costs to be considered when renting a home are:
- Water and electricity deposit (Dhs.2,000 for villas, Dhs.1,000 for apartments) paid directly to Dubai Electricity & Water Authority (DEWA) and fully refundable on cancellation of the lease.
- Real estate commission – around 5% of annual rent (one-off payment).
- Maintenance charge – varies, but could be around 5% of annual rent (may be included in the rent).
- Municipality tax – 5% of annual rent.
- Fully refundable security deposit – Dhs.5,000-Dhs.10,000.

If you're renting a villa, don't forget that you may have to maintain a garden and pay for extra water. It's worth asking the landlord or the previous tenants what the average DEWA bills are for a particular property. With your landlord's permission you could have a borehole installed to save money on water bills. To have a well dug and a pump fitted, expect to pay around Dhs.3,000.

Often the more popular accommodation has waiting lists that are years long. To secure an immediate tenancy many people offer the landlord 'key money': a down payment of several thousand dirhams to secure the accommodation (in other words, jump the queue).

Purchasing A Home

Property-Owner Visa
Until mid-2008, property owners in Dubai were eligible for residency permits that were valid as long as he or she owned the property. That rule no longer exists, although property owners are still able to apply for investor-based residency, without the help of the developer.

In 2002, the rules surrounding property purchase were opened up allowing foreign nationals to purchase freehold property in Dubai, but only in certain developments. A property boom ensued, with villas selling out within minutes, even though construction hadn't even started. The majority of properties have been bought by investors looking to make a bob or two in resale or renting, although plenty of residents have bought their dream homes in Arabian Ranches and Emirates Hills. Although prices have shot up, what you get for your money is still pretty good compared with some other cities around the world. One thing buyers have been frustrated by is the constant delays. At the time of writing, the future of Dubai's property market is in question. Confidence in the market has dropped, thanks to the current global recession. As a result, prices seem to be coming down and mortgages are becoming harder to obtain. As with buying any property, legal assistance is recommended and many legal firms in Dubai now have departments that deal specifically in real estate law.

Escrow Accounts

Trust accounts became mandatory in late 2007 for new, off-plan properties. Projects started after August 2007 cannot accept payment directly from buyers. Instead, buyers will pay into trust (or escrow) accounts, monitored by the Land Department, with money only released when building commitments are met. The move is designed to stop developers from disappearing with investors' money, and assure buyers that their 20m pool won't end up a 5m pond.

The Process

Once you find your dream home, it is worth seeking legal advice to help you in the purchase process. As a start, you have to be at least 21 years old to purchase property in Dubai.

For new, off-plan developments, it's worth speaking directly to developers and visiting their presentation centres and show homes. You may have to register in order to be eligible for new launches and often this is done at the sales centre where you give basic details and a copy of your passport. On the day of the launch you need to take your passport and copies and complete the contracts. You also have to pay a deposit or down payment at this stage, which is usually 10% of the purchase price, but may be up to 25%. Often, only a cheque is accepted. Further payments are then scheduled depending on the timescale of the development, normally around 15% every six months until completion, although many developers are offering more enticing payment plans in an effort to lure potential investors.

If you're buying as an investment, check if there are any limitations on reselling. Joint ownership is possible, but only with next of kin (mother, father, husband, wife, son, daughter) and both parties must be present to complete the formalities. It's important that you do your homework before you begin the purchasing process as not all mortgage lenders will give finance on all developments.

If you're buying from an individual (secondary market) the process is a bit different, and you'll need to use the services of a real estate broker. Once you've picked the property, you'll need to sign a memorandum of understanding (MOU) between yourself and the seller. This document, usually signed by both parties in conjuction with a 10% deposit, is basically a sales agreement and outlines the terms and conditions of the deal. The MOU will also determine when the final transfer will take place. Secondary sales are finalised at one of two locations. For properties that have yet to be completed, property transfers happen at the developer's office. For completed and registered properties, transfers take place at the Land Department offices in Deira. The Real Estate Regulatory Authority (RERA) recently announced laws that will bring a new level of transparency and security to the sometimes confusing real estate market. At the time of writing, these laws had yet to be executed.

Main Developers

Abyaar Real Estate Development	04 324 2144	www.abyaar.com
ARY	04 226 3535	www.arymarinaview.com
B&M FZ CO	04 299 6968	www.larivieratower.com
Continental Properties	04 222 5586	www.continentalrs.com
Damac Properties	04 332 2005	www.damacproperties.com
Dubai Properties	04 390 0094	www.dubai-properties.ae
Emaar Properties PJSC	04 367 3333	www.emaar.com
ETA Star Property Developers LLC	04 268 7222	www.etastar.com
First Group ▶ p.123	04 409 7500	www.thefirstgroup.com
Fortune Group	04 331 6789	www.fortunegroup.ae
Global Capital Partners	04 438 0665	www.globalcappartners.com
Nakheel Properties	04 390 3333	www.nakheel.ae
Saba Real Estate	04 330 0086	www.saba-re-com
Trident International Holdings	04 883 0555	www.tihglobal.com

Mortgages

Soon after the government announced the granting of freehold status of residential property to expats, mortgage plans were introduced for those wishing to purchase. Until autumn 2008, financing companies offered up to 90% of the purchase price or valuation, depending on the credit rating of the borrower. Since the global credit crunch reached the region in late 2008, most financing companies have become much

Getting Out Early

When arranging your home finance, check whether there are penalties for early redemption of the mortgage – they could be up to 2% of the mortgage value. Life insurance isn't always mandatory, but some banks insist you take out one of their policies which may involve a medical at their chosen Dubai clinic which can be inconvenient if you're arranging the mortgage from overseas.

INVEST AT THE FOREFRONT OF
OPPORTUNITY

All images are for illustrative purposes only

The First Group invites you to invest in lucrative emerging property markets. With bespoke developments in the most prestigious locations across the UAE, the First Group offers you unmatched possibilities for a secure and rewarding investment.

THE FIRST GROUP

INVEST NOW... SECURE YOUR FUTURE

CALL +971 4 511 8792 (UAE) OR +44 870 042 2888 (UK)

For more details visit www.thefirstgroup.com

Crunch Time
*At the end of 2008,
the previously blazing
Dubai property market
was decidedly chilly,
with some developers
reporting zero sales
over the last few
months. Optimists
are predicting that it's
just a minor hiccup in
an otherwise strong
market; pessimists
say that property will
never recover. Watch
this space.*

more conservative with their lending. Expect to receive loans no greater than 75% of the purchase price.

Mortgages must be paid back in monthly instalments within a maximum of 25 years (though 15 year mortgages are more popular), and rates are comparable to international norms, although the rate is often a little higher for non-residents. The mortgage amount depends on the chosen mortgage plan and is limited to an amount no greater than 60 times the monthly household income (husband and wife's combined), although these parameters might change in the future. Most banks that offer mortgages offer a 'pre-approved home finance', meaning you can get the go ahead for a mortgage before you actually choose a property, which speeds up the process (as well as gives you peace of mind during your home hunting). When buying a home on the secondary market, sellers and agents will often require that you obtain a mortgage pre-approval before signing the MOU (see Buying Property, p.121). Before deciding on which bank to borrow from, keep in mind that most banks only lend to certain developers, so be sure you are not requesting a loan from a bank that doesn't work with your developer of choice.

A tightening of regulations introduced in 2008 now means that mortgages taken out on properties in Dubai have to be sold by registered financial institutions, and be insured. The credit crunch has also seen many banks in the UAE scale back or even freeze their mortgage lending.

Mortgage Providers		
Abu Dhabi Commercial Bank (ADCB)	02 696 2222	www.adcb.com
Amlak Finance PJSC	04 427 4500	www.amlakfinance.com
Barclays Bank	04 362 6888	www.barclays.com
Dubai Bank	04 332 8989	www.dubaibank.ae
Dubai Islamic Bank	04 295 9999	www.alislami.ae
Emirates Bank International	04 225 6256	www.emiratesbank.ae
HSBC Bank Middle East	800 4722	www.hsbc.ae
Lloyds TSB Bank Plc ▶ p.109	04 342 2000	www.lloydstsb.ae
Mashreqbank	04 217 4800	www.mashreqbank.com
National Bank of Dubai (NBD)	04 310 0101	www.nbd.com
RAK Bank	04 224 8000	www.rakbank.ae
Tamweel	04 295 2259	www.tamweel.ae

Other Purchasing Costs

Most property owners will pay a maintenance charge to cover the upkeep of the building, gardens and any shared facilities. In some developments, this charge is fixed, but other developers charge between Dhs.6 and Dhs.15 per square foot per year. In a big villa, this could add up to quite a substantial amount. Another consideration is the transfer fee. If you're buying on the secondary market, the developer will require a percentage of the sale price. This is usually around 2% but can be as high as 7%. The buyer is responsible for this fee, but it may be possible to negotiate with the seller to share the cost. The buyer and seller will also owe a fee to the real estate agent (if one was used), and this is likely to be around 2% of the selling price. Be wary of 'all inclusive prices' and always demand to see a breakdown of every fee before you sign an MOU. You will also pay lawyer's fees, if you have opted to use a lawyer.

Real Estate Law

A law was passed in March 2006 allowing non-GCC expats the right to buy 99 year leasehold and freehold property in designated areas. This means that expatriates can

Housing

now register title deeds with the Dubai Land Registry. So, you get the land as well as the building on it.

Keep in mind that laws are constantly changing, and it's important that you get advice from a law firm specialising in real estate before you sign on the dotted line. Sale and purchase contracts should be reviewed thoroughly by your lawyer. Hadef Al Dhahiri & Associates (www.hadalaw. com) and Trench & Associates (www. trenchlaw.com) have dedicated real estate departments.

The term 'freehold' doesn't mean the same as in most other countries. For example, there may be restrictions on selling the property or making any structural changes to it. In some areas, you may not even be able to paint the outer walls.

Most developments levy annual service charges, and significant transfer fees when selling the property. Problems may also arise in the event of the owner's death, since under Shariah law (which UAE courts will apply, particularly in family law matters) it may not necessarily be transferred to the spouse. Your lawyer may be able to establish an offshore company which may avoid application of Shariah law.

Be aware that the market here is underdeveloped, so risks are potentially higher. But, if you have plans to stay in Dubai long-term, and can afford the down payment, buying can be a much better option than renting. Just don't forget to factor in maintenance, finance fees and other transfer costs. The best advice when purchasing in Dubai is to get a good lawyer.

Moving Tips

- Get more than one quote – companies will often match lower quotes to get the job.
- Make sure that all items are covered by insurance and get item specific insurance for your valuables.
- Make sure that you have a copy of the inventory and that each item in each box is listed.
- While you may not want to tell the packers how to do their jobs, it's much easier to insist on items being repacked if you're not happy than having to claim for them.
- It may sound odd but take photos of the process as it goes along, then if you do have to make a claim there'll be photographic evidence.
- Any customs restricted goods (DVDs, videos or books) should be carried with you, it's much easier to open a suitcase in an air-conditioned airport than empty a box outside in the sun.

Dubai Creek apartments

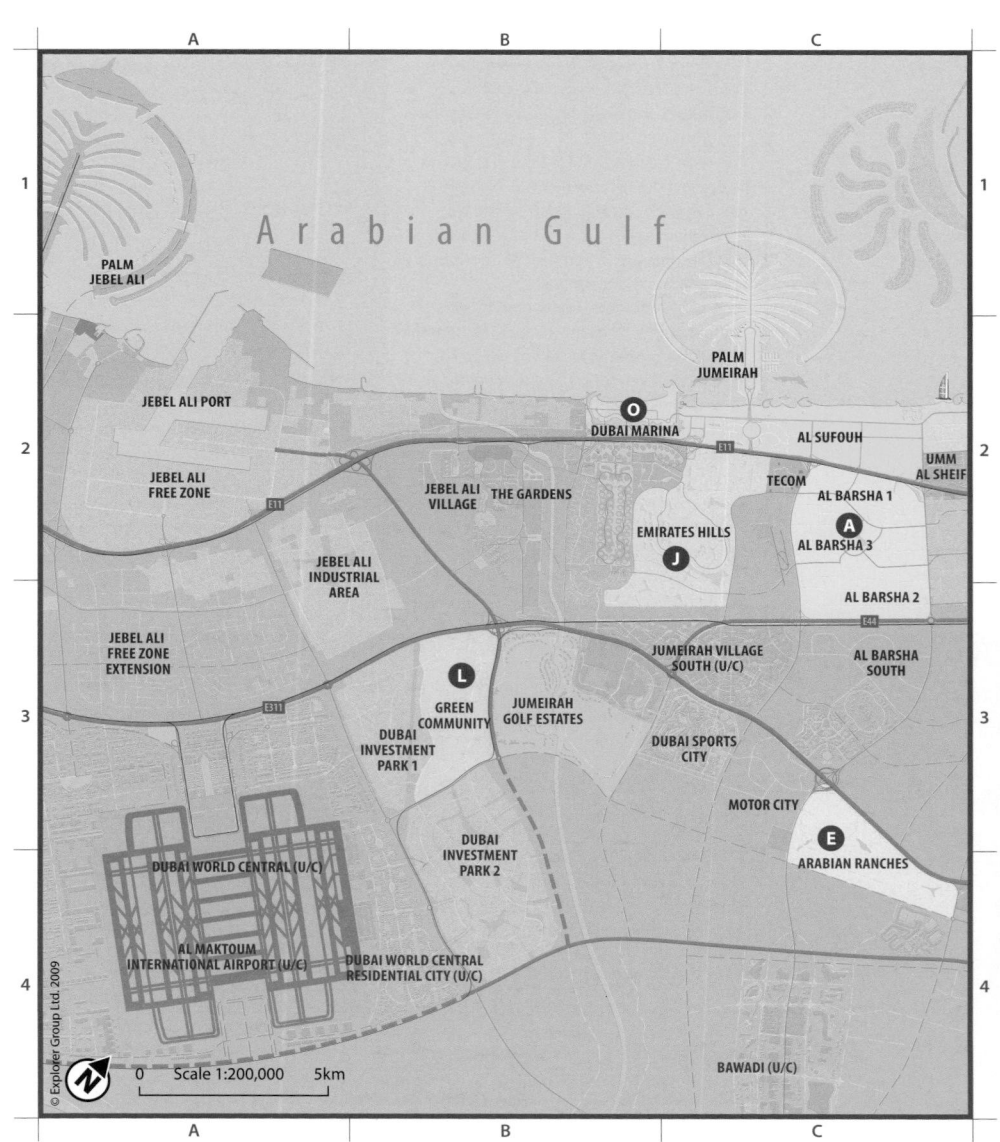

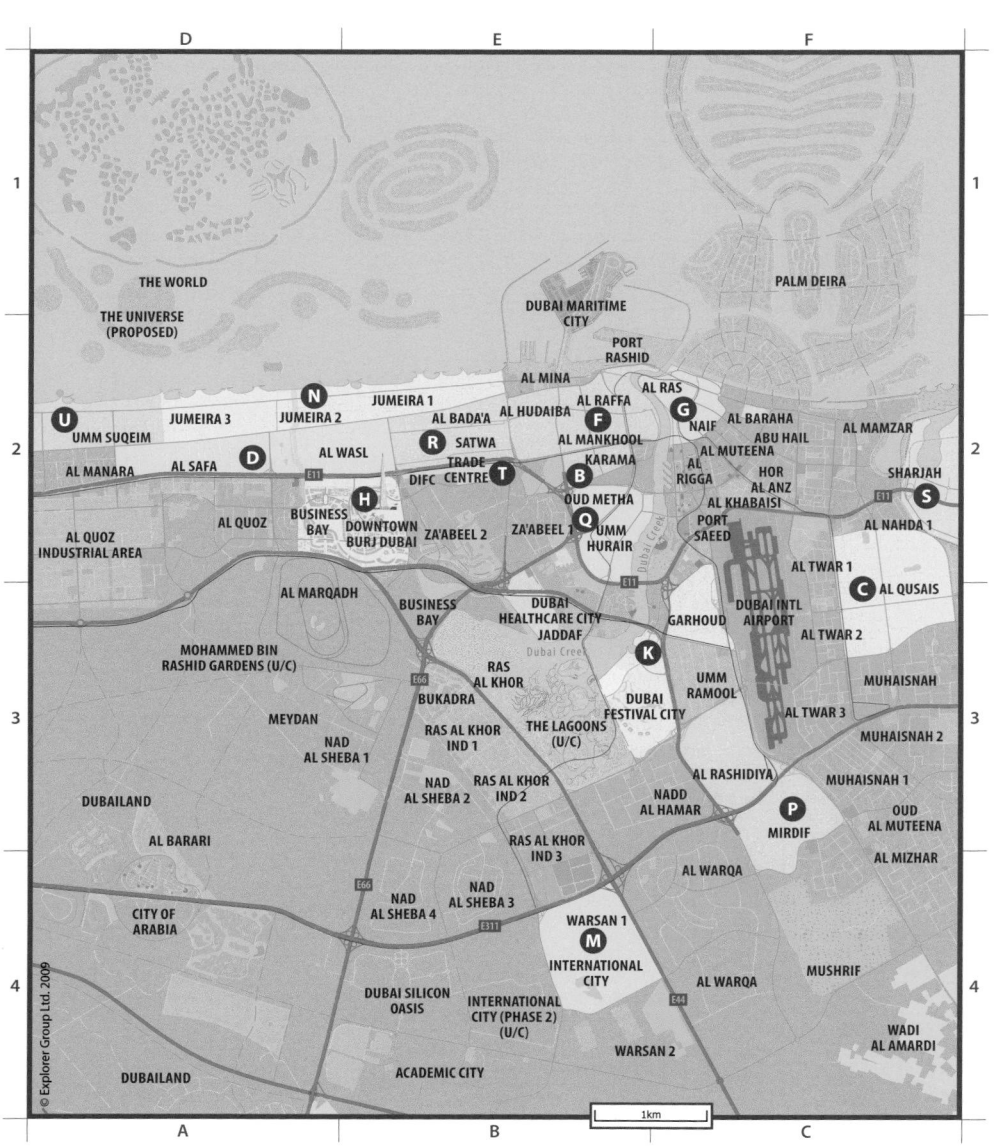

Area ⓐ p.126
See also Map 5

Al Barsha

Al Barsha has two distinct zones, each with their own accommodation options. The main area offers large villas with big gardens, while Al Barsha 1, near Mall of the Emirates, is home to a growing number of apartment blocks. Both are particularly handy for Media and Internet City workers but the E44 and E311 highways make most of Dubai accessible.

Best Points
Villas are larger and often much better value than in other areas on this side of town. Access to Sheikh Zayed Road is easy, and Mall of the Emirates is nearby.

Accommodation

Accommodation is mainly in the form of fairly new, three to five bedroom villas. Around 75% of the houses are locally owned and inhabited, the neighbours are quiet and the villa area is popular with families. Prices for villas start at Dhs.200,000 for a three bedroom and go up to Dhs.350,000. You could pay up to Dhs.575,000 for a four-bedroomed place. Apartments in Al Barsha 1 start from around Dhs.60,000 for a one bedroom and Dhs.130,000 for a two bedroom, but get snapped up quickly.

Worst Points
Some parts of the area are a bit isolated and lacking in convenient shopping and leisure facilities.

Shopping & Amenities

Mall of the Emirates houses a huge Carrefour. There's a Lulu's Hypermarket nearby, and an Organic Foods & Café in the Greens. You'll find a few 'corner shops' in the area and two petrol stations.

Entertainment & Leisure

Apart from numerous cafes, two foodcourts and a ski slope, the nearby Mall of the Emirates also houses the Kempinski Hotel which has its own restaurants and bars. The Marina and Madinat Jumeirah are only a short drive away.

Healthcare

The only private clinic in the area is the Medical Specialist Centre (04 340 9495) in the new Khoury Building near Sheikh Zayed Road. The nearest government clinic is in Umm Suqeim, and the nearest emergency hospital is Rashid Hospital (see p.180).

Education

There are a few schools in Al Barsha, including Dubai American Academy and Al Mawakeb. Many other schools can be found in nearby areas, such as Wellington International School off Sheikh Zayed Road, JESS in Arabian Ranches and Dubai College in Al Sufouh.

Travelling Times
Airport – 40 mins
Media City – 10 mins
Trade Centre – 20 mins

Traffic & Parking

Traffic isn't bad although Interchange 5 and the traffic lights near the Greens are hotspots. Sheikh Zayed Road is affected by slow traffic during rush hour. It's easy to get onto the E44 or E311. Parking is easy; finding a taxi less so.

Safety & Annoyances

In general, Al Barsha is safe. Street lighting is almost non-existent, however. Massive power lines run through the area, which might put people some people off.

Area ⓑ p.127
See also Map 8

Al Karama

Near the heart of downtown Dubai lies Karama, its convenient location means it is a thriving commercial area with plenty of amenities. The price you pay is a lack of peace and quiet and lots of traffic. There are many low-cost restaurants, supermarkets, shops and the Karama Market (p.471), which sells a wide range of goods. Reasonable rents make Karama a good choice for Dubai residents on a budget.

Residential Areas

Best Points

Right in the centre of Dubai, Karama is a convenient place to live with masses of shops and restaurants on your doorstep. The rest of Bur Dubai and Deira is only a short, inexpensive taxi ride away.

Accommodation

Most accommodation is in low-rise blocks with apartments ranging from studios to three bedrooms. Prices can be as low as Dhs.30,000 for a one bedroom in the older buildings. The most desirable buildings are along Zabeel Road or in the area along Trade Centre Road, opposite Spinneys. You can get two and three-bedroom apartments for around Dhs.120,000 and Dhs.200,000 respectively, but in a new building with facilities you could pay up to Dhs.200,000 and Dhs.400,000. Availability tends to be in the newer buildings – the older, cheaper apartments are snapped up through word of mouth.

Shopping & Amenities

Everything is on your doorstep here. On Trade Centre Road there is a Spinneys and a Union Co-Op. There are plenty of small grocery shops, a fish market and of course the well known Karama Market. The recently expanded BurJuman Mall provides good shopping, while cheap-and-cheerful Avenue (p.475) and Sana (p.481) are nearby. There are also beauty salons, barbershops, laundries, video rental shops and independent fitness clubs. The area is near the central post office as well as several banks and ATMs.

Worst Points

Parking is limited, even for residents, and traffic in the evenings gets pretty congested, especially around Karama Market.

Entertainment & Leisure

There is not much in the way of greenery, but there are several small public areas between buildings and next to the main shopping area. Zabeel Park (p.283) is close and can be accessed via a footbridge. Karama has an incredible, diverse selection of restaurants to suit all budgets. Eating out, takeaways and home deliveries from the Arabic, Indian, Filipino, Sri Lankan and Pakistani restaurants around Karama Market and along Trade Centre Road are popular. For bars, Karama houses one of Dubai's perennial guilty pleasures – the Rock Bottom Café (p.528) – while the Trade Centre area with its cafes, restaurants (many licensed), bars and nightclubs is only a five-minute cab ride away.

Travelling Times

Airport –15 mins
Trade Centre – 5 mins
Media City – 25 mins

Healthcare

Karama is convenient for many reasonably priced medical centres, doctors and dentists and is also just a few minutes away from Rashid Hospital for emergencies. For more information on healthcare facilities see (p.178).

Education

Although there are no popular schools or nurseries in the area, there are plenty of options close by and reaching them should be relatively easy.

Karama Market

Traffic & Parking

Traffic is a nightmare at peak times. Parking is limited and driving around in heavy traffic looking for a spot is frustrating. It's best to walk, and it's very easy to get round Karama on foot. Keep your wits about you though on the busy roads and remember it is not a very child-friendly area in terms of traffic.

Safety & Annoyances

Karama is busier than many other residential areas and there is significant traffic noise. Roads are packed and trying to get in or out of the area during busy times is a hassle.

Area **C** *p.127*
See also Map 14

Al Qusais (including Al Twar & Al Nahda)

Al Qusais is situated on the edge of Dubai. The area's biggest selling point is the lower rents. It's very close to the border with Sharjah so if you're commuting in and out of Dubai be prepared for a lot of traffic. The main street has developed considerably and is now home to several supermarkets and small shopping centres as well as an increasing number of flashy government buildings.

Best Points

Cheap accommodation compared with other parts of Dubai, easy parking with plenty of free spaces and limited local traffic problems.

Accommodation

Accommodation is mainly apartment blocks around Al Nahda Road. These range from studios to four-bedroom places in new buildings with similar facilities to new buildings in Karama or Oud Metha. It is still possible to get a one bedroom for about Dhs.30,000, but more common is a three bedroom at upwards of Dhs.70,000. There are few villas in this area available for rent.

Worst Points

The traffic heading to Dubai can reach gridlock at peak times on the Dubai to Sharjah Road, and other roads such as Emirates Road (E311) can also get pretty congested.

Shopping & Amenities

There are several larger supermarkets and hypermarkets including Lulu's Hypermarket, Union Co-Op and Emirates Cooperative Society, as well as plenty of smaller supermarkets for convenience items. The Al Bustan Centre is home to a selection of shops. There are also a number of ATMs and lots of pharmacies.

Entertainment & Leisure

The Qusais nightlife isn't going to set your social calendar on fire, and most people head for nearby Deira for a good night out. Fantasy Kingdom in the Al Bustan Centre is a large amusement centre, and with plenty of open sandy areas and parks, this is a good area for kids. For eating out, there is a good choice of cheap restaurants serving Arabic, Indian and Pakistani food, as well as fast-food outlets such as Pizza Hut and Hardees.

Healthcare

There are several private clinics in Qusais as well as the Zulekha Hospital (04 267 8666).

Education

There are a number of schools under construction in the area that should attract students from other areas.

Travelling Times

Airport – 10-15 mins
Media City – 40 mins
Trade Centre – 20 mins

Traffic & Parking

The roads are good and most have footpaths. Traffic is not a problem and neither is parking in Qusais, although getting in and out of the area can be challenging at busy times. During rush hour it can get crazy on Sharjah-Dubai routes.

Safety & Annoyances

This is a pretty safe area, the only annoyance being some noise from aircraft and the problems with the traffic at rush hour.

Area **D** *p.127*
See also Map 7

Al Safa & Al Wasl

These residential areas are separated from the beachside districts of Jumeira and Umm Suqeim by Al Wasl Road, with everything between Safa Park and Satwa officially known as Al Wasl, while Al Safa 1 & 2 lie between Safa Park at the north and Al Manara Street, which comes off Interchange 3. Housing is mainly large villas at high prices. Facilities are very good, and while you will usually need a car even to go to the local shops, just about everything you need is only a few minutes away.

Best Points
This is a quiet area (especially around the roads off or behind Al Wasl) and close to many areas of the city including Bur Dubai, Dubai Marina, Jumeira and the beach. There are all kinds of shops, amenities and facilities close at hand.

Worst Points
The lack of small 'corner shops' that can be reached on foot, and (depending on the location of your house) most journeys need to be done by car.

Accommodation

Safa consists mostly of villas, usually three bedroomed, but bigger villas are available. Styles range from independent villas to villas in small, older compounds with unique character and established greenery. There are also some attractive new compounds (although there are a few that are a bit prison-like in their austerity). At the top end there are the massive local family homes. You do find some old bungalows, but these are predominantly occupied by local families. Safa 1 and 2 are where most rental villas are found. Prices for both areas start from around Dhs.350,000 and go up, up and up.

Shopping & Amenities

Most houses are only a few minutes drive from one or more of the large supermarkets or shopping centres, with the Safa area having Union Co-Op and Choithram supermarkets opposite Safa Park, the Spinneys Centre along Al Wasl Road towards Umm Suqeim and the Park n Shop centre half way between the two on Al Wasl Road. All three centres have smaller auxiliary shops in or around them with a variety of facilities including video rental, cafes, restaurants, takeaways, bookshops, ATMs, chemists, liquor shops, hair and beauty salons and florists.

In the centre of Al Wasl, just beside Sheikh Zayed Road, is the Mazaya Centre, with a Spinneys supermarket, a branch of Gulf Greetings as well as Homes R Us and Pier Import for home goods. Almost next door is the large Safestway supermarket. Beach Road in Jumeira is also just a few minutes away with shopping opportunities such as Palm Strip, Town Centre and Mercato. There is also a 24 hour pharmacy on Al Wasl Road, ATMs all over the place, banks in Jumeira, several veterinary clinics, a public library near Safa Park and a post office.

Entertainment & Leisure

The huge, verdant spread of Safa Park is a popular attraction (see p.282). A second smaller park, Al Safa 2 Park, is located on Street 8A near Umm Suqeim School for Girls in Safa 2, and is open for ladies and children only through the week and families only at the weekend. There are plenty of cafes in or around the supermarkets and shopping centres, and numerous popular takeaways and small restaurants around Park n Shop and in the Safa area.

Healthcare

Both Al Wasl Road and the nearby Jumeira Road have lots of medical centres, doctors and dentists, but these are mostly all private. There is one government clinic on Al Attar Road (Al Safa Clinic), and the excellent value Iranian Hospital is just down Al Wasl Road towards Satwa. For a list of hospitals see p.178.

Education

Safa 1 has several schools including Jumeirah English Speaking School, The English College, Emirates English Speaking School, Jumeirah College and Jumeirah Primary School as well as nurseries including Jumeirah International Nursery School and Kangaroo Kids. The proximity to Sheikh Zayed Road makes Wellington International School a popular choice, and the highway means access to other schools is easy too. For a list of schools see p.203.

Travelling Times
Media City – 20 mins
Trade Centre – 10 mins
Airport – 20 mins

Traffic & Parking

This is usually an easy area to move around in and get in and out of, although Al Wasl Road can get congested between Safa and Satwa at peak hours. Most villas have ample parking and there's usually plenty of room at the supermarkets. Walking is not a common way of getting around, but there are plenty of quiet streets for a stroll or walking the dog. And the open areas add a bit of space and provide places for kids to play. There are usually plenty of taxis swarming around Al Wasl Road but if you live in one of the back streets you will most likely have to give clear directions on how to get to your home.

Safety & Annoyances
This is a safe area, although there have been reported cases of petty theft. Keep doors and windows secure to deter opportunists.

Area **E** *p.126*

Arabian Ranches

One of Emaar's many residential developments, Arabian Ranches is located away from the centre of town, off the Emirates road near Dubai Autodrome. This is an all-villa project set among lush greenery, lakes and the Arabian Ranches Golf Course, with a range of luxury facilities that all add up to some pretty fine living. Although it is a bit out of town it is still just a 15 minute drive from shopping and dining options.

Best Points
This is one of the most popular areas for buyers and it isn't difficult to see why. It feels like a community: enclosed, safe and neighbourly with all the everyday facilities that you might need.

Accommodation
Arabian Ranches is made up of villas of various sizes from two bedrooms to four bedrooms, for which you won't get much change from Dhs.210,000. Most of the villas were bought by people who now live in them, rather than rent them out. Telephone, internet and TV services are provided by du. There is also a residents' committee that people who live in Arabian Ranches can join (www.arrcdubai.com).

Shopping
The Village Community Centre is conveniently located on the estate, housing Le Marche supermarket, a chemist, bookshop, petshop, laundry, bank, ATM, a liquor store, a DVD rental machine and several cafes, restaurants and fast-food outlets, most of which do home delivery.

Worst Points
It is still a bit of a construction site, with some roads not completed and trucks clogging up the roads.

Entertainment & Leisure
Around the estate are several pools, basketball hoops, tennis courts, BBQ pits and grassy areas. The shopping centre has a good range of cafes and restaurants, many of which offer takeaway and home delivery. There is also The Arabian Ranches Golf Course, an 18 hole golf course with a pro shop, a clubhouse and the Ranches Restaurant and Bar, offering views out over the golf course from their terrace. The Autodrome and Dubai Polo and Equestrian Club are close by and offer fun on four wheels, or four legs.

Healthcare
There are no local healthcare facilities and the nearest medical centres are in Umm Suqeim (government) or Al Barsha (private), while the nearest hospitals are probably in the Oud Metha/Umm Hurair area of Bur Dubai.

Travelling Times
Airport – 25 mins
Media City – 25mins
Trade Centre – 20 mins

Education
Apart from the branch of Jumeirah English Speaking School (JESS) next to the shopping centre, there is no other choice in the Ranches at present. Otherwise, it isn't too far to Al Barsha and Emirates Hills.

Traffic & Parking
Your main access road is the Emirates Road (E311), which can be a bit hair-raising and congested at times. Traffic builds up as you enter or leave the Ranches.

Area **F** *p.127*
See also Map 8

Best Points

Good access to central Dubai and everything you need within easy reach and the rare pleasure of being able to walk around – be it to the bank, shopping centre, restaurant or bar.

Worst Points

Not a very attractive area, with few open spaces. Also has a lack of community feel due to the fact that nearly all the buildings are blocks of flats with no shops or services in inner Mankhool. All amenities are mainly located on the roads surrounding this block, Bank Street and Trade Centre Road. Can be an unpleasant area for women at night.

Safety & Annoyances

Security is good, with guards and barriers at the entrance to each estate, though residents may get tired of being stopped every day.

Bur Dubai (including Al Mankhool)

Bur Dubai is a bit of a concrete jungle with mid-size apartment blocks and virtually no green spaces, but many of the apartments have excellent facilities and spacious interiors. Bur Dubai is also popular because of its convenient central location. One of the most popular areas is Al Mankhool (also known as Golden Sands), but there are also some nice apartment blocks in the Al Hamriya area (across Bank Street from the BurJuman Mall). Nearer the creek and further west towards the sea, the buildings are generally a lot older with fewer facilities and limited parking, although those with balconies facing in the right direction do have beautiful views of the creek.

Accommodation

The area is dominated by apartments in a mix of new and old medium-rise buildings, from studios to large flats with several bedrooms. Some of the larger apartments are used as company flats. Rents in the newer buildings have risen to nearly the same as in other areas of Dubai, but the older the accommodation the cheaper it gets. A two-bedroom apartment in a new building could set you back around Dhs.130,000 but for that you should expect excellent facilities. A one-bedroom apartment in an older building starts at Dhs.70,000 while a two bedroom will be around Dhs.95,000, depending on the age of the building and range of facilities offered.

Shopping & Amenities

There are two large Spinneys supermarkets in the area, as well as a Union Co-Op on Trade Centre Road, a Choithram on Mankhool Road and a huge Carrefour in Al Shindagha near the mouth of the creek. On and around Bank Street (Khalid Bin Al Waleed Road), there are a number of banks and ATMs, some smaller food stores, clothing shops, cafes, independent restaurants and sports stores. The BurJuman Centre (p.486) provides a huge range of shops and both Al Ain Plaza and Al Khaleej Centre on Mankhool Road are well known for computers and electronic goods. The souk area of Bur Dubai will stimulate the senses with its bright lights, noise, and hustle and bustle, or head to Karama for its market shops full of bargain designer copies and Arabian souvenirs.

Metro construction

Bur Dubai

Entertainment & Leisure

You're so centrally located in Bur Dubai that you are just a short cab ride away from some of Dubai's best nightlife areas. There are also some good outlets right on your doorstep: The Arabian Courtyard Hotel on Al Fahedi Street and the Ascot Hotel on Bank Street both have various outlets, with Waxy O'Conners (in the Ascot) worth a special mention for one of Dubai's liveliest Thursday nights and biggest (and cheapest) Friday brunches. There is also the Regent Palace Hotel on the Karama side of Trade Centre Road, where the Rock Bottom Café is always good for a night out and a great venue for live music. There are also many small independent eateries on Bank Street and further into Bur Dubai.

Healthcare

Both in Bur Dubai and in neighbouring Karama you can find a number of small medical centres. Rashid Hospital (government) is just a stone's throw away in Umm Hurair. Some popular private medical centres are just a few minutes away, including American Hospital and those in the newly opened, expansive Healthcare City (see p.177).

Education

There are no schools in the area itself, but the central location means that there is plenty of choice nearby (see p.203).

Travelling Times ◀
Airport – 15 mins
Media City – 25 mins
Trade Centre – 10 mins

Traffic & Parking

Bur Dubai has seen an increase in traffic and it's getting a lot more difficult to find parking, especially in the Mankhool area and the shopping areas in the heart of old Bur Dubai. Getting around the residential areas away from the main roads is not too bad during the day, but it gets congested at rush hours. The main roads get clogged up especially at traffic lights, but you'll soon find yourself little shortcuts which save loads of time. For pedestrians, it is generally a relatively safe area to get around as long as you stick to the pedestrian crossings at the traffic lights.

Safety & Annoyances

Women may feel uneasy walking the streets, especially in the evening when there seem to be quite a few people just loitering around. There are very few cases of anything sinister going on, and so there is not really anything to fear, but just as in any city in the world, it pays to keep your wits about you.

Area ❻ p.127 ◀
See also Map 11

Deira

Deira is not a hugely popular residential area for expats in higher income brackets, probably because of the horrendous traffic and general congestion. The heart of Deira is built up with a mix of old apartment blocks and hardly any open spaces or public greenery, while nearer the creek there are lots of new buildings offering modern upmarket apartments, many with spectacular views across the creek. Rents are relatively low in some of the more built up areas, while the creekside dwellings cost big bucks. One of the great things about Deira is the fact there are so many things to explore on your doorstep, such as the dhow wharfage and the atmospheric souks.

Best Points ◀
It is a good area for shopping and amenities, and the rents are generally cheaper than just over the creek in Bur Dubai.

Accommodation

Although Deira does have some areas with villas (Abu Hail, Al Wuheida), they are almost exclusively inhabited by Nationals, with the areas closer to the creek full of apartments where most expats in the area congregate. In the heart of Deira, you'll pay around Dhs.60,000 for a studio apartment and Dhs.160,000 for two bedrooms, but these often are in older buildings and are not what you might call salubrious.

The creekside area just north of Maktoum bridge offers a great standard of accommodation and is used by professional expats of all nationalities. There are many executive apartments with great views over the creek, impressive landscaping and good facilities – but prices here tend to be high, with a standard two-bedroom costing around Dhs.180,000 and a one-bedroom, furnished, serviced apartment costing upwards of Dhs.18,000 per month.

Shopping & Amenities

Deira has lots to offer with popular malls like Al Ghurair City (p.500), Reef Mall (p.505) and Deira City Centre (p.488) being the most popular. All have good supermarkets (Spinneys, Al Maya and Carrefour respectively) as well as many other shops. Being an older area of town, there are also plenty of smaller groceries, pharmacies, dry-cleaners and laundry services on most of the streets. Deira's main post office is close to Al Ghurair Centre and there are many banks on Al Maktoum Road.

Entertainment & Leisure

Within a small area, there's a good choice of hotels, including the InterContinental, Hilton and Sheraton Creek, the JW Marriott, Renaissance, Traders and Metropolitan Palace, all of which offer a great choice of dining outlets, bars and nightclubs. The traffic later in the evening will usually ease off, allowing you to get out and about a bit more easily.

For cheap eats, Al Rigga Street has a great range of independent restaurants along with some fast food places, and the Al Ghurair Centre has some particularly nice cafes on the terrace. Traffic and parking in this area can get a bit crazy on weekends at night. There are some pleasant walking areas by the creek and along the corniche towards Mamzar Park, which is gigantic and great for weekends, especially with the beach chalets available for daily rental.

Healthcare

Local healthcare is provided by Dubai Hospital near the corniche, while Dubai's foremost emergency hospital, Rashid Hospital, is just across Maktoum bridge in Umm Hurair. There is also the choice of many small private medical clinics, although the larger private hospitals tend to be located on the Bur Dubai side of the creek (see p.182).

Education

There are not many recognised expat schools in Deira – the area tends to attract more singletons looking for a city dwelling than people with kids looking for a family home.

Traffic & Parking

Dreadful. Congestion and bottlenecks over the bridge can double or triple your journey time. Even getting from A to B within Deira itself can be a challenge – if you are just going down the road it may easier to walk. Taxis are popular, especially since parking is difficult.

Safety & Annoyances

The main annoyance for people living in Deira is the traffic problems. Apart from that, it is a relatively safe place to live. Single women may find it is not quite as pleasant as other areas in Dubai, mainly due to unwanted attention from men seeking the company of a 'lady'.

Area **H** *p.127*
See also Map 7

Downtown Burj Dubai

The newest residential area of Dubai, and one of the more expensive to live in, Downtown Burj Dubai is centred around its namesake, currently the tallest building in the world. A great location midway between old and new Dubai, with enough bars, restaurants and shopping in the area that you may not feel the need to venture out of it. Popular with single professionals and couples looking for a convenient location and a higher class of surroundings.

Best Points ◀

This area is really coming to life so the longer you're here, the more you will have on your doorstep. You also have the kudos of living next door to the world's tallest building.

Accommodation

A mix of modern high-rise apartments and low-rise Arabic-style builds. The Address boasts some of the most exclusive living spaces in Dubai, but this title is sure to be short lived once the Armani Residences open in Burj Dubai. The Old Town development offers character in the form of Arabian-style complexes, built around courtyards and alleys, with swimming pools and cafes dotted throughout. Because the area is so new rents have not really settled but landlords are pushing for the high end of the rental scale. Expect to pay anything upwards of Dhs.135,000 for a one bedroom apartment.

Worst Points ◀

Because the area is so new there are still lots of empty apartments so it can feel like a bit of a ghost town, but this is unlikely to last long.

Shopping & Amenities

With the opening of Dubai Mall (p.489) came record-breaking shopping possibilities, but there are a number of more intimate shopping experiences available in the Old Town at Souk Al Bahar (p.505) and Al Manzil Souk. A further souk is still to open, near the Qamardeen Hotel. The souks have a number of interesting and useful shops but by and large they cater for the tourist market. They are still worth a wander, even if just to admire the architecture and enjoy the calm and cool. You'll certainly find them a welcome relief from the, at times, overwhelming mall. If the inconceivable should happen, and you feel the need for even more choice, the area's central location means that it's only a short drive to the shopping areas of Satwa, Karama and Jumeira, and to the bigger malls further down Sheikh Zayed Road.

For your weekly shop, the high-end of the market is catered for by Waitrose in Dubai Mall, with a small Spinneys next to the Al Manzil Hotel for convenience purchases. A new branch of Organic Foods & Café (p.506) is due to open shortly in Dubai Mall.

Entertainment & Leisure

As more and more buildings reach completion, so the nightlife potential is growing. The standard of the bars and restaurants here is five-star to match the location. Neos, the sky bar on the 63rd floor of The Address, is a sundowner must, Left Bank in Souk Al Bahar is already establishing itself as a favourite, and Nezeaussi (p.516) at the Al Manzil Hotel is a venue guaranteed for a lively Saturday night for sports fans.

Excellent restaurants are found in abundance in this part of town: try Asado at The Palace Hotel (p.592) for Argentinean steaks, Fazaris at The Address (p.560) for exquisite fusion food, and The Courtyard at Al Manzil (p.537) for a shisha in atmospheric surroundings. Coffee shops and cafes are dotted around the area, along with a couple of lower key restaurants such as The Great Kabab Factory in the Yansoon district and Nando's in Burj Residences (Tower 4).

The cinema, aquarium and Olympic size ice rink at Dubai Mall will also provide entertainment for people of all ages.

Keep a look out in 2009 for new venues opening in the area, particularly when the Armani Hotel and Dubai Mall Hotel are launched.

Healthcare

There are a number of pharmacies dotted around Old Town, souks and Dubai Mall, and Al Zahra Medical Centre in the neighbouring Trade Centre area offers family medicine

Residential Areas

Jumeirah Beach Residence

Emirates Hills

Dubai Marina

The Gardens

Discovery Gardens

Festival City

and dentistry. The nearest A&E departments are at Medcare and Iranian hospitals. For more information on healthcare services see p.177, and for hospitals, p.178.

Education

There are no schools in Downtown Burj Dubai, and children aren't particularly well catered for, although some of the apartment blocks and Old Town complexes have kids' pools and play areas. Across Sheikh Zayed Road, there are schools and nurseries in Al Wasl, or, traffic depending, Al Satwa is a short drive. For more information, see p.203.

Traffic & Parking

Travelling Times
Airport – 15 mins
Media City – 20 mins
Trade Centre – 5 mins

Parking is not a problem and is unlikely to be so while so many of the apartments are empty. Getting in and out of Downtown Burj Dubai is generally traffic free, although which ever way you leave the area you are subject to whatever the traffic situation is on Sheikh Zayed Road or Doha Street. Once Burj Lake is filled in, water taxis will be available around Old Town and Burj Dubai.

Safety & Annoyances

A very safe area. The main annoyances come from construction noise but this is reducing as more buildings reach completion. While pedestrians are generally well catered for with wide promenades, until the roads are fully constructed there are few crossings for those on foot, and those that exist are not yet operational.

*Area **J** p.126*
See also Map 5

Emirates Hills

Part of the burgeoning 'new Dubai', Emirates Hills is a desirable address with a range of villa-style houses in The Springs, The Lakes and The Meadows and apartments in The Greens. Tree-lined streets and pathways, attractively landscaped lakes, gardens and pool/recreation areas make it perfect for those who want to escape the chaos of city life and enjoy the peace and quiet of this surburb-style area (although there is the inevitable construction noise). Convenient for those working in Media and Internet Cities and Jebel Ali Free Zone, it is also popular for those working in the centre of Dubai, as the morning and evening commute only takes 20-30 minutes against the flow of traffic.

Emirates Hills

Accommodation

The Greens, on the edge of Emirates Hills, offers a range of one to four bedroom apartments, which are well appointed but a bit small for the money. A one bedroom rents for around Dhs.140,000 and a three bedroom for around Dhs.280,000. Generally, the style and quality of all houses in Emirates Hills is good, although they all look the same. Mid-range villas with two bedrooms rent from about Dhs.220,000 or sell at around Dhs.2.5 million. Even with the lack of individuality, for most people the advantage of being able to buy here and the community feel beats more spacious options available elsewhere. Telephone, internet and TV services are provided by du (see p.176).

Best Points
You can buy or rent here and the whole area is nicely landscaped, attractive, safe, and has that 'out of town' feel.

Worst Points
Insects. The lush landscaping has provided the perfect habitat for a thriving insect population including mosquitos and spiders, even some dangerous species, so care is needed. Also, you can get slow moving traffic in and out of Emirates Hills during rush hour. The junction between Barsha and The Greens is a bottleneck, but has been eased since the opening of the new interchange at the Marina.

Travelling Times
Airport – 35 mins
Media City – 15 mins
Trade Centre – 25 mins

Shopping & Amenities

The Greens has a range of shops, including Choithram and Organic Foods & Café. Within Emirates Hills you'll find three centres, each anchored by a supermarket. There's Choithram at the Springs end, a large Spinneys at Spinneys Town Centre in the middle and a Spinneys Market in the Meadows. Each centre has a Hayya! gym, a beauty salon, a pharmacy and ATMs. Between them all, you should find everything you need, from laundry services to fast food and fine dining or coffee shops to video rentals. Town Centre boasts stores such as Beyond the Beach, Mothercare, Pets Delight and Tavola.

Other nearby supermarkets include Spinneys (Dubai Marina), Géant (Ibn Battuta) and Carrefour (Mall of the Emirates).

Entertainment & Leisure

Each estate within Emirates Hills has a recreation area and swimming pool, offering pleasant places to relax and for kids to play. Two of Dubai's latest and greatest shopping malls are both about 10 minutes away and between them have a huge range of shops, cafes, restaurants and foodcourts, as well as leisure facilities such as Ski Dubai in Mall of the Emirates and the 21 screen cinema (including Dubai's first IMAX screen) at Ibn Battuta Mall. For eating out, there's the licensed Academy Restaurant and Bar at Montgomerie Golf Club, plus all the options at The Greens, Emaar Business Park and Dubai Marina.

Healthcare

There are currently no medical facilities in the vicinity – although there is a new private medical centre in Al Barsha, or the government clinic in Jebel Ali. Otherwise it's a bit of a drive to get to the main government and private facilities (see p.178).

Education

There are lots of new schools springing up, although demand is high and it can be tough to get in anywhere. Waiting lists for a place in the most sought-after schools and nurseries are long, and it is best to sign up well in advance. Schools already open include Emirates School, Dubai British School, Regent School and Dubai International Academy, while the Kids' Oasis in Emirates Hills is the only pre-school in the immediate area. For more information on schools see p.203.

Traffic & Parking

Within the area the traffic flow is fine, although speed bumps slow things down. Getting in and out through the new interchange on Sheikh Zayed Road can be a problem at rush hour. This is not helped by the fact that the work on the metro system is still not completed. The traffic lights where Sheikh Zayed Road meets the 'back road' past The Greens are a nightmare during peak hours. An alternative route onto the Al Khail Road (E44) can be a lot quicker. The main road through Emirates Hills has landscaped, shaded pavements which makes the area great for pedestrians and children. However, development started in 2008 on transforming the main road through The Springs into a six-lane highway connecting to Al Khail Road. Not only will this increase traffic (and noise) but means many residents will not be able to walk around as freely.

Safety & Annoyances

There really are few annoyances – apart from the traffic, and a bigger than normal insect population in some parts. In addition, the area is well guarded by security and is pleasant to stroll around.

*Area **K** p.127*
See also Map 13

Garhoud & Festival City

With its central location, range of villas and suburban feel, it's no surprise that Garhoud is such a popular residential area. It's handy for both central Dubai and downtown Deira, although this does mean that traffic can be a problem at peak times. Finding available accommodation isn't always easy, and there's not much in the way of new construction. Being only two minutes away from the airport means it's popular with airline staff and frequent travellers, but also that there is a chance of aircraft noise depending on the wind direction. Rents are slightly lower than some other central areas but they have began to creep up like everywhere else.

Residential homes in the Festival City area are all fairly new, but this is a desirable area to live, with all apartments being situated around a golf course.

Best Points

It is conveniently situated just 10 minutes from the Trade Centre, close to Deira, the airport and Sharjah. It is also home to some excellent entertainment options, including the Irish Village, Century Village and Aviation Club.

Worst Points

Traffic congestion in the area is very bad at peak times. The area's proximity to the airport means noise and fumes can be a problem.

Accommodation

Garhoud has some nice, older villas, usually with well-established gardens and plenty of character. They are also relatively cheap considering the central location. The price for a three bedroom ranges anywhere from Dhs.200,000 upwards, and will depend on the age of the villa. The biggest problem is finding somewhere vacant. Away from the airport, there are some newer villas, predominantly in large compounds, that are similar in standard and price to villas in other areas of Dubai. The usual size is four bedroom, which will rent for around Dhs.300,000 per year. The whole area is home to a mix of nationalities with airline staff monopolising the accommodation. There are some apartment blocks in the Garhoud area, although a lot of these are reserved for Emirates accommodation.

Apartments in the Festival City complex are quite luxurious and therefore not cheap, but if you have a good budget then it's your only chance this side of town to experience golf course living.

Shopping & Amenities

The small shopping street in Garhoud has two good supermarkets as well as a laundry, a pharmacy, photo shop, and an ATM. There are also several small restaurants that offer takeaway and delivery. Less than a 10 minute drive away is Deira City Centre (p.488) which offers everything from washing machines to wellington boots. Along Casablanca Road there are several car cleaners, tyre shops and petrol stations, while the area near Welcare Hospital has a massage centre, beauty salons and hairdressers.

Dubai Festival Centre is huge and has Marks & Spencer, IKEA, Ace Hardware, Plug-Ins and the gigantic HyperPanda hypermarket, as well as dozens of other shops.

Al Badia Hillside Village

Entertainment & Leisure

Kids will love the park in Garhoud; it has a skate ramp, a sandy football pitch and some good playground equipment. For indoor activities, Magic Planet in Deira City Centre is a large amusement centre, with an 11 screen cinema.

In terms of eating out, Garhoud residents are spoilt for choice – there are many excellent restaurants and bars in the Al Bustan Rotana, the Le Meridien Dubai, the Millennium Airport Hotel, Century Village and the Irish Village. It's one of the few residential areas where you can actually walk to the pub.

In Festival City, there are a host of unlicensed restaurants within the shopping mall, as well as some licensed outlets in the Crowne Plaza and the InterContinental. The Belgian Beer Cafe is deservedly popular (p.510).

Healthcare
Although there are no government clinics in the area, there are good private facilities such as Welcare Hospital, and two of the main government hospitals, Al Wasl and Rashid, are only a short distance away across the creek. See p.178.

Education
Several schools are located along the road on the southern edge of Garhoud including Deira International School, American School of Dubai and Cambridge International School. Many other schools are accessible, in areas like Umm Hurair, Al Twar, and Festival City. Yellow Brick Road Nursery and Montessori Nursery are in the neighbourhood. Within Festival City you'll find Deira International School and Universal American School. For more information on education see p.203.

Travelling Times
Airport – 2 mins
Trade Centre – 10 mins
Media City – 30 mins

Traffic & Parking
Now that it's been widened and equipped with a Salik gate, Garhoud Bridge is not as awful as it used to be for traffic congestion. One of the worst things about Garhoud is trying to find a parking spot, although the recent addition of parking meters may alleviate this somewhat. Taxis are easy to find, and the fare to the Trade Centre is about Dhs.25.

Safety & Annoyances
On the whole this is a great area, very peaceful and suburban, with wide roads, plenty of quiet streets and grassy areas suitable for children to play in or for people to walk, cycle or jog along. Crime is low, and the only main annoyances are some traffic congestion and the occasional noisy aircraft overhead.

Area ⓛ p.126

Green Community
The Green Community lives up to its name. An oasis of green in the desert, this new development is especially good for families, and homes are hard to come by. Built by Union Properties, the apartments and houses are sold on a 90 year leasehold (see www.up.ae for details). It's a bit out in the sticks (or sand), but it's the perfect choice for people working in the Jebel Ali Free Zone.

Best Points
The sprawling greenery and splendid peace and quiet.

Accommodation
There is a wide variety including villas, townhouses, and apartments. The original Green Community was so well received that developer Union Properties built a new phase – Green Community West. For a four-bedroom villa you can expect to pay around Dhs.350,000 in rent.

Worst Points
The distance is the real downer, especially as it makes travelling times and taxi fares a little on the high side.

Shopping & Amenities
The Market is the Green Community's new shopping centre (p.504). As well as a jewellers, clothes shops, and home furnishing outlets, there's a pharmacy, a florist, a dry cleaners, a card shop, a book shop, an optician, and a branch of Ace. It is also home to a Choithram supermarket, and Ibn Battuta mall is not too far away.

Entertainment & Leisure
The Courtyard by Marriott and the neighbouring Market are the focal points for dining out, with a number of coffee shops, good restaurants and places for a quick bite with

licensed outlets in the hotel. There's top-class golf courses nearby at Emirates Hills, Jebel Ali and Arabian Ranches.

Healthcare

The Green Community Medical Centre (04 885 3225) upstairs in The Market is a private clinic with full-time doctors, plus visiting specialists. The nearest government-run clinic is at Jebel Ali. For emergencies the Cedars Hospital within the Jebel Ali Free Zone is nearest – they have their own ambulance too. For government A&E care it's quite a trip to Rashid Hospital.

Education

New primary school The Children's Garden (349 8806) offers a bilingual curriculum in English/German or English/French. There are various primary & secondary schools nearby in Emirates Hills and Jebel Ali.

Travelling Times
Airport – 40 mins
Media City – 20 mins
Trade Centre – 30 mins

Traffic & Parking

Traffic within the Community itself is not a problem. Parking is adequate. The biggest headache is that there's only one main road, the E311 Emirates Road, linking the Green Community to Jebel Ali and the rest of Dubai. This road is often clogged with trucks that come to a standstill in the nearside lane. It will cost around Dhs.65 for a taxi to Trade Centre and up to Dhs.100 to the airport.

Safety & Annoyances

The Green Community is a great place for families, as the gated complex is very safe. Just don't let little ones wander into the water.

Area **M** p.127

International City

Despite its bad reputation, International City has quite a bit to offer its residents. Located east of the creek on the Dubai-Hatta road, the development houses over 400 apartment buildings grouped into several country-themed clusters. Nakheel has been working to green the area and several clusters are now covered with trees and tall grasses. Cafes, grocery stores and restaurants are slowly creeping into the neighbourhood as well.

Best Points
The most affordable housing in Dubai, surprisingly good commute times

Accommodation

This is perhaps the most affordable place to live in Dubai. International City is broken up into two main sections; the outlying country-themed clusters and the central area, known as the Central Business District (CBD). All of the country-themed buildings were built by Nakheel and have nearly identical floor plans. These Nakheel buildings comprise studios and one bedrooms, which are relatively large by Dubai standards. The CBD buildings were built by other developers and offer studios, and one and two bedroom apartments. Expect to pay around Dhs.55,000 for a studio, Dhs.80,000 for a one bedroom and Dhs.120,000 for a two bedroom.

Worst Points
Not much to do in terms of entertainment, uninspiring architecture, lack of greenery and an out-of-the-way location.

Shopping

There are no branded supermarkets within International City, but each cluster has several small grocery shops and there is a large Chinese grocery store in the China Cluster. Scattered throughout the development are several Lebanese and Indian restaurants, a surprisingly good pizza joint and a few authentic Chinese restaurants. Right next door sits the sprawling DragonMart, which carries everything from wigs to diamond-tipped stone saws. For weekly grocery shopping, Festival City and Uptown Mirdif are both only a 10 minute drive away.

Entertainment & Leisure

There are a floodlit basketball courts in the China, Russia and France clusters, and residents tend to play football on the grassed roundabouts. There are also quite a few takeaway spots that are worth investigating. For a big night out, Festival City (p.490) is only a 10 minute drive away.

Healthcare

There are no medical clinics within International City and the closest clinics are in Dubai Healthcare City in the Oud Metha area. The nearest public hospital is Rashid, with 24 hour emergency services. The private Welcare Hospital is even closer.

Education

The closest schools are in Mirdif, a 10 minute drive away. Also nearby are the Sharjah American International School in Al Warqa, and the Royal Dubai School in Muhaisnah. The nearest preschools and nurseries are also in Mirdif.

Travelling Times
Airport – 15 mins
Media City – 35 mins
Trade Centre – 15 mins

Traffic & Parking

There is hardly any traffic within International City, although the exit and entrance tend to get clogged during rush hour. With close access to both the Dubai-Hatta Road and Emirates Road, commutes to any part of town are usually a breeze.

Safety & Annoyances

Like most new developments in Dubai, International City is generally safe. All of the streets are floodlit and you can usually see families walking around late at night. Now that construction has slowed, there are fewer staring labourers wandering the streets. Traffic during peak commuting hours can put a damper on an otherwise good day.

*Area **N** p.127*
See also Map 7

Jumeira

The actual area of Jumeira occupies a prime nine-kilometre strip of coastline stretching south-west from the port area, but the name has been hijacked to such an extent that new residential and commercial developments bearing the Jumeira tag are cropping up for miles around. Even the Palm Jumeirah doesn't connect with Jumeira, but actually extends from the area of Al Sufouh. (Admittedly though, this whole stretch of beach is known as Jumeira Beach.) Jumeira itself is characterised by quiet streets lined with sophisticated villas, golden beaches (some free, some paid-for), and good access to lots of shopping.

Best Points
This is location, location, location – it's close to the beach, close to the shops, close to Dubai and close to many a resident's heart.

Accommodation

The ultimate location for that dream villa in the sun, Jumeira property attracts some of the highest rents in the city. There's a mixture of huge 'palaces', independent villas, and villas in compounds with shared facilities. It's all low-rise, and hardly an apartment in sight. For a three-bedroom, stand-alone villa you can expect to pay anywhere in the region of Dhs.300,000 to Dhs.350,000 depending on the age and specific location. You can however get the odd villa in an older compound for around Dhs.250,000.

Worst Points
In keeping with the rest of Dubai, traffic can be heavy at certain times of day, but it's bearable. The only other downside to living in this desirable area is the sky-high rents you have to pay for the privilege.

Shopping & Amenities

There are shopping centres all along Beach Road, the biggest of which is the popular Mercato with well-known brands and a Spinneys supermarket. There's also a big Union Co-Op and a Choithram opposite Safa Park, and the Spinneys Centre just the other side of Al Wasl Road. There's another Choithram supermarket on Beach Road as well as the large Spinneys near the mosque end. Just a few kilometres along the coast you've got Madinat Jumeirah, and it's not that far to the Mall of the Emirates. You'll find lots of laundries, dry cleaners and tailors dotted along Beach Road, as well as a high

Jumeira or Jumeirah?
According to the
'official' spelling used
by Dubai Municipality,
it's Jumeira, so that's
what we use when
referring to this area.
However, many hotels,
parks, clubs, schools,
and residential
developments have
added an 'h' to the
end, so don't be
surprised if you see
the two different
spellings side by side
throughout the book.

concentration of art galleries and boutiques. You've got Empost on Al Wasl Road for postal services, a few petrol stations, and plenty of banks and ATMs.

Entertainment & Leisure

There are plenty of independent restaurants and cafes, especially in the shopping centres along Beach Road. The Lime Tree Cafe is fabulous, although it can get a bit too busy on weekends and during lunchtimes. Not far up Beach Road is the Jumeirah Beach Hotel, the Burj Al Arab, and Madinat Jumeirah with a host of glittering gourmet delights and beautiful bars.

There are many beaches, although the public ones are crowded at weekends. The Jumeirah Beach Park charges Dhs.5 entry, but it is worth it for the lack of crowds and the additional facilities. Safa Park is nearby, and is undoubtedly one of the most picturesque parks in Dubai. Mercato Mall has an 11 screen cinema.

Healthcare

Al Safa Clinic (04 394 3468) opposite Safa Park (next to the library) is the nearest government health clinic. Emirates Hospital, opposite Jumeirah Beach Park, has a 24 hour walk-in clinic to deal with common ailments, but they do not accept emergency cases. The Neuro Spinal Hospital in the same building does have a 24 hour emergency department though. Jumeira is known for being home to countless beauty salons and private medical facilities, including dentists, physiotherapists and cosmetic surgery centres. For more information on hospitals, see p.178.

Education

There are numerous nurseries in Jumeira, and Jumeriah Primary School, Jumeirah College and Jumeirah English Speaking School are all in the neighbourhood. Easy access to road networks means even outlying schools are fairly easy to reach. For more details of these schools, see p.203.

Travelling Times
Airport – 20 mins
Media City – 20 mins
Trade Centre – 10 mins

Traffic & Parking

Although it's been widened in recent times, Jumeira Road (more commonly known as Beach Road) gets very busy at rush hour, with traffic leaving Internet and Media Cities often bringing things to a crawl in the evenings. Mercato's popularity usually leads to jams along that stretch too, especially on a Friday evening.

Getting from one side of Beach Road to the other can be tricky for both pedestrians and drivers. Speed bumps and cameras along the length of the road do have the desired effect of slowing most of the traffic down. Streetside parking if you're located behind Beach Road shouldn't be a problem, but if your villa is near Mercato you may find people parking across your drive at busy times.

Safety & Annoyances

Small pockets of construction are noisy. In general, roads and pavements are very good, and mostly well-lit, but the fast traffic, even in the suburbs, means you probably wouldn't want your kids playing out in the street.

Area ◉ *p.126*
See also Map 5

Marina, The Palm, JBR & Al Sufouh

Dubai Marina introduces modern luxury living to the area while Al Sufouh has a little more history. Not too long ago, the area was little more than a huge building site; however, large parts of it are now completed and it is starting to look a bit more 'lived in'. The Marina's official name is Marsa Dubai (marsa is Arabic for port or harbour), but it's unlikely that you'll hear anyone call it that. In 2008, the first set of residents moved on to the Palm Jumeirah, thus creating an entire new neighbourhood.

Residential Areas

Best Points ◀

One of the most desirable areas in Dubai at the moment, especially for its proximity to entertainment and leisure facilities. In Al Sufouh you can find palatial villas (with a price tag to match). This area is the perfect location for Media and Internet City and Knowledge Village.

Worst Points ◀

Rents and purchase costs are high and the massive development going on both in the Marina and around the entrance to the Palm means lots of noise and disruption. Traffic is building in the area and will increase once more people move onto the Palm and into the Marina.

Accommodation

In the Marina it's almost all apartments, with just a few townhouses. A two-bedroom apartment in Jumeirah Beach Residence will set you back more than a million dirhams to buy, while renting a similar property in JBR or the Marina costs from Dhs.240,000 upwards. Dubai Marina was the first freehold development in the UAE, and lots of people bought places purely for investment. In the many towers that make up the Jumeirah Beach Residence there are still some apartments available for purchase directly from developers, and many are available on the secondary market.

Al Sufouh, on the other hand, is all villas. Some are new, some are old, but most are expensive. For a decent four-bedroom villa you won't get much change from Dhs.450,000. People pay a lot for the privilege of living on Dubai's newest landmark, The Palm, and you can expect to pay upwards of Dhs.250,000 per year for a two-bedroom apartment. Don't even bother looking at villas on the fronds unless you've got a budget of at least Dhs.500,000.

Shopping & Amenities

On Marina Walk, alongside all the restaurants, there's a Spinneys supermarket, a pharmacy, a bookshop, a florist, and a liquor store, plus a number of ATMs. In the cooler months, Friday and Saturday are Marina Market day, with stallholders selling arts and handicrafts.

The Walk, which lines the two-kilometre stretch between JBR and the beach, is now a thriving promenade of shopping and dining activities, transforming this part of town into one of the best outdoor entertainment areas. There's more to come too – Dubai Marina Mall is set to open in 2009.

Ibn Battuta, Madinat Jumeirah, and Mall of the Emirates are just a few kilometres away too. There's only a bit of free beach left along this stretch, by the hotels at the Marina. This was slated to be turned into private beach parks for Jumeirah Beach Residence residents, but for now at least these plans look to have stalled, so the beaches remain open to all. However, the free beaches in Umm Suqeim and Jumeira are not too far. There's not much greenery to speak of in this area – the nearest park is near the beach in Umm Suqeim.

Along the Palm, if you're lucky enough to live in one of the frond villas you'll always have your own private beach just outside. If you're in one of the apartments, however, you'll have to use the same public beaches as everyone else.

Palm Jumeirah apartments

Entertainment & Leisure

Plenty of options: the older hotels on the coast (including the Ritz-Carlton and the Hilton Jumeirah), as well as newer hotels like Harbour Hotel & Residence, The Westin and Habtoor Grand, all have some excellent restaurants and bars. Marina Walk has a number of decent spots including Chandelier (p.537) and Johnny Rockets (p.530), and The Walk around Jumeirah Beach Residence is now positively teeming with places to eat. The Marina also has a health spa above the parade of shops in Marina Walk. Most hotels have beach clubs and leisure facilities, although it's not cheap to become a member, and many have waiting lists. There are many bars and restaurants at the Madinat, and the Hard Rock Café is next to Media City. A crop of new dining out options are now open on the Palm – of course there's the 19 food and beverage outlets within Atlantis, but then there are also a few restaurants open in the Shoreline Apartments area, like BidiBondi (p.510). The Emirates Golf Club is just over the road.

Healthcare

The nearest government clinic is Umm Suqeim, and the nearest government hospital is Rashid. The Neuro Spinal hospital opposite Jumeira Beach Park has round-the-clock A&E, and its own ambulance. In the other direction, the Cedars Hospital at Jebel Ali also offers 24 hour emergency care. There's a Welcare clinic in Knowledge Village, and several Drs Nicolas & Asp dental clinics in this part of town. For more information on hospitals, see p.178.

Education

There is Dubai College in Al Sufouh, as well as the American University of Dubai and the many educational establishments within Knowledge Village. There's also the Wellington International School and the International School of Choueifat in Al Sufouh. See p.203.

Travelling Times
Airport – 40 mins
Media City – 10 mins
Trade Centre – 20 mins

Traffic & Parking

Getting in and out of the area has been greatly improved by the opening of a new interchange near Media City. The morning and evening traffic around Internet City, Media City and Knowledge Village can get busy in certain hotspots. Parking depends on whether you have access to your building's car park, although there's an underground car park by Marina Walk.
In Al Sufouh you should have plenty of room to park outside your villa.

Safety & Annoyances

Security is good, with many apartment blocks having 24 hour security and underground parking. The biggest annoyance is the ongoing construction in the Marina, and the roads around the main bridge into Jumeirah Beach Residence, which can cause traffic delays and extra noise at night.

*Area **P** p.127*
See also Map 14 & 15

Mirdif & Rashidiya

For many years Mirdif was one of Dubai's best-kept secrets – a quiet neighbourhood, nice villas, low rents, and not as far out of town as it may appear. Alas, the secret is out; new residential and retail developments are cropping up, and rents have sky-rocketed. It's still cheaper than certain other areas, however.

Best Points
The rents are certainly lower here than in many other areas of Dubai, and both Mirdif and Rashidiya still have that local, neighbourhood surburb feel. Unfortunately though, rapid growth means that many of the open desert areas that surround this residential hotspot have been taken over by property development.

Accommodation

In Mirdif it's a mix of independent villas and small compounds, with the odd large compound community. The new, and rather large, Uptown Mirdiff development offers apartments on a 99 year leasehold basis as well as townhouses for sale and rent. If you can find one, a decent three-bedroom villa should cost around Dhs.190,000 to Dhs.250,000 a year and, depending on whether it's a stand-alone or in a compound, it may have a little garden or shared pool.
As you drive into Mirdif you can see two huge new developments on either side of Algeria Street. These should open for leasing sometime in 2009, and will add over 500 new villas and thousands of new apartments to the area. Mirdif residents can only hope that this new supply may lead to a decrease in rental prices in this area, where rents have quadrupled over the last four years.
The best advice when looking for a villa in Mirdif is to really look around – phone agents and ask them to show you whatever they have on their books. Dhs.200,000 can

146   **Dubai** Explorer

get you a pokey, dilapidated three-bedroom villa with space to park a car and nothing else, or a brand new, spacious four-bedroom villa with a garden and pool.

Al Warqa, which is the area directly south of Mirdif, has a lot of big (expensive) villas, but also many new apartment blocks that have been fairly reasonably priced. There are a few schools and small shops in this area.

Shopping & Amenities

Mirdif has several little clusters of shops, selling the basics, as well as the impressive Uptown Mirdif. You can do your grocery shopping in Spinneys (in Uptown Mirdif), in Westzone (on Street 83) or in Lifco (on Street 37). Just down the road in Rashidiya you'll find the Bin Sougat Mall (p.500), which has a small Spinneys, a pharmacy and an excellent stationery shop. The main post office serving the area is in Rashidiya. In Al Warqa there's a big 'Mars' supermarket, with an internet cafe behind it. Deira City Centre (p.488) is just 15 minutes away and Festival City is an easy 10 minute drive (p.490). Next to the big mosque on Mirdif's Street 15 there's a DVD rental shop and a place for internet access at Dhs.7 per hour. Rashidiya Library has a small selection of English language books, and you can also surf the web for Dhs.3 per hour. The Elyazia beauty salon in Mirdif offers pedicures and manicures, hair styling, waxing and more.

Uptown Mirdiff is the area's big draw. Its pleasant piazza-style courtyards are home to numerous stores including Mothercare, Early Learning Centre, Accessorize, Adidas, Beyond the Beach and Pumpkin Patch. There's also a pet shop, a Starbucks, a huge foodcourt, and several restaurants including Gourmet Burger Kitchen (p.530) and Pane Caldo (p.574). Arabian Plaza, a new mall on Airport Road, will open in 2009.

Entertainment & Leisure

Mirdif has its share of good independent restaurants such as Oregano (Italian) and Open House (Indian). Your takeaway options range from Chinese, pizza and Indian to a traditional chippy. Uptown has a huge foodcourt that's sure to undo all your hard work at the local Fitness First.

Mushrif Park is so big that you actually drive around it rather than walk, and it features a train, swimming pools and tennis courts. Rashidiya has a quiet park with lots of greenery and swings and slides, but it's ladies and children only except Fridays and holidays. The new Mirdif Park is now open on Street 26B and features two big

Mirdif

playgrounds, grassy areas, basketball and badminton courts, a football pitch and a tennis court. Dads, please take note that this park is for ladies and children only during the week.

Healthcare
Welcare Clinic is open in Uptown Mirdif and they offer a wide range of medical services (04 288 1302). Drs Nicolas & Asp Dental Clinic is also in the area (04 288 4411). Over Airport Road in Mizhar there is a branch of Dubai London Clinic (04 287 8530). Rashidiya Clinic is the nearest government health facility. The nearest government hospital is Rashid, with 24 hour emergency services.

Education
There is a choice of nurseries in Mirdif including Small Steps, Super Kids and Emirates British Nursery (p.206). Uptown Primary is recommended. Other new schools include the Sharjah American International School in Al Warqa, Royal Dubai School in Muhaisnah, and the American Academy for Girls in Mizhar. Star International Academy will open in Mirdif sometime in 2009.

Travelling Times
Airport – 5 mins
Media City – 30 mins
Trade Centre – 20 mins

Traffic & Parking
Within Mirdif and Al Warqa the traffic is minimal, although the main road through Mirdif is often used as a shortcut for Emirates Road traffic heading to Sharjah. There's no problem with parking as most villas have plenty of room out front or on the driveway (if it hasn't been dug up for roadworks). It's not easy to flag down a taxi in these areas so you will need to call for one (04 208 0808).

Safety & Annoyances
Mirdif is generally safe, but some people drive too fast around the neighbourhood streets. Burglaries do occur, mainly opportunist, so don't leave windows or patio doors open. Emirates Road gets clogged, and of course the airport is fairly close so aircraft noise can be a nuisance.

Area Q p.127
See also Map 10

Oud Metha & Umm Hurair
Oud Metha has the advantage of being centrally located, within easy reach of the highways, plenty of shops and restaurants within walking distance or just minutes by car, as well as Lamcy Plaza and the Wafi City complex of shops and restaurants. Accommodation is mainly in low-rise apartment blocks, which are not as densely packed in as in other 'inner-city' areas. There is a fair amount of construction going on, but you might need to look for a while to find a vacant apartment.

Best Points
Convenient central location with easy access.

Accommodation
It is all apartments in this part of town and they are usually in four-storey buildings. Sizes range from studio to four-bedroom although the most common are one and two. Annual rents range from Dhs.95,000 (if you're really lucky) to Dhs.150,000 (if you're in the new buildings) for a one bedroom, Dhs.160,000 to Dhs.180,000 for a two bedroom and around Dhs.230,000 and upwards for a three bedroom, obviously with facilities increasing and improving in the higher priced buildings.

Worst Points
Small-scale construction affects some residences with noise and blocking roads, but lack of accommodation is probably the biggest problem.

Shopping & Amenities
This small area is packed with all you'll need, including a large Lals supermarket inside Lamcy Plaza on the top floor, and plenty of good medium-sized supermarkets, convenient smaller groceries, pharmacies and a Spinneys Market in the area. There are also plenty of dry cleaners and laundries scattered through the area as well as some

good DVD rental stores and a post office counter in Lamcy Plaza. ATMs for many banks can be found in Lamcy Plaza and Wafi City along with branches for a couple of banks in the area, including National Bank of Dubai near Movenpick Hotel. Several of Dubai's churches can also be found in the area.

Entertainment & Leisure

The area around Lamcy Plaza has some great independent restaurants, such as Lemongrass and Lan Kwai Fong, and there are licensed restaurants in Movenpick, Grand Hyatt and the Wafi complex. These were joined in late 2007 by Dubai's latest luxury hotel, Raffles. Cheaper options include the foodcourt in Lamcy with some branches of local chains and the big fastfood names, and there are numerous local shawarma joints around Oud Metha. For bars and nightclubs there is the low key, fun-packed Jimmy Dix in the Movenpick, and The Mix at the Grand Hyatt, one of Dubai's superclubs.

For relaxation there are numerous health spas, Moroccan baths, hairdressers and beauty salons located in this area are as well as several social clubs. For the more energetic there are plenty of places offering sports and activities including Al Nasr Leisureland (home to a bowling alley and ice rink), the health clubs at Movenpick, Grand Hyatt and Wafi, many small gyms dotted around, and billiard halls.

There is a small park on Umm Hurair Road close to Dubai TV, while Creekside Park and Zabeel Park are both just five minutes away. In addition, there are amusement centres at Al Nasr Leisureland, Lamcy Plaza and Wafi City, Children's City at Creekside Park and the 12 screen Grand Cineplex cinema next to the Grand Hyatt.

Healthcare

Dubai's two main government hospitals, Rashid and Al Wasl, are both nearby, but there are also several popular private medical centres such as American Hospital, the Canadian Specialist Medical Centre and Dubai HealthCare City, home to many medical facilities and the newly opened City Hospital (p.186).

Education

The main street between Oud Metha and Umm Hurair is home to some of Dubai's largest schools such as the Indian High School and Dubai English Speaking School, a popular school for western children living all over Dubai. For more information on schools, see p.203.

Travelling Times
Airport – 10 mins
Media City – 20 mins
Trade Centre – 10 mins

Traffic & Parking

While traffic tends to be a bit of a headache in most central areas there is the benefit of various alternative access routes. The only regular places to watch out for slow traffic are by Lamcy Plaza and through the main roundabout in Umm Hurair coming from the Wafi interchange. The area has some good free parking, in shopping centre carparks, on side roads, and on empty patches of sandy ground. The municipality carpark close to Lamcy is now metered.

In rush hour, Sheikh Zayed Road suffers the usual problems towards Garhoud Bridge and Sharjah and towards Media City, but Maktoum Bridge (now metered with a Salik gate) can be a viable alternative to Garhoud at certain times of the day. The Floating Bridge is also a useful access bridge for this area.

Safety & Annoyances

Sometimes at weekends there can be traffic noise from cruising cars, but a good police presence is addressing the problem. Traffic and parking can be painful, but not as bad as in other congested areas.

Area **R** p.127
See also Map 7

Satwa

A mixture of accommodation and a great central location makes Satwa (and the adjoining neighbourhoods of Al Bada'a, Hudheiba & Al Jafilya) a popular choice. Sadly, in 2008 large parts of Satwa were being demolished to make way for the Jumeirah Garden City Project, and many residents living in the area's older villas were evicted. Towards the end of 2008, however, it was announced that there would be some delays to parts of this project. For that idyllic peaceful villa you'll probably need to head further along the coast to Jumeira, Al Wasl and Umm Suqeim, but for singles or couples, Satwa's lively bustle can be rather endearing, and its main street, Diyafah is a blissful pedestrian paradise compared with the rest of Dubai.

Best Points

The good central location, lots of facilities and amenities within walking distance, and many more places just a short drive away.

Worst Points

The traffic on Diyafah Street (both vehicular and pedestrian).

Accommodation

There is a selection of apartment blocks on Diyafah Street and Al Hudeiba Street (Plant Street), all of which are no higher than seven or eight storeys. In addition there are a number of low-rent rooms above shops around the one-way system. Surprisingly, you'll also find a fair few villas too, some old, traditional and run down, others more modern and expensive. For a two-bedroom apartment on Diyafah Street you can expect to pay around Dhs.170,000. Prices for smart villas, however, are not much cheaper than Jumeira – starting at roughly Dhs.250,000 for a three bedroom.

Shopping & Amenities

There are plenty of shops and supermarkets on Diyafah Street, while the nearest 'big' supermarkets include Spinneys on Beach Road and Safestway on Sheikh Zayed Road. Dune Centre on Diyafah Street has a few shops (including a place to hire formal evening wear should you ever need it), a DVD rental shop and an internet cafe. The new Al Ghazal Shopping Complex has more than 70 outlets offering fashion and homewares, plus a nail bar, pharmacy and health clinic.

The one-way system is one of the best areas in Dubai for cut-price textiles and tailors. The multitude of tailors located here are great for upholstery and cushions too. You just take along your measurements and they'll run you up some snazzy 'majlis' style cushions. For the handyman, DIY gear and tools abound and Satwa is one of the best places for car spares such as batteries, and small repairs – pull into the small car park next to the mosque construction site and you'll have half a dozen guys on the bonnet offering to fix your car. Just be prepared to haggle.

'Plant Street' (real name Al Hudeiba Street) has a number of shops that sell plants (surprisingly) as well as pots and other garden equipment as well as a range of picture framing and soft furnishing shops and a Lal's supermarket.

Entertainment & Leisure

Rydges Plaza on Diyafah Street has some popular casual favourites, including Aussie Legends, Billy Blues, Cactus Cantina and Il Rustico. The Jumeira Rotana has the ever-popular Boston Bar where ladies' nights certainly draw in the crowds, while the nearby Capitol Hotel is home to Henry J. Beans.

Diyafah Street has some great independent restaurants too, including Al Mallah and Sidra for yummy shawarmas, falafel and juice. There are a few Indian and Chinese places, plus KFC, Pizza Hut and Burger King. Also, in virtually any direction there are a whole range of enticing hotspots, be it in Jumeira, Bur Dubai or on Sheikh Zayed Road. Green spaces are in short supply, although Za'abeel Park is nearby (p.283).

Healthcare

The Iranian Hospital on Al Wasl Road is very close and has an excellent A&E department plus a walk-in GP service with free medication. Also, the Rashid government hospital isn't too far. The Neuro Spinal Hospital on Beach Road has a 24 hour A&E and its own ambulance, while the Belhoul Hospital on Diyafah Street specialises in surgery. The new Al Bada'a Clinic (government) is behind Chelsea Tower. There are also a number of pharmacies on the main roads. For more information on hospitals see p.178.

Education

While there aren't any popular expat schools within Satwa there are a number in Jumeira and Al Wasl, as well as various nurseries, which are easily accessible. See p.203.

Travelling Times
Airport – 15 mins
Media City – 20 mins
Trade Centre – 5 mins

Traffic & Parking

Diyafah Street gets pretty busy, especially in the evening rush hour, and on a Friday night when drivers and pedestrians seem to spend hours cruising up and down. The one-way system is constantly busy too, with too much lane swapping and reversing out into oncoming traffic. Diyafah Street and the one-way system have metered parking, but spaces can be hard to come by. However, there are a few sandy areas outside buildings where you can park.

Safety & Annoyances

Around some of the older areas there may be one or two undesirables, and occasional break-ins have been reported in older villas. You may get annoyed by the traffic on the main roads and by the sheer volume of cars and people around the one-way system. If you like neon lights and hustle and bustle though, this could be right up your alley.

Area ⑤ p.127
See also Map 12

Sharjah

Dubai's neighbouring emirate is an attractive location for many mainly due to the significantly lower rents, which can be up to half what you'd pay in Dubai. As you'd expect in any city, there's a wide range of accommodation options, from small apartments to big villas.

Best Points
The low rents are a real draw for people looking for budget accommodation. The city also has a fairly quiet, community feel.

Accommodation

Downtown it's all high-rise apartment blocks. Some have been around a few years and so facilities will be a little basic. Newer blocks command higher rents. As you venture out of town there are some big independent villas, and smaller, older villas too.
For a one-bedroom apartment in town you could pay as little as Dhs.50,000, while a three-bedroom villa can be found for Dhs.150,000.

Worst Points
At rush hour the E11 linking Sharjah and Dubai becomes the world's longest car park. Journey times of two hours are not uncommon. Sharjah is the only 'dry' emirate, so there's no bars or licensed restaurants, and the city is certainly not as liberal as Dubai, so you should behave and dress accordingly.

Shopping & Amenities

Dubai may be famous for its shopping, but Sharjah isn't bad either. Sharjah City Centre, Sharjah Mega Mall, and the Sahara Centre all feature a host of international brands and stores (such as M&S and Debenhams), and there are plenty of smaller shopping centres catering to all tastes and budgets. For a slightly more traditional shopping experience, the big Central Souk (aka Blue Souk) has rows of jewellery shops and stores selling Arabian knick-knacks and pretty much anything you could imagine. The Souk Al Arsah, in the Heritage Area, is another traditional Arabian market (although it now has a roof and doors and is pleasantly air conditioned). Sharjah also has fruit, vegetable and fish markets in Al Jubail beside the water, with many stalls offering a variety of fresh produce.
For your everyday shopping needs, there's a big Carrefour hypermarket in the City Centre mall and a Spinneys in the Sahara Centre. You'll also find plenty of small grocery stores dotted around the residential areas, as well as dry cleaners and laundries.

Entertainment & Leisure

Sharjah does have a reputation for being a bit quiet, and many expats head for Dubai at night. That said, Sharjah has its share of dining and leisure options, with a number of good independent restaurants. You'll also find branches of well-known chains and fast-food restaurants, and the shopping malls all have foodcourts.

A particularly popular option for expats in Sharjah is the Sharjah Wanderers Sports Club. It has a host of sporting and leisure facilities (including two grass pitches), and, perhaps most importantly, licensed bars and restaurants (yes, licensed, selling alcohol, in Sharjah). The club is only accessible to members, and guests of members. For more info visit www.sharjahwanderers.com.

Cinemas in Sharjah include the Star Cineplex at City Centre and Century Cinema at the Sahara Centre. For spending time outdoors, Sharjah has some big green parks, attractive corniches, and good beaches, and Al Qasba is a lovely spot for a leisurely stroll. The Heritage and Arts areas are certainly worth a visit, with plenty of art galleries and museums showing how life used to be.

Healthcare

Sharjah has a number of government health clinics for subsidised medical care, plus private clinics and hospitals. The two government hospitals with emergency facilities are the Qassimi (06 538 6444) and Kuwaiti hospitals (06 524 2111), while Al Zahra (06 561 9999), Zulekha (06 565 8866), and the Central Private (06 563 9900) are the main private hospitals with 24 hour emergency care.

Education

Sharjah English School is a primary school for English-speaking children (06 552 2779), and Wesgreen International School (06 537 4401) teaches the curriculum of England and Wales from kindergarten through to secondary. The Sharjah American International School (06 538 0000) teaches the American curriculum. The Lycée Georges Pompidou de Sharjah (06 552 3430) is a French school for children from 3 to 18 years old, and the German School Sharjah (06 567 6014) offers the German curriculum to the same age group. The Australian International School (06 558 9967) is on the Sharjah-Dubai border, just five minutes from Sharjah Airport.

Sharjah University City is home to a number of higher education institutions including the American University of Sharjah (06 515 5555). For more information, see p.220.

Travelling Times
Airport – 15 mins
Media City – 45 mins
Trade Centre – 25 mins
(on a clear run)

Traffic & Parking

Thousands of people make the journey between Sharjah and Dubai every day, and the roads simply can't handle the volume of traffic. The notorious E11 Al Ittihad Road links central Sharjah and central Dubai, crossing Dubai Creek at Garhoud Bridge, and for most of the morning it's nose to tail leaving Sharjah and the same in the other direction once evening arrives. The E311 Emirates Road is one alternative, but it's a long way round, and it too becomes very busy at rush hour. Traffic within Sharjah itself suffers as a result, with delays at the big interchanges.

Finding your way around is a challenge, and whoever's in charge of the signposts in Sharjah clearly has a sense of humour.

Parking downtown can be tricky, as there's not really enough to go round. Much of the roadside parking is metered too, and as the parking bays are 'end on', you really have to look out for people reversing out into the oncoming traffic. The local taxis are not always as clean or modern as those in Dubai, but they are significantly cheaper and fairly easy to flag down in the built-up residential areas. The main companies are Delta Taxi (06 559 8598) and Emirates Taxi (06 539 6666). One problem you may well encounter is that your driver has been in Sharjah for less time than you have, and therefore will have no idea where he's going.

Safety & Annoyances
Crime is not common. Downtown is a bit of a concrete jungle so not ideal for families, but out of town is quieter. Sharjah is catching up with the construction boom, so you may experience noise and disruption. The ultimate annoyance in Sharjah is the traffic.

Area **T** p.127
See also Map 7

Trade Centre

The strip between Trade Centre Roundabout and Interchange One is home to some of Dubai's biggest, brightest and boldest towers, both residential and commercial, plus some of the most impressive hotels in town. Being so close to all the action it's a popular area, and rents are high as a result. This part of Sheikh Zayed Road has often been compared to Hong Kong because of its architecturally splendid skyscrapers.

Best Points
The proximity to so many entertainment venues is a definite plus point as is the easy access to all of Dubai. There is even the possibility of a sea view if you're high enough and facing the right direction.

Worst Points
There is always traffic and lots of hustle and bustle, so it's not really a place to retreat.

Sheikh Zayed Road

Accommodation
It's pretty much all apartments in a mix of styles and luxury levels, but all are on the expensive side. Most should have some sort of leisure facilities in the building. Rents can be Dhs.170,000 for a one bedroom and Dhs.390,000 for a three bedroom.

Shopping & Amenities
While there didn't used to be any huge malls in the immediate vicinity (the nearest were probably Deira City Centre or Mercato on Jumeira Road), the opening of Dubai Mall has changed all that. There are also two decent shopping centres: the Crowne Plaza 'Holiday Centre', with a few clothes shops, an optician, pharmacy, and a fairly big Choithram supermarket; and the Boulevard at Emirates Towers, with a selection of designer clothes outlets, jewellery and perfume shops. There's also an optician, a nail bar, a men's spa and a cigar shop.

Otherwise, there are plenty of smaller shops catering to all your everyday needs. Many of the towers have grocery or convenience stores on the ground floor, and there are supermarkets such as Lifco for weekly shops. Spinneys on Trade Centre

Road or in Mazaya Centre and Safestway supermarket (which stocks US brands) aren't a million miles away. There's an MMI liquor store behind Pizza Hut and plenty of banks and ATMs including NBD on both sides, HSBC, Mashreqbank and a Thomas Cook money exchange. There's a machine to pay police fines in the Boulevard at Emirates Towers. The hotels have spas, gyms and leisure facilities (although they don't come cheap), and many residential and office towers will have some sort of fitness facilities.

The nearest post office is on Al Wasl Road, but Mail Box in the lobby of Al Durrah Tower offers a range of postal services and PO boxes, and you can rent a PO box at the Emarat garage on Al Safa Street. The new Satwa Park has sports facilities and a bit of greenery and Safa Park isn't too far away.

For car care, just down Al Safa Street there's a Grand Lube, plus repairs, tyres, and a car wash. Emarat, right next door, also has a car wash (reputedly the best in Dubai) and offers oil changes.

Entertainment & Leisure

With a high concentration of hotels and independent restaurants, the options are almost endless. Dining wise, at one end of the scale (and the street) you've got the five-star finery of the Fairmont, while at the other you'll find a range of coffee shops and cafes.

Some of Dubai's favourite bars, restaurants and clubs are along this strip, including Spectrum on One in the Fairmont, Teatro and Long's Bar in the Towers Rotana and Trader Vic's and Zinc in the Crowne Plaza. The Loft, run by the same people who run Lotus One, is a nightclub next to Fibber McGee's.

Arabica and Zyara are good cafes for local food and shisha and Saj Express is good for cheap Arabic food. French Connection has good food, tea, coffee and bakery products, plus free wireless web access if you're eating there. Shakespeare & Co is a favourite thanks to its unique bohemian decor and interesting outside space. There are also bowling lanes and a pool hall just by Interchange 1 on the Satwa side.

> ### Defence Roundabout
> You'll often hear Sheikh Zayed Road's Interchange One referred to as Defence Roundabout, as the army HQ was previously situated nearby. The current overhaul of this busy junction includes bridges, flyovers, and a new name – Burj Dubai Interchange – although the old Defence title will no doubt live on for many years.

Healthcare

Al Zahra Medical Centre in Al Safa Tower has a number of departments including family medicine and dentistry. The nearest emergency care is either Rashid or Iranian hospital or the private Neuro Spinal Hospital. The new Al Bada'a Clinic (government) is behind Chelsea Tower. The Doha Pharmacy near 21st Century Tower is open 24 hours and there are quite a few other pharmacies dotted around. For information on hospitals, see p.178.

Education

There are not may international schools in the area, apart from Wellington Primary, but several schools and nurseries can be found nearby in Satwa and Jumeira. See p.203.

Travelling Times
Airport – 10 mins
Media City – 20 mins

Traffic & Parking

Parking is not bad if you have a card to access your building's car park, otherwise it's either find a sandy spot between the towers (these are disappearing as more buildings go up) or pay for metered parking on the street. Traffic is a problem in this area, as the E11 Sheikh Zayed Road is a main thoroughfare linking Sharjah and 'old' Dubai with Jebel Ali, and Media and Internet Cities. During rush hour the traffic is crawling, towards Jebel Ali in the morning, and towards Sharjah in the evening. The two interchanges (Trade Centre Roundabout and Defence Roundabout) are busy too, especially the latter which is being upgraded. If you're on one side of Sheikh Zayed Road, it could take about 20 minutes to drive to the building directly opposite. Traffic is even worse if there's a major event or exhibition (such as Gitex) going on at the Trade Centre.

Safety & Annoyances

There are pavements but watch out for speeding drivers on the service roads. Until the Metro bridges open, the only way to cross Sheikh Zayed Road is via the bridge linking the Trade Centre with the Fairmont, or the pedestrian underpass further down near the Crowne Plaza. Living here can be a bit noisy if you're on one of the lower floors facing the road, although thundering trucks are not allowed on Sheikh Zayed Road.

Area ⓤ p.127
See also Map 6

Umm Suqeim

This is a desirable area mainly because it is close to the beach and all the amenities you could wish for, while still remaining relatively peaceful. Plus it is slightly cheaper than neighbouring Jumeira (only just). There are no high-rises either (not counting the Burj Al Arab hotel) and Umm Suqeim is within easy reach of the major road networks, and midway between the old centre of Dubai in Deira and the new Dubai emerging further along the coast towards the marina. This is an ever popular choice for expats with kids but the rents are on the steep side.

Best Points

Easy access to the beach, shopping, entertainment facilities and plenty of nice big villas – perfect for families.

Accommodation

Villas, villas, villas. Ranging from traditional, old single-storey dwellings and smart multi-bedroom villas to palatial mansions. If you're extremely lucky you may hear about an old (perhaps run-down) villa going for Dhs.275,000, but for this price you can expect to have to pay for any maintenance and repairs. In fact, you hear stories of people spending a fair amount to make their cheap villa more liveable, only for the owner to then up the rent once they see how nice it is. For a detached four or five-bedroom villa, you'll be paying at least Dhs.450,000.

Worst Points

The rents are high and the traffic on Beach Road can be bad at rush hour, but apart from that there is little else to criticise about the area.

Shopping & Amenities

The modern but traditional Souk Madinat Jumeirah is on the Umm Suqeim-Al Sufouh border and makes for a nice shopping trip. There's a well-stocked Choithram supermarket (04 348 1864) on Al Wasl Road, with a dry cleaners, a good little florist, and a shop that sells CDS, DVDs, and videos. You can also rent videos from here (but not DVDs). Outside there's an HSBC ATM, and Al Faisal Pharmacy (04 348 5102) next door, open 07:30-24:00 seven days.

Showcase Antiques (04 348 8797) opposite the Dubai Municipality building on Jumeira Road (known as Beach Road) has a big selection of furniture, decorative items, old doors and chests, and ancient weapons. Kids' clothes shop Stitches (04 348 6110) on Beach Road does school uniforms and there are various grocery stores, pharmacies, laundries, tailor's shops and Mercato Mall (p.496).

Spinneys Centre is also nearby (p.505), and the enormous Mall of the Emirates (p.494) is just across Interchange 4 on Sheikh Zayed Road.

There are long stretches of golden sandy beach open to the public – the section immediately north of the Jumeirah Beach Hotel is the nicest, and busiest as a result. There are new lifeguard centres being constructed at intervals along the beach. Walking and jogging around the residential areas is popular as they are pretty quiet, but the best place has to be the beach. There are also occasional areas of sand and scrub for dog walking, and one or two have goal posts for a kick-around. Umm Suqeim Park on the seafront is a pleasant oasis of green with a kids' playground, picnic areas, benches, a cafe, and toilets. It's open between 08:00 and 23:00 from Saturday to Wednesday, but only to ladies and children. On Thursday, Friday and holidays it is open from 08:00 to 23:30 for families only (no men on their own).

Umm Suqeim Library is primarily an IT centre with plenty of smart new PCs with internet access costing Dhs.3 per hour. You can also study for the International Computer Driving Licence (ICDL) here.

Entertainment & Leisure

With the Burj Al Arab, Jumeirah Beach Hotel, and Madinat Jumeirah all on the doorstep, the entertainment and dining options are plentiful. At the opposite end of the spectrum, but no less enjoyable, are places such as the Buqtair 'restaurant', a Portakabin opposite the fishing harbour in Umm Suqeim 1. The guys here do a mean fish curry made with the morning's catch. The Chalet Restaurant on Beach Road is great for traditional Arabic food and juices. The nearest cinema is at Mercato, and the Wild Wadi water park is next to the Jumeirah Beach Hotel.

Healthcare
The nearest hospital with a 24 hour emergency room is the private Neuro Spinal Hospital opposite Jumeirah Beach Park in Jumeira 2. For general medical care there is The Umm Suqeim Clinic (government) as well as many specialists and dentists along Beach Road including Advanced Chiropractic & Massage Clinic (04 348 8262) and the Euro American – Cosmetic Surgery and Telesurge Center (04 348 5575). For more information on hospitals, see p.178.

Education
The biggest secondary school is Emirates International School, but there are lots of other schools in nearby Jumeira. There are plenty of nurseries including Emirates British Nursery, Alphabet Street Nursery, British Curriculum Children's Nursery and Le Petit Poucet (a French nursery, 04 348 4451). For more information on schools, see p.203.

Travelling Times ◀
Airport – 25 mins
Media City – 5 mins
Trade Centre – 15 mins

Traffic & Parking
During rush hour and the school-run, Beach Road up to Media City is pretty busy, as is Al Wasl Road, but it does flow. Parking is fine off the main roads, but tricky now on Beach Road after it was widened by one lane each way.

Safety & Annoyances
Umm Suqeim is generally pretty safe and secure, and a great area for families, but there are the occasional instances of petty burglary so keep doors locked. Beach Road can be noisy and busy.

Developing Areas
There are several new areas in Dubai that, within a year or two, could become vast residential neighbourhoods.

Silicon Oasis, located off the Academic City Road, is a development containing hundreds of beautiful villas with gardens. Many of the villas are lived in by Emirates pilots. This area is considered to be quite far out of town, although it is just a 10 minute drive from Mirdif. There are a few small restaurants inside Silicon Oasis and in the nearby Academic City, and the Outlet Mall is just a quick trip over the other side of the Dubai-Al Ain Road. For more information, check out the community forum www.siliconoasis.org.

Jumeirah Lakes Towers (JLT) is a high-rise community made up of 79 towers, both residential and commercial. It is located directly across Sheikh Zayed Road from the Marina, and will be serviced by two Metro stations. When the lakes are completed there will be a promenade around them with cafes and shops.

International Media Production Zone (IMPZ) will eventually have many large studios for film production, although currently it is just home to a few apartment blocks.

Discovery Gardens is considered by some to be the 'upscale International City'. It consists of hundreds of nearly identical low-rise apartment blocks, and is very green. It is located near Ibn Battuta Mall and The Gardens.

TECOM is next door to The Greens, and at the moment it is mainly residential apartment blocks, but there are some office towers under construction. It will have its own Metro station, but unfortunately at the moment this area is a bit too much of a construction site, with no greenery, no pavements and no shops. Watch this space.

Residential Areas

Villa living

Moving Services

When hiring from abroad, Dubai employers sometimes offer help (such as a shipping allowance or furniture allowance) but the city is also well served by relocation specialists. If you're planning to arrive with more than a suitcase, you'll need to send your belongings by air or by sea. Air freight is faster but more expensive. Sea freight takes longer but it's cheaper, and containers can hold a huge amount.

Some well known removal firms are in Dubai, and if you use a reputable company you'll probably have fewer worries about breakages and loss. Everything you ship will need to be checked by customs and you must be present to collect your goods – air freight at Cargo Village in Garhoud and sea freight at Jebel Ali Port. Be sure to have your own copy of the inventory so that you know exactly what is in each box. And be patient.

Shipping goods by air can be expensive, so it may be worth only sending your bare essentials that you can't do without before you leave and will need as soon as you arrive. Also, depending on how much you ship, the entire process could be done at Cargo Village. Most of the big relocation companies will have warehouses there, or with affiliated companies. Head to the warehouse and fill out the customs information, and pay any applicable fees. You will then have to go across to Customs where you will pay any duty, plus a processing fee. Once this has been done, you can go back to the warehouse and collect your shipment. Before you can leave, you will have to head back over to Customs to have your goods x-rayed.

The process for sea freight is a little longer but some agencies will do the customs clearing for you, and arrange delivery to your home. In the hot summer months, you'll be glad of the reduced hassle. This is also true for some air freight companies.

Once your freight is ready for collection (you'll get a call or letter), go to the agent's office and pay the administration and handling charges. Keep these documents. The Bill of Lading number must be marked on all paperwork and entered into the customs computer system.

Then go to Dubai Customs House, on Al Mina Road. The staff are helpful and the procedure is fairly straightforward, so ignore the touts outside. When the papers have been stamped and the Port Clearance received (there are fees at each stage) head down to Jebel Ali Port.

Smooth Moves

- Get more than one quote – some companies will match lower quotes to get the job.
- Make sure that all items are covered by insurance.
- Make sure that you have a copy of the inventory and that each item is listed.
- Don't be shy about requesting packers to repack items if you are not satisfied.
- Take photos of the packing process, to use for evidence if you need to make a claim.
- Carry customs restricted goods (DVDs, videos or books) with you: it's easier to open a suitcase in an air-conditioned airport than empty a box outside in the sun.

Start Afresh

Prices for furniture and appliances in Dubai are pretty reasonable so it may make sense to furnish your new home with new items (see Home Furnishings, p.449). There's also a good second-hand market thanks to the transient nature of expat life in Dubai (see Second Hand Items, p.464 and p.160). When, and if, the time comes when you want to return home, you'll certainly be shipping a packed container.

Removal Companies

Ahmed Saleh Packing & Forwarding	04 285 4000	www.ahmedsalehpacking.com
Allied Pickfords ▶ p.159	04 408 9555	www.alliedpickfords.com
Crown Relocations ▶ p.83	04 289 5152	www.crownrelo.com
DASA International Movers	04 334 4545	www.dasadxb.com
Euro Movers	04 340 3920	www.euromovers-ae.com
Interem (Freight Systems Co Ltd) ▶ p.89	04 807 0584	www.freightsystems.com
Gulf Agency Company (GAC) ▶ p.161	04 881 8090	www.gacworld.com/dubai
ISS Worldwide Movers	04 303 8651	www.iss-shipping.com
Movers Packaging	04 267 0699	na
Southeast Shipping LLC	04 258 1815	na
Swift Freight International	04 881 9595	www.swiftfreight.com
Writer Relocations	04 340 8814	www.writercorporation.com

moving?

relax. we carry the load.SM

Door to door moving with Allied Pickfords

Allied Pickfords is one of the largest and most respected providers of moving services in the world, handling over 50,000 international moves every year.

We believe that nothing reduces stress more than trust, and each year thousands of families trust Allied Pickfords to move them. With over 800 offices in more than 40 countries, we're the specialists in international moving and have the ability to relocate you anywhere anytime. Move with Allied to Allied worldwide.

Call us now on +971 4 408 9555
www.alliedpickfords.com
general@alliedpickfords.ae

Your Chance to Earn Airmiles for using Allied Pickfords

The Careful Movers™

Create A Dream Home
New city, new house, new start – an interior designer can make your new abode look just like the one you've always pictured in your mind. See p.164.

If you need a truck to transport the boxes, there's an area at the sea end of Kuwait Street or in Al Quoz where you can hire one.

Jebel Ali is huge, so make sure you have the phone number of the warehouse and good directions; a day pass will be issued at the gate. At the warehouse, if the consignment has been stamped 'need to be inspected', load up and take it to the police inspection area by the main gate; it's up to the officer whether they'll be x-rayed or not. If there's any doubt about whether any of your DVDs, videos and books comply with UAE censorship laws, they'll be taken to the Department of Information and viewed. If they're passed you'll be notified when they are ready for collection, otherwise, they'll be destroyed. The release papers will be issued at the office where the inspection stamp was issued. If you need storage call Sentinel Storage in Al Quoz on 04 340 6962.

Relocation Specialists

If the mere thought of relocation raises your stress levels, there are a number of companies who will go that one step beyond shipping and removals. Relocation companies offer a variety of packages to help new expats settle into their new country. Depending on the company, services include orientation of a new city, accommodation finding (and sometimes furnishing), utility connection, and they can even help find a school if you are bringing the family. Some companies will also arrange shipping of goods from your home country to your new home. Relocation companies are becoming popular with expats who want the transition to their new life to be as smooth as possible, plus having inside help is always invaluable when choosing a home or school. Packages and costs can vary, so it is always wise to shop around. Have a rough idea of what kind of services you require, as it will make quotations much easier.

Relocation Companies

Company		Phone	Website
Allied Pickfords	p.159	04 408 9555	www.alliedpickfords.com
Crown Relocations	p.83	04 289 5152	www.crownrelo.com
Daily's Relocation		04 343 7428	www.dailys.ae
Dubai Luxury Homes		04 303 9300	www.dubailuxuryhomes.com
Echo Xpats		04 391 2252	www.echo-xpats.com
Enigma Relocation		04 394 6710	www.enigmadubai.com
Equate Relocations		04 884 6051	www.equaterelocations.com
Interem (Freight Systems Co Ltd)	p.89	04 807 0584	www.freightsystems.com
Global Relocations		04 352 3300	www.globalrelocations.com
Gulf Agency Company (GAC)	p.161	04 881 8090	www.gacworld.com/dubai
Gulf Relocation Services		04 801 9210	www.gulfrelocation.com
In Touch Relocations		04 321 5701	www.intouchdubai.com
Southeast Shipping		04 258 1815	na
The Specialists	p.117	04 329 5959	www.thespecialistsdubai.com
Writer Relocations		04 340 8814	www.writercorporation.com

Furnishing Accommodation

Other options **Home Furnishings & Accessories** p.450, **Second-Hand Items** p.464

Whether you're renting or you've bought somewhere, you'll need some furniture. Most properties, including rentals, are unfurnished, and don't even have basic white goods such as a cooker or fridge. Not all villas have fitted cupboards and wardrobes. Dubai is home to many furniture shops, ranging from Swedish simplicity at IKEA to rich Indian teak at Marina Gulf Trading. Alternatively, head to one of the carpentry workshops on Naif Road or in Satwa. For more information on where to buy beautiful furniture, see p.450.

Second-Hand Furniture

The population of Dubai is still fairly transitory, and with so many arrivals and departures, there's a constant stream of second-hand items out there. There are a number of small shops, mainly in Karama, Naif and Satwa that sell second-hand

GAC Dubai International Moving
Quality, Reliability, Flexibility

Relocation in itself is a challenge. And we believe that you already have enough to do without worrying about your forthcoming move. That's why when it comes to moving your home or office, GAC treats each item with care and every move with pride.

With more than 30 years of experience in moving household goods in and out of the Middle East, GAC provides comprehensive high quality door-to-door services for any relocation need. Moves are professionally planned, starting with a free initial survey and recommendations on the most efficient shipment mode. All necessary services, including professional export packing, custom built crating, forwarding and secure storage facilities are also provided. For reliable relocation services wherever you go, start your journey at **www.gacworld.com**.

 wherever you go

Gulf Agency Company (Dubai) L.L.C   P O Box 17401, Jebel Ali, Dubai, United Arab Emirates
Tel: + 971 4 881 8090   Fax: + 971 4 805 9342   Email: gacremov@emirates.net.ae

furniture, but you might find even better bargains from scouring online classifieds. Try www.dubizzle.com, www.expatwoman.com, www.websouq.com, or www. dubaidonkey.com. They have quite a large following and everything from white goods to living room furniture can be picked up. The Expat Woman website will often have notices for garage sales, where it's quite often possible to buy in bulk and prices can be negotiable. Supermarket noticeboards also carry listings for garage sales, or individual items with photos so you have a good idea what to expect before you view. Safa Park has recently launched a flea market (www.dubai-fleamarket.com). Held the first Saturday of every month, the market is open between 09:00 and 15:00. With bargains plentiful, this is a great place to pick up finishing touches to your new home, or even a few cheap books while you wait for your home-cinema to be delivered.

Furniture Leasing

Setting up a new life and home is an expensive business. Aside from rental or mortgage costs, it is unlikely that many expats will have shipped their entire home contents over here. Furniture rental, from firms such as Indigo Living (p.164), provides a solution for new arrivals. Having the option of renting furniture means it's possible to move into your new home earlier, and there is no initial rush to have the entire house furnished before you can move in. There is always the danger of not liking expat life, so renting furniture before you commit long term can work out as quite a money saver.

Ready-Made Homes

Following on from relocation companies, having the option to have your home furnished before you move in is quite attractive to some people. If your company is providing you with accommodation rather than an allowance, it may provide you with a furnished apartment or villa. Decor is likely to be quite neutral, so while you may not be too offended by the colour scheme, you may want to add personal touches. However, a number of companies will also kit out your home, so that when you step off the plane you can head straight to your own comfy bed.

Curtains & Blinds		
Aleena Curtains	050 252 9870	na
Avenue Interiors	04 340 8955	www.blinds.ae
Couture Interiors	04 323 5855	www.couture.ae
Everest Furniture Factory	04 338 6255	na
Feshwari Curtains	04 339 3559	www.feshwari.com
Indigo Living ▶ p.165	04 341 6388	www.indigo-living.com
Royal Blinds	04 347 4760	www.royalblinds.com
Sedar Emirates	04 345 4597	www.sedaremirates.com

Curtains & Blinds

Year-round sunshine is a draw for expats coming to Dubai, but not everybody can sleep with the sun beating through the window. Finding the right blinds or curtains can add a finishing touch to your room, ensure privacy if the house is overlooked, or stop you waking up with the sun. Some properties have windows built to standard sizes, which means you can buy ready-made options from shops such as IKEA and THE One. If these don't measure up though, there are several companies that will tailor and install curtains and blinds to fit your property, usually for a higher price than pre-made ones. IKEA also has a fabric store and offers a tailoring service for basic curtains and roman blinds at bargain prices.

Various Locations ◀ Dubai Blinds ▶ p.163
04 312 4086 | *www.dubaiblinds.com*
If you want to take the hassle out of getting your windows covered up, check out Dubai Blinds. A representative will come to your home to measure up and show samples, and, once ready, will return to fit your chosen drapes. The firm offers all styles of blinds, from roman through to wooden venetian, as well as curtains and shutters.

Interior Design

Moving into a brand new, empty apartment can be a hassle if you have arrived without any furnishings – but starting with a blank canvas can also provide an excellent opportunity to style up your home from scratch in a coordinated way. From art to hiring furniture, the companies listed below can help you get up and running.

Warehouse 3
Umm Sequim Rd
Al Quoz

House of the World

04 323 3482 | *www.houseoftheworld.com*

House of the World supplies works of art to designers and commercial and residential spaces, as well as tailored interior design for apartments and villas. It draws heavily on eastern influences. Founded in Ireland, the company moved to Dubai in 2005 and now has offices in Jumeirah Lakes Towers and a gallery in Al Quoz.

Showroom 45
Road 8, Street 19
Al Quoz

Indigo Living ▶ p.165

04 341 6388 | *www.indigo-living.com*

Indigo Design offers several services that come in handy for new arrivals. As well as selling furniture from its Al Quoz store, it also has an interior design section and rents out furniture on a short or long-term basis – a useful stop-gap or alternative to kitting out an empty apartment from scratch. There is another branch of Indigo Living at The Walk in Jumeirah Beach Residence.

Various Locations

MacKenzie Associates ▶ p.453

050 453 4232 | *www.dubaimurals.com*

Pep up your villa or apartment with some large murals, trompe l'oeil or special paint effects. MacKenzie Associates offers all of these services, as well as original artwork, and can take on large or small projects. From outdoor murals to large-scale paintings in children's bedrooms, and from intricate gold leaf designs to beautiful trompe l'oeil (trick of the eye) artworks, check out the website for ideas on how to make your home interior unique.

Household Insurance

Crime and natural disasters are not generally a big concern for Dubai's residents, but insuring your household goods against theft or damage is still wise. See the table below for a list of reputable insurance companies. To create a policy, the insurance provider will need your home address, a list of household items and valuation, and invoices for anything worth more than Dhs.2,500.

Cover usually includes theft, fire and storm damage. You can also insure personal items outside the home. Costs vary, but prices remained roughly the same over the last year. As a guideline you can expect to pay around Dhs.1,500 per 1.2sqm for building insurance, Dhs.250 for up to Dhs.60,000 worth of home contents and Dhs.850 for up to Dhs.60,000 worth of personal possessions.

Household Insurance		
AXA Insurance – UAE ▶ p.179, p.233	800 4845	www.axa-gulf.com
Greenshield Insurance	04 397 4464	www.greenshield.co.ae
HSBC Bank Middle East	800 4560	www.hsbc.ae
Millennium Insurance Brokers Co	04 335 6552	www.mibco-uae.com
National General Insurance	04 222 2772	www.ngi.ae
Oman Insurance	04 262 4000	www.tameen.ae
Royal & Sun Alliance Insurance (RSA)	04 334 4474	www.royalsunalliance.com

Some of our best customers never buy a thing...

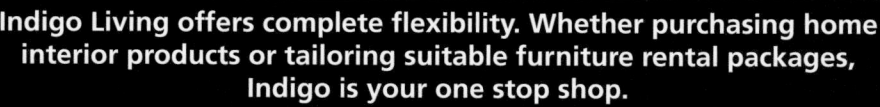

Indigo Living offers complete flexibility. Whether purchasing home interior products or tailoring suitable furniture rental packages, Indigo is your one stop shop.

Buy or rent, and discover that Expressive Living has never been easier!

Furniture Retail ▪ Rental Packages ▪ Accessories ▪ Project Solutions

• Showroom 45, 8 Road, Street 19, Al Quoz Industrial 1 (near Times Square Mall)
• P25 Sadaf, The Walk, Jumeirah Beach Residences 4

Tel: (971) 4 341 6388   Fax: (971) 4 341 6389
salesdubai@indigo-living.com   www.indigo-living.com

indigo
EXPRESSIVE LIVING

Baby Bounty

If you have visitors of the crawling variety but none of the essential baby-related equipment to hand, contact Rent-a-Crib (www.rentacrib. ae, 050 253 2535), which hires out all the gear you'll need, from car seats and strollers to cots and even toys.

Laundry Services

There are no self-service laundrettes, but laundries are everywhere. As well as dry cleaning and laundry, they all offer an ironing service. If you have specific instructions, make sure these are noted when you drop off your laundry – creases in trousers are standard, so if you don't want them pressed into your jeans, speak up. Compensation policies for lost or damaged items vary, but losses are rare, even in the places that look most disorganised. Large chains normally have a free pick-up and delivery service. The average laundry costs are reasonable. Expect to pay Dhs.8 for a shirt, Dhs.25 for a suit and Dhs.35 for a quilt.

Laundry Services		
Black & White	Oud Metha	04 337 5111
Butler's	Emirates Hills	04 366 3359
	Al Garhoud	04 282 0712
	Umm Suqeim	04 348 3186
Champion Cleaners	Deira	04 224 6403
	Al Garhoud	04 282 8297
	Umm Suqeim	04 394 0986
	Al Rashidiya	04 285 2822
	Jumeira	04 344 9727
	Trade Centre 1	04 351 2998
	Emirates Hills	04 368 4890
	Al Barsha	04 347 0761
	Jebel Ali	04 368 5564
Dubai Laundry	Al Karama	04 336 4158
	Jumeira	04 344 8177
Radiant Laundry	Deira	04 295 8367
	Bur Dubai	04 355 9958
	Jumeira	04 394 3058
Snow White Laundry	Al Rashidiya	04 289 4993
White Way	Mirdif	04 272 4165

Carpet Cleaners	
DDJ Building Mainenance & Cleaning LLC	050 880 9710
Modern Cleaning Methods	04 285 1668
Royal Carpet Cleaning & Painting	04 393 5038
Spotless	04 331 8827

Carpet Cleaners

Wall-to-wall carpets are rare in this part of the world, but many homes do sport loose rugs and carpets. When they're looking a bit grubby, the companies listed below can pay you a visit, give you a quote, and take the carpets away to be cleaned, returning them a couple of days later.

Domestic Help

Other options **Entry Visa** p.82

Domestic help is readily available in Dubai, whether full or part-time, and there are a number of options available, depending on your needs. Legally, a housemaid may only be employed by the individual who sponsors her, but in practice many maids take on cleaning or babysitting for other families; if you are caught you face a hefty fine but the law seems rarely to be enforced. If you are looking for someone part time, but want to stay within the law, see below for a list of domestic help agencies.

Domestic Help Agencies

When your busy lifestyle leaves no time for those tiresome household chores, help is just a phone call away. Many companies in Dubai provide cleaners and maids on an hourly basis, and for around Dhs.20 to Dhs.30 per hour they'll take care of all your sweeping, mopping, dusting, washing, and ironing. Most companies stipulate a minimum number of hours, usually two or three per visit. For an apartment, three hours a week should be enough, while bigger villas may need four or five hours worth of cleaning each week.

If you're considering sponsoring your own maid full-time, see p.87

Domestic Help Agencies	
Home Comfort Services	04 272 2135
Home Help	04 355 5100
Molly Maid	04 398 8877
Ready Maids	04 294 8345
Sky Maid Services	04 332 4600

Babysitting & Childcare

Babysitting & Childcare	
Home Help	04 355 5100
Ready Maids	04 294 8345
Sky Maid Services	04 332 4600

Childcare is the dilemma that faces all working parents. Options here are fairly limited, and there is no network of childminders. You could hire a full or part-time maid, if you can find someone who you are comfortable leaving the children with. Or another parent may be willing to take care of your child for a fee (while there are mums who do this in Dubai they don't advertise their services, so word-of-mouth is the way to go). The information board on www.expatwoman. com is a good place to start. Domestic help agencies also offer babysitting services. Ask around your neighbourhood to see if there is a maid who is available for evening babysitting, or try the nurseries – classroom assistants are often looking for extra work. A good place to find nannies is Trixabell (www.trixabell.com).

Domestic Services

Domestic Services		
Al Mezhar Landscaping	04 344 6055	Landscaping
Al Salam Sanitary & Electrical	04 261 5977	Electrician
Aquamani	04 360 3593	Pool maintenance
Berkeley Services	04 339 3111	General maintenance
Burooj 2000	04 288 7665	General maintenance
Cape Reed	04 341 7452	Landscaping
Clearview	04 295 1303	Landscaping
Cracknell Landscaping	04 344 5417	Landscaping
Desert Leisure	050 455 0328	Pool maintenance
Hassan Foulad Plumbing Works	04 285 9187	Plumbing
Hennessy Pools	050 453 6214	Pool maintenance
Hitches & Glitches	04 341 2888	General maintenance
Howdra	04 285 4308	Domestic services
Island King	04 334 6555	Pool maintenance
Royal Gardenscape ▶ p.445	04 340 0648	Landscaping
Speedy Home Repairs	050 298 8340	Electrician
Technomart	050 253 2247	Pool maintenance
Those Pool Guys	04 339 0418	Pool maintenance

Having maintenance work done is often just a matter of a phone call to the landlord. Otherwise, plumbers, handymen and electricians are easy to find. Smaller, local firms often advertise by slapping stickers on your gate or door. Burooj 2000 operates across Dubai and does plumbing, painting and air-conditioner servicing. Howdra is also city wide and offers maid and ironing services along with heavier work. Hitches & Glitches operates in the Meadows, Springs and Emirates Hills areas and can provide 24 hour general maintenance on an annual contract. For garden maintenance, try a service company like Berkeley, which will maintain your garden for a monthly fee. Alternatively, independent gardeners may knock on your door, and they usually charge around Dhs.250 per month, to water and tidy your garden every day. If you have a pool, for around Dhs.400 per month you can get twice weekly visits to clean it and balance the chemicals.

Garden & Landscape Services

With the boom in housing comes a boom in landscaping – now that expats can own their own villas, they are prepared to spend a bit more money on having a nice garden. Fake lawn is becoming a popular option for those who want a hassle-free garden; it stays green throughout the year and needs no watering (although it does need hosing down every few weeks to get rid of the dust). Clearview and Cape Reed both install fake lawn.

Pool Maintenance Services

If you are lucky enough to have your own swimming pool, knowing how to take care of it can be a bit daunting. Aside from regular cleaning, the pool will need the water changing and chemical levels balanced. While some people do attempt to do this themselves, it is always wise to get professionals to do it, especially with chemical balancing. Those Pool Guys or Island King are well established in Dubai, and word of mouth can turn up other companies such as Aquamani or Hennessy. Most pool maintenance companies will also be able to perform repairs from broken lights to filter changes.

Pets

The attitude towards pets in Dubai is mixed so it's sensible to keep your pet under control. Pets are prohibited from parks and beaches, so there aren't many places where you can walk your dog, other than the streets in your area. While uncommon, there are a number incidents of animal abuse, which can be reported to the municipality (04 289 1114). Dubai has several pet shops and they vary enormously in quality. Smaller outlets are usually not for the faint-hearted.

Pertaining To Cats & Dogs

Feline Friends (050 451 0058) is a non-profit organisation, aiming to improve the lives of cats by rescuing and rehoming stray cats and kittens. It has a 24 hour telephone answering service as well as a comprehensive website, www.felinefriendsuae.com. K9 Friends (04 347 4611) helps to rehome stray and injured dogs, many of which are abandoned family pets looking for a second chance. See www.k9friends.com for more information. Another useful website for pet owners is www.petdubai.com.

Cats & Dogs

Dubai has a significant problem with strays. Feline Friends (050 451 0058) and K9 Friends (04 347 4611) are hard-working animal charities that take in as many as they can, and they are always on the lookout for help (see p.170).

You should inoculate your pet annually against rabies, and register it with the municipality (04 289 1114), which will provide plastic neck tags. If the municipality picks up an animal without a tag, it is treated as a stray. You can have your pet microchipped, but with no national register the plastic tag is your best bet. The municipality's clampdown on strays has been successful and the UAE is now considered to be free from rabies (so pets can travel to the UK under the 'Pet Passport' scheme and are subject to a reduced quarantine in Australia and New Zealand). Most areas have street cats, which tend to be harmless and keep a lid on rodent problems. The municipality is currently working on trapping the cats and sterilising them before releasing them – it's the first authority in the region to do so. Feline Friends is active in trapping and sterilising street cats, and should be contacted if your area is overrun. Sterilised street cats usually have part of their ear removed.

You should check with your landlord what the pet policy is before you move in. When walking your dog, keep it on a short leash, as many people are frightened of them.

Birds & Fish

Birds are popular and are sold in all the pet shops. A wide variety of species is available, from budgies to macaws. For those interested in keeping fish, the pet shops of Dubai have a huge selection, and all the equipment you will need.

Pet Shops

The standard of pet shops in Dubai ranges from the passable to the awful. Pet lovers are better off avoiding the smaller ones, predominantly in Satwa, as they tend to pay little regard to the health or welfare of the animals. There are laws governing pet shops but the maximum penalty for those contravening them is the closure of the shop for a day – hardly a deterrent. It's illegal for puppies to be offered for sale before they are 16 weeks old but in many cases the papers have been altered and the animal is younger; the origin of the animals is also altered and many come from eastern European 'puppy farms' where conditions are inhumane. A much better option is to get your pet from K9 Friends or Feline Friends instead. All their animals have been sterilised and inoculated.

Vets & Kennels

Standards of care at Dubai's veterinary clinics are reasonably high. Prices do not vary dramatically, but the Deira Veterinary Clinic and Al Barsha Veterinary Clinic are a little cheaper than the rest. Dubai Municipality has a veterinary services department

Pets Boarding & Sitting

Boarding	
Al Zubair Animal Care	06 743 5988
The Doghouse	050 457 8874
Dubai Kennels & Cattery (DKC) ▶ p.169	04 285 1646
Petland Resort	04 347 5022
Poshpaws Kennels & Cattery	050 273 0973
Petsitting	
Creature Comforts	050 695 9480
Eve's Home Comforts Pet Sitting Service	06 524 4111
Pet Partner	050 774 2239
Pets At Home	04 331 2186

(04 289 1114), which treats and vaccinates animals and issues identity tags. It is located next to Mushrif Park. Kennels are generally of a good standard, although spaces are limited during peak times (summer and Christmas). An alternative is to use an at-home pet-sitting service – someone will come into your house at least once a day to feed and exercise your pet for a reasonable fee (for a bit extra they might even water your plants).

Bringing Your Pet To Dubai

Imported dogs and cats must be older than 120 days – this ensures that they are old enough to have had rabies vaccinations. Pets flying into Dubai must travel as cargo – animals are no longer permitted to travel as excess baggage. Dubai Kennels & Cattery (www.dkc.ae), The Doghouse (www.dubaidoghouse.com) and Snoopy Pets (050 477 8759) are pet relocation specialists that can help.

Otherwise, you need an import permit from the Ministry of Environment & Water, Vet Quarantine Section (04 222 8161). They will need to see the owner's passport and residence visa (or employment offer letter), the pet's vaccination certificate (showing rabies vaccination) and a government-issued health certificate. You also need proof that the animal has been microchipped. After receiving the import permit, you can book the flight. You must also present a certificate of good health to authorities on arrival. Animals will be taken to the Cargo Village in Garhoud for collection.

Pets Grooming/Training

Grooming		
Al Safa Veterinary Clinic	04 348 3799	na
Creature Comforts	050 695 9480	www.creaturecomfortsdubai.com
The Doghouse	050 457 8874	www.dubaidoghouse.com
Poshpaws Kennels & Cattery	050 273 0973	www.poshpawsdubai.com
Shampooch Mobile Pet Grooming	04 344 9868	www.shampooch.ae
Snoopy Pets	04 420 5348	na
Training		
Paws Canine Training Centre	050 784 5350	www.pawstraining.com

Taking Your Pet Home

The process can be quite lengthy, taking a minimum of seven months for the UK. All countries require a health certificate – this is issued by the Ministry of Environment & Water vet section and should be taken to the government vet at Cargo Village not more than seven days before departure. For this you will need the animal's vaccination card showing a valid rabies inoculation (some countries require additional vaccinations or blood tests). These must have been done not less than 30 days before departure and no later than the expiry date set out by the manufacturer.

You will also need an airline-approved travel box (available through Dubai Kennels & Cattery and The Doghouse). Most airlines allow animals to travel either as accompanied baggage or cargo, but check with the airline beforehand.

Veterinary Clinics

Al Barsha Veterinary Clinic	Beh Mall of the Emirates	04 340 8601
Al Safa Veterinary Clinic	Al Wasl Rd	04 348 3799
Al Zubair Animal Care	Sharjah	06 743 5988
Animal Care Centre Sharjah	Industrial Area No 6	06 543 6280
Deira Veterinary Clinic	Beh DNATA Bldg, Mistubishi Showroom	04 258 1881
Energetic Panacea	49 St, Off Al Wasl Rd	04 344 7812
European Veterinary Center	Sheikh Zayed Rd	04 343 9591
Jumeirah Veterinary Clinic	Off Al Wasl Rd	04 394 2276
Modern Veterinary Clinic	Al Wasl Rd	04 395 3131
Veterinary Hospital	Al Wasl Rd	04 344 2498

Electricity & Water

Dubai Electricity and Water Authority (DEWA) is the sole provider of water, electricity and sewerage. When you sign up for connection to your new home you will need to pay a deposit (Dhs.2,000 for a villa and Dhs.1,000 for an apartment), which is fully refundable when you leave the property. DEWA charges a standard rate per unit, currently 20 fils per unit for electricity, 3 fils per unit for water and 0.5 fils per unit for sewerage. Your DEWA bill also includes the municipality housing tax, which is 5% of the rental value of the property and covers refuse collection and utilities maintenance. Your DEWA bill will fluctuate depending on the time of year – the need for round the clock air conditioning in summer equals a high bill.

If you have a garden to water it will probably need doing twice a day in summer. It might be possible to have a borehole installed in your garden, meaning you have access to free groundwater. Installation will set you back around Dhs.1,000. Once it's done you should notice a marked decrease in your DEWA bill, although there is a chance of the borehole becoming brackish after a few years.

Electricity

The electricity supply in Dubai is 220/240 volts and 50 cycles and the socket type is the same as the three-pin British system. Many appliances are sold with two pin plugs which can either be changed or used with an adaptor which are widely available and can be bought for a couple of dirhams from Carrefour.

Water

Tap water is desalinated sea water and is generally considered safe to drink – although the government's Food & Environment Laboratory does warn of contaminated water in buildings which have poorly maintained pipes. Most people opt for mineral water, mainly because it tastes better. Bottled water is cheap, especially the locally produced brands. Most people end up buying a water cooler or pump (available from most large supermarkets), or leasing one from a water supplier, and using the four or five-gallon bottles of purified water to drink at home. Prices vary per company; some charge a deposit of around Dhs.30 for each re-useable bottle, and then Dhs.7 per refill, while Masafi recycles its bottles rather than re-using them and charges Dhs.12 per new bottle (plus one free bottle for every 10 you buy). Companies will deliver the bottles to your door, and collect your empties. Bottled water, both local and imported, is served in hotels and restaurants.

Water Suppliers

Al Madina Drinking Water Supply	04 267 0710
Al Rawi Pure Drinking Water	04 347 7112
Culligan International	800 4945
Desert Springs	800 6650
Falcon Spring Drinking Water	04 396 6072
Masafi	800 5455
Nestle Pure Water	800 4404
Oasis Drinking Water	04 884 5656

Gas

There are still no gas mains in Dubai, even though gas is the most popular method for cooking. Individual gas canisters need to be purchased and attached to the cookers. There are a number of gas suppliers. They can also connect up the supply, but let them know so that they can bring the pipes and regulators needed. Gas bottles come in three sizes: most houses use the medium size, the small are better in apartments and the large are really only for industrial use – they are enormous. The canisters initially cost around Dhs.300 and refills are usually Dhs.60 (keep your receipt so that you can get your deposit back). There is usually a gas van around your area at all times so chances are that if you run out of gas in the middle of cooking your chips, one call to your local gas man and he can be with you in less than 20 minutes.

Gas Suppliers

Honest Hands Gas	04 285 6586
Lahej Gas Distribution	04 337 6686
New City Gas Distributors	04 351 8282
Oasis Gas Suppliers	04 396 1812
Salam Gas	04 344 8823
Union Gas Company	04 266 1479

Sewerage

Much of Dubai now has mains sewers but there are areas where houses are still serviced by septic tanks. These are regularly emptied by municipality contractors, but should you have a problem, contact your landlord or local municipality office. All sewage has to be treated, hence the charges on the DEWA bill even for houses not on the main sewer network.

Rubbish Disposal & Recycling

Dubai's per capita domestic waste rate is extremely high, with some estimates saying that each household generates over 1,000kg of rubbish per year. Fortunately, rubbish disposal is efficient, with municipality trucks driving around each area and emptying skips daily. Just empty your household bins into the skips (there is usually one on every street). If you don't have a skip on your street, contact the municipality on 04 206 4234 to request one. Certain areas, such as Emirates Hills, have wheelie bins outside each house, where waste is collected from. Recycling efforts are poor but slowly improving. There are over 40 recycling points where you can dump your glass bottles, aluminium cans and paper. Most of these are in schools and shopping centres (such as at Spinneys in Emirates Hills), but there's also one in Deira (in the carpark near Samsung) and one at Knowledge Village. Emaar offers residents in its developments an excellent recycling collection service called Earth Watch (050 347 4576, earthwatch@emaar.ae).

Telephone

In 2007, the telecom industry in the UAE witnessed competition for the first time, with the entry of second operator, du. Currently, du provides internet, phone and television services to all Emaar properties. Mobile phone users can choose between du (prefix 055 or 056) and Etisalat (prefix 050); while du offers some good services, it has not been able to monopolise market share in the same way that Etisalat has. Both providers offer monthly or pay-as-you-go packages.

Landline Phones

To install a landline with Etisalat you must apply directly with a completed application form, a copy of your passport and residence visa, a no objection letter from your sponsor, and Dhs.250 (inclusive of first quarterly rental). Taking the number of the landline closest to your house can help pinpoint your location. Telephone calls between landlines in Dubai are free, but there is a nominal charge for calls to Jebel Ali. Depending on the time of day, calls to elsewhere in the UAE cost between Dhs.0.12 and Dhs.0.24 per minute; calls to mobiles cost between Dhs.0.18 and Dhs.0.24. Off-peak timings are 14:00 to 16:00 and 19:00 to 07:00, Saturday to Wednesday; and all weekend from 14:00 on Thursday to 07:00 on Saturday. Off-peak rates are applicable all day on public holidays. Off-peak timings for mobile calls are 14:00 to 16:00 and midnight to 07:00 every day. The tariffs for international calls vary from country to country but there is some variation in peak timings, depending on country. For more information on phone services with Etisalat, see www.etisalat.com.

du's landline service offers pay-by-the-second landlines and some great flat rates on long-distance calls. du provides services to many Emaar and Nakheel properties, both business and residential (such as Dubai Marina, Arabian Ranches, Emirates Hills, the Greens/Springs/Lakes, and Jumeirah

Cheap Calls Not Allowed

Sites like Skype.com that allow you to make cheap international calls via the internet have been blocked by the TRA (the local telecoms regulator). This has provoked anger, since the proxy is only supposed to block sites that offend the religious, political, moral or cultural values of the UAE, rather than ones that hurt the operators' profits. While it's not legal, some people download a proxy bypasser or VPN that allows them to access Skype.

Don't Forget The Prefix

You have to dial 050 for Etisalat mobile numbers even if you're dialling from one yourself. That's because mobile numbers from du begin with 055. Prefixes are as follows: 04 – Dubai, 02 – Abu Dhabi, 03 – Al Ain, 06 – Sharjah, 050 – Etisalat mobile, 055 and 056 – du mobile.

Dubai's **ONLY** Complete Street Atlas

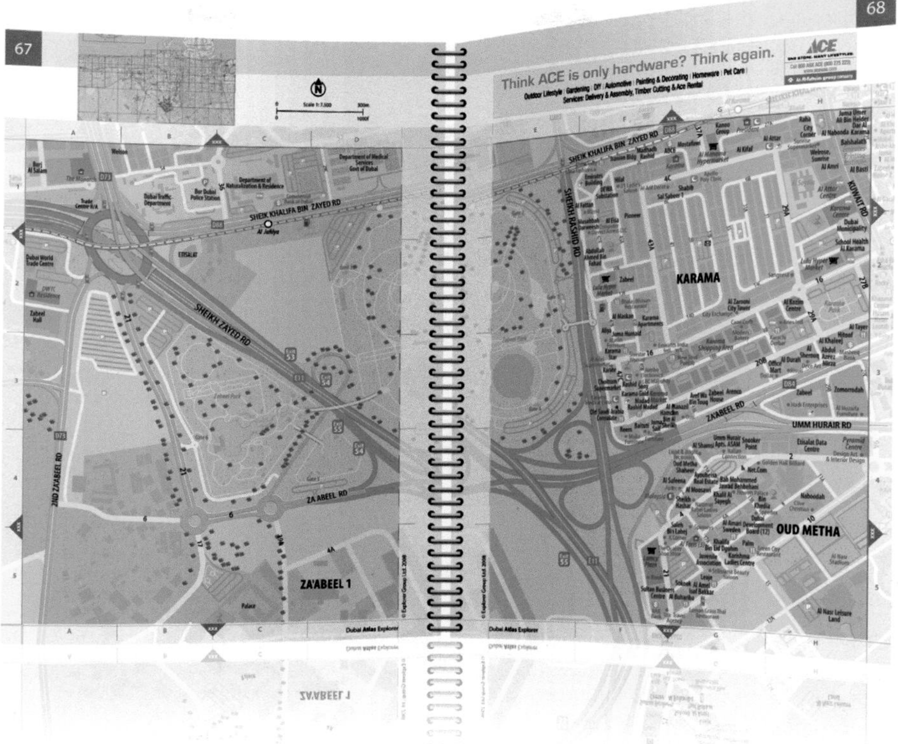

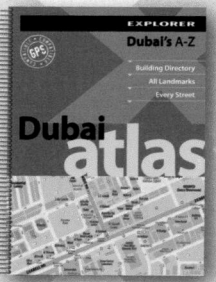

Featuring over 10,000 buildings, plus the new road naming system, this is the most comprehensive atlas for Dubai ever produced. You just got lost for the last time.

Dubai Atlas
The complete street atlas

EXPLORER

www.liveworkexplore.com

Area Codes & Useful Numbers

Abu Dhabi	02
Ajman	06
Al Ain	03
Directory Enquiries (du)	199
Directory Enquiries (Etisalat)	181
du Contact Centre (from du phones)	155
du Contact Centre (other phones)	04 369 9155
Dubai	04
Etisalat Contact Centre	101
Etisalat Information	144
Fault Reports (Etisalat)	171
Fujairah	09
Hatta	04
Jebel Ali	04
Mobile Telephones (du)	055
Mobile Telephones (Etisalat)	050
Operator	100
Ras al Khaimah	07
Sharjah	06
Speaking Clock	140
UAE Country Code	971
Umm Al Quwain	06
Ras al Khaimah	07

Islands). Currently, villas and apartments are equipped with multiple sockets for telephone, internet and TV signals. To apply, you will need a copy of your passport and tenancy agreement. The fees include a one-off installation charge (Dhs.200) plus line rental of around Dhs.15 per month. In addition, internet packages are available from 64 kbps to up to 2mbps. For more information on phone services with du, check their website: www.du.ae.

Internet

Other options **Websites** p.69, **Internet Cafes** p.506

Internet services in the UAE are provided by either Etisalat (through their subsidiary, Emirates Internet and Media, or EIM) or du; all internet usage, however is regulated by the Telecommunications Regulatory Authority (TRA). This means that many sites that are deemed to be offensive, either religiously, culturally or politically, are blocked and can't be accessed.

Through EIM, the internet is accessible from any standard Etisalat phone line using a 56k modem. You can also get an ISDN line (128 kbps) or an ADSL line (256-512 kbps). To get connected you will need a landline, a copy of your passport and residence visa, and a completed application. The initial charge is Dhs.100 for dial-up, Dhs.200 for ISDN (plus Dhs.415 for modem) and Dhs.200 for ADSL (plus Dhs.275 for modem). Rental charges are typically Dhs.20 per month, plus an hourly rate (Dhs.1.80 peak, Dhs.1 off-peak). You can also get broadband internet through EIM. There are various packages available based on speed, but for a 1Mbps connection with unlimited usage you pay Dhs.249 per month. Check www.emirates.net.ae for more details.

If you live in an Emaar property, your internet will be provided by du (www.du.ae). It offers a range of 'always on' internet packages to its Emaar residents, ranging from 64kbps (Dhs.75 per month) to 2mbps (Dhs.349 per month). There is a Dhs.200 installation fee. Check www.du.ae for details.

Dial & Surf

This facility allows you to surf without subscribing to the Etisalat internet service. All that's needed is a computer with a modem and a regular phone (or ISDN) line – no account number or password is required. In theory, you then simply dial 500 5555 to gain access. However, in practice it may not be quite so straightforward, since there are different set-ups depending on your software. If you have difficulties, contact the helpdesk (800 5244). The charge of 12 fils per minute is made for the connection and billed to the telephone line from which the call is made.

Bill Payment

Bills are mailed monthly and are itemised. du bills can be paid at the sales office in Media City, at one of the drop boxes dotted around Emaar developments, or via bank transfer or credit card. The bill can be checked online (www.telecom.dic.ae). You have 30 days from the date of the invoice to settle the bill. Etisalat bills can be paid online (www.e4me.ae for phone bills, www.eim.ae for internet bills), by phone banking, at Etisalat offices or at one of the payment machines in most shopping centres. You have 10 days to settle your landline bill, and 45 days to settle your mobile bill.

Bill Enquiry Service

It is possible to get the current amount due on your Etisalat phone bill – just dial 142 from the phone in question and you will be given the balance.

Postal Services

There is currently no postal delivery service to home addresses, although there are plans for Dubai's streets to be named so a home delivery system can be introduced. For the time being, everyone has their mail delivered to a PO box. Mail is first delivered to the Central Post Office and then distributed to clusters of PO boxes in various areas. To get your own, fill in the application form and pay the annual fee (Dhs.150); you will be given a set of keys (Dhs.10 per key) to access your own box. Many people have mail delivered to their company's PO box.

Sending Gifts Home

If you would rather not chance the post, Gift Express provides a selection of gifts that can be sent to most countries (www.giftexpress.ae).

Empost will send you notification by email when you receive registered mail or parcels in your PO box. For an extra Dhs.9 you can have the item delivered to your door. However, you might have to pay customs charges on international packages.

Letters and packages do occasionally go missing and, if the item has not been registered, there's little that you can do apart from wait – some turn up months after they are expected. Empost offers a courier service for both local and international deliveries. Delivery times are guaranteed and packages can be tracked. Registered mail is a relatively inexpensive alternative, and can also be tracked via the reference number.

Courier Services

Aramex	04 286 5000	www.aramex.com
DHL	04 299 5333	www.dhl.co.ae
Empost	04 282 6366	www.empostuae.com
Fedex UAE	800 4050	www.fedex.com
Immex – Immediate Courier Express	04 282 4444	na
TNT Dubai	800 4333	www.tnt.com
UPS	800 4774	www.ups.com

Radio

The UAE has a number of commercial radio stations broadcasting in a range of languages, including Arabic, English, French, Hindi, Malayalam and Urdu. Daily schedules can be found in the local newspapers.

There are six English language music stations, all operating 24 hours a day. Dubai 92 (92.0FM), Channel 4 (104.8 FM), Emirates Radio 1 (99.3FM & 100.5FM), Virgin Radio (104.4FM) and The Coast (103.2FM) all play a mixture of old and new popular music, and have regular news broadcasts. If you're more into ELO than Eminem, you might prefer Emirates Radio 2 (90.5FM & 98.5FM), which plays adult contemporary music mixed with news and talk shows.

Most shows are locally produced but there are some syndicated shows. Dubai 92 airs a number of dance music programmes at the weekend featuring international DJs. Dubai Eye (103.8FM) is Dubai's first major talk radio station, with a good mix of news, talk, and sport. There are some interesting shows with topics relevant to residents of Dubai. QBS Dubai (97.5FM & 102.6FM) focuses on radio plays and jazz music. Umm Al Quwain's Hum FM (106.2FM) broadcasts mainly in Hindi with a bit of English, and if you want to hear Arabic music, tune in to 93.9FM. You can also listen to the BBC World Service in English between 09:00 and 18:00 on 87.9FM.

Television

The local television channels in Dubai generally leave a little to be desired. There have however been developments and the revamped Dubai One (formerly Ch 33) now shows a respectable line up of British and American programmes. The MBC channels also have a good selection. You can catch some classic films from the 80s and 90s on MBC2, various children's programmes such as the *Tweenies*, *Bob the Builder*, *Barney* and *Tom and Jerry* on MBC3, and comedies, dramas, news and chat shows (such as *Oprah*, *Charmed*, *Frasier*, *Friends*, *Dead Zone*, *CBS News* and *60 Minutes*) on MBC4.

Most Dubai residents subscribe to one of the satellite networks (see below). Look out for *Entertainment Plus*, a supplement published on Wednesday inside *Gulf News*. It provides a comprehensive listing of what's on for the next week. You'll also find TV listings in *Time Out*, *Ahlan!* and *7Days*.

Satellite TV & Radio

Showbox
Showtime offers a Showbox service, with which you can pause live television and record your favourite shows on a digital box. You can also watch special previews of forthcoming movies, or virtual 'boxsets' of showtime series. Contact Showtime (www.showtimearabia. com) for more info.

Do your homework before you choose a satellite provider – your choice will depend on what kind of TV you just can't live without. For example, Sky News is only available on FirstNet, while MTV and VH1 are only available on Showtime. Popular British soaps *Eastenders* and *Coronation Street* are both available, but only on Orbit and Showtime respectively.

FirstNet was always the choice for Premiership football fans, but Showtime has had the rights since the start of the 2007/08 season. It's possible to flick between every Premiership match as Showtime spreads coverage on Saturdays and weekday nights across its channels. Pictures and commentary are taken from English channels. FirstNet is good for reality show addicts (catch up with current episodes of *American Idol*, *The Bachelor*, *For Love or Money* and *The Apprentice* on the Star World channel).

Showtime seems to be in the lead for popular American sitcoms, with the recent addition of *Desperate Housewives* and *Lost* to its schedules, but Brits might choose Orbit for BBC Prime and shows such as *The Weakest Link*, *Strictly Come Dancing* and *Changing Rooms* (it's also great for the kids shows on CBeebies).

Showtime is renowned for getting the best films sooner, although other providers also provide a variety of movie channels.

One new entrant in 2007 was City 7. It is the first UAE based, English language channel, and offers a mix of locally produced news and lifestyle shows and imported dramas and comedies. The news programmes feel a little like provincial news in the UK or US, and still tend to show an excessive reverence to the movements of the UAE's rulers, but do have a local flavour that is unavailable elsewhere in English. It is available (normally for free) from all of the above satellite providers.

Satellite Radio

Depending on your satellite provider, you may get some radio stations through your decoder. Various channels are available, including Virgin Radio from the UK and the BBC World Service.

You can also access a variety of music channels – from country to pop. You get 10 Music Choice channels on Showtime, and 20 on Orbit. For more information on Dubai's local radio stations, see p.175.

Satellite & Cable Providers		
Arabtec SIS	04 286 2616	www.sisuae.com
Bond Communications	04 343 4499	www.bondcommunications.com
Emirates Cable TV & Multimedia E-Vision	101	www.evision.ae
Eurostar Group	04 808 7777	www.adduniverse.com
FirstNet	03 766 1144	www.adduniverse.com
Orbit	04 405 9999	www.orbit.net
Showtime	04 367 7888	www.showtimearabia.com

General Medical Care

The general standard of healthcare in the UAE is high, both in the public and private sectors. As in most countries, private healthcare is seen as preferable (English speaking, shorter waiting times and more comfortable inpatient facilities) and is likely to be mandatory under new UAE laws. So even though residents qualify for subsidised state care, you might want to consider health insurance. Emergency treatment in government hospitals is free, regardless of nationality or whether you have a health card. When you get your health card (see p.85) it will list a clinic or hospital to which you are assigned, although you're not obliged to use this one.

Emergency Services

Rashid Hospital is the main hospital for medical emergencies and has a well-equipped accident and emergency (A&E) department. Dubai Hospital also has an emergency section. Al Wasl Hospital offers emergency services to women and children under the age of 12, and is especially recommended for maternity and paediatric emergencies, although they do not deal with trauma cases. The Iranian Hospital has a busy A&E. While finding a place to get emergency treatment is easy, getting there is more problematic as Dubai's paramedic services are under-developed, to say the least. Ambulance response times are variable but can be up to 30 minutes (compared with around four minutes in a large UK city like Birmingham).

Government Healthcare

In Dubai, the Department of Health and Medical Services (www.dohms.gov.ae) runs the following hospitals: Dubai, Rashid, Al Baraha (aka Kuwaiti), Maktoum and Al Wasl. Dubai Hospital is renowned as one of the best medical centres in the Middle East, while Al Wasl is a specialised maternity and paediatric hospital. DOHMS also operates a number of outpatient clinics. The Iranian Hospital, while not funded by the UAE government, also provides subsidised healthcare.

Private Healthcare

Dubai's various private hospitals and clinics have high standards. American Hospital (p.182), Welcare Hospital (p.186), Medcare and Al Zahra Private Hospital (p.182) are popular. But be aware that if you don't have the money, the Hippocratic oath can go out of the window. Your best bet is to make sure that you have health insurance, but at the same time not all companies cover treatment in all of Dubai's private hospitals so always check with your insurance company before receiving treatment.

Health Insurance

Employers in Dubai must pay a Health Benefits Contribution for all of their employees which covers the cost of their health card and contributes towards the public healthcare system. Your employer may also provide additional health insurance. Levels of cover vary depending on the policy – check what you're entitled to. Dental care and screening tests aren't usually provided as standard, and you may need to have been on the policy for a year before you can receive maternity cover.

Health Insurance Companies

Alliance Insurance Co (PP Healthcare)	04 605 1111	alliance-uae.com
Allianz Worldwide	04 702 6666	www.allianz.com
American Life Insurance Company (ALICO)	04 360 0555	www.alico-measa.com
AXA Insurance – UAE ▶ p.179	800 4845	www.axa-gulf.com
Greenshield Insurance	04 397 4464	www.greenshield.co.ae
Lifecare International (BUPA)	04 331 8688	www.bupa.com
Mednet	800 4882	www.mednet-uae.com
National General Insurance	04 222 2772	www.ngi.ae
Nextcare	04 286 9311	www.nextcare.co.ae
Oman Insurance	800 4746	www.tameen.ae

Pharmacies
Most pharmacies are open from around 09:00 to 22:00, Saturday to Thursday (although some close for lunch between 13:00 and 16:00). Most are also open on Fridays, from 16:00 to 22:00. There is a rota system for pharmacies to stay open 24 hours, so there is always at least one pharmacy in every emirate open round the clock. Call 04 223 2323 to find out which pharmacy is open, consult the daily papers, or check on the Dubai Municipality website (www.dm.gov.ae).

Free Breast Tests
All women in Dubai, be they nationals, expats or visitors, have access to free breast cancer screening. Call 04 219 5104 for more information and to arrange a screening.

Giving Blood
Like any other country in the world, the UAE relies on public donations to keep its blood banks topped up. If you'd like to give blood, many hospitals will be grateful to receive your donation – call your local one for details. Al Wasl Hospital has a dedicated blood donation centre – call 04 324 1111 for opening times and special collection locations. The website www.uaedonors.com is also a useful resource.

Main Government Hospitals
Government healthcare in the UAE is of a high standard and all expats qualify for subsidised care as long as they have a government health card. Refer to p.85 for more information on applying for your health card. The following major government hospitals offer a high level of treatment.

Nr Naif Rd
Al Baraha
Deira
Map 9 F2

Al Baraha Hospital
04 271 0000
Commonly referred to as the Kuwaiti Hospital, this large government hospital is situated on the Deira side of the Shindagha Tunnel, on the right-hand side. You're not likely to use this hospital for treatment, but you might need to come here for your blood test when processing your residency (Maktoum and Al Bahara Hospitals are the most common 'blood test' hospitals), or for a birth or death certificate.

Nr Fish Roundabout
Deira
Map 9 D3

Al Maktoum Hospital
04 222 1211 | *www.dohms.gov.ae*
Opened in 1949, this was the first modern healthcare facility in the region. The place is showing its age, but the facilities are adequate. Today however, the only reason you're likely to visit Maktoum Hospital is to go for the health test for your medical card (there are no emergency or surgical departments). You'll first have a blood sample taken, and then walk to another building to have the chest x-ray. Maktoum Hospital also has a department that carries out embalming. For more information on the medical test, see p.85.

What should you ask when choosing car insurance?

do they offer you a 24 hour claims service? / **we do**

if your car is in the workshop,
do they offer you a replacement? / **we do**

if you have an accident, will they bring
a replacement car to the accident location? / **we do**

will they let you open a claim with just one call? / **we do**

do we honestly believe that AXA gives
you the best service and cover available? / **we do**

can we prove it? / **we just did**

redefining / insurance
رؤية جـديـدة / للتأمين

AXA

For a motor quote call 800 4845

Oud Metha Rd ◄
Bur Dubai
Map 10 D4

Al Wasl Hospital

04 219 3000 | *www.dohms.gov.ae*

Al Wasl specialises in obstetrics, gynaecology, paediatrics and paediatric surgery. The hospital has an emergency department that provides 24 hour care, seven days a week to women and children up to the age of 12 years. This includes medical, surgical and non-trauma cases, it also includes women with serious problems relating to pregnancy and gynaecology. There is a walk-in clinic for emergencies, but trauma and orthopaedic cases cannot be treated here. You'll be charged Dhs.100 for a non-emergency case if you hold a valid heath card; if you don't hold a valid heath card you will be charged Dhs.200 to see a doctor. For expat residents admitted in an emergency without a valid heath card the charge is Dhs.100 a day as well as your medication bill on top. A deposit of Dhs.500 must be paid for the first five days if the patient came through the A&E but was not diagnosed as an emergency case. A deposit of Dhs.1,500 is required upon admission if you want a private room plus a Dhs.300 per day charge. If you don't have a valid heath card, non-emergency operations can cost anywhere from Dhs.2,000 to Dhs.6,000 based on the type of operation you require. Al Wasl is a popular choice for expat couples who are having a baby in Dubai and don't have medical insurance to cover the pre-natal care and delivery charges in a private hospital.

Nr Baraha Hospital ◄
Al Baraha
Map 9 F3

Dubai Hospital

04 219 5000 | *www.dohms.gov.ae*

Dubai Hospital has a number of outpatient clinics including gynaecology, orthopaedics, dermatology, paediatrics, ophthalmology, ENT (ear, nose and throat) and general medicine. They also undertake general surgery and cardiac surgery as well as dentistry. The A&E department will take patients whether you're a critical emergency or not. The charges for treatment are Dhs.50 to see a doctor if you have a valid heath card, Dhs.200 to see a doctor if you don't have a valid health card, and an additional charge of Dhs.300 per day for private rooms. Only emergency cases without a health card are exempt from charges. Other in-patients without a health card who were diagnosed as non-emergency upon admission will be charged Dhs.100 a day.

Al Wasl Rd ◄
Jumeira
Map 7 F1

Iranian Hospital

04 344 0250 | *www.irhosp.ae*

If you haven't already seen the mosaic-fronted Iranian Hospital then you may want to take a look – even if not from a medical point of view. The building itself – at the Satwa end of Al Wasl Road – is an impressive sight. The hospital is in fact affiliated to the Red Crescent Society of Iran and therefore isn't strictly a UAE government hospital. It offers its own health card and the fees are very reasonable. There are two cards: one for Dhs.100 and one for Dhs.250 which offer 20% and 40% discounts respectively for in-patient and out-patient services. In addition, some of the medicines which they prescribe are free. On the downside the hospital is rather busy.

Nr Maktoum Bridge ◄
Bur Dubai
Map 11 A2

Rashid Hospital

04 337 4000 | *www.dohms.gov.ae*

Rashid Hospital is the main government hospital for accident and emergency, trauma and intensive care patients and paramedic services in Dubai. They have inpatient and outpatient care for elective and emergency surgery and cover virtually all surgical treatments. The hospital provides diagnostic facilities including laboratory testing (haematology, biochemistry, bacteriology and serology), radiology testing (mammography, CT and MRI scan as well as a nuclear medicine unit) plus a well-equipped physiotherapy and social affairs unit.

Main Private Hospitals

In addition to the government-funded hospitals, Dubai has a growing number of private hospitals offering world-class medical care. Almost every conceivable treatment and procedure is available, to treat all conditions. Many private hospitals have 24 hour emergency departments too, and may even have their own ambulance. One other number worth noting is Health Call (see Private Clinics table below). The firm can send round a European or North American certified GP for house calls at short notice.

Private Health Centres & Clinics

Al Borj Medical Centre	Al Wasl	04 321 2220
Al Zahra Private Medical Centre ▶ p.xi	Trade Centre 1	04 331 5000
Allied Diagnostic Centre	Al Satwa	04 332 8111
Belhoul European Hospital	Al Satwa	04 345 4000
Cedars Jebel Ali International Hospital	Jebel Ali	04 881 4000
The Diabetes Endocrine Center	Umm Hurair	04 324 5555
Dr Akel's General Medical Clinic (GMC)	Jumeira	04 349 4880
Drs Nicolas & Asp Clinic ▶ p.193	Various Locations	04 394 7777
Dubai Bone & Joint Center ▶ p.197	Umm Hurair	04 423 1400
Dubai Herbal & Treatment Centre	Umm Hurair	04 335 1200
Dubai London Clinic	Jumeira	04 344 6663
Dubai Medical Village	Jumeira	04 395 6200
Dubai Physiotherapy Clinic	Jumeira	04 349 6333
French Medical Centre	Jumeira	04 349 5020
General Medical Centre	Jumeira	04 349 5959
German Heart Centre Bremen ▶ p.187	Umm Hurair	04 362 4797
German Medical Center	Umm Hurair	04 362 2929
Green Community Medical Centre	Jebel Ali	04 885 3225
Gulf American Clinic	Doha	04 344 2050
Health Call	Umm Hurair	04 363 5343
Health Care Medical Centre	Jumeira	04 344 5550
Manchester Clinic	Jumeira	04 344 0300
New Medical Centre	Deira	04 268 3131
Prime Medical Center	Various Locations	04 349 4545
Wellness Medical Centre	Jumeira	04 395 3115

Al Zahra Sq
Sharjah
Map 2 C2

Al Zahra Hospital ▶ p.xi
06 561 9999 | www.alzahra.com

Al Zahra Hospital in Sharjah operates a 24 hour GP clinic and emergency unit, with consultants on call around the clock. There is also Al Zahra Private Medical Centre (04 331 5000) situated in Al Safa Tower on Sheikh Zayed Road (Trade Centre 1) in Dubai. This offers outpatient services covering a range of medical and surgical disciplines including cardiology, dentistry, dermatology, ENT, family/general practice, gastroenterology, general and laparoscopic surgery, internal medicine, neurology, obstetrics & gynaecology, ophthalmology, orthopaedics, paediatrics and physiotherapy. They also offer various health packages and check-ups including Well Woman, Well Man, and Well Child assessments, cardiac fitness assessments, and maternity packages.

Oud Metha Rd
Opp Movenpick
Oud Metha
Map 10 E3

American Hospital ▶ p.185
04 336 7777 | www.ahdubai.com

The American Hospital has excellent facilities for both in and outpatients. It has top-of-the-range diagnostic equipment and the doctors and nurses are from all corners of

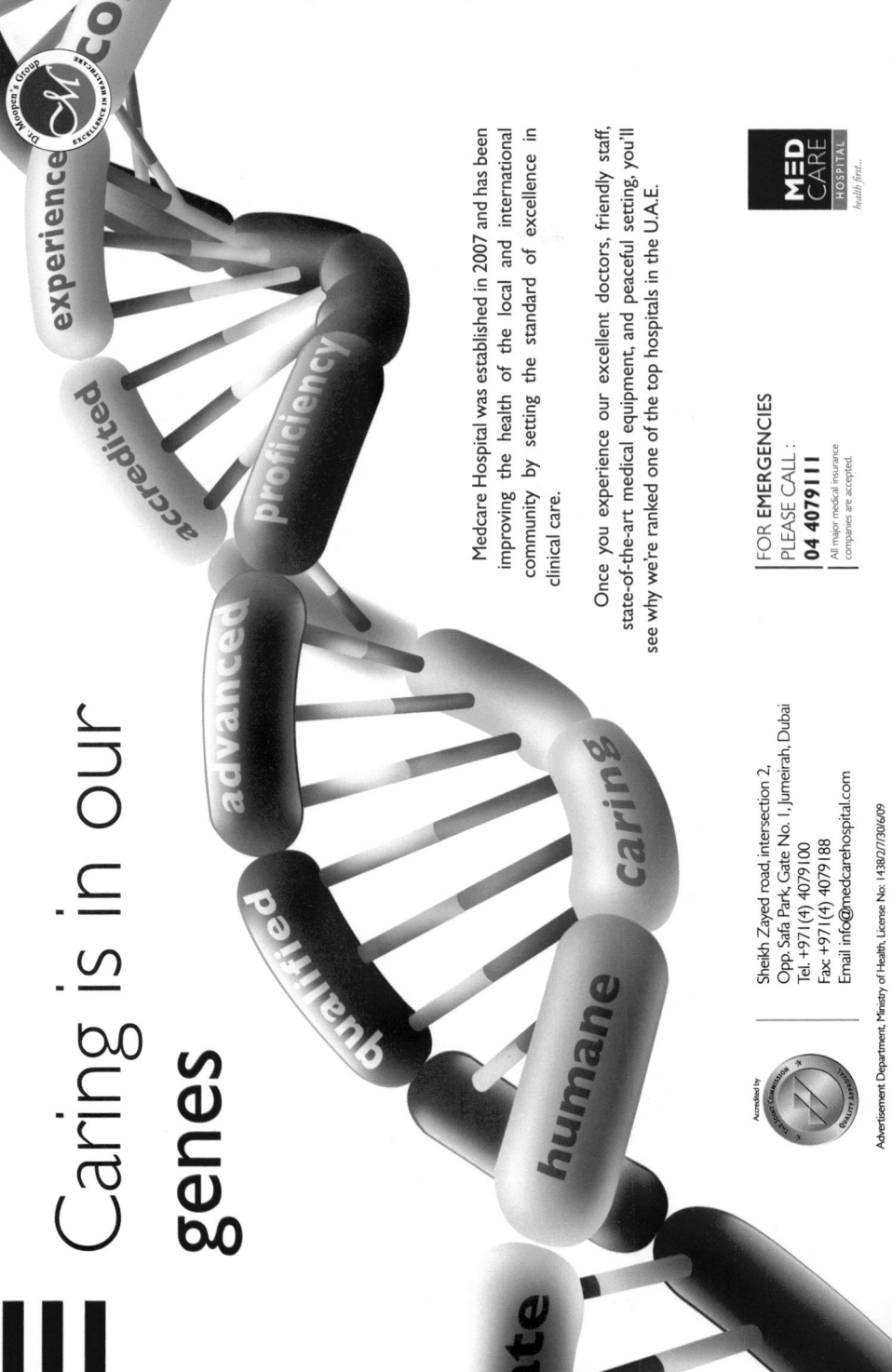

the world. The hospital has an A&E unit, operating rooms, intensive care and a neonatal intensive care. It offers maternity packages for prenatal care and delivery in the labour ward which is equipped with private rooms. In addition to gynaecology and obstetrics, the hospital's outpatient clinics include paediatrics, family medicine, internal medicine, cardiology, ophthalmology and an excellent neurology clinic. There is also a wide range of elective and emergency surgery available including reconstructive surgery, urology, orthopaedics, and microsurgery.

Diagnostics	
Al Shifa Al Khaleeji Medical Center	04 294 0786
Al Zahra Private Medical Centre ▶ p.xi	04 331 5000
Allied Diagnostic Centre	04 332 8111
American Hospital ▶ p.185	04 336 7777
Apollo Medical Diagnostic Centre	04 227 0001
Dr Leila Soudah Clinic	04 395 5591
German Heart Centre Bremen ▶ p.187	04 362 4797
Gulf Plastic Surgery Hospital	04 269 9717
Medcare Hospital ▶ p.183	04 407 9100
Medic Polyclinic	04 355 4111
Medical Imaging Department	04 309 6642
Welcare Hospital	04 282 7788

Al Khaleej Rd ◀
Deira
Map 9 E2

Belhoul Speciality Hospital

04 273 3333 | www.belhoulspeciality.com

The Belhoul Speciality Hospital has a new nephrology department offering four state-of-the-art dialysis machines for kidney disorders. The latest diagnostic equipment is also on offer such as MRI, CT scan, digital radiography, cath lab and gamma camera. Other specialities include ophthalmology, interventional cardiology and cardiac surgery, general and laparoscopic surgeries, dental work, gynaecology and obstetrics, and paediatrics. The hospital has an emergency room and its own ambulance (04 214 0333).

Off Jct 6 ◀
Sheikh Zayed Rd
Jebel Ali
Map 3 F2

Cedars Jebel Ali International Hospital

04 881 4000 | www.cedars-jaih.com

Cedars Jebel Ali International Hospital is situated near to the Jebel Ali Free Zone. Services include a 24 hour emergency clinic and dedicated ambulance, family medicine, paediatrics, gynaecology, dentistry, day surgeries, cardiology, dermatology, and a 24 hour pharmacy. To call its ambulance telephone 881 4000 or 881 8816.

Jumeirah Beach Rd ◀
Jumeira
Map 7 B1

Emirates Hospital

04 349 6666 | www.emirateshospital.ae

This hospital mainly deals with inpatient care and specialises in acute disorders. It does not deal with chronic illnesses such as cancer or diseases of the brain, nor does it admit trauma patients or have a maternity unit. The care that it does administer includes plastic surgery, gastric banding, gastric balloon, cardiology, osteoporosis pain management, paediatrics and diabetes. It also operates a 24 hour walk-in clinic. It is possible to book an appointment online.

Opp Safa Park Gate 1 ◀
Jumeira
Map 7 B2

Medcare Hospital ▶ p.183

04 407 9100 | www.medcarehospital.com

One of the newest hospitals in Dubai, the 60 bed private Medcare Hospital offers advanced medical care and emergency services, with a particularly strong maternity department. Facilities include an emergency department, 25 outpatient consultation rooms, intensive care unit, neonatal intensive care unit, delivery suites, endoscopy room and day surgery unit, as well as a high-tech diagnostic centre that has open MRI, CT scan, mammography, 4D ultrasound and fluoroscopy. Inpatient and outpatient care is offered, covering a range of specialties. Staff are qualified to international standards.

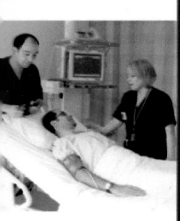

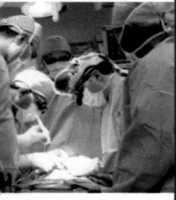

Feel better . Heal better

THE HOSPITAL
WHERE QUALITY AND TRUST MATTER

Medical Specialities

- Cardiac Surgery / Cardiac Catheterization • Cardiology
- Cardiopulmonary • Diabetes / Endocrinology
- Dietary Counseling • Endoscopy • ENT Surgery • Primary Care
- Gastroenterology / Hepatology • Hematology • General Surgery
- Internal Medicine • Medical Imaging • Nephrology / Dialysis
- Neurology • Neurosurgery • Obstetrics / Gynecology
- Oncology / Chemotherapy • Ophthalmology • Orthopedics
- Pathology & Laboratory • Pediatrics (children) • Dermatology
- Plastic, Cosmetic, Reconstructive and Maxillofacial Surgery
- Rheumatology • Sports Medicine & Physical Therapy
- Urology / Lithotripsy (Kidney Stones)
- 24 Hour Emergency Service

P . O . B o x : 55 66   Dubai - United Arab Emirates
Tel: +971-4-336-7777   Fax:+971-4-336-5176
Website: www.ahdubai.com

The first hospital in the Middle East to be awarded Joint Commission International Accreditation (JCIA).
The first private laboratory to be certified by the College of American Pathologists (CAP)

MOH 2015/29/31/8/2009

المستشفى الأمريكي
AMERICAN HOSPITAL
DUBAI

Delivering better health in the Middle East

Neuro Spinal Hospital

Jumeirah Beach Rd
Jumeira
Map 7 B1

04 342 0000

www.nshdubai.com

The Neuro Spinal Hospital has an emergency room that is open around the clock. The unit is prepared for all kinds of spinal, neurosurgical and neurological emergencies. There are also two other emergency rooms that are used for general examination and minor injuries. The hospital has 40 beds and a multi-national team of specialists, doctors and nurses. As well as spinal treatment facilities The Neuro Spinal Hospital has a stroke centre for treatment of acute cerebro-vascular accidents, and the hospital also has its own ambulance which can be dispatched by calling 04 315 7777.

Dermatologists	
Al Mousa Medical Centre	04 345 2999
Al Noor Poly Clinic	04 223 3324
Al Rustom's Skin & Laser Clinic	04 349 8800
Al Zahra Private Medical Centre ▶ p.xi	04 331 5000
Atlas Star Medical Centre	04 359 6662
Belhoul European Hospital	04 345 4000
Belhoul Speciality Hospital	04 273 3333
Dr Mohamed Al Zubaidy Clinic	04 227 7533
Dr Simin Medical Clinic	04 344 4117
Medcare Hospital ▶ p.183	04 407 9100
Medica	04 282 8338
Prime Medical Center	04 349 4545

The City Hospital

Dubai
Healthcare City
Umm Hurair
Map 10 E4

04 435 9999 | www.thecityhospital.com

The City Hospital became the first hospital to open in Dubai's flagship Healthcare City. It offers state-of-the-art facilities for all of its specialties, which include cardiology, dentistry, gynaecology, trauma and endocrinology. If you feel deserving of a different class of treatment to the rest of the hospital's patients (and have the wallet to match), you can take advantage of the VIP (very important patient) floor, which boasts luxury facilities akin to that of a top hotel. You can convalesce in a VIP, presidential or royal suite, plus have access to a VIP-only swimming pool, spa and gymnasium. Your own butler will bring you anything you want or need from the hospital's special menu.

Welcare Hospital

Nr Aviation Club
Al Garhoud
Map 11 C4

04 282 7788 | www.welcarehospital.com

The Welcare Hospital offers in and outpatient care in a modern and aesthetically pleasing atmosphere. It covers a wide range of surgical and medical services including cardiac surgery, dermatology, ENT, general and prosthetic dentistry, general surgery, neurology, obstetrics, gynaecology, paediatrics and neonatology, physiotherapy, plastic and cosmetic surgery and urology. Special services include a contact lens clinic, diabetic clinic, holiday dialysis, home call consultations (specialist and GP), laser treatment (eyes), MRI/LT scan and maternity packages as well as Well Man and Well Woman packages. Its prenatal and delivery care is considered to be one of the best in Dubai. Welcare also does postnatal packages for parents and their new baby, which is a nice way to meet other new mums.

Zulekha Hospital

Nr Dubai
Women's College
Al Qusais
Map 14 D1

04 267 8866 | www.zulekhahospitals.com

The Zulekha Hospital and diagnostic centre contains both outpatient and inpatient facilities, including a 24 hour emergency department and a fully equipped intensive care unit. Other speciality departments in the hospital include general surgery, orthopaedics, internal medicine, obstetrics and gynaecology, paediatrics, dermatology, cardiology, and neurology.

Heart Care Made in Germany

A distinguished team of senior cardiology consultants delivering superior, general and interventional cardiology treatment. Our experience and commitment is what makes a difference in quality health care.

Dr. Klaus T. Kallmayer MD, MA
Interventional Cardiologist

Dr. Caspar A. Boerner MD
Specialist Cardiologist

Dr. Helmut W. Lange MD
Specialist Cardiologist

■ **Efficient and hassle-free consultation and test process**

■ **Out and in-patient care offered in Dubai**

■ **A comprehensive range of Cardiology services**

■ **Expertise in complicated and critical cases**

German Heart Centre

Bremen

Branch of German Teaching Hospital located at: Dubai Healthcare City
Call + 971-4-362 47 97

Maternity

Other options **Maternity Items** p.458

Every expatriate child born in the UAE must be registered at the Ministry of Health within two weeks and hold a residence visa within four months of birth, otherwise you may not be able to take the child out of the country. See Birth Certificates & Registration (p.94) for more details about the process.

There are various considerations when deciding where to give birth. If you have your heart set on a water or home birth you may want to consider going home, since these options aren't available in the UAE. If you decide that you would rather have the baby in your home country, keep in mind that airlines do have restrictions on carrying heavily pregnant passengers, so check when their cut-off date is. However, if you do decide to have your baby here you will find the level of care is excellent. The *Dubai Red-Tape Explorer* lists the procedures you'll need to follow as well as the costs you can expect. The Al Wasl Hospital may lack some of the private hospital frills but it has an excellent reputation for maternity care and paediatrics. Before you decide on a government hospital check their policy regarding husbands and family members in the labour ward. Certain hospitals may not allow your husband to be with you in the labour ward (although he can be present at delivery and often, if you are persuasive and there are no local ladies admitted, they will allow access). All government hospitals now charge expatriates for maternity services and delivery, and costs vary depending on the package you choose. Private hospitals will be more expensive, although if you shop around you may be surprised to find that in some cases the difference between government and private is not as great as you might think. No matter which you choose, if you have medical insurance check that it covers maternity costs – some have a limitation clause (you need to have been with the insurer for at least 12 months before conception) and some may not cover any costs at all. Private hospitals offer maternity packages that include prenatal care, delivery and postnatal care for you and the baby. But remember that the price you are quoted by the hospital is for the basic, 'best case scenario' delivery, and if you have additional requirements, such as an epidural (when the anaesthetist must be present) or an assisted delivery (when the paediatrician must be present), you will be charged extra. If you give birth by caesarean section, the cost is usually significantly higher and the hospital stay is longer (five days, compared to two days for standard delivery). Maternity leave in the UAE is short compared to some other countries. Although a new mother is entitled to 45 days leave on full pay (whether this is calendar days or working days depends on your employer), a lot of employers here are not that flexible

Gynaecology & Obstetrics	
Al Aliaa Poly Clinics	04 349 3600
Al Diyafa Modern Medical Centre	04 345 4945
Al Wasl Hospital	04 219 3000
Al Zahra Private Medical Centre ▶ p.xi	04 331 5000
American Hospital ▶ p.185	04 336 7777
Belhoul European Hospital	04 345 4000
Dr Akel's General Medical Clinic (GMC)	04 349 4880
Dr Fakih Gynaecology & Obstetrics Center	04 349 2100
Dr Leila Soudah Clinic	04 395 5591
Dr Taher H Khalil Clinic	04 268 7655
Dubai Gynaecology & Fertility Centre	04 438 0610
Dubai London Clinic	04 344 6663
General Medical Centre	04 349 5959
German Clinic ▶ p.189	04 429 8346
Jumeirah Family Clinic	04 344 8844
Manchester Clinic	04 344 0300
Medcare Hospital ▶ p.183	04 407 9100
Medlink Clinic	04 344 7711
Prime Medical Center	04 349 4545
Royal Medical Centre	04 345 6780
Welcare Hospital	04 282 7788

Pediatrics
- **General Pediatrics**
- **ADHD** and Pediatric Neurology
- **Bronchial Asthma**

Gynecology/Obstetrics
- **Sinology** (diagnostic and treatment of breast cancer)
- **Endrocrinology**
- **Anti-Aging**
- **Check up Programs**
- **Minimal Invasive** Treatment Hysteroscopy & Laparoscopy
- **Urinary** Incontinence Treatment
- **Reconstructive & Tumor** Treatment
- **Hormone** Replacement Therapy
- **Menstrual & Breast Disorders**
- **Infertility & Contraception** (Consultancy only)
- **Screening** of Gyn. Tumours, Female Infertility, Recurrent Abortion & STD
- **Normal Delivery & Caesarean Section**
- **Obesity Treatment**
- **Doppler & Ultrasound examination incl.** 4D
- **Immunization** (e.g. HPV & Hepatitis)

WE CARE FOR YOUR **HEALTH AND BEAUTY**

Located at Dubai Healthcare City • Call us: 04 / 42 98 346

www.germanclinic-dubai.com

Maternity Hospitals & Clinics

Government	
Al Wasl Hospital	04 219 3000
Dubai Hospital	04 219 5000
Private	
Al Zahra Private Medical Centre ▶p.xi	04 331 5000
American Hospital ▶p.185	04 336 7777
Belhoul European Hospital	04 345 4000
Dr Akel's General Medical Clinic (GMC)	04 349 4880
Dr Fakih Gynaecology & Obstetrics Center	04 349 2100
Dr Leila Soudah Clinic	04 395 5591
Dubai London Clinic	04 344 6663
General Medical Centre	04 349 5959
Medcare Hospital ▶p.183	04 407 9100
Medlink Clinic	04 344 7711
Royal Medical Centre	04 345 6780
Welcare Hospital	04 282 7788

about giving further leave, even on an unpaid basis, so it's worth discussing this with your employer as early as possible. New dads are not entitled to any paternity leave (unlike the UK where you get two weeks), so will have to take annual leave if they want to help with the sleepless nights and nappy changing.

Having a baby in Dubai as opposed to returning to your home country for the birth has its advantages. The level of care in both the private and government hospitals is of a very high standard, both for prenatal, delivery and postnatal care. In addition if you stay in the country then you have the benefit of developing a relationship with your obstetrician during your prenatal care which will make the delivery all the more comfortable when the time comes (midwives, although they take an active role, are not qualified in Dubai to deliver babies and your obstetrician must deliver the baby). In addition, if you do decide to have your baby in Dubai you benefit from not being separated from your husband. Without paternity leave it's unlikely that your husband will be able to accompany you back home and stay until you and baby are ready to board a plane. Also there is no guarantee that you'll deliver on your due date so it makes the trip very hard to plan. Plus, if you have to have an emergency caesarean this could make the recovery period a lot longer and therefore delay your return to Dubai. Whatever you decide to do there are numerous mother and baby groups in Dubai that will help you to settle into your new role as a mother (see p.202).

Paediatrics

Most public and private hospitals and medical centres in Dubai have full time paediatricians on staff, with a growing number having devoted paediatric departments. The American Hospital and Welcare Hospital (both private) have teams of specialist paediatric doctors, while Al Wasl Hospital (government) has dedicated paediatric surgeons and neurodevelopment therapists that care for children with special needs and learning difficulties. The Dubai Community Health Centre (www.dubaicommunityhealthcentre.

Paediatrics

Belgium Medical Services	04 362 4711
Dr Abed Aydin	04 336 7777
Dr Anil Gupta	04 309 6488
Dr Ayman Beirute	04 282 7788
Dr Carole Chidiac	04 349 5020
Dr Ejaz Wasseem	04 344 7711
Dr Keith Nicholl	04 394 1000
Dr Michael Loubser	04 349 5959
German Heart Centre Bremen ▶p.187	04 362 4797
Health Call	04 363 5343
Isis – The French Pediatric Clinic	04 429 8450
Medcare Hospital ▶p.183	04 407 9100

org, 04 395 3939) also provides professional services such as speech therapy and social skills training for children with special needs.

Dentists & Orthodontists

Dentistry in Dubai is, like most other medical services, of a high standard and various practitioners offer dental surgery, cosmetic cleaning and check-ups. Prices match the high level of service and standard health insurance packages generally don't cover dentistry, unless it's an emergency treatment brought about by an accident. You may be able to pay an additional premium to cover dentistry, but the insurer may first want proof that you've had regular, six-monthly check-ups for the previous two or three years. If you have a health card, you're entitled to dentistry at your assigned hospital, and if your hospital doesn't have a dental section, they'll refer you to another public

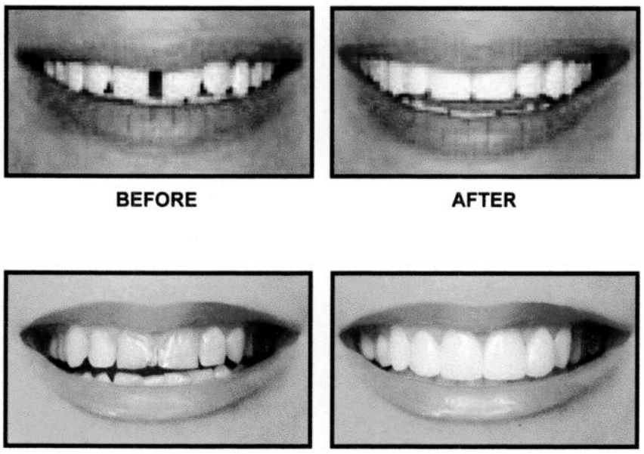

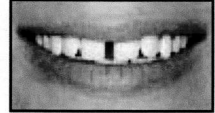
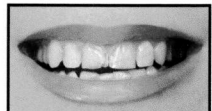

hospital that does, such as Rashid Hospital. You will be charged Dhs.100 for the visit, as well as for any other services that are performed, such as cleaning and filling. Service is generally professional and good, but the rates may not be any lower than at a private dental clinic.

For a standard filling you could be looking at paying anywhere between Dhs.50 and Dhs.1,000. If it is root canal treatment that you need, expect to part with anything from Dhs.600 to Dhs.3,000. A number of practices in Dubai, including Talass Orthodontic & Dental Center and the American Dental Clinic, specialise in cosmetic dentistry using crowns, veneers and teeth whitening to give you a dazzling smile to be proud of.

Dr Michael's Dental Clinic has a range of international dentists based in both its Jumeirah and Umm Suqeim branches, while Drs Nicolas & Asp has several dentistry and medical clinics, in Dubai Marina, Green Community, Jumeira, Mirdif and Dubai Healthcare City.

Dentists & Orthodontists	
Al Zahra Private	
Medical Centre ▶p.xi	04 331 5000
American Dental Clinic	04 344 0668
British Dental Clinic	04 342 1318
British Medical Consulting Centre	04 344 2633
Charly PolyClinic	04 337 9191
The Dental Center	04 375 2175
The Dental SPA Family	
& Cosmetic Dentistry	04 395 2005
Dr Michael's Dental Clinic	04 349 5900
Drs Nicolas & Asp Clinic ▶p.193	04 394 7777
Dubai London Clinic	04 344 6663
Dubai Sky Clinic ▶p.xii	04 355 8808
Emirates Hospital	04 349 6666
General Medical Centre	04 349 5959
Health Care Medical Clinic	04 344 5550
Jumeira Beach Dental Clinic	04 349 9433
Medcare Hospital ▶p.183	04 407 9100
Modern Dental Clinic	04 369 3625
Seven Dental Centre ▶p.181	04 395 2177
Swedish Dental Clinic	04 223 1297
Talass Orthodontic	
& Dental Center ▶p.191	04 349 2220
Tower Clinic	04 330 0220

Cardiology

Cardiology	
American Hospital ▶p.185	04 336 7777
Belhoul Speciality Hospital	04 273 3333
German Heart	
Centre Bremen ▶p.187	04 362 4797
Mayo Clinic	04 362 2900

The UAE has a high rate of death from heart disease – up to 40% of deaths in the country are linked to heart problems, according to recent figures released by the Ministry of Health. At the end of 2008, the MoH launched a year-long campaign to educate people about heart disease; particularly about contributing factors such as smoking, stress, high blood pressure and diabetes (of which there is a high prevalence in the UAE).

Opticians & Ophthalmologists

You're never far from an optician in Dubai, with most of the malls having at least one outlet. The bigger branches such as Al Jaber Optical in Deira City Centre (04 295 4400) and Yateem in the BurJuman Centre also carry out the eye test required for a driving licence (see Driving Licence, p.91). Most opticians stock a good range of contact lenses and the necessary solutions. Barakat Optical on Sheikh Zayed Road

Opticians & Ophthalmologists	
Al Zahra Private	
Medical Centre ▶p.xi	04 331 5000
American Hospital ▶p.185	04 336 7777
Atlanta Vision Clinic	04 348 6233
Barakat Optical	04 329 1913
Gulf Eye Centre	04 329 1977
Medcare Hospital ▶p.183	04 407 9100
Moorfields Eye Hospital ▶p.195	04 429 7888
Sharif Eye Center	04 423 3664
Welcare Hospital	04 282 7788

"CARING IS OUR CONCERN"

دكـتــورنيـقـولا وآسـب

DRS. NICOLAS & ASP

SPECIALISED DENTAL CARE FOR ALL THE FAMILY

NERAL DENTISTRY
E NICOLAS, USA
SVEN ASP, SWEDEN
OAN ASP, SWEDEN
TOMAS VON POST, SWEDEN
CLAS OSKARSSON, SWEDEN
CHRIS JOHANSSON, SWEDEN
E. IZABELA, POLAND
KARIM FEKIH, FRANCE
DIANE FARHANG, FRANCE
HELEN KHATIB, UK
RUBY GHAFFARI, USA
CATARINA FAERBOM, SWEDEN
FARMAN POUR, SWEDEN
FLORA RISSLER, SWEDEN
GAVIN VAN VLEDDER, SOUTH AFRICA
CYRIL COMA, FRANCE

THODONTICS (BRACES)
ROLF LINDMAN, SWEDEN
BRITTANY NICOL, AUSTRALIA
TANJA NAKOVICS, GERMANY
AHMAD ISMAIL, FRANCE

THODONTICS & CLEFT LIP & PALATE
SALAM AL - KHAYYAT, TURKEY

RGERY & IMPLANTS
DAVID ROZE, FRANCE

DODONTICS
DIANE FARHANG, FRANCE

OSTHODONTICS (CROWN & BRIDGE)
MAHER ATASSI, USA

EDIATRIC DENTISTRY
AGNES ROZE, FRANCE

AL MAXILLOFACIAL SURGERY
CHRISTER DAHLIN, SWEDEN
THOMAS TKOTZ, GERMANY
DIRK NOLTE, GERMANY

NTAL HYGIENE
TE PASZKOWSKA, POLAND
HLEH MAHTABPOUR, IRAN
JA OSTLING, SWEDEN

MOH: 2731/2/12/31/12/08

JUMEIRAH DENTAL : 04 394 7777

24/7 Emergency Hotlines
Dental: 050 551 7177 • Medical: 050 640 7695

GREEN COMMUNITY	MARINA WALK	MIRDIF	DHCC
DENTAL + MEDICAL	**DENTAL + MEDICAL**	**DENTAL**	**DENTAL**
04 885 4440	04 360 9977	04 288 4411	04 362 4788

enquiries@nicolasandasp.com

will even deliver disposable lenses. For a list of opticians see Eyewear (p.440).
For eye problems requiring specialist treatment, many hospitals and clinics offer consultations and are able to carry out appropriate treatment, especially Moorfields Eye Hospital, American Hospital and Welcare Hospital, which all have well-equipped ophthalmology departments. A number of clinics and medical centres offer laser eye surgery, such as Moorfields Eye Hospital, Al Zahra Private Medical Centre, the Gulf Eye Centre and the Atlanta Vision Clinic.

Alternative Therapies

There is a well-balanced choice of spiritual and holistic therapies available in Dubai. The Dubai Herbal & Treatment Centre (www.dubaihtc.com, 04 335 1200) offers a full range of Chinese, Indian and Arabic herbal medicines. The facility, which is unique in the GCC region, currently caters to outpatients only, but there are plans to expand the facility to offer inpatient services.

Natural medicine can be very specialised, so when consulting with someone make sure that you ask questions and explain your needs and expectations to ensure practitioners can help with your situation. Prices vary but are generally comparable to western medicine, and most insurance companies will not cover the costs. As always, word of mouth is the best way of establishing who might offer the most appropriate treatment (posting a query on www.expatwoman.com could turn up some recommendations).

There is also a range of clinics providing 'well-being' services, such as U Concept (www.uconcept6.com, 04 344 9060) in the Village Mall, Jumeira. U Concept offers a 'unique lifestyle service', combining personal training, nutritional advice, and a range of treatments. You can agree on a 12 week programme to help you achieve your personal health and fitness goals and cope with stress. It even advises on nutrition and helps you to put together a long term eating plan.

The UAE Ministry of Health grants licences to and administrates qualified practitioners of alternative medicine through its dedicated department for Traditional, Complementary and Alternative Medicine. On the following pages are some of the services offered, and the main practitioners in Dubai.

Acupressure & Acupuncture

Acupressure involves the systematic placement of pressure with fingertips on established meridian points on the body. This therapy can be used to relieve pain, soothe the nerves and stimulate the body, as determined necessary by the therapist. Acupuncture is an ancient Chinese technique that uses needles to access the body's meridian points. The technique is surprisingly painless and is quickly becoming an alternative or complement to western medicine as it aids ailments such as asthma, rheumatism and other serious diseases.

Acupressure & Acupuncture	
Cedars Jebel Ali International Hospital	04 881 4000
Dubai Herbal & Treatment Centre	04 335 1200
Dubai Physiotherapy Clinic	04 349 6333
Gulf American Clinic	04 349 8556
House Of Chi & House Of Healing	04 397 4446
King China Acupuncture Center	04 398 5548

Aromatherapy

Essential oils derived from plants and flowers can be used in many ways to add balance to your health. Specialists use oils when delivering massages as well as a number of other methods to address your needs. While no certification is required

Aromatherapy	
Cleopatra's Spa	04 324 7700
Essensuals Aromatherapy Centre	04 344 8776
The Haven Depilex	04 345 6770
Marie France Beauty Salon	04 344 8739
Talise Spa	04 366 6818

Quitting Is For Winners

Although it sometimes seems impossible to escape the smoke in Dubai, there are groups and organisations that exist solely to help people kick their addiction to nicotine. The number of Quit Smoking clinics provided by the Ministry of Health and private hospitals has increased since the smoking ban came into effect in 2007. Contact your local hospital (p.178) for more information on the schemes and support groups available.

to practise aromatherapy, it's a healthy decision to make sure your practitioner has studied plants and can make the best choices for you. For cosmetic and relaxing purposes alone, aromatherapy facials or massages are recommended, which many spas and salons offer. While these are intended to be for pleasure rather than health related, they can work wonders on your soul.

Healing Meditation

Art of Living	www.artoflivingme.org
Dubai Community Health Centre	04 395 3939
GMCKS Pranic Energy Healing Centre	04 336 0885
SSY (Siddha Samadhi Yoga)	04 344 6618

Healing Meditation
Meditation can offer inner peace as well as a disease-free mind and body. With various breathing techniques, movements and mantras, group and individual meditation sessions can be a powerful tool in healing and stress relief. Growing numbers of Dubai's residents are trying meditation as a means to unwind.

Homeopathy
Homeopathy aims to strengthen the body's defence system. Natural ingredients are used to address physical and emotional problems.

Homeopathy

Dr Ray's Medical Centre	04 397 3665
Dubai Herbal & Treatment Centre	04 335 1200
Holistic Healing Medical Centre	04 348 7172
Medlink Clinic	04 344 7711
Prime Medical Center	04 349 4545

The practice extracts elements from traditional medicines of various origins but was recently organised into a healthcare system in Europe. Practitioners undergo disciplined training and some are also western medical doctors.

Physiotherapy

Al Zahra Private Medical Centre	▶ p.xi	04 331 5000
American Hospital	▶ p.185	04 336 7777
Dubai Bone & Joint Center	▶ p.197	04 423 1400
Dubai Physiotherapy Clinic		04 349 6333
General Medical Centre		04 349 5959
Gulf American Clinic		04 344 2050
Health Care Medical Centre		04 344 5550
Medcare Hospital	▶ p.183	04 407 9100
OrthoSports Medical Center	▶ p.199	04 345 0601

Physiotherapy
Many Dubai residents lead an active lifestyle, working hard and then playing harder. But accidents and injuries do happen, so whether you got roughed up playing rugby, pulled something in the gym or simply tripped over the cat you'll be pleased to hear that the city has some excellent facilities to help you on the road to recovery. The OrthoSports Medical Center in Jumeira specialises in orthopaedic and sports medicine, offering physiotherapy, hydrotherapy and orthopaedic surgery to international standards.

Reflexology & Massage Therapy
Reflexology is a detailed scientific system, with Asian origins, that outlines points in the hands and feet that impact other parts and systems of the body. As well as stress reduction and improved health, the pressure applied to the points directly addresses issues in those specific corresponding parts of the body. While many spas and salons offer massage and reflexology, the listed centres have a focused approach to the holistic healing qualities of reflexology and massage. See p.402 for spas that offer massage.

Reflexology & Massage Therapy

Bliss Relaxology	04 286 9444
Cleopatra's Spa	04 324 7700
Dubai Herbal & Treatment Centre	04 335 1200
Dubai Physiotherapy Clinic	04 349 6333
Essensuals Aromatherapy Centre	04 344 8776
Feet First	04 349 4334
The Haven Depilex	04 345 6770
Healing Zone	04 394 0604
Herbalpan Ayurvedic Centre	04 321 2553
House Of Chi & House Of Healing	04 397 4446
Marie France Beauty Salon	04 344 8739
Thai Relaxation Therapy Centre	04 321 2345
Welcare Hospital	04 282 7788

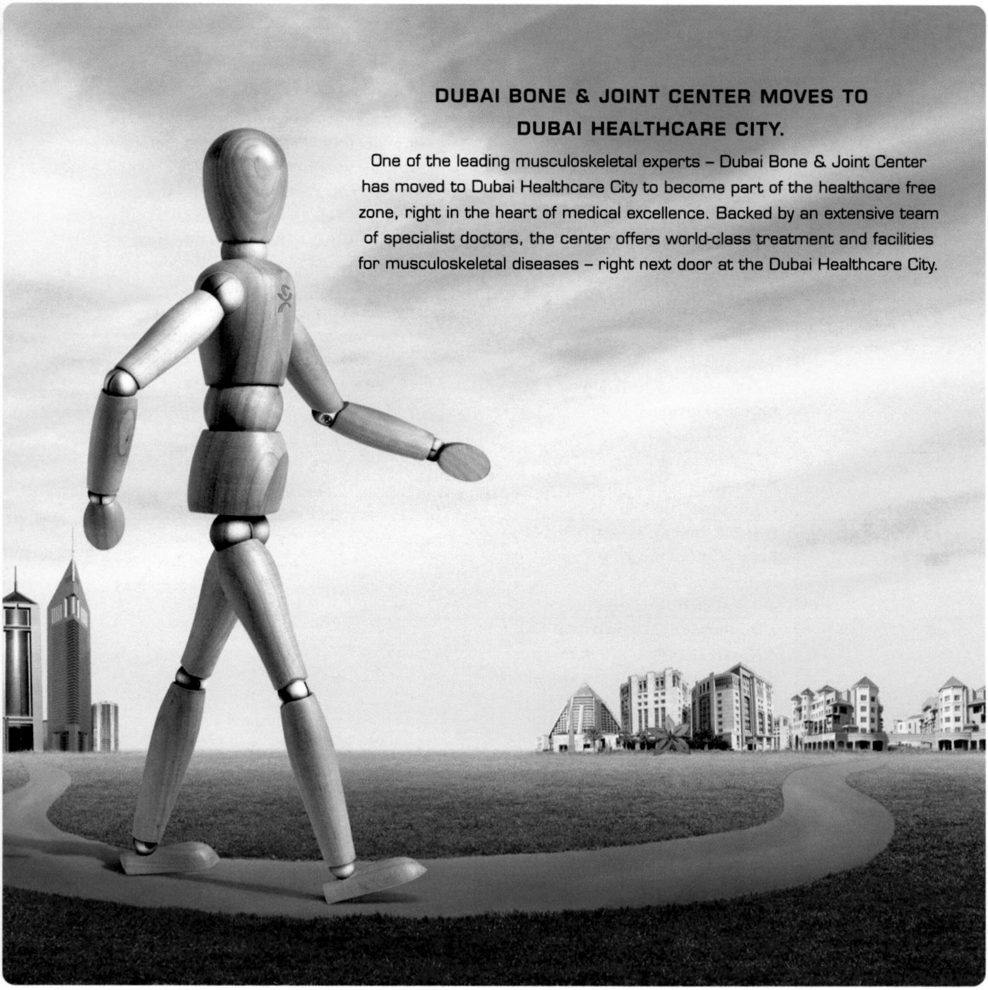

Back Treatment

Back problems plague many people, whether they are young and fit sports fanatics or sedentary people in their later life. Luckily, treatment is widely available in Dubai with excellent specialists from all around the world practising here.

Chiropractic and osteopathy treatments concentrate on manipulating the skeleton in a non-invasive manner to improve the functioning of the nervous system or blood supply to the body. Chiropractic therapy is based on the manipulative treatment of misalignments in the joints, especially those of the spinal column, while osteopathy involves the manipulation and massage of the skeleton and musculature. Craniosacral therapy aims to relieve pain and tension by gentle manipulations of the skull to balance the craniosacral rhythm. Pilates is said to be the safest form of neuromuscular reconditioning and back strengthening available. It is also a form of exercise that's gaining popularity. Check to see if your gym offers Pilates.

Back Treatment	
Advanced Chiropractic Health Center	04 348 8262
Al Zahra Private Medical Centre ▶ p.xi	04 331 5000
Canadian Chiropractic & Natural Health Centre	04 342 0900
Clark Chiropractic Clinic	04 344 4316
Dr Akel's General Medical Clinic (GMC)	04 349 4880
Drs Nicolas & Asp Clinic ▶ p.193	04 394 7777
Dubai Bone & Joint Center ▶ p.197	04 423 1400
Gulf American Clinic	04 349 8556
House Of Chi & House Of Healing	04 397 4446
Medcare Hospital ▶ p.183	04 407 9100
Neuro Spinal Hospital	04 342 0000
OrthoSports Medical Center ▶ p.199	04 345 0601
Osteopathic Health Centre	04 348 7366
The Pilates Studio	04 343 8252
Specialist Orthopaedic Surgery Centre	04 349 5528

Nutritionists & Slimming

With such a variety of dining options in Dubai, and with the emphasis very much on lounging and relaxing, it's easy to let your diet suffer and pile on the pounds. Thankfully, a number of slimming clubs and nutritionists are on hand to help:

- 8 Weeks To A New You (www.8weeks.net) is for people wanting to lose weight and improve their general health and wellbeing. The programme offers regular exercise sessions and individual nutrition consultation.
- Shapes at Knowledge Village (www.shapeshealthclub.com) describes itself as the biggest weight and inch-loss facility in the UAE. Nutritionists and dieticians will devise a personal diet and exercise plan, and the club offers a number of fitness classes each week to choose from.
- Hypoxi All Body Solutions is the only outfit in Dubai offering HypoxiTherapy. The method aims to help you lose cellulite and fat from your stomach, waist, hips, thighs and buttocks, achieved by exercise combined with vacuum suction. Loved by celebrities, this method is painless. There are a number of machines around Dubai, including at Emirates Towers (04 319 8662) and Le Meridien (04 702 2466).
- Right Bite (www.right-bite.com) offers a tailor-made healthy eating service. Low calorie, low fat and low cholesterol meals, devised by their own dieticians, are freshly prepared and delivered to your door.
- Good Habits (www.goodhabitsuae.com) helps people lose weight through healthy eating. Meetings are held every week at various locations all over Dubai, and often include food tasting and cookery demos. Exercise classes are also organised.

Nutritionists & Slimming	
8 Weeks To A New You	050 559 2852
American Hospital ▶ p.185	04 336 7777
Dubai London Clinic	04 344 6663
Emirates Hospital	04 349 6666
Eternal MedSpa Dubai	04 344 0008
Good Habits	04 344 9692
Hypoxi All Body Solutions	04 204 5032
Manchester Clinic	04 344 0300
Medcare Hospital ▶ p.183	04 407 9100
Right Bite	04 351 4453
Shapes Weight-Loss Club	04 367 2137
VLCC	800 8522
Welcare Hospital	04 282 7788

...be fit

orthopedic surgery • sports medicine • osteopathy • physiotherapy • hydrotherapy •

www.orthosp.com

ORTHOSPORTS
MEDICAL CENTER
THE SPORTS MEDICINE SPECIALISTS

BEACH ROAD JUMEIRA
TEL: 04-345 0601 FAX: 04-345 0028

- The Welcare Hospital (www.welcarehospital.com) provides a dietary counselling service, where a team of dieticians and nutritionists will educate and evaluate the patient's eating habits, and then point them in the right direction with a unique diet plan.
- The American Hospital (www.ahdubai.com) offers a food and nutrition service managed and provided by ADNH Compass. The hospital also runs a Diabetic Centre of Excellence.
- Emirates Hospital (www.emirateshospital.ae) has a weight reduction programme that uses liquid supplements and a very low calorie diet. The hospital has dietician and nutrition experts who specialise in medically supervised weight reduction programmes, obesity in children, obesity in diabetic patients and patients with high blood pressure or cholesterol. It also offers weight loss programmes through gastric band fitting.

Cosmetic Treatment & Surgery	
Al Rustom's Skin & Laser Clinic	04 349 8800
American Hospital ▶ p.185	04 336 7777
Belhoul European Hospital	04 345 4000
British Medical Consulting Centre	04 344 2633
Cosmesurge	04 344 5915
Drs Nicolas & Asp Clinic ▶ p.193	04 394 7777
Dubai Cosmetic Surgery ▶ p.201	04 348 5575
Dubai Medical Village	04 395 6200
Emirates Hospital	04 349 6666
Euro Gulf Medical Center	04 331 3544
Gulf Plastic Surgery Hospital	04 269 9717
Manchester Clinic	04 344 0300
Medcare Hospital ▶ p.183	04 407 9100
Welcare Hospital	04 282 7788

Cosmetic Treatment & Surgery

Dubai is becoming known as a destination for cosmetic surgery due to the heightened awareness of image through an influx of people, the rapid growth of the media and those with expendable money. The city now boasts a growing number of clinics that specialise in reducing, reshaping, removing and enlarging various parts of your anatomy. The private hospitals also offer cosmetic services including aesthetic and reconstructive surgery. Many of the independent clinics are located in Jumeira, especially along Beach Road. One of these is Dubai Medical Village (04 395 6200) whose dedicated team of surgeons offer a range of surgical procedures, eye care, and laser treatment including hair removal. If you want a bit of sprucing and don't fancy slicing, a lot of the cosmetic clinics will do Botox and other non-surgical treatments.

Counselling & Therapy

Even the most resilient of personalities can be affected by expat culture shock or homesickness. Whatever the origin of the stress, a new environment takes some getting used to, and can take its toll on your nerves. The good news is there are a number of support groups (p.202) where problems can be shared (and halved) and much needed ears bent. If your troubles run deeper, then you may benefit from some therapy and there are a number of counsellors and psychologists in Dubai that will help you deal with emotional problems. Many doctors will also treat cases of child psychology or children with behavioural issues such as ADHD. The Dubai Community Health Centre (www.dubaicommunityhealthcentre.org, 04 395 3939) is a non-profit organisation that offers workshops and other psychiatric services at competitive rates. The centre is the GCC region's first dedicated mental health centre, and also specialises in

Psychiatrists	
Belhoul European Hospital	04 345 4000
Belhoul Speciality Hospital	04 273 3333
British Medical Consulting Centre	04 344 2633
Counselling and Development Clinic	04 394 6122
Dr Adnand Clinic	04 398 9740
Dr Akel's General Medical Clinic (GMC)	04 349 4880
Dubai Community Health Centre	04 395 3939
Health Call	04 363 5343
Medcare Hospital ▶ p.183	04 407 9100
Prime Medical Center	04 349 4545
Welcare Hospital	04 282 7788

Our canvas...
your beauty...

Cosmetic Surgery Clinic

Facial Enhancment
Body Contouring
Breast Cosmetic Surgery
Botox and Fillers
Hair Transplant
Rhinoplasty
LPG (Cellulite Treatment)

Cosmetic Surgery Clinic | Cosmetic Dentistry Clinic | Skin Care Clinic | Cosmetic Laser Clinic

Laser Hair Removal
Tattoo Removal
Laser Veins Removal
Photo Rejuvination
Birthmarks Removal
Freckles & Age Spot
Melasma & Rosacea

Dubai Cosmetic Surgery
complete make-over experts

nfo@dubaicosmeticsurgery.com
www.dubaicosmeticsurgery.com

Al Wasl Rd., (Al Manara, Umm Suqueim area), Dubai, U.A.E
For more information please contact us on : 04 348 5575

educational psychology for children and adults, marriage and family counselling, as well as yoga and reiki programmes. In addition there are a number of psychiatrists in Dubai who deal with the diagnosis and treatment of more chronic mental illnesses.

Counsellors & Psychologists	
Belhoul European Hospital	04 345 4000
Counselling & Development Clinic	04 394 6122
Dubai Community Health Centre	04 395 3939
Health Call	04 363 5343
Human Relations Institute	04 331 4777

Table4six ◀
To help you meet new people, Table4six (www. table4six.net) will reserve a table at a Dubai restaurant and then invite six of its members to dinner. Upon joining you can specify your preferences, including how often you want to be invited.

Single Dubai Female ◀
The Bridget Jones Club Dubai is a social group of more than 400 single women that get together for various events and activities. They welcome members of all ages and nationalities and are always looking for suggestions on new activities. Visit www. thebridgets.com.

Support Groups

Living away from your family can be challenging, but there are support groups offering a hand through the difficult patches. There is also the Dubai Community Health Centre (04 395 3939) which provides space for support group meetings.

- ADHD (attention deficit hyperactive disorder). Meetings are held every other Sunday (04 335 5578).
- Adoption Support Group (04 360 8113). Meetings held once a month. Call Carol.
- Alcoholics Anonymous (AA) (04 344 1542 – 24 hour hotline). Information on weekly meetings can be found on www.aainarabia.com.
- All 4 Down's Syndrome (www.downsyndromedubai.com, 050 880 9228 – 24 hour hotline). Providing support to families whose lives have, in some way, been affected by Down's Syndrome. The group holds social mornings every Sunday between 10:00 and 12:00.
- Bullied children and their parents can learn how to deal with bullying as a family. Call Salomi on 050 657 0866.
- City of Hope (04 394 2650 or 050 651 6511). Not a support 'group' as such, but a project providing shelter for women and children of all nationalities who have been the victim of abuse. They are in the process of applying for a licence, but as yet remain 'unofficial'. The shelter is staffed entirely by volunteers, and the project is reliant on donations and support. Contact the above number from Saturday to Wednesday, 08:15 to15:30, or by emailing cityofhope18@gmail.com.
- Diabetic Support Group (04 309 6954). Based at the American Hospital Dubai.
- Mother 2 Mother (04 348 3754 or 050 452 7674). Support, friendship, fun and advice for all mothers, from those who are expecting to those who have already delivered.
- Overcomers Outreach (04 342 1302). A group for those affected directly or indirectly by the abuse of any mood altering chemical, or obsessive/compulsive behaviour.
- Pastoral Counselling (050 422 0251 or 04 297 3221). A support service available whatever the problem, with the aim of restoring the joy and significance of living.
- SANDS Support Group. A UK-based charity for those families experiencing pregnancy loss, either through still birth, neonatal death or late miscarriage. Contact June on 04 884 6309. SANDS also offers hospital and home visits.
- Special Families Support (04 360 5654) has monthly meetings for the families of special needs children. Call the above number or Gulshan on 050 454 1940.
- Multiple Sclerosis runs monthly meetings for suffers, care givers and family. Contact Coreen Dolan on 03 761 5668 or 03 709 5292.
- Mothers of Children With Special Needs is run by parents of special needs children offering support and information. Call Lilly 050 659 1707 for details of monthly meetings.
- Coping With Caregiving offers support specifically to professionals and family members involved in caring for elderly people with memory problems. Contact 04 395 3939 or ndemascarel@yahoo.com.

Support Groups	
Anxiety & Depression Support Group	04 365 8498
Breastfeeding Telephone Support Group	050 453 4670
Dubai Dyslexia Support Group	04 344 6657
Fertility Support Group	050 632 4365
Still Birth & Neo Natal Death Society	04 884 6309
Twins, Triplets or More!	04 288 1982
UAE Down Syndrome Support Group	800 369 647 687

Education

The education system is varied, with many international schools to choose from, and more opening every year. But, as there is no government-funded education for expat children, all these schools charge fees.

Other parents are always a good source of advice, as are company HR departments. Also, consider posting a query on one of the expat websites (see p.69) – just bear in mind that advice won't necessarily be objective. It's also a good idea to visit a few schools before you make your decision. Most of the top schools operate waiting lists and you may not be able to get your child into your first choice. You may also have to pay a fee to be registered on the waiting list, which is non-refundable.

After-school activities are common and include things such as gymnastics, swimming, ballet, Arabic classes, horse-riding, rugby, golf, football and tennis. Most are free. The school terms are similar to education systems in the UK and USA, with autumn (mid September to mid December), spring (early January to early April) and summer (mid April to early July) terms.

In most cases you will need the following documents in order to enrol your child:

- Application form
- Copies of student and parents' passports – both information page and residence visa stamp
- Passport photographs (usually eight)
- Copies of student's birth certificate
- School records for the past two years
- Current immunisation records and medical history
- Official transfer certificate from the student's previous school detailing his/her education.

Original transfer certificates must contain the following details:

- Date of enrolment
- Year of placement
- Date the child left the school
- School stamp
- Official signature

The Ministry of Education also requires the following documents for any student enrolling in any school in Dubai:

- Original transfer certificate (to be completed by the current school)
- Most recently issued original report card

If the student was attending a school anywhere other than the UAE, Australia, Canada, Europe or USA, the transfer certificate and the most recently issued original report card must be attested by the Ministry of Education, Ministry of Foreign Affairs and the UAE embassy in that country.

Nurseries & Pre-Schools

Some nurseries accept babies from as young as 3 months, although most prefer to take on children who are at walking age (around 12 months). Fees and timings vary dramatically so it's best to call around and visit a few nurseries to get an idea of what's available. As a general rule of thumb, most nurseries are open for four or five hours in the morning and charge anything from Dhs.3,000 to Dhs.12,000 per year.

The more popular nurseries have long waiting lists so you should enrol your child before it's even born. Some of the bigger primary schools also have nursery sections – if you've got a primary school in mind for your child, it's worth checking to see if they have a nursery, as this may help you secure a place a few years down the line.

There are a number of factors to consider when you are looking for a nursery and it is always a good idea to take your time to visit a number of schools.

Knowledge Village ◀
Knowledge Village (www.kv.ae) is a key part of Dubai's commitment to improving educational services and attracting more international students to the country, as well as providing opportunities for local students to study here rather than abroad (see p.218).

Try to drop in during the day so that you can have a look at the facilities while there are children in school. Many of the nurseries in Dubai operate morning hours which may rule them out if you are working. However many also run late classes for an extra fee, while a number of them have early-bird drop-offs as well as running term break classes and summer school. Another factor worth thinking about when selecting your child's nursery is whether or not the school provides meals – having to make a packed lunch every morning when you're trying to get ready for work may not be suitable for you.

> **Power To The People**
>
> Power Tutoring supports school-age students by providing specialised private tutoring after normal lesson hours. The organisation offers a variety of subjects and curriculums, including maths and English, and has focused exam and revision timetables. It also offers small group sessions or one-to-one study. Power Tutoring is located in Knowledge Village. For more information on what's on offer, call 04 364 3080 or visit www.powertutoring.com .

Al Manara St, Rd 8
Umm Suqeim
Map 6 D2

Alphabet Street Nursery
04 348 5991 | *www.alphabetstreetnursery.com*
Alphabet Street employs a mix of the Montessori teaching method and the Early Years & Foundation Stage Programme (UK), to develop each child's communication, control, and coordination. It offers flexible early morning drop off, with the possibility of a 07:30 start, and also provides holiday care during the holidays. Late class available until 17:30. Age range: 14 months to 5 years

Nr Choithram
Al Wasl Rd
Umm Suqeim
Map 6 C2

Baby Land Nursery
04 348 6874 | *www.babylandnursery.com*
Baby Land uses Montessori methods to encourage learning through play and exploration. Children participate in a series of practical activities especially designed to improve independence, concentration, hand-eye coordination, fine motor skills, patience and judgement. Baby Land offers late classes until 16:00 and a summer school. Age range: 12 months to 4.5 years

28-30 Umm
Al Sheif Rd
Jumeira
Map 6 F2

The Blossom Nursery
055 687 7379
With opening scheduled for 2009, The Blossom Nursery will focus on all-round development of children through varied methods of learning. Based on the International Early Years Curriculum, structured play programmes are set to include dance, drama, music, water play, and foreign languages. A 'smartbook' record will keep parents informed of their child's development, and there's a high priority placed on parent-staff interaction.

Villa 20a, St 33
Al Mankool
Bur Dubai
Map 8 D4

British Orchard Nursery
04 398 3536 | *www.britishorchardnursery.com*
This nursery follows the British national curriculum, and the guidelines of OFSTED, the schools regulator in the UK. Timings are from 08:00 to 12:30 and there are two out-of-school daycare clubs, Little Apples and Breakfast Club, which run from 07:30 to 17:00. Parents can also log on to a secure website and see what their children are up to through the in-class CCTV. There's another branch in Jumeira (04 395 3570).

Green Community
Dubai Investment Park
Map 2 A2

The Children's Garden ▶ p.213
04 885 3484 | *www.childrensgarden.ae*
Offering early years education to pre-schoolers from 2 to 5 years, Children's Garden features an innovative curriculum which focuses on the attainment of knowledge through creativity. Languages form an integral part of this and children will be taught in at least two languages, becoming fluent in both after three years. A Taaleem school, The Children's Garden is located in the Green Community, in custom-built premises.

Off Al Wasl Rd
Umm Suqeim
Map 6 B3

Emirates British Nursery
04 348 9996 | *www.ebninfo.ae*
Emirates British Nursery regards playtime as an important factor in a child's early development. Both locations (the other is in Mirdif, 04 288 9222) are spacious and well planned, with multilingual staff and an in-house nurse. A summer school (a lifesaver for working mums) is available during July and August. Late class available until 15:00. Age range: 11 months to 4 years.

Nr Jumeira
Post Office
Jumeira
Map 7 D2

Jumeirah International Nursery School
04 349 9065 | *www.jinschools.com*
One of the oldest nurseries in Dubai, Jumeirah International Nursery follows the standards set by UK Ofsted, and individual care and attention is given in a safe and balanced environment. Classes run from 08:00 to 12:30. Another branch off the Al Wasl Road near Jumeirah Primary School offers early drop-offs at 07:30 and late classes until 17:00 (04 394 5567). Age range: 18 months to 4.5 years.

Off Beach Rd
Umm Suqeim
Map 6 F2

Kids Cottage Nursery School ▶ p.207
04 394 2145 | *www.kids-cottage.com*
This cheerful nursery with good facilities offers an activities-based curriculum for children over the age of 12 months. Parents can check up on their kids via a webcam (access is password protected). Early class is available from 07:30. Age range: 12 months to 4 years.

Off Beach Rd
Umm Suqeim
Map 6 F1

Kids' Island Nursery
04 394 2578 | *www.kidsislandnursery.com*
Kids' Island aims to create a relaxed and caring atmosphere, in which children follow the British curriculum. The nursery is open all year round, thanks to the summer school. There are large, outdoor shaded play areas, an activity room and playroom. Late class available until 13:30. Age range is 13 months to 3 years. Another branch in Jumeira 3 called Cocoon Nursery (04 394 9394) is aimed at children between 3 and 4 years.

Burj Bungalow 24
St 17
Umm Suqeim
Map 6 B2

The Knightsbridge Nursery School
04 348 1666 | *www.theivychild.com*
The Knightsbridge Nursery School was founded in 2006. Located near Jumeirah Beach Hotel, it takes children from 4 months to 4.5 years old. Classes are based on the British curriculum and run for 50 weeks of the year. Opening hours of 07:30 to 18:00 make it convenient for working parents to drop off and pick up.

Nr Post Office
Al Wasl
Map 7 C2

Ladybird Nursery
04 344 1011 | *www.ladybirdnursery.ae*
Ladybird strikes an interesting balance between a traditional nursery and a Montessori school, by providing the usual bright and cheerful environment, toys, dressing up clothes and soft play. Late class available until 13:30. Age range: 18 months to 4.5 years.

KIDS COTTAGE NURSERY

DUBAI

Where
"Good Beginnings Never End."

* Warm, caring & friendly environment

* Experienced, qualified & dedicated teachers

* British Foundation Curriculum

* Spacious play areas & bike path

* Bright & well equipped classrooms

Kids Cottage Nursery
04-3942145
www.kids-cottage.com

Little Land Montessori

Beach Rd
Umm Suqeim
Map 6 D1

04 394 4471 | www.littleland-montessori.com
Jointly owned by a neonatal specialist and a qualified Montessori teacher, this professional team has created a relaxing environment. The six classes are split according to age. A late class is available until 14:00. Age range: 15 months to 4 years.

Little Woods Nursery

Villa 82
St 4C
Al Safa
Map 6 E2

04 394 6155 | www.littlewoodsnursery.com
Catering for infants aged 40 days to 4 years, this well-equipped Safa-based nursery has a strong emphasis on child learning through interaction with others and individual development, within a structured framework. Early morning drop-off and late pick-up are offered.

The Palms Nursery

Villa 45
St 25B
Jumeira
Map 7 A2

04 394 7017 | www.palmsnursery.com
Now in its new spacious home on Street 25B, Palms Nursery has six classrooms and seven outdoor play areas. The curriculum is intended to help children acquire the skills and values that enable them to develop socially, physically and emotionally. Late class available until 13:30. Age range: 22 months to 4 years.

Safa Kindergarten Nursery

Nr Shangri-La
off Sheikh Zayed Rd
Al Safa
Map 7 D3

04 344 3878 | www.safanurseries.com
This nursery follows the British curriculum with Montessori principles. Activities include educational play, singing, playhouse activities and water play. The choice of Arabic or French as a second language is introduced to children above the age of 3. Field trips to various locations are arranged throughout the year, and there are annual event days. Late classes run until 14:00. Age range: 2 to 4 years. Other branches: New Safa Nursery (04 29575).

Seashells Nursery

Nr Mall of the Emirates
Al Barsha
Map 6 A4

04 341 3404 | www.seashellsnursery.com
Seashells follows the British curriculum, has two indoor playrooms, an indoor gym, a project room for cooking and fun experiments, and outdoor shaded play areas. The children can join in library, show and tell, recycling activities and field trips. A holiday school programme is available. Age range: 18 months to 4 years.

Small World Nursery

Rd 16
Nr Beach Rd
Jumeira
Map 7 F1

04 349 0770 | www.smallworldnurserydubai.com
Small World offers a balanced educational structure, combining academic learning with physical education. The well-equipped facilities include sensorial areas like a sandy play space, discovery garden, swimming pool and outside play area. There is a late class until 13:30. There is another branch in Umm Suqeim called Child's Play (04 348 0788) which offers a mixture of the UK curriculum and Waldorf-Steiner philosophy, a swimming pool, and a late class until 15:00. Age range: 1 to 4.5 years.

Super Kids Nursery

Off Street 15
Mirdif
Map 15 B3

04 288 1949 | www.superkidsnursery.com
Super Kids is a small but popular nursery that serves the growing Mirdif community. The focus is on providing a warm, cosy 'home away from home' environment. Facilities include a large, shaded outside play area, an activity gym and a music room. Hot lunch and transport are optional extras. Early bird class from 07:30 and late class available until 17:00. Age range: 11 months to 4.5 years.

Education

Dubai Media City ◀
Al Sufouh
Map 5 C2

Tender Love & Care
04 367 1636 | *www.tenderloveandcare.com*
A popular option for people working in Internet and Media cities, this nursery has weekly activity plans and parents are notified of the monthly theme. Facilities include a gymnasium and garden. The nursery has a daily 'drop in' service, and a late class until 17:00. Age range: 18 months to 4.5 years.

Nr Irish Village ◀
Al Garhoud
Map 13 E1

Yellow Brick Road Nursery
04 282 8290 | *www.yellowbrickroad.ws*
This huge and very popular nursery (with a long waiting list) accommodates 180 children in nine classes and a dedicated baby room. Children are taught the British nursery curriculum as well as enjoying outdoor play and swimming in the paddling pool. A cooked breakfast and lunch is provided. Late class available until 18:00. There is another branch in Jumeira 2 called Emerald City Nursery (04 349 0848). Age range: 4 months to 4.5 years.

Primary & Secondary Schools

Primary school ages are from 4.5 years to 11 years, and secondary is from 11 years to 18 years. In addition to the documents listed on p.203, your child may also be required to take a short entrance exam and there may even be a physical examination and a family interview. Translated school certificates must have the student's name spelled exactly as it is found on the student's school record and passport. Most national curriculum syllabuses can be found in Dubai schools, covering GCSEs, A-levels, French and International Baccalaureate and CNEC as well as the American and Indian equivalent. Standards of teaching are usually high and schools have excellent facilities with extracurricular activities offered. The international schools will often employ teachers who have been trained in, and have teaching experience from, the country relevant to the curriculum being offered. You should think carefully about what curriculum you want your kids to study. If you're coming from the UK it makes sense to go for a school teaching the British curriculum as the transition should be seamless.

Likewise, if and when you return home (or move to another country) you want your child to be able to slot right back into the schooling system. The Ministry of Education regularly inspects schools to ensure rules and regulations are being upheld, and most schools insist on a school uniform.

Most schools are open from 08:00 to 13:00 or 15:00, from Sunday to Thursday. Ramadan hours are shorter – usually starting an hour or so later and finishing an hour earlier.

Primary school fees can range from Dhs.10,000 to Dhs.30,000 per year, while secondary school fees can range from Dhs.15,000 to Dhs.55,000 per year. Other costs may include a deposit or registration, medical fees, excursion fees, and arts and activity fees.

11A St ◀
Mizhar 1
Mirdif
Map 15 D2

Al-Mizhar American Academy for Girls ▶ p.213
04 288 7250 | *www.aag.ae*
American curriculum for girls from kindergarten to Year 12. Based in Mizhar (near Mirdif), the school is equipped with a range of facilities including swimming, basketball, football, volleyball, drama and a band. A swimming pool, gymnasium, well-resourced library, computer labs, interactive whiteboards, art studios, music studios, science labs, and a mini auditorium are all present. The girls-only policy is intended to encourage potential and avoid gender stereotypes found in co-ed schools. Age range: primary & secondary. Curriculum: American

American School Of Dubai

Building 30
Street 53B
Al Wasl
Map 7 E1

04 344 0824 | www.asdubai.org

The American School of Dubai is an independent, non-profit school offering top-quality education according to the American curriculum. The huge campus includes around 70 classrooms as well as two separate buildings for kindergartens. Other facilities include a media centre, swimming pool, computer labs, art rooms and two gymnasiums. Students partake in a range of sports including athletics, tennis, hockey, basketball and football, as well as activities like drama, sailing, scouts, dance and music. The school also partners with external companies to provide a range of recreational activites such as skiing, horse-riding, surfing and sailing. Age range: primary and secondary. Curriculum: American.

Australian International School

Opp Shj Univeristy
Malihard Rd
Sharjah
Map 2 C2

06 558 9967 | www.ais.ae

This school is run in partnership with the State of Queensland. Facilities have been customised to complement the Australian curriculum, and include large activity rooms, teaching areas for art and music, computer labs, a comprehensive library, conference rooms, a swimming pool and a multi-purpose hall and gym area. School clubs are encouraged in activities such as reading, chess, drama, music, arts and sports, and annual overseas trips are organised to broaden pupils' life experiences and social skills. Age Range: primary. Curriculum: Australian.

Cambridge International School

Opp mosque
5th Rd
Al Garhoud
Map 13 E2

04 282 4646 | www.gemscis-garhoud.com

With an attractive campus set in the popular suburb of Garhoud, Cambridge is equipped with excellent recreational facilities including a kindergarten playground, a swimming pool, tennis and volleyball courts, science and computer labs, music and art studios, a library and a canteen. The school currently has around 700 pupils, and a diverse range of professional staff. It follows the National Curriculum of England meticulously and to an extremely high standard, providing its students with an education that is recognised around the world. Age range: primary and secondary with foundation year. Curriculum: British.

Deira International School

Festival Centre
Dubai Festival City
Map 13 D2

04 232 5552 | www.disdubai.ae

DIS is one of the newer schools in Dubai, and one of two situated within the Dubai Festival City complex. It offers GCSE/IGCSE, A-levels and the British Baccalaureate programme and has the capacity for around 600 students. Facilities within the school include a gymnasium, a full-size track and football field, music rooms, computer and science labs, libraries, a large auditorium and a swimming pool. Although English is the language of instruction the school also offers strong Arabic and Islamic study programmes. Age range: primary with foundation year. Curriculum: British.

Dubai American Academy

Interchange 4
Sheikh Zayed Rd
Al Barsha
Map 6 A4

04 347 9222 | www.gemsaa-dubai.com

Dubai American Academy provides high quality education to students from more than 60 countries. The school offers the International Baccalaureate Diploma and an enriched American curriculum. In terms of facilities, there is a cafeteria, computer and science labs, gymnasium, library, swimming pool, athletics track and an auditorium. There's also an after-school programme from 14:45 to 15:45. Age range: primary and secondary school. Curriculum: American.

Education

Springs 3 ◀
Emirates Hills
Map 5 A4

Dubai British School ▶ p.213

04 361 9361 | *www.dubaibritishschool.ae*

Dubai British School is situated in several acres of land in the grounds of Emirates Hills. The curriculum is based on the British curriculum. The school strongly encourages pupils to participate in the many extra-curricular activities. Facilities at the school include a swimming pool, gymnasium and library. Age range: primary and secondary with foundation year. Curriculum: British.

Nr Internet City ◀
Al Sufouh
Map 5 E2

Dubai College

04 399 9111 | *www.dubaicollege.org*

Students at Dubai College are encouraged to develop their intellectual, physical, creative and social skills, and therefore the school boasts a diverse range of facilities. Sporting activities include athletics, rugby, football (soccer), netball, tennis and swimming, in addition to non-sporting activities such as music, public speaking and drama. There are currently just over 700 pupils at the school. Age range: secondary. Curriculum: British.

Nr St Mary's Church ◀
Oud Metha
Map 10 F3

Dubai English Speaking School

04 337 1457 | *www.dessdxb.com*

DESS first opened in a single room of a villa in 1963, and has since grown into a highly respected school with top-class facilities and around 700 pupils. The curriculum is based on the British curriculum and prepares students for secondary education either here or in the UK. Facilities and activities include computers, music, swimming, dance, a library and various sports. Age range: primary. Curriculum: British.

Emirates Hills ◀
Map 5 C4

Dubai International Academy

04 368 4111 | *www.diadubai.com*

Dubai International Academy follows an international curriculum taught in English. The International Baccalaureate programme consists of the primary years programme (PYP), middle years programme (MYP) and the diploma programme (DP). The school has more than 80 classrooms, as well as music, art, dance and drama rooms, science and computer labs, libraries, swimming pools, playing fields, basketball and tennis courts, and a cafeteria. Age range: primary. Curriculum: British (International Baccalaureate).

Meadows ◀
Emirates Hills
Map 5 A3

Emirates International School

04 362 9009 | *www.eischools.ae*

With campuses in both the Meadows and Umm Suqeim, Emirates International School aims to foster independent thinking with a balanced approach to education and an international curriculum. Facilities include fully equipped classrooms, computer and science labs, library, theatre and canteen. Extra curricular activities include drama, music, swimming and basketball. Age range: primary and secondary. Curriculum: International.

Off Shk Zayed Rd ◀
Al Safa
Map 6 F3

The English College

04 394 3465 | *www.englishcollege.ac.ae*

The English College has a long tradition of academic and sporting excellence. A varied extra-curricular programme offers activities such as chess, rugby, tennis, trampolining, and even rock climbing. Students are encouraged to explore their unique talents. The multicultural environment at the school promotes tolerance and understanding. Age range: primary and secondary. Curriculum: British.

Dubai
Investment Park
Jebel Ali
Map 2 A4

Greenfield Community School ▶ p.213

04 885 6600 | www.gcschool.ae

Located in Dubai Investments Park just beyond the Green Community, Greenfield Community School currently teaches the International Baccalaureate's Primary Years Programme (PYP), and Middle Years Programme (MYP), but will be extending to the Diploma Programme (DP) with the first graduating students anticipated in 2011. Class sizes are no greater than 24 pupils and student amenities include a well-stocked library, Wi-Fi connectivity throughout, and a swimming pool and gymnasium. An extensive after-school programme is available covering sport, music, ballet, and arts and crafts.

Nr Park N Shop
Al Wasl
Map 7 B2

Horizon English School

04 342 2891 | www.horizonschooldubai.com

Horizon opened in 1992 with just 15 pupils, and has expanded to a large complex complete with top-class facilities and over 300 children. Students are educated according to the British curriculum, and can choose from afternoon activities such as football, netball, rounders, karate, swimming, dancing, cooking and drama. Age range: primary. Curriculum: British. Other branches: Safa Horizon School (04 394 7879).

Btn Jct 4 & 5
Umm Suqeim
Map 5 E2

International School of Choueifat

04 399 9444 | www.iscdxb-sabis.net

The school system here is a unique method of education that allows students to learn more in a shorter time and with less effort. New students take placement tests to check whether they have attained certain standards in English and mathematics. Age group: primary and secondary with foundation year. Curriculum: British and American.

Jebel Ali
Map 4 C3

Jebel Ali Primary School

04 884 6485 | www.jebelalischool.com

This friendly primary school first opened its doors in 1977 and today educates close to 500 pupils in 22 classes. It occupies two sites, one for infants and one for juniors. Both have access to swimming pools and grassed areas. After-school activities include football, netball, golf, gymnastics, squash, drama, cooking, music and computers. Age range: primary. Curriculum: British.

Off Al Wasl Rd
Al Safa
Map 7 A2

Jumeirah College

04 395 5524 | www.gemsjc.com

Jumeirah College is registered with the DFES (Department for Education & Skills) in London. The school offers all the regular sporting and cultural extra curricular activities, as well as some more unconventional pursuits such as trampolining, ballet, waterskiing, horse riding, rock climbing, and karate. There are facilities for tennis, netball, swimming and there is a small, grassed playing field. The campus also has studios for art and ceramics, music rooms and drama facilities. Age range: secondary. Curriculum: British.

Nr Shk Zayed Rd
Al Safa
Map 7 A2

Jumeirah English Speaking School (JESS)

04 394 5515 | www.jess.sch.ae

At JESS there are four classes in each year group from Foundation I to Year 6. The campus is well equipped, with a gymnasium, music rooms, two playing areas, a football pitch and a swimming pool. Preference will be given to British passport holders, those holding debentures, and those with siblings higher up the school. Other branch: Arabian Ranches (04 394 5515). Age range: primary with foundation. Curriculum: British.

táaleem
inspiring young minds

Inspiring tomorrow's visionaries, today.

Taaleem inspires young minds to discover their
talents and pursue their passions.

The Taaleem family of schools:

Al-Mizhar, American Academy for Girls *Mirdif, Dubai*
American Curriculum (Girls only)
T + 971 (4) 288 7250 www.aag.ae

The Children's Garden *Green Community, Dubai*
Unique Tailor Made Multilingual Program
T + 971 (4) 885 3484 www.childrensgarden.ae

Dubai British School *The Springs, Dubai*
British National Curriculum
T + 971 (4) 361 9361 www.dubaibritishschool.ae

Greenfield Community School *Dubai Investments Park, Dubai*
IB Candidate School
T + 971 (4) 885 6600 www.gcschool.ae

My Nursery *Jumeirah, Dubai*
Bilingual Classical Arabic and English Curriculum
T + 971 (4) 344 1120 www.mynursery.ae

Raha International School *Al Raha Gardens, Abu Dhabi*
IB Candidate School
T + 971 (2) 556 1567 www.ris.ae

Uptown High School *Muhaisnah, Dubai*
IB Candidate School
T + 971 (4) 264 1818 www.uptownhigh.ae

Uptown School *Mirdif, Dubai*
IB World School
T + 971 (4) 288 6270 www.uptownprimary.ae

We encourage the apple of your eye to become
a visionary of tomorrow.

For more information visit www.taaleem.ae

The Visionary

Nr Park n Shop
Jumeira Rd
Al Safa
Map 7 A2

Jumeirah Primary School

04 394 3500 | *www.jumeirahprimaryschool.com*

Jumeirah Primary School is one of the most well-known primaries in Dubai, and provides a high quality education to children from Foundation Stage 1 to Year 6. Campus facilities include a well-stocked library, an active art department, a specialist music department, a discovery centre, modern computer facilities, gymnasium, swimming pool, playing fields and a seperate play area for the foundation stage. Age range: Primary with Foundation. Curriculum: British.

Street 17
Off Al Wasl Rd
Umm Suqeim
Map 6 B2

Kings' Dubai

04 348 3939 | *www.kingsdubai.com*

Kings' Dubai opened in 2004 and has around 300 pupils. The facilities include a purpose-built auditorium, gymnasium, swimming pool, games court and sports field. The school teaches the British National Curriculum, through an innovative and creative approach with specialist teachers of ICT, PE, music, French and Arabic. Age range: primary school with foundation. Curriculum: British.

Umm Suqeim
Map 6 B2

Raffles International School ▶ p.215

04 427 1200 | *www.rafflesis.com*

Raffles International School meets the educational needs of 1,500 students from over 70 different countries, offering studies from nursery and kindergarten through to Grade 9. The international school has two main campuses in Umm Suqeim, and six nurseries, in Arabian Ranches, Emirates Hills, The Lakes, The Springs and Old Town. All campuses have facilities to support Raffles' Centres of Excellence in science, arts and sports. The Middle School offers the IGCSE curriculum, while the High School offers British A-levels and American High School Diploma. Age range: 3 to 16. Curriculum: British/International.

The Greens
Emirates Hills
Map 5 D3

Regent International School

04 360 8830 | *www.risdubai.com*

The school's new complex at The Greens includes state-of-the-art technology, multimedia zones, library, computer, science and language labs. The sporting facilities range from a football pitch, playing fields and gymnasium to a swimming pool. The school also has an auditorium for the performing arts. Age range: primary and secondary with foundation year. Curriculum: British.

Off Airport Rd
Mirdif
Map 15 D3

Royal Dubai School

04 288 6499 | *www.royaldubaischool.com*

Royal Dubai School is a brand new school situated on six acres of land in Mirdif. It follows the British curriculum with an internationally recruited teaching team. School facilities are wide ranging and include music and drama studios, art and science rooms, ICT suites and a library. A large, multi-purpose sports hall has been built along with a sports field, a 25m swimming pool and covered play areas. Age range: primary with foundation year. Curriculum: British.

Al Qusais
Map 14 D1

The Sheffield Private School

04 267 8444 | *www.sheffieldprivateschool.com*

This is a GEMS managed school that follows the British curriculum. The school prides itself on a happy and supportive environment, especially among the youngest children, who have a separate play area up to the end of the second year. Facilities include music and art studios, an ICT lab, covered play areas, plus pools for swimming and wading. The school offers a wide variety of extra-curricular activities and school trips. Age range: primary with foundation year (eventually up to year 13). Curriculum: British.

Sowing the seeds of success, for life.

RAFFLES
INTERNATIONAL
SCHOOL

Raffles International School now open for registration.

Umm Suqeim Campuses – Kindergarten through Grade 8

The world of tomorrow will be a diverse and challenging place. Give your child the finest holistic education for personal and professional success at Raffles International School.

• State-of-the-art facilities • IGCSE curriculum • Teachers and instructors of the highest calibre
• Centres of excellence for science, the arts, and sports including FC Barcelona Soccer Academy
• Effective student to teacher ratio • A wide choice of second languages including French, German and Mandarin • Full Arabic and Islamic programme

Emaar Education offers world-class learning through Raffles International School – a leading international educator with a full spectrum of institutions from nursery to university.

Register your child today

Call 800 RAFFLES (800 723 3537) or +971 4 4271200.
Sunday to Thursday from 8 am to 4 pm

www.rafflesis.com

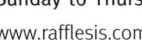

EMAAR
Education

Villa19
Street 43 A
Al Safa
Map 6 F2

St Andrews International School ▶ p.217

04 394 5907 | *www.british-ild.com*

St Andrews follows the International Primary Curriculum and a neuro-developmental programme, based on the belief that children learn better when they have personal coaching to help develop the main senses. Its staff includes occupational, play, speech and educational therapists as well as teachers. Age range: primary. Curriculum: international.

Opp Iranian Club
Oud Metha
Map 10 F3

St Mary's Catholic High School

04 337 0252 | *www.stmarysdubai.com*

Founded in 1968, St Mary's retains the discipline of convent education but welcomes the diversity of all religions at the school. In addition to various sports activities, other activities include drama, music, debating, cookery and chess. Age range: primary & secondary. Curriculum: British.

Nr Airport Terml 3
Al Twar
Map 14 B2

Star International School

04 263 8999 | *www.isbi.com*

Located near the new airport terminal building, Star International School follows the British curriculum, supplemented by the international primary curriculum. Day boarding is offered, so you can leave your child at the school under full supervision until 16:30. Age range: primary & secondary. Curriculum: British.

Festival City
Map 13 D2

Universal American School Dubai

04 232 5222 | *www.uasdubai.ae*

UASD follows a full American curriculum culminating with the American high school diploma. Arabic language classes are also included. The campus has a gymnasium, Olympic size track and football field, music rooms, art rooms, computer and science labs, libraries, a large auditorium and a swimming pool. Age range: primary & secondary. Curriculum: American.

Off Amman Street
Mirdif
Map 14 D3

Uptown High School ▶ p.213

04 264 1818 | *www.uptownhigh.ae*

Uptown High, a Taaleem school, opened in 2008. It aims to deliver an outstanding quality of teaching following the International Baccalaureate's Middle Years Programme (MYP) and Diploma Programme (DP), for students between 11 and 19 years of age. A variety of extra-curricular activities and overseas trips are organised for students. Age range: Middle and Secondary. Curriculum: International Baccalaureate.

Cnr Algeria Rd
& Rd 15
Mirdif
Map 15 B3

Uptown Primary School ▶ p.213

04 288 6270 | *www.uptownprimary.ae*

Uptown School, formerly Uptown Mirdiff, offers the International Baccalaureate Primary Years Program (PYP) and Middle Year Programme (MYP). The main language of instruction is English. The school also houses an early learning centre developed specially for the under 6s. Facilities include a swimming pool, gymnasium, library, computer labs, art studios, music rooms, safe play areas and science labs. Uptown School also caters for students with special needs and is staffed by qualified specialists. Age range: primary and middle years. Curriculum: International Baccalaureate.

Opp Mall of
the Emirates
Al Sufouh
Map 5 F2

Wellington International School

04 348 4999 | *www.wellingtoninternationalschool.com*

Wellington International School is a brand new GEMS-managed school with Prince Michael of Kent as its patron. Unique features in the school include an observatory,

British Institute
for
Learning Development
in association with the
St Andrews International School

The Creative Approach to Schooling

The British Institute's Sensational Learning Programme is based on the belief that children's learning capabilities can improve where children receive personal coaching to develop the sensory systems of the mind and body. Our research shows that intelligence and cognitive performance can significantly increase even within one year.

St Andrews College International, the parent company of the British Institute, is a registered international school with FES - the management company for the Royal Dutch Shell Schools - and uses the IPC - UK curriculum.

The IPC allows us to motivate children toward achieving academic skills and their personal goals. It also allows us to develop their 'talents' so the children can increase their ability for intellectual reasoning.

43a Street, Jumeriah 3
Dubai   PO Box 65725
Tel: 04-394 5907
Email: reception@british-ild.com

www.british-ild.com   **www.sta-college.com**

TV station, creative garden and ICT, art and music suites. Other facilities include a large sports hall, gymnasium, health and fitness studio, 25m indoor swimming pool, 300m running track, basketball and tennis courts and two climbing walls. Dance and drama are encouraged through a performing arts programme. Age range: primary & secondary. Curriculum: British.

Al Qusais
Map 12 C4

The Westminster School

04 298 8333 | *www.gemsws-ghusais.com*

The Westminster school is another GEMS managed school that takes children from key stage 1 (3 years) up to year 12 (16 years). The school has 120 classrooms and a multi-purpose auditorium. Laboratories for biology, chemistry and physics are provided for the more senior pupils along with three computer labs and three libraries. The school offers athletics, basketball, football, hockey, volleyball, gymnastics and table tennis. Children are educated to the highest standards, following the British curriculum. Age range: primary and secondary with foundation year. Curriculum: British.

The Gardens
Jebel Ali
Map 4 D3

The Winchester School

04 882 0444 | *www.thewinchesterschool.com*

The Winchester School started in 2003 and has students from many different countries. Facilities include a multi-purpose auditorium, a sports field, music, art and craft rooms, science and computer labs, a library and audiovisual rooms. For the younger children there's an air-conditioned play area and covered outside area. There are numerous extra-curricular activities including music, dance, drama, outdoor sports and indoor games. Age range: primary with foundation year. Curriculum: British.

University & Higher Education

Upon leaving school, children of expat families have traditionally returned to their home country to continue with higher education, but Dubai does have a growing number of internationally recognised universities and colleges offering degree and diploma courses in the arts, sciences, business and management, and engineering and technology. There are also a number of opportunities for post-graduate courses. Many institutions are based at Knowledge Village near Media and Internet Cities – for more info visit www.kv.ae. Dubai Academic City, on the outskirts of Dubai, will house a number of tertiary institutions and is due for completion by 2012.

Professional Training

A number of business schools have also opened recently, offering MBAs and other professional qualification for those looking to advance their careers. A number of UK institutions have shown enthusiasm in tapping in to this potentially lucrative market. The London Business School (www.london.edu/dubai-london) is based in DIFC, as is Cass (www.cass.city.ac.uk/mba/dubai, formerly known as City University Business School). The latter specialises in energy and Islamic finance. Warwick Business School (www.wbs.ac.uk) has been offering MBAs in Dubai since 2003.

Opp Dubai
Festival City
Al Garhoud
Map 13 E1

The American College Of Dubai

04 282 9992 | *www.centamed.com*

The American College of Dubai offers courses that will provide students with university-level credits allowing them to transfer to institutions in the US, UK, UAE, Canada, Europe, India, or elsewhere around the world. Additionally, associate degrees in the liberal arts, business, and information technology are also available.

FIRST
IMPRESSIONS?
120 fascinating portraits depicting the culture and unique infrastructure that contributes to Dubai's rich landscape.
IMPRESSIONSDUBAI
Also available for Abu Dhabi, Bahrain, Oman and Qatar.
EXPLORER
www.liveworkexplore.com

American University In Dubai

Sheikh Zayed Rd
Al Sufouh
Map 5 C2

04 399 9000 | *www.aud.edu*
With its impressive main building that is something of a landmark along Sheikh Zayed Road, the American University in Dubai is a well-established university with over 2,000 students of various nationalities. Courses offered include business, engineering, information technology, visual communication, interior design and liberal arts.

American University Of Sharjah

Sharjah Intl Airport St
Sharjah
Map 2 C2

06 515 5555 | *www.aus.edu*
The American University of Sharjah offers a wide range of undergraduate programmes in areas such as language, literature, communications, business, finance, and various engineering degrees. Postgraduate courses are also offered from the schools of Arts and Sciences, Architecture and Design, Business and Management, and Engineering.

British University In Dubai

Dubai Knowledge Village
Al Sufouh
Map 5 D2

04 391 3626 | *www.buid.ac.ae*
The British University In Dubai, established in 2004, is the region's first postgraduate research based university. BUID offers postgraduate degrees including MSC environmental design of buildings, MSC information technology and PHD programmes.

Esmod French Fashion University

Block 4
Academic City
Map 2 C3

04 429 1228 | *www.french-fashion-university.com*
The French Fashion University is the only University in the Middle-East fully dedicated to fashion. Accredited by the French Ministry of Education they carry three year BA courses, fashion workshops of three and six months, trend forecasting masterclasses, merchandising training sessions for retailers and individuals, and MBA in fashion management.

Heriot-Watt University Dubai

Academic City
Map 2 C3

04 361 6999 | *www.hw.ac.uk./dubai*
One of the UK's oldest universities, Heriot-Watt has now opened a campus at Academic City in Dubai (with an office at Knowledge Village). The university offers undergraduate and postgraduate courses in business, management, finance, accounting, and IT.

Manipal Academy Of Higher Education

Dubai Knowledge Village
Al Sufouh
Map 5 D2

04 429 1214 | *www.mahedubai.com*
Manipal Academy of Higher Education offers certificate programmes, bachelors and masters degree programmes in a range of subjects including information systems, media and communications, and fashion and interior design.

Middlesex University

Dubai Knowledge Village
Al Sufouh
Map 5 D2

04 367 8100 | *www.mdx.ac*
The UK's Middlesex University recently opened a campus at Knowledge Village. Students have the option of studying for single or joint honours degrees, in subjects including accountancy, business studies, tourism, human resource management, marketing and computing science.

Raffles Campus ▶ p.221

Street 30A
Umm Suqeim
Map 6 D2

04 427 1427 | *www.emaareducation.ae*
Raffles Campus runs a hospitality programme in collaboration with Australia's Box Hill Institute. Courses are offered on a full and part-time basis. Focus is on vocational qualifications, including a BTEC in hospitality, Certificate IV Hospitality (Supervision),

and Advanced Diploma of Hospitality Management. International work attachment is a feature of the latter two courses. The specialist campus has a training centre which includes front office, housekeeping, and food and beverage facilities for hands-on training.

Dubai
Knowledge Village
Al Sufouh
Map 5 D2

SAE Institute
04 361 6173 | www.sae-dubai.com
This respected Australian film, which has branches throughout the world, has an impressive multimedia training institute. SAE offers courses specialising in audio engineering, digital animation and filmmaking.

Dubai
Knowledge Village
Al Sufouh
Map 5 D2

University Of Wollongong (UOWD) ▶ p.223
04 367 2400 | www.uowdubai.ac.ae
The University of Wollongong offers a number of undergraduate and postgraduate programmes in business and IT, in addition to certificates and awards in accounting, banking and management. This Australian university used to be situated along Beach Road, but moved to Knowledge Village in 2005.

Special Needs Education
If your child has physical or learning difficulties, there are several organisations that can help. Some mainstream schools will try to accommodate children suffering from dyslexia, ADHD and other more manageable challenges but are rarely geared up to take students with other needs. Special needs schools operate without government assistance, and therefore rely on donations, sponsorship, grants and help from volunteer workers. All charge tuition fees.

- The Al Noor Centre For Children With Special Needs (04 394 6088, www.alnooruae. org) provides therapeutic support and comprehensive training to special needs children of all ages. The centre also equips its 220 students with work related skills.
- The Dubai Centre For Special Needs (04 344 0966, www.dcsneeds.ae) currently has 130 students, all of which have an individual programme, including physiotherapy, speech therapy and occupational therapy. A pre-vocational programme is offered for older students, which includes arranging work placements.
- Rashid Paediatric Therapy Centre (04 340 0005, www.rashidc.ae) includes physical, occupational and speech therapy. In the afternoons, therapists see children on an outpatient basis, and work on early intervention and assisting school children with motor, learning, speech and communication difficulties.
- There is a therapeutic horse riding programme for children with special needs – Riding For Tthe Disabled (www.rdad.ae). The team offers lessons to children from the various special needs schools around Dubai, providing much-needed physical and mental stimulation. Lessons take place at the Desert Palms Polo Club, and include a variety of gentle exercises and short outrides.

A Whole Lot Of Knowledge
Knowledge Village prides itself on creating an environment conducive to education, the business of education and networking. The operating rules and regulations are relatively straightforward and they simplify the application process for a one-year student's resident visa, too. Some of the tertiary institutions to be found here (in addition to those mentioned above) are: European University College Brussels, Institute of Management Technology, Islamic Azad University, Mahatma Ghandi University, UAE University, Royal College of Surgeons and the University of New Brunswick in Dubai. Find out more on www.kv.ae.

We've been here for 15 years and have over 2,735 graduates to prove it!

Choose wisely, choose well, choose UOWD

Visit **www.uowdubai.ac.ae**,
call **04 367-2400**,

or visit us at Block 15, Dubai Knowledge Village

UOWD
University of Wollongong in Dubai

An Academic Partner of
DIAC
DUBAI
INTERNATIONAL
ACADEMIC CITY
A member of
TECOM INVESTMENTS

Your Australian University in Dubai

- Dubai Autism Centre provides a support network for parents and teacher training for teaching autistic children (04 398 6862, www.dubaiautismcenter.ae).
- The Dyslexia Support Group is run by volunteer mums, and offers advice and support to families. Call 04 344 6657 or 04 344 0738 for more information.
- Senses is a Dubai-based residential and daycare centre for people with special needs, speak to Kerry on 04 394 8765 for more details.

Learning Arabic
Other options **Language Schools** p.366

English is so widely used in Dubai that you can get by without having to learn a single word of Arabic. However, some say that to enrich the cultural experience of your time in this part of the world, knowing some basic Arabic is helpful. Many expat children have Arabic lessons at school, so it can be useful to know a bit yourself. The language schools listed in the table all offer classes in Arabic, and most teach beginner, intermediate and advanced classes. Arabic classes are available both during the day and in the evenings, so you should be able to find one at a convenient time.

Learning Arabic		
Arabic Language Centre	04 308 6036	na
Berlitz	04 344 0034	www.berlitz.ae
Dar El Ilm School Of Languages	04 331 0221	na
El Ewla Language Academy	04 391 1640	na
Polyglot Language Institute	04 222 3429	www.polyglot.ae
Sheikh Mohammed Centre for Cultural Understanding	04 353 6666	www.cultures.ae
University of Wollongong (UOWD) ▶ p.223	04 367 2400	www.uowdubai.ac.ae

Modern schooling

Transportation

Other options **Getting Around** p.53, **Car** p.58

Options for public transport are somewhat limited, and most Dubai expats find that owning a car is essential. There's a comprehensive bus network operated by Dubai Municipality, but it gets busy and you'll often find yourself having to wait a while for a bus to come along that isn't too overloaded with people for you to get on board. The Municipality is moving fast towards a better public transportation system with Metro plans still moving forward and more buses on the roads to take care of the issue of overcrowding. Air-conditioned bus shelters, which feature high on the agenda, have already begun to be introduced. For information on Dubai's bus services, see p.57 or call 800 9090. Construction work on the Dubai Metro is well underway. This is a light rail network that should hopefully ease traffic congestion when it is finished (estimated completion date is 2009). For more information on the Metro project, see p.62.

Cash Only

In 2007, petrol stations adopted a 'cash only' policy whereas before you could pay for your petrol by debit and credit card. So make sure you have cash to hand before you fill up, and don't rely on there being an ATM at all petrol stations.

Taxi

Dubai has a fleet of around 5,000 licensed taxis, so it's pretty easy to flag one down during off-peak hours. You can also order one from Dubai Transport (www.dubaitransport.gov.ae) to come and pick you up where you are. This service used to work pretty well but has become unreliable due to a shortage of cabs. There is a satellite tracking system installed in all the cabs and an automated phone system – to order a taxi call 04 208 0808 and follow the instructions. The first time you call you'll be put through to an operator who will take down the directions to your house; your details are then stored on a database so the next time you call from your home number, simply press '1' on your phone and the taxi should be dispatched straight away. It's also possible to request a bigger taxi for trips to the airport when you might have lots of luggage, although you should book one of these in advance. The Toyota Camry is the standard car model used for taxis.

If needed, you can hire a Dubai Transport cab for longer periods. This costs about Dhs.500 for 12 hours (within Dubai). So-called 'hotel taxis' will be more expensive cars (and won't look like standard taxis). These tend to charge fixed rates which are more expensive than government taxis (which have meters), so you should always agree a price before you set off. Remember a landmark nearby your destination, and have the phone number of your destination handy in case your driver cannot find the way and needs guidance.

As of December 2008, taxis are exempt from paying Salik charges, so make sure you're not charged the extra Dhs.4 add on that used to be mandatory. For more information on taxis, see p.62.

Driving

The price of petrol has recently gone up several times, but in comparison with other countries it's still pretty cheap. This means that many people drive gas-guzzlers. Car prices are generally lower than in other countries, so you may have the opportunity to drive in style. Car pooling has not really taken off.

On the roads that connect Sharjah to Dubai the sheer volume of traffic results in gridlock nearly every morning and evening.

Most street parking in Dubai is now governed by parking meters. You pay Dhs.1 or Dhs.2 for one hour, depending on how busy the area is. After feeding your coins into the machine, you get a printed ticket that you must display on your dashboard. The price increases dramatically the longer you park in a spot, so you'll pay Dhs.5 for two hours, Dhs.8 for three hours, and Dhs.11 for four hours (the maximum). Parking is free from 13:00 to 16:00 and 21:00 to 08:00 daily and on Fridays and public holidays.

Dubai drivers are notoriously bad. You can expect lots of overtaking on the inside, dramatic lane-switching manoeuvres, sudden stops, and quite surprising levels of aggression. Your first few weeks of driving will be an ordeal, but you will quickly learn to drive defensively. The important thing is not to let the bad driving keep you from getting out and about – the sooner you get behind the wheel, the sooner you'll get used to it. For more information about driving and driving licences, see p.91.

Parking Cards

There are several different ways of purchasing pre-paid parking cards for use in parking meters, which save you money and the hassle of always needing the right change at the many paid parking areas in Dubai. The first way is through the post office where you can get pay-as-you-go cards you display in the car – for Dhs.42.50 you get Dhs.50 worth of parking and for Dhs.80 you get parking to the value of Dhs.100. Alternatively, you can buy a card from Dubai Municipality that can be used for an unlimited amount. Type A parking cards can be used in all parking areas – they cost Dhs.700 for three months, Dhs.1,300 for six months and Dhs.2,500 for a year. Type B parking cards restrict you to off-street parking in designated areas – they cost Dhs.450 for three months, Dhs.800 for six months and Dhs.1,500 for a year.

Salik

In 2007, the Salik road toll system came into effect. There are several gates: one at the Bur Dubai entrance to Garhoud Bridge, another on the Sheikh Zayed Road after Mall of the Emirates, one at Safa Park on Sheikh Zayed Road (between interchanges one and two), and another on Maktoum Bridge. The Maktoum Bridge crossing will be free whenever the Floating Bridge is closed (22:00 to 06:00, 22:00 to 09:00 on Fridays). There are no booths, and no need to stop as you drive through. Instead, drivers stick a tag to their windscreen, which is read by radio frequency as they pass through. Drivers initially must buy a 'welcome pack' costing Dhs.100: Dhs.50 for the tag and Dhs.50 for credit. It costs Dhs.4 each time, but if you travel between the Al Barsha toll gate and the Al Safa toll gate during one trip (and in the space of an hour) you will only be charged once. If your Salik card is out of credit you will be fined Dhs.50 for each gate you pass through. The kit can be bought from Emarat, EPPCO, ENOC, and ADNOC petrol stations, Dubai Islamic Bank and Emirates Bank. Salik fees no longer have to be paid by passengers in taxis. For more information about the toll gates, visit the Salik website, www.salik.ae, or call 800 72545 (800 SALIK).

Vehicle Leasing

Many people find that they have no other option (due to visa requirements) than to lease a vehicle, and while it may be easier in terms of repairs, re-registration and servicing, long term leasing can be expensive. Most leasing companies include the following in their rates: registration, maintenance, replacement, 24 hour assistance and insurance. Find out which car hire agent your company uses, as you might qualify for a corporate rate.

Leasing is generally weekly, monthly or yearly. Monthly lease prices range from Dhs.1,500 for a small vehicle such as a Toyota Yaris, Dhs.1,900 for larger cars

Vehicle Leasing Agents

Autolease Rent-a-Car	04 282 6565	www.autolease-uae.com
Avis	04 295 7121	www.avisuaecarhire.com
Budget Rent A Car	04 295 6667	www.budget-uae.com
Diamond Lease	04 343 4330	www.diamondlease.com
EuroStar Rent-a-Car	04 266 1117	www.eurostarrental.com
FAST Rent A Car	02 622 0088	www.fastuae.com
Hertz	04 282 4422	www.hertz-uae.com
National Car Rental ▶ p.227	04 335 5447	www.national-me.com
Thrifty Car Rental	800 4694	www.thriftyuae.com
United Car Rentals	04 285 7777	www.unitedcarrentals.com

What does great service mean to you?

Providing professional, friendly service is our most valuable asset - it's what sets us apart and it's what makes you feel special every time you interact with us.

Whether you need one car or a fleet of vehicles for your company, you can rely on us to take care of all your car rental and leasing requirements across the UAE.

Call us toll free on:
Dubai 800 3031
Abu Dhabi 800 3130

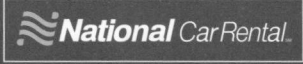

www.national-ae.com

like a Honda Accord, and Dhs.3,500 for a 4WD. As the lease period increases, the price decreases, so if you're considering keeping the car for a long period, it may not work out that much more expensive than buying.

Before you take possession of your leased car, check for any dents or bumps. While many companies will deliver the car to you, you might still have to visit the office to sort out all the paperwork. To hire any vehicle you will need to provide a passport copy, credit card and a valid driving licence (either your Dubai licence, your licence from your home country, or a valid international licence).

If you are just visiting Dubai (and have no Dubai driving licence), you might find that a valid international licence is more readily accepted than the licence from your home country. Many companies offer daily rentals – refer to the table above for the most reputable agents.

> **Tinted Windows**
>
> Currently, the government allows you to avoid the sun somewhat by tinting your vehicle's windows up to 30%. Some areas have facilities where you can get your car windows tinted but don't get carried away – remember to stick to the limit. Random checks take place and fines are handed out to those caught in the dark. Tinting in Sharjah is allowed for a fee of Dhs.100 and Ajman residents may tint for Dhs.200 per annum, but only if they are women.

Company Cars

Some people will be given a company car as part of their package, which will no doubt have been bought or leased by the company and therefore will be returned if you leave. Others are given a lease car by their employer when they first arrive (until they get their residency formalities sorted out and can buy a car). Some employees receive a transportation allowance as part of their salary package.

> **Second Opinion**
>
> *When buying a used car it's well worth having it checked over by a garage or mechanic. EPPCO/ Tasjeel, AAA and Max Garage offer a checking service. Alternatively, speak to the service department at the dealership where the car was originally bought. A thorough inspection will cost about Dhs.250.*

Buying A Vehicle

You must have a residence visa in order to own a car. Most insurance policies cover multiple drivers (as long as they have a valid UAE driving licence, either temporary or permanent), but check the small print before you let your spouse behind the wheel (see Certificates & Licences, p.91).

New Car Dealers

Most of the major car makes are available through franchised dealerships in Dubai, with big Japanese and American brands particularly well represented. Expat buyers may be pleasantly surprised by the low cost of new cars – for example, a Jeep Wrangler would cost around $24,000 (approx Dhs.88,150) in the US, over £16,000 (approx Dhs.88,000) in the UK, but as little as Dhs.74,000 here in Dubai. Similarly, the ubiquitous Toyota Land Cruiser would set you back roughly $56,000 (approx Dhs.205,680) in the US and a massive £45,000 (approx Dhs.250,000) in the UK, but Dubai prices start at around Dhs.110,000. For many, this lower initial cost, coupled with cheaper fuel and maintenance, means they can afford something a little more extravagant than they might drive at home.

> **Dodgy Drives**
>
> Finding a taxi in congested areas can be difficult, and in their frustration, many people are using illegal cabs. Be warned though that unlicensed taxis haven't had to meet the safety standards for their cars that legal cabs do. As these cabs are difficult to trace, there have also been cases where drivers have either been the victim of crimes or have perpetrated them.

UAE's Largest Used Automobile Retailer

The second hand car that makes a first impression.

Al-Futtaim Automall is proud to have the world's

most comprehensive used car warranty up to 3 years.

★ The world's most comprehensive Used Car Warranty up to 3 years   ★ Mileage Certificate
★ 99-Point Check   ★ Fully Reconditioned   ★ 30 day Exchange Pledge

New Car Dealers

AGMC	BMW, Rolls Royce, Mini	04 339 1555	www.bmw-dubai.com
Al Futtaim Motors	Lexus, Toyota	04 228 2261	www.toyotauae.com
Al Ghandi Automotive	Fiat, Lancia, Ssangyong	04 266 6511	www.alghandi.com
Al Habtoor Motors	Aston Martin, Bentley, Mitsubishi	04 269 1110	www.alhabtoor-motors.com
Al Majid Motors	Kia, Renault	04 269 5600	www.kia-uae.com
Al Naboodah Automobiles – Audi Showroom ▶ p.81	Audi	04 347 5111	www.nabooda-auto.com
Al Naboodah Automobiles – HQ ▶ p.81	Volkswagen, Porsche	04 338 6999	www.nabooda-auto.com
Al Rostamani Trading Company – Zuzuki	Suzuki	04 295 5907	www.alrostamani.com
Al Tayer Motors	Ferrari, Ford, Jaguar, Landrover, Lincoln, Maserati, Mercury	04 201 1001	www.altayer.com
Al Yousuf Motors	Chevrolet, Daihatsu	04 339 5555	www.aym.ae
Arabian Automobiles Nissan	Nissan, Infinity	04 295 1234	www.arabianautomobiles.com
Autostar Trading	Skoda	04 269 7100	na
Galadari Automobiles	Mazda	04 299 4848	www.mazdauae.com
Gargash Enterprises LLC – Mercedes Benz	Mercedes	04 209 9777	www.gargash.mercedes-benz.com
Gargash Motors	Alpha Romeo, Saab	04 266 4669	www.gargashme.com
Juma Al Majid Establishment	Hyundai	800 498 6324	www.hyundai-uae.com
Liberty Automobiles	Cadillac, Opel, Hummer	04 282 4440	www.libertyautos.com
Swaidan Trading	Peugeot	04 266 7111	www.swaidanpeugeot.com
Trading Enterprises	Chrysler, Dodge, Honda, Jeep, Volvo	04 204 7160	www.alfuttaim.ae

Used Car Dealers

Due to the relatively low price of cars and the high turnover of expats in the UAE, there is a thriving second-hand market. Dealers are scattered around town but good areas to start are Sheikh Zayed Road and Garhoud. Expect to pay a premium of between Dhs.5,000 and Dhs.10,000 for buying through a dealer (as opposed to buying from a private seller), since they also offer a limited warranty, insurance, finance and registration.

One of the biggest used-car dealers in Dubai is 4x4 Motors (www.4x4motors.com), with a large showroom near the airport. Despite the name, they sell saloon cars as well as 4WDs, and offer finance on all purchases. They have been well-established in Dubai for many years and are often the port of call for new residents looking to upgrade their vehicle of choice from what they used to drive in their home country. They often have 'nearly new' vehicles that are a year or less old and therefore cheaper than buying from a new car dealer.

Al Futtaim Automall (www.automalluae.com) has three sites in Dubai, and each car comes with a 12 month warranty and a 30 day exchange policy.

Off Road Motors (04 338 4866) on Sheikh Zayed Road also has a good selection of used cars (again, with saloons as well as 4WDs) as do Jumeirah Motors (next to the Mazaya Centre on Sheikh Zayed Road), Western Auto (branches at Al Awir and Deira), Target Auto (near Mazaya Centre), House of Cars (Sheikh Zayed Road), and Sun City Motors (branches near the airport, Al Awir, and Al Barsha).

The Al Awir complex has a website (www.usedcars.ae) with links to many of the dealers and the ability to search for cars by make, model or year. Al Awir is also home to

Golden Bell Auctions (www.goldenbellauctions.com), with sales held each Wednesday evening. All cars up for auction have to undergo a test at the nearby Eppco/Tasjeel garage, and all outstanding fines will have been cleared. The cars are put up for sale by banks and finance companies, showrooms, rental companies, taxi firms and individuals. There's a Traffic Department office on the site so buyers can register their new vehicles on the spot. You have to pay a refundable deposit that allows you to bid, and there are some real bargains to be had. However, you should never forget the handy Latin phrase caveat emptor – let the buyer beware. Take along someone who knows their cars, and give any vehicle a thorough going over before you get bidding.

Gulf News and Khaleej Times classifieds sections are a good starting place for second-hand cars. There are lots of ads placed by showrooms, but plenty of private ads too. Supermarket noticeboards are another good option. Alongside the adverts for cheap furniture and lost cats, you may just find a bargain motor being sold by an expat leaving town at the end of the week. Most Choithram supermarkets have noticeboards, and the ones at Spinneys are usually pretty big, as is the one at Park n Shop in Al Safa.

To Oman & Back
It is wise to check whether your insurance covers you for the Sultanate of Oman as, within the Emirates, you may find yourself driving through small Oman enclaves (especially if you are off road, near Hatta, through Wadi Bih and on the East Coast in Dibba – see Exploring, p.240). Insurance for a visit to Oman can be arranged on a short-term basis, usually for no extra cost.

Ownership Transfer

To register a second-hand car in your name you must transfer vehicle ownership. You will need to submit an application form, the valid registration card, the insurance certificate, the original licence plates and Dhs.20 to the Traffic Police, plus an NOC from the finance company, if applicable. The seller must also be present with their passport and residence permit (and copies) to sign the form.

Used Car Dealers

4x4 Motors – HQ	Al Awir	04 706 9666	www.4x4motors.com
Al Futtaim Automall ▶ p.229	Al Quoz	04 347 2212	www.automalluae.com
Auto Plus	Al Quoz	04 339 5400	www.autoplusdubai.com
Boston Cars	Al Awir	04 333 1010	na
Dynatrade	Al Awir	04 320 1558	www.dynatrade-uae.com
Exotic Cars	Al Quoz	04 338 4339	www.exoticcarsdubai.com
House Of Cars	Various Locations	04 343 5060	www.houseofcarsgroup.com
Jumeirah Motors	Al Wasl	04 343 4449	na
Motor World	Al Awir	04 333 2206	na
Off Road Motors	Al Quoz	04 338 4866	www.offroad-motors.com
Quartermile – HQ	Al Quoz	04 339 4633	www.quartermile.net
Reem Automobile	Al Wasl	04 343 6333	www.reemauto.com
Sun City Motors	Al Barsha	04 269 8009	www.suncitymotors.net
Target Auto	Al Wasl	04 343 3911	www.target-auto.com
Tony Edwards Motors	Al Quoz	04 338 3887	www.temllc.com
Western Auto	Deira	04 297 7788	www.westernauto.ae

Vehicle Finance

Many new and second-hand car dealers will be able to arrange finance for you, often through a deal with their preferred banking partner. Previously this involved writing out years and years worth of post-dated cheques, but most official dealers and main banks will now set up automatic transactions. Always ask about the rates and terms, and then consider going directly to one of the banks to see if they can offer you a better deal.

Vehicle Import

A requirement for cars imported by individuals or private car showrooms that were manufactured after 1997/98, is an NOC from the official agent in the UAE or from the

Vehicle Finance

Emirates Bank	04 316 0316	www.emiratesbank.ae
HSBC	04 228 8999	www.hsbc.ae
Lloyds TSB Bank ▶ p.109	04 342 2000	www.lloydstsb.ae
Mashreqbank	04 217 4800	www.mashreqbank.com
National Bank of Dubai (NBD)	04 310 0101	www.nbd.com
RAK Bank	04 213 0000	www.rakbank.ae

Ministry of Finance and Industry (if no official agent exists). This is to ensure that the car complies with GCC specifications. Additionally, if you are buying a vehicle from another emirate you have to export and import it into Dubai first. This means lots of paperwork, and you'll need your essential documents, the sale agreement, current registration and Dhs.60. You will be issued with a set of temporary licence (export) plates, which are valid for three days – enough time to submit a new registration application in Dubai. Note that export plates are not available for motorbikes.

Registration Costs ◀
Registration with long number plates, Dhs.70. Registration with short number plates, Dhs.50. Registration through a finance company may cost a little more for the convenience.

Vehicle Insurance

Before you can register your car you must have adequate insurance, and there are many insurance companies to choose from in Dubai. The insurers will need to know the usual details such as year of manufacture, and value, as well as the chassis number. If you got a real bargain of a car and feel it's worth much more than you paid, make sure you instruct the insurance company to cover it at the market value. However, if the value is higher than they would normally estimate, they may ask to inspect the vehicle. Take copies of your UAE driving licence, passport and the existing vehicle registration card.

Registration Service ◀
Companies
• AAA (04 266 9989) Dhs.150.
• Al Ghandi Shamel (04 333 1204), Dhs.200.
• Echo Car Registration Service (04 396 9929), Dhs.125.
• Emarat Shamil (800 4559), Dhs.200.
• EPPCO Tasjeel (800 4258), Dhs.200.
• Midland Cars (04 396 7521), Dhs.200

Annual insurance policies are for a 13 month period (this is to cover the one-month grace period that you are allowed when your registration expires). Rates depend on the age and model of your car and your previous insurance history, although if you're new in Dubai and insuring a car for the first time, very few companies will recognise any no-claims bonuses you have accrued in your home country. The rates are generally 4% to 7% of the vehicle value, or a flat 5% for cars over five years old. Fully comprehensive cover with personal accident insurance is highly advisable, and you are strongly advised to make sure the policy covers you for 'blood money' (see p.60 for more details). For more adventurous 4WD drivers, insurance for off-roading accidents is also recommended.

Vehicle Insurance

Al Khazna Insurance Company	04 294 4088	www.alkhazna.com
Arab Orient Insurance Company	04 295 3425	www.al-futtaim.com
AXA Insurance – UAE ▶ p.233	800 4845	www.axa-gulf.com
Emirates Insurance Company	04 299 0655	www.eminsco.com
Greenshield Insurance	04 397 4464	www.greenshield.co.ae
Nasco Karaoglan	04 352 3133	www.nascodubai.com
National General Insurance (Healthnet)	02 667 8783	www.ngi.ae
Oman Insurance	04 398 1710	www.tameen.ae

Registering A Vehicle

All cars must be registered annually with the Traffic Police. There is a one-month grace period after your registration has expired for you to re-register your car (hence the 13 month insurance period), but after that there'll be a Dhs.110 fine for each month the registration has expired. Please beware that some second-hand dealers may sell you a car that under normal circumstances would not pass the annual vehicle testing. However, with 'friends' at the test centre, they are able to get the car passed, leaving you stuck when you come to do it yourself the following year.

while your car
is in the workshop

THE AXA
"I want 365 days
of peace of mind"
ADVANTAGE.

**only AXA gives
you a replacement**

redefining / insurance
رؤية جديدة / للتأمين

The Process

In order to get licence plates for the vehicle, the car must first be tested, then registered with the Dubai Traffic Police. If you have purchased a new vehicle from a dealer, the dealer will register the car for you. You do not need to test a new vehicle for the first two years, although you must re-register it after one year. There are several ways to test your car. Ras Al Khor boasts a five-lane testing centre (Al Ghandi Shamel) that is run in conjunction with the Traffic Police. The centre is paperless and this saves you time in necessary procedures. EPPCO and Emarat offer a full registration service. For an additional fee they will collect your car, test and register it, and deliver it back to you in the same day. Alternatively, an express service, where you bring the car in and enjoy your complimentary drink in the air-conditioned waiting room while they do the process for you, is available. Emarat (04 343 4444) also has several full-registration and vehicle-testing service centres (called Shamil), where they will test and register your car with the police. You can also pay any traffic fines here.

Registration Service	
AAA	04 266 9989
Echo	04 396 9928
Emarat Shamil	800 4559
EPPCO Tasjeel	800 4258
Midland Cars	04 396 7521

Remember to take all your essential documents, insurance valid for 13 months, registration card, proof of purchase agreement and vehicle transfer or customs certificate (if applicable) and cash. Before the registration procedure can be completed, all traffic offences and fines against your car registration number must be settled. Try to check your fines before you get your car tested (you can do so on www.dubaipolice.gov.ae), as some of the larger fines cannot be paid at the test centre.

Traffic Fines & Offences

If you are caught driving or parking illegally you will be fined unless the offence is more serious, in which case you may be brought before the courts. You can also be fined Dhs.100 on the spot for being caught driving without your licence, so always keep it with you, along with your vehicle's registration card.

There was a clamp down on traffic offences in 2008 and as a result fines have been increased. New hi-tech cameras have also been introduced which have the ability to track your vehicle between traffic cameras – so if you speed up and reach the next camera too soon, you could also be fined. Penalties for speeding start at Dhs.400 if you exceed the maximum speed by 10km/h. If you exceed the limit by over 60km/h you could run the risk of a Dhs.1,000 fine, your vehicle could be confiscated and 12 points added to your licence. Fines for overtaking on the hard shoulder are Dhs.600 with six black points on your licence. If you run a red light you could be facing a Dhs.800 fine, eight points on your licence and a 30 day confiscation. Dangerous driving attracts Dhs.2,000, 12 points and your vehicle will be confiscated for 30 days. Parking tickets are Dhs.200 if issued. If the black points on your licence reach 24 points, within six months, your licence could be suspended.

Breakdowns

In the event of a breakdown, you will usually find that passing police cars will stop to help, or at least to check your documents. It's important that you keep water in your car at all times – the last thing you want is to be stuck in the middle of summer with no air conditioning while you wait for assistance. Dubai Traffic officers recommend, if possible, that you pull your car over to a safe spot. If you are on the hard shoulder of a highway you should pull your car as far away from the yellow line as possible and step away from the road until help arrives.

The Arabian Automobile Association (AAA) (04 266 9989 or 800 4900, www.aaauae.com) offers a 24 hour roadside breakdown service for an annual charge. This includes help in minor mechanical repairs, battery boosting, or help if you run out of petrol, have a flat tyre or lock yourself out. Mashreq Bank Visa card holders receive free AAA membership.

Recovery Services & Towing (24 hour)	
AAA	04 266 9989
AKT Recovery Service	04 263 6217
Dubai Auto Towing Services	04 359 4424
IATC Recovery	800 5200

The more advanced service includes off-road recovery, vehicle registration and a rent-a-car service. It's a similar concept to the RAC or AA in Britain, or AAA in the States. Other breakdown services that will be able to help you out without membership include IATC (it also offers annual membership), Dubai Auto Towing Services and AKT Recovery.

Black Points

In addition to a system of fines for certain offences, a black points penalty system operates. If you have a permanent licence and receive 12 black points in one year, your licence is taken away and your car impounded. Driving in a reckless manner or racing will earn you 6 points, as will parking in a handicapped zone or in front of a fire hydrant. Other major offences include overtaking where prohibited, jumping a red light and entering a road dangerously. If you do something particularly dangerous your licence can be taken away immediately. However, the rules are somewhat ambiguous, and erratically applied.

Traffic Accidents
Other options **Car** p.58

Many people who arrive in Dubai and become familiar with the roads by taking a taxi around the city often think they will never be able to drive here. This hesitation is understandable; firstly, the road systems seem somewhat complicated when you first arrive and secondly, you witness an inordinate amount of accidents ranging from numerous fender benders to many serious collisions. However, most people do eventually get behind the wheel and invariably find that within a few months they've adopted a very defensive method of driving. It's vital not to become complacent about driving in Dubai no matter how long you have been doing it. You should always exercise extra care and attention when on the roads as there are more than a few maniacs driving machines that simply have too much horsepower for them. Be vigilant and remember to use your mirrors (and indicators) at all times.

Blood Money

As the law currently stands, the family of a pedestrian killed in a road accident is entitled to Dhs.200,000 diya (blood) money. The money is usually paid by the insurance company unless there's any whiff of the driver having been under the influence of alcohol. However an amendment to the law is being considered to put a stop to the terrible trend among desperate lower-income workers of killing themselves to provide for their family. This will mean blood money is not automatically due if the victim was walking across a road not intended for use by pedestrians, such as Sheikh Zayed Road.

A total of 196 people were killed on Dubai's roads in the first nine months of 2008. That's an average of 22 deaths per month. The number of accidents rockets during the holy month of Ramadan, as many drivers are tired, hungry and irritable, and in an even bigger hurry than usual to reach their destination, especially in the late afternoon and evening.

If you are involved in an accident call 999. If the accident is minor and no one has been hurt you need to agree with the other driver where the blame lies and move your cars to the side of the road to avoid obstructing the flow of traffic. You can be fined Dhs.100 for failing to do so even if the accident wasn't your fault.

The Dubai Police Information Line (800 7777, Arabic and English) gives the numbers of police stations around the emirate. The police will assess the accident and once they have apportioned blame they will give you a copy of the accident report, if it is green then the other party is at fault but if it is pink then you are to blame for the accident. You will need to submit this form to the insurance company in order to process the claim, or to the garage for repairs. Garages are coming under increasing pressure not to accept any vehicle for repair without a police report of the accident. The police have also announced they will also fine rubberneckers Dhs.100 if caught driving slowly to gawp at accidents. For more details on traffic accidents and procedures see Accidents in General Information, p.60.

Agency Repairs

If you purchase a new vehicle your insurance should cover you for 'agency repairs,' that is, repairs at the workshop of the dealer selling the car, although this is not a guarantee and you may have to pay a premium. It's worth it though as your car's warranty (two to three years) may become invalid if you have non-agency repairs. Even if you buy a fairly new second-hand car (less than three years old) it may be an idea to opt for agency repairs, especially if the service history has only agency repairs, in order to protect the value of the car.

Vehicle Repairs

By law, no vehicle can be accepted for major 'collision' repairs without an accident report from the Traffic Police, although very minor dents can be repaired without a report. Basically, if it looks like you hit another vehicle and you don't have an accident report, the garage could get into trouble if they repair your car.

Your insurance company will usually have an agreement with a particular garage to which they will refer you. The garage will carry out the repair work and the insurance company will settle the claim. Generally, there is Dhs.500 deductible for all claims, but check with your insurance company for details of your policy.

If you purchase a new vehicle your insurance should cover you for 'agency repairs', that is, repairs at the workshop of the dealer selling the car, although this is not a guarantee and you may have to pay a premium. It's worth it though as your car's warranty (two to three years) may become invalid if you have non-agency repairs done on it. Besides accidents and bumps, you may also have to deal with the usual running repairs associated with any car.

Vehicle Repairs	
4x4 Garage – Sheikh Zayed Road	04 339 2020
AAA	04 347 0400
Central Motors	02 554 6262
House Of Cars	04 339 3466
Icon Auto Garage	04 338 2744
Max Garage	04 340 8200
X Centre	04 339 5033

Common problems in this part of the world can include the air-conditioning malfunctioning, batteries suddenly giving up and tyres blowing out. With the air-con it may just be a case of having the system topped up, which is a fairly straightforward procedure. Car batteries don't tend to last too long in the hot conditions, and you may not get much warning (one day your car just won't start), so it's always handy to keep a set of jump leads in the boot.

If you do manage to get your car started then it's worth taking a trip to Satwa; before you know it, your car will be surrounded by people offering to fix anything and everything. Haggle hard and you can get a bargain for simple repairs and spares – including that new battery.

When it comes to maps…
size does matter

Tank

4x4

Saloon

Whether you need the perfect pocket reference, or a jumbo atlas that offers pinpoint detail, Explorer has the right map for you. From the small city runaround to the mother of all maps - we've got it covered.

Explorer Maps
Never get lost again

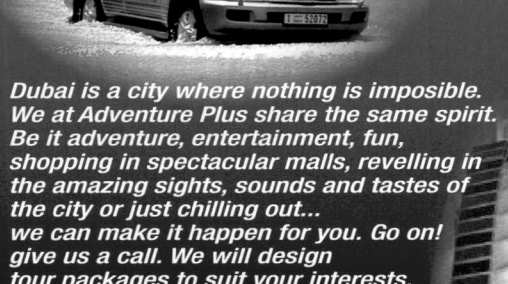

Exploring

Exploring

Exploring

Known as the City of Gold and the City of Lights, Dubai is a world class metropolis where east meets west, and old meets new. It is jam-packed with luxurious five-star hotels, it boasts some of the most innovative and biggest shopping malls, it is the region's most happening nightspot, and has a growing collection of heritage sites, museums and places of interest. There are also numerous photographic opportunities: mosques, palaces, dhows, camel and horse racing, sunsets, architecture and windtowers, to name just a few. Just remember to ask permission before taking photos of people, especially local women. As a cosmopolitan city, it has something for everyone, and just when you think you've seen it all, a new project is announced, whether it's the world's tallest building, the largest shopping mall, or a ski slope in the desert. The Checklist (right) highlights some of the best sites to explore, but you may also come across some other amazing places on your travels that are not listed here.

Dubai Creek is still considered to be the lifeline of the city – this is where it all started, when early settlers built their mud huts along the gleaming stretch of water that splits the city in two: Deira to the north and Bur Dubai to the south. Today, it is lined with skyscrapers and is a popular destination for visitors and residents – many of whom still commute across the creek on traditional wooden 'abras' (water taxis). The creek is 15 kilometres long, about 500 metres wide, and has five main crossing points: Al Shindagha Tunnel, Maktoum Bridge, Garhoud Bridge, Floating Bridge and Business Bay Crossing. More bridges are under construction to help ease traffic congestion across the creek, which itself is being extended out through Business Bay back to the sea again.

On the Bur Dubai side you'll find Oud Metha and Umm Hurair (residential, recreational and commercial areas), Satwa and Karama (original suburbs of old Dubai), and Jumeira and Umm Suqeim (both originally fishing settlements) along the coast. Further past Umm Suqeim on the way to Abu Dhabi is Dubai Marina – one of the centres of 'New Dubai' with hundreds of towers and several popular beach hotels, then Jebel Ali, the southern-most point of the city and famous for its port and free zone. The main road connecting Dubai and Abu Dhabi is Sheikh Zayed Road, a multi-lane highway lined with some impressive skyscrapers in the areas known as Trade Centre 1 and 2.

On the north side of the creek, you'll find Deira, one of the hearts of the city, Garhoud (near the airport), Rashidiya (an older residential and industrial area) and Mirdif. The maps at the back of this book will help you find your bearings wherever you decide to venture. In this chapter, each of Dubai's main areas is described in detail, including landmarks, attractions and shopping opportunities. Areas outside of the city are also covered; also see www.explorerpublishing.com for other leisure titles in the Explorer series.

GCC Easy As ABC

While Dubai and its surrounding emirates have many landscapes and horizons to discover, the other GCC countries are also worth visiting while you live in the region. Whether you want to get sporty in Qatar, check out the colourful heritage of Kuwait, find tranquility in the wilderness of Oman or join in the excitement of the grand prix in Bahrain there is a whole host of exploring to be done just a very short flight away. Pick up a copy of the respective Explorer guide and make the most of your trip or trips.

Cruising the creek

Lose Yourself At Madinat Jumeirah p.43

Inspired by traditional Arabian architecture, this stunning resort is a must for shopping, sightseeing and a night out. Explore the maze of alleyways of the traditionally styled, air-conditioned souk, leading to intimate open-fronted boutiques, classy cafes, and charming waterfront bars and restaurants with amazing views of the Burj Al Arab.

Watch World Class Sport

Dubai is becoming a popular destination for some of the world's sporting competitions, with parallel social events of note. The Dubai World Cup (p.75) offers high-class horseracing, hobnobbing and hats, the Dubai Tennis Championships (p.392) always attracts some top tennis legends, and the Rugby Sevens (p.395) has fast and furious action on the field and one of the best social nights off it.

Cruise Creekside Park p.281

The next best thing to a scenic flight over the city, the 45 minute ride by cable car travels the full length of Creekside Park suspended 30 feet in the air, and offers great views over the creek to the striking Deira skyline. Definitely one for the cooler months as the cars can get quite hot inside and there are no windows. Not advisable for those suffering from acrophobia.

Experience The Thrills Of The Desert p.288

While in Dubai, a trip to the desert is an absolute must. Surfing over the dunes in a car at impossible angles is great fun and part of the essential desert experience, along with a camel ride, climbing a sand dune, sand skiing, star gazing, eating your fill at the BBQ and learning how to belly dance. Plenty of tour operators offer various excursions at competitive prices, so be sure to shop around.

See The World At Global Village p.71

Increasing every year in size and duration, Global Village now has its own site just out of town on Emirates Road, and remains open for nearly five months of the year. Stands and stalls representing countries from around the world offer culture, shows, attractions, and traditional items and food for sale. There is enough to keep kids and adults entertained on multiple visits.

Enjoy A Dinner Cruise On The Creek p.540

Experience a truly memorable evening on Dubai Creek, taking in the atmosphere and the views of both the Bur Dubai and Deira sides of the creek from the best vantage point. Dining options vary from lunch, sunset and dinner cruises, and on board entertainment is often included (don't forget your camera).

Witness History In The Making

For a glimpse of craftsmen still practising their ancient skills, visit the dhow building yard in Jaddaf, just to the east of the Business Bay Bridge on the south side of the creek (Map 13 C2). Watch the mesmerising procedures of dhows being constructed without the aid of drawings or modern equipment, and all without nails.

Smoke Shisha
Join in the Arabic social tradition of hanging out at a shisha cafe (p.605). A hugely popular pastime with the locals (both men and women in places popular with the younger crowd), shisha consists of tobacco mixed with molasses and a variety of fruity flavourings, which is then smoked from a water pipe.

Step Back In Time At Dubai Museum p.271
This is a fantastic museum offering an enlightening stroll through Dubai's past. With displays depicting everything from the fascinating history of the emirate and how traditional life used to be before the discovery of oil just over half a century ago, to views of the wildlife and natural environment of the UAE.

Dive Into Dubai's Heritage
The former fishing village of Shindagha is now home to an increasing number of restored buildings, including the museums in Sheikh Saeed Al Maktoum's House (p.270) and the Heritage & Diving Villages (p.268), where you can also see traditional crafts, tribal dances and ceremonies. On the creekside, several local restaurants provide great surroundings for sampling typical Emirati and Arabic fare.

Get In Tents p.52
One of the best ways to see the natural beauty of the countryside of the UAE, camping gets you away from it all and closer to nature. In the tranquility of the mountains or the desert, you can camp almost anywhere you please, and a night under the clear star-studded Arabian skies is an unforgettable experience.

Explore Bastakiya p.267
Stroll through historical streets for a glimpse of Dubai's past with traditional windtowers, courtyard houses, museums and galleries that characterise this heritage-rich part of the city. Learn ancient facts at the nearby Dubai Museum (p.271), stop for a coffee at the Basta Art Cafe (p.599) or a meal in one of the area's great Arabic restaurants (p.629).

Hit The Slopes p.386
In the city whose imagination knows no bounds, it should come as no surprise to find an enormous ski slope towering above a shopping mall. There are a number of runs, all with real snow, and lessons are available for non-skiers and boarders. Alternatively, you could just go to the Snow Park for a spot of tobogganing and a snowball fight.

Do Buy p.71
Dubai Shopping Festival sees Dubai come alive with the ringing of a million cash registers, as shoppers flock to the city for great bargains. It is about much more than shopping though, with attractions, events and special entertainment in malls creating a buzz throughout the city.

Checklist

Learn About Local Culture At Jumeira Mosque p.274
Learn more about local culture, Islam and what goes on inside a mosque through organised tours held here four days a week (10:00 sharp). You don't need to book, but it would be wise to call beforehand to confirm. You should also adhere to the conservative dress code.

See Dubai By Bus p.287
Think you've seen it all? Think again. View Dubai from the upper floor of a double-decker bus, learning some fascinating facts about the city in the process. The Big Bus allows you to hop on and hop off at various attractions and traditional points of interest. Or try the amphibious Wonder Bus, which sails along the creek and then drives around some of Dubai's land-based attractions.

Shop In The Souks p.481
Still an essential part of life for many people, Dubai's souks should be visited at least once. Check out the Spice Souk (p.481) for the aromas, the colourful textile souk in Bur Dubai (p.483), the Fish Market in Deira (p.481) or Karama (p.471), and the Gold Souk (p.482) to discover why Dubai is called the City of Gold.

Experience The Glamorous Burj Al Arab
Venture into the glamour at the Burj and indulge yourself with Afternoon Tea at Sahn Eddar (p.605) or Sky View (p.605) – where they also do a cocktails (p.605), or a meal at the top class seafood restaurant Al Mahara (p.587), complete with simulated submarine ride. You can even make use of the special weekend packages during summer and stay the night in one of the amazing rooms.

Shop Till You Drop
Beat the heat, splash some cash and cut a dash in one of Dubai's many shopping malls. No matter where you're from, chances are that Dubai does shopping bigger and better. Skim through the Shopping Malls section (p.416) for detailed descriptions of each mall.

Stroll Along The Creekside p.281
Don't miss a walk around the heart of Dubai's trading heritage, exploring the atmospheric area around Dubai Creek. Stroll down the open corniche and past the cruise vessels towards the creekside souk on the Bur Dubai side, or head over to Deira to see dhows being loaded and unloaded on the wharf – the way boxes of assorted goods are left trustingly on the pavement is quite refreshing.

Cross The Creek By Abra p.249
Take in the panoramic views along both sides of Dubai Creek on a ride from Bur Dubai to Deira by traditional abra (water taxi). As well as being a great tourist attraction, these functional, traditional vessels are still used as everyday transport for people getting from one side of Dubai to the other.

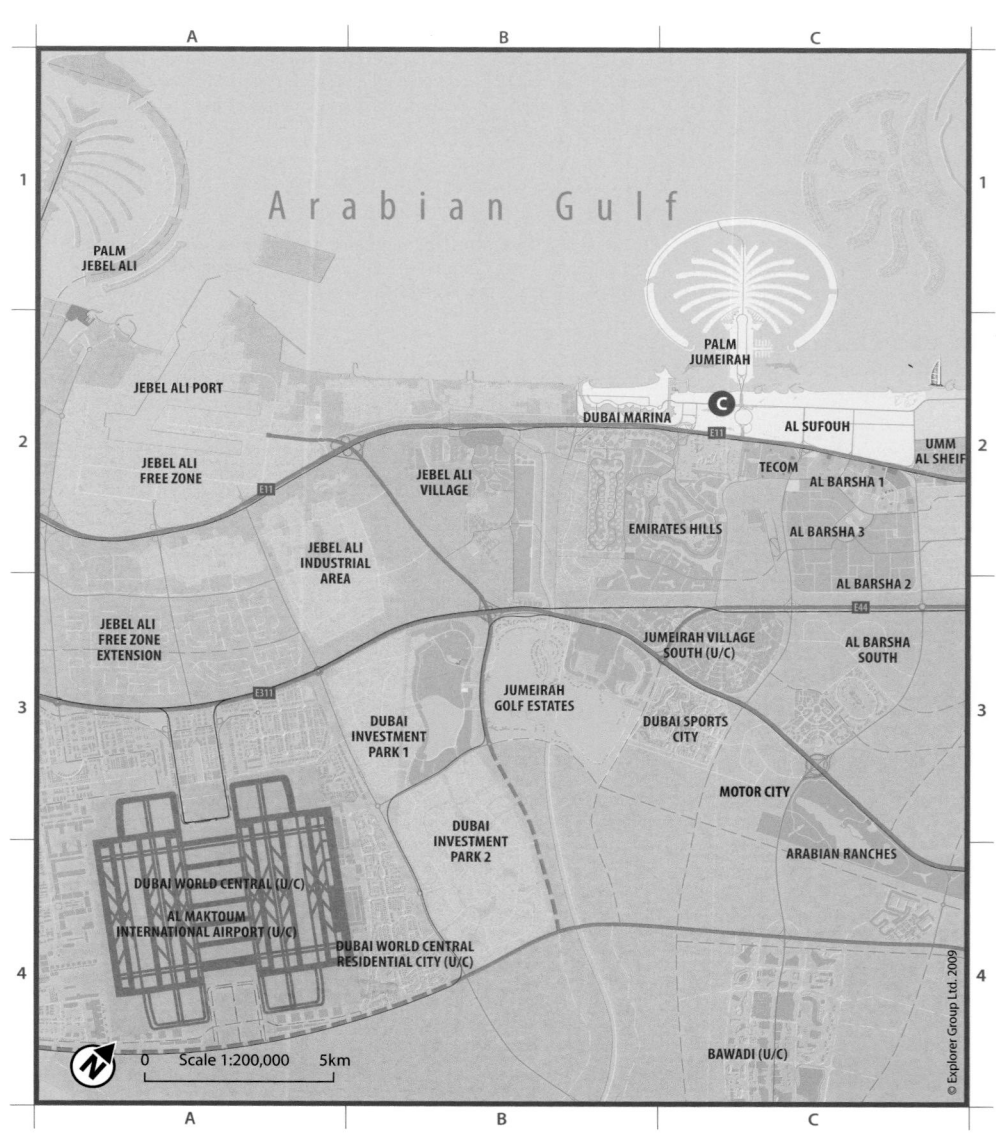

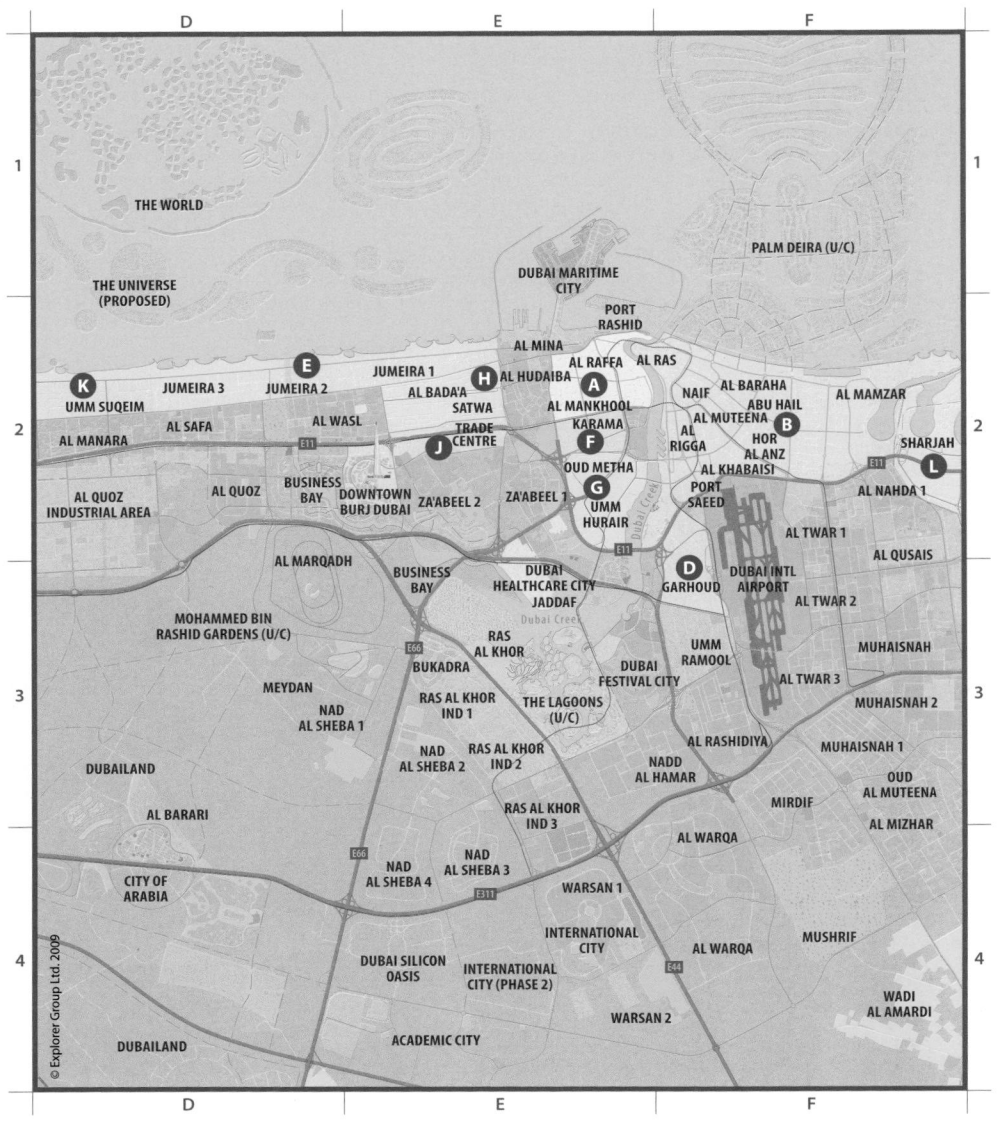

Area **A** *E2 p.245*
Maps 8 & 9

Bur Dubai

What was once just a flat, sandy area with a sprinkling of palm trees and barasti (palm) houses, is now the bustling heart of the city. Up until only a few years ago, Bur Dubai, and Deira across the creek, were the business districts of the city, but the development of office towers along the prestigious Sheikh Zayed Road, as well as future plans for Burj Dubai and Business Bay, are shifting the business focus to other areas. Bur Dubai is still a residential hotspot, with a multitude of nationalities living in various multi-storey apartment blocks. It also offers great shopping and entertainment options. For exploring, this is one of the best areas in Dubai with both Bastakiya and Shindagha offering atmospheric, historical sites that are great to stroll around, as well as Dubai Museum, the souks and the Bur Dubai corniche.

The Lowdown

The centre of Dubai's history and now the centre of its heritage – a great place to explore, especially on foot.

The Good

The fabulous Bastakiya area, the illuminating Dubai Museum, the atmospheric souks and a ride on an abra over the creek to Deira.

The Bad

Traffic in rush hour can be slow, especially with all the traffic lights, and you're more likely to strike gold in some areas than find a parking space at particular times of the day.

The Must Dos

A walking tour of the entire area, especially Bastakiya by day and the corniche at night.

Take Your Time

While in the area, take time to linger and absorb the unique sights, sounds and smells of Bur Dubai over a meal at Kan Zaman (p.537).

Residential

Despite the area being a bit of a concrete jungle, it remains very popular with expats of all nationalities. Mostly modern mid-rise buildings house various sizes and styles of apartments, which due to ever-rising rents are becoming increasingly populated by professionals. The quality of accommodation is generally excellent. Residents are well served by a comprehensive selection of shopping malls, supermarkets, smaller shops and other services, as well as restaurants, cafes, bars and nightclubs. There are no green or public spaces and the roads can get blocked with traffic at rush hour, but for its convenient central location, it is hard to beat. For more details, refer to Residential Areas (p.133).

Retail

Modern malls, such as BurJuman (p.486) and the smaller malls on Bank Street and Mankhool Road, contrast with the oldest souks in Bur Dubai near the creek to provide a complete range of shopping choices. Whether you like to buy designer labels, or have your own clothes made up from Indian silk, it's all available here. Likewise, food shopping ranges from bulk-buy bargains in discount stores in the souk, right up to gourmet dates from Bateel in BurJuman.

Places Of Interest

The area near the mouth of the creek, known as Shindagha, is a good starting point to explore Bur Dubai. Here you can visit Sheikh Saeed Al Maktoum's House (see p.270) and the Heritage & Diving Villages (p.268), a two-minute walk from each other, before following the creek inland to Dubai Museum and finishing in the Bastakiya area.

On your way through Bur Dubai, you will pass the busy Al Faheidi Street (p.471) near the Astoria Hotel, a great place to shop for electrical goods. Nearby, underneath wooden shaded walkways, is the Textile Souk (p.483) with every type of fabric imaginable. Facing Dubai Museum (p.271) is the 'Diwan', the Ruler's office and the highest administrative body of the

Bur Dubai Creekside

Dubai government. Built in 1990, the low white building is surrounded by black railings and combines modern materials with a traditional design, including windtowers. Located near the Diwan is the Grand Mosque, which can accommodate 1,200 worshippers and has 54 domes and a 70 metre minaret – presently the tallest in the city. It is possible to walk inland along the edge of the creek, past the Diwan to the Bastakiya district, which is one of the oldest heritage sites in the city (see p.267). Originally known as Bastakiya Chok (square), this area is gradually being reconstructed by Dubai Municipality to pay homage to the traditional local way of life and provide a great little area for tourists to explore the maze of small winding alleys.

From Bastakiya it is possible to follow the corniche up along the creekside where a number of luxury cruise boats moor (you can board one of these for a Dinner Cruise, see p.540 for more info). The relaxed atmosphere of this area, with its grassy parks often full of people (especially families and children), makes it a great place to view the flashy buildings on the Deira side of the creek and watch the water traffic. For more information on Dubai Creek, refer also to p.249.

Nearby, Bait Al Wakeel was built in 1934 as Dubai's first office building. It currently houses the fishing museum. Numerous embassies are located in this area, while further inland from the creek is the popular BurJuman shopping centre (p.486). Located on the busy crossroads of Khalid bin Waleed Road (or Bank Street, as it is popularly known), this already huge mall has been extended to triple its original size.

| **Photo Op** |
| To the south-west of Bur Dubai is Port Rashid, where you'll find the Dubai Ports Authority building. A large glass and chrome construction imaginatively designed like a paddle steamer, all the paraphernalia of a port can be glimpsed over the surrounding fence. |

Deira

Area B F2 p.245
Maps 9, 11, 12

The Lowdown
Deira is not dead! This is one of the oldest and most atmospheric parts of town. There's plenty to explore along the corniche, through the souks and in the heritage sites, and there are loads of restaurants and bars in the modern hotels along the creek.

The Good
The ambience of the souks and the corniche where the traditional trade from the dhows still plays a major role in this part of the city.

Although Deira has fallen out of favour as a residential area for many expats in recent years, with the creek now seeming to be a barrier as to how far people will move or even travel in search of entertainment, it is still an incredibly atmospheric area with plenty to explore. Narrow convoluted streets bustle with activity while gold, spices, perfumes and general goods are touted in numerous souks. The streets are full of people, especially in the evenings. As the oldest part of the city, there is plenty of heritage around, and while it can be a crazy place to navigate by car, you can avoid the frustrations of the snarled-up traffic if you visit at quieter times of the day. Alternatively, beat the block (and the nightmare of the Maktoum Bridge traffic) and arrive by abra.

Residential

Perhaps because of the traffic, the rapid southward expansion of Dubai and the opportunity to own property in the Emirates Hills areas, Deira is not as popular a residential area as it once was. Most accommodation is in apartments, with few villas to be found. It is mainly chosen by people seeking more reasonable rents. For more details, refer to Deira in Residential Areas (p.134).

Retail

Still a big draw for shopping locations, both modern and historical, Deira has one of Dubai's largest and most popular malls, in the shape of Deira City Centre (p.488). Shopping in the souks such as the Gold Souk (p.482) and the Spice Souk (p.483) is an essential part of any tourist's stay in Dubai, as well as being an integral aspect of life for many residents.

The Bad

Some of the worst traffic in Dubai, especially in rush hour and when trying to get over Maktoum Bridge, and parking can be tricky.

The Must Dos

Gold Souk, Spice Souk, Dhow Wharfage, Al Ahmadiya School & Heritage House, Deira Fish Market and the Dubai Creek Golf & Yacht Club.

Gold Linger

The Gold Souk is an Aladdin's cave of gold shopping. Bargaining is expected, and discounts depend on the season and the international gold rate. Dubai Shopping Festival and Dubai Summer Surprises are the main periods for low prices, when huge discounts attract gold lovers from around the world. Individual pieces can be made, or copies done to your own specifications, within a few days. Even if you aren't buying, an evening stroll through the Gold Souk, when it's glistening, is worth the experience.

Places Of Interest

Inland, near Garhoud Bridge, is Deira City Centre (p.488). Not only is it a gigantic shopping mall, but it also houses many restaurants and cafes and an 11 screen cinema. Its recent expansion has created 20 more outlets and despite the opening of several other massive malls in the city, City Centre shows no signs of slowing down.

Opposite City Centre and bordering the creek for about 1.5 km is an enticing stretch of carefully manicured greenery, home to the Dubai Creek Golf & Yacht Club (p.356). The impressive golf clubhouse is based on the shape of dhow sails (the image of this famous building is found on the Dhs.20 note), while the yacht club is aptly in the shape of a yacht. This is also the site of one of the city's top five-star hotels, the Park Hyatt Dubai, which features Mediterranean-style low buildings offering creek views and some great restaurants.

Bordering the creek are some awe-inspiring buildings that seemed years ahead of their time when they were built. The large golf ball that sits atop the Etisalat building is testimony to the unique imagination of Dubai's modern architecture. The sparkling glass building housing the National Bank of Dubai (known fondly as the 'pregnant lady') is a sculptural vision, standing tall like a magnificent convex mirror that reflects the bustling activity of the creek.

It is also in this area that you can find three of Dubai's finest five-star hotels: Hilton Dubai Creek, Sheraton Dubai Creek, and the SAS Radisson Dubai Creek (formerly the InterContinental), which recently celebrated its 30th anniversary. Between them, they offer many fantastic dining and nightlife opportunities.

Take a stroll along the dhow wharfage where local traders unload wooden dhows lazily docked by the water's edge, tightly packed with everything from fruit and vegetables to televisions and maybe even a car or two. Often you will find a stack of electrical goods trustingly left on the wharfage – a sight rarely seen elsewhere in the world. This slice of local merchant life is a reminder of Dubai's trading history and a photo opportunity not to be missed.

Take the pedestrian underpass to the left of the abra station on the Deira side to enter the oldest market in Dubai, now mainly selling household items. Nearby is the Spice Souk (p.483), where the aroma of saffron and cumin fill the air. You'll find every spice under the sun as well as loose frankincense and other perfumed oils and dried herbs sold for medicinal purposes. The souk spreads over a large area between Al Nasr Square and the Gold Souk (p.482), where street after street is paved with gold shops whose windows are laden with yellow and white gold and platinum. If it's rugs you want then Deira Tower on Al Nasr Square is worth a visit. About 40 shops offer a colourful profusion of carpets from Iran, Pakistan, Turkey and Afghanistan to suit everyone's taste and pocket. For further information on carpets and gold, refer to the Shopping section (p.416).

Closer still towards the sea, set back a little from the main roads by the creek, is a small area being renovated and developed into a tourist area by the Dubai Municipality. It contains the earliest school in the city, Al Ahmadiya School (now the Museum of Education), and the Heritage House next door (see p.267), an excellent example of an Emirati family home. These have been joined by a traditionally styled hotel with a small restaurant, an old-style mosque and a building housing several shops, all located around a small central courtyard renovated in the last few years. In the nearby lanes there are other buildings with preservation orders, awaiting reconstruction to add to the 'Al Souk Al Khabeer' area.

Dubai Municipality has also reconstructed Murabba'at Umm Rayool (the name comes from the Arabic word for 'leg', as the building stands on seven pillars, or legs). This was originally used as a weaponry store and was located on Baniyas Street, but the new building is on Union Square near the Deira taxi stand. This building style dates from 1894.

Another cultural attraction is Dubai's largest and busiest fish market (near the Hyatt Regency Hotel), where you can stock up on the freshest seafood in town at bargain prices. You can pay a 'wheelbarrow man' to follow you and carry your shopping, and someone else to gut your fish. Once you get used to the smell it's a lot of fun. A fish museum has recently been created at Deira Fish Market to give shoppers and tourists more information about the 350 species in the Arabian Gulf, the history of the fishing trade in the UAE, and the types of fishing boats and equipment used by fishermen. Along the seafront from the Hyatt Regency (itself one of Dubai's oldest landmarks and home to several superb restaurants including the revolving Al Dawaar (p.555), you will pass Al Hamriya Port as you continue on Al Khaleej Road, which has plenty of car parking and a spectacular corniche looking straight out over the ocean. In true Dubai style, the views are becoming interrupted by the construction on Palm Deira, the third and biggest of Nakheel's Palm Island projects, so make the most of them now. Palm Deira is set to cover over 80 square kilometres, making it almost as large as Greater London and bigger than Paris or Manhattan, but with the recent economic downturn, plans keep changing and downsizing. In addition, the 'Abu Hail Development Project' plans to transform the corniche area by replacing older buildings with smart new residential and commercial units, public utilities and tourist attractions.

Further still is Al Mamzar Beach Park (p.279). The road also follows past the park inland along the lagoon, with a path on the corniche, public beaches and a slipway to launch jet skis and speedboats into the water.

Dubai Creek

The creek has played a pivotal role in the development of Dubai. The earliest Dubai settlement was near the mouth of the creek, but when it was dredged to create a larger anchorage and to encourage trade, the growing town gradually crept further inland.

At present, Dubai Creek has five main crossing points – nearest to the sea is the Shindagha Tunnel, then further inland are Floating Bridge, Maktoum Bridge, Garhoud Bridge and finally, Business Bay Bridge.

Creek Tours

Bateaux Dubai ▶ p.541	04 399 4994
Danat Dubai Cruises	04 351 1117
Tour Dubai	04 336 8409

Maktoum Bridge can be raised to allow boats through (thereby diverting traffic), but this usually only happens late at night. Floating Bridge is open from 06:00 to 22:00, closing overnight to let boats through. There is also a pedestrian foot tunnel near Shindagha.

Creek Tours

A cruise on Dubai Creek is a wonderful way to enjoy views of new and old parts of the city side by side. Many of the tours are in traditional wooden dhows, but even these often have air conditioning inside to avoid the summer heat and humidity. In the cooler months, the top deck is the place to be. Prices per adult range from about Dhs.45 for a daytime trip or Dhs.150 for a bargain dinner cruise and up to Dhs.325 for a top-class evening cruise with fine food. For more information see the table (right), Boat Tours & Charters (p.284) and Dinner Cruises (p.340).

There are many parts of creekside Bur Dubai and Deira that are worth exploring on foot. On both sides, there are souks and corniches, and you can cross from one side to the other in a traditional water taxi (abra). This short boat ride makes a refreshing change from crossing the creek via one of the often-congested bridges, and it only costs only Dhs.1. It is estimated that around 15,000 people make the crossing every day. For visitors, an abra ride gives a unique perspective of the gleaming, mirrored buildings along the creek, which stand in contrast to the traditional domes and windtowers of 'old Dubai' on the Bur Dubai side. Official one-hour RTA tours of the creek cost Dhs.100 per abra, and are available from the stations, although you may get a slightly cheaper fare if you are prepared to haggle with boat drivers further up the creek – be sure to agree on the price in advance.

For details of areas to explore along the corniches, see p.246 (for the Bur Dubai side) and p.247 (for the Deira side).

Area **C** *C2 p.244*
Maps 4 & 5

Dubai Marina, Al Sufouh & Palm Jumeirah

Previously home to just a handful of waterfront hotels, Dubai Marina (or Marsa Dubai to use its official title) has seen some of the most intensive of all Dubai's construction in recent years. Hundreds of apartment buildings are popping up along every inch of the man-made marina, while Jumeirah Beach Residence (JBR) has squeezed over 40 towers into Dubai's last stretch of beach available to developers. The coast is home to a number of stunning five-star hotels, such as The Ritz-Carlton and One&Only Royal Mirage. The Hilton Dubai Jumeirah, Sheraton Jumeirah, and Le Meridien Mina Seyahi can also be found here along this strip, as well as Grosvenor House (04 399 8888), home to the hip Buddha Bar. Al Sufouh is home to Media City, Internet City and Knowledge Village (which are expanding all the time), but also has isolated clusters of villas and a peaceful air, despite the mad developments going on around it. The pinnacle of the area is the Palm Jumeirah with its lavish playground, Atlantis (p.315).

The Lowdown
A mainly residential area, with a good selection of eating and drinking options at the many hotels. Also good for those that like messing about on, or in, the water.

Residential

Apart from a few townhouses and villas, Dubai Marina is all apartments. Depending on the floor number and side of the building, some have great sea views, and are luxuriously finished. In Al Sufouh there are a few compounds of older villas (although these are very pricey) and new ones, too. The Palm Jumeirah (which vastly increased Dubai's coastline) features almost every type of accommodation going, which are rapidly being moved into, with the frond-end signature villas being among the most desirable.

The Good
You're never far from the sound of lapping waves.

The Bad
The building sites around the marina have more cranes, more dust, and more sun-blocking high-rise towers than anywhere else in Dubai.

Retail

There is increasingly more on offer for shoppers with big brand names such as Saks Fifth Avenue, Boutique 1 and Gallery One opening along The Walk (p.475) at Jumeirah Beach Residence, and the new Dubai Marina Mall (p.490) due to open in 2009.

Places Of Interest

Marina Walk is worth a meander, especially at night when diners sit out in front of the many restaurants, and you can gaze out over the gleaming yachts and glittering towers. On Friday and Saturday afternoons from October to April, Marina Walk hosts the Marina Market (p.482), with stalls selling clothing, jewellery, gifts and handicrafts. The Walk (p.475) at JBR has turned a building site into a pleasant community with shops and restaurants. JBR itself stretches along 1.7km of shoreline and there are fountains, grassy areas and benches should you need a rest from shopping or an evening stroll.

For beach lovers there is still a free stretch between the hotels, although JBR has claimed a slice for its beach club. Mina Seyahi Dubai (formally DIMC) is a prime location for sailing and boating in Dubai, and also hosts legs of the Off-Shore Powerboat Racing series, in which Dubai's own Victory Team are world-class contenders. On race days you can watch the high-octane action from the adjacent beach – it's quite a spectacle.

The Must Dos
The bars and restaurants with a view of the Gulf. Lots to recommend, including the Rooftop Lounge at The One&Only Royal Mirage, and the top deck of Bussola at The Westin Dubai Mina Seyahi for pizza and cocktails.

Check the calendar at www.minaseyahidubai.com. Since opening in September 2008, the Atlantis resort is proving a top draw as the first hotel open on Palm Jumeirah. Wander through The Avenues shopping arcade with views into the Lost Chambers aquarium (p.262), try the rides at Aquaventure waterpark (p.274) or dine in one of the restaurants run by Michelin-starred chefs. For more views out over this area, try the Sky View Bar (p.618) in the Burj Al Arab or Rooftop Lounge & Terrace (p.617) in the Royal Mirage.

Dubai Marina

Area **D** *F2 p.245*
Maps 11 & 13

The Lowdown
A small area with currently just a few attractions, but worth checking out for all its restaurants, pubs and bars. Dubai Festival City is adding more options as it expands.

The Good
A great place for eating out and entertainment – especially alfresco – including Century Village, Irish Village, Meridien Village and many others.

The Bad
Can be tough getting in and out of the area at certain times of the day due to the traffic on Garhoud Bridge and the Dubai-Sharjah Road.

The Must Dos
Irish Village is a great place to chill out with a pint outside on the fantastic terrace, while Century Village next door offers some great restaurants, all with alfresco dining.

Garhoud

The area of Garhoud (aka Al Garhoud) lies to the north of Garhoud Bridge, between the creek and Deira, and is bordered by the airport. The centre has a small, but pleasant and sought-after, residential neighbourhood, while surrounding this is the commercial area to the west bordered by Garhoud Road. The area has some well-known hotels, a few shops, Dubai Tennis Stadium, Century Village, Irish Village (p.624), the Aviation Club, and several large schools to the east.

Irish Village

Residential

Offering accommodation in a variety of villas, Garhoud is centrally located with good facilities and has a really nice atmosphere. Despite being only a few minutes from the airport, it is a quiet place to live and a great location from which to access most of central Dubai. Rents are reasonable for villas compared to Jumeira and Umm Suqeim, but are on the rise. For more details, refer to Garhoud under Residential Areas (p.140).

Retail

Although previously not one of Dubai's foremost shopping areas – although it is not far from Deira City Centre (p.288), Garhoud used to offer convenience for residents but nothing to attract shoppers from elsewhere. However, this changed with the opening of Festival Centre (p.490), one of the city's largest shopping and entertainment mega-projects. Since 2005, over 600 shops have opened in, as well as IKEA, ACE Hardware and the enormous HyperPanda hypermarket, and the potential in what is now Dubai's second largest shopping mall makes it well worth a trip.

Places Of Interest

Under Garhoud Bridge and alongside the creek is a popular spot for fishing, although the water may not be the cleanest. Also alongside the creek, the massive Dubai Festival City is bursting into life, with the opening of the golf club, bowling centre, private residences, office spaces, Festival Marina, hundreds of new shops in Festival Centre, and a host of popular chain restaurants and coffee shops opening along the Canal Walk. Even more is planned for the coming years, including more shops, restaurants, and a 'global' village. In the middle of Garhoud is Dubai Tennis Stadium, home to the star-studded annual Dubai Tennis Championships (p.392) and also doubling as a concert venue on occasion. It also has some very popular venues for eating out and socialising, with the licensed bars and restaurants all boasting alfresco dining in the pleasant landscaped courtyards and gardens of Century Village and the Irish Village (p.624), and at The Cellar (p.558) just across the lake in the Aviation Club. There are also three hotels in Garhoud with popular outlets including Le Meridien Dubai, Al Bustan Rotana Hotel and Millennium Airport Hotel. One landmark in Garhoud that will definitely catch your eye is a building shaped like the front half of an aeroplane, which rather appropriately is the training centre for Emirates. Located to the north-east, Dubai International Airport has undergone a multi-billion dollar expansion, culminating in the opening of the new Emirates Terminal 3. Garhoud has its very own park that is a haven of peace in a quiet part of the suburb. Entrance to the park is free, and this is one of the few free parks that allows men to enter during the week. It is quite small, and grassy areas are limited, but the children's play areas are huge and packed with the latest and greatest playground equipment.

Jumeira

Area **E** *D2 p.245*
Map 7

Jumeira is a highly desirable residential area, with good access to the beach and plenty of shopping. It's also something of a medical district, with loads of private clinics and surgeries offering everything from sports physiotherapy to tummy tucks. Jumeira Road (aka Beach Road) runs the whole length of Jumeira (around nine kilometres), and it's here that you'll find most of the shopping centres.

The Lowdown
Shops, sandy beaches, sunshine, socialising – Jumeira has it all, which is why it is the original expat area, and home to the infamous, coiffeured 'Jumeira Janes'.

Residential

The address of choice for Dubai's movers and shakers, Jumeira has some beautiful big villas with rents to match. There's nothing much higher than two storeys (apart from the shopping malls) and very few apartments. Villas are sometimes in compounds with a shared pool, but there are also many independent and semi-detached villas. Occasionally you will find an old villa with slightly more reasonable rent, but these are often snapped up quickly, and often before they even come onto the market (through word of mouth).

The Good
Picking from the many malls and shopping centres in Jumeira is tough, but for a shopaholic it's a dream come true. Plus you're just a stone's throw away from the beach and several excellent entertainment options.

Retail

So many shops, so little time. Drive along Beach Road and you'll pass plenty. While Mercato Mall (p.496) is impressive with its renaissance theme, well-known brands, multi-screen cinema and many dining options, the real clincher for Jumeira is the fact that you could almost be shopping on a high street thanks to the side-by-side mini malls. Start at Jumeira Plaza (p.503) and head towards Jumeira Mosque, (a five minute walk if it wasn't for all the retail opportunities that will hypnotise you). There are a number of boutiques and independent shops in the area that you won't find in other malls in Dubai, such as ladies fashion favourite Eve Michelle (04 342 9574) and the excellent school supplies shop White Star Wasco (04 342 2179).

The Bad
The widening of Beach Road means you can no longer pull over and park outside some of the shops and cafes – robbing the area of some of its character. Even with the extra lane, this road can get very busy, especially at rush hour.

Jumeira Mosque interior

Places Of Interest

Jumeira should have something to keep everyone busy. The beautiful Jumeira Mosque (p.274) is certainly worth a visit, and the Majlis Ghorfat Umm Al Sheef (p.268) makes an interesting diversion. For art lovers there are a couple of galleries (see p.264), and

The Must Dos
The Jumeira Mosque tour for an enlightening glimpse into the culture and religion of the country, a delicious, leisurely breakfast at the Lime Tree Café, and a stroll round along Jumeira Open Beach.

if it's beach you want there's plenty of it. The popular Jumeira Open Beach (by Dubai Marine Beach Resort & Spa) has showers and lifeguards, but unfortunately attracts a few voyeurs so you may prefer to try the more private Jumeira Beach Park (p.480). Jumeira is one of the few areas of Dubai that makes for a pleasant stroll and whether you walk along the beach or down the shop-laden Beach Road, the excellent Lime Tree Cafe (p.603) is a good pitstop.

Although there aren't really any major hotels in the area – the Burj Al Arab and Jumeirah Beach Hotel (which are actually in Umm Suqeim) are visible in the distance – Dubai Marine Beach Resort & Spa is the only beach hotel close to the centre of Dubai and is home to some of the city's most stylish venues such as Sho Cho (p.617) and Boudoir (p.626).

Area ⓕ E2 p.245
Maps 8 & 10

Karama

Karama is well known for having something for everyone. It is primarily a residential area, consisting of relatively low-cost flats in low-rise apartment blocks, but has a great shopping area, the Karama Shopping Complex, which is very popular with residents, and especially visitors to Dubai. It also has a particularly good range of inexpensive restaurants serving tasty cuisine from Arabic and Indian to Sri Lankan and Singaporean.

The Lowdown
A lively area with a community feel, great shopping, and scores of superb low-priced dining options – a must for any visitor to Dubai.

Residential

Karama is a good choice for people seeking reasonable rents and a central location. All sizes of apartments (from studio to three bedrooms) are available in the area's many low-rise buildings. It is one of the few places where you can feasibly get around on foot, as you have all kinds of shops and services right on your doorstep. Access to most of central Dubai is quick and easy. The noise and traffic may put some people off, but in terms of price and convenience it has many fans. For more details, refer to Residential Areas (p.128).

The Good
The shopping. There are plenty of great buys in Karama Shopping Complex and the surrounding streets, where bargain prices can be lowered further depending on your haggling skills.

Retail

The heart of Karama is an open-air shopping area consisting of two central streets lined with lots of small shops, all with their goods spilling out onto the pavements. This is a great area for buying anything from clothes or suitcases to kitsch fluffy camels or silver jewellery from Oman. The incessant approach from vendors offering 'copy watches, copy handbags, copy DVDs' can be annoying, especially if you are not interested in any of these items. The renovated fish and vegetable markets are also worth a visit for the atmosphere and some reasonably priced, fresh produce, or for cheap or second-hand furniture on the streets nearby. For more details, also refer to Karama Shopping Complex (p.471).

The Bad
Traffic and parking can get a bit crazy at night.

Places Of Interest

The Karama Shopping Complex is the main draw for most people. Combine a trip around the market with a cheap meal in one of the many roadside restaurants scattered around. Particularly good examples include Pakistani food at Karachi Darbar (p.584), Sri Lankan food at Chef Lanka (p.592), or Filipino food at Tagpuan (p.546). There are also numerous cheap Indian restaurants serving amazing value 'thali' set meals (for as little as Dhs.8) and lots of small Arabic restaurants for shawarma, falafel and fresh fruit juices. The area alongside Trade Centre Road, offers a slightly higher standard, at very reasonable prices. The nearby Zabeel Park (p.283) just across Al Qataiyat Road is linked by a footbridge from Karama to the area near Trade Centre Roundabout. This park is full of open green spaces in perfect contrast to Karama, as well as recreational areas for kids, a jogging track, a cricket pitch, a boating lake with lakeside restaurants and cafes and other facilities for adults.

The Must Dos
Eat in one of the cheap local restaurants for as little as Dhs.8 per person for a delicious meal, then go shopping for delightful kitsch like a mosque alarm clock, a shisha pipe or a wooden camel.

Area **G** E2 p.245
Maps 10, 11 & 13

The Lowdown
*It may be small,
but this area has a
surprisingly good
choice of leisure and
recreation for kids and
adults, great shopping
and numerous options
for eating out.*

The Good
*Exclusive brand names
at Wafi Mall, cheaper
shopping in Lamcy,
numerous leisure
opportunities and
some of Dubai's best
restaurants – including
many independent
restaurants where a
delicious, authentic
meal will cost under
Dhs.100 for two.*

The Bad
*Slightly hard to
navigate to because
of all the cloverleaf
junctions and hidden
slip roads, but you'll get
used to it.*

The Must Dos
*The Pyramids at
Wafi City has a great
health club as well as
some of Dubai's best
restaurants and bars,
while Jimmy Dix (p.613)
is a firm big night out
favourite. Creekside
Park is an explosion of
greenery and houses
numerous leisure
activities in a beautiful
setting overlooking
Dubai Creek.*

Oud Metha & Umm Hurair

Oud Metha and Umm Hurair are located in the centre of Dubai next to Karama, bordered by the creek to the north, Umm Hurair Road to the west and the E11 (Dubai-Sharjah Road) to the south and east. Within this area, popular for its good quality residential buildings, you'll find a great deal of top-quality shopping, entertainment, recreational, social and educational facilities. Some of Dubai's most popular shopping is found in Wafi City (p.499) in Umm Hurair and Lamcy Plaza (p.503) in Oud Metha, with both areas also offering some great eating out options. You'll also find some of the city's best leisure options with Creekside Park (p.281), Al Nasr Leisureland (p.363), WonderLand Theme & Water Park (p.261) and Wafi City.

Residential

A great central location with easy access to the highways. Accommodation is located mostly in Oud Metha where there are lots of new, low-rise apartment blocks and all the facilities you'll need within easy reach. For more details, refer to Oud Metha & Umm Hurair under Residential Areas (p.148).

Retail

Oud Metha has the lively Lamcy Plaza (p.503), which offers great shopping in a variety of stores throughout its five floors, and is home to Loulou Al Dugong's, a fabulous play area for young children. In Umm Hurair, Wafi Mall (p.499) is packed with some of Dubai's most exclusive names which pull in the punters, although it always manages to appear quiet and serene in contrast to the frenzy of other malls.

Places Of Interest

Just off Oud Metha Road are a string of social clubs from various countries and two of Dubai's churches. Nearby you'll find Rashid Hospital (the government emergency hospital), the private American Hospital and Al Nasr Leisureland. This complex offers a variety of facilities, including bowling (p.333), an indoor ice rink (p.363) and an amusement park, the Fruit & Garden Luna Park (p.261). As well as one of Dubai's most popular nightclubs, Chi@The Lodge (p.626), there are also some licensed restaurants just outside the park – try the excellent Khazana (p.553).

The area around Lamcy Plaza has some great independent restaurants, including Lemongrass (p.596), Lan Kwai Fong (p.539), Russian Home Restaurant (p.586) Italian Connection (p.572) and Sai Dham (p.554). The two hotels in the area, the Mövenpick and the Grand Hyatt, have been joined by one of Dubai's newest, Raffles (p.44), already home to some of the city's top restaurants, including Fire & Ice (p.562) and there is also the mighty shopping, leisure and entertainment complex, Wafi City (p.499).

Near Maktoum Bridge and the Dubai Courts you'll find Creekside Park (p.281). There is another, smaller park in Oud Metha on Umm Hurair Road near Maktoum Bridge. WonderLand Theme & Water Park (p.261) is a popular amusement park offering various rides and incorporating the SplashLand Water Park (p.276).

The Al Boom Tourist Village near Garhoud Bridge is a popular wedding venue for local couples. Visitors can sample local cuisine in Al Dahleez (p.534) or take a dinner cruise on one of the beautifully illuminated dhows.

Near Wafi City is the Grand Cineplex, an 11 screen cinema, and the impressive Grand Hyatt Hotel with its opulent lobby resembling a beautiful, lush tropical garden. Also in this area is Dubai Healthcare City, phase one of which is now open. It is a state-of-the-art medical facility being developed in conjunction with top international medical organisations, and will be completed by 2010.

Area ⊕ *E2 p.245*
Maps 7 & 8

The Lowdown
A central location, with its fair share of good-value eateries and interesting shopping – just what you need if you've overdone the malls.

The Good
The 'challenge' of bargain hunting in the little shops along Satwa Road and down Al Hudaiba Street (aka Plant Street).

The Bad
Not necessarily the place to come if you're looking for some peace and quiet.

The Must Dos
Visit while you can. Much of the area may shortly be demolished to make way for the Jumeirah Gardens, a residential and commercial development that will link up to the Business Bay hub and Creek extension.

Satwa

Satwa is an area of contrasts. At one end, quiet suburban streets house smart villas, while just a 15 minute walk away you'll reach Al Diyafah Street and Satwa Road, bustling thoroughfares lined with shops and plenty of inexpensive restaurants and cafes. When the weather is cool enough, it's a great area to wander around – the evenings get particularly busy, and Al Diyafah Street is the place for people to show off their expensive, customised cars.

Residential

There is a mixture of housing options, from a room above a shop to big, independent villas. Somewhere in the middle there are some decent apartments in low-rise blocks, but the central location means rents are not really on the low side.

Retail

Satwa is home to textiles and tailors. For a fraction of what you'd pay in a proper shop, you can choose your material and then let one of these guys knock up a made-to-measure masterpiece. There are also plenty of fascinating knick-knack shops selling

Iranian Mosque

mostly cheap tat, but a browse is always good for a laugh and there are some genuine bargains to be found. Plant Street is famous for pots and plants (hence the name), dodgy pet shops, and furniture upholstery shops and hardware stores. For grocery shopping, there are small 'corner shops', Lal's supermarket (Plant Street), a tiny branch of Union Co-op (just off Satwa Roundabout) and West Zone supermarket. For anything lacking in these, there's a Spinneys on Beach Road just a few minutes' drive away.

Places Of Interest

At the end of Al Diyafah Street nearest the sea is the Dar Al Ittehad (Union House), where the treaty to create the United Arab Emirates was signed on 2 December 1971. It is also the site of the UAE's largest flag (40m x 20m) on top of a 120m reinforced column – quite unmissable, especially at night.

At the other end of Al Diyafah Street (near the Rydges Plaza Hotel) is the permanently busy Satwa Road. Along here are numerous small shops selling mainly textiles, inexpensive clothes and general household items. You will also find a small area full of car repair shops. If you need a tyre change, new battery, or some minor repairs, this place is worth a visit – they can fix just about anything and everything, and bargaining on price is expected.

Plant Street is between Satwa Road and Al Wasl Road, and is very interesting to explore. This is the place to come at Christmas time, as they stock fir trees. On Al Wasl Road is the beautiful and intricate Iranian Mosque, with its distinctive blue tiles, arches and pillars mirroring the similarly patterned Iranian Hospital across the road. If it's greenery you're after, Satwa Park (p.282), in the shadow of the skyscrapers on Sheikh Zayed Road, and the smaller Al Khazzan (p.281) and Al Wasl Parks are oases of greenery with shade and benches. Sporty types can also try a spot of five-a-side football or basketball on the courts along Al Diyafah Street.

Area ➊ *E2 p.245*
Maps 7, 8 & 10

Trade Centre & Downtown Burj Dubai

This lively location is known for the striking architecture of its high-rise residential buildings, office towers, and top-class hotels. From the Trade Centre to Interchange One (known as Defence Roundabout) the Hong Kong-style stretch of Sheikh Zayed Road (SZR) – all 3.5 kilometres of it – is the subject of many a photo, as well as many after-hours tete-a-tetes in the various happening hotspots. While offering contrasting styles, the new Downtown Burj Dubai district has added to the area's architectural reputation with The Address, The Palace Hotel, and the ever-rising landmark, Burj Dubai, which will be another Dubai best, the world's tallest building at a rumoured final height of over 800 metres. With so many residents, tourists, and business people around, this area really buzzes at night, as the crowds flit from restaurants to bars to clubs. During the day there's shopping to be done, nowhere more so than Dubai Mall (p.489), the largest shopping mall in the Middle East.

The Lowdown
Dubai's 'strip', where people work hard and then play hard.

The Good
So much to do, and all on your doorstep. From this central location you are close to everything, from beaches and malls to nightlife and leisure activities.

Residential

Tall apartment blocks offer a variety of units and great views, but they don't come cheap. If you're high enough and facing in the right direction, you can see right over the top of Satwa and Jumeira to the sparkling ocean beyond. There are a number of executive apartments that include a housekeeping service. As time goes by, more and more buildings are muscling into this the area making the parking situation even more dire, but unfortunately not halting the skyscraping rents. The brand new, ironically named, Old Town offers a contrast to the style and size of buildings on SZR, with low-rise traditionally-styled Arabic architecture. For more information on living in the area see p.153.

The Bad
With traffic and a lack of pedestrian subways or overpasses, it could take you half an hour to reach a building on the other side of the road.

Retail

Around Trade Centre almost every building has at least a shop or a small selection of them on its ground floor, and many feature mini-shopping centres. The shopping destination of choice for many of Dubai's well-to-do is the Boulevard at Emirates Towers (p.489). With designer names and designer prices, you can always make do with a bit of window shopping. The Crowne Plaza is also home to The Holiday Centre which has a good (and much cheaper) selection of shops from bookstores to boutiques. The city's newest and largest, Dubai Mall (p.489), already houses 600 shops including flagship stores such as Hamleys and Waitrose, and with another 600 shops still to open, you'll never be short of choice. Once you're all shopped-out, there are the Olympic-size ice rink, fashion catwalk, 22 screen cinema and the enormous Dubai Aquarium (p.292) and Discovery

The Must Dos
Vu's Bar (51st floor of Emirates Towers Hotel) and Neos (63rd floor of The Address) are the ultimate places for sundowners in Dubai with amazing bird's eye views of the city.

Fairmont Hotel

Old Town & Burj Dubai

Centre to keep you entertained, so make sure you pace yourself. Souk Al Bahar (p.505) at The Palace Hotel, offers a selection of souvenir shops aimed at hotel residents, as well as upmarket retailers, but is worth a wander if only for a tranquil escape from Dubai Mall.

Places Of Interest

At the start of the Sheikh Zayed Road 'business district' is the landmark Dubai World Trade Centre and exhibition halls (illustrated on the Dhs.100 banknote). When it was completed in the 70s the 39 storey tower was by far the tallest building in Dubai. Although it has been surpassed in terms of size and grandeur by a multitude of statuesque skyscrapers, it remains a prominent landmark on this ever-expanding skyline. For a great view, especially in winter when it is less hazy, try the guided tour to the observation deck. Nearby the Emirates Towers are an impressive address for international business and pleasure in Dubai. At 355 metres, the office tower was the tallest building in the Middle East and Europe until it was beaten by Burj Dubai. The smaller tower, at 305 metres, houses the Emirates Towers five-star hotel. The views from Vu's cocktail bar (p.620) on the 51st floor are spectacular and the adrenaline-pumping lift ride is not to be missed. Behind the towers is the site of the Dubai International Finance Centre (DIFC), with the distinctive 'Gate' building. DIFC is home to Dubai's very own financial exchange. Just beyond the first interchange, and towering above the rest of the skyline is Burj Dubai, which at upwards of 700 metres and still under construction, is the world's tallest building, even before it's finished. It is due to be completed in 2009.

Area 🅚 D2 p.245
Map 6

The Lowdown
Golden beaches, smart villas, posh hotels, a 'souk' and a popular water park.

The Good
A wander around Souk Madinat Jumeirah with the iconic Burj Al Arab in the background.

The Bad
Sky-high rents means that living in a villa with a view of the Burj Al Arab is reserved for a few fortunates only.

The Must Dos
Pick a great bar in Al Qasr, Mina A'Salam or the Jumeirah Beach Hotel, then sit and sip a cocktail and watch the sunset.

Umm Suqeim

Umm Suqeim is a pleasant family neighbourhood with a good stretch of beach and some top-class leisure and entertainment facilities. It is also home to Dubai's iconic landmark, the Burj Al Arab (currently the tallest hotel in the world), which sits 280m off the coast on its own island. Although not nearly as tall, the area's other luxury hotels in the Madinat and next door, Jumeirah Beach Hotel, are no less impressive, with fine-dining restaurants and some real star bars. Souk Madinat Jumeirah (p.498) should be on every visitor's itinerary, and Wild Wadi Water Park (p.276) is a great place to cool down on a hot day.

Residential

Umm Suqeim is a great location for families, thanks to its low-rise villas, many with gardens and courtyards. Some villas are actually so large and luxurious they could be described as palaces. Being so close to Internet City and Media City means the area is popular with high-flyers, and the rents are sky-high too. See p.155.

Retail

Until fairly recently there was no real shopping to be had in Umm Suqeim, but that changed with the opening of Souk Madinat Jumeirah (p.276). Built to resemble a traditional Arabian market, the souk is a maze of alleyways featuring 75 shops and boutiques. For weary shoppers there's endless coffee shops, restaurants and bars.

Places Of Interest

The ultimate place of interest has to be the Burj Al Arab hotel (p.38). If your budget allows, you shouldn't miss the chance to sample its bars and restaurants, or even the health spa. If you prefer your leisure to be free-of-charge, there's plenty of public beach to enjoy – just turn up, pop your towel down and relax. However, if the beach is a little sedate and you fancy some aquatic fun for the whole family, it has to be Wild Wadi Water Park (p.276). For a spot of culture, see what's on at the theatre at the Madinat (p.634) or, in winter, catch an open-air cinema screening at Hydra (www.hydraopenair.com).

Area ⬤ F2 p.245
Map 12

The Must Dos
Wander around the Heritage Area and imagine that you've stepped back in time. Hats off to the local government for restoring and preserving this fascinating slice of history.

The Good
Sharjah is a city of culture, heritage and the arts, and also boasts an attractive corniche and lush green parks.

The Bad
Traffic! A 10 kilometre journey can take well over an hour, which may put you off visiting in the evenings.

The Lowdown
Quieter than Dubai, but still plenty to see and do, especially for arts and culture lovers.

Tone It Down
Sharjah is more conservative than Dubai, both in terms of dress code and behaviour. Wearing revealing clothing or kissing and canoodling might earn you some disapproving stares, if not a stern talking to from the police. Bear this in mind when exploring the area.

Sharjah

Before Dubai's rise to prominence as a trading and tourism hotspot, its neighbour, Sharjah, was one of the wealthiest towns in the region, with settlers earning their livelihood from fishing, pearling and trade. The city grew inland from the original creekside town, and the creek remains a prominent landmark today. Sharjah is worth a visit for its various museums and great shopping. In 1998, UNESCO named Sharjah the cultural capital of the Arab world due to its commitment to art, culture and preserving its traditional heritage.

> ## Close Neighbour
> Sharjah is, of course, a separate city, and emirate, but it is within easy reach (traffic depending) of Dubai, it does have its fair share of things to see and do, and it is home to many people who work in Dubai. Therefore, it appears here as an extended 'main area' of Dubai, with its good points and bad points listed, and details some of the sights and attractions to tempt you over the border.

Residential
Downtown is mainly apartment blocks, while further inland and along the coast you'll find a mixture of villas old and new. Rents in Sharjah are generally cheaper than those in Dubai, meaning many Dubai workers live in Sharjah and make the short trip in each day. Short, that is, in terms of distance (less than 10 kilometres 'creek-to-creek'), but because so many thousands hit the road at the same time, journey times can be infuriatingly long.

Retail
Big shopping centres and malls are well represented in Sharjah, with the biggest being Sharjah City Centre, Mega Mall and the Sahara Centre. All the big shops and brands are here, and you may be pleasantly surprised to find fewer shoppers than in Dubai's malls. Sharjah also has numerous good souks, with the Central Souk, aka Blue Souk (p.482) and Souk Al Arsah (p.483) particularly worth a mention. Beside the creek, the fruit and vegetable markets provide some real atmosphere and colour.

Places Of Interest
Sharjah is built around Khalid Lagoon, (popularly known as the creek), and the surrounding Buheirah Corniche surrounding is a popular spot for a stroll in the evening. From various points on the lagoon, small dhows can be hired to see the lights of the city from the water. One place you shouldn't miss is Sharjah Heritage Area (p.268), the fascinating old walled city that is home to numerous museums and the traditional Souk Al Arsah (p.483). The nearby Arts Area (p.258) is a treat for art lovers with galleries and more museums. Another must is Al Qasba (p.273), with a canal, performance spaces and waterside restaurants. The city's latest attraction is Sharjah Aquarium (p.262). Another worthy weekend stop-off is the Sharjah Desert Park, for the Natural History Museum, Arabian Wildlife Centre and Children's Farm and the newest addition Sharjah Botanical Museum – see p.273 for more.

Sharjah Corniche

My
destination
takes me on a journey
to the**past**

Old fishing boats sailing smoothly, a lasting legacy of this historic emirate.
A precious pearl of inspiration, a rich treasury of timeless tradition.

Sharjah my destination

For more information and to receive a copy of our brochure call **800 Shj (745)** or visit **www.sharjahtourism.ae**

الشارقة
Sharjah

Amusement Centres

Other options **Amusement Parks** p.261

Creekside Park
Umm Hurair
Map 11 A3

Children's City

04 334 0808 | *www.childrencity.ae*

Children's City is an educational project that offers kids their own learning zone and amusement facilities, by providing hands-on experiences relating to theory they have been taught at school. There's a planetarium focusing on the solar system and space exploration, a nature centre for information on land and sea environments, and the Discovery Space, which reveals the miracles and mysteries of the human body. It is aimed at 5 to 12 year olds, although items of interest are included for toddlers and teenagers.

Opp Sharjah Airport
Al Dhaid Rd
Sharjah
Map 2 C2

Discovery Centre

06 558 6577 | *www.discoverycentre.ae*

This colourful centre features a wide range of activities suitable for toddlers and children up to the age of 13, including a soft-play area for the very tiny tots. Children can explore the themed areas and experiment and interact with the exhibits. The underlying aim is to teach youngsters about the biological, physical and technological worlds in a practical way. There is good pushchair access, an in-house cafe and ample parking. Children under 2 years get in for free. Kids under 12 pay Dhs.5 and over 13s, Dhs.7. Family tickets are also available. Open from 09:00 to 14:00 Sunday to Wednesday, 16:30 to 20:30 on Thursdays, and 15:30 to 20:30 Friday and Saturday. Hours are subject to change, so call to check times.

Wafi Mall
Umm Hurair
Map 10 E4

Encounter Zone

04 324 7747 | *www.waficity.com*

With a range of activities for all ages, Encounter Zone is a great stop-off if you want to reward your kids for being good while you have shopped up a storm in Wafi's many boutiques. Galactica is for teenagers and adults and features an inline skating and skateboarding park. Lunarland is for kids aged 1 to 8, and is packed with activities designed especially for younger children, including a small soft-play area for little ones. Prices range from Dhs.3 to Dhs.27, or you can buy a five-hour pass for Dhs.45. Open from 10:00 to 22:00 Sunday to Wednesday and from 10:00 to midnight on Thursday and Friday.

Hamarain Centre
Deira
Map 11 E1

Extreme Fun

04 262 1110 | *www.dubaishoppingmalls.com*

Previously known as City 2000, this is a small centre with lots of video games and a few rides. Entrance is free and all machines are operated by Dhs.1 tokens. Most take two tokens, except for adult simulator games that take three. If all that fun leaves you famished, head to the foodcourt.

Al Bustan Centre
Al Qusais
Map 14 B1

Fantasy Kingdom

04 263 0000 | *www.al-bustan.com*

Themed as a medieval castle, Fantasy Kingdom offers adventure and excitement for the little ones. The centre has a 24,000 square foot indoor play area, which is divided into sections for different age groups. Younger children can enjoy the merry-go-round, cars to ride and the soft-play area, while older kids can play interactive games, video games, bumper cars, pool and air hockey. There is also a children's cafeteria.

Deira City Centre
Deira
Map 11 C3

Magic Planet

04 295 4333 | *www.deiracitycentre.com*

These blaring, boisterous play areas are located in Deira City Centre and Mall of the Emirates (04 341 4000) next to the foodcourts, and are hugely popular for kids accompanying their mums and dads on long shopping trips. There are various rides, including merry-go-rounds, a train, bumper cars and the latest video games. For tinier tots there is a large activity play gym and a small soft-play area. Entrance is free, and you use the facilities on a 'pay as you play' basis (by loading cash onto a plastic card). For unlimited fun and entertainment, you can buy a Dhs.50 special pass. If hunger pangs start interfering with playtime, there are many outlets in the foodcourts where you can refuel.

Amusement Parks

Other options **Amusement Centres** p.260, **Water Parks** p.274

Kids' Play Areas

When high temperatures drive you indoors, it's good to know that most malls have an indoor play area that should keep kids busy for ages. Most have various facilities and activities to suit a spectrum of ages. Some recommended venues are: Fun Corner – Bin Sougat Mall (04 286 2848), Umm Suqeim (04 394 0315), Reef Mall (04 227 6620); LouLou Al Dugong's – Lamcy Plaza (04 335 2700); Magic Planet (p.260); and Peakaboo – Village Mall (04 344 7122) and Mall of the Emirates (04 347 0622).

Sahara Centre
Sharjah
Map 2 C2

Adventureland

06 531 6363 | www.adventureland-sharjah.com
Located on the first floor of the Sahara Centre, you may think this is just another 'amusement corner' to keep the kids happy while you recover from a hard day's shopping, but you'd be wrong. Adventureland is a fully fledged indoor funfair, with an impressive variety of rides and attractions to keep all ages happy. The Quantum Leap ride shouldn't be missed – it's fast and thrilling and not for the faint-hearted, but there's also plenty of sedate rides for the little ones. The centre also features 100 video games and simulators, an internet cafe, a climbing wall, billiards, bowling and a sports cafe. They also have a party room, and offer a number of packages catering to children's parties.

Al Nasr Leisureland
Oud Metha
Map 10 E2

Fruit & Garden Luna Park

04 337 1234 | www.alnasrleisureland.ae
This fruity little park offers many attractions that are suitable for everyone, and is an ideal venue for a birthday party. Activities include rides, go-karts, bumper cars and a rollercoaster, and you can combine a visit here with use of the other facilities of Al Nasr Leisureland. Entrance fees are set at Dhs.10 for adults and Dhs.5 for children under the age of 5.

Zabeel Park
Zabeel
Map 10 B1

Stargate

Set to open at Zabeel Park in March 2009, Stargate is built to resemble a spaceship that has crash-landed. Primarily aimed at 4 to 14 year olds, it promises to become a family 'edutainment' centre, with spaces for learning, shopping, dining and exercising, in addition to high speed rides and roller coasters. For more details, see local press.

Nr Creekside Park
Umm Hurair
Map 13 C1

WonderLand Theme & Water Park

04 324 1222 | www.wonderlanduae.com
With both an amusement theme park and the SplashLand Water Park (p.276), WonderLand will keep the most demanding of youngsters happy. The theme park offers indoor and outdoor rides and slides for people of all ages, including The Space Shot, Freefall and Action Arm as well as play areas, trampolines, video and arcade games. Parties and events can be catered for and go-karting and paintball are also available (see Paintballing on p.377). A multi-million dollar renovation of WonderLand is on the cards to be completed by the end of 2010, but the start date has not yet been announced. Check the website or call before you set out.

Aquariums & Marine Centres

Atlantis The Palm
Palm Jumeirah
Map 2 A3

Dolphin Bay ▶ p.76

04 4426 1030 | *www.atlantisthepalm.com*

Playing with a bottlenose dolphin on the Shallow Water Interaction package at Dolphin Bay is an unforgettable experience. Touching, hugging, holding 'hands', playing ball and feeding are all encouraged, under supervision of the marine specialists. A 90 minute session, will set you back Dhs.385 per person (with significant discounts for hotel guests) and is open to all ages. Your family and friends can watch and take photos from the beach for Dhs.100, but this also grants them access to Aquaventure, Lost Chambers and the private beach. More options are promised for early 2009, such as a deep water experience, where visitors can swim and snorkel alongside the mammals with the aid of an underwater scooter.

The Dubai Mall
Downtown Burj Dubai
Map 7 D4

Dubai Aquarium

04 362 7500 | *www.thedubaimall.com*

Part of Dubai's legacy for record breaking architectural feats, at three storeys high the Dubai Aquarium holds the Guinness World Record for the world's largest acrylic viewing panel. Aside from being tagged with a slightly pointless record, the magnitude of this spectacle can be viewed at a variety of angles from different floors of the mall and from inside the 270° walk-through tunnel. The 50 metre long aquarium will eventually house over 33,000 aquatic animals, with more than 85 species including sharks and rays. The aquarium is free to view, and there is a charge of Dhs.50 for visitors to the interactive Discovery Centre and Tunnel Experience.

Creekside Park
Umm Hurair
Map 11 A3

Dubai Dolphinarium ▶ p.263

04 336 9773 | *www.dubaidolphinarium.ae*

Despite the controversy surrounding its opening, the dolphinarium has proved to be a popular addition in Creekside Park (p.281). The main attraction is the seal and dolphin show which runs three times a day at 11:00, 17:00 and 20:00, except on Tuesdays and Saturdays when the 20:00 show does not run. During the show you will meet the three resident black sea bottlenose dolphins and the four northern fur seals, and afterwards you can have your picture taken with them, or even get up close and personal with them in the water. Prices start from Dhs.100 for an adult and Dhs.50 for a child, but a whole range of group and family discounts are available.

Atlantis The Palm
Palm Jumeirah
Map 2 A3

Lost Chambers ▶ p.ii - p.iii

04 426 0000 | *www.atlantisthepalm.com*

The ruins of the mysterious lost city provide the theme for the aquarium at Atlantis. The maze of underwater halls and tunnels provide ample opportunity to get up close to the aquarium's 65,000 inhabitants, ranging from sharks and eels to rays and piranhas, as well as multitudes of exotic fish. The entrance fee is Dhs.100 for adults and Dhs.70 for 7 to 11 year olds. Hotel guests get in for free, and while you can see quite a lot from the windows in the hotel, it is worth splashing out for the views inside.

Al Khan
Sharjah
Map 2 C2

Sharjah Aquarium

06 556 6002 | *www.sharjahaquarium.ae*

Although eclipsed by the two aquariums that also opened in Dubai in 2008, and a littler smaller, Sharjah Aquarium is the city's newest attraction and draws big crowds. Situated next door to Sharjah Maritime Museum at the mouth of Al Khan Lagoon, its location allows visitors to walk along the sea outside the centre as well as viewing

GOVERNMENT OF DUBAI

سلدية دبي
DUBAI MUNICIPALITY

DUBAI DOLPHINARIUM

**Located at Creek Park, Gate 1,
in the heart of Dubai**

Show timings:

Mon	Tue	Wed	Thu	Fri	Sat
11:00am	11:00am	11:00am	11:00am	11:00am	11:00am
5:00pm	5:00pm	5:00pm	5:00pm	5:00pm	5:00pm
8:00pm	No show	8:00pm	8:00pm	8:00pm	No show

Contact: 04 3369773
www.dubaidolphinarium.ae

Online booking: www.timeouttickets.com

Creative Art Centre

life underwater inside. When complete, there will be over 250 species on show in tanks filled with coral and plants, as well as many interactive displays. Another great attraction in Sharjah, well worth combining on a day out there with some of the other museums. Opening times vary, check the website. Closed Sunday and Tuesday.

Art Galleries
Other options **Art** p.424, **Art & Craft Supplies** p.424

While there's nothing like the Tate Gallery or the Louvre in Dubai, there are a number of galleries that have interesting exhibitions of art and traditional Arabic artefacts, and more are springing up, particularly around the Al Quoz area. Most operate as a shop and a gallery, but some also provide studios for artists and are involved in the promotion of art within the emirates. The Majlis Gallery, The Courtyard and the XVA Gallery are all worth visiting for their traditional and unusual architecture alone. They provide striking locations in which you can enjoy a wide range of art, both local and international. Take a look at *Time Out* magazine for details of weekly exhibitions and events, or contact the galleries directly.

Artsawa
Hasa Rd
Al Quoz
Map 6 C4

04 340 8660 | *www.artsawa.com*
Opened in October 2008, Artsawa is one of a group of art galleries newly opened in Dubai. It will host up to 15 exhibitions annually, making it one of the most active art platforms in the region. Focusing on the promotion of contemporary Arab art in a variety of mediums including collage, etching, installation, painting, photography, sculpture and video, Artsawa will also hold educational events aimed at engaging the local and international communities. The large warehouse location in Al Quoz past Time Square provides a great space for visitors to interact with the exhibitions.

Basement
Street 8
Al Quoz
Map 6 C3

04 341 4409 | *www.basementdubai.com*
Another new addition to the art scene in Al Quoz, Basement is located behind Time Square shopping mall. This contemporary gallery showcases the work of emerging and established artists (primarily Iranian) and the exhibitions boast the use of a diverse range of media, in new and traditional formats.

Creative Art Centre
Beh Jumeirah Rd
Jumeira
Map 7 D1

04 344 4394 | *artcentr@emirates.net.ae*
A large gallery and shop with eight showrooms set in two villas, Creative Art Centre has a wide range of original art, framed maps, and Arabian antiques and gifts. The selection of antiques includes Omani chests and old doors, much of it 'rescued' in Oman by the gallery owners and then restored in-house. There's also a good selection of old weapons and silver. Lynda Shephard, the managing partner, is a well-known artist in both Oman and Dubai and some of her works can be purchased here. The gallery offers a picture-framing service, and they specialise in the restoration of antiques and

furniture. The centre can be found set back from Beach Road (take the turning inland between Choithram supermarket and Town Centre shopping mall).

Four Seasons Ramesh Gallery

Al Zomorrodah Bldg
Karama
Map 10 E1

04 334 9090 | *www.fourseasonsgallery.com*
Originally opened in 1970, this company has one of the largest selections of art and photography in Dubai. Located in Block A of the Zomorrodah Building on Zabeel Road in Karama, just along from the main post office, the gallery is in one end of the store, which is now largely devoted to selling contemporary furniture. There is a large selection of different types of art exhibited, and for sale, with a mixture from both local and international artists, as well as some interesting photos of Dubai's history.

Green Art Gallery

Villa 23 St 51
Jumeira
Map 7 E1

04 344 9888 | *www.gagallery.com*
Housed in an attractive single-storey villa just a stone's throw from Beach Road behind Dubai Zoo, Green Art Gallery features original art, limited edition prints and hand-crafted work by artists from all over the world. In particular, the gallery draws on those influenced and inspired by the heritage, culture and environment of the Arab world and its people. The managing partners also encourage local artists of all nationalities by guiding them through the process of exhibiting and promoting their work. This is a 'proper' art gallery, with large white minimalist walls and lots of floor space, and makes a great stop-off if you fancy some peace and quiet and a little culture. Seasonal exhibitions are held from October to May.

Hunar Art Gallery

Villa 6 St 49a
Rashidiya
Map 2 C3

04 286 2224 | *www.hunargallery.com*
This gallery exhibits international fine art. Beautifully decorated Japanese tiles, Belgian pewter and glass pieces fill the spaces between ever-changing, contemporary local and world art. Some artists (usually either local artists or those particularly popular at the gallery) receive more regular showings, but typically there is a diverse array of artists shown. Exhibitions last for around a month, and each one displays either a theme, an artist or a group. The gallery will also, on occasion, display the works of talented local scholars. Many of the pieces in the gallery can be purchased, but if the piece you buy is part of an exhibition, you can only take it home after the event.

The Majlis Gallery

Al Faheidi St
Bur Dubai
Map 8 F2

04 353 6233 | *www.majlisgallery.com*
Set in traditional surroundings in the old Bastakiya area of the city (close to Al Faheidi Roundabout), The Majlis Gallery is a converted Arabic house, complete with windtowers. Small whitewashed rooms lead off the central courtyard and host a variety of exhibitions by contemporary artists. In addition to the fine art collection, there's an extensive range of handmade glass, pottery, fabrics, frames, unusual pieces of furniture and other bits and bobs. The gallery hosts exhibitions throughout the year, but is worth visiting at any time. Open Saturday to Thursday.

Miraj Islamic Art Gallery

582 Jumeirah Rd
Jumeira
Map 6 F1

04 394 1084 | *www.mirajislamicartcentre.com*
Miraj holds a fantastic collection of Islamic art objects from silver, metalware and marble, to intricate astrolabes, painstakingly crafted carpets and textiles, and displays of calligraphy and engraving. Just up the road is Saga World (04 395 9071), a souk-style, high-end department store, where you can buy a range of Middle Eastern and Indian handcraft products similar to those on display in the gallery.

Opera Gallery

Bldg 3, DIFC
Trade Centre 2
Map 7 E3

04 323 0909 | *www.operagallery.com*

Part of an international chain, Opera Gallery opened in November 2008 in Gate Village Building 3 in Dubai International Financial Centre. They have a permanent collection of international art on display and for sale, mainly European and Chinese, with visiting exhibitions changing throughout the year. The permanent collection also includes several masterpieces, so look out for the odd Dali or Picasso.

The Third Line

Nr The Courtyard
Al Quoz
Map 6 E3

04 341 1367 | *www.thethirdline.com*

Showcasing the work of contemporary Middle Eastern artists, The Third Line also has a gallery in Doha. In addition to monthly exhibitions, the gallery hosts 'alternative programmes' which include film screenings, debates and international multimedia forum, all with the intention of promoting interaction between artists and the public. Closed Fridays.

Total Arts Gallery

The Courtyard
Al Quoz
Map 6 E3

04 347 5050 | *www.courtyard-uae.com*

Dubai's biggest gallery occupies two floors of The Courtyard in Al Quoz. It usually exhibits works of art from a variety of cultures and continents, although there is a leaning towards regional talent (particularly Iranian). There are over 300 paintings on permanent display, and regular shows of traditional handicrafts and antique furniture. One of the main attractions is the beautiful cobbled courtyard itself, surrounded by different facades combining a variety of building styles from around the world.

XVA Gallery

Bastakiya
Bur Dubai
Map 9 A2

04 353 5383 | *www.xvagallery.com*

Located in the centre of the maze-like alleyways of Bastakiya, this is one of Dubai's most interesting art galleries. Originally a windtower house, it is now fully restored and worth a visit for its architecture and displays of local and international art or for a snack in the tranquil shaded courtyard. The gallery focuses on paintings and hosts many different exhibitions throughout the year. From November to April, the gallery hosts free film screenings on Thursday evenings. XVA can also lay claim to the title of Dubai's hippest hotel – there are eight guest rooms located on the upper floors, where you can chill out in rooftop rocking chairs and gaze over the minarets to the lights of Bur Dubai and beyond.

Heritage Sites

Other options **Museum** p.270

Old Dubai features many fascinating places to visit, all of which offer glimpses into the past when the city was nothing more than a small fishing and trading port. Many of the pre-oil heritage sites have been carefully restored, paying close attention to traditional design and using original building materials. Take an ambient stroll through the Bastakiya area, characterised by the many distinctive windtowers, and marvel at how anyone could have survived in Dubai before air-conditioning.

Aside from Dubai, many other areas also offer history fans opportunities to learn more about the region's fascinating past.

Ramadan Timings

During Ramadan, timings for many companies in Dubai change significantly. For museums and heritage sites, they usually open slightly later in the morning than usual, and close earlier in the afternoon. Check before you go.

Al Khor St Al Ras ◀
Deira
Map 9 A1

Al Ahmadiya School & Heritage House

04 226 0286 | *www.dubaitourism.ae*

Al Ahmadiya School was the earliest regular school in the city and a visit is an excellent opportunity to see the history of education in Dubai. Established in 1912 by Mr Ahmadiya for Dubai's elite, this building was closed in 1963 when the school relocated to larger premises. Situated in what is becoming a small centre for heritage in Deira (Al Souk Al Khabeer), it is just behind the Heritage House, an interesting example of a traditional Emirati family house and the former home of Mr Ahmadiya, which dates back to 1890. Both buildings were renovated and converted into museums with the same excellent care and attention as Dubai's other heritage sites. They opened in March 2000, and are now great places for a peek into how life used to be in Dubai's past. Admission to both is free.

Nr Al Hisn Fort, Kalba ◀
East Coast
Map 1 F2

Al Hisn Kalba

09 277 4442 | *www.sharjah-welcome.com*

As you drive along the coast road in Kalba town, you come to the restored house of Sheikh Sayed Al Qassimi, which overlooks the sea. The house is located at the end of a large grassy expanse with swings and small rides for children. On the opposite side of the road is Kalba's Al Hisn Fort, which houses the town's museum and contains a limited display of weapons. Entrance fee: Dhs.3 for individuals; Dhs.6 for families.

Btn Al Diwan R/A &
Al Faheidi R/A ◀
Bur Dubai
Map 9 A2

Bastakiya

The Bastakiya area is one of the oldest heritage areas in Dubai and certainly one of the most atmospheric. The neighbourhood dates back to the early 1900s when traders from the Bastak area of southern Iran were encouraged to settle there by tax concessions granted by Sheikh Maktoum bin Hashar, the ruler of Dubai at the turn of the century. The area is characterised by traditional windtower houses, built around courtyards and clustered together around a winding maze of alleyways. The distinctive four-sided windtowers (barjeel in Arabic), that can be seen on top of the traditional flat-roofed buildings, are one of the earliest forms of air conditioning.

The whole area is a great place to explore for a few hours, strolling around the peaceful and shaded narrow lanes really takes you away from the bustle of Bur Dubai just streets away. Many buildings have been restored and converted into art galleries, shops, cafes, including Dubai's smallest and most unique guesthouse, a traditionally styled Arabic restaurant, Calligraphy House, Philately House and offices for several non-governmental organisations such as the Sheikh Mohammed Centre for Cultural Understanding (p.270), the Journalists' Association and the World Wildlife Fund. To cater to the growing number of tourists visiting this area, a new tourism office was opened in 2006.

An ongoing reconstruction project is gradually turning Bastakiya into a pedestrian conservation area with more and more buildings being restored, creating a hub for artists in the city, with galleries, workshops, studios, and will host art events and festivals. Maps of the area (in English and Arabic) are situated opposite Al Musalla Post Office on Al Faheidi Street and also near Al Diwan Roundabout.

Nr Fujairah Fort ◀
Fujairah
Map 1 F2

Fujairah Heritage Village

This 6,000 square metre heritage village depicts life in the UAE before oil was discovered, with displays of fishing boats, simple dhows, clay, stone and bronze implements and pots, and hunting and agricultural tools. The heritage village is close to Ain Al Madhab Gardens, which are situated in the foothills of the Hajar Mountains just outside Fujairah City. The gardens are fed by mineral springs and this warm sulphur laden water is used in two swimming pools (separate for men and women). Private chalets can be hired on a daily basis. The entrance fee is Dhs.5.

Town Centre
Hatta
Map 1 F2

Hatta Heritage Village

***04 852 1374** | www.dubaitourism.ae*

Opened to the public in 2001, Hatta Heritage Village is located an hour's drive south east of Dubai city and three kilometres from Hatta Fort Hotel. It is constructed around an old settlement and was restored in the style of a traditional mountain village. Explore the tranquil oasis, the narrow alleyways and discover traditional life in the mud and barasti houses. Hatta's history goes back over 3,000 years and the area includes a 200 year-old mosque and the fortress built by Sheikh Maktoum bin Hasher Al Maktoum in 1896, which is now used as a weaponry museum. Entry is free.

Nr Al Shindagha
Tunnel
Al Shindagha
Map 9 A1

Heritage Village & Diving Village

***04 393 7151** | www.dubaitourism.ae*

Located near the mouth of Dubai Creek, the Heritage and Diving Villages focus on Dubai's maritime past, pearl diving traditions and architecture. The museum is staffed by real potters and weavers who display their craft the way it has been practised for centuries. There are also a number of shops clustered in one corner selling the usual range of souvenirs. As you wander through, local Arabic women serve up traditionally cooked bread and fried 'doughnuts' – one of the rare opportunities you'll have to sample genuine Emirati cuisine. Camel rides are available most afternoons and evenings. The village is very close to Sheikh Saeed Al Maktoum's House, and is part of the area of Shindagha currently being developed into a cultural centre. Buildings in the area are being renovated and reconstructed to recreate the traditional and simple life in Dubai as it was before modernity took hold. It's particularly lively here during the Dubai Shopping Festival and Eid celebrations, with performances such as traditional sword dancing.

Off Jumeira Rd
Jumeira
Map 7 B1

Majlis Ghorfat Um Al Sheef

***04 394 6343** | www.dubaitourism.ae*

Constructed in 1955 from coral stone and gypsum, this simple building was used by the late Sheikh Rashid bin Saeed Al Maktoum as a summer residence. The ground floor is an open veranda (leewan or rewaaq), while upstairs the majlis (Arabic for meeting place) is decorated with carpets, cushions, lanterns and rifles. The roof terrace was used for drying dates and even sleeping and it originally offered an uninterrupted view of the sea, although all you can see now are villa rooftops. The site has a garden with a pond and traditional falaj irrigation system, using stone and gypsum channels to direct water from a well. In another corner there's a barasti shelter constructed entirely from palm branches and leaves. The structure has a windtower, designed to channel any available wind down into the building, the Middle East's early and efficient attempt at air conditioning. The Majlis is located just inland from Beach Road on Street 17, beside HSBC bank and Jumbo Electronics – look for the brown Municipality signs. Entry is Dhs.1 for adults and free for children under 6 years. Closed Friday mornings.

Nr Arts Area
Sharjah
Map 2 C2

Sharjah Heritage Area

***06 568 1738** | www.sharjahmuseums.ae*

The beautifully restored heritage area in Sharjah is a great place for people with an interest in local history. The area includes a number of old buildings: Al Hisn Fort (Sharjah Fort); Sharjah Islamic Museum; Sharjah Heritage Museum (Bait Al Naboodah); the Maritime Museum; the Majlis of Ibrahim Mohammed Al Midfa and the Old Souk (Souk Al Arsah). Here you will see traditional local architecture and life described, depicted and displayed as it was over 150 years ago and right up to more recent times. The Majlis of Ibrahim Mohammed Al Midfa, situated between the souk and the waterfront, is a peaceful majlis famous for its round windtower, the only one of its kind in the UAE. Toilets can be found at each venue and there's an Arabic coffee shop in the shady courtyard of Souk Al Arsah.

Heritage Village

Sheikh Mohammed Centre For Cultural Understanding

Bastakiya
Bur Dubai
Map 9 A2

04 353 6666 | *www.cultures.ae*

Located in the Bastakiya area, the cultural centre of Dubai, SMCCU was established to help visitors and residents understand the customs and traditions of the UAE through various activities. These include tours in Jumeira Mosque, (see p.274), a walking tour around the Bastakiya, Arabic courses, cultural awareness programmes and weekly coffee mornings where it is possible to meet UAE Nationals to learn about all aspects of Emirati life. The centre itself is also worth a look for the majlis-style rooms around the courtyard and great views through the palm trees and windtowers.

Sheikh Saeed Al Maktoum's House

Nr Heritage &
Diving Villages
Al Shindagha
Map 9 A1

04 393 7139 | *www.dubaitourism.ae*

The modest home of Dubai's much-loved former ruler was once strategically located at the mouth of Dubai's creek but now lies close to the Bur Dubai entrance to Al Shindagha Tunnel. Dating from 1896, this carefully restored house-turned-museum is built in the traditional manner of the Gulf coast, using coral covered in lime and sand-coloured plaster. The interesting displays in many rooms show rare and wonderful photographs of all aspects of life in Dubai pre-oil. There is also an old currency and stamp collection and great views over the creek from the upper floor. Entry is Dhs.2 for adults, Dhs.1 for children and free for under 6s.

Museums

Other options **Art Galleries** p.264, **Heritage Sites** p.266

For residents and visitors alike, a visit to one of the museums or heritage sites in the UAE is a great opportunity to discover the culture and history of the country, as well as to catch a glimpse of a fast disappearing way of life. Dubai Municipality plays an active role in preserving Dubai's past and is currently overseeing a huge renovation project which includes 230 of Dubai's old buildings; completion is expected in 2009. Dubai Museum is a gem, while neighbouring Sharjah offers a multiple cultural attractions.

Ajman Museum

Opp Etisalat
Ajman
Map 2 C1

06 742 3824 | *www.am.gov.ae*

Ajman Museum is interesting and well arranged, with displays described in both English and Arabic. The museum has a variety of exhibits, including a collection of passports (Ajman used to issue its own) and depictions of ancient life, but it's the building itself that will most impress visitors. Housed in a fortress dating back to around 1775, and a former residence of the ruler of Ajman, the museum is a fascinating example of traditional architecture, with imposing watchtowers and traditional windtowers. The fortress served as a police station before becoming the museum in the early 1980s. Entry is Dhs.5 for adults. Morning opening times are 09:00 to 13:00 then 16:00 to 19:00 in the evening. Closed on Fridays.

Al Mahatta Museum

Nr Dept of
Immigration
Sharjah
Map 2 C2

06 573 3079 | *www.sharjahmuseums.ae*

This museum is a must for plane spotters and anyone interested in the history of aviation. Home to the first airfield in the Gulf in 1932, Sharjah played an important role as a primary stop-off point for the first commercial flights from Britain to India, and the museum looks at the impact this had on the traditional way of life in Sharjah. Four of the original propeller planes have been fully restored and are on display. Entry is Dhs.5 for adults and Dhs.10 for families, and it can be found behind Al Estiqlal Street.

Nr Bastakiya
Bur Dubai
Map 9 A2

Dubai Museum

04 353 1862 | www.dubaitourism.ae

Located in Al Faheidi Fort, one of Dubai's oldest buildings, dating back to 1787, Dubai Museum is a highly creative, appealing and well thought-out museum. It is well worth a visit for residents and visitors to get an overview of Dubai and its history. The fort was originally built as the residence of the ruler of Dubai and for sea defence, then renovated in 1970 to house the museum. The site has also been expanded to include a large area under the courtyard of the old fort. All parts of life from Dubai's past are represented in an attractive and interesting way: walk through a souk from the 1950s, stroll through an oasis complete with falaj, see the way of life in a traditional Emirati house, get up close to the wildlife of the UAE, learn about the archaeological finds from the area or go 'underwater' to discover the part the sea has played in Dubai's growth with its pearl diving and fishing industries. Even if museums aren't your thing, you will find it interesting and informative. It's highly recommended for the whole family.

Opp Ruler's Palace
Fujairah
Map 1 F2

Fujairah Museum

09 222 9085

This interesting museum offers an insight into Fujairah's history and heritage which, despite being less colourful than its neighbouring emirates, is interesting nonetheless. You can see permanent exhibitions on traditional ways of life including the not-so-distant Bedouin culture. There are also artefacts which were found during archaeological excavations throughout the emirate. Some of the items uncovered by local and foreign archaeologists include weapons from the bronze and iron ages, finely painted pottery, carved soapstone vessels and silver coins. The museum is closed on Saturdays. Entry fee is Dhs.5.

Nad Al Sheba
Racecourse
Nad Al Sheba
Map 16 A3

Godolphin Gallery

04 318 5555 | www.godolphin.com

The Godolphin Gallery celebrates the Maktoum family's private racing stable, and houses the world's finest collection of racing trophies. The gallery is refurbished every year and incorporates interactive touch-screen consoles, photographs, video presentations and memorabilia from over 10 years of the Godolphin racing stable. Adjacent to Nad Al Sheba Club in the Al Quoz Stables, the gallery is open throughout the racing season from its start in November until the end of April.

Nr Police HQ
Ras Al Khaimah
Map 1 E1

National Museum of Ras Al Khaimah

07 233 3411 | www.rakmuseum.gov.ae

Housed in an impressive fort, the former home of the present ruler of Ras Al Khaimah, this museum has mainly local natural history and archaeological displays, plus a variety of paraphernalia from pre-oil life. Upstairs you can see an account of the British naval expedition against Ras Al Khaimah in 1809, a model of a 'baggala' (a typical craft used in the early 1800s), and excellent examples of silver Bedouin jewellery. Look out for fossils set in the rock strata of the walls of the fort – these date back 190 million years. The building has battlements, a working windtower, and ornate, carved wooden doors.

Entrance fees: Adults Dhs.2; children Dhs.1. If you wish to use your camera you need a photo permit costing an extra Dhs.5. The museum is located behind the Police Headquarters in the old town close to the bridge. From Dubai, turn left at the second roundabout after the Clock Roundabout once in RAK and the museum is 100 metres on your right. Open September to May from 10:00 to 17:00, and from June to August from 08:00 to 12:00 and 16:00 to 19:00. The museum is closed on Tuesdays.

Sharjah Archaeological Museum

Nr Cultural R/A
Sharjah
Map 2 C2

06 566 5466 | *www.sharjahmuseums.ae*

This hi-tech museum offers an interesting display of antiquities from the region. Linked to a conference centre and used as an educational venue for local schoolchildren, the museum has installed computers in each hall to provide in-depth information on the exhibits. Using well-designed displays and documentary film, the museum traces man's first steps and progress across the Arabian Peninsula through the ages, and one area features the latest discoveries from excavation sites in the UAE. It is worth a visit for archaeology and history lovers. The museum is closed on Sunday, and for part of the afternoon on other days, so call before you visit to check times.

Sharjah Art Museum

Sharjah Arts Area
Sharjah
Map 2 C2

06 568 8222 | *www.sharjahmuseums.ae*

Opened in April 1997, Sharjah Art Museum dominates the arts plaza area. It was purpose built in a traditional style, chiefly to house the personal collection of over 300 paintings and maps of the ruler, HH Dr Sheikh Sultan bin Mohammed Al Qassimi. Permanent displays include the work of 18th century artists, with oil paintings and watercolours depicting life from all over the Arab world, while other exhibits change frequently. There's also an art reference library, bookshop and coffee shop, and the museum hosts various cultural activities. The museum is closed on Mondays and Friday mornings; Wednesday afternoons are for ladies only. Adult entry costs Dhs.5 and Dhs.10 for families.

Sharjah Desert Park

Jct 8 Sharjah–East
Coast Rd
Sharjah
Map 2 C2

06 531 1411 | *www.sharjahmuseums.ae*

Located 25 kilometres outside the city, Sharjah Desert Park comprises of the Natural History Museum, the Arabian Wildlife Centre, the Childrens' Farm and the recently opened Sharjah Botanical Museum. The facilities are excellent, excellent care is given to the animals, and it's an excellent venue for an enjoyable, interactive and educational day out. The fascinating Natural History Museum combines learning with entertainment, unfolding through five exhibition halls that to expose you to the earth's secrets. Exhibits include a 35 metre diorama of the UAE's natural habitat and wildlife; a stunning geological UV light display; a hall showing the interaction between man and his environment, including the museum's best known exhibit: a mechanical camel. At the Arabian Wildlife Centre you get the chance to see many reptiles, birds, mammals and creepy crawlies., including indigenous and endangered species, and most famously, the Arabian leopard. There is also a breeding centre on site, but this is not open to the public. There is also a Children's Farm (06 531 1127) where animals such as donkeys, camels, goats, cows and sheep can be fed and petted. Picnic areas are available, plus cafes and shops. It's great fun for all ages, and a place that you will want to visit again and again. Closed on Tuesdays. Entry costs Dhs.5 for children, Dhs.15 for adults, Dhs.30 for families, and includes access to everything.

Sharjah Heritage Museum

Sharjah
Heritage Area
Sharjah
Map 2 C2

06 568 0006 | *www.sharjahmuseums.ae*

Also known as Bait Al Naboodah, this two-storey building was once owned by the late Obaid bin Eesa Al Shamsi (nicknamed Al Naboodah), and is a reconstruction of a family home (bait) as it would have been around 150 years ago. Three generations of the Al Naboodah family lived here until 1972. The home is built around a large courtyard, as were many traditional Arabic houses at the time. Each room shows various items such as clothing, weapons, cooking pots and goatskin water bags. You can get a good background knowledge of the house and its history by watching the short documentary film when you first arrive. Entry costs Dhs.5 for adults and Dhs.10 for families.

Sharjah
Heritage Area
Sharjah
Map 2 C2

Sharjah Islamic Museum

06 568 3334 | *www.sharjahtourism.ae*

Sharjah Islamic Museum is home to a collection of Islamic masterpieces and manuscripts, representing the cultural history of Muslims over 1,400 years. Housed in a 200 year old building, the displays are from HH Dr Sheikh Sultan bin Mohammed Al Qassimi's private collection, and include examples of Islamic crafts such as ceramics, manuscripts, jewellery and textiles. In the Honoured Ka'aba Hall there is an impressive collection of gold-plated Qurans and a replica of the curtain that covers the Ka'aba Stone at Mecca. There is also a Science Hall, particularly fascinating for its map of the globe, the first of its kind made by Al Shareef Al Idrisi (born 1099AD), which appears upside down compared to modern maps. The museum is open during holy days and public holidays. Wednesday afternoons are for ladies and children under 12 only. Closed on Mondays and Friday mornings. Entrance is Dhs.5 for adults and Dhs.10 for families.

Sharjah
Heritage Area
Sharjah
Map 2 C2

Sharjah Maritime Museum

06 556 6002 | *www.sharjahmuseums.ae*

This museum is a must for anyone with interested in nautical history and the development of seafaring in the Middle East, with displays featuring fishing, trading, pearl diving and the construction of the many types of boats native to the UAE. Each room in the museum informs visitors about a different aspect of marine industry. One room contains scale models of the larger ships while in the open courtyard, at the centre of the museum, and also just outside the entrance, there are full-size boats with names and descriptions.

Corniche St
Sharjah
Map 2 C2

Sharjah Museum of Islamic Civilization

06 565 5455 | *www.islamicmuseum.ae*

This brand new museum is housed in a magnificent building which used to be Souk Al Majarrah. With vaulted rooms, impressive galleries and halls, the architecture alone makes a visit worthwhile, but with over 5,000 Islamic artefacts, and reams of information of Arab-Islamic life, this is one of the best places to learn about Islam and Islamic culture. The museum is organised according to five themes: the Islamic religion, Islamic art, artefacts, craftsmen and weaponry, each in it's own gallery; the Temporary Exhibition Gallery hosts a programme of visiting exhibitions. There is a cafe, gift shop and prayer room on site. Entry for adults is Dhs.5; children are free.

Nr TV Station
Sharjah
Map 2 C2

Sharjah Science Museum

06 566 8777 | *www.sharjahmuseums.ae*

Opened in 1996, this museum is the only interactive science museum in the UAE and offers visitors exhibits and demonstrations, covering subjects such as aerodynamics, cryogenics, electricity, colour and a guided tour of the universe in the planetarium. There's also a children's area where the under 5s and their parents can learn together. Those who are inspired to learn more can visit the Learning Centre, which offers more in-depth programmes on many of the subjects covered in the museum. There is also a cafe and gift shop. School groups are more than welcome. Entry costs Dhs.2 for children aged 2 to 12 years; and Dhs.3-5 for over 12s. Family entry (two adults and four kids) costs Dhs.8-15. Groups of 20 or more receive a 20% discount.

Other Attractions

Btn Al Khan &
Khalid Lagoons
Sharjah
Map 12 F3

Al Qasba

06 556 0777 | *www.qaq.ae*

The beautiful Al Qasba is a kilometre-long canal linking Al Khan Lagoon and Khalid Lagoon, with lots of attractions and eateries along its banks. The emphasis is on culture, with an ever-changing calendar including Arabian poetry and film (with English subtitles), art exhibitions and classes, musical events and theatrical performances, either in the dedicated venues or outdoors on the walkways beside the canal. The Tent of Wonders is a permanent 'big top' featuring shows by performers from around the world. There are shops and stalls selling Arabian treasures and souvenirs including woodwork, metalwork and pottery, embroidery, sculpture, and Islamic calligraphy and engraving. When you get hungry, restaurants and cafes with outdoor terraces serve Arabic, Asian and Mediterranean cuisine. Motorised abras provide boat tours up and down the canal, but perhaps the biggest draw, and certainly the most visible, is the Eye of the Emirates – a 60 metre high observation wheel with air-conditioned pods offering amazing views over Sharjah and across to Dubai and beyond. See the website for details of events.

Religious Sites

Jumeira Rd
Jumeira
Map 7 F1

Jumeira Mosque

04 353 6666 | www.cultures.ae

Jumeira Mosque, located at the beginning of Beach Road, is easily the most beautiful in the city and perhaps the best known. Its image features on the UAE's Dhs.500 banknote. The mosque is especially breathtaking when lit at night. Non-Muslims are not usually permitted entry to mosques, but the Sheikh Mohammed Centre for Cultural Understanding (p.270), through its 'Open Doors, Open Minds' programme, organises tours on (Saturday, Sunday, Tuesday and Thursday mornings at 10:00 sharp). Visitors are guided around the mosque and told all about the building, and then the hosts give a talk on Islam and explain the prayer rituals that all Muslims undertake. At the end of the hour-long tour there's a question-and-answer session with the guides. For both visitors and residents this tour provides a fascinating insight into the culture and beliefs of the local population, and is thoroughly recommended during your time in Dubai. Men and women are required to dress conservatively – that means no shorts and no sleeveless tops. Women must also cover their hair with a head scarf or shawl, and all visitors will be asked to remove their shoes before entering. Cameras are allowed and, in fact, picture-taking is encouraged. There is a registration fee of Dhs.10 per person, and large groups are able to book their own private tour.

Water Parks

Other options **Amusement Parks** p.261

Atlantis The Palm
Palm Jumeirah
Map 2 A3

Aquaventure ▶ p.275

04 426 1000 | www.atlantisthepalm.com

Aquaventure is the ultimate destination for thrill seekers: to get the adrenaline pumping try the Leap of Faith, a 27 metre near-vertical drop that shoots you through a series of tunnels surrounded by shark-infested waters. Alternatively, The Rapids will take you on a tumultuous journey down a 2.3 kilometre river, complete with waterfalls and wave surges. For the little ones, there is Splashers, a water playground. Open daily from 10:00 until sunset. Entrance for those over 1.2m is Dhs.285, and Dhs.220 for those under. Children younger than 2 years old and Atlantis hotel guests get in for free.

North of UAQ
on the RAK Rd
Umm Al Quwain
Map 1 B1

Dreamland Aqua Park ▶ p.xiii

06 768 1888 | www.dreamlanduae.com

With over 25 water rides spread across 250,000 square metres of green, landscaped grounds, Dreamland Aqua Park is one of the largest water parks in the world. Adrenaline junkies will not be disappointed with rides such as the Black Hole, the

DROP INTO AQUAVENTURE

AQUAVENTURE, THE LARGEST WATER-THEMED ATTRACTION
IN EUROPE AND THE MIDDLE EAST, IS OPEN TO ATLANTIS
DAY VISITORS. ENJOY WARM, TEMPERATURE CONTROLLED
WATER, SLIDE DOWN THE 27.5 METRE ZIGGURAT THROUGH
SHARK-FILLED WATERS. SPEED THROUGH RAPIDS, TIDAL
WAVES AND UNDERWATER TUNNELS AND TAKE YOUR PICK
OF HEART-PUMPING RIDES.

FOR AED 285, YOU CAN ENJOY A GREAT DAY OUT WITH ACCESS TO
AQUAVENTURE AND A BEAUTIFUL 700 METRE PRIVATE BEACH.

OPEN DAILY FROM 10AM – SUNSET. NO PRE-BOOKING NECESSARY.
VISIT ATLANTISTHEPALM.COM

ATLANTIS
PALM JUMEIRAH, DUBAI

DON'T FORGET TO BREATHE

Kamikaze, and the four 'twisting dragons'. For a more leisurely experience there's the lazy river, a wave pool, and a high-salinity pool for floating about. The Aqua Play area has 19 games and attractions for the whole family, and if you prefer not to get wet you can burn rubber on the 400 metre go-kart track. There's a variety of cafes and restaurants, including Saj Zaman, a Lebanese cafe, as well as a licensed pool bar and shisha majlis. Overnight accommodation is also available, either in a tent (provided for you) or a 'cabana' hut. Admission costs Dhs.100 for adults and Dhs.70 for children under 12, while children under 4 go free. The park is open all-year-round (log on to the website for timings). Fridays, Saturdays and holidays are reserved for families only.

WonderLand
Umm Hurair
Map 13 C1

SplashLand

04 324 1222 | *www.wonderlanduae.com*
The waterpark within WonderLand offers fun for kids or adults with nine rides including slides and twisters, a lazy river, an adults' pool and a children's activity pool with slides, bridges and water cannons. Alternatively, you can just relax by the pool and sunbathe. Lockers and changing rooms are available. Refer to WonderLand Theme & Water Park (p.261) for more details of what is available.

Nr Burj Al Arab
Jumeira
Map 6 B1

Wild Wadi Water Park ▶ p.277

04 348 4444 | *www.wildwadi.com*
Don't miss this world-class waterpark themed around the adventures of Juha, the mythical friend of Sinbad. Spread over 12 acres beside Jumeirah Beach Hotel, and with the Burj Al Arab towering nearby, the park has 23 aquatic rides and attractions to suit all ages and bravery levels. One of the first you'll encounter is the Wipeout, a permanently rolling wave giving you the chance to show off your body-boarding skills. Less taxing and altogether more relaxing is Juha's Journey, where you just sit back (in either single or double rubber rings) and float through a changing landscape. For thrill-seekers there's the Jumeirah Sceirah – the tallest and fastest freefall water slide outside North America.

Depending on how busy it is you may have to queue for some of the rides, but the wait is always worth it. There are two cafes serving drinks and snacks, and once you've paid the entrance fee there is no limit to the number of times you can ride. The park opens at 11:00. The closing time depends on the time of year – 18:00 from November to February, 19:00 from March to May and September to October, and 21:00 from June to August. Admission is Dhs.195 for adults and Dhs.165 for children under 1.1m in height. There is also a 'sundowner' rate (for the last three hours of opening), when adults pay Dhs.165 and children pay Dhs.135. Two new rides will be added in 2009, Tantrum Alley and Behemoth Bowl, both downhill slides with plenty of spinning. The park will be closed from January 22 to February 11 in preparation for the construction of the rides.

Zoos, Wildlife Parks & Open Farms
Other options **Mushrif Park** p.281

Nr Traffic Police
Al Ain
Map 1 E3

Al Ain Wildlife Park & Resort

03 782 8188
Located at the foot of Jebel Hafeet, this 400 hectare wildlife park has one of the largest animal collections of both local and exotic species. Conditions for the animals are very modern, far superior to Dubai Zoo, and some of the highlights include gazelle and Arabian oryx in large numbers and giant tortoises. The zoo is open daily 09:00 to 22:00. The reptile house is open 16:00 to 21:00, and there is a bird show which starts at 18:30. Entrance is Dhs.15 for adults, Dhs.5 for children and it's free for those under 6 years. Within the zoo there is a free train which transports visitors around.

TONNES OF WATER PER SECOND.

DAYS A WEEK.

FLOWRIDERS AT WILD WADI.

LET THE FUN FLOW

Wild Wadi
WATERPARK

Sharjah Desert Park ◀
Sharjah
Map 2 C2

Arabian Wildlife Centre

06 531 1999 | www.sharjahmuseums.ae

This centre is home to lots of animals, birds, reptiles and endangered species, such as the Arabian leopard. For more, see the entry for Sharjah Desert Park on p.272.

Sharjah Desert Park ◀
Sharjah
Map 2 C2

Children's Farm

06 531 1127 | www.sharjahmuseums.ae

A great place for a day out for families, especially when combined with the Arabian Wildlife Centre. For more information, see the entry for Sharjah Desert Park on p.272.

Jumeira Beach Rd ◀
Jumeira
Map 7 E1

Dubai Zoo

04 349 6444 | www.dubaitourism.ae

Originally a small private collection of animals, Dubai Zoo was taken over by the Municipality in 1971 and underwent expansion and refurbishment in the mid 1980s. This is an old-fashioned zoo, with lions, tigers, giraffes, monkeys, deer, snakes, bears, flamingos, giant tortoises and other animals housed behind bars in small cages. The curator and his staff do their best, with the woefully inadequate space and resources, to look after the animals. Attempts are occasionally made to offload animals by handing them over to other zoos, but despite this the numbers are actually increasing as the zoo takes in dangerous and exotic creatures seized in Dubai. The zoo has around 1,200 animals, and space is so tight that cages have even been extended vertically. Visitor numbers are increasing too, with over 400,000 a year on average, and you may find some visitors' treatment of the animals as troubling as the conditions. An early attempt at barrier-free cages was abandoned after people attempted to feed the animals, and threw their rubbish into the enclosures. It could be said that the bars are there now to protect the animals from the public as much as the other way round. For many years there has been talk of relocating the zoo to much bigger premises – first near Mushrif Park, and more recently to a site within Dubailand – but up to now the plans have never materialised. It can only be hoped that the authorities make good on their promises and build a new zoo very soon with sufficient space and facilities. Until then, those with a more modern attitude to animal welfare are advised to steer clear, and to try Al Ain Wildlife Park & Resort (p.276) or the Arabian Wildlife Centre (above) instead. Entry costs Dhs.2 per person, while under 2s go free. Closed on Tuesdays.

Jumeira Beach Park

Jumeira Open Beach

Beaches

Other options **Swimming** p.391, **Beach Clubs** p.396

If you love the sea breeze in your hair and sand between your toes, you'll be happy to know that there are many beautiful beaches in Dubai. You have a choice between public beaches (limited facilities but no entry fee), beach parks (good facilities and a nominal entrance fee, see below), and private beaches (normally part of a hotel or resort – see Beach Clubs on p.396 in the Activities chapter).

Options for public beaches include the area around Al Mamzar Beach Park (p.279), which has a cordoned-off swimming area, chalets, jet skis for hire and free beaches along the lagoon to the south. South of Dubai Creek, you'll come to Jumeira Open Beach (Map 7 E1), which is great for soaking up the sun, swimming and people watching. Moving further south brings you to the small beaches between Dubai Offshore Sailing Club (Map 6 F1) and Jumeirah Beach Hotel (Map 7 C1), previously popular for kite surfers and paramotors. Those looking for more natural beaches used to go to Jebel Ali, but this previously quiet area is now also being developed with construction of Palm Jebel Ali and Dubai Waterfront, which means that just all but the smallest, scrappiest bit of beach has been closed to the public. For new options only a little further from town, and great for kitesurfing, drive south of Jebel Ali and turn right at the first major junction, actually in Abu Dhabi emirate, where the beaches are still quiet, and as yet, undeveloped.

Regulations for the public beaches seem to be getting more strict. Dogs are banned from the beaches, and so is driving. Officially, other banned beach activities include barbecues, camping without a permit and holding large parties. Contact the Public Parks & Recreation Section (04 336 7633) for clarification.

Beach Parks

Other options **Parks** p.280

A visit to one of Dubai's beach parks is a perfect way to spend the day – the warm waters, white sandy beaches and stretches of lush greenery will transport you a hundred miles from the stresses of city life.

Both Al Mamzar Beach Park (below) and Jumeira Beach Park (p.280) are busy at weekends, especially during winter, although Al Mamzar rarely feels crowded because it is so huge. Both parks have a ladies' day when men are not allowed (ladies may enter with their young sons, however). Remember where you are and dress appropriately – swimming costumes and bikinis are totally acceptable, as long as you wear both the top and bottom halves.

Timings often change during Ramadan, when parks usually open and close later in the day. Both parks have lifeguards on duty – when they raise the red flag, it is unsafe to swim and you should take the opportunity to work on your tan instead.

Al Mamzar Beach Park

Nr Hamriya Port
Al Hamriya
Map 12 D1

04 296 6201 | www.dm.gov.ae

With its four clean beaches, open grassy spaces and plenty of greenery, Al Mamzar Beach Park is a popular spot and well worth a visit, even for people who don't live in Deira. A large amphitheatre is located near the entrance and paths wind through picnic areas and children's playgrounds. The well-maintained beaches have sheltered areas for swimming and changing rooms with showers. Kiosks near each beach sell food and other small necessities you may have left at home, while near the entrance is a basic restaurant and a coffee shop. Air-conditioned chalets, complete with a barbecue area, can be rented on a daily basis for Dhs.150-Dhs.200. There are also two swimming pools and lifeguard patrols.

To get around the park you can hire bicycles or take a train tour. During the Dubai Shopping Festival (p.71) there are activities organised here as well as shows for kids in the amphitheatre. Sadly, the previously clear views out to sea are now becoming a little obstructed by the construction on the Palm Deira. Entrance fees are Dhs.5 per person or Dhs.30 per car (including all occupants). Pool fees are Dhs.10 per adult, Dhs.5 per child. Wednesday is family day, which means no single males are allowed.

Nr Jumeirah
Beach Club
Jumeira
Map 7 B1

Jumeira Beach Park

04 349 2111 | *www.dm.gov.ae*

With azure seas, a one-kilometre stretch of golden sand and palm trees for shade, Jumeira Beach Park is a popular destination. You can hire a sunbed and parasol for Dhs.20, but they do sometimes run out so get there early or take your own. At either end of the beach there's a cafe selling snacks and drinks, as well as another drinks shop and an icecream parlour. There are showers along the beach and toilets too. Lifeguards are on duty from 08:00 to sunset, after which swimming is not permitted. Away from the beach there are plenty of grassy areas and landscaped gardens, children's play areas, and barbecue pits available for public use. Cycling is not allowed (except for small children) and neither is rollerblading. The park can get really busy at weekends and in the evenings, especially on public holidays when there's a good atmosphere with friends and families getting together for a barbie. Entry is Dhs.5 per person and Dhs.20 per car. Mondays are for women and children only. Open daily from 07:00, closing at 22:30 Sunday to Wednesday, and at 23:00 Thursday to Saturday and on holidays.

Nature Reserves

End of Dubai Creek
Ras Al Khor
Map 16 C2

Ras Al Khor Wildlife Sanctuary

04 206 4240 | *www.wildlife.ae*

This is the only nature reserve within the city where greater flamingos and other shore birds and waders can be spotted. On an average winter day up to 15,000 birds, including 1,500 flamingos, can be seen. Dubai Municipality takes great precaution to protect these birds and their ecosystem, so you'll see police patrolling the area around the clock. A guide to the sanctuary and information on the different visiting birds is available at all hides. One of the hides is situated beside Ras Al Khor Road, the other two off Oud Metha Road. All are manned, have their own carparks, and are free to visit for small parties. Groups of more than 10 may need to contact the Environment Department at Dubai Municipality (04 206 4240) to arrange permits.

Parks

Other options **Beaches** p.279

Dubai has a number of excellent parks, and visitors will be pleasantly surprised by the many lush green lawns and the variety of trees and shrubs which create the perfect escape from the concrete jungle of the city. In winter months, the more popular parks can be very busy at weekends. Most have a kiosk or cafe selling snacks and drinks, alternatively take a picnic or use the barbecue pits provided (remember to take your own wood or charcoal, and food). Creekside Park has an amphitheatre and often holds concerts during public holidays or special occasions, including events during the Dubai Shopping Festival (details are announced in local newspapers two or three days before). Regulations among the parks vary, with some banning bikes and rollerblades, or limiting ball games to specific areas. Pets are not permitted and you should not take plant cuttings. Some parks have a ladies' day when entry is restricted to women,

Parks, Beaches & Gardens

girls and young boys (check the individual entries) and certain smaller ones actually ban anyone other than ladies through the week, while allowing families only at the weekends. As with the beach parks, opening hours change during Ramadan. Entrance to the smaller parks is generally free, while the larger ones charge up to Dhs.5 per person. Contact the Dubai Municipality by email at publicparks@dm.gov.ae or by telephone on 050 858 9887 for more info.

Al Khazzan Park

Btn Sheikh Zayed Rd
& Al Wasl Rd
Al Wasl
Map 7 D2

050 420 2893

Al Khazzan is a small, often overlooked, family park recognisable by its large, decorated water tower. The park has a pleasant shaded area which overlooks the children's playground. Located between Sheikh Zayed Road and Al Wasl Road, the park is open daily from 08:00 to 22:30. Admission is free, with ladies-only entrance Saturday to Wednesday, and families only on Thursday and Friday.

Creekside Park

Nr WonderLand
Umm Hurair
Map 11 A3

04 336 7633 | www.dm.gov.ae

Situated in the heart of the city but blessed with acres of gardens, fishing piers, jogging tracks, BBQ sites, children's play areas, mini-golf, restaurants and kiosks, this is the ultimate in park life. There's also a mini falaj and a large amphitheatre. Running along the park's 2.5km stretch of creek frontage is a cable car system which allows allowing visitors an unrestricted view from 30 metres in the air. From Gate Two, four-wheel cycles can be hired for Dhs.20 per hour (you can't use your own bike in the park). Rollerblading is allowed, and there are no ladies-only days. Newly opened is Dubai Dolphinarium (p.262). Entrance fee: Dhs.5. Cable car: adults Dhs.25; children Dhs.15. Children's City: adults Dhs.15; children Dhs.10.

Mushrif Park

Al Khawaneej Rd
Mushrif
Map 15 C4

04 288 3624 | www.dm.gov.ae

Situated just past Mirdif on Airport Road, nine kilometres past Dubai Airport, Mushrif Park is a huge park full of activities and facilities. The grounds are extensive, and although it is a 'desert park', there are many large stretches of beautiful green lawn. There are three swimming pools in total: two large pools (one for men, one for women, with no mixing allowed), and a smaller pool for young children that is situated next to the ladies' pool. There are numerous playgrounds dotted around the park, featuring slides, swings, roundabouts and climbing frames, and a central plaza complete with fairground rides and trampolines. There is also an animal enclosure where you can get up close and personal with horses, camels, goats and even a turkey – pony and camel rides are available, starting from Dhs.5 for a short ride. An interesting feature of the park is a mini-town, where you can wander around miniature houses themed on different building styles from around the world. There is also a train that tours the park in the afternoons (Dhs.2 per ride). No bikes or rollerblades are allowed inside the park, but you can drive around it. Entry costs Dhs.3 per person or Dhs.10 per car. Swimming pool entrance is Dhs.10 per adult and Dhs.5 per child. A membership scheme is available.

Nad Al Sheba Park

Off Nad Al Sheba Rd
Nad Al Sheba
Map 2 B3

One of the lesser-known parks located in a quiet and beautiful area of the city, this park provides a place for leisure for local people living in the area, and is worth making the trip if you'd like to escape the crowds. There is plenty of greenery and trees making it easy to find a spot to curl up in the shade. The park is also well equipped with a jogging track and a separate cycling track, a football pitch, basketball and volleyball courts, and different play areas for children of 3-6 years and 7-12 years. Facilities for visitors with disabilities to the park are also provided. Open from 07:30 to 23:00 every day, the park allows women and children only during the week, but it open to everyone at weekends. Entry is free.

Off Airport Rd
Rashidiya
Map 13 F4

Rashidiya Park

This pretty and peaceful park is where you'll find plenty of expat mums from Mirdif, Rashidiya and the surrounding areas. It has several large grassy areas, divided by paved walkways. There are also two comprehensive play areas for children, featuring a good mix of climbing frames, miniature playhouses, slides, swings and see-saws. Although the play areas are not very shady, there are plenty of other shaded areas in the park where you can go to escape the sun for a while. There is a little shop next to the entrance, selling drinks, snacks and a range of cheap plastic toys that go down well with children. Entrance is free. Saturday to Wednesday is reserved for women and children only – the park gets much busier on weekends when families are allowed.

Nr Jct 2 Al Wasl Rd
Al Wasl
Map 7 B2

Safa Park

04 349 2111 | www.dm.gov.ae
Spot the giant Ferris wheel opposite Jumeira Library and you've found Safa Park. This huge, artistically divided and beautiful park offers electronic games for teenagers in its large pavilion, plus (at weekends) bumper cars, a big wheel, a mini-train ride, 'Traffic Garden' (buggies and a course), a big trampoline cage and a merry-go-round. It also has volleyball, basketball and football pitches, tennis courts, an obstacle course, barbecue sites, expanses of grassy areas and several play areas with swings. In the centre of the park is an Arabic garden and a lake promenade with waterfall feature, where boats can be hired. The lake is home to a bevy of friendly ducks who love being fed, so remember to take along all your old bits of stale bread. You are not allowed to take your own bicycle into the park, but you can hire one inside (Dhs.100 deposit and Dhs.30 for one hour). Rollerblading is allowed. A popular feature of the park is the running track around its perimeter – you don't have to pay to use this and in the early evenings it is very busy with runners and walkers. The track is specially sprung to help you avoid high-impact sports injuries. There is also a permanent ladies' garden within the park where men are not allowed. The park also has a Birds' Promenade and a Plant Nursery, and at certain times of the year is home to various exhibitions and the Dubai Flea Market (p.481). During the exhibitions, the entrance fee may rise to Dhs.10, but normally entry costs just Dhs.3, with children under 3 years going in for free.

Beh Al Moosa Towers
Trade Centre 1
Map 7 E2

Satwa Park

04 329 0989
This community park opened its gates in 2006 and, while certainly not on the scale of Safa or Zabeel Parks, it does offer some welcome relief and relaxation in the shadows of the SZR skyscrapers. The park has tennis and basketball courts, a grass football pitch, and a running track around its perimeter. There's plenty of shade, seating, and grassy areas, and the kids' play area has the usual array of colourful slides and climbing frames.

Nr Jumeirah
Beach Hotel
Umm Suqeim
Map 6 C1

Umm Suqeim Park

04 348 4554
This ladies' park is closed to men except for weekends. It is fairly large and has three big playgrounds with some great equipment that kids will love. There are also plenty of shady, grassy areas so that mums can sit and rest while the kids let off steam. In the middle of the park there is a popular coffee shop. Entrance is free.

Nr Trade Centre R/A
Zabeel
Map 10 B1

Zabeel Park

Providing an oasis of greenery in the heart of downtown Dubai, Zabeel Park serves the communities of Karama, Bur Dubai, Satwa and the Trade Centre area. It is also the first park in the Middle East with a 'technology theme', and features three zones: alternative energy, communications and technology. Covering 51 hectares, the huge green area is taken up by recreational areas, a jogging track, a mini cricket pitch, a football field, boating lake, and an amphitheatre. There are a number of restaurants and cafes within the park for some refreshment and a bite to eat. The newest attraction is Stargate (p.261), a themed area of the park due to open in 2009, which is built to resemble a spaceship that has crash-landed. It promises to become a family 'edutainment' centre, with spaces for learning, shopping, dining and exercising. The park is open from 08:00 weekly, closing at 23:00 Sunday to Wednesday, and at 23:30 Thursday to Saturday. On public holidays the park stays open until midnight. Mondays are reserved for ladies only. Entry costs Dhs.5 (it's free for children up to 2 years). People with disabilities can gain free access.

Safa Park

Creekside Park

Safa Park

Zabeel Park

Tours & Sightseeing

As you might expect from a city that is staking its future on the tourism industry, Dubai has numerous tour operators offering an exciting range of city, desert and mountain trips. The following information covers the most popular tours given by the main operators. If there is something specific you have in mind, many operators can tailor a tour to your needs.

When booking your tour, it is useful to book three or four days in advance. Some operators will request a 50% deposit, while others are happy for you to pay the driver the full amount when he picks you up. You can usually expect to pay about Dhs.150 for a half-day city tour, and around Dhs.300 for a desert safari, but prices do vary between operators. Tours usually depart from set pick-up points, such as major hotels, although some operators will actually pick you up from your house. Wear cool, comfortable clothing, and take a hat and sunglasses. Desert or mountain tours require strong, flat-soled shoes, and if you're going into the desert in the cooler months, take a jacket as the temperature can drop considerably after sunset. One last word on desert or mountain tours: these trips often involve some pretty extreme driving over sand dunes or through wadis. If you are pregnant, elderly, sick, are travelling with young children or suffer from motion sickness, inform the tour company so that they can arrange a more gentle route for you.

Boat Tours & Charters

Other options **Dhow Charters** p.290, **Speedboating** p.390, **Creek Tours** p.249, **Dinner Cruises** p.540

Al Wasl Cruising & Sport Fishing ▶ p.285

Various Locations

04 268 1468 | www.cruiseindubai.com

Al Wasl has a variety of vessels available for trips around the UAE. Deep sea fishing boats can be hired and trips tailored to suit your preferences. Smaller yachts are available for day cruises around Dubai's coast and creek, and luxury yachts can be chartered allowing you to decide on your own route. Watersports such as wakeboarding, parasailing, and banana boat rides are all available with yacht charters, and dhow dinner cruises are also offered.

Bateaux Dubai ▶ p.541

Nr British Embassy
Bur Dubai
Map 9 B3

04 399 4994 | www.bateauxdubai.com

The sleek Bateaux Dubai provides parties of up to 300 people with unobstructed sightseeing from all seats, and offers charters for corporate events and private parties. The vessel can be chartered daily with advance bookings, including weekends and holidays. Daily sightseeing and dinner cruises (p.540) are also available.

Bluesail Dubai

Nr British Embassy
Bur Dubai
Map 9 B3

04 882 3129 | www.bluesailyachts.com

Bluesail has two 42ft sailing yachts available for private charter and corporate development events including professionally facilitated team building and 'Match Race' incentive days. Bluesail specialises in marine training but also offers private motor boat charters on their new 21ft/200hp and 34ft/450hp speedboats, taking in the creek and Dubai's coastline – see Speedboating (p.390). All vessels are fully insured and equipped with the required safety equipment.

Bristol Middle East Yacht Solution

Marina Walk
Dubai Marina
Map 5 B2

04 366 3538 | www.bristol-middleeast.com

This Dubai Marina-based company offers charters and packages on boats of all kind, from luxury yachts to its old wooden dhow, Captain Jack. Its boats can be hired for any

event, including romantic outings for two, right through to weddings and birthday parties. Fishing trips and watersports can be organised too, and Bristol also puts together land and air tours.

Fujairah Intl
Marine Club
Fujairah
Map 1 F2

Charlotte Anne Charters
09 222 3508 | *www.charlotteannecharters.com*
The Charlotte Anne was built in Denmark in 1949 and has been chartering in Arabian waters for more than a decade. Built entirely of oak, the ship operates exclusive, live-aboard charters to the Musandam region of northern Oman, with particular emphasis on scuba diving at some of the finest, and as yet untouched, dive sites in the region.

Nr British Embassy
Bur Dubai
Map 9 B3

Danat Dubai Cruises
04 351 1117 | *info@ddcgroup.ae*
Boasting a top speed of 18 knots, this 34 metre catamaran is available for group charters, product launches and wedding receptions, and has a capacity of 300 passengers (170 for sit-down functions). Onboard facilities include a dancefloor, music system, video monitors, sun deck and two enclosed air-conditioned decks.

Mina Seyahi Dubai
Al Sufouh
Map 5 B2

Dusail
04 398 9146 | *www.dusail.com*
Dusail Yacht Charter provides coastline tours aboard their 50ft flagship luxury yacht, Andorra, as well as deep sea, reef or fly fishing packages, and rentals of motor and rigid inflatable boats. Morning cruises depart from Mina Seyahi Dubai at 10:30, returning at 12:30, while the sunset cruises set sail at 15:30 for two hours. Light snacks and soft drinks are offered onboard while guests relax and enjoy uninterrupted views of Dubai's coastline.

Mina Seyahi Dubai
Al Sufouh
Map 5 B2

El Mundo
050 452 3202 | *www.elmundodubai.com*
El Mundo is a 60ft catamaran that can be chartered for all manner of occasions, including romantic cruises, corporate events, lunch/dinner cruises around the Palm Jumeirah and 'Fun In The Sun'. Longer charters for snorkelling, dolphin watching or trips to Musandam are also available. Other vessels include Andora a 60ft luxury yacht, and the smaller, 20ft, Nina Marina II.

Various Locations

ENJOY Yachting
050 465 0425 | *www.uaeyachting.com*
ENJOY Yachting offers a variety of scheduled and bespoke trips allowing visitors and residents to sample the beautiful waters of the Gulf. Embarking from a number of locations throughout Dubai, a private boat charter makes a great romantic trip for two, or could be just the place for a business meeting or presentation with a difference. A sunset trip is also a popular choice. Additionally, perhaps the coolest way to beat Dubai's traffic jams is to ring for your very own powerboat taxi service, with various pick-up and drop-off points between the creek and Dubai Marina. These fast (50kmph) powerboats can be hired from as little as Dhs.500 per hour, inclusive of a skipper (English, German and Arabic speaking) and soft drinks.

Nr Palm Jebel Ali
Jebel Ali
Map 3 A1

Jebel Ali Golf Resort & Spa ▶ p.533
04 883 6000 | *www.jebelali-international.com*
Club Joumana, at the Jebel Ali Golf Resort & Spa, can arrange one or two-hour boat trips for up to seven people on their 36ft fishing boat. Departure is from the private marina at the resort in the morning or afternoon. Prices and timings are available on request.

Al Sufouh Rd
Al Sufouh
Map 5 C1

Le Meridien Mina Seyahi Beach Resort & Marina

04 399 3333 | www.lemeridien-minaseyahi.com

Le Meridien Mina Seyahi operates a variety of charter cruises from their marina. A number of boats are available for trips of different lengths and activities include deep-sea fishing, trawling and sightseeing. Prices are available upon request and all rates include a skipper and equipment.

Wafi Residence
Umm Hurair
Map 10 E4

Ocean Group

050 624 0684 | www.oceanindependence.com

Ocean Group (which incorporates Cavendish White and Ocean Independence) provides luxury yacht charters, including everything from short blasts to exclusive overnight stays, and even holidays on the water. Hiring one of its fleet is definitely a good way to impress business partners or friends. Many cruising options are available (including charters all over the world), and it provides full catering services. Corporate enquiries are also welcome. The company has a large selection of craft for sale and also do new builds.

Nr Radisson SAS Hotel
Deira Creekside
Map 9 C3

Tour Dubai ▶ p.543

04 336 8409 | www.tour-dubai.com

Tour Dubai offers a one-hour creek tour aboard a traditional dhow, including pre-recorded commentary of the area, the country's history and places of interest. Commentary is available in English. There are four departures a day: 11:30, 13:30, 15:30 and 17:30, for Dhs.45. Transfers are available on request at an additional charge. The company offers a variety of other tours, including private dhow charters (see p.290).

Bus Tours

Various Locations

Art Bus

04 341 7303 | www.artinthecitydubai.com

The Art Bus runs a hassle-free bus service from The Jam Jar (p.331) to art galleries and exhibitions all over Dubai during major art festivals. Look out for services during Art Dubai in March 2009, as well as during other major exhibitions.

Wafi Mall
Umm Hurair
Map 10 E4

The Big Bus Company

04 340 7709 | www.bigbustours.com

It's not a mirage, there really are eight open air London double-decker buses roaming the streets of Dubai. There's live commentary in English, which includes little known facts such as in 1968 there were only 13 cars in Dubai. It's wise to break the tour at their recommended stops and then hop on the following bus once you've finished exploring. Prices are Dhs.200 for adults; Dhs.100 for children aged 5 to 15; free for children under 5 years; and families are Dhs.500 (two adults and two children). Tickets are valid for 24 hours and the service runs daily with departures every hour from 09:00 to 17:00.

BurJuman
Bur Dubai
Map 8 F4

Wonder Bus Tours

04 359 5656 | www.wonderbusdubai.net

The Wonder Bus is an amphibious bus capable of doing 120kph on the road and seven knots on water. The trips are two-hour mini tours of Dubai, concentrating on the creek, and covering Creekside Park and Dubai Creek Golf & Yacht Club, under Maktoum Bridge towards Garhoud Bridge, then up the boat ramp and back to BurJuman. The bus is air conditioned and can take 44 passengers, and life jackets are supplied if you're nervous. Prices: adults Dhs.125; children Dhs.85 (ages 3-12); families Dhs.390 (two adults, two children). There are three departures daily: usually 11:30, 14:30 and 17:00, but this is subject to change depending on the tide.

Camel Rides

When in Arabia, riding a camel is like riding a London bus – it's a must-do and a bumpy ride too. You could opt for a short camel ride as part of a desert tour (see Main Tour Operators on p.294 or a hotel and beach resort package, but for a more memorable experience you should go on a longer guided camel ride in the sand dunes. On such tours there are stops for rests, refreshments and photos, so that you can remember your experience long after the aches subside.

Hilton Al Ain
Al Ain
Map 1 E3

Al Ain Golden Sands Camel Safaris

03 768 8006 | www.hilton.com

Al Ain Golden Sands Camel Safaris offer a selection of tours that include a camel ride over the dunes of Bida Bint Saud. The rides usually last one to two and a half hours, and all tours include transfers from Al Ain, Arabic coffee and dates, and soft drinks.

Activity Tours
If you're an adrenaline junkie, get in touch with Absolute Adventure (p.294), Desert Rangers (p.337), Desert Rose Tourism (p.296), Mountain High (p.322), Off-Road Adventures (p.298) or Voyagers Xtreme (p.298) – all of these tour operators offer a great range of activity tours.

Desert & Mountain Safaris

Desert safaris are easily the most popular tour available, perhaps because a good safari offers many activities in one day. Starting with an exciting ride up and down some of the desert's biggest dunes, you can try sand skiing before watching the sun set over the desert. After driving a short distance to a permanent Bedouin-style camp, you are treated to a sumptuous barbecue, followed by shisha, belly dancing, camel rides and henna painting. You can vary the length of your safari, choosing to stay overnight or combine it with a trip into the mountains, if desired. However, a safari to the mountains is highly recommended, if only to see how the landscape changes from orange sand dunes to craggy mountains within the space of a few kilometres. The approximate cost for a desert safari is Dhs.150-Dhs.300 (overnight up to Dhs.500). Many companies offer these types of tour; below is a selection of typical itineraries you can choose from.

Dune Dinners

Enjoy some thrilling off-road desert driving before settling down to watch the sun set behind the dunes. Starting around 16:00, the tour passes camel farms and fascinating scenery, that provide great photo opportunities. At an Arabian campsite, enjoy a delicious dinner and the calm of a starlit desert night, returning around 22:00.

Full-Day Safari

This day-long tour usually passes traditional Bedouin villages and camel farms in the desert, with a drive through sand dunes of varying colours and heights. Tours often visit either Fossil Rock or the mesmerising Hajar Mountains. A cold buffet lunch may be provided in the mountains before the drive home.

Hatta Pools Safari

Hatta is a quiet, old-fashioned town nestled in the foothills of the Hajar Mountains, famed for its fresh water rock pools that you can swim in. The full-day trip usually includes a stop at the Hatta Fort Hotel, where you can enjoy the pool, landscaped gardens, archery, clay pigeon shooting and nine-hole golf course. Lunch is served either in the hotel, or in the mountains. The trip costs between Dhs.260-Dhs.350.

Mountain Safari

This full-day tour takes you to the east coast, heading inland at Dibba and entering the spectacular Hajar Mountains. You will travel through rugged canyons onto steep winding tracks, past terraced mountainsides and old stone houses. It returns via Dibba, where the journey homewards stops off at Masafi Market on the way.

Dubai's best selling map

Whether you're a map person or not, this pocket-sized marvel will help you get to know the city like the back of your hand.

Dubai Mini Map
The city in your pocket

EXPLORER

Overnight Safari
This 24 hour tour starts at about 15:00 with a drive through the dunes to a Bedouin-style campsite. Dine under the stars, sleep in the fresh air and wake to the smell of freshly brewed coffee, before heading for the mountains. The drive takes you through spectacular rugged scenery, past dunes, along wadis (dry riverbeds), before stopping for a buffet lunch and returning to Dubai.

Dhow Charters

Other options **Boat Tours & Charters** p.284, **Dinner Cruises** p.540

An evening aboard a dhow, either on Dubai Creek or sailing along the coast, is a wonderfully atmospheric and memorable experience. Contact one of the companies below to find out more about dhow charters. Alternatively, large independent groups can charter a dhow from the fishermen at Dibba on the east coast, to travel up the coast to Musandam (p.306). If you're prepared to haggle you can usually knock the price down substantially, especially if you know a bit of Arabic. Expect to pay around Dhs.2,500 per day for a dhow large enough to take 20-25 people, or Dhs.100 per hour for a smaller one. You'll need to take your own food and water, as nothing is supplied onboard except for ice lockers suitable for storing supplies. Conditions are basic, but you'll have the freedom to plan your own route and to see the beautiful fjord-like scenery of the Musandam from a traditional wooden dhow. The waters in the area are beautifully clear and turtles and dolphins can often be seen from the boat, although sometimes unfavourable weather conditions can seriously reduce visibility for divers. If you leave from Dibba (or Daba), Omani visas are not required, even though you enter Omani waters. It is also possible to arrange stops along the coast and it's worth taking camping equipment for the night, although you can sleep on board. This kind of trip is ideal for diving but you should hire any equipment you may need before you get to Dibba (refer to the *UAE Underwater Explorer* for dive shop rentals, and see Diving on p.344). If diving is not your thing, you can just spend the day swimming, snorkelling and soaking up the sun.

Nr Garhoud Bridge
Umm Hurair
Map 13 C1

Al Boom Tourist Village

04 324 3000 | www.alboom.ae
Al Boom Tourist Village operates nine dhows on the creek, ranging from single-deckers with room for 20 people, right up to the huge triple-decker Mumtaz with a capacity of 350 passengers. Al Boom claims that this is the biggest dhow currently operating on the creek. They offer a variety of packages, so prices vary accordingly. As well as the usual dinner cruises, late-night trips can also be arranged.

Salahuddin Rd
Sharjah
Map 2 C2

Al Marsa Tours

06 544 1232 | www.musandamdiving.com
Al Marsa has two purpose-built dhows that are suitable for divers and tourists. You can relax on the sundeck for a day trip and discover fishing villages, or go on an overnight voyage and explore the Musandam fjords. Prices for divers cost Dhs.520 from 08:00 to 17:00 (including two dives, light breakfast, lunch and tea break, plus Dhs.20 for diving equipment). Non-divers must pay Dhs.425 for a full day and Dhs.325 for a half day from 11:00 to 16:00.

Baital Khair Bldg
Nr NMC Hospital
Al Qusais
Map 12 C4

Creek Cruises

04 393 9860 | www.creekcruises.com
The Malika Al Khor and Zomorrodah dhows can be chartered for any occasion and are suitable for groups of 20 to 150 people for dinner, and more for cocktail parties when

seating is not required. Facilities include an air-conditioned deck, majlis, sound system and dance floor. The charter fee is Dhs.1,500 per hour for dinnertime (minimum two hours), Dhs.1,200 for lunchtime and Dhs.1,000 for breakfast. Catering can be provided from Dhs.80 per person.

Opp Dubai
Municipality HQ
Deira
Map 9 C4

Creekside Leisure

04 336 8407 | www.tour-dubai.com

Creekside Leisure offers a variety of charter packages that range from romantic dinners for two, to corporate hospitality for up to 200 guests. The dhows are licensed and can provide catering, live entertainment and business facilities. A two-hour dinner cruise costs Dhs.225 for adults or Dhs.125 for children, which includes a welcome drink, food and soft drinks.

Dibba
East Coast
Map 1 F1

Khasab Travel & Tours

04 266 9950 | www.khasabtours.com

Sailing north from Dibba (no Omani visa is required) the cruise follows the coastline where steep rocky cliffs rise out of the sea. You'll pass small fishing villages that are accessible only by boat, and will hopefully see dolphins and turtles. Prices start at Dhs.200 per adult for a full-day cruise including lunch and refreshments.

Helicopter & Plane Charters

Other options **Plane Tours** p.292, **Flying** p.351

Dubai Intl Airport
Garhoud
Map 11 F4

Aerogulf Services Company

04 220 0331 | www.aerogulfservices.com

Viewing Dubai from the air is an exhilarating experience and a great way to get a unique perspective of the city. Helicopter tours show you dhows, the creek, parks, palaces and beaches. The tours operate during daylight hours. Starting rates are Dhs.3,200 for a half-hour tour for four people that takes you out over Palm Jumeirah, or you can charter a chopper from Dhs.6,800 per hour and choose your route.

Heritage Tours

Other options **Heritage Sites** p.266

To find out what life was like in Dubai before the discovery of oil and the frenetic pace of development, try a heritage tour in the Bastakiya area (see Sheikh Mohammed Centre For Cultural Understanding on p.270. You will walk through narrow alleyways in old areas, where houses were built close together to maximise shade, and see how, in the days before air conditioning, buildings included windtowers to catch the slightest breeze. Many old buildings have been restored and converted into art galleries and museums, which further illuminate the fascinating and not too distant past of the region.

Hot Air Ballooning

Other options **Plane Tours** p.292, **Flying** p.351

Nr Bin Sougat Centre
Rashidiya
Map 13 F4

Balloon Adventures Dubai

04 285 4949 | www.ballooning.ae

Operating four of the most advanced and largest hot air balloons in the world, with an overall capacity of up to 82 people, Balloon Adventures offer tours for individuals and groups. Flights begin first thing in the morning between October and May in order to catch the sunrise, and afterwards you can go off-road driving over the dunes with their experienced drivers as part of the trip. Price per person is Dhs.950.

Pearl Coast Hotel
Al Barsha
Map 6 A3

Desert Rangers
04 422 0044 | *www.desertrangers.com*
Desert Rangers operates balloon trips that enable you to sample the absolute stillness and silence as you float over the desert. With flights available at dawn or dusk, you can watch the ever-changing colours of the sand dunes below as they react to the first or last flickers of sunlight. You'll finish this memorable experience with refreshments on landing. It's advisable to book early as these are popular tours. From October to May (please enquire about September flights), pick-up time for the morning balloon safari is 05:00. The cost is Dhs.950 per person. Flights are subject to weather conditions on the day.

Dune Centre
Satwa
Map 8 A2

Voyagers Xtreme
04 345 4504 | *www.turnertraveldubai.com*
A great way to celebrate birthdays, anniversaries or product launches, daily flights for up to 12 people operate every morning over the city, mountains or desert, taking off from Dubai Internet City or Fossil Rock with a fully certified pilot. Voyages Xtreme are happy to tailor flights for individuals or corporates, so you can combine a balloon ride with an overnight stay in the desert or dune driving. Trips are weather permitting. Prices start from Dhs.880 per person, but call for the latest information.

Plane Tours
Other options **Flying** p.351, **Helicopter & Plane Charters** p.292, **Hot Air Ballooning** p.291

What better way to view the sights of Dubai or the desert than from the air? Aerial tours are an expensive, but truly memorable way to experience unobstructed views and take some awe-inspiring aerial photos of the many fantastic dunes, buildings and landmarks that make Dubai famous. Cessna tours require at least three people, at a cost of Dhs.900 per person, and a tour in a private jet will set you back around Dhs.1,600. For further information, see the company entries below, refer to Helicopter & Plane Charters (p.291) or Hot Air Ballooning (p.291) for other options, or try the following companies: Gulf Ventures (p.296), Heli Dubai (224 4033), Sunflower Tours (p.298) or Voyagers Xtreme (p.298).

Fujairah Intl Airport
Fujairah
Map 1 F2

Fujairah Aviation Academy
09 222 4747 | *www.fujaa.ae*
An enthralling bird's-eye view of Fujairah's coastline, rugged mountains, villages and date plantations is available from the Fujairah Aviation Academy. Flights can accommodate one to three people at a cost of Dhs.960 per hour which includes all passengers. There is an additional administration cost of Dhs.100 per person. For more information call the Aviation Centre and select option one ('student admissions') from the English menu.

Jebel Ali Hotel
Jebel Ali
Map 3 A1

Seawings
04 883 2999 | *www.seawings.ae*
Get a different perspective of Dubai from an eight-seater Cessna 208 Caravan seaplane. This unique flying experience begins at the Jebel Ali Golf Resort & Spa (p.409), and gives you a breathtaking seagull's-eye view of the city's attractions, soaring past and over Dubai Marina, the Jumeirah and Jebel Ali Palms, The World and downtown Dubai, before touching down smoothly again on the water at Jebel Ali. Prices start at Dhs.895 for a seat on the half-hour flight, or you can opt for an upgrade with the extended, more luxurious Gold, Silver or Diamond tours and charters.

Shopping Tour ◄

Dubai has a well-deserved reputation as the shopping capital of the Middle East. From designer clothes, shoes and jewellery in the malls, to electronics, spices and textiles in the souks, everything is available. This half-day tour (available with most of the main tour operators) takes you round some of the hottest shopping spots in Dubai. Whether or not you walk away with some bargains depends on your haggling skills, so start practising.

Sightseeing Tours

Dubai By Night

Enjoy the early evening lights with a tour of the city's palaces, mosques and souks (see p.294 for tour operators). See the multitude of shoppers of all nationalities, and streets alive with traditional charm, before dinner at one of Dubai's many excellent restaurants.

Dubai City Tour

This is a half-day overview of old and new Dubai. Usual sights include souks, the fish market, mosques, abras, Bastakiya windtower houses and thriving commercial areas with striking modern buildings. Available from most tour operators (see p.294).

Mosque Tours

For an insight into Islam and a closer look at the amazing architecture of a mosque, you can book a mosque tour through a number of tour operators or directly through the Sheikh Mohammed Centre For Cultural Understanding (p.270). You will visit the impressive Jumeira Mosque, with tours starting at 10:00, four days a week.

Tours Outside Dubai

Abu Dhabi Tour

The route from Dubai passes Jebel Ali Port, the world's largest man-made seaport, on the way to Abu Dhabi, capital of the United Arab Emirates. Founded in 1761, the city is built on an island. Visit the Women's Handicraft Centre, Heritage Village, Petroleum Exhibition and Abu Dhabi's famous landmark – the corniche. (Full day).

Liwa Tour

The oasis of Liwa, a couple of hours from Abu Dhabi, offers an opportunity to experience the desert at its most unspoilt. Liwa borders the biggest sand desert in the world – the Rub Al Khali or Empty Quarter. It is worth seeing for the awesome landscape and the strange tranquility of such an area. This tour is only offered by a few operators – Off-Road Adventures (p.298) and Voyagers Xtreme (p.292), while Orient Tours (p.298) offers it as part of package tours.

Stuck in Liwa

Seawings

Tour Operators
Almost all tour operators offer the usual tours: city tours, desert safaris and mountain safaris. Some, however, offer more unique activities, such as fishing or diving trips, trips to see the Empty Quarter in Liwa, helicopter tours and desert driving courses. The main tour operators and those that offer something a little bit different are listed on p.294. Other tour companies are listed in the table on p.298.

Ajman & Sharjah Tour

Ajman is one of the famous places that built dhows, and the museum is worth a visit before driving to the neighbouring emirate of Sharjah, where you can shop to your heart's content at the souks. Finish with a wander around the restored Bait Al Naboodah house to see how people lived before the discovery of oil. (Half day)

Al Ain Tour

Known as the Garden City, there are many historical attractions here, from one of the first forts to be built by the Al Nahyan family over 175 years ago, to prehistoric tombs at Hili, said to be over 5,000 years old. Other attractions include Al Ain Museum, the camel market, the falaj irrigation system, which is still in use, and the souk. (Full day)

Ras Al Khaimah Tour

Drive up country along the so-called Pirate Coast through Ajman and Umm Al Quwain. Explore ancient sites and discover the old town of Ras Al Khaimah and its museum. The return journey passes natural hot springs and date groves at Khatt, via the striking Hajar Mountains. (Full day)

East Coast Tour

Journey east to Al Dhaid, a small oasis town known for its fruit and vegetable plantations. Catch glimpses of dramatic mountain gorges before arriving at Dibba and Khor Fakkan on the east coast. Enjoy a refreshing swim, then visit the oldest mosque in the UAE. This tour usually visits the Friday Market for a browse through cheap carpets, clay pots and fresh local produce. (Full day)

Main Tour Operators

Nr Golden Tulip Hotel
Dibba
Map 1 F1

Absolute Adventure

04 345 9900 | *www.adventure.ae*

For a revitalising weekend doing something different, Absolute Adventure offers dormitory-style camping (food and washing facilities are included), in a traditional stone bungalow just off Dibba beach in Omani territory (no visa required, but you may need your passport at the border checkpoint). Choose from a range of adrenalin-pumping activities in unspoilt surroundings such as treks exploring ancient ruins and secret caves, sea kayaking, snorkelling, mountain biking and motor hang gliding. Activity prices start at Dhs.250. Overnight accommodation costs from Dhs.1,250 for up to 6 people and Dhs.150 per extra guest – you can even rent out the whole house. Dinner costs Dhs.100 per person. See the website for more details or contact Paul on 050 625 9165.

Emirates Holiday
Bldg, Shk Zayed Rd
Business Bay
Map 7 B3

Arabian Adventures

04 303 4888 | *www.arabian-adventures.com*

Offering a remarkably comprehensive range of tours and activities for business or pleasure, Arabian Adventures is a one-stop operator for all your touring needs. It organises itineraries for complete trips and can provide specific services. The tours available include desert safaris, city tours, sand skiing, dhow cruises, camel riding, wadi and dune bashing.

Pearl Coast Hotel
Al Barsha
Map 6 A3

Desert Rangers

04 422 0044 | *www.desertrangers.com*

In addition to the standard range of desert and mountain safaris, Desert Rangers offers many more exciting activities and tours. The scope of their activities is huge and covers camel trekking, sand boarding, canoeing, raft building, deep sea fishing, dhow cruises,

camping, hiking, rock climbing, desert driving courses, dune buggying and helicopter tours of Dubai. It also specialises in initiative tests, corporate events, team building and multi-activity trips for children.

Desert Rose Tourism

Green Community
Jebel Ali
Map 2 A4

04 813 5111 | *www.holidayindubai.com*
Desert Rose Tourism offers city discovery tours with a personal guide/driver as an escort. It's ideal if you are new to Dubai and don't know your way around, as the chauffeur service is available 24 hours a day (050 644 8820). They also arrange various trips that showcase the best of the UAE and Oman – choose from a Bedouin desert safari, a dhow dinner cruise, a camel safari or many other activities. For further information, visit the website.

Dream Explorer Dubai ▶ p.297

Saeed Tower
Trade Centre 1
Map 8 A4

04 331 9880 | *www.dreamexplorerdubai.com*
A new arrival to the tour scene, Dream Explorer offers tours in the desert and mountains in the usual Landcruisers or in Hummers, as well as jet boating tours (see p.364). Desert options include the normal desert safaris with barbecue dinners, sandboarding trips and a luxury option which combines an afternoon desert drive with a visit to Bab Al Shams Desert Resort for the evening, with an Arabic dinner extravaganza at Al Hadheerah.

Dubai Tourist & Travel Services

Nr Splash Al
Abbar Bldg
Bur Dubai
Map 11 A1

04 336 7727 | *www.dxbtravels.com*
An international company founded in 1976, DTTS offers Dubai, Abu Dhabi and Al Ain city and shopping tours, creek dinner cruises, cultural tours to Sharjah and Ajman, East Coast tours, desert safaris, mountain tours to Hatta, sand skiing, camel riding and overnight safaris.

Gulf Ventures

Nr Gold Souk
Deira
Map 9 B1

04 404 5880 | *www.gulfventures.ae*
Gulf Ventures is one of the longest established tour companies in Dubai and is very knowledgeable about culture, history and the lay of the land. It offers a great variety of exciting and informative tours over a wide area of the UAE and Oman, including Bedouin camps, creek cruises, tours around the east coast, plus activities such as fishing, polo and ballooning, and a wide range of city tours.

Net Tours

Various Locations

04 266 6655 | *www.nettoursdubai.com*
Net Tours offers all that Dubai can bestow in terms of adventure; from mountain tours to theme parks and dhow cruises to desert safaris. Delve into Dubai's history, trek through the Ras Al Khaimah mountains or try sand skiing, on a wide range of tours. Five desert campsites just 45 minutes from Dubai, allow you to explore the dunes before settling in a Bedouin haven for an 'authentic' Arabian adventure that comes complete with air conditioning, toilets, internet, satellite connection and even a VIP lounge.

Oasis Palm Tourism ▶ p.295

Royal Plaza Bldg
Al Rigga Rd
Al Rigga
Map 9 B4

04 262 8889 | *www.opdubai.com*
Oasis Palm's desert safaris, dhow dinner cruises and wadi trips come with the typical guarantee of the desired Arabian adventure, alongside the promise of great service

and a memorable experience. The east coast tours will take you through the Hajar Mountains and the strawberry garden in Al Dhaid to one of the oldest mosques in the UAE. They also offer diving trips to the beautiful Khor Fakkan, the 'creek of two jaws', and four-hour deep sea fishing trips.

Off-Road Adventures

Shangri-La Hotel
Trade Centre 1
Map 7 E3

050 628 9667 | *www.arabiantours.com*

As its name suggests, this company offers a wide range of off-road excursions, including desert trips (with dinner at an Arabian camp), wadi and mountain drives, overnight camping, and expeditions to Liwa and the Empty Quarter. In addition to off-road tours it also arranges watersports and airborne activities, and can offer tailor-made packages for groups.

Orient Tours

Nr Le Meridien
Fairway
Garhoud
Map 11 C4

04 282 8238 | *www.orienttours.ae*

Orient Tours offers tours to all major cities in the UAE, including trips to the horse and camel races, desert safaris, sea safaris around Musandam, off-road trips to Hatta and day tours of the majestic dunes of the Empty Quarter in Liwa. It offers corporate events and is happy to organise private events for special occasions, catering to individual needs. Established in 1982, Orient Tours has branches in Dubai, Sharjah, Abu Dhabi, Muscat and Salalah.

Planet Travel Tours & Safaris

Airport Rd
Garhoud
Map 11 D3

04 282 2199 | *www.planetgrouponline.com*

Planet Travel Tours & Safaris offer various tours in and around Dubai, as well as along the east coast and to the major cities of the UAE. Within Dubai they offers coach tours, heritage tours and shopping tours, outside of the city it offers safaris and desert tours.

Sunflower Tours ▶p.299

Zabeel Rd
Karama
Map 10 E1

04 334 5554 | *www.sunflowerdubai.com*

Sunflower Tours offers the full range of usual desert and city tours, but it also runs camel safaris, fishing trips and helicopter tours. For something really different, book a crab hunting trip with them, or a diving trip to explore the splendour of Musandam and Khasab.

Voyagers Xtreme

Dune Centre
Satwa
Map 8 A2

04 345 4504 | *www.turnertraveldubai.com*

Voyagers Xtreme provides a range of adventurous activities over land, air and sea. For a trip to remember, try its 'One Wild Week in the Emirates' tour. You will visit places such as the Empty Quarter, Al Ain, the Hajar Mountains, Fossil Rock, the east coast, Dibba, Musandam and Wadi Bih, and enjoy activities as diverse as mountain biking, trekking, desert driving, hot air ballooning, snorkelling and sky diving.

Other Tour Operators

Adventure Plus ▶p.238	04 272 5272	www.johertravels.com
Arabianlink Tours	06 282 4477	www.arabianlinkholidays.com
Emirates Oasis Tourism	04 268 0041	www.emiratesoasis.net
Khasab Travel & Tours	04 266 9950	www.khasabtours.com
Lama Desert Tours	04 334 4330	www.lama.ae
Leisure Time	04 332 7226	leisure1@eim.ae
Quality Tours	04 297 4000	www.quality-tour.com
SNTTA Travel & Tours	04 282 9000	www.sntta.com

Get ready for an experience of a lifetime!

Discount up to 40%

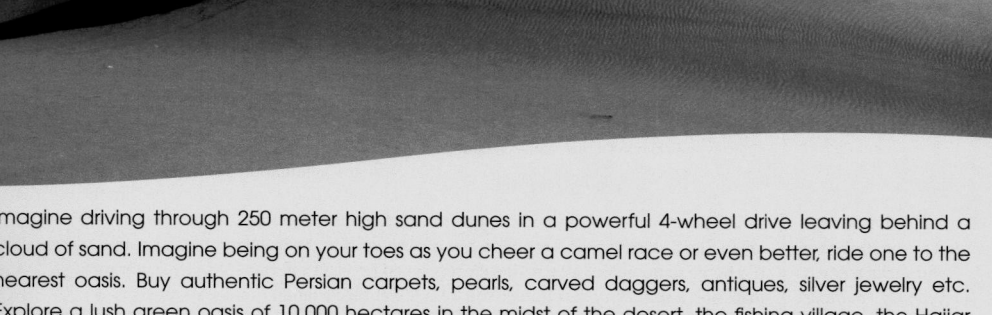

Imagine driving through 250 meter high sand dunes in a powerful 4-wheel drive leaving behind a cloud of sand. Imagine being on your toes as you cheer a camel race or even better, ride one to the nearest oasis. Buy authentic Persian carpets, pearls, carved daggers, antiques, silver jewelry etc. Explore a lush green oasis of 10,000 hectares in the midst of the desert, the fishing village, the Hajjar mountain range, or a 300-year old abandoned town. Imagine an expedition into the deep sea as you fish, or sit at the shore with an electric torch as you crab hunt. Experience romance, as you revel in the traditional Arabian hospitality with belly dancers swinging to cheer you. Time to live your fantasies with Sunflower Tours… and enjoy an experience of a lifetime!!!
Visit us at www.sunflowerdubai.com
and download our Tours & Safaris brochure for more details.

Concept Creation and Brand Consultants - Printmasters International +971 4 282 8181

Sunflower Tours
www.sunflowerdubai.com

Destination Management Company
Tel. +9714 3345554 | Fax +9714 3344566 | P.O. Box 29488 Dubai-UAE | e-mail: tours@sunflowertours.ae | www.sunflowerdubai.com

Out Of Dubai

Other options **Weekend Breaks** p.315

Dubai may have everything from ski slopes and souks to boutiques and beaches, but there are a number of interesting and varied areas outside the city that deserve a place in your weekend plans. There are six other emirates in the UAE, all of which warrant exploration. Also within the Dubai enclave, the small town of Hatta is worthy of at least a day trip. While Dubai may be home to skyscrapers and sophisticated living, the landscapes you can discover beyond this modern metropolis are of the more rugged variety. Impressive mountain ranges, sprawling deserts, and winding wadis are all waiting to be discovered – all you need is a copy of the fantastic *UAE Off-Road Explorer*, which details 26 awe-inspiring routes across the UAE.

Abu Dhabi Emirate

Big Sister

Just an hour or so away (depending, of course, on where you start from) Abu Dhabi is the perfect weekend getaway for Dubai residents who fancy a change of pace. While life may be a bit slower, the shopping and social scene is burgeoning. For more information on what the capital emirate has to offer pick up a copy of Abu Dhabi Mini Visitors' Guide.

Dubai is often mistaken as the capital of the UAE thanks to the 'Sydney Syndrome', but in actual fact, it is further south where you'll find the true king of the desert, Abu Dhabi. Oil was discovered in Abu Dhabi before Dubai (1958 compared to 1966), and in far greater quantities, and today accounts for 10% of the world's known crude oil reserves. No surprise then that Abu Dhabi is the richest emirate in the UAE and its main city has the skyline to prove it. In recent years there has been a greater commitment to tourism with a number of developments attracting a greater number of tourists. While there isn't much you can get in Abu Dhabi that you can't find in Dubai, its slightly slower pace makes a refreshing change from its frenetic neighbour. The city itself lies on an island shaped liked a scorpion and is connected to the mainland by causeways. It is home to numerous internationally renowned hotels, a selection of shiny shopping malls and a sprinkling of culture in the form of heritage sites and souks. Shoppers may be pleasantly surprised to find the malls much less busy than in Dubai, goods and services are often a little cheaper too. There are often good deals to be had on hotel breaks too, and quite a few restaurants offer 'all you can eat and drink' deals for much less than you pay in Dubai.

Abu Dhabi is marketed as the cultural capital of the UAE and is home to an annual jazz festival, a film festival, a music and arts festival, and hosts numerous art exhibitions throughout the year. Find out more from the Authority for Culture & Heritage (www.adach.ae).

In the cooler months, the newly renovated and extended corniche is a lovely spot for a stroll, and on weekend evenings the area comes alive with families meeting up to enjoy a barbecue and shisha.

Al Raha Beach Hotel

Al Raha Corniche
Abu Dhabi
Map 1 D2

02 508 0555 | www.ncth.com

This elegant boutique hotel located in Al Raha, near the airport, offers excellent service and unsurpassed comfort in an idyllic beach setting. Choose from one of the 110 luxury rooms or one of 24 beautiful villas (two, three or four bedrooms) for a really relaxing break. The hotel boasts uninterrupted sea views, a private health club with swimming pool, sauna and steam room, and a state-of-the-art spa. Book yourself into one of the magnificent Royal Suites for the ultimate in luxury and a taste of the high life.

Danat Resort Jebel Dhanna

250km west of
Abu Dhabi
Jebel Dhanna
Map 1 D2

02 801 2222 | www.danathotelgroup.com

Located 250 kilometres west of the city of Abu Dhabi, the secluded location of this five-star beach resort is a world away from the hustle and bustle of city life. Apart from beautifully furnished deluxe guest rooms and private waterfront villas, Jebel Dhanna offers a huge range of leisure activities including tennis, squash, golf (on a nine-hole sand course), a temperature-controlled swimming pool and a beautiful stretch of beach where you can enjoy watersports. It's a good base from which to visit the pristine Sir Bani Yas Island, a natural wildlife reserve just off the coast of Abu Dhabi, and the hotel can organise trips for you.

Corniche Rd
Abu Dhabi
Map 1 D2

Emirates Palace

02 690 9000 | www.emiratespalace.com

Abu Dhabi's answer to the Burj Al Arab is the ultimate in luxury, and perhaps even more ostentatious than its more famous rival. With 12 restaurants, 390 rooms and suites, and an amazing collection of pools and a private beach, all set in 200 acres of lush gardens, it is an incredible place to visit if you want to treat yourself to a weekend of pure indulgence. All of the rooms come with plasma screens, Wi-Fi, a private balcony or terrace, and butler service. If you're feeling flash you can book yourself into one of the opulent Palace Suites, enjoy your own Jacuzzi and rain shower, indulge with Hermès bathroom products, and order a limousine to take you to and from the hotel.

Btn Dubai &
Abu Dhabi
Jazira
Map 1 D2

Golden Tulip Al Jazira Hotel & Resort

02 562 9100 | www.goldentulipaljazira.com

The Golden Tulip has original architecture and a seven kilometre man-made channel connecting the main hotel to the beach resort, where you can stay in luxury bungalows. The hotel is fully equipped with everything needed for a relaxing retreat. Each room has a large terrace overlooking the swimming pool or the impressive sea channel. There is a special pool for children and a private beach with various watersports. Guests have a number of dining options, from light snacks to a la carte menus.

Corniche Rd West
Abu Dhabi
Map 1 D2

Hilton Abu Dhabi

02 681 1900 | www.hilton.com

This 10 storey luxury hotel is located on Abu Dhabi's Corniche Road near the financial and business district and several shopping malls. Choose from king or twin, Guest, Deluxe or Executive rooms and suites, all of which have views of either the sea, the landscaped gardens or the city. There are three swimming pools and a private beach, as well as a wide range of watersports. Enjoy good vibes and casual food at Hemingways (which incorporates the Tequilana Discotheque), cocktails, fusion food and live music at The Jazz Bar and Dining, alfresco eating at Coconut Bay or Vasco's, Mediterranean at La Terrazza, a taste of Austria at Vienna Plaza, authentic far eastern and Lebanese food at Royal Orchid and Mawal respectively, and delectable Italian dishes at the world-renowned restaurant chain, BiCE.

Al Bateen St
Abu Dhabi
Map 1 D2

Hotel InterContinental

02 666 6888 | www.intercontinental.com

Adjacent to the marina, this hotel is surrounded by lush parks and gardens. With five restaurants, four bars and 330 deluxe rooms offering views of the city and the Arabian Gulf, the hotel draws many conference and business visitors. Following the hotel's recent renovation many of the outlets are worth a visit, and the pool, health club and spa are excellent.

Nr Abu Dhabi
Co-op Society
Abu Dhabi
Map 1 D2

Le Meridien Abu Dhabi

02 644 6666 | www.starwoodhotels.com/lemeridien

Located in the heart of Abu Dhabi, this hotel has a vast choice of accommodation from standard five-star rooms to studios, residence, diplomatic and deluxe suites, and even a presidential suite. The hotel is famous for its health club and spa, private beach, and Culinary Village with 15 excellent food and beverage outlets. There is a children's swimming pool and numerous activities on offer including tennis, squash and volleyball.

Liwa Oasis

A couple of hours south of Abu Dhabi by car lies the Liwa Oasis, which is situated on the edge of the infamous Rub Al Khali desert (also known as the Empty Quarter). Covering parts of Oman, Yemen, a good chunk of Abu Dhabi emirate and most of southern Saudi Arabia, the Rub Al Khali is actually the largest sand desert in the world. If you appreciate spectacular scenery and enjoy a spot of camping, a trip into the dunes here is possibly one of the most rewarding experiences in the country. The scale is hard to describe, but imagine standing at the top of a 300 metre-high dune (if you can reach the top) and looking out over a 'sea' of sand that stretches to the horizon in every direction. It's desolate and remote, but quite breathtaking and thoroughly recommended. The driving is hard and should only be attempted by experienced off-roaders, in groups, with all the necessary equipment. If you're not up to the challenge yourself, many of the tour companies listed on p.298 organise trips.

Mezaira'a
Liwa
Map 1 E3

Liwa Hotel

02 882 2000 | www.danathotelgroup.com

The majestic Liwa Hotel overlooks the Rub Al Khali desert, one of the most stunning panoramas in the world. In contrast to the miles and miles of dunes, the hotel is a luxurious retreat set among lush, landscaped gardens. Facilities include a beautiful pool (a modern oasis in the desert), a sauna, Jacuzzi and steam room, as well as tennis and volleyball courts. Kids will love the playground and children's pool. There are several food and beverage options, from international and Arabic cuisine at Al Mezoon to the swim-up Al Nakheel Pool Bar.

Al Ain

Al Ain is Abu Dhabi emirate's second city. It lies on the border with Oman, with whom it shares the Buraimi Oasis. The shady oasis is a pleasant stretch of greenery among the harsh surroundings, and the palm plantations have plenty of examples of the ancient falaj irrigation system. Al Ain has a variety of sights and attractions to interest visitors. Hili Archaeological Garden is the source of many ancient finds, most of which are now displayed in Al Ain Museum. The museum is worth a visit, with displays of traditional Bedouin life and photographs showing how much the area has changed. The camel market is also a must. Arrive early to see the traders haggling over these grunting ships of the desert.

Jebel Hafeet, around 15km to the south of Al Ain, is a rather dramatic mountain that rises abruptly from the surrounding flat terrain. A silky smooth road allows you to reach the very top and survey Al Ain and the desert beyond. At the base of the jebel is the surprising sight of Green Mubazzarah, a landscaped park of rolling grassy hills, trees, hot springs, and waterfalls. Accommodation is also available in chalets, either within the park, or around a man-made lake where you can rent pedalos. Reservations can be made by calling 03 783 9555, and prices are around Dhs.500 per night for a single chalet or Dhs.900 for a double.

Al Sarooj District
Al Ain
Map 1 E3

Hilton Al Ain

03 768 6666 | www.hilton.com

Located near the heart of Al Ain, this ageing hotel, built in 1971, is a good base from which to explore the zoo, museum, Jebel Hafeet and the Hili Tombs. The 202 guestrooms, suites and villas overlook landscaped gardens, while its five bars and

restaurants, floodlit tennis/squash courts, a health club and a nine-hole golf course offer plenty to do. Dining options offer you choices from around the world, including Persian and Italian.

Al Niyadat Rd
Al Ain
Map 1 E3

InterContinental Al Ain Resort

03 768 6686 | www.interconti.com

One of the most impressive inland resorts in the UAE, this hotel has landscaped gardens, swimming pools, luxurious guestrooms, deluxe villas and a Royal Villa with a private Jacuzzi. Especially good for families, the hotel has a training pool, family pool, a shaded babies' pool, a large children's playground and a soft-play area. The many restaurants and bars, and luxurious spa also make this a great day-retreat.

Jebel Hafeet
Al Ain
Map 1 E3

Mercure Grand Jebel Hafeet

03 783 8888 | www.mercure.com

Situated near the top of the imposing Jebel Hafeet, this hotel offers the best views of Al Ain from all of its simply decorated rooms. As you sample great Mediterranean food in La Belvedere, you can enjoy amazing views of the city by night. The hotel also has some superb sports and leisure facilities, including three swimming pools with water slides, mini golf and a children's playground.

Ajman

Ajman is the smallest of the seven emirates, its centre being about 10 kilometres from Sharjah, although the two towns merge along the beachfront. Ajman also has two inland enclaves, one at Masfut on the edge of the Hajar Mountains and one at Manama between Sharjah and Fujairah. Ajman was historically known for having one of the largest dhow building centres in the region, but it's harder to see them being built nowadays, with boats now made from modern materials. The quiet emirate has some great beaches and a pleasant corniche, and an increasing number of facilities to tempt the visitor, including the Kempinski Hotel Ajman, and the Ajman City Centre mall offering a good selection of retail outlets and a cinema, while the old souk is a traditional reminder of a slower pace of life. The developers are making their way up the coast too, with Al Ameera Village – a project featuring heritage-styled residential buildings, a mall and a hotel, on Emirates Road.

The Corniche
Ajman
Map 2 C1

Kempinski Hotel Ajman ▶ p.305

06 714 5555 | www.ajmankempinski.com

Just a short drive out of frenetic Dubai is the tranquility and calm of Ajman and its renowned leisure resort, Kempinski Hotel Ajman. Relax on half a kilometre of private beach with unobstructed views out to sea or around the superb pool complete with adjoining children's pool. The hotel has 185 seaview rooms and a diverse range of international restaurants, cafes and bars, plus a gallery and grand ballroom. The Laguna Club is a comprehensive health and fitness club offering a gym and a range of sports activities, and there is also a spa offering indulgent massages and beauty treatments.

East Coast

Even if you're only in the UAE for a short time, a trip to the east coast is worth the effort. From Dubai you can get there in under two hours, and the drive takes you through the interesting scenery of the rugged Hajar Mountains. The coast and the mountains and wadis inland provide plenty of opportunities for sampling the great outdoors, from snorkelling and scuba diving to camping and off-road driving. The diving off the east coast is considered better than that off Dubai, with increased visibility and more attractive underwater scenery around rocky islands and reefs, and many diving

*B*reak

AWAY

The weekend is all about that much deserved break from our daily routines. Why not magnify this pleasure by lounging in a luxurious world of comfort? Experience a slice of paradise where lush surroundings, superior service and unrivalled pampering become the rewards for your escape.

Sheikh Humaid Bin Rashid Al Nuaimi Street
P.O. Box 3025 • Ajman • United Arab Emirates
Tel +971 6 714 5555 • Fax +971 6 745 1222
ajman.kempinski@kemp-aj.com
www.kempinski-ajman.com
www.kempinski.com

KEMPINSKI - A COLLECTION OF INDIVIDUALS

schools operating out of Dubai often head east with their students. Snoopy Island is a favourite spot for snorkelling, where you're guaranteed to see a host of exotic fish species, and perhaps turtles and small sharks if you're lucky.

Bidiyah

The site of the oldest mosque in the UAE, Bidiyah is located roughly half way down the east coast, north of Khor Fakkan. The mosque is made from gypsum, stone and mud bricks finished off with plaster and its original design of four domes supported by a central pillar was considered unique, but the shape was changed to stepped domes during the recent renovation. The building is believed to date back to the middle of the 15th century. Officially called Al Masjid Al Othmani, it was restored in 2003, and this ancient mosque now looks quite smart and new. The mosque is still used for prayer, so non-Muslim visitors have to satisfy themselves with a photo from the outside. Built next to a low hillside with several restored watchtowers on the ridge behind, the area is now lit up at night with coloured light. The village of Bidiyah is one of the oldest settlements on the east coast and is believed to have been inhabited since 3000BC.

> **East Coast Made Easy**
>
> To reach the UAE's east coast from Dubai takes about an hour and a half by road. The most popular route is to pick up the E88 that runs from Sharjah to Masafi, and then turn left to Dibba or right to Fujairah. A quieter alternative is the S116, which heads south-east out of Sharjah, past Fossil Rock and through the Hajar Mountains, hitting the coast at Kalba. It's faster than the E88, it's smooth, it's got tunnels, great scenery, and is so quiet you'll wonder why no-one else seems to know about it yet.

Dibba Castle ◀

Hidden away in the Omani part of Dibba (aka Daba), adjacent to the vast area of farms and plantations, Dibba Castle is an interesting place to have a poke around. Built over 180 years ago, it has been restored and while there aren't a lot of artifacts on show, you can access all the rooms, and climb up all towers, where you'll get great views over the castle and the area around it. It is signposted off the road past the UAE border check post.

Bithnah

Set in the mountains about 12 kilometres from Fujairah, the village of Bithnah is notable mainly for its fort and archaeological site. The fort once controlled the main pass through the mountains from east to west and is still impressive. The village can be reached from the Fujairah-Sharjah road, and the fort through the village and wadi. The archaeological site is known as the Long Chambered Tomb or the T-Shaped Tomb, and was probably once a communal burial site. It was excavated in 1988 and its main period of use is thought to date from between 1350 and 300BC, although the tomb itself is older. Fujairah Museum has a detailed display of the tomb that is worth seeing, since the site itself is fenced off and covered against the elements. The tomb can be found by taking a right, then a left hand turn before the village, near the radio tower.

Dibba

Located at the northern-most point of the east coast, on the border with Musandam (part of Oman), Dibba is made up of three fishing villages. Unusually, each part comes under a different jurisdiction: Dibba al Hisn is part of Sharjah, Dibba Muhallab is Fujairah and Dibba Bayah is Oman. The three Dibbas share an attractive bay, fishing communities, and excellent diving locations – from here you can arrange dhow trips to take you to unspoilt dive locations in the Musandam (see also Dhow Charters, p.290). The Hajar Mountains provide a wonderful backdrop, rising in places to over 1,800 metres. There are some good public beaches too, where your only company will be the crabs and seagulls, and where seashell collectors may find a few treasures. Since the RAK border crossing closed, going via Dibba is the only way to access the stunning gorge drive through Wadi Bih.

Fujairah

Fujairah was actually part of Sharjah until 1952, making it the youngest of the seven emirates. Its independence makes it the only emirate located entirely on the east coast, and with its golden beaches bordered by the Gulf of Oman on one side and the Hajar Mountains on the other, it's definitely worth a visit. The town is a mix of old and new. Overlooking the atmospheric old town is a fort, which is reportedly about 300 years old, and which will eventually house the artefacts currently on display in the Fujairah Museum once its restoration is complete. The surrounding hillsides are dotted with ancient forts and watchtowers, which add an air of mystery and charm. Most of these also appear to be undergoing restoration work, too. Fujairah is also a busy trading centre, with its modern container port and a thriving free zone attracting major companies from around the world.

Off the coast, the seas and coral reefs make a great spot for fishing, diving and watersports. It is also a good place for birdwatching during the spring and autumn migrations since it is on the route from Africa to Central Asia. The emirate has started to encourage more tourism by opening new hotels and providing more recreational facilities. Since Fujairah is close to the mountains and many areas of natural beauty, it makes an excellent base to explore the countryside and discover wadis, forts, waterfalls and even natural hot springs. An excellent tourist map has been produced by the Fujairah Tourism Bureau (09 223 1554). To get a copy of this map, visit the Tourism Bureau at Fujairah Trade Centre, 9th Floor, Office No. 901, on Sheikh Hamad Bin Abdullah Road (call ahead for opening times, as these are subject to change).

On Friday afternoons during winter, crowds gather between the Hilton Hotel and the Khor Kalba area to watch 'bull butting'. This ancient Portuguese sport consists of two huge bulls going head to head for several rounds, until after a few nudges and a bit of hoof bashing, a winner is determined. It's not as cruel or barbaric as other forms of bullfighting, but animal lovers may still want to avoid it. A new wire fence protects spectators from any angry runaways.

Fujairah Fort

Part of the east coast's rich heritage, Fujairah Fort has undergone a major renovation programme. Although you cannot enter the fort itself, the surrounding heritage buildings are open for viewing. Carbon dating estimates the main part of the fort to be over 500 years old, with other sections being built about 150 years later. The museum next door is worth a look too and has commentaries translated into English.

Hajar Mountains

East Coast Beach

Saudi Arabia ◀

The Kingdom of Saudi
Arabia has some
incredible scenery,
fascinating heritage and
archaeological sites, and
diving locations that are
among the best in the
world. Sadly, due to the
difficulty in obtaining
visas and the present
security concerns, most
expats are unlikely to ever
experience this diverse
and intriguing country.
Recent press reports
suggest that the Kingdom
will issue more tourist
visas in order to boost
the tourism industry,
and give better access to
business travelers now
that it is part of the WTO.
Until then, take a look at
www.sauditourism.gov.sa
and www.saudinf.com to
see what you're missing.

Kalba

Just to the south of Fujairah you'll find Kalba, which is part of the emirate of Sharjah and renowned for its mangrove forest and golden beaches. It's a pretty fishing village that still manages to retain much of its historical charm. A road through the mountains linking Kalba to Hatta has recently been completed, creating an interesting alternative to returning to Dubai on the Al Dhaid-Sharjah road.

Khor Kalba

South of the village of Kalba is Khor Kalba, set in a beautiful tidal estuary (khor is the Arabic word for creek). This is the most northerly mangrove forest in the world, the oldest in Arabia and home to a variety of plant, marine and birdlife not found anywhere else in the UAE. The mangroves flourish in this area thanks to a mix of saltwater from the sea and freshwater from the mountains, but worryingly they are receding due to the excessive use of water from inland wells. For birdwatchers, the area is especially good during the spring and autumn migrations when special species of bird include the reef heron and the booted warbler. It is also home to the rare white collared kingfisher, which breeds here and nowhere else in the world. There are believed to be only 55 pairs of these birds still in existence. A canoe tour by Desert Rangers (p.342) is an ideal opportunity to reach the heart of the reserve and you can regularly see over a dozen kingfishers on a trip. There is also the possibility of seeing one of the region's endangered turtles. The reserve is a unique area so please treat it with respect.

Khor Fakkan

Khor Fakkan lies halfway down the east coast between Dibba and Fujairah. It is a popular and charming town, set in a bay and flanked on either side by two headlands, hence its alternative name Creek of the Two Jaws. It is a favourite place for weekend breaks and day trips and has an attractive waterfront and beach. The iconic 70s style Oceanic Hotel (09 238 5111) is a popular choice, and there are plenty of good fishing and diving sites nearby. Khor Fakkan is part of the emirate of Sharjah, and above the Oceanic Hotel the Ruler of Sharjah's Palace is visible high up on the hilltop. The town has a modern port, and its position on the Gulf of Oman means visiting ships don't have to undergo a further 48 hour journey through the Strait of Hormuz to the west coast. The nearby old harbour is an interesting contrast to the modern port. There are some great dive sites just a few minutes from Khor Fakkan, including Shark Island, Martini Island and the Car Cemetery. See the *UAE Underwater Explorer* for more details. Set inland in the mountains is the Rifaisa Dam which was built to contain flood water and feed the towns below. Local legend has it that when the water is clear, a lost village can be seen at the bottom of the dam.

Al Aqah ◀
Fujairah
Map 1 F2

Fujairah Rotana Resort & Spa ▶ p.309

09 244 9888 | *www.rotana.com*

Located between the Hajar Mountains and the Indian Ocean, the Fujairah Rotana Resort & Spa opened in 2007. It has 250 guest rooms and suites each with its own balcony and view over the sea, and spread around a pool and gardens. The hotel also offers a variety of dining options (from Mediterranean to Middle Eastern), spas, a private beach, watersports, a kid's pool, a kid's club (including a 'graffiti' room), and conference facilities.

Al Ghourfa Rd ◀
Fujairah
Map 1 F2

Hilton Fujairah Resort

09 222 2411 | *www.hilton.com*

The Hilton Fujairah, set on the north end of Fujairah corniche within sight of the grand Hajar Mountains, is a relaxing resort with all the facilities needed for a wonderful

Fujairah
Rotana
Resort & Spa – Al Aqah Beach

Wish you were here

Welcome to the pearl of the Indian Ocean,
Fujairah Rotana Resort & Spa, Al Aqah. Our resort provides the
ultimate serene setting. Whenever the mood strikes, you can relax in
the finest rooms, enjoy an astounding array of recreational facilities,
including unlimited water sports and desert tours or choose from the
amazing dining experiences to indulge in delectable cuisine from
around the world. For business, discover a new dimension to your
next event. From hosting small meetings, to orchestrating group
seminars, we pride ourselves on developing unique experiences.
The Fujairah Rotana Resort & Spa will be without a shadow of
doubt a truly relaxing and inspirational experience.

P.O. Box: 1856, Fujairah, United Arab Emirates
T: +971 (0)9 244 9888, F: +971 (0)9 244 9800, fujairah.resort@rotana.com

rotana.com

weekend away. If you get tired of lounging by the temperature-controlled swimming pool, or activities such as tennis, snooker, basketball or the watersports offered on the private beach, you could always explore the rugged splendour of the surrounding mountains. The hotel is great for families, and there is a safe play area for children.

Al Aqah
Fujairah
Map 1 F2

Le Meridien Al Aqah Beach Resort

09 244 9000 | *www.lemeridien-alaqah.com*

About 15 kilometres south of Dibba, the award-winning Le Meridien Al Aqah Beach Resort is a very popular weekend retreat for Dubai residents, and is just a two-hour drive away. All the rooms have views over the Indian Ocean, and the grounds are characterised by lush foliage and a mountain backdrop. It is particularly geared up for families, with the Penguin Club, kids' pool, and outdoor and indoor play areas. There's an extensive spa at Le Mirage Health Club, a dive centre, and entertainment options include a cinema, restaurants and bars, which serve a range of Thai, Indian and European cuisine.

Al Aqah
Fujairah
Map 1 F2

Sandy Beach Hotel & Resort

09 244 5555 | *www.sandybm.com*

The appealing Sandy Beach Hotel is positioned on an idyllic bay amid a stretch of golden sand running along the Indian Ocean. About 30 minutes from Fujairah and an hour and a half from Dubai it is ideally situated for a short break. The ocean and beach are clean and beautiful and there is a Five-Star Padi Dive Centre within the hotel. This is an ideal spot from which to explore Snoopy Island. Choose from a one or two-bedroom chalet, or a double or twin room.

Hatta

Hatta is a small town in the Hajar Mountains about 100 kilometres from Dubai city and 10 kilometres from the UAE-Oman border. Hatta is still within the UAE though, in an enclave of Dubai emirate, and is home to the oldest fort in the emirate, which was built in 1790. There are also several watchtowers on the surrounding hills. On the drive there you'll pass row after row of carpet shops which are great for practising your bargaining skills and for picking up a new rug for your home. The town of Hatta has a sleepy, relaxed feel, and apart from the Hatta Heritage Village and the dam, where there is always water, there is little to see or do.

However, beyond the village into the mountains, is one of the UAE's must-do trips to visit the Hatta Pools, where you can swim in cool water all year round in deep, interestingly shaped canyons that have been carved out by rushing floodwater. For more details on this trip and attractions in the area, see the *UAE Off-Road Explorer*. The Hatta Fort Hotel is an ideal weekend destination, see below for more details.

Dubai-Hatta Rd
Hatta
Map 1 F2

Hatta Fort Hotel ▶ p.311

04 852 3211 | *www.hattaforthotel.com*

Hatta Fort is a perfectly isolated mountain retreat in tranquil gardens that is fully equipped with numerous facilities and activities. The extensive grounds cover 80 acres of land with a beautiful oasis of greenery. In it, the 50 spacious chalet-style rooms and suites all come with patios overlooking the impressive Hajar Mountains, making it the perfect antidote to Dubai's hectic city living. A good range of sports and leisure facilities will leave you refreshed and relaxed, including two swimming pools, a children's pool, a bar, conference facilities, gift shop, the Senses Beauty Salon, a driving range and chipping green, floodlit tennis courts, archery and clay pigeon shooting, a restaurant, and a coffee shop in an open-air gazebo. Tours are also offered to the nearby mountains.

Stellar Cellar ◄

*The Al Hamra Cellar,
although owned by
MMI (www.mmidubai.
com), is a tax-free liquor
store that is well worth
the trip. You won't find
dodgy booze past its
sell-by date; instead,
you can browse a wide
range of fine wines, spirits
and beers in a pleasant
environment at tax-free
(and very competitive)
prices. Call 07 244 7403
for more info.*

Ras Al Khaimah

Ras Al Khaimah (RAK) is the most northerly of the seven emirates, but thanks to
the new Emirates Road extension you can make the trip from Dubai in less than an
hour. With the majestic Hajar Mountains rising just behind the city, the Arabian Gulf
stretching out from the shore as well as the desert starting just to the south near the
ghaf forest and area of farms at Digdagga, RAK has possibly the best scenery of any city
in the UAE. A creek divides the city into the old town (Ras Al Khaimah proper) and the
newer Al Nakheel district.

If you're visiting for the day you should make time to visit the souk in the old town
and the National Museum of Ras Al Khaimah (p.271), which is housed in an old fort.
Manar Mall is a large shopping and leisure complex, housing a cinema complex, family
entertainment centre, a watersports area and dining options overlooking the creek and
mangroves. The town is quiet and relaxing, and is a good starting point for exploring
the surrounding mountains, visiting the ancient sites of Ghalilah and Shimal, the hot
springs at Khatt and the camel racetrack at Digdagga. Also part of the emirate, the
town of Masafi, inland towards the east coast, is the source of the bottled water of the
same name.

Off the E11 ◄
South of RAK
Map 1 E1

Al Hamra Fort Hotel

07 244 6666 | *www.alhamrafort.com*

With traditional Arabic architecture, and set amongst acres of lush gardens along a
strip of sandy beach, this hotel offers a peaceful get-away, just an hour's drive from
Dubai. Offering a range of watersports and activities, including two floodlit golf
courses and an onsite dive centre, there is plenty to keep you entertained, and the
eight themed eateries offer a wide variety of cuisine and atmosphere. There is also a
kid's club and babysitting service, making it ideal for families too.

Bin Dahir Rd ◄
Nxt to Etisalat
Ras Al Khaimah
Map 1 E1

Hilton Ras Al Khaimah

07 228 8888 | *www.hilton.com*

The biggest draw of this city hotel is the Hilton Ras Al Khaimah Beach Club, which
is just down the road from the four-star hotel and has attractive leisure facilities.
With three pools and a pool bar, there is also a beach with plenty of watersports
on offer. For a weekend spent relaxing by the mountains in a quiet part of the
UAE, this is well worth a trip. The luxury Hilton Ras Al Khaimah Resort & Spa (www.
hiltonworldresorts.com, 07 228 8888) has opened next to the beach club, offering a
more pampered stay.

Umm Al Quwain

Umm Al Quwain is the second smallest of the emirates, and has the smallest
population. Nestled on the coast between Ajman and Ras Al Khaimah, it's a quiet place
where not much has changed over the years. The main industries are still fishing and
date cultivation. The emirate has six forts and a few old watchtowers around the town,
and a lagoon with lots of mangroves and birdlife, which is a popular weekend spot
for boat trips, windsurfing and other watersports – it is the new home of Dubai Water
Sports Association (050 492 7445, www.dwsa.net).

The emirate has not escaped the attention of the developers though, and a project
currently underway will see over 9,000 homes and a marina emerge on the shore of
the Khor Al Beidah wildlife area. What impact this will have on the delicate ecosystem
and abundant plant and animal life remains to be seen. Another project under
development is the massive Al Salam City on the Emirates Road. When completed it
will feature residential districts, towers, commercial units and a shopping mall, and will
be home to over half a million residents.

The area north of the lagoon is known for being the activity centre of the region, with a variety of distractions to suit all tastes. Umm Al Quwain Aeroclub (p.352) offers flying, skydiving, paramotoring and microlighting, and can also arrange 10 minute air tours, either in a Cessna or a microlight, at very reasonable prices. Emirates Motorplex (www.motorplex.ae) hosts all types of motorsport events, including the Emirates Motocross Championship which takes place here on a specially built track. One of the most popular attractions here is Dreamland Aqua Park (p.274). Another favourite destination for Dubai residents is the adjacent Barracuda Beach Resort (below), which is particularly popular thanks to its well-stocked duty-free liquor store.

Nr Dreamland
Aqua Park
Umm Al Quwain
Map 1 E1

Barracuda Beach Resort
06 768 1555 | *www.barracuda.ae*
Many Dubai residents are familiar with the Barracuda Beach Resort, as it is the location of one of the most popular 'hole in the walls' – a place where you can buy tax-free booze. But it is also a pleasant beach resort that is ideal for a quick getaway, particularly if you want to combine it with a booze run. The facilities are built for relaxation; the pool, Jacuzzi and children's pool are all situated next to the tranquil lagoon. If you want more activity, the Dreamland Aqua Park (p.274) is right next door.

After UAQ
Hospital R/A
Umm Al Quwain
Map 1 E1

Flamingo Beach Resort
06 765 0000 | *www.flamingoresort.ae*
Situated within the popular Umm Al Quwain Tourist Club, Flamingo Beach Resort is never going to grace the pages of The Leading Hotels of the World, but it is cheap. The pool area includes a Jacuzzi and a children's pool. The resort is surrounded by an unpolluted, shallow lagoon interspersed with many green islands that attract a variety of birdlife, including migrating flamingos. You can try a number of watersports activities including paragliding, fishing and cruising the coral reefs in a glass-bottomed boat

Nr Palma Beach Hotel
Umm Al Quwain
Map 1 E1

Imar Spa
06 766 4440 | *www.imarspa.com*
The perfect girly weekend getaway, this five-star ladies-only spa haven is in the heart of Umm Al Quwain, in a peaceful, seaside setting. The hotel has a small private beach and terrace for sun lounging and a fabulous temperature-controlled pool and saltwater aqua therapy pool. The hotel offers limited but pleasant accommodation (with only five rooms – two twin rooms and three singles) so booking in advance is advised. Facilities include a gym and workout space, hammam, funky hair salon and an immaculate spa with a seemingly endless choice of treatments.

Imar Spa

Weekend Breaks

There are plenty of amazing places to escape to outside Dubai, and many are quite different. With adventurous outdoor activities, peaceful desert resorts and posh, luxury hotels that are willing to cater for your every need, you can put up your feet and relax or take the time to explore hidden parts of the country. Pick up a copy of *Weekend Breaks in the UAE & Oman* from Explorer Publishing and start planning your get-away. For some tasters of the hotels, see the mini reviews listed in the areas in the Out Of Dubai section on p.300. Outside the UAE, the other countries around the Gulf offer some very different destinations to keep you occupied. See below for details of the countries and some ideas of where to stay.

Bahrain

For a change of pace, head to nearby Bahrain, it is just a 50 minute flight away and small enough to be explored in a weekend. With traditional architecture, miles of souks, excellent shopping and some truly outstanding bars and restaurants, you can choose from a cultural escape or fun-packed break. Formula 1 fans won't want to miss the Grand Prix that usually takes place in March or April, with hotels booked up months in advance – see the *Bahrain Mini Visitors' Guide* for more on what to do there.

Off Sheikh Hamad
Causeway
Manama

Novotel Al Dana Resort
+973 1729 8008 | *www.novotel-bahrain.com*
The only city beach resort in Bahrain, the Novotel offers three restaurants, a lounge bar, a large outdoor pool, a small private man-made beach, indoor and outdoor play facilities for children and a health club including a steam room, sauna, Thai and aromatherapy massages. Watersports equipment available for hire on the beach includes jet skis, water skis, banana boat, windsurfers and kayaks.

Seef
Manama

The Ritz Carlton Bahrain Hotel & Spa
+973 1758 0000 | *www.ritzcarlton.com*
The hotel has one of the best beaches in Bahrain, in a man-made lagoon surrounded by lush gardens. The 600 metre private beach sweeps round the lagoon with its own island and private marina. As one would expect from one of the country's premier five-star hotels, it has nine quality dining venues and comprehensive business facilities. Hotel residents have access to all of the club facilities, including the racquet sport courts, the luxurious Ritz-Carlton Spa and watersport activities.

Dubai

Crescent Rd
Palm Jumeirah
Map 2 A3

Atlantis The Palm ▶ p.ii - p.iii
04 426 1000 | *www.atlantisthepalm.com*
Dubai's newest addition is a grand one: sitting proudly on the crescent of the Palm Jumeirah, Atlantis doesn't do anything on a small scale. Over 1,500 rooms, a huge spa, 17 food outlets and Aquaventure (p.274), the region's largest waterpark (complete with a vertical slide into a shark-infested pool) make this a must-visit resort.

Off the
Dubai-Al Ain Rd
Map 1 E2

Al Maha Desert Resort & Spa
04 303 4222 | *www.al-maha.com*
Set within the 225 square kilometre Dubai Desert Conservation Reserve, with breathtaking views across picturesque dunes and rare wildlife, this luxury getaway describes itself as 'the world's first Arabian eco-tourism resort' and was named as one of the worlds' best ecotourism models by *National Geographic* in 2008. Al Maha is designed to resemble a typical Bedouin camp, but conditions are anything but basic. Each suite

is beautifully crafted and has its own private pool. Guests are welcome to dine on their own veranda, with impeccable, yet discreet, butler service, or in the elegant restaurant. Activities include horse riding, camel trekking and falconry. There is also a superb spa.

Nxt to
Endurance Village
37km from Arabian
Ranches R/A
Map 1 E2

Bab Al Shams Desert Resort & Spa

04 809 6100 | www.jumeirahbabalshams.com
Bab Al Shams ('The Gateway to the Sun'), is a beautiful desert resort built in the style of a traditional Arabic Fort. Each of its 115 rooms is decorated with subtle yet stunning Arabian touches, and pristine desert dunes form the backdrop. Al Hadheerah (p.534), an authentic, open-air, Arabic desert restaurant, is highly recommended. There is a kids' club, a large swimming pool (complete with swim-up bar), and the luxurious Satori Spa (p.409).

Jebel Ali

Nr Palm Jebel Ali
Jebel Ali
Map 3 A1

Jebel Ali Golf Resort & Spa ▶ p.533

04 883 6000 | www.jebelali-international.com
Just far enough out of Dubai to escape the city's hustle and bustle, this fully equipped resort offers 392 luxurious rooms in resplendent surroundings, with a peaceful atmosphere – the perfect place for a weekend break (or longer). The two distinct properties, the Jebel Ali Hotel and The Palm Tree Court & Spa, are set in 128 acres of lush, landscaped gardens, with an 800 metre private beach, a marina and one of the region's first golf courses. Guests can also enjoy horse riding, shooting and a variety of watersports. Although the trunk of Palm Jebel Ali (still undergoing construction) is only 400 metres away, it doesn't detract from the experience for those looking for a tranquil escape. The Palm Tree Court & Spa is undergoing renovation and extension work until November 2009.

Kuwait

Kuwait is not always immediately considered as a weekend break destination (no alcohol, don't forget), but the colourful (and somewhat tainted) heritage of this small, yet rich, country means it is still worth a visit. Kuwait may be one of the world's smallest countries but its 500 kilometre coastline has long golden beaches that remain refreshingly tranquil. From the Grand Mosque to the Kuwait Towers there are many architectural splendours to explore, while Al Qurain House, which still shows the scars of war with its immortal bullet holes, gives you a fascinating insight into the troubled times of the Iraqi invasion. There is also Green Island, an artificial island linked by a short bridge and home to restaurants, a children's play area and a great alternative view of Kuwait's shoreline. For more information and inspiration, check out the *Kuwait Complete Resident's Guide*.

Fahaheel 64009
Mangaf

Hilton Kuwait Resort

+965 2225 6222 | www.hilton.com
Located in Mangaf, this resort has one of the best beaches and health clubs in the country. There are 143 rooms, four suites, 80 chalets, 61 studios and apartments, 52 Presidential Villas and 12 Royal Villas, plus four restaurants, two cafes, one coffee shop and two poolside bars. The resort also has a watersports pavilion and a dive centre.

King Fahad Highway
Sabahiyah

Sea Shell Julai'a Hotel & Resort

+965 84 4444
Formerly the Kempinski Julai'a Resort, this five-star hotel is under new management from Seashell Hotels & Resorts. It has three pools, including a ladies' pool, a health club, The Underground billiards club equipped with a PlayStation and billiards table, and

two restaurants – one poolside and one beachside. Choose from one of the 74 chalets or the 40 hotel rooms, or treat yourself to your own Royal Chalet, complete with private swimming pool.

Visas ◀

Oman

Just a few hours from Dubai, you'll find the countless attractions of Oman. It's a peaceful and breathtaking place, with history, culture and spectacular scenery. The capital Muscat has enough attractions to keep you busy for a good long weekend, including beautiful beaches, some great restaurants and cafes, and the mesmerising old souk at Mutrah. Out of the capital you will find many historic old towns and forts, and some of the most stunning mountain and wadi scenery in the region. Salalah in the south has the added bonus of being cool and wet in the summer.

A flight from Dubai to Muscat takes 45 minutes, but when you factor in check-in times and clearing customs it's not much quicker than driving. There are daily flights from Dubai with Emirates and Oman Air, while Air Arabia flies from Sharjah. Regular flights direct to Salalah from Dubai are also available. There is also a bus service from Dubai to both Muscat and Salalah, taking six and 16 hours respectively, and costing from Dhs.50 for Dubai to Muscat (www.ontcoman.com).

For further information on what Oman has to offer both visitors and residents, refer to the *Oman Mini Visitors' Guide*, *Oman Off-Road Explorer* and the *Oman Trekking Explorer* – all from Explorer Publishing.

Musandam

The UAE's northern neighbour, Musandam, is an isolated enclave belonging to the Sultanate of Oman, and its capital Khasab is a quaint fishing port largely unchanged by the modern world. The region is dominated by the Hajar Mountains, which run through the UAE and the rest of Oman.

It is sometimes called the 'Norway of the Middle East', because the jagged mountain cliffs plunge directly into the sea and the coastline is littered with inlets and fjords. Just metres off the shore are beautiful coral beds with an amazing variety of sea life, including tropical fish, turtles, dolphins, occasionally sharks, and even whales on the eastern side. This area offers some of the best dive sites in the Middle East, and as such is becoming increasingly popular with divers. A dhow trip into the fjords is a great way to sample the beauty of Musandam – on a full-day trip you'll see isolated coastal villages, get a chance to swim and snorkel in the calm waters, and hopefully see dolphins frolicking beside your boat. Khasab Travel & Tours operates a number of dhows, with day trips costing around Dhs.200 per person including lunch, soft drinks, and an informative guide. Call their Dubai office on 04 266 9950. Alternatively, get down to the harbour in Khasab and bargain hard with the independent dhow owners to arrange your own private cruise.

To get there by road, turn right about 30km north of Ras Al Khaimah, at the Shams Roundabout, turn right and follow the road as it loops around to the UAE exit post (unfortunately at busy periods this is a real bottleneck). You'll have to park the car and battle your way to one of the three windows,

Visas for Oman are required whether entering by air or road, and different regulations apply depending on your nationality and how long you want to stay. Nationalities are split into two groups – check out the Royal Oman Police website, www.rop.gov.om, for full lists (click on 'Directorates', then 'DG of Passports'). People in group one can get a visit visa at the border – it's usually free for visitors but Dubai residents are likely to incur a Dhs.30 charge for single entry or Dhs.100 for multiple entry. Residents from group two, however, will need to get a visa from the Oman consulate or embassy in advance, which may take a few days to process. The charges are the same for both groups. Oman does have a common visa facility with Dubai, meaning people on a Dubai visit visa will not need a separate visa to visit Oman.

Al Hoota Cave

Now open to the public, this cave has a large chamber with some amazing rock formations, an underground lake and a fascinating ecosystem. Facilities include a train that transports you into the cave, knowledgeable Omani guides, a restaurant and a natural history museum. Photography is not allowed. All visitors need to book at least 24 hours in advance, as only a limited number of people are allowed into the cave at a time. (+968 24 490 060, www.alhootacave.com)

making sure you grab an exit form to fill in as you queue – on Eid weekends you may be there over an hour. Then drive just a few hundred metres to the Oman entry point where you fill in an entry form and pay for your visa, if applicable. Finally there's a checkpoint where cars are occasionally searched for prohibited goods such as alcohol. The officers won't empty the car though, so with a little careful packing. The road then follows the scenic coastline until it reaches Khasab, passing some great beaches on the way. The visa/nationality rules for entering this region of Oman are the same as those outlined earlier, but again, you're advised to check with the embassy if in any doubt.

Shati Al Qurm ◄
Muscat

InterContinental Muscat

+968 24 680 000 | *www.interconti.com*
This is an older hotel that has recently undergone a major facelift. The InterContinental continues to be popular for its outdoor facilities, international restaurants and regular entertainment in the form of dinner theatres and visiting bands. Alfresco restaurant Tomato is a must-try. Trader Vic's, with its legendary cocktails, is perennially popular. All of the rooms have views of Qurm Beach, landscaped gardens or the mountains.

Barr Al Jissah ◄
Muscat

Shangri-La's Barr Al Jissah Resort & Spa

+968 24 776 666 | *www.shangri-la.com*
Al Waha is the largest of the hotels within Shangri-La's Barr Al Jissah Resort, with 262 bedrooms, and has been built for families. Kids will love the Little Turtles club, where they can play in air-conditioned comfort or outdoors. The hotel has numerous swimming pools, including a rubber-cushioned toddlers' pool and a kids' pool in the shape of a mushroom. For something more grown up, Al Bandar is aimed primarily at business customers and offers deluxe facilities, while the exclusive Al Husn is a six-star hotel with everything you'd expect from a luxury resort.

Zighy Bay ◄
Dibba

Six Senses Hideaway Zighy Bay

+968 26 735 555 | *www.sixsenses.com*
Located in a secluded cove, shared only by a fishing village, the Six Senses Hideaway is a little slice of paradise near the Musandam border. It is accessible in three ways: by 4WD on a rather bumpy road that cuts over the hills down to Zighy Bay, by speed boat into the bay or, believe it or not, by paragliding. The resort has been designed in true rustic style (without compromising on luxury of course) and is made up of individual pool villas. Guests have the option to dine in their villa, eat in the main restaurant, have an intimate dinner atop the stone wine tower or enjoy breathtaking views in the mountainside restaurant.

Qatar

Qatar once had something of a sleepy reputation, but things are changing fast. The amount of development and investment in the country means it is becoming increasingly popular with visitors. With an attractive corniche, world-class museums and cultural centres, and plenty of hotels with leisure and entertainment facilities, the capital Doha makes a perfect weekend retreat. The Doha Asian Games in December 2006 attracted thousands of visitors and put Qatar firmly in the spotlight; many new hotel, retail, leisure and entertainment projects were built especially for the event. Away from the city, the inland sea (Khor Al Udaid) in the south of the country also makes a great day trip, usually as part of an organised tour. The *Qatar Complete Resident's Guide* has details of all these activities and many more.

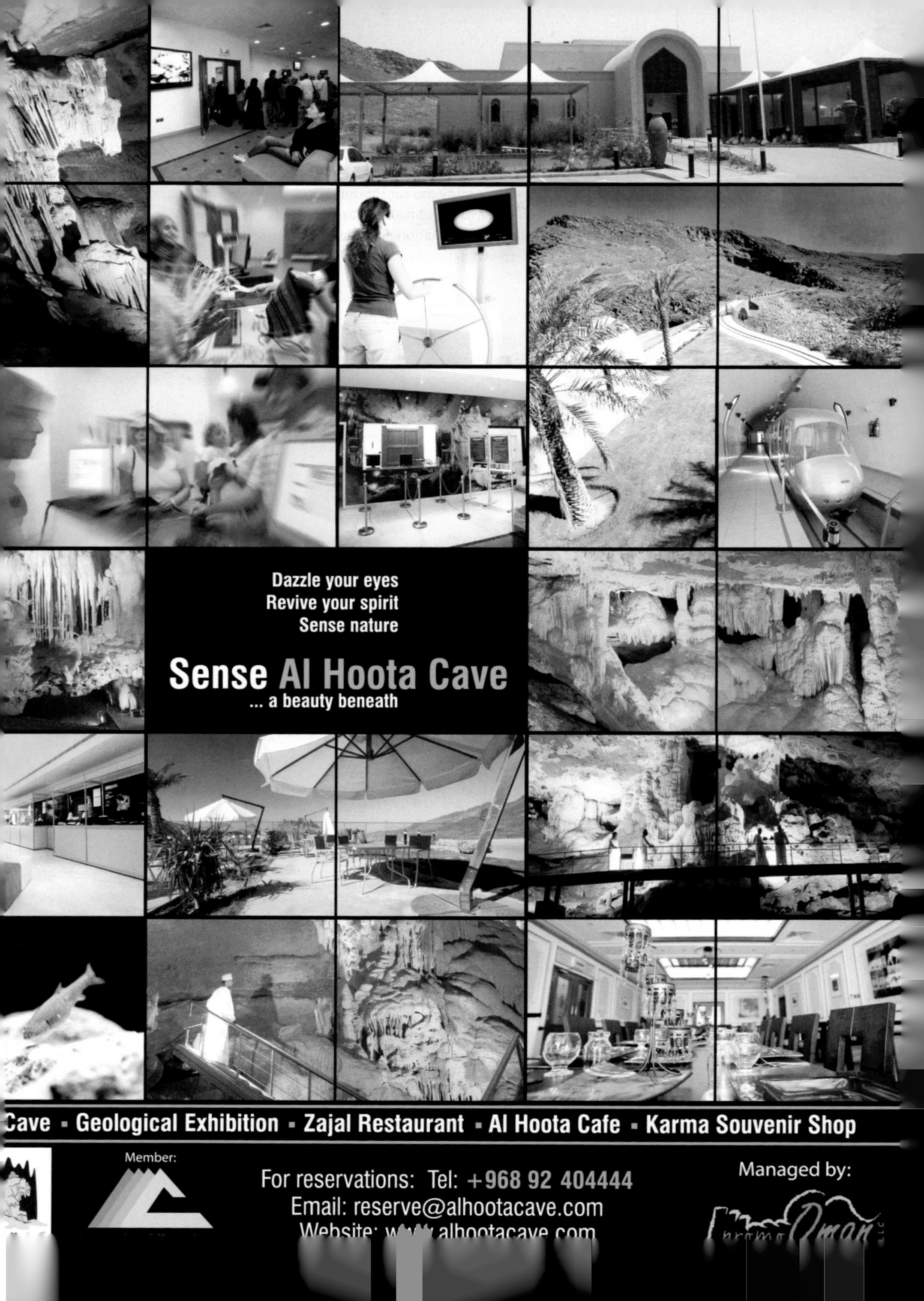

Dazzle your eyes
Revive your spirit
Sense nature

Sense Al Hoota Cave
... a beauty beneath

Cave ▪ Geological Exhibition ▪ Zajal Restaurant ▪ Al Hoota Cafe ▪ Karma Souvenir Shop

Corniche Rd ◀
Doha
Map 1 A2

Mövenpick Hotel Doha
+974 429 1111 | www.moevenpick-hotels.com

This modern hotel boasts the breathtaking corniche as its vista, where guests can enjoy a morning jog or afternoon stroll. Popular with business travellers, this boutique-style hotel also attracts tourists with its excellent restaurants and leisure facilities which include a swimming pool, whirlpool and steam bath.

Corniche West ◀
Bay Lagoon
Doha
Map 1 A2

Ritz-Carlton Doha
+974 484 8000 | www.ritzcarlton.com

The opulent Ritz-Carlton is a perfect stop-off point if you are sailing in the region, with its 235 slip marina and clubhouse. You can expect five-star touches as standard at this resort which takes opulence to another level. All of the 374 rooms and suites have breath-taking views over the sea or marina. The beach club provides a great selection of water sports while the luxurious spa offers every imaginable pampering treatment. You'll be spoilt for choice with nine restaurants all serving a range of excellent international and local cuisine, and you can finish the night off with either a cigar at Habanos or a cocktail at the Admiral Club.

Weekend Breaks – Other Hotels

Location	Name	Phone	Website
Abu Dhabi	Beach Rotana Hotel & Towers	02 697 9000	www.rotana.com
	Hilton Baynunah	02 632 7777	www.baynunah.hilton.com
	Mafraq Hotel	02 582 2666	www.mafraq-hotel.com
	Millennium Hotel	02 626 2700	www.milleniumhotels.com
	Sheraton Abu Dhabi Hotel & Resort	02 677 3333	www.sheraton.com
Al Ain	Al Ain Rotana Hotel	03 754 5111	www.rotana.com
Barka	Al Sawadi Beach Resort	+968 26 795 545	www.alsawadibeach.com
Dubai	Al Qasr Hotel	04 366 8888	www.madinatjumeirah.com/al_qasr
	Jumeirah Beach Hotel	04 348 0000	www.jumeirahbeachhotel.com
	Mina A'Salam	04 366 8888	www.madinatjumeirah.com
	The Palace at One&Only Royal Mirage	04 399 9999	www.oneandonlyroyalmirage.com
	Ritz-Carlton, Dubai	04 399 4000	www.ritzcarlton.com
Fujairah	Al Diar Siji Hotel	09 223 2000	www.aldiarhotels.com
Khasab	Golden Tulip Resort Khasab	+968 26 730 777	www.goldentulipkhasab.com
	Khasab Hotel	+968 26 730 271	www.khasabhotel.net
Muscat	Al Bustan Palace InterContinental	+968 24 799 666	www.al-bustan.intercontinental.com
	Al Falaj Hotel Muscat	+968 24 702 311	www.omanhotels.com
	Beach Hotel	+968 24 696 601	www.omanbeachhotel.com
	The Chedi Muscat	+968 24 524 400	www.chedimuscat.com
	Crowne Plaza Hotel Muscat	+968 24 660 660	www.cpmuscat.com
	Grand Hyatt Muscat	+968 24 641 234	www.muscat.grand.hyatt.com
	Hotel Muscat Holiday	+968 24 487 123	www.muscat-holiday.com
	Radisson SAS Hotel Muscat	+968 24 487 777	www.muscat.radissonsas.com
Nizwa	Falaj Daris Hotel	+968 25 410 500	www.falajdarishotel.com
Ras Al Khaimah	Ras Al Khaimah Hotel	07 236 2999	www.rakhotel.net
Salalah	Hilton Salalah	+968 23 211 234	www.salalah.hilton.com
	Holiday Inn Salalah – Crowne Plaza Resort Salalah	+968 23 235 333	www.holiday-inn.com
Sohar	Sohar Beach Hotel	+968 26 841 111	www.soharbeach.com
Sur	Sur Plaza Hotel	+968 25 543 777	www.surplazahotel.com

Explore OMAN

Exhilarating Soft Adventure

Discover Oman's incredible natural beauty, fascinating culture and warm welcoming people. Experience miles of unspoilt sandy beaches, dive and fish in the warm waters of the Indian Ocean. Explore Oman's interior, camp among the vast desert dunes or the invigorating mountain ranges. Trek through the hills and valleys, climb the dramatic cliff faces and uncover the secret caves and underwater lakes. With easy access by road and air from around the Gulf Region, Oman offers a wealth of exciting activities. Are you ready to try?

SULTANATE OF OMAN

www.omantourism.gov.om

Oman Tourism, Dubai Media City
Tel: +971 4 369 2314, Fax: +971 4 391 8490
E-mail: oman@afkarmarketing.com

WNNLimited

Holidays From Dubai

One of the best things about living in Dubai is its central location and easy access to some wonderful holiday destinations that you may not have had the opportunity to visit had you stayed in your home country. The following holiday hotspots are just some of the amazing places that you can visit with ease from Dubai.

Mountain High

Founded by Dubai resident Julie Amer, Mountain High organises an exhilarating range of adventure challenges such as worldwide mountain treks, cycling holidays, walking, and Himalayan expeditions to Nepal, Tibet and India. You can also opt for something calmer with their range of holistic and well-being treatments. For more info, call 050 659 5536 or log on to their website www.mountainhighme.com.

Flight time: *3 hours*
Time difference:
2 hours behind
Best time to visit:
Apr – May; Sep – Oct

Cyprus

It's hard to believe that this idyllic Mediterranean island is such a short flight from Dubai. Three main towns, Larnaca, Limassol and Paphos, each offer unique accommodation and leisure options, and capital city Nicosia is great for shopping and nightlife. Whether you choose to rent a self-catering apartment or stay in a luxurious hotel with full-board, a holiday in Cyprus is a huge change from Dubai. You can drive up mountains for crisp, cool air and some awesome views, and explore quiet local villages off the beaten track.

Flight time: *4 hours*
Time difference:
2 hours ahead
Best time to visit:
Oct – Apr

Egypt

Egypt is undoubtedly an ideal trip for history fans. It's one of the oldest civilisations in the world and home to famous historical sites such as the pyramids and sphinx. It also has some amazing scenery: there is the White Desert in the west, the Red Sea in the east, and, of course, the Nile. Cairo is a busy city with an active nightlife, and the resort town of Sharm El Sheikh is a popular spot for diving holidays at luxurious beach resorts.

Flight time: *4 hours*
Time difference:
2 hours behind
Best time to visit:
Apr – Jun; Sep – Oct

Greece

Postcard-perfect vistas of whitewashed chalets against a backdrop of azure skies and sea are what you can expect from Greece. A wide variety of accommodation options means you can either settle in a beach hotel or be a bit more adventurous and island hop for a couple of weeks between Corfu, Crete, and Mykonos among others.

Flight time: *3 hours*
Time difference:
2 hours ahead
Best time to visit:
Oct – Feb

India

India is a land of contrasts, from the beautiful beaches of Goa to the vibrant city of Mumbai or the imposing mountains of Kashmir. Goa is probably the top holiday spot, thanks to its palm-fringed white beaches and luxurious hotels. Alternatively, travel to Agra for architecture, handicrafts and jewellery, as well as the legendary Taj Mahal, or the rose pink city of Jaipur. Daily flights are operated by Emirates, Air India and Air Arabia.

Flight time: *3 hours*
Time difference:
2 hours behind
Best time to visit:
Oct – Apr

Jordan

Jordan is packed with religious and historical sites, incredible architecture, and friendly, welcoming people. You can brush up on your history by visiting the Bronze Age Citadel of Amman and a city hewn out of bare rock at Petra. If it's sun and luxury you're after, Jordan boasts an excellent choice of five-star hotels and resorts. And with Emirates, Air Arabia and Royal Jordanian Airlines all offering direct flights, it's ideal for a quick getaway.

Flight time: *5 hours*
Time difference:
1 hour behind
Best time to visit:
Aug – Mar

Kenya

The epic beauty of Africa and the opportunity to spot the big five on a wildlife safari is just a five-hour flight away. For a once-in-a-lifetime experience, head there between August and October to witness the annual migration, when you can observe over two million wildebeest moving over the great plains of the Masai Mara – a sight best seen from above in a hot air balloon. Both Emirates and Kenyan Airlines operate a daily flight to Nairobi.

Flight time: *3.5 hours*
Time difference:
2 hours behind
Best time to visit:
Oct – Apr

Lebanon

Lebanon's blossoming development as a vibrant tourist destination has suffered some knockbacks recently with conflicts both internally and externally. But never a nation to take things lying down, it is doing everything possible to rebuild itself, but it's probably still best to check the current safety situation before picking it for your next holiday.

Flight time: *7 hours*
Time difference:
4 hours ahead
Best time to visit:
Apr – Oct

Malaysia

This natural paradise is a unique and beautiful place to visit, with hundreds of little islands, plenty of almost-untouched little villages and jungles, interesting communities and exotic wildlife. It also has one of the world's most progressive cities: Kuala Lumpur is bustling and attracts expats and visitors from around the globe. Emirates operates a codeshare with Malaysian Airlines, and there is a daily flight from Dubai.

Flight time: *4 hours*
Time difference:
1 hour ahead
Best time to visit:
Dec – Apr for good weather;
Nov – Apr for diving

Maldives

The Maldives is undoubtedly a destination best suited to those who are looking for a relaxing beach holiday rather than an action-packed adventure. That said, many of the luxurious beach resorts offer a range of exciting watersports that will keep adrenaline junkies happy, and this one of the premier dive locations in the world. Resorts tend to be tailored, either to families or couples only.

Flight time: *8 hours*
Time difference:
3 hours behind
Best time to visit:
Feb – Jun; Sep – Oct

Malta

Malta is a country rich in history, with its oldest temple dating back to 3600BC. The medieval city of Madina (which you tour by horse and carriage), and the beautifully preserved 16th century city of Valletta are the historical highlights. There are many excellent beach resorts and hotels, as well as a lively offering of bars, restaurants and nightlife. Emirates flies direct to Malta daily.

Flight time: *6 hours*
Time difference: *None*
Best time to visit:
Nov – Apr

Mauritius

Since Emirates started offering direct flights four times a week, Mauritius has become hugely popular. It is not a massive island, but it has enough variety for you to explore something different each day. From the endless white beaches to the clear blue seas rich with marine life, and from the hustle and bustle of Port Louis (and some great shopping), to the lush, tropical greenery of the inner countryside, Mauritius is an island of contrasts.

Flight time: *7 hours*
Time difference:
4 hours behind
Best time to visit:
Oct – Apr

Morocco

Whether you visit Casablanca, Marrakesh, Tangier or Rabat, the cities of Morocco have a similar thread running through them – a perfect balance of African and Middle Eastern cultures, with some great shopping (both traditional and modern), excellent nightlife, and superb cuisine. Marrakesh is known for its traditional Berber villages, markets and festivals while Casablanca is busy and industrialised.
Emirates operates a daily flight to Casablanca.

Flight time: *5 hours*
Time difference:
1 hours behind
Best time to visit:
Jun – Aug

Russia

Hidden for so long behind the iron curtain, it is now one of the most up-and-coming destinations for the curious traveller. Culturally, Moscow is a powerful city with a history of artistic and literary achievement. Perhaps one of Russia's most interesting aspects is the fusion of the old-fashioned, way of life, with the young, vibrant lifestyle that followed the demise of the Soviet Union in 1991. Emirates fly daily to Moscow.

Holiday Specialists

MMI offer a range of personalised package deals including short breaks exploring exotic destinations in Asia, to longer trips enjoying relaxation and luxury in Europe or experiencing Africa's amazing wildlife on safari. They can also arrange tailor-made holidays perfectly designed to suit your needs (www.mmitravel.com).

Flight time: 4.5 hours
Time difference: None
Best time to visit:
Year round

Seychelles

Enjoying balmy weather throughout the year, the Seychelles are a perennially attractive holiday destination. The 115 islands that make up the Seychelles Archipelago feature beautiful white sands and vivid turquoise waters. Because it is a natural haven for wildlife, there is an emphasis on eco-tourism. Accommodation ranges from acceptable three-star hotels to luxurious five-star beach resorts.

Flight time: 8.5 hours
Time difference:
2 hours behind
Best time to visit:
Year round

South Africa

Whether you choose the vibrant, cosmopolitan city of Johannesburg, the tropical, coastal beauty of Durban or the stylish, Mediterranean-influenced Cape Town, South Africa is a fantastic holiday destination and often referred to as 'a world in one country'. The list of things to do here is almost endless: whale watching, surfing, a wildlife safari or wine tasting through the Cape. Flights are available with Emirates to Johannesburg and Cape Town, Etihad to Johannesburg from Abu Dhabi, and with Qatar Airways from Dubai.

Flight time: 4 hours
Time difference:
2 hours ahead
Best time to visit:
Oct – Mar

Sri Lanka

The beauty of Sri Lanka, apart from the short flight time and negligible time difference, is that you can either have a fantastic holiday on a small budget, or a luxurious holiday of a lifetime. Capital city Colombo has its attractions, although most holiday makers head for the beautiful beach resorts. Emirates offers direct flights to Sri Lanka on a daily basis, and low-cost airline Air Arabia offers return flights for under Dhs.1000.

Flight time: 6 hours
Time difference:
3 hours ahead
Best time to visit:
Aug – Feb

Thailand

It used to be big with backpackers but now Thailand is a popular holiday destination for all. It is blessed with beautiful beaches and numerous luxury resorts in areas such as Phuket and Koh Samui, while Bangkok is a bustling city with a dynamic population and a vibrant nightlife. Emirates operates several daily flights direct to Bangkok, from where you can catch a connecting flight to Phuket and Koh Samui.

Flight time: 4 hours
Time difference:
2 hours behind
Best time to visit:
Apr – Jun; Sep – Oct

Turkey

Perfectly placed between contrasting cultures of east and west, Turkey is an extremely popular holiday destination with beautiful landscapes, great weather, sun, sea and mountains, and one of the most reasonably priced. Istanbul is an amazing city, with an impressive cultural heritage. Alternatively, visit the bazaar and the mosques in Bursa, and the Bodrum at Halicarnassus where Herodotus, the 'father of history' was born.

Travel Agencies		
Absolute Adventure	04 345 9900	www.adventure.ae
Africa Connection	04 339 0232	www.africa.ae
Airlink	04 282 1050	www.airlinkuae.com
Al Futtaim Travel	04 261 1115	www.access2travel.com
Al Naboodah Travel	04 294 5717	www.uaetraveler.com
Al Rostamani Travel	04 295 6777	www.alrostamanitravel.com
Al Tayer Travel Agency	04 223 6000	www.altayer-travel.com
Arabian Pacific Travel & Tourism	050 397 8387	www.arabianpacific.com
DNATA	04 316 6666	www.dnata.com
Emirates Holidays	04 343 9999	www.emirates-holidays.com
Kanoo Travel	04 393 3633	www.kanoogroup.com
MMI Travel	04 404 5858	www.mmitravel.com
Signature Travels	04 344 4272	www.signaturetravel.com
SNTTA Travel & Tours	04 282 9000	www.sntta.com
Turner Travel & Tourism	04 345 4504	www.turnertraveldubai.com

Holidays

Turkey

Jordan

Kuala Lumpur

Morocco

India

The No. 1 off-road guide to the UAE

The ultimate accessory for any 4WD, *UAE Off-Road Explorer* helps drivers to discover this region's 'outback'. Just remember your 4WD was made for more than just the school run.

UAE Off-Road Explorer

What your 4WD was made for

Activities

Activities

Sports & Activities

Believe it or not, life in Dubai is not all shopping malls, restaurants and five-star hotels. Warm winters provide the perfect environment for all manner of outdoor activities, while a host of diversions are available to take your mind off the extreme heat and humidity of the summer.

Traditional sports such as tennis, golf, football and cricket are widely available and both recreational and competitive leagues are becoming more and more common. Many sports clubs offer tennis and squash leagues, as well as five-a-side football.

Duplays, a recent newcomer to the Dubai recreation scene, organises leagues for several sports, including football, touch rugby and ultimate frisbee. Its website, www. duplays.com, lists all of the current leagues and organises them by skill level and location, so players can find a league that is convenient and enjoyable. Individual prices for each league range from Dhs.250 to Dhs.500 for eight weeks of play. To find out about upcoming leagues and one-off events, register yourself on the website. For the more adventurous, the UAE's surprisingly varied geography lends itself perfectly to skydiving, rock climbing, mountain biking, dune bashing and wadi driving.

Activity Finder

A new website, www.adrenalinesportslive.com, allows users to upload descriptions and photographs of local adrenaline sports locations. The content isn't always great, but people new to Dubai might find helpful information for their sport of choice. Thanks to a sprawling coastline of crystal clear waters, watersports are particularly popular as well, with scuba diving, snorkelling, sailing, surfing, water-skiing, and kitesurfing being firm favourites.

With so many different nationalities and cultures at play in Dubai, most sports, activities and interests are covered. Sometimes word of mouth is the best way of discovering that there are others that share your passion. If you can't find an existing club, you could always start your own.

Aerobics & Fitness Classes

Step, pump, aqua and conventional aerobics classes are offered at many beach, health and sports clubs. For a complete list of up to date classes, times and instructors, check with the clubs – see the table below for more details. Prices vary from club to club but average around Dhs.30 per class for members and Dhs.40 for non-members.

Aerobics & Fitness Classes

Name	Phone	Web	Type of Class
The Aviation Club	04 282 4540	www.aviationclub.ae	Body Balance Body Combat Body Pump Spinning, Step
The Big Apple	04 319 8660	www.jumeirahemiratestowers.com	Body Pump, Spinning
Club Olympus Fitness & Spa	04 209 1234	www.dubai.regency.hyatt.com	
Dimension Health & Fitness Centre	04 407 6704	www.metropolitandubai.habtoorhotels.com	Aerobics
Fitness First ▶ p.397	04 358 0344	www.fitnessfirst.ae	Body Attack Body Balance Body Combat, Body Jam Body Pump, Body Step, Dancing Pilates, Spinning, Tai Chi, Yoga
Fitness Planet Unisex Gym & Health Club	04 269 9773	www.bgroupme.com	Aerobics
Hayya!	04 362 7790	www.hayya.ae	Aerobics, Pilates, Powerpump, Yoga
Healthy 4 U	050 157 3552	www.outstandinghealth.co.uk	Personal Training
Lifestyle Health Club	04 603 8825	www.sofitel.com	Aerobics
Nautilus Fitness Centre	04 331 4055	www.crowneplaza.com	Powerpump Tae-Bo, Yoga Belly-Dancing
Pharaohs' Club	04 324 0251	www.pyramidsdubai.com	Body Pump Spinning, Step
Quay Healthclub	04 366 8888	www.madinatjumeirah.com	Body Balance Body Pump, Spinning
Shapes Weight-Loss Club & Health Spa	04 367 2137	www.shapeshealthclub.com	Aerobics

Aqua Aerobics

With so many fantastic swimming pools at hotels and health clubs, aqua aerobics is more a pleasure than a chore. It's also a good workout for people with knee or lower back injuries, osteoporosis sufferers and pregnant women. You can get your aqua aerobics fix at the Pharaohs' Club (04 324 0000), the Quay Healthclub at Madinat Jumeirah (04 366 8888), and the Dubai Ladies Club (04 349 9922).

Archery

Sharjah Wanderers
Golf Club
Sharjah
Map 2 C2

Dubai Archers Club

050 450 9819 | www.dubaiarchers.com

Small, friendly and informal, the Dubai Archers Club meet at Sharjah Wanderers Golf Club on Fridays. Experienced archers play till 10:30am while there are two sessions for beginners at 10:30 to 12:30 and 14:30 to 16:30pm. Coaching is available and club equipment is on hand for novices. Non Sharjah Wanderers club members pay Dhs.50 for the entry fee, including the hire of equipment. Call Simon on 050 450 9819 for more details.

Dubai-Hatta Rd
Hatta
Map 1 F2

Hatta Fort Hotel ▶ p.311

04 852 3211 | www.jebelali-international.com

Existing since 1981, Hatta Fort Hotel has an archery range 25 metres long, with eight targets. Archery fans can enter the hotel's annual competition, with the Dubai Archers Club (above) also holding its annual archery tournament at this venue. Assistance is available at the hotel for this challenging sport.

Nr Jebel Ali Golf
Resort & Spa
Jebel Ali
Map 2 A4

Jebel Ali Shooting Club

04 883 6555 | www.jebelali-international.com

As well as five outdoor floodlit clay-shooting ranges, Jebel Ali Shooting Club also boasts indoor and outdoor archery ranges with equipment for both men and women. Well worth the 45 minute drive from Dubai, the outdoor range is huge at 5,000 square metres and can accommodate up to 12 archers at the same time. There's also an indoor and outdoor shooting academy with professional coaching for both individuals and groups. Check the website for summer and winter timings. It is closed on Tuesdays throughout the year.

Art Classes

Other options **Art & Craft Supplies** p.425, **Art Galleries** p.264

Villa 504b
Jumeira Road
Nr Beach Park
Jumeira
Map 6 F1

Bead Palace & Accessories

04 395 2771 | www.dubaikidz.biz

Located in Jumeirah 3 on Beach Road, Bead Palace & Accessories is a full service bead store which carries a great selection including semi-precious beads, Czech and Japanese seed beads, and Austrian Swarovski crystals. It also offers a wide range of classes and workshops for kids and teens which run throughout the year. It is open Saturday to Thursday from 10:00 to 19:00, and on Friday from 14:00 to 18:00.

Jumeirah Town
Centre
Jumeira
Map 7 D1

Café Ceramique

04 341 5008 | www.cafe-ceramique.com

Part cafe, part art studio, Café Céramique offers a novel art and eating experience. Pick a tasty bite from the menu and a blank piece of pottery, and get creative. Once you've finished your masterpiece it'll need glazing and firing – the cafe takes care of this for you, and you're given a time and date on which to pick up your pot. Events offered include Art4fun Workshops and the Kidz4art Summer Camp. A second branch can be found in Mall of the Emirates (04 341 0144).

Mall of the Emirates
Al Barsha
Map 6 A3

Dubai Community Theatre & Arts Centre (DUCTAC)
04 341 4777 | *www.dubaitheatre.org*

Located at Mall of the Emirates, The Dubai Community Theatre & Arts Centre (DUCTAC) is a modern, non-profit-making cultural and arts facility serving the varied communities within Dubai. In addition to a 540 seat two-level theatre and a 190 seat studio theatre/rehearsal space, it features art galleries, classrooms and studios for painting, sculpture, photography, calligraphy, pottery, dance and much more. Several artist-led classes are held at the centre and the website has lists each class with the relevant contact information. With a cafe, art supplies shop and lending library, DUCTAC has become a hub for art in Dubai.

Check the website for upcoming performances, exhibitions, and workshops. DUCTAC is open daily 09:00 to 22:00, and 14:00 to 22:00 on Fridays.

Slimming Made Easy

If you can't stand the thought of going to the gym, try HypoxiTherapy. The training system is said to lose cellulite and fat by exercise combined with vacuum suction. The method is immediate and painless, can be directed where you want to lose weight, and shows visible results after the first session. The treatment is gaining popularity and you can try it at both The Aviation Club (04 282 4122) in Garhoud and Club Active Plus (04 336 0001) in Oud Metha.

Nr Town Centre
Jumeira
Map 7 D1

Dubai International Art Centre
04 344 4398 | *www.artdubai.com*

As one of the first art-centred establishments to reach Dubai, this centre is a haven of artistic tranquillity. Classes are offered in over 70 subjects, including painting and drawing, dressmaking, etching, pottery and photography. Courses last from six to eight weeks, and prices vary according to the materials required. The DIAC also holds regular exhibitions showcasing the members' works. Annual membership fees start at Dhs.350, with Dhs.450 for family membership and Dhs.120 for those under 18. Classes are open to non-members too.

Jumeirah Centre
Jumeira
Map 7 F1

Elves & Fairies
04 344 9485 | *www.elvesandfairies.org*

This craft shop for adults and children specialises in stencils, rubber stamps and face painting. It also deals in decorative paint effects and stock paints, glazes, colourwashes, varnishes and brushes, as well as cross-stitch, mosaics and decoupage. It runs regular workshops for children and adults on all things crafty, including the popular new activity of scrapbooking.

St 17a
Beh Dubai Garden Ctr
Al Quoz
Map 6 B4

The Jam Jar
04 341 7303 | *www.thejamjardubai.com*

At The Jam Jar you'll be equipped with unlimited paint, brushes, music and drinks, and let loose to freely express yourself on canvas. Whether you've never painted before or are something of a closet Picasso, inspiration, creativity and fun is what it's all about. Private painting parties can be arranged, and The Jam Jar hosts regular exhibitions and competitions. The 'Jam-To-Go' service even brings the experience to you – a novel idea for your next garden party or corporate event. It is open on Friday and Saturday from 14:00 to 21:00, and weekdays from 10:00 to 21:00, closed on Sundays.

Baseball

Nr Nad Al Sheba Club
Nad Al Sheba
Map 2 B3

Dubai Little League

050 293 3855 | www.eteamz.com/DubaiLittleLeague

Dubai Little League is a non-profit organisation run by parent volunteers. Every year it fields over 20 baseball teams, consisting of 350 boys and girls between the ages of 4 and 18, and this year it has a new all-girls slow pitch softball programme. Previous experience or knowledge is not necessary, it's all about learning to play as a member of a team and enjoying some outdoor exercise. Registration costs Dhs.500 which includes season fees, team picture, uniform and year end trophy.

Basketball

Basketball courts can be rented at the Aviation Club and Dubai Country Club, or you can go down to Safa Park (04 349 2111) and get regular pick up games on Wednesday, Thursday and Sunday evenings. You'll also find courts beside Diyafah Street in Satwa, near Rydges Plaza hotel. Duplays also organises a league for both recreational and competitive players (www.duplays.com).

Various Locations

Basketball Academy Dubai

050 457 1706 | www.badubai.com

Aimed at teaching and promoting basketball in Dubai, the Basketball Academy holds classes, free-play events and camps for children of all ages and skill levels. All of the highly qualified staff are properly trained in instructing children. Classes focus on everything from basic hand-eye coordination to advanced court strategy.

Beauty Training

Other options **Beauty Salons** p.401

Wafi Pyramids
Umm Hurair
Map 10 E4

Cleopatra & Steiner Beauty Training Centre

04 324 0250 | www.cleopatra-steiner.com

This is the Middle East's first internationally endorsed training facility, and offers long and short term courses in health, beauty and holistic therapy. Courses include anatomy and physiology, body massage, nail and skin treatments, reflexology, hairdressing and aromatherapy. It has recently included Spa Management to the list of courses. Qualifications are recognised by CIDESCO, CIBTAC, and City & Guilds.

Belly Dancing

Other options **Dance Classes** p.339

Belly dancing is not only an ancient Arabic art but also great fun and a good way to keep fit. The Ballet Centre (04 344 9776) holds belly dancing lessons on various mornings and evenings, and the Nautilus Fitness Centre (04 331 4055) at the Crowne Plaza teaches oriental belly dancing on Sunday and Tuesday evenings. You can also try Shapes Health Club in Knowledge Village, where classes cost Dhs.35 and are open to all (04 367 2137). Groups of seven or more ladies can also arrange lessons at home from Isabella (050 651 2273).

Oops!

Did we miss anything out? If you have any thoughts, ideas or comments for us to include in the Activities section, drop us a line, and if your club or organisation isn't in here, let us know and we'll give you a shout in the next edition. Visit www.liveworkexplore.com and tell us whatever's on your mind.

Birdwatching

Other options **Environmental Groups** p.349, **Birdwatching** p.333

Thanks to the ever-increasing greenery, Dubai attracts many bird species not easily found in Europe or the rest of the Middle East. Over 80 species breed locally, and during the spring and autumn months, over 400 species have been recorded on their migration between Africa and Central Asia. The many parks and golf clubs are often the best birdwatching sites, where parakeets, Indian rollers, little green bee eaters and hoopoe can easily be spotted. Other species found in the Emirates include the striated scops owl, chestnut bellied sandgrouse, Saunders' little tern and Hume's wheatear. Outside Dubai, the mangrove swamps in Umm Al Quwain and Khor Kalba are good places for birdwatching. Khor Kalba is the only place in the world where you can spot a rare subspecies of the white-collared kingfisher. Canoe trips through the mangroves can be arranged by tour companies, see Desert Rangers (p.335). The Ras Al Khor Wildlife Sanctuary at the end of Dubai Creek is the only wildlife park within the city and a great place to see many types of resident and migratory birds, including the famous flamingos, from the three bird hides. See p.280 for more details.

Various Locations ◀ Emirates Bird Records Committee
050 642 4358 | *www.uaeinteract.com/nature*
The Emirates Bird Records Committee puts together information about birds in the UAE and maintains a checklist. A weekly round up of bird sightings and a monthly report is available via email upon request.

Boot Camp Training

Boot Camps are hardcore fitness programmes for gym-goers in a rut, or those that want to get super fit. They normally take place at sunrise on public beaches and parks, and tend to involve burly men telling flabby expats to jog, sprint, squat and heave.

Various Locations ◀ Fitness O2
050 955 6129 | *www.fitness02.com*
The bootcamp programme at Fitness 02 combines the standard military-inspired training as other courses, but mixes in a few Thai boxing moves (non contact) to get you kicking and swinging (and possibly imagining your instructor on the receiving end). Each four-week course costs Dhs.950 and includes 12 sessions.

Various Locations ◀ Physical Advantage
04 311 6570 | *www.physicaladvantage.ae*
Famous for its Military Bootcamp, this is an outdoor training programme designed to challenge all aspects of health and fitness. It costs Dhs.950 for a four-week course with three sessions a week. They also have a GI Jane boot camp for ladies only. Exercises include jogging and sprinting along the beach, squats, sit ups, push ups and running with a 'gun' (usually plastic piping filled with sand). A basic fitness test in the first session decides which section you should be in.

Bowling

Beh American ◀ Al Nasr Leisureland
Hospital
Oud Metha *04 337 1234* | *www.alnasrleisureland.ae*
Map 10 E2 Al Nasr Leisureland has an eight-lane bowling alley with various fast food outlets and a bar that serves alcohol. Booking is recommended since there are regular league games that take place during the week. The entrance fee is Dhs.10, and each game costs Dhs.7

which includes shoe rental. Annual membership for bowling costs Dhs.1,600 for males, Dhs.1,250 for females and Dhs.750 for kids accompanied by parents.

Dubai Bowling Centre

Al Hadiqa St
Al Quoz
Map 7 B3

04 339 1010 | www.bowlingdubai.com

This state of the art bowling and recreation centre is the newest and biggest of its kind in Dubai and the Northern Emirates. With 24 Brunswick lanes for recreational and professional bowling, the bowling arena has leagues for serious players as well as those who bowl for fun. They cater for professional tournaments, corporate events and are in the process of constructing a 24,000 square foot gym and spa. They also have Action Zone – a gaming area for kids, a Booster juice shop and a Mugg & Bean coffee shop.

Dubai International Bowling Centre

Opp Al Shabab Club
& Century Mall
Al Mamzar
Map 12 B3

04 296 9222 | www.dubaibowlingcentre.com

The biggest bowling centre in Dubai, this modern venue has 36 state-of-the-art computerised lanes, which are enjoyed by recreational and competitive bowlers alike. Several of Dubai's clubs and leagues are based here and the centre hosts regular competitions. The range of facilities is excellent and includes an equipment shop, snooker and billiards, amusements and video games, and a number of cafes and dining options.

Bridge

Dubai Ladies Bridge Club

Dubai Intl Women's
Club
Jumeira
Map 7 D1

050 684 8544

Ladies-only bridge mornings are held at 09:00 on Sundays and Wednesdays. Registration ends at 08:45, and games start promptly at 09:00. For further details, contact Marzie Polad on 050 659 1300 or Jan Irvine on 050 645 4395.

Bungee Jumping

For adrenaline junkies, bungee jumping is available in Dubai at certain times of the year. During the Dubai Shopping Festival (DSF) there are various attractions and funfairs dotted around town, and the one on Al Seef Road by the creek usually has bungee. For more information, check the daily press for details as DSF approaches.

Camping

Other options **Off-Road Driving** p.376, **Outdoor Goods** p.461

Constant sunshine and an awe-inspiring array of locations make camping a much-loved activity in Dubai and the UAE. In general, warm temperatures and next to no rain means you can camp with much less equipment and preparation than in other countries, and many first-timers or families with children find that camping becomes their favourite weekend break. For most, the best time to go is between October and April, as in the summer it can get unbearably hot sleeping outside.
Choose between the peace and tranquillity of the desert, or camp among the wadis and mountains next to trickling streams in picturesque oases. Many good campsites are easily accessible from tarmac roads so a 4WD is not always required.
Although the UAE has low rainfall, care should be taken in and near wadis as flash floods can and do occur (remember, it may be raining in the mountains miles from where you are).

Sports & Activities

The UAE Off-Road Explorer

Got A 4WD?

The UAE offers SUV owners a real chance to push their vehicles to the limits and experience nature first hand. From dune bashing and wadi driving to hiking and mountain biking, *The UAE Off-Road Explorer* will give you all you need to know about your local wilderness.

You should consider taking the following equipment:
- Tent
  - Lightweight sleeping bag (or light blankets and sheets)
  - Thin mattress (or air bed)
  - Torches and spare batteries
- Cool box for food
- Water (always take too much)
- Camping stove, or BBQ and charcoal if preferred
- Firewood and matches
- Insect repellent and antihistamine cream
- First aid kit (including any personal medication)
- Sun protection (hats, sunglasses, sunscreen)
- Jumper/warm clothing for cooler evenings
- Spade
- Toilet rolls
- Rubbish bags (ensure you leave nothing behind)
- Navigation equipment (maps, compass, Global Positioning System (GPS)
- Mobile phone (fully-charged)

For the adventurous with a 4WD, there are endless possibilities for camping in remote and beautiful locations all over the UAE. The many sites in the Hajar Mountains (in the north near Ras Al Khaimah or east and south near Hatta or Al Ain), and the huge sand dunes of Liwa in the south are highly recommended. These routes require some serious off-road driving but offer a real wilderness camping experience. For more information on off-road adventuring and places to camp, refer to the *UAE Off-Road Explorer*.

Nr Golden Tulip Hotel
Dibba
Map 1 F1

Absolute Adventure

09 345 9900 | www.adventure.ae

For companies looking to give their employees a treat while enhancing teamwork and problem solving skills, Absolute Adventure organises corporate camping trips. Departing from their base in Dibba, a boat takes large groups to a nearby cove where they'll camp in tents and participate in team-building activities. All of the equipment and food is taken care of, including sunshades, shower tents and toilet tents.

Canoeing

Other options **Kayaking** p.364, **Outdoor Goods** p.461

Canoeing is a great way to access hidden places of natural beauty and get close to marine and bird life in the UAE. At Khor Kalba Nature Reserve on the east coast, tours are available and canoes can be hired. If you have your own canoe, other worthwhile areas to visit include the coastal lagoons of Umm Al Quwain, selected areas around Ras Al Khaimah and mangrove-covered islands north of Abu Dhabi. Many of these areas are on their way to becoming protected reserves, so treat them with respect and do not litter. Adventurous paddlers occasionally go to the Musandam in sea-touring canoes where it is possible to visit secluded bays and view spectacular rocky coastlines with fjord-like inlets and towering thousand metre cliffs. Also see Khor Kalba in the Exploring section on p.308.

Pearl Coast Hotel
Beh MOE
Al Barsha
Map 6 A3

Desert Rangers

04 422 0044 | www.desertrangers.com

Desert Rangers offers canoe expeditions through the mangroves at Khor Kalba Nature Reserve. Only a basic level of fitness is required and this is a suitable activity for people of all ages. A guide accompanies you on your trip. Trips usually cost Dhs.300 per person (Dhs.150 per person if you provide your own transport) and Dhs.210 for kids.

Caving
Other options **Out of Dubai** p.300

The cave network in the Hajar Mountains is extensive and much of it has yet to be explored. Some of the best caves are located near Al Ain, the Jebel Hafeet area and just past Buraimi near the Oman border. Many of the underground passages and caves have spectacular displays of curtains, stalagmites and stalactites, as well as gypsum flowers. At present there are no companies offering guided tours, and caving is limited to unofficial groups of dedicated cavers. Within the region, caving ranges from fairly safe to extremely dangerous, but either way you should always be well-equipped and accompanied by an experienced leader.
Check weather forecasts to find out about recent rainfalls and be warned that flash floods occur regularly at certain times of the year. The Hajar Mountain range continues into the Sultanate of Oman, where it is higher and even more impressive. In Oman, the range includes what is believed to be the second largest cave system in the world, as well as the Majlis Al Jinn Cave – the second largest chamber in the world. A word of warning though, no mountain rescue services exist, therefore anyone venturing out into mountains should be reasonably experienced, or go with someone who knows the area.

Chess
Other options **Scrabble** p.383

Nr Al Shabab Club
Hor Al Anz
Map 12 B3

Dubai Chess & Culture Club
04 296 6664 | *www.dubaichess.com*
This club is involved in all aspects of chess and cultural programmes. Members can play chess at the club seven nights a week and competitions are organised on a regular basis. International competitions are also promoted including the Dubai International Open, Emirates Open and Dubai Junior Open, attracting representatives from Asia, Arabia and Europe. Annual membership is Dhs.100 for Nationals and Dhs.200 for expats.

Rapelling off Jebel Hafeet

Climbing
For those who feel at home on vertical cliffs or hanging from rocky precipices, excellent climbing can be found in various locations around the UAE, including Ras Al Khaimah, Dibba, Hatta and the Al Ain/Buraimi region. The earliest recorded rock climbs were made near Al Ain and Buraimi in the late 1970s; since then more than 600 routes have been climbed and named. These vary from short outcrop routes to difficult and sustained mountain routes of alpine proportions. New routes are generally climbed 'on sight', with traditional protection. Most are in the higher grades – ranging from (British) Very Severe, up to extreme grades (E5). Due to the nature of the rock, some climbs can feel more difficult than their technical grade would suggest. Many routes, even in the easier grades, have loose rock, poor belays and difficult descents,

often by abseil, making them unsuitable for total novices. However, there are some easier routes for new climbers, especially in Wadi Bih and Wadi Khab Al Shamis. To meet like-minded people head to Wadi Bih where you're sure to find climbers nearly every weekend, or go to the indoor climbing wall at Pharaohs' Club (below), where most of the UAE climbing fraternity hangs around (ahem). For more information contact John Gregory on 050 647 7120 or email arabex@eim.ae. Another excellent resource is www.globalclimbing.com, which features a wealth of information for anyone interested in climbing in the UAE.

Dubai World Trade Centre
Trade Centre 2
Map 10 A1

Climbing Dubai
04 306 5061 | www.climbingdubai.com

Climbing Dubai has daily climbing programmes, outdoor climbing tours and international climbing expeditions. Currently based outdoors at Horizon School Dubai, next to Safa Park Gate 4, they have an eight metre climbing tower. The group seeks to attract new climbers and promotes walk-ins at the evening sessions which cost Dhs.50 and include all necessary equipment. The club is also completing a massive new climbing wall at the Dubai World Trade Centre Club on Sheikh Zayed Road.

Pearl Coast Hotel
Beh MOE
Al Barsha
Map 6 A3

Desert Rangers
04 422 0044 | www.desertrangers.com

Desert Rangers offers rock climbing trips to well-established locations throughout the Emirates that are suitable for absolute beginners or experienced climbers. Trips include instruction, all necessary safety equipment and lunch. The cost is Dhs.400 per person, and there is a minimum of four people per trip.

Wafi Pyramids
Umm Hurair
Map 10 E4

Pharaohs' Club
04 324 0251 | www.pyramidsdubai.com

The indoor climbing wall at Pharaohs' Club lets climbing enthusiasts improve their skills, and offers a range of courses for kids and adults of all abilities, as well as public sessions for experienced climbers. It also boasts the highest climbing wall in Dubai. Lessons cost Dhs.55 per hour, need to be booked in advance, and are limited to six people per instructor. The wall consists of varied climbing routes, and crash mats are present for bouldering.

Cookery Classes

Many hotel restaurants hold occasional cookery demonstrations or classes, so look out for events advertised in the media. The Shangri-La (04 343 8888, p.45) can organise classes for groups of 10 or more people, speak to someone in the F&B department for more info. The Blue Elephant (04 282 0000, p.596) in Al Bustan Rotana holds Thai cooking classes the first Monday of every month, and Sushi Sushi (04 282 9908, p.579) has been known to provide classes as well. Gordon Ramsay's Verre at the Hilton Dubai Creek (04 227 1111, p.41) also stages occasional demonstrations and master classes.

Dubai Media City
Al Sufouh
Map 5 C2

Cooking Sense
04 882 1295 | www.cooking-sense.com

In addition to being a cookery school for all age groups, this is also a place to learn healthy cooking to lead a healthy life. The school offers classes in cooking, baking, cooking with and for children, cooking as a corporate event, table decoration, business etiquette over a meal and special diets for certain conditions (diabetes, obesity and heart diseases) . The school also organises classes in cooperation with consulting specialists like well known chefs, physicians, beauticians and etiquette consultants. They have separate classes for adults, kids, teens, mothers, beginners and the advanced.

Tavola

Century Plaza
Jumeira
Map 7 E1

04 351 8310 | tavola@tavola.ae

If cake decorating is your thing, at Tavola an authorised Wilton method instructor will convert you to a much-envied pro. Located at Century Plaza on Jumeria Beach Road, they hold classes on Sundays and Wednesdays from 09:30 to 12:30. A whole course consists of four sessions and costs Dhs.700.

Crab Hunting

Flamingo Beach Resort Hotel

Umm Al Quwain
Map 1 E1

06 765 0000 | www.www.flamingoresort.ae

This might be the perfect setting for an inexpensive family daytrip. Only an hour drive from Dubai, the guides at Flamingo Beach Resort will take you and your family out on a rickety old boat at sunset and teach you how to spear crabs. The hunt is easy and exciting and the hotel will cook your catch for you when it's all over.

Lama Desert Tours

Al Sayegh Bld
Oud Metha Rd
Oud Metha
Map 10 E2

04 334 4330 | www.lama.ae

This unusual tour takes you to Umm Al Quwain where you head out to sea to hunt crabs, and then enjoy a dinner consisting of your own catch of the day. The cost is Dhs.280 per person (minimum six people) and includes return transfers, soft drinks, snacks and the traditional (if you can call crabs traditional) dinner.

Cricket

With such a mixture of nationalities and cultures in Dubai, cricket is a passion shared across many communities. Many organisations have their own cricket teams for inter-company competitions and the sport is becoming more popular in schools. There are also several small-scale training centres such as the Emirates Cricket Training Centre (050 497 3461). International matches are regularly hosted in the Emirates, especially at the grounds in Sharjah where it's possible to see some of the world's best teams in action.

Chevrolet Insportz Club

Cnr Street 17
Beh Garden Centre
Al Quoz
Map 6 B3

04 347 5833 | www.insportzclub.com

This indoor sports centre located behind Dubai Garden Centre near Interchange Four is a handy little club with cheap prices and good equipment and facilities. There are three main net courts with a scoreboard, and one side court, available for playing a social game, as part of a league, or just for practice. There's also a small outlet for refreshments. Contact the centre for booking inquiries and prices.

Last Man Stands

Zabeel Park
Zabeel
Map 10 B1

056 605 2905 | www.lastmanstands.com

This international cricket T20 club has established itself in Dubai. The first league started in the autumn of 2008 and there will be a new season twice a year, every year. The current league has eight teams of highly competitive players, and there are plans for a second, more recreational league. Registration fees vary depending on sponsorship.

Cycling

Other options **Sports Goods** p.468, **Mountain Biking** p.374, **Bicycle** p.56

Dubai is not a very bicycle-friendly city but there are plenty of areas where you can ride, and it can be a great way to explore as well as keep fit. The pedestrian areas on

Mountain biking

both sides of the creek are pleasant places for a spin, especially in the evening, and riding through the souks can also be an experience. Clubs and groups of cyclists generally ride at the weekends, and early mornings and evenings when roads are quieter and the temperatures are cooler. If you have no choice but to ride in busy areas, exercise a lot of care and attention. Although helmets are not legally required, it is recommended that you wear one considering how crazy Dubai traffic can be. Outside the city limits the roads are flat until you near the mountains. Jebel Hafeet near Al Ain, the Hatta area of the Hajar Mountains, and the central area in the mountains near Masafi down to the coast at either Fujairah or Dibba, offer interesting paved roads with better views. The new road from Hatta through the mountains to Kalba on the east coast is probably one of the most scenic routes in the country.

Various Locations ◄

Dubai Roadsters

04 339 4453 | www.wbs.ae

To join Dubai Roadsters you need nothing more than a safe bike, cycling helmet, pump and spare tubes. The average distance covered on a Friday ride is 65 to 100 km, while weekday rides are about 30 to 50km. There are no membership fees. Email wolfi@wbs.ae to be added to the club's mailing list.

Dance Classes

Other options **Music Lessons** p.375, **Salsa Dancing** p.381, **Belly Dancing** p.332

Whether it's the polka, salsa or bharatnatyam, all dancing tastes are catered for in Dubai. In addition to established dancing institutions, many health clubs, restaurants and bars hold weekly sessions in flamenco, salsa, samba, jazz dance, ballroom and more. Some health clubs also offer dance-based aerobic classes (see p.329).

Al Ghurair City ◄
Deira
Map 9 D4

Al Naadi Club

04 205 5229 | wilson@alghurairgroup.com

Ballet lessons leading to Royal Academy of Dancing examinations are taught by Sally Bigland, who also teaches Latin American dance to adults. Karate classes for boys and girls aged 6 and older, and swimming lessons for children and adults are also on offer. Tennis and squash is available seven days a week.

Beh Jumeira Plaza ◄
Jumeira
Map 7 F1

The Ballet Centre

04 344 9776 | www.balletcentre.com

The Ballet Centre offers Royal Academy Ballet and Imperial Society of Teachers Tap classes. The centre also has classes for modern, Spanish, Irish and jazz dancing, and not forgetting belly dancing too. For aerobics fans, there are various sessions for all levels of fitness.

Various Locations ◄

Ceroc Dubai

04 367 2217 | www.cerocarabia.com

Ceroc modern jive is a stylish partner dance similar to salsa but with no tricky footwork. This makes it very easy to learn, and unlike other partner dances it can be danced to many different musical styles such as club and chart hits, old classics, swing, Latin & rock n roll. Regular classes, workshops, social dance nights and private tuition are available. Partners are rotated regularly so there's no need to bring one, and no special footwear or clothing is required. Prices are Dhs.45 per person for the evening.

Dance Dubai

Dubai Knowledge Village
Al Sufouh
Map 5 D2

050 157 3061 | *www.dancedubai.com*
A large part Russia's rich heritage is dancing and is brought to Dubai at St Petersburg State University in Knowledge Village. It offers classes, lectures, private lessons and workshops given by Russian professional dancers, in disciplines ranging from ballroom to Latin for both children and adults. For more details you can contact Mr Anton on 050 157 3061.

Dance Horizons

Various Locations

04 360 7691 | *dancehorizons@gmail.com*
This specialist ballet school offers the Royal Academy of Dance Examination syllabus for beginners and advanced dancers. There is a Specialized Music and Movement programme for children aged 4 years and older. Classes are held at Horizon School and Safa School in Jumeira (near Safa Park) in fully equipped ballet studios with sprung floor, barres and mirrors, and are led by highly qualified, RAD registered, teaching staff.

Disco Dance Dubai

Various Locations

055 820 2642 | *discodancedubai@hotmail.com*
This fun programme teaches future pop divas dance routines and moves from the likes of Britney and *High School Musical*. The RAD and IDTA trained director, Becky Kerrigan, offers two seperate classes for girls aged 4 to 7 and 8 to 11. Each class starts with an aerobic warm-up and stretching exercises – great for instilling fitness into your child's future.

Dubai Liners

Various Locations

050 654 5960 | *difromdubai@yahoo.com*
Although traditional line dancing involves a strong country and western music theme, Dubai Liners teaches a more modern version, using a wide variety of music including disco, rock 'n' roll, salsa, jazz, R&B, waltz and ballads. Classes are held on Saturdays, with classes for beginners from 09:30 to 11:30 and for intermediate students from 11:00 to 13:00. People of all ages and fitness levels are welcome. Contact Diana for more details.

Swing Dancing

Various Locations

050 428 3061 | *www.lindyswing.com*
Swing, or to give it its correct name, Lindy Hop, was invented by New York's African American community in the 1930s. It is an energetic partner dance involving intricate footwork and jazz steps from dances like the Charleston. With music from jazz greats like Count Basie and Duke Ellington to dance to, swing has enjoyed a huge resurgence over the last decade. Call Des on 050 428 3061 for details of classes and events.

Turning Pointe Dance Studios ▶ p.341

Various Locations

04 338 8413 | *www.turningpointe.ae*
This dance centre has over 19 studios throughout Dubai, catering to people living in Emirates Hills, Arabian Ranches, Jumeira, Bur Dubai, Mirdif and many more areas. It specialises in classes for children from the age of 3 up to 19. The centre is affiliated to the Royal Academy of Dance (RAD) in London, teaching its ballet syllabus and offering its Graded Examinations, alongside the Imperial Society of Teachers of Dance (ISTD) syllabus with examinations in modern, jazz, tap and disco/freestyle.

Desert Driving Courses

Other options **Off-Road Driving** p.376

For those who want to master the art of driving a 4WD in the desert without getting stuck (and learn how to get yourself out when you do), several organisations offer desert driving courses with instruction from professional drivers. Vehicles are provided on some courses, while others require participants to bring their own (this is usually cheaper). Picnic lunches and soft drinks are often included as part of the package.

Getting unstuck

Opp Municipality
Garage
Al Rashidiya
Map 13 E2

Al Futtaim Training Centre

04 285 0455 | www.traininguae.com

The Desert Campus Training Course gives off-road driving enthusiasts the knowledge and experience to venture safely into the desert. It starts with a three hour classroom session covering the basics of your vehicle and is followed by five hours of supervised off-road driving where you take your own 4WD up and down the dunes.

Pearl Coast Hotel
Beh MOE
Al Barsha
Map 6 A3

Desert Rangers

04 422 0044 | www.desertrangers.com

Desert Rangers offers lessons for anyone wanting to learn how to handle a car in the desert. If you are just starting out you'll be taught the basics of venturing off-road. There are also advanced classes that tackle challenging dune scenarios.

Al Qusais
Map 14 B1

Emirates Driving Institute

04 263 1100 | www.edi-uae.com

The Emirates Driving Institute offers a one day desert driving course for Dhs.500 (Saturday to Thursday), or Dhs.550 on Fridays. A vehicle can be hired for Dhs.1,000 (Saturday to Thursday) or Dhs.1,100 on Fridays. The institute also offers a one day defensive driving course for Dhs.500, or Dhs.600 on Fridays. Participants receive certificates on completion of all courses. Call to find your nearest branch.

Shangri-La Hotel
Trade Centre 1
Map 7 E3

Off-Road Adventures

050 628 9667 | www.arabiantours.com

Off-Road Adventures provides exciting safari tours with a focus on safety, exclusivity and personnel expertise. In addition to off-road driving courses, the company also arranges fun drives, treasure hunts, camping tours, camel safaris and sand boarding.

Jebel Ali Shooting
Club
Jebel Ali
Map 3 A2

OffRoad-Zone ▶ p.343

04 339 2449 | www.offroad-zone.com

OffRoad-Zone's driver training course has simulated obstacles that let drivers learn the rules of the road in a controlled environment. From deep water crossings and loose rocks to sandy descents and logs, the course has every kind of terrain covered. All of the instructors have years of experience and are patient enough for the slowest of learners. You can bring your own 4WD or rent one from OffRoad-Zone for the day.

OffRoad-Drive
by OffRoad-Zone.com

Circular Ramp

Water & Rocks

Exciting 10 Challenges

Vertical Logs

Vertical Hills

Extreme driving

Soft Sand

Large Logs

The Most Unique and Fun Driving Experience...

- Improve Your 4x4 Driving Skills
- Ideal For Team & Corporate Events
- Shooting, Archery & Catering Packages
- Minutes From Jebel Ali Golf Resorts & Spa

Drive our 4x4s in a Safe and Secure Environment, At Jebel Ali International Shooting Club
20 minutes from Dubai

Rent I Lease I Buy I Service I Modify I OffRoad Drive NEW

04 339 2449 | 055 RENT 4X4 (055 7368 494)

www.OffRoad-Zone.com

Diving

Other options **Snorkelling** p.388

The UAE's coastal waters are home to a variety of marine species, coral life and even shipwrecks. You'll see some exotic fish, like clownfish and seahorses, and possibly even spotted eagle rays, moray eels, small sharks, barracuda, sea snakes and stingrays. Most of the wrecks are on the west coast, while the beautiful flora and fauna of coral reefs can be seen on the east coast.

There are many dive sites on the west coast that are easily accessible from Dubai. Cement Barge, Mariam Express and the MV Dara wrecks are some of the more popular dive sites. Off the east coast, a well-known dive site is Martini Rock, a small, underwater mountain covered with colourful soft coral, with a depth range of three to 19 metres. North of Khor Fakkan is the Car Cemetery, a reef that has thrived around a number of cars placed 16 metres below water. Visibility off both coasts ranges from five to 20 metres.

Another option for diving enthusiasts is to take a trip to Musandam. This area, which is part of the Sultanate of Oman, is often described as the 'Norway of the Middle East' due to the many inlets and the way the sheer cliffs plunge directly into the sea. It offers some spectacular dive sites. Sheer wall dives with strong currents and clear waters are more suitable for advanced divers, while the huge bays, with their calm waters and shallow reefs, are ideal for the less experienced. Visibility here is between 10 and 35 metres. If you plan to travel to Khasab, the capital of the Musandam, you may not be able to take your own air tanks across the border and will have to rent from one of the dive centres there. You may also require an Omani visa. Alternatively, from Dibba on the UAE east coast, you can hire a fast dive boat to take you anywhere from five to 75 kilometres up the coast. The cost ranges between Dhs.150 and Dhs.500, for what is usually a two-dive trip.

There are plenty of dive companies in the UAE where you can improve your diving skills. Courses are offered under the usual international training organisations.

Nr Khor Fakkan Souk
East Coast
Khor Fakkan
Map 1 F1

7 Seas Divers

09 238 7400 | *www.7seasdivers.com*

This PADI dive centre offers day and night diving trips to a variety of sites around Khor Fakkan, Musandam and Lima Rock. Training is provided from beginner to instructor level, in a variety of languages including Arabic, English, German, Dutch, Italian and Russian. The centre provides diving equipment for you to buy or rent.

Al Wasl Rd
Nr Iranian Hospital
Jumeira
Map 7 F1

Al Boom Diving

04 342 2993 | *www.alboomdiving.com*

Al Boom's Aqua Centre on Al Wasl Road is a purpose-built school with a fully outfitted diving shop. There's a variety of diving courses on offer. PADI courses are available for beginners, certified divers, juniors, speciality, rescue and pros. Prices start from Dhs.100 for the Try Dives beginner courses and go up to Dhs.6,000 for pro courses.

Street 40a
Al Quoz
Map 7 A4

The Desert Sports Diving Club

www.desertsportsdivingclub.com

This is Dubai's only independent diving group. Made up of diving enthusiasts, members meet once a week at the clubhouse near Sheikh Zayed Road to plan weekly dives. The group has two boats docked in Dubai and one at the east coast. The types of dives that the members do range from fun training dives to extreme deep water technical dives.

The ultimate boating guide

Dubai Yachting & Boating

Guaranteed to float your boat

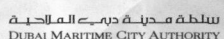

DUBAI MARITIME CITY AUTHORITY

Divers Down

Oceanic Hotel
Khor Fakkan
Map 1 F1

09 237 0299 | *www.diversdown.ae*

Divers Down is a PADI Five Star Gold Palm Resort that offers courses from beginner to instructor level, and organises pleasure dives three times a day in the tropical waters of the Gulf of Oman. The centre is open seven days a week, and transport is available. Check the website for rates and diving information.

Emirates Diving Association

Heritage Village &
Diving Village
Al Shindagha
Map 9 A1

04 393 9390 | *www.emiratesdiving.com*

Based at the Heritage & Diving Village by Dubai Creek, the aim of this non-profit organisation is to conserve, protect and restore the UAE's marine resources by promoting the importance of the environment. The association looks after the well-being of UAE corals as part of its coral monitoring project, and organises annual Clean-Up Arabia campaigns. A quarterly newsletter, Divers for the Environment, details their current activities and the website has lots of useful info. Divers are encouraged to join, with membership costing just Dhs.100 per year.

Nomad Ocean Adventures

Nr the Harbour
Al Biah
Dibba
Map 1 F1

050 885 3238 | *www.discovernomad.com*

Nomad offers a range of trips and excursions. For qualified divers a single dive with all equipment included starts from Dhs.320, while beginners can try the Discover Scuba Diving programme for Dhs.400. The company can also organise all manner of tailor-made trips that, in addition to offering diving (both scuba and snorkelling), can incorporate dhow trips and overnight stays at traditional Arabian camps. For details speak to Christophe on the number listed, or try the Oman office: +968 99 834 256

The Pavilion Dive Centre

Jumeirah
Beach Hotel
Umm Suqeim
Map 6 B1

04 406 8827 | *www.thepaviliondivecentre.com*

This PADI Gold Palm IDC Centre is run by PADI Course Directors and offers an extensive range of courses from beginner to instructor. Daily dive charters for certified divers are available in Dubai, and dive charters to Musandam can be organised upon request. A day trip in Musandam inclusive of full equipment, two dives, dhow, light breakfast and lunch is priced at Dhs.740 or Dhs.640 without equipment. Courses offered include Discover Scuba Diving (Dhs.300), Open Water (Dhs.2,350), Adventures in Diving (Dhs.1,850), Instructor Development IDC (Dhs.3,000) and several others.

Sandy Beach Diving Centre

Sandy Beach
Hotel & Resort
Fujairah
Map 1 F2

09 244 5555 | *www.sandybm.com*

This dive centre is managed by Sandy Beach Hotel and offers a qualified team of instructors and support staff. It is open all year round for diving and accommodation, and the retail store stocks diving gear. The famous Snoopy Island, alive with hard corals and marine life, is an excellent spot for snorkelling and scuba diving.

East Coast marine life

Scuba 2000

Al Badiyah Beach
Dibba
Map 1 F1

09 238 8477 | *www.scuba-2000.com*

This east coast dive centre is open all year round and provides daily trips to dive sites at Dibba and Khor Fakkan. Standard courses are available for beginners and advanced divers. Costs range from

Sports & Activities

Dhs.500 for Discover Scuba to Dhs.2,350 for the Open Water diving course. Teaching materials are available in a variety of languages.

Al Khail Rd
Al Barsha
Map 2 B3

Scuba Dubai

04 341 4940 | www.scubadubai.com

For those wishing to arrange their own diving and snorkelling trips, equipment can be rented from Scuba Dubai on a 24 hour basis. Weekend rates are the same as renting for one day because the shop is closed on Fridays. Note that original diving certification must be shown for all scuba equipment rentals. Scuba Dubai is open from 09:00 to 20:30 Saturday to Wednesday, 09:00 to 19:00 on Thursday and is closed Fridays.

Sana Building
Al Karama
Map 8 E4

Scubatec

04 334 8988 | scubatec@eim.ae

Scubatec is a Five Star IDC licenced by PADI and TDI. Lessons are provided in Arabic, English, German or Urdu, and the company offers a full range of courses from beginner to instructor level. A variety of dive trips is available in Dubai and on the east coast.

Sharjah Wanderers
Sports Club
Sharjah
Map 2 C2

Sharjah Wanderers Dive Club

06 566 2105 | www.sharjahwanderers.com

Sharjah Wanderers Dive Club is part of Sharjah Wanderers Sports Club, which means that members automatically get to benefit from other sporting and social activities. The club is a member of the British Sub Aqua Club and follows its training, certification and diving practices. Clubhouse facilities include a training room, social area, equipment room, compressors, dive gear and two dive boats.

Dragon Boat Racing

Le Meridien Mina
Seyahi
Al Sufouh
Map 5 C1

Dubai Flying Dragons

www.dubaidragons.com

Fancy getting out of bed before the sun rises for a bit of on-water action, Chinese style? If so, Dubai Flying Dragons has your name all over it. Training sessions in the ancient eastern sport of dragon boat racing are held several mornings a week, or if you can't face the early start, on a Saturday evening. It's a good way to be sociable (through regular get togethers) as well as to get yourself extremely fit. For serious paddlers there is also the opportunity to participate in international dragon boat competitions.

Mina Seyahi Dubai
Al Sufouh
Map 5 B1

Dubai Sea Dragons

055 584 0588 | www.dubaiseadragons.com

Dragon boating is a group activity that gives adrenaline junkies a much sought after boost. The independent club holds training at the Mina Seyahi Dubai (formally DIMC) Marina from 08:30 on Monday and Wednesday, 17:00 on Monday and Wednesday evenings and at 07:30 on Saturdays. A junior crew for Grade 8 to Grade 11 high school students is now available on Saturdays at 07:30 and Wednesday evenings at 17:00.

Drama Groups

DUCTAC
Mall of the Emirates
Al Barsha
Map 6 A3

Drama Workshops Dubai

050 986 1761 | www.dramaworkshopsdubai.com

With classes for both children and adults, acting teacher and director Kemsley Dickinson organises several workshops that focus on the different aspects of acting. Classes are held at DUCTAC and private tuitions for individuals and groups are available, as are corporate packages.

Dubai Drama Group

DUCTAC
Mall of the Emirates
Al Barsha
Map 6 A3

050 509 4211 | *www.dubaidramagroup.com*
Being a community theatre for over 20 years, the DDG has recently enjoyed a renaissance. Members range from actors, singers and dancers, to behind the scenes personnel like directors, costumiers, writers and scene shifters. Four productions are staged each year, and there are workshops, monthly social events, and an internet forum. Annual membership is Dhs.100.

DUCTAC

Scenez Group

Dubai Media City
Al Sufouh
Map 5 C2

04 391 5290 | *www.scenezgroup.com*
Dubai's arts scene is promising, and new ways to get involved occasionally spring up. Scenez Group offers budding talent the opportunity to get involved in theatre and production through its workshops and events. Young actors between 6 and 16 can experience the world behind the scenes and onstage with courses featuring scriptwriting, costume design, acting and mime. Previous performances have included *The Wizard of Oz* at The Dubai Community Theatre & Arts Centre (DUCTAC). There are even workshops in juggling and clownery.

Dune Buggy Driving

Other options **Quad Bikes** p.378, **Karting** p.364

Bouncing over the dunes in a buggy is exhilarating, addictive, and definitely one of the best ways to experience the desert. Desert Rangers (below) offer dune buggy tours, where you can enjoy all the thrills and spills of this extreme sport in the safest possible way – they provide training, all the safety equipment you'll need, and an experienced leader to guide you through the dunes.

Arabia Horizons Tours

110 Snow White Bld
Omar Al Khattab St
Deira
Map 9 D3

04 234 7477 | *www.arabiahorizons.com*
Utilising golf cart-like, 800cc buggies, these tours follow a nature trail through the desert. The buggies are easier to drive than traditional buggies, and the guide tends to start off slow so you can get a feel for the vehicle. Both morning and night trips are available and pick up and drop off is included. The night trip includes dinner at a Bedouin-style camp.

Desert Rangers

Pearl Coast Hotel
Behind MOE
Al Barsha
Map 6 A3

04 422 0044 | *www.desertrangers.com*
After a brief safety lecture you will be taken on a buggy drive through a series of desert dunes. This is not to be mistaken for quad biking which has clocked up a few unsurprising accidents over the years. Safaris can be combined with a BBQ dinner at a campsite for Dhs.525 per person. A half day dune buggy safari (excluding dinner) costs Dhs.425 per person or Dhs.324 per person if two people share a buggy.

Dream Explorer ▶ p.297

Saeed Tower 1
Sheikh Zayed Rd
Trade Centre 1
Map 7 E3

04 331 980 | *www.dreamexplorerdubai.com*
Dream Explorer provides drivers with custom-designed, twin-seat 1500cc dune buggies and all the necessary safety equipment. Half day tours follow exciting trails through

the desert and include stops for refreshments. The tours can be combined with private barbecues and overnight camps.

Environmental Groups

Other options **Voluntary & Charity Work** p.102

People don't generally chain themselves to palms or dunes in Dubai, but over the last few years environmental issues have gradually become more important in the UAE. However, as is always the case, far more needs to be done by all sections of the community. Leading the way, HH Sheikh Mohammed bin Rashid Al Maktoum, Crown Prince of Dubai, has established a prestigious international environmental award in honour of HH Sheikh Zayed bin Sultan Al Nahyan, late President of the UAE. The award, which was first presented in 1998, goes to an individual or organisation for distinguished work carried out on behalf of the environment.

On an everyday level there are increasing numbers of glass and plastic recycling points around the city. *The Khaleej Times* sponsors bins for collecting newspapers for recycling; these are easily spotted at a variety of locations, but mainly outside shopping centres.

In addition, the government of Dubai is gradually taking action with school educational programmes and general awareness campaigns. However, overall, there seems to be very little done to persuade the average person to be more environmentally active, for instance by encouraging the reduction of littering.

If you want to take action contact one of the environmental groups that operate in the Emirates such as the Emirates Environmental Group or the flagship Arabian Leopard Trust. They always need volunteers and funds.

Emirates Academy
Opp Wild Wadi
Jumeira
Map 6 B2

Dubai Natural History Group

04 349 4816 | www.enhg.org

Dubai Natural History Group was formed to promote interest in flora, fauna, geology, archaeology and the natural environment of the emirates. Meetings are held on the first Sunday of each month and speakers give lectures on a range of natural history topics. Regular trips are organised and the group maintains a library of natural history publications. Annual membership costs Dhs.100 for families and Dhs.50 for individuals.

Villa No JMR 68
Btn Dubai Zoo & Beach
Centre
Jumeira
Map 7 E1

Emirates Environmental Group

04 344 8622 | www.eeg-uae.org/newsupdate.htm

This is a voluntary, non-governmental organisation devoted to protecting the environment through education, action programmes and community involvement. Current members include individuals and corporate members, schools and government organisations. Activities include regular evening lectures on environmental topics and special events such as recycling collections and clean-up campaigns. Annual membership costs Dhs.100 for adults and Dhs.25 for juniors and Dhs.30 for students.

Fencing

Mina A'Salam
Umm Suqeim
Map 6 A1

Dubai Fencing Club

050 794 4190 | www.dubaifencingclub.com

The Dubai Fencing Club is the first club of its kind in the UAE, providing individual and group training sessions in épée and foil for adults and juniors of any level. Training is conducted by experienced fencing coaches. All fencers receive the necessary basic equipment such as masks, gloves and weapons. For advanced fencers, the club offers three fencing paths with electrical scoring systems and electrical weapons. The club meets in the Quay Health Club at Mina A'Salam Hotel.

International Fencing Club Of Dubai

Metropolitan Hotel
Sheikh Zayed Road
Map 7 B3

050 626 7440 | *www.fencingdxb.com*

Located in the Dimension Club of the Metropolitan Hotel on Sheikh Zayed Road, this club of fencing enthusiasts formed in 2003 with the hope of promoting the sport in Dubai. Since then, membership has grown considerably and the club utilises its more experienced members to teach newcomers and beginners. The club has equipment for beginners, three metallic pistes and all electrical signalisation.

Fishing

Other options **Boat Tours & Charters** p.284, **Crab Hunting** p.338

Fishing has become popular in the region recently, and the government has introduced regulations to protect fish stocks off the coast. However, you can still fish, as long as you have the right permit or you charter a licensed tour guide. The most productive fishing season lasts from September to April, although it is still possible to catch sailfish and queenfish in the summer. Fish commonly caught in the region include king mackerel, tuna, trevally, bonito, kingfish, cobia and dorado. Beach or surf fishing is popular along the coast, and in season you can even catch barracuda from the shore. Any beach along the Dubai coastline will work, and you should try from the end of the promenade on the Jumeira Beach Corniche. The creek front in Creekside Park is also popular, although you may want to think twice eating your catch. Alternatively, on a Friday, you could hire an abra for the morning (either at the Bur Dubai or Deira landing steps) and ask your driver to take you out to the mouth of the creek. Always agree on a price before you leave. You could also consider a deep-sea fishing trip with one of the charter companies listed. For more competitive anglers, the UAQ Marine Club (www.uaqmarineclub.com) sponsors a fishing competition twice a year in April and October. The event caters to families and there is plenty to occupy the children while the adults are out finding the biggest catch. Call 06 766 6644 for more details.

> **Licence To Krill**
>
> Unless you set off with a registered fishing charter, you'll need to obtain a fishing licence from the Dubai government. There are different permits for leisure boats and offshore fishing, but both are free and can be had through the government portal, www. dm.gov.ae. For details on how to get your hands on the yearly permit, call 04 206 4260.

Bounty Charters

Mina Seyahi Dubai
Al Sufouh
Map 5 B1

050 552 6067 | *bountycharters@hotmail.com*

Bounty Charters has a fully equipped 36 foot Yamaha Sea Spirit game fishing boat captained by Richard Forrester, an experienced game fisherman from South Africa. The company offers full day sailfish sessions, half day bottom fishing or night fishing charters as well three to five-day trips to the Musandam Peninsula.

Club Joumana

Jebel Golf Resort
& Spa
Jebel Ali
Map 3 A1

04 804 8058 | *www.jebelali-international.com*

Four and eight-hour fishing trips are available for up to seven people per boat. The captain, tackle, equipment, soft drinks, water, pastries and croissants are included as part of the package as you try to catch barracuda, lemonfish, trevally, hammour and kingfish. Call for prices.

Dubai Creek Golf & Yacht Club

Baniyas Rd
Opp Deira City Centre
Deira
Map 11 C3

04 295 6000 | www.dubaigolf.com

Take a trip on the club's Sneakaway Yacht into the Arabian Gulf and experience big game sports fishing. The fully equipped 32ft Hatteras carries up to six passengers and rates include tackle, bait, ice, fuel and a friendly crew. Trips cost Dhs.3,500 for four hours, Dhs.4,000 for six hours and Dhs.4,500 for eight hours.

Dubai Voyager

Fishermen Port 2
Umm Suqeim
Map 6 B1

04 348 1900 | www.dubaivoyager.com

Based at the Fishing Village in Umm Suqeim, this company operates a fleet of reliable and fully equipped fishing boats, captained by qualified and experienced South African crew. Full safety gear is installed. Soft drinks, water, ice, bait and all fishing gear are supplied. Rates are Dhs.2,300 for four hours (morning or afternoon), Dhs.2,800 for six hours (morning or afternoon) or Dhs.3,300 for eight hours (full day).

Le Meridien Mina Seyahi Beach Resort & Marina

Al Sufouh Rd
Al Sufouh
Map 5 C1

04 399 3333 | www.lemeridien-minaseyahi.com

Fishing trips take place on the custom-built Ocean Explorer and Ocean Luhr. Sailfish are the main prize, and Le Meridien Mina Seyahi supports the tag and release scheme. While you are welcome to bring your own gear, the boats are fully equipped with 20, 30 and 50lb class tackle.

Oceanic Hotel

Beach Rd
Khor Fakkan
Map 1 F1

09 238 5111 | www.oceanichotel.com

Fishing trips from the hotel head to a favourite local spot where catches are guaranteed. For hotel guests, the catch of the day can then be cooked according to your taste by the hotel chef (a nominal cleaning fee is charged). Non-guests can take their catch home with them. The cost for a boat with a maximum of five people is Dhs.600 and trips leave from 14:00 onwards.

Flower Arranging

Other options **Flowers** p.442, **Gardens** p.446

Ikebana Sogetsu Group

Opp Syrian
Consulate
Al Waheda
Deira
Map 9 A4

04 262 0282 | fujikozarouni@hotmail.com

Ikebana is the art of Japanese flower arranging. Dubai's Ikebana Sogetsu Group was formed by Sogetsu members in 2000, and attempts to deepen cultural understanding among the city's multinational society through exhibitions, demonstrations and workshops. Classes are taught by Fujiko Zarouni, a qualified teacher from Japan.

Flying

Other options **Hot Air Ballooning** p.291, **Plane Tours** p.292

Dubai Flying Association

UAQ Airport
Umm Al Quwain
Map 1 E1

04 351 9691 | www.fly-dxb.com

The Dubai Flying Association (DFA) is a registered, non-profit group that aims to provide flying time to members at cost price. Membership costs Dhs.500 per annum and the association welcomes UAE Private Pilot Licence holders to join. The DFA has also taken up operations at Umm Al Quwain Airfield, but please note that the DFA is not a flying school and does not offer sightseeing or pleasure flights.

Emirates Flying School

Dubai International Airport
Terminal 2
Al Garhoud
Map 14 A1

04 299 5155 | *www.emiratesaviationservices.com*

This flying school is the only approved flight training institution in Dubai. With six Piper aircraft, the school offers private and commercial pilot's licences, and will convert international licences to UAE licences. The average cost for a Private Pilot Licence course is Dhs.38,000. Gift vouchers (Dhs.900) are available for those interested in experiencing flying for the first time.

Fujairah Aviation Academy

Fujairah Intl Airport
Fujairah
Map 1 F2

09 222 4747 | *www.fujaa.ae*

Fujairah Aviation Centre is accredited with Civil Aviation Authorities in the UAE and UK. Facilities include single and twin-engine training aircraft, an instrument flight simulator and a workshop for repairs. Training is offered for Private and Commercial Pilot Licences, instrument rating and multi-engine rating. The centre also offers pleasure flights and sightseeing tours, and has aircraft available for hire to licence holders.

Jazirah Aviation

Dubai-Ras Al Khaimah Highway
Ras Al Khaimah
Map 1 F1

07 244 6416 | *www.jac-uae.net*

Approved by the General Civil Aviation Authority, Jazirah Aviation club is dedicated solely to microlight/ultralight flying. They offer flight training courses as well as pleasure flights lasting from 10 minutes to an hour. A complete Microlight Pilot's Licence course, with around 25 hours flying time, costs Dhs.15,000.

Micro Aviation Club

UAQ Airport
Umm Al Quwain
Map 1 E1

055 843 5254 | *www.microaviation.ae*

Micro Aviation Club offers training courses in microlight flying, paragliding and paramotoring. Their office is located at Dubai Men's College, within Dubai Academic City. Courses start from Dhs.3,500, with an annual registration fee of Dhs.250.

Umm Al Quwain Aeroclub

17km North of UAQ On RAK Rd
Umm Al Quwain
Map 1 E1

06 768 1447 | *www.uaqaeroclub.com*

The club offers flying, skydiving, skydive boogies, paramotors and helicopter training. The facilities include a variety of small aircraft, two runways, eight hangars with engineering services, a pilot's shop and a briefing room. Sightseeing tours are available in Cessna aircraft, with prices starting from Dhs.350 for 30 minutes.

Football

Like most places around the world, football (or soccer) is a much-loved sport here in the UAE, and evenings and weekends will often witness impromptu games in parks, open areas, and even on the beach. If you fancy a kick-around, InSportz in Al Quoz has indoor five-a-side pitches, and some university campuses are willing to rent out their outdoor and five-a-side pitches. More details below, or see Sports Clubs on p.400. Gaelic Football fans should contact Dubai Celts GAA – their details can be found in Gaelic Games on p.354.

Dubai Amateur Football League

Various Locations

www.dxb.leaguerepublic.com

The Dubai Amateur Football League, also known as the 'Expat League', hosts 23 teams in two divisions. Teams take part in relatively competitive 11-a-side league and cup games between September and April at various locations, and seven-a-side games during the summer. If you're keen to pull on those boots once more, check out the different teams via the website.

Sports & Activities

Various Locations

Dubai Football Academy
04 282 4540 | www.esportsdubai.com

The Dubai Football Academy provides comprehensive training to youngsters in a fun and enjoyable environment, with training sessions held at various locations including the Dubai Country Club and Jumeirah Primary School. Players are encouraged to join one of the teams competing in the Dubai Junior Football League. The course duration for one term is 20 weeks and costs Dhs.1,350 (one lesson per week) or Dhs.2,500 (two lessons per week). Full details of prices, schedules and venues can be found on the website, or alternatively contact academy director Terry Kidd on 050 286 1041.

Duplays
Duplays (www.duplays.com) is quickly becoming the largest sports organisers in the city. It regularly hosts five-a-side indoor and seven-a-side outdoor leagues that sometimes have more than 150 teams. Sign up on the website to receive notifications via email.

Various Locations

Dubai Irish
050 465 1087 | hayes_conor@yahoo.ie

Dubai Irish consists of players of all nationalities and participates in the Dubai Amateur Football League. Despite competing in the more competitive division one, the team welcomes players of all skill levels to come out and train with them. The location and time of the training sessions varies from week to week during the season depending on that week's game schedule.

**Jebel Ali
Shooting Club**
Jebel Ali
Map 3 A2

Dubai Women's Football Association
050 702 7841 | www.dubaiwfa.com

Women's football is a popular sport in Dubai, with DWFA hosting 16 teams across two leagues. Catering to women of all abilities, the first division is suited to more experienced players, while the second division is ideal for those yet to master their skills. Players must commit to two nights a week for training and matches throughout the season. There are two seasons a year running September to December and January to May. There is also a one day tournament held each year. If you're interested, but unsure of your ability, head to one of the weekly training sessions where you can be assessed and assigned a team. Players must be 16 or over to participate.

Various Locations

International Football Academy
04 337 1698 | www.intlfootballacademy.com

The International Football Academy offers high standards of football training by experienced FA-qualified coaches. Boys and girls of all ages are welcomed, with the academy providing tailored coaching programmes to schools and local communities as well as existing teams. Children not already affiliated with a team can also join programmes at one of the many venues listed on the website. The aim is to increase footballing skills, confidence and team building.

Various Locations

UAE English Soccer School Of Excellence
050 476 4877 | www.soccerkidsdubai.com

The ESSE now operates at eight locations in Dubai, including Safa Park, Jumeirah Primary School, Trade Centre Apartments and the Lakes Club at Emirates Hills. They have over 575 students enrolled, and the fees for each training session range from Dhs.35 to Dhs.45, depending on the age of the child and how many sessions you sign up for. Kids from 4 to 17 are welcome, and training takes place at various times throughout the week except Fridays. Speak to James on the above number for more info. The ESSE schedule coincides with the school terms and camps are organised during the holidays.

Gaelic Games

Safa Park
Al Wasl
Map 7 B2

Dubai Celts GAA
www.dubaicelts.com
Dubai Celts GAA holds games and organises training in men's and ladies' Gaelic football, hurling and camogie. In addition to monthly matches within the UAE, international tournaments are held in Bahrain (November) and Dubai (March) each year. Training sessions are held every Saturday at 16:00.

Gardening
Other options **Gardens** p.446

Sheikh Rashid Rd
Villa 52
Street 6C
Jumeira
Map 7 B2

Dubai Gardening Group
04 344 5999 | bomi@eim.ae
The Dubai Gardening Group was established in 2000 and aims to share its love and knowledge of gardening in a friendly and informal atmosphere. During the cooler months, trips to greenhouses, nurseries and members' gardens are arranged. Speakers, who are experts in various fields, address the meetings and, where possible, give practical demonstrations.

Golf
Dubai is fast becoming one of the world's premier golfing destinations, with excellent weather and top class facilities. The number of international standard courses grows every year, with recent additions including Al Badia within Festival City, the Els Club and the Arabian Ranches Golf Club (see below).

Emirates Golf Club hosts the annual Dubai Desert Classic tournament, which is part of the European PGA Tour and attracts such big names as Tiger Woods, Ernie Els, Ian Woosnam and Colin Montgomerie. There are also several local monthly tournaments and annual competitions open to all, such as the Emirates Mixed Amateur Open, the Emirates Ladies' Amateur Open (handicap of 21 or less), and the Emirates Men's Amateur Open (handicap of five or less).

Dubai Golf operates a central reservation system for those wishing to book a round of golf on any of the major courses in the emirate. For further information visit www.dubaigolf.com or email booking@dubaigolf.com.

The future looks good for Dubai's golfers too: Nakheel is working with Greg Norman to develop six new courses based within residential communities, and Golf World at Dubailand promises four 18 hole courses plus an academy and driving ranges.

Coast Road (E11)
Ras al Khaimah
Map 1 E1

Al Hamra Golf Club ▶ p.357
07 244 7474 | www.alhamragolf.com
Although it's a bit of a drive, this links style course is quickly gaining popularity as a nice break from the city's courses. The main attraction, a 7,267 yard, par 72 course designed by Peter Harradine, surrounds a huge lagoon and features several interconnected lakes. Prices are much more reasonable than courses in Dubai and the quality of play is just as high. The club also houses a golf academy, driving range and par-three course. Both the first nine holes of the championship course and the par three course are floodlit.

Arabian Ranches
Map 2 B3

Arabian Ranches Golf Club
04 366 3000 | www.arabianranchesgolfdubai.com
Designed by Ian Baker-Finch in association with Nicklaus Design, this par 72 grass course uses the natural desert terrain and features indigenous shrubs and bushes. Facilities include a golf academy with floodlit driving range, an extensive short game practice area,

EXPERIENCE TROON GOLF®

and GPS on all golf carts. Within the clubhouse is the Ranches Restaurant & Bar (p.565) as well as 11 luxury guest rooms overlooking either the golf course or the lake. Bookings can be made via the website and reservations are open 24 hours, seven days a week.

Golf in Dubai

Dubai Creek Golf & Yacht Club

Baniyas Rd
Opp Deira City Centre
Deira
Map 11 C3

04 295 6000 | *www.dubaigolf.com*

Dubai Creek Golf & Yacht Club has recently undergone a major redevelopment, with a challenging new front nine redesigned by Thomas Björn. The par 71 championship course is open to all players holding a valid handicap certificate, and those who are new to the game are encouraged to join the golf academy manned by PGA-qualified golf instructors. There is also a new nine-hole par three course, a floodlit driving range and extensive short game practice facilities, and the iconic clubhouse has undergone extensive refurbishment too.

Emirates Golf Club

Interchange 5
Sheikh Zayed Rd
Emirates Hills
Map 5 C2

04 380 2222 | *www.dubaigolf.com*

Emirates Golf Club has two 18 hole championship courses to choose from. The 6,857 yard, par 71 Majlis Course was the first grass course in the Middle East and plays host to the annual Dubai Desert Classic (p.394). The Faldo Course reopened in October 2006 after undergoing a major redesign by Nick Faldo and IMG Design. The club also offers the Peter Cowen Golf Academy, along with two driving ranges, dedicated practice areas and a beautiful clubhouse.

The Els Club Dubai ▶ p.355

Dubai Sports City
Dubailand
Map 2 C3

04 425 1010 | *www.elsclubdubai.com*

Situated in Sports City, this is every golfer's dream come true. The 7,538 yard, par 72 signature course was designed by golf's international ambassador – Ernie Els. Memberships are available, and the first round of memberships sold out within hours. The club includes a Butch Harmon School of Golf for players of all ages and skill levels, and a mediterranean club house, managed by internationally renowned Troon Golf.

Four Seasons Golf Club

Al Rebat St
Festival City
Map 13 D3

04 601 0101 | *www.fourseasons.com/dubaigolf*

This course was designed by world-renowned designer Robert Trent Jones II. Lying at the heart of the Festival City project beside the creek, this golf resort enjoys great views over the Dubai skyline. The 7,250 yard, par 72 championship course has extensive water features including 11 lakes, as well as a very plush clubhouse, and the grass used is salt-tolerant, meaning it can be irrigated with sea water.

Jebel Ali Golf Resort & Spa ▶ p.533

Nr Palm Jebel Ali
Jebel Ali
Map 3 A1

04 804 8058 | *www.jebelali-international.com*

Situated in the landscaped gardens of the Jebel Ali Golf Resort & Spa, this nine-hole, par 36 course offers golfers the opportunity to play alongside peacocks and with views of the Gulf. Renowned for its good condition all year round, the Resort Course is also home to the Jebel Ali Golf Resort & Spa Challenge, the curtain raiser to the annual Dubai Desert Classic (p.394).

A taste of links golf

AL HAMRA GOLF CLUB AND RESORTS

Al Hamra golf club provides you with the first taste of "Links Style" golf in the Middle East, meandering along the shores and rolling waves of the Arabian Gulf, it is a truly unique experience for the region.

www.alhamragolf.com

E-mail: enquiries@alhamragolf.com Tel: +971 7 2447474

The Montgomerie Golf Club
04 390 5600 | www.themontgomerie.com

The Montgomerie is set on 200 acres of land and was designed by Colin Montgomerie and Desmond Muirhead. The 18 hole, par 72 course has some unique characteristics, including the mammoth 656 yard 18th hole. Golfing facilities include a driving range, putting greens and a swing analysis studio, while the newly opened clubhouse boasts guest rooms, a spa, and various bars and restaurants. The club also has a well maintained par three course that is floodlit – perfect for mid-week games after work.

Sharjah Golf & Shooting Club
06 548 7777 | www.golfandshootingshj.com

Offering a range of membership options, Sharjah Golf & Shooting Club is a great option for a spot of out-of-town golf. Members are discounted on aerobics classes, swimming classes and on all personal training packages. Members can also avail discounts at the shooting range, restaurant and hair salon. The club sponsors a Junior Development Programme for youngsters interested in improving their game, and floodlights have been added to the course for night play.

UAE Golf Association
04 368 4988 | www.ugagolf.com

This non-profit organisation is the governing body for amateur golf in the UAE. It is overseen by the General Authority of Youth & Sports and actively supports junior players and the development of the national team. The Affiliate Membership rate is Dhs.200 for a year, and the UGA Handicap Scheme costs Dhs.595. The website has a comprehensive calendar of forthcoming events.

Gymnastics/Trampolining
Other options **Kids' Activities** p.365

Dubai Olympic Gymnastics Club
050 765 1515 | www.uae-gymnastics.com

Dedicated to the advancement of gymnastics as a sport in Dubai, this gym utilises low teacher-student ratios to provide personal training for its members. Geared specifically towards children, courses correspond to school terms and punctuality and commitment are key aspects of the programme. Classes are available for gymnasts of all levels.

DuGym
050 553 6283 | www.dugym.com

DuGym offers gymnastics and trampoline coaching to children of all ages and abilities. Established by Suzanne Wallace in 2000, the club now operates at 15 locations including the GEMS World Academy, Jumeirah English Speaking School and Emirates International School. Classes are held from Sunday to Thursday. Contact Suzanne on the above number for more details.

My Gym
04 394 3962 | www.mygymuae.com

If you are looking for innovative ways to get the kids active, My Gym offers a variety of event. Programmes rang from 'Mommy and Me' for babies aged six weeks and up to gymnastics, dance and general fitness alongside fun-filled private birthday parties and camps; children up to the age of 13 can participate. A two hour per week class and play session will cost Dhs.1,000 for 10 weeks. Parents can also participate in classes with their children if preferred, but independent classes are offered.

Do you have talent?

The region's largest events supplier
is looking for fresh, enthusiastic, new talent!
Successful candidates will be offered
either full time or freelance work.

• *Aerialists* • *Jugglers* • *Balloon Artists*
• *Face Painters* • *Singers* • *Dancers*
• *Instrumentalists* • *Stiltwalkers*
• *Comedians* • *Unicyclists*
• *Fire Eaters* • *Carvers...etc*

Show us what you've got!

To set up an audition time, e-mail
talent@flyingelephantuae.com
or call **+ 971 4 347-9170**

Flying Elephant

The region's largest events supplier of corporate and family entertainment

Call 800-PARTY (72789)
www.flyingelephantuae.com

Hashing

Other options **Running** p.379

Sometimes described as drinking clubs with a running problem, the Hash House Harriers are a worldwide family of social running clubs. The aim of running in this setup is not to win, but to merely be there and to take part. The original club was formed in Kuala Lumpur in 1938 and is now the largest running organisation in the world. Hashing consists of running, jogging or walking around varied courses, often cross-country, laid out by a couple of 'hares'. It's a fun way to keep fit and meet new people, since the clubs are invariably very sociable affairs.

Various Locations

Barbie Hash House

04 348 4210 | *hasher@deserthash.net*

Meeting on the first Wednesday of every month (except in summer), this is a girls only gathering with a Barbie theme, which means pink dress code with a tiara. Each time around 20 to 25 members get together for a social evening that involves hashing, champagne, a meal and singing their Barbie song. Call for details.

Various Locations

Creek Hash House Harriers

050 451 5847 | *www.creekhash.net*

This is a men only hash that meets each Tuesday in a different location. Start times are usually 45 minutes before sunset and runs last 40 to 50 minutes. Further information can be obtained from Ian Browning on the above number or John Harrington (050 645 0587).

Various Locations

Desert Hash House Harriers

050 454 2635 | *www.deserthash.org*

The Desert Hash House Harriers meet every Sunday evening at various locations around Dubai. Runs start an hour before sunset and last about 50 minutes. Fees are Dhs.50 for men and women and include food and beverages.

Various Locations

Moonshine Hash House Harriers

050 879 6576

Moonshine Hash House Harriers run once a month on the night of the full moon. The run/walk creates a thirst, which is then quenched upon return to the alehouse for traditional hash ceremonies. Fees are Dhs.10 per hash. Contact Mo on the above number for details.

Hiking

Other options **Out of Dubai** p.300,
Outdoor Goods p.461

Despite Dubai's flat terrain, spectacular hiking locations can be found just an hour outside the city limits. To the north, the Ru'us Al Jibal Mountains contain the highest peaks in the area and stand proud at over 2,000 metres. To the east, the impressive Hajar Mountains form the border between the UAE and Oman, stretching from the Musandam Peninsula to the Empty Quarter desert, hundreds of kilometres to the south.

Most of the terrain is heavily eroded due to the harsh climate, but there are still places

Trail Network

Keen trekkers can check out the UAE Trekking group on Facebook. The casual group organises hikes throughout the Emirates and Oman. The *UAE Off-Road Explorer* also details several hikes throughout the country that are accessible by both 4WD and 2WD vehicles. If you'd like to push the geographical limits, pick up a copy of *Oman Trekking*, which details many routes in Oman on separate route cards.

where you can walk through shady palm plantations and lush oases. Routes range from short, easy walks leading to spectacular viewpoints, to all-day treks over difficult terrain, and can include major mountaineering. Some hikes follow centuries old Bedouin and Shihuh mountain paths, a few of which are still being used.

One of the nearest and easiest places to reach is the foothills of the Hajar Mountains on the Hatta Road, near the border of Oman. After passing through the desert, the flat stark, rugged outcrops transform the landscape. Explore any turning you like, or take the road to Mahdah, along which you'll find several options.

Other great areas for hiking and exploring include Al Ain and its surroundings, many places in the mountains in and around Musandam, and the mountains near the east coast. The mountains in the UAE don't generally disappoint, and the further off the beaten track you get, the more likely you are to find interesting villages where residents live much the same way as they did centuries ago.

For somewhere a bit further afield see the *Oman Trekking*, a guide book from Explorer Publishing with pull-out maps covering major signed routes in Oman.

As with any trip into the UAE 'outback', take sensible precautions. Tell someone where you are going and when you should be back and don't forget to take a map, compass, GPS equipment and robust hiking boots. Don't underestimate the strength of the sun – take sunscreen and, most importantly, loads of water.

For most people, the cooler and less humid winter months are the best season for serious mountain hiking. Be particularly careful in wadis (dry riverbeds) during the wet season as flash floods can immerse a wadi in seconds. Also note that there are no mountain rescue services in the UAE, so anyone venturing out into the mountains should be reasonably experienced or accompanied by someone who knows the area.

Pearl Coast Hotel
Behind MOE
Al Barsha
Map 6 A3

Desert Rangers

04 422 0044 | www.desertrangers.com

Desert Rangers offer hikes for individuals and groups of up to 100 people by dividing them into smaller teams and taking different trails to the summit. A variety of routes are offered according to age and fitness. Locations include Fujairah, Dibba, Masafi, Ras Al Khaimah and Al Ain, with prices starting at Dhs.275 per person.

Hockey

Other options **Ice Hockey** p.363

Various Locations

Dubai Hockey Club

055 966 8762 | www.dubaihockeyclub.com

Dubai Hockey Club (DXBHC) is made up of men and woman of all abilities and from all around the world (members hail from Ireland, England, Australia, Holland, South Africa and Canada). Matches take place on Sunday and Wednesday evenings at two locations: a new astro pitch or a floodlit five a-side all weather pitch. The club also plays in local tournaments on grass as well as arranging friendly matches throughout the year. Annual international tours are also organised to locations such as Singapore, Hong Kong and the UK.

Sharjah Wanderers
Sports Club
Sharjah
Map 2 C2

Sharjah Wanderers Hockey Club

06 566 2105 | www.sharjahwanderers.com

The club was born as a part of the Sharjah Contracts Club in 1976. The hockey section became the first mixed team in the Gulf, and has always retained a strong mixed club atmosphere. The approach at the club is to play sport within a friendly, but competitive, environment.

Horse Riding
Other options **Polo** p.378

The Desert Equestrian Club
Nr Municipality Vet
Al Khawaneej
Map 2 C2

050 309 9770

Horse lovers will be hard pushed to beat the excitement of being out there among the dunes, galloping over sandy tracks with the camels. Riders will be back at the stables before sundown, gritty, exhilarated and with colour in their cheeks, ready to give the horses a much-needed hose down. If you've got your own horse, the Desert Equestrian Club offers livery services for Dhs.1,500 a month, while accomplished riders can pay Dhs.100 to take one of the stable's horses out for a jaunt (accompanied by a member of staff so there's no fear of not finding your way back). Those keen to learn can take a private lesson for Dhs.80 for adults (approximately 30 minutes long) and Dhs.50 for children under 16. During the hottest months, the hours are from 06:00 until 08:00 and from 18:00 until 21:00, Monday to Saturday. Contact Anna on the above number for bookings or further information.

Dubai Polo & Equestrian Club
Arabian Ranches
Map 2 B3

04 361 8111 | www.poloclubdubai.com

Located near the Arabian Ranches off Emirates Road, this riding centre has five horses, air-conditioned stables and a beautiful paddock. Three instructors give half-hour private lessons from Tuesday to Sunday, and one-hour desert rides can be arranged for experienced riders. The stables are closed during the summer months.

Emirates Equestrian Centre
Nr Camel Race Track
Nad Al Sheba
Map 2 C3

04 336 1394 | www.emiratesequestriancentre.com

The Emirates Equestrian Centre has 147 horses and the facilities include an international size floodlit arena, riding school, dressage and lunging rings. It's also possible to take along children and small toddlers and let them have a ride. The club hosts at least two competitions and three riding school shows per month, as well as gymkhanas from October to May. The centre also has regular clinics and stable management courses.

Jebel Ali Equestrian Club
Jebel Ali Village
Jebel Ali
Map 4 C3

04 884 5101 | www.jaec-me.com

Fully qualified instructors teach children and adults, from beginner to advanced levels, at Jebel Ali Equestrian Club. For more experienced riders, dressage, jumping and hacking are on offer, and gymkhana games, with competitions, are held on a regular basis. Newcomers can try a one-day lesson, after which a 10 lesson package will cost Dhs.800 for children and Dhs.1,000 for adults, plus a Dhs.120 annual registration fee.

Jebel Ali Golf Resort & Spa ▶ p.533
Nr Palm Jebel Ali
Jebel Ali
Map 3 A1

050 189 0425 | www.jebelali-international.com

Located at Jebel Ali Golf Resort & Spa, this riding centre has 10 horses and air-conditioned stables. The riding instructors give private lessons for 45 minutes from Tuesday to Sunday, and one hour desert rides can be arranged with Ms Tiki for experienced riders.

Riding For The Disabled
Desert Palms Polo
& Country Club
International City
Map 2 C3

050 450 4204 | www.rdad.ae

RDAD is a non-profit charity which uses therapeutic horse riding and hippotherapy to attain a variety of therapeutic goals for those suffering from disabilities including autism, cerebral palsy, Down's syndrome, spina bifida and learning disabilities. RDAD presently has 50 riders from 11 countries, eight horses, around 45 volunteers and two NARHA certified therapeutic riding instructors. Their aim is to improve poise, posture, strength and flexibility while boosting confidence. Classes are usually 45 minutes long but will vary according to the attention span, age and disability of the rider. Classes are held at the Desert Palm (p.40).

Sharjah Equestrian & Racing Club

Al Dhaid Rd
Jct 6
Sharjah
Map 2 C2

06 531 1155 | www.forsanuae.org.ae

This riding centre was built in 1984 under the supervision of Sheikh Sultan bin Mohammed Al-Qassimi, member of the Supreme Council and Ruler of Sharjah. Facilities include a floodlit sand arena and paddock, a grass show jumping arena, hacking trails into the desert and a new training centre. The club houses 250 horses, and riding must be arranged by appointment. Annual membership is Dhs.1,000 per person, or Dhs.2,000 for a family. Membership benefits include discounted riding lessons, plus preferential rates at the club's hotel, chalets and recreational facilities.

Ice Hockey

Other options **Ice Skating** p.363

Dubai Mighty Camels Ice Hockey Club

Al Nasr Leisureland
Oud Metha
Map 10 E2

050 450 0180 | www.dubaimightycamels.com

Ice hockey has been a fixture on the local sports scene ever since Al Nasr Leisureland opened in 1979. The club presently has over 120 adult members and has regular social get-togethers from September to May. The club also hosts an annual tournament in April, which regularly attracts up to 20 teams from the Gulf, Europe and the far east.

Dubai Sandstorms Ice Hockey Club

Al Nasr Leisureland
Oud Metha
Map 10 E2

050 775 8713 | www.dubaisandstorms.com

This club was established to provide boys and girls (6 to 18 years) with the opportunity to play ice hockey. The club's emphasis is on teamwork and sportsmanship, and previous experience is not necessary. Practice sessions are held twice a week and matches are played against teams from Dubai, Abu Dhabi, Al Ain and Oman. For further details email Isabelle Jones at sandstormspresident@gmail.com.

Ice Skating

Other options **Ice Hockey** p.363

Al Nasr Leisureland

Behind American
Hospital
Oud Metha
Map 10 E2

04 337 1234 | www.alnasrleisureland.ae

Open to the public (except when in use by clubs), the rink is part of the Leisureland complex that comprises a bowling alley, tennis courts, squash courts, fastfood outlets, arcade games and shops. Entrance fees are Dhs.10 for adults and Dhs.5 for children under 10, while skate rental charges are Dhs.5 for two hours. Call before you go to make sure the ice rink is free and not booked for an event.

Galleria Ice Rink

The Galleria
Residence
Deira
Map 9 D1

04 209 6550

Fees for public sessions are Dhs.25 per person (including skate hire) or Dhs.15 if you have your own skates. Membership rates start at Dhs.300 per month, or Dhs.1,200 per year, and members are entitled to unlimited skating. Lessons are available for non-members and start at Dhs.100 for a half hour lesson.

Jetskiing
Other options **Speedboating** p.390

Officially, jetskiing has been shut down in Dubai, primarily to maintain the peace and quiet, and also to protect swimmers and avoid accidents. Keen jetskiers have been waiting for the Municipality's review of the situation for some time. However, in the meantime, unofficial operators are still hiring out jetskis from Mamzar Lagoon. If you do manage to get your hands on a machine in Dubai waters, it may be worth checking that your medical insurance covers you for this potentially dangerous sport before you rev away, as accidents do happen. You may also want to consider whether you have any personal liability insurance in case you injure a third party.

Karting
Other options **Dune Buggy Driving** p.348

Arabian Ranches Interchange
Dubailand
Map 2 C3

Dubai Autodrome
04 367 8700 | www.dubaiautodrome.com
Wannabe Alonsos of any age or gender should head to this new kartdrome to burn some rubber and let off steam. After a safety briefing you'll take to your powerful 390cc kart (there are smaller 120cc karts for the kids) and hit the tarmac on the exciting 1.2km circuit. Each kart has a transponder allowing you to see the overall winners and losers, and lap times. With overalls, gloves and helmets supplied, it's a great option for parties or team-building exercises. Those with their very own karts can also use the track at certain times of the week, and full garaging and maintenance packages are available.

Nr Jebel Ali Golf Resort & Spa
Jebel Ali
Map 1 E2

Emirates Kart Centre
050 559 2131 | www.emsf.ae
Operated by the Emirates Motor Sports Federation, this kart centre has a floodlit, 0.8km track with straights, hairpins and chicanes. Professional and junior karts are available, and you can take part regularly without buying any equipment. The centre is open seven days a week.

Kayaking
Other options **Canoeing** p.335

Al Aqah
Fujairah
Map 1 F1

Sandy Beach Hotel & Resort
09 244 5555 | www.sandybm.com
The Beach Hut at Sandy Beach offers a variety of watersports equipment for rent or sale. For those who want to paddle out to Snoopy Island, single kayaks are available for hire at Dhs.40 per hour, or you could go for a two-seater for Dhs.60. It's a great way to see the abundant marine life (including the occasional turtle and shark) without getting too wet.

Kickboxing
Other options **Martial Arts** p.371, **Thai Boxing** p.393

Emirates Towers
Trade Centre 2
Map 7 F3

Raifet N Shawe
050 495 4446 | rifshawe@emirates.net.ae
Raifet Shawe has been teaching kickboxing professionally for around 10 years. Currently a Black Belt 4th Dan in karate and kickboxing and a black belt in judo, his methods of teaching include forms of karate, kickboxing and muay thai. Classes

are thorough, concise and most importantly, enjoyable. Beginners will find themselves learning quickly, especially if attending his three weekly classes held at the Big Apple gym in the Emirates Towers (04 319 8660). Group classes are held on Mondays, Wednesdays and Saturdays from 17:30 to 18:30. Rates are reasonable and class length is usually an hour. Contact him directly for further information or to set up private classes.

Fun in the desert

Kids' Activities

Various Locations ◀ DuGym Gymnastics Club
050 553 6283 | www.dugym.com

DuGym offers gymnastics and trampoline coaching to children of all ages and abilities. Established by Suzanne Wallace in 2000, the club now operates at 15 locations including the GEMS World Academy, Jumeirah English Speaking School and Emirates International School. Classes are held from Sunday to Thursday. Contact Suzanne on the above number for more details.

Off Tunis St ◀ Junior Gym Bus
Exit 60
Al Qusais
Map 14 C4

04 254 3070 | www.juniorgymbus.com

Junior Gym Bus is a unique and stimulating innovation promoting fitness in children and encouraging them to partake in sport activities. A converted school bus is driven to the daycare centre or preschool, and parked outside where certified instructors teach gymnastics and basic motor skills to the children. The floors and walls are padded with foam and carpeted for safety. Rates include monthly payments of Dhs.200 per month as a member or a fee of Dhs.65 per session as a non-member. An annual registration fee of Dhs.120 per child is also applicable.

Cooper Health Clinic ◀ Kid-Fit
Al Wasl Rd
Umm Suqeim
Map 6 C2

04 348 6344 | kidfitdubai@gmail.com

Kid-Fit is a licensed physical education curriculum designed to introduce healthy lifestyle habits to children aged 2 to 5. They encourage healthy habits and regular exercise, sound nutrition and sufficient rest. Children are taught about their bodies and how they work – covering topics such as the heart, lungs, muscles, bones, brain and mouth.

Jumeira Rd ◀ My Gym
Villa 520
Jumeira
Map 6 F1

04 394 3962 | www.mygymuae.com

If you are looking for innovative ways to get the kids active, My Gym offers a range of activities to keep your tots on their toes. My Gym offers a variety of events. Programmes range from 'Mommy and Me' for babies aged six weeks and up, to gymnastics, dance and general fitness. They also organise fun-filled private birthday parties and camps. A two hour per week class and play session will cost Dhs.1,000 for 10 weeks. Parents can also participate in classes with their children if preferred, but independent classes are offered.

Various Locations
Physical Advantage
04 311 6570 | www.physicaladvantage.ae

If your kids seek a challenge, try out Physical Advantage's Military Bootcamp Programmes which are designed for 6 to 15 year olds. The Cadets Bootcamp programme will test all aspects of your child's health and fitness while teaching them discipline and health education. Timings and locations for courses vary according to the age group your child belongs to. A single session costs Dhs.100, and a two week course (four sessions) costs Dhs.300.

Kitesurfing
Other options **Beaches** p.279

Kitesurfing is an extreme sport that is swiftly gaining popularity. It's not windsurfing, it's not wakeboarding, it's not surfing and it's not kite flying. In fact, it's a fusion of all these disciplines, with a few other influences thrown in for good measure. At the moment kiting is allowed on the stretch of beach near the old Wollongong University premises, but is most popularly practised at the Jebel Ali Public Beach, on the left-hand side of the Jebel Ali Hotel. You'll need a licence too. The rules and regulations are prone to change without warning, so check with the Dubai Kite Club for the latest info.

Mina Seyahi Dubai
Al Sufouh
Map 5 B1
Dubai Kite Club
050 618 0612 | www.dubaikiteclub.com

Dubai Kite Club regulates the sport of kitesurfing, mountain board kiting, power kiting and display kiting. To kitesurf in Dubai you are now required to hold a licence – the police carry out spot-checks and may punish offenders. Membership of DKC (Dhs.200 per year) automatically grants the licence, plus a number of other benefits such as third party liability insurance. To join you'll need passport copies and photos, a medical certificate from a clinic confirming that you're fit enough to participate in an extreme watersport, and a completed application form (available on the website). Take everything along to the office at Mina Seyahi Dubai and your membership card/licence will be ready within a week. For the latest information call the number above. You may also want to check out www.fatimasport.com when looking to buy equipment.

Language Schools
Other options **Learning Arabic** p.224

Kitesurfing

Opp Our Own English High School
Umm Hurair
Map 10 E3
Alliance Française
04 335 8712 | www.afdubai.com

The Alliance Française is a non-profit organisation supported by the French Government, with the goal of promoting French language and culture. The Alliance in Dubai offers special morning classes for ladies, afternoon classes for children and evening classes for everybody. It also offers Arabic language classes for foreigners. In addition, it offers evening French language classes for adults at the Lycée Georges Pompidou in Sharjah. Terms run from September to June, but intensive courses are also held during the summer for both adults and children. Alliance Française offers DEL/DALF and TEF degrees.

Arabic Language Centre

Dubai World Trade Centre
Trade Centre
Map 10 A1

04 308 6036 | alc@dwtc.com

A division of the Dubai World Trade Centre, this language school was established in 1980 to teach Arabic as a foreign language. Courses, from beginner to advanced levels, are held five times a year, last 30 hours, and cost Dhs.1,800 (inclusive of all materials). Specialist courses can be designed to meet the requirements of the hotel, banking, hospital, motor and electronics industries.

Berlitz

Nr Dubai Zoo
Jumeira
Map 7 E1

04 344 0034 | www.berlitz.ae

The Berlitz method has helped more than 41 million people acquire a new language. A variety of language courses are offered and can be customised to fit specific requirements, such as 'English for banking' or 'technical English'. Instruction is in private or small groups, from kids to adults. Additional training includes translation and self-teaching. See the website for more details.

British Council

Dubai English Speaking College
Dubai Academic City
Map 2 C3

04 337 0109 | www.britishcouncil.org

The British Council is the world's largest education and cultural relations organisation. In the UAE there are three centres, in Dubai, Abu Dhabi and Sharjah. In addition to teaching English to adults, children, professionals and teacher training programmes, the British Council administers professional, academic and vocational examinations, and advises students looking for study opportunities in the UK. Students are supported by learning zones which provide multimedia learning resources, including a lending library and audio books, videos and DVDs, and access to the internet. From a creative perspective, the British Council is active in supporting arts, music, science and sports projects which help young people from the UAE and the UK to connect with each other. Call toll free 800 225 522 or visit the website for more info.

Dar El Ilm School Of Languages

Dubai World Trade Centre
Trade Centre
Map 10 A1

04 331 0221 | darelilm@eim.ae

Now in its 18th year, Dar El Ilm offers language courses to students of all ages and abilities, with an emphasis on making learning fun. Adult and children's tuition is offered in English, French, German, Italian, Spanish and Arabic. With fees starting at Dhs.1,600, adult courses last 15 hours and run eight times during the academic year. Lessons for children are also offered at Dhs.85 per hour.

El Ewla Language Academy

Dubai Knowledge Village
Al Sufouh
Map 5 D2

04 391 1640 | elewlainfo@partners.kv.ae

El Ewla, meaning 'the first' in Arabic, is a language and training institute. El Ewla's language programmes (Arabic, English, French) are offered to individuals, companies and government institutions. Classes focus on every language aspect including grammar, vocabulary, use of idioms and improving your accent and pronunciation. Special exam programmes and corporate packages are also available.

ELS Language Center ▶ p.369

Al Hai Bld
Port Saeed
Deira
Map 11 D3

04 294 0740 | www.elsmea.com

Sessions at ELS last four weeks and prices range from Dhs.2,100 for the standard 48 hour session, to Dhs.4,000 for a super intensive 100 hour session. Unlike traditional forms of English language instruction, ELS concentrates on applying language patterns through group work and problem solving. Along with their standard programmes, they offer a children's programme, TOEFL training and business English courses.

Dubai Knowledge Village
Al Sufouh
Map5 D2

Eton Institute Of Languages
04 360 2955 | www.eton.ac

'Dubai's leading institute of languages' boasts courses in 31 different languages from Pashto to Swahili. Their instructors are native-fluent and especially trained in motivating, guiding, and inspiring their students to achieve their language goals. In addition, they offer a diverse range of courses including etiquette training, workshops in cultural sensitivity, orientation in the UAE, as well as soft skills training. Course fees start from Dhs.1,000. Visit at Dubai Knowledge Village or call on the toll free number: 800 3866

Nr Sea View Hotel
Bur Dubai
Map 8 E2

Goethe-Institut German Language Center
04 359 0529 | www.goethe.de/dubai

The Goethe-Institut is Germany's cultural institution and operates worldwide. The Dubai centre provides German language courses, from beginner level upwards. Tailor-made courses can be designed to meet the specific need of educational and corporate institutions and companies. The centre also offers classes for teenagers and individual courses, as well as internationally recognised exams.

Sultan Business Ctr
Nr Lamcy Plaza
Oud Metha
Map 10 D2

Inlingua
04 334 0004 | www.inlingua.com

Part of an international language system, the Dubai office of Inlingua conducts courses in French, Spanish, German and English. Courses are broken up into seven levels and new students will need to take a placement test to determine where they belong. Classes are held in the evening, and each two month course meets three days a week for two hours at a time. Each level costs Dhs.2,000 inclusive of materials.

Al Maktoum St
Al Masaeed Bld
Deira
Map 9 C3

Polyglot Language Institute
04 222 3429 | www.polyglot.ae

Polyglot Language Institute offers courses in modern languages, as well as secretarial and computer skills for individuals and companies. Courses offered include Arabic, general and business English, French, Spanish, Italian, German, TOEFL preparation, office skills, typing, and secretarial and computer studies. Courses last six to 10 weeks and all materials are provided. Course costs range from Dhs.1,450 to Dhs.1,750.

Libraries
Other options **Books** p.428, **Second-Hand Items** p.464

Opp Our Own English High School
Umm Hurair
Map 10 E3

Alliance Française
04 335 8712 | www.afdubai.com

The Alliance Française multimedia library has over 12,500 French books (including a children's section), plus 50 daily, weekly and monthly French newspapers and magazines, 18,000 French documents, 2,000 videotapes, 150 CD-ROMs, 100 audio CDs and 3,000 DVDs. A library membership for a year including books and magazines costs Dhs.500, while a multimedia membership including videos and DVDs costs Dhs.800.

Pyramid Building
Nr Burjuman
Al Karama
Map 8 F4

Archie's Library
04 396 7924 | abcl180@hotmail.com

Archie's Library is stocked with 45,000 English fiction, non-fiction, classic, cooking, health and fitness, and management books. A selection of children's books and comics

is also available, along with the latest magazines. The annual membership fee of Dhs.75 (plus a Dhs.100 refundable deposit) entitles you to borrow four books at a time for 14 days. Reading charges vary from Dhs.1 to Dhs.7 according to the book. The library is open 365 days a year, and they also have a branch in Sharjah (06 572 5716).

Various Locations

Dubai Municipality Public Libraries
04 226 2788 | www.libraries.ae

The Municipality is in the process of rebranding some of Dubai's public libraries as e-Libraries; look out for the big brown road signs directing you to the nearest branch. The e-Library in Umm Suqeim was the first, with many of the books having made way for banks of shiny new PCs – it is now home to an ICDL training and test centre. The ICDL (International Computer Driving Licence) is a computer skills competency standard recognised around the world. Covering all aspects of computer use (such as file management, word processing and spreadsheets), students take seven tests (one theoretical and six practical), and upon passing the course will receive a personalised certificate, or 'licence'. Contact the Umm Suqeim branch for details of fees and timings. Libraries also offer internet access – Dhs.3 for one hour, or Dhs.5 for two hours, but members pay nothing.

Some of Dubai's libraries do still have selections of English language books to borrow. The Al Ras and Safa branches are perhaps your best bet. Library membership costs Dhs.210, but Dhs.150 of that is refundable. Family membership is Dhs.260 (including a refundable Dhs.200). To apply you'll need passport and visa copies and photos.

The libraries website has a facility allowing you to search the entire catalogue, and you can even apply for membership online by uploading your photos and scanned copies of your passport. Current branches: Al Ras (04 226 2788), Hatta (04 852 1022), Hor Al Anz (04 266 1788), Rashidiya (04 285 8065), Safa (04 394 7279), Umm Suqeim (04 348 9572), Union House (04 345 2929).

Nr Dubai Cinema
Deira
Map 11 E1

Juma Al Majid Cultural & Heritage Centre
04 262 4999 | info@almajidcenter.org

This is a non-profit reference library and research institute that focuses on Islam. It has a collection of 500,000 cultural media items that range from historical to current world issues, plus 3,000 periodicals and out of print publications. Books cannot be taken home, but you can use the reading room or make photocopies. There's no fee to use the library.

DUCTAC
Mall of the Emirates
Al Barsha
Map 6 A3

The Old Library
04 341 4777 | www.theoldlibrary.ae

The Old Library, established in 1969, is the oldest English language library serving the expatriate community in Dubai. It is now part of the Dubai Community Theatre & Arts Centre (DUCTAC), located near Magic Planet on the second level of the Mall of the Emirates. The library has a collection of over 13,000 adult fiction and reference books as well as an extremely well-stocked children's section and specialist sections for romance and the Middle East. Reading sessions for children are conducted on Saturday mornings. The Old Library is a non-profit making organisation run entirely by volunteers. New volunteers are always welcome to train as librarians or to assist with maintaining the book collection. Donations of second-hand books are encouraged, as funds raised from book sales and subscriptions are used to cover operational expenses and the purchase of new books. The library is open from 10:00 to 18:00 Saturday to Thursday and closed on Fridays and public holidays.

Sports & Activities

Martial Arts

Whether you're a black belt Bruce Lee wannabe or just fancy trying your hand at karate, there are various fitness centres in Dubai where you can hone your martial arts skills. Choose from disciplines like judo, which is a great form of self defence, or aikido, which combines joint locks and throws with the body movements of sword and spear. Check with the club to find out which martial arts are taught.

Marina Walk
Dubai Marina
Map 5 B2

Angsana Spa & Health Club Dubai Marina

04 368 4356 | *www.angsanaspa.com*

Angsana Spa & Health Club is best known for its spa, which was awarded the Gold Award for Best Spa by Travel Awards in 2006, but they also offer a great Thai boxing class. If you crave a good old boost of fitness, be sure to give them a call and arrange to attend their class every Saturday at 19:00. The instructors have plenty of experience and are masters of motivation. Classes cost Dhs.60 per person for a group lesson, although individual classes can be arranged too.

Dubai Karate Centre
Al Safa
Map 7 A2

Dubai Aikido Club

04 344 4156 | *www.aikido.ae*

Aikido is a self defence martial art that also trains the mind. The Dubai Aikido Club was established in 1995 and is affiliated with the International Aikido Association. Classes for both children and adults are held throughout the week at the Dubai Karate Centre. The membership fee is Dhs.300 for kids and Dhs.400 for adults. For further information contact John Rutnam, the chief instructor, on the above number or on his mobile: 050 795 2716.

Al Raizi Boys School
Training Hall
Nr Medcare Hospital
Al Safa
Map 7 A2

Dubai Karate Centre

050 855 7996 | *www.dubaikarate.com*

At the Dubai Karate Centre, a team of black belt, JKA qualified instructors teach shotokan, taekwondo, aikido, muay thai and judo, and there are also courses in self defence. The club is a member of the Japanese Karate Association (JKA) and offers tuition for everyone from beginners to black belts. There is a registration fee of Dhs.100 and monthly membership fees are Dhs.300 and up.

DUCTAC
Mall of the Emirates
Al Barsha
Map 6 A3

EBMAS School Of Self Defense

055 605 8128 | *www.ebmas-selfdefense.com*

EBMAS is a form of self-defense that is taught in more than 40 countries world wide, and students have been taught in Dubai since 2006. The organisation teaches both armed and unarmed self defense classes from its base within DUCTAC at Mall of the Emirates. Classes are available for all, but the centre also runs special courses for women, children, as well as offering private tutorials and group sessions. The school operates on Sundays and Wednesdays from 20:30 to 21:30.

Nxt to Choithram
Supermarket
Al Karama
Map 10 D1

Golden Falcon Karate Centre

04 336 0243 | *www.goldenfalconkarate.com*

Established in 1990, this karate centre is affiliated with the International Karate Budokan and UAE Judo, Taekwondo & Karate Federation. The centre is open throughout the week and students can choose class times to suit their schedules. Official certificates are issued from international headquarters to successful candidates. Membership prices are between Dhs.120 and Dhs.250 per month (excluding fees charged on registration, uniforms and transport), depending on how many days a week you plan to train.

Al Riffa Plaza
Nr Ramada R/A
Bur Dubai
Map 8 F3

Golden Fist Karate Club

04 355 1029 | *http://goldenfistkarate.net*

Golden Fist provides training in a number of martial arts, including karate and kung fu, with students receiving official certificates upon passing each grade. The club offers flexible timings and classes run throughout the day and well into the evening. A nine-month black belt crash course is also available. You can sign up for between two and six classes a week, with the monthly fee ranging from Dhs.100 to Dhs.200 (plus a Dhs.30 admission fee). Discounts are available if you pay in advance.

The Ballet Centre
Jumeira
Map 7 F1

Taekwondo

04 344 9776 | *www.balletcentre.com*

The Ballet Centre's taekwondo arm is run by Fabun, a 7th dan black belt. This form of martial art teaches children and adults mental calmness, courage, strength and humility, courtesy, integrity, perseverance, self-control and indomitable spirit. Lessons take place on Sundays, Tuesdays and Thursdays. The membership fee is Dhs.825 for three months (12 classes) and includes a Dhs.100 registration fee and one free trial class.

Mini Golf

Other options **Golf** p.354

Nr Tennis Stadium
Al Garhoud
Map 13 E1

The Aviation Club

04 282 4540 | *www.aviationclub.ae*

This nine-hole pitch and putt course is located between the tennis stadium and the clubhouse. With manicured fairways and greens, each hole is a reasonable challenge for beginners and accomplished golfers. The course offers putting variety, and holes differ from 40 to 82 yards. Free for members, non-members can play mini golf for Dhs.150.

Dubai-Hatta Rd
Hatta
Map 1 F2

Hatta Fort Hotel ▶ p.311

04 852 3211 | *www.jebelali-international.com*

Set against the backdrop of the Hajar Mountains, the Hatta Fort Hotel has a mini golf course, a chipping green, and a driving range where golfers can practise their swings. Guests at the hotel can use the course for free, but visitors need to pay. Prices are available upon request.

Hyatt Regency
Deira
Map 9 D1

Hyatt Golf Park

04 209 6802 | *www.dubai.hyatt.com*

The Hyatt offers a nine-hole pitch and putt grass course (Dhs.30 for one round) or an 18 hole crazy golf course (Dhs.15 per person). For the pitch and putt you'll need your own clubs, and golf balls are rented at Dhs.15 each. Clubs and balls are provided for the crazy golf though. The park is floodlit in the evenings and the clubhouse overlooks a small lagoon. No membership is required.

Mother & Toddler Activities

There are a number of mother and baby or toddler activity groups in Dubai that are great when you are a new mum and a million miles away from your friends and family support network.

Opp Choithram
Al Garhoud
Map 13 E1

Kidz & Mumz

050 451 0225 | *shalini@eim.ae*

The aim of this group is to allow mums and their children to engage together in creative and educational activities such as arts and crafts, games, reading, writing, story telling, and cooking and baking. The 'MumZ Forum' also allows the grown-ups to discuss different aspects of their children's development. The current age group of the 'kidz' is between 2 and 5.

Mothers & Miracles

Le Meridien Mina Seyahi
Al Sufouh
Map 5 C1

050 794 1439 | *rjvrensburg@hotmail.com*

Mothers & Miracles offers a structured, interactive learning programme, designed to stimulate children between 3 months and 3 years, in the areas of intellect, emotions, creativity, physical movement, social interaction and music. The programme, developed by a leading early childhood educationalist, encourages the active participation of the parent in each session, guiding and encouraging the child through each activity. For more details, contact Ronel by phone or email above.

Mums & Tots Group

Wafi Mall
Umm Hurair
Map 10 E4

050 656 5837 | *anncassidy100@hotmail.com*

This well-established, informal mums' group has been going for over 15 years. All mums (and dads) are welcome, and the focus is on meeting like-minded people and making friends. The meetings take place in a huge hall that is crammed with toys to keep the kids busy while mums chat over coffee. This group is highly recommended, especially if you're new to Dubai or new to motherhood. Contact Ann for more info and directions. The cost is Dhs.20 per meeting, which includes tea and coffee, biscuits, and snacks for the kids.

Motocross

Other options **Quad Bikes** p.378, **Motorcycling** p.373

Dubai Motocross

Behind Kart Club
Jebel Ali
Map 2 A4

050452 7844 | *www.mydubaimotocross.com*

Dubai Motocross (DMX) runs classes for Cadets, Juniors, 65cc, 85cc, 125cc and adults. The new Jebel Ali Motocross Park features two tracks (one for juniors and one for seniors) along with other facilities that make it fun for the whole family to enjoy a day at the track. The club organises 12 individual championship events per year, with an entry fee of Dhs.100 for members and Dhs.200 to Dhs.250 for non-members.

Motorcycling

Other options **Motocross** p.373

Harley Owners Group (HOG) Dubai

Various Locations

www.hogdubai.com

If you're a true motorcycle aficionado at heart, this club is holding up a sign with your name on it. Meeting up at the crack of dawn (06:00) and leaving promptly at 06:30, these proud Harley-owners enjoy weekly organised rides to various destinations for breakfast. They also participate in many rallies around the Middle East including the Middle East HOG Rally in Fujairah. Check out the website for more information on recent news and events. Those wishing to become members can attend a monthly meeting or an 'open' event.

Catching air

Al Muraqqabat St
Above Al Tayer Motors
Deira
Map 11 D1

UAE Motorcycle Club

04 296 1122 | *www.uaedesertchallenge.com*

The UAE Motorcycle Club is the UAE's FIM representative. Regular motocross and off-road enduros are held between September and April, and activity centres at the DMX Club and in Umm Al Quwain host quad and drag races. Call the number or keep an eye on the website for details of upcoming events.

Motorsports

Nr Arabian Ranches
Dubailand
Map 2 C3

Dubai Autodrome

04 367 8700 | *www.dubaiautodrome.com*

The home of motorsport in Dubai, the Autodrome (part of Dubailand, on Emirates Road) has six different track configurations, including a 5.39km FIA-sanctioned GP circuit, state-of-the-art pit facilities and a 7,000 seat grandstand. The venue hosts a variety of events throughout the year, including rounds of the FIA GT Championship.

Nr Aviation Club
Al Garhoud
Map 13 E1

Emirates Motor Sports Federation

04 282 7111 | *www.emsf.ae*

For rally and racing enthusiasts in the UAE, the Federation organises a variety of events throughout the year ranging from the 4WD 1000 Dunes Rally to the Champions Rally for saloon cars. Other events include road safety awareness campaigns and classic car exhibitions. Federation membership is Dhs.200 per year, although non-members can enter races for a fee. Check the website for a full calendar of events.

Mountain Biking

Other options **Cycling** p.338

Away from the cities, the UAE has a lot to offer outdoor enthusiasts, especially mountain bikers. On a mountain bike it's possible to see the most remote and untouched places that are not even accessible in 4WDs. For hardcore, experienced mountain bikers there is a good range of terrain, from the super-technical rocky trails in areas like Fili and Siji, to mountain routes like Wadi Bih, which climb to over a thousand metres and can be descended in minutes.
The riding is mainly rocky, technical and challenging. Even if you are an experienced biker, always be sensible and go prepared – the sun is strong, you will need far more water than you think, and it's easy to get lost. You'll find wide, knobby tires work much better on the loose, sharp rocks. For further information on mountain biking in the UAE, including details of possible routes, refer to the *UAE Off-Road Explorer*.

Various Locations

Dream Adventure

050 951 5794 | *www.dreamadventure.ae*

Whether you're an amateur or a pro, Dream Adventure has a package especially for you. You have a choice of three mountain biking tour packages, which are designed according to level of difficulty from easy, moderate to pro-level. Half-day trips (three hours) cost Dhs.350 and a full-day tour (six hours) costs Dhs.800 including lunch. Call the above number for reservations and private bookings.

Various Locations

Hot Cog MTB

050 840 5901 | *www.hot-cog.com*

Hot Cog MTB is an active group of enthusiasts who ride every weekend, all over the country, all year round. They also camp, hike and barbecue, and new riders are always welcome. Visit their website for more information.

Music Lessons

Other options **Music, DVDs & Videos** p.459, **Dance Classes** p.339, **Singing** p.384

Dubai Music School

Stalco Building
Zabeel Rd
Al Karama
Map 10 E1

04 396 4834 | www.glennperry.net

Dubai Music School offers guitar, piano, organ, violin, brass, drums, singing and composing lessons for beginners and serious amateurs. Lessons last for one hour, and students take Trinity College of Music examinations to get certification. Monthly fees range from Dhs.200 to Dhs.395, and there's a Dhs.50 registration fee.

Juli Music Centre

Al Wadi Building
Nr Safestway
Sheikh Zayed Road
Map 7 C3

04 321 2588

In addition to selling a wide variety of musical instruments including new and used pianos, brass, woodwind, strings, and percussion, Juli Music Centre also offers tutoring to students of all experience levels. Contact the shop for details of fees and which instruments are offered.

Jumeirah Music Center

Jumeirah Plaza
Jumeira
Map 7 F1

04 349 2662 | www.jumeirahmusic.com

Opened in 2004, the Jumeirah Music Centre now boasts more than 300 members. Lessons are offered in piano, guitar, flute, violin, drums, and voice. All children are welcome to audition for the choir, which puts on a big concert every year. Music lessons are also available to adults.

THE Music Institute

Dubai Knowledge
Village
Al Sufouh
Map 5 D2

04 390 0786 | www.themusic-uae.com

TMI offers a variety of musical instruments as well as teaching music theory, from its base at Knowledge Village. Courses on offer include piano, violin, guitar and drums, together with musical theory. A branch at Jumeirah Beach Residence offers the same classes in addition to woodwind instruments such as flute and saxophone. Classes are available for all ages, and are tailored to ability and the free time you have to practice. In addition to individual classes, THE Music Institute also offers group lessons on guitar and violin. There are practice rooms available to hire in between lessons, and recitals to show off your new skills.

Sruthi Music & Dance Training Center

Sana Fashion Bld
Al Karama
Map 8 E4

04 337 7398 | www.sruthimusic.com

Lessons are available for a variety of instruments including piano, electric organ, guitar, drums, violin, accordion and tabla, and students can register with Trinity College of Music and take exams in Dubai. Lessons are also offered in Carnatic and Hindustani vocals, as well as dance from Indian styles such as Bharatnatyam or Kathak, to western dance styles like disco and jive.

The Vocal Studio

Various Locations

050 698 0773 | www.bravodubai.com

The Vocal Studio offers vocal instruction and a range of singing related activities for adults and youngsters. The centre offers ABRSM and Trinity College of Music syllabus exam preparations, and grades range from beginner to advanced. Students are also encouraged to take part in recitals and concerts, and are also featured in musical productions with visiting international guest artists. For more information email info@bravodubai.com.

Netball

UAE Tennis Academy
Mirdif
Map 15 A2

Dubai Netball League

050 450 6715 | www.dxbnetball.com

There are over 22 teams in three divisions at the club, and players range from beginners to experts. Matches are played from September to May on Wednesday nights. During the season, players are selected for the Inter-Gulf Netball Championships, a tournament that features teams from throughout the Gulf. Although they currently play at the UAE Tennis Academy in Mirdif, they plan on moving to the new courts at Silicon Oasis.

Off-Road Driving

Other options **Desert Driving Courses** p.342, **Camping** p.334

With the vast areas of virtually untouched wilderness in the UAE, wadi and dune bashing are very popular pastimes. To protect the environment from damage, you should try to stick to existing tracks rather than create new tracks across virgin countryside. While it may be hard to deviate from the track when wadi bashing, dunes are ever changing so obvious paths are less common. Although the sandy dunes may look devoid of life, there is a surprising variety of flora and fauna that exists.

> **Course Work**
>
> OffRoad-Zone (p.342) has recently opened a driving centre at the Jebel Ali Shooting Club. The purpose-built course simulates various obstacles that you might find while off-roading, including deep water, loose rocks and steep descents. Contact 055 7368 494, for visit www.offroad-zone.com for more information.

Dune bashing, or desert driving, is one of the toughest challenges for both car and driver, but once you have mastered it, it's also the most fun. Driving in the wadis is usually a bit more straightforward. Wadis are (usually) dry gullies, carved through the rock by rushing floodwaters, following the course of seasonal rivers. The main safety precaution to take when wadi bashing is to keep your eyes open for developing rare, but not impossible, thunderstorms – the wadis can fill up quickly and you will need to make your way to higher ground pretty quickly to avoid flash floods.

If you want a wilderness adventure but don't know where to start, contact any of the major tour companies (see Tour Operators, p.294). All offer a range of desert and mountain safaris. If you're really keen, have a go at a desert driving course (p.294). For further information and tips on driving off-road check out both the *UAE Off-Road Explorer* and *Oman Off-Road Explorer*. These fabulous books feature a multitude of detailed routes, stunning satellite images, striking photos, useful reference material and essential off-road directories.

Orchestras & Bands

Other options **Singing** p.384, **Music Lessons** p.375

Horizon English
School
Al Wasl
Map 7 B2

Dubai Chamber Orchestra

04 349 0423 | www.dubaiorchestra.org

The Dubai Chamber Orchestra was founded by a group of musicians residing in the UAE. The group comprises many different nationalities and meets regularly to rehearse. Its aim is to give at least two public performances a year. There are currently over 40 members from more than 15 countries. For more information, send an email to enquiries@dubaiorchestra.org.

Horizon English School
Al Wasl
Map 7 B2

Dubai Wind Band

04 348 3631

This is a gathering of over 50 woodwind and brass musicians. Abilities range from beginners to grade eight plus, and all levels and ages are welcome. The band is in popular demand during December for seasonal singing and music engagements at clubs, malls and hotels. For further information, contact Peter Hatherley-Greene. Alternative number: 050 651 8902.

Dubai College
Al Sufouh
Map 5 E2

UAE Philharmonic Orchestra

www.uaephilharmonic.com

The UAE Philharmonic Orchestra was founded by conductor and artistic director Philipp Maier to start promoting the need of an orchestra within the United Arab Emirates. Originally called Dubai Philharmonic Orchestra DPO, the UAEPO consists of musicians resident in the UAE from 21 different countries and performs regularly at private events, public concerts and corporate functions. The UAE Philharmonic Orchestra is the only full orchestra in the UAE and represents a major step towards orchestral culture and musical education within the UAE.

Paintballing & Laser Games

Other options **Shooting** p.383

Dubai Autodrome
Arabian Ranches
Map 2 C3

Laserdrome Dubai

04 436 1422 | www.dubaiautodrome.com

With the use of laser guns to defeat each other, it's paintballing without the mess and bruises. Laserdrome is at Dubai Autodrome (p.364) and a definite fun activity to enjoy with friends and family. Players wear special vests that detect their enemies' lasers. At the end of each round, contestants can not only see how many times they got shot, but also who shot them. It costs Dhs.80 per person for 20 minutes.

Paintballing

If you want to maintain a great work environment, why not take your office mates on a team building exercise? Paintballing is sure to improve, boost or destroy relations in the office. Find out if you're brave enough to smoke out the 'silent but deadly' types. Note of caution: It is advisable for the boss to wear extra padding.

WonderLand Theme & Water Park
Umm Hurair
Map 13 C1

Pursuit Games

04 324 4755 | www.paintballdubai.com

This is a fun game for teenagers and adults where bullets are replaced by paintballs. Club experts break groups up into two teams and give safety demonstrations before equipping participants with overalls, facemasks, special guns and paintballs. Costs start at Dhs.85 for a two-hour game, and include 100 paintballs and gear. Bookings are required.

Parasailing

Want an aerial view of the Palm Jumeirah but can't afford a helicopter? Then pop down to the beach for a spot of parasailing. The area around the Marina is the place to be – the Sheraton Jumeirah Beach (04 399 5533) has a watersports and activity centre, and Nautica 1992 (050 426 2415) operates from the Habtoor Grand. Summertime Marine Sports (04 331 1483) also offer flights from the open beach near Le Meridien Mina Seyahi. All use specially designed boats with winches and a launch pad on the back, meaning you no longer have to sprint down the beach (or get dragged through the sand) in order to get airborne – all very sensible. You can expect to pay around Dhs.250 for a 15 to 20 minute ride, or Dhs.350 for a tandem ride.

Photography

Gulf Photo Plus (www.gulfphotoplus.com) and UAE Photo (www.uae-photo.com) are web-based communities where local photography enthusiasts can exchange tips and ideas, post their pictures, and buy and sell equipment. Competitions, workshops, exhibitions and events are held at regular intervals throughout the year.

Polo

Other options **Horse Riding** p.362

Arabian Ranches
Map 3 B3

Dubai Polo & Equestrian Club

04 361 8111 | www.poloclubdubai.com

With two full-size pitches, this club at Arabian Ranches is a regular venue for both local and international polo events. A wide selection of polo coaching is offered, from beginner to advanced level, and ranging from 40 minute lessons to six-day courses. The club has over 300 stables and livery is available. Keep an eye on the website or call the club for details of forthcoming events.

Camel Polo

For a fun twist on the game, head to the Dubai Polo & Equestrian Club for a spot of camel polo. It might not be as fast-paced as the real thing, but you'll come away with plenty of stories. Any group of eight or more people is welcome to reserve a session. Call 04 404 5861 for reservations.

Sheikh Maktoum Rd
Abu Dhabi
Map 1 D2

Ghantoot Racing & Polo Club

02 562 9050 | www.grpcuae.com

With seven international standard polo fields (three of which are floodlit), two stick and ball fields, three tennis courts, a swimming pool, gym, sauna and restaurant, this club has first-class facilities for the entire family. They have 200 polo ponies which are supported by six fully equipped stables, five paddocks and an outdoor training ring. Non-members are welcome to dine at the restaurant or to watch polo matches that take place between October and April.

Quad Bikes

Other options **Motocross** p.373, **Dune Buggy Driving** p.348

Quad bikes are available to hire from a number of firms operating around the 'Big Red' sand dune on the Dubai-Hatta road; after a bit of haggling you should pay around Dhs.100 for half an hour. You won't necessarily be allowed out into the dunes unaccompanied as most have their own fenced-off area, but for an extra fee you may be given permission to tackle the big stuff on your own. Beware though – unlike dune buggies, quad bikes have no roll cages or seatbelts, so be careful hurtling over sand dunes when you've no idea what's on the other side.

Rollerblading & Rollerskating

Other options **Parks** p.280, **Beaches** p.279

Dubai's many parks provide some excellent locations for rollerblading. Creekside Park (p.281) and Safa Park (p.282) have wide pathways, few people and enough slopes and turns to make it interesting. Alternatively, check out both sides of Dubai Creek, the seafront near the Hyatt Regency Hotel or the promenades at the Jumeira Beach Corniche and in Deira along towards Al Mamzar Beach Park (p.279), where the views are an added bonus. Aggressive inline skaters can catch air and grind rails at both Rampworks (p.384) and the Springs Village skate park (p.384).

Rowing

Mina Seyahi Dubai
Al Sufouh
Map 5 B1

Dubai Rowing & Sculling Club (DRSC)
04 318 1804 | www.minaseyahidubai.com
The Dubai Rowing & Sculling Club was founded in 2005 at the Dubai Water Sports Association (DWSA) complex on the creek, but moved to Mina Seyahi Dubai when DWSA closed. The club has coxed fours and both double and single sculls, and also has two ergometers. Rowing usually takes place early morning, and other activities include regular regattas, indoor rowing competitions, coaching camps and social events.

Rugby

The Sevens
Dubai-Al Ain Rd
Nad Al Sheba
Map 2 C3

Dubai Exiles Rugby Club
050 459 8603 | www.dubaiexiles.com
The Exiles is Dubai's most serious rugby club and has become a bastion for the sport. The club has a 1st and 2nd XV team that competes in the AGRFU leagues, as well as veterans, U19s, ladies, girls U17s and a minis and youth section.
The Exiles also host the annual Dubai International Rugby 7s Tournament, which attracts international teams from all the major rugby playing nations. For further information on playing rugby call the club, or email enquiries@ dubaiexiles.com.

Exiled Exiles
2007 saw the last ever rugby game played on the Exiles ground in Al Awir. However, Exiles moved to their new grounds at The Sevens, a custom-built rugby stadium on the Al Ain Road, which was completed in time to host the 2008 Rugby 7s tournament.

The Sevens
Dubai-Al Ain Rd
Nad Al Sheba
Map 2 C3

Dubai Hurricanes
050 626 6107 | www.dubaihurricanes.com
Originally formed as a purely social outfit, Dubai Hurricanes now compete in the Dubai 7s tournament. The club sports a ladies' team and invites new players of all abilities to join their ranks. Training sessions are every Monday and Wednesday at 19:00. Contact 1st team captain, Chris Gregory for more details. The club is based at their new grounds on the Al Ain road.

Running

Other options **Hashing** p.360

For over half the year Dubai's weather is perfect for running and many groups and clubs meet up for runs on a regular basis. There are several major running events, usually held annually, such as the Round the Creek Relay Race, the Dubai Marathon, and the epic Wadi Bih Race. In the latter, each runner in a five-member team runs a portion of the 70km route between Ras Al Khaimah on the west coast to Dibba on the east. The terrain is arduous, featuring mountains that top out at over a

7s action

thousand metres (depending on the erratic rules at the border posts on the day itself). For more information on the Round the Creek Relay Race, contact John Harringon (050 645 0587) and for more information on the Wadi Bih Race, email John Young at jcyoung@eim.ae. The Dubai Marathon is usually run in January every year, and aside from the official marathon-distance run around the city of Dubai, there is also a 10km road race and a 3km charity run. For more information, or to register online, visit www.dubaimarathon.org.

Various Locations ◄

Dubai Creek Striders

04 321 1999 | *www.dubaicreekstriders.com*

This medium to long-distance running club organises weekly outings on Friday mornings. Distances and routes differ each week, but normally consist of 10km runs during the summer and 32km winter training runs that form part of the build up to the annual 42.2km Dubai Marathon. The club chairman, Malcolm Murphy, can be reached via the above number. Otherwise, check the website for details of the weekly training runs and forthcoming events.

Safa Park ◄
Al Wasl
Map 7 B2

Dubai Road Runners

050 624 3213 | *www.dubai-road-runners.com*

Come rain or shine, 100% humidity or 50°C temperatures, Dubai Road Runners meet every Saturday at 18:30 outside gate four of Safa Park. The object of the meeting is to run a 3.5km or 7km loop around the park. A Dhs.5 entrance fee is charged, and for an added bit of fun runners predict their times, with a prize being awarded to the winner. Additional runs and events are organised too – check the website for the full schedule.

Uptown School ◄
Mirdif
Map 15 B3

Mirdif Milers

050 652 4149 | *www.mirdifmilers.blogspot.com*

This friendly group meets for group training runs every Monday evening at 19:00 outside Uptown Primary School. It also organises various longer runs leading up to marathons and half marathons taking place in the region, and has an active social programme.

Various Locations ◄

Stride For Life

050 657 7057 | *www.strideforlife.com*

This is an aerobic walking and running programme designed to allow people of all abilities and fitness levels to take part in regular, enjoyable, safe exercise. After an initial one-on-one meeting to assess lifestyle and current fitness, an exercise programme is recommended and you then attend the group sessions that take place three times a week (Saturday, Monday and Wednesday) at various locations. Stride for Life also teaches Nordic walking, conducts mall walking programmes on behalf of several malls around Dubai, and puts together focused 'training journeys' for novices, in preparation for first time participation in long distance events (half and full marathons). At present these are either at the Lakes Club or Safa Park. Progress is tracked continuously, and members receive computerised feedback monthly, plus a follow up meeting every 12 weeks. The fees are very reasonable – if you join for a year it works out at about Dhs.10 per session or Dhs.1,600 for a one year membership.

Sailing

Other options **Boat Tours & Charters** p.284

Temperatures in winter are perfect for sailing, and taking to the sea in summer serves as an escape from the scorching heat. Membership in one of Dubai's sailing clubs allows you to participate in club activities and to rent sailing and watersports equipment. You can also use the leisure facilities and the club's beach, and moor your boat at an additional cost. There's a healthy racing scene for a variety of boat types, and long distance races such as the annual Dubai to Muscat race, held in March. The traditional dhow races are also an exciting spectacle. See Dhow Racing – Annual Events (p.74) for more details.

> ### Float Your Boat
>
> *Dubai Yachting & Boating* has advice on buying and mooring a boat, details of local marinas, local rules and regulations, handy maps, suggested cruising areas and a comprehensive contacts directory. With so much invaluable information, this is the ultimate resource for boaters old and new.

The Atrium Centre
Khalid Bin Waleed St
Bur Dubai
Map 8 F3

Bluesail Dubai
04 882 3129 | www.bluesailyachts.com
Bluesail are the most highly qualified Royal Yachting Association tidal sailing school in the Middle East, offering RYA power and tidal sail training for all levels of ability, from novice through to Yachtmaster. They have 42ft sail yachts and a new 21ft Yamaha powerboat, which are used for instruction. Bluesail's Fast 42 yachts are entered in the Middle East's racing calendar annually, so budding race crew are encouraged to apply for tuition. Each of the Bluesail instructors is RYA Yachtmaster Ocean qualified.

Behind Dubai
Marina Mall
Dubai Marina
Map 5 A2

Dubai Marina Yacht Club
04 362 7883 | www.dubaimarinayachtclub.com
There are currently over 200 births dotted throughout the Dubai Marina, and all of them are controlled by the Dubai Marina Yacht Club. Both members and non-members can charter the club's 43ft motor yacht. Sail boats can not use the births, in the Marina, however, because of the many bridges.

Umm Suqeim Beach
Umm Suqeim
Map 6 F1

Dubai Offshore Sailing Club
04 394 1669 | www.dosc.ae
DOSC is a Royal Yachting Association Training Centre, providing dinghy and keelboat courses throughout the year. Members can take advantage of marina moorings, storage, launch facilities, and sail training, alongside an active social calendar.

Mina Seyahi Dubai
Al Sufouh
Map 5 B1

Jebel Ali Sailing Club
04 399 5444 | www.jebelalisailingclub.com
This club is recognised by the RYA to teach and certify sailing and powerboat licences, and to instruct in kayaking. Races are held on most Fridays for toppers, lasers, catamarans and cruisers. Topper coaching takes place every Wednesday afternoon, while cadet club takes place on Thursdays. Annual club membership is available.

Salsa Dancing
Other options **Dance Classes** p.339, **Belly Dancing** p.332

Dubai Marine Beach
Resort & Spa
Jumeira
Map 7 F1

El Malecon
04 346 1111 | www.dxbmarine.com
Sunday night is salsa night at Malecon, with lessons available between 20:00 and 21:00 and costing Dhs.35 for one hour. If you're dining in the restaurant classes are free of charge, making this a cheap and enjoyable way to burn off the calories.

Various Locations

Salsa Dubai
050 848 7188 | www.salsanight.com
Salsa Dubai is fronted by Phil, who has 13 years experience in Cuban, New York and Spanish dance styles. Classes are tailored to the individual, so everyone can progress

at their own speed. Members also have the opportunity to learn the famous La Rueda Cuban dance. Nights out are organised at Latin venues to enjoy live bands. Call the above number or check the website for more details on classes and locations.

Capitol Hotel
Al Satwa
Map 8 B2

Savage Garden
04 346 0111 | www.capitol-hotel.com

Savage Garden is a Latin American restaurant and nightclub that sports a Latino band and food. You can also partake in salsa and merengue dance classes. Daily classes (except Sundays) are offered from 20:00 to 21:00 for beginners and 21:00 to 22:00 for intermediate and advanced dancers. Classes cost Dhs.40 per hour.

Sand Boarding & Skiing

Sandboarding is not as fast or smooth as snowboarding, but it can be a lot of fun. Head out into the desert in your 4WD, climb a big dune and feel the wind rush past you as you carve down the sandy slopes. Boards are usually standard snowboards. Some sports shops sell sandboards, but they are really nothing more than cheap, basic snowboards. As an alternative for children, a plastic sled or something similar is just as much fun. All major tour companies (p.294) offer sandboarding experiences, along with basic instructions, and will also provide 4WD taxi services back to the top. Sandboarding can be done as part of another tour or you can opt for a half day session, which costs between Dhs.175 and Dhs.200.

Scouts & Guides

The English College
Al Safa
Map 6 F3

1st Dubai Guides
050 286 7501

A member of British Guides in Foreign Countries, this guide group caters to girls aged 10 to 14. With more than 30 members from eight countries, these guides teach girls the importance of decision making and responsibility. They meet each Sunday from 17:30 to 19:30 to play games and sports and do community work and arts and crafts. They also do one overnight camping trip every school term. Membership costs Dh.150 each term. Contact Jain at the above number.

> **Scout Volunteers**
>
> Scouts and Guides groups are gaining popularity in Dubai and with each new group comes a need for adult volunteers. If you have experience with scout or guide groups, or you have a child that was once a member, call Mary Dunn (04 348 9849) or Dawn Tate (050 654 2180) to see how you can help out.

Various Locations

British Guides In Foreign Countries
04 348 9849 | www.bgifc.org.uk

Various groups for girls of different age ranges include Rainbows (5 to 7), Brownies (7 to 10), Guides (10 to 14), and Young Leaders and Rangers (14 to 26). For more information call Jane Henderson (04 340 8441) for the Jumeira packs, Liz Smith (04 395 4640) for the UAE Senior Section, or Mary Dunn (04 348 9849), the Dubai District Commissioner.

Various Locations

Scouts Association (British Groups Abroad)
050 654 2180 | www.scoutbase.org.uk

The Scout Association aims to encourage the development of youngsters through weekly activities and outings. The scout groups are broken up by age: Beavers (6 to 8), Cubs (8 to 10½), Scouts (10½ to 14), Explorer Scouts (14 to 18) and Scout Network (18 to 25). Activities for younger groups include games, badge activities, sports, competitions and outings. For general enquiries, the group contact is Dawn Tate.

Scrabble

Other options **Chess** p.336

Al Maskam Bld
Al Karama
Map 10 D1

Dubai Scrabble League

050 653 7992 | alicoabr@eim.ae

This club meets once a week for friendly games between players of all levels. Regular competitions are held, and players also attend competitions in Bahrain, Singapore and Bangkok. The UAE Open (held every year in March or April) is the qualifier for the Gulf Open held in Bahrain. For more information, contact Selwyn Lobo.

Scrapbooking

Various Locations

Creative Hands

04 348 6568 | www.dubaiscrapbookingshop.com

Primarily an online store based out of Dubai, the shop also offers workshops and cropping sessions at various locations around the city. At the time of writing, Creative Hands didn't have a physical location, although plans are in the works to set up a shop before 2010. The owner, Ms Annais, is very helpful and clearly enjoys the craft.

Umm Al Sheif St
Villa 2, Opp Spinneys
Umm Suqeim
Map 6 F2

Paper Lane

04 395 5337 | www.dubaiscrapbookstore.com

One of the city's biggest scrapbooking shops, Paper Lane carries all the materials you need to create a memorable album. Their massive inventory is constantly rotating and scrapbookers can check up on new arrivals on their blog, www.paperlane.blogspot.com. The experts at Paper Lane also host classes for every age group and skill level.

Times Square
Al Quoz
Map 6 C3

Paper@ARTE

www.arte.ae

Held on the second Friday of every month, Paper@ARTE is a part of the larger Arte Souk, held at the Times Square Center on Sheikh Zayed Road in Al Quoz. Scrapbookers of all ages and skill levels are welcome and the programme runs like a workshop with experienced teachers to help you along the way. Creative Hands (above) is present and brings along supplies for patrons to buy and use.

Shooting

Other options **Paintballing & Laser Games** p.377

Dubai-Hatta Rd
Hatta
Map 1 F2

Hatta Fort Hotel ▶ p.311

04 852 3211 | www.jebelali-international.com

Clay pigeon shooting is one of many activities offered by Hatta Fort Hotel, which is located just an hour's drive from Dubai. More frequently visited as an overnight retreat from the hustle and bustle of Dubai, the hotel also features a rock pool and Friday barbecue for guests or day visitors. See Hatta Fort Hotel (p.310) in Weekend Breaks for more information.

Nr Jebel Ali Golf
Resort & Spa
Jebel Ali
Map 2 A4

Jebel Ali Shooting Club

04 883 6555 | www.jebelali-international.com

The Jebel Ali Shooting Club has five floodlit clay shooting ranges that consist of skeet, trap and sporting. Professional shooting instructors give comprehensive lessons and experienced shooters are welcome to try their hand at clay shooting or archery. Members and non-members are welcome. Refreshments are available at Shooters restaurant (p.532) and corporate or group activities can be arranged.

Activities

Ras Al Khaimah Shooting Club

Al Duhaisa
Nr RAK Airport
Ras Al Khaimah
Map 1 F1

07 236 3622 | *rakshooting@rakshooting.com*

This club welcomes interested parties that want to learn how to shoot, whether it's shotguns or long rifles. The club boasts a 50m indoor and 200m outdoor rifle range, and has a canteen selling snacks and soft drinks. If you ring them you may want to have an Arabic speaker standing by. Otherwise, just drop by the next time you're in RAK.

Singing

Other options **Music Lessons** p.375

Dubai Harmony

Various Locations

seewhy@eim.ae

Barbershop-style singing varies greatly from other kinds of group singing. Finding the right part for your voice is the initial step, but any woman with average singing ability, with or without music or vocal training, will find a part that fits her vocal range. Dubai Harmony has 50 female members who get together for weekly rehearsals.

Dubai Singers & Orchestra

JESS
Al Safa
Map 7 A2

04 349 1896 | *www.dubaisingers.info*

This is a group of amateur musicians who meet regularly to create music in a variety of styles, including requiems, choral works, Christmas carols, musicals and variety shows. Membership is open to everyone and no auditions are required, except for solo parts. Membership fees are low and sheet music is provided. If you're interested in joining, send an email to dubaisingers@gmail.com.

Skateboarding

Rampworks Skate Park

Beh Dubai Garden Centre
Al Quoz
Map 6 B3

050 440 5857 | *chris@rampworks.com*

This is the Middle East's first air-conditioned indoor park for skateboarders and in-line skaters. Rates are Dhs.10 per hour from Saturdays to Tuesdays and Dhs.15 per hour from Wednesdays to Fridays including holidays. Membership is also available. Under 18s must get their parents to sign a liability waiver and helmets are mandatory. The park also has gaming facilities, a pool table and a chill-out lounge, and is open from 10:00 to midnight daily. For more info, call Chris on the above number.

Springs Village Skate Park

Springs 7
Emirates Hills
Map 4 E3

Thanks to Emaar's initiative to make their community a better place to live, future Tony Hawkes have been given a skate park nearer to home. Emirates Hills residents and 'Hayya! Club' members are able to enjoy this great facility for free. The skate park has four ramps of different sizes with obstacles and two half pipes. With a spot for non-skaters to enjoy the view, 20 skaters can give it their all, all at the same time. Guest charges are Dhs.15 during the weekend and Dhs.10 during the week. The skate park is open daily from 06:00 to 22:00.

Skiing & Snowboarding

Dubai Ski Club

Ski Dubai
MOE, Al Barsha
Map 6 A3

www.dubaiskiclub.com

To coincide with the opening of its first ski slope, Dubai got its very own ski club to go with it. The club now has over 1,400 members. Skiers and snowboarders meet at 18:00 every last Saturday of the month next to Ski Dubai's ticket counter for social skiing or

live it, love it
...log on

www.liveworkexplore.com

- Communities
- Updates
- Competitions
- Discounts
- Explorer expeditions
- Shop online

EXPLORER

snowboarding, race training and races, followed by apres ski. Membership benefits include a reduced fee for the slope pass and use of the 'advance booking' lane when purchasing tickets, plus regular special offers on equipment, clothing, accessories and holidays. Membership costs Dhs.300.

Ski Dubai

Mall of the Emirates
Al Barsha
Map 6 A3

Ski Dubai ▶ p.387

04 409 4000 | www.skidxb.com

When temperatures outside are melting your sunglasses, go sub-zero with a visit to Ski Dubai. The huge tube extending behind and above the Mall of the Emirates is home to five slopes to suit all skill levels, from gentle beginner slopes to the world's first indoor 'black' run. There's also a 90m long quarter pipe to get some serious air, and don't forget the largest indoor snow park in the world – perfect if you fancy a snowball fight in the middle of July. The slope has both chair lifts and tow lifts, and there's a well-stocked retail shop selling skis, boards, and clothing. Strict rules ensure only suitably skilled skiers and boarders can take to the slopes, but for those that don't make the grade, lessons are offered with qualified instructors.

Entrance to the Snow Park is Dhs.80 for adults and Dhs.75 for children. Prices for a two-hour Slope Pass start at Dhs.180 for adults and Dhs.150 for kids, and this includes all equipment and clothing (except gloves).

Skydiving

17km North of UAQ
on RAK Rd
Umm Al Quwain
Map 1 E1

Umm Al Quwain Aeroclub

06 768 1447 | www.uaqaeroclub.com

In addition to pilot training, helicopter flying, hangar and aircraft rental, paramotors and microlights, the club also operates as a skydive school and boogie centre. You can enjoy an eight level accelerated free fall parachute course including 10 AFF Jumps (Dhs.8,000) and train for your international parachute licence. Alternatively, try a tandem jump with an instructor from 12,000 feet for Dhs.1,000.

Snooker

Sana Building
Al Karama
Map 8 E4

Billiard Master

04 335 2008 | www.uaebilliard.com

Billiard Master has 18 billiard tables in spacious surroundings and two private snooker tables. The club organises annual inter-club leagues as well as international tournaments. They are also the official organiser of the Billiards Championships in Dubai. Other facilities include computer games and an internet cafe.

Nr Post Office
Al Karama
Map 10 F1

Dubai Snooker Club

04 337 5338 | www.dubaisnooker.com

The Dubai Snooker Club has 14 snooker tables and 13 pool tables, along with three private snooker rooms that can be rented by groups. Tables are rented out at Dhs.20 per hour, and the club organises five tournaments a year. The club is open to the public, with no membership required.

You'll never really leave

Whether it's skiing, snowboarding, tobogganing or just plain fun, you'll find it all at Ski Dubai. With over three-football fields of snow, Ski Dubai will leave a lasting impression. What won't be so easy is getting the experience out of your head.

SKI DUBAI

an unforgettable snow experience

Snorkelling

Other options **Diving** p.344

Snorkelling is a great way to see the varied marine life in the Arabian Gulf or on the east coast at popular places such as Snoopy Island, near Sandy Beach Hotel. Another good spot is the beach north of Dibba village where the coast is rocky and coral can be found close to the shore. Closer to home, the sea off Jumeira Beach has a fair amount of marine life. Most hotels or dive centres rent equipment (snorkel, mask and fins) but costs vary greatly so shop around. Check out the *UAE Underwater Explorer* for further information on where to go snorkelling in the UAE.

Beach Rd
Khor Fakkan
Map 1 F1

Oceanic Hotel

09 238 5111 | *www.oceanichotel.com*

The Oceanic Hotel, on the UAE's east coast, offers a boat ride out to Shark Island, or guests can snorkel and swim off the hotel beach. Equipment hire is Dhs.35 per hour for guests, and the boat trip is Dhs.35. Visitors are obliged to pay an entrance fee of Dhs.150 for adults (including lunch or dinner buffet, use of the beach and pool) and Dhs.75 for children. Snorkelling on Shark Island costs Dhs.70 per person (including the boat and equipment).

Al Aqah
Fujairah
Map 1 F1

Sandy Beach Hotel & Resort

09 244 5555 | *www.sandybm.com*

For those who want an exhilarating snorkelling experience, the Beach Hut at Sandy Beach is a good place to start. Snoopy Island, the house reef, is just off their private beach and is an excellent place to enjoy the underwater world. Equipment is available for sale, or you can rent an entire set for Dhs.30 per hour, or Dhs.60 for the day. Kayaks are also available for hire. Entry to the hotel costs Dhs.100 from Thursday to Saturday, and Dhs.75 for the rest of the week.

Al Badiyah Beach
East Coast
Dibba
Map 1 F1

Scuba 2000

09 238 8477 | *www.scuba-2000.com*

This east coast centre offers snorkelling from the beach or by boat ride to Snoopy Island, Shark Island or Al Badiyah Rock. Snorkelling trips to these destinations cost Dhs.170 and are inclusive of equipment, refreshments and the boat. The centre also has other watersports facilities, including diving, pedal boats and canoes.

Al Khail Rd
Al Barsha
Map 2 B3

Scuba Dubai

04 341 4940 | *www.scubadubai.com*

For those wishing to arrange their own diving and snorkelling trips, equipment can be rented from Scuba Dubai on a 24 hour basis, collecting one day and returning the next. Rates for Thursday, Friday and Saturday are the same as renting for one day because the shop is closed on Fridays. Note that original diving certification must be shown for all scuba equipment rentals. Scuba Dubai is open from 09:00 to 20:30 Saturday through Wednesday, 09:00 to 19:00 on Thursday and is closed Fridays.

Social Groups

Other options **Support Groups** p.202

With its cosmopolitan population, it's hardly surprising that Dubai has a large number of social and cultural groups for people from all walks of life. Some are linked to an embassy or business group, and can be an excellent way of meeting like-minded people or even for business networking. See the Business Councils & Groups table in Residents (p.100) for more details. If your particular interest or background is not covered, now is the perfect opportunity to fine tune your organisational skills and to start something new. The 'expat mum' population is also alive and well in Dubai with various Mother and Toddler groups (p.372), and check out www.expatwoman.com for more information.

Social Groups	
British Community Assistance Fund	04 337 1413
Club for Canadians	04 355 6171
Egyptian Club	04 336 6709
German Speaking Women's Club	050 459 1885
Indian Association	04 351 1082
Italian Cultural Association	050 558 2716
Norwegian Centre	04 337 0062

Various Locations ◀

American Women's Association Of Dubai
www.awadubai.org

The AWA is a volunteer group offering information programmes, social functions, common interest groups, and charitable activities while fostering fellowship among American women in Dubai. The organisation is open to women who are United States citizens, legal residents, or spouses of US citizens.

Various Locations ◀

The Bridgets
04 360 2826 | *www.thebridgets.com*

The Bridgets is a social group for single women in Dubai to meet and make like-minded friends. They currently have over 400 members of approximately 20 nationalities ranging in age from 21 to 65. The club was established a few years ago and organises various events such as a desert safari, cruise to the Musandam peninsula, belly dancing lessons, salsa classes and dinners at various restaurants. They also run a book club and have two events a month – a brunch and evening drinks. Women of all ages and nationalities are welcome and the club is open to suggestions from members for events and activities. For more information on becoming a member email the club or check out the website.

Various Locations ◀

Dubai Caledonian Society
050 552 3831 | *www.dubaicaledoniansociety.com*

The society provides a social focal point for Scottish expats in Dubai as well as raising money for Scottish and local charities. There are four main events every year – the St Andrew's Ball in November, the Burns Supper in January, The Chieftain's Ball in May, and the Welcome Back Ceilidh in September. Every first Sunday of the month the committee and members meet in the St Andrew's Snug in Rydges Plaza. Anyone can join, even non-Scots.

Various Locations ◀

Dubai Irish Society
www.irishindubai.com

Dubai Irish Society has been in existence for over 30 years and aims to promote Irish culture, social events and sporting interests to its members and to a wider public. DIS organises events such as the St Patrick's Day Ball, Rose Ball and other social and cultural events as per members' requests. The website has more details, and those interested in membership can email keith@dubaiirishsociety.com.

Various Locations

Dubai Manx Society

04 394 3185 | www.dubaimanxsociety.com

The Dubai Manx Society is a non-profit making social and cultural organisation, dedicated to bringing the traditions of the Isle of Man to Dubai. Originally formed in 1911, the international society now has branches all over the world. The website has details of forthcoming events and membership.

Al Futtaim Training
Centre
Al Rashidiya
Map 13 E2

Dubai Toastmasters Club

050 47 4083 | www.dubaitoastmasters.org

Toastmasters is a worldwide, non-profit organisation which offers its members opportunities to hone their public speaking, leadership, creative thinking, evaluation and effective listening skills. The club provides a supportive and positive learning environment that fosters self-confidence and personal growth. They meet on the first and last Monday of every month from 19:00 to 21:30. Contact V.P. Menon for more details.

Mugg & Bean
Uptown Mirdif
Mirdif
Map 15 C2

Matinee Girls – The Evening Club

www.matineegirlsclub.blogspot.com

Ideal for women in the Mirdif, Warqa, Al Mizhar and Garhoud area, this group meets monthly at the Uptown Mirdif Mugg & Bean. It's a purely social group and is geared towards both professional and stay-at-home women who need a break from the daily routine. Potential members can join the group through the website.

Softball

Metropolitan
Downtown Burj Dubai
Map 7 B3

Dubai Softball League

050 651 4970 | www.dubaisoftballleague.com

The Dubai Softball League runs from September to December, and from January to May, and the only criteria is that you are over 16 years of age. Dubai usually hosts the biannual Middle East Softball Championships, held in November and April. It attracts 30 teams with over 500 players from around the Gulf. Entrance is free and food and beverages are available. Membership costs Dhs.100 per player per season. Check the website for team and fixture details.

Speedboating

Other options **Boat Tours & Charters** p.284

The Atrium Centre
Khalid Bin Waleed St
Bur Dubai
Map 8 F3

Bluesail Dubai

04 882 3129 | www.bluesailyachts.com

You and up to four friends can experience a thrilling two-hour ride aboard either a 21ft, 200hp or 34ft, 450hp speedboat. The Bluesail skipper will even give you the wheel following a safety and tactics briefing. A short leisurely trip down the creek is followed by a high-octane blast out into the Gulf. All vessels are fully insured and equipped with the required safety equipment.

Umm Suqeim
Fishing Marina 2
Umm Suqeim
Map 6 B1

Dream Explorer ▶ p.297

04 331 9880 | www.dreamexplorerdubai.com

Dream Explorer is the first tour operator in Dubai to offer Jetboating. Instead of using the traditional propeller, the jetboat uses a propulsion system similar to that of a jet ski, allowing it to make nimble manoeuvres including fish tails and 270° spins. Jetboat rides last 30 minutes and leave every hour from the marina to the right of the Burj al Arab.

Sports & Activities

Squash
Other options **Sports & Leisure Facilities** p.396

Various Locations

Dubai Squash League
04 343 5672 | www.dubaisquash.org

The squash league has been active in Dubai and Sharjah since the 1970s and is run by the UAE Squash Rackets Association. About 300 competitors play three 10 week seasons at over 30 clubs. The league meets every Monday evening and each team fields four players. Contact Shavan Kumar (04 343 5672), Chris Wind (050 688 7421) or Andy Staines (04 339 1331) for more details.

Summer Camps & Courses
With more and more kids in Dubai during the summer holidays, many hotels, clubs and organisations have added summer camps and activities to their annual schedule. Most language schools run summer courses for kids (see Language Schools, p.366), if you want your kids to put their time off to good use. If you'd rather see them having fun over the holidays, many leisure clubs offer summer camps that focus on sports, arts and crafts, so if you have a leisure club in your area, contact them to see what they have on offer. Alternatively, contact Active Sports (www.activeuae.com), as they arrange sporty summer camps at various venues around the city.

Surfing
Other options **Kitesurfing** p.366, **Beaches** p.279

Surfin' UAE

Scott Chambers offers surfing lessons off Jumeira Beach near the Burj Al Arab. Times and dates depend on the conditions. You can hire a board if you don't have your own. Call 050 504 3020 or email scott@surfingdubai.com.

Dubai is a reasonably good surfing location, and there is a dedicated group of surfers keeping their eye on the weather and tides from November to June. Swells are on the small side, but every now and again bigger waves hit the coast. Check out www.surfersofdubai.com for information on locations, current conditions, where to buy boards and where to meet up with fellow surfers. A popular destination is Oman (especially Masirah Island), where the open ocean and conditions make for more exciting swells.

Swimming
Other options **Sports & Leisure Facilities** p.396, **Beaches** p.279

Dubai has some great swimming spots, whether it's at a public beach, beach club or one of the beach parks. The water is relatively clean with pleasant temperatures most of the year, although during the summer it can feel like stepping into a bath. Be warned that rip tides and undertows can catch out even the strongest swimmer, so be especially careful and never ignore flags or signs ordering you not to swim. You might also run into jellyfish around the end of the summer. If you don't fancy roughing it on the beach, many hotels and clubs have swimming pools that are open for public use for a day entrance fee. Swimming lessons are widely available from health and beach clubs. For children's lessons, check with your school whether they offer any extra-curricular swimming coaching.

Swimming Lessons
Active Sports Academy	050 559 7055	www.activeuae.com
DubaiSwim	050 282 2819	www.dubaiswim.com
Excel Sports	050 748 5631	www.excelsportsuae.com
Speedo Swim Squads	04 394 4898	www.speedodubai.net
Supersports Dubai	04 399 4826	www.supersportsdubai.com

Table Tennis

Other options **Sports & Leisure Facilities** p.396

Table tennis can be played for Dhs.20 per hour, including equipment, at Insportz (04 347 5833) just off Sheikh Zayed Road behind Dubai Garden Centre (booking is required). Several of the old leisure clubs also provide table tennis, although the equipment is usually a bit rusty. There is a UAE Table Tennis Association based in Dubai (04 266 9362), which can provide some information on how to get into leagues and high level competitions, but unfortunately most of the local clubs only accept UAE Nationals.

Tennis

Other options **Sports & Leisure Facilities** p.396

Dubai is firmly established on the international tennis circuit, with the annual $1,000,000 Dubai Tennis Championships attracting the best players in the world (p.72). There are plenty of venues around the city to enjoy a game. Outdoor courts are available at most health and beach clubs, many of which are floodlit. There are also indoor courts for hire at InSportz (04 347 5833).

Atlantis The Palm
Palm Jumeirah
Map 2 A3

The Atlantis Tennis Academy ▶ p.275

04 426 0000 | www.atlantisthepalm.com

The Atlantis Tennis Academy offers some of the best facilities and training in Dubai. The world class professional coaching team leads a full range of programmes for children, teenagers and adults at all levels. The excellent facilities include state-of-the-art court surfaces and video technology for technique analysis, helping you to perfect your killer shot. The academy also organises social events such as tournament afternoons, so you can put your fine-tuned skills into action. Email tennisacademy@atlantisthepalm.com for more information.

Nr Tennis Stadium
Al Garhoud
Map 13 E1

The Aviation Club

04 282 4540 | www.aviationclub.ae

The Clark Francis Tennis Academy at The Aviation Club offers a variety of lessons and activities for all ages and abilities. A 15 week coaching course costs Dhs.800 as part of a group, or Dhs.1,400 for individual coaching. The club boasts a range of modern facilities, including eight floodlit Decoturf tennis courts. It also hosts the Aviation Cup and the annual Dubai Tennis Championships.

American University in Dubai
Al Sufouh
Map 5 C2

Dubai Tennis Academy

04 344 4674 | www.dubaitennisacademy.com

The Academy offers world class training with experienced internationally qualified coaches all year round, for tennis players of all ages and abilities. The Academy's full time adult and junior programmes include private lessons, group clinics, competitions, ladies' tennis mornings and school holiday sports camps. A personal progress report and video analysis are also available.

Int 5, Shk Zayed Rd
Emirates Hills
Map 5 C2

Emirates Golf Club

04 380 2222 | www.dubaigolf.com

The Emirates Tennis Academy is open to members and non-members, and offers coaching for all ages and skill levels. The centre has four courts, and coaching is provided by qualified USPTR professionals. The academy also has two teams in the ladies' Spinneys League and one in the men's Prince League.

Sports & Activities

Thai Boxing

Other options **Martial Arts** p.371

Montana Centre
Za'abeel Rd
Al Karama
Map 10 F1

Colosseum

04 337 2755 | www.colosseumuae.com

This health and fitness club was the first to introduce the martial art of Muay Thai (Thai boxing) to the UAE. Classes are held daily, with personal training sessions also available for children over the age of 8. The price per lesson is Dhs.40, but slightly less if you sign up for lessons in advance. Personal classes are Dhs.200 per session. Colosseum also organises competitions between different clubs in the area.

Water fun

Triathlon

Various Locations

Dubai Triathlon Club

050 774 6581 | www.dubaitriclub.net

During the winter season (October to April), the Dubai Triathlon Club organises the Dubai Triathlon Series that comprises three or four triathlons, aquathons or duathlons. Membership is not required, but all interested participants are invited to register via email.

Wakeboarding & Waterskiing

Nr Yacht Club
Umm Al Quwain
Map 1 E1

Dubai Water Sports Association

050 492 7445 | www.dwsa.net

Though no longer located at the creek, the DWSA still provides wakeboarding and waterskiing lessons out of their new home in Umm Al Quwain. A 15 minute lesson costs Dhs.100 and those interested can contact Henri at the above number.

Watersports

Jebel Ali Golf Resort & Spa
Jebel Ali
Map 3 A1

Club Joumana ▶ p.533

04 804 8058 | www.jebelali-international.com

Operating from the Aqua Hut on Jebel Ali Golf Resort and Spa's private beach, the club offers watersports including windsurfing, waterskiing, kayaking, catamaran and laser sailing, and banana boat rides. Special rates are available for guests and club members. Non-residents are charged an additional fee for access to the beach and pools.

39a Road
Off Jumeirah Rd
Jumeira
Map 6 D1

Dubai Surfski & Kayak Club

050 550 3771 | www.dskc.net

Those with a penchant for a paddle can take full advantage of the Dubai Surfski and Kayak Club's range of activities for all levels of ability. The club has a paddling school that offers training for surf ski or kayak beginners. For the more advanced, there are individual private coaching sessions. The focus of the sessions is to develop fitness and technique while encouraging safety, with sessions on the Kite Beach at the Dubai Surfski and Kayak club. The club itself runs a range of activities and challenges, including the DSKC Squall which takes place on the last Friday of every month at the Mina Seyahi and involves a 10km course along the Palm, finishing at Bussola Beach.

Racing at the Autodrome

Spectator Sports

Dubai has been expanding its repertoire of sporting events on two fronts. In an effort to retain a sense of culture in an increasingly international city, the UAE government has made clear efforts to promote traditional sports. The best example of this can be found in the Friday camel races held throughout the country. On the other front, Dubai has steadily been promoting huge international events with massive prizes that not only satisfy the local population, but draw sporting enthusiasts from around the world.

Camel Racing

This is a chance to see a truly traditional local sport up close. Apart from great photo opportunities and the excitement of the races, you can also have a browse around the shops; most race tracks have camel markets alongside (they are dark and dusty but should not be missed). The best buys are the large cotton blankets (used as camel blankets), which make excellent bedspreads, throws and picnic blankets, and only cost around Dhs.40. It is also interesting to see the old traders sitting on the floor of their shop, hand weaving camel halters and lead-ropes.

Races take place during the winter months, usually on Thursday and Friday mornings, at tracks in Dubai, Ras Al Khaimah, Umm Al Quwain, Al Ain and Abu Dhabi. Often, additional races are held on National Day and certain other public holidays. Races start early (about 07:30) and are usually over by 08:30. Admission is free.

Ras Al Khaimah has one of the best racetracks in the country at Digdagga, situated on a plain between the dunes and the mountains, about 10km south of the town.

The camel racetrack in Dubai used to be near Nad Al Sheba, but it has now been moved to make way for the Meydan development. To find the new location (it's always a good place to take visitors), head up the Al Ain Road, past the Dubai Outlet Mall, until you reach the Al Lisali exit. Turn right off this exit and you will see the big track on your right. Races are usually early on a Friday morning, but you should see plenty of camels being exercised throughout the day in the cooler months.

Robotic Jockeys

The law now prevents children from riding camels in races. In their place robotic jockeys have been tried and tested. The operators follow the race in 4WD while directing the jockeys by remote control.

Golf

Dubai Desert Classic

04 380 2112 | www.dubaidesertclassic.com

One of the highlights of the Dubai sporting calendar, this European PGA Tour event at the end of January and start of February is popular among both players and spectators. Tiger Woods won the 2006 competition with Henrik Stenson taking the title off him in 2007, only for Woods to regain his crown in 2008. Tickets for the event at Emirates Golf Club sell out fast, so check the website regularly for details.

Emirates Golf Club
Emirates Hills
Map 5 C2

Horse Racing

Dubai Racing Club

04 327 0077 | www.dubairacingclub.com

A visit to Dubai during the winter months is not complete without experiencing a race night at Nad al Sheba. This racecourse is one of the world's leading racing facilities,

Nad Al Sheba
Racecourse
Nad Al Sheba
Map 16 A3

with top jockeys from Australia, Europe and the USA regularly competing throughout the season (October – April). Racing takes place at night under floodlights and there are usually six to seven races each evening. The start time is 19:00 (except during Ramadan when it is 21:00). The clubhouse charges day membership on race nights; prices change, so check the Nad al Sheba's website for details. Everyone can take part in various free competitions to select the winning horses, with the ultimate aim of taking home prizes or cash. Hospitality suites, with catering organised on request, can be hired by companies or private individuals. The dress code for the public enclosures is casual, while racegoers are encouraged to dress smart-casual in the clubhouse and private viewing boxes. General admission and parking are free and the public has access to most areas with a reserved area for badge holders and members. Nad al Sheba also plays host to the world's richest horse race, the Dubai World Cup, every March (see p.73).

Nad Al Sheba is approximately 5km south-east of Dubai, signposted from Sheikh Zayed Road at the Metropolitan Hotel junction and then from the roundabout close to the Dubai Polo Club and Country Club. You can also catch a slightly more raw form of horse racing at Jebel Ali racecourse, near the Greens, every other Friday afternoon during the season.

Motorsports

Emirates Rd
Nr Arabian Ranches
Dubailand
Map 2 C3

Dubai Autodrome

04 367 8700 | www.dubaiautodrome.com

Dubai Autodrome is a purpose-built motorsports facility that stages a number of large motorsports events throughout the year, as well as smaller meets on a more regular basis. It hosts the annual Dubai Motorsports Festival, as well as Grand Racing, a family-oriented day of thrilling track events. Check the events calendar on their website for more information.

Rugby

The Sevens
Dubai-Al Ain Rd
Al Awir
Map 2 C3

Dubai Rugby 7s

04 321 0008 | www.dubairugby7s.com

One of the biggest events in the UAE, sport or non-sport related, the Dubai Rugby 7s never fails to attract massive crowds. The two-day event is the first stop in the IRB Sevens World series and plays host to the top 16 sevens teams in the world. The first day of the event sees regional teams go head to head while the second day lets the big boys take the pitch. Compared to 15-a-side rugby, sevens often proves more exciting for fans due to its fast pace and high scores. Tickets regularly sell out weeks in advance so make sure you plan early. The tournament is held at the new rugby grounds called 'The Sevens' near Silicon Oasis on the Al Ain Road.

Tennis

Dubai Tennis Stadium
Al Garhoud
Map 13 E1

Dubai Tennis Open

04 282 4122 | www.dubaitennischampionships.com

The Dubai Duty Free Tennis Open takes place every February at the Aviation Club in Garhoud, and is a great opportunity to catch some of the top players in the game at close quarters. The $1,000,000 event is firmly established on the international tennis calendar, and features both men's and ladies' tournaments. Tickets for the later stages sell out in advance so keep an eye out for sale details, although entrance to some of the earlier rounds can be bought on the day.

Sports & Leisure Facilities

Wherever you are in Dubai, there is a wide variety of sport and leisure facilities available. As well as health clubs in hotels, there are many local neighbourhood gyms, often filled with serious workout fanatics. While facilities tend to be mixed, prices are generally a fraction of health club membership fees. Depending on the gym, its size, location and facilities you may find that the annual membership is at least half that of the beach clubs. Sports clubs, however, are more geared to the hard work involved with getting in shape whereas beach clubs have a little luxury thrown in for good measure. Refer to the Beach Clubs and Health Clubs table on p.398 for full details of various clubs in Dubai, including their membership rates and amenities offered.

Beach Clubs

Other options **Beaches** p.279

Beach clubs are very popular with families on weekends, and you can swim, play sports or just lounge in the sun in a peaceful environment. Most include some excellent food and beverage outlets, so people tend to stay for the day. Generally beach clubs require you to be a member before you can use their facilities, although many also have day guest rates. Day rates sometimes include lunch, which often is a buffet so that you can get your money's worth by stuffing your face. For listings of rates and facilities of Dubai's beach clubs, see the Club Membership Rates & Facilities Table (p.398).

Gyms

Boulevard at
Emirates Towers
Trade Centre 2
Map 7 F3

The Big Apple

04 319 8660 | www.jumeirahemiratestowers.com

Located in the Emirates Towers, Big Apple caters to professionals that work in the DIFC. Both single and couple's memberships are available for one, three and six months or one year. Prices range from Dhs.6,390 for a yearly couple's membership to Dhs.585 for a one month single membership. Classes are available, but cost extra. Non-members can also join the classes for a slightly higher fee. The gym's equipment is all branded and there are plenty of cardio machines, so waiting is rarely a problem.

Towers Rotana
Trade Centre
Map 7 E3

Bodylines Leisure & Fitness Club

04 343 8000 | www.rotana.com

Located in Rotana hotels throughout the city, Bodylines provides its clients with an upscale workout environment that caters more towards older adults. Each gym has a full set of branded cardio equipment as well as free weights and weight machines. Fitness classes are available, as are personal trainers.

Various Locations

Fitness First ▶ p.397

04 363 7444 | www.fitnessfirst.ae

With eight branches located across the city, Fitness First is quickly taking over the Dubai health club scene. Compared to other health clubs of the same caliber, the memberships here are less expensive. All of the branches are large and some have pools. Several types of classes are offered at no extra fee for members. Most of the locations tend to get crowded after work and on the weekends, so if you don't like the 'social gym' atmosphere, you might want to look elsewhere. Promotions are common, so check the website for your nearest branch and current deal. Locations include: Ibn Battuta Mall (04 366 9933), Uptown Mirdiff (04 288 2311), Burjuman Centre (04 351 0044), Dubai Festival City (04 375 0177), Al Mussalla Towers (04 397 4117), Al Hana Centre (Ladies Gym, 04 398 1866; Mixed, 04 398 9030), Dubai Media City (04 424 3999) and DIFC (04 363 7444).

FitnessFirst

Looking for a healthier lifestyle?
Join the club

Impressive Clubs in the Middle East offering:

→ State of the art Exercise Machines by Technogym

→ Cardio Theatre throughout the Club

→ Extensive Free Weights Area

→ FREE Group Exercise Classes consisting of RPM®, BODYPUMP®, BODYATTACK®, BODYCOMBAT®, BODYBALANCE®, BODYJAM®, BODYSTEP®, Yoga, Pilates and more...

→ 1:1 Personal Training by World Class Fitness Professionals

→ Member's Lounge with complimentary drinks, free DVD's and wireless internet access

World's No.1 Health Club Chain

Watch out for upcoming Fitness First Clubs across the Middle East

Call 800-FITNESS

YES! WE CARE

Fitness First in the Middle East - U.A.E. - Dubai: Ibn Battuta Mall 04 3669933 • UPTOWN Mirdiff 04 2882311 • BurJuman Centre 04 3510044 • Dubai International Financial Centre 04 3637444 • Dubai Festival City 04 3750177 • Al Mussalla Towers 04 3974117 • Al Hana Centre 04 3989030 • Dubai Media City (Platinum) 04 4243999
LEBANON: Downtown Beirut +961 1 999901/2 • Taj Tower Hamra +961 1 751666
JORDAN: Mecca Mall (+962) 6 5863046 • Abdoun (Platinum) (+962) 6 5863046
BAHRAIN: Bahrain World Trade Centre (+973) 13322200

www.fitnessfirst.com

Fitness First, UAE is a franchise owned and operated under license by Awwal Fitness Limited

Club Membership Rates & Facilities

DUBAI

Beach Clubs	Location	Area	Map Ref	Phone
Club Joumana	Jebel Ali Golf Resort & Spa	Jebel Ali	3 A1	883 6000
Club Mina	Le Meridien Mina Seyahi Beach Resort	Al Sufouh	5 C1	399 3333
Dubai Marine Beach Resort & Spa	Off Jumeirah Rd, beh Palm Strip	Jumeirah	7 F1	346 1111
Elixir Spa & Health Club	Habtoor Grand Resort & Spa	Dubai Marina	5 B1	399 5000
Pavilion Marina & Sports Club	Jumeirah Beach Hotel	Umm Suqeim	6 B1	406 8800
Ritz-Carlton Beach & Health Club	Ritz-Carlton, Dubai	Dubai Marina	5 A1	399 4000

Health Clubs	Location	Area	Map Ref	Phone
Al Nasr Fitness Centre	Al Nasr Leisureland	Oud Metha	10 E2	337 1234
Assawan Health Club	Burj Al Arab	Umm Suqeim	6 B1	301 7777
Aviation Club	Nr Tennis Stadium	Al Garhoud	13 E1	282 4122
Taj Health Club	Taj Palace Hotel	Deira	11 C1	223 2222
Big Apple	Boulevard at Emirates Towers	Trade Centre 2	7 F3	330 0000
Body Connection Health Club	Rydges Plaza Hotel	Al Satwa	8 A3	398 2222
Bodylines Jumeira	Jumeirah Rotana	Al Satwa	8 A2	345 5888
Bodylines Leisure & Fitness Club	Towers Rotana Hotel	Trade Centre 1	7 E3	343 8000
Bodylines Leisure & Fitness Club	Al Bustan Rotana Hotel	Al Garhoud	13 E1	705 4571
Club Olympus Fitness & Spa	Hyatt Regency Hotel	Deira	9 D1	209 6802
The Club	Dubai World Trade Centre Apartments	Trade Centre 2	7 F3	306 5050
Colosseum Muay Thai Health Club	Montana Centre Bld, Za'abeel Rd	Al Karama	10 F1	337 2755
The Creek Health Club	Sheraton Dubai Creek Hotel & Towers	Creekside, Deira	9 B4	207 1711
Dimension Health & Fitness Centre	Metropolitan Hotel	Downtown Burj	7 B3	407 6704
Creek's Gym	Dubai Creek Golf & Yacht Club	Al Garhoud	11 C3	205 4567
Fitness First ▶ p.397	Various Locations	Dubai	na	363 7444
Fitness Planet	Atrium Apartments Bld	Hor Al Anz	12 A3	269 9773
Griffins Health Club	JW Marriott Hotel	Deira	11E1	607 7755
Hayya!	Various Locations	Dubai	na	362 7790
The Health Club	Emirates Towers Hotel	Trade Centre 2	7 F3	330 0000
Hiltonia Health & Beach Club	Hilton Dubai Jumeirah	Dubai Marina	5 A1	399 1111
Inter-Fitness Dubai	Radisson SAS Hotel, Dubai Deira Creek	Creekside, Deira	9 C3	222 7171
Lifestyle Health Club	Sofitel City Centre Hotel	Deira	11 C3	603 8825
Natural Elements Spa & Fitness	Le Meridien Dubai	Al Garhoud	13 E1	702 2430
Nautilus Health Centre	Metropolitan Palace Hotel	Deira	11 C2	227 0000
Pharaohs' Club	Pyramids, Wafi City	Umm Hurair	10 E4	324 0000
The Quay Healthclub	Madinat Jumeirah	Umm Suqeim	6 A1	366 8888
u Concept	The Village Mall	Jumeirah	7 F1	344 9060
Willow Stream Spa & Health Club	Fairmont Dubai	Trade Centre 1	8 A4	311 8800

Club Membership Rates & Facilities

Membership Rates				Gym							Activity				Relaxation				
Male	Female	Couple	Family	Day Pass	Treadmills	Exercise bikes	Step machines	Rowing machines	Free weights	Resistance machines	Tennis courts	Swimming pool	Squash courts	Aerobics/Dance Exercise	Massage	Sauna	Jacuzzi	Plunge pool	Steam Room
14500	14500	21000	26000	300	1	1	1	1	✓	✓	4FL	✓	2	–	✓	✓	✓	–	✓
35000	35000	55000	55000	250	10	4	1	2	✓	18	4FL	✓	–	✓	✓	✓	✓	✓	✓
14000	14000	17000	19800	300	5	5	2	1	✓	13	2FL	✓	4	✓	✓	✓	✓	✓	✓
30000	30000	50000	70000	225	8	3	2	2	✓	25	2FL	✓	2	✓	✓	✓	✓	✓	✓
40500	40500	60750	87750	500	9	8	2	3	✓	23	7FL	✓	3	✓	✓	✓	✓	✓	✓
40000	40000	55000	85000	–	3	6	3	2	✓	10	4FL	✓	2	✓	✓	✓	✓	✓	✓
3500	3500	5000	6000	–	4	5	–	–	✓	✓	4	✓	✓	–	–	✓	–	–	–
35000	35000	50000	65000	300	5	8	3	2	✓	15	–	✓	1	✓	✓	✓	✓	✓	✓
8750	7750	11250	12000	250	9	5	3	3	✓	16	6FL	✓	2	✓	✓	✓	✓	✓	✓
5000	5000	8125	10125	150	5	3	1	1	✓	7	–	✓	–	✓	✓	✓	✓	✓	✓
3885	3885	6390	–	55	8	3	4	2	✓	11	–	✓	–	✓	–	–	–	–	✓
2500	2500	3800	4000	–	2	2	2	2	✓	9	–	✓	–	–	✓	✓	✓	✓	✓
2500	2500	3500	4000	125	1	1	–	–	✓	2	–	✓	–	✓	–	✓	–	✓	–
3000	3000	4700	5700	65	3	1	2	2	✓	9	–	✓	–	✓	✓	✓	✓	✓	✓
4500	3600	5700	6700	120	6	6	2	2	✓	9	3	✓	2	✓	✓	✓	✓	✓	✓
4500	4500	7000	–	150	8	4	2	2	✓	10	3	✓	2	✓	✓	✓	✓	✓	✓
5050	4150	7800	9300	90	6	3	2	2	✓	12	4FL	✓	3	✓	–	✓	✓	✓	✓
2400	2400	3800	–	50	5	3	–	2	✓	10	–	✓	–	–	✓	✓	✓	✓	✓
3600	3600	5300	6800	–	2	2	2	–	✓	1	1	✓	–	–	✓	✓	✓	–	✓
2800	2500	4000	4000	75	6	4	2	2	✓	19	1	✓	–	✓	✓	✓	✓	✓	✓
4800	4800	7200	–	70	6	5	3	3	✓	✓	–	✓	–	–	✓	–	–	–	✓
Various Rates, Depends on Package				100	40	20	25	3	✓	30	–	✓		✓		✓			✓
3390	3390	–	–	40	10	9	2	2	✓	36	–	–	–	✓	✓	✓	✓	–	✓
3575	2530	5060	–	99	7	6	4	2	✓	✓	–	✓	2	✓	✓	✓	✓	✓	✓
4500	4500	6750	9000	45	8	4	8	2	✓	8	4FL	✓	2	✓	–	✓	✓	–	✓
7390	7390	9880	–	120	8	3	2	2	✓	11	–	✓	–	–	✓	✓	✓	✓	✓
10500*	10500*	15750*	18750*	250	4	2	2	2	✓	2	–	✓	–	–	✓	✓	–	–	✓
3850	2825	5600	–	100	5	4	2	2	✓	10	1FL	✓	2	✓	✓	✓	✓	✓	✓
4000	3200	6000	–	90	8	6	2	1	✓	14	1FL	✓	2	✓	✓	✓	✓	✓	✓
9550	9550	16000	24000	250	3	4	1	2	✓	15	–	✓	2	✓	✓	✓	✓	✓	✓
4000	3500	6000	6000	70	10	4	2	3	✓	22	3FL	✓	2	✓	✓	✓	✓	✓	✓
6600	6600	9600	12000	130	7	8	4	2	✓	18	3	✓	2	✓	✓	✓	✓	✓	✓
16000	16000	20000	–	–	9	8	3	3	✓	12	5FL	✓	✓	✓	–	✓	–	–	✓
Per Session 300 – 350			–	–	2	2	–	1	✓	5	–	–	–	–	✓	–	–	–	–
7000	7000	12000	–	200	5	4	2	2	✓	13	–	✓	–	✓	✓	✓	✓	✓	✓

* Half-yearly membership

Family membership is based on parents+2 children

Town Centre ◀
Emirates Hills
Map 4 F4

Hayya!

04 362 7775 | *www.hayya.ae*

Membership at a Hayya! health club used to be reserved for residents of the Emirates Hills, the Springs, the Lakes or the Meadows. The family-oriented health club has recently opened its doors to anyone. There are four branches located in the Springs, the Meadows, the Lakes and one in Old Town. Each branch has a pool and workout area, and some include restaurants, cafes and children's pools. The clubs frequently offer promotions for couples and families.

Sports Clubs

Other options **Beach Clubs** p.396

Most of the following clubs offer a range of sporting activities, and feature a variety of facilities like swimming pools, tennis and squash courts, and golf courses. Many also have workout facilities. For details of individual sports refer directly to listings in this section of the guide.

Cnr Street 17 ◀
Beh Garden Ctr
Al Quoz
Map 6 B3

Chevrolet Insportz Club

04 347 5833 | *www.insportzclub.com*

Insportz is Dubai's first indoor sports centre and features five multi-purpose courts, a cricket coaching net and cafeteria, all within the comfort of air-conditioned surroundings. Sports available include table tennis, cricket, football, basketball and hockey, and prices (inclusive of equipment) start from Dhs.30 for children and Dhs.40 for adults. There's also a complete coaching programme for juniors. The club can also be booked for functions such as a kids' party or a corporate get-together with a difference.

Nxt to Indian ◀
High School
Oud Metha
Map 10 E2

India Club

04 337 1112 | *www.indiaclubdubai.com*

Opened in 1964, this club currently has 6,500 members and seeks to provide facilities for sports, entertainment and recreation, and to promote business. Facilities include a gym, separate steam rooms and saunas for men and women, badminton, squash and tennis courts, table tennis, basketball hoops, a swimming pool and a variety of indoor games.

Nr Sharjah ◀
English School
Sharjah
Map 2 C2

Sharjah Wanderers Sports Club

06 566 2105 | *www.sharjahwanderers.com*

This is a popular club supported by the expat community in Sharjah, Dubai and the Northern Emirates. Facilities include floodlit tennis courts, football, rugby and hockey fields, squash courts, swimming pool, gym, library, snooker, darts, aerobic classes, yoga, dancing for kids, netball and a kids' play area. Memberships are available and this is one of the only places in Sharjah were people can enjoy a post workout drink.

Nr Grand City Mall ◀
Al Quoz
Map 2 B3

Top Sport

04 340 7688 | *topsport@eim.ae*

Best known for its boxing gym, this surprisingly clean club in Al Quoz has a five-a-side football pitch, basketball course, weight room and indoor tennis courts. Memberships are available and cost Dhs.1,250 for six months, and members have free access to all of the facilities. Non-members can also use the facilities but need to book at least one week in advance.

Well-Being

Whether it's a pampering session at a health spa, receiving meditation guidance from a guru, or a limbering body massage: whatever your definition of well-being there's a good chance that someone, somewhere in Dubai will have the necessary facilities and skills to have you feeling and looking better in no time.

Mobile Beauty

If you dread the thought of sitting in a beauty salon, there are quite a few mobile hairdressers that will come to your house. It's best to get a recommendation from a friend, but here are a few names and numbers to get you started: Gemma 050 283 3445, Vicky 050 770 5366 and Maureen 050 535 3382. Comfort Beauty (04 332 6844) also offers manicures, pedicures and waxing.

Unbeweavable!
You can find a few salons specialising in afro hair, braiding and extensions near the fish roundabout in Deira. Elyazia Beauty Center (04 422 6149, www.nbeautywoman. com), in International City, specialises in relaxing, weaving, dreadlocks and afro hair treatments.

Beauty Salons

Other options **Health Spas** p.402, **Beauty Training** p.332, **Perfumes & Cosmetics** p.463

Beauty is big business in Dubai. Salons are very popular and there is a huge variety to choose from offering every type of treatment imaginable. Services range from manicures, pedicures, waxing and henna, to the latest haircuts, styles and colours. Alternatively, you can arrange for a stylist to come to your house if you want to be truly decadent. The quality and range of treatments vary greatly, so trial and error or word of mouth is probably the best way to find a good salon.

In hotels you'll find both male and female stylists working alongside each other, but in establishments located outside hotels, only female stylists are permitted to work in ladies' salons. These salons are very private and men are not permitted inside – even the windows are covered.

There are also numerous salons aimed primarily at Arabic ladies and they specialise in henna designs, so look out for a decorated hand poster in salon windows. The traditional practice of painting henna on the hands and feet, especially for weddings or special occasions, is still very popular with UAE Nationals. For tourists, a design on the hand, ankle or shoulder can make a great memento – it will cost about Dhs.30 and the intricate brown patterns fade after two to three weeks.

Hairdressers

Dubai has a wide range of options for getting a cut, colour or restyle. At one end you have the small barber shops where gents can get a haircut (and relaxing head massage) for as little as Dhs.10, with the option of a shave with a cut-throat razor for a few extra dirhams. Ladies should be able to find salons where a basic haircut starts at around Dhs.40. At the other end of the scale you have upmarket boutiques and salons offering the latest styles and treatments to men and women, where you could pay Dhs.300 or more for a cut and blow dry. Many of the shopping malls have hairdressers, as do some of the bigger hotels. Roots in Jumeira and Al Barsha is popular, as is Hair Corridor. A new

Hairdressers		
Carla K. Styling Centre	Trade Centre 1	04 343 8544
Cut Shape	Al Satwa	04 398 6008
Essentials	Al Wasl	04 398 8723
Franck Provost	Various Locations	04 341 3245
Glamour	Bur Dubai	04 396 8826
The Gold Salon	Trade Centre 1	04 321 1423
Hair Corridor	Al Wasl	04 394 5622
The Hair Shop	Trade Centre 2	04 332 6616
Hair@Pyramids	Umm Hurair	04 324 1490
Hairworks	Umm Suqeim	04 394 0777
Jen's Hair Studio	Marsa Dubai	04 800 5367
Lamcy Hair & Beauty Centre	Oud Metha	04 335 1101
MariaDowling	Bur Dubai	04 345 4225
Pastels	Various Locations	04 394 7393
Patsi Collins Hair Beauty Nails	Al Garhoud	04 286 9923
Reflection Hair & Beauty	Al Wasl	04 394 4595
Roots Salon	Various Locations	04 331 7555
Sisters Beauty Lounge	Jumeira	04 342 0787
SOS Beauty Salon	Jumeira	04 349 1144
Ted Morgan Hair Group	Palm Jumeirah	04 430 8190
The Edge Hair & Beauty	Umm Hurair	04 324 0024
Toni & Guy	Trade Centre 2	04 330 3345
Top Style Salon	Al Garhoud	04 282 9663
Zouari	Al Sufouh	04 399 9999

concept that recently touched down at the Grosvenor House is JetSet, a ladies wash and blow-dry salon (so no cutting or colouring) with a cool airline-themed interior. If you are looking for a bridal hair stylist contact Maria Dowling on 04 345 4225 (for more information on weddings see p.470).

Health Spas

Other options **Sports & Leisure Facilities** p.396, **Massage** p.412

The Aviation Club
Al Garhoud
Map 13 E1

Akaru Spa

04 282 8578 | *www.akaruspa.com*

The Akaru Spa opened in the summer of 2005 with autumnal colours and natural decor, such as wooden fittings, orange walls and glass features, creating a truly tranquil retreat. There is a Turkish Room with sauna and dim lighting, as well as fruit juices and water on tap. Exotic treatments range from specialised facials and wraps to Microdermabrasion and Sunvision. During the cooler months they offer Sky Therapies including Sky Facial, Aromatic Sky Massage and Face and Body Experience which are administered on the rooftop terrace. Also on the indulging menu is Thalgo (La Beaute Marine), a range of specialised body marine treatments that utilise the riches of the ocean, with a whole host of benefits for your skin.

Park Hyatt Dubai
Creekside
Deira
Map 11 B4

Amara Spa

04 602 1234 | *www.dubai.park.hyatt.com*

The Amara spa is something of a breath of fresh air in Dubai's spa world. While the city's spa scene is certainly sublime, it tends to follow the same formula – a paradise retreat with dimmed lighting, rose petals, candles and hypnotic music. Amara, however, is something different. Not to say that the aforementioned approach isn't heavenly but what sets this spa apart is the treatment rooms. After you arrive at the grand spa entrance there is no communal changing room or wet area, instead you are escorted directly to your treatment room which acts as your personal spa. Here you have all the facilities of a changing room (toilet, shower, hairdryer, wardrobe) as well as a relaxation corner. After your treatment, or during if you are having a scrub or wrap, you can treat yourself to a shower under the sun in your very own private outdoor shower (very liberating) with a relaxation area for you to dry off under the warm rays. The treatments are usually packaged, which is definitely a good thing as you won't be in a hurry to leave.

Dubai Polo &
Equestrian Club
Arabian Ranches
Map 2 B3

Angsana Spa

04 361 8251 | *www.angsanaspa.com*

Angsana promises to be a 'sanctuary for the inner self', offering privacy and tranquillity in a retreat-like atmosphere. The promise is delivered. The minimalist Asian surroundings feature rich, dark wood, while incense, exotic oils, low light and soft music set the tone for relaxation. The impeccably trained staff work wonders on stressed, aching bodies, turning tight muscles into putty and sending overworked minds to cloud nine. Unique massages, ranging from Balinese to Hawaiian, and of course Thai, are certainly at the higher end of the scale in terms of price, but the quality of treatment ensures value for money. This Singaporean and Thai affiliate brand of Banyan Tree certainly has brought its highly reputed standards to Dubai. Other locations include Dubai Marina (04 368 4356), Emirates Hills (04 368 2222) and The Montgomerie (04 360 9322). All spas have male and female areas; the Dubai Marina location also features a health club with outdoor pool and mixed and female-only gyms.

Well-Being

Akaru Spa

Sheraton Jumeirah Beach Resort
Dubai Marina
Map 4 F1

Armonia Spa
04 399 5533 | www.sheraton.com/jumeirahbeach

Upon arriving at the spa you'll be greeted at reception and offered a complimentary beverage or juice while waiting for your treatment. You then begin with a refreshing welcome ritual, including a warm herbal aromatic foot massage using sea salt, rose petals, dried herbs, peppermint oils, and pebbles. The wood-themed interior, candles, and relaxing music help set the mood. Treatments on offer include facials, full-body massages and luxurious body wraps for both men and women. Recommended is the Well-Being massage, a 60 minute pampering session with a gentle body massage that incorporates treatment of the face and scalp. The massage may be a little too gentle for some, so don't be afraid to tell your therapist to increase the pressure if required. The spa is on the small side, and facilities not as comprehensive as some other spas in town, but this is certainly a good place to come for facials and massages.

Burj Al Arab
Umm Suqeim
Map 6 B1

Assawan Spa & Health Club
04 301 7480 | www.burj-al-arab.com

The Assawan Spa is situated on the 18th floor of the breathtaking Burj Al Arab. Unsurprisingly it's an elaborate affair with a mosaic domed ceiling and ornately tiled corridors. The personal service here is excellent; you are pampered from the minute you walk through the door. The Spa has female only and mixed environments, including a state of the art gym with studios (where you can take part in everything from yoga to aerobics), saunas, steam rooms, plunge pools and two wonderfully relaxing infinity pools decorated in mosaic and gold leaf tiles. You can literally swim up to the edge of the pool, put your nose to the window, and enjoy the amazing views of the Palm and the World islands.

For pure unadulterated indulgence try the caviar body treatment – at Dhs.680 it's a bit pricey but worth it. Also on offer is a 'men only' range including massage, facial, manicure, pedicure and more. If you really want to feel like royalty then this spacious and seriously sublime spa is a dream come true. You will feel like a princess, or indeed a prince.

Wafi Pyramids
Umm Hurair
Map 10 E4

Cleopatra's Spa
04 324 7700 | www.waficity.com

Tucked away behind the members only door of the Pharaohs' Club, Cleopatra's Spa may not have the grand entrance that some hotel spas share, but what it lacks in ostentation it makes up for in occasion. You will be led from the modest reception (literally led by the arm, which is both attentive and awkward), to the changing rooms which have all the necessary goodies but are more operational than opulent. The relaxation area, however, is more of an ancient Egyptian affair with drapes, silk cushions and majlis-style seats. There is also a small plunge pool with Jacuzzi and sauna. The treatment rooms are all comfortable, softly lit and basked in luxurious touches with the obligatory hypnotic tunes. The spa menu should satisfy all, with everything from massages (including pregnancy) and facials to body wraps and anti-ageing miracles. The big bonus is that if you book a package you get a pool pass which allows you to float round the lazy river at the Pharaohs' Club's idyllic tree-shaded pool area. There is also a separate spa for men, and while this may not be the most splendid of spas, a visit to Cleopatra's is pure pleasure.

Dragonfly Spa

BurJuman
Bur Dubai
Map 8 F4

04 351 1120 | www.burjuman.com

Set amid the hustle of Fitness First at Burjuman shopping mall, Dragonfly is a haven for shoppers and gym bunnies alike. The three flights of stairs to reception really do lead guests to believe they are escaping the outside world. The treatment menu is extensive and focuses on Chinese and Japanese shiatsu styles. Arriving guests are announced by the large gong at reception, before being transported to the treatment suites. Dark woods and traditional ornaments line the walls and treatment rooms which are spacious and low-lit. There is also a chill-out space for guests to relax after their treatment with some soothing green tea. For a real treat, book in to the Crystal Suite, a massive treatment room adorned with crystals, a private bathroom and relaxation space.

Dubai Marine Spa

Dubai Marine Beach
Resort & Spa
Jumeira
Map 7 F1

04 346 1111 | www.dxbmarine.com

Although it is not as plush as some others in Dubai, the spa at Dubai Marine offers an excellent array of treatments. This is a rather compact spa and the changing rooms are on the small side, but the treatment rooms are comfortable and fragrantly scented. The treatments available range from Guinot, Thalgo and La Phyto facial and body treatments in addition to the Ionithermie slimming treatment, manicures and pedicures. Particularly pleasurable is the hot stone massage that can also be combined with a facial, manicure and pedicure. It involves the use of essential oils chosen for their calming, relaxing and grounding effects designed to uplift and relax the body. Also on offer are full and half-day packages and a limited range of treatments for men.

Elche

Beh Jumeirah Plaza
Jumeira
Map 7 F1

04 349 4942 | www.elche.ae

Elche is Jumeira's only organic beauty salon. They use 100% organic herbs, flowers, vegetables and fruits home-grown in Hungary. Traditional know-how and contemporary scientific techniques combine to give Elche a unique advantage in Dubai's spa landscape. Warm tones decorate the interior of the villa, and are accented by sensuous music and a delicious aroma of fresh ingredients. The certified Hungarian beauty and massage therapists are specially trained to efficiently utilise Elche products. Amongst 80 products, a special range is developed to cope with Dubai's harsh climate. A health questionnaire assesses your skin, determining the treatment for your skin type. Finally, your skin is evaluated and Elche products are recommended. Their two-hour Cleansing facial is fiercely popular with a unique paprika mask. Whether it's a facial, or a Yumeiho Japanese massage, a visit to is always welcomed with a smile. Innovative monthly offers and a loyalty and membership program are available.

Elixir Spa & Health Club

Habtoor Grand
Resort & Spa
Dubai Marina
Map 5 B1

04 399 5000 | www.habtoorhotels.com

Don't be fooled by first impressions with this spa (the reception area is located by the main entrance to the pool/beach and can be very busy and the changing rooms are located off a main corridor) – the six large treatment rooms are the height of relaxation and luxury. There is also a dry float room, rasul mud chamber and nail station plus wet spa facilities and recovery area stocked with herbal teas. The spa offers a wide range of treatments, including Karin 02 Herzog skincare treatments from Switzerland. The therapists spend time going over your treatment to ensure the required results and you emerge feeling well pampered and relaxed.

Eternal MedSpa Dubai

Jumeirah Rd, Villa 5
Opp Jumeirah
Beach Park
Jumeira
Map 7 C1

04 344 0008 | *www.eternalmedspa.com*

The medspa concept is relatively new to Dubai and combines the pampering and decor of a spa with treatments performed by medical professionals. Eternal Medspa offers the same non-surgical treatments that are usually performed at cosmetic surgery and dermatology clinics. Several options are available, including fillers, thermage treatments and health coaching. The spa regularly promotes treatments through special offers, and patients can book treatment packages to suit their specific needs.

Express Unwind

Trafalgar Bld
CBD 7
International City
Map 2 C3

04 430 8304 | *www.expressunwind.com*

Compared to the pampering softness of most other spa treatments, Thai massage is more of a forceful body workout. The Thai staff at this small spa in International City are experts at the art form, which combines firm stretching and body contortion. Don't go expecting a gloriously relaxing hour of soft touches and little whispers in your ear. Instead, expect to have all of your aches and knots pulled out of you by well-trained hands. The simple decor is identical to something you'd find in Thailand and the tiny treatment rooms are only a bit bigger than the floor mat you'll be kneaded on. This is the type of massage you could get every two weeks without having to explain the massive hole in your wallet to your husband.

Givenchy Spa

One&Only
Royal Mirage
Al Sufouh
Map 5 C1

04 315 2140 | *www.oneandonlyresort.com*

The emphasis in this serene setting is on understated decor, with plenty of neutral colours, natural light and soft music in the treatment rooms. The relaxation room is a haven of tranquillity and an ideal spot to savour the sensations after your treatment. While they offer a variety of massages and facials, their speciality is the Canyon Love Stone Therapy, an energy-balancing massage using warm and cool stones. The volcanic stones have been specially selected, are 'charged' in the moonlight and cleansed with salt. The stones are placed on specific points around the body, and then used to massage the skin. Other massages are available, such as Swedish, lymphatic drainage, slimming and sports massages. For high-level pampering, you could try one of the body treatments, which include peels, wraps and oil baths. Only Givenchy products are used in this spa, and all are gentle and safe.

The Grand Spa

Grand Hyatt Dubai
Umm Hurair
Map 13 C1

04 317 1234 | *www.dubai.grand.hyatt.com*

The spa may not be the biggest in Dubai but what it lacks in size it makes up for in atmosphere and attention to detail. The changing room and adjacent relaxation area have dark wooden floors and walls and are lit by rows of candles. The wet area is drizzled in rose petals and houses a Jacuzzi, plunge pool, sauna and steam room as well as spacious showers. The treatment rooms are medium in size but very comfortable, and the tranquil tunes help transport you to a higher plane. The treatments on offer range from facials, all designed with preservation and attainment of youth in mind, to massages with specialist 'aromasoul' treatments using essential oils. They also have fusion packages that allow you to combine a massage, body or hand/foot treatment, facial and a lifestyle enhancer such as pilates, circuit training, and joint flexibility – perfect for unadulterated top-to-toe indulgence.

H2O

Emirates Towers
Trade Centre 2
Map 7 F3

04 319 8181 | *www.jumeirahemiratestowers.com*

Tucked away on the lower floor of the Emirates Towers, H20 is a compact, sophisticated men-only spa that offers a range of treatments, with a particular emphasis on aromatherapy. The interior is all dim lighting and dark wood panels, inducing a calming, tranquil atmosphere that lowers the stress levels at once. The hour-long H20 signature treatment uses a combination of oils and massage techniques to de-stress and revitalise the weary, while other options cater to specific requirements. There's also a flotation pool and oxygen bar to supplement the massages, while the range of Aromatherapy Associates oils and products is available to purchase on your way out.

The Haven Depilex

Villa 1, Street 332
Jumeira
Map 7 F1

04 345 6770 | *www.depilexonline.com*

The Haven is a holistic clinic dedicated to relaxation and rejuvenation for the mind, body and soul. Housed in a converted two-storey villa, the mesmerising scents, earthy decor and gentle background music will transport you into a relaxed state the moment you enter. Downstairs is a beauty and hair salon, while the candle-lit stairs lead you up to the simple and welcoming treatment rooms. There are none of the trappings of a hotel spa (steam room, Jacuzzi and relaxation area), but The Haven benefits from a wonderfully intimate aura. It offers a wide range of treatments including Thai yoga massage, Ayurvedic treatments, reflexology, aromatherapy and yoga. They also offer the increasingly popular hot stone massage. During this treatment the smooth stones are used as an extension of the therapist's hands, allowing a deeper penetrating massage that releases tension, increases circulation and induces a deep state of relaxation. No doubt you will slowly drift into a blissful sleep and when you surface in the comfortable surroundings it will be as if you have woken from a wonderful dream.

The Health Club

Emirates Towers
Hotel
Trade Centre 2
Map 7 F3

04 319 8888 | *www.jumeirahemiratestowers.com*

As well as unisex gym facilities, a refreshing outdoor swimming pool and a sun terrace, The Health Club at Emirates Towers offers a range of spa treatments for ladies only. Treatments include aromatherapy, Swedish and Shiatsu massage, facials, and manicures and pedicures. All can be tailored to suit individual needs – from perking up the young and sporty to the perfect treat for the weary mother-in-law, there's something for everyone. The signature Pure Indulgence Exclusive 4 U full body massage is relaxation heaven, employing varied techniques and oils to perfectly match your state of mind and body. Tanning sessions can be booked to give you a pre, post or mid-holiday boost, while steam and sauna rooms are situated in the luxurious locker rooms to help round off the cleansing rituals.

Heavenly Spa

The Westin Dubai
Mina Seyahi Beach
Resort & Marina
Al Sufouh
Map 5 C1

04 399 4141 | *www.starwoodhotels.com*

Housed in the massive new European-style Westin in Al Sufouh, this is the newest Heavenly Spa in the successful international chain. Similar to other luxury spas in the immediate area, the service leaves nothing to be desired. The chaperones are neither neglectful nor intrusive and the clean, contemporary decor still manages to feel warm and inviting, helping to clear your mind for the gorgeous treatments that await. The spa's signature treatment is the Heavenly Massage, which uses four hands moving in sync. The effect is unlike anything you're likely to experience again, unless you make this a regular occurrence.

Lime Spa

Desert Palm Dubai
Al Awir Rd
Al Awir
Map 2 C3

04 323 8888 | www.desertpalm.ae

The Desert Palm resort is one of Dubai's best-kept secrets – tucked away on a private polo estate just past Dragonmart, this 24 room boutique hotel has two great restaurants, a bar and one of the city's most beautiful spas. Lime is more of a retreat than a spa, and with any treatment you get use of the facilities for the day, so you can linger in the relaxation rooms or lounge around the pool. The spa itself has six treatment rooms, all naturally lit by large windows overlooking the polo fields. The couples' treatment room has its own plunge pool and private relaxation area. The communal relaxation area is a sublime place to enjoy a cup of herbal tea after your treatment – the heated beds are heavenly. A range of massages and facials are available at the spa, all drawing on colour therapy to tailor each treatment to the needs of each individual. Highly recommended, not just for a specific treatment, but for a full-on, girly spa day out.

Natural Elements Spa & Fitness

Le Meridien Dubai
Al Garhoud
Map 13 E1

04 702 2550 | www.lemeridien.com

It may not be in one of Dubai's upper-luxury hotels (although the Le Meridien is a leading five-star hotel), but Natural Elements Spa is definitely worth a visit. They have a total of nine treatment rooms, two of which are 'wet' – one containing a hydrotherapy bath and one that is equipped for luxury spa manicures and pedicures. Before or after your treatment, you can relax in what is undoubtedly one of the spa's most unique features: the Aroma Heat Cave. This beautiful cocoon of relaxation has a (faux) starlit sky, large comfortable loungers and special aromatherapy fragrances throughout. The spa menu offers a huge range of services, from hot stone massages and luxury hand and foot treatments, to facials and grooming rituals. Products used are from Pevonia Botanica, renowned for their natural, holistic treatment properties.

Oriental Hammam – Health & Beauty Institute

One&Only
Royal Mirage
Al Sufouh
Map 5 C1

04 315 2130 | www.oneandonlyresorts.com

Having battled through the Dubai traffic you feel instantly relaxed arriving at the One & Only Royal Mirage, which is the ultimate in Arabian luxury. Welcomed by the attentive staff, you are put at ease as they explain the Oriental Hammam Experience. The surroundings are elegant but not overly opulent, with a warm traditional feel. A variety of wraps, robes and slippers are available in the changing rooms where soft pipe music and relaxing fragrances set the mood. The Hammam and Spa is an impressive area with mosaic arches and intricate carvings on the high domes. The 50 minute treatment involves a variety of different experiences, including being bathed, steamed, washed with black soap, vigorously scrubbed with a loofah and massaged on a hot marble table which sounds invasive but manages somehow to be wonderfully invigorating and leaves your skin feeling as soft as cream. Also included in this treatment is free use of the Jacuzzi, plunge pools and the sensually sleep-inducing relaxation room.

Raffles Amrita Spa

Raffles Dubai
Umm Hurair
Map 10 D4

04 324 8888 | www.dubai.raffles.com

As you might expect from Raffles Hotel, the Amrita Spa offers the height of decadent indulgence. On arrival you are shown into your treatment room which has a private changing room on the side, complete with power shower, fluffy towels and luxury toiletries. Atmospheric lighting, relaxing music, a heated treatment bench with

Raffles Amrita Spa

warmed towels await you whichever treatment you chose. The Desert Oasis comes highly recommended, combining a mud wrap treatment followed by a full body massage. For the ultimate spa experience try Dubai Decadence – a full six hours of head-to-toe pampering including a steam bath, body scrub, hot stone massage, facial, manicure and pedicure. Afterwards lie back in the relaxation lounge and pretend for a few more minutes that you don't have to go home. Male and female hair and beauty salons, a gym, pool, sauna, steam bath and whirlpool are also available, should you wish to delay your departure further. The spa specialises in couples packages in which you and your partner can indulge together in a treatment specially designed to promote togetherness and unity. Look out for romantic packages around February for an unforgettable Valentine's treat.

Ritz-Carlton, Dubai
Dubai Marina
Map 5 B1

Ritz-Carlton Spa
04 318 6184 | www.ritz-carlton.com

While the Ritz-Carlton is certainly a majestic hotel, its spa is somewhat understated. The large treatment rooms push all the right buttons – spacious with bamboo features, running water, dimmed lights, hypnotic background music and highly professional service. If you're a member then you have the benefit of a private pool outside with a healthy spa menu and beds that have the required sink-in comfort for true relaxation. Non-members though are limited to the facilities inside the spa, the design of which seems a little ill conceived. This spa is on the petite size with a changing room, shower room (with an open entrance), and the treatment rooms all leading off a central corridor. While there is a wet room with Jacuzzi, sauna and steam room, the small relaxation area has just three beds, and feels a little claustrophobic. The range of treatments is impressive nonetheless, with an excellent selection of Balinese massages and facials, hot stone therapy, aroma body treatments, spa baths and signature spa packages.

Al Mamzar Centre
Deira
Map 12 B4

Royal Waters Health Spa
04 297 2053 | therwspa@eim.ae

Located on the top floor of the Al Mamzar Centre, with separate entrances for men and women, you will receive a warm welcome from the friendly and knowledgeable staff waiting to advise you on the vast range of treatments available for health, relaxation and beauty. The spa has simple tiled decor with soft lighting and tranquil music. There are lockers and showers available and a sauna and steam room. Walk through the well-equipped gym and up on the roof you'll find the swimming pool with views of the bustling area below. You can sit and take in the surroundings as you wait for your treatment in the relaxation area. The spa offers treatments for cellulite and stretch marks, and they have a wonderful hydrotherapy circuit designed to leave you refreshed after a hard day.

Satori Spa

Bab Al Shams Desert Resort & Spa
Map 1 E2

04 809 6232 | www.jumeirah.com

The spa's location in the middle of the desert adds to the all natural feeling that you immediately get when you walk through the doors. Satori's treatments are worth every penny. A combination of smooth, long strokes and kneading movements makes the Satori Reviver an invigorating treatment that manages to both de-stress and revive you during 50 minutes of uninterrupted pampering. Aromatherapy Associates is the oil of choice here, and a beguiling scent surrounds you as you are kneaded and massaged into a state of semi-conscious bliss. The treatment rooms feature a window with a wooden blind, which is quite unusual for spas in Dubai which are usually cosseted away in the deep innards of a hotel. Here, the sense of being close to the desert in its natural state seeps into the gently lit room, and the quiet tinkle of spa music empties your mind of everything but the rhythmic strokes of the therapist.

SensAsia Urban Spa

The Village Mall
Jumeira
Map 7 F1

04 349 8850 | www.sensasiaspas.com

Tucked away in The Village Mall, SensAsia may not have all the trimmings of some five-star spas, but what it lacks in the way of plunge pools and Jacuzzis it makes up for in the 60+ minutes you spend in a heightened sense of bliss. The hot stone massage is particularly sensational, with your choice of aroma, strength of massage and the temperature control of the stones in your hands (literally – you hold hot stones in your palms throughout the treatment). This spa is not spacious (the changing room has only one shower but it's one of the best you'll ever have), but with treatments from Bali, Thailand and Japan, space is of little concern. And with names like 'Urban Unwind', and 'Gorgeous Geisha', you'll want to make space in your diary every month.

The Spa at Jebel Ali Golf Resort & Spa ▶ p.533

Jebel Ali Golf Resort & Spa
Jebel Ali
Map 3 A1

04 883 6000 | www.jebelali-international.com

The Spa at the Jebel Ali Resort caters mainly to hotel guests, although the influx of new residents in the nearby areas could change that. An excellent level of service is offered for both men and women, in intimate and well-presented surroundings. There is a communal area with an invigorating shower, sauna, Jacuzzi and steam room (just be warned the shower leaves you not only refreshed but shivering). The changing areas are a little small but equipped with Elemis goodies, and the tranquil after-treatment area overlooks the beach. Recommended is the Royal Hammam Ritual, a 90 minute treatment in a steamy marble room that involves black soap, a henna mask, some exuberant exfoliating and a rasul mud mask before a darn good wash down. This style of pampering is literally from head to toe. Just leave any shyness at the marble door – but not your partner, if you're brave enough to try the couple's option.

The Spa at Shangri-La

Shangri-La Hotel
Trade Centre 1
Map 7 E3

04 343 8888 | www.shangri-la.com

The emphasis here is to restore the balance of Yin and Yang in the body with the five elements – fire, water, metal, wood and earth. The signature Chi Balance massage is 50 minutes of blissful stimulation and relaxation. The health club includes a rooftop swimming pool, tennis courts, a squash court plus a gym. Relaxation facilities include separate spas for men and women, each with plunge pool, sauna, steam room and nine treatment rooms. A salon and barber, juice bar and boutique complete the package. Surroundings are minimalist and the treatment rooms are a little on the clinical side, while the communal areas lean more towards fitness club than spa, with too many open spaces and not enough privacy. That said, it's ideal for a healthy break for those working on the Sheikh Zayed Road strip.

Atlantis The Palm
Palm Jumeira
Map

The Spa At Atlantis ▶ p.411
04 426 1020 | www.atlantisthepalm.com

You'll enter this spectacular spa with the highest of expectations; after all, this is the resort that hosted the glitziest celebrity party in Dubai's history. And disappointment is definitely not on the menu here – from the minute you walk into the boutique area (where you can sample a wide range of products used in the spa, and load up on girly goodies) up until the end of your treatment, when you're sipping green tea in the relaxation lounge, it's a heavenly experience. Even though it has 27 treatment rooms, it doesn't feel like a big spa; perhaps because of the personal touch. Whether you choose a massage, a facial, a Bastien Gonzalez manicure or pedicure, or one of the delectable Spa Journeys, your therapist has one clear focus: you. Highly recommended.

The Palace –
The Old Town
Downtown Burj Dubai
Map 7 D4

The Spa At The Palace
04 428 7888 | www.thepalace-dubai.com

You couldn't find a more suitable address for the Spa at the Palace; after a treatment here you will leave feeling like royalty. Upon arrival you are met by friendly staff who welcome you and give you a tour of the facilities. There are five spacious treatment suites, two Oriental bath houses, monsoon showers and two Hydrospa bath tubs with therapy jets. The entire spa is a haven of tranquility surrounded by beautiful mosaic designs on the walls, and before long you will have forgotten the hustle and bustle of your busy Dubai lifestyle. Sink in to a welcoming Hydrospa bath tub or unwind in the steam room until you are called for your treatment – there is a huge range on offer, but for a unique regional experience, try the Hammam. Once your treatment is finished, your therapist will show you to the Relaxation Lounge, where you can enjoy some refreshments.

Taj Palace Hotel
Deira
Map 11 C1

Taj Spa
04 211 3101 | www.tajpalacedubai.com

This is a relaxing and tranquil spa with a mystic and romantic atmosphere. They offer modern Ayurvedic treatments as well as popular European and far eastern ranges and natural therapies. The therapists concentrate on the body as well as the mind and methods are based on the ancient science of Ayurveda (fused with modern technology). Massage techniques, movements, herbal selection and products used are tailored to the individual guest, supporting the holistic principle that each individual has a unique body type and will therefore have different balancing needs. The changing rooms are welcoming and have a sauna and steam room, while the relaxation area is hard to tear yourself away from thanks to the spacious and sumptuous surroundings blessed with sink-in sofas and armchairs.

The Harbour Hotel &
Residence
Dubai Marina
Map 5 B2

Timeless Spa
04 319 4000 | www.emirateshotelsresorts.com

Once inside this Asian-inspired spa, you can delve straight into your treatments or spend a few minutes using the sauna, steam room and Jacuzzi – your therapist will explain which will complement your treatments best. Before you start, you'll relax in an inviting lounge area with reclining chairs while you sip on ginger tea and fill out an information sheet to help your therapist shape your treatments. There are separate areas for men and women and each treatment room has soft lighting, ambient music, and a bed in the centre of the room. You'll find a comprehensive range of treatments here (sports massages, facials and even a massage used for Hawaiian royalty), which use products like Sodashi and Babor. For head-to-toe pampering try the 90 minute Timeless Traditions signature body treatment for Dhs.600 which uses date extract and includes a magnificent Swedish massage.

SPA

THE ATLANTIS SPA PRESENTS A MEMORABLE EXPERIENCE,
AWAKENING YOUR SENSES WITHIN AWE-INSPIRING AND
SERENE WATER SURROUNDINGS. SET OVER TWO MAGNIFICENT
FLOORS, THE 27 TREATMENT ROOMS PROVIDE THE ULTIMATE
PRIVACY FOR BOTH HIS AND HER RELAXATION TIME.
EXCLUSIVE THERAPIES WITH MANICURES AND PEDICURES
BY BASTIEN GONZALEZ AND GLAMOROUS PRODUCTS SUCH
AS NATUROPATHICA AND DANIELE DE WINTER, ALL AVAILABLE
FOR YOUR PURE INDULGENCE.

FOR MORE INFORMATION CALL +971 (4) 426 1020 OR
VISIT ATLANTISTHEPALM.COM

ATLANTIS

PALM JUMEIRAH, DUBAI

DON'T FORGET TO BREATHE

Madinat Jumeirah
Umm Suqeim
Map 6 A2

Talise Spa
04 366 6818 | *www.jumeirah.com/talise*

You'll find yourself relaxing the second you walk through the huge Arabic doors at Talise. This regal spa is made up of luxurious lounges and treatment rooms connected by garden walkways. The rooms themselves are exotic and well-appointed with warm shades and ambient music. The welcoming staff truly set this spot apart, advising on products and technique before your individually designed treatment. The range of therapies is extensive but not overwhelming, with a focus on body treatments using natural oils. A true destination spa, take advantage of the steam room, sauna and plunge pools before or after your appointment, or read a magazine while sipping on ginger tea sweetened with honey in one of the chill out rooms. Yoga, including the popular classes held under the stars, is also available.

Fairmont Dubai
Trade Centre 1
Map 8 A4

Willow Stream Spa & Health Club
04 311 8800 | *www.fairmont.com*

In keeping with the eclectic decor of The Fairmont Dubai, Willow Stream is decorated in a luxurious Greco-Roman style, with beautiful mosaics and sleek white pillars. There is a comprehensive selection of top-to-toe spa and beauty treatments using Phytomer and Aromatherapy Associates product lines. The added bonus is being able to select spa packages for that ultimate pampering session. After a friendly welcome you'll be guided to the changing rooms where there are showers, a steam room, sauna and Jacuzzi. Soft, white towels and subtle candlelight create a wonderful sense of calm. Before or after your treatment you can use the fitness centre, the outdoor swimming pools or simply relax with a herbal tea or fresh juice. When you are ready for your treatment the knowledgeable staff will talk you through the process and give you advice so you can continue the good work at home.

Massage
Other options **Health Spas** p.402, **Reflexology & Massage Therapy** p.196, **Sports & Leisure Facilities** p.396

Soothing for the body, mind and soul, a massage could be a weekly treat, a gift to someone special, or a relaxing way to get you through a trying time at work. Numerous massage techniques are available, but prices and standards vary, so it's worth doing your research into what's on offer. A full body massage will cost in the range of Dhs.100 to 300 for a one-hour session. Massages, in addition to a variety of other treatments, are available at most spas in Dubai, see Health Spas on p.402.

Nail Bars

Aroushi Beauty Salon	Opp Lamcy Plaza	Oud Metha	04 336 2794
Essential Image Salon	Sheikh Zayed Rd	Al Wasl	04 343 3321
The Hair Shop	Sheikh Zayed Rd	Trade Centre 2	04 332 6616
N.Bar	Various Locations	na	04 346 1100
The Nail Bar	Aviation Club	Garhoud	04 282 1617
Nail Express	Nr Welcare Hospital & Irish Village	Garhoud	04 283 3828
Nail Moda	Wafi City	Umm Hurair	04 327 9088
Nailstation	Town Centre	Jumeira	04 349 0123
NStyle Nail Lounge	Various Locations	na	04 341 3300
Pretty Lady	Mankhool Rd	Satwa	04 398 5255
Tips & Toes Nail Haven	Jumeirah Beach Residence	Dubai Marina	04 429 3477

Reiki

Reiki is a healing technique based on the belief that energy can be channelled into a patient. Translated as 'universal life force energy', Reiki can emotionally cleanse, physically invigorate and leave you more focused.

Various Locations

Pookat Suresh Reiki
04 285 9128

The Pookat Suresh Reiki centre offers various degrees of attunement. In the first degree, a series of four attunements are taught by a traditional master with the aim of channelling a higher amount of universal life force energy. The second degree level teaches powerful absentee healing.

Tai Chi

Musalla Towers
Khalid bin Al Walid St
Bur Dubai
Map 8 F3

House Of Chi & House Of Healing
04 397 4446 | www.hofchi.com

Tai Chi has been practised in China for over 2,000 years. It is a soft martial art that is today practised by 20% of the world's population. Tai Chi is particularly beneficial to the elderly or those with impaired motor skills, since it emphasises correct posture and balance thus making it a safe exercise option for people with frail bones.

Yoga

Many health and fitness clubs offer yoga classes as part of their weekly schedule, catering to all levels of experience. Check the table on p.329 for a list of health club phone numbers or see below for some centres dedicated to yoga. Art of Living courses (www.artofliving.org) are also offered at various locations throughout Dubai. Ring 04 334 0105 for details of where and when.

Karama Centre
Al Karama
Map 10 E1

Al Karama Ayurvedic & Yoga Centre
04 335 5288 | www.alkaramahealthcare.com

Operating for over 18 years, this centre is run by qualified professionals with expertise in the traditional systems of Ayurveda, herbal beauty care, yoga and meditation. They have all the necessary facilities to take care of healing, rejuvenation and beauty care. Separate areas are available for men and women.

White Crown Bld
Trade Centre 1
Map 7 F2

Gems Of Yoga
04 331 5161 | www.gemsofyogadubai.com

Gems of Yoga mixes yoga and art through yogasanas, mudras, pranayam, meditation and other stress release techniques. The centre also offers classes such as weight-watchers, desktop yoga, prenatal and postnatal yoga, therapeutic yoga, animal yoga for children, and Ashtanga Vinyasa power yoga from Mysore. Prices range from Dhs.50 per hour to Dhs.15,000 for annual enrolment. 'Yoga@home' packages are also available.

Various Locations

Zen Yoga
04 367 0435 | www.yoga.ae

Zen Yoga offers full-time yoga and Pilates classes in three centres: Emirates Hills, Dubai Media City, and The Village Mall on Beach Road. Studios are pristine and airy with mirrored walls to help you check your posture. Facilities include changing rooms, showers and lockers. Instructors are all highly trained and professional. Zen donates 10% of its profits to charity.

THE AVENUES

THE AVENUES IS A TRULY UNIQUE SHOPPING EXPERIENCE.
SURROUNDED BY CELEBRITY RESTAURANTS AND A 13 MILLION
LITRE MARINE HABITAT, THE AMBASSADOR LAGOON.
YOU CAN CHOOSE FROM THE FINEST BRANDS OF JEWELRY,
WATCHES, DESIGNER CLOTHING AND ACCESSORIES INCLUDING
THE FIRST 'LEONARD PARIS' BOUTIQUE AND THE ONLY 'THE
COUNTER' SUNGLASS STORE IN DUBAI.

KEEP STROLLING AND YOU WILL DISCOVER EXCLUSIVE ATLANTIS
MEMENTOS AND TOYS IN THE 'LEGENDS OF ATLANTIS'. WITH
OVER TWENTY FIVE HIGH QUALITY BOUTIQUES YOU WILL BE
SPOILT FOR CHOICE.

FOR MORE INFORMATION CALL +971 (4) 426 1000
OR VISIT ATLANTISTHEPALM.COM

ATLANTIS
PALM JUMEIRAH, DUBAI

DON'T FORGET TO BREATHE

Shopping

Shopping

Need Help? Just Ask ◀

Be picked up by a resident shopaholic and taken on a guided tour of Dubai's shopping hotspots. To arrange a tailor-made shopping trip, contact Dubai VIP Services on 04 311 6675 or visit www.dubai vipservice.com.

Fashion Tips ◀

If you simply can't decide what shoes go with your new outfit, or if your wardrobe needs a total revamp, you can contact Kelly Lundberg on 050 396 2296 or visit www. divine.ae for personal shopping advice. Kelly will provide tailor-made consultations for each client, whether you are looking for a specific outfit for an event, or you need to update your look.

Shopping

Dubai provides innumerable opportunities to indulge in a spot of retail therapy. The city is either a shopaholic's dream or nightmare – depending on who's paying the bill. The rapid development that Dubai continues to experience is inextricably linked to shopping, and with each new development comes a new mall. The retail sector is taken very seriously, and its contribution to the emirate's economy is not underestimated. The Dubai Shopping Festival, a month dedicated to consumerism, takes place annually (postponed only once, in 2006, as a mark of respect following the death of Sheikh Maktoum Bin Rashid Al Maktoum).

Shopping in Dubai revolves around the malls, both big and small (see p.437), but it is also well worth checking out the ever-expanding number of independent stores, as there are some real gems. Practicality plays a large part in the mall culture, and during the hotter months they are oases of cool in the sweltering city – somewhere to walk, shop, eat and be entertained – where you can escape the searing heat for a few hours. From the smaller community malls dotted around the city, to the mega malls that have changed the skyline, shopping opportunities abound and with most shops open until 22:00 every night, there's enough time to browse. The popularity of the malls is evident by the crowds that they pull, particularly at the weekends. It takes a brave and dedicated shopper to tackle them on a Friday evening.

In common with many countries, the cost of living is increasing and while some of what is available is still cheaper than elsewhere, groceries seem to be more expensive every week. While average prices for most items are comparable, there are not many places that can beat Dubai's range and the frequency of the sales. Cars are, on the whole, a good buy and petrol, though prices are going up, is still cheap enough to make large 4WDs practical for the school run. Electronics can be cheaper but it depends what you are used to; and Dubai is the world's leading re-exporter of gold. The variety of goods on sale is staggering and there is very little that is not available. For most items there is enough choice to find something to fit any budget, from the streets of Karama with its fake designer goods, to the shops in the malls that sell the real thing.

Always On Sale

The Dubai Shopping Festival is now more about promotions, with raffles and scratch-and-win offers rather than great discounts. Then again, discounts are available throughout the year during the many sales that take place so frequently, so you may never need to pay full price for anything! The annual shopping festival will run from January 15 to February 15, 2009, for more info see the website www. dubaishoppingfestival.com.

What & Where To Buy – Quick Reference

Shopping

Some of Dubai's most interesting shops are the independent ones (see p.478) that are springing up all over the city – they may take a bit of looking for but it is usually worth it, as what they sell is invariably more original than anything the malls have to offer. The various shopping areas, the closest that Dubai has to high streets, are great for their eclectic mix of shops. There are few other places where you can shop for fabric while waiting for your car windows to be tinted. One of the few retail sectors where Dubai is lacking is second-hand shops (see Second-Hand Items on p.467), although there are a few linked to various charities. With the population still being largely transitory, there is no shortage of second-hand goods, many of which are advertised on the notice boards in supermarkets, in the classified section of newspapers, and on websites (such as www.expatwoman.com).

Further afield, the modern malls of Sharjah are an alternative to what Dubai has to offer, the brands are pretty much the same but they are convenient for those living on that side of the city. Sharjah's souks, and the Al Arsah Souk (p.483) in particular, are more traditional than those in Dubai and are great for unique gifts. Sharjah is also renowned for its furniture warehouses, especially those selling Indian pieces, such as Lucky's, Pinky's and Khan's. Ajman is developing as the population grows, and has its own City Centre and an area with garment factories and their outlet shops. The traffic to both emirates can get pretty heavy and they are more traditional, with many companies still working split shifts ie. closing between 13:00 and 16:00.

Online Shopping

The popularity of online shopping is increasing around the world, and in an expat city like Dubai, where many residents long for the products they can get in their home countries, it is great to be able to order online. The variety of goods available, and possibly the bargain prices, make this an attractive option for anything you can't find locally. However, not all companies will ship to the UAE and if they do, the shipping charges can be prohibitive. The increasing popularity of PayPal is causing problems for many residents as the facility is only available to those with a US or UK credit card. There are often ways around this, and many sites will accept other forms of payment. eBay is a good example of a site where PayPal is preferred, making it potentially inaccessible here, but some vendors are usually willing to be flexible, especially if you explain the situation.

There should be no problems buying from sites like Amazon, although its branded packaging may sometimes be opened at customs. If you are buying DVDs or videos Benson's World (www.bensonsworld.co.uk) has much cheaper shipping rates and they use plain packaging, so often the DVDs come straight to your post box without going through the censor. Companies without representation in the region will sometimes agree to sell directly to individual customers, so it is worth emailing them. It is possible that if the UAE is not listed as a country that the site deals with, it is because they have not had customers here before, so you may get a positive response if you contact them.

There are a number of local businesses and organisations with an online presence. For electrical goods, Jacky's Electronics (www.jackys.com) has a fairly comprehensive site with good online deals; Magrudy's website (www.magrudy.com) allows for both buying and reserving books; www.uaemall.com is a site which sells items from a number of companies. There are also sites based here that will arrange delivery of gifts both here and internationally, for example, www.giftexpressdubai.com, or www.papagiftexpress. com, which deals with India, Sri Lanka and the UAE.

Access to the second-hand market is available through sites such as www.dubizzle. com, www.expatgossip.com, www.expatwoman.com, www.souk.ae, www.souq.com and www.websouq.com.

Aramex (see also Shipping below) can provide a 'Shop & Ship' service which sets up a mailbox in both the UK and US, great for dealing with sites which do not offer international shipping. They also offer the Web Surfer card, a prepaid MasterCard for use online – as this can be set up through the mailboxes it is a solution to PayPal problems.

Refunds & Exchanges

The policies on refunds and exchanges vary from shop to shop. There is more chance of success with faulty goods rather than with those where you have changed your mind, and it is more common to be offered an exchange or credit note rather than a refund. Even with tags attached, many stores will not even consider an exchange unless you have the receipt. For some items, such as those in sealed packages, shops insist that the packaging should be intact so that the item can be resold. This is ok if the item was unwanted however it has been known for claims for faulty goods to be rejected as the packaging has been damaged but how could you know if it was faulty if you hadn't opened it?

If you are having no success with customer services, ask to speak to the manager, as the person on the shop floor is often not authorised to deviate from standard policy whereas managers may be more flexible.

Consumer Rights

The Consumer Protection Department (part of the UAE Ministry of Economy) was recently established to safeguard the interests of shoppers. The department keeps track of retail prices and has been known to reject planned price increases for staple goods. Consumers wishing to complain about a retailer can do so by completing the complaint form on the website www.economy.ae, by sending an email to consumer@economy.ae, or by calling the freephone hotline on 600 522225. The hotline, however, is manned by non-English speakers so you may be better off sticking to the other methods. In Dubai, the Consumer Rights Unit within the Dubai Economic Department (700 4000, www.dubaided.gov.ae), primarily deals with unfit food, but can be contacted to report faulty goods or to complain if a guarantee is not honoured.

No Going Back?

Buying a gift to send back home? Marks & Spencer (p.476) is one of the few international retailers that allows refunds and exchanges on goods bought overseas. So if granny in Scotland would have preferred a woolly scarf to those flip-flops you bought her, she can take them back to her local store, providing she has the receipt.

Shipping

The large number of both international and local shipping and courier agencies make transporting anything from a coffee pot to a car feasible. Both air freight and sea freight are available; air freight is faster but more expensive and not really suitable for large or heavy objects, whereas sea freight may take several weeks to arrive but it is cheaper and, as it is possible to rent containers, size and weight are not as much of an issue.

With so many companies to choose from it is worth getting a few quotes and finding out what will happen when the goods arrive; some offer no services at the destination while others, usually the bigger ones, will clear customs and deliver right to the door. For smaller items, or those that have to be delivered quickly, air freight is better, and the items can be tracked; again, it is worth shopping around for deals, especially during Dubai Shopping Festival or Dubai Summer Surprises. Empost (286 5000), the Emirates Postal Service, offer both local and international courier and air freight services – their prices are competitive and packages can be tracked.

Several of the courier companies can arrange for items to be delivered to Dubai, and Aramex (286 5050) offers a great service called 'Shop & Ship', for those wishing to buy online. If the site doesn't offer international delivery or their postage rates are high, for a one-off payment of US$35, Aramex will set up a mailbox for you in both the UK and the US. They will arrange for delivery up to three times a week and packages can be tracked; rates for the first half kilo are US$8 and US$5.50 for additional half kilos.

AMOUAGE

LYRIC

story of the rose

Amouage is available at all Paris Gallery stores, Dubai Duty Free,
Abu Dhabi Duty Free, Sharjah Duty Free and Emirates Airlines in UAE

THE GIFT OF KINGS   WWW.AMOUAGE.COM

How To Pay

You'll have few problems parting with your money. Credit cards (American Express, Diners Club, MasterCard and Visa) and debit cards (Visa Electron) are accepted in all the shopping malls, supermarkets, and many of the independent shops. However, you can no longer pay for your petrol with credit or debit cards – it's either cash or a petrol card. Cash is easily accessible, and you're never far from an ATM. While credit cards are great in shops with fixed prices, if you're looking to get the most from your bargaining skills, use cash. Cash is preferred in the souks and smaller shops – try to have a variety of denominations, because it is better to hand over close to the exact amount. US dollars and other foreign currencies are accepted in some larger shops (and in the airport duty free shops), but you're likely to get a better deal if you use dirhams.

Buyer Beware ◀

Traps for the unwary shopper do exist in Dubai. Some of the international stores sell items at prices that are far more expensive than in their country of origin (you can even still see the original price tags). This can be as much as 30% higher – so beware.

Bargaining

Other options **Markets/Souks** p.481

Bargaining is still common practice in the souks and shopping areas of the UAE. Whether you find it fun or not, it is expected and you'll need to give it a go to get the best prices. Before you take the plunge, try to get an idea of prices from a few shops, as there can often be a significant difference for the same item, and decide how much you are willing to spend.

Once you've picked out exactly what you want, start by making the vendor aware that you are a resident and not a tourist, and that if the prices are good, you will come back to shop again. No matter how much you want the item, try to stay laidback and vaguely disinterested. The initial bid should usually be around half of what the vendor is offering. When this is rejected keep going until you reach an agreement or until you have reached your limit. If the price isn't right, say so and walk out – the vendor will often follow and suggest a compromise price. The more you buy, the better the discount and you should find that it improves further if you become a regular customer. When the price is agreed, a verbal contract has been created and if you back out, don't be surprised if you get an angry earful from the vendor.

While common in souks, bargaining isn't appreciated in malls and independent shops; many do operate a set discount system and the price shown may be 'before discount'.

Harvey Nichols

Shopping

Gold Souk

Al Diyafah Street

Electronics shop

Five Green

Al Ghurair City

Traditional lanterns

What & Where To Buy

With so much choice there should be little problem finding what you need. From antiques to the latest technology, and from tools to toys, the aim of this section is to let you know what's out there and the best places to buy.

Alcohol

Other options **On the Town** p.607, **Liquor Licence** p.92

In Dubai, it is legal for anyone over the age of 21 to buy alcohol at licensed bars, restaurants and some clubs, for consumption on the premises. This does not apply to all the emirates. However, if you wish to drink at home you will need a liquor licence (see p.92). Liquor licences are only issued to non-Muslims earning over Dhs.4,000 per month and are only valid for use in the emirate in which they were issued; the amount that you can spend each month on alcohol is determined by your monthly salary.

There are two companies that operate liquor stores in Dubai: African & Eastern (A&E) and Maritime & Mercantile International (MMI). Both have branches in several locations around the city, the most handy being the ones near supermarkets. The selection is decent, and prices are not so bad: wine costs from around Dhs.20 and upwards; vodka from Dhs.60; whisky from Dhs.80; and beer from Dhs.4 to Dhs.8 per can or Dhs.100 to Dhs.135 per case. There is a catch however; alcohol is subject to 30% tax on top of the marked prices and, although this is not included in your allowance, it can be a bit of a shock at the till. The alcohol available at the airport is similar in price to the shops in town, but you don't pay the tax.

In the time-honoured tradition of there being a way round everything, there are a number of 'hole in the wall' stores close to Dubai that sell duty-free alcohol to members of the public, even if you don't have a licence. Prices are reasonable and there is no tax. You can pick up a cheap bottle of plonk from around Dhs.20, and most international brands of beer, wine and spirits are available. MMI-owned Al Hamra Cellar is around an hour's drive from Dubai and they have an amazing selection of wines, beers and spirits. Unlike some of the other hole-in-the-wall stores, Al Hamra Cellar has properly chilled storage facilities, and there is no danger of anything you buy there being past its sell-by date. You can buy wines that have been specially selected by wine guru Oz Clarke, as well as award-winning wines from around the world. To get there, drive along the Emirates Road, heading out of Dubai, until you reach the roundabout at the very end, then turn left and Al Hamra Cellar is on your right hand side seven kilometres down the road. Barracuda Beach Resort (www.barracuda.ae) and Centaurus International (www.centaurusint.com) are other tax-free, licence-free outlets. You don't need to worry about being busted buying booze illegally, but you should be careful when driving home, because it is the transporting of alcohol that could get you into trouble, especially if you are stopped within the borders of the Sharjah emirate. There have been reports of random police checks on vehicles driving from Ajman into Sharjah. Also, if you have an accident and you're found to have a boot full of liquor, your day could take a sudden turn for the worse.

Take A Break

Head for the hills of Oman or the thrills of the UAE – Just one weekend away can make a world of difference to those with busy Dubai lifestyles. Pick up a copy of **Weekend Breaks in Oman & the UAE** for inspiration: it has reviews of over 50 hotels as well as expert tips on what to see and do once you get there.

Alcohol

African & Eastern (A&E) ▶ p.423	Various	See p.508	www.aneme.ae
Al Hamra Cellar ▶ p.313	Ras Al Khaimah	07 244 7403	www.mmidubai.com
Barracuda Beach Resort	Umm Al Quwain	06 768 1555	www.barracuda.ae
Centaurus International (RAK)	Ras Al Khaimah	07 244 5866	www.centaurusint.com
MMI ▶ p.93, p.313, p.621	Various	See p.517	www.mmidubai.com

enjoy the finest fruits of the harvest all year round

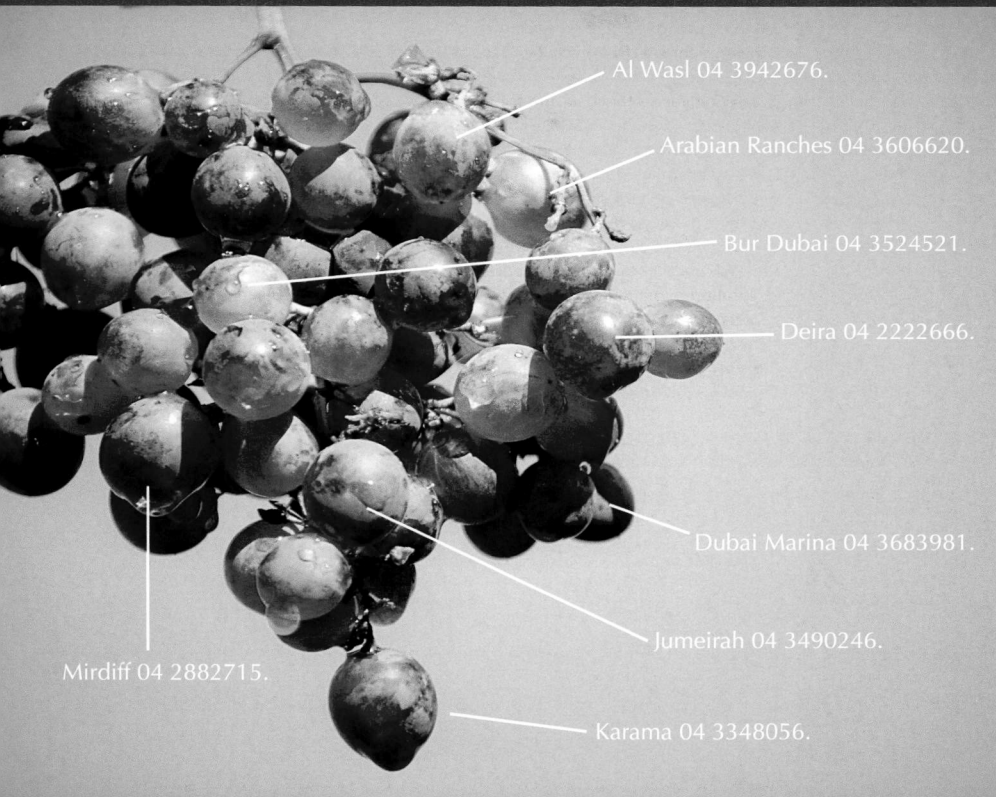

Al Wasl 04 3942676.

Arabian Ranches 04 3606620.

Bur Dubai 04 3524521.

Deira 04 2222666.

Dubai Marina 04 3683981.

Jumeirah 04 3490246.

Mirdiff 04 2882715.

Karama 04 3348056.

The cream of the crop at 8 conveniently located stores around Dubai.

Arte Soukh
Pick up art and crafts,
made by local artists,
at Times Square Center
a few times a month.
There are one hundred
stalls selling a range
of items including
photography, jewellery
and a variety of art.
For more information,
including dates, visit
www.arte.ae.

Art

Other options **Art Galleries** p.264, **Art & Craft Supplies** p.424, **Art Classes** p.330

The art scene in Dubai, quiet for so long, is now enjoying rapid growth. There are galleries and exhibitions displaying traditional and contemporary art by Arabic and international artists working in a range of media.

Aquarius sells locally inspired, often light-hearted, silk paintings and antique furniture. The Majlis Gallery, in a traditional windtower house, is a great venue for fine art, handmade glass, pottery and other unusual pieces. For cutting edge art, check out Five Green or XVA Gallery, while the Art Source in the Al Ghazal Mall in Satwa stocks a range of original artwork – a framing service is also offered. You can also find information on art auctions, as well as information on art fairs and gallery openings, at www.artinthecity.com.

If your knowledge of art isn't up to speed Chrystel Sandra Livolsi is an art consultant who can provide advice on your purchases. For more information call 050 157 6937, or send an email to chrystel@livolsiartgroup.com.

Souk Madinat Jumeirah has the largest concentration of boutiques selling art, glass and photographs, both originals and reproductions. The style and subjects are diverse, from traditional to modern, and Arabic to international.

Many of the galleries and showrooms have a framing service or can recommend one. There are some excellent framing shops on Plant Street in Satwa (map 7 F2) and in Karama Market (map 10 D1) – they can frame anything from prints to sports jerseys.

Art			
Aquarius	Jumeira	04 349 7251	na
Art & Culture	Deira	04 221 9339	na
Art In The City	Various	na	www.artinthecity.com
The Art Source	Al Wasl	04 345 3887	www.theartsource.ae
Artspace Gallery	Trade Centre 2	04 323 0820	www.artspace-dubai.com
Creative Art Centre	Jumeira	04 344 4394	na
Dubai Murals ▶ p.452	Various	050 453 4232	www.dubaimurals.com
Five Green	Oud Metha	04 336 4100	www.fivegreen.com
Gallery One	Umm Suqeim	04 368 6055	na
House of the World	Al Quoz	04 323 3482	www.houseoftheworld.com
Kenza Art Gallery	Umm Suqeim	04 368 6603	na
The Majlis Gallery	Bur Dubai	04 353 6233	www.majlisgallery.com
Mirage Glass	Jebel Ali	04 880 4360	www.mirage-glass.com
Miraj Islamic Art Gallery	Jumeira	04 394 1084	www.mirajislamicartcentre.com
Mondo Art Gallery	Al Barsha	04 341 3001	www.mondoarte.net
Nakkash Gallery	Al Garhoud	04 282 6767	www.nakkashgallery.com
Profile Gallery	Jumeira	04 349 1147	na
Sharjah Art Museum	Sharjah	06 568 8222	www.sharjahmuseums.ae
Soho Gallery	Bur Dubai	04 397 5637	na
The Third Line	Al Quoz	04 341 1367	www.thethirdline.com
Total Arts Gallery	Al Quoz	04 347 5050	www.courtyard-uae.com
XVA Gallery	Bur Dubai	04 353 5383	www.xvagallery.com

Art & Craft Supplies

Other options **Art Galleries** p.264, **Art** p.424, **Art Classes** p.330

There are a number of shops selling a good range of art and craft supplies. Prices can be rather expensive for some speciality items, such as mosaic tiles for example, but are reasonable for art materials. There is enough choice to keep most artists happy, from paints and crayons for children, to top quality oils. Emirates Trading, near Maktoum Bridge, stocks everything from children's crayons to industrial spray booths, and they are suppliers for Windsor & Newton and Daler products. Elves & Fairies, upstairs in the Jumeirah Centre, have a huge range of decorative stamps and stencils. Wasco White Star, in the Beach Centre, has a selection of reasonably priced craft supplies, many of which are suitable for children's projects and difficult to find elsewhere. The Holiday Centre on Sheikh Zayed Road houses a few good art and craft supplies shops, such as Creations Art, and there are also some excellent shops within the Bin Sougat Mall in Rashidiya. For DIY picture-framers, Rafi Frame Store (aka Al Warda Gallery) in Karama is the place to find the necessary equipment, including mountboard.

Art & Craft Supplies			
Al Hathboor General Trading	Trade Centre 1	04 337 3364	www.alhathboor.com
The Art Source	Al Wasl	04 345 3887	www.theartsource.ae
Art Stop	Jumeira	04 349 0627	na
Creations Art	Trade Centre 1	04 331 1047	www.artdubai.com
Dubai International Art Centre	Jumeira	04 344 4398	www.artdubai.com
Dubai Library	Al Rashidiya	04 286 2400	www.dubailibrary.com
Elves & Fairies	Jumeira	04 344 9485	www.elvesandfairies.org
Emirates Trading Est.	Various	See p.513	www.emiratestrading.ae
Kazim Gulf Traders	Jumeira	04 349 3347	na
Rafi Frame Store	Karama	04 337 6989	www.dubaiframes.com
Wasco White Star	Jumeira	04 342 2179	na

Baby Items

The basic baby items are all available in Dubai and, while you may not find the range you would back home, you should find the majority of the things you need.

The supermarkets all stock formula, jars of food, nappies and wipes; many also sell bottles and feeding equipment. Choithram has the best selection of formulas, stocking popular UK brands SMA and Cow & Gate. If you can't find what you are looking for, ask a shop assistant because they sometimes keep certain brands behind the counter. They also have a good range of jars of baby food – they may cost double what they would back home but they are great for when you can't face cooking. Large pharmacies sell baby essentials and some have breast pumps.

For nursery essentials, Baby Shop, Goodbaby and Mothercare all sell bottles, buggies, car seats, changing bags, cots, prams, rocking chairs, travel cots and pretty much everything else you'll need. Toys R Us has recently doubled the size of its baby department and now stocks a wide range, from pushchairs to baby bottles, cots to travel accessories. The quality of the items is good and most conform to international safety standards. Britax and Maxi Cosi car seats are widely available and should fit most cars; all shops will offer to help fit car seats but the staff are often trained in the mechanics of how the seat fits in rather than whether it is the most suitable.

The quality of cot mattresses may vary. Mothercare can order specific sizes but plan ahead so that you get it in good time. The range of slings is pretty limited and backpacks to put your baby in are hard to find, so you may want to order these items from overseas or look online at Kid Eternity.

Mamas and Papas products can be found in Harvey Nichols in Mall of the Emirates and in Mercato Mall and Wafi. The brand is also expected to have its own shop in Dubai Mall. DubaiBabies stocks a range of products and gift ideas for babies and parents. You can pick up gift sets, vouchers or feeding and bathing accessories here. There is a stand

Second-Hand Stuff

Second-hand baby stuff is widely available in Dubai – you just need to know where to look. There are classifieds listings on www.expatwoman. com and www.expat gossip.com, and then of course there's always the supermarket noticeboards.

in Mercato Mall but you can also purchase items online, with free delivery (see www. dubaibabies.com for more details).

IKEA has a small range of nursery furniture such as cots, changing tables and bathtubs. They also do a selection of cot sheets and blankets and some baby-safe toys.

Worth waiting for are Baby Shop's sales which they have several times a year. Goodbaby has the largest selection of buggies and prams, including Cam, Quinny and Phil & Teds. Mothercare provide an ordering service for items that you've seen online or in a UK catalogue but the delivery time is a minimum of four weeks and often longer. Just Kidding sells a range of baby items, furniture and clothes from Europe, including Bugaboo buggies, Little Company bags and Stokke high chairs. It's not for the budget conscious, but worth a browse.

Baby Items

Babyshop	Various	See p.510	www.babyshopstores.com
Carrefour	Various	See p.511	www.carrefouruae.com
Choithram	Various	See p.512	www.choithram.com
DubaiBabies	Online	050 457 9698	www.dubaibabies.com
Goodbaby	Trade Centre Rd, opp Spinneys	04 397 5653	www.goodbabydubai.com
Harvey Nichols	Mall of the Emirates	04 409 8888	www.harveynichols.com
IKEA ▶ p.451	Festival Power Centre	800 4532	www.ikeadubai.com
Just Kidding	Al Quoz	04 341 3922	www.justkidding-me.com
Kid Eternity	Online	050 151 3825	www.kid-eternity.com
Mamas & Papas	Various	See p.517	www.mamasandpapas.co.uk
Mothercare	Various	See p.517	www.mothercare.com
Textura Interiors	Mercato	04 344 2899	www.textura-interiors.com
Toys R Us	Various	See p.522	www.toysrus.com

Beachwear

Other options **Clothes** p.435, **Sports Goods** p.467

For the amount of time spent on the beach or by the pool in Dubai, it's not surprising that there are several specialist and designer beachwear shops where a swimsuit can cost as much as a good night out. With year-round sunshine there is no real off-peak season, so end-of-season sales are a bit unpredictable. Join the Beyond the Beach mailing list though, and they'll send you advance notice of their December sales.

UV protective items are a must for children and a good idea for adults. There are limited ranges in Beyond the Beach, UV swimsuits for kids at Woolworths all year round, and a number of the larger stores and department stores carry them seasonally. Debenhams has a great range of fashion swimwear (including a full range of beach accessories, like hats, sarongs, beach towels and matching flip-flops). Heatwaves sell a good range for both adults and children, and if they don't have much stock you can leave your name and they'll let you know when a new delivery arrives. The Uniform Shop has some UV suits (they also carry Baby Banz sunglasses and hats), as does Picnico on Beach Road. Hamac's ranges include Vilebrequin swimming shorts for men and boys.

Beachwear

Al Boom Marine	Various	See p.508
Bare Essentials	Jumeirah Centre	04 344 0552
Beyond The Beach	Various	See p.510
Debenhams	Various	See p.513
Hamac	Various	See p.515
Havaianas	Souk Al Bahar	04 420 0150
Heatwaves	Various	See p.515
Oceano	Palm Strip	04 346 1961
OndadeMar	Atlantis The Palm	04 422 6996
Picnico General Trading	Jumeirah Rd	04 394 1653
The Uniform Shop	Spinneys	04 394 1477
Woolworths	Various	See p.522

Bicycles

Once you've experienced the traffic in Dubai it may not seem like the most bicycle-friendly city, but there is an active cycling scene. Both mountain biking and road cycling are popular and the equipment needed for them is available; the range is adequate but can be expensive. For serious cyclists, there are an increasing number of shops, and brands, in town – all offer a good selection of bikes and all the paraphernalia and safety equipment that you'll need, and they also repair and service bikes. Newest arrivals include the Kona range near Lamcy Plaza and Rage, in Festival Centre and Dubai Mall, which sells Giant and the sought-after Santa Cruz range of bikes. 360 Lifestyle in Oud Metha stocks a wide range of the excellent Specialized bikes, clothing and accessories (and also has a smaller range on show inside Studio R in Ibn Battuta, 04 366 9890), and there is a Trek shop in the Metropolitan Hotel. Bike 'n' Rack (on Al Khail Road) also stocks Giant and a range of Thule bike racks, the Cannondale shops stock Cannondale, Fuji, Mongoose and Schwinn, and Wolfi's stocks Scott, Felt, Merida and Storck.

For the casual cyclist, Toys R Us and a number of sports shops sell more basic models at reasonable prices. Go Sport has a large bike section and workshop in their store in Mall of the Emirates. If you're after a bit of nostalgia, the 'sit-up-and-beg' models – popular with gardeners and delivery cyclists – can be found in the smaller bike shops all over the city (check out Karama and Satwa). Children's bicycles are widely available in bike and sports shops, and toy shops like Baby Shop, Toys R Us and Goodbaby have a range for tiny Lance Armstrong wannabes. Magrudy's also carries a small range of bikes both big and small – kids' models like their hot-pink trike complete with flower basket and handlebar tassles will take you right back to childhood. If you want to make cycling a family activity, Cannondale has a selection of children's seats, priced from Dhs.150 to Dhs.300, which they will fit for you. Both adult's and children's helmets are available at the main retailers.

Bicycles		
360 Lifestyle	Al Nasr Palace, Oud Metha	04 337 3013
Babyshop	Various	See p.510
Bike 'n' Rack	Ras Al Khor	04 333 3556
Carrefour	Various	See p.511
Cycle Sport	Al Barsha	04 341 5415
Go Sport	Various	See p.514
Goodbaby	Trade Center Rd, Opp Spinneys	04 397 5653
Kona Bike Shop	Oud Metha	04 335 0999
Magrudy's ▶ p.429	Various	See p.516
Prozone	Various	See p.519
Rage Bike Shop	Festival Centre	04 375 0231
Sun & Sand Sports	Various	See p.521
Toys R Us	Various	See p.522
Trek	Metropolitan Hotel	04 407 6641
Wolfi's Bike Shop	Btn Jct 2-3, Al Quoz	04 339 4453

Cuddly camels

Paul Frank

Books

Other options **Libraries** p.368, **Second-Hand Items** p.464

Book lovers of all ages are well catered for in Dubai. There are a number of English language bookshops with huge ranges of books, from the latest bestsellers to obscure reference books. The logic behind the shelving system can be a little eccentric and although you'll be able to find out if a book is in stock, finding the actual item, even for the staff, can be a bit hit-and-miss. Prices of books vary but generally compete with online prices.

Magrudy's has a good range of titles and can order specific books for you. They also have a website (www.magrudy.com) on which you can order and reserve books. Kinokuniya Bookstore in The Dubai Mall stocks a variety of foreign titles including a fantastic range of Japanese titles. The popular international chain Borders opened its first Dubai store in Mall of the Emirates in late 2006, and added two more branches in 2007 in Deira City Centre and Dubai Festival Centre. Jashanmal Bookstore carries an impressive range for all ages and Virgin Megastore has an interesting selection worth checking out – both have branches around Dubai. Books Plus has an excellent range of books both for adults and children, including fiction, travel, hobbies and interests. Book Worm, in the Park n Shop complex is especially good for children. They carry a huge range of children's books, and if you know about a book that children will love, they'll consider ordering it for the shop.

With Dubai's many transitory residents trying to keep their clutter (and book collections) to a minimum, the second-hand book shops have a wide choice, including a large selection of fiction, and a fast turnover. Many of their books have only been read once, and it's considerably cheaper than buying new books. Both House of Prose in Jumeira and Ibn Battuta and Book World in Karama and Satwa, buy and sell, and also have a buy-back service, where they'll give you back 50% of what you paid on books you've bought from them, regardless of how long ago it was.

There are regular charity book sales, the most notable being the ones organised by Medecins Sans Frontiers (www.msfuae.ae). They are held several times throughout the year, usually in the Dune Centre in Satwa.

Books

Book Park Trading	Hyatt Regency Hotel	04 273 1361	na
Book World	Various	See p.510	na
Book Worm	Beh Park n Shop	04 394 5770	na
Books Gallery	The Village Mall	04 344 5770	na
Books Plus ▶ p.493	Various	See p.511	na
Borders ▶ p.495	Various	See p.511	www.bordersstores.com
Carrefour	Various	See p.511	www.carrefouruae.com
Culture & Co	API Tower, Trade Centre 1	04 331 3114	www.culturecodubai.com
Dubai Library	Bin Sougat Centre	04 286 2400	www.dubailibrary.com
Géant ▶ p.479	Ibn Battuta Shopping Mall	04 368 5858	www.geant-dubai.com
House of Prose	Various	See p.515	na
Jashanmal ▶ p.431	Various	See p.515	www.jashanmal.ae
Kinokuniya Bookstore	The Dubai Mall	04 434 0111	na
Magrudy's ▶ p.429	Various	See p.516	www.magrudy.com
Spinneys	Various	See p.520	www.spinneys.com
Titan Book Shop	Various	See p.521	na
Virgin Megastore ▶ p.497	Various	See p.522	www.virgin.com
Wasco White Star	Beach Centre	04 342 2179	na
White Star Bookshop	Beach Centre	04 344 6628	na

Books make us who we are.

Magrudy's™
bringing you only the best

Camera Equipment

Other options **Electronics & Home Appliances** p.439

From single-use cameras to darkroom equipment, photographers have got plenty of places to include on their shopping lists. In common with market forces the world over, digital models dominate the shelves. They are available in all the electronics shops, hypermarkets, and photo processing outlets; all the major brands are represented. The jury's still out on whether cameras here are cheaper than elsewhere, it really depends on where else you are looking; the prices in Singapore are often lower, and in most of Europe they will be higher. Within Dubai, prices will vary between the larger outlets, where prices are fixed, and the electronics shops of Bur Dubai. However, while you might be able to bag a bargain from the independent retailers using your superior powers of negotiation, you'll have more protection buying from the larger outlets. The most important consideration, if you are buying the camera to take to another country, is to ensure that your warranty is international: don't just take the retailer's word for it, actually ask to open the box and read the warranty to make sure.

For specialist equipment and a good range of film cameras, the main outlets are Grand Stores and Salam Studio. Grand Stores sells Fuji, Nikon, Canon and Mamiya; Salam Studio carries Bronica, Leica, Minolta and Pentax; they both sell a selection of filters, tripods and studio equipment. The alternative to buying locally is to use an online retailer. B&H Photo, in New York, is extremely popular, and although shipping is expensive you can group together with a few friends for a big order, and spread the delivery costs (www.bandhphoto.com).

For second-hand equipment, www.gulfphotoplus.com has an active equipment noticeboard (as well as being a great source of information and a good networking site for locally based photography enthusiasts).

Should your equipment need to be repaired, Grand Stores offers a repair service. HN Camera Repairs offer an in house repair service for all makes of camera.

Camera Equipment			
Grand Stores	Various	See p.515	www.grandstores.com
HN Camera Repairs	Jumeirah Centre	04 349 0971	na
Jacky's Electronics	Various	See p.515	www.jackys.com
Jumbo Electronics	Various	See p.516	www.jumbocorp.com
MK Trading Co	Deira	04 222 5745	na
National Store	Khan Saheb Bld, Al Fahidi St	04 353 6074	www.nationalstore.ae
Plug-Ins	Various	See p.516	www.pluginselectronix.com
Salam Studio & Stores	Wafi Mall	04 324 5252	www.salams.com
Sharaf DG	Various	See p.520	www.sharafdg.com
United Colour Film (UCF)	Al Qusais	04 267 5599	www.ucfq.com

Car Parts & Accessories

Wherever there are cars, there will be accessories for them and Dubai is no exception. ACE and Carrefour have large departments selling everything from steering wheel covers to fridges which run off the car battery. For those who enjoy tinkering with what's under the bonnet, there are a myriad of tools available in larger stores and in the smaller shops in Satwa. Off-road enthusiasts should also check out AAA for specialist sand tracks and heavy duty jacks and winches – if your car is fitted with a GPS system they can rescue you from the most remote dune or wadi. GPS systems are available from Picnico and Abdulla Mohammed Ibrahim Trading (who recommend the

" *Today a Reader*
Tomorrow a Leader "

JASHANMAL BOOKSTORES

Garmin brand), and even from more mainstream shops like Plug-Ins, Carrefour and Sharaf DG.

Car stereos are widely available, and are sold by most electronics shops, with some of the car dealerships stocking alternative models for their cars. To have them fitted, head either to the workshops of Rashidiya or Satwa, or AAA and the dealers – it should cost around Dhs.500 if you are providing all the parts.

Many car owners try to beat the heat by having their car windows tinted. The legal limit is 30% tint; if you get your windows tinted any darker you could be fined, and your car won't pass its annual inspection. The options range from the Dhs.75 plastic film from the workshops in Satwa, to Dhs.1,300 to Dhs.1,500 at After Dark (covered a by a ten-year warranty), and up to Dhs.5,000 at V-Kool (also covered by warranty, and its clear film is more heat resistant than the tinted one). Al Quoz and Rashidiya are the places to head if you're looking to customise your car by increasing its performance. Drivers really wishing to pimp their ride will be thrilled to hear that West Coast Customs (as featured on the MTV series) now has a showroom and workshop in Al Quoz.

Car Parts & Accessories

AAA	Nr Honda Trading Enterprises	04 266 9989	www.aaadubai.com
Abdulla Mohammed Ibrahim Trading (Amit)	Al Ras	04 229 1195	www.amitdubai.net
ACE	Various	See p.508	www.aceuae.com
After Dark	Nr Lamcy Plaza	04 337 8337	www.afterdark-uae.com
Carrefour	Various	See p.511	www.carrefouruae.com
Picnico General Trading	Jumeirah Rd	04 394 1653	na
Plug-Ins	Various	See p.519	www.pluginselectronix.com
V-Kool Emirates	Jebel Ali Free Trade Zone	04 340 0092	www.v-kool.com
West Coast Customs	Nr 3rd Interchange, Shk Zayed Rd	04 347 2888	www.wcc-me.com
Yellow Hat ▶ p.433	Times Square	04 341 8592	www.yellowhat.ae

Cards & Gift Wrapping

Other options **Books** p.428, **Art & Craft Supplies** p.424

The standard greetings cards and wrapping paper are widely available, but there are also alternatives. Carlton Cards and Gulf Greetings cover most occasions and the supermarkets carry limited selections. Marks & Spencer greeting cards are good quality. For something a bit different, the Susan Walpole shops have a good selection, as do Magrudy's and THE One; there are small gift wrapping counters in several of the malls. For gift wrapping paper that won't break the bank try IKEA and Woolworths, or for elaborate wrapping that will really add a special touch to your gift, try Paper Moon. There are handmade cards available, most readily at craft fairs. Cadorim, in The Village Mall, offer a gift wrapping service (boxes and paper) and they also have a selection of cards.

Cards & Gift Wrapping

Al Fahidi Stationery	Various	See p.508
Cadorim	The Village Mall	04 394 3333
Carlton Cards	Various	See p.511
Carrefour	Various	See p.511
Emirates Trading Est.	Various	See p.513
Farook International Stationary	Meena Bazaar	04 352 1997
Gulf Greetings	Various	See p.515
IKEA ▶ p.451	Festival Power Centre	800 4532
Marks & Spencer	Various	See p.517
Paper Moon	Various	See p.518
Susan Walpole	Various	See p.521
THE One	Various	See p.521
Titan Book Shop	Various	See p.521
Virgin Megastore ▶ p.497	Various	See p.522
Woolworths	Various	See p.522

Think Car Think 🤠 YellowHat
Japan

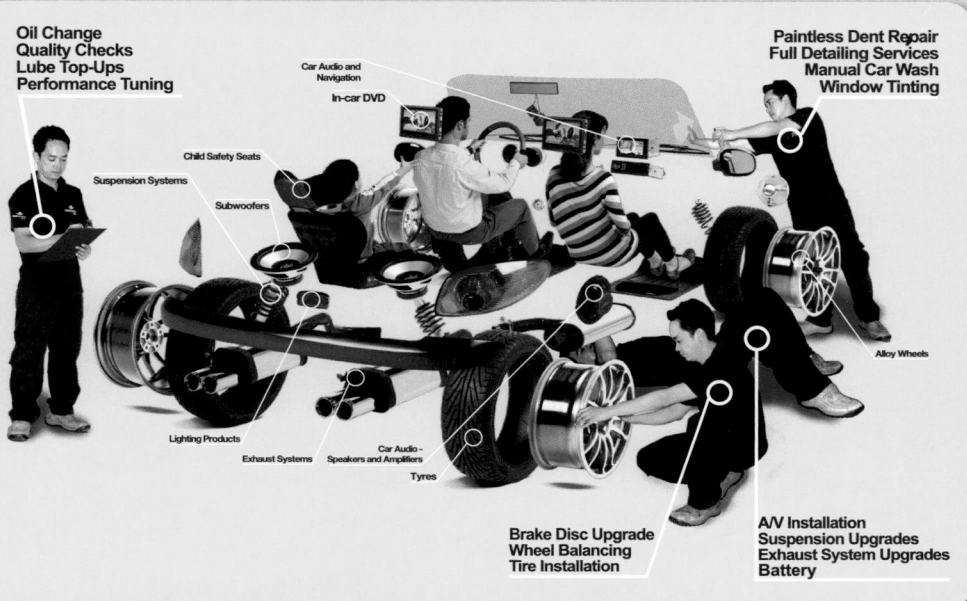

Oil Change
Quality Checks
Lube Top-Ups
Performance Tuning

Car Audio and Navigation
In-car DVD

Child Safety Seats
Suspension Systems
Subwoofers

Paintless Dent Repair
Full Detailing Services
Manual Car Wash
Window Tinting

Alloy Wheels

Lighting Products
Exhaust Systems
Speakers and Amplifiers
Car Audio - Speakers and Amplifiers
Tyres

Brake Disc Upgrade
Wheel Balancing
Tire Installation

A/V Installation
Suspension Upgrades
Exhaust System Upgrades
Battery

YellowHat - the ultimate car accessory superstore now in the UAE.

YellowHat. Japan's leading car accessory store for the past 50 years with more than 500 stores, promises to deliver nothing less than Japan quality and experience to the U.A.E. market.

Nadd Al Hamar Branch - Services Available
7 Power Wash Bays - 3 TOTAL Rapid Oil Change Bays - 4 Audio Visual Bays - 3 Tyre Bays
PLUS a huge range of other services like tint application, battery change, dent removal,
A/C refilling, wheel alignment, auto-detailing, engine flushing and more ...

WWW.YELLOWHAT.AE

Times Square Center Branch   Tel - 04 341 85 92   **Nadd Al Hamar Branch**   Tel - 04 289 80 60

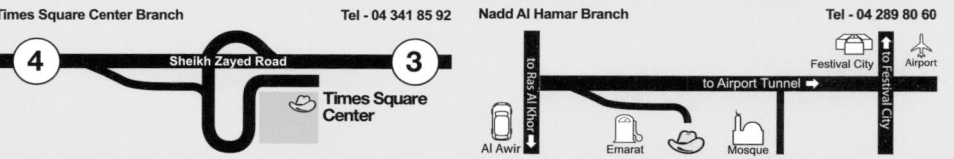

(4) Sheikh Zayed Road (3)
Times Square Center

to Ras Al Khor
to Airport Tunnel ➡
Festival City
Airport
to Festival City
Al Awir
Emarat
Mosque

Carpets

Other options **Bargaining** p.420, **Souvenirs** p.466

Carpets are one of the region's signature items. The ones on sale here tend to be imported from Iran, Turkey, Pakistan and Central Asia. The price of a carpet depends on a number of factors such as its origin, the material used, the number of knots, and whether or not it is handmade.

The most expensive carpets are usually those hand-made with silk, in Iran. The higher the quality the neater the back, so turn the carpets over – if the pattern is clearly depicted and the knots are all neat, the carpet is of higher quality than those that are indistinct. Try to do some research so that you have a basic idea of what you are looking for before you go, just in case you happen to meet an unscrupulous carpet dealer who could take advantage of your naivety. Fortunately, crooked carpet conmen are few and far between, and most will happily explain the differences between the rugs and share their extensive knowledge with you. National Iranian Carpets have a section on their website (www.niccarpets. com) about the history and development of carpets from the various regions.

Ask to see a selection of various carpets so that you can get a feel for the differences between hand-made or machine-made, silk, wool or blend carpets. Of course, asking may not be necessary, since the moment you walk through the doors the carpet vendor will undoubtedly start unrolling carpets and laying them out at a furious pace! Carpets range in price from a few hundred dirhams to tens of thousands of dirhams. It is always worth bargaining to get a better price – make sure the seller knows you are not a tourist, and remain polite at all times to maximise the success of your haggling. Deira Tower on Al Nasr Square has a huge number of carpet outlets under one roof, and the Blue Souk in Sharjah (see p.482) also has a great range. Occasionally you might get a travelling carpet seller ringing your doorbell – he usually drives around an area in his old and battered pickup that is packed to the roof with carpets. The quality isn't great, and even if you show the slightest interest he'll be back to ring your doorbell time and time again.

Carpetland is a one-stop-shop for whatever type of carpet you are after, whether your heart is set on a Persian antique, or having shagpile laid in the bedroom, you'll be spoilt for choice. Other options, if you are looking for something practical rather than decorative, are Fabindia, IKEA, Carrefour or THE One.

Carpets		
Al Orooba Oriental	BurJuman	04 351 0919
Carpetland	Opp Al Nasr Cinema	04 337 7677
Carrefour	Various	See p.511
Fabindia	Al Mankhool Rd	04 398 9633
Gemaco	Nr Ace Hardware, Shk Zayed Rd	04 338 9500
IKEA ▶ p.451	Festival Power Centre	800 4532
Kashmir Gallery	Al Ghurair City	04 222 5271
National Iranian Carpets	Various	See p.518
Persian Carpet House	Crowne Plaza	04 332 1161
Pride Of Kashmir	Various	See p.519
Quem Persian Carpets	Sheraton Dubai Creek Hotel & Towers	04 228 1848
Red Sea Exhibition	Beach Centre	04 344 3949
THE One	Various	See p.521
Total Arts Gallery	The Courtyard	04 347 5050

Carpets

Cars

Other options **Buying a Vehicle** p.228

Cars are one of the best buys in Dubai, with prices much lower than you'd usually pay in your home country. Your time in Dubai may be the only chance you have to drive a really luxurious car, rather than a more practical model, so if you've always fantasised about driving a Rolls Royce Silver Shadow, this could be the time. It is almost de rigueur to own a four-wheel drive, even if the only off-roading you do is to park on the pavement. Fortunately, compared to the rest of the world petrol is still pretty cheap here, so it is affordable to fill up even the thirstiest of fuel-guzzlers.

All the major car dealers are represented (see p.230) and, to make owning a car even more attractive, the interest rates for car loans are fairly low. If you are buying a new car and are after a bargain, there are usually special offers during the Shopping Festival and Ramadan.

The second-hand car market is thriving (see p.231). There are garages across the city, and the Used Car Market at Al Awir is worth a look. If you would prefer to buy privately, check out the classified ads or the noticeboards at the supermarkets.

The conditions are tough for cars here, especially if they have been used in the desert, so it is a good idea to have the car vetted by a garage before you hand over your money. AAA, in Al Quoz (04 347 0400) and Rashidiya (04 285 8989), look at everything from the engine to the paintwork.

Factory Outlets

There's a Benetton factory shop (04 335 2761) near Maktoum Bridge and Adidas factory shops on Airport Road (04 282 0211) and near Lamcy Plaza (04 335 4403), among others. There is also a factory outlet in Jebel Ali Free Zone (04 881 8817). Prices are not always lower than they are in the retail shops, so you'll probably get better bargains if you wait for the sales. The new Outlet Mall (p.502) is the best bet for bargain hunters.

Clothes

Other options **Sports Goods** p.467, **Beachwear** p.426, **Kids Clothes** p.455, **Lingerie** p.457, **Shoes** p.465, **Tailoring** p.469

Dubai is a haven for well-dressed shopaholics, with all the malls housing a high concentration of clothes shops. Whether you are a designer diva or a bargain babe, in Dubai it is nearly impossible to have a 'bad shopping day' where you leave tired, but empty-handed. Not only is the range of clothes amazing, but several times a year there are sweeping sales when you'll end up paying so little for a designer frock that you might as well buy two!

For those events when only the very best will do, the Boulevard at Emirates Towers is the place. Having chosen the creation to be seen in, be it by Alexander McQueen, Stella McCartney, Marni or Prada, the selection of Lulu Guinness bags and Jimmy Choo shoes will enable you to complete your ensemble without having to venture beyond this enclave of exclusivity. Then again, Saks Fifth Avenue in BurJuman, and Harvey Nichols in Mall of the Emirates, are both worth a visit (or many visits) to bag yourself some cutting-edge couture. Via Rodeo, also at Mall of the Emirates, houses outlets for Dolce & Gabbana, Emporio Armani and Versace, among others. Other designer names that you will see as you scour Dubai's many shopping malls include Karen Millen, Kenneth Cole, Calvin Klein,

Clothes		
Amichi	Mercato	04 349 0999
Armani Exchange	Deira City Centre	04 294 3057
Armani Jeans	Mercato	04 344 2118
Ayesha Depala Boutique	The Village Mall	04 344 5378
Banana Republic	Deira City Centre	04 294 1163
Bebe	BurJuman	04 355 4007
Benetton	Various	See p.510
Bershka	Various	See p.510
Bhs	Various	See p.510
BinHendi Boutique	Various	See p.510
Bossini	Various	See p.511
Boutique 1	Various	See p.511
Burberry	Various	See p.511
Calvin Klein	Various	See p.511
Carrefour	Various	See p.511
Cartoon Fashion	Al Ghurair City	04 221 6461

Clothes

Century 2000	Nr Al Nasr Cinema	04 336 6654
Cerruti	Mercato	04 344 4041
Chanel	Various	See p.512
Christian Lacroix	BurJuman	04 351 7133
Club Monaco	Various	See p.512
Coast	Various	See p.512
Danier	Various	See p.512
Debenhams	Various	See p.513
Diesel	Various	See p.513
DKNY	Various	See p.513
Donna Karan	BurJuman	04 351 6794
Dorothy Perkins	Various	See p.513
Elle	Various	See p.513
Escada	BurJuman	04 359 1117
Esprit	BurJuman	04 355 3324
Etoile	Wafi Mall	04 324 0465
Evans	Various	See p.514
Eve Michelle	Magrudy's	04 342 9574
Fabindia	Al Mankhool Rd	04 398 9633
Factory Fashions	Lamcy Plaza	04 336 2699
FCUK	Various	See p.514
Five Green	Garden Home Center, Oud Metha	04 336 4100
Fleurt	Mercato	04 342 0906
Forever 21	Various	See p.514
G2000	Various	See p.514
Gap	Various	See p.514
Géant ▶ p.479	Ibn Battuta Shopping Mall	04 368 5858
Gerry Webber	Various	See p.514
Gianfranco FERRE'	Various	See p.514
Ginger & Lace	Wafi Mall	04 324 5699
Giordano	Various	See p.514
Guess	Various	See p.514
H&M	Various	See p.515
Hang Ten	Various	See p.515
Harvey Nichols	Mall of the Emirates	04 409 8888
Hugo Boss	Various	See p.515
HyperPanda	Festival Power Centre	04 232 5566
Jaeger	Wafi Mall	04 324 9838
JC Penney	BurJuman	04 351 5353
Jennyfer	Various	See p.515
Karen Millen	Various	See p.516
Kitsch Boutique	Souk Al Bahar	04 367 4504
Kookai	Deira City Centre	04 295 2598
Lacoste	Deira City Centre	04 295 4429
Levis	Various	See p.516
Levis Outlet	Various	See p.516
Liwa	Various	See p.516
Liz Clairborne	Bur Dubai	04 351 4917
Luxecouture	The Village Mall	04 344 7933
Mango	Various	See p.517
Marks & Spencer	Various	See p.517

Donna Karan, Hugo Boss, Paul Smith, Ralph Lauren and Christian Lacroix. Vying for the crown of Dubai's most exclusive mall, BurJuman and Wafi City both have designer labels in abundance in their many exclusive boutiques; although both also have some high-street shopping such as Marks & Spencer in Wafi and Bhs in BurJuman. The Mall of the Emirates and the colossal Dubai Mall are the big rollers and both hold a broad range of stores offering a huge variety of designer names and high-street brands. The Designers at Debenhams range at the Mall of the Emirates appeals to designer tastes but a limited budget with an exclusive selection of men's and women's clothing from Jasper Conran, Pearce Fionda and John Rocha. Eve Michelle (Magrudy's Mall) has a loyal following for its range of exclusive European creations for ladies. If you are into street chic, Five Green (p.480) will be a regular hangout – every corner of this unique space is dedicated to cutting-edge clothing, art and music.

The newly opened Dubai Mall will soon feature renowned department store Bloomingdales and stores from well-known designers such as Marc by Marc Jacobs, Dolce and Gabanna and Jean Paul Gaultier. For everyday clothing, the choice is unlimited. Debenhams, Marks & Spencer, H&M, Zara, Woolworths (the South African one, not the UK one), Mango, Promod, River Island, Topshop, Massimo Dutti, Monsoon, Next... the list goes on and on, and these all have more than one branch around Dubai.

For something a little different, you can get beautiful hand-crafted fabrics and traditional Indian clothing at Fabindia (see also p.478) on Al Mankhool Road, or Melangè in Jumeirah Plaza.

Men needn't feel left out or poorly dressed: Maktoum Road (between the Clock Tower Roundabout and Al Khaleej Palace Hotel) is lined with

Clothes

Marlboro Classics	Various	See p.517
Massimo Dutti	Various	See p.517
Max	Various	See p.517
Max Mara	BurJuman	04 351 3140
Melangé	Jumeira Plaza	04 344 4721
Mexx	Various	See p.517
Mexx for Less	Lamcy Plaza	04 334 0096
Miss Sixty	Various	See p.517
Moka	Jumeirah Centre	04 349 3800
Monsoon	Various	See p.517
Mr Price	Lamcy Plaza	04 336 6656
New Look	Various	See p.518
New Yorker	Festival Centre	04 232 9744
Next	Various	See p.518
O'de Rose	999 Al Wasl Rd	04 348 7990
Oasis	Various	See p.518
Oltre	Deira City Centre	04 299 0011
Oui	Wafi Mall	04 324 2167
Ounass	Various	See p.518
Peacocks	Various	See p.519
Pierre Cardin	Various	See p.518
Polo Ralph Lauren	Various	See p.519
Priceless	Dubai Outlet Mall	04 425 9818
Principles	Various	See p.519
Promod	Various	See p.519
Pull & Bear	Various	See p.519
Raoul	Various	See p.519
Reem's Closet	Mazaya Centre	04 343 9553
Replay	BurJuman	04 355 3324
RHS	Various	See p.520
River Island	Various	See p.520
Rodeo Drive	Various	See p.520
S*uce	Various	See p.520
Saks Fifth Avenue	Various	See p.520
Sana Fashion	Various	See p.520
Splash	Various	See p.520
Stadium	Deira City Centre	04 295 0261
Stradivarius	Various	See p.521
Ted Baker	BurJuman	04 355 3842
Ted Lapidus	Twin Towers	04 227 2789
The White Company	Various	See p.521
Topman	Various	See p.522
Topshop	Various	See p.522
Via Rodeo	Mall of the Emirates	04 341 0113
Wallis	Various	See p.522
Warehouse	Deira City Centre	04 294 0811
Woodland	Century Mall	04 296 7890
Woolworths	Various	See p.522
XOXO	BurJuman	04 355 3324
Zadig & Voltaire	The Walk, JBR	04 423 3768
Zara	Various	See p.522

stores selling men's designer clothing, and there are also plenty of options inside the Twin Towers Mall in Deira. There are a couple of suit shops along Al Diyafah Street in Satwa. Of course, most of the shops loved by women also have excellent men's sections, such as Debenhams, Marks & Spencer, Next, Zara and Massimo Dutti. Bargain hunters will love Dubai... the choice is huge. Try Sana Fashions, Carrefour and Géant for really good bargains – they receive regular deliveries of factory seconds and retailer overruns, and there are plenty of well-known brands available if you get there early, such as Gap, George and Cherokee. Lamcy Plaza is a real bargain-hunter's mall – Mexx for Less, Peacocks and Factory Fashions (stocking overruns from Adams and Pumpkin Patch) are all excellent, as are Jennyfer and Mr Price. The new Dubai Outlet Mall (p.502) is a welcome addition to the shopping scene, with a number of brands offering end-of-line stock at reduced prices.

The Karama Market is perhaps the main contender for bargain shopping in Dubai: with rows and rows of shops selling designer labels, both the genuine article and some quite convincing knock-offs. There's also some pretty dreadful tat on offer and some of the clothing isn't suitable for even the most liberal of customers.

Petite & Plus Sizes

If you are frequently frustrated by the standard range (UK 8 to 16) of clothing sizes found in stores because items are always a little bit too big or a little bit too small, you will be relieved to know that retailers in Dubai are increasingly offering petite and plus-size lines. Petite ranges are available in Debenhams, Splash and Marks & Spencer, while Bhs, Debenhams, Liz Claiborne, Marks & Spencer, Splash and Woolworths all carry plus-size collections (look out for Evans in Debenhams and Scarlett's in Splash).

For more exclusive lines for the fuller figure, try Irene Sieber, Oui Plus and Samoon (all in Wafi), or Charisma in the Beach Centre in Jumeira.

It's not only women who are frustrated at not being able to find clothes that fit. Men looking for larger sizes should head to Big & Tall (04 397 3873) on Bank Street. They cater for waist sizes from 40 plus and shirts up to 6XL.

Computers

Other options
Electronics & Home Appliances p.439

In terms of technology, Dubai is no slacker – the latest computer equipment is easy to find and there's even a mall dedicated to it (Al Ain Mall in Bur Dubai).

Every year Dubai hosts GITEX (the Gulf Information Technology Exhibition), the largest IT exhibition in the region. Alongside GITEX is the phenomenally popular GITEX Computer Shopper – a great place to bag the latest technology at lower prices (www.gitex.com).

If you can't wait until GITEX, computer equipment is on sale in a surprising number of outlets, from Carrefour to CompuMe, and all the main manufacturers are represented. CompuMe has a great website where you can order products online (www.compume.com).

The market is dominated by PCs, but Macs are available from a growing number of stores including CompuMe, PACC, Virgin Megastore, the Mac Store in Ibn Battuta and iStyle in Dubai Festival Centre. The UAE government has been cracking down on the sale of pirated software, and consequently the software and hardware that is available is genuine and should be of good quality. If you have a poorly PC, contact St George Computers who provide all the assistance you need with faulty equipment and upgrades. For more information call Lee on 050 456 282.

> ### ℹ Shoes & Clothing Sizes
>
> Figuring out your size isn't rocket science, just a bit of a pain. Firstly, check the label – international sizes are often printed on them. Secondly, check the store – they will often have a conversion chart on display. Otherwise, a UK size is always two higher than a US size (so a UK 10 is a US 6). To convert European sizes into US sizes, subtract 32 (so a European 38 is actually a US 6). To convert European sizes into UK sizes, a 38 is roughly a 10. As for shoes, a woman's UK 6 is a European 39 or US 8.5 and a men's UK 10 is a European 44 or a US 10.5. If in doubt, ask for help.

Computers

Computers			
Al Faris Computers	Bur Dubai	04 393 3444	na
Aptec Gulf LLC	Mezzanine Flr, Al Safi	04 336 6885	www.aptecme.com
Carrefour	Various	See p.511	www.carrefouruae.com
CompuMe	Various	See p.512	www.compume.com
Explorer Computers	Deira	04 228 9625	na
GBM Distribution	Jebel Ali	04 883 5652	www.gbmd.com
Interdev Information Systems	Computer St, Bur Dubai	04 351 4153	www.interdev-me.com
iStyle	Various	See p.515	na
Jumbo Electronics	Various	See p.516	www.jumbocorp.com
PACC	Karama	04 337 0070	na
Plug-Ins	Various	See p.519	www.pluginselectronix.com
Redington Middle East	The Atrium Ctr, Khalid Bin Waleed St	04 359 0555	www.redingtongulf.com
Seven Seas Computers	Bin Lahej Building, Oud Metha	04 308 3555	www.sscomp.co.ae
Sharaf DG	Various	See p.520	www.sharafdg.com
Virgin Megastore ▶ p.497	Various	See p.522	www.virgin.com

Electronics & Home Appliances

Other options **Camera Equipment** p.430, **Computers** p.438

From blenders to plasma TVs, electronics are a staple of the retail sector. All the major brands are available, along with some of the lesser-known brands. If it's advice you need, you'll have to choose your store carefully – some shop assistants have excellent product knowledge while others simply read off the main selling points from the display. The good news is that there's a lot of competition, so prices are reasonable and most dealers offer warranties.

A word on warranties: some retailers offer an extended warranty system where, by paying a little bit extra you can get a year or even two added onto your warranty. Just remember to make sure your warranty is an internationally valid one if you're planning on taking your electronic items back to your home country during the life of the warranty.

Prices are often cheaper in Dubai than they are elsewhere, but it's worth your while checking whether the items will work in all areas of the world. You should also find out whether you will have to pay any import duty if you take the item back to your home country. If you're interested in second-hand items, keep checking the adverts placed on supermarket noticeboards and online classifieds (a good one worth visiting is www.expatwoman.com).

Electronics & Home Appliances

Agiv (Gulf)	Al Quoz	04 223 2228	www.agivgulf.com
Al Futtaim Electronics	Al Khabaisi	04 359 9979	www.al-futtaim.com
Al Ghandi Electronics	Deira	04 337 6600	www.alghandielectronics.com
Al Sayegh Brothers Trading	Deira	04 227 4142	www.alsayeghbrothers.com
Archimedia	Karama	04 337 0181	www.archimedia-me.com
Axiom Telecom	Various	See p.509	www.axiomtelecom.com
Bang & Olufsen	Various	See p.510	www.bang-olufsen.com
Better Life	Various	See p.510	www.betterlifeuae.com
Carrefour	Various	See p.511	www.carrefouruae.com
Elekta Gulf	Jebel Ali	04 883 7108	www.elekta.net
Eros Electricals	Various	See p.514	www.erosgroup.com
G & M International	Deira	04 266 9000	www.gnminternational.com
HyperPanda	Festival Power Centre	04 232 5566	www.panda.com.sa
Jacky's Electronics	Various	See p.515	www.jackys.com
Jashanmal ▶ p.431	Various	See p.515	www.jashanmal.ae
Jashanmal and Company	Deira	04 266 5964	www.jashanmal-uae.com
Juma Al Majid	Deira	04 266 0640	www.al-majid.com
Jumbo Electronics	Various	See p.516	www.jumbocorp.com
Mohd Hareb Al Otaiba	Deira	04 269 1575	www.alotaibagroup.com
The New Store	Jumeira	04 353 4506	na
Oasis Enterprises	Deira	04 282 1375	na
Oman National Electronics	Bur Dubai	04 351 0753	na
Plug-Ins	Various	See p.519	www.pluginselectronix.com
Radio Shack	Various	See p.519	www.radioshack.com
Samsung Electronics	Various	See p.520	www.samsung.com
Scientechnic	Deira	04 266 6000	www.scientechnic.com
Sharaf DG	Various	See p.520	www.sharafdg.com
Sounds Middle East Trading L.L.C.	Bur Dubai	04 397 6615	www.soundsme.com
Universal Electricals	Deira	04 282 3443	www.universal-uae.ae
Viking Electronics	Deira	04 223 8167	na
VV & Sons	Bur Dubai	04 353 2444	www.vvsons.com

Eyewear

Other options **Sports Goods** p.467

Unless you want to spend your life in Dubai squinting against the year-round sunshine, you'll need to get yourself a good pair of sunglasses. From Dhs.10 knock-offs in Karama to Dhs.7,000 designer creations in exclusive opticians, and everything in between, you'll probably have trouble choosing just one pair. Most people have sunglasses for driving with good quality lenses and others they don't mind getting sandy at the beach.

You can buy sunglasses in fashion shops, hotel lobbies, opticians, pharmacies, petrol stations, sports shops and supermarkets, so you'll never be far from a replacement pair if you lose, break or forget yours. If you're looking for protection as well as style, the lenses need to be dark and protect against both UVA and UVB. The range of sunglasses for children is improving, with Baby Banz and Kidz Banz available in both Picnico, on Beach Road, and The Uniform Shop, in Spinneys Centre, Umm Suqeim. For adults, a quality pair of sunglasses, which offer a good level of protection, will cost anywhere from Dhs.100 and up. Major brands like Oakley, Ray Ban, Police and Polaroid are widely available.

Eyewear		
Al Jaber Optical Centre	Various	See p.508
Barakat Opticals	Various	See p.510
City Optic	Deira City Centre	04 295 1400
Dubai Opticals	Various	See p.513
Fashion Optics	Jumeirah Beach Hotel	04 348 6559
Grand Optics	Various	See p.515
Grand Sunglasses	Deira City Centre	04 295 5334
Gulf Optics	Various	See p.519
Lunettes	Jumeirah Centre	04 349 2270
Lutfi Opticals Centre	Wafi Mall	04 324 1865
Optic Gallery	Deira City Centre	04 295 3825
Optic Art	BurJuman	04 352 8171
Optic Centre ▶ p.441	Various	See p.518
Pearle Opticians	Various	See p.519
Picnico General Trading	Jumeirah Rd	04 394 1653
Solaris	Various	See p.520
Sunglass Hut	Wafi Mall	04 324 4277
Top Visions Optics	Al Diyafah St	04 398 4888
The Uniform Shop	Spinneys	04 394 1477
Yateem Opticians	Various	See p.522

For prescription glasses, the choice is just as good, with opticians in virtually every mall. Lenses cost from Dhs.80 up to Dhs.2,000 for single focus and from Dhs.150 to Dhs.5,000 for bifocal. There are a dizzying selection of frames, with most of the designer names available, and prices are from around Dhs.350 to Dhs.9,000 (some cost as much as Dhs.18,000 – just make sure you don't sit on them). There is a fairly comprehensive selection of contact lenses on sale, both single focus and bifocal. Prices range from Dhs.120 for a month's supply of daily single focus, to Dhs.200 for six bifocal monthly lenses.

Many opticians will do an eye test for free, particularly if you go on to buy glasses from them, but others may charge Dhs.20 to Dhs.50. As with any service, it's worth asking around to get some recommendations.

Flowers

Other options **Gardens** p.444

For a city in the desert, flowers are remarkably abundant. Dubai's position as an international hub means that they are transited through the airport. This has led to the opening of the Dubai Flower Centre where as well as providing cool storage, flowers are sold wholesale (www.dubaiflowercentre.com).

The larger supermarkets have in-house florists (Carrefour, Choithram, Park n Shop and Spinneys) where the prices are usually towards the lower end of the scale; bouquets start from around Dhs.65. The quality is fairly good but the varieties available are usually limited to basics. Specialist florists often have more exotic ranges to

مــركــز الــعــدســات
OPTIC CENTRE

SHARJAH —————————————————————————————

Optic Centre	Mega Mall	06-5740559
Optic Centre	Clock Tower	06-5631545
Optic Centre	Al Zahra Street	06-5625051
Optic Centre	Co-Op Society (Halwan)	06-5663323
Optic Centre	Al Zahrah Street	06-5637408

DUBAI —————————————————————————————

Optic Centre	Lamcy Plaza	04-3354006
Optic Centre	Co-Op Society (Jumeirah)	04-3943723
Optic Centre	Co-Op Societ (Ghusais)	04-2631038
Optic Centre	Al Aweer	04-3331872
Optic Centre	J B R - Marina	04-4243871
Optic Centre	Lamcy Plaza Mirdiff (Opening Shortly)	

ABU DHABI —————————————————————————————

Inter Optic	Khalifa Street	02-6269183
Inter Optic	Abu Dhabi Mall	02-6455114
Inter Optic	Marina Mall	02-6816557

choose from but here the sky can be the limit in terms of price. Most stores produce arrangements for formal functions, including weddings.

If you need to send flowers, many of the florists can arrange delivery; Intraflora and Gift Express can both arrange for overseas delivery. Local online options include www. emiratesflorist.com, www.flowersdubai.com and www.uaegiftshop.com, all of which deliver within the UAE.

Artificial flowers are widely available but the quality varies enormously. Home Centre and Homes r Us, in the Mazaya Centre, both have good ranges of good quality artificial flowers, and THE One has a fabulous selection of gorgeous artificial flowers; Blooms is the shop to head for if you are looking for silk flowers.

Flowers

Art & Flower	Trade Centre 2	04 343 3288	na
Blooms	Jumeirah Rd, Nr Dubai Zoo	04 344 0912	na
Carrefour	Various	See p.511	www.carrefouruae.com
Choithram	Various	See p.512	www.choithram.com
Dubai Garden Centre	Btn 3rd & 4th interchange	04 340 0006	www.dubaigardencentre.com
Floramex	Al Qusais	04 267 5850	www.floramex-uae.com
Gift Express	Jumeirah Centre	04 342 0568	www.giftexpressdubai.com
Home Centre	Various	See p.515	www.homecentre.net
Homes r Us	Mazaya Centre	04 321 3444	www.lalsgroup.com
Intraflora	Sheikh Zayed Road	04 332 5333	www.intraflorame.com
Oleander	Jumeirah Rd, next Mercato	04 344 0539	www.oleander.co.ae
Park n Shop	Al Wasl Rd	04 394 5671	www.parkshopdubai.com
Planters	Opp Hamrain Centre	04 266 6427	www.planters.info
Spinneys	Various	See p.520	www.spinneys.com
Swissflora	Al Quoz	04 340 1944	www.swissflora.com
THE One	Various	See p.521	www.theoneplanet.com

Food

Other options **Health Food** p.448

The cosmopolitan nature of Dubai results in a huge amount of choice for consumers, and this is most apparent in the amazing array of foodstuffs available. As well as basic staples, many supermarkets specialise in foods from a particular country or region: for example, Safestway on Sheikh Zayed Road stocks a great range of American products,

Food

Al Maya Supermarket	Various	See p.509	www.almayagroup.com
Carrefour	Various	See p.511	www.carrefouruae.com
Choithram	Various	See p.512	www.choithram.com
Géant ▶ p.479	Ibn Battuta Shopping Mall	04 368 5858	www.geant-dubai.com
HyperPanda	Festival Power Centre	04 232 5566	www.panda.com.sa
Lifco	Various	See p.516	www.lifco.com
Lulu Hypermarket	Various	See p.516	www.luluhypermarket.com
Organic Foods & Café	Various	See p.518	www.organicfoodsandcafe.com
Park n Shop	Al Wasl Rd	04 394 5671	www.parkshopdubai.com
Safestway	Shk Zayed Rd	04 343 0412	na
Spinneys	Various	See p.520	www.spinneys.com
Union Co-Op	Various	See p.522	na
Waitrose	The Dubai Mall	04 362 7500	www.waitrose.com

Spinneys keeps the Brits happy with their Waitrose range as well as other British products, and Carrefour keeps just about everybody happy by stocking products from France, the UK, USA, South Africa, the Philippines, Thailand and India, among others. Apart from the gigantic hypermarkets and well-stocked supermarkets, all areas have a few 'corner shops' that are good for bread, milk and other daily essentials. Most petrol stations have 24 hour convenience shops that sell a basic range of food items.

Eat Your Greens
Fresh and Simple
sources fresh fruit,
vegetables and
prepared salads from
a range of suppliers
within the UAE.
Deliveries are made
to different areas on
set days throughout
the week. To sign up,
register online at www.
freshandsimple.net.

Gardens

Other options **Flowers** p.440, **Hardware & DIY** p.448

For a city on the edge of the desert, Dubai is amazingly green. A surprisingly large number of plant species thrive here, although not without help. With very little annual rainfall and rapidly diminishing groundwater, if you want to create your own oasis, it's going to need plenty of water. If you are living near the coast you may be able to save on the DEWA bill by having a well bored in your garden and a pump installed. Keep an eye on it though, if your plants start to wilt it means the water may have become saline. For many, the answer is to have an irrigation system installed so that watering the garden is as easy as turning on the tap. Many residents have a gardener (an industrious chap who rides around a particular area on his bicycle and services several gardens every day). When you move into an area, you'll have gardeners touting for your business not long after the delivery trucks have left. Alternatively you can get a garden service, such as Berkeley.

Even if you are living in an apartment the world of horticulture is open to you and pots are widely available so you can turn your balcony into a mini garden to be proud of. To buy plants, you should definitely visit the nursery area (currently to your right just before the Garhoud Bridge, as you head towards Deira, but there are plans to move it to the Academic City area). They sell a great range of plants, pots, soil and compost. As with any informal shopping in Dubai, the more you buy the better the discount. Plant Street, in Satwa, also has a number of nurseries that are great for basics but the range is limited. You'll see a number of independent nurseries in various areas with prices roughly the same as in the nursery area. Of course, the larger retailers like IKEA, Spinneys and Carrefour sell plants too, as well as a range of gardening equipment. For budget tools, Plant Street is hard to beat, with rakes for around Dhs.10. Serious gardeners might find ACE a good source of gardening tools and furniture, and it also stocks a particularly good range of irrigation equipment.

The Dubai Garden Centre, between Junctions Three and Four on Sheikh Zayed Road, has you need for gardens. It sells everything from plants and furniture to tools and irrigation systems, and is staffed by knowledgeable people who can tell you why your wisteria is wilting. If you are starting your garden from scratch (freehold buyers pay attention), it offers a landscaping and planting service. Royal Gardenscape, in Al Quoz and Mirdiff, has a great selection of products for hard landscaping like natural stone paving slabs.

If it's just garden furniture you're after, try ACE, Carrefour, IKEA, or Home Centre. You can pick up wooden garden furniture quite reasonably, but if you can't store it properly during the harshest months of summer you will probably have to revarnish it every year or two. Parasol in Al Quoz also stocks a range of quality outdoor furniture. Once you've got your garden all green and kitted out with some comfy garden furniture, you are well on your way to making the most of the idyllic alfresco lifestyle that is common in Dubai. All you need now is a good barbecue, which can be found in hypermarkets, supermarkets, hardware stores and garden centres. Prices start at around Dhs.25 for a disposable model, and range up to Dhs.20,000 for a state-of-the-art, six-burner beast.

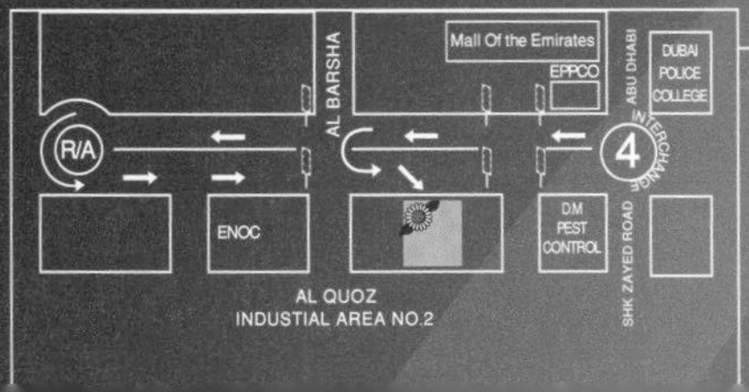

If you decide to splash out and install your own pool, you can choose between an above-ground or below-ground pool. Above-ground pools, available in Carrefour and Toys R Us, are cheaper and portable, although not very sturdy for the long term. Although it's a big investment (starting from around Dhs.65,000 for a fibreglass pool and Dhs.85,000 for a concrete one), getting a below-ground pool is worth it in the long run. There are several companies that, for a monthly fee, will take care of routine pool maintenance for you (such as Those Pool Guys).

Gardens			
ACE	Various	See p.508	www.aceuae.com
Berkeley	Trade Centre 1	04 339 3111	na
Carrefour	Various	See p.511	www.carrefouruae.com
Dubai Garden Centre	Btn 3rd & 4th interchange	04 340 0006	www.dubaigardencentre.com
Floramex	Al Qusais	04 267 5850	www.floramex-uae.com
Hennessey	Al Quoz	04 347 0379	www.hennesseyllc.com
Home Centre	Various	See p.515	www.homecentre.net
IKEA ▶ p.451	Festival Power Centre	800 4532	www.ikeadubai.com
In-Step Trading Co.	Deira	04 285 5996	na
Parasol	Umm Suqeim St	04 347 9003	www.parasoldubai.com
Royal Gardenscape ▶ p.445	Various	See p.520	www.royalgardenscape.com
Spinneys	Various	See p.520	www.spinneys-dubai.com
Stone Gallery	Al Quoz	04 347 2525	na
Suncoast	Sheikh Zayed Road, nr BMW showroom	04 339 4730	www.suncoastllc.com
THE One	Various	See p.521	www.theoneplanet.com
Those Pool Guys	Al Quoz	04 339 0418	www.thosepoolguys.com
Union Co-Op	Various	See p.522	na

The Emirates High Street

Use your Skywards air miles, or your credit card, to purchase a variety of products online at The Emirates High Street. The new venture from Emirates airlines offers delivery to over 60 countries, so you can send gifts back home or pick them up from a few locations near Dubai International airport. For more information see www.emirateshighstreet.com.

Gifts

With so many expats enjoying a high standard of living in Dubai, with more disposable income to spend on gadgets and luxuries for themselves, it can be difficult to buy gifts as many people already seem to have everything. Fortunately, Dubai has all bases covered with gift items that range from small to large, cheap to expensive, run-of-the-mill to bizarre, and practical to indulgent. Lifestyle, Harvest Home, Magrudy's, Susan Walpole and The Warehouse all stock some interesting pieces with broad appeal. Debenhams and Next have some good toys for big boys as well as other gift-worthy items. If you are looking for something really special, Raffles Boutique sell a good range of tasteful souvenirs and gifts. Many malls have little stalls selling novelty gift items and Arabian knick-knacks.

You'll have no worries if you need to buy a gift for a child, as Dubai is full of toy stores (see also p.456) and bookshops (p.69). For something different, try Stuck on You, an Australian franchise selling labels and personalised items for children (www.stuckonyou.biz).

For extra-special gifts, try Rivoli. And if your budget stretches to jewellery, then what could be more exciting than giving something beautiful wrapped up in the distinctive packaging from Tiffany & Co?

If online gift shopping is your thing, Gift Express (www.giftexpressdubai.com) delivers a range of items within the UAE and overseas. And Blue Banana (www.bluebanana.ae) is a gift service that specialises in adventure package gift certificates; you can even give someone the gift of flying in a MiG-25 to the edge of space, if you have a spare Dhs.58,000 to spend. If you want to send Christmas presents to family members back home, you can order on Amazon (www.amazon.com or www.amazon.co.uk) and have it all delivered for you.

Most shops issue gift vouchers. Debenhams issues vouchers but does not accept those issued in overseas branches of Debenhams, Marks & Spencer will accept vouchers issued in the UK (there are two types of voucher issued, and the Dubai branch of M&S will only accept the ones for franchise branches).

Gifts

Bateel	Burjuman	04 355 2833	www.bateel.ae
Debenhams	Various	See p.513	www.debenhams.com
Dreamdays	Online	04 266 9906	www.dreamdays.ae
Gift Express	Jumeirah Centre	04 342 0568	www.giftexpressdubai.com
Harvest Home Trading	Jumeirah Centre	04 342 0225	na
Lifestyle	Various	See p.516	na
Marks & Spencer	Various	See p.517	www.marksandspencerme.com
Melangé	Jumeira Plaza	04 344 4721	na
Music Room	Beach Centre	04 344 8883	na
Next	Various	See p.518	www.alshaya.com
Quick Dubai	Dubai Internet City	04 391 3133	www.quickdubai.com
Raffles Boutique	Wafi Mall	04 324 8888	www.wafi.com
Rivoli	Various	See p.520	www.rivoligroup.com
Sunny Days Trading	Jumeirah Centre	04 349 5275	na
Susan Walpole	Various	See p.521	na
Tiffany & Co.	Various	See p.521	www.tiffany.com
Virgin Megastore ▶ p.497	Various	See p.522	na
Warehouse	Jumeira Plaza	04 344 0244	na
Woolworths	Various	See p.522	www.woolworths.co.za

Handbags

Local ladies love their handbags and the humble handbag has become a major status symbol, especially since it is often the only item visible when dressed in the long black abaya. As a result, you can get some amazing creations (both in terms of craftmanship and in price) at various exclusive boutiques around Dubai. For the latest Louis Vuitton or Tod's handbag, head for BurJuman where both have stores.

If you're addicted to designer handbags but don't have the money to support your habit, various shops in Karama sell knock-offs. The price for a really good copy handbag is not that cheap at around Dhs.300 to Dhs.400 but sometimes the quality is so good that it is nearly impossible to distinguish between the copy and the real thing. Shop owners selling copy handbags are the focus of a crackdown to stamp out this illegal trade, and as, a result, if you want to view the handbags you will be taken into a back room so that you can see them behind closed (and sometimes even locked) doors. If you are looking for the real

Handbags

Accessorize	Various	See p.508
Bally	Mall of the Emirates	04 341 0280
Benetton	Various	See p.510
Boutique 1	Various	See p.511
Burberry	Various	See p.511
Carrefour	Various	See p.511
Coach	Various	See p.512
Debenhams	Various	See p.513
Elegance	Wafi Mall	04 324 2266
Eve Michelle	Magrudy's	04 342 9574
Ginger & Lace	Various	See p.514
Louis Vuitton	Various	See p.516
Mapochette.com	Dubai Internet City	04 344 5029
Monsoon	Various	See p.517
Next	Various	See p.518
Tod's	Various	See p.522

thing, you could always sign up to the designer bag hire service www.mapochette.com. You can rent a range of the most fashionable bags online, for a day, or up to three days, including bags by Manolo Blahnik, Christian Dior and Jimmy Choo. Bags cost from Dhs.625 a day for a Gucci Indy Top Handle to Dhs.150 a day for Ted Baker Vallary clutch. For the less label-conscious, handbags are sold in most fashion, luggage, and accessories shops, including Accessorize, Monsoon, Benetton, Next, Debenhams, Bally and even Carrefour.

Hardware & DIY
Other options **Outdoor Goods** p.461

With a number of companies offering handyman services (see Domestic Services on p.167), it may be easier and cheaper to find a 'man who can' rather than invest in the tools and materials you need for DIY jobs. However, if you enjoy tinkering with tools and doing odd jobs around the house, there are plenty of outlets where you can buy your toolkit. Both ACE and Speedex on Sheikh Zayed Road stock comprehensive ranges of tools, along with all the nails, nuts, bolts and screws you need. Carrefour has a DIY section and in Satwa there are numerous independent shops selling everything from the rustiest nail to the shiniest drill bit. Dragon Mart, in International City, has a section for builder's merchants and here you can find baths, tiles, power tools and other hardware items.

Hardware & DIY			
ACE	Various	See p.508	www.aceuae.com
Carrefour	Various	See p.511	www.carrefouruae.com
Dragon Mart	International City Emirates Rd	04 368 7205	www.chinamexmart.com
Speedex	Nr Oasis Centre	04 339 1929	na

Hats
The Dubai World Cup is not just the highlight of the horse racing season, it is the fashion event of the year, when no outfit is complete without a hat. Some shops, including Debenhams, have hats year round, great for weddings, but most shops stock them between January and March. Oasis Fashions creations tend toward the full-on feathery and flowery and are aimed at race goers. Eve Michelle stocks a selection of designer hats in different styles for those looking to make a bold statement. Their main collection arrives in time for the races with a small selection available year round. Sunny Days sells hats year round, made by local milliner Lynn Holyoak, whose stunning creations are very reasonably priced. Malls, including BurJuman and Wafi, get in on the act by hosting displays in the run up to World Cup night. For high-street style, Accessorize has hats for all seasons, with accessories to match.

If you are looking for something functional rather than fashionable, options are rather limited but the beachwear shops have small collections. Beyond the Beach and Stadium have surfwear styles, while Heatwaves has UV protective models for adults and children.

Hats		
Accessorize	Various	See p.508
Beyond The Beach	Various	See p.510
Debenhams	Various	See p.513
Eve Michelle	Magrudy's	04 342 9574
Heatwaves	Various	See p.515
Oasis	Various	See p.518
Stadium	Various	See p.521
Sunny Days Trading	Jumeirah Centre	04 349 5275

Health Food
Other options **Food** p.442

The range of health and speciality food is increasing, and although prices are generally high it is worth shopping around as costs vary from shop to shop. Shops selling sports supplements, energy bars and protein powders are often classified as health food shops and some are now diversifying into selling speciality foodstuffs.

Good Health, at the Nutrition Centre, sells both and they have a small selection of gluten-free and wheat-free products. Nutrition Zone specialises in vitamins, health supplements and detoxifying products from Holland & Barrett. They also carry a range of health food, grains, gluten and wheat-free products, as well as Green & Blacks chocolate and some ecological household products. Their prices are reasonable and below those of the supermarkets for many items. The main supermarkets stock increasing varieties of speciality foods and they all carry products for diabetics, Choithram has possibly the widest range; it also stocks dairy-free, gluten-free and wheat-free products ranging from bread to icecream. Spinneys carries a limited selection of organic fruit and vegetables and, through their

Health Food		
Carrefour	Various	See p.511
Choithram	Various	See p.512
GNC	BurJuman	04 352 6771
Healthy Eating	Nr Princeton Hotel	04 286 5777
Nutrition Centre	Jumeirah Centre	04 344 7464
Nutrition World	Palm Strip	04 345 0652
Nutrition Zone	Various	See p.518
Organic Foods & Café	Various	See p.518
Park n Shop	Al Wasl Rd	04 394 5671
Planet Nutrition	Various	See p.519
Spinneys	Various	See p.520

partnership with Waitrose, an organic range which includes beans, pulses, biscuits and fruit juice. They also stock some items from Waitrose's 'Perfectly Balanced' calorie and fat counted range. Park n Shop's health food range includes breads made from spelt or rye flour which are less allergenic than wheat; they even make spelt hot cross buns and mince pies. Carrefour's range is increasing and, as well as the basic range that most supermarkets carry, have some own-brand organic products.

Organic Foods and Café go to the source for every item in their stores and their product range is constantly evolving. Some products are quite expensive but they carry a good selection, including bread, seafood, frozen meals, and fresh produce. Many products are cheaper than in the supermarkets and not available elsewhere. The cafes, attached to the Satwa and Emirates Hills stores, use only products that they stock in the shops and many of the dishes are suitable for vegetarians and vegans.

Dubai hosts the annual Middle East Natural & Organic Products Expo, which sees over 300 companies from 35 countries exhibiting a range of natural products and treatments. See www.globallinksdubai.com for details.

Home Furnishings & Accessories
Other options **Hardware & DIY** p.448, **Furnishing Accommodation** p.162

Interior Desires
If your interior design is lacking inspiration, then there are some excellent glossy magazines available to lend a hand. Emirates Home, Identity *and* Inside Out *may inspire you to transform your home into a palace fit for a sheikh.*

This is one of Dubai's most buoyant retail sectors, perhaps because the seemingly unlimited supply of new villas and apartments all need to be furnished. For more and more people, Dubai is home rather than a limited-term posting, and this has led to an increased interest in home furnishings and accessories.

Most tastes are catered for, from ethnic pieces to the latest designer concepts and specialist children's furniture stores. IKEA, in an enormous showroom in the Festival Power Centre, is perhaps the city's best known furniture store, and sells some great furniture at great value. Its selection is suitable for most budgets, and it sells everything from Dhs.1 tealight holders to Dhs.20,000 kitchens. On a slightly higher-end level, THE One covers all aspects of home furnishing and is great for Christmas decorations. Marina Gulf stocks a good range of Arabian-style furniture and accessories, from lamps and bedding to chests and huge dining tables. They also have a warehouse outlet in Al Quoz. And So To Bed is one of the UK's top bedlinen shops. The Dubai branch is opposite BurJuman and although it is not for the budget shopper, it sells some beautiful beds and bed linen. Another British company renowned for quality is The White Company, now with several branches. Royal Furniture Mall has recently opened a huge store near Sharjah which has large showrooms featuring various styles of furniture. Cottage Chic, in the Holiday Centre next to the Crowne Plaza, packs a good selection of home furnishings into its small shop space, including items from Rachel Ashwell's Shabby Chic range.

For top-class Italian leather furniture try Natuzzi, who have opened their largest international branch between Junctions Two and Three on Sheikh Zayed Road. The craftmanship is of such a high standard that their products can be classed as investment furniture rather than something to change when you redecorate.

Memoires, in Wafi Mall, is quite a spectacular retail experience. Selling a variety of antiques and knick-knacks for the home, it is sublimely decorated in 'medieval' style with a maze-like layout of themed rooms, and the end result is more like that of a museum than a store.

If you want to add some exotic touches to your home, there are plenty of items from India and the Far East. Safita Trading has a good range at competitive prices. Panache Interiors in Jumeira Centre offers design services, interior decoration, ready made home accessories and goodies made of natural fibres that make great gifts.

The industrial area between Junctions Three and Four of Sheikh Zayed Road is home to a number of furniture warehouses, many of which sell pieces crafted from Indonesian teak. For authentic warehouse shopping, try Lucky's and Pinky's – these hot, dusty warehouses located near the Sharjah border are piled to the rooftops with higgledy-piggledy pieces of Indian teak furniture. Don't be put off though – prices are excellent and after a good polish the furniture looks fabulous. Fabindia on Al Mankhool Road stocks an interesting range of hand-crafted bed linen, table linen, fabrics and accessories from India.

Home Furnishings & Accessories

@home	Mercato	04 344 3783
Aati	Al Manzil Bld	04 337 7825
Al Huzaifa Furniture	Zomoroddah Bld, Karama	04 336 6646
Al Jaber Gallery	Various	See p.508
And So To Bed	Nr BurJuman	04 396 2022
Antique Museum	Nr Kanoo, Al Quoz 3	04 347 9935
Apollo Furniture	Sheikh Zayed Rd	04 339 1358
Art Of Life	The Courtyard	04 340 6755
Bafco Trading	Trade Centre Rd, Splash Bld	04 335 0045
Bayti	Deira City Centre	04 294 9292
Bedrooms 4 kids	Al Hana Centre	04 398 9640
Bhs	Various	See p.510
Bombay	Various	See p.510
Carpe Diem	Villa 145 A, Jumeira	04 344 4734
Carre Blanc	Deira City Centre	04 295 3992
Carrefour	Various	See p.511
Casa Marakesh	Wafi Mall	04 342 0981
Chen One	Century Plaza	04 342 2441
Cottage Chic	Holiday Centre Mall	04 331 3308
Cozy House	Al Quoz	04 340 4596
Daiso	Lamcy Plaza	04 335 1532
Desert River	Centro Mall, Plant Street	04 345 4541
Design Diva	Al Quoz	04 347 6507
Elegan Art	Gold & Diamond Park	050 688 4593
Ethan Allen	Jumeirah Rd (Nxt to Century Plaza)	04 342 1616
Exotic Grove Furniture	Btn 3rd & 4th Interchange, Al Quoz	04 347 9664
Exotica	Nr Spinney's warehouse, Al Quoz	04 340 2966
Fabindia	Al Mankhool Rd	04 398 9633
Fauchar	Wafi Mall	04 324 6769
Feshwari	Various	See p.514
Georg Jensen	Wafi Mall	04 324 0704
Grand Stores	Various	See p.515
Guess Home	BurJuman	04 355 3324
Habitat	Various	See p.515
Harvest Home Trading	Jumeirah Centre	04 342 0225
Home Centre	Various	See p.515
Homes r Us	Mazaya Centre	04 321 3444
ID Design	Various	See p.515
IKEA ▶ p.451	Festival Power Centre	800 4532

OTTAVA
pendant lamp
Dhs **149**

Visit Space.

Just one word describes the vastness of space –
never-ending. Our customers have something similar to say
about our store. Even our home products make your house
look bigger. They come in minimalist designs
and with features that make IKEA products
perfect for every home. So, to bring home 'space'
visit the spacious IKEA store.

Home Furnishings & Accessories

Interiors	Umm Hurrair Rd, opp Dubai TV	04 337 0116
Irony Home	The Village Mall	04 342 2145
Jotun Paints	Al Quoz	04 339 5000
KA International	Dubai	04 345 9988
Kas	Mercato	04 344 1179
Kidz Inc.	Al Quoz	04 340 5059
Kitchens & Beyond	Al Garhoud Rd	04 283 1331
KKids	Jumeira Plaza	04 344 4753
Liwa	Various	See p.516
Lucky's	Ind Area 11, Sharjah	06 534 1937
Marina Gulf Trading	Al Barsha Rd	04 347 8940
Marlin	Various	See p.517
Memoires	Wafi Mall	04 324 3001
Move-in Emirates	Al Quoz 4	04 340 1994
Natuzzi	Al Quoz	04 338 0777
Pan Emirates	Nr Oasis Centre, Al Quoz	04 324 8061
Panache Furnishing	Jumeirah Centre	04 344 3677
Persepolis	Karama	04 334 2824
Petals	The Courtyard	04 340 2201
Pier Import	Mazaya Centre	04 343 2002
Pinky's	Sharjah	06 534 1714
Pride Of Kashmir	Various	See p.519
Royal Furniture Factory Outlet	Nxt to Hyundai Showroom, Sharjah – Dubai Rd	04 297 1224
Safita Trading Est.	Beh Pepsi Cola	04 339 3230
Sara – Villeroy & Boch	Various	See p.520
Showcase Antiques	Opp Dubai Municipality	04 348 8797
Tanagra	Various	See p.521
Tavola	Various	See p.521
Textura Interiors	Jumeirah Town Centre	04 363 8861
THE One	Various	See p.521
The White Company	Various	See p.521
Warehouse	Jumeira Plaza	04 344 0244
Western Furniture	Nr Maktoum Bridge	04 337 7152
Wicker	Zabeel Road, Shk Rashid Bld	04 337 5544
Woolworths	Various	See p.522
Zara Home	Various	See p.522
Zen Interiors	Essa Lutfi Bld, Al Barsha	04 340 5050

Genuine antiques are available but very rare (and therefore very expensive). Many antique pieces come from Oman and Yemen; Al Jaber Gallery is known for genuine Emirati pieces. Children's furniture is a growth market. IKEA has a great range of reasonably priced kids' furniture, and its range of bunkbeds is consistently popular. It's good to visit even if you are not buying; while you browse around your kids can play with all the display toys. Kidz Inc. are the sole agents for Haba – this German, hand-made, wooden furniture doesn't come cheap but all pieces meet European and American safety standards and come with a five-year warranty. Especially good is the range of themed beds (think pirate ships and flowery glades), with matching furniture and accessories.

Feshwari can custom-make furniture for you, from sofas and beanbags to ottomans and cushions. It specialises in designer upholstery fabrics (such as Designers' Guild, Sheila Coombes, Andrew Martin and Jim Thompson silk), curtains and blinds. Plant Street in Satwa has a couple of fabric shops that can reupholster just about anything, should you have furniture that is beginning to look a little bit tired and curtain shops who will make to measure and even install them.

For accessories rather than large pieces of furniture, there are plenty of shops that will help you add the finishing touches to your home. House of the World provide advice on interior design and offer a range of art and photography to suit your stylish surrounds. Zara Home's fresh, European designs are now available in a number of malls. Next (Mall of the Emirates and Deira City Centre) has a small home accessories section at the back of the shop. Debenhams is good for homeware, bedding and kitchenware – this is where you can buy the entire range of Jamie Oliver's cookware. Kitchenalia junkies will love Tavola and Harvest Home, which have some unusual items you hadn't realised you couldn't live without.

For something unique, Mackenzie Associates can assist you with some amazing finishing touches to your home, including murals, trompe l'oeils and sculptures (see p.164).

The transient nature of some of Dubai's population results in an active second-hand furniture market. Items are advertised in the classified sections of the local newspapers but the supermarket noticeboards are the best source; they are also where to keep an eye out for garage sales.

Jewellery & Watches
Other options **Markets/Souks** p.481

Dubai is the world's leading re-exporter of gold and you'll find at least one jewellery shop in even the smallest malls, and large areas dedicated to shops selling it. From trinkets for toddlers to multi-million dirham gold and diamond creations, Dubai has it all. Gold is available in 18, 21, 22 or 24 carats and is sold according to the international daily gold rate. This means that for an identical piece, whether you buy it in Emirates Towers or the Gold Souk, there will be very little difference in the price of the actual gold. Where the price varies is in the workmanship that has gone into a particular piece. While gold jewellery may be the most prevalent, silver, platinum, precious stones, gems and pearls are all sold, either separately or crafted into jewellery. Most outlets can make up a piece for you, working from a diagram or photograph. Just ensure that you are not obliged to buy it if it doesn't turn out quite how you had imagined.

Many of the world's finest jewellers are represented in Dubai. Cartier and Tiffany & Co are well known as creators of some beautiful jewellery and watches. Fabergé jewellery is amongst the elite collection in Saks Fifth Avenue's jewellery department. Graff and De Beers are among the world's top diamond retailers and produce pieces just waiting to become a girl's best friend.

The Gold Souk is great in terms of choice. A traditional gift is a pendant with your name spelled out in Arabic, or some jewellery crafted with black pearls. The recently expanded Gold & Diamond Park (at junction four on Sheikh Zayed Road) has branches of many of the same shops but in a calmer, air-conditioned atmosphere. You can still barter, and there is an added bonus of cafes to wait in while the jeweller makes any alterations. This is also a good spot to head for if you are looking for engagement or wedding rings and, like the outlets in the souk, you are able to commission pieces.

Jewellery & Watches		
Al Fardan Jewellery	Various	See p.508
Al Futtaim Jewellery	Various	See p.508
Al Liali	Various	See p.509
BinHendi Jewellery	Various	See p.510
Breitling Watches	Various	See p.511
Cartier	Various	See p.512
Chopard	Wafi Mall	04 324 1010
Citizen	Nr Fish R/A	04 271 5607
Claire's	Various	See p.512
Damas Jewellery	Various	See p.512
De Beers	Various	See p.512
Debenhams	Various	See p.512
Eve Michelle	Magrudy's	04 342 9574
For Love 21	Deira City Centre	04 294 3038
Fossil	Various	See p.514
Golden Ring	Deira City Centre	04 295 0373
Guess	Various	See p.515
Mahallati Jewellery	Various	See p.516
Mansoor Jewellery	BurJuman	04 355 2110
Marks & Spencer	Various	See p.517
Montblanc	Various	See p.517
Next	Various	See p.518
Omega	Various	See p.518
Paris Gallery	Various	See p.518
Philippe Charriol	BurJuman	04 351 1112
Prima Gold	Various	See p.519
Pure Gold	Various	See p.510
Raymond Weil	Deira City Centre	04 295 3254
Rivoli	Various	See p.520
Rolex	Mall of the Emirates	04 341 1222
Ruane Jewellers	Wafi Mall	04 327 9212
Silver Art	Deira City Centre	04 295 2414
Swarovski	Wafi Mall	04 324 0168
Swatch	Various	See p.521
TAG Heuer	Various	See p.521
Tanagra	Various	See p.521
Tiffany & Co	BurJuman	04 351 1784
Watch House	Various	See p.522

Costume jewellery and watches can be found in most department stores as well as Eve Michelle and the beautiful Swarovski range in Tanagra. Accessorize and For Love 21 have a great range of every-day pieces which echo the colours and fashions of the season, and Next and Fat Face have a small range of mostly silver pieces. For children, Claire's Accessories is like an Aladdin's cave for girly girls, with inexpensive jewellery and hair accessories.

All the major brands of watches are available in Dubai, so whether you're in the market for a Rolex, Breitling, Tag Heuer, Swatch, Casio or Timex, you have many models to choose from.

Kids' Clothes
Other options **Clothes** p.435

Finding kids' clothing in Dubai is child's play – from high-end designer fashion (Christian Lacroix and Armani) down to factory seconds from Sana, there is something to suit all tastes and budgets. In the middle, there are great children's departments in Debenhams, Marks & Spencer, Next and Woolworths. For babies and younger children, Mamas and Papas, Mothercare, Woolworths and Next carry the essentials and have some great outfits at reasonable prices. Okaidi and Pumpkin Patch sell bright, colourful and practical clothes that children love – the beauty of these clothes is that they are designed for children rather than trying to make them look like miniature adults. Monsoon's ranges are great for party clothes and especially loved by little girls. Online store Kid Eternity (www.kid-eternity.com) offers a range of clothing brands that are not widely available in Dubai.

The majority of children's clothes shops also stock shoes and there are some specialist stores. Pablosky stocks a range of colourful shoes for babies and children while Magrudy's and Shoe Mart have children's sections.

For party costumes check out Early Learning Centre or Toys R Us, year round, and Mr Ben's in Al Ghazal Mall. You can also pick up costumes at the supermarkets and hypermarkets in the run up to festive events like Halloween and Christmas; the craft fairs

Kids' Clothes

Adams	Various	See p.508
Bòboli	BurJuman	04 351 4579
Dar Al Tasmim Uniforms	Various	See p.513
Debenhams	Various	See p.513
Factory Fashions	Lamcy Plaza	04 336 2699
Gap	Various	See p.514
Géant ▶ p.479	Ibn Battuta Shopping Mall	04 368 5858
H&M	Various	See p.515
Hamleys	The Dubai Mall	04 339 8889
Ladybird	Dubai Festival City	04 206 6575
Limited Too	Various	See p.516
Lola et moi	Palm Strip	04 345 4774
Mamas & Papas	Various	See p.517
Marks & Spencer	Various	See p.517
Monsoon	Various	See p.517
Mothercare	Various	See p.517
Next	Various	See p.518
Okaidi	Various	See p.518
Peacocks	Various	See p.519
Prémaman	BurJuman	04 351 5353
Pumpkin Patch	Various	See p.519
Saks Fifth Avenue	Various	See p.520
Sana Fashion	Various	See p.520
Shoe Mart	Various	See p.520
Woolworths	Various	See p.522
Zara	Various	See p.522

are another good source. If all else fails, buy the material and have a costume made by one of the city's numerous tailors (see p.469).

Children grow out of their clothes so quickly that it's worth waiting for the sales or head to the Outlet Mall; prices are often greatly reduced and you can restock their wardrobe at a fraction of the cost.

Buying school uniforms in Dubai is both easy and hard; easy because your school will have an official outfitter where you can go and buy all the items you'll need, and hard because most of the time the uniforms are only available in one shop. That means that a few days before a new term, you may find yourself fighting over the last size five shirt with other mums who have also left it to the last minute.

Kids' Items

Dubai is a child-friendly city, not least because there is a high concentration of shops selling toys. There is something for everyone, from hi-tech baby learning laptops to cheap plastic tat (which your kids will probably prefer, despite your best intentions), but remember that not all toys conform to international safety standards and therefore should only be used under supervision.

Baby Shop, the Toy Store and Toys R Us cater to all age groups from babies to teens, and sell international brands including Little Tikes and Fisher Price. Early Learning Centre and Imaginarium stock a range of educational products and toys that stimulate play and imagination. Magrudy's sells toys for younger children, including Little Tikes and the Whoozit range, as well as a good range of games and puzzles. Renowned store Hamleys has recently opened a sizeable shop at The Dubai Mall; the UK brand offers a great variety of well-crafted toys for children. Park n Shop has a great toy department with some good 'pocket money' toys as does Book Worm. For educational and wooden toys, try the little shop on the ground floor of Children's City, IKEA and Haba – they all carry good quality toys that are built to last. For inexpensive birthday presents and stocking fillers, Carrefour and Géant both have toy departments, and the little shops around Karama and Satwa are excellent for cheap toys (just don't expect them to last a long time). Hobby Centre will appeal to all those who prefer a little more interactive action with their toys, from build-your-own, wind-up vehicles to remote-controlled planes and cars. This is the place for serious model enthusiasts. Those who prefer to get their entertainment from a TV and a games console will not be disappointed by what the city has to offer – most electronics stores stock a wide range of games for the various platforms. Try Geekay and Carrefour which have a good selection.

Toys R Us

Toys R Us has a huge range catering to children of all ages. The opening of an in-house branch of Ladybird, offering everyday children's wear from the UK, is a welcome addition. As well as toys and a staggering variety of dolls, there are bikes for both adults and children, baby essentials including buggies and car seats and an area for DVDs, videos and computer games. Check out the huge flagship store at Dubai Festival Centre (p.490) and the new opening in Times Square Centre (p.505).

Kids' Items		
Adams	Various	See p.508
Armani Junior	Mercato	04 342 0111
Babyshop	Various	See p.510
Book Worm	Beh Park & Shop	04 394 5770
Carrefour	Various	See p.511
Children's City	Creekside Park, Umm Hurair	04 334 0808
Dar Al Tasmim Uniforms	Various	See p.513
Dragon Mart	International City	04 368 7205
Early Learning Centre	Various	See p.513
Géant ▶ p.479	Ibn Battuta Shopping Mall	04 368 5858
Geekay	Deira City Centre	04 295 2140
Goodbaby	Trade Centre Rd, opp Spinneys	04 397 5653
Hobby Centre	Airport Rd, Nr Volvo Showroom	04 295 5512
HyperPanda	Festival Power Centre	04 232 5566
IKEA ▶ p.451	Festival Power Centre	800 4532
Imaginarium	Wafi Mall	04 324 8055
Just Kidding	Al Quoz 4	800 5878
Kidz Inc Haba	Al Quoz	04 340 5059
Lego Store	Jebel Ali Village	04 368 5217
Little Me	Palm Strip	04 345 6424
Lola et moi	Palm Strip	04 345 4774
Magrudy's ▶ p.429	Various	See p.516
Mamas & Papas	Various	See p.517
Mothercare	Various	See p.517
Ovo Kids	Deira City Centre	04 295 5900
Park n Shop	Al Wasl Rd	04 394 5671
Pumpkin Patch	Various	See p.519
Toy Store	Mercato	04 349 3490
Toys R Us	Various	See p.522
The White Company	Various	See p.521

Lingerie

Lingerie		
Bare Essentials	Jumeirah Centre	04 344 0552
Bendon	Mall of the Emirates	04 341 3373
Bhs	Various	See p.510
Carrefour	Various	See p.511
Debenhams	Various	See p.513
K-Lynn	Mall of the Emirates	04 341 0083
La Belleamie	Beach Centre	04 349 3928
La Perla	Various	See p.516
La Senza	Various	See p.516
Marks & Spencer	Various	See p.517
My Time	BurJuman	04 351 3881
Nayomi	Various	See p.518
Saks Fifth Avenue	Various	See p.520
Secrets Boutique	Bin Sougat Centre	04 285 6602
Triumph	Various	See p.522
Women'secret	Various	See p.522
Woolworths	Various	See p.522

Lingerie

Other options **Clothes** p.435

Dubai has a huge range of lingerie outlets. Nayomi is a regional retailer selling a range of functional and sexy underwear. They offer a bridal chest full of lacy, frilly, silky goodies, including the ultimate in bedroom glamour – high-heeled fluffy slippers. Top European brands are also available, such as Agent Provocateur at Saks Fifth Avenue and Janet Reger in the Boulevard at Emirates Towers. Bendon caters to women of all sizes. In the same mall, K-Lynn is a well-known Lebanese boutique carrying lines to suit everyone. Secrets Boutique in the Bin Sougat Centre specialises in bras in larger sizes. It may be worth visiting their website, www. secretsgroup.com, before you head over to the shop. If you want a fitting you should also call in advance. Debenhams, Marks & Spencer and Woolworths are famed for their lingerie, from every day basics to sets for special occasions, and they all offer fitting services. Debenhams stocks the renowned Floozie collection, as well as a small Calvin Klein range. La Senza has a super-girly and fun selection of reasonably priced lingerie and pyjamas.

Luggage & Leather

Dubai residents tend to travel a lot, so luggage is widely available. At the lower end, Carrefour is a great starting point with its huge selection and reasonable prices. Just a tip though… so many Dubai travellers buy their luggage from Carrefour that you might have a bit of trouble identifying your suitcase among the hundreds of other Carrefour suitcases on the conveyor belt. Sports shops sell good ranges of kit bags and trolley bags, usually in bright, sporty colours.

At the higher end of the luggage market, designer labels are widely available. Try BurJuman for Aigner, Bally, Tod's and Louis Vuitton. Or if you like the labels but not the prices, a good rummage around Karama can unearth some quite convincing knock-offs. Some labels also have stores in the Outlet Mall. Leather clothing is not overly popular in such a warm climate, but people often buy leather coats and accessories for when they take a trip to colder climes. For reasonably priced leather jackets imported in bulk from the subcontinent, try Karama. For more luxurious options, stores like Timberland (which now has a branch in Dubai Mall), Massimo Dutti, and other designer boutiques are a good bet.

Luggage & Leather		
Aigner	Various	See p.508
Aristocrat	BurJuman	04 355 2395
Bally	Mall of the Emirates	04 341 0280
Benetton	Various	See p.51
Calonge	Al Ghurair City	04 228 4232
Carrefour	Various	See p.511
Chanel	Various	See p.512
Francesco Biasia	Mercato	04 349 9622
Furla	BurJuman	04 352 2285
HyperPanda	Festival Power Centre	04 232 5566
IKEA ▶ p.451	Festival Power Centre	800 4532
Jashanmal ▶ p.431	Various	See p.515
La Valise	Deira City Centre	04 295 5509
Leather Palace	Various	See p.516
Louis Vuitton	Various	See p.516
Mohd Shareif	BurJuman	04 355 3377
Timberland	The Dubai Mall	04 434 1291
Porsche Design	Various	See p.519
Sacoche	Deira City Centre	04 295 0233
Sun & Sand Sports	Various	See p.521
THE One	Various	See p.521
Tod's	Various	See p.522

Leather furniture is available in most home furnishing outlets, but Natuzzi specialise in leather. Its enormous store, between junctions two and three on Sheikh Zayed Road, has something for most tastes. IKEA and THE One also have leather collections.

Maternity Items

Fortunately, pregnant women no longer have to suffer months of dressing in large, shapeless smocks, or wearing their husband's shirts over leggings. These days, with many retailers jumping on the maternity fashion bandwagon, mums-in-training can look as stylish as everyone else. Dorothy Perkins and Topshop are great for fun, fashionable items, and Debenhams, Marks & Spencer, Mothercare, Mamas and Papas and Woolworths also stock good selections of maternity clothes.

Maternity Items		
Arabian Home Health Care	Oud Metha	04 335 1230
Babyshop	Various	See p.510
Chocolate & Pickles	Wafi Mall	04 327 92 77
Debenhams	Various	See p.513
Dorothy Perkins	Various	See p.513
Formes	Wafi Mall	04 324 4856
Great Expectations	Palm Strip	04 345 3155
Harvey Nichols	Mall of the Emirates	04 409 8888
Jenny Rose	Various	See p.517
Just Kidding	Al Quoz	04 341 3922
Mamas & Papas	Various	See p.517
Marks & Spencer	Various	See p.517
Mothercare	Various	See p.518
New Look	Various	See p.518
Pumpkin Patch	Various	See p.518
Topshop	Various	See p.519
Toys R Us	Various	See p.522
Woolworths	Various	See p.522

Formes, Great Expectations and Jenny Rose carry the latest styles, and might be the best places to find speciality items such as swimwear, underwear and evening wear.

As well as buggies and nursery furniture, Just Kidding carries Noppies maternity wear from Holland. The Pumpkin Patch store in the Mall of the Emirates now also stocks a limited maternity range – hold out for the sales if you can.

For other maternity items, like cool packs, creams and bras, you'll have to shop around in Mothercare, Baby Shop, Debenhams, Marks & Spencer or Jenny Rose – ranges vary and may be limited. Baby Shop and Mothercare stock a range of breast pumps, or you could try one of the larger pharmacies if you want a really heavy duty one (you can also rent one, try Susi on 050 658 8905). Storage bags for breast milk are widely available (Playtex, Medela, and Avent brands). Boppy breastfeeding pillows are available in Toys R Us, and Arabian Home Health Care, opposite Rashid Hospital, also stock pillows for breast feeding – you need to ask for them when you go in.

Other essential accessories for pregnancy are available here – one example is a 'Bump Belt', which redirects your car seatbelt under your bump, which can be found in Mothercare and some Spinneys (p.507).

Medicine

Other options **General Medical Care** p.177

The UAE has a more relaxed policy on prescription drugs than many other countries and most can be bought over the counter. If you know what you need it cuts out the hassle of having to see a doctor just so that you can get a prescription. Pharmacists are willing to offer advice, although they may be reluctant to suggest antibiotics. Always tell the pharmacist if you have any pre-existing conditions or are taking other medication, as they don't always ask.

Certain medications do require a prescription, and some medications (such as codeine and temazepam) are banned here even though they are widely available over the counter in other countries. It's a crime to have these medicines in your possession or to take them, unless you can produce an official prescription from your doctor in your home country (but even then you might end up at the police station while it is translated into Arabic). So unless it is absolutely necessary and there's no alternative, avoid medications that are banned in the UAE.

Supermarkets and petrol station convenience stores sell basic medications such as Panadol or ENO. They also stock basic first aid equipment such as plasters, gauze and antiseptic cream. You might find it frustrating that certain common medications from your home country are not available here (such as Gaviscon for infants, for example). You can however bring these into the country for your own personal use. There are pharmacies all over the city and a number are open 24 hours a day.

Medicine

Al Wasl Pharmacy	Jumeira	04 344 8333
Boots	Various	See p.511
Life Pharmacy	Al Barsha	04 347 3451
Safa Society Pharmacy	Al Wasl	04 394 6618

Mobile Phones

Other options **Telephone** p.172

Every mall seems to have at least one or two outlets selling mobile phones (but usually more). Major electronics shops sell the leading brands but the mobile specialists are Axiom Telecom and Cellucom, both of which have servicing and repair facilities and issue their own warranties, as well as the standard ones from manufacturers – Cellucom's also covers accessories.
While there's no real market for second-hand mobile phones, they are sometimes advertised on supermarket noticeboards, websites and in the newspapers. As models become obsolete so quickly, and basic handsets are so cheap, buying a used phone is not the preferred option. For convenience, the major retailers can now also issue subscriptions to Etisalat and du's pay-as-you-go schemes.

Mobile Phones

Aptec Mobiles	Various	See p.509	www.aptecmobiles.com
Axiom Telecom	Various	See p.509	www.axiomtelecom.com
Carrefour	Various	See p.511	www.carrefouruae.com
Cellucom	Various	See p.512	www.cellucom.com
Jacky's Electronics	Various	See p.515	www.jackys.com
Jumbo Electronics	Various	See p.516	www.jumbocorp.com
Plug-Ins	Various	See p.519	www.pluginselectronix.com
Sharaf DG	Various	See p.520	www.sharafdg.com

Music, DVDs & Videos

Unless you're a music connoisseur with particularly eclectic tastes, you should be able to find music here that will satisfy you. The advantage to shopping for music in such a multi-cultural society is that you can open yourself up to new genres – Arabic dance music for example, is very popular. Everything has to go through the censor, so any music or DVDs deemed offensive will not be sold here, unless it can be edited to make it more acceptable.

Vinyl fans and those into electronic mixing should head for speciality shop Ohm Records – everything they stock comes from independent labels. They also sell processors and turntables, as well as record bags and a select line of street wear.

Ohm Records offer a selection of DVDs and videos which are mainstream, very

Music, DVDs & Videos

Al Mansoor	Wafi Mall	04 324 4141
Al Meher Recordings	Bur Dubai	04 353 1278
Carrefour	Various	See p.511
Diamond Audio Vision	BurJuman	04 352 7671
Disco 2000	Spinneys	04 394 0139
Géant ▶ p.479	Ibn Battuta Shopping Mall	04 368 5858
Ohm Records	Opp. Burjuman Centre	04 397 3728
Plug-Ins	Various	See p.519
Spinneys	Various	See p.520
Virgin Megastore	Various	See p.522

Hollywood, with few independent films. Bollywood films are extremely popular and available in most shops. Of course, online shopping is an alternative and you should be able to get more variety on sites such as Benson's World (www.bensonsworld.co.uk) and Amazon (www.amazon.com and www.amazon.co.uk). Amazon's postal charges are often more expensive, and its packaging is branded so may occasionally be opened by an inspector at the post office, although this is happening less frequently. Benson's World send your DVDs in plain packaging, so they are often delivered directly to your post box without passing through the censor.

Retailers generally won't order titles not on the lists approved for the UAE. Diamond Audio Vision has a fairly good range and often has sales; they will try to order items listed in the catalogues but are not always reliable. Disco 2000 have a pretty good range, especially BBC and children's titles; they also have a rental section. Magrudy's have a selection of BBC titles and can order from the catalogue. Carrefour has good value bargain bins and although they are usually filled with mainstream Hollywood titles, there are occasional gems and the odd BBC children's title. In common with the rest of the world, video is being phased out, and DVD is now prevalent.

Musical Instruments
Other options **Music Lessons** p.375, **Music, DVDs & Videos** p.459

Good musical equipment was hard to find in Dubai, but things are changing. Juli Music, on Sheikh Zayed Road, stocks a good range of instruments and can also arrange lessons. Particularly useful is its 'hire before you buy' policy. Sowira Pianos offer rental and sales on a range of new and used pianos. The Music Room is run by an experienced music teacher, and has the widest range of sheet music in Dubai. Here you'll find a range of instruments including clarinets, flutes, violins, trumpets and guitars, and their associated accessories. The store is an agent for Steinway & Sons pianos, but if you don't have the space it also stocks Kawai grand, upright and digital pianos. Prices for pianos are considerably lower than elsewhere in the world. Thomsun Music House stocks a wide range of mainly Yamaha instruments, from pianos to drum kits and guitars, and they also sell mixing desks and equipment for digital music-making (there is a branch in Ibn Battuta called Thomsun Pure Music). Carrefour, Géant and the larger supermarkets stock basic keyboards and guitars, which are fine for beginners.

Musical Instruments

Carrefour	Various	See p.511
Fann Al Sout Music	Nr Fish R/A	04 271 9471
Géant ▶ p.479	Ibn Battuta Shopping Mall	04 368 5858
House of Guitar	Karama Shopping Complex	04 334 9968
JS Music	Ibn Battuta Shopping Mall	04 366 9715
Juli Music	Trade Centre 1	04 321 2588
Jumeirah Music Equipment	Jumeira Plaza	04 344 3855
Melody House Musical Instruments	Opp. Hamarain Centre	04 227 5336
Mozart Musical Instruments	Karama Shopping Complex	04 337 7007
The Music Chamber	Crowne Plaza Ctr, Shk Zayed Rd	04 331 6416
The Music Institute	Various	See p.521
Music Room	Beach Centre	04 344 8883
Sadek Music	Souk Madinat Jumeirah	04 368 6570
Sowira Pianos	Mazaya Centre	04 343 9188
Thomsun Music	Various	See p.521
Zak Electronics	Zabeel Rd	04 336 8857

Climb Every Mountain

Global Climbing is a brand new company created to meet all UAE residents' climbing needs. As well as importing climbing and caving equipment into Dubai, its new website, www. globalclimbing.com, will also have route information and useful climber tips.

Outdoor Goods

Other options **Sports Goods** p.467, **Hardware & DIY** p.448, **Camping** p.334

With miles of desert, mountains and coastline, and year-round sunshine, spending time in the great outdoors is a popular pastime in the UAE. With temperatures cooler on higher ground, the hardiest adventurers are still out there in the heat of the summer. For everyone else, the cooler months are ideal for exploring.

While there are no specialist camping shops, the basic gear is readily available in Carrefour, Go Sport, Géant, ACE and Picnico. Items are suitable for weekend campers, but would not withstand extremes, so if you are intending anything more strenuous you should consider ordering kit online. Go Sport produce their own range of camping equipment as well as importing ranges from other suppliers.

Caveman Make Fire produce a range of barbecues and heaters which you can pick up at Géant or Spinneys and Hyper Panda, or you can also have them delivered free of charge. Picnico are outdoor specialists, stocking a good range of Coleman and Campingaz equipment like cooler bags, tents and accessories. They also stock GPS systems and rock climbing gear. They have one of the largest ranges of hydration packs, and are stockists for Dakine (kite surfing kit) sea kayaks and angling equipment. GPS equipment can also be found in Sharaf DG – the Times Square branch has the biggest selection. For outdoor sports enthusiasts there are a number of options (see Sports Goods on p.467). Fishing equipment is also widely available from shops such as Al Hamur Marine, Go Sport and Picnico.

Serious climbers and hikers should consider getting their boots and equipment from overseas, as a very limited range of boots are available and are often aimed more towards the fashion market. While hydration packs (backpacks that you can fill with water, complete with a long tube and mouthpiece) are becoming more widely available in sports shops, anything larger than a day pack should be bought overseas. Hiking accessories for those people with small children, such as backpack carriers, are not widely available here and should be bought online or from overseas.

Outdoor Goods

ACE	Various	See p.508	www.aceuae.com
Al Hamur Marine	Jumeira	04 344 4468	
Carrefour	Various	See p.511	www.carrefouruae.com
Caveman Make Fire	Online	04 347 6167	www.cavemanmakefire.com
Géant ▶ p.479	Ibn Battuta Shopping Mall	04 368 5858	www.geant-dubai.com
Go Sport	Various	See p.514	na
Harley-Davidson UAE	Shk Zayed Rd	04 339 1909	www.harley-uae.com
Picnico General Trading	Jumeirah Rd	04 394 1653	na
Sharaf DG	Various	See p.520	www.sharafdg.com
ULO Systems Ltd	Sharjah	06 531 4036	www.ulosystems.com

Party Accessories

Other options **Parties At Home** p.629, **Party Organisers** p.629

Party accessories are available, on a small scale, in most supermarkets and toy shops but there are several specialist stores that stock everything for children's or adults' parties. If you want a party at home but without the bother, there are a number of companies who will do it for you. You can always have children's parties at one of the various play centres around town, if your house won't stand up to an afternoon of messy toddlers buzzed up on too much sugar.

The Party Centre, in Garhoud, is enormous and stocks pretty much everything you will need, no matter what the occasion. This is a one-stop shop for decorations and party accessories, and they even sell children's fancy dress outfits. Partyzone in the Beach Centre, Jumeirah Plaza and The Balloon Lady, in Jumeira Plaza, cover the basics. Carrefour, Park n Shop and Toys R Us all sell themed party essentials, such as paper cups, gift bags, balloons and plates. The range isn't huge and tends to be either Winnie the Pooh, Barbie or Mickey Mouse, so if your child has a preference you may have to order online.

For certain occasions, like Halloween and Easter, specialist shops and even supermarkets (Park n Shop, Carrefour and Spinneys) really get into the spirit of things, selling a range of costumes, sweets and accessories. Costume ranges tend to be a bit limited though. In Disguise, in Satwa, has a slightly bigger selection or you can shop online for costumes, party accessories and weird and wacky gifts at www.bonkers.ae. Purchases are delivered to your door within two days. Mr Ben's costume closet, in Al Ghazal Mall, is dedicated to fancy dress, with costumes for children and adults available for purchase and hire. Fabric is inexpensive and it doesn't cost much to hire the services of a tailor, so you can easily have a costume made.

For that all-important birthday cake, the choice is great. For adult's cakes, try Lenôtre, Coco's or Boulevard Gourmet at the InterContinental for some yummy options. For children, you can get a customised cake made at Park n Shop (choose from one of their designs or take your own picture in and they will scan it onto edible paper and put it on top of your cake). Baskin Robbins makes a range of icecream party cakes, or Caesars does some elaborately iced creations.

For party entertainment, Flying Elephant can provide bouncy castles, soft-play areas and more. Tumble Time are bouncy castle specialists, and Harlequin provide marquees, tables and chairs and even outdoor cooling units.

Party Accessories

Andy the Entertainer	Various	050 840 1770	www.andystuartentertainments.com
Balloon Lady	Jumeira Plaza	04 344 1062	www.balloonladyuae.com
Baskin Robbins	Various	See p.510	www.baskinrobbins.com
Boulevard Gourmet	Radisson SAS Hotel	04 205 7317	na
Caesars	Karama Centre	04 335 3700	www.caesars-uae.com
Café Ceramique	Jumeirah Town Centre	04 344 7331	www.cafe-ceramique.com
Carrefour	Various	See p.511	www.carrefouruae.com
Coco's	Shk Zayed Rd	04 332 6333	na
Elves & Fairies	Jumeirah Centre	04 344 9485	www.elvesandfairies.org
Flying Elephant ▶ p.359	Jct 3, Shk Zayed Rd	04 347 9170	www.flyingelephantuae.com
Fun Island	Arbift Tower, Office#1801	04 227 8273	www.funislanddubai.com
Gulf Greetings	Various	See p.515	www.gulfgreetings.com
The Jam Jar	St 17a, Beh Dubai Garden Ctr	04 341 7303	www.thejamjardubai.com
Lenôtre	Spinneys	04 349 4433	www.lenotre.fr
Magrudy's ▶ p.429	Various	See p.516	www.magrudy.com
Mr Ben's Closet	Al Ghazal Mall	04 345 3577	www.mrbendubai.com
Papermoon	Mina Rd, off Al Diyafah St	04 345 4888	na
Park n Shop	Al Wasl Rd	04 394 5671	www.parkshopdubai.com
The Party Centre	Party Centre Bld, opp Welcare Hospital	04 283 1353	www.mypartycentre.com
Partyzone	Beach Centre	04 344 4158	na
Planet Hollywood	Wafi Mall	04 324 4777	www.planethollywood-dubai.com
Spinneys	Various	See p.520	www.spinneys.com
Toys R Us	Various	See p.522	www.toysrus.com
Tumble Time	Various	04 348 8542	www.tumbletimedubai.com

Planet Hollywood, Café Céramique and The Jam Jar all cater for children's parties, as do many of the hotel clubs. For entertainment at an adult's party, try Andy the Entertainer – his acts range from the amazing (magic tricks and fire eating) to the bizarre (encasing his whole body in a big balloon).

Perfumes & Cosmetics
Other options **Markets/Souks** p.481

Perfumes and cosmetics are big business here, from the local scents like frankincense and oudh, to the latest designer offerings. The department stores and local chains (such as Areej and Paris Gallery) stock the most comprehensive ranges of international brand perfumes and cosmetics.

The Body Shop, MAC and Red Earth are found in many of the city's malls, while Boots now has several branches. This sector has been joined by Pixi Cosmetics in Mall of the Emirates. L'Occitaine is also worth seeking out for their natural skincare products.

Larger supermarkets and pharmacies all stock skincare products and some make-up. Anti-allergenic ranges are available at some of the larger pharmacies. Most needs are covered but if yours aren't, specialist retailers often have online shopping facilities.

Local perfumes and scents tend to be strong and spicy – shops selling these products can often be smelled before they are seen as many burn incense in the doorways. Amouage produces some of the world's most valuable perfumes, with scents made with rare ingredients.

Perfumes & Cosmetics		
Ajmal Perfumes	Various	See p.508
Amouage ▶ p.419	Paris Gallery	04 295 5550
Arabian Oud	Various	See p.509
Areej	Various	See p.509
The Body Shop	Various	See p.511
Boots	Various	See p.511
Debenhams	Various	See p.513
Jashanmal ▶ p.431	Various	See p.515
L'Occitaine	Various	See p.516
Lush	Deira City Centre	04 295 9531
MAC	Various	See p.516
Make Up Forever	Wafi Mall	04 324 2364
Makeup etc.	Mazaya Centre	04 343 3531
Mikyajy	Various	See p.517
The Nature Shop	Deira City Centre	04 295 4181
Paris Gallery	Various	See p.518
Pixi Cosmetics	Mall of the Emirates	04 341 4747
Rasasi	Various	See p.519
Red Earth	Various	See p.519

They can be found in airports and on board Emirates flights as well as in Paris Gallery outlets. Ajmal and Arabian Oud outlets are found in most malls, but they cater to the Arab population and don't always have English-speaking shop assistants on duty. Prices for perfumes and cosmetics are similar to those in some other countries, although certain nationalities might find perfume is cheaper here than in their home country. There are no sales taxes, so there is rarely a difference between Duty Free and shopping mall prices.

Pets
Other options **Pets** p.168

Pets		
Animal World	Jumeira	04 344 4422
Pet Land	Al Quoz	04 338 4040
Pet Zone	Trade Centre 1	04 321 1424
Pet's Delight	Various	See p.519
Retail Pet Store	Al Barsha	04 341 8085

Most supermarkets carry basic ranges of cat, dog, bird and fish food, although the choice is limited. If yours is a particularly pampered pet you might end up bringing some special treats home with you after your next trip. If your pet has specific dietary requirements, many of the veterinary clinics (p.170) carry specialist foods.

Pet shops are a bit on the dismal side here – standards are low and animals are usually in tiny cages without water for long periods. The pet shops along Plant Street in Satwa are notoriously the worst offenders and animals purchased there are often malnourished and diseased. Dubai Municipality has laid down regulations and if they are contravened the shop will be closed down for a day; hardly a strong motivation for these shops to clean up their acts. Even the pet shops that most animal lovers can bear to go into have a long way to go before standards are acceptable. Petland, in Al Quoz, Petzone on Sheikh Zayed Road, and Animal World, on Jumeira Beach Road, are the most acceptable. All sell a range of pet accessories, food, animals, birds and fish.

If you are looking for a family pet, consider contacting Feline Friends or K9 Friends (see p.168) who have hundreds of cats and dogs looking for homes.

Portrait Photographers & Artists

Many of the photography shops in Dubai also have a portrait studio where you can get attractive family or individual portraits done. Alternatively, there are several independent portrait photographers that can take beautiful pictures of you and your family – the advantage of using an independent photographer is that they can do the portraits at the location of your choice, be it in your home or garden or on the beach. Many shopping malls have 'roving' portrait painters who set up a stall from time to time. They can either do a genuine likeness (working from a sitting or a photo), or a caricature. Try Souk Madinat Jumeirah and Deira City Centre. See also Wedding Items (p.470).

Portrait Photographers & Artists		
Belina Muller	050 769 7650	na
Charlotte Simpson	050 428 3660	www.hotshotsdubai.com
Darrin James Photography	04 374 7299	www.djphotography.net
Henk Bos	050 626 3724	www.henkbos.com
Karen Bullock	050 458 1846	na
Riot Art	04 422 4166	www.riot-art.com
Robeya Photography	050 494 4297	www.robeya.com
Stu Williamson Photography	04 348 8527	www.stuwilliamson.com
Studio Al Aroosa	04 344 1663	www.studioalaroosa.com
Sue Johnston	050 564 5519	www.imageoasisdubai.com

Second-Hand Items

Other options **Books** p.69, **Cars** p.434, **Furnishing Accommodation** p.160

There is an active second-hand market in Dubai, as people are always leaving, redecorating or downsizing and need to get rid of their stuff. Supermarket noticeboards are a great place to start, as many people post 'for sale' notices with pictures of all the items. Garage sales are also popular on Fridays and you'll notice signs going up in your neighbourhood from time to time.

For the Dhs.3 entry fee into Al Safa Park you can peruse the flea market which has stalls filled with furniture, books, clothing and a broad range of unwanted items and homemade crafts. The flea market is set up on the first Saturday of every month near Gate 5 (for more information see www.dubai-fleamarket.com). There are also a number of websites with classifieds sections. Try www.

Second-Hand Items		
Al Noor Shop	Nr Interchange 4, Shk Zayed Rd	04 340 4844
Book World	Various	See p.510
Dubai Charity Association	Al Rigga Rd	04 268 2000
Dubai Charity Centre	Beh Choithrams, Karama	04 337 8246
Holy Trinity Thrift Shop	Holy Trinity, Oud Metha Rd	04 337 8192
House of Prose	Various	See p.515
Rashid Pediatric Therapy Centre	Al Barsha	04 340 0005

expatwoman.com, www.dubizzle.com, www.souq.com, and www.websouq.com. There are a number of second-hand shops, often linked to churches and special needs schools, but the opening hours can be somewhat eccentric. The Holy Trinity Thrift Shop gives you back 50% of what your items sell for, so you can even make money out of being charitable. It is good for high-quality items and books in particular, and proceeds go towards a number of orphanages supported by the church. The Al Noor shop raises funds for the Al Noor School for Special Needs and is good for second-hand clothing. All donations in good condition are accepted. The Dubai Charity Centre (04 337 8246), behind Choithram in Karama, is the biggest of the charity shops. This store supports the students who attend The Dubai Centre for Special Needs, and finances a number of places for those who are unable to afford them. It stocks a good range of clothes, books and toys. The Rashid Paediatric Therapy Centre, behind the American Academic School in Al Barsha, has a decent range of items and raises money for projects at the centre.

If you are looking to clear some space on your bookshelves, Book World in Karama and Satwa, and House of Prose which has branches in Jumeira Plaza and Ibn Battuta, both buys books in good condition that they will be able to sell. Any books bought from them will be worth 50% of the purchase price if returned in good condition.

Shoes

Other options **Clothes** p.435, **Beachwear** p.426, **Sports Goods** p.467

The choice of shoes available in Dubai is enormous, unless you are a woman with outsized feet. Designer labels like Jimmy Choo and Gucci mingle with middle-of-the-range creations from Bally, Milano, Faith and Nine West, which also mingle with cheap-as-chips flip-flops and sandals in the big hypermarkets. Apart from the dedicated shoe shops, department stores like Debenhams, Marks & Spencer and Woolworths all have shoe departments. For stylish shoes that won't break the budget, Shoe Mart, Brantano Shoe City and Avenue all carry fashionable and practical shoes, as do the many shoe shops in Karama Market. You'll probably find that sports shoes are cheaper than in your home country,

Shoes		
ALDO	Various	See p.509
Aqua Shoes	Al Ghurair City	04 221 3340
Avenue	Opp BurJuman	04 397 9983
Bally	Mall of the Emirates	04 341 0280
Brantano	Various	See p.511
Carrefour	Various	See p.511
Cesare Paccioti	Wafi Mall	04 324 3227
City Shoes	Karama Centre	04 337 8010
Clarks	Various	See p.512
Debenhams	Various	See p.512
Domino	Various	See p.513
Ecco	Various	See p.513
Escada	BurJuman	04 359 1117
Eve Michelle	Magrudy's	04 342 9574
Faith	Various	See p.514
HyperPanda	Festival Power Centre	04 232 5566
Jimmy Choo	Boulevard at Emirates Towers	04 330 0404
Kenneth Cole	Mall of the Emirates	04 341 0320
Magrudy Shoe Shop	Magrudy's	04 344 4192
Manolo Blahnik	BurJuman	04 351 5551
Marelli	Al Ghurair City	04 227 0933
Mario Bologna	BurJuman	04 352 9726
Marks & Spencer	Various	See p.517
Milano	Various	See p.517
Nine West	Various	See p.518
Pablosky	Various	See p.518
Peacock	Shk Hamdan Colony	04 396 2299
Philippe Charriol	BurJuman	04 351 1112
PrettyFIT	Various	See p.519
Rockport	Deira City Centre	04 295 0261
Shoe Bazar	Al Faheidi St	04 353 0444
Shoe City	Various	See p.520
Shoe Mart	Various	See p.520
Spring	Various	See p.521
Stadium	Various	See p.521
Tod's	Various	See p.522
Topshop	Various	See p.522
Valencia	Various	See p.522
Vincci	Various	See p.522
Woodland	Century Mall	04 296 7890
Woolworths	Various	See p.522

but you might not be able to get the latest styles. Stadium is good for active-wear shoes and sandals. Birkenstocks are widely available and Scholl shoes can be found in shoe shops and larger pharmacies. Pharmacies also stock supports, powders and specialist plasters.

For children's shoes, Magrudy's Shoe Shop stocks Clarks, Start-Rite and Elephanten, and they provide a foot measuring service. Pablosky has branches in many of the malls, and Ecco stocks a good range of children's shoes. Because of the weather, children spend a great deal of time in sandals, which are widely available. If you are planning a trip to colder climes, it can be hard to find good winter shoes for little feet – so if you see a pair, grab them.

Souvenirs
Other options **Carpets** p.434

From fridge magnets to antique wooden wedding chests, the range of souvenirs available is incredible. Many souvenirs are regional rather than local, and many are mass produced in India, Pakistan and Oman.

Souvenir and gift shops are widely available, and there is at least one outlet in every mall. The best prices are to be had in the souks and shopping areas, where bargaining is encouraged and expected – make sure the vendor knows you are not a tourist, and be firm but reasonable while you haggle. Being rude won't help. The more you buy, the better the discount, and if the vendor gets to know you over time he will give you special discounts on every visit.

The Antiques Museum in Al Quoz is full of souvenirs, although not all of them are from the UAE. The warehouse stocks a broad range of items from souvenir T-shirts to furniture, pashminas and Omani silver, the prices are less than in tourist hotspots like Souk Madinat Jumeirah, and wandering through its passageways and secret rooms is an added treat. As you would expect, camels feature heavily in the souvenir shops; wooden carvings, camel pot stands, and even carvings made from camel bones are all widely available and are great as novelty presents. Perhaps the frontrunner for the 'tackiest souvenir' prize are plastic alarm clocks in the shape of a mosque – they only cost Dhs.10 and they wake you up with a loud call to prayer.

Coffee pots are symbols of Arabic hospitality and another popular souvenir item. Prices vary enormously from Dhs.100 for a brand new, shiny one, to several thousand dirhams for a genuine antique.

Souvenirs

Traditional silver items, such as the Arabic dagger (khanjar), are excellent souvenirs, and are available both framed and unframed. Of course, you shouldn't attempt to transport a khanjar back home in your hand luggage. Silver wedding jewellery is chunky and ornate, and is often framed. Wooden items are popular and representative of the region. Trinket boxes (often with elaborate carvings or brass inlays) start from around Dhs.10. Elaborate Arabic doors and wedding chests, costing thousands, are also popular. The doors can be hung as art, or converted into tables or headboards.

While carpets are a good buy, it is worth doing some research before investing. For a smaller, cheaper option, many shops sell woven coasters and camel bags, or you can buy a Persian carpet mouse pad.

You can hardly walk through a mall or shopping area without being offered a pashmina – they are available in an abundant range of colours and styles. Most are a cotton/silk mix and the ratio dictates the price. It is a good idea to check out a few shops before buying as prices vary and, as with most items, the more you buy the cheaper they are. For a decent quality pashmina, prices start from around Dhs.50.

Shisha pipes make fun souvenirs and can be bought with various flavours of tobacco, such as apple or strawberry. Both working and ornamental examples are on sale, prices start from around Dhs.75 in Carrefour. If you are into smells, the heavy local perfume and incense make good gifts and are widely available in outlets like Arabian Oud.

For book lovers, there are a number of great coffee table books with stunning photos depicting the diversity of this vibrant city. Grab a copy of *Dubai: Tomorrow's City Today*, *Impressions Dubai*, or *Images of Dubai and the UAE*. *Dubai Discovered* is a concise pictorial souvenir of Dubai and is available in five languages (English, Japanese, French, German and Russian).

If you've scoured the souvenir shops in Dubai and still can't find what you're looking for, head for Souk Al Arsah in Sharjah (p.483), where you can shop for traditional items in a traditional setting.

Souvenirs

Al Jaber Gallery	Various	See p.508	www.aljabergallery.com
Antique Museum	Nr Kanoo, Al Quoz 3	04 347 9935	na
Arabian Oud	Various	See p.509	www.arabianoud.com
Carrefour	Various	See p.511	www.carrefouruae.com
Creative Art Centre	Beh Jumeirah Rd	04 344 4394	na
Falcon Gallery	Mina Road, Near Port Rashid	04 345 3369	www.falcongallery.com
Jad Hafs Novelties Gift Shop	BurJuman	04 352 2550	na
Showcase Antiques	Opp Dubai Municipality	04 348 8797	www.showcaseantiques.net

Sports Goods
Other options **Outdoor Goods** p.461

The development of Sports City (part of Dubailand) will rocket Dubai into the sports limelight. Sport is already big business in Dubai, and whatever you are into, chances are that it is played here. Basic equipment is well covered – the many sports shops stock clothing and footwear, as well as equipment for 'core sports' like running, basketball, cricket, football, swimming, badminton, squash and tennis.

Go Sport, at Ibn Battuta and Mall of the Emirates, has the most comprehensive collection of sports goods. Apart from equipment for the above sports, they also stock cycling, camping, equestrian and golfing gear. Stadium combines active-wear clothing labels with serious sports equipment – they are stockists for New Balance footwear and have large Speedo and Reebok collections. You can also pick up Lorna Jane active wear and Capezio dancewear from Active Living LLC (contact Belinda Reardon for more information, 050 352 7446). Sun & Sand Sports have outlets all over the city, and the larger branches have Nike, Columbia and Timberland departments. They also stock home gym equipment, from treadmills to rowing machines, as well as a limited range of pool and snooker tables (although the specialists for pool and snooker tables and equipment are Knight Shot Inc.).

Golf is extremely popular and clubs, balls and bags are available in most sports shops. Golf House and the pro shops are the best places for decent kit.

Sports Goods

Sports Goods		
Adidas	Various	See p.508
Al Boom Marine	Various	See p.508
Alpha Sports	Deira City Centre	04 295 4087
Carrefour	Various	See p.511
Dubai Surfski Kayak Club	Umm Suqeim	050 813 3207
Emirates Sports Stores	Wafi Mall	04 324 2208
Go Sport	Various	See p.514
Golf House	Various	See p.514
Intersport	Times Square	04 341 8214
Knight Shot Inc.	Nr Mazaya Centre, Shk Zayed Rd	04 343 5678
Magic Swell	www.magicswell.com	na
Magrudy's ▶ p.429	Various	See p.516
Picnico General Trading	Jumeirah Rd	04 394 1653
Profit Free Sports	Nr Lamcy Plaza	04 337 3799
Prozone	Various	See p.519
RHS	Various	See p.520
Royal Sporting House	Deira City Centre	04 295 0261
Scuba Dubai	DWTC Apts, Block C	04 341 4940
Skechers	Various	See p.520
Speciality	BurJuman	04 352 0106
Sport One Trading	BurJuman	04 351 6033
Stadium	Various	See p.521
Sun & Sand Sports	Various	See p.521
ULO Systems Ltd	Sharjah	06 531 4036
Wheels Trading	Sahara Tower, Shk Zayed Rd	04 331 7119
Wolfi's Bike Shop	Btn Jct 2-3	04 339 4453

The clubs that organise specialist sports, such as Dubai Surfski Kayak Club (www.dskc.net), can often be approached for equipment. Kite surfing is a sport that has become popular very quickly and the equipment is now being stocked in shops; Al Boom Marine stocks North Kites at the Jumeira Beach Road showroom, and Picnico, next door, stocks Dakine. Al Boom also stocks equipment for other watersports, including waterskiing and diving. Magic Swell (www.magicswell.com), is an online shop which sells a wide range of watersport accessories such as wetsuits, harnesses and helmets. Profit Free Sports is a factory outlet for Sun & Sand Sports and is great for end-of-range clothes, shoes and equipment. Stadium and Adidas also have factory shops – the Stadium factory shop is on Sheikh Zayed Road and there are some excellent bargains to be had; and Adidas has factory shops on the Airport Road and near Lamcy Plaza, but although their prices are slightly lower than in their retail stores, the difference is not huge. Karama Market has several sports shops with decent ranges that are often cheaper than the bigger stores – just remember, if the item you are buying is much cheaper than normal, it could be a fake.

Stationery

Whether you are looking for a pencil sharpener or professional standard plotting paper, there are stationery shops all over the city. For basic school and personal stationery, Carrefour and Union Co-Op carry extensive ranges, particularly at the beginning of the school year. Dubai Library Distributors and Kazim Gulf Traders should have everything

Stationery		
Books Plus ▶ p.493	Various	See p.511
Carrefour	Various	See p.511
Compu-Me	Various	See p.512
Dubai Library Distributors	Various	See p.513
Emirates Trading Est.	Various	See p.513
Kazim Gulf Traders	Jumeirah Centre	04 349 3347
Montblanc	Various	See p.517
Office Mart	Orange Bld Zabeel Rd	04 335 9929
Office Outlet	Umm Suqeim Bld Shk Zayed Rd	04 338 8444
Union Co-Op	Various	See p.522
World of Pens	Jumeirah Town Centre	04 349 1022

that you will need for personal or home office use. Offices are well served by Emirates Trading Est., Office Mart and Office Outlet, all selling wide ranges of stationery. If a ballpoint pen just isn't appropriate, World of Pens and Mont Blanc stock luxury models that will add style to your signature.

What & Where To Buy

Tailoring

Al Aryam Tailor	Satwa	04 349 2434
Ali Eid Al Muree	Jumeirah Beach Rd	04 348 7176
Couture	Deira	04 269 9522
Dream Boy	Bur Dubai	04 352 1840
Dream Girl	Various	See p.513
Eves	Nasser Square	04 228 1070
First Lady	Al Faheidi St	04 352 7019
Future Tailors	Satwa	04 349 8723
Garasheeb	Karama Shopping Complex	04 396 8900
Kachins	Carpet Souk	04 352 1386
Khamis Abdullah Trading & Embroidery	Al Rashidiya	04 285 2543
La Donna	Al Wahida Rd	04 266 6596
Ma Belle	Opp Buy & Save Supermaket	04 269 6500
Monte Carlo	Behind York Hotel	04 352 0225
Montexa	Satwa	04 349 4037
Oasis	Various	See p.518
Regency Tailors	Bur Dubai	04 352 4732
Royal Fashions	Karama	04 396 8282
Stitches	Jumeira	04 342 1476
Tailorworks	Satwa	04 349 9906
Vanucci Fashions	Al Qusais	04 263 2626
Whistle & Flute	Satwa	04 342 9229
Yoginir'z Tailoring & Fashion Design	Musalla Rd, nr Dubai Museum	04 355 5105

Tailoring

Other options **Clothes** p.435, **Textiles** p.469, **Bur Dubai** p.133, **Souvenirs** p.466

There are so many tailors in Dubai, and word of mouth is the best way to find a good one. They can be found in most areas, but the area around the Dubai Museum in Bur Dubai, or the main street in Satwa, are good places to start. A good tailor will be able to make a garment from scratch (rather than just make alterations), either from a photo or diagram or by copying an existing garment. If they don't get the garment spot on, they will happily make the necessary alterations.

Dream Girl tailors, in Meena Bazaar and Satwa, have huge followings and they are great for all tailoring jobs from taking up trousers to making ball gowns. Skirts cost around Dhs.50 and dresses from around Dhs.80, depending on how basic the pattern is. For those living on the Deira side, Khamis Abdullah Trading & Embroidery, in Rashidiya, is one of the least expensive in town, with skirts starting from around Dhs.30.

Dream Boy, near the museum, is good for shirts and suits, as are Kachins and Whistle & Flute; shirts usually start from Dhs.30 and suits from around Dhs.500.

Textiles

Other options **Souvenirs** p.466, **Tailoring** p.469

Abdulla Hussain	Al Ghurair City	04 221 7310
Al Masroor (Gents)	Deira City Centre	04 295 0832
Damas (Ladies)	Al Ghurair City	04 221 6700
Deepak's	Plant St	04 344 8836
Feshwari	Various	See p.514
IKEA ▶ p.451	Festival Power Centre	800 4532
Meena Bazaar Fashions	Bur Dubai	04 353 9304
Mostafawi	Deira	04 225 5678
Ratti	Al Fahidi St nxt to Giordano	04 353 8143
Regal Traders	Various	See p.519
Rivoli Textiles	Bur Dubai	04 335 0075
Royalex	Bur Dubai	04 351 8800
Yasmine (Ladies)	Al Diyafah St	04 398 8476

You have three options if you are looking for fabric: the Textile Souk (near Al Fahedi Street), Satwa, or the shopping malls (most of which have at least one fabric outlet). Prices start from a few dirhams for a metre of basic cotton. The Textile Souk can get busy and parking is difficult, but the sheer range of fabrics makes it worth while. Deepaks, in Satwa, is renowned for its huge selection of fabrics and helpful staff. There are several haberdashery shops in the same area should you wish to buy matching buttons, bows or cotton.

Plant Street in Satwa is the place to go for upholstery fabrics; IKEA and Fabindia also stock a range of fresh and vibrant fabrics that can be used for cushions, curtains or bedding.

Wedding Items

If you are planning a Dubai wedding, you can either choose to work with a wedding planner (see also p.95) or do it yourself. For books and magazines on etiquette, traditions and fashion for weddings, Magrudy's has a large selection, and Marks & Spencer has a limited range of books.

For the latest off-the-peg wedding gown fashions, Saks Fifth Avenue has a fabulous department stocking designer dresses by Vera Wang and Reem Acra. They keep some gowns in stock, but others can be ordered (allow around four months for delivery). The bride will attend a number of fittings; alterations are done in-house and are up to couture standards. The Wedding Shop also sells off-the-peg dresses in a range of styles.

There are several specialist bridal designers with workshops in Dubai. Arushi is renowned as one of the best. The bride can either provide the fabric or it can be selected during the first meeting with the designer. Gowns take around one month to make, but as Arushi is so popular, there is often a waiting list. If you want to get your dress made but are on a tighter budget, some of the city's tailors are able to work from pictures to create your ideal dress. Bridal accessories and shoes are available at Saks Fifth Avenue and The Wedding Shop.

For the groom, there are several shops where formal wear can be hired, including The Wedding Shop and Elegance and Formal Wear, on Al Diyafah Street.

Bridesmaid's dresses are sold in the children's department of Saks Fifth Avenue. Debenhams and Monsoon both sell suitable ranges, as does Cocomino; if the style or shade you are looking for aren't available, have them made up by a tailor. Monsoon also sells hair accessories and pretty shoes suitable for young bridesmaids.

Wedding guests have many options when it comes to choosing the ideal outfit. Mothers of the bride and groom, and guests, are well catered for at Debenhams and Monsoon, among many others.

The Wedding Shop sells everything but the cake, and is a great place to get your confetti, guest books and photo albums. Amal & Amal and Chic Design both make bespoke wedding stationery, and Cadorim and Enigma do tailor-made favour and ring boxes. Magrudy's and Susan Walpole stock invitations, guest books and photo albums. As well as offering wedding planning services, several of the hotels can be commissioned to make the wedding cake; Lenôtre also creates them. Most of the city's florists can turn their hands to wedding bouquets and arrangements, discuss your requirements with them to find out what will be available.

Debenhams and THE One both offer wedding list services. For any items that you can't find here, www.confetti.co.uk accept international orders.

Wedding Items		
Amal & Amal	Jumeirah Centre	04 344 4671
Cadorim	The Village Mall	04 394 3333
Cocomino	Bin Sougat Centre	04 286 1514
Debenhams	Various	See p.513
Dream Girl	Various	See p.513
Elegance	Al Diyafah St	04 349 1613
Eve Michelle	Magrudy's	04 342 9574
Formal Wear	Al Diyafah St	04 345 5185
House of Arushi	Beach Rd, Opp Dubai Zoo	04 344 2277
Lenôtre	Spinneys	04 349 4433
Magrudy's ▶ p.429	Various	See p.516
Marks & Spencer	Various	See p.517
Monsoon	Various	See p.517
THE One	Various	See p.521
Saks Fifth Avenue	Various	See p.520
The Wedding Shop	Jumeirah Centre	04 344 1618
Wedding.ae	Saleh Bin Lahej Bld, opp Lamcy Plaza	04 336 7878

Colourful lanterns

Places To Shop

The following section features Dubai's main shopping areas and malls. The information for each mall includes a directory of stores. Information on a selection of the city's smaller malls and souks have also been provided.

Areas To Shop

Other options **Bur Dubai** p.133, **Karama** p.253, **Satwa** p.150

Nr Astoria Hotel
Bur Dubai
Map 8 F2

Al Faheidi Street

Central to Bur Dubai's traditional shopping area, and bordering the Textile Souk, Al Fahedi Street is the location of Dubai's electronics souk. This area is always busy but it really comes to life at night – if you're not sure if you're in the right place, just head for the neon lights. Electronics shops abound with top global brands such as Canon, JVC, LG, Panasonic, Philips and Sony available. Prices are negotiable and competitive but the vendors know the value of what they're selling. Don't make your purchases at the first shop you go into; rather, take the time to look around at the range and prices available. Although goods are often cheaper here, if you are making a big purchase it may be worth it to pay that little bit extra and buy from a major retailer, so that you have more security if something goes wrong.

Al Fahedi Street is part of the commercial area that runs from the Bastakiya area all the way to Shindagha and takes in Dubai Museum and the Textile Souk. A great place to wander round in the cooler evenings, it's perfect for a bit of local colour and some great shopping. This area has a good range of inexpensive places to eat, including some fantastic vegetarian restaurants near the museum, as well as various outlets at the nearby Astoria and Ambassador hotels.

Nr Karama Park
Karama
Map 10 D1

Karama Shopping Complex

Karama is an older residential district, and it has a big shopping area that is one of the best places to find a bargain. The main shopping area is the Karama Complex, a long street running through the middle of the district. It is lined by veranda-covered shops on both sides, and most display some goods outside to entice you in. The area is best known for bargain clothing, sports goods, gifts and souvenirs. While you wander round, you will quickly become aware of the reason for Karama's popularity and notoriety, as you will be offered 'copy' watches and handbags at every shop. If you show any interest you will be whisked into a back room to view the goods – if you have a specific model in mind, ask and they may be able to get it for you. If you're not interested, a simple 'no thank you' will suffice, or even just ignore the vendor completely – it may seem rude, but sometimes it's the only way to cope with the incessant invitations to view 'copy watches, copy bags'. Prices are negotiable in many of the shops in Karama; exceptions include the Benetton luggage shop and City Shoes (near Emirates Bank) and their prices are fixed, but very reasonable and they always have special offers.

Much of the clothing comes from the Far East, so check the sizes before you buy – they tend to be on the smaller side. There's always a huge range of T-shirts, shoes, shorts, and sunglasses at very reasonable prices. There are several shops selling gifts and souvenirs, from toy camels to mosque alarm clocks and stuffed scorpions to pashminas – Gifts Tent is one of the larger outlets and has a wide range, including every colour of pashmina imaginable – they are happy to take most of them out so you can find exactly the right shade.

With loads of small, inexpensive restaurants in the area serving a range of cuisines, you won't go hungry; Shezan, near Choithram, has good Indian and Chinese food. For fresh produce, head for the large fish, fruit and vegetable market.

Downtown Burj Dubai
Map 7 D4

Downtown Burj Dubai & Dubai Mall
www.thedubaimall.com

Although parts of the Downtown still feel quite deserted, the buzz around the opening of The Dubai Mall (p.489) and the new hotel The Address (p.38) has sparked a growing interest in this vibrant area teaming with new restaurants and shops. The area is only just starting to dust off the sand and make its mark on the shopping circuit.
Dubai Mall opened 600 stores in November 2008 and it will eventually hold 1200 shops. Those keen to spend won't be disappointed with the extensive store listing, but it is worth keeping in mind that the mall is still within its opening phases and many of the outlets still have 'coming soon' facades. Nonetheless, those looking for high-street fashion will be happy with its range of favourites like Topshop, GAP and Marks & Spencer. Dubai Mall also caters for the high end market with a range of designer stores such as Tiffany & Co., Chanel, Dior, and Jimmy Choo. Well-known American department store Bloomingdales is also on its way. The mall offers a huge array of entertainment options with an aquarium, cinema and ice rink. This colossal mall is a big addition to Dubai's retail market and the area is already coping with an increase in traffic.
For a more laidback atmosphere, Souk Al Bahar and Dukkan Souk Al Manzil both feature a number of shops selling Arabian wares such as carpets, ornaments, paintings, jewellery, clothes and perfumes. Designed to resemble traditional market areas, both feature large archways, winding passageways and a mix of stores. You'll also find that there are a number of useful outlets catering for residents such as banks, a branch of Jacky's electronics and a Spinneys at Souk Al Bahar. Many of the shops cater to tourists but those looking for a quiet wander, after fuelling up in the many cafes and alfresco restaurants, will find a few international brands and the odd funky boutique like Kitsch (p.435). The souks never feel too busy and most folk seem to head here for the views of the Burj Dubai and the range of eateries. To round off a day's shopping, try Urbano for waterside Italian dining (once the Burj Lake is filled), The Meat Co. (p.593) for great South African steaks, or The Mezza House for Arabic cuisine with an international flavour. For a pit-stop of a different class try Tonino Lamborghini or treat yourself at New York's gourmet cafe Dean & DeLuca.

Btn Trade Centre & Jumeira
Al Satwa
Map 7 E2

Satwa

Satwa, one of Dubai's original retail areas, has something of a village feel about it. Primarily arranged over four roads, the area is best known for its fabric shops and tailors, but in reality, it's like Aladdin's cave.
Parts of Satwa have been marked for demolition, and many houses and retail spaces have already been demolished. There appears, however, to be a slow down in the process and many of the retail outlets seem to have escaped intact. Shops in the area tend to cater to the lower end of the market and are great fun to look around. Popular reasons to visit Satwa include buying traditional majlis seating and getting your car windows tinted. The pick of the fabric shops is Deepaks, with an amazing range, reasonable prices and helpful staff.
Shop around, because whatever you are looking for there's bound to be more than one outlet selling it and prices vary. If you want to brighten up your house or garden, there are a number of shops on 'Plant Street' with good indoor and outdoor plants. This is also the street for upholstery and paint, with Dulux, Jotun and National Paints' outlets and several upholstery shops. Animal lovers are probably better off giving the pet shops a wide berth – conditions are awful, despite regulations, and the animals are often in a sorry state.
Al Diyafah Street is a great place for an evening stroll. There's an eclectic mix of shops and fastfood outlets but, for some reason, there is a fairly high shop turnover so don't count on finding the same outlets twice. Al Mallah, the popular Lebanese restaurant,

recognisable by its green umbrellas and neon lighting, is highly recommended for delicious and authentic local food (the best falafel in Dubai). Along Al Diyafah Street you'll also find an off-road motorbike gear shop and a shop hiring formal evening wear, both men's and women's.

Satwa is renowned for its fastfood outlets and reasonably priced restaurants. Ravi's is an institution in Dubai, serving good Pakistani food at incredible prices; Mini Chinese has been going for years and serves great Chinese food, and if you're looking for healthy food, the Organic Foods and Café, opposite Rydges Plaza, has rapidly established itself as one of the city's best speciality outlets. Rydges Plaza Hotel has a number of popular, licensed bars and restaurants.

Satwa is also home to some great salons, where you can get various treatments at low prices. They might not be as smooth as the upper-end salons, but they are great for a quick treatment. Try Pretty Lady (04 398 5255) or Honeymoon (04 398 3799).

**Btn Trade Centre
& Jebel Ali**
Trade Centre 1
Map 7 F3

Sheikh Zayed Road

More than just the highway connecting Abu Dhabi and Dubai, Sheikh Zayed Road, between the Trade Centre and Jebel Ali, is rapidly developing into the city's largest shopping district. The area is a mixture of industrial and retail units which house some of the city's larger independent stores.

Beginning at the Trade Centre end, this portion of the highway is flanked by some of Dubai's tallest buildings. While they are interesting to look at in themselves, it is worth checking out what is happening at ground level. On the left side are Emirates Towers (home to Boulevard at Emirates Towers – see p.501), a number of sports shops and an Axiom Telecom repair centre; while on the right are the Holiday Centre, Lifco supermarket, and a number of cafes and fastfood outlets.

The left-hand side of the stretch between Junction One (Defence Roundabout) and Junction Two (Safa Park) is home to Emaar's new Downtown district and the Burj Dubai (p472). This area should become one of the key shopping districts especially since it is near the massive Dubai Mall (p.489). On the right-hand side are Safestway supermarket, the Mazaya Centre and a number of used-car dealers.

After Junction Two, the right-hand side of the road is residential while on the left-hand side there are a number of retail outlets and car dealerships. Behind the Pepsi factory is Safita, which sells well-priced wooden Indian furniture. For those looking to make improvements to their homes, ACE and Speedex (both p.448) will have the equipment to do the job. The area between Junctions Three and Four has some real gems waiting to be discovered. Innovative Kidz sells furniture, puzzles and toys for children – it's not cheap but everything is built to last. Just Kidding (p.456) has all the latest baby equipment, furniture and fashion from Europe as well as maternity wear. The Courtyard, near the Spinneys warehouse, is home to a collection of interesting shops and galleries; there's even a coffee shop. This is also the area to head for if you have green fingers or enjoy the alfresco lifestyle; Dubai Garden Centre has everything for the garden pretty much covered. The Gold & Diamond Park, right by junction four, has almost as much to offer as the Gold Souk, but you can browse in air-conditioned comfort.

Those feeling the heat should head to Mall of the Emirates (p.494) where you can indulge in a spot of shopping and skiing. There is little else other than high rise-buildings but there are a few shops around the Greens, including a branch of Organic Foods & Café (p.506). Dubai Marina is where you'll find the weekend Marina Market (www.marinamarket.ae) during the cooler months, and The Walk, a new outdoor shopping area beneath the Jumeirah Beach Residence. Marina Mall is under construction too. It's then not far to Ibn Battuta Shopping Mall. After that you'll be hard pressed to part with your cash until you reach Abu Dhabi; be sure to have a copy of the *Abu Dhabi Residents' Guide* on hand when you arrive.

Mirdif
Map 15 C2

Uptown Mirdif

Bearing in mind that three years ago the only shopping that could be done in Mirdif itself was getting milk and bread from Ali Akhbar's cornershop, it's hardly surprising that Uptown Mirdif has fast become the centre of eating, socialising, and of course shopping for many a Mirdif dweller. With a Spinneys, an A&E, a money exchange, a bank (Lloyds), a pharmacy and a florist, it is well-equipped to meet all your daily needs. But it is also home to the kind of shops full of things you just have to have, whether you need them or not. Bedu, La Senza, Pumpkin Patch, Adams, Mothercare, Kamiseta, and Beyond the Beach will keep you and the kids dressed to the nines, and you can kit yourself out with the best shoes, bags and accessories from Brantano, Aldo, Claire's Accessories and Nine West. There's also a huge Paris Gallery which is stocked full of beautiful things, and it seems that it has yet to pull the crowds, so it's great if you like to do your shopping in solitude. Cosmetics chain Faces also has a branch here, and it's almost impossible to walk in and walk out without having spent a fortune on must-have goodies by Benefit or Urban Decay.

If you've just moved into a new villa in the area, or you want to spruce up your old one, 2XL has some lovely furniture and their kitchen section is full of great gadgets that you just know will turn you into an award-winning chef. Howard's Storage World and Stokes are also great for kitchen stuff.

The cafe culture that was once the sole pleasure of Jumeira Janes has finally arrived in Mirdif – Uptown has a Caribou Coffee where you can play boardgames, browse in the bookshop, or read magazines, a Central Perk (yes, it's just like the one in the TV show and features an excellent healthy food menu), a Starbucks, a Mugg & Bean and a Le Pain Quotidien. In terms of other food outlets, there's Gourmet Burger Kitchen (shame on you if you haven't tried their blue cheese burger yet), Da Shi Dai for innovative Chinese cooking with not a shake of MSG in sight, and Pane Caldo for interesting Italian yummies in a cool setting. And then of course there's the foodcourt – probably one of the best in Dubai, with Mcdonalds, Burger King, KFC and Hardees all fighting for your chicken nugget cravings, as well as Pizza Hut, Da Gamas, ARZ Lebanon, Zaatar W Zeit, Automatic, a Chinese takeaway, an Indian takeaway, and a branch of Fresh, where you can get the ultimate paradox: healthy fast food.

After all that eating, you can burn it all off in the Mirdif branch of Fitness First, or you can take a course of slimming therapy with nutritionists VLCC (they can also sort out your skin and hair).

Even if you don't have a penny to spend, Uptown has a sense of community that attracts plenty of families in the late afternoon, so expect to see the neighbourhood kids riding their bikes, scooting round on scooters, or impressing their mates in their new heelies.

Al Faheidi Street

Karama Market

Jumeirah Beach Residence
Dubai Marina
Map 5 A2

The Walk, Jumeirah Beach Residence

04 435 1111 | www.dubairetail.ae

The Walk offers a fresh approach to shopping in Dubai, moving away from glitzy mall interiors to street-side shops and cafes. The fully pedestrianised area that stretches 1.7 kilometres along the beachfront should provide a solution to an age old gripe – there aren't enough places to walk in Dubai. Situated within the Jumeirah Beach Residence (JBR) residential complex, retail outlets and restaurants service the JBR community as well as providing a meeting point for beach strollers, wandering window shoppers and guests from the nearby hotels. Outlets are located either on the ground level or on the plaza level of the six clusters of towers called Murjan, Sadaf, Bahar, Rimal, Amwaj and Shams. The plaza level of each cluster can be accessed from large staircases, or by the lifts at ground level and in the carpark.

Fashionistas will be happy with the massive branch of Boutique 1 that has recently opened which sells men and women's fashion and accessories, furniture and cosmetics. Saks Fifth Avenue, which only carries men's fashion and accessories, has also opened here. Other outlets include a broad range of restaurants, fashion, jewellery and home furnishings stores and a supermarket. There does seem to be an overabundance of jewellery shops and elaborate homeware stores, but there are also a few options that are convenient for nearby residents such as Al Maya Supermarket. Many of the outlets are yet to open and new stores keep appearing – you will need to become a regular if you want to keep up-to-date with new store openings. In the afternoons, people congregate in the cafes along The Walk (particularly popular are Le Pain Quotidien and Starbucks) and there are plenty of restaurants to dine in come the evening. Parking is available along the beach near Bahar, or you can also park in designated areas of the Murjan carpark. Many of the shops open at 10:00 and close at 22:00.

Department Stores

Department stores are now a standard feature of Dubai's larger malls. This is an expanding sector – with famous department store Bloomingdales set to enter the fray. The scope of department stores is representative of Dubai's shopping scene, from the epitome of chic, Saks Fifth Avenue, in BurJuman and at The Walk, to Avenue, which caters for the more budget conscious.

Opp BurJuman
Bur Dubai
Map 8 F4

Avenue

04 397 9983

This independent store, on the other side of Trade Centre Road from BurJuman, is good for those on a budget. Selling men's, women's and children's clothes and shoes, lingerie, luggage, some items for the home, sunglasses and watches, Avenue has the basics covered. This may not become one of your regular stops, but it is worth a look.

Various

Debenhams

See p.513 | www.debenhams.com

A stalwart of the British high street, Debenhams has three stores in Dubai: Deira City Centre, Ibn Battuta and Mall of the Emirates. The stores all stock perfumes and cosmetics, clothing for men, women and children, and homeware. There are a number of brands with concessions within the stores, including Evans for plus-size clothing, Liz Claiborne, Oasis and Dorothy Perkins. There's a good selection of homeware, including Jamie Oliver's cookware. Debenhams is renowned for selling good quality items at reasonable prices. This ethos continues in the Designers at Debenhams ranges by John Rocha, Jasper Conran and Pearce Fionda – a great way for the budget conscious to own designer chic. Fans of Italian fashion will be happy to know that the Ibn Battuta and Mall of the Emirates branches stock Motivi.

Saks Fifth Avenue

Ibn Battuta
Shopping Mall
Jebel Ali
Map 4 D2

Fitz & Simons
04 368 5598
www.fitzandsimons.com
This bright and spacious store sells quality European brands, with a guarantee that each collection will be limited, keeping it exclusive. Fashion for ladies and men is on offer here as well as lingerie, kitchenware, and home decor accessories. The store's brands include Gerry Weber, Oui and Olsen, Camel Active and Windsor Man, Luisa Cerano, Sem Per Lei and Windsor Woman. Casa Marrakesh has interesting home accessories.

Mall of the Emirates
Al Barsha
Map 6 A3

Harvey Nichols
04 409 8888 | *www.harveynichols.com*
Dubai simply couldn't call itself a luxury destination without its own Harvey Nichols. Since the largest Harvey Nick's, as it is affectionately called, outside the UK opened in February 2006, Dubai's label junkies have taken to their local branch like designer-coat-wearing ducks to Gulf waters. It contains a large selection of high-rolling fashion (for men, women and kids), food, beauty and homeware brands. Here's where you'll find Jimmy Choo, Diane Von Furstenburg, Juicy Couture, Hermes and Sergio Rossi, rubbing shoulders with other swish brands. On the top floor is the popular restaurant Almaz by Momo (04 409 8877), which is a great place for a mid-shop pit stop.

Various

Jashanmal ▶ p.431
See p.515 | *www.jashanmal.ae*
One of Dubai's original department stores, with branches in Al Ghurair City, Mall of the Emirates and Wafi City. Jashanmal is the importer for several brands including Burberry, Clarks shoes and Mexx. With books, cameras, fashion, gifts, houseware, household and kitchen appliances, and luggage, the stores are worth a look. For other branches, see the directory on p.515.

Various

Marks & Spencer
See p.517 | *www.marksandspencerme.com*
One of the best known brands from the UK, M&S, as it is also known, sells clothes and shoes for men, women and children, along with a small, but ever popular, selection of food. This store is famous for its underwear, worn by a good portion of women in Britain, and has a reputation for quality. The Dubai stores carry selected ranges which include Per Una – high street chic – as well as more classic lines. The cafe is a great place to sit and relax; the food is good and the portions generous, particularly the children's menu. The Dubai Festival Centre is the largest M&S outside the UK. As well as offering fashion and homeware, the DFC shop also has an espresso bar, a restaurant and a bakery. Other branches can be found in Wafi (p.499) and the Al Futtaim Centre (next to Reef Mall, p.505) in Deira. For contact details see the directory on p.517.

Various

Next
See p.518 | *www.next.co.uk*
Next is a popular British chain that has 11 stores in the UAE. On sale are a range of high-quality clothes for men, women and children, as well as shoes, underwear,

accessories and homeware. It's a great place to go clothes shopping for all occasions. The kids' clothing section is great for children of all ages. For branches, see the directory on p.518.

Saks Fifth Avenue

Bur Juman
Bur Dubai
Map 8 F4

See p.520 | www.saksfifthavenue.com

Anchoring the extension to BurJuman is the second-largest Saks Fifth Avenue outside the US. The name is synonymous with style, elegance, and the good life, encapsulated here in two floors of paradise for the label conscious. Even in Dubai's cultured retail sector, this store has an added air of sophistication. The first level is all about pampering, with cosmetics and perfumes, designer sunglasses and the Saks Nail Studio; it also houses the D&G Boutique, the children's department (Petit Bateau, and designer clothes for little ones), the men's store, and the chocolate bar and cafe. The second level is dedicated to shopping – you'll find the designer boutiques here including Christian Dior, Jean Paul Gaultier and Prada. This is where to head for accessories, jewellery – including Tiffany and Fabergé – and an exclusive bridal salon which stocks Vera Wang gowns. For those looking for something a little different, head for Agent Provocateur (lingerie with a twist) – ignore the discreet exterior, the lingerie on display inside is anything but. The Fifth Avenue Club is a personalised shopping service, where members can browse the store with the guidance of a consultant. A smaller branch has opened at The Walk, Jumeirah Beach Residence which only caters for men (04 435 5681).

Stadium

Various

See p.521 | www.rshlimited.com

With branches in several of the larger malls, Stadium (previously known as Studio R) sells a selection of brands that cater to those with an active lifestyle. With a range of well-known clothing labels (Quiksilver, Rockport and Union Bay), and sports brands (Adidas, New Balance, Reebok and Speedo), Stadium has created its own niche. It also stocks Teva, which make a range of practical sandals. The store has sales throughout the year when prices are heavily discounted. Other branches are listed in the directory on p.521.

Hypermarkets

Carrefour

Various

See p.511 | www.carrefouruae.com

There are branches of this French hypermarket chain throughout the city, all of which are enormous. As well as aisles piled high with all sorts of foodstuffs, each branch carries fairly comprehensive ranges of electronics, household goods, luggage, mobile phones, and white goods. Camping gear and car accessories are also on sale here, in addition to clothes and shoes for men, women and children, garden furniture, hardware, music, DVDs and videos, and stationery. The range of products is enormous – the store offers a good range of French products (it's the best place to get crusty, freshly baked French sticks) and it has a small health food section. Carrefour is renowned for its competitive pricing and special offers. For other branches, see the directory on p.511.

Géant ▶ p.479

Ibn Battuta
Shopping Mall
Jebel Ali
Map 4 D2

04 368 5858 | www.geant-dubai.com

Géant is at one end of Ibn Battuta Shopping Mall. It has a good range of products that are similar to that of Carrefour. A massive number of items are stocked here and there's a good electronics section. In addition to food, you can pick up clothes, household goods, outdoor goods and stationery, as well as a selection of DVDs. The store is a great bonus for anyone living in Jebel Ali and Dubai Marina.

Festival Power Centre
Festival City
Map 13 D2

HyperPanda
04 232 5566 | *www.panda.com.sa*
At an enormous 175,000 sq ft, HyperPanda is owned by the Saudi-based Savola Group and located at Festival Power Centre. It may not have the selection of produce found in other hypermarkets, but it did have the first hypermarket healthcare department in the UAE (there is now one at the Mall of the Emirates store) and a strong electronics department. The parking is good and allows easy access to other outlets.

Various

Lulu Hypermarket
See p.516 | *www.luluhypermarket.com*
The Lulu Hypermarkets, in Al Barsha, Karama and Qusais, are great for those on a budget. These stores, especially the smaller branch, which is in Karama, have an Aladdin's cave quality about them. There's not much that they don't sell, from luggage and electronics to food and clothing. Each store stocks a good range of home appliances and have an area set aside with lots of colourful saris. For other branches, see the directory on p.516.

Independent Shops
This is a blossoming sector of the retail market. These independent stores and boutiques are opening, predominantly in converted villas, all over the city; Jumeira Beach Road is seen as the most popular address, although many more can be found in the more traditional shopping areas.

The Village Mall
Jumeira
Map 7 F1

Ayesha Depala Boutique
04 344 5378 | *www.ayeshadepala.com*
Ayesha studied at London's prestigious, Central St Martins College of Art & Design, and is now based in Dubai. Her boutique holds all of her own creations. Pick up glamorous couture frocks, shimmering fabrics and feminine accessories. As well as items fit for the catwalk, the store offers a bridal service, ready-to-wear pieces and vintage dresses and accessories.

Various

Boutique 1
See p.511
A regular feature on any fashion hunters' shopping trips, Boutique 1 offers a broad mix of high-end fashion by international designers. As well as a store in Emirates Towers and The Outlet in Dubai Outlet Mall, a new colossal branch of the store has recently opened at The Walk, Jumeirah Beach Residence, which has a cafe, gallery, spa, and a cosmetics, and furniture section. Boutique 1 offers a range of high-end (high-priced) garments for men and women. See the directory on p.508 for details of other branches.

Al Mankhool Rd
Bur Dubai
Map 8 E2

Fabindia
04 398 9633 | *www.fabindia.com*
Beginning as a company that exported Indian handcrafted soft furnishings and clothes, Fabindia is now one of India's leading retail chains. The products are made in villages, creating a livelihood for many and supporting rural communities. The branch in Dubai is one of only two outside India. The clothing range for men and women combine Indian and western styles – from capri pants to kurtas, the cotton-based designs are guaranteed to add a splash of colour to any wardrobe. You can also pick up soft furnishings and a beautiful range of rugs and hard-wearing dhurries to liven up dreary white floor tiles. The rolls of fabric, sold by the metre, are a great alternative to standard upholstery. The prices are very reasonable, especially as everything is handcrafted; shirts from around Dhs.40, large table cloths from Dhs.120 and quilts from Dhs.300.

Welcome to 🦅 Géant

أهلاً وسهلاً بكم في جيـان

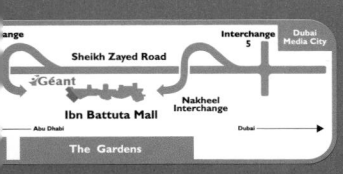

Garden Home Center
Oud Metha
Map 10 F2

Five Green

04 336 4100 | *www.fivegreen.com*

This is the best independent clothes shop in Dubai. Styled as an urban living boutique, it's the place to go for cutting-edge fashion and art. Street chic jeans, printed tees, shirts and trainers from labels including Paul Frank, GSUS and Boxfresh mix with creations from Dubai-based designers. The soundtrack to your retail experience is provided by top US labels like BBE, Compost and Soul Jazz. Five Green's inspiring space plays host to a number of exhibitions throughout the year from both home-grown and international talent. It may be expensive, but it is a unique spot in Dubai.

The Village Mall
Jumeira
Map 7 F1

Luxecouture

04 344 7933 | *www.shopluxecouture.com*

Luxecouture is yet another sparkly gem in this Beach Road retail heaven. Buyers from this fresh, stylish store regularly head to New York on buying trips to ensure Dubai's discerning shoppers stay on trend. Get a slice of red carpet glamour with dresses from Carmen Marc Valvo, bags by Goldenbleu, and individually designed jewellery pieces. Two more branches are due to open at The Walk, Jumeirah Beach Residence and Souk Madinat Jumeirah.

999 Al Wasl Rd
Umm Suqeim
Map 6 C2

O'de Rose

04 348 7990 | *www.o-derose.com*

Surely one of the most enchanting additions to the city's shopping scene, O'de Rose arrived this year with a feminine flounce. The gorgeous boutique, in a spacious villa, is lovingly devoted to clothing, art and furniture, with embellished kaftans, clutch bags and homeware at every turn. Minimal it is not. You'll find a diverse range of pieces here from all over the world; a trip to O'de Rose is as good as a mini-break – with better souvenirs.

Various

Ounass

See p.518

Its name means 'people' in Arabic, and Ounass appeals to sophisticated party people of Dubai with lines from Diane Von Furstenburg, Marchesa and Alberta Ferretti. As well fashionable creations and designer treats, shoppers can also pick up original pieces by Arabic artists. The walls in this modern store are lined with artwork, so you can pick up something beautiful for your home as well as your wardrobe.

Mazaya Centre
Al Wasl
Map 7 D3

Reem's Closet

04 343 9553 | *www.reemscloset.com*

This is what Dubai fashionistas have been waiting for. This boutique, tucked away in the decidedly non-flashy Mazaya Centre off Sheikh Zayed Road, is a second-hand haven, packed to the rafters with quality designer clobber at astonishing prices. Bring in the 'it bag' you've tired of, pick up some vintage pieces or discover a nearly new item from just last season, buyers and sellers alike will struggle to spend just five minutes inside this unique store. The mix of items accepted here includes designer pieces and items off the high street; what is essential is that each item offers the same quirky high-fashion that gets items flying off the racks. What you won't find are Karama's finest genuine fakes – quality control is uncompromised so you can buy with confidence.

Various

S*uce

See p.520 | *www.shopatsauce.com*

You can't pick up your basic white T-shirt or simple plastic flip-flops at this shop. The items at S*uce are anything but basic, but you can peruse the funky accessories, pick

Fish Market

up quirky high-fashion and individual pieces at this eclectic boutique. Fashionistas head here for token buys that are less likely to be seen on anyone else. You'll find clothes by international designers such as Chloè, Sass & Bide, and the odd piece of arty interior design. The store also offers a loyalty card, and personal shopper for those needing advice on the seasons key buys.

Various ◄

Sana Fashion
See p.520

Sana Fashion is renowned for branded clothing at bargain basement prices, it is worth sorting through the racks to find its hidden gems. There are regular deliveries, especially in the run up to Eid and Diwali, but if you see something you like, buy it – chances are it'll be gone before you go back. The store is spread between two shops, and over two floors. The huge ladies department has racks of everything from lingerie to linen trousers – prices start at around Dhs.20 and go up to around Dhs.120. The children's department, girls on the ground floor and boys upstairs, caters for newborns up to teens. The men's section has a good range of casual and formal wear and prices are super reasonable with shirts starting at around Dhs.30 and trousers starting from around Dhs.50.

Many of Sana's products are seconds and overruns from factories in the UAE and India, so stock depends on what's available; if you persevere this is a great value store, particularly for children's clothing.

Markets/Souks
Other options **Bur Dubai** p.133, **Bargaining** p.420, **Deira** p.134

Souks are traditional trading areas, some more formally demarcated than others. In keeping with tradition, bargaining is expected and cash is the best bargaining tool. Parking around the Gold Souk, Spice Souk and Textile Souk is limited so it is better to go to these areas by taxi or, if you are visiting all three, park on one side of the Creek and take an abra (water taxi) to the other side – great value at Dhs.1 each way. Markets are an increasingly popular concept in the city; they are usually based around crafts and are often seasonal. The Marina Market is the first to take place on a regular basis. The Dubai Flea Market (www.dubai-fleamarket.com) in Safa Park, held on the first Saturday of every month, is also a good spot to pick up secondhand items. Craft fairs are held throughout the year, mainly in the Mazaya Centre and Times Square Centre.

Nr Shindagha Tunnel ◄
Deira
Map 9 C1

Fish Market

The Fish Market in Deira is hard to ignore if you're in the area, especially during the hotter months – maybe not the best place to visit if you don't like the smell of fish. To get the freshest fish for your evening meal, and to experience the vibrancy of this working market, head down early in the morning or late at night as the catch is coming in. There is an incredible range of seafood on display. The emphasis is on wholesale but the traders are usually more than happy to sell to individuals and, for those of a squeamish disposition, the fish can be cleaned and gutted for you.

As well as the market there's a seafood restaurant and a museum dedicated to the history of the fishing village Dubai used to be.

Dubai – Hatta Rd
Nr Used Car Market
Nad Al Sheba
Map 2 C3

Fruit & Vegetable Market

There are a number of small fruit and vegetable markets around the city, like the one in Karama. The main market is now located off Emirates Road in Al Awir. It is a wholesale market but, like the Fish Market, the traders are usually happy to sell by the kilo rather than the box. There is a huge variety of produce on offer and it is usually fresher than in the supermarkets. Be sure to haggle, you can often tell if you have paid more than the trader thinks the goods are worth if they give you freebies. The location is not overly convenient for most people but it is worth a look if you are out that way. It is well signposted as you drive along the Dubai-Hatta Road. Mornings are the best time to visit.

Baniyas Rd
Deira
Map 9 B1

Gold Souk

This is Dubai's best-known souk and a must-do for every tourist. There is a huge number of shops and many of them have branches in other parts of town. Whether you are looking to make a special purchase or just want to window shop, a wander through the Gold Souk is a great experience. The meandering lanes are lined with shops selling gold, silver, pearls and precious stones. These can be bought as they are or in a variety of settings. This is definitely a place to try your bargaining skills but don't expect a massive discount. Gold is sold by weight according to the daily international price and so prices will be much the same as in the shops in malls – the price of the workmanship is where you will have more bargaining power. Most of the outlets operate split shifts, so try not to visit between 13:00 and 16:00 as many outlets will be closed. The Gold Souk is always busy, and it is shaded, but there is added sparkle when you visit in the evenings, as the lights reflect on the gold and gems.

If you are more interested in buying than enjoying the souk experience, the Gold and Diamond Park, by junction four on Sheikh Zayed Road, has a far calmer atmosphere. There are branches of many of the outlets which are also found in the Gold Souk but here they are quieter and the whole area is air conditioned. There's also a cafe if you'd like a break while you decide which pieces you can't live without.

Marina Walk
Dubai Marina
Map 5 B2

Marina Market

050 244 5795 | *www.marinamarket.ae*

This venture is the brainchild of Roslynne Bourguignon, a long-term expat who couldn't believe Dubai didn't have any outdoor markets similar to those common in the UK. Originally a Friday affair, the Marina Market now operates on a Friday and Saturday, from October to April at the picturesque Marina Walk. It features around 50 stalls selling a range of items, predominantly crafts, clothing and home accessories. The setting makes this an enjoyable place to head at the weekend, as you can wander around the stalls before adjourning to one of the cafes or restaurants. Things get started at 11:00 and wind up around 19:00. The organisers recently expanded the concept and added outdoor weekend markets at two further locations – Uptown Mirdif and Burj Dubai Old Town. See the website for more details.

Nr Corniche
Sharjah
Map 2 C2

Sharjah Central Souk

www.sharjah-welcome.com

Situated beside the lagoon, the Sharjah Central Market, or Blue Souk, is an unmissable sight. Consisting of two long, low buildings running parallel to each other and connected by footbridges, the souk is intricately decorated and imaginatively built according to Islamic design.

Each building is covered and air-conditioned to protect shoppers from the hot sun, with one side selling a range of gifts, knick-knacks, furniture, carved wood and souvenirs, and the other given over almost entirely to jewellery stores. There are over

600 individual shops, and the upper floors have a traditional souk feel with narrow passages and staircases. The souk also has shops selling a fabulous range of carpets from all over the world. For visitors and residents, a half-hour trip into the Blue Souk can easily turn into half a day.

Nr Bank St
Sharjah
Map 2 C2

Souk Al Arsah

www.sharjah-welcome.com

This is probably the oldest souk in Sharjah. It has been renovated in recent years, so although the shops are still in a style reminiscent of old market places, the souk is covered (to provide shelter from the sun) and air-conditioned. Around 100 tiny shops line a labyrinth of peaceful alleyways, selling goods such as silver jewellery, perfumes, spices, coffee pots and wedding chests. There is a small coffee shop where you can get Arabic coffee and sweets. Shop closing times do vary, with some closing by 20:30 and others remaining open until 22:00.

Nr Gold Souk
Deira
Map 9 B2

Spice Souk

With its narrow streets and exotic aromas, a wander through the Spice Souk is a great way to get a feel for the way the city used to be – it makes the modern city that Dubai has become seem a long way away. The number of spice shops is diminishing, due in part to hypermarkets like Carrefour having areas dedicated to spices and supermarkets selling a wider range. Most of the stalls sell the same range and the vendors are usually happy to advise on the types of spices and their uses. This is unlikely to be where you do your shopping on a regular basis, but the experience of buying from the Spice Souk is more memorable than picking a packet off a shelf. You may even be able to pick up some saffron at a bargain price. The shops operate split shifts but, whether you visit in the morning or the evening, this is a bustling area of the city.

Nr Abra Station
Bur Dubai
Map 9 A2

Textile Souk

The Textile Souk, in Bur Dubai, is stocked with every fabric and colour imaginable. The textiles are imported from all over the world, with many of the more elaborate coming from the subcontinent and the Far East. There are silks and satins in an amazing array of colours and patterns, velvets and intricately embroidered fabrics; basic cotton can sometimes be harder to find but you can always try Satwa (p.150). Prices are negotiable and there are often sales, particularly around the major holidays, Eid and Diwali, and the shopping festivals. It is worth having a look in a few shops before parting with your

Spice Souk

cash as they may have different stock and at better prices. The mornings tend to be a more relaxed time to browse. Meena Bazaar is the shop that most taxi drivers head for if you ask for the Textile Souk; it has an amazing selection of fabrics from raw silk to metallic net and plain cotton but, be prepared to haggle. Rivoli has a range of textiles for men on the ground floor and for women upstairs. The assistants are keen to offer the 'best discount' but it is always worth haggling to see if the price will drop further. Rivoli also runs a tailoring shop in Karama where you will get a discount on pieces made with fabric from the shop. There are a number of tailoring shops around the Textile Souk, including a branch of Dream Girl (p.513) which is renowned for its service. Before choosing a tailor, check out their finished pieces as some are better at certain styles of clothing.

Shopping Malls

Shopping malls are not just places to shop; a definite mall culture exists here and they are places to meet, eat and mingle. Many malls provide entertainment and people of all ages can spend hours in them. Recent changes to the law have resulted in a smoking ban in all of Dubai's malls (and some of the bars attached to them) which has been welcomed across the city.

With so much choice out there, malls make sure they can offer something unique to shoppers to draw the crowds. In terms of architecture, Ibn Battuta is remarkable – six distinct architectural styles reflecting the sights of Egypt, China, India, Persia, Tunisia and Andalusia. Mall of the Emirates has got their unique selling point covered – a community theatre and a huge ski slope has made this one of the busier malls. Deira City Centre is the old kid on the block and yet is still consistently popular because of its excellent range of outlets, huge cinema multiplex and wide range of food outlets. Wafi City and BurJuman have cornered the market for exclusive boutiques and designer labels. Despite the choice of shopping centres on offer, there are more in the pipeline particularly in Dubai Marina, with Dubai Marina Mall nearing completion and The Walk, Jumeirah Beach Residence's outlets growing by the month. The latter is currently growing into a popular meeting spot for residents and curious window shoppers as its high-street appeal offers a change to mall hopping. Special events are held during Dubai Shopping Festival, Dubai Summer Surprises and Ramadan, with entertainment for children and some special offers in the shops. These are peak shopping times and an evening in the larger malls at this time is not for the faint-hearted. Most of the malls have plenty of parking – often stretched to the limits at the weekends; all have taxi ranks and many are handy for bus routes.

Shopping Malls		
Al Ain Centre	Bur Dubai	04 351 6914
Al Bustan Centre	Al Qusais	04 263 0000
Al Ghazal Complex & Shopping Mall	Al Wasl	04 345 3053
Al Ghurair City	Deira	04 222 5222
Al Hana Centre	Al Satwa	04 398 2229
Al Khaleej Centre	Bur Dubai	04 355 5550
Al Manal Centre	Deira	04 227 7701
Al Mulla Plaza	Al Qusais	04 298 8999
Al Rais Center	Bur Dubai	04 352 7755
Beach Centre	Jumeira	04 344 9045
Bin Sougat Centre	Al Rashidiya	04 286 3000
Boulevard at Emirates Towers	Trade Centre 2	04 319 8999
BurJuman ▶ p.487	Bur Dubai	04 352 0222
Century Mall	Al Mamzar	04 296 6188
Century Plaza	Jumeira	04 349 8062
Deira City Centre ▶ p.x	Deira	04 295 1010
The Dubai Mall	Downtown Burj Dubai	04 362 7500
Dubai Outlet Mall	Nad Al Sheba	04 367 9600
Galleria Shopping Mall	Deira	04 209 6000
Gold & Diamond Park	Al Quoz	04 347 7788
Hamarain Centre	Deira	04 262 1110
Holiday Centre Mall	Trade Centre 1	04 331 7755
Ibn Battuta Shopping Mall	Jebel Ali	04 362 1900
Jumeira Plaza	Jumeira	04 349 7111
Jumeirah Centre	Jumeira	04 349 9702
Jumeirah Town Centre	Jumeira	04 344 0111
Karama Centre	Karama	04 337 4499
Lamcy Plaza	Oud Metha	04 335 9999
Magrudy's Shopping Mall	Jumeira	04 344 4193
Mall of the Emirates ▶ p.xv	Al Barsha	04 409 9000
Mazaya Centre	Al Wasl	04 343 8333
Mercato	Jumeira	04 344 4161
Palm Strip	Jumeira	04 346 1462
Reef Mall	Deira	04 224 2240
Saga World	Umm Suqeim	04 395 9071
Souk Madinat Jumeirah	Umm Suqeim	04 366 8888
Spinneys	Umm Suqeim	04 394 1657
Times Square	Al Quoz	04 341 8020
Twin Towers	Deira	04 221 8833
The Village Mall	Jumeira	04 344 4444
Wafi Mall	Umm Hurair	04 324 4555

Small but indispensable…

Perfectly proportioned to fit in your pocket, this marvellous mini guidebook makes sure you don't just get the holiday you paid for but rather the one that you dreamed of.

Dubai Mini Visitors' Guide
Maximising your holiday, minimising your hand luggage

Main Shopping Malls

BurJuman ▶ p.487

04 352 0222 | www.burjuman.com

BurJuman is a firm favourite in Dubai, and has always been renowned for its blend of designer and high-street brands, attracting many a well-heeled shopper. The newer area, anchored by Saks Fifth Avenue, has attracted even more big names. Other outlets exclusive to the mall include Valentino and Hermes. The original area houses many famous brands, as well as some interesting smaller shops. There is a Fitness First gym with a pool on site too.

BurJuman has been active in organising activities for the Dubai Shopping Festival and Dubai Summer Surprises and is also heavily involved with the Safe & Sound breast cancer awareness programme; during October (breast cancer awareness month) it gets decked out in pink ribbon and organises a walkathon to raise money for this worthy cause.

Insider Tip
For gift-wrapping, head to the Customer Service Counter on level two.

The outlets within the mall are a mixture of clothing, electronics, home decor and sports goods. There are a few shops on the ground level that are often overlooked, including ACE (hardware & DIY store) and a pharmacy. There's also branches of Yo! Sushi, and Dôme on the same level.

Within the mall, there are enough designer shops to keep even the most dedicated fashionista happy, including Fendi, Just Cavalli and Christian Dior. For everyday fashion, Massimo Dutti and Zara lead the way. If you are into music or DVDs, the independent music shops sell a good range and they often have sales. There is a branch of Virgin Megastore for those with more mainstream tastes – you can also pick up tickets here for local events. Home decor stores include THE One and Zara Home.

There are two foodcourts and numerous cafes, well arranged for people watching, including the popular Pavillion Gardens on the third floor and Paul on the ground floor, where you can dine outside during the cooler months. There is a taxi rank outside the mall and plenty of underground parking but it does get pretty full at peak times.

BurJuman

HERE I COME
BurJuman

burjuman.com 04-352 0222

Head straight for the finest in shopping indulgence. Over 300 elite names reside in absolute luxury to truly spoil you for choice. Along with chic dining and stylish pampering, enjoy the serene elegance of it all.

BURJUMAN

Deira City Centre

04 295 1010 | *www.deiracitycentre.com*

A stalwart of Dubai's mall scene, this is a great place to go to get a feel for the real cosmopolitan nature of the city. Deira City Centre is popular with residents and visitors alike, particularly at the weekends. The three floors offer a huge and diverse range of shops where you can find anything from a postcard to a Persian carpet. There's an 11 screen cinema, a children's entertainment centre, a jewellery court, a textiles court and an area dedicated to local furniture, gifts and souvenirs. Deira City Centre is anchored by a huge Carrefour hypermarket, a Debenhams department store, and a large Magrudy's bookshop (beyond the cinema). Most of the high street brands are represented, including the more recent additions, Gap, Next, Pull and Bear, Club Monaco, New Look and River Island in the new extension,

Insider Tip

* The Starbucks on the top floor of Debenhams is a haven from the crowds and noise of the mall.
* There is a left luggage area on the second floor, near the men's prayer room at the Debenhams end, which is great if you don't want to be weighed down by bags while you browse.

and a number of designer boutiques which are mainly on the top floor. The City Gate section (on the same level as car parks P2 and P3) is dominated by electronics retailers, although there is also a pharmacy and information desk. The mall has two foodcourts: one on the first floor, around the children's entertainment area, serving mainly fast food, and one on the second floor, featuring several good sit-down restaurants. Bin Hendi Avenue features some excellent restaurants, including the Noodle House and Japengo. There are a number of coffee houses, including Paul and three Starbucks, so you're never far from a caffeine kick. The facilities for mothers and babies are tucked away on the top floor, near the entrance to car park P4, and in the centre of the ground floor. There are four car parks but its popularity means that, at weekends, spaces are scarce. P4 is usually the quietest of the carparks. The taxi ranks are in the City Gate section.

Deira City Centre

The Dubai Mall

04 362 7500 | *www.thedubaimall.com*

Anyone who thinks Dubai has enough shopping malls to cater to its relentless shoppers will be stunned by this colossus. In true Dubai style, Dubai Mall has already accumulated its fair share of records since its opening. With nearly 600 stores trading on its opening day, The Dubai Mall is said to be the world's largest-ever single-day mall opening in retail history – it will eventually house over 1,200 stores, including 160 eateries. The huge shopping and entertainment complex houses an extensive range of stores, as well as an Olympic size ice skating rink, a catwalk for fashion shows, an enormous aquarium, a 22-screen cinema, an indoor theme park called SEGA Republic, a luxury hotel, and a children's 'edutainment' centre.

Situated next to Burj Dubai, the large mall is in itself a landmark. Its enormous exterior has been designed to look like an aircraft hanger and inside you'll find cathedral-like atriums for exhibitions and performances.

The shopping highlights are manifold, but unique to Dubai Mall are the regional flagship stores for New York department store Bloomingdales, French department store Galleries LaFayette, the world-renowned toy shop Hamleys and UK's luxury food retailer Waitrose. You'll find all of the haute couture designer brands along Fashion Avenue and there is a sprawling gold souk with over 220 gold and jewellery outlets. When you need to check your funds, you'll also find branches of the major banks on the ground floor. For refreshment there is a vast array of fastfood outlets, cafes and restaurants. It may be a good idea to check the store listings on the website before you tackle this mall as many of the outlets are yet to open. For a complete contrast, cross the wooden bridge over the Burj Lake and you'll find yourself in Souk Al Bahar (p.505). The tranquility of its dimly lit passageways offer a more relaxing stop after the onslaught of the mall.

Dubai Mall

Dubai Marina Mall

www.dubaimarina.ae

This mall is scheduled to open by the end of 2008, but construction is still in full swing. Located in Dubai Marina's thriving community, and within walking distance of the huge residential complex Jumeirah Beach Residence, the mall's 160 outlets will service the area's growing community with a broad range of outlets and entertainment. Aside from its retail offerings, the mall will also include the Gourmet Tower which will offer world-class cuisine with waterfront views and an eight-screen cinema.

Festival Centre

04 232 5444 | *www.festivalcentre.com*

Dubai Festival Centre is a large complex that features around 600 retail outlets (including 25 flagship stores) and 100 restaurants including 40 alfresco dining options. The need for retail therapy can be sated by the broad range of fashion, electronics and homeware outlets spread over 2.9 square feet of retail space. Festival Power Centre is the first dedicated household shopping complex in the world. It houses some of the biggest names in homeware, such as The White Company and The Red Carpet, as well as electronic stores, including Al Falak Electronics. In addition, it is home to HyperPanda (p.478), the largest IKEA in the UAE, and boasts a large Plug-Ins as well as the largest ACE store outside of North America, so it is an ideal stop when you've moved into a new home, or just looking to spruce up your existing abode. You'll also find a branch of the Dubai London Clinic here, a pharmacy, banks and dry cleaners.

The Power Centre is linked to Festival Waterfront Centre by a 25,000 square foot marketplace selling gold from all over the world. The Festival Waterfront Centre has dramatic water features, performance spaces and many international brands. Most of this bright and airy mall might feel a little less crowded than others in Dubai, but that may be because everyone is in IKEA. The mall also features a flagship Toys R Us store, Brit favourite Marks & Spencer and designers like Marc by Marc Jacobs.

It's not just shopping though; Fitness First gym, Grand Cinema and a ten-lane bowling alley are on site so this is a place where you can happily spend an entire day, before dining (choose from family favourites at Romano's Macaroni Grill, Steam Sum Dim Sum and everything in between) then relaxing in one of the licensed bars.

Festival Power Centre

Places To Shop

Art Friday at Dubai Marina

Fabric Souk

Fruit & vegetable market

Textile Souk

Al Diyafah Street

Ibn Battuta Shopping Mall

04 362 1900 | *www.ibnbattutamall.com*

Ibn Battuta is huge, but you can pick up maps from the information kiosks that will help you find your way around. Named after 14th century explorer Ibn Battuta who spent 29 years travelling throughout the Middle East and Asia, the mall is divided into six zones, each based on a country that he visited (China, India, Egypt, Tunisia, Andalusia and Persia). Each zone has distinctive architecture representative of that country. Guided tours that illuminate the mall's more unusual features, such as the full-size replica of a Chinese junk and Al Jazari's Elephant Clock, are available.

There are a good range of outlets with mostly international brands represented. There are several anchor stores, including Debenhams and Géant hypermarket. Shops are loosely grouped: China Court is dedicated to entertainment, with several restaurants and a 21 screen cinema – this has the UAE's first IMAX screen, which is often used to show regular films as well as blockbusters.

The fashion conscious should head for India Court for the likes of Fitz & Simons, H&M, River Island and Topshop. Persia Court is styled as the lifestyle area, anchored by Debenhams – when you get to Starbucks, look up to see the ceiling detail. Egypt Court is for sporty types; Tunisia Court is anchored by Géant, so this is where to head for the weekly shop, and finally, Andalusia Court covers life's necessities such as banking, dry cleaning, key cutting, and DVD and video rental.

The foodcourts are at either end of the mall. There are several restaurants in China Court (including the excellent Finz) and a group of fastfood outlets in Tunisia Court.

There are several restaurants and coffee shops dotted around in other areas of the mall. To reward the kids for trailing round after you, there's a Fun City in Tunisia Court. ATMs can be found in most of the courts so refuelling your wallet shouldn't take too much effort.

It is an enjoyable mall to wander around but because of its size it can be a long way back if there's something you've missed, and the taxi points are by the entrance to each court so if you really can't face walking back to the car with all that shopping, you could always get a cab. There are 10 car parks, so parking shouldn't be a problem; the numerical order of the car parks is a little eccentric, so remember which zone you came in through.

Persia Court

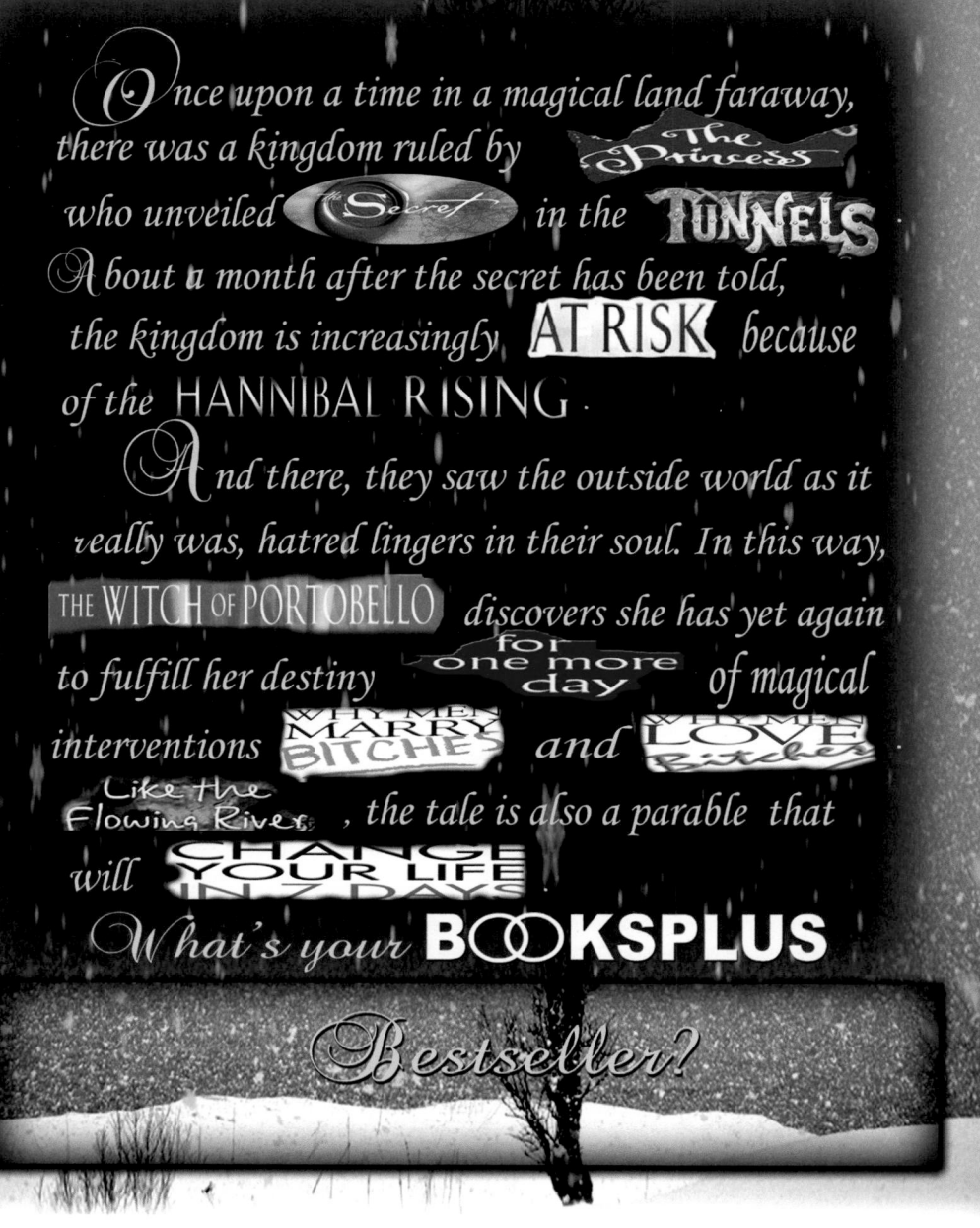

Once upon a time in a magical land faraway, there was a kingdom ruled by *The Princess* who unveiled *The Secret* in the *TUNNELS*. About a month after the secret has been told, the kingdom is increasingly *AT RISK* because of the HANNIBAL RISING.

And there, they saw the outside world as it really was, hatred lingers in their soul. In this way, THE WITCH OF PORTOBELLO discovers she has yet again to fulfill her destiny *for one more day* of magical interventions *WHY MEN MARRY BITCHES* and *WHY MEN LOVE Bitches*. Like the Flowing River, the tale is also a parable that will CHANGE YOUR LIFE IN 7 DAYS. What's your B**OKSPLUS**

Bestseller?

Mall of the Emirates
04 409 9000
www.malloftheemirates.com

This is Dubai's most renowned mall. It's a big one, so you will need to grab a map as you go in, and if you see a shop that you want to go into don't put it off until later – it will be too far to go back. Mall of the Emirates is more than a mall, it's a lifestyle destination. It houses a indoor ski slope (Ski Dubai, see p.386), the Kempinski Mall of the Emirates Hotel (p.42) and the Dubai Community Theatre & Arts Centre (p.632).

There are over 400 outlets selling everything from forks to high fashion here. The mall is anchored by Carrefour hypermarket, Dubai's largest branch of Debenhams, Harvey Nichols (London's trendiest department store),

Via Rodeo

and Centrepoint, which is home to Baby Shop, Home Centre, Lifestyle, Shoemart and Splash. There is also a Cinestar cinema where you can treat yourself to a film in Gold Class which involves enormous leather armchairs and waiter service throughout. Nearby, the huge Magic Planet includes a bowling alley, a myriad of games and rides, just in case the kids haven't used up enough energy walking round the mall.

Label devotees should head for Via Rodeo to get their fix of designer labels such as Burberry, Dolce & Gabanna, Salvatore Ferragamo, Tod's and Versace. If you're more into street chic, there are two H&M stores and Fat Face as well as Phat Farm, the New York clothing line that will add a bit of bling to your wardrobe, and Forever 21. With skiing now possible in Dubai, a whole new area of fashion has opened up; check out Rampage and Staff for the coolest slope styles.

You're spoiled for choice when it comes to homeware, with Home Centre, Marina Gulf, BoConcept, B&B Italia, THE One, and Zara Home, to name but a few.

For entertainment, head to Virgin which has a bookshop and many international magazines alongside CDs, DVDs, mobile phones and computers. You'll also find a range of Apple products and accessories.

Of course, you'll need to keep your energy up so it's fortunate there is a wide range of dining options from the Swiss chalet feel of Après (p.556) to the three separate foodcourts.

Whatever you're looking for, you'll want to come back again and again, not least because you're unlikely to make it round in one day. Should you fancy a marathon shopping trip, Mall of the Emirates is open from Sunday to Wednesday 10:00 to 22:00, Thursday to Saturday: 10:00 to midnight and Carrefour opens 09:00 to midnight every day. And don't forget there's always mall walking here to keep you fit.

BIGGEST CHOICE OF BOOKS

MAGIC CHOICE OF BOOKS

EXCITING CHOICE OF BOOKS

Phenomenal choice of books

UNBEATABLE CHOICE OF BOOKS   IN FULL COLOUR

SPECIAL CHOICE of books

THRILLING CHOICE OF BOOKS

Encyclopedic choice of Books

BALANCED CHOICE OF BOOKS

FANTASTIC CHOICE OF BOOKS

BORDERS®

YOUR PLACE FOR KNOWLEDGE AND ENTERTAINMENT

Mercato

04 344 4161 | *www.mercatoshoppingmall.com*

Mercato is the largest mall in Jumeira, with over 90 shops, restaurants, a cinema and cafes. As you drive along the Jumeira Beach Road, the Renaissance-style architecture really makes the mall stand out, and once inside, the huge glass roof provides a lot of natural light enhancing its Mediterranean feel.

The mall is anchored by Spinneys which has a dry cleaners, photo lab and music shop; a large Virgin Megastore (that has a decent book department) and a new Gap outlet which replaced Home Centre. There are also a few good options for kids such as Early Learning Centre and Armani Junior. You'll also find a good mix of designer boutiques and high-street brands in the mall and shops range from the reasonably priced Pull and Bear, to the more exclusive Hugo Boss. With Topshop and Next on site, Mercato makes many British expats feel at home while Massimo Dutti and Mango have cornered the European market. Shoes and accessories are covered by favorites like ALDO and Nine West, while cosmetics can be picked up at MAC.

The layout is more interesting than many of the malls and it's worth investigating the 'lanes' so you don't miss anything.

There is a foodcourt and a number of cafes and restaurants, including Paul, a French cafe renowned for its patisserie, and Bella Donna, an Italian restaurant where you can dine alfresco. The cinema and large Fun City play area near the food court should keep most of the family occupied. There is a mother and baby room, tucked away near Costa Coffee on the upper floor, in addition to ATMs, a money exchange, and a branch of HSBC (they don't handle money but can offer advice and do the paperwork) and a shoe repair shop.

Mercato

MUSIC
DVDs
BOOKS
GAMES
ELECTRONICS
MULTIMEDIA
BOUTIQUE

Mall of The Emirates • Deira City Centre • Mercato • Burjuman • Abu Dhabi Mall

Souk Madinat Jumeirah

04 366 8888 | *www.madinatjumeirah.com/shopping*

Part of the Madinat Jumeirah complex, which also incorporates the Mina A'Salam and Al Qasr hotels, Souk Madinat Jumeirah really doesn't feel like a mall. It's a recreation of a traditional Middle Eastern marketplace, complete with narrow alleyways and authentic architecture. The blend of outlets is unlike anywhere else in Dubai, with boutique shops, galleries, cafes, restaurants and bars. It is one of Dubai's hotspots, so spend some time wandering through the souk before enjoying an evening out dining, drinking and dancing.

The layout, in keeping with traditional souks, can be a little confusing. There are location maps throughout and the main features are signposted (the signposts are quite subtle – look up). If you're really lost, a member of staff will be able to point you in the right direction.

The souk is best appreciated if you have time to walk around and enjoy the experience. During the cooler months the doors and glass walls are opened to add an alfresco element and there is shisha on offer in the courtyard.

With an emphasis on unique brands, there are a large number of speciality outlets which aren't found anywhere else in Dubai. The souk is home to the greatest concentration of art boutiques in the city including Gallery One (selling photos with a local flavour) and Mirage Glass. The stalls in the outside areas sell souvenirs, some tasteful and some tacky. There are more than 20 waterfront cafes, bars and restaurants to choose from, including some of Dubai's hottest night spots – you'll find The Meat Co (p.593), Trader Vic's (p.586), Jambase (p.613) and BarZar (p.609) here to name a few. There's also the impressive Madinat Theatre (www.madinattheatre.com) which has seen international and regional artists perform everything from ballet to comedy.

Souk Madinat Jumeirah

Wafi Mall

04 324 4555 | www.waficity.com

Wafi is possibly Dubai's most exclusive mall. Part of the larger Wafi City, with its Egyptian theme and designer boutiques, this mall really stands out. The distinctive building has three pyramids forming part of the roof and a large stained glass window. Two of the pyramids are decorated with stained glass, depicting Egyptian scenes – best viewed during daylight.

Wafi has been extended several times since it opened and the latest revamp included the five-star Raffles Dubai hotel, a new underground carpark and 90 new shops, including the largest Topshop in the UAE and popular LA retailer Kitson. The layout makes this one of the more interesting malls to wander around, and it rarely feels busy. There are often exhibitions held throughout and the atrium features a giant tree at Christmas – it even snows. For something a little different, the new underground souk, Khan Murjan, is an impressive addition to Wafi with its magnificent stained glass ceiling (64 metres), long curved arches and over 150 stalls. You'll find a broad mix of items including jewellery, antiques, perfume and souvenirs, but it's particularly good if you wish to spice up your home with traditional arts and crafts. You can pick up fabulous pieces here and there are workshops where artisans can create pieces onsite. When you've worked up an appetite perusing the many stalls, you'll find several places for you to fuel up in.

Wafi seems to become more exclusive with each extension and the store directory now reads like a who's who in design, be it jewellery or couture. Imaginarium, a children's toy shop, has some great traditional toys and a separate kid-sized door. There's a large Marks & Spencer and a branch of Jashanmal to browse in when you're taking time out from the likes of Nicole Farhi or Versace.

There are also a number of cafes and restaurants, including Biella, where you can enjoy your meal in the alfresco dining area. The children's entertainment area, Encounter Zone, is very popular and has age-specific attractions.

If you feel the need for pampering, or an evening out, head across to the Pyramids complex where there are some excellent bars, restaurants, a club and a renowned spa.

Khan Murjan

Other Shopping Malls

Al Ghazal Complex & Shopping Mall

Cnr Al Diyafah St
& Al Wasl Rd
Al Wasl
Map 8 A2

04 345 3053

The Al Ghazal Centre is a new low-key shopping hub just finding its place on the Dubai shopping map. It's situated in a large office building and can often feel deserted, but the ground floor is used occasionally at weekends for craft fairs featuring stalls with jewellery, photography and home accessories, which get the crowds through the doors. Although the mix of stores won't rival the big players in town, what is on offer is enough smaller stores to make it a worthwhile pit stop for those little essentials and treats. Head to Alina Baby's Dream and Bambini for kid's clothes, Damas for jewellery, or pick up costumes at Mr Ben's Closet. You can also visit Giordano for high-street clothes or get your toes pampered at NStyle.
Other outlets include: Barocco, Brazil One, Century 2000, Century Home, Claire's, Cutest Fashion, Daphne, Dazzle, FAE, Gulf Optiks, Le Carmen, Little Luxuries, Marble Slab, Redstar, Revolution, S.O.S, and Watch Me.

Al Ghurair City

Al Riqqa Rd
Deira
Map 9 D4

04 222 5222 | *www.alghuraircity.com*

Al Ghurair City is Dubai's oldest mall, the one that set the ball rolling. If you are in Deira, chances are that you will head to Deira City Centre but, for a change of scene, Al Ghurair is worth a look. It was refurbished in 2003, and now houses an eight-screen cinema, a Spinneys, and a good range of shops. The layout of the two-storey mall has the maze-like quality of a souk. There are a number of international brands, including Bhs, Book Corner and Mothercare, along with smaller boutiques. When you need a break, there are coffee shops and food outlets, and a Fun Corner to keep children occupied.
Other outlets include: Aldo, Bhs, Bossini, Esprit, FCUK, French Connection, Guess, La Senza, Mexx, Nine West, Paris Gallery, Plug-ins, Red Earth, Starbucks, Sun & Sand Sports, Swatch and Triumph.

Beach Centre

Jumeira Rd
Nr Dubai Zoo
Jumeira
Map 7 E1

04 344 9045

Located on Jumeira Beach Road, this unassuming mall is home to a number of interesting independent shops selling everything from books to furniture and jewellery. Notably, the mall includes two branches of White Star Bookshop, one stocks craft materials and the other specialises in teachers' supplies. It also houses Charisma, an independent plus-size womens' clothes shop, and the Music Room, at the back on the second floor has the largest supply of sheet music in Dubai and a selection of instruments. With Kuts 4 Kids, a children's hairdressers, and an opticians, pharmacy and Cyber Café, this is a good community mall.
Other outlets include: Bossini, Crystal Gallery, Dubai Desert Extreme, Kids to Teens, Party Zone, Sports House, Studio Al Aroosa, Yateem Opticians.

Bin Sougat Centre

Airport Rd
Rashidiya
Map 13 F4

04 286 3000

Located on Airport Road in Rashidiya, this mall is really convenient for Mirdif dwellers. The long, two-storey building, with impressive glass skylights, is packed with outlets selling everything from beanbags to paint brushes. Spinneys is the anchor store with all the essentials, including a pork section and readymade meals, an in-house photo processors, a dry cleaner, DVD rental and two ATMs. For creative types, there is a branch of Emirates Trading, an art supplies store with a great range of professional standard equipment, as well as Brush & Bisque-It, where you can paint your own designs onto ceramic items which are then fired for you. Dubai Library Distributors is excellent for stationery, especially school stuff. The Balloon Lady, on the first floor, is a whole shop dedicated to party supplies, from balloons to fancy dress outfits. If you are looking for furniture, head to the basement for Orient Curios Furniture where they keep larger pieces including wardrobes and cabinets. Or for something a little more unusual, RelaxSit sells beanbag chairs for adults and children. There is a small branch of Jumbo Electronics, concentrating mainly on mobile phones but they are able to order other items for you. Cocomino is the pick of the children's clothes shops – if you have to dress up your little one for a wedding this is a good place to start as its lines are fairly formal. If you are looking for pampering, try Nugoosh (follow the henna footprints), a ladies salon which offers henna, facials, body waxing and hairdressing. Secrets Boutique is the city's first lingerie shop dedicated to larger sizes. The range is limited but it's still a welcome addition to the retail scene.

Most culinary tastes are catered to, with branches of Costa Coffee, Pizza Express, Dôme, Automatic restaurant and Gazebo Indian Restaurant. There is ample parking both in front and behind the mall, although it is hard to find a space at certain times on Fridays when the mosque next door is busy.

Other outlets include: Al Ansari Money Exchange, Al Jaber Optical, Baskin Robbins, Damas Jewellers, Dubai Leisure Holidays, House of Translation, KFT (fabric and carpets), Lily's flower shop, London Café, Kuts 4 Kids, Network Zone, San Marco and Union National Bank.

Boulevard at Emirates Towers

Sheikh Zayed Rd
Trade Centre 2
Map 7 F3

04 319 8999 | *www.jumeirahemiratestowers.com*

The Boulevard houses some of Dubai's most exclusive boutiques, popular restaurants and bars. The area links the Emirates Towers Hotel and Emirates Towers Offices, and is accessible from both. Boutiques include Cartier, Gucci, Yves Saint Laurent, and Boutique 1 (which stocks Stella McCartney, Alexander McQueen, Prada and Jimmy Choo shoes – so exclusive it has its own entrance from the carpark). If you're into more than shopping, there's also a health club and 1847, a men-only spa.

Should you need to recharge, there are cafes (some with wireless internet access), licensed restaurants (Scarlett's and The Noodle House), and the ever-popular early evening hangout, The Agency.

This is one of the first malls in Dubai to introduce paid parking, at a costly Dhs.10 per hour, but if you have to think before paying for parking, this is not the mall for you.

Other outlets include: Ajmal, Areej, Azza Fahmy, Bottega Veneta, Bvlgari, Damas, D. Porthault, Emporio Armani, Ermenegildo Zegna, Europcar, Flower@the towers, Lanvin, N-Bar, Paper Room, Rodeo Drive, Sergio Rossi.

Dragon Mart

Nr International City
Dubai-Hatta Rd
Al Awir
Map 2 C3

04 368 7205 | *www.chinamexmart.com*

Central to what will become Dubai's China Town, Dragon Mart is part of International City; a residential and commercial development beside the Hatta Road. It is reportedly the largest concentration of Chinese traders outside China. The centre is open from 10:00 to 23:00, but many of the shops don't open till 17:00, so the mornings are quiet. The huge number of outlets sell a mix of anything made in China. The mall is divided into zones by commodity, but these demarcations have been blurred. From building materials to toys, household items to quad bikes, everything is available, and cheaper than elsewhere in the city. The quality isn't great, but if you're looking for something cheap and for the short haul, you can't go wrong.

At over one kilometre in length, it takes about three hours to have a good look round. There is no foodcourt as such, although there is a restaurant, a cafe, and several little foodstands at regular intervals – helpful for when those hunger pangs strike as you make the great trek around this vast retail space.

Dubai–Al Ain Rd
Route 66
Map 2 C3

Dubai Outlet Mall

04 367 9600 | *www.dubaioutletmall.com*

In a city where the emphasis in on excess, it is refreshing (not only for the wallet) to find a mall dedicated to saving money. Dubai's first 'outlet' concept mall may be quite a way out of town, but bargain-hunters will find it's worth the drive. Only 20 minutes down the Al Ain road, it is quickly becoming the place for hard-up fashionistas and frugal families to stop off and spend up. Big discounts on major retailers and labels are available with price tags seemingly missing a zero; think T-shirts for under Dhs.30 and Karama-esque prices for Marc Jacobs handbags. High street shops including Massimo Dutti and Dune sit alongside designer names such as Tommy Hilfiger and DKNY, with city style and sports casual equally catered for. Pick up trainers from Adidas, Nike and Puma, reduced eyewear from Al Jaber or Magrabi, jewellery from Damas, cosmetics from Paris Gallery and a range of electronics and homewares from more than 10 different outlets.

In addition to more shops than you can shake a credit card at, several pharmacies, and even a barber, you'll also find a few spots to refuel including Starbucks, Stone Fire Pizza Kitchen and Automatic as well as the usual foodcourt suspects. And to keep the little ones engaged there's Chuck E Cheese's – a US institution serving up ample portions of food and entertainment.

Other outlets include: Adams, Aldo, Converse, Diesel, Espirit, Fashion For Less, G-Star, Giordano, Guess, Kenneth Cole, Levi's, Mango, Monsoon, Nine West, Phat Farm, Pierre Cardin, Planet Nutrition, Price Less, Pumpkin Patch, Replay, Samsonite, Sports Direct Outlet, Stadium and Timberland.

Emirates Towers Boulevard

Dubai Outlet Mall

Jumeira Rd ◀
Nr Jumeira Mosque
Jumeira
Map 7 F1

Jumeira Plaza

04 349 7111 | www.dubaishoppingmalls.com

The 'pink mall' on Jumeira Beach Road has an interesting range of independent shops that are definitely worth a browse. It is dominated on the ground floor by a children's play area and the Dôme Cafe; the play area is really only suitable for younger children. Downstairs, there's an eclectic mix of outlets selling everything from furniture to greeting cards. House of Prose is a popular second-hand book shop, there are a number of home decor, trinket and card shops, and a small branch of the Dubai Police – great for paying fines without having to queue. Upstairs, Aquarius sells silk paintings of local scenes; and Melangé has an interesting selection of clothing, jewellery and soft furnishings from India. Those not wishing to browse the shops can sit and watch the fish in the water feature on the ground floor.

This is a busy area and parking spaces can be hard to find; there is parking under the mall but the entrance is quite tight, especially for larger cars or four wheel drives.

Other outlets include: Art Stop, Balloon Lady, Blue White, Falaknaz Habitat, Girls' Talk Beauty Centre, Kashmir Craft, KKids, Susan Walpole, Safeplay and The Warehouse.

Jumeira Rd ◀
Nr Jumeira Mosque
Jumeira
Map 7 F1

Jumeirah Centre

04 349 9702 | www.dubaishoppingmalls.com

This mall seems to pack a lot in to a small space. There are branches of several established chains including Benetton, Mothercare, Stadium and Sun & Sand; and a number of independent shops. The stationery shop, Kazim, on the ground floor, has a good range of stationery and art supplies. Upstairs, independent shops abound and include Elves & Fairies (a crafts and hobbies shop), Panache (for accessories made only from natural materials), Sunny Days (a boutique selling a range of gift items), and the Wedding Shop that does exactly what it says on the door.

There are also some interesting clothes shops, and a gallery here. Harvest Home has shops on both levels selling an interesting range of gifts and kitchenalia. The branch of the Coffee Bean & Tea Leaf has a terrace where you can enjoy an alfresco coffee.

Other outlets include: Blue Cactus, Caviar Classic, Cut Above, Harvest Home, HN Camera Repair, Kazim Gulf Traders, Lunnettes, Mothercare, Nutrition Centre, Photo Magic, Rivoli, Sunny Days, The Barber Shop, The Wedding Shop and Thomas Cook.

Jumeira Rd ◀
Jumeira
Map 7 D1

Jumeirah Town Centre

04 344 0111 | www.towncentrejumeirah.com

Town Centre is a community mall on Jumeira Beach Road, next to Mercato. With an interesting blend of outlets, this is the place to head to for a little time out. There are several cafes, including Café Céramique where you can customise a piece of pottery while you dine. For those after a bit of pampering, there's Feet First (reflexology and massage for men and women), Kaya Beauty Centre, Nail Station and SOS Salon. There are also clothing shops including Heat Waves (for beachwear) and DKNY, a large branch of Paris Gallery, an Empost counter and an Etisalat machine.

Other outlets include: Al Jaber Optical, Bang & Olufsen, Bateel, Books Plus, Bayti, Calonge, Damas, Marie Claire, Nine West, Nutrition Zone, Papermoon, Paris Gallery, Simply Healthy and World of Pens.

Nr EPPCO HQ
Oud Metha
Map 10 D2

Lamcy Plaza

04 335 9999 | www.lamcyplaza.com

Home to five floors of open-plan shopping, with a wide range of outlets, Lamcy is consistently popular. As the only mall open at 09:00 seven days a week, it's the place to head for if you need a Friday morning shopping fix. It can be a bit tricky to find your way around at first, with the escalators from the first to second floors hidden away behind a shoe shop, but once you get the hang of it Lamcy is great for shopping in many different stores without having to walk for miles.

Entertainment dominates the ground floor, with a huge foodcourt and Loulou Al Dugong', a play area for children There is also a pharmacy, a money exchange, a florist and a post office counter, as well as a fascinating feng shui shop that is crammed with interesting knick-knacks. Towards the back of the ground floor (behind Paris Gallery), there's a photo developing outlet, a key cutting service and a driving school.

The first floor is for women's fashion and shoes and includes Dorothy Perkins (good value fashion), Guess, Monsoon and Hush Puppy. The second floor is great for mums and kids, with Mothercare, Pumpkin Patch and Adams. Mexx for Less, as the name suggests, sells discounted Mexx clothing for men, women and children, and Peacocks and Mr Price sell reasonably priced fashion. Factory Fashions is well worth a look as it carries Adams and Pumpkin Patch overstocks.

Men and sporty types should head for the third floor where there are several men's clothing and sports shops. This is the destination for bargain hunters too; Daiso is a Japanese store where almost everything costs Dhs.6 – there are some great bargains to be had here but you'll have to sort through quite a bit of tacky stuff first. The top floor is dedicated to the Hypermarket which sells everything from kitchenware and bedding to clothes and groceries.

Parking is limited and Lamcy offer a unique service to combat it; if you have to park further away, look out for a red people carrier with Lamcy written on it, it offers a pick-up and drop-off service to the mall.

Other outlets include: Al Jaber Optical Centre, Adams, Aldo, Athlete's Foot, Books Plus, Bhs, Bossini, City Sports, Dorothy Perkins, Giordano, Golf House, Guess, Hang Ten, Hush Puppies, La Senza, Mothercare, Mexx For Less, Nine West, Peacocks, Pumpkin Patch, Rivoli, Shoe Mart, Swatch and Watch House.

Jumeira Road
Jumeira
Map 7 F1

Magrudy's Shopping Mall

04 344 4193 | www.magrudy.com

The Magrudy's Shopping Mall, on Beach Road between Jumeirah Centre and Spinneys, comprises a collection of shops around a central courtyard. The shaded ground floor packs a lot into a small area. The Magrudy's Gift Shop sells a good selection of cards (this is where to look for seasonal decorations), gifts and stationery. The children's shop has bikes, books, toys and games all under one roof and for more reading material head to the renovated Magrudy's book shop, also home to the shoe and school uniform departments.

There's also a small health food shop and a pharmacy. Eve Michelle is a clothes and accessories shop with a loyal customer base – a great place to find a hat for the races. It's also where you will find clothes by European designers including Fenn Wright Manson, Tuzzi and Frank Usher. The patisserie, Gerard, is a popular place to sit outside and enjoy a coffee – the croissants are legendary. Above the shops are a number of medical practices and a beauty salon.

Green Community
Jebel Ali
Map 2 A4

The Market

04 885 3500 | www.up.ae

Located in the Green Community, The Market has proved to be a welcome addition to the area among residents who previously had quite a trek to get their supplies. Among the stores on offer is Choithram supermarket, ACE (hardware and DIY store), Damas jewellery, Emirates Bank, and Athlete's Foot, as well as an impressive range of other outlets and cafes. Other outlets include: Ace Hardware, Books Plus, Grand Optics, Hour Choice, Jumbo Electronics, Karisma, McDonald's, Mothercare, Gulf Greetings, Oriental Stores and Plug-ins.

Places To Shop

Jumeira Rd ◀
Opp Jumeira Mosque
Jumeira
Map 7 F1

Palm Strip

04 346 1462 | *www.dubaishoppingmalls.com*

Palm Strip is across the road from Jumeira mosque, and is more of an arcade than a mall. Upmarket boutiques dominate; there are also speciality shops for Arabic perfumes (Rusasi), maternity wear (Great Expectations) and chocolate (Jeff de Bruges). There are two beauty salons and a walk-in branch of N-Bar. Zara Home has an outlet selling bright and stylish accessories. Palm Strip is often quiet during the day, getting a little more lively in the evenings with the popular Japengo Café. If the shaded parking at the front is full, there's an underground carpark, with access from the side. Other outlets include: Beyond the Beach, Elite Fashion, Gulf Pharmacy, Hagen-Dazs, Little Me, Mask, My Time Ladies Salon, Oceano and Starbucks.

Salahuddin St ◀
Deira
Map 9 D4

Reef Mall

04 224 2240 | *www.reefmall.com*

This surprisingly large mall is anchored by Home Centre, Lifestyle, Splash and Babyshop. Among many other outlets are branches of Cellucom, i2, and Athlete's Foot. There's a huge Fun City here, a great place where everyone from toddlers to teens can burn off a bit of energy. There's a small foodcourt, several cafes and a supermarket. Other outlets include: Aldo, The Athlete's Foot, Babyshop, Bossini, Cellucom, Charles & Keith, Damas, Digi 4 U, Grand Optics, Giordano, Karisma, McDonald's, Nayomi, Nine West, Oasis Greetings, Splash, The Coffee Bean & Tea Leaf, Dome Café.

Al Wasl Rd ◀
Umm Suqeim
Map 6 F2

Spinneys Centre

04 394 1657 | *www.spinneys-dubai.com*

This small mall, just off Al Wasl Road, centres around a large Spinneys supermarket. There are a small number of other shops including Early Learning Centre and Mothercare, Tavola (for kitchenalia), and Disco 2000, which is one of Dubai's better music and DVD shops. There are branches of both MMI and A&E, along with cafes and a large Fun Corner play area for children. It gets quite busy at weekends and the small carpark is nearly always full. Other outlets include: Arabella Pharmacy, Areej, Arts Palace, Axiom Telecom, Baskin Robbins, Beyond the Beach, Books Plus, Café Havana, Champion Cleaners, Damas, Emirates Bank, Gulf Greetings, Hair Works, The Healing Zone, Marina Gulf Trading, Photo Magic, Starbucks and Uniform Shop.

The Old Town Island ◀
Downtown Burj Dubai
Map 7 D4

Souk Al Bahar

04 362 7011 | *www.theoldtown.ae*

This Arabian-style mall is similar to the souk at Madinat Jumeirah (p.498), but this is a much more intimate affair. Although many of the outlets serve the tourist market, Souk Al Bahar also has shops for the more discerning shopper. Designer style can be found at Roccobarocco and Kitsch Boutique, with Indian designer labels at Samsaara and Manish Malhotra. For exclusive beachwear head to Pain de Sucre, and pick up a pair of famously comfortable flip-flops at Dubai's only Havaianas store. Marina Interiors or Sia sell contemporary home furnishings and interior design, or try Pride of Kashmir, Fortix or Emad Carpets for a more Arabian look. Sadek Music has a wide array of eastern and western instruments. For information on other shopping possibilities in Downtown Burj Dubai see p.472.

Sheikh Zayed Rd ◀
Btn Jct 3 & 4
Al Quoz
Map 6 C3

Times Square

04 341 8020 | *www.timessquarecenter.ae*

This relatively small mall is bright, modern. The large branch of Sharaf DG is the big draw with deals on electronics. You'll also find a large Intersport, several home stores, Toys R Us and even V-Moto should you feel the need to pick up a scooter on a Saturday afternoon. The Chillout ice lounge (not licensed) is a unique spot to have a sub-zero drink while wearing boots and a coat. In addition to the foodcourt, there is also the world's first Lamborghini Café, Caribou Coffee and Extreme Freshies Café where you can eat lunch while watching snowboarding on the screens. There's also a pharmacy, mini supermarket and ATM. Other outlets include: Bayti, InWear, Joe Bloggs, JYSK, Ladybird, Sanrio (Hello Kitty), Sharaf DG, Trek, Toys R Us, Watch Square and Yellow Hat.

Jumeira Rd
Jumeira
Map 7 F1

The Village Mall

04 344 4444 | *www.thevillagedubai.com*

The Village Mall, with its Mediterranean theme, has more of a community feel than many of the malls in Dubai. The niche boutiques are great if you're looking for something a bit different, whether it's clothing or something for the home. With pampering opportunities for both men and women, and Sensasia Urban Spa (p.409), this is one of the more relaxing malls. Peekaboo, the children's play area, is bright and fun for younger children – they also run activities. There are a number of places to eat, including Shakespeare & Co, Thai Time, and the Village Kitchen. Other outlets include: Books Gallery, Boots, Cadorim, Candella Clothing, Edouard Rambaud Designs, Irony Home, Julian Hairdressing for Men, Lollipop, Magrabi Optical, Offshore Legends, OXBOW Sportswear, Peekaboo, S*uce, Sisters Beauty Lounge and Tayyiba Beachwear.

Supermarkets & Hypermarkets

Various

Al Maya Supermarket

See p.509 | *www.almayagroup.com*

Although medium in size, Al Maya supermarket is an anticipated addition to the outlets at The Walk, Jumeirah Beach Residence. A store has recently opened up on the plaza level of the Amwaj cluster of towers and another is due to open in Sadaf. The JBR branch offers all the essentials and there is a good range of fresh vegetables, fish and meat. For more branches see p.508.

Various

Choithram

See p.512 | *www.choithram.com*

With 12 branches, Choithram is technically Dubai's largest supermarket chain. The stores are renowned for stocking items that can't be found elsewhere but, unfortunately, they are also known for being expensive. You'll find a selection of British, American and Asian products, as well as a range of baby food. They also have excellent freezer sections, although you'll pay top dollar for your favourite foods from home.

Various

Lifco

See p.516 | *www.lifco.com*

Although not the largest of the city's supermarkets, Lifco stocks a great range of items in terms of convenience. It is a good place to go for fresh olives. They regularly have items on special, where you can buy two or three items banded together for a discount.

Various

Organic Foods & Café

See p.518 | *www.organicfoodsandcafe.com*

A welcome addition to Dubai's food shopping options, Organic Foods & Café has a product range that's under constant review. All items are organically produced, so prices for fresh items can be expensive, although other items are competitively priced. You can dine in at the Satwa branch until 22:00 and 21:00 and in The Greens, where there are also regular coffee mornings for mums and new arrivals in Dubai. Stores sell bread, vegetables, seafood, coffee, tea and body care products.

Places To Shop

Al Wasl Rd
Al Wasl
Map 7 A2

Park N Shop

04 394 5671 | www.parkshopdubai.com

Although it is small, and just one shop (rather than a chain), Park n Shop is worth a trip simply because it has the best bakery and butchery in the city. The bakery sells a range of wheat-free breads (made with alternatives such as spelt), as well as a range of delicious, delectable and incredibly fresh goodies, including reputedly the best jam doughnuts in Dubai. Famous for its birthday cakes, come Christmas time this is where you'll get your mince pies. The butchery sells a range of marinated cuts ideal for the barbecue, and they also have a Christmas ordering service for your turkey and ham. Prices are competitive and they have products you won't always find elsewhere.

Various

Spinneys

See p.520 | www.spinneys.com

With branches across Dubai, from Mirdif to the Marina, you're never far from this well-known store. Products are competitively priced (although many items are more expensive in Spinneys than they are at one of the larger hypermarkets). They have a great range of South African and Australian, as well as British and American items. They stock a selection of Waitrose products (a supermarket renowned in the UK for its quality), and the freezer section and vegetarian options are both good. Also worth a try are items from the deli counter which are great for picnics, along with the ever popular roasted chickens.

Various

Union Co-op

See p.522

This local chain sells a diverse range of goods. They have some of the best fruit and vegetables, and because they are always busy, the turnover is quick and the produce fresh. There is a bulk-buy section, which can save you money as long as you can eat your way through a box of cucumbers before they go soft. Some branches incorporate 'Hot Breads' bakeries, selling a freshly baked range of pies, cakes, samosas and croissants. The big branch on Al Wasl Road is open 24 hours a day.

Lomography cameras

Shoes in the souk

Accessorize	Deira City Centre (04 295 0725), Mall of the Emirates (04 340 9052), Uptown Mirdif (04 288 8403), Wafi Mall (04 327 9001)
ACE	BurJuman (04 355 0698), Festival Centre (04 206 6700), Green Community (04 885 3208), Shk Zayed Rd (04 338 1416)
Adams	Al Ghurair City (04 223 7004), BurJuman (04 351 0068), Deira City Centre (04 294 5576), Lamcy Plaza (04 337 6002), Mercato (04 349 2272), Uptown Mirdif (04 288 8424)
Adidas	Al Ghazal Complex & Shopping Mall (04 345 3818), Al Ghurair City (04 227 8936), BurJuman (04 359 0995), Deira City Centre (04 295 4151), Dubai Outlet Mall (04 426 4927), Festival Centre (04 232 5690), Ibn Battuta Shopping Mall (04 366 9777), Mall of the Emirates (04 347 7007), Uptown Mirdif (04 288 1280)
African & Eastern (A&E)	Arabian Ranches (04 360 6620), Bur Dubai Spinneys (04 352 4521), Marina Walk (04 368 3981), Maktoum Rd (04 222 2666), Mirdif (04 288 2715), Karama (04 334 8056), Al Wasl, Spinneys (04 394 2676), Spinneys nr Ramada (04 359 0730), Spinneys, Jumeira Beach Rd (04 349 0246)
Aigner	BurJuman (04 351 5133), Deira City Centre (04 295 4149), Mall of the Emirates (04 341 4747)
Ajmal Perfumes	Al Dagaya Nr Kuwaiti Mosque, Deira (04 235 1500), Al Ghurair City (04 222 7991), Bin Sougat Centre (04 285 7717), BurJuman (04 351 5505), Deira City Centre (04 295 3580), Emirates Co-operative, Al Awir (04 264 4381), Emirates Towers Hotel (04 330 0600), Gold Souq (04 226 9939), Hamarain Centre (04 269 0102), Mall of the Emirates (04 341 4151), Murshad Bazaar Shop, Deira (04 226 6274), Satwa Rd (04 344 1010), Union Co-op (04 394 7992), Wafi Mall (04 327 9998)
Al Boom Marine	Jumeirah Rd (04 394 1258), Ras Al Khor nr Coca Cola (04 289 4858)
Al Fahidi Stationery	Al Faheidi St, Bur Dubai (04 353 5861), Al Ras (04 225 5993), Murshid Bazaar, Deira (04 226 5508), Nasr Square (04 222 8641)
Al Fardan Jewellery	Deira City Centre (04 295 3780), InterContinental Dubai Festival Centre (04 222 9687), Mall of the Emirates (04 341 4241)
Al Futtaim Jewellery	BurJuman (04 351 1275), Deira City Centre (04 295 2906), Festival Centre (04 206 6960), Lamcy Plaza (04 334 7004), Mall of the Emirates (04 341 4499)
Al Jaber Gallery	Deira City Centre (04 295 4114), Gold Souk (04 226 2966), Ibn Battuta Shopping Mall (04 366 9795), Mall of the Emirates (04 341 4103), Souk Madinat Jumeirah (04 368 6511)
Al Jaber Optical Centre	Al Ghurair City (04 224 9444), Bin Sougat Centre (04 286 1180), Deira City Centre (04 295 4400), Emaar Town Centre, Emirates Hills (04 360 7466), Ibn Battuta Shopping Mall (04 366 9806), Jumeirah Town Centre (04 342 9933), Lamcy Plaza (04 336 0773), Mall of the Emirates (04 341 1322), Meena Bazaar Fashions (04 355 9393), Mercato (04 349 3938), Shk Zayed Rd (04 331 1955), The Palace – The Old Town (04 420 0588)

Shopping Directory

Al Kamda ◄ Al Wasl (04 343 0808), Deira (04 266 4200)

Al Liali ◄ Al Ghurair City (04 222 8844), Arabian Ranches (050 978 0805),
BurJuman (04 351 1075), Dubai Outlet Mall (04 425 5966), Festival Centre (04 232 6700),
Gold & Diamond Park (04 341 7745), Springs (04 360 6839),
Ibn Battuta Shopping Mall (04 368 5384), Jebel Ali Golf Resort & Spa (04 883 6684),
Jumeirah Centre (04 342 0909), Mall of the Emirates (04 341 4080),
Mazaya Centre (04 321 2711), Mercato (04 344 5055),
Souk Madinat Jumeirah (04 368 6220), Spinneys (04 359 5164),
Spinneys Trade Center Rd (04 359 9200), Uptown Mirdif (04 288 4495)

Al Maya Supermarket ◄ Al Mamzar (04 262 4949), Al Murooj (04 321 5552),
Jumeirah Beach Residence (04 437 0166), Reef Mall (04 222 9898)

ALDO ◄ Al Ghurair City (04 223 8851), Deira City Centre (04 295 7885),
Festival Centre (04 232 6196), Ibn Battuta Shopping Mall (04 368 5243),
Lamcy Plaza (04 334 8486), Mall of the Emirates (04 341 0360), Mercato (04 344 7995),
Uptown Mirdif (04 288 6808)

ALDO Accessories ◄ Al Ghurair City (04 225 7950), Festival Centre (04 232 6162),
Ibn Battuta Shopping Mall (04 368 5426), Mercato (04 344 7628),
Reef MFall (04 234 9017), The Palace – The Old Town (04 420 0353),
Uptown Mirdif (04 288 6830)

Aptec Mobiles ◄ Al Ghurair City (04 227 9925), Arabian Ranches (04 360 8040),
Danat Al Khaleej Bld, Deira (04 271 3331), Lamcy Plaza (04 335 7147)

Arabian Oud ◄ Al Bustan Centre (04 263 6784), Al Ghurair City (04 229 7507),
Al Manal Centre 1 (04 227 3392), Al Manal Centre 2 (04 227 6900),
BurJuman (04 352 9988), Deira City Centre (04 295 6767),
Dubai Concorde Hotel & Residence (04 229 6900), Dubai Outlet Mall (04 426 4904),
Gold Souk (04 225 8334), Hamarain Centre (04 297 6870),
Ibn Battuta Shopping Mall (04 368 5638), Souk Al Bahar (04 420 0120),
Wafi Mall (04 324 4117)

Areej ◄ Emirates Towers Hotel (04 330 3340), Meadows Village (04 360 7770),
Ibn Battuta Shopping Mall (04 366 9985), Mall of the Emirates (04 409 8888),
Mercato (04 344 6894), Spinneys (04 394 6303)

Axiom Telecom ◄ Al Ghurair City (04 224 8808), Bin Sougat Centre (04 285 7552),
BurJuman (04 351 2112), Century Mall (04 296 6547), Deira City Centre (04 295 1888),
Dubai International Financial Centre (DIFC) (04 370 0322),
Dubai Internet City (04 391 8725), Trade Center Rd (04 331 6657),
Emirates Hills (04 360 7848), Festival Centre (04 232 6557), Grand Cineplex (04 324
2777), Hyatt Regency Hotel (04 273 3765), Ibn Battuta Shopping Mall (04 366 9960),
Jebel Ali (04 887 2293), Jumeirah Town Centre (04 342 2996),
Mall of the Emirates (04 340 6746), Mercato (04 342 0083),
Nr Al Manzil Hotel (04 420 3662), Shk Zayed Rd (04 321 0600), Bur Dubai (04 355 1305),
Spinneys, Umm Suqeim (04 394 2272), The Dubai Mall (04 434 1314),
Wafi Mall (04 324 1394)

Babyshop
Abu Hail Center (04 266 1519), Al Ghurair City (04 223 9731), Karama (04 337 8075), Mall of the Emirates (04 341 0604), Reef Mall (04 224 3343), The Dubai Mall (04 339 8878), Trade Centre Rd (04 359 9953)

Bang & Olufsen
BurJuman (04 355 1162), Jumeirah Town Centre (04 342 2344)

Barakat Opticals
Umm Suquem (04-3954006), Dubai Festival City (04-2325650), Jumierah Beach Residence (04-4270565), Dubai Outlet Mall (04-4259816), Jumeira Plaza (04-3499945), Dubai Mall (04-3398181)

Baskin Robbins
Al Ain Centre (04 352 3585), Al Ghurair City (04 222 5910), BurJuman (04 355 5651), Carrefour, Al Shindagha (04 393 2316), Century Mall (04 296 7061), Deira City Centre (04 295 1326), Festival Centre (04 232 5644), Gold Souk (04 225 1804), Hyatt Regency Hotel (04 271 3958), Ibn Battuta Shopping Mall (04 368 5227), Jumeirah Centre (04 349 6176), Lamcy Plaza (04 335 0663), Mall of the Emirates (04 340 2677), Reef Mall (04 223 9825), Sh Zayed Rd (04 332 9104), Spinneys, Umm Suqeim (04 394 3199), Union Co-Op Nr Safa Park (04 394 3121), Wafi Mall (04 324 3224)

Benetton
Deira City Centre (04 295 2450), Factory Outlet (04 335 2761), Jumeirah Centre (04 349 3613), Mall of the Emirates (04 341 4646)

Bershka
Deira City Centre (04 295 8440), Mall of the Emirates (04 341 0224), Mercato (04 344 8645)

Better Life
Al Ittihad Rd, Deira (04 268 0656), Karama (04 337 6804), The Walk, Jumeirah Beach Residence (04 424 3749), Mall of the Emirates (04 341 0716)

Beyond the Beach
Emaar Town Centre (04 360 8877), Green Community (04 885 3244), Grosvenor House (04 399 3241), Le Royal Meridien Beach Resort & Spa (04 399 5481), Mercato (04 349 0105), One & Only Royal Mirage (04 315 2177), Palm Strip (04 345 1650), Sheraton Jumeirah Beach Resort & Towers (04 399 3109), Spinneys (04 394 2977), Uptown Mirdif (04 288 7416)

Bhs
Al Ghurair City (04 227 6969), BurJuman (04 352 5150), Ibn Battuta Shopping Mall (04 368 5404), Lamcy Plaza (04 335 8334), Mall of the Emirates (04 341 1152)

BinHendi Boutique
Burj Al Arab (04 348 1104), Madinat Jumeirah (04 368 6545), Palm Strip (04 346 1933), Wafi Mall (04 324 0329)

BinHendi Jewellery
Burj Al Arab (04 348 1104), BurJuman (04 355 1664), Deira City Centre (04 295 2544), Festival Centre (04 232 9086), Ibn Battuta Shopping Mall (04 368 5404), Jumeirah Beach Hotel (04 348 7030), Mall of the Emirates (04 341 0711)

Bombay
Mall of the Emirates (04 341 1220), Mercato (04 344 5994), Wafi Mall (04 324 5255)

Book World
Karama (04 396 9697), Satwa (04 349 1914)

Books Plus ◄ Arabian Ranches (04 360 6198), Academic City (04 429 1393),
Dubai Marina (04 368 3986), Festival Centre (04 232 5563),
Green Community (04 885 3250), Greens (04 367 4388),
Ibn Battuta Shopping Mall (04 368 5375), Jumeirah Town Centre (04 344 2008),
Lamcy Plaza (04 334 9514), Reef Mall (04 222 7547), Spinneys,
Umm Suqeim (04 394 0278), Spring Community Centre (04 360 5703),
Uptown Mirdif (04 288 6735)

Boots ◄ Al Diyafa St, Al Satwa (04 398 9913), Al Wasl Hospital (04 324 0114),
Burj Residence (04 420 0339), Deira City Centre (04 294 3990),
Dubai International Financial Centre (DIFC) (04 370 0112),
Ibn Battuta Shopping Mall (04 368 5936), Mall of the Emirates (04 340 6880),
Nr Dubai Festival Centre (04 332 7884), Opp Safa Park (04 394 6339),
The Village (04 349 9112)

Borders ◄ Deira City Centre (04 294 3344),
Dubai International Financial Centre (DIFC) (04 425 0371),
Mall of the Emirates (04 341 5758)

Bossini ◄ Al Ghurair City (04 221 5917), Al Manal Centre (04 222 1167),
Beach Centre (04 349 0749), BurJuman (04 351 6917), Cosmos Lane,
Meena Bazaar (04 352 4817), Ibn Battuta Shopping Mall (04 368 5534),
Lamcy Plaza (04 335 9999), Reef Mall (04 224 7555)

Boutique 1 ◄ Emirates Towers (04 330 4555), Jumeirah Beach Residence (04 425 7888)

Brantano ◄ Deira City Centre (04 295 0437), Mall of the Emirates (04 341 3394),
Uptown Mirdif (04 288 7386)

Breitling Watches ◄ Deira City Centre (04 295 4109), Dubai Duty Free (04 206 6444),
Festival Centre (04 232 8106),
Le Meridien Mina Seyahi Beach Resort & Marina (04 399 3090),
Mall of the Emirates (04 341 1165), Ritz-Carlton, Dubai (04 399 4942),
Sheraton Dubai Creek Hotel & Towers (04 228 4739),
The Westin Dubai Mina Seyahi Beach Resort & Marina (04 399 7441),
Wafi Mall (04 324 3530)

Brendon ◄ Dubai Festival Centre (04 232 66 36), Mall of the Emirates (04 341 3373),
The Dubai Mall (04 339 85 32)

Burberry ◄ BurJuman (04 351 3515), Deira City Centre (04 295 0347),
Mall of the Emirates (04 340 5559), The Dubai Mall (04 339 8357)

Calvin Klein ◄ Deira City Centre (04 295 0194), Festival Centre (04 232 6406),
Mall of the Emirates (04 341 0810), The Dubai Mall (04 434 1461)

Carlton Cards ◄ Deira City Centre (04 294 8707), Lamcy Plaza (04 336 6879),
Mall of the Emirates (04 340 6789)

Carrefour ◄ Al Shindagha (04 393 9395), Century Mall (04 203 5699),
Deira City Centre (04 295 1600), Mall of the Emirates (04 409 4899)

Cartier
BurJuman (04 355 3533), Emirates Towers Hotel (04 330 0034),
Atlantis The Palm (04 330 0034)

Cellucom
Al Diyafah Rd, Al Satwa (04 345 1445), BurJuman (04 359 8796),
Deira City Centre (04 295 5818), Festival Centre (04 232 9870),
Green Community (04 885 3497), Greens (04 885 3497),
Ibn Battuta Shopping Mall (04 368 5151), Mall of the Emirates (04 341 0503),
Reef Mall (04 234 9290), The Dubai Mall (04 339 8577)

Chanel
BurJuman (04 355 7388), Wafi Mall (04 324 0464)

Choithram
Al Garhoud (04 282 5494), Al Rais, Bur Dubai (04 352 4012), Al Wasl Rd (04 394 3852),
Deira Tower (04 223 2488), Emirates Lakes (04 380 1010),
Green Community (04 885 2299), Holiday Centre Mall (04 331 1377),
Hyatt Regency Hotel (04 209 6455), Jebel Ali (04 884 6242),
Nr Karama fish market (04 337 1021), Jumeirah Beach Rd (04 344 2424),
Bur Dubai (04 352 0435), Springs (04 360 6626), The Greens (04 366 3160),
Umm Suqeim (04 348 1864)

Claire's
Al Ghazal Complex & Shopping Mall (04 346 2990), Al Ghurair City (04 221 5542),
Deira City Centre (04 295 7277), Emaar Town Center, Emirates Hills (04 360 7814),
Festival Centre (04 232 5854), Ibn Battuta Shopping Mall (04 368 5941),
Lamcy Plaza (04 334 0721), Mall of the Emirates (04 340 7575), Mercato (04 344 9520),
Uptown Mirdif (04 288 5274), Wafi Mall (04 324 2830)

Clarks
Al Ghurair City (04 227 7780), Deira City Centre (04 294 8266),
Festival Centre (04 232 6090), Mall of the Emirates (04 340 3449),
Wafi Mall (04 324 4800)

Club Monaco
Deira City Centre (04 295 5832), Wafi Mall (04 327 9225),
Emirates Towers Hotel (04 330 1020), Mall of the Emirates (04 409 8897),
The Dubai Mall (04 339 8670)

Coach
Deira City Centre (04 294 0011), Ibn Battuta Shopping Mall (04 368 5900),
Mall of the Emirates (04 340 7575)

Coast
BurJuman (04 352 5773), Festival Centre (050 304 3698),
Mall of the Emirates (04 341 4442), Mercato (04 344 9321)

CompuMe
Al Bustan Centre (04 263 0285), Al Ghazal Complex & Shopping Mall (04 346 2442),
Al Ghurair City (04 228 0003), Bin Sougat Centre (04 286 2188),
BurJuman (04 352 5566), Deira City Centre (04 295 3848), Festival Centre (04 213 6213),
Gold & Diamond Park (04 347 9663), Green Community (04 885 2117),

Damas Jewellery
Hamarain Centre (04 268 8167), Holiday Centre Mall (04 332 2272),
Ibn Battuta Shopping Mall (04 366 9944), Jumeirah Town Centre (04 342 0460),
Spinneys, Umm Suqueim (04 394 0638), The Dubai Mall (04 339 8846),
Uptown Mirdif (04 288 6253)

Danier
The Dubai Mall (04 434 0820), Festival Centre (04 206 6966)

Dar Al Tasmim Uniforms
Al Rashidiya (04 285 9624), Spinneys, Umm Suqeim (04 394 1477)

De Beers
Dubai International Financial Center DIFC (04 370 0023),
Mall of the Emirates (04 341 2121), Wafi Mall (04 327 9222)

Debenhams
Deira City Centre (04 294 0011), Ibn Battuta Shopping Mall (04 368 5884),
Mall of the Emirates (04 340 7575)

Diesel
BurJuman (04 351 6181), Deira City Centre (04 295 0792),
Dubai Outlet Mall (04 425 5806), Festival Centre (04 232 6442),
Mall of the Emirates (04 341 1395), Mercato (04 349 9985)

DKNY
BurJuman (04 351 3788), Deira City Centre (04 295 2953),
Festival Centre (04 232 6123), Mall of the Emirates (04 341 4343)

Domino
Al Ghurair City (04 228 9058), BurJuman (04 352 3340),
Mercato (04 344 9407), Wafi Mall (04 324 5812)

Dorothy Perkins
Ibn Battuta Shopping Mall (04 368 5900), Lamcy Plaza (04 334 0740),
Mall of the Emirates (04 340 7575)

Dream Girl
Karama (04 337 7287), Al Satwa (04 349 5445), Meena Bazaar Fashions (04 352 1841)

Dubai Library Distributors
Bin Sougat Centre (04 286 2400), Nad Al Rashida Bldg, Al Rashidiya (04 285 9756),
Naif Rd (04 222 4005), Nasr Lootha Old Bldg, Al Qusais (04 261 5192),
Satwa Rd (04 331 6635), Al Muteena St (04 262 5552),
Salahudhin Rd, Al Yasmeen Bldg (04 297 3661), Shk Zayed Rd (04 339 4966)

Dubai Opticals
Al Khaleej Centre (04 356 4767), BurJuman (04 351 0051),
Deira City Centre (04 295 4303), Dubai Outlet Mall (04 426 4944),
Festival Centre (04 232 5692), Ibn Battuta Shopping Mall (04 368 5540),
The Walk, Jumeirah Beach Residence (04 435 5790), Mall of the Emirates (04 341 4090),
Palm Strip (04 346 1931), The Dubai Mall (04 434 1282)

Early Learning Centre
Al Ghurair City (04 228 1873), Al Manzil Hotel (04 360 8150), BurJuman (04 359 7709),
Deira City Centre (04 295 1548), Mall of the Emirates (04 341 4177),
Mercato (04 344 8463), Souk Madinat Jumeirah (04 368 6519),
Spinneys Uptown Mirdiff (04 394 1204), The Dubai Mall (04 339 8199), Uptown Mirdif
(04 288 6792), Wafi Mall (04 324 2730)

Ecco
Al Ghurair City (04 221 3340), Deira City Centre (04 295 2797),
Festival Centre (04 232 5809), Mall of the Emirates (04 341 3838),
Mercato (04 344 3374), Reef Mall (04 224 2252)

Elle
Deira City Centre (04 295 1551), Ibn Battuta Shopping Mall (04 366 9950),
Reef Mall (04 222 2323)

Emirates Trading Est.
Bin Sougat Centre (04 284 4594), Nr Al Nasr Cinema (04 337 5050),
Nr Jumeirah Town Centre (04 344 1052)

EROS Electricals ◄ Karama (04 335 0141), Al Khubaisi, Deira (04 265 9484),
Al Mussalla Rd, Bur Dubai (04 397 0982) Baniyas Rd, Deira (04 222 2971),
Deira City Centre (04 295 8885), Mall of the Emirates (04 341 3141), Opp Hamarain
Centre, Deira (04 266 6216)

Espirit ◄ BurJuman (04 355 3324), Deira City Centre (04 295 0542),Festival Centre (04 375 0561),
Mall of the Emirates (04 341 1399), The Dubai Mall (04 425 5835)

Evans ◄ Al Ghurair City (04 222 8261), Deira City Centre (04 294 0011),
Ibn Battuta Shopping Mall (04 368 5900), Mall of the Emirates (04 340 7575)

Faith ◄ Deira City Centre (04 294 0011), Ibn Battuta Shopping Mall (04 368 5951),
Mall of the Emirates (04 340 7575)

FCUK ◄ Al Ghurair City (04 227 3848), Deira City Centre (04 295 0413),
Festival Centre (04 232 9293), Mall of the Emirates (04 341 1116)

Feshwari ◄ Al Hudheibah Rd, Al Satwa (04 344 5426), Shk Zayed Rd (04 339 3559)

Forever 21 ◄ Deira City Centre (04 295 2031), Ibn Battuta Shopping Mall (04 368 5232),
Mall of the Emirates (04 341 3412)

Fossil ◄ BurJuman (04 352 8699), Deira City Centre (04 295 0108),
Lamcy Plaza (04 334 8073), Nasr Square (04 228 9593)

G2000 ◄ Al Ghurair City (04 221 5023), BurJuman (04 355 2942), Lamcy Plaza (04 336 0588),
Mall of the Emirates (04 347 9992), Dubai Festival Centre (04 232 5923)

GAP ◄ BurJuman (04 352 0120), Mercato (04 342 0145), The Dubai Mall (04 339 8784),
Wafi Mall (GAP Kid's and Baby) (04 327 91 97)

Gerry Webber ◄ Deira City Centre (04 295 4914), The Dubai Mall (04 339 8950)

Gianfranco FERRE' ◄ BurJuman (04 355 1845), Deira City Centre (04 295 5035),
Mall of the Emirates (04 341 0919), Mercato (04 344 0895), The Dubai Mall (04 434 1409)

Ginger & Lace ◄ Wafi Mall (04 324 5699), Ibn Battuta Shopping Mall (04 368 5109)

Giordano ◄ Al Ghurair City (04 223 7904), BurJuman (04 351 3866), Deira City Centre (04 295 0302),
Dubai Outlet Mall (04 426 4955), Festival Centre (04 232 6999),
Ibn Battuta Shopping Mall (368 5453), Jumeirah Beach Residence (04 423 3741),
Karama Centre (04 336 8312), Mall of the Emirates (04 341 0117),
Wafi Mall (04 324 2852)

Go Sport ◄ Ibn Battuta Shopping Mall (04 368 5344), Mall of the Emirates (04 341 3251),
Uptown Mirdif (04 288 8132)

Golf House ◄ BurJuman (04 351 4801), Deira City Centre (04 295 0501),
Ibn Battuta Shopping Mall (04 366 9895), Lamcy Plaza (04 334 5945),
Mall of the Emirates (04 341 0611)

Grand Optics ◄ Al Shindagha Carrefour (04 393 6133), Deira City Centre (04 295 4699), Mall of the Emirates (04 341 0351)

Grand Stores ◄ BurJuman (04 352 3641), Deira City Centre (04 294 3070), Dubai Outlet Mall (04 426 4915), Garhoud (04 286 8010), Maktoum St (04 221 3700), The Dubai Mall (04 339 8690), Dubai Festival Centre (04 232 6302), Ibn Battuta (04 368 5353), Mall of the Emirates (04 341 4555)

Guess ◄ BurJuman (04 355 3324), Deira City Centre (04 295 7646), Dubai Festival Centre (04 375 0183), Mall of the Emirates (04 341 1177), The Dubai Mall (04 339 8881)

Gulf Greetings ◄ Al Khaleej Centre (04 355 7387), BurJuman (04 351 9613), Deira City Centre (04 295 9627), Ibn Battuta Shopping Mall (04 368 5068), Lulu Centre, Al Qusais (04 298 8633), Mall of the Emirates (04 347 6888), Mazaya Centre (04 343 7433), Mercato (04 349 0085), Spinneys, Umm Suqeim (04 394 0397), Wafi Mall (04 324 5618)

Gulf Optics ◄ Al Nasir Square (04 228 4328), Al Sabkha (04 226 0502), Meena Bazaar, Bur Dubai (04 353 5260), Al Ghazal Mall, Jumeira (04 346 0061), Dubai Mall (04 434 0120)

H&M ◄ Deira City Centre (04 295 7244), Ibn Battuta Shopping Mall (04 364 9819), Mall of the Emirates (04 341 5880), Mall of the Emirates (04 341 5440)

Habitat ◄ Jumeira Plaza (04 344 7456), Nr Spinneys Distribution Centre, Al Quoz (04 340 4996)

Hamac ◄ Dubai Marine Beach Resort & Spa (04 345 1167), Jumeirah Beach Hotel (04 406 8169)

Hang Ten ◄ BurJuman (04 351 9285), Deira City Centre (04 295 5449), Mall of the Emirates (04 341 3322)

Heatwaves ◄ Jumeirah Town Centre (04 342 0445), Le Meridien Dubai (04 399 3161)

Home Centre ◄ Mall of the Emirates (04 341 4441), Reef Mall (04 222 7755)

House of Prose ◄ Ibn Battuta Shopping Mall (04 368 5526), Jumeira Plaza (04 344 9021)

Hugo Boss ◄ BurJuman (04 355 7845), Deira City Centre (04 295 5281), Festival Centre (04 232 6411), Mall of the Emirates (04 341 0630), Mercato (04 342 2021), Twin Towers (04 227 7177)

ID Design ◄ Mall of the Emirates (04 341 3434), Sharjah Rd (04 266 6751)

iStyle ◄ Festival Centre (04 232 9979), Ibn Battuta Shopping Mall (04 366 9797)

Jacky's Electronics ◄ Al Garhoud (04 282 1822), Century Mall (04 296 8829), Deira City Centre (04 294 9480), Mall of the Emirates (04 341 4858) Ibn Battuta Shopping Mall (04 368 5080)

Jashanmal ◄ Al Ghurair City (04 227 7780), The Village Mall (04 344 5770), Mall of the Emirates (04 340 6789), Wafi Mall (04 324 4800)

Jenny Rose ◄ BurJuman (04 352 1706), Mall of the Emirates (04 341 0577)

Jennyfer ◄ Al Ghurair City (04 227 1208), Ibn Battuta Shopping Mall (04 368 5125)

Jumbo Electronics	Karama (04 336 9208), Al Qusais (04 261 6626), Mall of the Emirates (04 341 0101), Opp Ramada Hotel (04 352 3555), Shk Zayed Rd (04 332 8315), Wafi Mall (04 324 2077)
Karen Millen	Deira City Centre (04 295 5007), The Dubai Mall (04 339 8608)
La Perla	BurJuman (04 355 1251), Mall of the Emirates (04 341 3070)
La Senza	BurJuman (04 352 17 91), Lamcy Plaza (04 335 3580), Mall of the Emirates (04 340 7004)
Leather Palace	Al Ghurair City (04 222 6770), BurJuman (04 351 5251), Hamarain Centre (04 266 7176), Mall of the Emirates (04 341 0814)
Levis	BurJuman (04 351 6728), Deira City Centre (04 295 9943), Mall of the Emirates (04 341 4050)
Levis Outlet	Al Khaleej Centre (04 359 6770), Mall of the Emirates (04 341 4747)
Lifco	Mirdif (04 288 8975), Nr Al Moosa Tower, Trade Center Rd (04 332 7899), Nr Welcare Hospital, Al Garhoud (04 286 8685)
Life Style	Al Barsha (04 347 3451), Al Bustan Centre (04 261 6585), Al Ghurair (04 224 8362), Century Mall (04 429 67710), Dubai Health City (04 362 4802), Hamarain Centre (04 297 0105), Mankhool Towers (04 3529229), Naser Square (04 422 21445), Palm Strip Shopping Mall (04 344 1122), Residential Oasis, Al Gusais (04 258 6774)
Lifestyle	Bur Dubai (04 351 0177), Ibn Battuta Shopping Mall (04 348 5699), Mall of the Emirates (04 341 0523), Reef Mall (04 222 7915)
Limited Too	Ibn Battuta Shopping Mall (04 368 5936), Mall of the Emirates (04 340 7575)
Liwa	BurJuman (04 351 5353), Deira City Centre (04 295 3988)
Liz Claiborne	Deira City Centre (04 294 0011), Ibn Battuta Shopping Mall (04 368 5900), Mall of the Emirates (04 340 7575)
L'Occitaine	Festival Centre (04 232 6050), Ibn Battuta Mall (04 368 5505), Mall of the Emirates (04 340 4309), Uptown Mirdiff (04 288 2692)
Louis Vuitton	BurJuman (04 359 2535), Mall of the Emirates (04 341 4462)
Lulu Hypermarket	Al Barsha (04 341 8888), Deira (04 298 8876), Nr Dubai Municipality, Karama (04 336 7070), Opposite Zabeel Park (04 334 6333)
MAC	BurJuman (04 351 2880), Deira City Centre (04 295 7704), Ibn Battuta Shopping Mall (04 368 5966), Mercato (04 344 8014), Wafi Mall (04 324 4112)
Magrudy's	Call Centre (04 344 4009) Locations: BurJuman, Dubai Festival Centre, The Dubai Mall Deira City Centre, Ibn Battuta Shopping Mall, Jumeira Beach Rd
Mahallati Jewellery	Gold Souk (04 226 7023), Mall of the Emirates (04 341 0787), Mercato (04 344 4771)

Mamas & Papas
Mercato (04 344 0981), Mall of the Emirates (04 409 8888), Wafi Mall(04 324 0230)

Mango
BurJuman (04 355 5770), Deira City Centre (04 295 0182),
Dubai Outlet Mall (04 425 9879), Mall of the Emirates (04 341 4324),
Mercato (04 344 7195)

Marina Gulf Trading
Mall of the Emirates (04 341 0314), Souk Madinat Jumeirah (04 368 6050),
Spinneys, Umm Suqeim (04 394 2541), Al Barsha Rd (04 347 8940)

Marks & Spencer
Festival Centre (04 206 6466), Salahuddin St, Deira (04 222 2000),
Wafi Mall (04 324 5145)

Marlboro Classics
Ibn Battuta Shopping Mall (04 368 5590), Festival Centre (04 232 6035)

Marlin
Port Rashid Rd, Karama (04 334 6664), Shk Zayed Rd (04 338 6866)

Massimo Dutti
BurJuman (04 351 3391), Deira City Centre (04 295 4788),
Mall of the Emirates (04 341 3151), Mercato (04 344 7158)

Max
Abu Hail Center (04 266 8660), Ibn Battuta Shopping Mall (04 368 5435),
Khalid Bin Al Waleed St, Bur Dubai (04 397 5111)

Mexx
Deira City Centre (04 295 4873), Mall of the Emirates (04 341 1990)

Mikyajy
Deira City Centre (04 295 7844), Mall of the Emirates (04 341 4277),
Souk Madinat Jumeirah (04 368 6529)

Milano
Al Ghurair City (04 222 8545), Deira City Centre (04 294 0011),
Ibn Battuta Shopping Mall (04 368 5981), Mall of the Emirates (04 340 7575),
Mercato (04 344 9517), Uptown Mirdif (04 288 8124)

Miss Sixty
Mall of the Emirates (04 311 4600), Wafi Mall (04 324 1998)

MMI
Al Hamra Cellar (07 244 7403), Cellar Saver Karama, Nr Enoc Garage (04 335 1722),
Dnata Airline Bld (04 294 0390), Dubai Silicon Oasis (DSO) (04 326 4583),
Green Community (04 8854550), Ibn Battuta Shopping Mall (04 368 5626),
Khalid Bin Waleed St (04 393 5738), Mall of the Emirates (04 341 0371),
Shk Zayed Rd (04 321 1223), Spinneys, Trade Center Rd (04 352 3091),
Umm Suqeim (04 394 0351)

Monsoon
BurJuman (04 355 2205), Deira City Centre (04 295 0725), Lamcy Plaza (04 335 7375),
Mall of the Emirates (04 341 0479), The Dubai Mall (04 339 8953),
Uptown Mirdif (04 288 8403), Wafi Mall (04 327 9801), Festival Centre (04 232 6601)

Montblanc
BurJuman (04 355 7377), Deira City Centre (04 295 4308), Ibn Battuta Shopping
Mall (04 368 5584), Mall of the Emirates (04 341 4451), Wafi Mall (04 324 8825)

Mothercare
Al Ghurair City (04 223 8176), BurJuman (04 352 8916), Deira City Centre (04 295 9061),
Emmar Town Center, Emirates Hills (04 360 7816), Ibn Battuta Shopping Mall (04 368
5921), Jumeirah Beach Residence (04 424 3822), Jumeirah Centre (04 349 4019),
Lamcy Plaza (04 334 0742), Mall of the Emirates (04 340 7575),
Spinneys, Umm Suqeim (04 394 0228), Uptown Mirdif (04 288 4519)

Mr Price ◀ Reef Mall (04 224 0244), Lamcy Plaza (04 336 6656)

National Iranian Carpets ◀ AL Nasr Square, Deira Tower (04 221 9800), Deira City Centre (04 295 0576), Mall of the Emirates (04 341 1904), Souk Madinat Jumeirah (04 368 6002)

Nayomi ◀ Al Ghurair City (04 227 2337), Ibn Battuta Shopping Mall (04 366 9832), Lamcy Plaza (04 335 8841), Mercato (04 344 9120), Wafi Mall (04 324 5141)

Next ◀ BurJuman (04 351 0026), Deira City Centre (04 295 5025), Ibn Battuta Shopping Mall (04 368 5971), Lamcy Plaza (04 335 0262), Mall of the Emirates (04 340 3898), Mercato (04 344 8016)

New Look ◀ BurJuman (04 355 6578), Deira City Centre (04 295 9542), The Dubai Mall (04 434 0737)

Nine West ◀ Al Ghurair City (04 221 1484), BurJuman (04 351 6214), Deira City Centre (04 295 6887), Ibn Battuta Shopping Mall (04 368 5097), Jumeirah Town Centre (04 344 0038), Lamcy Plaza (04 337 4575), Mall of the Emirates (04 341 0244), Mercato (04 349 1336)

Nutrition Zone ◀ Ibn Battuta Shopping Mall (04 368 5390), The Walk, JBR (04 438 0667), Jumeirah Town Centre (04 344 5888), The Dubai Mall (04 339 9868)

Oasis ◀ Deira City Centre (04 294 0011), Ibn Battuta Shopping Mall (04 368 5956), Mall of the Emirates (04 340 7575), Wafi Mall (04 324 9074)

Okaidi ◀ BurJuman (04 351 9340), Dubai Festival Centre (04 232 5053), Mall of the Emirates (04 347 1411)

Omega ◀ Deira City Centre (04 294 3233), Mall of the Emirates (04 341 3122)

Optic Centre ◀ Al Aweer (04 333 1872), Co-op Society, Jumeirah (04 334 3723), Co-op Society, Ghusais (04 263 1038), The Walk, JBR (04 424 8871), Lamcy Plaza (04 333 4006)

Organic Foods & Café ◀ Al Satwa (04 398 9140), The Greens (04 361 7974)

Ounass ◀ Boulevard at Emirates Towers (04 330 0617), Madinat Jumeirah (04 368 6167), Wafi Mall (04 324 9870)

Pablosky ◀ BurJuman (04 359 6330), Ibn Battuta Shopping Mall (04 368 5085), Mercato (04 344 7816)

Paper Moon ◀ Al Ghurair City (04 223 4415), Al Mina Rd, Al Satwa (04 345 4888), Jumeirah Town Centre (04 344 5998)

Paris Gallery ◀ Al Bustan Centre (04 261 1288), Al Ghurair (04 211 1166), BurJuman (04 359 7774), Burj Al Arab (04 348 8222), Deira City Centre (04 294 5550), Hamarain Centre (04 268 8122), Ibn Battuta Shopping Mall (04 368 5500), Jumeirah Town Centre (04 342 2555), Lamcy Plaza (04 336 2000), Uptown Mirdiff (04 288 8333), Wafi Mall (04 324 2121)

Pierre Cardin ◀ Century Mall (04 296 6040), Dubai Festival Centre (04 232 6296), The Dubai Mall (04 434 1356), Dubai Outlet Mall (04 425 5808), Hamarain Centre (04 265 3551), Ibn Battuta Mall (04 366 9864), Lamcy Plaza (04 335 9033), Uptown Mirdif (04 288 5174)

Peacocks — Ibn Battuta Shopping Mall (04 368 5931), Lamcy Plaza (04 337 7321)

Pearle Opticians — Ibn Battuta Shopping Mall (04 347 7057), Mall of the Emirates (04 368 5926)

Pet's Delight — Arabian Ranches (04 361 9184), Emirates Hills (04 361 7767)

Planet Nutrition — Deira City Centre (04 294 5889), Dubai Outlet Mall (04 425 9819)

Plug-Ins — Al Ghurair City (04 228 3657), BurJuman (04 351 3919), Festival Centre (04 206 6777), Souk Madinat Jumeirah (04 368 6131)

Polo Ralph Lauren — BurJuman (04 352 5311), Mall of the Emirates (04 341 4200)

Porsche Design — Atlantis The Palm (04 422 0311), Deira City Centre (04 295 7652), Jumeirah Beach Hotel (04 348 0648), Mall of the Emirates (04 341 0899)

PrettyFIT — Deira City Centre (04 295 0790), Mercato (04 344 0015)

Pride Of Kashmir — Deira City Centre (04 295 0655), Mall of the Emirates (04 341 4477), Mercato (04 342 0270), Souk Madinat Jumeirah (04 368 6110)

Prima Gold — BurJuman (04 355 1988), Deira City Centre (04 294 4244)

Principles — Deira City Centre (04 294 0011), Ibn Battuta Shopping Mall (04 368 5906), Mall of the Emirates (04 340 7575)

Promod — BurJuman (04 351 4477), Deira City Centre (04 295 7344), Mall of the Emirates (04 341 4944), Mercato (04 344 6941)

Prozone — Jebel Ali (04 882 1660), Shk Zayed Rd (04 339 1333)

Pull & Bear — Deira City Centre (04 295 3525), Mall of the Emirates (04 341 4234), Mercato (04 344 7214)

Pumpkin Patch — Al Ghurair City (04 234 0931), BurJuman (04 351 0445), Dubai Outlet Mall (04 425 9843), Festival Centre (04 232 6620), Jumeirah Beach Residence (04 427 0384), Lamcy Plaza (04 337 1006), Mall of the Emirates (04 341 3633), The Dubai Mall (04 339 8662), Uptown Mirdif (04 288 7629)

Pure Gold — Ibn Battuta Shopping Mall (04 368 5071), Mercato (04 349 2400)

Radio Shack — Deira City Centre (04 295 2127), Mall of the Emirates (04 341 3337)

Raoul — Festival Centre (04 232 6099), Mall of the Emirates (04 341 0282)

Rasasi — Al Ghurair (04 222 9109), BurJuman (04 351 2757), Deira City Centre (04 295 0670)

Red Earth — Al Ghurair (04 227 9696), Bin Sougat Centre (04 285 8653), Deira City Centre (04 295 1887), Mercato (04 344 9439)

Regal Traders — Al Satwa (04 353 2320), Bur Dubai (04 355 1742)

RHS ◄ Jumeirah Centre (04 344 1756), Lamcy Plaza (04 336 5651)

River Island ◄ Deira City Centre (04 295 4146), Ibn Battuta Shopping Mall (04 368 5961),
Mall of the Emirates (04 340 9115)

Rivoli ◄ BurJuman (04 355 5191), Ibn Battuta Shopping Mall (04 368 5583),
Mall of the Emirates (04 341 3122), Mercato (04 344 6918), Wafi Mall (04 324 6675)

Rodeo Drive ◄ Al Bustan Rotana Hotel (04 282 4006), Boulevard at Emirates Towers (04 330 3500),
BurJuman (04 355 5204), Mall of the Emirates (04 340 0347),
Atlantis The Palm (04 422 0190)

Royal Gardenscape ◄ Al Quoz (04 340 0648), Uptown Mirdiff (04 288 3049)

S*uce ◄ Jumeirah Centre (04 344 4391), The Village Mall (04 344 7270),
XVA Bur Dubai (04 353 8468)

Saks Fifth Avenue ◄ BurJuman (04 351 5551), Dubai Marina (04 435 5681)

Samsung Electronics ◄ Bur Dubai (04 334 4973), Salahuddin Rd, Deira (04 266 0640)

Sana Fashion ◄ Abu Hail (04 266 2919), Karama (04 337 7726)

Sara – Villeroy & Boch ◄ BurJuman (04 351 7775), Deira City Centre (04 295 0408), Wafi Mall (04 324 0100)

Sharaf DG ◄ Deira City Centre (04 294 8483), Ibn Battuta Shopping Mall (04 368 5115),
Times Square, Al Quoz (04 341 8060)

Shoe City ◄ Deira City Centre (04 295 0437), Dubai Outlet Mall (04 426 4917), Mall of the Emirates
(04 341 3394), Uptown Mirdiff (04 288 73 86)

Shoe Mart ◄ Lamcy Plaza (04 337 9811), Nr Jumbo Showroom, Bur Dubai (04 351 9560)

Skechers ◄ BurJuman (04 359 3557), Festival Centre (04 232 6191),
Ibn Battuta Shopping Mall (04 368 5126), Mercato (04 344 3119)

Solaris ◄ Deira City Centre (04 294 9959), Ibn Battuta Shopping Mall (04 368 5913),
Mall of the Emirates (04 340 7842)

Spinneys ◄ Al Ghurair City (04 222 2886), Bin Sougat Centre (04 286 2442),
Burj Residence (04 360 3980), Damascus St, Al Qusais 2 (04 261 8264),
Dubai Marina (04 367 48010), Dubai Silicon Oasis (04 326 4575),
Emirates Hills Town Centre (04 360 6511), Festival Centre (04 232 6201),
Al Qusais 1 (04 258 6729), Mazaya Centre (04 321 2225),Meadows Village (04 360 6484),
Mercato (04 349 6900), Mirdiff 2 (04 288 2182), Al Manzil Hotel (04 422 2307),
Hudaiba, Satwa (04 358 0556), Nr Lamcy Plaza, Oud Metha (04 335 7321),
Nr Ramada Htlm, Bur Dubai (04 355 5250), Souk AL Bahar (04 420 3644),
Trade Centre Rd, Nr BurJuman (04 351 1777), Umm Suqeim (04 394 1657),
Uptown Mirdiff (04 288 0335)

Splash
Nxt to BurJuman (04 351 1130), Deira City Centre (04 295 0553), Mall of the Emirates (04 341 0644), Nr Maktoum Bridge (04 335 0525), Reef Mall (04 222 2512)

Spring
Ibn Battuta Shopping Mall (04 368 5244), Lamcy Plaza (04 334 7952), Mall of the Emirates (04 341 0311), Reef Mall (04 228 4462)

Stradivarius
Deira City Centre (04 294 1221), Mall of the Emirates (04 341 3999)

Stadium
BurJuman (04 351 3435), Deira City Centre (04 295 0261), Ibn Battuta Shopping Mall (04 366 9890), Jumeirah Beach Hotel (04 348 0830), Lamcy Plaza (04 336 5651)

Sun & Sand Sports
Al Ghurair City (04 227 5758), Bank St (04 351 6222), BurJuman (04 351 5376), Deira City Centre (04 295 5551), Ibn Battuta Shopping Mall (04 366 9777), Jumeirah Centre (04 349 5820), Mall of the Emirates (04 341 0933), Souk Madinat Jumeirah (04 368 6120)

Susan Walpole
Mall of the Emirates (04 341 3227), Mercato (04 344 8551)

Swatch
Al Ghurair City (04 224 8556), BurJuman (04 359 6109), Deira City Centre (04 295 3932), Ibn Battuta Shopping Mall (04 368 5580), Mall of the Emirates (04 341 4453),Wafi Mall (04 324 0518)

TAG Heuer
BurJuman (04 355 9494), Wafi Mall (04 324 6060)

Tanagra
Deira City Centre (04 295 0293), Wafi Mall (04 324 2340)

Tavola
Mall of the Emirates (04 340 2933), Spinneys Umm Suqeim Centre (04 394 8150), Town Center Emirates Hills (04 361 8787)

Ted Baker
BurJuman (04 355 3842), Dubai Festival Centre (04 232 6053), Deira City Centre (04 295 6174), The Dubai Mall (04 434 0623)

The Body Shop
Al Ghurair City (04 228 9494), Deira City Centre (04 295 0701), Festival Centre (04 232 5551), Ibn Battuta Shopping Mall (04 368 5456), Jumeirah Centre (04 344 4042), Lamcy Plaza (04 337 0831), Mall of the Emirates (04 341 0551), The Dubai Mall (050 614 1439), Wafi Mall (04 324 5435)

THE One
BurJuman (04 351 4424), Jumeira Rd (04 345 6687), Mall of the Emirates (04 341 3777), Wafi Mall (04 324 1224)

The Music Institute
Knowledge Village (04 390 0786), Jumeirah Beach Residence (04 424 3818)

The White Company
Deira City Centre (04 295 6182), Festival Centre (04 232 5506), Mall of the Emirates (04 341 0493), Wafi Mall (04 327 9110)

Thomsun Music
Salahuddin St, Deira (04 266 8181), Wafi Mall (04 324 2322)

Tiffany & Co.
BurJuman (04 351 1784), Deira City Centre (04 295 3884), Mall of the Emirates (04 341 0655), Atlantis The Palm (04 422 0187)

Titan Book Shop
Holiday Centre Mall (04 332 8343), Radisson SAS Hotel, Dubai Deira Creek (04 227 1372)

Tod's ◀ BurJuman (04 355 4417), Mall of the Emirates (04 341 3033)

Topman ◀ Deira City Centre (04 295 1804), Ibn Battuta Shopping Mall (04 344 2677),
Wafi Mall (04 327 9929)

Topshop ◀ Deira City Centre (04 295 1804), Ibn Battuta Shopping Mall (04 368 5946),
Mercato (04 344 2677), Wafi Mall (04 327 9929)

Toys R Us ◀ Festival Centre (04 206 6552), Marks & Spencer, Deira (04 224 0000),
Times Square, Al Quoz (04 341 8383)

Triumph ◀ Deira City Centre (04 295 2756), Mercato (04 344 4707)

Union Co-op ◀ Abu Hail Rd (04 262 9191), Al Twar (04 261 3100), Nr Safa Park (04 394 5999),
Nr Police Station, Al Rashidiya (04 286 2434), Trade Centre Rd, Karama (04 398 0944),
Satwa (04 331 2314)

Valencia ◀ Baniyas Centre, Al Maktoum St (04 223 2772), Deira City Centre (04 295 0990),
Mall of the Emirates (04 341 3020), Twin Towers (04 227 6012)

Vincci ◀ BurJuman (04 351 7246), Deira City Centre (04 295 7684)

Virgin Megastore ◀ BurJuman (04 351 3358), Deira City Centre (04 295 8599),
Mall of the Emirates (04 341 4353), Mercato (04 344 6971)

Wallis ◀ Deira City Centre (04 294 0011), Ibn Battuta Shopping Mall (04 368 5976),
Mall of the Emirates (04 340 7575)

Watch House ◀ BurJuman (04 352 8699), Mall of the Emirates (04 341 0354)

Women's Secret ◀ BurJuman (04 359 9447), Deira City Centre (04 295 9665)

Woolworths ◀ Deira City Centre (04 295 5900), Ibn Battuta Shopping Mall (04 368 5104)

Yateem Opticians ◀ Al Diyafah Rd, Al Satwa (04 345 3405), Al Ghurair City (04 228 1787),
Boulevard at Emirates Towers (04 330 3301), BurJuman (04 352 2067)

Zara ◀ BurJuman (04 351 3332), Deira City Centre (04 295 3377),
Mall of the Emirates (04 341 3171)

Zara Home ◀ BurJuman (04 359 5598), Mall of the Emirates (04 341 4184), Palm Strip (04 346 0020)

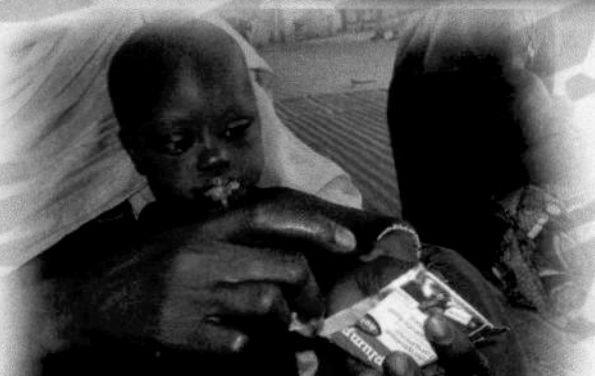

Therapeutic Feeding    Essential Medicines 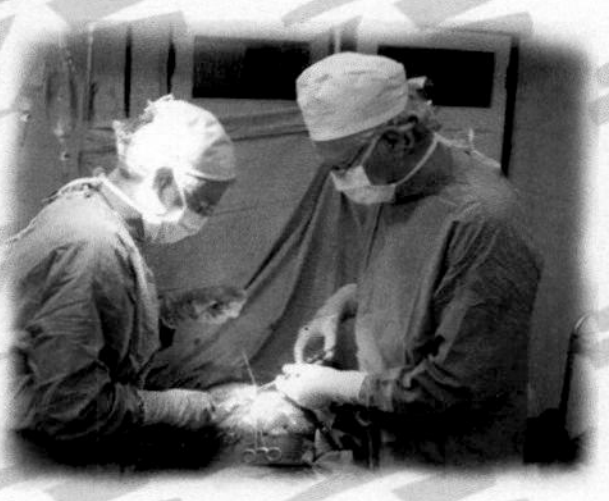   Surgery

MEDECINS SANS FRONTIERES
أطبــاء بــلا حــدود

Providing emergency medical
relief in over 70 countries.

help us help the helpless

CULINARY JOURNEY

COME AND JOIN US IN A CULINARY JOURNEY
EXTRAORDINAIRE. AWAKEN YOUR TASTE BUDS FROM
FINE DINING, CELEBRITY CHEF'S MENUS TO FAMILY
RESTAURANTS AND AL FRESCO SETTINGS. THE RESORT
BOASTS AN ASTOUNDING 17 UNIQUELY DESIGNED
RESTAURANTS, BARS AND LOUNGES TO FULFIL EVERY
TASTE AND BUDGET.

FOR BOOKING AND ENQUIRIES CALL + 971 (4) 426 2626 OR
VISIT ATLANTISTHEPALM.COM

ATLANTIS
PALM JUMEIRAH, DUBAI
DON'T FORGET TO BREATHE

Going Out

Going Out

*Serving
The Community*

*Most fastfood outlets
deliver, but you can
also order through
Room Service,
which publishes
a list of menus
from participating
restaurants
(www.roomservice-
uae.com). Delivery time
is between 30 minutes
and an hour, with a
minimum order of
between Dhs.60 and
Dhs.80, depending on
your location. There's
also a Dhs.25 delivery
charge per outlet. Call
toll free on 800 4788.*

Going Out

As you'd expect from a bustling multicultural metropolis, Dubai has a wide range of options when it comes to eating, drinking, and socialising. With almost 400 independent reviews, this Going Out section covers restaurants, cafes, bars, pubs and clubs, and provides details of cinemas, theatres and live entertainment venues throughout the city. From Arabic to Vietnamese, and from Indian to Italian, the city really does dish up the world on a plate. And whether you're after five-star finery or cheap and cheerful you'll find somewhere to suit.

Bar flies won't be disappointed either, with plenty of high-class hangouts and no-nonsense pubs to choose from, while big-name DJs and regular dance events keep clubbers more than happy. The live entertainment scene does lag behind other cities somewhat, but with the opening of new theatres and venues, and more international names such as George Michael and Kylie being lured over to perform, it is improving all the time.

Emirati Etiquette

Although it's definitely not expected in Dubai's Arabic restaurants, it is traditional to eat Emirati cuisine with your right hand, for reasons that might put you off your dinner. In very authentic places, there are also no chairs, little in the way of cutlery and sometimes even no tables. Al Hadheera at Bab Al Shams (p.534) is one place offering such a genuine experience. Every aspect of the restaurant, from the main course to the traditional desserts, and even the cooking and dining methods, is rooted firmly in tradition.

Eating Out

Many of Dubai's most popular restaurants are located within hotels and leisure clubs, and no doubt their popularity is partly down to the fact that these are virtually the only outlets where you can drink alcohol with your meal. Look out for the Alcohol Available icon next to the reviews. There's quite a hefty mark-up on drinks, with a decent bottle of wine often costing as much as your meal.

The city has some superb independent restaurants and cafes that shouldn't be ignored just because they don't serve booze. Bottled water also seems to rocket in price in the five-star venues, and if you ask for water you'll often be given an imported brand, costing up to Dhs.40 a bottle. You should specify 'local' water when ordering, but even then you can expect to pay Dhs.10 or Dhs.20 for a bottle of water that costs less than Dhs.2 in the supermarket.

Cuisine List – Quick Reference

American	p.530	Italian	p.568	Russian	p.586
Arabic & Lebanese	p.532	Japanese	p.576	Seafood	p.587
Chinese	p.538	Korean	p.580	Singaporean	p.591
Dinner Cruises	p.540	Latin American	p.580	Spanish	p.591
European	p.542	Mediterranean	p.581	Sri Lankan	p.592
Far Eastern	p.544	Mexican	p.583	Steakhouses	p.592
Filipino	p.546	Moroccan	p.584	Tex Mex	p.595
Fish & Chips	p.547	Pakistani	p.584	Thai	p.595
French	p.547	Persian	p.585	Turkish	p.597
German	p.548	Pizzerias	p.586	Vegetarian	p.598
Indian	p.550	Polynesian	p.586	Vietnamese	p.598
International	p.555	Portuguese	p.586		

Restaurant Or Bar?

With so many competing bars and restaurants in Dubai, many venues try to be all things to all people. Bars have restaurants and restaurants have bars, clubs and cafes have a la carte food and you'll find pubs in five-star surroundings. This means that while a certain outlet may be famed for its late-night activities, it may also have an excellent restaurant. For a list of bars with good food see p.538, for restaurants with good bars see p.528, and for bars and restaurants that transform into nightclubs, see p.626.

Hygiene

Food and drink outlets are subject to regular checks by Dubai Municipality, and unclean outlets are warned to either scrub up or shut down. You can be fairly confident that wherever you eat will meet basic health and hygiene requirements.

Special Deals & Theme Nights

Many Dubai restaurants and bars dedicate one evening a week to a promotion. Details of some of the best deals can be found in All You Can Eat & Drink on p.528.

Another Dubai institution is Friday Brunch – for a set price you get to take multiple visits to a huge buffet serving both breakfast food (British fry-ups alongside continental and local choices) and lunch with roasts, curries and international dishes. For more on Friday Brunch and a list of recommended outlets, see p.606.

Ladies' Nights (p.620) are big in Dubai – usually on Tuesdays or Wednesdays, ladies get a few free drinks in various locations around town – a bit of careful planning and you can go the whole night without paying for a single drink. And of course, wherever there are crowds of tipsy ladies, the fellas are never far behind.

Tax & Service Charges

Look out for the small print at the bottom of your menu – you may spot the dreaded 'prices are subject to 10% service charge and 10% municipality tax'. In most hotel restaurants and bars these extras are already included, but in an independent outlet they may appear as an additional charge. The 10% service charge is perhaps incorrectly named as often it isn't passed on to the staff, and you have no option of withholding it if you receive poor service. If you want to reward the waiting staff directly then the standard rule of a 10-12.5% tip will be appreciated, but give them cash personally, or your tip may go straight in the till.

Restaurant Listing Structure

Dubai is growing, and with it the choice of venues for dining, drinking and dancing. Reviewing every outlet would fill a whole book in itself (check out the beautiful restaurant and bar guide *Posh Nosh, Cheap Eats & Star Bars* also by Explorer Publishing), so the Going Out section features a select 400 venues. Each review attempts to give an idea of the food, service, decor and ambience, while those venues that really excel get a yellow star (see left). Primarily the restaurants have been categorised by cuisine (in alphabetic order) but if you want to go out for a specific occasion, see 'Alfresco' (p.530), 'Cocktails' (p.599), 'Karaoke' (p.620), 'Live Music' (p.632), 'Night of Romance' (p.548) and 'Sports Bars' (p.610).

If you want to plan your evening around a particular location – maybe you have guests in town and you want to dine in their hotel or at a hotel nearby – then simply turn to the index at the back of this book. Each of the hotels will have a list of all its outlets and their cuisine, or you can turn to the Restaurant or Bar section on p.530.

As a rule, non-English names retain their prefix (Al, Le, La and El) in their alphabetical placement, while English names are listed by titles, ignoring prefixes such as 'The'.

Quick Reference Icons

- Alfresco Option
- Have a Happy Hour
- No Credit Cards Accepted
- Kids Welcome
- Live Music
- Serve Alcohol
- Will Deliver

Privilege Cards

With so much choice it's no surprise that many places offer privilege cards to keep you coming back. The benefits vary so call to find out what you get and whether you have to pay for the card. The Wafi Advantage Card is a favourite as it gives discounts on shopping and restaurants, and it's free. Dine In by Hyatt is another popular loyalty scheme – for every Dhs.10 you spend, you get Dhs.1 Collected points are converted into rewards that can be used in Hyatt outlets across Dubai.

Vegetarian Food

Vegetarians should be pleasantly surprised by the variety of cuisine available in restaurants in Dubai. Due to the large number of the population from subcontinent who are vegetarian by religion, numerous Indian restaurants offer a range of cooking styles and tasty vegetarian dishes. Try Saravana Bhavan (p.554) and Aryaas (p.550) in Karama. In other restaurants (even in steakhouses), you'll find at least one or two vegetarian options. Also Arabic food (p.532), although dominated by meat in the main courses, offers a staggering range of mezze that are mostly vegetarian.

Dubai's cafes are also great for vegetarian food. Of particular note are the Lime Tree Café, (p.603) THE One (p.604) and Celebrities (p.558), which offers fine dining and a completely separate vegetarian menu. One notable restaurant is Magnolia (p.598) in Madinat Jumeirah, which offers high-class organic, vegetarian food.

A word of warning: if you are a strict veggie, confirm that your meal is completely meat free. Some restaurants cook their 'vegetarian' selection with animal fat or on the same grill as the meat dishes. Also, in some places you may need to check the ingredients of seemingly vegetarian items.

Dinner & Drinks

Dubai has a number of restaurants that deserve a special mention for their bars. For example Trader Vic's (p.618) is primarily a restaurant but is also renowned for its cocktail bar. Other eateries that are worth visiting for a drink include Bussola's upstairs terrace (p.569), Malecon (p.580), Seville's (p.592) and Spectrum on One (p.566). For a great wine selection, try The Cellar (p.558).

Street Food

Other options **Arabic/Lebanese** p.532

Shawarma is a popular local snack consisting of rolled pita bread filled with lamb or chicken carved from a rotating spit, vegetables and tahina sauce. You'll see countless roadside stands offering shawarma for as little as Dhs.3 each, and they make a great alternative to the usual fast-food staples. In residential areas, the small cluster of shops beside a mosque is often a good place to look for your local shawarma outlet. These cafes and stands usually sell other dishes, such as falafel (or ta'amiya), which are small savoury balls of deep-fried chickpeas, also sold separately or in a pita bread sandwich. Many also offer freshly squeezed fruit juices for around Dhs.10. For a really unique version, check out Al Shera'a Fisheries Centre, next to Marks & Spencer in Deira (04 227 1803), the only place in town that offers fish shawarmas.

All You Can Eat & Drink

While the concept of 'all you can eat and drink' may sound a little on the cheap and nasty side, in Dubai buffet deals are the best of both worlds. For an all-inclusive price you can stuff your face, get very tipsy and the food is of an a la carte standard. Some of the best deals are offered by Flavours on Two (p.562), Pergola (p.565), Spice Island (p.566), Five Dining (p.562) and Bamboo Lagoon (p.545).

Discount Delights

The Entertainer, a book full of 'buy one, get one free' vouchers could also save you thousands of dirhams on a year of wining and dining. Call 04 390 2866 or visit www.theentertainer.ae for more information. You should always check the expiry date on the book before you buy it.

American

Other options **Tex Mex** p.595

Sheikh Issa Tower
Sheikh Zayed Rd
Trade Centre 1
Map 7 F3

Applebees

04 343 7755 | *www.applebees.ae*

Applebee's is an all-American family restaurant where huge portions are offered up by enthusiastic, smiley staff in a bright, welcoming setting. Big screen TVs are scattered around the restaurant showing the latest US sports and the walls are filled with photos and souvenirs of the US of A. The menu consists of all you'd expect, with the focus on Tex-Mex grills, burgers and sandwiches, but there are also sufficient options to keep vegetarians happy. The desserts are particularly impressive and the kids' menu has plenty to choose from. To finish off, the Oreo milkshake is a fine way to end your calorie overload. Wrap up warm though – the air conditioning here works a bit too well.

> **Alfresco**
>
> As soon as it's cool enough (typically October until May), diners head outside. Popular spots include Al Mallah (p.535), Barasti (p.609), Boardwalk (p.558), Bussola (p.569), Century Village (various), Madinat Jumeirah (various), Medzo (p.582) and The Terrace (p.568).

Saleh Bin Lahej Bld
Garhoud
Map 11 C4

Chili's

04 282 8484 | *www.chilis.com*

If you're looking for a fast-paced meal in a buzzing atmosphere, then get down to Chili's. Decorated with Americana knick-knacks, the restaurant is bright with TVs, music, and plenty of seating in booths or at the 'bar'. The varied menu offers soups, salads, steaks, fajitas and sandwiches. There's a low-carb menu and inexpensive kids' dishes, along with table activities to keep them busy. Home delivery and takeaway are also available. Other Locations: Al Ghurair City (04 229 6760); BurJuman (04 352 2900); Deira City Centre (04 295 9559); Dubai Internet City (04 390 1495); Jumeirah Beach Centre (04 344 1300); Mall of the Emirates (04 341 3344); Sahara Centre, Sharjah (06 531 8890); Dubai Home Delivery (04 282 8303).

Uptown Mirdif
Mirdif
Map 15 B2

Gourmet Burger Kitchen

04 288 9057

This popular chain follows a simple formula – good juicy meat, fresh produce, an eclectic choice of toppings and sauces, and wholesome fries, all served in a pleasant loungey setting. Take your pick from the blackboard menu which includes avocado and bacon, chilli, cajun, blue cheese, Jamaican and lamb. Unusually, vegetarians are well catered for with three choices: falafel, aubergine and goat's cheese, and portabella (mushrooms, sweet red peppers, rocket). There are miniature burgers for kids, fresh juices and GBK milkshakes available in five flavours. They do deliveries, and there's another branch in Dubai International Financial Centre (800 287437).

Interchange 5
Sheikh Zayed Road
Al Sufouh
Map 5 C2

Hard Rock Café

04 399 2888 | *www.hardrock.com*

The distinctive gigantic guitar that sits atop the Hard Rock Café's entrance sets the tone for this well-known chain. Rock and roll memorabilia adorns all the walls, while the TVs in every corner cycle through various music videos. The menu is typical American/Tex-Mex fare with huge starters and even larger main courses, with kids' choices complete with crayons. In keeping with the American theme, the enthusiastic service comes with a smile, and the staff will ensure that your glass remains filled.

Juma Al Majid Centre
Jumeira
Map 7 E1

Johnny Rockets

04 344 7859 | *www.johnnyrockets.com*

This 1950s inspired American diner on Beach Road, with its blast-from-the-past decor and coin-operated jukeboxes, transforms a casual meal with friends and

family into a novelty experience. A variety of fresh hamburgers and chilli, cooked in an open kitchen, go great alongside their must-have shakes. Although not ideal for vegetarians, the reasonable prices, apt portions, impromptu outpouring of dance by the friendly staff and speedy service are sure to brighten up anybody's evening. Other locations: Mall of the Emirates (04 341 2380) and Dubai Marina (04 368 2339).

Planet Hollywood
Wafi City
Umm Hurair
Map 10 E4

04 324 4777 | www.planethollywood-dubai.com

With bright colours, lots of space and super-friendly staff, this Dubai branch of the popular chain is a good place for lunch or dinner with the kids. The menu is pretty much as you would expect – huge, American-style portions of carb-carnivore combos with some healthy and vegetarian options, but generally calorie-laden. The kids' menu will definitely put smiles on faces and have your little ones jumping with joy while the Friday brunch is particularly popular thanks to the movies, toys and face painting.

Ruby Tuesday
Rimal Building
Jumeirah Beach
Residence
Dubai Marina
Map 5 B2

04 424 3771 | www.rubytuesday.com

With its subtly lit booths overlooked by oil paintings, you'll find a private space ideal to relax with friends and family, or meet business contacts. High quality Angus beef burgers and steaks are the speciality, and the affordable menu also includes ribs and seafood. You can supplement your choice from the extensive salad bar. A kids' menu and mini hamburgers are on offer, and there are plenty of chocolaty desserts to choose from. It also does takeaway and delivers to Jumeirah Beach Residence. Other branches are in Jumeira Beach Park Plaza (04 342 8015) and Dubai Mall.

Shooters ▶ p.533
Jebel Ali Shooting
Club
Jebel Ali
Map 3 A2

04 883 6555 | www.jebelali-international.com

Shooters is a peaceful retreat popular with club members and guests from nearby Jebel Ali Golf Resort & Spa. This modern western saloon with denim-clad waiters is surprisingly quiet despite the gunfire (a glass wall gives unobstructed views of the five floodlit shooting ranges below). The menu is simple yet sophisticated, mainly offering fish and steak. King-size prawns and lobster tails are firm favourites but save room for the tempting traditional American desserts.

Arabic & Lebanese
Other options **Turkish** p.597, **Persian** p.585, **Moroccan** p.584

Al Basha
Habtoor Grand
Resort & Spa
Dubai Marina
Map 5 B1

04 399 5000 | www.habtoorhotels.com

It isn't the heavy feet of the belly dancer causing the light rumble underfoot, it's the construction next door. Nevertheless, Al Basha offers fine Lebanese food with enthusiastic service – book a late table, the live music starts from 21:30. You can order al a carte, but the set menus are wide-ranging with wafer-thin pitta, cheese rolls and grilled meat starting from Dhs.220 per person up to Dhs.350 with prawn and lobster. Be warned, alcohol is pricy at Dhs.50 for a bottle of Heineken.

Emirati Cuisine

The Department of Tourism & Commerce Marketing is working closely with the Emirates Culinary Guild and a few chefs to revive Emirati cuisine in Dubai's restaurant scene. Truly local food has several distinct flavours, thanks to the country's trading past. Look out for tangs of cinnamon, saffron and turmeric along with nuts (almonds or pistachios), limes and dried fruit in the different mouthfuls.

JEBEL ALI GOLF RESORT & SPA
Dubai's Only True Resort

Middle East's Leading Golf Resort

A MEMBER OF

JEBEL ALI INTERNATIONAL
HOTELS

Dubai's Best Beach, Spa & Golf Resort

In addition to its lush gardens and breathtaking views over the golden shores of the Arabian Gulf, the 5-star Jebel Ali Golf Resort & Spa features a pristine private beach, spa and 9-hole golf course, complete with practice facilities and a golf academy. This award-winning resort provides everything for a relaxing beach, golf or spa holiday including 13 restaurants and bars, three temperature-controlled swimming pools with underwater music, horse riding lessons, camel rides, fishing trips, watersports, and seaplane flights over Dubai's coastline departing from the resort's private marina. Choose between Jebel Ali Hotel and Palm Tree Court & Spa.

For more information please call +971 4 883 6000
E-mail: jagrs@jaihotels.com ● www.jebelali-international.com

Al Boom
Tourist Village
Umm Hurair
Map 13 C1

Al Dahleez
04 324 3000 | *www.alboom.ae*

Who hasn't wondered about the Al Boom Tourist Village when crossing the Garhoud Bridge? Inside you'll find Al Dahleez, an Arabic dining experience where diners can have it both ways – one restaurant, two buffets, one price. On one side you have authentic Arabic cuisine; on the other, international. Mix and match or stick with one. For an extra charge, you can add barbecue to your buffet experience. It's a good place to take out-of-town visitors for a taste of the region's culinary delicacies, and there are plenty of locals on hand to attest to the authenticity of the food and experience.

Stretch In Style

If you're feeling a bit flash (or are on a stag or hen party), you can rent a stretch Hummer or Lincoln from Dubai Exotic Limo so that you can arrive at your destination in style. See p.61.

Habtoor Grand
Resort & Spa
Dubai Marina
Map 5 B1

Al Dhiyafa
04 399 5000 | *www.habtoorhotels.com*

Imagine brass ceiling fans, the warm red glow from table lamps, a tantalising aroma of roasting meats and you have recreated the ambience of Al Dhiyafa. While the buffet food themes change daily, the splendid array of fresh, imaginative food remains constant, in particular the excellent selection of starters, but make sure you leave room for the meat-fest to follow. Attentive service from friendly waiters will guarantee a delightful evening and if you manage to sample some of the desserts, you will definitely leave replete.

Metropolitan Palace
Hotel
Deira
Map 11 C2

Al Diwan
04 205 1336 | *www.habtoorhotels.com*

If it isn't the traditional Lebanese food that entices you, it's the charm of the Lebanese waiters. Decorated in red and gold, the restaurant sways to ethnic Arabic music. Red and white wines from France and Italy, Montecristo Cigars and Beluga caviar indicate that this cosy restaurant is for a special night out. Must tries include the Hommous Al Diwan and the sumptuous Oriental Mix Grill, which truly define great Lebanese food. A belly dancing show takes place every night from 23:00.

Bab Al Shams
Desert Resort & Spa
Map 1 E2

Al Hadheerah
04 809 6100 | *www.jumeirahbabalshams.com*

Walking through the traditional souk sets the mood for a delightful dining experience. All sorts of traditional Arabic (including Emirati) food are available at the buffet, with mezze served at your table on arrival. Between the belly dancing, whirling dervish, singing, falcon display and legendary scenes acted out on the surrounding hillside, all ages are entertained and diners can enjoy the grilled seafood and steak, kebabs, rice dishes and of course desserts on offer. Henna painting and shisha are available for an extra charge. Prices start from Dhs.375 for adults and Dhs.225 for children.

Nr Al Nasr
Leisureland
Oud Metha
Map 10 E2

Al Koufa
04 335 1511 | *www.alkoufa.com*

Al Koufa is a popular restaurant and nightspot, especially with the Arabic population. The interior is massive, so it's nice to tuck yourself away at one of tables around the side until the place fills up. It normally starts livening up around 23:00, often with live performances (which are recorded for broadcast on local TV). The menu offers great Arabic food and fruit juices, including the usual range of mezze, breads and manakish, as well as some dishes not typically found including the odd Emirati dish. There is a cover charge of Dhs.30 if you plan on being there when the show starts.

Al Diyafah St
Satwa
Map 8 A2

Al Mallah
04 398 4723

Among the multitude of small Arabic joints across Dubai, this one stands out. Situated on one of the busiest streets in town, Al Mallah offers great pavement dining with an excellent view of the world cruising by in customised cars. The shawarmas and fruit juices are excellent, the cheese and zatar manoushi exceedingly tasty, and it has possibly the biggest and best falafel in Dubai. The incongruous 'Diana' and 'Charles' shakes are also recommended.

Al Mallah

Boulevard at Emirates Towers
Trade Centre 2
Map 7 F3

Al Nafoorah
04 319 8088
www.jumeirahemiratestowers.com

Al Nafoorah is a crisp, colonial and busy Lebanese restaurant, perfect for either a power lunch or an elegant dinner. The food is excellent and the menu is extensive, with pages and pages of mezze and mains to tantalise, so come in a group and share the wide selection. After dinner, you can take a stroll round The Boulevard, or sit out on the terrace, in awe of the towers looming above, while you smoke shisha.

Al Kawakeb Bld
Sheikh Zayed Rd
Trade Centre 2
Map 7 E3

Al Safadi
04 343 5333

This spacious restaurant may not have five-star trappings, but in Dubai that's not necessarily a bad thing. If you've had your fill of well-polished eateries and want to experience a more 'come as you are' style of local cuisine, then Al Safadi hits the spot. It's pretty basic, but what it lacks in imagination it makes up for in quality. The lights are bright and the customer turnover high, but relaxed dining is available outside where you can watch the world go by as you eat or smoke shisha. Another branch is on Al Rigga Road in Deira (04 227 9922).

Metropolitan Palace Hotel
Deira
Map 11 C2

Al Shindagah
04 227 0000 | www.habtoorhotels.com

Al Shindagah translates as 'the captive' and most of this restaurant's cosmopolitan diners are snared by bountiful lunchtime and Iftar buffets or the prospect of decent hotel food at any time of the day or night. During Ramadan the focus shifts from international to Middle Eastern food with dishes such as Kouzi, a whole sheep on a bed of rice, and a dizzying array of exotic mezze and desserts – the Um Ali (bread-butter pudding) must be the yummiest in town. The buffet is Dhs.258 for two people and includes soft drinks.

Ramadan Timings

During Ramadan, opening and closing times of restaurants change considerably. Because eating and drinking in public is forbidden during daylight hours, many places only open after sunset then keep going well into the early hours. Restaurants in some hotels remain open, but will be screened off from public view. Live entertainment is not allowed, so while some nightclubs remain open, all dancefloors are closed.

Ritz-Carlton Dubai
Dubai Marina
Map 5 A1

Amaseena
04 399 4000 | www.ritzcarlton.com
For a truly memorable outdoor Arabian experience, spend the evening in your own private majlis in the luxurious grounds of the Ritz-Carlton. A torch-lit entrance, night air filled with sounds of the oud, the aroma of shisha, and exotic belly dancing under the stars make this a truly magical setting. The food – an all you can eat Arabic buffet – is excellent, with hot and cold mezze, tasty kebabs and a range of small, but sweet desert dishes – although at over Dhs.200 per person, plus drinks, it's not a bargain. Closed during summer.

Beach Centre
Jumeira
Map 7 E1

Automatic
04 349 4888
The Automatic chain has been delivering great quality Arabic food throughout the Middle East for over 25 years. The usual vast range of mezze is accompanied by mountainous plates of salad, with tasty main courses including grilled meat, fish and kebabs. The atmosphere is minimalist in style but still clean and bright, with family friendly amenities and good service attracting a mixed clientele.
Other locations: Jumeirah Tower (04 321 4465), Al Abbas Building (04 359 4300), Al Khalij Centre (04 355 0333), Al Riqqa St (04 227 7824), Bin Sougat (04 286 3022), Abu Hail Centre (04 265 0101), Jebel Ali Free Zone (04 881 0800).

JW Marriott Hotel
Deira
Map 11 E1

Awafi Arabic Café
04 607 7977 | www.marriottdiningatjw.ae
If you can get over the slight whiff of chlorine, this is a lovely setting for a laid-back bite to eat. Situated around the Marriott's rooftop pool you can enjoy top-quality Arabic food underneath the stars with atmospheric traditional music sound tracking your evening. The menu includes the usual fare, with an ample selection of hot and cold mezze, grilled items, and a selection from the tandoor oven. For those with a sweet tooth, the dessert selection is limited, although you can enjoy a natural sugar rush by picking a delicious fresh juice or fruity shisha.

Grand Hyatt Dubai
Umm Hurair
Map 13 C1

Awtar
04 317 1234 | www.dubai.grand.hyatt.com
The decor at this sophisticated Lebanese restaurant is the epitome of opulent Arabic elegance, with booths tastefully swathed in gold muslin, impeccably dressed tables and low lighting from ornate lanterns effusing an ambience of refined luxury. Smiling and helpful waiters hover attentively while you choose from an appealing selection of well-presented mezze. The main courses do not quite live up to the same standard, and can quite confidently be ignored in favour of double helpings of the tasty starters and traditional desserts. A band accompanies the refined clink of cutlery and after 22:00 a brightly attired belly dancer takes to the stage.

Bastakiya
Bur Dubai
Map 9 A2

Bastakiah Nights
04 353 7772 | bastakr@eim.ae
There are some meals where mood is almost as important as the food itself. Bastakiah Nights, a haven in the concrete jungle of Bur Dubai, combines the two effortlessly. As you enter the heavy wooden doors you are reminded that, despite the glitzy malls and luxurious hotels, this is still very much Arabia. The food is delectable, and you can choose from fixed menus or the

Cultural Meals
Bastakiya (p.267) is a great place to eat while soaking up local culture. This traditional part of the city is best experienced by strolling through the streets, visiting the museums and dining at one of the many cafes. A cultural and culinary experience rolled into one.

various a la carte offerings. This is a magical place where local cuisine mingles with authentic local culture. There's no alcohol on the menu, but you'd be a fool to let that put you off.

Cafe Arabesque

Park Hyatt Dubai
Deira
Map 11 B4

04 602 1234 | www.dubai.park.hyatt.com

Cafe Arabesque has a wide selection of fantastic Lebanese, Syrian and Jordanian dishes – and a marvellous view of the creek to match. Buffet tables piled high with cold mezze kick-start the feast, while on the a la carte menu it's hard to choose which of the succulent wood-fired kebabs to opt for. Take your time in this romantic, softly lit restaurant, and watch the dhows on the creek pass gently by. Add a loved one for good measure, and the perfect evening is all yours.

Chandelier

Marina Walk
Dubai Marina
Map 5 B2

04 366 3606 | inquiry@chandelier-uae.com

Set in the vibey Marina Walk, Chandelier has a modern interior and a pleasant outdoor section. The alfresco lounge area overlooking the fountain has comfy seating with views out over the marina, making it a great spot for shisha after your meal. The food is good, with the menu offering an interesting mix of fare, and a full range of (non-alcoholic) cocktails and juices. Service here is renowned as being leisurely, but as this is a great place to linger over a meal or a shisha, this is no great burden.

The Courtyard

Al Manzil Hotel
Downtown Burj Dubai
Map 7 D4

04 428 5888 | www.almanzilhotel.com

Smoke authentic shisha in this dimly lit, atmospheric Arabic outdoor restaurant, where you can sit amid the arches and vegetation. Choose from an assortment of cold and hot mezzes, soups and mixed grills. Five items from the mezze menu cost Dhs.90 or individual portions can be ordered at Dhs.18. Dishes include hummus, Persian yoghurt and falafel. A broad a la carte menu is also available if you fancy poultry, fish or steak. Fully licensed, the hotel bars around The Courtyard ensure a plentiful array of alcoholic beverages. Shisha flavours include rose and apple, and Wi-Fi is also available.

Fakhreldine ▶ p.573

Mövenpick Hotel
Bur Dubai
Oud Metha
Map 10 D3

04 336 6000 | www.moevenpick-hotels.com

It's disappointing when you go to a five-star Lebanese restaurant and the (very expensive) mixed grill tastes identical to the Dhs.15 dish from your local street cafe. No such worries with Fakhreldine – from your first dip into their creamy hummus to the last crumb of Arabic sweets, the quality is apparent and the bill isn't too painful. The extensive menu gives you the opportunity to try new dishes that you won't easily find elsewhere, yet features old favourites for less adventurous tastes. The decor is impressive, as is the gyrating belly dancer, making this a restaurant worth the glad-rags.

Kan Zaman

Heritage Village
& Diving Village
Al Shindagha
Map 9 A1

04 393 9913 | www.alkoufa.com

With some of the best night views of Dubai creek, Kan Zaman offers an excellent Arabic menu and a rare chance to try some local food. As well as a full range of the usual Arabic mezze and mains on offer, there are also some traditional Emirati dishes. Local breads are served either with honey and dates or cheese, and the starters are good to share. Portions are large, but prices are low so it's great for groups to share a host of different dishes. There is seating available inside, but the outdoor dining with waterfront views draws the crowds night after night.

Atlantis The Palm
Palm Jumeirah
Map 2 A3

Levantine ▶ p.524
04 426 2626 | www.atlantisthepalm.com

The spacious Levantine at Atlantis could be Dubai's ultimate upscale Lebanese dining venue. The sumptuous surroundings result in higher prices than the norm, but the popular set menus provide a delicious spread of hot and cold mezze, mains and desserts. An extensive a la carte menu allows the more adventurous to try new dishes. The wine list includes a large selection from Lebanon, while a belly dancing show every hour and shisha area in the upstairs bar complete the experience.

> **Bar Food**
>
> There are quite a few bars around town that are renowned for the quality of their food. Some worth considering for both drinks and dinner include Boudoir (p.626), Barasti (p.609) Left Bank (p.614), Carter's (p.610), Ginseng (p.612), Lotus One (p.614) and Sho Cho's (p.617).

Century Village
Garhoud
Map 13 E1

Mazaj ▶ p.549
04 282 9952 | www.centuryvillage.ae

A great place to go if you crave the fruity aroma of shisha smoke in the night air and the tunes of a live Lebanese band, Mazaj is one of Dubai's most renowned hookah hangouts. The restaurant has an authentically styled interior, while outside, the dining area is in the fairy lit courtyard and leafy trees of Century Village. If you are here for food, you might be best advised to stick to the starters (which are wonderful), with enough on the menu to keep a leisurely evening going. Main courses, however, are pretty standard kebab house fare, although generous nonetheless.

Jumeira Road
Nr HSBC
Jumeira
Map 7 C1

Reem Al Bawadi
04 394 7444 | aymanshj@eim.ae

The interior of this popular venue is traditionally decorated, with three majlis areas near the entrance where you can enjoy shisha and coffee before or after your meal. The menu features all the usual Arabic fare plus some speciality dishes not found in many other restaurants around Dubai. The restaurant doesn't serve alcohol, but is always busy because of its reputation for good food and great shisha. A definite cultural experience, it's a perfect spot for newcomers or visitors to grab a slice of real Arabia.

Chinese
Other options **Far Eastern** p.544

Radisson SAS Hotel
Dubai Deira Creek
Deira
Map 9 C3

The China Club ▶ p.37
04 205 7333 | www.interconti.com

Nestled in a hidden corner, you may have to search for The China Club, but once you find it you'll be greeted with a chic space with subtle touches of Chinese authenticity. The extensive menu is a mix of recognisable favourites and new creations like the sea scallop dim sum. The knowledgeable staff can steer you through the choices but the peking duck, which the waiter hand carves at the table, is recommended. Lunchtimes boast a Dhs.95 tasting menu, while the Friday brunch for Dhs.140 (excluding alcohol) is one of the best value and delicious deals in Dubai.

Al Maktoum Rd
Nr Clock Tower R/A
Deira
Map 11 C2

China Sea
04 295 9816

China Sea is a hidden gem, offering authentic Chinese food at reasonable prices. One side of the restaurant is a display area of fish and crabs in tanks and at the back the workings of the kitchen are visible behind large glass windows. Even the noodles are prepared in full view; chefs start with a block of dough, and with skilled stretching and folding, quickly produce a pile of fresh fine noodles. Private rooms for karaoke are also available for hire.

Deira City Centre
Deira
Map 11 C3

China Times

04 295 2515 | *www.binhendi.com*

China isn't too far away with this Chinese eatery, located in the hustle and bustle of Deira City Centre. Chinese music, water statues and a striking collaboration of red and black, contrasted with the traditional white and blue vases, induce a peaceful ambience. A tempting sushi bar accounts for only a quarter of the enticing menu, which packs an assortment of dim sum, stir-frys, and noodles. Affordable prices, kind staff and the 'special of the day' will lure you back for a wholesome lunch or dinner. Also located at Jumeirah Plaza (04 344 2930).

Uptown Mirdif Mall
Mirdif
Map 15 B2

Da Shi Dai

04 288 8314 | *www.da-shi-dai.ae*

An oriental fusion of contemporary interior design and traditional Chinese cuisine inspires a tranquil dining experience. Neutral shades, combined with warm lighting and classical music, are complemented with fresh dishes prepared by Chinese master chefs. Delicately arranged dishes like crystal prawns and kung po chicken introduce the 'lighter side of Chinese dining', with a selection for vegetarians too. Alfresco dining, reasonable prices and a fast friendly service guarantee a plan brewing for a return visit. There is another branch at Jumeirah Beach Residence (04 426 4636).

Ramada Hotel
Bur Dubai
Map 8 F3

Dynasty

04 351 9999 | *www.ramadadubai.com*

Dynasty serves good but not dazzling Chinese cuisine. Szechuan, Cantonese and Peking dishes, with their characteristic degrees of spice, allow diners with diverse tastes to enjoy variations on a cuisine. A choice of four set menus enables the novice to experiment without committing to the comprehensive (but not overwhelming) a la carte menu. Ultimately, like many hotel Chinese restaurants, the superior environment does not necessarily guarantee food or service of a very high standard.

The Address
Downtown Burj
Dubai
Downtown Burj Dubai
Map 7 D4

Hukama

04 436 8888 | *www.theaddress.com*

More fine dining Chinese than comforting carb-fest, this sophisticated offering from The Address will wow with views and its imaginative take on traditional cuisine. If the weather (and mosquitoes) allow, book a table on the terrace, where you'll be confronted by Burj Dubai in all its dizzying glory. The menu consists of the usual and the unexpected (such as wontons on soy infused crushed ice) but the staff can make excellent recommendations. The vegetable rice might sound ordinary but with delicate pieces of tempura it's an ideal accompaniment. Hukama may be on the pricey side, but for formal, modern dining with vistas to die for it's worth it.

Hukama

Nr Lamcy Plaza
Oud Metha
Map 10 D2

Lan Kwai Fong

04 335 3680

If you judge a good Chinese restaurant by the number of Chinese inside, then Lan Kwai Fong is worth exploring. Located between Lamcy

Plaza and the Mövenpick Hotel, the restaurant's exhaustive menu includes a vast array of dim sum, clay pot, seafood, meat, duck and noodle dishes. The interior is a little dated, yet typical of any local suburban Chinese restaurant. Lan Kwai Fong is an unpretentious, inexpensive Chinese restaurant suitable for informal dining occasions.

Shangri-La Hotel
Trade Centre 1
Map 7 E3

Shang Palace
04 405 2703 | *www.shangri-la.com*

Choose to people-watch from the balcony overlooking the Shangri-La's bustling entrance, or take a quieter position inside the circular dining room. The food is delicious and the attentive and knowledgeable staff are available to guide newcomers through the numerous options. Familiar dishes are well prepared, and set menus are available. With shark fin soup, live seafood, dim sum and then some, this is certainly a place for something different. A well-stocked bar also makes this a suitable venue in which to start an evening, or round one off.

Festival Centre
Dubai Festival City
Map 13 D2

Steam Sum Dim Sum
04 232 9190 | *www.festivalcentre.com*

Vibrant fuchsia overtones, plush cushions and flickering candlelight will make you think you've entered a trendy bar – minus the bar. You'll be seated promptly and have your tastebuds refreshed by an impressive selection of Asian-inspired mocktails and teas. Once cocooned in your private lounge you may have to flip a coin to choose from over twenty varieties of fried and steamed dim sum which arrive stacked in labelled bamboo steamers, or from the tasty noodles and salads. A good choice for fun, no fuss dining.

Mina A'Salam
Umm Suqeim
Map 6 A1

Zheng He's
04 366 6730 | *www.madinatjumeirah.com*

Zheng He's superb take on Chinese delicacies, together with its exquisite waterside spot, ensure Dubai's more affluent dwellers enjoy a taste of the orient. Exciting combinations used in dim sum and mini starters are complemented well with tangy dips and sauces. Traditional dishes with a twist are too good to pass up, while marinated fish and stir-fried meat are taken to new heights and the duck is arguably the best in town. The wine list is as thick as it is pricey, but in terms of culinary experience you certainly get what you pay for.

Dinner Cruises
Other options **Boat Tours & Charters** p.284, **Dhow Charters** p.290, **Creek Tours** p.249

Radisson SAS Hotel
Dubai Deira Creek
Deira
Map 9 C3

Al Mansour Dhow  ▶ p.37
04 222 7171 | *www.radissonsas.com*

This two-hour trip features dinner aboard a traditional dhow operated by the Radisson SAS, ensuring the standard of food and service is excellent. Setting sail at 20:30 daily the relaxing cruise takes in the iconic sites along the Dubai Creek amid background music of the live oud player. Reasonably priced at Dhs.185 per adult, the cruise includes an extensive traditional buffet, with optional soft drinks and a reasonably priced wine selection. Shisha pipes are available on the outdoor upper deck, and can add to the atmosphere of watching both sides of the creek from a new vantage point.

Nr British Embassy
Bur Dubai
Map 9 B3

Bateaux Dubai ▶ p.541
04 399 4994 | *www.bateauxdubai.com*

From the moment you're welcomed aboard the sleek, glass-topped Bateaux Dubai, you become aware this is no ordinary creek cruise. The intimately lit interior reveals cosy tables sporting crisp white table linen and silver cutlery, and a baby grand piano. No

matter where you sit, the full-length windows afford splendid views of the city beyond, and between courses you are encouraged to go out on deck and enjoy the open air. Diners choose three courses from the small, but varied international menu, and the quality of the food (and drink) lives up to the five-star surroundings. A top pick for a romantic dinner or tourist treat. Departure is prompt so don't get left behind.

Baital Khair Bld ◀
Nr NMC Hospital
Al Qusais
Map 12 C4

Creek Cruises

04 393 9860 | *www.creekcruises.com*

Whether you're the trendiest of talent spotters, the laziest of couch potatoes or the biggest of bar crawlers, you can't live in Dubai and not go on a dinner cruise. You might think it cheesy, or it should be reserved for tourists in white socks but the fact is the Dubai Creek is this city's most natural landmark. Sip your drink, fill up at the standard 'authentic' Arabian buffet, enjoy the live music and belly dancer, be mesmerised by the creekside sights and just go with the flow.

Opp Dubai ◀
Municipality HQ
Deira
Map 9 C4

Creekside Leisure

04 336 8407 | *www.tour-dubai.com*

This floating majlis is an authentic dhow with a delightful upper deck, where guests can recline on traditional Arabic-cushioned seating and relax with a drink, watching the world drift by. Downstairs in an air-conditioned, glass-sided cabin, a good international buffet (with an Arabic slant) is served halfway through the two-hour cruise. The route takes passengers to the mouth of the creek at Shindagha, before turning around and cruising to the Maktoum Bridge then back to its original mooring by the Twin Towers in Deira.

Nr British Embassy ◀
Bur Dubai
Map 9 B3

Danat Dubai Cruises

04 351 1117 | *info@ddcgroup.ae*

After boarding the luxury Danat vessel you head down the creek towards Shindagha with drink in hand (try to bag one of the sofas on the front deck for the best view). Whenever you feel hungry you can go back inside for the buffet – admittedly not the most spectacular range of dishes, but the food is secondary to the experience here. Cheerful staff do a great job of seeing to everyone's needs, which can be a tall order when the boat is full. Apart from their dinner cruise, which lasts for two and a half hours, Danat also offers a daily sundowner cruise.

Nr Nasr Cinema ◀
Oud Metha
Map 10 E2

Tour Dubai ▶ p.543

04 336 8409 | *www.tour-dubai.com*

Explore the creek during the day alongside the busy abras or after the sun goes down on a traditional dhow. For larger groups, of up to 40 people, a lounge bar allows relaxed conviviality. Majlis seating, regular dining and cocktail receptions are on offer, while bigger boats and buffet meals are also available. Alternatively, for a romantic evening, charter a personal dhow, complete with your own butler, roses for your partner, champagne, five-star dining and a limousine to pick you up and drop you off home.

European

Other options **German** p.548, **Spanish** p.591, **Russian** p.586, **Portuguese** p.586, **Pizzerias** p.586, **Mediterranean** p.581, **Italian** p.568, **French** p.547

The Monarch Dubai ◀
Trade Centre 2
Map 8 A4

Empire

04 501 8888 | *www.themonarchdubai.com*

With its refreshing attention to detail, the newly opened Empire is sure to please those looking for subtle elegance when dining. Seating for about 40 ensures that diners are

TOUR *Dubai*

Dubai's First
Arabian Dhow Cruises

Floating Functions - A unique experience for every event.

- Sail on the creek with Dubai's premier Dhow cruise operator
- Exclusive Dhow charters - Fully licenced to serve beverages
- Dhow capacities ranging from 30 to 280 guests
- Choice of catering options - Arabic entertainment options
- Fitted with Govt. approved safety equipment

DAILY DINNER CRUISES
- 2 Hours Cruising - 5 Star Buffet Dinner
- Incl. Mineral water / Soft Drinks
Transfers can be arranged on request

GUIDED CREEK TOURS
Four times daily : 11.30, 13.30, 15.30, 17.30
Pre-recorded commentary in English
Incl. Mineral water or soft drink

Also available: Safaris & Sightseeing Tours

Tel: 04 3368407 / 9 Fax 04 3368411
Email:admin@tour-dubai.com Web:www.tour-dubai.com

well attended, with discrete visits from the chef and sommelier to offer any assistance with the menu, which changes daily. The carefully selected wine list emphasises the importance of selection over volume. The chic atmosphere, attentive service and exquisite food ensure that Empire will not remain a secret for long.

Hilton Dubai Creek
Deira
Map 11 C1

Glasshouse Brasserie

04 227 1111 | www.hilton.com

Managed by the same team behind Gordon Ramsay's Verre, Glasshouse is a chic brasserie serving up modern Mediterranean cuisine at very reasonable prices. The interior is stylish yet surprisingly casual, with glass walls, dark woods, tasteful colours and Mondrian-style paintings creating a sophisticated atmosphere. The excellent staff serve up all dishes from the superb menu attractively presented, with a blend of tastes that amaze for the price. And if any more encouragement was needed, the incredible value continues on Monday and Wednesday nights with house wine and spirits for Dhs.10 a glass all night, if you order two courses, as well as business lunches and Friday brunch.

Park Hyatt Dubai
Deira
Map 11 B4

Traiteur

04 602 1234 | www.dubai.park.hyatt.com

After a delightful aperitif in the lofty bar, descend into this elegant restaurant, with its modern decor and gleaming white table settings. If weather permits opt for the cosy terrace, overlooking the impressive marina and creek beyond. Traiteur was designed with exquisite taste, offering simple yet excellently presented dishes, such as shellfish on ice, seafood platter, Angus beef, oysters and all things decadent. The accompanying wine list is equally opulent and the deserts are as sweet as they sound. Despite a pay-day bill, this restaurant is worth waiting all month for.

Far Eastern

Other options **Filipino** p.546, **Chinese** p.538, **Japanese** p.576, **Vietnamese** p.598, **Thai** p.595, **Singaporean** p.591, **Polynesian** p.586, **Korean** p.580

Raffles Dubai
Umm Hurair
Map 10 D4

Asiana Restaurant

04 314 9888 | www.dubai.raffles.com

Noble House may have the city's culinary tongues wagging, but its less assuming, same-floor neighbour, Asiana, is possibly the more accessible of the two. Enjoy a seriously delicious feast of Asian inspired dishes created with that special Raffles touch (the pad thai is remarkable), and savour the beautiful views over the city. In cooler

Traiteur

Glasshouse

months you can dine out on the balcony; while you'll miss the breathtaking decor of the interior, you'll be able to make the most of the view. For a classy Asian lunch or dinner, with excellent service, in a high-end restaurant but with non-exorbitant prices, Asiana ticks all the right boxes.

JW Marriott Hotel
Deira
Map 11 E1

Bamboo Lagoon

04 607 7977 | www.marriottdiningatjw.ae

The Bamboo Lagoon's staggering range of exquisite fusion cuisine demands a repeat visit. There's sushi, tempura, teriyaki, curries, steaks, stir-fries, grills, seafood, rice and noodle dishes galore. The bottomless buffet with numerous stalls offers diverse dishes with an abundance of bamboo, straw, water features, dainty bridges and other oriental trappings dominating the decor. At 21:00 a band takes to the stage and grass-skirted singers serenade diners with low key renditions of tropical Polynesian tunes and entertaining cover versions.

Jumeirah
Beach Hotel
Umm Suqeim
Map 6 B1

Beachcombers

04 406 8999 | www.jumeirahbeachhotel.com

Located right on the beach with fantastic views of the Burj Al Arab, this breezy seaside shack hosts atmospheric far eastern buffets every night. There are live cooking stations for stir-fries and noodles, and overall there is a huge range of delicious Oriental cuisine – the peking duck, curry hotpots and satay are highly recommended. Although the food is excellent, and the staff are friendly and skilled, what you will remember most about Beachcombers is the idyllic location.

One&Only
Royal Mirage
Al Sufouh
Map 5 C1

Eauzone

04 399 9999 | www.oneandonlyroyalmirage.com

For a truly romantic evening, dine outside at Eauzone, underneath softly lit canopies and beside a network of waterways. The tasty Thai and Japanese fusion menu comes in moderately sized portions – between each course opt for one of the unusual sorbets, such as chili and raspberry, or the selection of sake. The well-versed staff are on hand to explain the menu. Large groups should try the teppanyaki station which starts from Dhs.225 per person for up to six people.

Habtoor Grand
Resort & Spa
Dubai Marina
Map 5 B1

Munchi

04 399 5000 | www.habtoorhotels.com

Munchi offers great Thai food and sushi in a relaxed environment. The bamboo hut-style restaurant is situated in the green gardens of the hotel, and features an attractive patio dining area next to a small babbling brook. Inside the decor is smart, all browns and creams, with an elegant bar area upstairs. The starter sharing platter, for Dhs.100, is a great way to get the juices flowing. There's live cooking for the showpiece dishes, and the adept staff helpfully explain how to match sauces with the appropriate dish.

Boulevard at
Emirates Towers
Trade Centre 2
Map 7 F3

The Noodle House

04 319 8088 | www.jumeirahemiratestowers.com

The Noodle House is a refreshingly relaxed affair. Just turn up and wait for the first available spot at one of the long communal tables. You order by ticking your desired dishes on the notepads (after some advice from the clued-up staff, if required). The mouthwatering food is well priced, with big portions of soups, noodles and stir-fries served up in record speed. The modern decor, open kitchen and zingy cocktails add to the vibrant atmosphere. Other branches are located in the Souk Madinat Jumeirah (04 366 6730), which has the added bonus of a terrace for alfresco eating, and Deira City Centre (04 294 0085).

Clubhouse Al Nafura
Shoreline Apartments
Palm Jumeirah
Map 2 A3

Veda Pavilion

04 361 8845 | www.emiratesleisureretail.com

Chic yet comfortable, this is a great place to head after a day on the beach. The substantial drinks list and the far eastern inspired menu are suited to casual lunches, dinners with groups of friends, or just a lazy beer on the poolside terrace. From here you can experience the much sought-after views of the Burj Al Arab and the Arabian Gulf for a snip of the price of owning a place on The Palm. Don't expect the most authentic flavours, but the portions are generous and a Thai green curry with rice and jasmine tea will set you back only Dhs.50.

Jebel Ali Golf
Resort & Spa
Jebel Ali
Map 3 A1

White Orchid ▶ p.533

04 804 8604 | www.jebelali-international.com

Some of the best eastern flavours in Dubai are served up at this contemporary Asian restaurant. The menu focuses on predominantly Thai and Japanese dishes, and you can mix and match between great sushi platters and hot green curries, or try something from the teppanyaki table. The decor is styled on a Thai bamboo hut, there's a spacious outdoor terrace, and service is impeccable. The location of the hotel, some 20 minutes from Dubai Marina, is the only downside, but if delicious Asian is your thing it's definitely worth the trip.

Grand Hyatt Dubai
Umm Hurair
Map 13 C1

Wox

04 317 1234 | www.dubai.grand.hyatt.com

Wox takes the concept of noodle houses to the next level. Here you can choose to sit around the noodle bar or at one of the individual tables – either way you will get to enjoy the sights, sounds and smells of live cooking. Just place your order from the simple (but comprehensive) menu and sit back while your meal is prepared in a flurry of sizzling woks and steaming pots. All your favourite Asian noodle and rice dishes are there, bracketed nicely by some interesting appetisers and desserts. The food prices are surprisingly reasonable, but the alcoholic beverages will definitely take their toll on your final bill.

Radisson SAS Hotel
Dubai Deira Creek
Deira
Map 9 C3

Yum! ▶ p.37

04 222 7171 | www.radissonsas.com

An open kitchen, airy setting and fragrant aroma welcome you to Yum! at the Radisson in Deira. Catering to an especially busy lunch crowd, the focus is on fresh, high quality Asian food cooked swiftly. Delicious and good-sized dishes are offered from Thailand, Malaysia and other regions, with healthy options highlighted on the menu for the body conscious. Surprisingly affordable dishes offer proof that it is still possible to get tasty, fresh, healthy food at reasonable prices in a clean, licensed restaurant.

Filipino

Other options **Far Eastern** p.544

Karama Shopping
Complex
Karama
Map 10 E1

Tagpuan

04 337 3959 | www.bridgewaygroup.com

Tagpuan (meaning meeting place in Tagalog) brings traditional Filipino fare to Dubai. The tiny tables inside the small restaurant can fill up pretty quickly, but the outside area on the terrace offers more space, weather permitting. The menu offers a range of simple but tasty versions of Filipino home favourites including adobong pusit (squid), tapa (fried marinated beef), fried tilapia (fish) or pinakbet (mixed vegetables including bitter gourd). Prices are good value, especially the daily combo of two dishes with rice for Dhs.15.

Restaurants

Fish & Chips

You may not find a 'chippy' on every street corner in Dubai, but if you're really hankering for some good old fish and chips there are a few choices at your disposal. The Fish & Chips Room (04 427 0443) in Jumeirah Beach Residences is a newcomer on the fish and chips scene, and already has a legion of loyal fans, plus they stay open until the wee hours of the morning. Fish Supper,

La Maison d'Hôtes

the renowned chippy in Bin Sougat Mall in Rashidiya, has closed down but will reopen soon in the Arabian Plaza mall on the Al Khawaneej Road (so breathe a sigh of relief, Mirdif dwellers). The Irish Village (p.624), Barasti Bar (p.609), The Boardwalk (p.558) and the Dhow & Anchor (p.622) also deserve a special mention for the quality of their fish and chips.

French

Le Meridien Dubai
Garhoud
Map 13 E1

Café Chic

04 282 4040 | *www.lemeridien-dubai.com*
To call this outstanding gem of a restaurant a cafe does it a disservice. Dishes such as pressed duck liver coated with pistachio, or a lamb rack adorned with parmesan polenta, black olive and citrus essence are hardly the fodder of your average cafe, and neither is the faultless service, the parade of beautifully presented amuses bouches, or the outstanding dessert selection. Nudging upwards of Dhs.600 for dinner for two with wine represents excellent value for money when you consider the authentic and outstanding food you'll have delighted over.

Villa 18
Street 83B
Nr Al Rabee
Kindergarten
Jumeira
Map 7 D1

La Maison d'Hotes

04 344 1838 | *www.lamaisondhotesdubai.com*
La Maison d'Hôtes' decor is Middle East meets Morocco, with its covered terrace with chunky wood furniture and cushioned benches, but in taste it's refreshingly Français. Starters include fresh salads, homemade soups, delectable foie gras, beef carpaccio and goats' cheese numbers, while mains include succulent duck, beef, fish, and pasta. Vegetarians be warned – this is French territory, and the menu is more meaty than leafy. Open for lunch from 12:30 to 15:00 and dinner from 20:30, it's reasonably priced gourmet food, which is all very French and all very good, especially the desserts.

Emirates Golf Club
Emirates Hills
Map 5 C2

Le Classique

04 380 2222 | *www.dubaigolf.com*
Le Classique, the dining equivalent of championship golf at Emirates Golf Club, asks gentlemen to dress in coat and tie. Beginning with beverages in the handsome lounge, well-dressed patrons move into the lavish dining room set comfortably under a silk tented ceiling featuring a large chandelier. Velvet panels and Roman shades adorn vast windows adding to an environment reminiscent of Hollywood's finest country-club sets. A talented pianist sings old standards and honours requests. In that romantic setting the professional staff serve from a creative and delicious menu assembled by Le Classique's veteran chef.

Atlantis The Palm
Palm Jumeirah
Map 2 A3

Rostang – The French Brasserie ▶ p.524
04 426 2626 | www.atlantisthepalm.com

Step through the doors and past the traditional bakery at this spacious French brasserie and you'll quickly forget that you're in the basement of the massive Atlantis hotel. Wood trim, leather bench seating and dim lighting perfectly mimics the decor of a French bistro from the 1930s. The food is just as reminiscent. Two-star Michelin chef Michel Rostang's menu is full of comforting dishes that shy away from experimentation and concentrate on preparation and presentation. Fish and seafood play heavily on the menu but there's enough selection to please anyone.

> **Night Of Romance** i
>
> Dubai is overflowing with excellent eateries and beautiful bars. If you are looking for a truly romantic experience check out the following intimate spots perfect for candlelit liaisons: Tagine (p.584), Pierchic (p.589), Vu's (p.583), Medzo (p.582), Teatro (p.568) and La Baie (p.588).

Jebel Ali Golf
Resort & Spa
Jebel Ali
Map 3 A1

Signatures ▶ p.533
04 804 8604 | www.jebelali-international.com

This restaurant has something for everyone in terms of choice. Although a bit on the expensive side, the experience is well worth that extra dirham or two. The atmosphere is sophisticated both inside and out and, whether the weather permits alfresco dining or not, you'll feel like you are dining under the stars. The staff are very knowledgeable about all aspects of the comprehensive menu and can help the less-experienced guests with the most delicious of choices. An elegant restaurant with a well selected wine list makes this worthy of special occasion status.

Century Village
Garhoud
Map 13 E1

St Tropez ▶ p.549
04 286 9029 | www.centuryvillage.ae

This bistro at the Century Village offers a truly authentic French meal. The sight of frog's legs and snails on the menu gives you a good idea of what to expect. The food is delicious, simple and fresh, with a home-cooked feel. The main courses are dominated by hearty meat dishes with an impressive selection of steaks, but save room for a dessert as the creme brulee is a treat. The interior of the restaurant, with walls oddly filled with photos of celebrities, is a bit cramped, so it's best to opt for the terrace if weather permits.

Hilton Dubai Creek
Deira
Map 11 C1

Verre
04 227 1111 | www.hilton.com

Gordon Ramsay's reputation precedes him, and this is definitely the case at Verre, his first foray outside the UK. You enter through sliding glass doors, but your first impressions of the decor – understated dark wood furniture and simple white table linen – may leave you wondering what all the fuss is about. However, Ramsay is a chef, not an interior designer, and at Verre it's all about the food. The exciting and enticing menu is not huge, but contains some stunning culinary creations (although vegetarians are advised to steer clear). Faultless service, the delightful canapes and between-course palate cleansers make this a truly memorable dining experience, albeit an expensive one.

German

Jumeira Rotana
Satwa
Map 8 A2

Brauhaus
04 345 5888 | www.rotana.com

This is a perennial favourite among the German expat community and for those seeking authentic Bavarian food in a comfortable, informal setting. Brauhaus' semi-

THE AVIATION CLUB

CENTURY VILLAGE

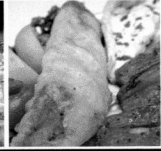

| INDIAN | LOUNGE | FISH & CHIPS | FRENCH STEAK HOUSE | CHINESE | PERSIAN |

THIS CHARMING RESTAURANT COMPLEX WITHIN THE GROUNDS OF
THE AVIATION CLUB IS THE PERFECT VENUE FOR DINING AND ENTERTAINMENT.
BE IT A BUSINESS LUNCH, AN INTIMATE DINNER OR TO MEET WITH FRIENDS,
CENTURY VILLAGE HAS IT ALL.
THE TWELVE LICENSED OUTLETS OFFER SUPERB CUISINE
FROM AROUND THE WORLD IN AUTHENTIC SETTINGS.

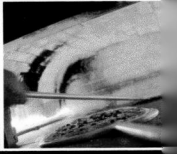

| LEBANESE | PORTUGUESE | JAPANESE | CAFÉ | ITALIAN | OVEN BAKED SPECIALTIES |

THE WORLD ON YOUR PLATE...

WWW.CENTURYVILLAGE.AE

The Aviation Club, P.O. Box: 55400, Dubai, U.A.E. Tel. 04 282 4122 Fax. 04 282 4751 www.aviationclub.ae

private wood-panelled booths are the most sought after tables, which will groan with all manner of schnitzels, plump bratwursts and eye-watering sauerkraut. This is substantial fare, a million miles away from nouvelle cuisine, but is fresh, well cooked and the result is a warming hearty glow. A range of good imported German beers complements the effect.

Der Keller

Jumeirah Beach Hotel
Umm Suqeim
Map 6 B1

04 406 8999 | *www.jumeirahbeachhotel.com*
From pretzels to schnitzels, frankfurters to fondue, the deservedly popular Der Keller delivers immense portions of the finest German cuisine and draft beverages in a cosy pseudo-subterranean setting with a view of the Burj. Try to resist devouring the fresh bread that forms the centrepiece of your table, as the starters are as big as mains and the mains bigger than Austria. Plus, you wouldn't want to miss the desserts, which taste as delicious as they look.

Hofbräuhaus

JW Marriott Hotel
Deira
Map 11 E1

04 607 7977 | *www.marriottdiningatjw.ae*
Sometimes the copy is better than the original and that could be the case with the food and experience at JW Marriott's Hofbräuhaus – it may even be better than you'd get in Munich. From the sauerkraut to the white sausage with sweet mustard and the strudel, everything is top notch. Add in the beer hall decor, Bavarian garb for the staff and traditional accordion music, and you have a recipe for a fun night out. Several German beers are on tap, along with a full selection of wines and spirits.

Indian

Other options **Sri Lankan** p.592, **Pakistani** p.584

Aangan

Dhow Palace Hotel
Bur Dubai
Map 8 E3

04 359 9992 | *www.dhowpalacehoteldubai.com*
Housed in the Dhow Palace, Aangan is a welcome addition to Dubai's growing Indian restaurant roster. Traditionally decorated in rich wood with many elaborate ornaments nailed to the walls, the atmosphere and live in-house music combine to boast the authentic quality of the food. Savour their range of biryanis, special curries and kebabs from their charcoal-smoked clay oven, as well as some of the most divine Indian desserts outside Delhi.

> ### Bargain Bhajis
>
> With a large population from the Indian subcontinent, Dubai is home to a host of good independent Indian eateries. The areas around Karama Shopping Complex and along Trade Centre Road are good starting places for some seriously cheap chow. Don't be put off by the streetside locations – give them a try and you just might stumble upon some of the city's best fare.

Antique Bazaar

Four Points by Sheraton Bur Dubai
Bur Dubai
Map 8 F3

04 397 7444 | *www.starwoodhotels.com*
The impressively decorative, and aptly named, Antique Bazaar offers an exhaustive menu of curried delights to ever-present musical accompaniment. The background music progressively builds to foreground music, as the perfectly languid sitar player is joined by a vivacious band fronted by gyrating singers. When in full swing, the stage show is a memorable cultural experience, but does detract from the great food, which is as pleasing and exotic as the decor and dancing. Arrive early for conversation, late to party.

Aryaas

Kuwait St
Karama
Map 10 E1

04 335 5776
Unassuming Aryaas is at the quieter end of Kuwait Street. With only an M&M machine and a few pictures to disrupt the prison-like austerity of the clean canteen tables,

Restaurants

Spice Island

Asiana Restaurant

Jebel Ali Golf Resort & Spa

St Tropez

Sho Cho

Left Bank at Souk al Bahar

it aims to impress with super cheap 100% vegetarian food, rather than the decor. Fortunately, the plan works, and this chain of restaurants has been serving up no-frills Indian fare since 1959. The house speciality is thali: small pots of different flavours into which you dip as much naan bread or rice as you can physically handle. For around Dhs.10 it will provide enough food to leave you comatose for the afternoon with a satiated grin that says it all.

Wafi City
Umm Hurair
Map 11 E4

Asha's

04 324 4100 | www.waficity.com

Indian superstar Asha Bhosle has put a lot of love into this beautiful restaurant. Decked out in Indian summer reds, yellows and oranges, the atmosphere is enhanced by beaded curtains, low-level lighting, intimate booths and a majestic terrace. Start in the bar and get your tastebuds tingling with one of the signature cocktails; then enjoy the offerings of the eclectic menu which includes Indian classics, Asha's very own signature dishes inspired by her travels, and some fusion choices concocted by the resident chef. Excellent service and consistent quality make Asha's one of Dubai's must-dos.

Sheraton Hotel
& Towers
Deira
Map 9 B4

Ashiana

04 207 1733 | www.sheraton.com

Enter to an enchanting aroma of masala-infused Indian cuisine and the soothing beat of the tabla. A dimly lit cosy setting sets the tone for a menu packed with fairly pricey Indian specialities for vegetarians, meat-lovers, seafood fiends and all who desire spice. The refined beverage menu and wine list are a great accompaniment with the high-quality tandoor-cooked meals. Helpful staff and poppadoms you can't get enough of will lighten up any lunch (13:00 to 15:00) or dinner (19:30 to 23:30). A live band croons from 20:30 everyday, so don't forget to request a song.

Opp Ramada
Continental Hotel
Hor Al Anz
Map 12 A3

Foodlands

04 268 3311

It might be one of the numerous cheap and cheerful independent restaurants in town, but Foodlands deserves a special mention thanks to the excellent quality of its awesome array of Indian, Persian and Arabic dishes. You can see the mastery in action through the large window between the kitchen and the restaurant, which serves to get your mouth suitably watering before your fresh, sizzling meal (kebabs, naans and tasty vegetarian dishes) is presented before you.

Nr Meena Plaza Hotel
Bur Dubai
Map 8 E3

Gazebo

04 359 8555

Indian food at its very best, Gazebo impresses with authentic dishes packed with flavour. The elegantly clad staff are genuinely friendly and the service is top notch. Choosing from the vast menu is a challenge, but it has a fantastic selection of charcoal grilled specialities like the chunky chicken kebabs and marinated leg of lamb, masses of mouth-watering curries and stacks of biryanis. The salads and side dishes are all bursting with freshness, the breads tasty and the lassis and fresh fruit kulfis deliciously sweet accompaniments. All in all it's a great value Indian experience.

Taj Palace Hotel
Deira
Map 11 C1

Handi

04 223 2222 | www.tajpalacehotel.co.ae

You can get a mean curry at Handi – and no ordinary curry at that. The elaborate silver thali dish offers four curries and kebabs for Dhs.90, including biryani, salad, dessert and lassis. The lamb curry with cashew and cardamom, or the chicken with tomato and fenugreek are so savoury you're bound to order more. For biryani lovers there is a special treat – individual copper pots are sealed to keep the flavour in, and when the seal is broken the aroma will transport you to Rajasthan. The decor is rich and elegant with private dining rooms available and live Indian music.

Al Hudda Building
Nr Al Tayer Motors
Garhoud
Map 13 C1

India Palace
04 286 9600 | sfcdxb@eim.ae

Stepping through the elaborately carved wooden doors you'll be transported back to the time of the Moghul Dynasty. Low lighting, traditional sitar music and ornate wooden panelling create a tranquil respite, while upstairs there are private booths for a more intimate dining experience. A mouth-watering selection of starters complements a wide range of sturdy curries, fragrant rice dishes and vegetable accompaniments while a delectable grill selection will appeal to hungry carnivores. After dinner spend your many left over dirhams on handmade bangles and necklaces at the craft stall.

Grand Hyatt Dubai
Umm Hurair
Map 13 C1

iZ
04 317 1234 | www.dubai.grand.hyatt.com

iZ's dark, contemporary interior might be one of the most beautifully designed spaces in Dubai. What would otherwise be a massive room is broken up by hardwood screens, metal sculptures and private rooms. The perfectly prepared Indian dishes are presented in a manner similar to tapas, with tandoori items served by the piece, so you'll need to order at least two per person. The curries are a bit larger, but don't expect heaped bowls of gravy. The emphasis is on perfect flavour combinations and the kitchen does a great job of creating a gourmet Indian cuisine that doesn't veer too far from tradition.

Building One
Burj Residences
Downtown Burj Dubai
Map 7 D3

Jaipur
04 422 6767 | www.theroyalorchid.com

While the extravagant tableware harkens back to the royalty of the maharajas, the friendly service sets a relaxing atmosphere to enjoy delicious food. Samosas, tandooris and other familiar dishes are available alongside lesser-known specialities from Rajasthan and northern India. A busy delivery system for the Burj Residences means that the ingredients are always fresh, even when the restaurant itself has space during the week. A terrace is available for alfresco dining, which offers great views of the mighty Burj Dubai.

Al Nasr Leisureland
Oud Metha
Map 10 E2

Khazana
04 336 0061 | cyclonic@emirates.net.ae

Indian celebrity chef Sanjeev Kapoor's spacious, popular eatery specialises in cuisine from the north of his home country. All dishes are well prepared and served in big portions, but the prawn curry and chicken tikka are famous. Other delicacies include grilled tandoori seafood, a variety of rice dishes and some hearty gravy-based dishes with meat and fish, as well as Anglo-Indian novelties like 'British Raj Railroad Curry'. With such excellent food and its relaxing ambience, it's no surprise that Khazana is so popular.

Bab Al Shams
Desert Resort & Spa
Map 1 E2

Masala
04 809 6100 | www.jumeirahbabalshams.com

Set amid the enchanting courtyards of Bab Al Shams Resort (p.46), Masala serves up top Indian food in beautiful surroundings. Tables are arranged in alcoves around the central kitchen from where the slapping of naans accompany the sounds of tabla and sitar that drift through the corridors. Outside, you can dine gazing up at the peaceful night sky. The menu offers tasty versions of all you might expect from the tandoor, curries and rice dishes, as well as some more unusual finds. Packed at the weekends, the traffic-free drive means it can take less time to get to than some places in central Dubai. To do it properly, arrive late afternoon to walk around the resort, enjoy the sunset with a sundowner in hand at the Al Sarab Lounge, then linger over a superb, relaxed dinner – you'll go home feeling like you've actually been on holiday.

One&Only
Royal Mirage
Al Sufouh
Map 5 C1

Nina

04 399 9999 | www.oneandonlyroyalmirage.com

Even if Indian food isn't your favourite you'd be a fool to miss Nina. You're immediately struck upon entering by its high ceilings, luscious red and orange Bollywood decor and soothing deep beats, it is a great place for a candlelit dinner for two. Not overwhelming, the menu is complemented by a good wine list and the food is exquisite with all the usual suspects, from the restaurant's signature dish, butter chicken, to frogs legs and Rambutan, which are brought carefully to your table by the rather reserved waiters. This won't be the cheapest curry you've had and not that you would ever need a reason to visit the lovely Royal Mirage Hotel, but if you did this is definitely it.

Marina Walk
Dubai Marina
Map 5 B2

The Rupee Room

04 390 5755 | www.therupeeroom.com

Occupying a prime spot along the popular Marina Walk, The Rupee Room offers a wide selection of north Indian dishes in relaxed surroundings. The indoor dining area spills out on to the covered walkway, and a wooden staircase leads to the mezzanine level. The glass-fronted kitchen allows you to keep an eye on the action between courses which often includes a great little trio of live musicians. Weather permitting, the best tables are those outside, providing marina views and the chance to watch the world go by.

Saleh Bin Lahej Bld
Oud Metha
Map 10 D2

Sai Dham

04 336 6552 | www.sai-dham.com

Pushing open the heavy wooden doors at Sai Dham reveals a surprising gem of a restaurant. With gold textured walls, stylish wooden furniture, attractively clad and polite waiters, the tardis-like interior defies expectations from outside, and the food is definitely up there with the best in the independent hot bed of Oud Metha. Serving superb, concept vegetarian food that 'celebrates purity', they use no garlic or onion, and only gentle spices, so the fresh taste of all ingredients comes through, and the huge range on the menu has something for everyone; even non-vegetarians will really enjoy the food. A bargain for the level of food and experience.

Opp Karama Park
Karama
Map 10 E1

Saravana Bhavan

04 334 5252

Taking its name from the much-loved hotel Saravana Bhavan in Chennai, India, this unassuming restaurant in Karama is arguably the best of the area's south Indian restaurants. Squeezing in as many customers as possible over its two floors, Saravana prefers elbow-to-elbow dining on tables decorated only with a bottle of mineral water. The menu is long enough to keep demanding Indian expats interested but it's the thalis that draw big crowds – for around Dhs.12 you can get a plate packed with colour and flavours, dal and chapatti. Fine Indian food doesn't come much cheaper.

Al Murooj Rotana
Hotel & Suites
Trade Centre 2
Map 7 E3

Zaika

04 321 1111 | www.rotana.com

The atmosphere is intimate at this upmarket Indian restaurant, set in a characterful split-level rotunda building. Private booths occupy the upper level, Buddha statues and candles sit among the tables down the spiral stairs on the lower level, and eastern music fills the air. An interesting a la carte selection based on traditional Indian flavours is underpinned by some excellent set menus, where you can work your way through spicy starters, a soup course, a delicious array of main dishes and authentic Indian sweets. Service is attentive yet unhurried.

International

Dubai Creek Golf & Yacht Club
Deira
Map 11 C3

Academy
04 295 6000 | www.dubaigolf.com
Millions of people watch golf courses on TV screens. Surely it's much better to sit in the Academy snack bar and look through the surrounding glass at the beautiful Dubai Creek golf course? You'll be closer to the real thing and even closer to professional staff serving a wide assortment of international appetisers, sandwiches, salads, main courses, and beverages of all sorts. The cheerful colour scheme fits in well with the view of luscious green and happy golfers.

> ### High Class Pig Outs
> Buffet restaurants often get a bad press for offering cheap chow in even cheaper surroundings. In Dubai, however, buffets are more like ready-made a la carte meals, and should by no means be discounted. Even better, they are often a more affordable way of stuffing your face with first-class fodder. The following are a few of Dubai's best buffet restaurants: Al Dawaar (p.555), Al Muna (p.555), Cascades (p.558), The Market Café (p.563), The Market Place (p.563), and Meridien Village Terrace (p.564).

Hyatt Regency
Deira
Map 9 D1

Al Dawaar
04 317 2222 | www.dubai.regency.hyatt.com
If you think a revolving restaurant is more tack than taste, Al Dawaar may change your mind. There is nothing corny about this surprisingly sophisticated eatery, which features minimalist decor, immaculate white tablecloths and un-buffet-like buffet food. The buffet is ample rather than over the top, with dainty starters, a la carte-style main dishes and an unrivalled dessert table. As the restaurant turns slowly (one revolution takes an hour and 45 minutes), you can enjoy the changing views over Deira and out to sea.

Bab Al Shams Desert Resort & Spa
Map 1 E2

Al Forsan
04 809 6100 | www.jumeirahbabalshams.com
Al Forsan boasts impressive decor, with polished concrete floors, deep red walls, rich tapestries and chunky, dark wood furniture. You can fill your plate from the petite but delectable buffet featuring a good range of Arabic dishes as well as some more suitable for conservative tastes. The a la carte menu is similarly small but comprehensive, and features a great children's menu. It may take a while before Dubai's convenience-driven public cottons on to the idea of a 45 minute drive to Bab Al Shams for dinner, but the Al Forsan experience is well worth it.

Mina A'Salam
Umm Suqeim
Map 6 A1

Al Muna
04 366 6730 | www.madinatjumeirah.com
While the thought of yet another buffet restaurant may put you off your dinner, Al Muna has the best of both worlds. It offers a mouthwatering array of international cuisine with everything your stomach desires and more, as well as a 24 hour a la carte menu catering to those who want a more personal experience. The only problem with the latter is that you have to watch as other patrons chow down while you wait (for a little too long) for your delicate choices to arrive. This may be a buffet but like everything in the Madinat it comes in a nice posh package with elegant decor and an inviting terrace to match.

Après

Al Muntaha

Burj Al Arab
Umm Suqeim
Map 6 B1

04 301 7600
www.burj-al-arab.com

If you weren't at the top of the Burj Al Arab, with an unrivalled view of Dubai's coastline, you would be forgiven for thinking this restaurant's decor is a bit tacky considering the price tag attached to the menu. The menu is less surprising than the decor, with the usual suspects in a European fine-dining line-up. While the food is certainly good, the atmosphere akin to a private member's club and the view breathtaking, you have to wonder whether you're paying for the name over the door more than the dining experience served behind it.

Après ▶p.557

Mall of the Emirates
Al Barsha
Map 6 A3

04 341 2575 | www.emiratesleisureretail.com

To accompany its first indoor ski resort, Dubai now has its very own alpine ski lodge in the shape of Après. There's a large restaurant, a comfortable bar area, and the lodge lounge complete with a cosy fireplace and an unrivalled view of the slope. The varied menu offers wholesome fare including steaks, fondue and excellent pizzas – perfect for respite and replenishment after the snow or shops. During the day Après is popular with shoppers and families, but at night the vibe is more suitable to both chilling and partying. The wide-ranging cocktail list certainly helps you to do both.

Arboretum

Al Qasr Hotel
Umm Suqeim
Map 6 A2

04 366 8888 | www.madinatjumeirah.com

Tempting variety, excellent presentation, an impressive setting and delicious flavours come together to put Arboretum at the top of the all-you-can-eat list. After tackling the Asian, Middle Eastern and western salads and appetisers you'd be forgiven for thinking the meal was over, but a wide variety of seafood, meat and pasta dishes (with a live-cooking station) still awaits. By this time you really will be full, which is a shame because the desserts are absolutely fantastic. The a la carte menu is available 24 hours a day, with the buffet available at traditional meal times.

Blades

Four Seasons
Golf Club
Dubai Festival City
Map 13 D3

04 601 0101 | www.fourseasons.com

Blades is a typical fancy restaurant: subtle lighting, enviable furniture, delicious food (Asian noodles, steaks and tasting platters feature prominently), and excellent service – so far, so fine dining. The twist, however, is that it is also child friendly; a kids' menu serves healthy (yet still appealing) meals, food is eaten off unbreakable plates with special kids' cutlery, and the waitress will bring over a colouring book with crayons to keep them busy. Great for parents who lack a babysitter, but want to escape the usual chicken-nuggets-and-plastic-toys nightmare of eating out with their children.

Blue Orange

The Westin Dubai
Al Sufouh
Map 5 C1

04 399 4141 | www.westin.com

Certainly not for candlelit dinners, Blue Orange at the Westin is a no frills, lively restaurant, open 24 hours. Breakfast buffet is from 06:00 to 10:00, lunch 12:00 to 15:00

FIRST FLOOR - MALL OF THE EMIRATES

Contact us 04 341 2575

and dinner 18:00 to 23:00. It is a vibrant, open kitchen and at these times the chefs can prepare your meal in front of you. From Japanese sushi to Arabic mezze, Chinese dim sum to Belgian waffles, Blue Orange is an unforgettable culinary trip around the world, with something for everyone. The staff are friendly, polite and very accommodating of children. Prices are average for this part of town but this pleasant, contemporary and stylish restaurant is a splendid family friendly new addition to the Marina.

The Boardwalk

Dubai Creek Golf & Yacht Club
Deira
Map 11 C3

04 295 6000 | *www.dubaigolf.com*
Positioned on wooden stilts over the creek, Boardwalk offers patrons a spectacular view virtually unmatched in Dubai. The menu is of a comprehensive array of starters, salads, meats, seafood, and vegetarian dishes, as well as desserts. Servings are generous and well presented while the drinks list contains a standard array of wines and beers and a huge selection of cocktails and mocktails. Equally suitable for both intimate dinners and large groups, unfortunately the restaurant doesn't take reservations but you can always grab a drink at QD's (p.616) while you wait.

Cascades

Fairmont Dubai
Trade Centre 1
Map 8 A4

04 332 5555 | *www.fairmont.com*
Cascades is situated in the Fairmont's breathtaking lobby; transparent elevator pods and water-features cascade serenely all around walls bedecked with windows, mirrors and spotlights. The food is ample and well presented with a variety of international dishes to suit every palate. Beware of the devilishly tempting desserts and cocktails. Open 24 hours a day, Cascades is ideal for a trendy dinner, a business lunch, an extended brunch or a spot of indulgent tippling, nibbling and elevator watching.

Celebrities

One&Only Royal Mirage
Al Sufouh
Map 5 C1

04 399 9999 | *www.oneandonlyroyalmirage.com*
This elegant restaurant offers romantic views of softly lit gardens from tables peppered with rose petals or iridescent stones. As the lounge singers sing Lady in Red, peruse the well-priced European menu – there is plenty to tempt you whether it is the pan-seared sea bass or the baked rack of lamb. Mains are dainty, but filling, and you'll be served the odd amuse bouche. The attentive staff make great recommendations, and you can also try the tasting menu for Dhs.245.

The Cellar ▶ p.559

The Aviation Club
Garhoud
Map 13 E1

04 282 9333 | *www.aviationclub.ae*
Lively yet elegant, straightforward but sophisticated, grand but economical – The Cellar offers a lovely dining experience. The international menu has both favourites and innovations while the wine list, with special bargains on Saturday and Sunday evenings, shows a surprisingly unusual range. Diners enjoy their own space, sometimes created by soft gauze curtains, in a well-lit room of soaring arches and stained glass. The outside space is relaxed with just a glimmer, and whisper, of the more raucous Irish Village across the pond.

Chalet

Jumeira Road
Nr Jumeirah Beach Hotel
Jumeira
Map 6 C1

04 348 6089
The interior is clean and modern, with no more than a dozen tables packed into the compact space (beware the unisex toilet which embarrasses first-timers who think they've walked into the wrong bathroom). The menu takes diners on a world tour, with stops in China for noodles and India for curries, but most people are here for the sturdy Arabic offerings including shawarma and the usual mezze suspects. On any

...delightfully delectable gastronomy

Saturday Brunch. Wine Evenings. Friday Brunch.
Contact Chris at 04 282 9333

The Aviation Club - P.O.Box 55400, Dubai, U.A.E - Tel. 04 282 4122 - Fax. 04 282 4751 - www.aviationclub.ae

given evening you'll see a real mixed bunch of punters including neighbourhood locals and expats, clued-up tourists discovering another side of Dubai, and sandy sunbathers fresh from the beach.

Radisson SAS Hotel
Dubai Media City
Al Sufouh
Map 5 C2

Chef's House ▶ p.561

04 366 9111 | www.radissonsas.com

For a good mix of Asian styles in a contemporary setting, try Chef's House. The a la carte menu features a cross section of south-east Asian, Indian and Middle Eastern dishes, while various themed buffet nights and a Saturday brunch are on offer too for all-you-can-eat options. The decor is contemporary, with an open kitchen. Ice cream fans will be in their element, with a range of exotic flavours to try including red bean, coconut lemongrass and rhubarb.

Al Bustan Rotana
Garhoud
Map 13 E1

Choices

04 282 0000 | www.rotana.com

Lights that look like upside-down chocolate truffle cups cast a warm glow over the very comfortable and elegant dining areas at Choices. This all-day dining restaurant hosts a differently themed buffet each night of the week, including Shanghai, French, Mexican, seafood and international. Whichever takes your fancy, it's all inclusive of unlimited selected beer, house wine and soft drinks, which are regularly topped up by attentive staff. Breakfast and lunch buffets are also served, and an a la carte menu is available at all other times.

Novotel World
Trade Centre
Trade Centre 2
Map 7 F3

Entre Nous

04 332 0000 | www.novotel.com

Entre Nous is a big, bright, airy restaurant with few distinguishing features, but what it lacks in character, it makes up for with its excellent, value-for-money themed buffets. Every day, for just Dhs.135 (or Dhs.185 with alcohol included), you can fill your plate with tasty, high-quality fare; the barbecue (Mondays), Asian (Tuesdays) and seafood nights (Thursdays) are all recommended. Most of the clientele are business people from the Trade Centre area, but if you're in the neighbourhood, Entre Nous puts on a great spread.

Qamardeen Hotel
Downtown Burj Dubai
Map 7 D4

Esca

04 428 6888 | www.qamardeenhotel.com

Situated directly beneath the lobby of the Qamardeen Hotel, this place has a sharp, designer atmosphere, with a huge metallic oven behind the live cooking station and 10 metre-high curtains hanging down from the lobby above. Food is buffet style, with international offerings for breakfast and lunch. Dinner always has an Italian theme, and includes dishes like minestrone soup, lasagne, pizza, seafood, pasta and steak. The buffets change daily and an a la carte menu is also available. It has a spacious and reflective atmosphere; you can also sit outside near the palm trees and pool. The evening buffet costs Dhs.149, excluding drinks.

The Address
Downtown Burj Dubai
Map 7 D4

Fazaris

04 436 8888 | www.theaddress.com

The menu at Fazaris is 12 pages of mouthwatering, globetrotting fare covering dishes from Japan, south-east Asia, India, Arabia and the Mediterranean, so there is literally something for everyone. The main restaurant is cavernous and bright, while the atmosphere outside on the terrace is quieter and more romantic, with view of The Palace hotel and the iconic Burj Dubai. However, insect repellent is a must in mosquito season. The food is excellent (if you can ever manage to decide what to order) and is accompanied by an extensive wine list to suit most budgets.

Destination
new Dubai

Welcome to the Radisson SAS Hotel, Dubai Media City located in the bustling media hub in the heart of 'New Dubai'. The 246 Standard, Business Class and Executive Suites offer contemporary design, chic interiors and state-of-the-art advanced technology. The hotel offers extensive choice of restaurants, bars and 12 meeting rooms catering for up to 150 delegates with awe-inspiring facilities. Close proximity to the beach, Wild Wadi, Emirates Golf Club and the city's vibrant shopping areas make it the perfect destination to mix business with pleasure.

Radisson SAS Hotel, Dubai Media City
PO Box 211723, Dubai, United Arab Emirates
Tel: +971-4-366-9111, Fax: +971-4-361-1011
info.mediacity.dubai@radissonsas.com
mediacity.dubai.radissonsas.com
events.radissonsasdmc.com

Radisson SAS
HOTEL, DUBAI MEDIA CITY

Fire & Ice – Raffles Grill

Raffles Dubai
Umm Hurair
Map 10 D4

04 314 9888 | *www.dubai.raffles.com*

This conceptual restaurant, with its exposed brick walls and dark-wood furniture has two set menus. The more extreme of the two, Ice, is a seven course exploration of unusual consistencies, such as the foie gras on a bed of what can only be described as popping candy, crab cakes with a bubble bath-esque topping and a steak that could be mistaken for liver. Each course comes with its own wine and, for Dhs.1,000 you'll want all seven glasses. The Fire menu is somewhat tamer, and at Dhs.500 for three courses, the food as well as the price tag is much easier to swallow.

Five Dining

Jumeira Rotana
Satwa
Map 8 A2

04 345 5888 | *www.rotana.com*

This lively, but relaxed, venue hosts a compact, well-chosen buffet with mouthwatering, fresh cooked food. The theme changes daily and includes the usual favourite cuisines including seafood, delighting customers with succulent fish cooked to order. A live cooking station for pasta adds to the choice. An enjoyable evening is ensured by friendly, knowledgeable waiters who create an ambience more suitable for groups than romancing couples, guaranteeing a busy atmosphere ideal for the mid-market price range.

Flavours On Two

Towers Rotana
Trade Centre 1
Map 7 E3

04 343 8000 | *www.rotana.com*

If you're looking for something a little more lively, this stylish, busy 'dinner brunch' venue is a fabulous experience. Every night of the week sees a different culinary take on the cuisine of various countries, including the UK (Tuesday) and Italy (Friday). Choose from a wide range of well-prepared dishes including cold starters, hot grills and spectacularly delicious desserts you simply have to make room for. Free-flowing alcohol is included in the very reasonable cover charge, and for a small supplement you can also upgrade to champagne, so expect lots of entertaining antics as the evening goes on.

Inferno Grill

Marina Walk
Dubai Marina
Map 5 B2

04 343 7710 | *dubai-marina.com*

With a terrace that offers a stunning night-time view of the marina, this is the perfect spot to relax over dinner. Although the service can be a little disorganised at times, the

Boardwalk

Inferno Grill

vista and the menu make this worth a visit. The menu selection should keep everyone happy, with steaks, seafood, pizza and a variety of delicious grilled Lebanese-style meats, plus a good selection of fresh juices and mocktails. Prices are reasonable, and if you decide to eat inside the achingly modern restaurant, you'll be treated to live music.

Traders Hotel
Deira
Map 11 E1

The Junction

04 265 9888 | www.shangri-la.com

Traders Hotel in Deira is owned and operated by the Shangri-La group, and this ground-floor restaurant certainly reflects the quality and attention to detail of its better known corporate kin. The Junction's speciality is the buffet, with breakfast and lunchtime deals at reasonable prices, while weekend evenings are reserved for a themed buffet. Friday is seafood night, and the prawns are particularly recommended, with numerous methods of cooking on offer including battered, barbecue and tandoori. With great tasting desserts to finish, Deira residents and visitors may want to add this to their favourites list.

Al Nasr Leisureland
Oud Metha
Map 10 E2

Keva

04 334 4159 | www.alnasrleisureland.ae

Keva boasts trendy Asian-inspired decor, slick furnishings, and a truly international menu, which includes everything from butter chicken to lamb chops and sushi, and good cocktails. There's a quiet dining area or a more buzzy bar lounge for those readying themselves for Chi@The Lodge (p.626) next door. Keva offers a different theme each night of the week; there's even free mojitos for ladies on Tuesday nights when the sax player joins the resident DJ.

Hyatt Regency
Deira
Map 9 D1

The Kitchen

04 317 2222 | www.dubai.regency.hyatt.com

As the name suggests this restaurant has an open kitchen, which is truly open and not sheltered by glass, accompanied by simple dark wood furniture and dividers to create intimate dining. The warm farmhouse bread sets the tone and the menu is a selective mix of Thai, Lebanese and European divided into styles of cooking – wok, charcoal grill, wood burning oven and tandoor. Everything is simply delicious, including the devilish desert station where over-indulgence is a must.

Grand Hyatt Dubai
Umm Hurair
Map 13 C1

The Market Café

04 317 1234 | www.dubai.grand.hyatt.com

Not exactly a buffet, not exactly a typical a la carte eatery, this bustling and popular restaurant does what it says on the tin – it's a market-style restaurant. Diners wander from station to station selecting their style of food as well as their specific starters, mains, desserts and drinks. Mix and match or stay within the Italian, Asian, Arabic or international cuisines on offer. It's a different twist on a buffet – more creative, more fun, but the bottom line is great food and great service. Plus, you'll enjoy the decor of the Grand Hyatt's greenhouse layout, which is part rainforest and part underwater fantasy.

JW Marriott Hotel
Deira
Map 11 E1

The Market Place

04 607 7977 | www.marriottdiningatjw.ae

This restaurant is friendly and welcoming with relaxed, bistro-style decor in a large, open-plan setting. No sooner have you sat down than the waiter brings what will undoubtedly be the first beverage of many – drinks are free-flowing and you won't sit with an empty glass for long. Drinks aside, it is the food that distinguishes this buffet restaurant which has with several live-cooking stations and a most impressive buffet of starters and desserts. The various theme nights all have one thing in common; superb five-star cuisine in seemingly endless supply.

Le Meridien Dubai
Garhoud
Map 13 E1

Meridien Village Terrace
04 217 0000 | *www.lemeridien-dubai.com*

Beautifully lit at night, the large Meridien Village Terrace manages to feel intimate for couples but is also great for groups. Each night there is a different culinary theme, be it Caribbean, Mexican, BBQ or Arabic, and there's always plenty of delicious staples such as roast beef on offer for those with a specific hankering. Numerous live-cooking stations keep the food wonderfully fresh, and a great choice of drinks are replenished with alarming regularity. It may be yet another buffet in Dubai but the variety, value, quality and setting is an absolute treat capable of wooing even the most pretentious of foodies.

The Monarch Dubai
Trade Centre 2
Map 8 A4

Mizaan
04 501 8888 | *www.themonarchdubai.com*

This restaurant offers hotel guests a number of cuisines from around the world, but it need not be overlooked by Dubai residents. The menu truly does have a flavour of international cuisine from Indian and Thai inspired curries through to grilled Mediterranean vegetables, fillet of beef and a gingerbread butter pudding. A real league of nations awaits the diner. A most pleasant surprise is the well constructed wine list that is exceptional value compared to similar venues in Dubai.

Atlantis The Palm
Palm Jumeirah
Map 2 A3

Nasimi ▶ p.524
04 426 2626 | *www.atlantisthepalm.com*

As beachside restaurants go, this has to be the cream of the crop. Considering its location in the fantastical surroundings of Atlantis, on the crescent of the Palm Jumeirah, Nasimi surprises with its simplicity – it offers a small, yet delectable menu of seafood and meat dishes, all expertly prepared, relaxing decor and one of the best alfresco settings in the city. The large terrace stretches along both sides of the restaurant, offering views of either the swimming pool or the Palm, and you could easily while away a long, sunny afternoon here.

The Montgomerie
Dubai
Emirates Hills
Map 5 B3

Nineteen
04 363 1275 | *www.themontgomerie.com*

Still need convincing that golf is cool? Head to Montgomerie's flagship restaurant, Nineteen, where slick, pared-back modernism sends members-only fustiness the way of wooden clubs. Situated in a miniature White House, the restaurant would be pitch black save for a pink back-lit bar, 70s kitsch lampshades, and subtle lights that single out your table. In contrast, the show kitchen is loud, proud and slightly out of context. Choose from a perfectly balanced Thai-influenced menu and, like a pro perfecting his swing, see the food get better with each course.

The Harbour Hotel
& Residence
Dubai Marina
Map 5 B2

The Observatory
04 319 4000 | *www.emirateshotelsresorts.com*

Describing itself as a gastro-lounge, this new venue is half-bar and half-restaurant, and enjoys dizzying 360° views from its 52nd floor location. In the restaurant the mood is dark and cosy, with smoked mirrors, black table linen and flickering candles. The lighting is dimmed to the point of near-blackout, all to minimise glare and maximise the killer views. The short and simple menu favours fish and meat, but the dishes themselves are anything but plain, with ingredients presented in imaginative combinations. Some of the descriptions are a touch misleading so don't be afraid to ask the staff exactly what you can expect. In the bar things are more colourful, and a couple of telescopes allow you to look down on the neighbours while enjoying a pre-dinner cocktail or a nightcap.

Restaurants

Hilton Jumeirah
Dubai Marina
Map 5 A1

Oceana
04 399 1111 | www.hilton.com

Your first decision should be what night to visit Oceana, a difficult choice thanks to the interchanging themes of equal temptation, while your second will be what delicious dish to devour. If, for example, you choose fish night, forgoing Arabic, French and Mexican, there are up to 30 superb options to satisfy your piscean yearning. The decor is akin to glamorous dining rooms of 1930s cruise ships – lots of chrome and wood with Art Moderne furniture and lighting fixtures that ensure visibility while still providing shadowed privacy.

Al Murooj Rotana Hotel & Suites
Trade Centre 2
Map 7 E3

Pergolas
04 321 1111 | www.rotana.com

Perfect for a romantic evening, Pergolas offers a wide array of international buffet-style cuisine based around theme nights each day of the week. The restaurant's stylish terrace (more popular during the cooler months) is overlooked by fairytale architecture. The decor changes throughout the week to reflect themes, including Seafood and Orient Express evenings with live cooking stations. The a la carte menu is broad, but unavailable on theme nights. Reasonably priced, an all-you-can-eat brunch is available on Fridays for Dhs.179. Reservations necessary on theme nights.

Four Points by Sheraton Bur Dubai
Bur Dubai
Map 8 F3

Promenade
04 397 7444 | www.starwood.com

The Promenade resides in the hotel lobby of the Four Points Sheraton and promotes itself as a 'chic French-styled cafe'. On selected days and during lunch and dinner times, it offers guests a chance to watch their food being cooked at the live-cooking stations but the selection of dishes from the a la carte menu is limited and the international buffet is basic. The food, however, is well presented and the staff are attentive and responsive. The mains are rather expensive but the various cuts of meat and the selection of shellfish and fish are cooked on the grill to specific requirements, which will appeal to fussy diners.

The Desert Course
Arabian Ranches
Map 2 B3

Ranches Restaurant
04 366 3000 | www.arabianranchesgolfdubai.com

Set within the elegant golf club building, Ranches serves home cooked, unpretentious fare in comfortable surroundings. The outdoor terrace offers a more intimate dining experience overlooking the golf course. This is the perfect choice for family dining as the menu offers something for everyone, with a particular focus on British traditional dishes. Bookings are essential for the Tuesday night quiz, while themed buffets provide a more international flavour with curries, carvery and grills alongside live cooking stations and a great choice of hearty desserts.

Atlantis The Palm
Palm Jumeirah
Map 2 A3

Saffron ▶ p.524
04 426 2626 | www.atlantisthepalm.com

After an unforgettable opening night party and fireworks display, Atlantis has a lot to live up to. Saffron boasts one of the hotel's expansive live cooking station buffets, featuring international and Asian-themed dishes. It's a colourful, energetic restaurant whose sheer size means there's no danger of a cosy, intimate meal and at times you feel like you're in an upmarket canteen. While the selection of food is certainly impressive, the sheer scale of things means that quality may not quite live up to the a la carte standard you'd get if you ordered off menu. The live cooking stations are the best bet, with Mongolian barbecue and lovely gloopy Chinese noodle soups cooked straight to order.

Mall of the Emirates
Al Barsha
Map 6 A3

Seasons
04 341 2483 | *restaurants.malloftheemirates@kempinski.com*
Swiftly swarming every area in Dubai, Seasons is a chain of cafes serving healthy dishes to hungry shoppers and lunch-breakers. The menu offers the usual array of soups, salads and sandwiches, as well as items from the grill. Gadget geeks will love the service system: you're given a buzzer/pager which flashes when you need to trot up and collect your food. With a bright and fresh interior, Seasons is a healthy and reasonably priced alternative to typical flyby lunch and dinner options. Other branches are at Dubai Internet City (04 391 8711) and Ibn Battuta (04 368 5630).

Mall of the Emirates
Al Barsha
Map 6 A3

Sezzam
04 341 3600 | *www.sezzam.com*
Sezzam's open-plan concept may seem a little confusing, but once you've got the hang of it you could eat here every night of the week and have a different experience every time. There are three kitchens: 'Bake' serves up pizzas, lasagne and roasts; 'Flame' offers grilled meats and seafoods; and 'Steam' serves up Asian cuisine. There is also a special area if you want to drink alcohol. Confusion aside, the food, once you get it, is excellent and even the fussiest of diners should be able to find something tasty.

Metropolitan Palace
Deira
Map 11 C2

Sketch
04 227 0000 | *www.habtoorhotels.com*
Maybe it's dishes like the fillet steak with spicy chocolate sauce (Dhs.129) or the hammour with pea tzatsiki (Dhs.89) that lend a slight quirkiness to Sketch. Then again, maybe it's the incongruously large spotlights, which cast the scarlet walls with a theatrical glow, that make this Deira eatery feels like it might be run by a group of experimental artists. Either way, this is a refreshing spot with an intimate vibe and an excellent cocktail list.

Fairmont Dubai
Trade Centre 1
Map 8 A4

Spectrum On One
04 332 5555 | *www.fairmont.com*
A firm fine dining favourite in Dubai, Spectrum on One attracts a lot of repeat diners thanks to its deliciously varied menu. Divided into some of the world's most delicious regions – India, China, Thailand, Europe, Japan and Arabia – you need a good half hour to absorb the menu so thankfully the equally diverse bread basket provides sumptuous sustenance. In spacious surroundings, with inventive interior dividers creating intimate spots for couples and room for groups to mingle, whatever you do save some room for the desserts – the molten chocolate is a must.

Renaissance Hotel
Deira
Map 11 E1

Spice Island ▶ p.567
04 262 5555 | *www.renaissancehotels.com*
A trip to the all-you-can-eat Spice Island buffet creates a few dilemmas, with Indian, Mexican, Chinese, Thai, Mongolian and Japanese food all begging to make their mark on your palate from live cooking stations. There's a choice of alcoholic and non-alcoholic drinks packages to choose from, and the kids will be more than content too, thanks to a designated play area. And if you still have room for dessert after your round-the-world feast, there's a fine selection of sweet treats and an extensive cheese board. Tough decisions indeed.

Le Meridien Mina
Seyahi
Al Sufouh
Map 5 C1

Tang
04 399 3333 | *www.lemeridien-minaseyahi.com*
Knowledgeable staff guide you through this Alice in Wonderland restaurant, while frozen nitrogen cocktails announce that the exquisite offerings were designed in conjunction with NASA scientists. Many dishes are available in sampler sizes, encouraging diners

to experiment. Specific wine suggestions for each dish and palate cleansers between courses maximize the 'molecular gastronomy' experience. With a small menu providing a surprisingly large variety (but not for vegetarians) Tang is a must-do for those who think they've done it all. Science meets magic, deliciously unique.

Teatro

Towers Rotana
Trade Centre 1
Map 7 E3

04 343 8000 | *www.rotana.com*

Embark on a global culinary journey from the moment the lift doors open and you step into the eclectic space that houses this perennially popular restaurant and bar. Teatro offers a true fusion of cultures and tastes, with menu offerings from Japan, China, India and Europe. Whether you go for pizza, noodles, sushi or a curry, the food is guaranteed to please; you can also choose one of the chef's special taster menus. The decor is dark, moody and modern, and if you book early enough in advance you should request a table by the window for views over Sheikh Zayed Road. One word of warning: the air conditioning is always on, so don't forget your pashmina.

The Terrace

Park Hyatt Dubai
Deira
Map 11 B4

04 602 1234 | *www.starwoodhotels.com*

Tucked into a far corner of Deira, the aging Sheraton Deira still exudes enough charm to make it a worthwhile visit. As the hotel's main restaurant, The Terrace comfortably sits behind the entryway in a massive, tree-lined atrium. Faux columns along the walls create isolated booths perfect for both an intimate date and a raucous evening with friends. The buffet and live cooking stations change based on the nightly theme and the selection is extensive, fresh and varied.

Wavebreaker

Hilton Jumeirah
Dubai Marina
Map 5 A1

04 399 1111 | *www.hilton.com*

Between the pool and the beach at the Hilton Jumeirah is the Wavebreaker bar. Serving snacks, light meals, kids' meals and a variety of mocktails and cocktails, it is a great place to get away from it all. The staff are friendly and laid back, just like the setting itself, and the sandwiches and snacks are big enough to satisfy any appetite. There's a playground and bouncy castle nearby to keep the kids amused, while you can sit and watch the beach action from a distance. Try going at sunset, when it's quiet, cool and the view stunning.

Italian

Other options **Mediterranean** p.581, **Pizzerias** p.586

Al Fresco

Crowne Plaza
Trade Centre 1
Map 7 F3

04 331 1111 | *www.crowneplaza.com*

Don't leave Al Fresco just for the hotel guests. It is a great little taste of Italy in the heart of Dubai. The pastas are authentic and the risottos have a modern flare, but make sure you leave room for dessert as the tiramisu is deliciously traditional. The casual feel, resaonable prices and small outdoor area make it a cosy nook on Sheikh Zayed Road, great for a birthday or large group but not so suitable for fine dining romancing.

Andiamo!

Grand Hyatt Dubai
Umm Hurair
Map 13 C1

04 317 1234 | *www.dubai.grand.hyatt.com*

The most eye-catching feature of Andiamo! is the colourful, fiery mosaic surrounding the pizza oven, hinting at the fresh-baked delights within. This chic Italian features Miro-style lamps, with an abundance of mirrors, wood and stark colours offset by black-clad serving staff dashing around like smiley ninjas. The starters are pretty,

delicious and generous while pizzas are thin, crispy, fresh and tasty. The clientele are mainly hip young things and the ambience so relaxed, you could easily forget to check the prices which are a little above average.

Mercato
Jumeira
Map 7 D1

Bella Donna

04 344 7701 | www.binhendi.com
Located within a Venetian piazza styled mall, Bella Donna has a slight 1920s feel to it. The decor is minimalist with blacks and whites adorning the walls, tables and menus. Reasonably priced Italian

Bussola

fare is served up by friendly staff willing to recommend their favourite dish. Pasta is homemade on the premises and pizzas range from classics like margarita to more unusual capricciosa that comes with a cooked egg and potatoes, and although there is no kids menu there is plenty on offer to keep them happy – and full.

Hilton Jumeirah
Dubai Marina
Map 5 A1

BiCE

04 399 1111 | www.hilton.com
Put the book down and make a reservation now. With excellent food and a delightful atmosphere, BiCE is hugely popular and rightly so. Live piano music complements the 1930s art deco furnishings, while the huge windows offer stellar views over the pool. The menu offers a great mix of traditional Italian comfort food and nouvelle cuisine, with good-sized portions to satisfy almost every appetite, and flavours for the most discerning palates. Discreet and observant staff can offer advice on all aspects of the menu, including the extensive wine list which changes every few months. It's tricky, but try to save room for dessert.

Wafi Mall
Umm Hurair
Map 10 E4

Biella

04 324 4666 | www.waficitirestaurant.com
After building up an appetite at the mall, shoppers can unwind and fill up on Biella's consistently tasty food. The staff are friendly and attentive, and the open kitchen provides glimpses of the chefs preparing unpretentious, varied Italian favorites. The menu is extensive, with salads, appetisers, pastas and mains, but pizza rightfully gets top billing here. If you are not ready for a full meal, you can recharge inside or on the terrace with an authentic Italian coffee and cake.

The Westin Dubai
Mina Seyahi
Al Sufouh
Map 5 C1

Bussola

04 399 4141 | www.starwoodhotels.com/westin
After a short buggy ride from the hotel to the beach you'll be welcomed at Bussola by friendly, helpful staff. The interior is light and airy, with smart wooden furnishings and floor-to-ceiling windows, so you can't help but appreciate the shoreline vistas. Alternatively, the outdoor terrace gets you even closer to the sea. A Sicilian influence on the menu means the choices are slightly more adventurous than your standard Italian fare, but all are delicious nonetheless. Save room for dessert because the chef's creations are art on a plate. For a slightly more laid-back night out, the open-air first-floor veranda serves cocktails and pizza to a backdrop of sparkling sea views and chill-out tunes.

**Jumeirah
Beach Hotel**
Umm Suqeim
Map 6 B1

Carnevale

04 406 8999 | *www.jumeirahbeachhotel.com*

Located on the mezzanine level of the Jumeirah Beach Hotel, the recently remodelled Carnevale provides up-market Italian food to a steady stream of moneyed hotel guests. The convenient location within the hotel is a big draw, as are the views of the Burj Al Arab from the adjoining indoor terrace. Despite its dark, Venetian-themed interior, families and children are welcome and well catered for. The extremely attentive staff ensure that dishes are swiftly served.

Le Meridien Dubai
Garhoud
Map 13 E1

Casa Mia

04 282 4040 | *www.lemeridien-dubai.com*

With more than 400 types of Italian wine kept safely in a temperature-controlled room, you'll find plenty of reasons to slip in to the Mediterranean style of relaxing over your meal. Casa Mia has maintained its high standards and delicious food over the years, which means that reservations are a must for dinner. Portions are generous, and many dishes are available either as a main course or as a side dish, allowing you to broaden your selection from the extensive menu.

Radisson SAS Hotel
Dubai Media City
Al Sufouh
Map 5 C2

Certo ▶ p.561

04 366 9111 | *www.dubai.radissonsas.com*

Located in the commercial zone that is Dubai Media City, Certo's roomy interior is uninspiring save for the floor-to-ceiling, glass encased wine cellar. The restaurant does however redeem itself with a surprisingly creative menu, including deliciously described signature and classic Italian dishes. It's not worth making a special trip for unless you are in the area, but the combination of excellent food and attentive, helpful staff make an otherwise bland environment worth visiting if you are a media or IT mogul.

Al Bustan Rotana
Garhoud
Map 13 E1

Come Prima

04 282 0000 | *www.rotana.com*

The Pasta Basta night at Come Prima works on so many levels. Firstly there's the antipasti table, packed with an array of Italian delicacies such as marinated mussels, carpaccio, seafood salad, sun dried tomatoes and a whole host of beautiful breads. Secondly there's the perfectly thin and crispy pizzas that melt in your mouth. Then there are the 13 types of pasta which you can mix and match with your choice of sauce. Next is the trio of deserts to end a meal worth breaking your diet for. And the best thing, it won't break the bank at Dhs.119 with unlimited house wine, beer and soft drinks.

**Ibis World
Trade Centre**
Trade Centre 2
Map 7 F3

Cubo Pasta

04 332 4444 | *www.ibishotel.com*

Cubo Pasta dishes up serviceable Italian fare to hungry Trade Centre conference goers. Arrive early to snag a prime spot against the wall or you might be banging elbows with a delegate at the next table, as the chic interior is strangely airy, yet cramped at the same time. Wednesdays and Thursdays are busiest as there's a good value all-you-can-eat-and-drink buffet. There's pizza, secondi and the pasta comes in every shape and texture but the innovative antipasti is the highlight.

JW Marriott Hotel
Deira
Map 11 E1

Cucina

04 607 7977 | *www.marriottdiningatjw.ae*

With its faux-Tuscan farm decor, Cucina adds a touch of the rustic to Dubai's usual glitz. A solidly traditional Italian menu provides high culinary standards and a reasonably priced wine list, helping you keep the budget in check. The pizzas are very good and pasta dishes, while not exemplary, are still honest to Italian kitchens. If you like an old fashioned sing-a-long, then be sure to get there in time for the staff's renditions of classic Italian tunes.

Da Vinci's

Millennium
Airport Hotel
Garhoud
Map 13 E1

04 282 3464 | *www.millenniumhotels.com*

This rustic Italian trattoria favours wholesome decor with checked tablecloths, quirky Leonardo related flair, and even a dummy pianist. The interior is three-tiered and spacious enough to accommodate smokers, non-smokers and large parties. Discounts are offered for early evening dining and there is a great value three-course business lunch special. There is a reasonable choice of no-fuss pasta, pizza, meats, fish, soups and Mediterranean starters which may not be especially inspiring but are suitably hearty. The drinks are affordable and the wine list well populated.

Don Corleone

Metropolitan Hotel
Sheikh Zayed Road
Map 7 B3

04 343 0000 | *www.habtoorhotels.com*

A 'traditional' Italian right down to its red and white checked table cloths and plastic vines, Don Corleone may not have reached kitschdom yet, but it's not far away. The restaurant, like the hotel, has been around a few years and the decor may not be as modern as some Dubai diners have come to expect. It does have a cosy feel though, and there is a terrace for alfresco eating on winter evenings. The antipasti are fine, as are the meat and fish dishes, but the stars of the slightly limited menu are the excellent home-made pasta dishes.

Focaccia

Hyatt Regency
Deira
Map 9 D1

04 317 2222 | *www.dubai.regency.hyatt.com*

Home is where the heart is at Focaccia, from freshly-baked bread and hand-made pasta to the decor, reminiscent of a palatial Italian casa. Book ahead to reserve a table in the kitchen, library, dining room, or cellar or to catch a glimpse of the sea from the terrace. Tasty pasta dishes rule the menu but don't miss the desserts, which are delicious and boldly presented. Brunch offers choices from the neighbouring Iranian restaurant and pub for Dhs.135 or Dhs.175 depending on alcohol options.

Frankie's

Oasis Beach Tower
Dubai Marina
Map 5 A1

04 399 4311 | *www.frankiesitalianbarandgrill.com*

Co-owned by Frankie Dettori and Marco Pierre White, this bar and restaurant is a tasty illustration of the burgeoning marina, and a follow up to the pair's London restaurant. Grab a vodka martini and thin-crust pizza in the bar or head into the main restaurant for Italian classics and new favourites such as duck ravioli. The Friday bubbly brunch (Dhs.390) is a set menu including excellent mini dishes like eggplant lasagne and sea bass carpaccio. With a sultry interior, pianist and even a waitress called Babes, this is no one-trick pony.

Il Rustico

Rydges Plaza Hotel
Satwa
Map 8 A3

04 398 2222 | *www.rydges.com*

This little gem is a genuine Italian restaurant both in look and feel, with a Mediterranean tiled floor, dark brown wooden doors and intimate seating. The food is very good and the chef's larder contains everything you could want from pasta, pizzas and salads, all of which are freshly made on the premises, and the desserts taste as good as they look. It may not be the poshest of restaurants, or the finest of dining, but Il Rustico is a cosy corner of Italy in a little corner of Rydges Plaza hotel.

Italian Connection

Nr Lamcy Plaza
Oud Metha
Map 11 D4

04 335 3001

Providing a refreshing change from usual hotel Italian restaurants, Italian Connection is a friendly neighbourhood cafe-restaurant in Oud Metha. Run by an Italian family with a flair for interior design, it is colourful and fresh, just like the food. From a menu packed with choice, the pasta is made daily and comes with tasty sauces, while the pizzas are just the way they should be – thin, crisp and delicious. Popular at lunchtime with business people in the area, it is more relaxed in the evening, when you are under no pressure to do anything but linger in pleasant surroundings and enjoy great Italian food.

La Moda ▶p.37

Radisson SAS Hotel
Dubai Deira Creek
Deira
Map 9 C3

04 222 7171 | *www.radissonsas.com*

La Moda quite rightly deserves its recommendations for great Italian food. The decor may seem a little too trendy, but the food is unpretentious and generous in portion. The ambience indoors is lively, and big tables make it perfect for an evening of pizza swapping with friends. The small but pretty terrace is more romantic, so be sure to sample the extensive wine (or champagne) selection. Aside from pizzas, La Moda has a tasty selection of meat and seafood dishes together with a daily buffet for those who find the choice too much.

La Veranda ▶p.573

Mövenpick Hotel
Bur Dubai
Oud Metha
Map 10 D3

04 336 6000 | *www.moevenpick-hotels.com*

With undoubtedly one of the best value all-you-can-eat deals in town, La Veranda is well-known to many for the buffet night, but it is worth a visit at other times of the week. On Tuesday nights, the place gets packed with hungry diners in search of a bargain Italian feast, and Dhs.109 gets you access to the stacked, delicious antipasti buffet, unlimited pasta and pizzas, as well as bottomless red and white house wine. The a la carte menu offers a good range of starters and mains, with seafood dishes and pizzas cooked in their wood-fired oven.

La Veranda

Jumeirah
Beach Hotel
Umm Suqeim
Map 6 B1

04 406 8999 | *www.jumeirahbeachhotel.com*

For unpretentious fare, head over to La Veranda's cosy wooden tables with marina views and fans whirling overhead. The restaurant has the feel of an impromptu beachside cabin and the restrooms are back in the hotel some distance away. A variety of inexpensive Italian pizza, pasta and seafood is served up in large portions by animated staff. Children will enjoy the Sinbad comic book menu which includes typical treats like burgers and fish fingers.

Luciano's

Habtoor Grand
Dubai Marina
Map 5 B1

04 399 5000 | *www.habtoorhotels.com*

The Habtoor Grand's high standards continue with this reasonably-priced poolside Italian which provides good quality, family-friendly dishes. The usual suspects like lasagne are executed very well, so don't feel guilty about sticking with favourites; you'll be pleasantly surprised. If you don't mind a slight chlorine smell and the weather is conducive, ask for a table outside underneath the fairy-light bedecked palm trees, which help screen the hotel.

Mosaico

Emirates Towers
Trade Centre 2
Map 7 F3

04 319 8088 | *www.jumeirahemiratestowers.com*

Open 24 hours a day, this upmarket Italian restaurant is nestled inside Emirates Towers. Chef Marco Torasso blends Italian flavours with Spanish flamboyance, creating a mood

Fabulous Food – Swiss Style.

Enjoy true Swiss hospitality at the Mövenpick Hotel Bur Dubai. Allow our chefs to tantalise your taste buds with specially created cuisine fusions across five restaurants and three bars.

A cosy atmosphere and traditional pub grub awaits at our Somerset's English pub and the roof top offers itself for al fresco fondue and raclette dining. Between the tasty Italian at the La Veranda restaurant, sweet delights at Café Espresso or international dining at the atrium style lobby Fountain restaurant there truly is something for every taste.

Whether you are entertaining clients, friends or family the Mövenpick Hotel Bur Dubai is the unrivalled home of Swiss hospitality.

Mövenpick Hotel Bur Dubai
19th Street, Oud Metha, P.O. Box 32733
Dubai, United Arab Emirates
Phone +971 4 336 60 00, Fax +971 4 336 66 26
hotel.burdubai@moevenpick.com

www.moevenpick-hotels.com
True Excellence in Swiss Hospitality.

MÖVENPICK
Hotel Bur Dubai

ideal for families or business meetings. A Mediterranean buffet incorporates starters like seafood and tapas cooked at live cooking stations, mains like pasta and pizzas made to your preference, with honey-drizzled profiteroles for dessert. Polish it off with a glass or three of traditional Italian wine.

One&Only
Royal Mirage
Al Sufouh
Map 5 C1

Olives

04 399 9999 | *www.oneandonlyroyalmirage.com*

Sturdy wicker furniture, lots of archways, indoor foliage and white ceramic tiles on the walls help to set the scene in Olives. While diners can order a la carte, most people are here for the buffet of Italian and Mediterranean favourites. Tasty pizzas and pasta are made to order, and there's even a shawarma stand. Be sure to leave room for the impressive dessert selection. When the cooler months allow, there's a lovely outdoor terrace overlooking the gardens and pool area.

Uptown
Mirdif Mall
Mirdif
Map 15 B2

Pane Caldo

04 288 8319 | *www.pane-caldo.ae*

Enjoy the superb antipasti and desserts in this bright and trendy trattoria while people-watching in Uptown Mirdif. With a decor so white and funky, eating at Pane Caldo is like dining in an iPod. The staff are welcoming and there's a take-away service that includes freshly baked bread, sauce and pasta. Touted as a 'different' Italian, the menu is innovative and varied enough to suit every taste. Don't be too tempted by the pizza oven, the menu abounds with tastier treats.

Dusit Thani Dubai
Trade Centre 2
Map 7 E3

Pax

04 343 3333 | *www.dusit.com*

Pax does traditional Italian dishes in less than traditional sizes to give punters a pick 'n' mix of tastes. It is a style they call bocconcini (little delicacies). With appetisers starting at Dhs.15, and most mains costing less than Dhs.70, a hearty feed is not prohibitively expensive. Pax is on the 24th floor with a number of tables facing out onto Sheikh Zayed Road. In line with the hotel's Thai ownership, service is cheery and polite without being obtrusive, and the atmosphere feels relaxed despite the interior designer's faux-renaissance efforts at austerity.

Bab Al Shams Desert
Resort & Spa
Map 1 E2

Pizzeria Le Dune

04 809 6100 | *www.jumeirahbabalshams.com*

Perfect for a romantic getaway Pizzeria la Dune brings the smells and tastes of rustic Italy to the heart of the desert. Like the journey to get there, the restaurant's interior is a long hall and the serene setting provides a secluded venue to enjoy intimate dining. Upon arrival, the welcoming antipasti buffet offers a taste of everything but save room for the tiramisu trio – one of which appropriately contains Arabic coffee, the perfect pick-me-up for the long trek home.

Four Seasons
Golf Club
Dubai Festival City
Map 13 D3

Quattro

04 601 0101 | *www.fourseasons.com/dubaigolf*

Discerning diners pay attention: this superior culinary experience may just be Dubai's greatest hidden gem. Quattro features sweeping views from the terrace or breathtaking decor from the interior; ensconce yourself in one of the subtly lit alcoves with your special someone for an unforgettable romantic evening. The menu features contemporary Italian creations that make it hard to choose; non-deciders can opt for the chef's degustation menu. A large wine list complements the delectable dishes perfectly, and the knowledgeable staff can make a recommendation if you don't know your chardonnay from your chenin blanc. Unmissable.

Atlantis The Palm
Palm Jumeirah
Map 2 A3

Ronda Locatelli ▶ p.524
04 426 2626 | www.atlantisthepalm.com

With roaring flames creating a warm welcome at the entrance, Ronda Locatelli is the new Italian run by celebrity chef, Giorgio Locatelli. The cavernous interior seats hundreds in raised alcoves or at tables surrounding the centrepiece of the restaurant, a huge stone-built wood-fired oven, which cooks up pizzas and other dishes. Curving wooden frames separate the seating while lights are suspended from the ceiling under huge wheels. The casual menu offers a good range of starters, pasta and mains, as well as a range of small dishes that are perfect for sharing. Already one of the busiest venues in Atlantis, evenings are packed and family friendly early on, then changing to a more adult atmosphere later. Prices are quite reasonable for such a connected restaurant.

Dubai International
Financial Centre
(DIFC)
Trade Centre 2
Map 7 F3

Sana Bonta
04 425 0326 | www.difc.ae

Sana Bonta's main attraction is its cool decor and heroic invitation to iPod users to bring their playlists to broadcast to other diners. There's no Wi-Fi but there's WIGIG – a proudly sporadic chef's special: 'When it's gone it's gone.' It was gone, but the choice is generally sufficient as all dishes are customisable with a tickable menu. The food quality is reasonable but watch out for the arabiatta, which needs a fire-risk warning and the starters, which are scandalously skimpy.

Souk Madinat
Jumeriah
Umm Suqeim
Map 6 A1

Segreto
04 366 8888 | www.madinatjumeirah.com

Tucked away in the heart of the Madinat, candle-lit lamps lead you through the walkways to this hidden gem, offering quality Italian fare. Start the evening with a glass of prosecco on the terrace by the canal, then head into the stylish, modern interior. Segreto has a modern feel, and is equally suited to dinner with friends as a romantic dinner a deux due to clever table layout. The food is aesthetically appealing, if a little on the bland side, and the portions are more suited to a catwalk model than a rugby lad – but at least you feel a little like a celebrity in a top-secret eatery.

Marina Walk
Dubai Marina
Map 5 B2

Stefano's Restaurant
04 422 2632 | www.reginapasta.com

Stefano's is an opportunity to delight in home-cooked classic Italian dishes in a relaxed alfresco setting. Dining tables and sofas fill Stefano's position along the water's edge at Marina Walk, offering excellent views. The menu combines traditional items such as bruschetta, spaghetti and pizza calzone together with fresh juices and shisha. Food recommendations include Antipasti Stefano followed by beef bresaola. This casual, relaxed restaurant is perfect for coffee, a quick lunch, afternoon juice, evening meal or night-long shisha.

Dubai Outlet Mall
Dubai-Al Ain Rd
Route 66
Dubailand
Nad Al Sheba
Map 2 C3

Stone Fire Pizza Kitchen
04 425 5817 | www.stonefirekitchen.com

The world's first Stonefire Pizza Kitchen serves the most original pizza in the UAE – and is so Dubai. Not only does it produce superb Italian fare from the freshest ingredients, it goes beyond to proffer bizarre but sublimely successful fusions of contrasting cuisines. The Norwegian Salmon white pizza with caviar and avocado is delectable and their brave chef is deservedly proud of his 'top-secret-recipe' pad thai pizza and molten chocolate lava cake creations – imaginative five-star food in a bargain mall.

Sheraton Hotel
& Towers
Deira
Map 9 B4

Vivaldi

04 207 1717 | www.sheraton.com/dubai

Surely a contender for one of the most romantic restaurants in Dubai, this gem is perched over the sparkling Dubai Creek. With spectacular views from both inside the warmly lit restaurant and the two outdoor terraces, you won't know whether to watch the abras glide by or the chefs at work in the open kitchen. Attentive yet unintrusive staff coupled with an experimental Italian menu and comprehensive wine list will have you coming back to try all the delicious selections on offer.

Japanese

Other options **Far Eastern** p.544

Al Bustan Rotana
Garhoud
Map 13 E1

Benihana

04 282 0000 | www.rotana.com

You'll need to reserve a table to get in to Benihana's all you can eat sushi night, including Asahi beer and house wine. Benihana does the basics very well, with an assortment of sushi and sashimi, as well as hot dishes for those who want to experiment with sushi, but stay with some more familiar treats. Desserts of fruit and green tea chocolate fountain might seem unusual, but if it's good, reliable, all-you-can-eat sushi, this it the best place to come.

Al Kawakeb Building
Trade Centre 2
Map 7 E3

Bento-Ya

04 343 0222 | www.bentoya.info

Bento-Ya is a compact, double storey restaurant, that's great for a quick, casual dinner or lunch. The Japanese chef lures in an impressive number of fellow expatriates, which is a good indicator of how genuine your meal is going to be (irrespective of the decor). Happily, everything is as expected, with very fresh, good quality options. Come for authentic platters of maki, great sushi and bento boxes filled with various meats (try the teriyaki pan-fried beef), fish and egg dishes. The average price of a meal for two with soft drinks is Dhs.100-200.

Sheraton Hotel
& Towers
Deira
Map 9 B4

Creekside

04 207 1750 | www.sheraton.com/dubai

A warm welcome awaits at this above-average Japanese venue inside the Sheraton Creek. Depending on the day (sushi and teppanyaki theme nights, as well as regular all-you-can-eat evenings, happen on a regular basis) and your mood, you can choose to sit around one of the teppanyaki stations, at the sushi bar, or at a table. If weather permits you can also dine on the terrace and enjoy views of the creek. The food is expertly prepared, and the teppanyaki tables let you watch the charismatic chefs create succulent dishes.

Boulevard at
Emirates Towers
Trade Centre 2
Map 7 F3

ET Sushi

04 319 8088 | www.jumeirahemiratestowers.com

ET Sushi fits perfectly with the buzz of Emirates Towers, offering a wide range of decent Japanese food for lunching business people or for dining after work. The decor inside is traditional, and the atmosphere very business-like, with seating around the conveyor belt in sight of the impressive chefs slicing sashimi and preparing sushi, or 'outside' at tables in The Boulevard. There is a very wide range of sushi – and if you can't see what you're after spinning around on the belt, you can order from the menu. As the sister restaurant of the tokyo@thetowers (p.579) run by the same management, the kitchen also does masses of other options: grilled, fried and cold dishes and desserts. A good place for a quick meal before going for drinks elsewhere in the area, or for karaoke in Harry Ghattos.

Kiku

Haru Robatayaki

Rimal Building
Jumeirah Beach
Residence
Dubai Marina
Map 5 B2

04 437 0134
www.haru.ae

Haru has found a great location on The Walk to hide away and still draw a crowd. Knowledgeable, friendly staff are rightly proud of their work. They serve up authentic, fresh and delicious Japanese food from sushi and soba to amazing grilled specialties ('robatayaki') with signature sauces. Bright lights and Japanese pop music keep the feel upbeat in the actual restaurant, while the indoor terraced seating allows for a more relaxed meal in all weather. Other locations include the Green Community (04 885 3897) and there are rumours of Haru opening at Souk Al Bahar. A delivery service is also available.

Kiku

Le Meridien Dubai
Garhoud
Map 13 E1

04 702 2703 | *www.lemeridien-dubai.com*

One of Dubai's most popular Japanese joints, Kiku is regularly packed with Japanese guests (always a good sign), sushi lovers and novices looking to expand their cuisine catalogue. The restaurant has a choice of dining areas from the traditional private tatami rooms to the teppanyaki bar, sushi counter and tables. The diverse menu offers standard staples such as sushi, sashimi, tempura and teppanyaki which sit alongside some more unusual delicacies. Particularly worth trying are the set meals which are surprisingly good value considering the number of dishes that arrive at your table.

Minato ▶ p.37

Radisson SAS Hotel
Dubai Deira Creek
Deira
Map 9 C3

04 222 7171 | *www.radissonsas.com*

Bordering the creek hides Dubai's oldest Japanese restaurant preaching good tidings of sushi, sashimi and teppanyaki. Intricately painted vases, rice paper doors and soft lighting sway a personal yet traditional Japanese atmosphere. A sushi bar, tatami rooms, and teppanyaki tables, with live performances by Chef Sam Okita, liven up pricey dishes like black cod sashimi, alongside flavourful cocktails. sushi and sashimi buffets on Monday and Thursday from 19:00 to 23:30 are not to be missed. Reservations and a smart casual dress code are recommended.

Miyako

Hyatt Regency
Deira
Map 9 D1

04 317 2222 | *www.dubai.regency.hyatt.com*

One of Dubai's oldest restaurants, Miyako has been serving up delicious Japanese fare since 1980. Small yet chic, it combines a laid-back ambience with a genuinely exciting menu. While the restaurant's speciality is a delicate seafood broth served in a paper bowl and heated over a naked flame (the mystery is how the paper doesn't catch fire), it is the marvellously tender slivers of teppanyaki – wagyu, salmon and hammour

– that may well convince you to become one of the regular patrons of this elegantly low-key gem.

Atlantis The Palm
Palm Jumeirah
Map 2 A3

Nobu ▶ p.524

04 426 2626 | *www.atlantisthepalm.com*

The godfather of sushi, Nobuyuki Matsuhisa, has arrived in Dubai, and has upped the ante for sushi in the city. Japanese food aficionados will be delighted with the exceptional quality, attention to detail and huge menu of sushi, sashimi and tempura. The uninitiated will quickly feel at home thanks to the helpful, friendly staff. Wave-inspired curves flow throughout this funky restaurant, and the accompanying bar, in keeping with the Atlantis theme. The experience of eating here is not restricted to celebrities and those with friends in high places, and you're always welcome, as long as you can get a reservation and your wallet can take the hit.

Above Safestway
Al Wasl
Map 7 C3

Noodle Sushi

04 321 1500 | *seawfood@yahoo.com*

Conveniently located on Sheikh Zayed Road, Noodle Sushi is one of the four themed restaurants surrounding Sea World. The decor is striking, in black and bamboo tones, and you can sit at the live sushi station and watch the artistry, or order from a varied menu. The menu includes reasonably priced bento (complete Japanese meals in lacquered boxes), as well as a wide assortment of sushi, sashimi and tempura. If one of your group is not a big fan of Japanese food the staff will arrange for a meal to be brought from the Sea World section.

Crowne Plaza
Trade Centre 1
Map 7 F3

Sakura

04 331 1111 | *www.dubai.crowneplaza.com*

Sakura offers one of Dubai's widest varieties of delicious Japanese food, from sushi and teppanyaki to the less well-known shabu shabu. The sushi is basic but done well, and the teppanyaki is a great show with delicious flavours. The two buffet nights each week are excellent value, with both sushi and teppanyaki (vegetables, seafood and meat) available. Seating is available at the cooking tables themselves, standard tables, or in one of the private tatami rooms – great for enjoying sake.

Jumeirah
Town Centre
Jumeira
Map 7 D1

Sumo Sushi & Bento

04 344 3672 | *www.sumosushi.net*

Japanese food has become popular around the world and while there are many outlets in this city that cater to the rarefied tastes of its diners, there's also something reassuringly fuss-free about chowing down a bento box at Sumo. You can almost imagine a harried Tokyo executive eating a lunch much like yours: sweet and sticky beef atop a mound of glutinous rice and steamed vegetables, washed down with a little cup of green tea. It's simple, healthy stuff and while Sumo might not win any awards for culinary excellence, the food here does what it says on the tin and it does it rather well.

Grand Hyatt Dubai
Umm Hurair
Map 13 C1

Sushi

04 317 1234 | *www.dubai.grand.hyatt.com*

A stroll through the oasis-like lobby leads you to the almost secret hideaway that is Sushi, an appropriately petite venue for lovers of sushi and sashimi. Artfully prepared in the open kitchen, portions are determined by the number of pieces you feel like indulging in. This is evidently a popular venue for far eastern expats looking for some home style food which gives you some reassurance that the careful preparation and the melt in your mouth morsels are indeed high quality.

Restaurants

Century Village ◀
Garhoud
Map 13 E1

Sushi Sushi ▶ p.549
04 282 9908 | www.centuryvillage.ae

An intimate venue located in Century Village, this Japanese restaurant is decorated in a modern style with low lighting and comfy couches. There is also a fabulous outdoor terrace for cooler evenings. Offering a very comprehensive menu of sushi and sashimi, non-sushi eaters are equally well catered for with alternative Japanese dishes. Tuesday night allows you to choose all the sushi you can eat from the conveyor belt for Dhs.169. With good food, reasonable prices, and an enjoyable atmosphere, this is a popular choice. Reservations are recommended, especially on Tuesdays.

Boulevard at
Emirates Towers ◀
Trade Centre 2
Map 7 F3

tokyo@thetowers
04 319 8008 | www.jumeirahemiratestowers.com

This ultra-modern restaurant has some stylish Japanese garden features running along the corridor next to elegantly partitioned tatami rooms, with seating on traditional floor cushions. You can also dine by the windows overlooking the mall, at the sushi bar or at the teppanyaki table. The buzzing atmosphere is added to by the busy chef clanging cooking utensils and entertaining the diners around him. The menu is good, featuring a wide range of all the Japanese usuals, and for something different the 'ankimo' and 'spider' are must tries. The teppanyaki table serves up hot, freshly grilled food, and other staples such as tempura, grilled dishes and bento lunch sets are also worth trying.

Oasis Beach Tower ◀
Dubai Marina
Map 5 A1

Wagamama
04 399 5900 | www.wagamama.ae

Modelled on a traditional Japanese ramen bar, Wagamama's contemporary, streamlined design works well for a quick bite. Orders are taken and electronically sent to the kitchen where they are immediately and freshly prepared; if you want to linger over your meal, it is wise to order one course at a time. The menu is extensive and covers a wide variety of generously served noodle and rice dishes plus a few curries and warming soups. The friendly hustle and bustle atmosphere is created by the shared seating at long tables with benches. Other branches are at Crowne Plaza (p.38) and The Greens (04 361 5757).

Ascot Hotel ◀
Bur Dubai
Map 8 F2

Yakitori
04 352 0900 | www.ascothoteldubai.com

For those in search of authentic Japanese food, Yakitori is a good bet. The restaurant is in the style of a Japanese diner, in red and black. The extensive menu offers an unrivalled choice, which clearly delights the almost entirely Japanese clientele. Aficionados will enjoy the usual sushi and tempura, as well as a variety of noodle choices, set meals, and the signature yakitori dish. You may find venues with a more subtle ambience, but very rarely with such a choice of quality food.

Dubai Internet City ◀
Al Sufouh
Map 5 C2

Yo! Sushi
04 36254 70/1 | www.yosushi.com

Fresh sushi prepared before your eyes and whizzed around a conveyor belt to the first lucky taker is destined to be a success, as it is in Yo! Sushi's four trendy branches. Sushi addicts and first-time experimenters will all find something here, with both traditional and unconventional sushi available. Friendly staff explain the types of sushi and the restaurant's system, with different coloured plates indicating the price of the dish (from Dhs.9-19). Fresh, fun and easy sushi with bottomless miso soup and green tea. Branches are also in Dubai Festival City (04 232 9396), BurJuman (04 359 5479) and DIFC (800 967 8744), with further openings in Mirdif and Dubai Mall expected.

Korean

Other options **Far Eastern** p.544

Seoul Garden Restaurant

Zomorrodah Building
Karama
Map 10 E1

04 337 7876 | *seoulgarden@empal.com*

Here you sit tucked away in your own private room and each table is equipped with the traditional Korean barbecue – which you should definitely put to good use by ordering at least one beef dish. Your waiters are literally at your fingertips as a table-mounted button brings a friendly and helpful smile upon command. Cool ginger tea and a sweet melon dessert accompany every meal and provide a unique and satisfying finish.

Sumibiya ▶ p.37

Radisson SAS Hotel
Dubai Deira Creek
Deira
Map 9 C3

04 222 7171 | *www.radissonsas.com*

The Japanese clientele are a reassuring portent of quality at this yakiniku (Korean grilled meat) eatery which, lying tucked away in a corner of the Radisson SAS Deira Creek, might easily be overlooked in favour of more attention-grabbing places. It shouldn't. While the minimalist decor remains elegantly modest, the gas grill in the middle of every table cries out for diners to infuse the place with laughter as they tackle the art of searing, grilling and charcoaling bite-size morsels of food. It's informal, fun, and all of it is tasty; if your food is overdone, you only have yourself to blame.

Latin American

Other options **Mexican** p.583

Beach House Cabana

Clubhouse Azraq
Shoreline Apartments
Palm Jumeirah
Map 2 A3

04 361 8856 | *www.emiratesleisureretail.com*

This laidback restaurant is a good spot to go to with friends. Sitting in low lighting, inside intimate booths or on bar stools, the staff will potter about you adding dishes to your table. Share a moderate selection of hot and cold tapas like tacos filled with chili con carne, or opt for mains like beef and pinto beans with corn bread. There is also a good selection of cocktails. Prices are reasonable at around Dhs.30 for tapas dishes and Dhs.90 for mains.

El Malecon

Dubai Marine Beach
Resort & Spa
Jumeira
Map 7 F1

04 346 1111 | *www.dxbmarine.com*

Malecon's graffiti-covered turquoise walls and low lighting creates a sultry Cuban atmosphere that builds up during the evening, helped along by the live music and some of best Salsa dancers in town. Big windows overlook the glowing Dubai Marine lagoon and while the menu isn't massive (the signature paella is the best choice), the clientele is pretty delicious. With neighbouring venues bringing in the crowds as the clock ticks on, Malecon is a great place to start the night, dip into en route or end a liquid shoreline sojourn.

Sumibiya

Latino House

Al Murooj Rotana Hotel & Suites
Trade Centre 2
Map 7 E3

04 321 1111 | www.rotana.com

Smart, sexy and seductive, this restaurant embodies a stylish Brazilian business man, instead of a greasy Benidorm waiter. Romantic and dimly lit, Latino House uses heavy drapes, large chairs and marble to further intoxicate before you even see the food on offer. Succulent steaks, modern twists on South American classics and imaginative new creations make up the small but tempting menu. Throw in attentive service, dancing on Mondays and a golf buggy ride and you might have found your new favourite restaurant.

Pachanga

Hilton Jumeirah
Dubai Marina
Map 5 A1

04 399 1111 | www.hilton.com

Choose from the shadowy Havana-style bar, Brazilian barbecue, Mexican lounge or stylish Argentinean terrace that surround the central dancefloor and transport you to the Latin American destination of your choice. The welcoming service begins with guacamole prepared at your table, then dishes from all over Latin America offer diners a wide selection. Their seafood is delicious but the real delicacies are for meat-eaters. Tango nights on a Wednesday make it the busiest night of the week.

Mediterranean

Other options **Italian** p.568, **Spanish** p.591

At Home – Mediterranean Dining Room & Lounge

Four Points by Sheraton Sheikh Zayed Road
Trade Centre 2
Map 7 E3

04 354 3333 | www.starwoodhotels.com/fourpoints

With a small but well thought out menu, At Home is a great new addition to Dubai's eateries. Located on the mezzanine floor of the Four Points Sheraton, the restaurant overlooks the bustle of Sheikh Zayed Road, where you can gaze out at the traffic from a comfy armchair while perusing the decent-sized wine list. The menu is Mediterranean influenced, with good seafood choices including an impressive paella – if you can tear yourself away from the pizza that is.

az.u.r

The Harbour Hotel & Residence
Dubai Marina
Map 5 B2

04 319 4000 | www.emirateshotelsresorts.com/the-harbour

At first glance, the rather clinical modern decor may be off putting, but az.u.r (pronounced 'as you are') hides a cornucopia of wholesome high-end dishes using organic food wherever possible. It offers a range of hearty meat, fish and seafood dishes, super fresh vegetables and even organic wine. The food is excellent with rich combinations of ingredients, although the vegetarian section is small. The service is knowledgeable and friendly, and there's a great Marina view from the terrace.

Conservatory

Al Manzil Hotel
Downtown Burj Dubai
Map 7 D4

04 428 5888 | www.almanzilhotel.com

For light and airy dining, The Conservatory is a pleasant spot tucked away in the Al Manzil hotel. An uncomplicated and reasonably priced buffet featuring European, Arabic and Asian flavours complements the spacious and stylish indoor seating and the outdoor courtyard dining. This restaurant is a relaxing oasis, perfect for a quiet lunch or a laidback evening meal, but as you fill your plate with the tasty assortment remember to save room for the selection of desserts – they are a taste sensation.

Finz

Ibn Battuta
Jebel Ali
Map 4 D2

04 368 5620 | www.ibnbattutamall.com

Tucked away in the China court, the warm Mediterranean welcome is enough to get you past the not-so-romantic mall setting. Sink into the mock-leather seating and be prepared for an eclectic mix of Portuguese, Italian, Spanish and South American fare. Although this place is famous for its delicacies of the ocean, be sure to try their Portuguese signature dish Espetada. The tangy fresh fruit mocktails make up for the fact that the place is unlicensed. This may not be the perfect location for a romantic meal for two, but Finz could spin you into an oblivion of Mediterranean melts.

Kaleidoscope ▶ p.524

Atlantis The Palm
Palm Jumeirah
Map 2 A3

04 426 2626 | *www.atlantisthepalm.com*

The atrium-like setting of buffet restaurant Kaleidoscope provides nice, leafy views outside the large windows, where there is some seating. However, it's inside where you'll want to be, where under the stained glass skylight, the food stations offer a real mix of international cuisine. Italian food is well represented with delicious antipasti, pizzas and pasta dishes while at the Asian station, clanging pans and sizzling woks serve up a mix of stir-fries, noodles and dim sum. There's also a range of Indian curries and tandoori items, roasts, salads, and even a mini sushi conveyor belt. With so much on offer, you've really got to pace yourself to be able to sample one of the dozens of desserts.

La Villa

Sofitel City Centre
Port Saeed
Map 11 C3

04 294 1222 | *www.accorhotels.com*

For a complete change of scenery, take the short walk from busy Deira City Centre to the tranquil south of France at La Villa. Warm yellow walls bearing murals, prints, and paintings enclose beautifully appointed tables with fresh flowers under subtle lighting. The food is prepared with the freshest ingredients, and comes by way of the gracious staff. The Business Lunch, served Saturday to Wednesday, is a hit with diners who can then round off their meal with a winning dessert and choice of satisfying beverages.

Majlis Al Bahar

Burj Al Arab
Umm Suqeim
Map 6 B1

04 301 7600 | *www.burj-al-arab.com*

This pricey beachside spot is owned by the Burj al Arab and offers front row seats to the iconic hotel's nightly light show. Book through the hotel then get whisked away on a golf cart upon arrival. The mainly meaty Mediterranean cuisine isn't exceptional but the mini barbecues are a novel attraction and good for friends to share, while the salads are well executed. Desserts are limited and the wine is over-priced but for views to make your friends jealous Majlis al Bahar fits the (large) bill.

Medzo

Wafi City
Umm Hurair
Map 11 E4

04 324 4100 | *www.wafi.com*

For year-round terrace dining, Mediterranean style, head to Medzo. Outdoor air conditioning units make this an alfresco option even in the summer – with a little imagination, you could be eating out on the Amalfi coast. There is a good range of regional food on the menu, including superb seafood starters and mains, classic pastas, tender meat dishes and interesting pizza toppings, plus a varied wine menu. Service is swift and discreet, and if you're not in the mood for outdoors, the inside dining area gives a more intimate, sophisticated dining experience.

Olive House

No. One Tower
Sheikh Zayed Rd
Trade Centre 1
Map 7 E3

04 343 3110

Olive House is a marvellous corner of the Mediterranean on Sheikh Zayed Road. Its tables are always full though diners come and go, having eaten sandwiches, pizzas, mezze or salads and, almost surely, icecream. All of the delicious dishes also pass over the counter in a busy takeaway trade. The friendly and prompt service makes this an ideal place for a quick meal, especially given the reasonable prices and the convenient location. While this strip of Sheikh Zayed Road may be home to numerous eateries, Olive House is one of the finest in terms of simple, fresh and delicious cuisine.

One&Only
Royal Mirage
Al Sufouh
Map 5 C1

Rotisserie

04 399 9999 | *www.oneandonlyresort.com*

This all-you-can-eat buffet offers a mix of Arabic and Mediterranean dishes that certainly meet expectation from the Royal Mirage resort. Ranging from Arabic mezze to an excellent lamb tagine, the only problem is finding room to sample everything on offer. Ask for a table outside or by the window so you can enjoy the authentic surroundings and views over the grounds – the tables inside are spaciously placed to give you privacy and easy access to the buffet, but lack atmosphere.

Ritz-Carlton Dubai
Dubai Marina
Map 5 A1

Splendido

04 399 4000 | *www.ritzcarlton.com*

You really do get more bang for your dirham at Splendido and the reasonably priced wine list is a great bonus. The food is thoroughly enjoyable without changing the course of Italian cuisine. It is however, far beyond run of the mill pastas and risottos, with an enormous dessert menu finishing off the generous proceedings. Splendido represents great value and an enjoyable night for friends and family alike.

Jumeirah
Beach Hotel
Umm Suqeim
Map 6 B1

Villa Beach

04 406 8999 | *www.jumeirahbeachhotel.com*

Possibly one of the most upmarket beach shacks you'll set foot in, this restaurant serves up beautiful Mediterranean fare within cork-popping distance of the lapping sea and Burj Al Arab. The open, wooden-decked terrace and hanging lanterns that blow in the breeze give Villa Beach a laidback feel, but the food and service is anything but. Delicious dishes such as warm goats cheese, prosciutto and figs, tender steaks, fresh seafood and Bailey's tiramisu are complemented by a varied wine list, and the service is worthy of a fine-dining venue.

Emirates Towers
Trade Centre 2
Map 7 F3

Vu's

04 319 8088 | *www.jumeirahemiratestowers.com*

A stylish and elegant eatery, this is fine dining at its best and with one of the most sensational views in town. The cuisine is modern European, so you'll find a variety of original offerings with recognisable influences. The menu is finely compiled with dishes certain to impress: you can start with caviar linguine and move on to the signature dishes lobster or roast pigeon. Each plate is exquisitely presented in more manageable portions than you might find elsewhere. Be warned, the location and quality might be sky high but so are the prices.

Mexican

Other options **Tex Mex** p.595

Umm Al Sheif St
Nr Spinneys Centre
Umm Suqeim
Map 6 F2

Maria Bonita's

04 394 4523

In a city with so many hotel restaurants, Maria Bonita stands out as a friendly, well-worn neighbourhood eatery. Serving traditional Mexican (of which there aren't so many choices in town) and Tex-Mex dishes, it draws its customers back time and time again. Though you will have to sacrifice having a cerveza with your meal, the flavourful nachos, quesadillas and fajitas plus the laid back atmosphere make it more than worthwhile. Enjoy dining on the patio or inside, watching the tortilla machine churn out the flat bread. There is also another branch called Casa Maria (04 885 3188) in The Green Community.

Moroccan
Other options **Arabic/Lebanese** p.532

Marrakech

Shangri-La Hotel
Trade Centre 1
Map 7 E3

04 405 2703 | www.shangri-la.com

In keeping with the Shangri-La's high standards, this upmarket eatery offers a tempting menu of Moroccan fare for discerning diners. Smooth arches and lamps add to the sense of tranquility, while a rather strident duo belts out traditional tunes on a small stage. Starters such as 'wedding pie' with pigeon, crushed almonds and icing sugar, are served on beautiful blue ceramic tableware. For mains try the lamb tagine with fluffy, fragrant rice. After all those carbs, a light orange salad is the perfect ending.

Shoo Fee Ma Fee

Souk Madinat
Jumeirah
Umm Suqeim
Map 6 A2

04 366 6730 | www.madinatjumeirah.com

The views at many Madinat outlets are breathtaking, but as you walk out onto the terrace at Shoo Fee Ma Fee you'll find the postcard-perfect vista mesmerising. The menu places an emphasis on authentic Moroccan cuisine, and it must be the only place in Dubai where you can choose between roasted goat leg (for two), camel kofta or a mixed platter of grilled lamb, chicken and camel. Vegetarians: you might not like it. After your meal, you can relax in the comfortable upstairs area and enjoy pastries, shisha and live entertainment.

Tagine

One&Only
Royal Mirage
Al Sufouh
Map 5 C1

04 399 9999 | www.oneandonlyroyalmirage.com

Tagine is special. Duck down and enter through the tiny carved wooden doorway into a beautiful Moroccan den of embroidered hangings, glowing lanterns and sultry music. The food is deliciously authentic. Start with a tasty mezze plate or Moroccan harira soup, then choose from delicious speciality couscous, tajine or kebab main dishes. The meat is so tender it almost melts on first bite. A dessert accompanied by sweet mint tea, impressively poured from a great height, finishes things off in style. Request an intimate cushioned booth for a truly memorable setting.

Pakistani
Other options **Indian** p.550, **Sri Lankan** p.592

Karachi Darbar

Karama
Shopping Centre
Karama
Map 10 E1

04 334 7272

Quite possibly the cheapest place in Dubai for tasty, good quality food, this Indo-Pakistani chain is a perennial favourite. The simple decor, plain menus, and utilitarian settings may not pull visitors in off the street, but that's their loss. With the Pakistani dishes on the menu, it adds a little something different in comparison to the range usually offered by restaurants from the subcontinent. Dining options and facilities around town do differ, but some, like the Karama branch, offer dining outside which makes for good people watching with your curry.
Branches at: Karama Shopping Centre, near the large car park (04 334 7272); Bur Dubai, near HSBC (04 353 7080); Qusais Road (04 261 2526); Naif Road, near Hyatt Regency Hotel (04 272 3755); Satwa (04 349 0202); Hor Al Anz, behind Dubai Cinema (04 262 5251); Al Qusais, Sheikh Colony (04 263 2266); Rashidiya (04 285 9464).

Restaurants

Nr Satwa R/A
Satwa
Map 8 A3

Ravi's

04 331 5353

Ravi's has gained something of a legendary status among western expats and seems to be on a lot of tour guides' itineraries, despite being one of the cheapest eateries in town. This 24 hour diner offers a range of Pakistani curried favourites and rice dishes, such as biryani and butter chicken, alongside more quirky dishes like fried brains. The venue is basic and, while most people opt for the choice of eating outside, dining is also available in the main restaurant or in the quieter family section.

Persian

Other options **Arabic/Lebanese** p.532

Shahrzad

Al Durrah Tower
Sheikh Zayed Rd
Trade Centre 1
Map 7 F3

Al Borz

04 331 8777

One of Tehran's best kebab houses has crossed the Gulf and set up shop on Sheikh Zayed Road, providing Dubai residents the chance to sample its famous kebabs and rich rice specialities. The lunch buffet, including soups and desserts, is an ideal introduction to Iranian cuisine and is moderately priced. A family setting and large portions make Al Borz popular with Iranians and those who love Persian fare. The takeaway and delivery service is good.

Nr Rydges Plaza
Satwa
Map 8 A3

Pars Iranian Kitchen

04 398 4000 | *pars@eim.ae*

The first thing you'll notice is the huge, garish sign pulsating above the restaurant but Pars offers a traditional laid-back atmosphere a million miles from the modernity suggested by the neon. The menu is limited, with favourites including hummus, moutabel, tabbouleh, and a selection of grilled meats and kebabs. A delightful front garden, enclosed by a fairy light-entwined hedgerow, is home to low tables and soft, Arabic-cushioned bench seats, perfect for enjoying a leisurely shisha. Another branch in the Wilson building (04 398 8787), near the Dubai World Trade Centre, offers slightly more luxurious indoor dining. Pars can also be found in the food court at the Mall of the Emirates.

Pharaohs' Club
Umm Hurair
Map 10 E4

Persia Persia

04 324 4100 | *www.wafi.com*

Surrounded by cosy alcoves, Persia Persia's large dining area on the top floor of the pyramid is understated, simple yet elegant, and nicely lit. A terrace outside has views over the tree tops. Waiting staff are elegantly attired, pleasant and extremely attentive. The wide-ranging menu offers flavour-packed appetisers that are great for sharing, alongside several varieties of kebabs and other mains including lamb stew, an Iranian favourite, and duck with walnut and pomegranate in a sweet and sour sauce. Prices are not cheap, but the food is generally very good and it is already a regular hangout for many Iranians – always a good sign.

Hyatt Regency
Deira
Map 9 D1

Shahrzad

04 317 2222 | *www.dubai.regency.hyatt.com*

It takes a special kebab to warrant a trip through the maddening traffic to the beautifully renovated Hyatt Regency, and Shahrzad's offerings won't disappoint. Compared to the

Pizzerias	
800Pizza (T)	800 74992
Biella	04 324 4666
Cosi	04 345 4848
Casa Mia	04 282 4040
Cucina	04 607 7977
Il Rustico	04 398 2222
Italian Connection	04 335 3001
La Moda	04 391 2550
Oregano Pizza	04 374 6059
Papa John's (T)	04 335 2523
Pastamania	04 390 8672
Pizza Company	04 345 4848
Pizza Express (T)	04 355 2424
Pizza Hut (T)	800 6500
Pizzeria Uno Chicago Grill	04 294 8799
Round Table Pizza (T)	04 881 0808
Stefano's	04 422 2632
Tiger Pizza (T)	04 374 6059

hotel's contemporary lobby, Shahrzad's interior seems a bit dated, but the live Persian music and shiny, copper-clad open kitchen more than make up for it. Start with the bizarre but delicious Ash Irishta noodle soup, then move on to the equally tasty appetiser platter before digging in to some of the best kebabs in town. Prices are a bit steep, but well worth it.

Pizzerias
Other options **Italian** p.568

Sometimes nothing else on the menu can compete with a good pizza, and you'll find a decent variety in Dubai. The table on the left lists places where you'll find good, reliable fare – obviously you'll get pizzas at most Italian restaurants (see p.568), but those listed really stand out. Competition is fierce and opinion is divided on who does the best, but the only way to really know is to sample them for yourself.

Of course, takeaway pizzas are pretty good too – a few favourites are marked with a 'T' in the table.

Polynesian
Other options **Far Eastern** p.544

Souk Madinat
Jumeirah
Umm Suqeim
Map 6 A2

Trader Vic's
04 366 5646 | www.tradervics.com

Trader Vic's is a Dubai rite of passage. Until you've been through the doors and experienced the vibey atmosphere, you just can't consider yourself a seasoned night-lifer. You can linger over a delicious, Asian-inspired meal, munch your way through some moreish snacks (crispy wontons, prawns and other oriental finger foods), or just savour a few of their famously exotic cocktails (served in shrunken heads or adorned with feathers). There are two locations, one at the Crowne Plaza on Sheikh Zayed Road (04 331 1111) and another at the Madinat, complete with waterside terrace.

Portuguese

Sheikh Zayed Rd
Nr Crowne
Plaza Hotel
Trade Centre 1
Map 7 F3

Nando's
04 321 2000 | www.nandos.com

Worldwide chain Nando's is famous for its peri-peri chicken, which ranges from the mild to the extra hot with a sideline of curly fries. The menu is limited and the service a little rusty but the takeaway downstairs is a good option for residents of the neighbouring towers (extra points for the 'poultry in motion' slogan on the delivery bikes). Other locations are near Al Ghurair City (04 221 1992), The Greens Centre (04 360 8080), and Burj Residences (04 422 4882).

Russian

Nr Lamcy Plaza
Oud Metha
Map 10 D2

Russian Home Restaurant
04 334 6050

The Russian Home Restaurant lacks a bit of atmosphere, but is open 24 hours a day and is a great place to go for. Russian home cooking. Relax in diner-style booths while perusing the huge menu. Famous dishes like borsht are available, but there is also a good selection of other dishes including mashed potato, cabbage, dumplings and filled breads. The non-alcoholic drinks range from the mundane to the downright unusual, like 'kvas' which is made by fermenting yeast and rye flour. The service is very friendly, despite the language barrier.

Troyka

Ascot Hotel
Bur Dubai
Map 8 F2

04 352 0900 | www.ascothoteldubai.com

There are few surprises left in Dubai, but this place is definitely one of them. Troyka offers old-world Russian charm in a unique setting, complete with winter wonderland murals. The low ceilings, dim lighting, red roses and candles add to the intimate mood. The Tuesday night buffet is all-inclusive and comprises time-honoured delicacies from Russian cuisine. A band plays every night from 22:30 and an extravagant live Vegas-style cabaret begins at 23:30.

Seafood

Al Bandar

Heritage Village
& Diving Village
Al Shindagha
Map 9 A1

04 393 9001 | www.alkoufa.com

Its idyllic location on the edge of the creek is score one for Al Bandar, a terrific venue offering good international seafood for a more dress-down clientele. This is the perfect venue to ease guests and visitors into the Arabian experience and certainly a breath of fresh air from the overwhelmingly plush restaurants in five-star hotels that can be stifling at times. The choice of seafood is pleasantly varied and the prices all cheap and cheerful. Tradition is the theme with the added photographic thrill of the resident camels nearby.

Al Mahara

Burj Al Arab
Umm Suqeim
Map 6 B1

04 301 7600 | www.burj-al-arab.com

Your visit to Al Mahara starts with a simulated submarine ride that takes you 'under the sea' to dine among the fish. 'Disembark' and you'll see the elegant restaurant is curled around a huge aquarium. The menu is almost exclusively seafood, with creations prepared by some of Dubai's top chefs. The menu boasts sublime flavours and presentation; this is fine dining at its finest, with prices to match. Gentlemen are required to wear a jacket for dinner.

Amwaj

Shangri-La Hotel
Trade Centre 1
Map 7 E3

04 405 2703 | www.shangri-la.com

Although it doesn't get the constant media attention like the city's celebrity-chef restaurants, Amwaj is a fine-dining must. The restaurant's contemporary aquatic decor isn't quite perfect, and is probably the only thing holding it back from becoming the city's number one. The chef is an expert at combining seemingly contrasting flavours into dishes that work so well you'll find yourself licking the plate. Priding itself on its perfectly prepared seafood, Amwaj's meat and vegetarian dishes are equally impressive. The menu isn't cheap, but compared to its main competitors, it might be the best deal in town.

Beach Bar & Grill

One&Only
Royal Mirage
Al Sufouh
Map 5 C1

04 399 9999 | www.oneandonlyroyalmirage.com

Walk through the gorgeous Royal Mirage and head towards the beach. Here you'll find an opulent and romantic beach bar with candle-lit tables on a terrace overlooking the beach and Palm Jumeirah. Seafood lovers must make a trip here; fish is caught on the day and is cooked simply but with style. Dishes are beautifully presented and the excellent wine menu is worth careful consideration. Although the terrace is large, guests are never too close to their neighbours, and the setting has romance written all over it. Seafood platters to share, and surf and turf options are available for people who simply can't pick just one dish.

The Dhow

Le Meridien
Mina Seyahi
Al Sufouh
Map 5 C1

04 399 3333 | www.lemeridien-minaseyahi.com

The large portions, good selection of wine and the gentle sway of this softly lit restaurant moored in the marina, encourage you to take your time and enjoy the scene. The staff will only disturb you long enough to explain the menu which offers a broad range of seafood cooked in a variety of styles. Try the large seafood platter with lobster or the range of fresh sushi. Although pricey, for a relaxed, romantic evening this restaurant is a perfect choice.

Fish Market ▶ p.37

Radisson SAS Hotel
Dubai Deira Creek
Deira
Map 9 C3

04 222 7171 | www.radissonsas.com

The real draw here is the open fish market theme which lets diners pick specific items from a large bank of fresh, raw seafood and vegetables. Choose anything from gigantic tiger prawns and Omani lobster to tiny boori fish and red snapper. While the fish is being prepared, you can entertain yourself with the view over the creek and a complimentary plate of french fries. Although you can choose how you want your fish prepared, there isn't much variety and the restaurant tends to rely on its novelty rather than cooking expertise. If fresh fish is what you're after, however, it's worth a visit.

Jimmy's Killer Prawns

BurJuman
Bur Dubai
Map 8 F4

04 355 5182 | www.jimmyskillerprawns.ae

Jimmy's Killer Prawns is a hidden treat for all seafood lovers. Located on the third floor of BurJuman (p.486) this casual restaurant boasts a spacious outdoor terrace among the rooftop garden as well as tables inside the glasshouse. The menu predominantly offers prawn platters though other seafood, sushi and non-seafood dishes are on offer. Servings are reasonably priced and generous with starters priced around Dhs.50 and mains Dhs.60-100. The house special, Jimmy's Prawn Promise, is a must for new patrons.

La Baie

Ritz-Carlton Dubai
Dubai Marina
Map 5 A1

04 399 4000 | www.ritzcarlton.com

La Baie is a chic, expensive, French restaurant specialising in fish with exciting monikers. The carte du jour is so captivating that you won't notice how few choices there are, the food so imaginatively presented that you won't want to eat it, and the dishes so inventive they depart from the description of ingredients listed on the menu. The wine list is extensive but expensive and the serene balcony offers pleasant sea air or cigarettes depending on how the wind blows.

Mahi Mahi

Wafi Mall
Umm Hurair
Map 10 E4

04 324 4100 | www.wafi.com

The modestly spectacular Mahi Mahi fish restaurant is Dubai's prize catch. There's live mud crab from Africa, feisty langoustines from Norway, fresh red snapper, local helwayoo, hammour and more, offered in a choice of delicious sauces from the across the blue planet. The portions are plentiful and served with panache and organic vegetables in a beautiful setting with welcoming smiles. The Mahi Mahi fish's name translates as 'strong strong' in Hawaiian, which is a great description for such a fantastic restaurant.

Jumeirah Beach Hotel
Umm Suqeim
Map 6 B1

Marina

04 406 8999 | www.jumeirahbeachhotel.com

Negotiating the long walkway extending from Jumeirah Beach Hotel justifies a ride in one of the ever-available carts. In the restaurant, guests inspect the shiny fish recumbent in icy displays and the even more gorgeous, though less edible, fish swimming in their sparkling tanks. Since the glass of the restaurant effectively blocks the view enjoyed outside, patrons concentrate on the fish, cooked largely under Asian influence. Afterwards, head upstairs to 360° (p.608), for vistas, shisha, music and drinks.

Atlantis The Palm
Palm Jumeirah
Map 2 A3

Ossiano ▶ p.524

04 426 2626 | www.atlantisthepalm.com

Fine dining doesn't get much more sumptuous than Ossiano, where three Michelin star chef Santi Santamaria serves up Catalan-inspired seafood dishes. Glistening chandeliers and the underwater theme, with floor-to-ceiling views of the enormous Ambassador Lagoon, provide a formal, but romantic, setting for guests to enjoy simple, delicate dishes. Ossiano offers first-rate food, with exceptional service in a stylish setting, but it all comes at a premium price with degustation menus costing Dhs.650 and Dhs.750 or a chef's surprise menu starting at Dhs.950 per person.

Al Qasr Hotel
Umm Suqeim
Map 6 A2

Pierchic

04 366 8888 | www.madinatjumeirah.com/al_qasr

Pierchic could quite possibly be Dubai's most amazing restaurant, which is a rather bold statement considering its array of awe-inspiring adversaries. There are good reasons, however, for staking this claim. Firstly, the breathtaking location – Pierchic is situated at the end of a long wooden pier that juts into the Arabian Gulf and affords front-row seats of an unobstructed Burj Al Arab. Secondly, the superior seafood is meticulously presented and delicately cooked. And thirdly, the first-class wine menu reads like a sommelier's wishlist. However, if you're not a fan of rich, fancy food that comes in small packages then you might think you're not getting value for money (it doesn't come cheap). Just remember that what you're paying for are the incredible surroundings, especially if you request a table on the terrace where you can soak up the atmosphere as the waves dance beneath you.

Marina

Souk Madinat
Jumeirah
Umm Suqeim
Map 6 A2

Pisces

04 366 8888 | *www.madinatjumeirah.com*

Pisces is a plush seafood restaurant with modern decor, pleasingly professional service and creatively delicious food, always artistically presented. The attentive staff glide between beautifully set tables arranged spaciously to maintain intimacy. Pisces' perfectly presented fish is exactly what one would expect at a virtually perfect restaurant. Once you have finished, be sure to visit the outdoor bar upstairs that will give you a breathtaking view of the Madinat waterways in all their man-made glory.

Crowne Plaza
Trade Centre 1
Map 7 F3

Reef

04 331 1111 | *www.crowneplaza.com*

This unpretentious seafood buffet, while a little lacking in ambience, offers a lavish choice of seafood and at Dhs.160 is superb value for money. The range of cold and hot seafood, desserts and cheeses is broad, and quality is high. The grill also features whole lobster at a fraction of what you might pay elsewhere. Service is attentive, and the upgrade to unlimited alcohol for Dhs.50 is surprisingly reasonable. Visit with friends for a fun and satisfying evening – end up at Zinc nightclub (p.628) which is located downstairs.

Renaissance Hotel
Deira
Map 11 E1

Sails ▶ p.567

04 262 5555 | *www.renaissancehotels.com*

Sails may look a little dated with styling reminiscent of a P&O ferry, but the food is good and reasonably priced. At the market-style counter choose your fish or seafood and hand it over to the chef who will cook it to your liking and recommend sides and sauces to accompany it. For variety, it's hard to complete with Sails' neighbour, Spice Island (p.566), but there's choice enough with 14 different types of seafood, plus a good salad and dessert selection. Open for breakfast, lunch and dinner, the evening seafood buffet runs from Wednesday to Sunday, with surf 'n' turf on Mondays and Tuesdays.

Mall of the Emirates
Al Barsha
Map 6 A3

Salmontini

04 341 0222 | *restaurants.malloftheemirates@kempinski.com*

If you like salmon and snow this unique eatery might just be your idea of heaven. Located in a cosy cranny of the Mall of the Emirates, the lilac, pink and slate chic interior of Salmontini is fashioned around large windows overlooking Dubai's indoor ski slope. Choose from every imaginable working of Scottish salmon, from smoked and grilled to cured and poached. Prices are not cheap, but they do offer all-inclusive deals on different nights of the week.

Above Safestway
Al Wasl
Map 7 C3

Sea World

04 321 1500 | *www.seaworld-dubai.com*

This is a top-notch venue offering the freshest seafood in pleasantly decorated surroundings, so don't be put off by the giant red neon lobster that flashes outside, or its location above a supermarket. It's a simple concept: choose your 'catch' from the market stall, and have it cooked to perfection by the talented chefs. The service is excellent, easily rivalling the best five-star hotels, but the real surprise is the price, which is considerably lower than you'd pay for the same thing elsewhere.

> **Celebrity Chefs**
>
> Does food prepared by famous hands really taste better? To find out head to Frankie's (p.571) to sample Marco Pierre White's menu, Verre (p.548), Gordon Ramsey's restaurant, or at Atlantis try Matsuhisa Nobu's offering (p.578), Ronda Locatelli (p.575), Santi Santamari's Ossiano (p.589) and Michel Rostang's French restaurant (p.548). For a more reasonably priced option try Sanjeev Kapoor's Khazana (p.553).

Al Murooj Rotana Hotel & Suites
Trade Centre 2
Map 7 E3

Waterside Seafood Restaurant

04 321 1111 | www.almuroojrotanahoteldubai.com/

True to its name, even if the water is courtesy of Al Murooj's maze of pools and walkways, Waterside is all about the sea. There is a small fish market where you can select your fresh fish and the way in which you would like it cooked, and the attentive and knowledgeable staff are on hand with their worthy recommendations. The restaurant is relatively small, with window enclaves perfect for romancing couples and when weather permits there is a terrace available.

Mina A'Salam
Umm Suqeim
Map 6 A1

The Wharf

04 366 6730 | www.madinatjumeirah.com

The Wharf is fronted by magical (though man-made) waterways, where abras transfer guests from one elegant eatery or beautiful bar to the next. Both the outdoor deck, adorned with sailing paraphernalia, and the spacious interior, with an equally nautical atmosphere, are appealing. Sadly, The Wharf's cuisine is not as mesmerising. There's steak and a smattering of Arabic dishes, alongside plentiful pizza, but you've come expecting an ocean's worth of seafood not Sinbad's leftovers. Even the live lobster and crabs sizzling on the grill behind seem a little put out. To compound the contradictions, the bill crashes down on your table and stares up with a smirk.

Singaporean

Other options **Far Eastern** p.544

Grand Hyatt Dubai
Umm Hurair
Map 13 C1

Peppercrab

04 317 1234 | www.dubai.grand.hyatt.com

This is certainly one of Dubai's best Asian restaurants. The authenticity of the noodles and chili crab will make you feel like you're sitting in the middle of Newton's Circus in Singapore. Exceptional service that seems to be the hallmark of the Grand Hyatt will make you feel completely at ease. You will be paying the five-star prices, but when you're eating five-star dinners, with service to match, you probably don't mind so much.

Nxt to Open House Restaurant
Karama
Map 8 F4

Singapore Deli Café

04 396 6885 | singapuredeli@yahoo.co.uk

From bowls of steaming noodles to traditionally cooked nasi goreng, the authentic Asian dishes available at Singapore Deli Café are consistently excellent. The casual atmosphere and the high standard of home-style cooking draws a large crowd of regular customers, including many Indonesians and Malaysians who come for a taste of home. Prices are very reasonable, and this is one independent eatery that should definitely be on your must-do list if you're a fan of good Asian food.

Spanish

Other options **Mediterranean** p.581

Al Qasr Hotel
Umm Suqeim
Map 6 A2

Al Hambra

04 366 8888 | www.madinatjumeirah.com/al_qasr

Al Hambra's exposed brickwork and vaulted ceilings make for a more than passable Spanish restaurant, and the food, which fuses Andalusia with Morocco, is very good. Vegetarians are left with a skimpy choice, but for everyone else the seafood paella is a must. A duo of talented mariachis provides the mood to accompany your meal, and may have you stopping off to rent the *Desperado* DVD on the way home. It's not cheap, and you may want to save it for special occasions, but Al Hambra could just become your new favourite Spanish restaurant in Dubai.

Wafi City
Umm Hurair
Map 10 E4

Seville's

04 324 7300 | www.waficityrestaurants.com

The atmosphere at Seville's is both warm and buzzing. All ages gather for lunch or dinner at this Spanish restaurant to catch up with family and friends. You can share tapas or feast on the heartier dishes available. Live music adds to the friendly ambiance and the rustic decor lends itself to the cosy, homely feel. Reasonable prices and efficient service helps keep the atmosphere busy, whilst the outdoor terrace creates a tranquil spot for alfresco food and drink.

Sri Lankan

Opp Lulu
Supermarket
Karama
Map 10 E1

Chef Lanka

04 335 3050

Chef Lanka is the best chance to try Sri Lankan food in Dubai. It is a smart, clean little restaurant offering good value and great tasting food. There is a 'thatched' hut housing the daily buffet, but authentic dishes are cooked to order in the kitchen, allowing you to specify the spiciness. Alternatively, eat from the buffet for just Dhs.8 at lunch or Dhs.20 at dinner. It also does a mean nasi goreng.

Steakhouses

Other options **American** p.530

The Palace –
The Old Town
Downtown Burj Dubai
Map 7 D4

Asado

04 428 7888 | www.accorhotels.com

A combination of moody lighting, passionate music, and a meat lovers' dream menu cement Asado's top steakhouse position. The terrace provides a direct view of the Burj Dubai. Try an Argentinean 'stuffed cake' to feel right at home, but perhaps leave the whole roast goat for the heartier of appetite. Asado's reputation for the quality of its meat and varied choice is well deserved, while the ski lodge decor will encourage you to curl up with a glass of something special from the enormous wine list.

Fairmont Dubai
Trade Centre 1
Map 8 A4

The Exchange Grill

04 332 5555 | www.fairmont.com

Peer around the glass partition at Exchange Grill and you're confronted by excess – outsized leather armchairs, modern art installations and a floor-to-ceiling chandelier, offering visitors an even more exciting dining and leisure destination since its refurbishment. The menu strikes a balance between the classic and the innovative, and both lunch and dinner menus offer the best quality beef making it a real treat for meat lovers and fans of fine dining alike.

Asado

JW Marriott Hotel
Deira
Map 11 E1

JW's Steakhouse

04 607 7977

www.marriottdiningatjw.ae

Set in an intimate, out-of-the-way part of the hotel, JW's Steakhouse meets your expectations from the moment you walk through the door. Chefs can be seen cleaving huge chunks of meat in the open kitchen and once you are shown to your stately leather armchair, a huge menu offering an impressive range of steaks and seafood awaits. Salads are prepared fresh at your table and desserts, simple and generous, are worth it, if you can face them after all the meaty excess.

Creek Golf Club
Deira
Map 11 C3

Legends Steakhouse

04 295 6000 | *www.dubaigolf.com*

Membership of the golf club is not a requirement in order to savour Legends' relaxing atmosphere, deep comfortable seats and good quality food. The finely prepared, imaginative international cuisine includes a range of steaks and seafood, and is accompanied by an extensive wine list. The decor is modern, with a ceiling that stretches right to the top of the building's distinctive white sails. In the cooler months seating is also available on the large veranda, with great views overlooking the creek.

Le Meridien Dubai
Garhoud
Map 13 E1

M's Beef Bistro

04 702 2700 | *www.lemeridien-dubai.com*

Choose from light and airy inside dining or terrace seating with garden views. M's Beef Bistro is an unpretentious upper-end affair with an opulent feel, offering excellent service and cuisine, in the mid-price range. Ideal for a smart lunch or dinner, the wine list is comprehensive and the menu offers excellent steaks and French dishes; look out for le classiques including traditional french onion soup, burgundy snails and crepe suzette among the extensive chargrilled angus beef selection.

Grand Hyatt Dubai
Umm Hurair
Map 13 C1

Manhattan Grill

04 317 1234 | *www.dubai.grand.hyatt.com*

Compared to the opulent lobby and indoor rainforest of the Grand Hyatt, Manhattan Grill seems like the ultimate in low-key chic. Soft lighting, plush seating, smooth music and skilled staff make this one of the finest fine dining venues in town; not forgetting, of course, the raison d'etre – a selection of succulent, melt-in-your-mouth steaks. Non-meat eaters can take their pick from the seafood and vegetarian dishes, but the steaks are the stars of the show. Quality like this doesn't come cheap, but each mouthful adds weight to the old adage 'you get what you pay for' – Manhattan Grill is fancy, but worth it.

Souk Al Bahar
Downtown Burj Dubai
Map 7 D4

The Meat Co

04 420 0737 | *www.themeatco.com*

The Meat Co at Souk al Bahar appears tucked away from the crowds, which isn't a bad thing considering the construction work going on in Old Town. Take a seat on the expansive terrace for unrivalled views of the Burj Dubai and sit back with something from the extensive wine list while deciding where in the world you would like your steak to come from, what type of cut and how you would like it basted. The meat is aged, ensuring plenty of flavour, but the addition of the fiery peppercorn sauce is recommended. Another branch is at Souk Madinat Jumeirah (04 368 6040).

Dubai Polo
& Equestrian Club
Arabian Ranches
Map 2 B3

The Palermo Restaurant

04 361 8111 | *www.poloclubdubai.com*

By driving up to Dubai Polo Club and dining at Palermo you really feel that you are stepping away from city life. A quiet, elegant dining room and excellent food prove the drive was worth it. An original array of appetisers lead onto a solid choice of mains, where the quality of the meat and seafood will not disappoint. Perfect for an intimate meal, or even a business dinner, this cosy restaurant relaxes you in a way that only escaping the city can.

Radisson SAS Hotel
Dubai Deira Creek
Deira
Map 9 C3

Palm Grill ▶ p.37

04 222 7171 | *www.radissonsas.com*

Palm Grill cooks up juicy steaks in an open-plan kitchen to the accompaniment of a live pianist and pre-recorded open fire. The low ceiling, low lighting and fat-cushioned chairs foster a grand but intimate vibe – if you don't sit near the tinkling ivories. The steaks are a tender delight and cooked precisely to order and big enough to satisfy the most ravenous meat lover. On Thursdays, a giant roast is paraded around temptingly but the mignon remains the real star.

Desert Palm Dubai
Dubai-Hatta Rd
Map 2 C3

Rare Restaurant

04 323 8888 | *www.desertpalm.ae*

Located in one of Dubai's few boutique hotels, Rare is slowly gaining attention as one of the best steakhouses in the city. Although it isn't cheap, the menu has a large enough selection to please both the serious carnivore and the picky gourmand. With cuts from around the world, including the exclusive wagyu sirloin, meat lovers will have every reason to make a return visit. Book a table outside on the gorgeously contemporary terrace overlooking the polo fields, and take advantage of the hotel's isolated setting.

Emirates Towers
Trade Centre 2
Map 7 F3

The Rib Room

04 319 8088 | *www.jumeirahemiratestowers.com*

Diners tuck into large portions of steak and seafood among friendly chatter, amber lighting, dark wood and a flash of red. Leave room between your ribs for the tasty wagyu beef with peppercorn sauce or a large plate of surf and turf; you will be tempted with pretzels hanging from a stand, and a tasty amuse bouche. Fine wine and premium steak doesn't come cheap, but the staff will happily explain the many methods and accompaniments for your well-cooked meal.

Al Bustan Rotana
Garhoud
Map 13 E1

Rodeo Grill

04 282 0000 | *www.rotana.com*

Smoke a Montecristo cigar, sip a cool draught ale, and choose your selection from the grill while you relax in the snug little bar, where the chef works from an open kitchen. Attentive staff serve exceptional steaks from the exclusive a la carte menu, including the Chairman's Reserve striploin and fillet mignon. Desserts include New York cheesecake and chocolate mud pie. For a small restaurant (you should reserve), the wine list is huge. It's expensive, but a steak-lover's heaven.

Atlantis The Palm
Palm Jumeirah
Map 2 A3

Seafire ▶ p.524

04 426 2626 | *www.atlantisthepalm.com*

A restaurant of substance, the warm colours at Seafire contrast nicely with the rest of Atlantis, while the smell of leather and cosy alcoves conspire to create a well-established space that belies its youth. The menu is also well-executed with seafood and steak reigning supreme; start with oysters served on shaved ice before moving onto the impressive choice of meat cuts and side dishes. The signature dessert, a trio of chocolate treats, is worth waiting for. The staff's recommendations are spot on and you might need their help to steer through the lengthy wine list. While on the pricey side as you'd expect, this is already a contender for the best steakhouse in the city.

Crowne Plaza
Trade Centre 1
Map 7 F3

Western Steakhouse

04 331 1111 | *www.crowneplaza.com*

Western Steakhouse is great for meat lovers to line their stomachs before a night on the mai tais at Trader Vic's bar upstairs or Zinc nightclub. Centrally located within the Crowne Plaza Hotel, this unpretentious venue is a refreshing change with its homely atmosphere and decor. It's not the most glamorous night out for your money, but serves up large portions of great quality fare in a comfortable setting. If red meat is not your thing, the seafood and vegetarian selection should be enough to choose from.

Tex Mex

Other options **Mexican** p.583, **American** p.530

Arabian Courtyard
Hotel & Spa
Bur Dubai
Map 9 A2

Barry's Bench

04 351 6646 | *www.jackberrys.com/barrysbench*
Tucked away in a corner and run independently of the hotel, Barry's Bench's location in the Arabian Courtyard affords two things: views over the fort of Dubai Museum and its dhow, and windtowers – and the all-important drinks licence. Chow down on top quality Tex-Mex while supping a cold cerveza or one of their fantastic margaritas. Decorated in true Tex-Mex style, the expansive menu offers everything from Mexican-style breakfasts to a selection of fajitas, burritos, grills, burgers and decadent desserts. As you'd expect, portions are podgy, though always piping hot and packed with flavour. A quicker version is served up in Time Square's food court (04 341 8118).

Rydges Plaza Hotel
Satwa
Map 8 A3

Cactus Cantina

04 398 2274 | *www.cactuscantinadubai.com*
This ever-popular venue is a safe bet for sure-fire Tex-Mex fare. The food is tasty, with the emphasis leaning more toward the Tex than the Mex (refried beans and melted cheese with everything). Don't forget your appetite, as the portions are muy grande. With booths around the edges, plenty of tables squeezed into the floor space and a decor a few years past its prime, this isn't a good choice for an intimate meal. The lively atmosphere is aided by a pumping soundtrack and energetic staff. Weekends see the joint jumping, with crowds attracted by value-for-money meal deals and generous jugs of moreish margaritas.

Jumeirah
Beach Hotel
Umm Suqeim
Map 6 B1

Go West

04 406 8999 | *www.jumeirahbeachhotel.com*
This Tex-Mex eatery calls for a smart-casual dress code (but no cowboy boots). The well-priced menu offers a good variety, including the signature angus beef, which complements a drinks menu boasting everything from pints to vintage champagnes. A live band plays from 19:30 every night (except Sundays) so reserve a spot indoors or on the terrace with the accommodating staff if you fancy a dining experience with a Western twist.

Thai

Other options **Far Eastern** p.544

Dusit Thani Dubai
Trade Centre 2
Map 7 E3

Benjarong

04 343 3333 | *www.dusit.com*
Supposedly the Dusit's signature restaurant, this Thai eatery is a little on the cold side. This is not a reference to the over exuberant air conditioning, but rather the atmosphere – or lack there of. The decor is in a regal Thai style, and the food is deliciously concocted and perfectly presented. The staff are cordial, but verging on lackadaisical, resulting in a lack of pizzazz. There is no denying that the menu is tempting, with classics and a few inventive twists, and if you love Thai food you'll certainly enjoy it, but you can't help thinking that there are better places in town.

Blue Elephant

Al Bustan Rotana
Garhoud
Map 13 E1

04 282 0000 | *www.rotana.com*

Bringing the outdoors indoors, Blue Elephant is a lush space of greenery, bamboo and waterfalls. Both the decor and Thai cuisine are best suited to evening dining but the restaurant is open for lunch should you feel a daytime urge for noodles or a stir-fry. The buffet nights on Mondays, Tuesdays, Thursday and Saturdays offer the chance to sample spring rolls, prawn crackers, fragrant curries, spicy salads and delicate rice dishes while enjoying unlimited beer, house wines and soft drinks.

Lemongrass

Nr Lamcy Plaza
Oud Metha
Map 10 D2

04 334 2325

Located across from Lamcy Plaza, Lemongrass ranks among the better (and certainly cheaper) Thai restaurants in Dubai. The innovative and user-friendly menu offers a typical range of starters, soups, salads, noodles, curries, stir-fries and desserts, and for those who can't take the heat, spice levels can be tailored to individual preferences. While the food delivers fresh and authentic flavours, servings could be more generous. There's no alcohol, but the refreshing fruit mocktails more than compensate. The setting is bright, inviting and comfortable, and the service polite and unobtrusive. There's another branch at Ibn Battuta Mall (04 368 5616).

PaiThai

Al Qasr Hotel
Umm Suqeim
Map 6 A2

04 366 8888 | *www.madinatjumeirah.com*

From the abra ride through the Madinat's canals, to the brightly lit venue itself, Pai Thai is an experience to remember. Outdoor seating (available in the winter months) is a delightful way to enjoy the views, while the spacious interior keeps you cool on the hottest of evenings. The nouvelle cuisine is a delicious change of pace from Dubai's standard Thai restaurants. Most classic Thai dishes are available for purists, but the real beauty here is the opportunity to try a twist on a familiar favourite, with the menu holding new choices for almost every palate.

Royal Orchid

Marina Walk
Dubai Marina
Map 5 B2

04 367 4040 | *orchid04@eim.ae*

The Royal Orchid offers good quality Thai and Chinese food at reasonable prices. There's a two-tier interior dining area and an outdoor terrace overlooking the marina for the cooler months. The staff (and there are lots of them) are friendly and willing to help you choose from the extensive menu. A good option is the Magic Wok, where the chef will prepare your favourite meat, fish or vegetables in your chosen sauce. Portions are on the large side so arrive hungry and try a starter, like the stir-fried black pepper chicken wings. Also handy for a takeaway or delivery if you live in the area.

Smiling BKK

Al Wasl Rd
Nr Jumeira
Post Office
Jumeira
Map 7 C2

04 349 6677

This outstanding Thai pad is a rare and beautiful thing: a restaurant that serves great food with a side of good humour. The cheekily named dishes (some are too rude to print) are reasonable at around Dhs.30 but it's the atmosphere that sets Smiling BKK apart. With gossip mag pages for place mats, walls full of photos and ingenious theme nights such as 'sing for your supper', you're guaranteed to leave grinning.

Hungry In Hatta?

If you're out and about in the hills of Hatta, Café Gazebo at the Hatta Fort Hotel (04 852 3211) is the perfect lunch-time refuelling stop. Set in the lush grounds of this mountainside property, it serves a range of light meals, sandwiches and soups and non-guests are welcome. It's open from 07:00 to 20:00, and lunch is served from 11:00 to 16:00. You can also buy a day pass and enjoy the hotel's pool and facilities.

Le Meridien Dubai
Garhoud
Map 13 E1

Sukhothai

04 702 2307 | www.lemeridien-dubai.com

With dark wood-panelled walls and authentic Thai artefacts, this charming restaurant is a great venue for a romantic occasion or a special treat. The menu is extensive, offering all the usual favourites including curries and a good seafood selection, and the food is top notch although not cheap. Service from the traditionally dressed waiting staff is attentive but not intrusive. The restaurant has an outdoor seating area, which is quite pleasant in the cooler weather, but the atmosphere and ambience inside is so good it would be a shame to miss it any time of the year.

The Secret Is Out

Al Sahra Desert Resort is set to be the first development to open within Dubailand. One attraction already up and running is Jumana – Secret of the Desert (p.634), a visual extravaganza performed on a huge stage set on a lake. The show draws on Arabian folklore and fable, and offers a unique spectacle of song, theatre and dance using state-of-the-art technology. See www.alsahra.com for details.

Wafi City
Umm Hurair
Map 11 E4

Thai Chi

04 324 4100 | www.waficityrestaurants.com

The dilemma starts at the front door – whether to sit in the Thai-inspired bamboo lounge or the regal dinner room straight out of China. Regardless of your seating choice, the menu is at your disposal with double the choices of appetisers, meats, poultry, seafood and vegetarian options from both the Thai and Chinese kitchens. Like many Asian restaurants, the appetisers are better than the mains, but Thai Chi has good food in a great location, making it a regular for many of Dubai's out-on-the-towners.

Park Hyatt Dubai
Deira
Map 11 B4

Thai Kitchen

04 602 1234 | www.dubai.park.hyatt.com

Thai Kitchen is set around four live-cooking areas where all the ingredients are displayed and prepared by the chefs. The decor is stylish and modern with dark walls and teak wood floors contrasting well with the large soft lights. Although relatively small, the menu consists of a good range of Thai delicacies each prepared to maximise the rich authentic flavours. Portions are purposely small so that you can order a variety to share. Well worth a visit, especially given the grand surroundings of the Park Hyatt.

The Palace –
The Old Town
Downtown Burj Dubai
Map 7 D4

Thiptara

04 428 7888 | www.thepalace-dubai.com

The menu at Thiptara is select but the quality is excellent. The seafood is impeccably fresh, but if you need convincing you can select your own dinner from the lively lobster tank. The cooking comes with a kick, so if you're not a spice fan ask for less fiery recommendations. The extensive wine list includes special vintages for those with very deep pockets. The sleek decor has an Eastern flavour, and with views of the Burj Dubai (and soon its lake), this is a hard location to beat for impressing visitors and business associates.

Turkish

Other options **Arabic/Lebanese** p.532

Taj Palace Hotel
Deira
Map 11 C1

Topkapi

04 223 2222 | www.tajhotels.com

Topkapi is one of only two Turkish restaurants in Dubai but aside from the Istanbul-style interior and waiters in traditional garb, this has many Arabic adversaries in town. The usual fare of mezze dominates the menu although there is a bit of a Turkish twist. What does score bonus points is the pleasing decor with an open kitchen and cushion-laden benches adding to the proceedings. The food is average but the prices are certainly affordable and the everyday buffet is a particular bargain. The staff are extra-friendly, knowledgeable and all wearing a permanent smile.

Vegetarian

Hoi An

Al Qasr Hotel
Umm Suqeim
Map 6 A2

Magnolia
04 366 6730
www.madinatjumeirah.com/al_qasr
Tucked away in the furthest corner of the Madinat, next to the Talise Spa, Magnolia is Dubai's first fine dining vegetarian restaurant. You don't have to be vegetarian to dine here – open-minded non-vegetarians will also enjoy the experience. Complimentary appetisers, between-course amuses-bouches and main courses are imaginatively concocted using home-grown vegetables and herbs and are accompanied by a range of delicious fresh juices and cocktails. There's also a wine list if you need something sinful to counteract the spa cuisine.

Vietnamese
Other options **Far Eastern** p.544

Shangri-La Hotel
Trade Centre 1
Map 7 E3

Hoi An
04 343 8888 | *www.shangri-la.com*
Named after an ancient Vietnamese port renowned for its silk, jewellery and spice trade, Hoi An proudly reflects this exotic influence and offers traditional Vietnamese ingredients combined and presented with a unique, western twist. Novices can opt for a set meal, which with the excellent guidance of well-informed staff, allows for a gourmet experience. The decor is stately-home-meets-far-eastern-tea-house, where the traditional orange walls and bright turquoise shutters blend unobtrusively with the elegant wooden tables well-placed on rugs. As Hoi An is a compact restaurant, it is always busy and the overriding ambience is of eating in a private dining room, particularly appropriate for quieter business occasions or an intimate dinner.

Grand Hyatt Dubai
Umm Hurair
Map 13 C1

Indochine
04 317 1234 | *www.dubai.grand.hyatt.com*
A fusion of exotic flavours awaits the adventurous diner at Indochine. This popular restaurant serves a blend of Vietnamese, Thai, Cambodian and Laosian dishes, offering some exciting and unusual a la carte choices, especially the imaginative salads and expertly seasoned soups. The predominantly dark wood and bamboo decor is cleverly counter-balanced by the high ceilings, tall windows and well-placed tables, giving an ambience of air and space. Dining is limited to the evening only, and booking is recommended.

Cafes & Coffee Shops

Other options **Afternoon Tea** p.605

Whether you're taking a break from shopping or work, catching up with friends, or fancy a quiet spot to sit and read the paper, you'll be spoilt for choice by the variety of venues around Dubai to grab a quick cuppa and a light bite to eat. The following section encompasses cafes and coffee shops, internet cafes and shisha cafes.

Cocktails

If you're partial to multi-hued drinks with exotic names, here's a selection of Dubai's coolest and classiest bars that will leave you stirred but not shaken: Bahri Bar (p.608), Crossroads Cocktail Bar & Terrace (p.612) Ginseng (p.612), Koubba (p.613), Malecon (p.580), Neos (p.616) QD's (p.616), Trader Vic's (p.618), Uptown (p.620) and Vu's Bar (p.620).

Dubai Marina Yacht Club
Dubai Marina
Map 5 A2

25/55

04 362 7883 | *www.dubaimarinayachtclub.com*

The name of the cafe-bistro at the stylish new Dubai Marina Yacht Club sticks with the nautical theme – 25° 55° is the latitude and longitude of Dubai. Sit on the terrace for a marina-side view, or inside if you want a drink while you dine. The menu is fresh, tasty and wholesome; staples like pasta, sandwiches and salads are rounded off nicely by desserts such as warm strawberries in Pimm's. Early morning weekend breakfasts are popular, and the neighbouring 25/55 To Go enables you to stock up on healthy supplies for the day. Open to non-members.

JW Marriott Hotel
Deira
Map 11 E1

Atrium Café

04 607 7977 | *www.marriottdiningatjw.ae*

The Atrium Cafe is another in a long line of good eateries in the bustling JW Marriott. Offering the best in business cafe sophistication with its leather seats, international newspapers and beautifully presented cake and sandwich counter, the cafe also excels in offering a relaxed space for everyone. A good choice of tasty and well-packed gourmet sandwiches, salads, attractive cakes, croissants and brioches, and the choice of the hot and cold a la carte menu, make this elegant coffee house the right choice for breakfast and for lunch.

Bastakiya
Bur Dubai
Map 9 A2

Basta Art Café

04 353 5071 | *bastaartcafe@yahoo.com*

This courtyard cafe is a quiet sanctuary amid the frenetic Bastakiya area. Sit on majlis-style low cushions, or under one of the white cotton canopies while you look through the menu. The food really stands out from other Dubai cafes and is prepared with healthy eating in mind. Each dish has a description of the vitamins and minerals it contains, as well as the calorie count. A sister outlet is located in the Arabian Ranches (04 362 6100), with wicker tables and chairs creating a similarly rustic atmosphere. Works of art hang in pride of place, with various artists being showcased (and sold) each month.

Marina Walk
Dubai Marina
Map 5 B2

Bert's Cafe

04 422 4126

Serving healthy juices and simple cafe fare, Bert's is a good option for a quick bite. Its waterfront location in Dubai Marina is doubly appealing: outside spacious loungers let you soak up the sun and admire the snaking water while inside the low leather couches and subterranean feel bring to mind a London DJ bar designed for long, lazy lunches. The vibe is relaxed, with live music at weekends, open mic nights during the week, sport on unobtrusive screens and an attempt to recreate someone's library around the back. The smoothies, made with fresh fruit and frozen yoghurt, are recommended. There's another branch in the Greens Centre.

Café Ceramique

Jumeirah
Town Centre
Jumeira
Map 7 D1

04 344 7331 | www.cafe-ceramique.com

This popular cafe is a great place to spend an hour unleashing your creative side. Choose an item from the vast selection of pottery, select your colours, and get to work with an array of brushes, sponges and stencils. The finished article is then glazed in-house to be collected at a later date. The menu, although offering plenty of choice, is of the snack variety with salads, bagels, sandwiches and desserts. Children's birthday parties are catered for and hectic but come mid-week, grab a mag or paper, have a light lunch and let your inner artist out. There's another branch in Mall of the Emirates (04 341 0144).

Café Havana

Spinneys
Umm Suqeim
Map 6 F2

04 394 1727 | www.binhendi.com

This spot is very consistent, offering good cafe-style food with a Middle Eastern twist. It has a range of outlets across Dubai, including Deira City Centre (04 295 5238) and Ibn Battuta (04 366 9923). An ideal step up from your lunchtime shopping centre foodcourt, Café Havana affords a high quality, reasonably priced menu with great service. For the waistline conscious, the salads make for an excellent lunch or you could just take some time out from shopping with a coffee or smoothie.

Costa ▶ p.601

Mercato
Jumeira
Map 7 D1

04 344 5705 | www.mmidubai.com

Despite being a chain, Costa is still able to offer patrons a good quality brew as well as an ideal location for a get together and a chat. Fashionable bucket seats allow you to take the weight off your feet and relax as your goodies arrive at your table. Fresh pastries, salads, sandwiches and other snacks complement the long list of trendy tea and coffee blends. Outlets can be seen all over the city, from the new Emirates Terminal 3 to Madinat Jumeirah.

Counter Culture

The Harbour Hotel
& Residence
Dubai Marina
Map 5 B2

04 319 4000 | www.emirateshotelsresorts.com

Deli delights lie within this little known gem, with its leather chairs, wooden shelves and contemporary colour scheme. Counter Culture serves up fresh bread baked on the premises (you can watch), daily hot and cold specials, huge salads, chunky sandwiches and homemade icecream. The range of iced teas, juices and milkshakes served in pleasing plastic tumblers should sort out any Dubai dehydration too. Best of all, this unassuming 24 hour eatery is reasonably priced and licensed so if you fancy a late night beer and a good feed it's a tasty safe bet.

Elements

Wafi Mall
Umm Hurair
Map 10 E4

04 324 4252 | www.thomaskleingroup.com

Every inch of wall space is crammed with paintings giving Elements the feel of an industrial art warehouse. Its relaxed vibe has made it a favourite with longstanding regulars since opening in 2003. Lunchtime is always busy with the three-course buffet and shisha at Dhs.45. Evenings are popular too with the menu serving everything from sushi and tapas to pasta and Arabic dishes, but the main draw is the ever-full shisha terrace. Due to its popularity, the cafe operates a waiting list, so grab a coffee and peruse the art while you wait for a table.

Epicure

Desert Palm Dubai
Dubai-Hatta Rd
Map 2 C3

04 323 8888 | www.desertpalm.ae

Open every day from 07:00 until late, this licensed gourmet deli is undoubtedly one of Dubai's best-kept secrets. It is located within the lush green surrounds of the Desert

THE BEST COFFEE IS MADE BY EXPERTS NOT MACHINES.

There's More Than Just Coffee In Your Costa Cup.
Hand making a cup of coffee is an art. It takes time and skill to perfect.
That's why every single barista, in every single Costa store is professionally
trained in the art of coffee by our experts. It's a little thing, but it makes a
big difference, because it means you'll get a perfect cup of coffee every time.
Come In Store Today & Start Your Love Affair With Costa.

COSTA COFFEE

WE MAKE IT BETTER

Palm polo estate (p.40), and is part of the new onsite boutique hotel. Enjoy freshly baked bread and pastries, fruit compotes and organic berries, and a range of cooked breakfasts while you gaze out over the swimming pool and polo fields. A delicious range of lunch dishes and light snacks is also available.

The Palace –
The Old Town
Downtown Burj Dubai
Map 7 D4

Ewaan

04 428 7888 | *www.thepalace-dubai.com*

This might be the most archetypically Dubai shisha joint in town. Surrounding the palm-lined swimming pool in the Arabian-themed Palace Hotel (p.44), Ewaan's private cabanas sit directly beneath the towering Burj Dubai. Customers can stretch out on Arabic seating while an oud player gently picks in the background and attentive staff serve up shisha and tasty mezze. Despite its swanky location, the prices are surprisingly affordable. To make it even better, this little gem has yet to be discovered and reservations are rarely needed.

Wafa Tower
Trade Centre 1
Map 7 E3

French Connection

04 343 8311 | *farida@fcdubai.com*

Two floors, wide windows, cheerful decor and lots of sunshine make French Connection an excellent location for a quick bite or a leisurely coffee, while using the free Wi-Fi on your laptop. The breakfasts range from pastries and breads to the full English affair. There are a wide selection of salads and tasty sandwiches made from a variety of breads. And of course, the well prepared coffees will keep you going from early to late. If you have a sweet tooth you will be in awe of the cakes and pastries, which are freshly prepared in the bakery. There's another branch behind Spinneys next to BurJuman.

Magrudy's
Jumeira
Map 7 F1

Gerard's

04 344 3327 | *gerard07@eim.ae*

An institution in the Jumeira cafe scene, the courtyard setting gives this popular coffee spot its unique atmosphere. It is where the yummy mummies head between the school run and the first exercise class of the day. As the day progresses the core clientele slowly changes, and by evening it is popular meeting place with Emirati men to discuss the day's activities over coffee with friends. There's a good selection of croissants, pastries and chocolate covered dates, and takeaway trade is brisk. Another location is at Al Ghurair City (04 222 8637).

Bank St
Nr York International
Bur Dubai
Map 8 F2

Hakaya Cafe

04 352 8213

Tucked away from burly Bank Street, this comfy first-floor cafe quietly overlooks the neon-lit action below, and feels like a treehouse for shisha-smoking grown-ups – mainly because there's a huge plastic tree shooting up the middle of it. The menu is seriously eclectic, offering everything from pasta, pepper steak and pizza to every fruit juice and flavoured coffee imaginable. Go after 22:30 and you'll find live Arabic music and the venue at its smokiest.

Epicure

Cafes & Coffee Shops

Festival Centre
Dubai Festival City
Map 13 D2

IKEA ▶ p.451

800 4532 | www.ikeadubai.com

The IKEA restaurant serves up unpretentious food at low prices. With canteen-style self service, each day of the week brings a different Meal of the Day, Soup of the Day and Vegetarian Meal. The standard dishes (including Swedish meatballs) are available most days, and there's a range of pre-packed salads, sandwiches, cold plates and great breakfasts. Take the edge off your shopping-induced hunger with a coffee and muffin combo for just Dhs.7. The daily kids' meal usually offers simple choices like chicken nuggets and chips.

Mall of the Emirates
Al Barsha
Map 6 A3

Japengo Café

04 341 1671 | www.binhendi.com

Japengo Café offers a Japanese-western hybrid menu that impresses with top-notch food and drink in a bright, minimalist setting. The meals are excellent and include sushi, salads, sandwiches, hot dishes and fresh juices. Crab cakes and chicken dumplings are a treat and the assorted yakitori is superb – even better washed down with a fresh kiwi juice. The portions are generous and the prices reasonable, although drinks and water are a bit more expensive. Lunch or dinner, this is no fuss fare with a little flare. Other Locations include Ibn Battuta (04 362 1900), Wafi Mall (04 324 5411), Dubai Ladies Club, Jumeira (04 349 6878), Palm Strip (04 345 4979), Souk Madinat Jumeirah (04 368 6575) and Dubai Festival City (04 232 6220).

Nr Jumeira Mosque
Jumeira
Map 7 F1

Lime Tree Cafe

04 349 8498 | limetree@eim.ae

Set in a converted villa, this cafe has become a Dubai institution. The decor features trendy plastic chairs, dark wood tables and lime-green walls, with chalk boards touting the day's home-cooked meals. Enjoy an alfresco coffee break on the patio or the upstairs balcony, if the weather is not too sticky. With a definite nod towards Mediterranean cuisine, there's paninis filled with roast vegetables, halloumi cheese and roast chicken, as well as delicious couscous salads, satay kebabs and the best quiches in the city. Don't leave without sharing an enormous slice of carrot cake. There's another branch in China Court of Ibn Battuta mall (04 366 9320).

Boulevard at
Emirates Towers
Trade Centre 2
Map 7 F3

Lipton T-Junction

04 330 0788 | www.thomaskleingroup.com

The modern decor, bursting with orange and yellow tones, gives a cheerful welcome to T-Junction patrons. This tea bar leans heavily on the tea theme, and tea, in its many forms, finds its way into nearly every drink and dish on the menu. If you're peckish, try the salads or sandwiches, some of which feature chicken cooked in green tea (interesting and quite pleasant). The signature drinks should not be missed – Spice Cha' (Assam tea infused with sweet spices), Cha'latte (Assam tea infused with ginger and orange) or Berry T-Licious (a blend of teas and berry juices).

Nr Welcare Hospital
Garhoud
Map 11 C4

More

04 283 0224 | www.morecafe.biz

Known for its non-boozy brunches, outstanding sandwiches and imaginative salads, More attracts both families and fashionable media types. The stylish industrial interior, speedy service and extensive menu makes it one of the most popular weekend spots in town. Try the strawberry juice with balsamic vinegar and the spinach salad with pumpkin and feta. You won't regret it. You can eat outside at the Al Murooj Rotana branch (04 343 3779), while the new Gold & Diamond Park restaurant (04 323 4350) is more spacious, but similarly stylish.

Late & Lively

In addition to the dedicated clubs reviewed here, Dubai's nightlife scene also includes several bars and restaurants which transform late evening into lively joints with hopping dancefloors. These include Aussie Legends (p.622), Boston Bar (p.610), Boudoir (p.626), El Paso (p.612), Malecon (p.580), Rock Bottom (p.628) and Scarlett's (p.617).

Nr Jumeira Mosque
Jumeira Rd
Jumeira
Map 7 F1

THE One

04 345 6687 | www.theoneplanet.com

Tucked away on the first floor of THE One, this small cafe is decorated in the same funky style seen throughout the store. The extensive menu is imaginative (but does offer reliable classics if you're not feeling particularly adventurous) and the food is always of high quality. The freshly squeezed juices are fabulous and the cakes outstanding. There's also a kids' menu with pizza and sandwiches. With friendly and attentive service, this is a perfect spot for refuelling mid-shop, or for catching up with friends over a relaxed, reasonably priced lunch.

Grand Hyatt Dubai
Umm Hurair
Map 13 C1

Panini

04 317 1234 | www.dubai.grand.hyatt.com

As a place to meet up with friends or business associates for a lunch on the run, you can't go wrong with Panini. Set among the tropical indoor 'rainforest' in the impressive lobby of the Grand Hyatt, complete with lush greenery and jungle mist, the surroundings are spectacular. The food may not be out of this world, but it's fine for a quick bite. The signature paninis are a little plain so consider this when choosing your fillings, and order a zesty, freshly squeezed fruit juice to liven up your lunchtime.

Fairmont Dubai
Trade Centre 1
Map 8 A4

Pronto

04 332 5555 | www.fairmont.com

Hotel lobby cafes often get bad press, leaving them frequented only by hotel guests waiting for their tour guide or business people sitting for hours over one coffee. Fairmont's Pronto, however, should not be pigeonholed into Dubai's lacklustre hotel cafe culture. Its deli-style cuisine is worthy of a lingering lunch, with sushi and Arabic selections, alcohol and incredible cakes. Not only are the sofas comfy and the staff forever smiling, but they also offer complimentary Wi-Fi during lunch. Whoever said you should never mix business with pleasure had obviously never been to Pronto.

Al Attar Tower
Trade Centre 2
Map 7 E3

Shakespeare & Co.

04 331 1751 | shakesco@eim.ae

Shakespeare & Co would probably be more at home on a Parisian side street than behind a giant skyscraper on Sheikh Zayed Road. Its unique eccentricity, a shabby chic decor that mixes floral designs with lace and wicker, makes a refreshing change from the superficial qualities of so many Dubai eateries. The food is an equally eclectic mix, combining Arabic, Moroccan and continental dishes with a splendid selection of sandwiches and some of the finest smoothies in town. Other locations include The Village Mall (04 344 6228), Al Wasl Road (04 394 1121), Gulf Tower (04 335 3335) and Downtown Burj Dubai (04 434 0195).

JW Marriott Hotel
Deira
Map 11 E1

Vienna Café

04 607 7977 | www.marriottdiningatjw.ae

This small cafe has a slightly fusty Austrian charm. There's lots of wood panelling and delicate tablecloths not readily associated with Deira. Still, it blends well with the grandeur of the JW Marriott. With a passing array of people either entering or leaving the hotel, coming and going on business, or just ambling around the shopping complex, this makes a wonderful place to sit and enjoy a slow cuppa and watch the world go by. There is also a good selection of food on offer, from light salads to steaks.

Shisha Cafes

Shisha Cafes		
Al Koufa	Oud Metha	04 335 1511
Awafi Arabic Café	Deira	04 262 4444
Elements	Umm Hurair	04 607 7760
Fakhreldine	Oud Metha	04 336 6000
Hakaya Cafe	Bur Dubai	04 335 6100
Kan Zaman	Al Shindagha	04 393 9913
Mazaj	Garhoud	04 282 9952
QD's	Deira	04 295 6000
Reem Al Bawadi	Jumeira	04 394 7444
Samari Café	Satwa	04 345 4511
Shakespeare & Co.	Trade Centre 2	04 331 1751
Shoo Fee Ma Fee	Umm Suqeim	04 366 8888

Shisha Cafes
Other options **Arabic/Lebanese** p.532

Despite regular media murmurings about a ban on shisha smoking outside, it's common to see people, male and female, young and old, relaxing in the evening with a coffee or juice and a shisha pipe. For visitors and residents, even non-smokers, it's a popular experience. Many of the Arabic cafes and restaurants around town have shisha available; it often makes a pleasant end to a meal, especially when outdoors in the cooler months. If you fancy buying your own then Karama market (p.471) and the souks (p.481) are a good place to start, but most souvenir shops and larger supermarkets also sell them.

Afternoon Tea
Other options **Cafes & Coffee Shops** p.599

The Monarch Dubai
Trade Centre 2
Map 8 A4

Arcadia
04 501 8888 | *www.themonarchdubai.com*
For an afternoon of refinery at Dubai's most notable address – 1 Sheikh Zayed Road – try The Monarch's high tea selection. The relaxing, comfortable atrium area of this tasteful hotel is the perfect place to be ensconced with your scones. The experience starts with a refillable tower of finger sandwiches and a bottomless teapot, before moving on to freshly baked scones and Devonshire cream, and rounded off with an interesting patissier's platter – all for Dhs.120. If you like a glass of sparkle with your sandwiches, you can upgrade to the Indulgent option for an extra Dhs.25.

Ritz-Carlton Dubai
Dubai Marina
Map 5 A1

The Lobby Lounge
04 399 4000 | *www.ritzcarlton.com*
Dubai's very own Tea at the Ritz is an exquisite experience from the moment you step into the austere lobby until you lick the last morsel of cream from your lips. Delicate finger sandwiches and dainty pastries, succulent scones with clotted cream and a selection of jams, a fabulously colonial selection of teas and the fine china are all deliciously regal. It may feel exclusive, but all are welcome, and you can even swap your brew for a hot chocolate. In addition there is an all-day menu, as well as an inviting cocktail list.

Burj Al Arab
Umm Suqeim
Map 6 B1

Sahn Eddar
04 301 7600 | *www.burj-al-arab.com*
It may be an expensive cuppa but this is an experience that no visitor or Dubai resident should miss. The 'ultimate afternoon tea' begins with a glass of bubbly and continues with course after course of dainty sandwiches, fine pastries and the rather unusual addition of a course from the carvery. Sahn Eddar's first floor location looks back along the causeway towards the real world, but you can choose to take tea in the Skyview Bar (below) to enjoy the stunning vistas 200m above the sea.

Burj Al Arab
Umm Suqeim
Map 6 B1

Skyview Bar
04 301 7600 | *www.burj-al-arab.com*
Afternoon tea is fancy enough, but afternoon tea at the Burj Al Arab takes being posh to a whole new level. The Skyview Bar offers a luxurious version of the English traditional tea every afternoon from 14:00 until 18:00, in two sittings. Sit back and savour the view while a waiter piles vast quantities of finger sandwiches, mini buns,

cakes and biscuits on to your table, accompanied by a pot of tea and a glass of champagne. Once you've finished any layer on your four-tiered tray, it will be refilled for you (sadly the champagne dries up after the first glass). This experience will set you back Dhs.350, and you have to book well in advance, but it is undeniably worth it.

Internet Cafes

There are a number of cafes and eateries around town with PCs available for customers to use, or with Wi-Fi connections allowing you to use your own. Most charge for the privilege, with prices around Dhs.15-20 per hour, but you may find places where the connection is free if you're eating and drinking. Current hotspot locations include: French Connection, Sheikh Zayed Road; Coffee Bean & Tea Leaf, Beach Road; Spot Café, Bur Dubai, Bert's (p.599) and More Cafe (p.603).

Bakeries

Bakeries in Dubai offer a wonderful range of pastries, biscuits and Lebanese sweets. Arabic breads include 'borek', flat pastries, baked or fried with spinach or cheese, and 'manakish', which is hot bread, sometimes doubled over, and served plain or filled with meat, cheese or 'zatar' (thyme seeds). Biscuits are often filled with ground dates or pistachios.

Friday Brunch

An integral part of life in Dubai, Friday brunch is a perfect event for a lazy start to the weekend, especially once the really hot weather arrives. Popular with all sections of the community, it provides Thursday night's revellers with a gentle awakening, and often much-needed nourishment. For families, brunch is a pleasant way to spend the day, with many venues organising fun activities for kids, allowing parents to relax while filling themselves with fine food and drinks. Different brunches appeal to different crowds; some have fantastic buffets, others are in spectacular surroundings, while some offer all you can eat at amazing prices.

Fruit Juices

Other options **Cafes & Coffee Shops** p.599

Fresh juices are widely available from shawarma stands and juice shops. They are delicious, healthy and cheap, and made on the spot from fresh fruits like mango, banana, kiwi, strawberry and pineapple. Yoghurt is also a popular drink, often served with nuts, and the local milk is called 'laban' (a heavy, salty buttermilk that doesn't go well in tea or coffee). Arabic mint tea is available. Arabic coffee however (thick, silty and strong), is extremely popular and will have you buzzing for the rest of the day.

Friday Brunch		
Al Muntaha	Umm Suqeim	04 301 7600
Al Qasr	Jumeira	04 346 1111
Alpha	Garhoud	04 702 2640
Aquara Terrace	Dubai Marina	04 362 7883
Beachcombers	Umm Suqeim	04 406 8999
The Boston Bar	Satwa	04 345 5888
Carters	Oud Metha	04 324 4777
The Cellar ▶ p.559	Garhoud	04 282 9333
Certo ▶ p.561	Al Sufouh	04 366 9111
Double Decker	Trade Centre 2	04 321 1111
Frankie's	Dubai Marina	04 399 4311
Glasshouse	Deira	04 227 1111
The Irish Village ▶ p.623	Garhoud	04 282 4750
JW Marriott	Deira	04 607 7977
Legends	Deira	04 295 6000
Long's Bar	Trade Centre 1	04 343 8000
Lotus One	Trade Centre 2	04 329 3200
The Market Place	Deira	04 607 7977
More Cafe	Garhoud	04 283 0224
Organic Foods & Café	Satwa	04 398 9140
Pax	Trade Centre 2	04 343 3333
Planet Hollywood	Umm Hurair	04 324 4777
Rock Bottom	Bur Dubai	04 396 3888
Spectrum On One	Trade Centre 1	04 332 5555
Spice Island	Deira	04 262 5555
Waxy O'Conner's	Bur Dubai	04 352 0900
Yalumba	Garhoud	04 702 2328

Dressing Up

Generally speaking shorts and T-shirts are a no-no for Dubai's bars and restaurants, and even some pubs will frown at your beach-bum attire. While trainers aren't strictly outruled it will depend on the whole ensemble. Dubai's dress code is on the smarter side – more beautiful than bohemian – so shine your shoes when you're stepping out.

On The Town

Dubai has plenty to offer once the sun sets. This section covers it all, including details of cultural entertainment such as theatre and movies, as well as bars, pubs and nightclubs.

Social nights out in Dubai tend to start late, with people usually not leaving home until after 21:00. Even on weeknights, kick off is surprisingly late. Arabic nightclubs or restaurants, where there is usually live music and belly dancing, are largely deserted before 23:00.

Both nights of the weekend, Friday and Saturday, are particularly busy, but you will also find many promotions and theme nights held during the week to pull in the crowds. Ladies' nights are particularly popular (see p.620).

In general, cafes and restaurants close between 23:00 and 01:00, with bars and nightclubs split between those that close 'early' at 01:00 and those that go on until 03:00.

Single In The City

Dubai, like many cities, is not the easiest place to meet people if you're single. However, help is at hand: Table 4 Six (www.table4six.net) is a social service that will match you with like-minded people for a group dinner, and there is also The Bridgets (p.389) – a raucous club for single girls.

Spectrum On One

Door Policy

Even with the mix of nationalities in Dubai, there are certain bars and nightclubs that have a 'selective' entry policy. Sometimes the 'members only' sign on the entrance needs a bit of explaining. Membership is usually introduced to control the clientele frequenting the establishment, but is often only enforced during busy periods.

At quieter times, non-members may have no problems getting in, even if not accompanied by a member. Some places seem to use the rule to disallow entry if they don't like the look of you or your group. Large groups (especially all males), single men and certain nationalities are normally the target. You can avoid the inconvenience, and the embarrassment, by breaking the group up or by going in a mixed-gender group. If you do find yourself being discriminated against it's not worth arguing with the doorman – it won't work. Most companies do everything to avoid bad publicity, so try taking the issue up with the local media instead.

Dress Code

While many bars have a reasonably relaxed attitude towards dress code, some places will not allow you in if you are wearing shorts and sandals, while others require a collared shirt and have a 'no jeans or trainers' policy. In general, nightclubs are more strict, so dress to impress.

Bars

DUI

Drinking and driving is illegal in Dubai. There is zero tolerance; if you are caught with even a hint of alcohol in your system you will be sent to prison. Be responsible and always take a taxi – they're cheap, reliable and plentiful or book Safe Driver (04 268 8797) to take you and your car home.

Jumeirah Beach Hotel
Umm Suqeim
Map 6 B1

360°
04 406 8769 | www.jumeirahbeachhotel.com
Like a static carousel for grown-ups, 360° is a two-tiered circular rooftop, rebelliously partying above the more demure Marina seafood restaurant (p.589). With a bar at its heart, the place boasts striking panoramic views of the Arabian Ocean and light-throwing Burj that will put even the grumpiest expat in a decent mood. Late afternoon arrivals (it opens at 16:00) can laze on a catalogue of white seating, including beanbags, low cubic couches and wooden reclining benches, as they suck on colourful shisha. House DJs spin come the weekends, while scruffily chic stylistas sup cocktails – until they start spinning too.

Boulevard at Emirates Towers
Trade Centre 2
Map 7 F3

The Agency
04 319 8088 | www.jumeirahemiratestowers.com
Proving that wine bars aren't just a fad, The Agency continues to attract the crowds. If overwhelmed by the 33 page wine menu, try one of the 'flights' (a selection of four different wines) to get yourself in the swing. The cafe facade and the dark wood and brick interior could be from any great wine-producing region, as could the tasty tapas-style snacks. A great place to warm up for a big night out, it can get a little too cosy. There's another branch at Madinat Jumeirah (04 366 6730) but the food menu isn't as extensive.

Le Meridien Dubai
Garhoud
Map 13 E1

Alpha
04 702 2640 | www.alphaclub.ae
Alpha's high, white space was formerly home to a Greek restaurant and its design elements still prevail (check out the ceiling murals in the bathrooms). You'll also find a packed schedule of international DJs, special events, drink deals and even a late Friday brunch with live music. Attracting a low-key but still style-conscious crowd, this bar-club is raising the city's music standards with regular house nights (Thursdays) and urban gigs on Tuesdays. Keep an eye on local listings for one-off events.

Mina A'Salam
Umm Suqeim
Map 6 A1

Bahri Bar
04 366 6730 | www.madinatjumeirah.com
Imagine you had the chance to design the perfect bar. You might start with a stunning view, say, windtower rooftops, rustling palm trees, meandering canals, the towering Burj Al Arab and the sparkling ocean beyond. The bar itself might have rich furnishings in brown and gold, comfortable seating, and ornate lanterns providing intimate lighting. On the menu you'd make sure a comprehensive cocktail selection was accompanied by wines, beers, and delicious nibbles. You'll probably never get the chance to build your dream bar but that doesn't matter, because someone else did, it's at Mina A'Salam and it's called Bahri Bar.

Shangri-La Hotel
Trade Centre 1
Map 7 E3

Balcony Bar
04 343 8888 | www.shangri-la.com
Overlooking the imposing main entrance and chic lobby of the Shangri-La, Balcony Bar is a sophisticated little place to grab a fancy cocktail or aperitif. Dark, masculine wooden panelling dominates, with black leather armchairs and glass-topped coffee tables surrounding the bar. The drinks list is extensive, and the cocktails are

competently mixed and artfully presented. For the more extravagant pocket, there are some eye-wateringly expensive champagnes and vintage whiskies, while teetotallers can choose from a basic selection of booze-free beverages.

The Bar

Hyatt Regency
Deira
Map 9 D1

04 317 2222 | www.dubai.regency.hyatt.com

The patience-defying Deira traffic may not make it worth a trip in itself, but if you have planned your evening at the often overlooked Hyatt Regency, The Bar is a good spot to whet your whistle. Encased in glass and furnished with a mix of high tables, bar stools and low, soft leather armchairs, the interior is unobtrusive and relaxed much like the rest of the hotel. The well-stocked (and staffed) bar dispenses some interesting aperitifs and after-dinner liqueurs, as well as decent cocktails, wines and bottled beers.

Bar Zar

Souk Madinat
Jumeirah
Umm Suqeim
Map 6 A2

04 366 6348 | www.madinatjumeirah.com

This two-floor bar is slick and fashionable, with the upper floor open in the middle so you can peer over at the talent below (the band that is). The faux brick walls, art-house prints, friendly staff, small terrace and laid-back sofas all add up to a funky bar with a relaxed urban feel. The drinks are eclectic – with beer cocktails (champagne or Smirnoff Ice with Guinness), traditional, yet potent, long drinks and lagers aplenty. The food also pleases with bar snacks such as crab cakes, burgers, spring rolls, bangers and mash, and fish and chips.

Barasti

Le Meridien Mina
Seyahi
Al Sufouh
Map 5 C1

04 399 3333 | www.lemeridien-minaseyahi.com

You can turn up to beachside Barasti in your flip-flops or Friday finery which makes it a favourite on the expat scene. The underrated menu is divided by cuisine with tasty seafood, ribs and steak taking a starring role. Undeniably balmy in the summer, once the weather cools you'll be fighting for a sun lounger, beach bed, bar stool or just a spot on the wooden deck, so get there early for sundowners. The big screens, split

The Agency

level seating, views, live music, frozen cocktails and friendly crowd make this a reliable spot for a good night out.

InterContinental Dubai Festival City
Dubai Festival City
Map 13 D2

Belgian Beer Cafe
04 701 1111
www.intercontinental.com/dubai
This spot attracts everyone from Francophiles to locals with its inevitably large selection of beer and an impressive menu. The main draw are the moules frites, mussels served in your choice of sauce with thin, crisp fries, and lots of bread for mopping up the juices. You'll also find steaks, Belgian sausages, chocolate mousse and tempting waffles. The traditional decor is refreshing, with Victorian-style tiles and chunky furniture. It fills up fast, adding to that post-work vibe, with a packed bar and plans being made over 8% beer while the sun sinks over the creek and Dubai skyline.

Sporting Life
The glitz and glamour of Dubai's bars is all very well, but sometimes you just want a joint where you can catch the big match and enjoy a pint with your mates. These venues are recommended for supping and spectating: Aussie Legends (p.622), Boston Bar (p.610), Champions (p.611), Double Decker (p.622), Dubliners (p.624), El Paso (p.612), Fibber Magee's (p.624), Irish Village (p.624), Nezesaussi (p.616), The Underground (p.624) and Scarlett's (p.617).

Clubhouse Al Manhal
Shoreline Apartments
Palm Jumeirah
Map 2 A3

BidiBondi
04 427 0515 | *www.emiratesleisureretail.com*
You'd expect a laid back vibe from an Aussie bar, and that's exactly what you get at BidiBondi. This new offering on Palm Jumeirah offers both indoor and alfresco space, with a beach diner feel nicely complemented by poolside tables. The somewhat themed menu offers hefty burgers, sandwiches and salads plus bar snacks, breakfast and kids' specials. There is also a great range of mocktails, cocktails, beers and wines. More a spot for a weekend lunch than romantic liaison, BidiBondi is a great neighbourhood bar – if you're lucky enough to live in this neighbourhood.

Novotel World Trade Centre
Trade Centre 2
Map 7 F3

Blue Bar
04 332 0000 | *www.novotel.com*
The Blue Bar is a bit of a find for those who like jazz, or indeed those who have spent the day trawling through the exhibition halls at the Trade Centre. Dark wood, low lighting and smoky atmosphere create the perfect setting for the weekly live jazz band on Thursdays. Get there early for a seat and mix with the business crowd from Trade Centre, but stay for the band at around 21:30. Bar bites accompany a small but well-chosen drinks list. Live music is also played Wednesday and Friday.

Jumeira Rotana
Satwa
Map 8 A2

The Boston Bar
04 345 5888 | *www.rotana.com*
This American-style pub could be accused of being a bit dingy but is great for after-work drinks, watching sports, or just ending a long day. The menu also has some tasty surprises in store with winning fish and chips. Theme nights include sports on Saturday and Sundays, a tricky yet popular Monday quiz, Tuesday ladies' night, Wednesday two-for-one, Thursday ladies' night, and a Friday breakfast binge. The variety of the Boston Bar makes it difficult to choose a day, so it's best to try all seven. Maybe just not all in one week.

Wafi City
Umm Hurair
Map 11 E4

Carters
04 324 4100 | *www.waficitirestaurants.com*
A convivial watering hole frequented on any given evening by small herds on the hunt, this is both a great bar for singles and a relaxed place where families or couples

can enjoy decent no-fuss dining. The rhythmic swish of oversized wooden ceiling fans, hunting trophies in glass display cases and various colonial-style ephemera lend it a slightly 'themed' quality which thankfully does not extend to the food. The grub has improved in recent years and it would be fair to say it's the kind of stuff you're likely to get in any decent gastro-pub. Add the large bar, live music and popularity on a weekend and you're in for a good time.

Karaoke Queens & Kings

If you fancy yourself as a bit of a crooner and want to share your talent with the unsuspecting public, Dubai has two karaoke bars of note. Harry Ghatto's (p.612) and Hibiki Music Lounge (p.612) are both popular for a fun night out. Double Decker (p.622) also hosts karaoke after its Friday brunch. Ear plugs are optional but recommended.

Traders Hotel
Deira
Map 11 E1

Chameleon
04 265 9888 | www.shangri-la.com
Chameleon is a vibrant cocktail bar with liquid refreshment and entertainment on tap. The reasonably priced beverages range from sophisticated martinis to cheekily named cocktails, and include an assortment of signature colourful Chameleon drinks. The split-level venue is stylishly lit, with seating available at dining tables, bar stools or comfy circular couches. Depending on which night you visit, the music may be provided by a live pianist or a hip DJ, occasionally accompanied by live bongo and saxophone players.

JW Marriott Hotel
Deira
Map 11 E1

Champions
04 607 7977 | www.marriottdiningatjw.ae
This is just what you'd expect from a sports bar: big screens for viewing your favourite sports (including Grand Prix and American football), pool tables, quiz nights, karaoke, great US-style pub grub, and even a live DJ spinning the hits on Thursdays. It's a perfect place to meet friends and enjoy the diversion of your choice, and it helps that the staff are friendly and knowledgeable too. If you like hustle and bustle, go later as things heat up. The daytime food deals make this a good choice for lunch as well.

Emirates Towers
Trade Centre 2
Map 7 F3

Cigar Lounge
04 330 0000 | www.jumeirah.com
The cigars at the Cigar Lounge are housed in a room-sized humidifier, with prices for a single smoke ranging from Dhs.50 to Dhs.500. The staff are friendly but unable to provide much guidance for the novice. If you can snag a couch there are shimmering views of Sheikh Zayed Road to be had, but the skyline is obscured somewhat by gigantic wood-panelled air-conditioners. The clientele are mainly moneyed hotel guests and although the trip up in the glass elevator is an experience, the overall ambience is that of an airport with no planes.

Fairmont Dubai
Trade Centre 1
Map 8 A4

Cin Cin
04 332 5555 | www.fairmont.com
Cin Cin is one Dubai bar that wouldn't be so out of place in a bohemian behemoth of a city as opposed to this humble desert dwelling. Perhaps it's the arrogant impracticality: designed around a central pillar, the bar feels like a very circular, very narrow, very stylish, very well-lit… corridor. Modish furnishings, warehouse-high wine shelves, and walls fashioned like falling water create a backdrop as bling as Beyonce in a diamond-encrusted catsuit. It's easy to get carried away ordering imaginative cocktails and fine wines but brace yourself for the bar bill – this is expense account territory.

Raffles Dubai
Umm Hurair
Map 10 D4

Crossroads Cocktail Bar & Terrace

04 314 9888 | www.dubai.raffles.com

Somewhere in the enormous Crossroads cocktail menu, a new classic is hiding. The Dubai Sling, an imaginative mix of coriander, chilli, fig and lemon, is the drink of choice for surveying the nearby sparkling skyline. Outside boasts water features, linen cushioned seating and raised areas and you'll find rich, Asian-inspired decor indoors. With extremely knowledgeable staff, well-executed bar snacks and a dizzying choice of drinks, you probably won't mind paying above average prices for the experience.

> **Booze With A View**
>
> As soon as temperatures cool off, (typically from October to May) the city's chic set head straight outside to soak up Dubai's alfresco bar scene, complete with beautiful views. Kick off the evening with a beer at the Belgian Beer Cafe (p.610) or glass of wine at the romantic Rooftop Terrace (p.617), followed by martinis at stylish Sho Cho's (p.617), mojitos at Uptown (p.620), and an open-air bop at 360°(p.608). Just remember to glug enough water between cocktails.

Dubai Marine Beach
Jumeira
Map 7 F1

El Paso

04 304 8120 | www.dxbmarine.com

Quiz nights, party nights, ladies' nights, football nights, and live music – what more could you want from a good all-round bar? How about great service and excellent drinks? El Paso continues to draw a regular crowd of expats who meet and mingle to enjoy the relaxing but vibrant atmosphere. For dinner, stay for the Tex-Mex or move on to one of the other outlets at the Dubai Marine Beach Resort (p.40). Open from noon until 03:00, the bar is a good place to start or finish an evening.

Wafi City
Umm Hurair
Map 10 E4

Ginseng

04 324 8200 | www.ginsengdubai.com

If you fancy yourself as Dubai's answer to Carrie Bradshaw then Ginseng was made for you. Great for a girl's night out, it is dressier than neighbouring Seville's and Carter's but still relaxing. The menu is full of tempting Asian treats that lend themselves to sharing – especially the platters which you may be in danger of fighting over rather than just picking at. The cocktail menu, however, is the real draw with a variety of sweet and strong concoctions that slip down a little too easily. Two for one drink deals on Tuesdays and menu discounts on Mondays.

Boulevard at Emirates Towers
Trade Centre 2
Map 7 F3

Harry Ghatto's

04 330 0000 | www.jumeirahemiratestowers.com

The singing in this small karaoke bar starts at 22:00, so you've got plenty of time beforehand to muster up some Dutch courage. You'll find a great drinks list, although there is only a limited range of bar snacks and light meals to soak up the alcohol. There are over 1,000 songs to choose from, so whether you croon like Sinatra or rap like Eminem you'll find your anthem. The hostesses regularly take the stage and belt out a number to encourage the crowd, although with so many eager (and amazingly talented) participants, this hardly seems necessary.

Hyatt Regency
Deira
Map 9 D1

Hibiki Music Lounge

04 209 6701 | www.dubai.regency.hyatt.com

Take an escalator past the ice-rink and venture beyond the tassel-strung doors to find a hidden karaoke lounge. The cosy interior features a small stage, comfy seating areas, and a central bar. There are also three private rooms, with Japanese, Singaporean, and Thai themes, for those special occasions or for crooners not ready for a public performance. Singers have around 8,000 songs to choose from, and the audience can follow the action on monitors. With a nightly happy hour from 19:30 to 22:00, this friendly bar offers a great night out to its mixed clientele.

Radisson SAS Hotel
Dubai Media City
Al Sufouh
Map 5 C2

Icon Bar ▶ p.561

04 366 9111 | www.radissonsas.com

Icon is just that – a symbol for stylish post-work boozers everywhere. It's in Media City, so there's lots of styled hair, confident laughter and small groups sniggering about their absent boss. The carefully styled ambience – red leather chairs, sequined drapes and expensive looking ceramics – is book-ended by big screens showing football. The bar nibbles are good if a little small; you can pick from sandwiches, imaginative salads and jacket potatoes. There's also a choice of pizzas, fired downstairs at Certo (p.570), should you be planning a long night of office gossip.

Hilton Dubai Creek
Deira
Map 11 C1

Issimo

04 227 1111 | www.hilton.com

Issimo brings a touch of James Bond to Deira. The long, narrow bar has a retro-futuristic feel with stark chrome, black leather, and large slanted Japanese-style panels. The menu features a superb selection of martinis and cocktails (all worryingly without prices). The wonderful Mangolini, a mango and champagne creation, is as notable as the Dhs.85 bill that follows it. Issimo's clientele is an interesting blend of moneyed hotel guests, Mafioso lookalikes, and hip young clubbers.

Souk Madinat
Jumeirah
Umm Suqeim
Map 6 A2

Jambase

04 366 8888 | www.madinatjumeirah.com

Meet, dine, drink and dance – the perfect combination for a good night out. Situated just off the main entrance to the Madinat, Jambase's tempting drinks selection is enough to kick off a good night. Although food plays second fiddle, generous portions and a varied menu selection lead on to a night of dancing to the live band. The dark wooden interior and rustic lighting lend a 50s style jazz bar ambience and the fusion of cultures is felt in both the food and the music, harkening back to jazz bars of New Orleans to the Cape of South Africa.

Mövenpick Hotel
Bur Dubai
Oud Metha
Map 10 D3

Jimmy Dix ▶ p.573

04 336 6000 | www.moevenpick-hotels.com

For a friendly, unpretentious bar and nightclub with a relaxed dress code, you can always count on Jimmy Dix for a good crowd and lively atmosphere. The DJ and talented live band always satisfy the crowds, especially on their Thursday Thump weekend party. The food is unexpectedly good – a mix of Tex-Mex, grills, sausage and mash, and burgers making this a great one-stop shop for eating, drinking, and partying. Jimmy Dix is also one of the homes of the Laughter Factory, Dubai's thriving circuit of funnymen (p.632).

Al Qasr Hotel
Umm Suqeim
Map 6 A2

Koubba

04 366 8888 | www.madinatjumeirah.com/al_qasr

One of the most stunning views in Dubai awaits you from the terrace of this sumptuous cocktail bar, and on a balmy winter's evening you'd be hard pressed to find a better spot for showing off to out-of-town visitors. The ever-changing light show of the Burj Al Arab, the abras drifting by on the canal, and the balconies and windtowers of Al Qasr hotel all create a magical setting. Just off the terrace is the Armoury Lounge, where you can indulge in Cuban cigars surrounded by wooden screens, lavish carpets, and antique Indian weaponry.

Souk Al Bahar
Downtown Burj Dubai
Map 7 D4

Left Bank ▶ p.615

04 368 4501
www.emiratesleisureretail.com

Step through the thick, opaque glass doors and it'll take a minute for your eyes to adjust to the darkness. Once they do however, you'll feel as though you've been dropped into a secret lounge in the hippest section of New York. The black on black wallpaper, red velvet booths and white leather couches combine to create one of the best decorated bars in the city. The ornate food presentation and expertly prepared cocktails fit well with the swanky surroundings, and the 'small plates' menu begs to be explored with a cocktail in hand.

Dancing Outside The Box

Should you fancy wigging out to something slightly more alternative while out on the town, check out the Step On club nights at Chi@The Lodge (p.626). Offering some British flavour with indie, rock and whatever DJ Mark Evans fancies, these are great nights when you can jump around and feel like you're back at the student union.

Souk Madinat Jumeirah
Umm Suqeim
Map 6 A2

Left Bank ▶ p.615

04 368 6171 | www.emiratesleisureretail.com

Whether you sit indoors or out at Left Bank sets the tone for the evening; choose neon or nightsky. Sip on a cocktail as you peruse the menu of sharing platters and mains. Prices are slightly high for understated bar food, but the casual industrial style interior, group seating and waterside dining make it a good place to catch up with friends. Hungry diners should opt for the enormous Tiger beer battered fish and chips while the strawberry creme brulee with basil icecream is a real treat.

Ritz-Carlton Dubai
Dubai Marina
Map 5 A1

Library Bar & Cigar Lounge

04 399 4000 | www.ritzcarlton.com

The first thing that may strike you about the Library Bar is the lack of books. That aside, with the dark wood, comfy sofas and dimmed lighting could be in the study of an English country house. Situated just off the lobby, the bar serves light bites, main meals and a good range of cocktails including the house special Ritz Martini – a delicious blend of vodka and fresh strawberries. It's a relaxing location perfect for pre-dinner drinks or a late nightcap; of course, you could even choose a cigar.

Towers Rotana
Trade Centre 1
Map 7 E3

Long's Bar

04 343 8000 | www.rotana.com

Long's Bar is ideal to kick-start a brash night out, as there seems to be a party no matter how early you arrive – it's even buzzing during Ramadan. A firm favourite with long time expats and glammed-up flirty singles alike, Long's is often crowded and smoky but dull moments are not on the menu: there are happy hours, theme nights, a brunch and two ladies' nights. The pub grub is decent and varied and the steak and ale pie is so big it deserves bullhorns.

Dubai International Convention & Exhibition Centre
Trade Centre 2
Map 7 F3

Lotus One

04 329 3200 | www.lotus1.com

Uber-cool, hip and happening, super-trendy – whatever you want to call those places that draw in the 'it' crowd, Lotus One is at the top of the it-list. The glass and wood floors, shiny chrome bar and intimate tables for two with swinging chairs complement the progressive tunes courtesy of a groovy house DJ, bestowing a style that blends Philip Stark with Café Del Mar. Beyond the bar and obscured from view by wooden dividers is the spacious restaurant with a menu that jumps from Asian to Aussie but finds a commonality in exquisite quality.

DUBAI

1ST FLOOR WATERFRONT, SOUK AL BAHAR, DOWNTOWN BURJ DUBAI
Contact us on 04-368 4501

WATERFRONT PROMENADE, SOUK MADINAT JUMEIRAH
Contact us on 04-368 6171

ABU DHABI

2ND FLOOR WATERFRONT, SOUQ QARYAT AL BERI, BETWEEN THE BRIDGES
Contact us on 02-558 1680

Radisson SAS Hotel
Dubai Media City
Al Sufouh
Map 5 C2

Media Lounge ▶ p.561

04 366 9111 | www.dubai.radissonsas.com

With curvy 70s style chairs, criss-crossed windows and dangling metal decoration, the Media Lounge lives up to its name as a quiet but trendy hangout for creative types. Advertising execs stop by to brainstorm over frothy coffees or juices by day, or snap open their laptops and take advantage of the Wi-Fi. By sundown, you'll find the frazzled post-work crowd unwinding over an aperitif or cocktail. Head up the stairs and you'll find the more lively sister bar, Icon (p.613). Decent snacks are available, or you can order pizzas from Certo (p.570).

The Address
Downtown Burj Dubai
Map 7 D4

Neos

04 427 0515 | www.theaddress.com

Seriously glamorous, this sky high bar on the 63rd floor (you need to take two elevators) boasts views and drinks to make your jaw drop. With huge wall to wall windows, the staggering height makes it impossible to play it cool as you stare out at Burj Dubai and the city beyond. Drag your eyes from the twinkling vista and you'll see modern chandeliers, a touch of 1920s art deco and throne-like chairs. Such a setting deserves an impressive drinks list and Neos doesn't disappoint. There's a Dhs.100 cover charge after 22:00 at weekends.

Al Manzil Hotel
Downtown Burj Dubai
Map 7 D4

Nezesaussi

04 428 5888 | www.almanzilhotel.com

Celebrating the sport and cuisine of the tri-nations, Nezesaussi has quickly established itself as one of Dubai's favourite sports bars. Rugby paraphernalia tastefully adorns the walls, and with 13 big screens you're guaranteed a view of the game wherever you sit. But with great food and a comprehensive menu this venue will appeal to more than just sports fans. Meaty mains include South African sausages, New Zealand lamb and Australian steaks; the trophy chicken pie is also a winner. Open until 02:00 at weekends.

Crowne Plaza
Trade Centre 1
Map 7 F3

Oscar's Vine Society

04 331 1111 | www.crowneplaza.com

Wine cask tables and dim lighting set the mood for indulging in full-bodied reds and ripe cheeses. Oscar's knowledgeable staff can recommend wines to suit your preferences, and the cheese master can explain the day's selection. Special offers (including an unlimited wine buffet for Dhs.149 on Wednesday) make the wine more affordable if you're after more than just one glass. The food is very French and very meaty, so if you enjoy andouillete (tripe sausage) and boudin noir (blood sausage), you'll love it. If not, stick to the cheese platter and save your money for the wine.

Creek Golf Club
Deira
Map 11 C3

QD's

04 295 6000 | www.dubaigolf.com

The food at QD's is more along the lines of elegant bar snacks than full-on dining, but food is not the main draw – QD's is all about location. Pull up a comfortable chair on the banks of the creek, so close to the water's edge that you can almost dip your toes in, and watch the passing abras and dhow cruises while the sun sets. It also has an excellent cocktails list and as the night wears on, it plays host to a live band who keep the fun-loving, shisha-smoking crowd entertained until the early hours.

The Aviation Club
Garhoud
Map 13 E1

Rainbow Room

04 282 4122 | www.aviationclub.ae

It may be slightly obscured between its more famous neighbours, the Aviation Club and The Cellar, but the Rainbow Room is back and fighting its corner following a worthwhile refurbishment. With a pretty wooden deck around the outdoor swimming pool as well as a spacious lounge, it's a great spot for a cool drink and quick bite from the limited but sturdy menu of salads, sandwiches, chicken, beef and fish entrees. More chilled retreat than buzzing hotspot, it livens up when it hosts Laughter Factory comedy evenings (p.632).

Rooftop Lounge & Terrace
04 399 9999
www.oneandonlyroyalmirage.com
One of the most spectacular hotels in Dubai hosts one of the most chilled-out bars in the city. Rooftop is a hangout for the beautiful people, which means you can expect to pay high prices for your tall drinks (although if you go during happy hour, your sundowners will be cheaper). That aside, it offers a superb view of The Palm and boasts Arabic cushion seats that are cleverly placed, promoting interaction between the clientele. If you want to kick back your kitten heels and relax under the stars with superstar style cocktails then this is the place.

Scarlett's
04 319 8768 | www.jumeirahemiratestowers.com
Tucked away in Emirates Towers, Scarlett's has long been a favourite of both tourists and expats. The numerous big screens are great for sports fans, while the terrace in the shopping mall provides some respite from the big game bustle.
The menu is extensive, varied and very reasonably priced while the service is good enough to satisfy the crowd. Scarlett's is great for big groups who want to eat, drink and be merry with deals on throughout the week and one of most popular ladies' nights in town on Tuesdays.

Sho Cho
04 346 1111
www.dxbmarine.com
This resort is home to a number of party places that share an impressive alfresco setting around a sparkling azure lagoon. It may be a Japanese restaurant but the delicate and imaginative dishes (that tend to be a little on the pricey side) are not the real reason the beautiful set flock to Sho Cho's shoreline. As the clock ticks towards midnight the ample terrace begins to fill and the happy house mixes with hints of hardcore and traces of trance. It's not quite in the ranks of Ibiza but the atmosphere has definitely got that sunshine holiday appeal.

Live Music
Dubai's live music scene is currently the busiest it's ever been. From impromptu jam sessions to tight (or laughable) cover bands, these days you're spoilt for choice. Check out the sounds thumping from Aussie Legends (p.622), Bar Zar (p.609), Barasti (p.609), Blue Bar (p.610), Go West (p.595), Hard Rock Café (p.530), Irish Village (p.624), Jambase (p.613), Jimmy Dix (p.613), Malecon (p.580), Rock Bottom (p.628), and Trader Vics (p.618).

Rooftop Lounge & Terrace

Burj Al Arab
Umm Suqeim
Map 6 B1

Skyview Bar

04 301 7600 | *www.burj-al-arab.com*

This is the place to go for a posh night out – a single cocktail can easily run into triple figures, you have to book well in advance, and there is a minimum spend of Dhs.275 per person just to get in. But it is worth it, especially for special occasions or to impress visitors when they come to visit you in Dubai. The views are, as you would expect, amazing; for the best views, try to get there as the sun is going down.

Hilton Jumeirah
Dubai Marina
Map 5 A1

Studio One

04 399 1111 | *www.hilton.com*

Welcome to the sport watcher's paradise. Tongue-wrenchingly over-salted burgers and greasy fries are the perfect accompaniment to a night in front of the big game. TVs are scattered around the bar at unusual angles to provide punters with a multi-screen sport marathon. If the unashamedly promoted brand of beer plastered all over the walls doesn't get you in the mood, then the endless supply of popcorn will. The price of booze isn't off-putting, and the selection is good.

Radisson SAS Hotel
Dubai Media City
Al Sufouh
Map 5 C2

Tamanya Terrace ▶ p.561

04 366 9111 | *www.radissonsas.com*

More comfortable than one would expect from a mid-city outdoor venue, Tamanya Terrace welcomes business visitors, tourists and media locals in a trendy mix of concrete and chrome. There's music in the form of a DJ, but that's for laters. Tamanya tends to tempt punters as a stopping-off point after work and as night falls the cocktail bar gets busy with fun and merriment flowing. Good views, not bad nibbles, decent drinks – it all works just fine after a long day's slog.

Renaissance Hotel
Deira
Map 11 E1

Tiki Bar ▶ p.567

04 262 5555 | *www.renaissancehotels.com*

Sitting so close to Spice Island (p.566), one of Dubai's most enduring all-you-can-eats, is likely to prove tough competition for any bar, and its proximity means most people opt for the more appealing package next door. Despite that, this is still a welcoming – if slightly sad and quiet – little place to grab a tropical cocktail if you happen to be in the vicinity and in need of coconut-infused cheer. Deira has some hidden gems that tend not to get the same kind of attention lavished on the latest big openings, but if you're going off the beaten track you could do worse than to start – or end – your evening at Tiki.

Crowne Plaza
Trade Centre 1
Map 7 F3

Trader Vic's

04 331 1111 | *www.crowneplaza.com*

This tropical chain is a great party spot. You can come for dinner (Asian-inspired dishes, great seafood plus some fantastic bar snacks) or just prop up the bar with one of the famously strong cocktails which are served in glass bowls and ceramic skulls. Either way, it won't be long before you're dancing to the live Cuban band and vowing to take salsa lessons before the year's out. There's another branch in Madinat Jumeirah (04 366 5646) with outdoor dining but the same frantic, festival feel.

Oasis Beach Tower
Dubai Marina
Map 5 A1

Trader Vic's Mai-Tai Lounge

04 399 8993 | *www.tradervics.com*

The more sophisticated cousin of Dubai's other Trader Vic's (above), this large bar is decked out in a similar style to its Polynesian relatives. Mai-Tai offers the same criminally strong cocktails (a tiki puka puka is a must-try if you can handle it) and serves up tasty, if expensive, bar snacks, but the spacious dancefloor provides a more clubby

Explore more!

Discover the best of the UAE with Explorer guides...

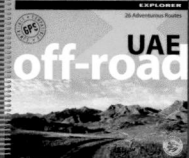

feel. Wagamama's (p.579) is just next door so you'd be wise to line the stomach with something substantial before hitting the enormous and totally tropical cocktail list.

Jumeirah
Beach Hotel
Umm Suqeim
Map 6 B1

Uptown Bar

04 406 8999 | www.jumeirahbeachhotel.com

With its location on the 24th floor affording great views of the Burj Al Arab, Uptown has always been a great place to admire the city over a sundowner or two. Nowadays, with Burj Dubai and the rest of the burgeoning downtown skyline, the views are even more impressive, and while the interior is classy enough – in a James Bond kind of way – the terrace is still one of the best places to take visitors or to enjoy a pre or post-dinner drink when dining in the area. There's an extensive menu of cocktails and other beverages, and tapas and bar snacks are also available.

Wafi City
Umm Hurair
Map 11 E4

Vintage

04 324 4100 | www.waficityrestaurants.com

Vintage is a cheese and wine aficionado's dream, with the menu a veritable telephone directory of all things cheese and grape. Wines range from the most respectable plonk to a dazzling array of costly vintages, burgundies and champagnes but, despite the exclusive list, this feels more like a friendly local than a stuffy wine bar. Don't overlook the food; there are some fantastic cheese and cold meat platters that come with fresh bread. Vintage is a small space, so reservations and smoke-free dining are not an option, and you may need to arrive early or very late to bag a sofa.

Emirates Towers
Trade Centre 2
Map 7 F3

Vu's Bar

04 319 8088 | www.jumeirahemiratestowers.com

The elevator ride to the 51st floor is itself an experience and when the lift opens you are invited into an intimate bar that feels like a private members' club. The window space is somewhat restricted but still gives you a fabulous view across Dubai's sprawling metropolis. A comprehensive choice of imaginative cocktails and a bulging beer and wine list should ensure no one goes thirsty. Vu's is far from cheap, but for sophisticated sundowners in a sleek space and showing off to out-of-towners, it takes some beating.

Grape Stuff

Ideal for wine buffs and novices, the MMI wine society (www. mmidubai.com) offers monthly wine offers, tastings, dinners, and talks by some of the world's top wine experts. It's free to join, and members receive a monthly e-newsletter with details of events, features and favourite wines.

Karaoke Bars

There are a few places in Dubai where you can show off your vocal abilities or just belt out a comedy version of *Ice Ice Baby*. Harry Ghatto's (p.612) in Emirates Towers is a popular haunt with the small space filling fast, while the post-brunch karaoke sessions at Double Decker (p.622) range from the sublime to the ridiculous. For a unique night, try 'curryoke' at It's Mirchi (04 334 4088) in the Ramee Royal Hotel, Bur Dubai, which serves up Indian fare with an enormous multi-language song book. On the other side of the creek, Hibiki (p.612) is less glam, but the private rooms are a good option if you're a bit shy.

Ladies Nights

Lucky ladies in this fair city can go out almost any night of the week and enjoy free drinks. Of course, this isn't a charitable venture by Dubai's bar scene; where ladies are drinking, the men and their wallets inevitably follow. Tuesday is the biggest ladies' night with many bars and pubs offering at least two free drinks. The most legendary venues are Scarlett's (p.617), Long's Bar (p.614) and Waxy O'Conner's (p.625), but Boudoir (p.626) is very lady friendly with free bubbly, cocktails or shots throughout the week.

Pubs

Other options **Bars** p.608

You can't expect authenticity from Dubai's pubs, but then when they're mostly in hotels, in the desert, in the Middle East, that won't come as a surprise. What you can look forward to is some inviting, friendly spots with a decent selection of draught and bottled beers, and reliably good bar grub. Many of these mostly ersatz English and Irish places are popular when there's a big game on. And they're all comfortable, raucous and smoky enough to feel enough like the real thing.

Wine Lists

You will find that the majority of fine dining restaurants in Dubai have excellent wine lists but there are a few places that deserve a special mention for their cellars. These include The Agency (p.608), The Cellar (p.558), Pierchic (p.589), Spectrum on One (p.566), Teatro (p.568), Verre (p.548) and Vintage (p.620). All you have to do is keep track of the dirhams (wine can be pricey) and make the right choice.

Rydges Plaza Hotel
Satwa
Map 8 A3

Aussie Legends

04 398 2222 | www.rydges.com

In the style of a friendly, chilled-out local, Aussie Legends offers regular appearances from live bands and musicians. The small dance floor is sometimes known to kick off quite early on a weekend evening, and the pool table is so popular you may wait all night for a game. As well as a wide variety of drinks, the menu offers a good range of satisfyingly tasty pub grub. With a weekly quiz night and numerous sporting events shown on the large screen TVs, this can be a great place to watch the big match in a lively atmosphere.

Sofitel City Centre
Port Saeed
Map 11 C3

Churchill's

04 294 1222 | www.accorhotels.com

While it might not be the kind of place you go out of your way to visit, Churchill's has one distinct advantage – it is attached (via the Sofitel Hotel) to Deira City Centre (p.488) so when shopping loses its appeal you can nip in for a quick half. As close as you can get to a traditional English pub, there are TVs, pool table, dartboard, dodgy carpets, wooden booths and obligatory tabletop nuts. The food is what you would expect – burgers, fish and chips, pies, chicken and some worthy desserts.

Jumeirah Beach Hotel
Umm Suqeim
Map 6 B

Dhow & Anchor

04 406 8999 | www.jumeirahbeachhotel.com

Slightly reminiscent of a traditional, if miniature, British pub, the Dhow & Anchor is a popular watering hole. Be warned that the compact bar can get crowded and smoky, particularly during happy hour or when a major sporting event is showing on the huge plasma TV. There's a small, rather plain seating area, so if dining try the attractive outdoor terrace, which allows glimpses of the Burj Al Arab through the palm trees. The drinks menu includes some interesting cocktails and the usual beers, wines and spirits, while the pub grub staples include terrific curries, pies, and fish and chips.

Al Murooj Rotana
Trade Centre 2
Map 7 E3

Double Decker

04 321 1111 | www.rotana.com

Double Decker is themed upon London transport, with memorabilia scattered around the pub. Perennially popular, it is packed on Fridays with revellers attracted by its

---

THE AVIATION CLUB

...irrepressibly Irish

TOBACCONIST

THE IRISH VILLAGE

04 282 4750

The Irish Village
Dubai

reasonably priced brunch. Thankfully, the two levels ensure plenty of room for patrons to eat, drink and have a dance. Weekly karaoke sessions, ladies' night offers and a big screen for sports ensure there is something for everybody. The large central bar is home to a good drinks menu, including plenty of cocktails. Upmarket pub grub includes plenty of stodgy choices and tasty sharing platters for a light bite.

Safe Driver

If you've enjoyed a few drinks with dinner then leave the car and contact Safe Driver. Not only will you be breaking the law if you drive after even one drink, but this clever service means you avoid the hassle of picking up the car in the morning. Simply call 04 268 8797 with your location and the time you wish to be picked up. A driver will then take you and your car home then be on his merry way.

Le Meridien Dubai
Garhoud
Map 13 E1

The Dubliner's

04 702 2508
www.lemeridien-dubai.com

This Irish pub is cosy, and lively, and a great venue for business or pleasure. Sit inside to partake in the weekly quiz, listen to music and watch football or sit outside on the romantic patio to enjoy the night air and conversation. The menu has many delectable choices and the dishes are fresh, tasty and reasonably priced. Save room for the Bailey's cheesecake. The pub includes some of the best beer choices in Dubai and an extensive selection of cocktails.

Beh White Swan Bldg
Trade Centre 1
Map 7 F2

Fibber Magee's

04 332 2400 | www.fibbersdubai.com

Pubs on foreign shores often strive for that all-important 'rustic' feel, and many fail miserably. Fibber Magee's, though, pulls it off with aplomb. Awkwardly positioned TV screens, dark wood furniture, the unique smell of years of smoke and drink-soaked carpets, and a well-stocked drinks cabinet appease and pub withdrawal symptoms immediately. Live televised sport, DJ, themed entertainment evenings (including the Easy Tiger quiz on Tuesdays), great value food and drink promotions makes Fibber's a popular choice for a no nonsense pint.

The Aviation Club
Garhoud
Map 13 E1

The Irish Village ▶ p.623

04 282 4750 | www.aviationclub.ae

Should you fancy fish and chips (in Guinness batter) or a steak with your favourite ale to wash it down, you can get it in a warm, relaxed environment at the 'IV'. The inside covers sizeable ground but cubby holes and wooden beams give it a cosy feel and, outside, wooden benches aplenty sit on cobbled stone, bordered by trees lit by multicoloured bulbs. Be it for a quick pint, a hearty meal, a knees-up, a hair-of-the-dog fry up or a spot of local talent (musical that is), the Irish Village is like a dear old friend.

Under Age

The law in Dubai states that drinkers must be 21 or over. If you're lucky enough to look like you barely remember the 80s, make sure to carry some form of ID that shows your age – a passport or driving licence is best. Even if you think you're flattering your slightly wrinkled self, it's better to be safe than sorry. Otherwise you'll be on lemonade all night, or worse still, left outside alone.

Habtoor Grand
Dubai Marina
Map 5 B1

The Underground

04 399 5000
www.habtoorhotels.com

This pub has a theme based around – you guessed it – the London Underground and the bar is even made to look like a Tube carriage. The order of the day in

this popular pub is beer, burgers and ball sports which attract a large crowd of regulars who don't mind paying Dhs.36 for a pint. There are numerous screens dotted throughout to ensure you can get a good view of the live sports action (which ranges from everything from football and rugby to baseball and boxing). There's also a dog-eared dartboard and pool tables to while away the time in between.

Four Points by Sheraton Bur Dubai
Bur Dubai
Map 8 F3

Viceroy Bar & Cocktail Lounge
04 397 7444
www.starwoodhotels.com
Despite the colonial pretensions of its name, the Viceroy is a very familiar-looking pokey British pub with authentic tobacco smoke, a clientele of white middle-aged men and a television tuned to a different sports channel in every corner. Happy hour is every day 12:00-19:00. If you can handle the perpetual

Double Decker

cigarettes while eating, the reasonably priced, generously portioned food is a decent range of British, Tex-Mex, Thai and curry, the latter no doubt imported from the Indian restaurant next door.

Ascot Hotel
Bur Dubai
Map 8 F2

Waxy O'Conner's
04 352 0900 | www.ascothoteldubai.com
Love it or hate it, this faux Irish pub serves a purpose. If you're from the British Isles and homesickness strikes then get a taxi to Waxy's. Its legendary weekend brunch (Dhs.85 for five drinks, full English breakfast with pork bacon and sausages then carvery) pulls in the punters, including – allegedly – rapper Fifty Cent when he was in town. At 18:00 the lights go down, the music goes up and the party starts. While you might not be mixing with high society, you'll have a good time and a hangover to remember.

Quiz Nights

If you want to test your brain power and knowledge of useless trivia then head to one of Dubai's many quiz nights. Try Boston Bar (p.610) or Player's Lounge (04 398 8840) on Mondays or try Tuesdays at Fibber Magee's, which features a plasticine model making round. For Mexican food head to El Paso (p.612) at Dubai Marine Resort & Spa on Wednesdays. There's even live music afterwards. Prizes range from bottles of booze and bucks (Dhs.700 for first place at Boston Bar) to the more unusual (a massage at the Gold Souk) but regulars go for the glory rather than the gold.

Quiz Nights	
Aussie Legends	04 398 2222
The Boston Bar	04 345 5888
Champions	04 607 7977
The Dubliner's	04 702 2508
El Paso	04 304 8120
Fibber Magee's	04 332 2400
Ranches Restaurant	04 366 3000

Nightclubs

Other options **Belly Dancing** p.332, **Dinner Cruises** p.540

Fairmont Dubai
Trade Centre 1
Map 8 A4

400

04 332 4900 | *www.the400nightclub.com*

Home of dark corners and big bar bills, this downtown club isn't to everyone's taste but serves a purpose for fans of excessive hair gel, plastic surgery and loud music. Negotiate the doormen, enter the underground venue via a stately staircase then get involved in the Arabic, house and R&B music, watching out for popping champagne corks. You can't help but notice when someone orders something special; the bottle is paraded around the club on a velvet cushion surrounded by sparklers. What credit crunch?

Jumeirah
Beach Hotel
Umm Suqeim
Map 6 B1

The Apartment Lounge & Club

04 406 8000 | *www.jumeirahbeachhotel.com*

Look out, another champagne cork is popping and yet more photos are being taken for local society mags. Yes, you have arrived at The Apartment, home to a few high rollers and many beautiful people. This is the place for moving and mingling, served with lashings of bubbles. With two decadent rooms for different styles of music, the soundtrack leans towards house, hip-hop and R&B.

Dubai Marine
Beach Resort
Jumeira
Map 7 F1

Boudoir

04 345 5995 | *www.myboudoir.com*

This exclusive spot can be as difficult to get into as a lady's chamber but once you get past the doormen – as long as you are appropriately dressed – you will be treated to a Parisian-style club that's perfect for dangerous liaisons. Expect lots of opulent fabrics in hedonistic hues, hypnotic tunes and moody lighting. Theme nights promote different types of music including house, latino and R&B, in addition to great free drinks deals throughout the week for ladies.

Al Nasr Leisureland
Oud Metha
Map 10 E2

Chi@The Lodge

04 337 9470 | *www.lodgedubai.com*

Chi@The Lodge is always busy with its indoor and outdoor dancefloors, lots of seating, large screens and VIP 'cabanas'. The regular theme nights with fancy dress are popular and this is also home of the legendary 'Cheese' nights with DJ Tim Cheddar. If you needed more reasons to go, it's easy to get taxis outside, there's often a shawarma stand in the carpark and entrance is free before 22:30 on most nights. Keep an eye on listings magazines for upcoming events, live music and offers at this fun favourite.

One&Only
Royal Mirage
Al Sufouh
Map 5 C1

Kasbar

04 399 9999 | *www.oneandonlyroyalmirage.com*

Kasbar manages to combine the best of both worlds – the mystique and luxury of regal Arabia and the feel of an exclusive dance party. In keeping with the Arabian decor of the Royal Mirage, this is a sultry, candlelit nightclub perfect for liaisons. There is an air of old-school romance emanating from the three levels linked by a spiral staircase. The main floor attracts toe-tappers, while the mezzanine space overlooks the dancefloor, and the basement is a chill-out lounge.

Grand Hyatt Dubai
Umm Hurair
Map 13 C1

MIX

04 317 1234 | *www.dubai.grand.hyatt.com*

Touted as Dubai's only superclub, MIX has three floors of hedonistic late-night entertainment. There is a sprawling dancefloor, a lounge area, two VIP rooms, a cigar bar and a sound-proofed live music room. Various local and international DJs earn the

SANCTUARY

BREAKING ALL PRECONCEIVED BOUNDARIES OF CLUBBING
IN DUBAI, WITH WEEKLY LINE UP OF EVENTS, UNIQUE PARTY
THEMES, THEATRICAL PERFORMANCES AND WORLD CLASS
SERVICE, SANCTUARY SHOWCASES DJ TALENT FROM THE
WORLD'S MOST IN-DEMAND ARTISTS. CHOOSE FROM EXCLUSIVE
LOUNGES, THE VELVET ROOM, THE TERRACE AND THE MAIN
ROOM, DANCE AREA.

OPEN DAILY FROM 9.30PM FOR MORE INFORMATION
CALL +971(4) 426 0561 OR VISIT ATLANTISTHEPALM.COM

ATLANTIS
PALM JUMEIRAH, DUBAI
DON'T FORGET TO BREATHE

respect of Dubai's hip crowd by belting out loud and large tunes (mostly house – but if that's not your bag you'll find some R&B upstairs). MIX can accommodate 800 clubbers – great on busy Thursday nights but during the week even a decent-sized crowd of 300 can seem lost in such a huge space.

Wafi City
Umm Hurair
Map 10 D4

Plan B
04 324 4777

Taking over the location once occupied by the much-loved Planetarium, the guys at Wafi took the opportunity to reinvent the space again and in 2007 the aptly named Plan B opened its doors. The VIP room upstairs serves champagne and sushi, but the focus is on dancing and not dining. Aimed at people looking for a relaxed late night hang-out (no cover charge or ridiculous drinks prices), Plan B is a refreshing change to Dubai's increasingly exclusive nightlife. The music is wide ranging, with happy hour enlivening the fervour of Saturday nights.

Regent Palace Hotel
Bur Dubai
Map 8 F4

Rock Bottom
04 396 3888 | *www.ramee-group.com*

You've probably heard the rumours: Rock Bottom is the sleazy, sweaty home of the legendary Bullfrog cocktail and a cracking cover band, and a place where you somehow 'end up' without ever planning to go. However, this Bur Dubai stalwart has a lot more to offer; head over early evening for a quiet, reasonably priced dinner or game of pool and you'll be surprised to find a respectable crowd before the fun-seekers hit. Whatever reason you end up in Rock Bottom, it's an essential Dubai experience and one you'll inevitably repeat – even if it's by accident.

Atlantis The Palm
Palm Jumeirah
Map 2 A3

Sanctuary ▶ p.627
04 426 2626 | *www.atlantisthepalm.com*

You'd expect something special from Atlantis, but you wouldn't expect a suspended catwalk in a nightclub. That's what you get at Sanctuary, along with lashings of cool. This brand new space is modern, glam and packed with a mixed crowd from hotel guests to dedicated clubbers. It's open every night of the week but Fridays are when it kicks off with a blend of house, R&B and Arabic music, and the outdoor terrace fills up early.

Dhow Palace Hotel
Bur Dubai
Map 8 E3

Submarine
04 359 9992 | *www.dhowpalacehoteldubai.com*

Located in the basement of the otherwise unremarkable Dhow Palace, Submarine has filled a bit of the alternative dance void that appeared when the now-legendary iBO closed its doors. The dancefloor doesn't start to fill up until midnight, but early arrivals can take advantage of the reasonably priced drink menu. If it wasn't for the prime music blasting out of the crisp sound system, the spaceship-meets-submarine decor might be a little hard to swallow. If you can't stand another thump of typical Dubai club music, Submarine's DJs will quickly remind you how diverse the genre can be.

Crowne Plaza
Trade Centre 1
Map 7 F3

Zinc
04 331 1111 | *www.crowneplaza.com*

Zinc's up-for-it marketing remains hyperactive, while the soundtrack is R&B, house and hip-hop, with Housexy (Ministry of Sound) and Kinki Milinky ferrying over some of the UK's hot-shot DJs. Design-wise, there are shiny flatscreens, louche lounge areas and glitzy mirrored walls, as well as an enlarged dancefloor that's sectioned off by a mammoth bar. Smaller bars ensure the path from dancefloor to fresh drink (from the new champagne, wine and cocktail list) is as smooth as possible.

Parties At Home

Kids' Parties

There are several companies in Dubai that can do all the cooking, decorating and cleaning up for you, leaving you with more time to tell witty after-dinner anecdotes. Harlequin (www.harlequinmarquees.com) offers marquees, tables and chairs, and even outdoor coolers for those summer garden parties. Flying Elephant (www.flyingelephantuae.com) helps with party decorations and venue equipment, as well as excellent children's party plans. For a novel outdoor party idea, you can get your very own shawarma stand set up in the garden, complete with shawarma maker. Several Arabic restaurants provide this service, which works out as a very reasonable and easy way to sustain hordes of party guests.

Shooting Stars

Shooting Stars is an adventure video production company that produces keepsake videos. Using the latest digital technology, it can turn your child into the star of their very own video blockbuster: a popular choice is My Arabian Adventure (the background tape is filmed in the dunes at Hatta). It's a unique and unusual gift to send back to the grandparents. For more information contact Shooting Stars on 04 394 1377 or 050 798 8209, or check out www.shootingstar.biz.

Caterers

Caterers	
Emirates Abela	04 282 3171
Intercat	04 334 5212
Lime Tree Cafe	04 349 8498
Maria Bonita's	04 394 4523
Metropolitan Catering Services	04 881 7100
Okku	04 501 8444
Open House	04 396 5481
Sandwich Express	04 343 9922
Something Different	04 267 1639
West One	04 398 7177

For parties, special occasions, and business lunches or dinners, there are numerous options for arranging outside catering, allowing you to relax and enjoy yourself and concentrate on anything but the cooking. In addition to specialist companies, many hotels and restaurants have catering departments, so pick your favourite and ask if they can help out.

Depending on what you require, caterers can provide just the food or everything from crockery, napkins, tables, chairs and even waiters, doormen and a clearing up service afterwards. You don't even have to stay at home to order catering for a function – how about arranging a party in the desert? Costs vary according to the number of people, dishes and level of service required.

For a list of hotel numbers, check out the table on p.46. For restaurants and cafes, browse this section of the book.

Party Organisers

Other options **Party Accessories** p.461

Flying Elephant ▶ p.631, p.359
04 347 9170 | *www.flyingelephantuae.com*

Whatever your party planning needs, Flying Elephant will be happy to comply. It offers everything from adding special effects for a product launch to providing entertainment for your child's first birthday party. It has a wide variety of products to complete every occasion, be it balloons and decorations or the Gulf's largest outdoor confetti blaster. Flying Elephant also offers theme decoration, theme parties, balloon printing and balloon decoration/sculpting.

Mad Science
04 337 7403 | *www.madscience.org/uae*

In addition to offering after-school activity programmes and workshops, Mad Science organises entertainment for special events and kids' birthday parties. Ideally suited to children between 5 and 12 years, the interactive, science-based shows last around an hour, and the kids get to take home a goody bag containing educational experiments.

Cinemas

Movie-going is popular in Dubai, although screenings are limited to the mainstream – you won't find too many art house offerings. Dubai has seen an explosion in the number of screens available over the past couple of years; the biggest cinemas include a 12 screen complex in Mall of the Emirates (p.494) and a 21 screen outlet in Ibn Battuta Shopping Mall (p.492) – the latter even has the region's first IMAX screen. Mall of the Emirates also boasts the luxurious Gold Class option for selected films, with a smaller theatre, enormous leather armchairs and waiter service throughout the movie. Dubai Festival Centre (p.490) also offers a premium cinema experience with Grand Class for the same Dhs.100 ticket price.

Cinema timings can be found in the daily newspapers, as well as in the *Entertainment Plus* supplement in *Gulf News* and *Time Out* every Wednesday. At weekends, there are extra shows at midnight or 01:00 – check press for details.

There are some common cinema annoyances widely moaned about in expatriate circles – freezing air conditioning, people talking on their mobiles or to the people sitting next to them, people switching seats mid-movie, Arabic subtitles (usually this is no problem, but if you're watching an English language film that contains some foreign language, there is no space for English subtitles so you miss out on some of the dialogue), and of course the heavy hand of the censor.

A definite cinematic highlight is Dubai International Film Festival. Improving year on year, the event runs for a week in December across various locations and showcases an impressive mix of mainstream, world and local cinema, from shorts to full features. There's also usually a good range of talks and seminars from actors and directors, including George Clooney who showed up in 200, and Nicholas Cage in 2008. See www.dubaifilmfest.com for more details.

Alternative Screenings

While most of the cinema multiplexes only show big Hollywood movies, several bars and clubs put on screenings of older, foreign and independent films, usually early in the week and free of charge. Check out Movies Under the Stars at Wafi City (04 324 4100), Beach Bar at Jumeirah Beach Club Resort & Spa (04 344 5333), or the Cine-Club Alliance Française auditorium (04 335 8712).

It is also worth looking in local listings magazines for details of one-off screenings at some of the city's more progressive art spaces, such as The Jam Jar (p.331).

Cinemas

Name	Location	Phone	Website	Map Ref
CineStar	Deira City Centre	04 294 9000	www.cinestarcinemas.com	11 C3
	Mall of the Emirates	04 341 4222	www.cinestarcinemas.com	6 A3
Grand Cinecity	Al Ghurair City	04 228 9898	www.century-cinemas.com	9 D4
Grand Cineplex	Nr Grand Hyatt	04 324 2000	www.grandcinemas.com	13 C1
Grand Festival Cinemas	Dubai Festival Centre	04 232 8328	www.grandcinemas.com	13 D2
Grand Megaplex Cinemas/IMAX	Ibn Battuta Shopping Mall	04 366 9898	www.grandcinemas.com	4 D2
Grand Mercato	Mercato	04 349 9713	www.grandcinemas.com	7 D1
Grand Metroplex	Metropolitan Hotel	04 343 8383	www.grandcinemas.com	7 B3
Lamcy Cinema	Lamcy Plaza	04 336 8808	na	10 D2
Plaza Cinema	Nr Carrefour, Al Ghubaiba Bus Station	04 393 9966	na	9 A1

Corporate Events

Themed Events,
Decoration & Mascots

Commercial &
Retail Installations

Corporate
Family Days

Team Building

Event
Management

MICE Events

Staff Parties

Flying Elephant

The region's largest events supplier of corporate and family entertainment

Call 800-PARTY (72789)
www.flyingelephantuae.com

Comedy

Comedy nights in Dubai are popular with the expat crowd. The Laughter Factory organises monthly events, with comedians from the UK's Comedy Store coming over to play various venues throughout the Gulf. In Dubai these venues include Zinc (p.628) at the Crowne Plaza, Jimmy Dix (p.613) at the Movenpick, Rainbow Room at the Aviation Club (p.616), and the Courtyard Marriott (p.46) at the Green Community. Keep an eye on www.thelaughterfactory.com for details of future shows. There are also several one-off events featuring comedians from around the world. Remember that a lot of comedy is regional, so unless you're familiar with the comedian's country, you might not get the joke.

Beats, Beanbags
& A Barbie

During the cooler winter months, Peanut Butter Jam at Wafi City's Rooftop Gardens (04 324 4100) is a must-do for all music fans. Resident and guest bands and performers play live music from 20:00 until midnight, with beanbags to relax on and a barbecue.

Concerts & Live Music

Dubai hosts a number of concerts each year, and as it grows bigger it attracts bigger names. Past acts to play include Kylie, Elton John, Robbie Williams, Mariah Carey, Sting, and George Michael. These big name acts usually play at outdoor venues such as the Tennis Stadium, Dubai Autodrome, Dubai Festival City and the amphitheatre at Media City. The amphitheatre has hosted Desert Rhythm, Dubai's very own music festival celebrating cultural diversity in music. A key event for all music lovers anticipating the rise of live music in Dubai, it has featured a variety of smaller acts alongside big names such as Paul Weller, Kanye West, Mika, Ziggy Marley, Joss Stone and Madness. Another event that goes from strength to strength is the annual Dubai Desert Rock Festival (www.desertrockfestival.com), and in 2008 it gave the region's rock fans a two-day, multi-band ear bashing with Muse headlining.

In addition to artists at the height of their fame, Dubai also plays host to a string of groups that may be past their prime, but are nevertheless able to provide some good entertainment (think Human League, Tony Hadley, Go West and Deacon Blue). There's also been a recent rise in the number of alternative and slightly lesser-known (basically 'more cool') acts coming over to some new sun. Groove Armada, 2ManyDjs and Soulwax (all part-band, part-dance acts) have all played in Dubai Autodrome, Fun Lovin' Criminals and Arrested Development have also played live to enthusiastic audiences. Keep an eye on 9714, a promotion, events and marketing company, and general 'arts collective' for information on more upcoming gigs (www.9714.com).

Theatre

Other options **Drama Groups** p.347

The theatre scene in Dubai has always been rather limited, with fans relying chiefly on touring companies and the occasional amateur dramatics performance. However, as the city grows so does its thirst for culture, and with an increase in modern facilities over the past couple of years, theatre lovers are finally finding something to cheer about. The Madinat Theatre at Madinat Jumeirah hosts a variety of performances, from serious stage plays to comedies and musical performances. Bigger events can be accommodated in the Madinat Jumeirah's arena – recent events include the production of *Stomp* and *The Nutcracker* ballet performed by Ballet Russe, The Classical Ballet Company of Wales. Dubai's theatre space has been bolstered further with the opening of the Dubai Community Theatre and Arts Centre (DUCTAC), see below. Young budding thespians can receive training in acting, mime, scriptwriting and costume design through the Scenez Arts & Drama Academy. Call 050 356 2709 for details.

Mall of the Emirates
Al Barsha
Map 6 A3

Dubai Community Theatre & Arts Centre (DUCTAC)

04 341 4777 | *www.dubaitheatre.org*

The Dubai Community Theatre & Arts Centre (DUCTAC) is the latest, and certainly the biggest, arts facility in the region. In addition to rehearsal spaces, workshops, exhibition

live it, love it
...log on

www.liveworkexplore.com

- Communities
- Updates
- Competitions
- Discounts
- Explorer expeditions
- Shop online

halls, a cafe, and a library, the complex features two fully equipped theatres. The Centrepoint Theatre can seat 543 people, while the smaller Kilachand Studio Theatre has a capacity of 196 people. Between them, the theatres aim to present a variety of entertainment; from drama, opera and classical music, to comedy and children's shows. Check the website for details of upcoming events and performances.

Al Sahra
Desert Resort
Off Dubai-Al Ain Rd
Map 2 B3

Jumana – Secret Of The Desert ▶ p.635

04 367 9500 | www.alsahra.com

In addition to the range of events on offer at the Madinat Theatre, a jaw-dropping contribution to Dubai's cultural scene comes from the Al Sahara Desert Resort in Dubailand. Jumana – Secret of the Desert is a remarkable show that uses around 60 acrobats and dancers in an amphitheatre capable of seating 1,200. The vibrant production uses water as a backdrop to the performance and boasts the use of fireworks, large scale water effects and video projection (not to mention Omar Sharif's voice as the storyteller) in a rich, awe-inspiring show depicting Arabian folklore. Visit the website for further details.

Souk Madinat
Jumeirah
Umm Suqeim
Map 6 A2

Madinat Theatre

04 366 8888 | www.madinattheatre.com

Housing a theatre within a huge complex that includes luxury hotels and a shopping centre may seem like something of an afterthought, but the Madinat Theatre is far from mediocrity – not only is it worthy of stand-alone status thanks to its well-planned design and space (424 seats no less), but its programme has been suitably impressive. From 'treading the boards' classics to musicals and innovative comedy shows, make sure you keep your eyes open for what's coming into town next and chances are you won't be disappointed.

DUCTAC

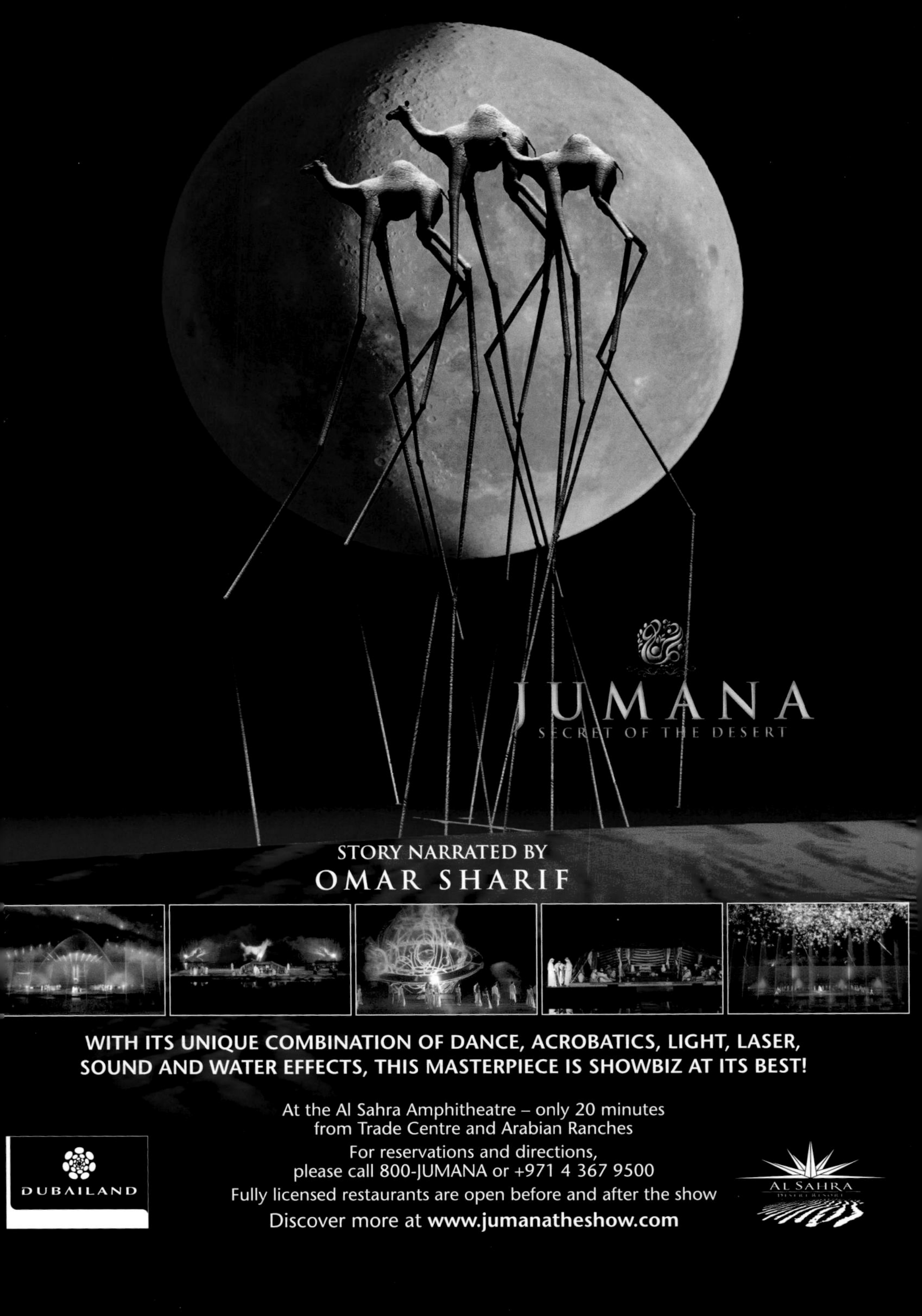

JUMANA
SECRET OF THE DESERT

STORY NARRATED BY
OMAR SHARIF

WITH ITS UNIQUE COMBINATION OF DANCE, ACROBATICS, LIGHT, LASER, SOUND AND WATER EFFECTS, THIS MASTERPIECE IS SHOWBIZ AT ITS BEST!

At the Al Sahra Amphitheatre – only 20 minutes
from Trade Centre and Arabian Ranches

For reservations and directions,
please call 800-JUMANA or +971 4 367 9500

Fully licensed restaurants are open before and after the show

Discover more at **www.jumanatheshow.com**

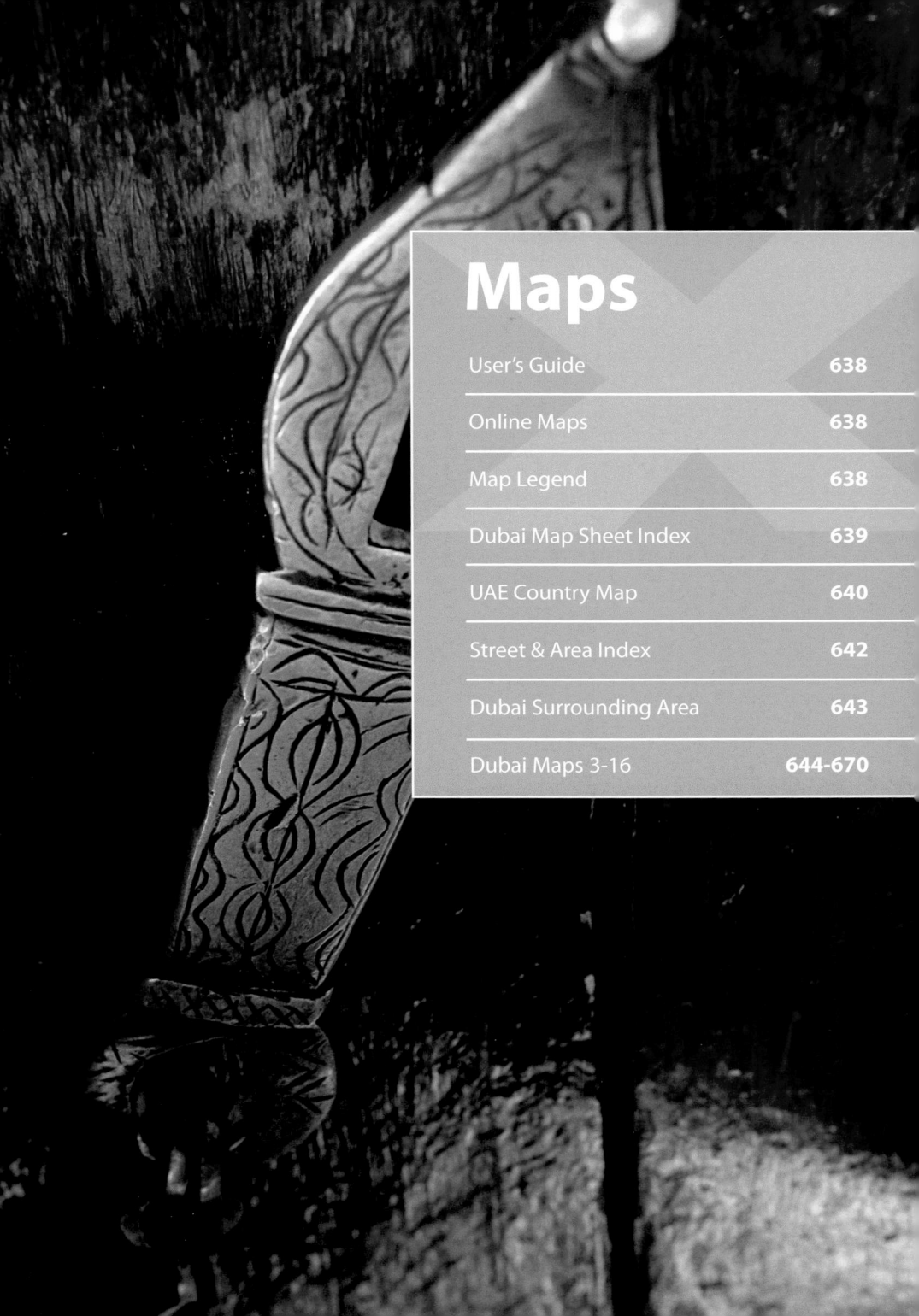

Maps

User's Guide

Dubai's ever-growing infrastructure can make it challenging to get around. The city is also in the process of overhauling its sign system, meaning those directions you got from your friend two weeks ago might not make sense tomorrow. The best way to think of Dubai's road system is as a series of parallel highways running the length of the city (north-south), with interconnecting main roads running from the sea (west) to the desert (east).

The map on the opposite page acts as an index to the entire map section. Map 1 is an overview of the entire UAE, while Map 2 is an overview of Dubai. Map 3 through to Map 7 and Map 12 through to Map 16 cover the city on a scale of 30,000:1, meaning one millimetre on the map is equivalent to 30 metres. Maps 8 to 11 are more detailed, with a scale of 15,000:1. The overview map (Map 2) is shown at a scale of 400,000:1

When navigating the city, keep in mind that street names are nearly non-existent and your best bet in finding your destination is by locating landmarks. With this in mind, these maps have all of the common landmarks used by residents marked on them. To give better visualisation, most of the maps have been oriented parallel to Dubai's coastline rather than the customary north orientation.

Mighty Maps

*If the thought of folding a map makes your head spin, you need to get yourself a **Mighty Map**. These cloth cartographical wonders can be stuffed into any pocket and are virtually indestructable. They have all the information you need to never get lost again.*

Need More?

This weighty book will provide you with all you need to know to get the most out of Dubai, but for when you need something a little more convenient in size, you can also buy the *Dubai Mini Map*. The whole city can slot in your back pocket, handy for when you need to travel light but still navigate your way around. It's part of a series of Mini Maps that includes cities as diverse as London, Amsterdam, New York and Shanghai. If you require something bigger, pick up a copy of the *Dubai Map* from any petrol station. It's all-encompassing detail makes it a necessity for any glove box. If you're a real map nut, you'll love the *Dubai Atlas*, which not only shows every street in the city, but labels each building. To make navigating even easier, the *Dubai Atlas* index lists and locates every street and building.

Map Legend

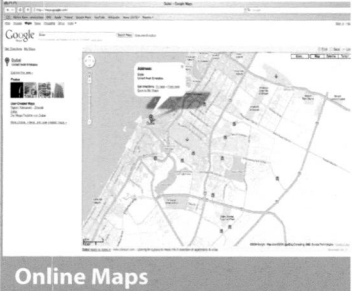

Online Maps

If you want to surf for maps online, www. ae.map24.com and www.maporama. com are worth a look. Hardcore map fans though are recommended to try Google Earth (http://earth.google.com). This amazing program (you download it from the site) combines satellite imagery, detailed maps, and a powerful search capability, allowing you to fly between various points on the globe and zoom in for incredibly detailed close-up views. Google Earth's satellite images of Dubai are a bit out of date, but still immensely helpful.

Hotel		Highway
Education		Major Road
Park/Garden		Secondary Road
Hospital		Other Road
Shopping	D96 E11	Road Number
Heritage/Museum		Metro (u/c)
Industrial Area		Salik Toll Gate
Built-up Area/Building		Hospital/Clinic
Land		Mosque
Pedestrian		Fire Station
Beach		Police Station
Mangrove		Golf Course
		Petrol Station
		Post Office
		Airport
		Embassy
		Library
		Visitor Attraction
	T28	Taxi Icon

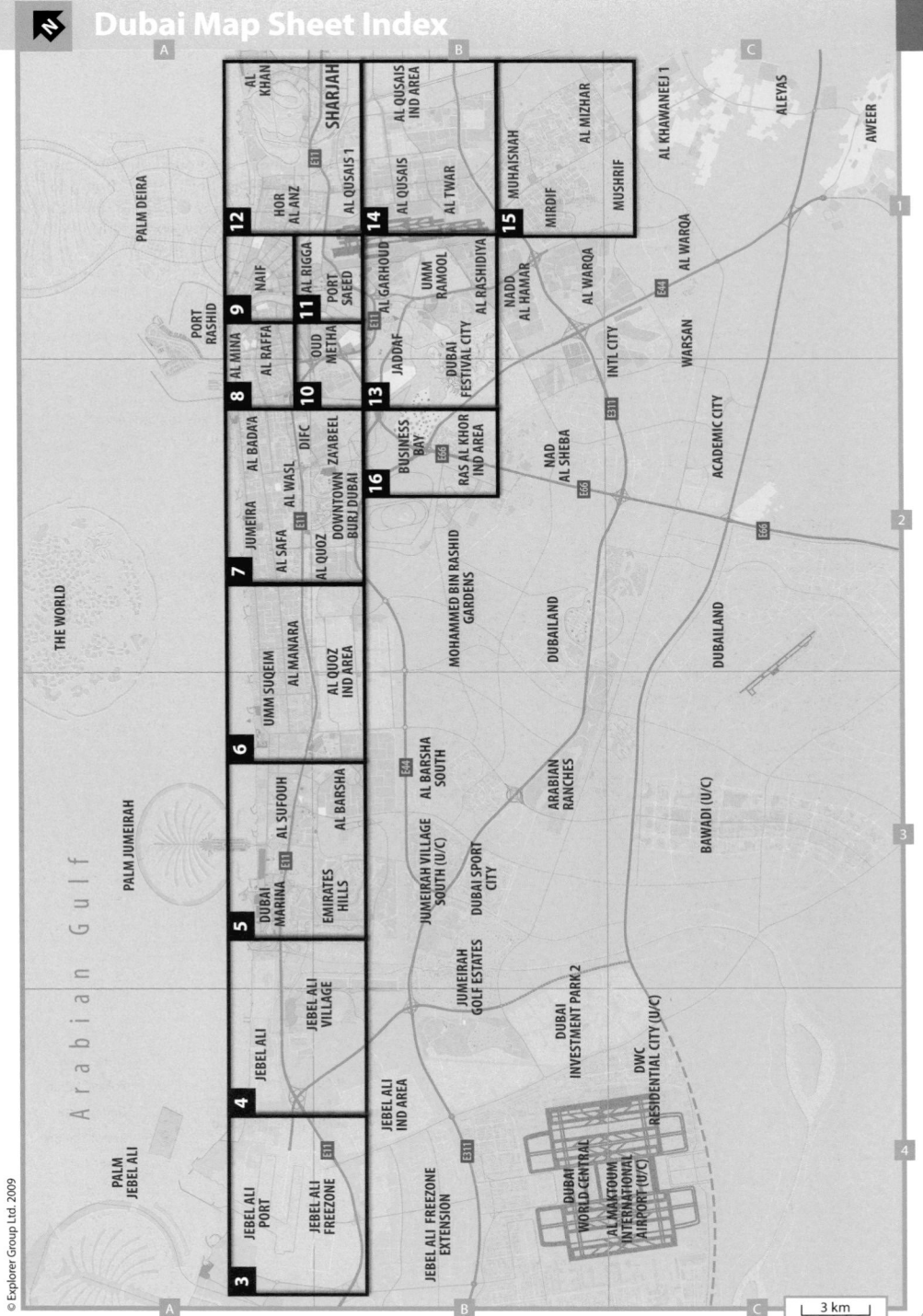

Arabian Gulf

PALM DEIRA

THE WORLD

PALM JEBEL ALI

PALM JUMEIRAH

A

SHARJAH

AL KHAN

HOR AL ANZ

12 NAIF

PORT RASHID

9 AL RAFFA
AL MINA **8**

11 AL RIGGA
PORT SAEED

OUD METHA
10

JUMEIRA
AL BADAA **7**
AL WASL
AL SAFA
AL QUOZ
DOWNTOWN ZA'ABEEL
BURJ DUBAI

UMM SUQEIM
AL MANARA **6**
AL QUOZ IND AREA

AL SUFOUH
5 AL BARSHA
DUBAI MARINA
EMIRATES HILLS

JEBEL ALI VILLAGE

4 JEBEL ALI

JEBEL ALI IND AREA

JEBEL ALI PORT
3 JEBEL ALI FREEZONE

PALM JEBEL ALI

JEBEL ALI FREEZONE EXTENSION

AL BARSHA SOUTH

JUMEIRAH VILLAGE SOUTH (U/C)
DUBAI SPORT CITY

JUMEIRAH GOLF ESTATES

DUBAI INVESTMENT PARK 2

B

AL QUSAIS IND AREA

AL QUSAIS 1

AL QUSAIS
AL TWAR **14**

AL GARHOUD **13**
UMM RAMOOL
AL RASHIDIYA

JADDAF
DUBAI FESTIVAL CITY

BUSINESS BAY
16 RAS AL KHOR IND AREA

NADD AL HAMAR

NAD AL SHEBA

MOHAMMED BIN RASHID GARDENS

DUBAILAND

ARABIAN RANCHES

BAWADI (U/C)

DWC RESIDENTIAL CITY (U/C)

DUBAI WORLD CENTRAL
AL MAKTOUM INTERNATIONAL AIRPORT (U/C)

C

AL KHAWANEEJ 1

ALEVAS

AWEER

AL MIZHAR

MUSHRIF
15 MIRDIF
MUHAISNAH
MUSHRIF

AL WAROA

AL WARQA

INTL CITY
ACADEMIC CITY

WARSAN

DUBAILAND

1

2

3

4

© Explorer Group Ltd. 2009

www.liveworkexplore.com

3 km

639

Map **1**   **UAE Country Map**

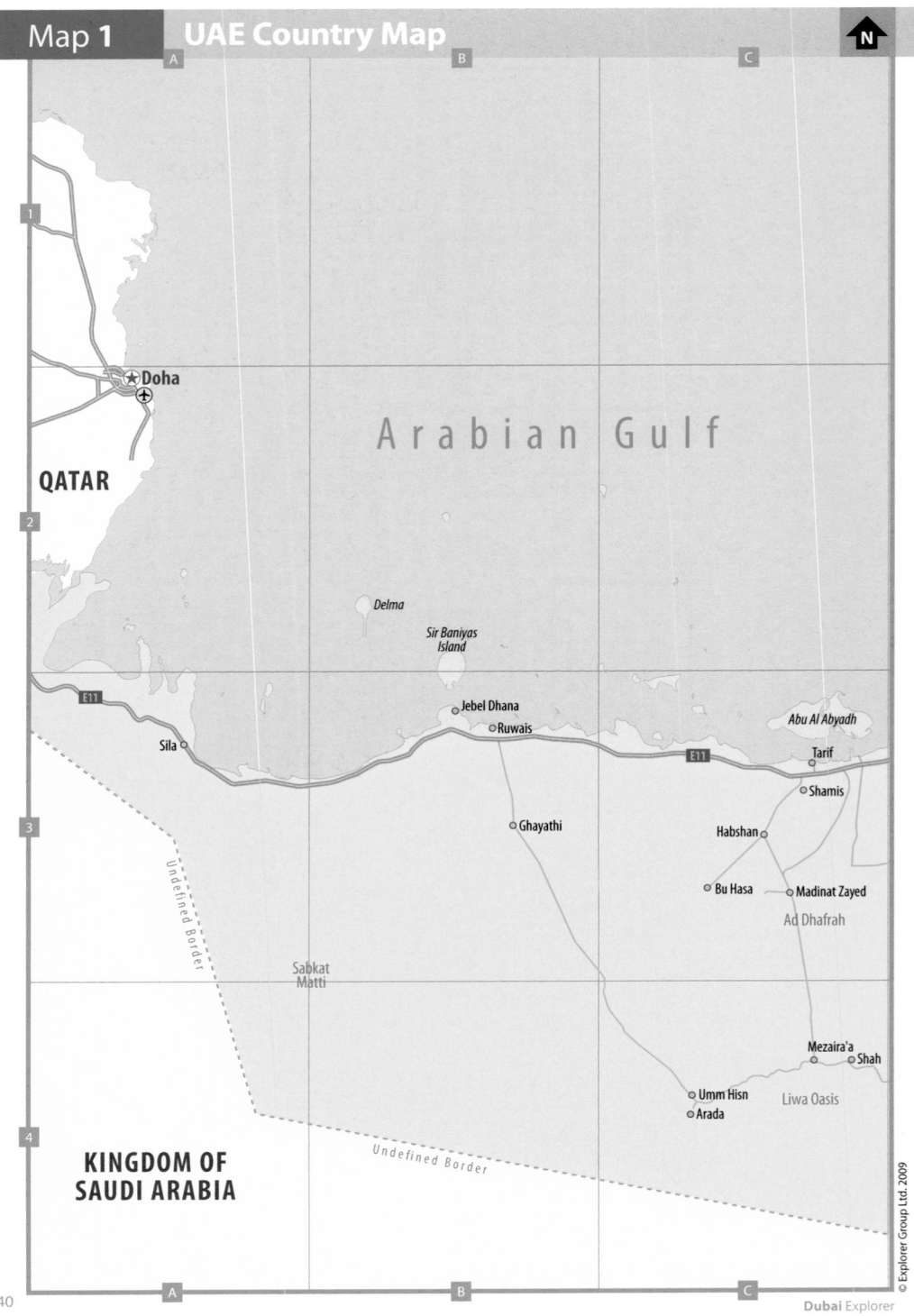

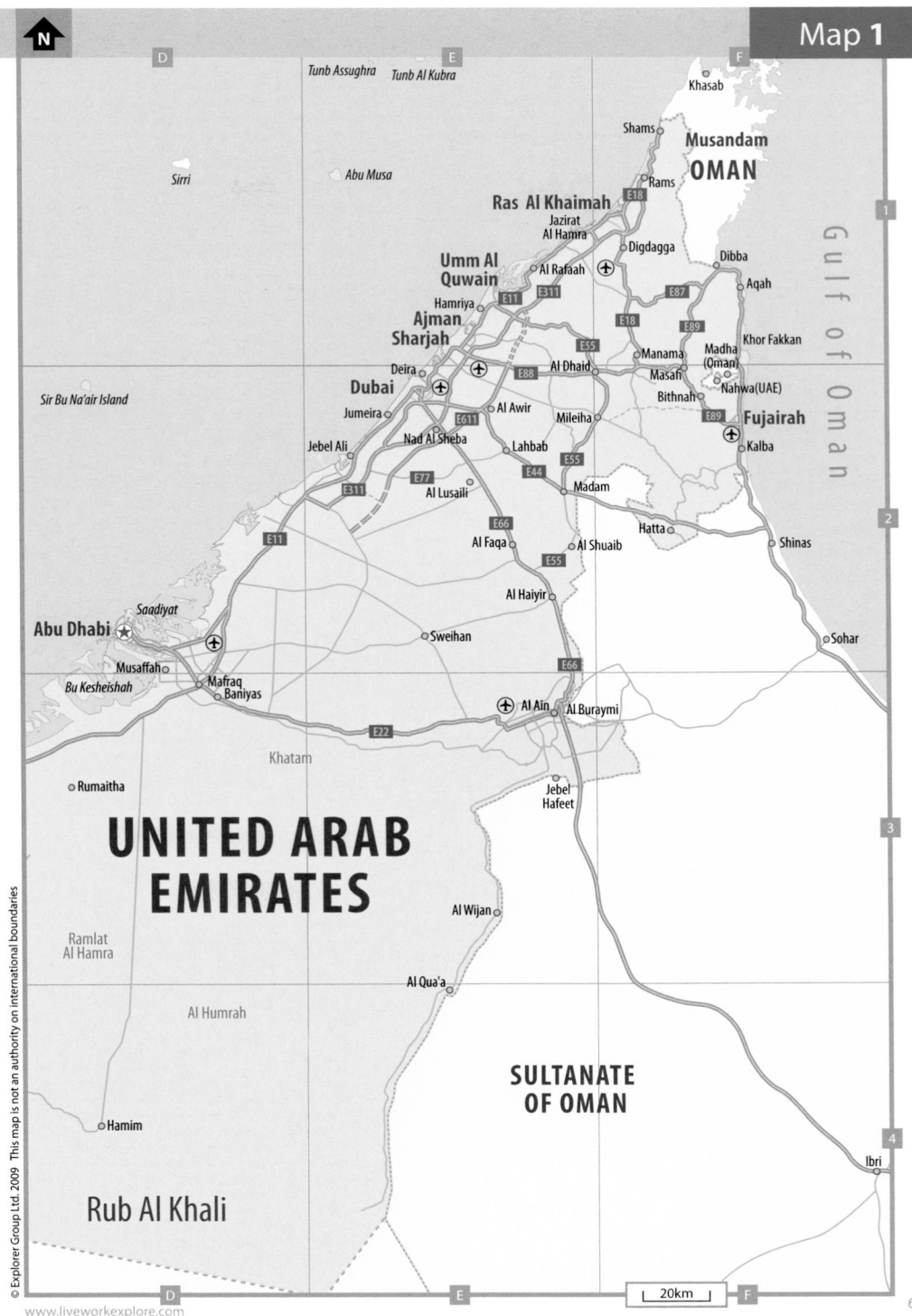

Map **1**

N

D

E

F

Tunb Assughra   Tunb Al Kubra

Khasab

Shams

Musandam
OMAN

Sirri

Abu Musa

Rams

1

Ras Al Khaimah

Jazirat
Al Hamra

Diggaga

Dibba

**Umm Al
Quwain**

Al Rafaah

E18

Aqah

E87

Hamriya

E11

E311

E18

**Ajman
Sharjah**

E89

Khor Fakkan

Manama

Madha
(Oman)

Sir Bu Na'air Island

Deira

Al Dhaid

Masafi

Nahwa(UAE)

Dubai

E88

Bithnah

Fujairah

Jumeira

Al Awir

Mileiha

E89

Jebel Ali

Nad Al Sheba

E611

Kalba

Lahbab

E311

E77

Al Lusaili

E44

E55

Madam

Hatta

Al Faqa

E66

2

E11

E55

Shinas

Al Shuaib

Al Haiyir

Abu Dhabi

Saadiyat

Sweihan

Sohar

Musaffah

Bu Kesheishah

Mafraq
Baniyas

E66

E22

Al Ain

Al Buraymi

Khatam

Rumaitha

Jebel
Hafeet

**UNITED ARAB
EMIRATES**

3

Ramlat
Al Hamra

Al Wijan

Al Humrah

Al Qua'a

**SULTANATE
OF OMAN**

Hamim

4

Ibri

Rub Al Khali

G u l f   o f   O m a n

20km

Street & Area Index

Area Names	Map Ref	Street Names	Map Ref	Street Names	Map Ref
Abu Hail	12-A2	Abu Backer Al Siddique Rd	9-F4	Dubai - Al Ain Rd	16-B4
Al Bada'a	7-F2	Abu Hail Rd	12-A2	Dubai - Sharjah Rd	12-A4
Al Baraha	9-E2	Airport Rd	11-D4	Emirates Hill Rd	5-B3
Al Barsha 1	5-E3	Airport Tunnel	14-A3	Emirates Rd	14-B4
Al Garhoud	13-E2	Al Attar St	7-B2	Financial Center Rd	7-E4
Al Jafiliya	8-C3	Al Baraha St	9-E3	First Industrial St	12-F4
Al Karama	8-E4	Al Diyafah St	8-A1	Garden Cross Rd	4-E2
Al Mamzar	12-D3	Al Ghubaiba Rd	8-F1	Gardens Boulevard	4-E3
Al Manara	6-C3	Al Hadiqa St	7-B2	Hadeed Rd	6-E3
Al Mankhool	8-D3	Al Hibab Rd	3-E4	Interchange 1	7-D3
Al Mina	8-B1	Al Ithihad Rd	11-C3	Interchange 10	3-A4
Al Muraqqabat	11-D1	Al Khail	13-B1	Interchange 2	7-B3
Al Muteena	9-E4	Al Khaleej Rd	8-F1	Interchange 3	6-D3
Al Nahda 1	12-C4	Al Khan Corniche St	12-F3	Interchange 4	6-A3
Al Quoz	7-A4	Al Khan St	12-E3	Interchange 5	5-B2
Al Quoz Ind Area 1	6-D4	Al Khawaneej Rd	15-D3	Interchange 6	4-C2
Al Quoz Ind Area 3	6-E4	Al Mafraq Rd	6-A4	Interchange 7	4-A2
Al Raffa	8-E2	Al Maktoum Rd	11-C1	Interchange 8	3-E4
Al Rashidiya	13-E4	Al Manara Rd	6-D2	Interchange 9	3-C4
Al Rigga	9-C4	Al Mankhool Rd	8-B3	Jumeira Rd	6-D1
Al Safa 1	7-A2	Al Meena	12-F1	Khalid Bin Al Waleed Rd (Bank St)	8-F3
Al Satwa	7-E2	Al Mina Rd	8-B2	Kuwait Rd	8-D2
Al Sufouh 1	5-E2	Al Muteena St	9-D3	Marina Drive North	5-A2
Al Wasl	7-C2	Al Nahda St	12-D4	Marina Drive South	5-A2
Bur Dubai	8-F1	Al Quds St	12-A4	Marrakech St	13-E2
Business Bay	16-B1	Al Rasaas Rd	6-C4	Meadows Drive	5-B3
Deira	9-C2	Al Rasheed Rd	9-E3	Meydan Rd	7-B3
DIFC	7-E3	Al Rebat St	13-D3	Nad Al Hamar Rd	13-E4
Downtown Burj Dubai	7-D4	Al Rigga Rd	9-C4	Nad Al Sheba Rd	16-A4
Dubai Festival City	13-D4	Al Safa St	7-C2	Naif Rd	9-C2
Dubai Marina	5-A2	Al Satwa Rd	7-E2	Omar Bin Al Khattab Rd	9-D3
Emirates Hills 1	5-B3	Al Seef Rd	9-B3	Oud Metha Rd	10-F2
Hor Al Anz	12-A3	Al Sufouh	5-C2	Ras Al Khor Rd	13-A4
Jaddaf	13-B2	Al Thanya Rd	6-C2	Riyadh Rd	10-F4
Jebel Ali	4-D1	Al Wahda St	12-F3	Rolla St	8-F2
Jumeira 1	7-E1	Al Wasl Rd	6-B2	Saheel Rd	5-A2
Meydan	16-A4	Al Wuheida Rd	12-B2	Salahuddin Rd	9-D4
Mirdif	15-B2	Algeria St	15-C2	Second Industrial St	14-F1
Naif	9-D3	Amman St	12-C4	Sharjah Ring Rd	14-F3
Oud Metha	10-E2	Baghdad St	12-C4	Sheikh Khalifa Bin Zayed St	8-C4
Palm Deira	12-A1	Baniyas Rd	9-B1	Sheikh Rashid Rd	13-C1
Palm Jebel Ali	1-E2	Beirut St	14-C2	Sheikh Zayed Rd	7-E3
Palm Jumeirah	2-A3	Bukadra Interchange	16-B2	Tariq Bin Ziyad Rd	11-A1
Port Rashid	8-C1	Burj Dubai Boulevard	7-D4	Third Industrial St	14-F2
Sharjah	12-D3	Business Bay Bridge	13-D2	Tripoli St	15-A3
Trade Centre 1	7-F2	Cairo St	12-B3	Tunis Rd	15-D1
Trade Centre 2	7-F3	Casablanca Rd	13-E1	Umm Amara Rd	7-C2
Umm Hurair 2	10-F3	Corniche Rd	9-C1	Umm Hurair Rd	10-F1
Umm Ramool	13-E3	Damascus St	14-B2	Umm Suqeim Rd	6-A2
Umm Suqeim 1	6-E2	Difaf Rd	5-C2	Za'abeel Rd	10-C2

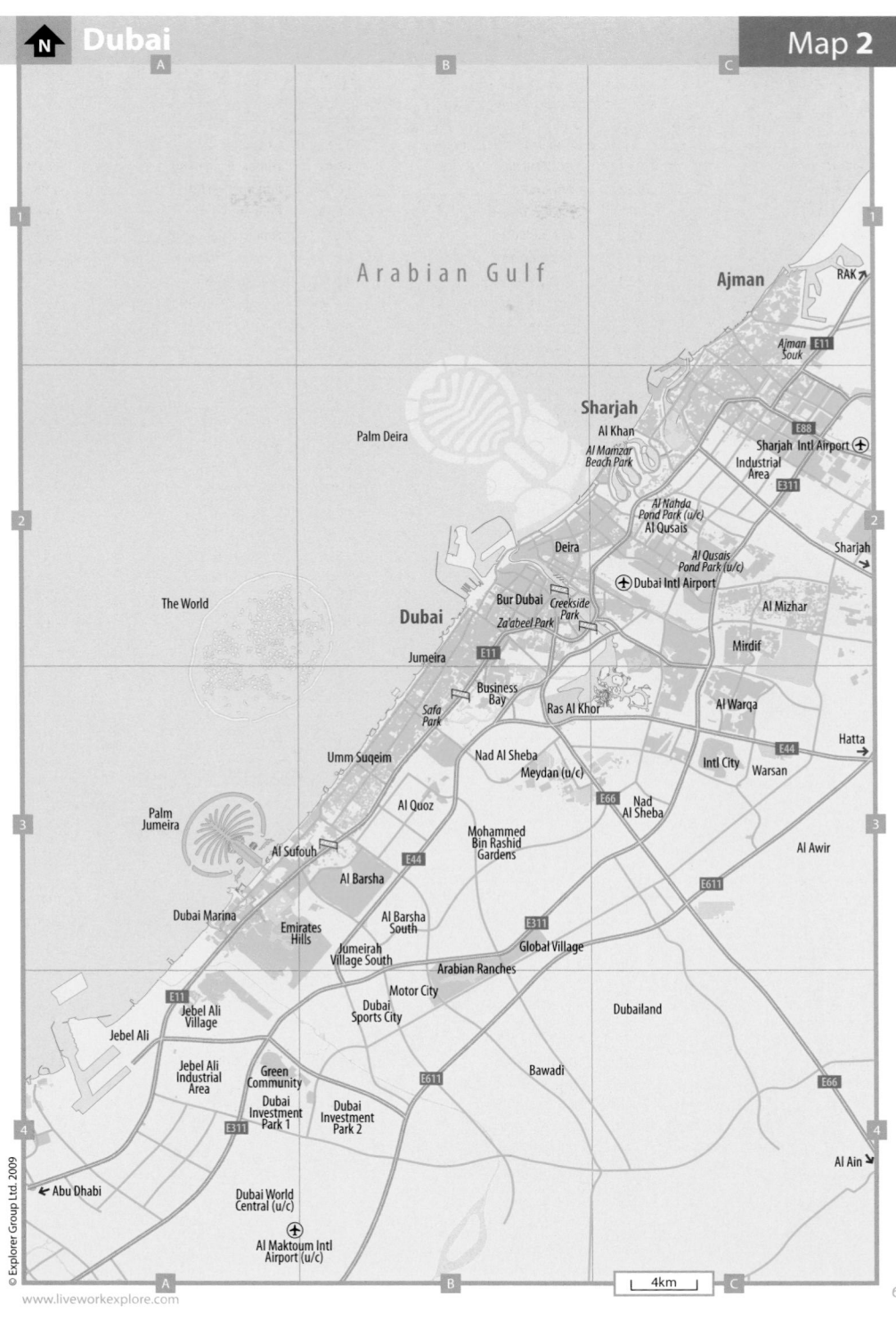

A   B   C

Arabian Gulf

1

Ajman   RAK ↗

Ajman Souk E11

Sharjah

Palm Deira   Al Khan

Al Mamzar Beach Park

Sharjah Intl Airport ✈

Industrial Area   E88

E311

Al Nahda Pond Park (u/c)   Sharjah ↗

The World   Deira   Al Qusais

Al Qusais Pond Park (u/c)

✈ Dubai Intl Airport

2

Dubai   Bur Dubai   Creekside Park   Al Mizhar

Za'abeel Park   Mirdif

Jumeira   E11

Business Bay   Al Warqa

Safa Park   Ras Al Khor

Umm Suqeim   Nad Al Sheba   Intl City   Hatta →

Meydan (u/c)   Warsan   E44

3   E66   Nad Al Sheba

Palm Jumeira   Al Quoz

Al Sufouh   Mohammed Bin Rashid Gardens   Al Awir

Al Barsha   E44

Dubai Marina   Al Barsha South

Emirates Hills   E311   Global Village

Jumeirah Village South   Arabian Ranches   E611

E11   Motor City

Jebel Ali Village   Dubai Sports City   Dubailand

Jebel Ali   Bawadi

Jebel Ali Industrial Area   Green Community   E611   E66

Dubai Investment Park 1   Dubai Investment Park 2

4   E311   Al Ain ↘

← Abu Dhabi   Dubai World Central (u/c)

✈ Al Maktoum Intl Airport (u/c)

4km

Map **3**

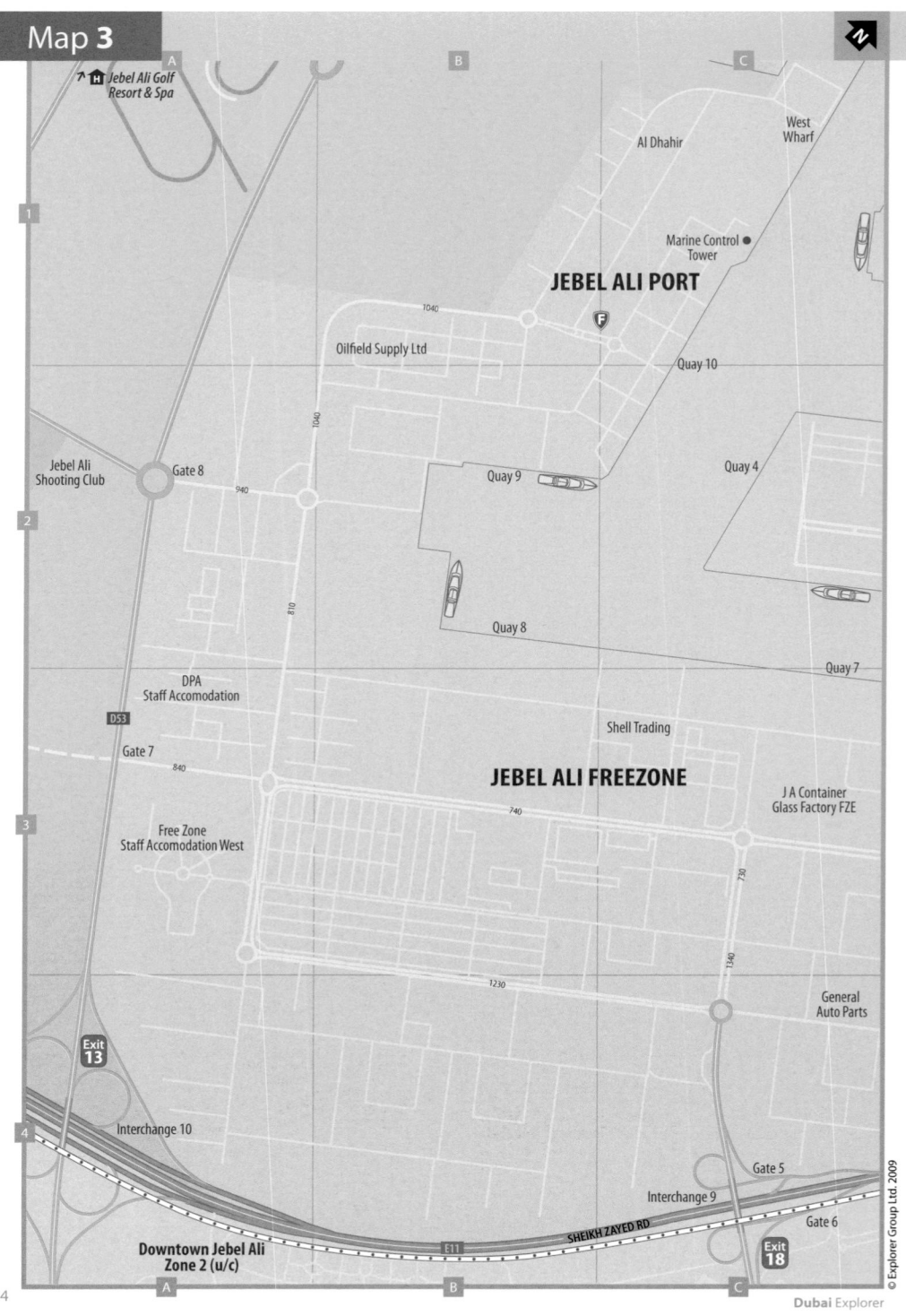

Jebel Ali Golf Resort & Spa

Al Dhahir

West Wharf

Marine Control Tower

JEBEL ALI PORT

1040

Oilfield Supply Ltd

Quay 10

Jebel Ali Shooting Club

Gate 8

940

1040

Quay 9

Quay 4

810

Quay 8

Quay 7

DPA Staff Accomodation

Shell Trading

D53

Gate 7

840

JEBEL ALI FREEZONE

J A Container Glass Factory FZE

Free Zone Staff Accomodation West

740

730

1340

1230

General Auto Parts

Exit 13

Interchange 10

Gate 5

Interchange 9

Gate 6

Exit 18

Downtown Jebel Ali Zone 2 (u/c)

E11

SHEIKH ZAYED RD

Map **3**

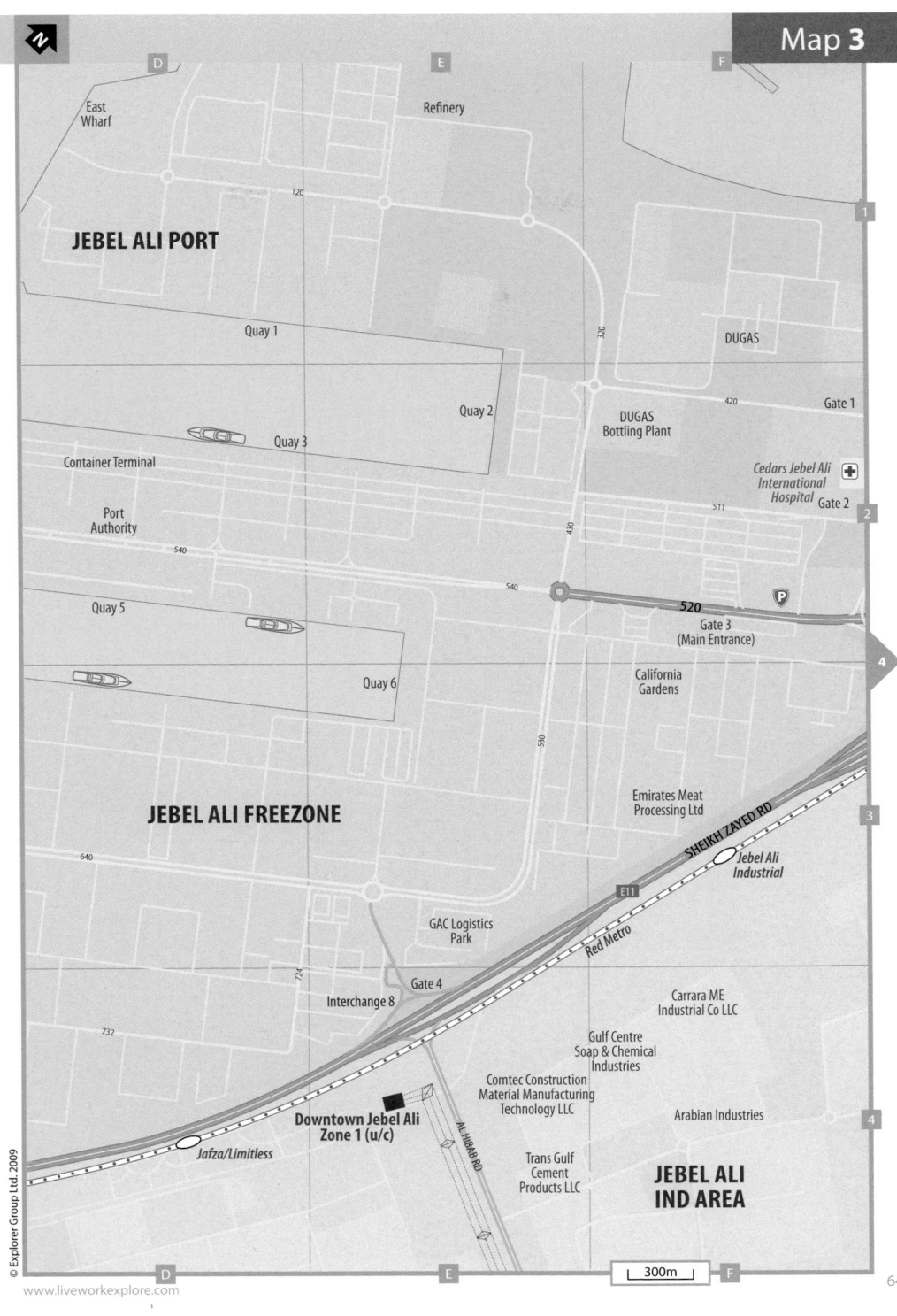

East
Wharf

Refinery

JEBEL ALI PORT

120

Quay 1

DUGAS

320

420

Gate 1

Quay 2

DUGAS
Bottling Plant

Quay 3

Container Terminal

*Cedars Jebel Ali
International
Hospital* Gate 2

511

Port
Authority

540

430

540

520

Quay 5

Gate 3
(Main Entrance)

California
Gardens

Quay 6

530

Emirates Meat
Processing Ltd

JEBEL ALI FREEZONE

*Jebel Ali
Industrial*

SHEIKH ZAYED RD

640

E11

Red Metro

GAC Logistics
Park

Gate 4

Carrara ME
Industrial Co LLC

724

Interchange 8

732

Gulf Centre
Soap & Chemical
Industries

Comtec Construction
Material Manufacturing
Technology LLC

Arabian Industries

AL HIBAB RD

**Downtown Jebel Ali
Zone 1 (u/c)**

Jafza/Limitless

Trans Gulf
Cement
Products LLC

**JEBEL ALI
IND AREA**

300m

© Explorer Group Ltd. 2009

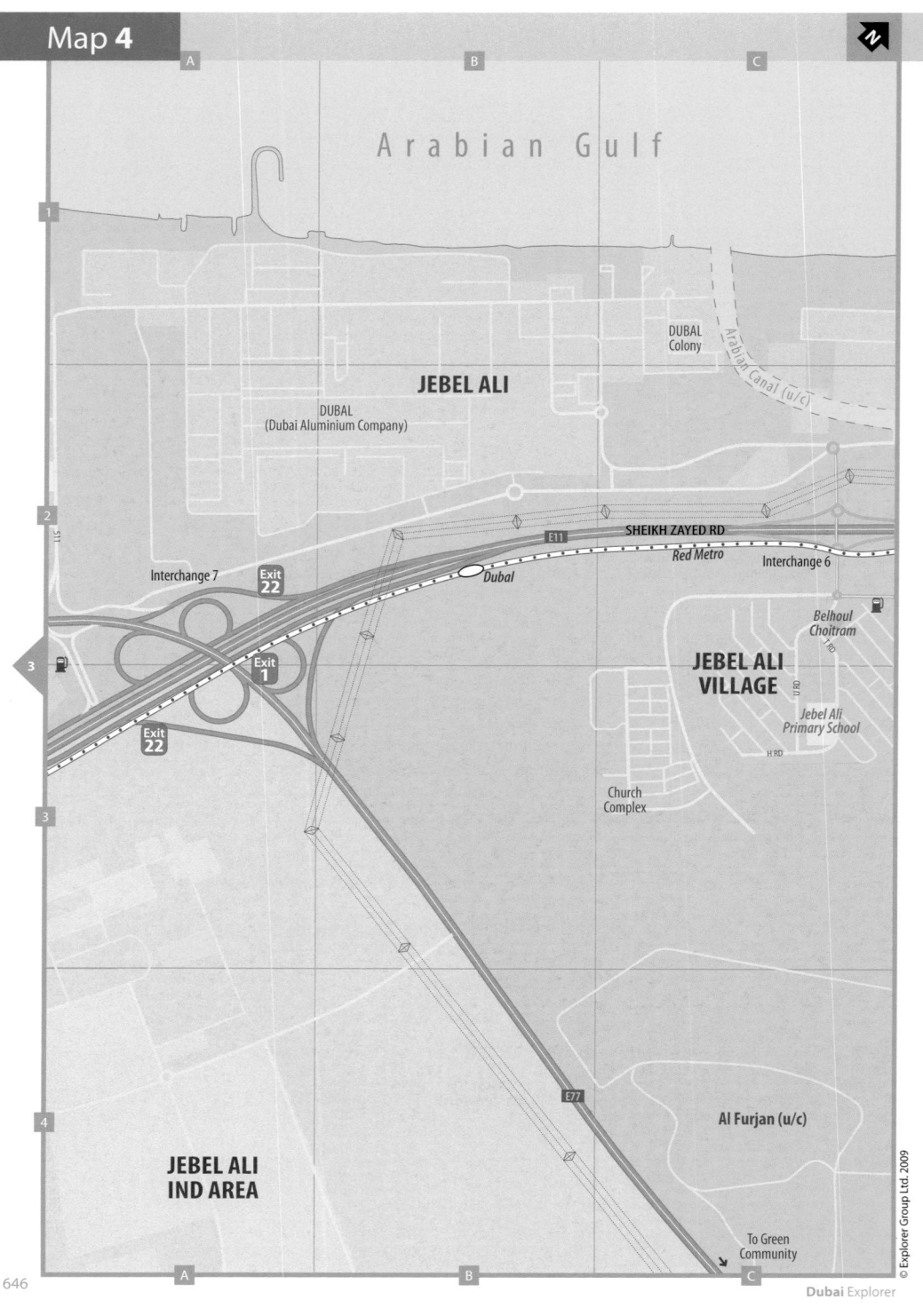

Map **4**

Arabian Gulf

DUBAL Colony

Arabian Canal (u/c)

JEBEL ALI

DUBAL
(Dubai Aluminium Company)

SHEIKH ZAYED RD

E11

Interchange 7

Exit **22**

Exit **1**

Exit **22**

Dubal

Red Metro

Interchange 6

Belhoul Choitram

T RD

JEBEL ALI VILLAGE

U RD

Jebel Ali Primary School

H RD

Church Complex

JEBEL ALI IND AREA

E77

Al Furjan (u/c)

To Green Community

S11

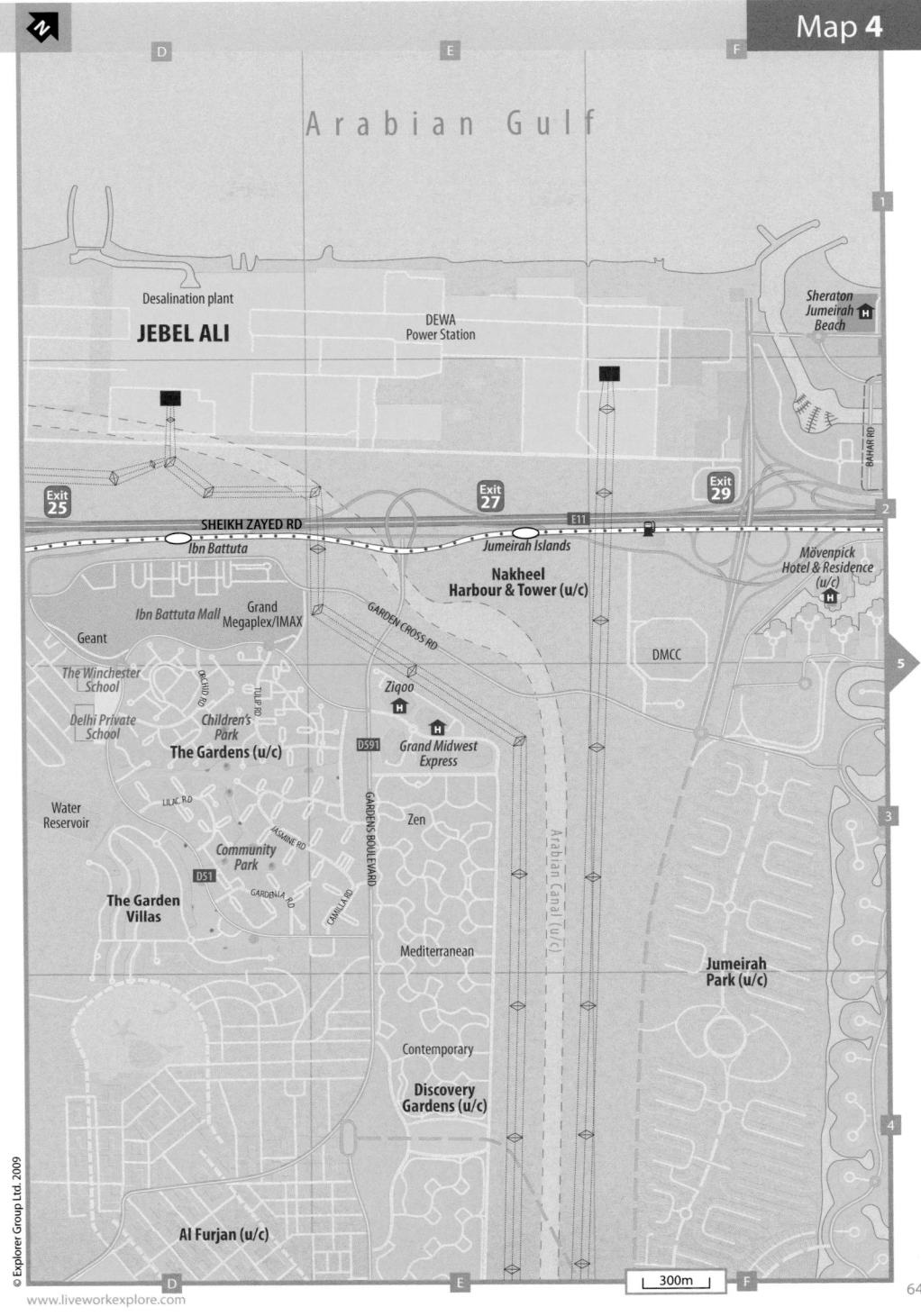

Map **4**

Arabian Gulf

Desalination plant
JEBEL ALI

DEWA
Power Station

Sheraton
Jumeirah
Beach

BAHAR RD

Exit
25

Exit
27

E11

Exit
29

SHEIKH ZAYED RD

Ibn Battuta

Jumeirah Islands

**Nakheel
Harbour & Tower (u/c)**

Mövenpick
Hotel & Residence
(u/c)

Ibn Battuta Mall

Grand
Megaplex/IMAX

GARDEN CROSS RD

Geant

DMCC

The Winchester
School

ORCHID RD

TULIP RD

Ziqoo

Delhi Private
School

Children's
Park

D591

Grand Midwest
Express

The Gardens (u/c)

Water
Reservoir

LILAC RD

JASMINE RD

GARDENS BOULEVARD

Zen

Arabian Canal (u/c)

Community
Park

D51

GARDENIA RD

CAMILLA RD

**The Garden
Villas**

Mediterranean

**Jumeirah
Park (u/c)**

Contemporary

**Discovery
Gardens (u/c)**

Al Furjan (u/c)

300m

Map 5

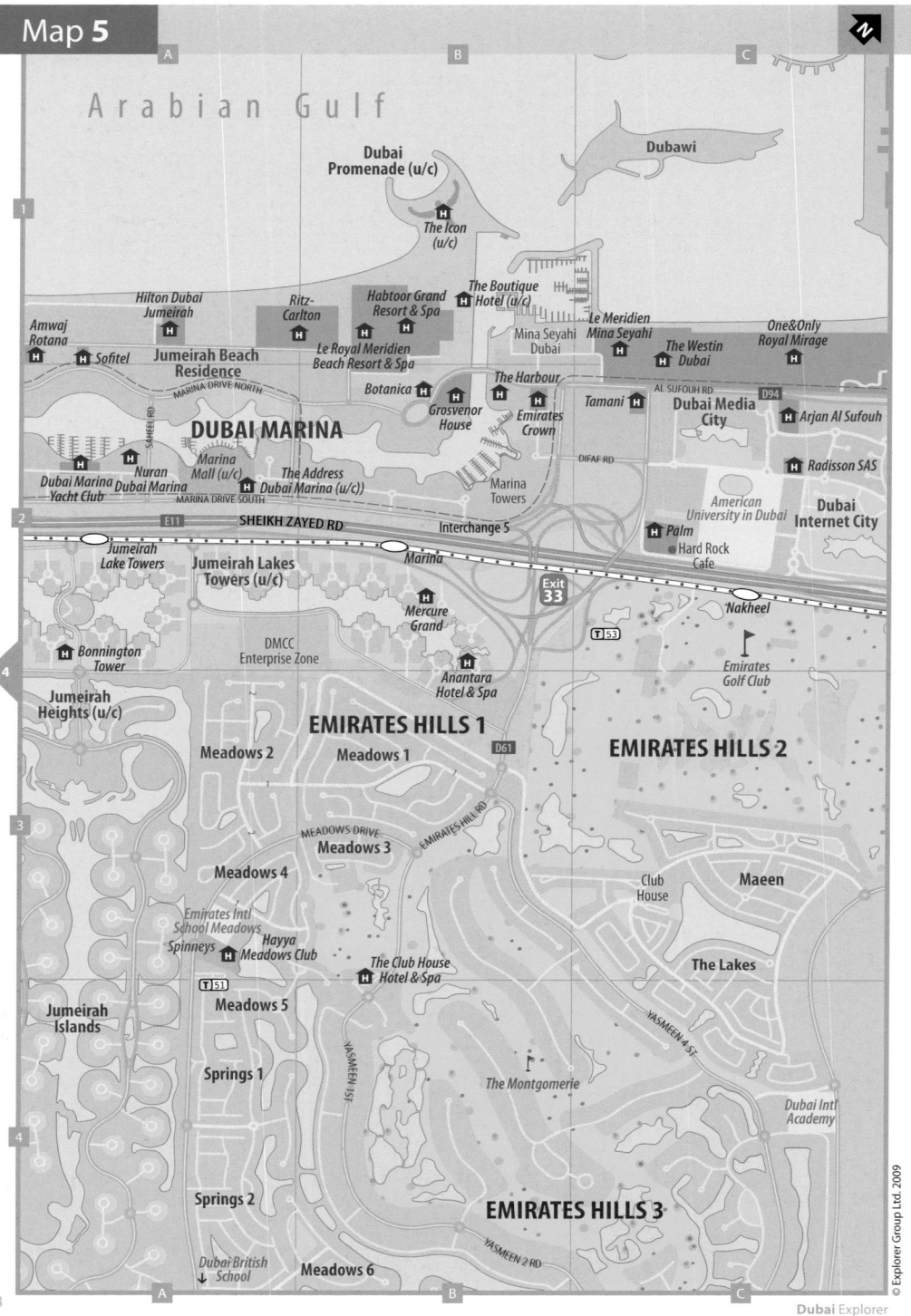

Arabian Gulf

Dubai Promenade (u/c)

Dubawi

The Icon (u/c)

Hilton Dubai Jumeirah

Ritz-Carlton

Habtoor Grand Resort & Spa

The Boutique Hotel (u/c)

Le Meridien Mina Seyahi

One&Only Royal Mirage

Amwaj Rotana

Sofitel

Jumeirah Beach Residence

Le Royal Meridien Beach Resort & Spa

Mina Seyahi Dubai

The Westin Dubai

MARINA DRIVE NORTH

Botanica

The Harbour

AL SUFOUH RD

Arjan Al Sufouh

SABHEEL RD

DUBAI MARINA

Grosvenor House

Emirates Crown

Tamani

Dubai Media City

Radisson SAS

Dubai Marina Yacht Club

Nuran

Dubai Marina

Marina Mall (u/c)

The Address Dubai Marina (u/c)

MARINA DRIVE SOUTH

DIFAF RD

Marina Towers

American University in Dubai

Dubai Internet City

E11

SHEIKH ZAYED RD

Interchange 5

Palm

Hard Rock Cafe

Jumeirah Lake Towers

Jumeirah Lakes Towers (u/c)

Marina

Exit 33

Nakheel

Bonnington Tower

Mercure Grand

T 53

Emirates Golf Club

DMCC Enterprise Zone

Jumeirah Heights (u/c)

Anantara Hotel & Spa

EMIRATES HILLS 1

EMIRATES HILLS 2

Meadows 2

Meadows 1

D61

MEADOWS DRIVE

Meadows 3

EMIRATES HILL RD

Club House

Maeen

Meadows 4

Emirates Intl School Meadows

Spinneys

Hayya Meadows Club

The Lakes

The Club House Hotel & Spa

T 51

Jumeirah Islands

Meadows 5

YASMEEN 1 ST

YASMEEN AL ST

Springs 1

The Montgomerie

Dubai Intl Academy

Springs 2

EMIRATES HILLS 3

YASMEEN 2 RD

Dubai British School

Meadows 6

© Explorer Group Ltd. 2009

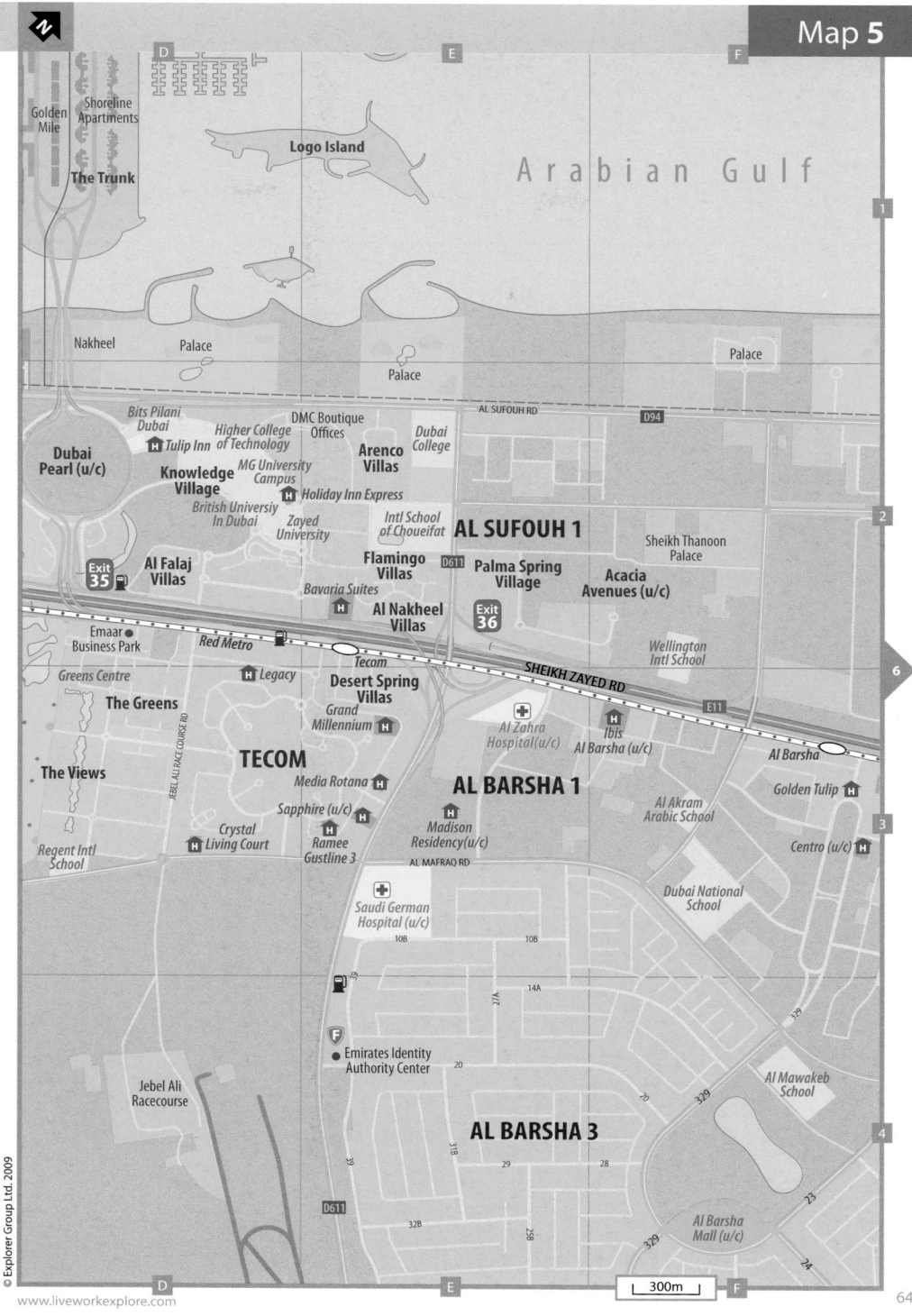

Map **5**

Golden Mile

Shoreline Apartments

The Trunk

Logo Island

Arabian Gulf

Nakheel Palace

Palace

Palace

Palace

AL SUFOUH RD

D94

Bits Pilani Dubai

Tulip Inn

Higher College of Technology

DMC Boutique Offices

Dubai College

Dubai Pearl (u/c)

Knowledge Village

MG University Campus

Arenco Villas

Holiday Inn Express

British Universiy In Dubai

Zayed University

Intl School of Choueifat

AL SUFOUH 1

Sheikh Thanoon Palace

Exit 35

Al Falaj Villas

Flamingo Villas

D611

Palma Spring Village

Acacia Avenues (u/c)

Bavaria Suites

Al Nakheel Villas

Exit 36

Wellington Intl School

Emaar Business Park

Red Metro

Tecom

SHEIKH ZAYED RD

E11

Greens Centre

Legacy

Desert Spring Villas

Al Zahra Hospital (u/c)

Ibis Al Barsha (u/c)

Al Barsha

The Greens

Grand Millennium

TECOM

JEBEL ALI RACE COURSE RD

Media Rotana

AL BARSHA 1

Al Akram Arabic School

Golden Tulip

The Views

Sapphire (u/c)

Centro (u/c)

Regent Intl School

Crystal Living Court

Ramee Gustline 3

Madison Residency(u/c)

AL MAFRAQ RD

Dubai National School

Saudi German Hospital (u/c)

10B

10B

39

14A

27A

Emirates Identity Authority Center

20

Al Mawakeb School

329

Jebel Ali Racecourse

39

31B

29

28

70

329

AL BARSHA 3

32B

25B

329

Al Barsha Mall (u/c)

74

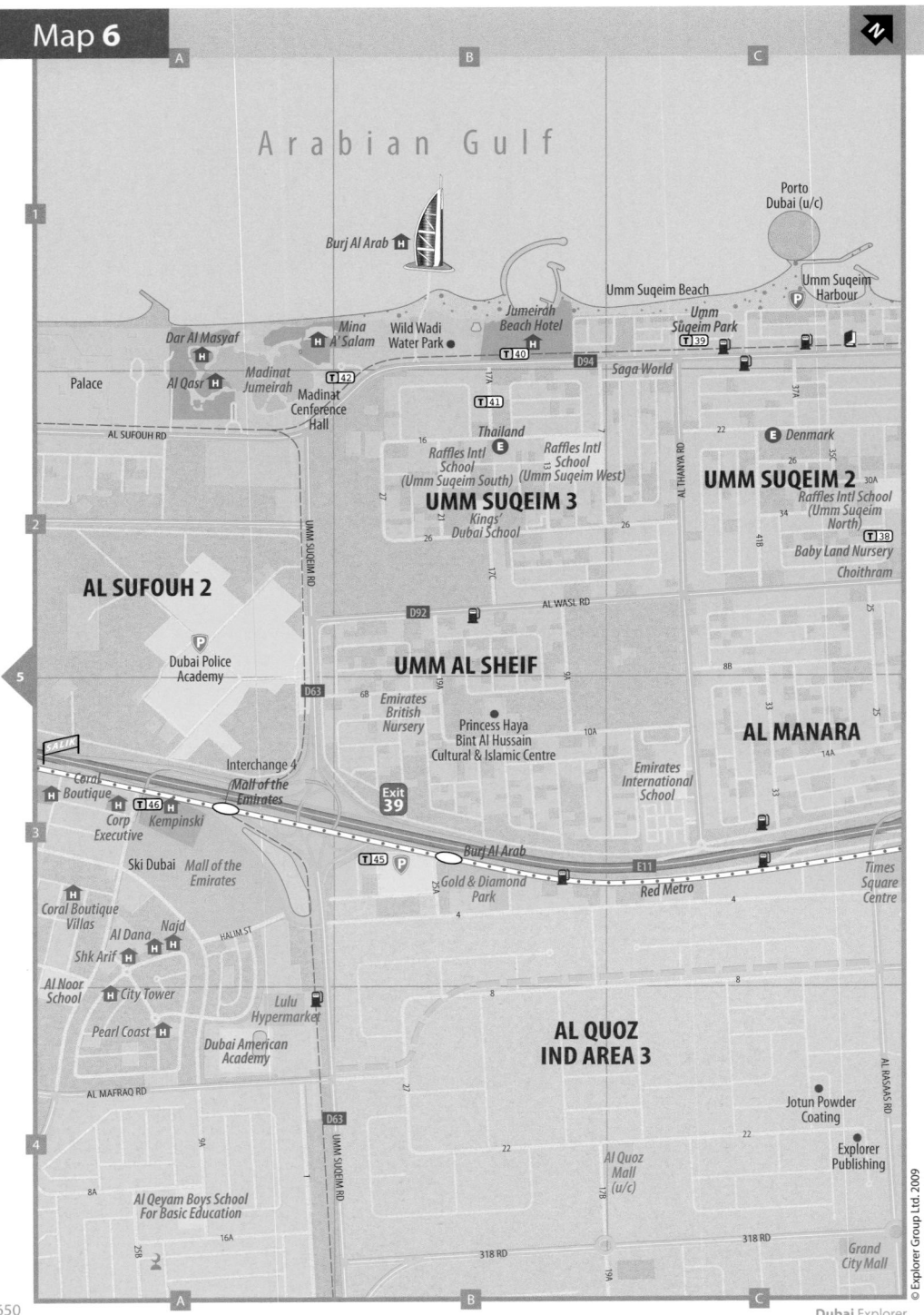

Map **6**

Arabian Gulf

Porto
Dubai (u/c)

Burj Al Arab H

Umm Suqeim Beach

Umm Suqeim
Harbour

Dar Al Masyaf

Mina
A'Salam

Wild Wadi
Water Park

Jumeirah
Beach Hotel

Umm
Suqeim Park

T 39

Palace

Al Qasr H

Madinat
Jumeirah

Madinat
Conference
Hall

T 42

T 40 H

D94

Saga World

AL SUFOUH RD

T 41

Thailand

Raffles Intl
School
(Umm Suqeim South)

Raffles Intl
School
(Umm Suqeim West)

E Denmark

UMM SUQEIM 2

16

E

Raffles Intl School
(Umm Suqeim
North)

T 38

Baby Land Nursery

Choithram

27

21

UMM SUQEIM 3

Kings'
Dubai School

26

26

17X

AL SUFOUH 2

D92

AL WASL RD

P

Dubai Police
Academy

D63

UMM AL SHEIF

6B

Emirates
British
Nursery

Princess Haya
Bint Al Hussain
Cultural & Islamic Centre

10A

AL MANARA

33

25

14A

5

Coral
Boutique H

Interchange 4
Mall of the
Emirates

Emirates
International
School

33

Exit
39

H T 46 H

Corp
Executive

Kempinski

Burj Al Arab

T 45 P

E11

Times
Square
Centre

Ski Dubai

Mall of the
Emirates

Gold & Diamond
Park

Red Metro

Coral Boutique
Villas

Al Dana

Najd

HALIM ST

Shk Arif H H

Al Noor
School

H City Tower

Pearl Coast H

Lulu
Hypermarket

Dubai American
Academy

AL QUOZ
IND AREA 3

Jotun Powder
Coating

Explorer
Publishing

AL MAFRAQ RD

D63

Al Qeyam Boys School
For Basic Education

8A

16A

25B

318 RD

Al Quoz
Mall
(u/c)

318 RD

Grand
City Mall

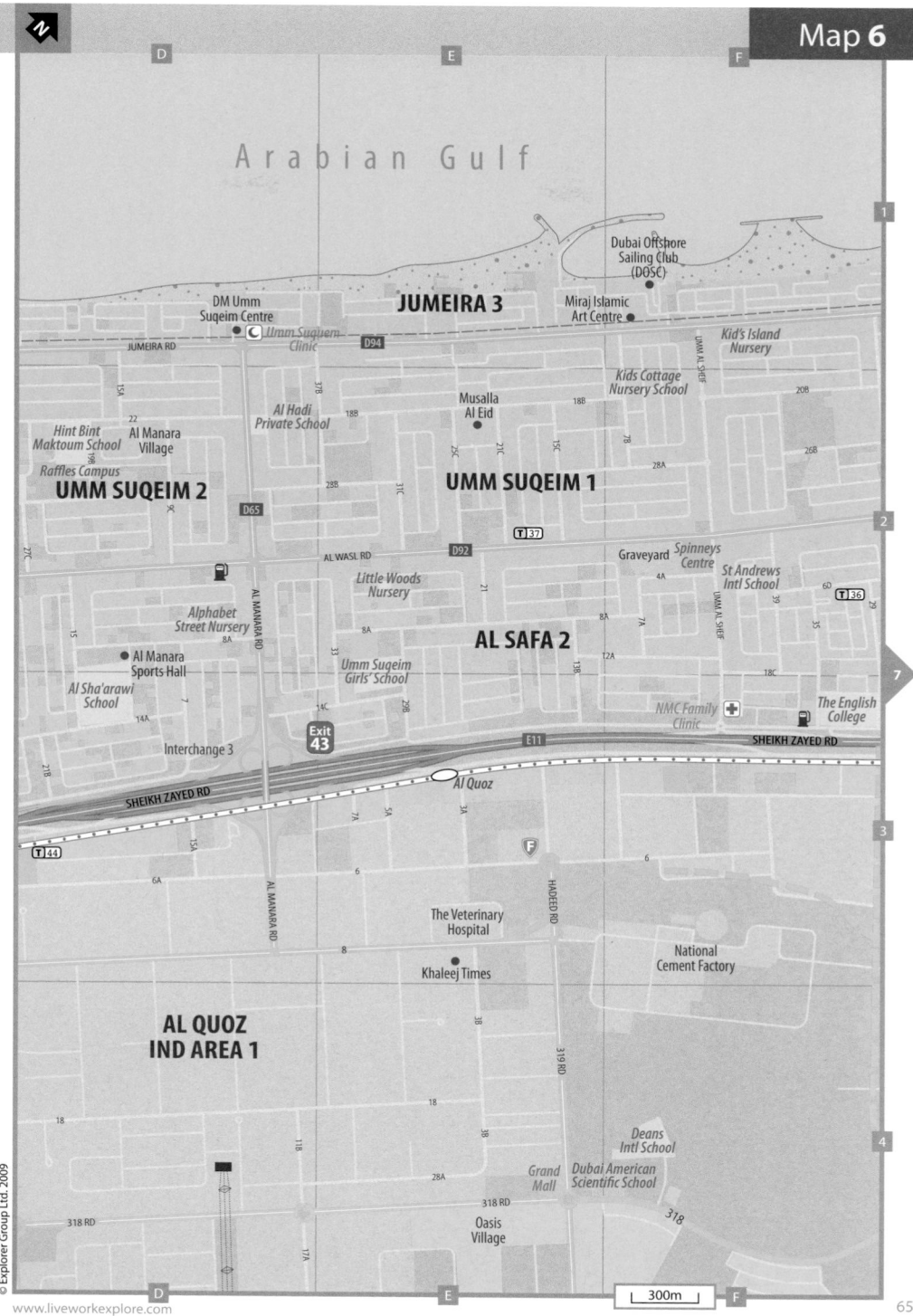

Map **6**

Arabian Gulf

JUMEIRA 3

Dubai Offshore
Sailing Club
(DOSC)

DM Umm
Suqeim Centre

Miraj Islamic
Art Centre

Kid's Island
Nursery

JUMEIRA RD

D94

Umm Suqeim
Clinic

Kids Cottage
Nursery School

UMM AL SHEIF

20B

Hint Bint
Maktoum School

Al Manara
Village

Al Hadi
Private School

Musalla
Al Eid

18B

18B

26B

13A

22

19B

37B

28A

7B

Raffles Campus

UMM SUQEIM 2

D65

28B

25C

21C

15C

UMM SUQEIM 1

9C

31C

Al Sha'arawi
School

AL WASL RD

D92

T 37

Little Woods
Nursery

21

Graveyard

Spinneys
Centre

St Andrews
Intl School

60

T 36

29

Alphabet
Street Nursery

8A

33

Umm Suqeim
Girls' School

8A

AL SAFA 2

7A

T2A

UMM AL SHEIF

4A

39

35

18C

Al Manara
Sports Hall

15

8A

13B

7

14A

7

14C

29B

18C

NMC Family
Clinic

The English
College

21B

Exit
43

E11

SHEIKH ZAYED RD

Interchange 3

SHEIKH ZAYED RD

Al Quoz

T 44

15A

7A

5A

3A

6A

6

F

6

HADEED RD

The Veterinary
Hospital

National
Cement Factory

8

Khaleej Times

**AL QUOZ
IND AREA 1**

18

11B

18

3B

28A

319 RD

Deans
Intl School

Grand
Mall

Dubai American
Scientific School

318 RD

318

318 RD

17A

Oasis
Village

300m

Map 7

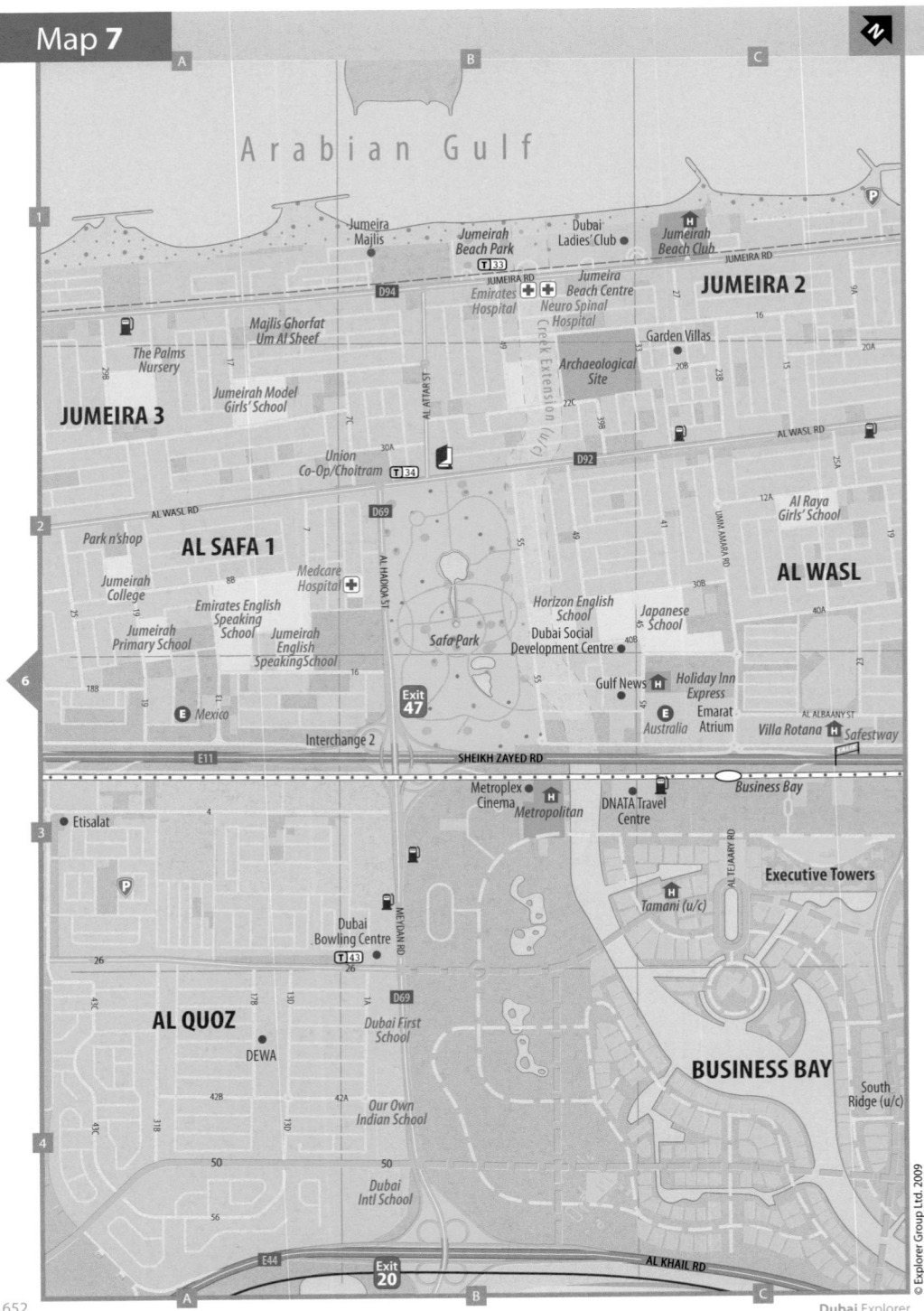

Arabian Gulf

Jumeira Majlis

Jumeirah Beach Park

Dubai Ladies' Club

Jumeirah Beach Club

JUMEIRAH RD

T 33

D94

JUMEIRA RD

Emirates Hospital

Jumeira Beach Centre

Neuro Spinal Hospital

JUMEIRA 2

Majlis Ghorfat Um Al Sheef

Garden Villas

The Palms Nursery

Archaeological Site

JUMEIRA 3

Jumeirah Model Girls' School

AL ATTAR ST

Union Co-Op/Choitram

AL WASL RD

T 34

D92

AL WASL RD

Park n'shop

Al Raya Girls' School

AL SAFA 1

Medcare Hospital

AL WASL

Jumeirah College

Emirates English Speaking School

Horizon English School

Japanese School

AL HADIQA ST

UMM AL SHEIF RD

Jumeirah Primary School

Jumeirah English SpeakingSchool

Safa Park

Dubai Social Development Centre

Holiday Inn Express

Exit 47

Mexico

E

Gulf News

Emarat Atrium

Interchange 2

Australia

E

Villa Rotana

Safestway

AL ALBAANY ST

E11

SHEIKH ZAYED RD

Business Bay

Metroplex Cinema

Metropolitan

DNATA Travel Centre

Etisalat

Executive Towers

P

Tamani (u/c)

AL TEJAARY RD

MEYDAN RD

Dubai Bowling Centre

T 43

AL QUOZ

D69

Dubai First School

BUSINESS BAY

DEWA

South Ridge (u/c)

Our Own Indian School

Dubai Intl School

E44

Exit 20

AL KHAIL RD

© Explorer Group Ltd. 2009

Dubai Explorer

Map **7**

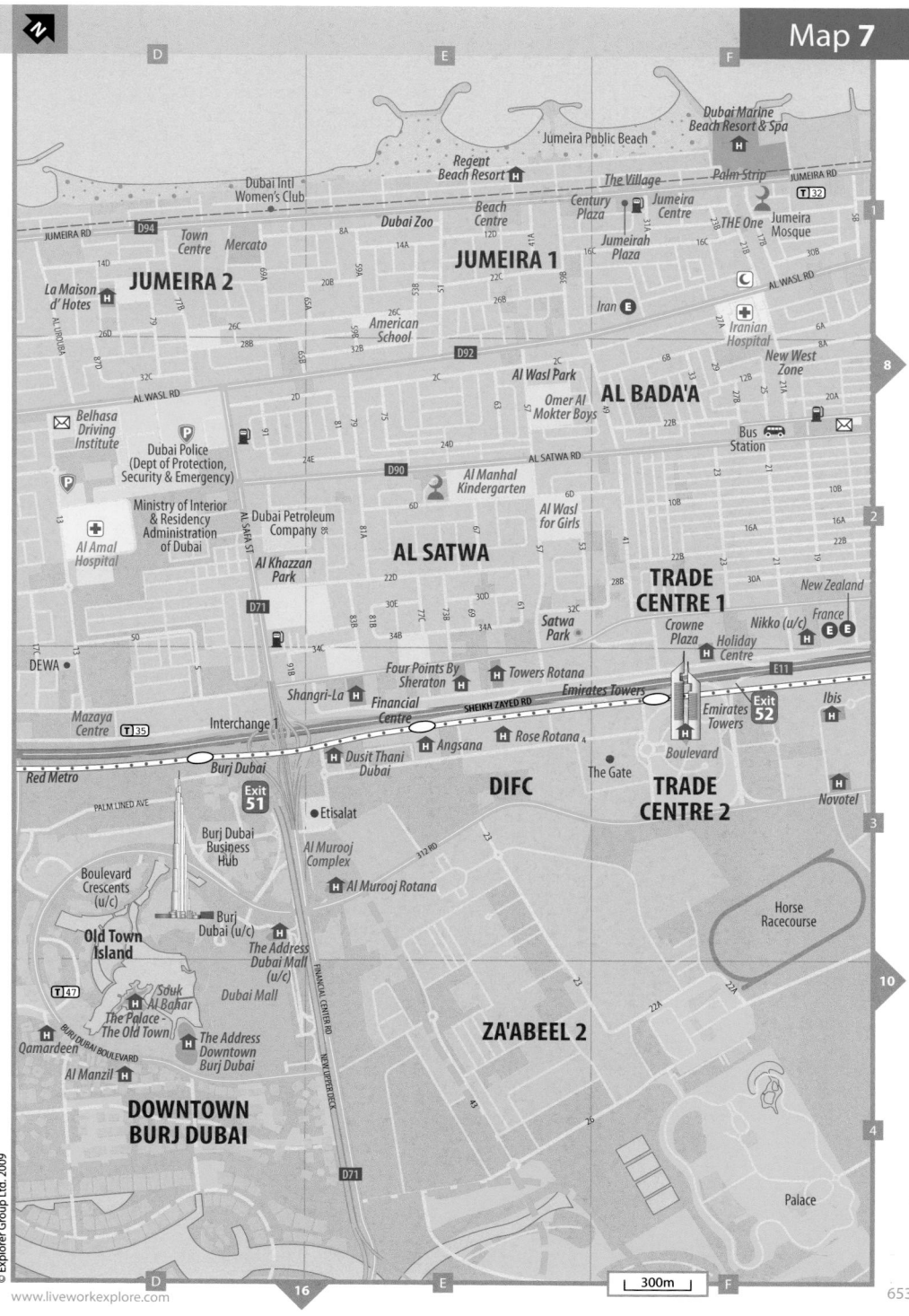

Dubai Marine Beach Resort & Spa

Jumeira Public Beach

Regent Beach Resort

The Village

Palm Strip

JUMEIRA RD

T 32

Dubai Intl Women's Club

Beach Centre

Century Plaza

Jumeira Centre

THE One

Jumeira Mosque

JUMEIRA RD

D94

Town Centre

Mercato

Dubai Zoo

JUMEIRA 1

Jumeirah Plaza

AL WASL RD

La Maison d' Hotes

JUMEIRA 2

American School

Iran

Iranian Hospital

New West Zone

AL URUBA

D92

Al Wasl Park

AL BADA'A

Bus Station

AL WASL RD

Omer Al Mokter Boys

Belhasa Driving Institute

Dubai Police (Dept of Protection, Security & Emergency)

Al Manhal Kindergarten

Al Wasl for Girls

D90

Ministry of Interior & Residency Administration of Dubai

Dubai Petroleum Company

AL SATWA

AL SARA ST

Al Amal Hospital

Al Khazzan Park

TRADE CENTRE 1

New Zealand

D71

Satwa Park

Crowne Plaza

Nikko (u/c)

France

DEWA

Holiday Centre

Four Points By Sheraton

Towers Rotana

Emirates Towers

E11

Ibis

Mazaya Centre

T 35

Shangri-La

Financial Centre

SHEIKH ZAYED RD

Emirates Towers

Exit 52

Interchange 1

Dusit Thani Dubai

Angsana

Rose Rotana

Boulevard

Red Metro

Burj Dubai

Exit 51

The Gate

TRADE CENTRE 2

Novotel

PALM LINED AVE

Etisalat

DIFC

Burj Dubai Business Hub

Al Murooj Complex

312 RD

Boulevard Crescents (u/c)

Al Murooj Rotana

Horse Racecourse

Old Town Island

Burj Dubai (u/c)

The Address Dubai Mall (u/c)

T 47

Souk Al Bahar

Dubai Mall

ZA'ABEEL 2

The Palace - The Old Town

The Address Downtown Burj Dubai

FINANCIAL CENTER RD

Qamardeen

BURJ DUBAI BOULEVARD

NEW UPPER DECK

Al Manzil

DOWNTOWN BURJ DUBAI

D71

Palace

300m

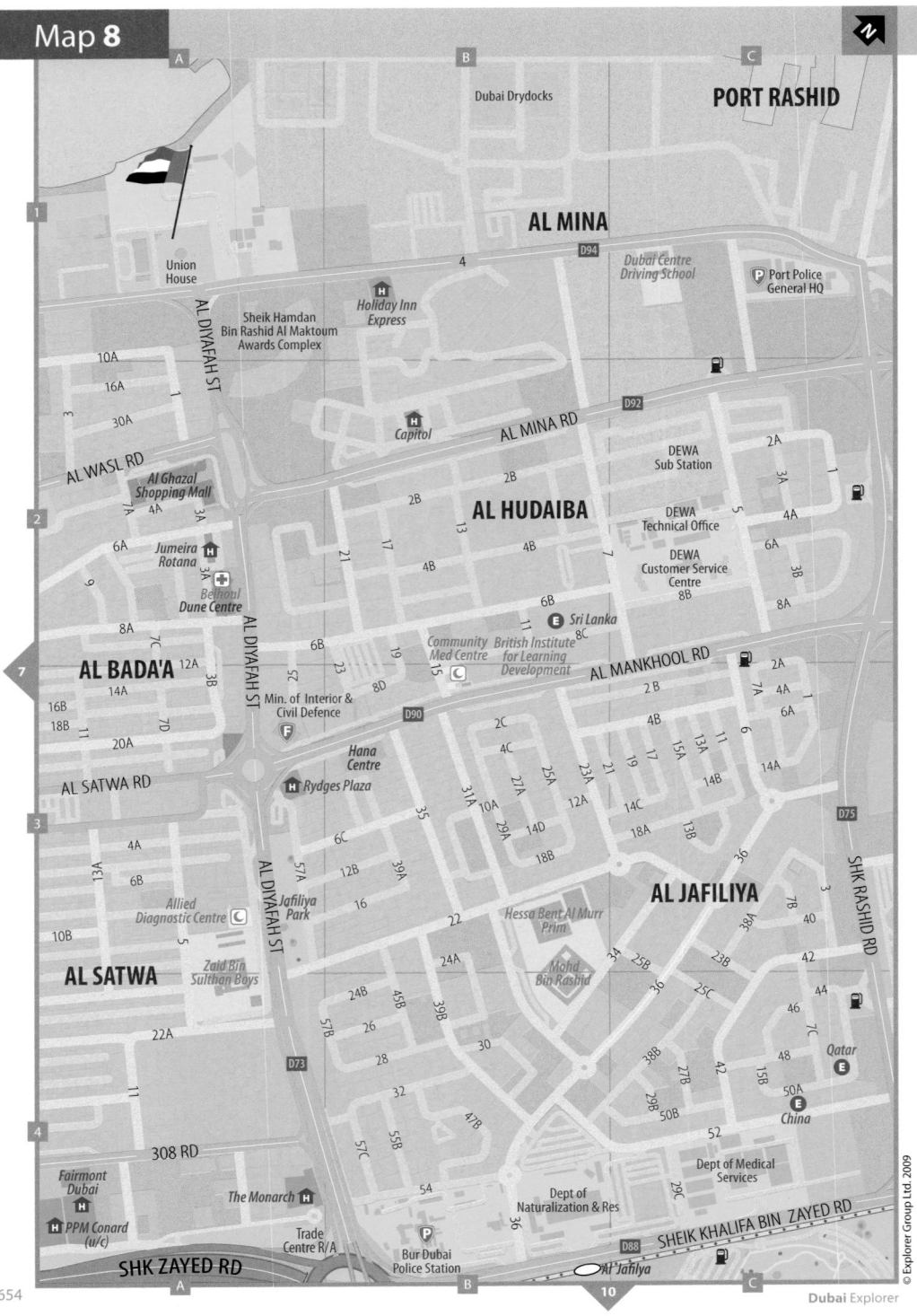

Map **8**

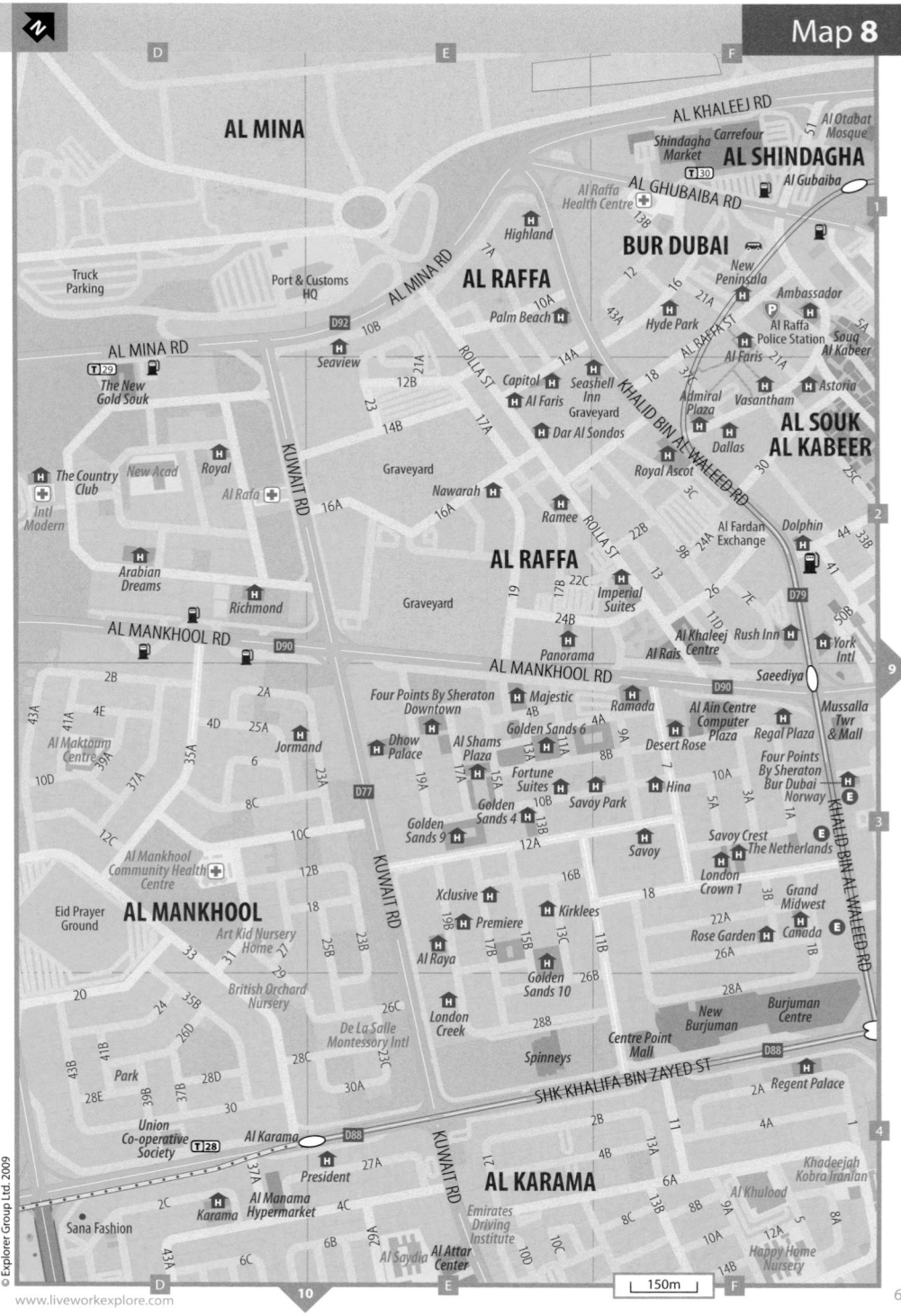

Map **8**

AL MINA

AL KHALEEJ RD

Al Otabat Mosque

Shindagha Market Carrefour AL SHINDAGHA

T 30

Al Raffa Health Centre AL GHUBAIBA RD Al Gubaiba

Highland 138

BUR DUBAI

7A AL RAFFA

Truck Parking

Port & Customs HQ

AL MINA RD

12 New Peninsula

Palm Beach 10A 16 21A Ambassador

43A Hyde Park Al Raffa Police Station Souq Al Kabeer

D92 10B Seaview 14A 18 3C Al Faris 21A Astoria

AL MINA RD 21A Capitol Seashell Inn Admiral Plaza Vasantham

T 29 12B Al Faris Graveyard Dallas

The New Gold Souk 23 17A Dar Al Sondos Royal Ascot AL SOUK AL KABEER

14B 30 25C

New Acad Graveyard

The Country Club Royal Nawarah Al Fardan Exchange Dolphin 44 338

Intl Modern Al Rafa 16A Ramee Al Fardan Exchange 41

Arabian Dreams 16A 22B Imperial 13 26 7E D79

Richmond 19 17B 22C Imperial Suites 9B 24A Al Khaleej Centre Rush Inn York Intl

AL MANKHOOL RD 24B Centre Al Rais

D90 Panorama Al Rais Saeediya

2B Four Points By Sheraton Downtown Majestic Ramada Al Ain Centre Computer Plaza Mussalla Twr & Mall

4E 2A 4B Golden Sands 6 4A 9A Desert Rose Regal Plaza

Al Maktoum Centre 4D 25A Dhow Palace Al Shams Plaza 13A 11A 8B Four Points By Sheraton Bur Dubai

10D 37A 6 23A 19A 17A 15A Fortune Suites Hina Norway

8C Jormand 10B Savoy Park 10A 5A 3A

12C 10C Golden Sands 9 13B 12A Savoy Savoy Crest The Netherlands

Al Mankhool Community Health Centre 12B 16B London Crown 1 Grand Midwest

Eid Prayer Ground AL MANKHOOL 18 Xclusive 18 22A Rose Garden Canada 1B

Art Kid Nursery Home 27 25B 19B Premiere Kirklees 11B 26A

British Orchard Nursery 33 31 17B 15B 13C 28A

20 24 35B 26C Al Raya Golden Sands 10 26B New Burjuman Burjuman Centre

43B 41B 26D 28B London Creek Centre Point Mall D88

Park 39B 37B 28D De La Salle Montessory Intl Spinneys Regent Palace

28E 30 28C 30A SHK KHALIFA BIN ZAYED ST 2A

Union Co-operative Society Al Karama D88 President 2B 11 4A 1

T 28 37A 27A 4B 13A

2C Al Manama Hypermarket 4C AL KARAMA 6A Al Khulood Khadeejah Kobra Iranian

Karama 6B 26A 8C 13B 8B 9A 8A

Sana Fashion 43A 6C Al Saydia Al Attar Center 10D 10C 10A 12A Happy Home Nursery

14B

© Explorer Group Ltd. 2009

150m

Map **9**

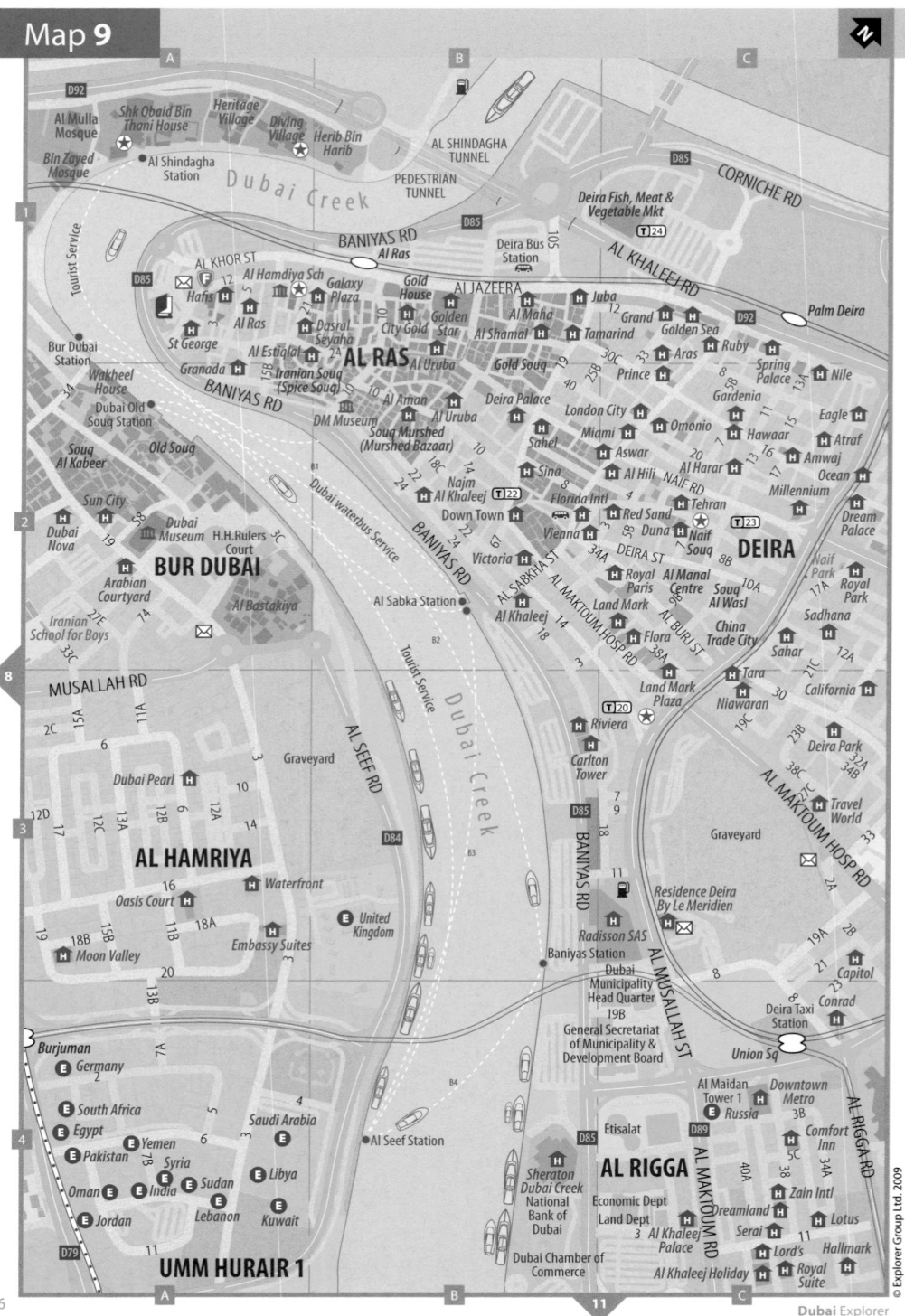

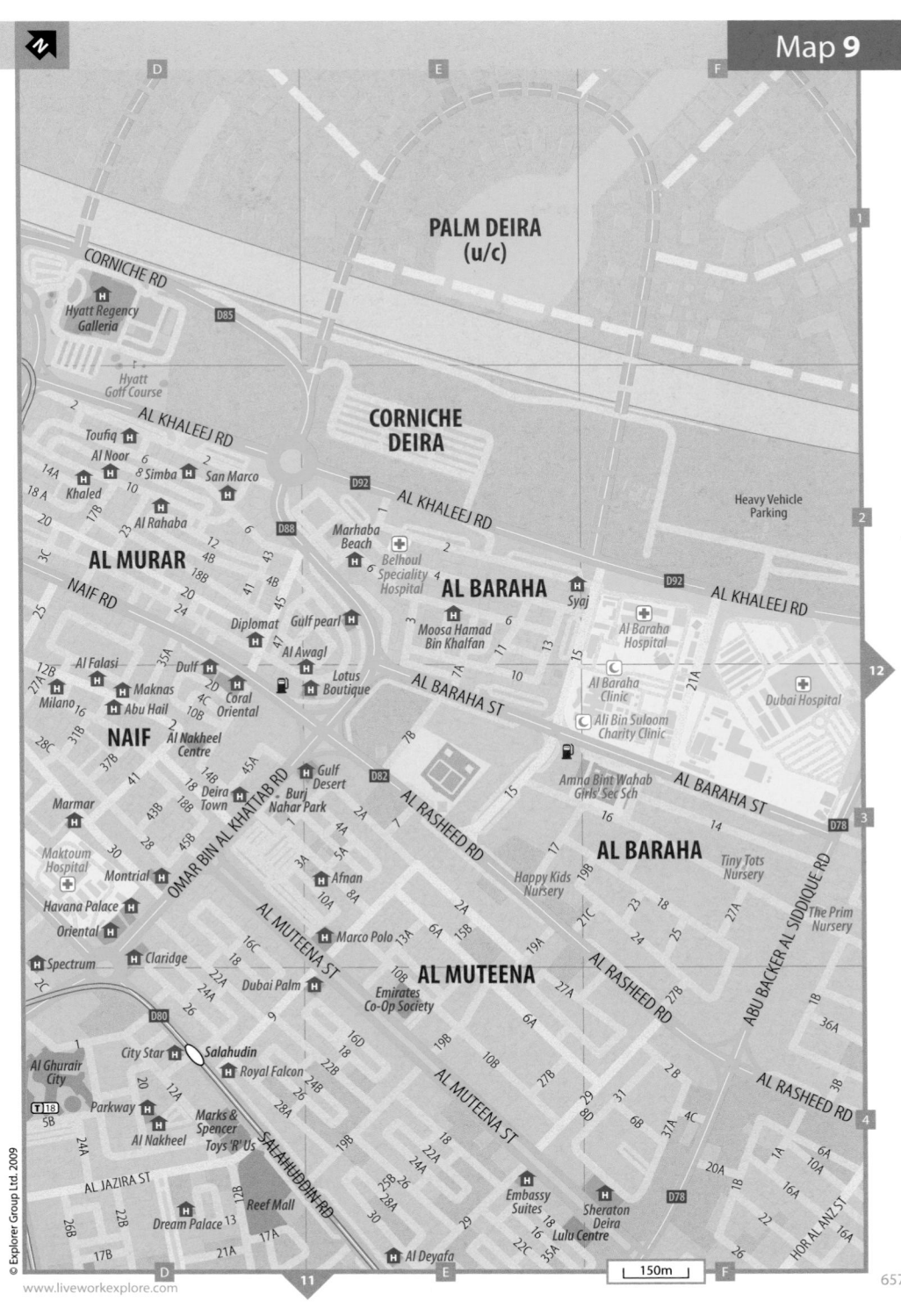

Map **9**

N

CORNICHE RD

Hyatt Regency
Galleria

D85

Hyatt
Golf Course

PALM DEIRA
(u/c)

Heavy Vehicle
Parking

AL KHALEEJ RD

CORNICHE
DEIRA

D92

Toufiq
Al Noor   2
14A   8 Simba   San Marco
18 A   Khaled   10
20   17B   23 Al Rahaba   12
3C   4B
AL MURAR   18B   41   4B
                          24   45
NAIF RD   Diplomat   Gulf pearl
                          Al Awagl
12B   Al Falasi   35A   Dulf
27A   2D
4C   4C
Milano 16   Coral   10B
31B   Oriental
NAIF   Al Nakheel
28C   37B   Centre
       41   14B   45A
Marmar   18   18B
       43B   28   45B
Maktoum
Hospital   30   Montrial
Havana Palace
Oriental

Spectrum   Claridge
2C   16C
              18   22A
              24A
              26
D80
City Star   Salahudin
Al Ghurair   20   12A
City   Parkway
T 18   Al Nakheel
5B   24A
AL JAZIRA ST   12B
26B   22B   Dream Palace 13
       17B   21A   17A

D88
Marhaba
Beach
Belhoul
Speciality
Hospital
2   Moosa Hamad
     Bin Khalfan
3   11   13
AL BARAHA   6
AL BARAHA ST   10
7B
D82
Gulf
Desert
Burj
Nahar Park
4A
2A   7
3A
5A
Afnan
8A
10A
Marco Polo 13A
             2A
18   10B   6A   15B
22A   **AL MUTEENA** 19A
Dubai Palm Emirates
9   Co-Op Society 6A
     16D
18
22B   19B
Royal Falcon 24B
       28A   26
Marks &
Spencer   19B
Toys 'R' Us   5B   26
       30
Reef Mall   28B
             29

Syaj
D92   AL KHALEEJ RD
Al Baraha
Hospital
15
Al Baraha
Clinic
21A
Ali Bin Sulaom
Charity Clinic
Amna Bint Wahab
Girls' Sec Sch
15   16
17   **AL BARAHA**
      19B   23   18
21C   24   25
27A   27B
        2B
AL RASHEED RD   6A
             10B
27A
6A
     19B   10B
            27B
AL MUTEENA ST
       18
       22A
       24A
5B 26   28A
Embassy 18
Suites   16
Al Deyafa 22C 35A Lulu Centre
Sheraton
Deira
D78

Dubai Hospital

12

AL BARAHA ST
D78   3
14
Tiny Tots
Nursery
The Prim
Nursery
27A
1B
36A
AL RASHEED RD
3B
1A   6A
      10A
20A   1B   16A
             22
AL HOR AL ANZ ST
26   16A

ABU BACKER AL SIDDIQUE RD
SALAHUDDIN RD
OMAR BIN AL KHATTAB RD

Map **10**

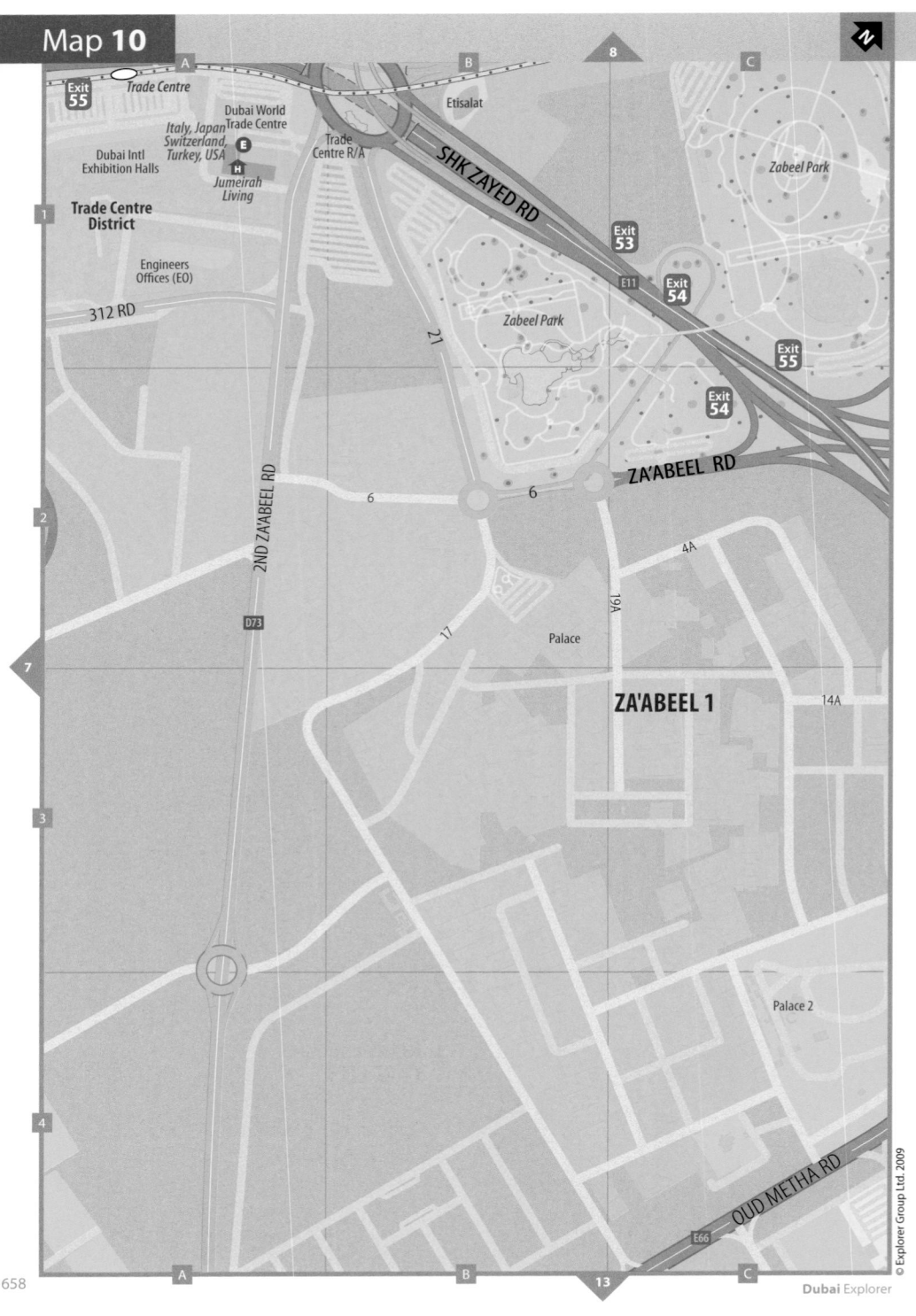

Dubai Explorer

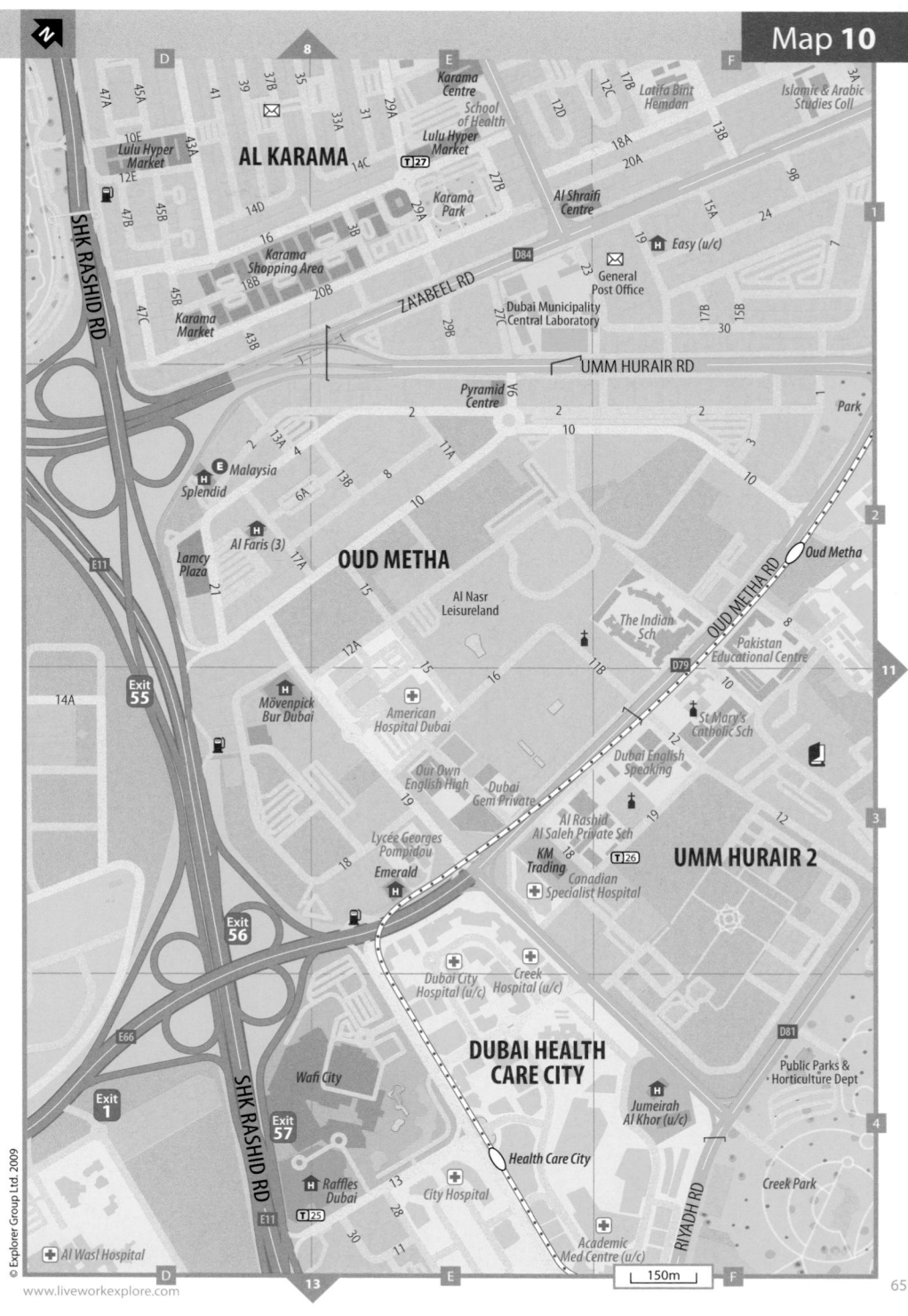

Map **10**

Islamic & Arabic Studies Coll

Karama Centre

School of Health

Lulu Hyper Market

AL KARAMA

Latifa Bint Hemdan

Lulu Hyper Market

Karama Park

Al Shraifi Centre

Easy (u/c)

Karama Shopping Area

Karama Market

ZA'ABEEL RD

Dubai Municipality Central Laboratory

General Post Office

UMM HURAIR RD

Pyramid Centre

Park

Malaysia

Splendid

Al Faris (3)

Lamcy Plaza

OUD METHA

Al Nasr Leisureland

The Indian Sch

OUD METHA RD

Oud Metha

Pakistan Educational Centre

Mövenpick Bur Dubai

American Hospital Dubai

St Mary's Catholic Sch

Our Own English High

Dubai Gem Private

Dubai English Speaking

Al Rashid Al Saleh Private Sch

Lycée Georges Pompidou

Emerald

KM Trading

Canadian Specialist Hospital

UMM HURAIR 2

Dubai City Hospital (u/c)

Creek Hospital (u/c)

DUBAI HEALTH CARE CITY

Public Parks & Horticulture Dept

Wafi City

Jumeirah Al Khor (u/c)

Creek Park

Raffles Dubai

City Hospital

Health Care City

Academic Med Centre (u/c)

Al Wasl Hospital

SHK RASHID RD

Exit 55

Exit 56

Exit 57

Exit 1

RIYADH RD

Exit 11

150m

Map **11**

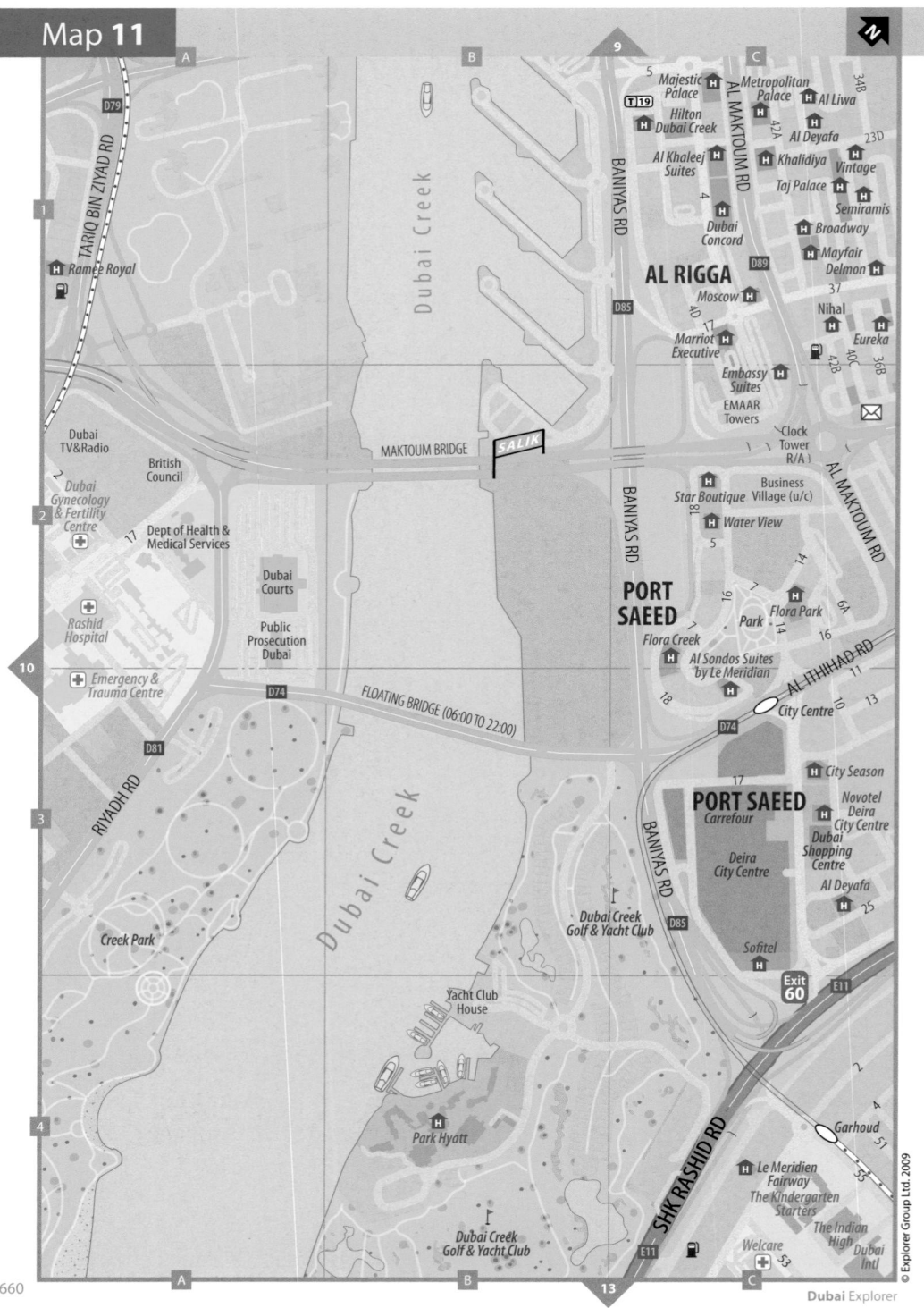

9

5 Majestic
Palace

T 19

Metropolitan
Palace
Al Liwa

34B

AL MAKTOUM RD

Hilton
Dubai Creek

42A

Al Deyafa

23D

Al Khaleej
Suites

Khalidiya

Vintage

4

Taj Palace

Semiramis

Dubai
Concord

Broadway

Mayfair
Delmon

AL RIGGA

D89

37

Moscow

Nihal

40

17

Eureka

Marriot
Executive

40C

42B

36B

Dubai
TV&Radio

Embassy
Suites

British
Council

EMAAR
Towers

Clock
Tower
R/A

2

Dubai
Gynecology
& Fertility
Centre

MAKTOUM BRIDGE

SALIK

2

17

Dept of Health &
Medical Services

BANIYAS RD

Star Boutique

Business
Village (u/c)

18

Water View

Dubai
Courts

5

14

Rashid
Hospital

Public
Prosecution
Dubai

16

**PORT
SAEED**

7

Flora Park

6A

Park

14

10

Flora Creek

16

Emergency &
Trauma Centre

D74

FLOATING BRIDGE (06:00 TO 22:00)

Al Sondos Suites
by Le Meridian

AL ITIHHAD RD

11

D81

18

City Centre

10

13

RIYADH RD

D74

City Season

3

Dubai Creek

17

Novotel
Deira
City Centre

PORT SAEED
Carrefour

BANIYAS RD

Dubai
Shopping
Centre

Deira
City Centre

Al Deyafa

25

Creek Park

Dubai Creek
Golf & Yacht Club

D85

Sofitel

Exit
60

E11

Yacht Club
House

Dubai Creek

2

4

Garhoud

51

4

Park Hyatt

SHK RASHID RD

55

Le Meridien
Fairway

The Kindergarten
Starters

The Indian
High

Dubai Creek
Golf & Yacht Club

E11

Welcare

Dubai
Intl

53

13

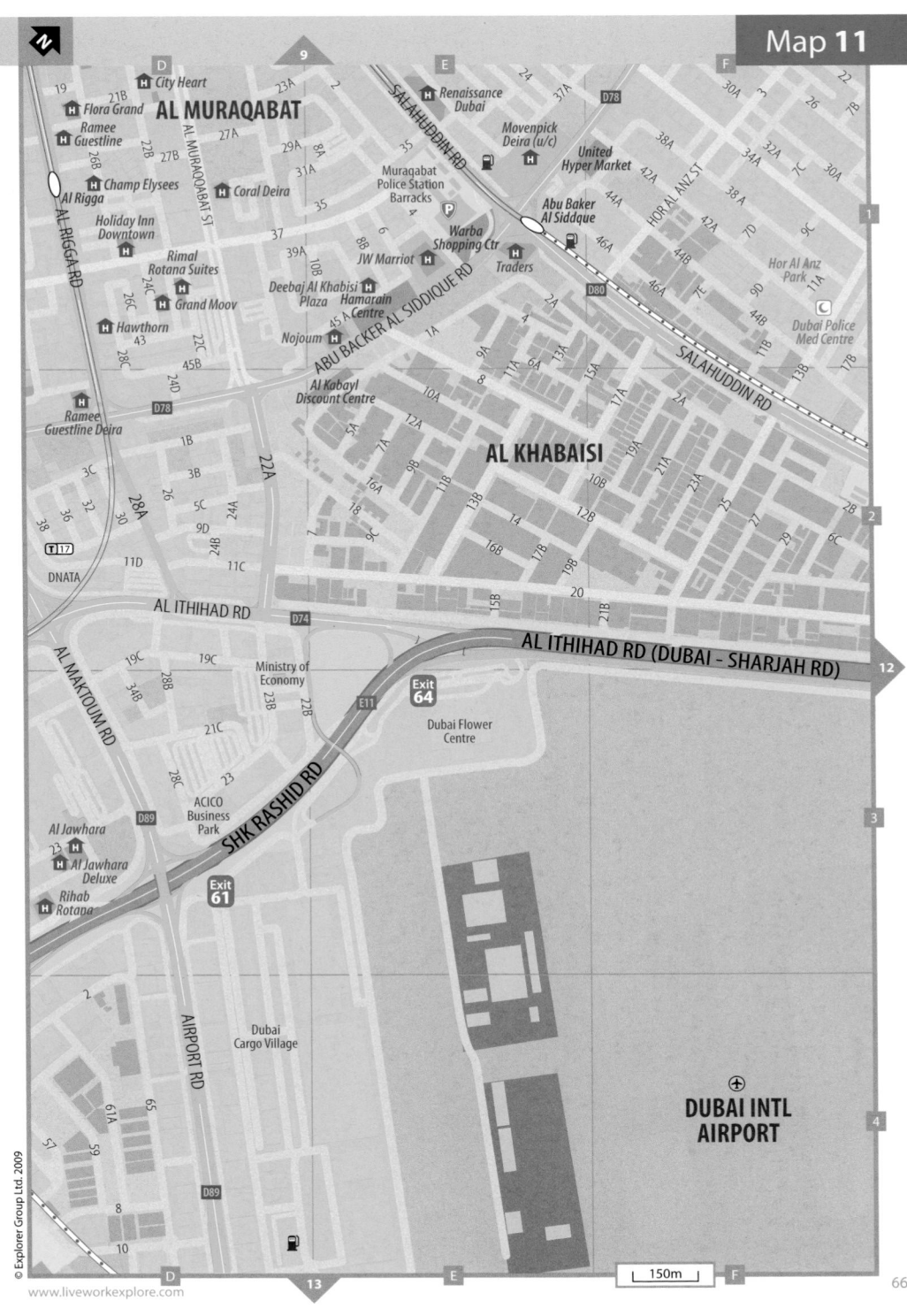

Map **11**

AL MURAQABAT

City Heart
Flora Grand
Ramee Guestline
Champ Elysees
Al Rigga
Holiday Inn Downtown
Rimal Rotana Suites
Grand Moov
Hawthorn
Ramee Guestline Deira

Coral Deira

Renaissance Dubai
Movenpick Deira (u/c)
United Hyper Market

Muraqabat Police Station Barracks
JW Marriot
Warba Shopping Ctr
Traders
Deebaj Al Khabisi Plaza
Hamarain Centre
Nojoum
Al Kabayl Discount Centre

Abu Baker Al Siddque

SALAHUDDIN RD

ABU BACKER AL SIDDIQUE RD

AL KHABAISI

Hor Al Anz Park
Dubai Police Med Centre

AL RIGGA RD

AL MURAQABAT ST

DNATA

AL ITHIHAD RD

AL ITHIHAD RD (DUBAI - SHARJAH RD)

Ministry of Economy
Exit 64
Dubai Flower Centre

SHK RASHID RD

AL MAKTOUM RD

ACICO Business Park
Al Jawhara
Al Jawhara Deluxe
Rihab Rotana

Exit 61

AIRPORT RD

Dubai Cargo Village

⊕
DUBAI INTL AIRPORT

150m

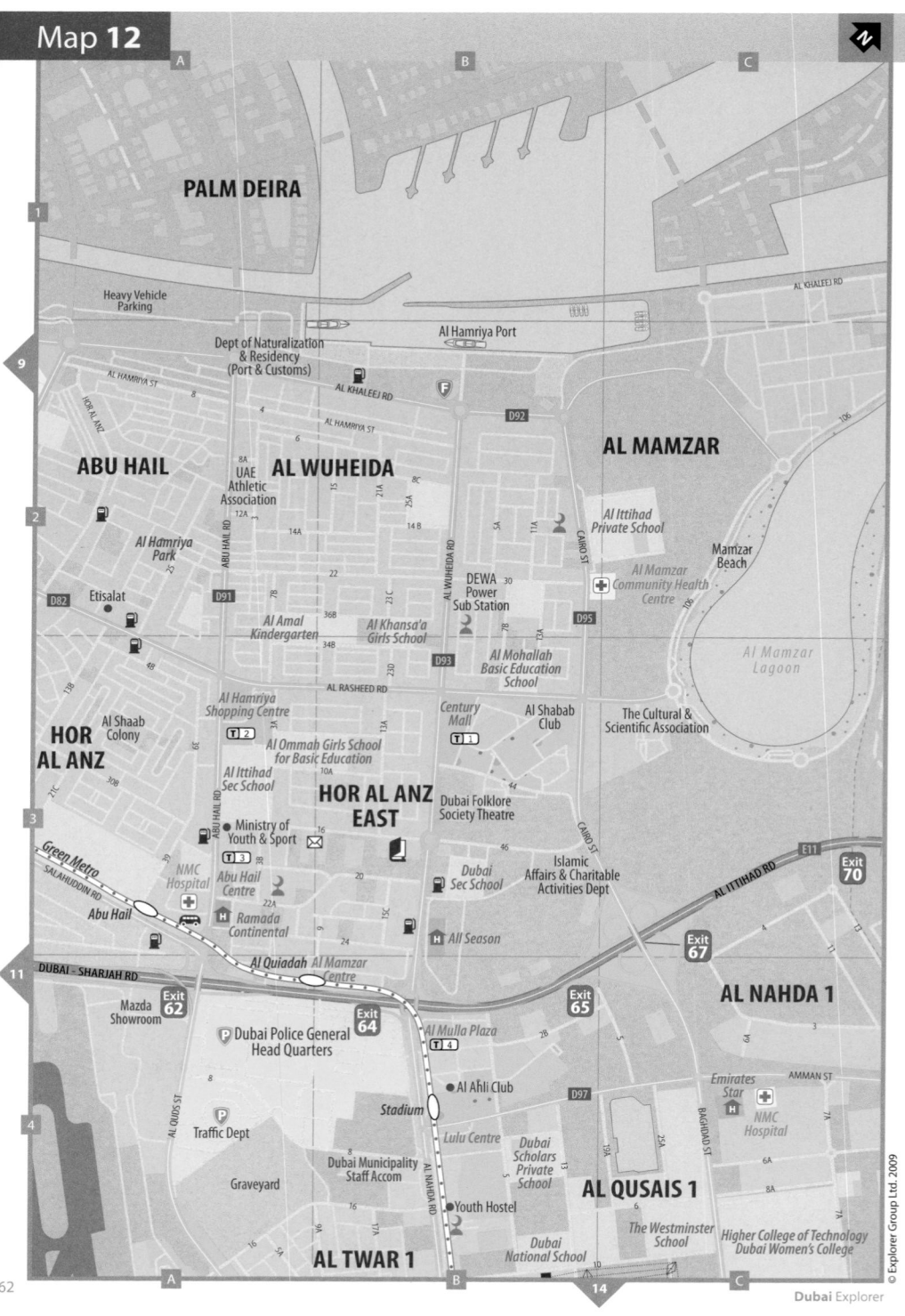

Map **12**

PALM DEIRA

Heavy Vehicle Parking

Dept of Naturalization & Residency (Port & Customs)

Al Hamriya Port

AL KHALEEJ RD

AL HAMRIYA ST

AL KHALEEJ RD

D92

ABU HAIL

UAE Athletic Association

AL WUHEIDA

AL MAMZAR

Al Hamriya Park

Al Ittihad Private School

Mamzar Beach

Etisalat

D82

D91

DEWA Power Sub Station

Al Mamzar Community Health Centre

D95

Al Amal Kindergarten

Al Khansa'a Girls School

Al Mamzar Lagoon

HOR AL ANZ

Al Shaab Colony

AL RASHEED RD

D93

Al Mohallah Basic Education School

Al Hamriya Shopping Centre

Century Mall

Al Shabab Club

The Cultural & Scientific Association

Al Ommah Girls School for Basic Education

Al Ittihad Sec School

HOR AL ANZ EAST

Dubai Folklore Society Theatre

Green Metro

SALAHUDDIN RD

Ministry of Youth & Sport

NMC Hospital

Abu Hail Centre

Dubai Sec School

Islamic Affairs & Charitable Activities Dept

E11

AL ITTIHAD RD

Exit 70

Abu Hail

Ramada Continental

All Season

Exit 67

DUBAI - SHARJAH RD

Al Quiadah

Al Mamzar Centre

Exit 65

AL NAHDA 1

Mazda Showroom

Exit 62

Exit 64

Al Mulla Plaza

Dubai Police General Head Quarters

Al Ahli Club

D97

Emirates Star

AMMAN ST

NMC Hospital

Stadium

Lulu Centre

Dubai Scholars Private School

AL QUSAIS 1

Traffic Dept

Dubai Municipality Staff Accom

Graveyard

Youth Hostel

The Westminster School

Higher College of Technology Dubai Women's College

AL TWAR 1

Dubai National School

AL NAHDA RD

AL QUDS ST

BAGHDAD ST

© Explorer Group Ltd. 2009

Dubai Explorer

Map **12**

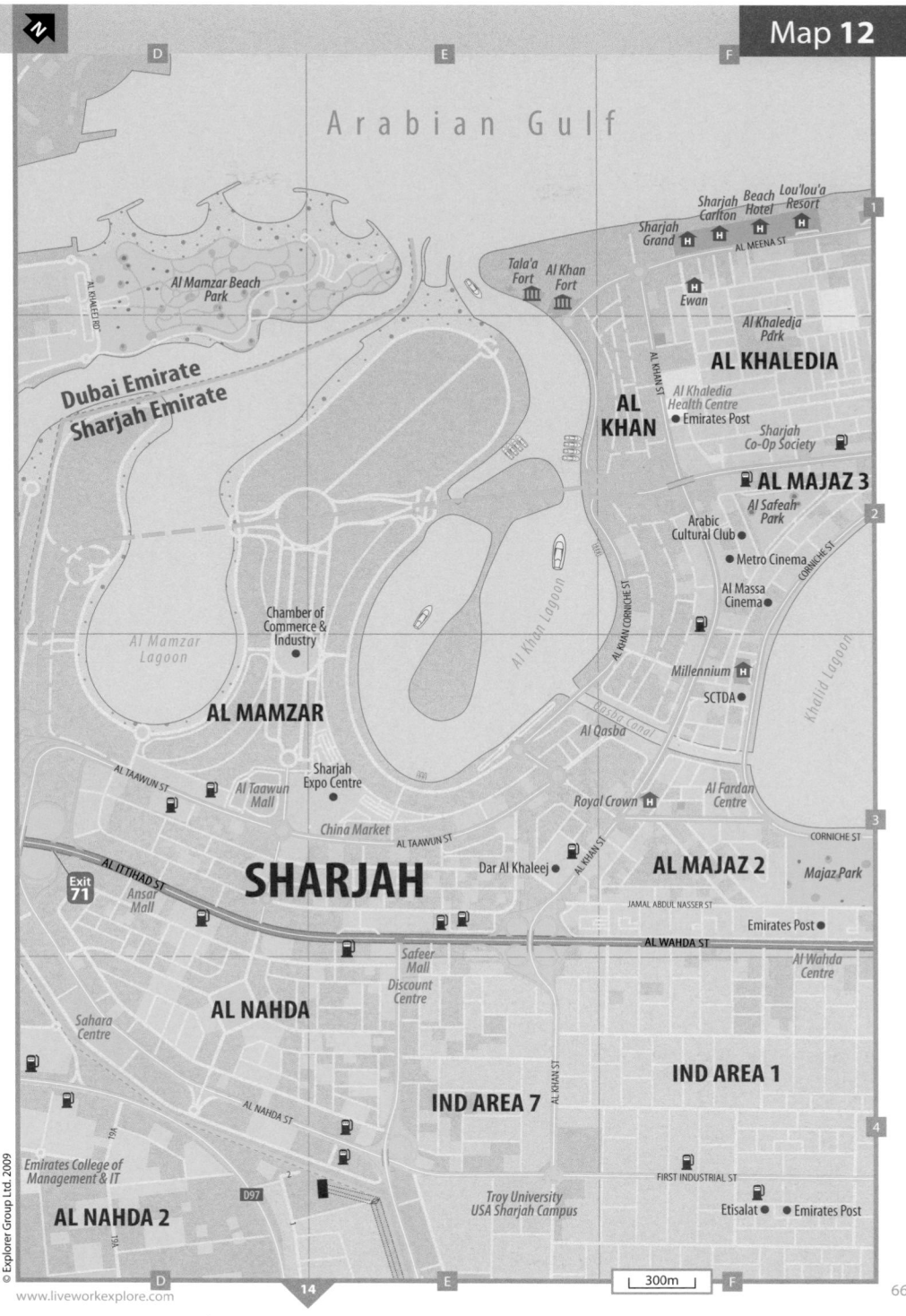

Arabian Gulf

Sharjah Carlton
Beach Hotel
Lou'lou'a Resort
Sharjah Grand
AL MEENA ST

Ewan

Tala'a Fort
Al Khan Fort

Al Khaledja Park

AL KHALEDIA

AL KHAN

Al Mamzar Beach Park

AL KHALEED RD

Dubai Emirate
Sharjah Emirate

Al Khaledia Health Centre
Emirates Post
Sharjah Co-Op Society

AL MAJAZ 3

Al Safeah Park

Arabic Cultural Club
Metro Cinema

Al Massa Cinema

CORNICHE ST

AL KHAN CORNICHE ST

AL KHAN ST

Chamber of Commerce & Industry

Al Mamzar Lagoon

Al Khan Lagoon

Millennium
SCTDA

Khalid Lagoon

AL MAMZAR

Al Qasba

Al Fardan Centre

Sharjah Expo Centre

AL TAAWUN ST

Al Taawun Mall

China Market

AL TAAWUN ST

Royal Crown

CORNICHE ST

SHARJAH

Dar Al Khaleej

AL KHAN ST

AL MAJAZ 2

Majaz Park

AL ITTIHAD ST

Exit 71

Ansar Mall

JAMAL ABDUL NASSER ST

Emirates Post

AL WAHDA ST

Al Wahda Centre

Safeer Mall Discount Centre

AL NAHDA

Sahara Centre

IND AREA 7

AL KHAN ST

IND AREA 1

AL NAHDA ST

Emirates College of Management & IT

D97

Troy University USA Sharjah Campus

FIRST INDUSTRIAL ST

AL NAHDA 2

Etisalat
Emirates Post

300m

14

Map **13**

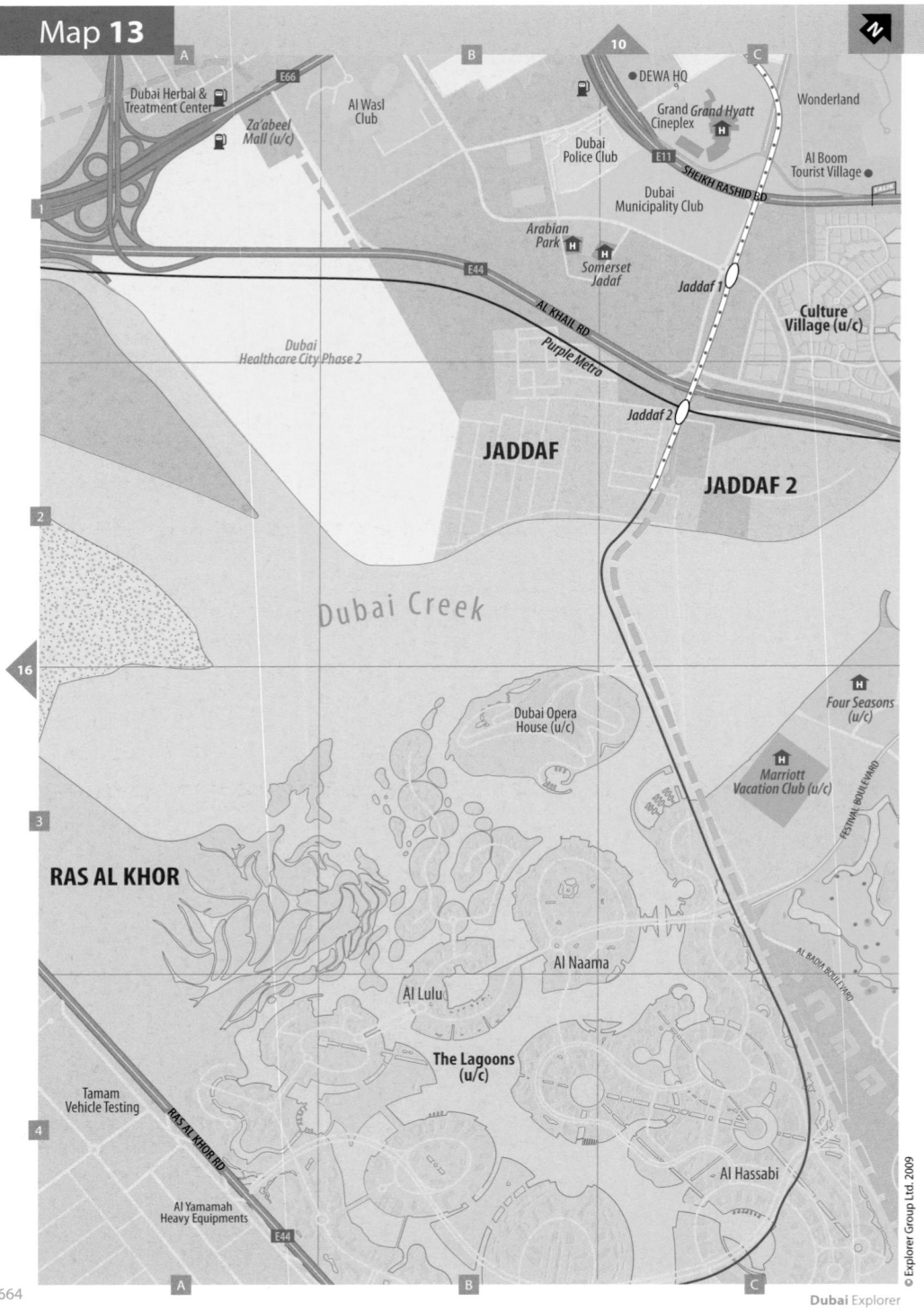

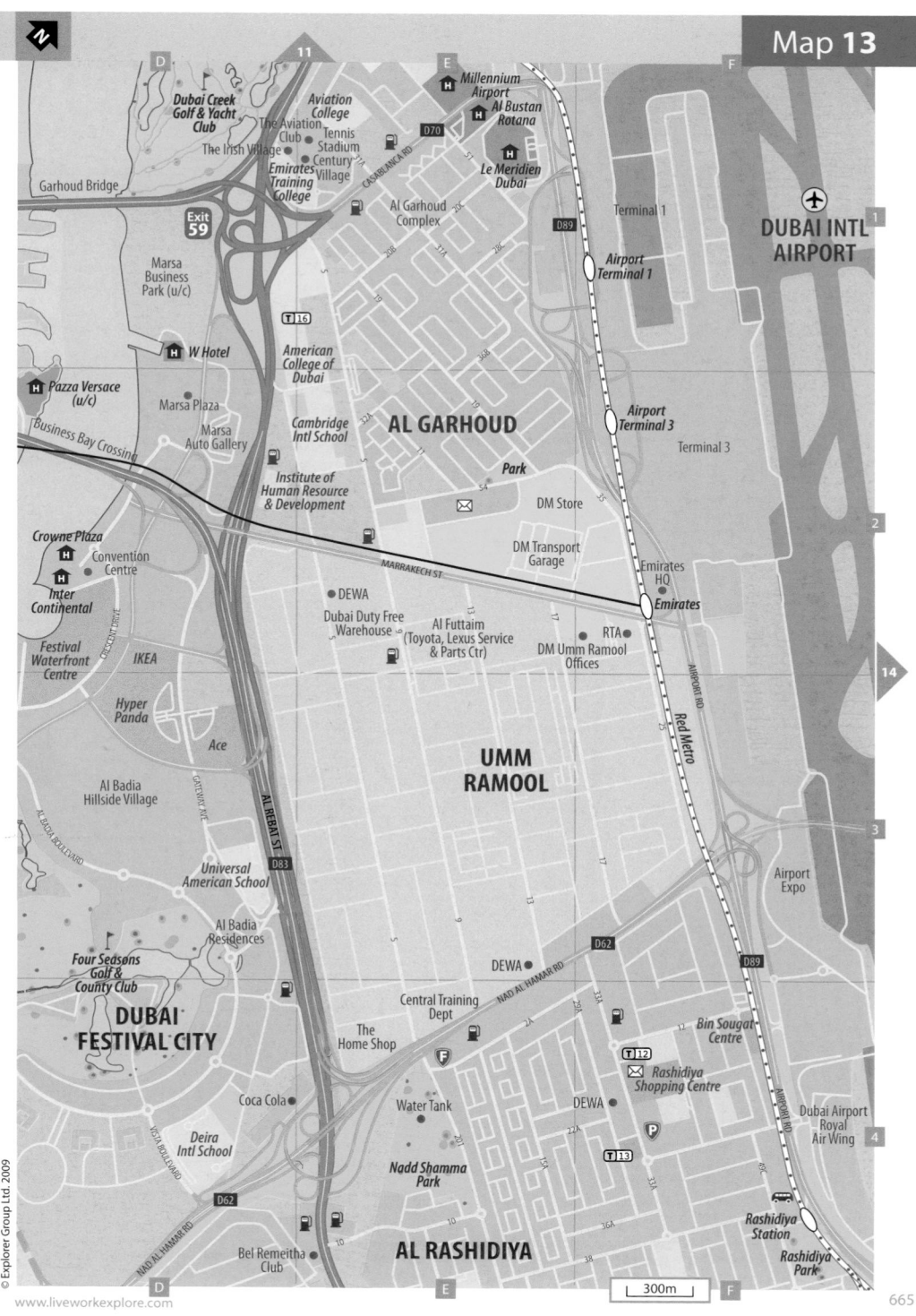

Map **13**

DUBAI INTL AIRPORT

Terminal 1

Airport Terminal 1

Airport Terminal 3

Terminal 3

Dubai Creek Golf & Yacht Club

The Aviation Club

The Irish Village

Emirates Training College

Garhoud Bridge

Exit 59

Marsa Business Park (u/c)

Aviation College

Tennis Stadium

Century Village

Al Garhoud Complex

Millennium Airport

Al Bustan Rotana

Le Meridien Dubai

Marsa Plaza

Marsa Auto Gallery

W Hotel

American College of Dubai

Cambridge Intl School

Pazza Versace (u/c)

Business Bay Crossing

Institute of Human Resource & Development

AL GARHOUD

Park

DM Store

DM Transport Garage

Crowne Plaza

Convention Centre

Inter Continental

Festival Waterfront Centre

IKEA

Hyper Panda

Ace

DEWA

Dubai Duty Free Warehouse

Al Futtaim (Toyota, Lexus Service & Parts Ctr)

MARRAKECH ST

Emirates HQ

Emirates

RTA

DM Umm Ramool Offices

Red Metro

AIRPORT RD

UMM RAMOOL

Al Badia Hillside Village

Universal American School

Al Badia Residences

Four Seasons Golf & County Club

DUBAI FESTIVAL CITY

Coca Cola

Deira Intl School

DEWA

Central Training Dept

The Home Shop

Water Tank

Nadd Shamma Park

NAD AL HAMAR RD

DEWA

Airport Expo

Bin Sougat Centre

Rashidiya Shopping Centre

Dubai Airport Royal Air Wing

Bel Remeitha Club

AL RASHIDIYA

Rashidiya Station

Rashidiya Park

300m

Map **14**

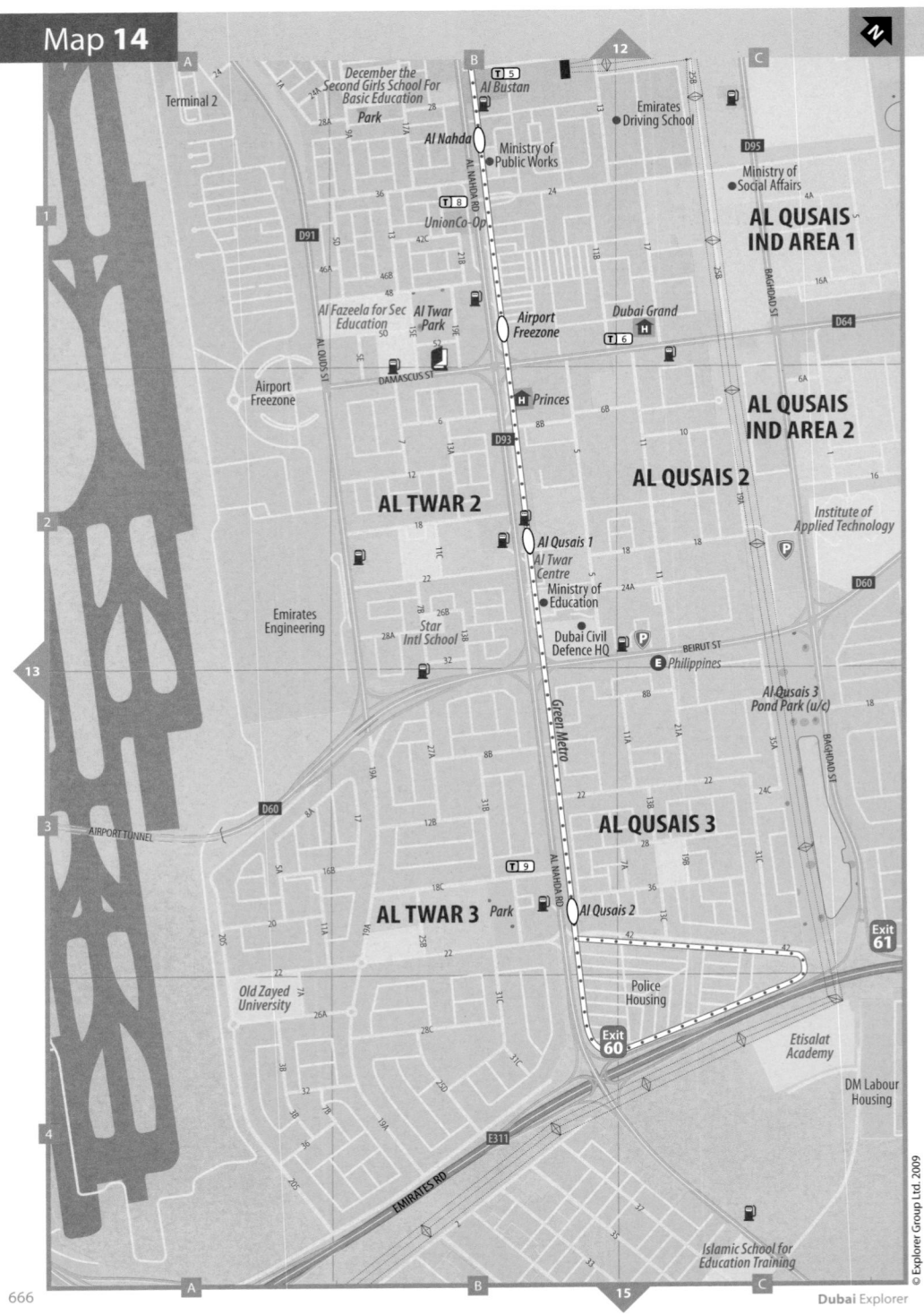

Terminal 2

December the
Second Girls School For
Basic Education
Park

Al Bustan
T 5

Emirates
● Driving School

Al Nahda

Ministry of
● Public Works

Ministry of
● Social Affairs

D95

AL QUSAIS
IND AREA 1

D91

T 8

UnionCo-Op

Al Fazeela for Sec
Education

Al Twar
Park

Airport
Freezone

Dubai Grand

T 6
H

D64

Airport
Freezone

DAMASCUS ST

D93

H *Princes*

AL QUSAIS
IND AREA 2

AL TWAR 2

AL QUSAIS 2

AL QUSAIS
IND AREA 2

Institute of
Applied Technology

D60

Emirates
Engineering

Al Qusais 1
Al Twar
Centre
Ministry of
● Education

Star
Intl School

Dubai Civil
Defence HQ

BEIRUT ST

P

E ● Philippines

Al Qusais 3
Pond Park (u/c)

Green Metro

AL QUSAIS 3

AIRPORT TUNNEL

D60

T 9

AL TWAR 3 *Park*

Al Qusais 2

Exit
61

Old Zayed
University

Police
Housing

Exit
60

Etisalat
Academy

DM Labour
Housing

E311

EMIRATES RD

Islamic School for
Education Training

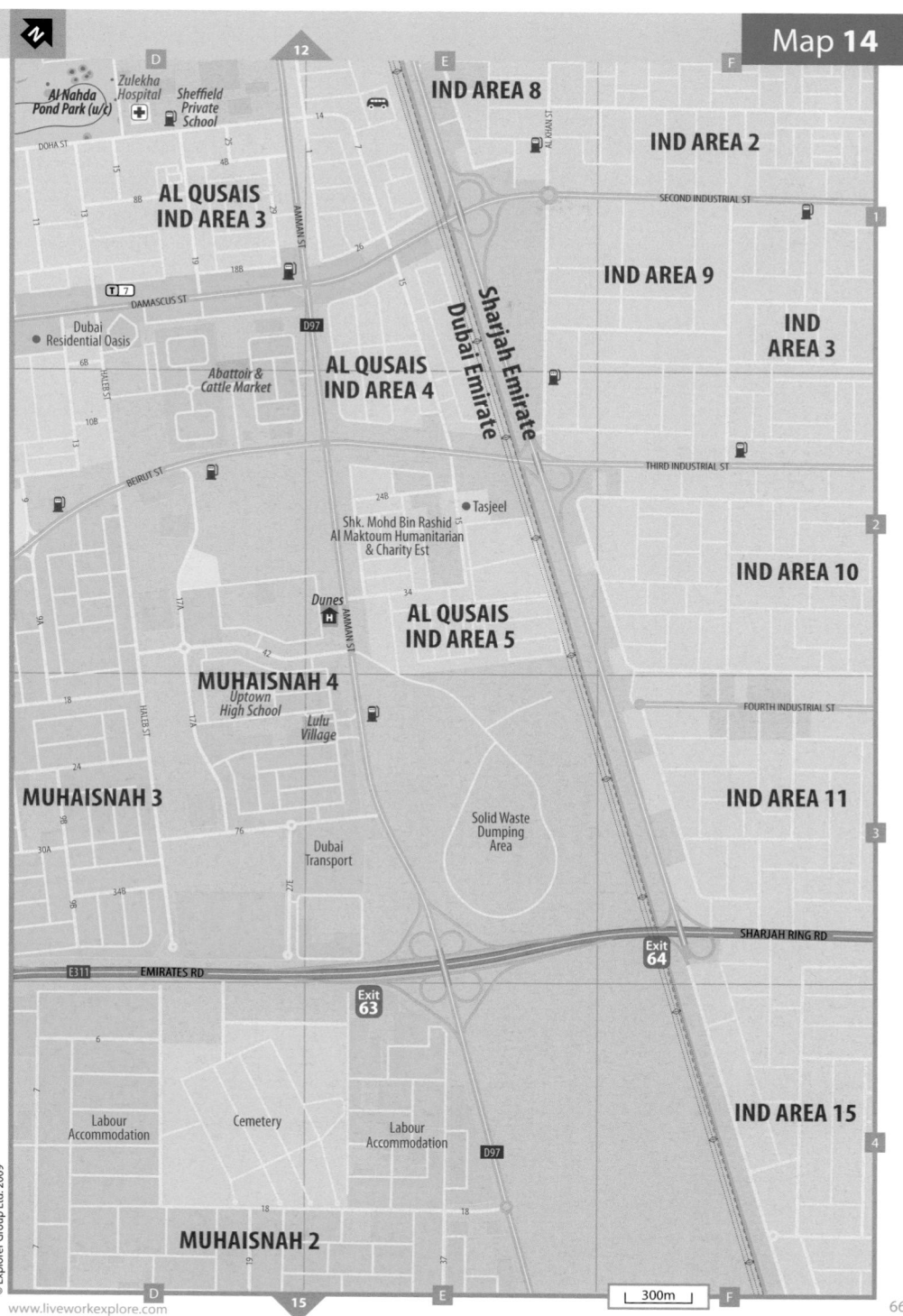

Map **14**

IND AREA 8

IND AREA 2

IND AREA 9

IND AREA 3

IND AREA 10

IND AREA 11

IND AREA 15

AL QUSAIS
IND AREA 3

AL QUSAIS
IND AREA 4

AL QUSAIS
IND AREA 5

MUHAISNAH 4

MUHAISNAH 3

MUHAISNAH 2

Al-Nahda
Pond Park (u/c)

Zulekha
Hospital

Sheffield
Private
School

Dubai
Residential Oasis

Abattoir &
Cattle Market

Shk. Mohd Bin Rashid
Al Maktoum Humanitarian
& Charity Est

Tasjeel

Dunes

Uptown
High School

Lulu
Village

Dubai
Transport

Solid Waste
Dumping
Area

Labour
Accommodation

Cemetery

Labour
Accommodation

Sharjah Emirate
Dubai Emirate

SECOND INDUSTRIAL ST

THIRD INDUSTRIAL ST

FOURTH INDUSTRIAL ST

SHARJAH RING RD

EMIRATES RD

DOHA ST

DAMASCUS ST

BEIRUT ST

AMMAN ST

AL KHAN ST

HALEB ST

Exit 64

Exit 63

T 7

D97

E311

300m

Map **15**

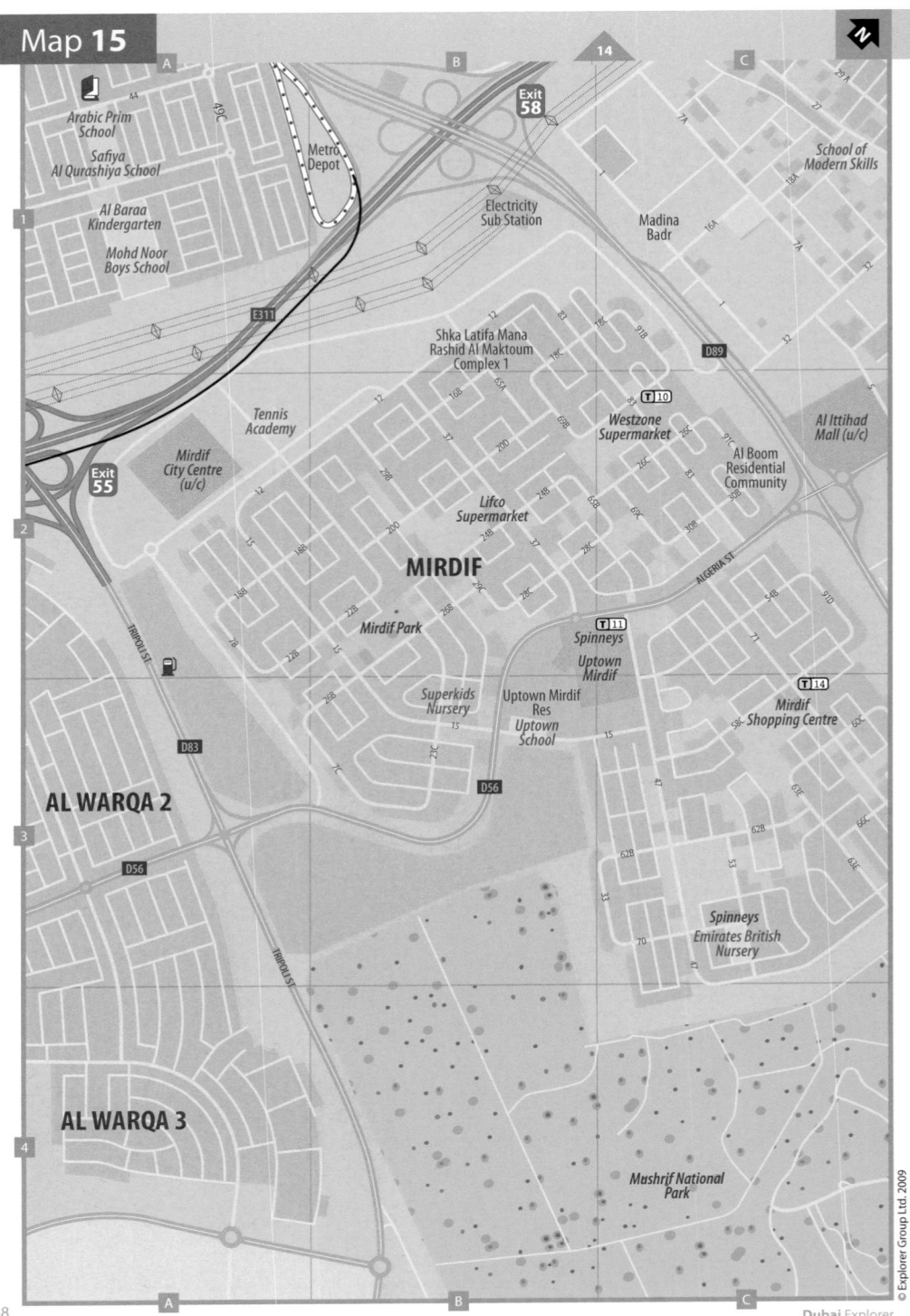

14

Exit **58**

A

B

C

Arabic Prim School

Safiya Al Qurashiya School

Al Baraa Kindergarten

Mohd Noor Boys School

Metro Depot

Electricity Sub Station

Madina Badr

School of Modern Skills

E311

Shka Latifa Mana Rashid Al Maktoum Complex 1

D89

1

Tennis Academy

T 10

Westzone Supermarket

Al Boom Residential Community

Al Ittihad Mall (u/c)

Exit **55**

Mirdif City Centre (u/c)

Lifco Supermarket

MIRDIF

2

ALGERIA ST

TRIPOLI ST

Mirdif Park

T 11

Spinneys

Uptown Mirdif

T 14

Mirdif Shopping Centre

Superkids Nursery

Uptown Mirdif Res

Uptown School

D83

D56

AL WARQA 2

D56

3

Spinneys Emirates British Nursery

AL WARQA 3

TRIPOLI ST

4

Mushrif National Park

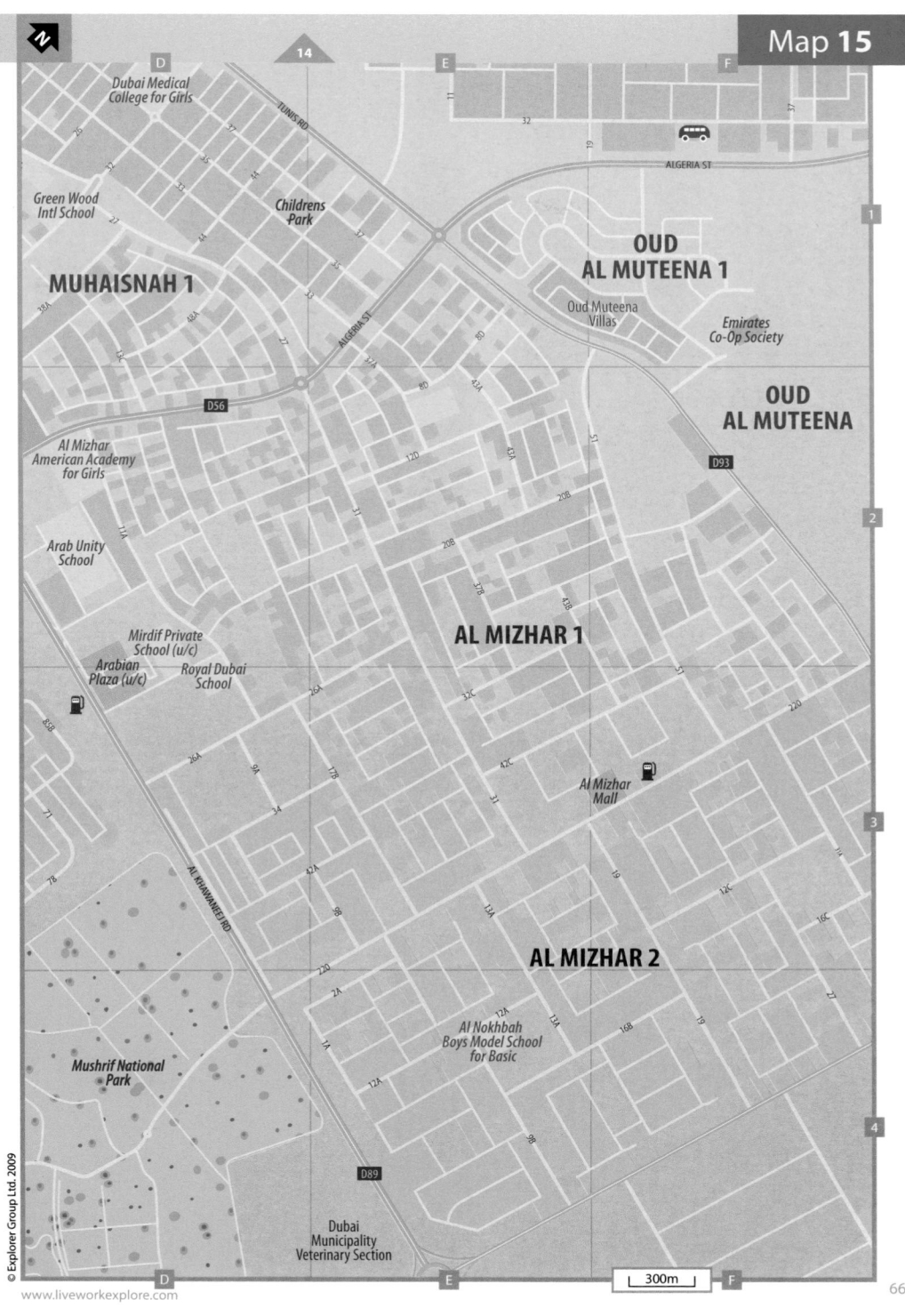

Map **15**

N

14

D

E

F

Dubai Medical
College for Girls

TUNIS RD

Green Wood
Intl School

Childrens
Park

ALGERIA ST

MUHAISNAH 1

**OUD
AL MUTEENA 1**

Oud Muteena
Villas

Emirates
Co-Op Society

1

D56

**OUD
AL MUTEENA**

Al Mizhar
American Academy
for Girls

D93

2

Arab Unity
School

Mirdif Private
School (u/c)

AL MIZHAR 1

Arabian
Plaza (u/c)

Royal Dubai
School

AL KHAWANEEJ RD

Al Mizhar
Mall

3

AL MIZHAR 2

Al Nokhbah
Boys Model School
for Basic

Mushrif National
Park

D89

4

Dubai
Municipality
Veterinary Section

300m

© Explorer Group Ltd. 2009

D

E

F

Map **16**

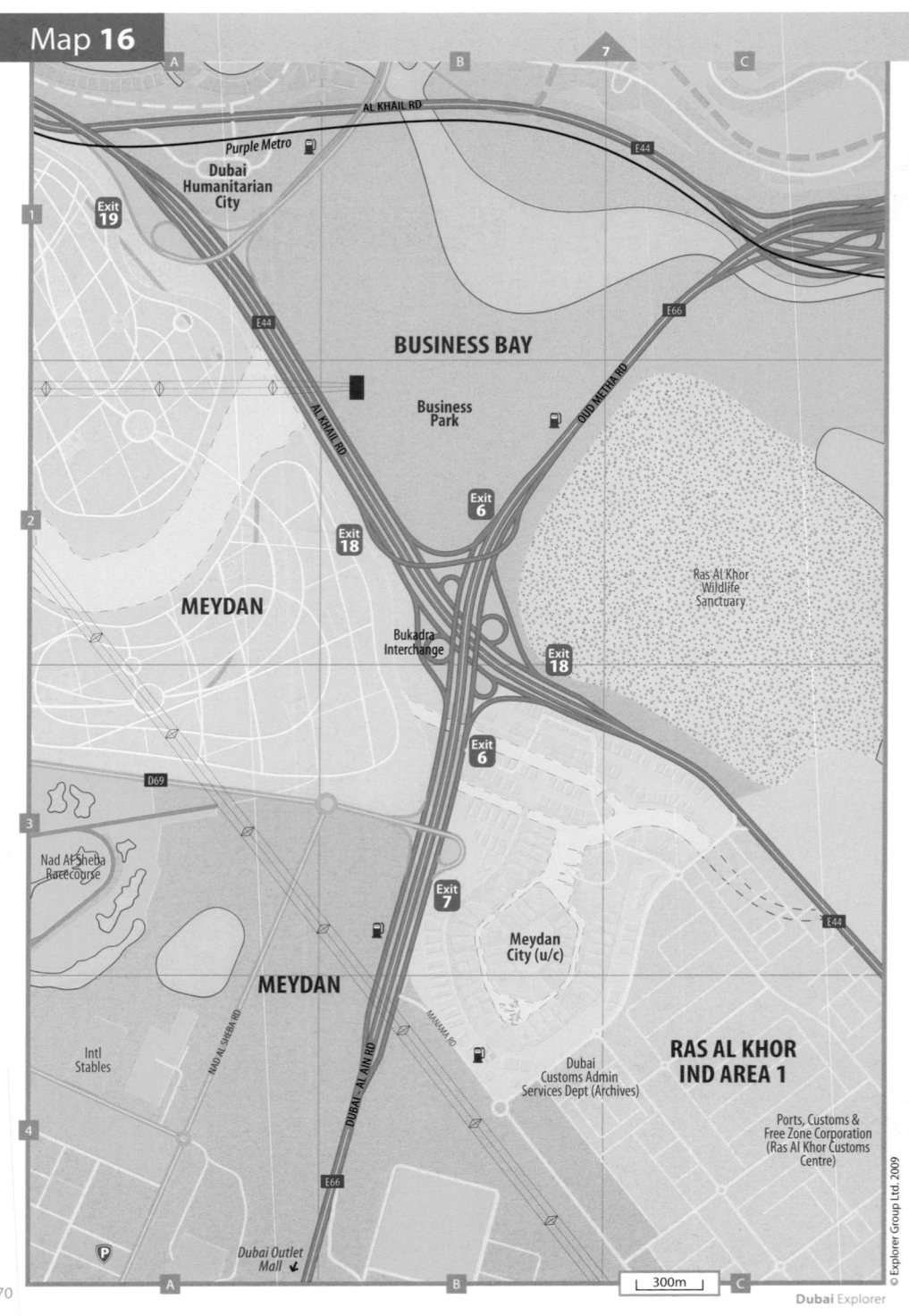

A   B   **7**   C

AL KHAIL RD

Purple Metro

Dubai Humanitarian City

Exit **19**

E44

1

E44

AL KHAIL RD

BUSINESS BAY

E66

OUD METHA RD

Business Park

Exit **6**

Exit **18**

MEYDAN

Ras Al Khor Wildlife Sanctuary

Bukadra Interchange

Exit **18**

2

Exit **6**

D69

Exit **7**

3

Nad Al Sheba Racecourse

E44

Meydan City (u/c)

NAD AL SHEBA RD

DUBAI – AL AIN RD

MANAMA RD

MEYDAN

RAS AL KHOR IND AREA 1

Intl Stables

Dubai Customs Admin Services Dept (Archives)

Ports, Customs & Free Zone Corporation (Ras Al Khor Customs Centre)

4

E66

P

Dubai Outlet Mall ↓

300m

A   B   C

Index

Index

Index

Index

Index

Residents' Guides

Mini Guides

Mini Maps

Photography Books

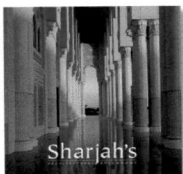

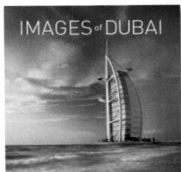

Maps

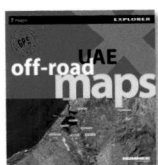

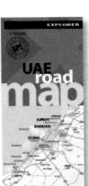
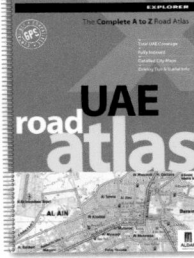

Activity and Lifestyle Guides

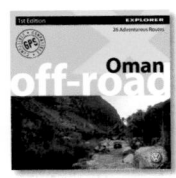

Check out
www.**live**work**explore**.com/shop